A Companion to Russian Cinema

Wiley Blackwell Companions to National Cinemas

The Wiley Blackwell Companions to National Cinemas showcase the rich film heritages of various countries across the globe. Each volume sets the agenda for what is now known as world cinema while challenging Hollywood's lock on the popular and scholarly imagination. Whether exploring Spanish, German, or Chinese film, or the broader traditions of Eastern Europe, Scandinavia, Australia, and Latin America the 20–25 newly commissioned essays comprising each volume include coverage of the dominant themes of canonical, controversial, and contemporary films; stars, directors, and writers; key influences; reception; and historiography and scholarship. Written in a sophisticated and authoritative style by leading experts they will appeal to an international audience of scholars, students, and general readers.

A Companion to German Cinema, edited by Terri Ginsberg & Andrea Mensch

A Companion to Chinese Cinema, edited by Yingjin Zhang

A Companion to East European Cinemas, edited by Anikó Imre

A Companion to Spanish Cinema, edited by Jo Labanyi & Tatjana Pavloviæ

A Companion to Contemporary French Cinema, edited by Raphaëlle Moine, Hilary Radner, Alistair Fox & Michel Marie

A Companion to Hong Kong Cinema, edited by Esther M. K. Cheung, Gina Marchetti, and Esther C.M. Yau

A Companion to Russian Cinema, edited by Birgit Beumers

A Companion to Nordic Film, edited by Mette Hjort and Ursula Lindqvist

A Companion to Russian Cinema

Edited by

Birgit Beumers

WILEY Blackwell

This edition first published 2016
© 2016 John Wiley & Sons, Inc.

Registered Office
John Wiley & Sons, Ltd, The Atrium, Southern Gate, Chichester, West Sussex, PO19 8SQ, UK

Editorial Offices
350 Main Street, Malden, MA 02148-5020, USA
9600 Garsington Road, Oxford, OX4 2DQ, UK
The Atrium, Southern Gate, Chichester, West Sussex, PO19 8SQ, UK

For details of our global editorial offices, for customer services, and for information about how to apply for permission to reuse the copyright material in this book please see our website at www.wiley.com/wiley-blackwell.

The right of Birgit Beumers to be identified as the author of the editorial material in this work has been asserted in accordance with the UK Copyright, Designs and Patents Act 1988.

All rights reserved. No part of this publication may be reproduced, stored in a retrieval system, or transmitted, in any form or by any means, electronic, mechanical, photocopying, recording or otherwise, except as permitted by the UK Copyright, Designs and Patents Act 1988, without the prior permission of the publisher.

Wiley also publishes its books in a variety of electronic formats. Some content that appears in print may not be available in electronic books.

Designations used by companies to distinguish their products are often claimed as trademarks. All brand names and product names used in this book are trade names, service marks, trademarks or registered trademarks of their respective owners. The publisher is not associated with any product or vendor mentioned in this book.

Limit of Liability/Disclaimer of Warranty: While the publisher and authors have used their best efforts in preparing this book, they make no representations or warranties with respect to the accuracy or completeness of the contents of this book and specifically disclaim any implied warranties of merchantability or fitness for a particular purpose. It is sold on the understanding that the publisher is not engaged in rendering professional services and neither the publisher nor the author shall be liable for damages arising herefrom. If professional advice or other expert assistance is required, the services of a competent professional should be sought.

Library of Congress Cataloging-in-Publication Data

Names: Beumers, Birgit, editor.
Title: A companion to Russian cinema / edited by Birgit Beumers.
Description: Chichester, West Sussex ; Malden, MA : John Wiley & Sons, Inc., 2016. |
  Series: Wiley Blackwell companions to national cinemas | Includes bibliographical references and index.
Identifiers: LCCN 2016002848 (print) | LCCN 2016005050 (ebook) | ISBN 9781118412763 (cloth) |
  ISBN 9781118424735 (pdf) | ISBN 9781118424704 (epub)
Subjects: LCSH: Motion pictures–Soviet Union–History and criticism. |
  Motion pictures–Russia (Federation)–History and criticism.
Classification: LCC PN1993.5.R9 C64 2016 (print) | LCC PN1993.5.R9 (ebook) | DDC 791.430947–dc23
LC record available at http://lccn.loc.gov/2016002848

A catalogue record for this book is available from the British Library.

Cover image: Poster for Aleksei Balabanov's "Ya Tozhe Khochu/Me Too." Reproduced with permission of Sergei Selianov, CTB Film Company.

Set in 11/13pt Dante by SPi Global, Pondicherry, India
Printed and bound in Malaysia by Vivar Printing Sdn Bhd

1   2016

Contents

Notes on Contributors — viii
Acknowledgments — xv
Notes on Transliteration and References — xvi

    Introduction — 1
    Birgit Beumers

Part I Structures of Production, Formation, and Exhibition — 21

1 The Film Palaces of Nevsky Prospect: A History of St Petersburg's Cinemas, 1900–1910 — 23
Anna Kovalova

2 (V)GIK and the History of Film Education in the Soviet Union, 1920s–1930s — 45
Masha Salazkina

3 Lenfilm: The Birth and Death of an Institutional Aesthetic — 66
Robert Bird

4 The Adventures of the *Kulturfilm* in Soviet Russia — 92
Oksana Sarkisova

5 Soiuzdetfilm: The Birth of Soviet Children's Film and the Child Actor — 117
Jeremy Hicks

Part II For the State or For the Audience? Auteurism, Genre, and Global Markets — 137

6 The Stalinist Musical: Socialist Realism and Revolutionary Romanticism — 139
Richard Taylor

7	Soviet Film Comedy of the 1950s and 1960s: Innovation and Restoration Seth Graham	158
8	*Auteur* Cinema during the Thaw and Stagnation Eugénie Zvonkine	178
9	The *Blokbaster*: How Russian Cinema Learned to Love Hollywood Dawn Seckler and Stephen M. Norris	202
10	The Global and the National in Post-Soviet Russian Cinema (2004–2012) Maria Bezenkova and Xenia Leontyeva	224

Part III Sound – Image – Text — 249

11	The Literary Scenario and the Soviet Screenwriting Tradition Maria Belodubrovskaya	251
12	Ideology, Technology, Aesthetics: Early Experiments in Soviet Color Film, 1931–1945 Phil Cavendish	270
13	Learning to Speak Soviet: Soviet Cinema and the Coming of Sound Lilya Kaganovsky	292
14	Cinema and the Art of Being: Towards a History of Early Soviet Set Design Emma Widdis	314
15	Stars on Screen and Red Carpet Djurdja Bartlett	337
16	Revenge of the Cameramen: Soviet Cinematographers in the Director's Chair Peter Rollberg	364

Part IV Time and Space, History and Place — 389

17	Soldiers, Sailors, and Commissars: The Revolutionary Hero in Soviet Cinema of the 1930s Denise J. Youngblood	391
18	Defending the Motherland: The Soviet and Russian War Film Stephen M. Norris	409
19	Shooting Location: Riga Kevin M. F. Platt	427

| 20 | Capital Images: Moscow on Screen
Birgit Beumers | 452 |

Part V Directors' Portraits **475**

21	Boris Barnet: "This doubly accursed cinema" *Julian Graffy*	477
22	Iulii Raizman: Private Lives and Intimacy under Communism *Jamie Miller*	500
23	The Man Who Made Them Laugh: Leonid Gaidai, the King of Soviet Comedy *Elena Prokhorova*	519
24	Aleksei Gherman: The Last Soviet Auteur *Anthony Anemone*	543
25	Knowledge (Imperfective): Andrei Zviagintsev and Contemporary Cinema *Nancy Condee*	565

Appendix Chronology of Events in Russian Cinema and History	585
Bibliography	614
Index	631

Notes on Contributors

Anthony Anemone is a literary historian and film critic who writes about modern Russian literature and cinema. Educated at Columbia University and The University of California, Berkeley, he has taught at Colby College, The College of William and Mary, and, since 2007, at The New School. His essays and reviews have been published in *Slavic Review*, *The Slavic and East European Journal*, *The Russian Review*, *The Tolstoy Studies Journal*, *Revue des Etudes Slaves*, *Wiener Slawistischer Almanach*, and in numerous books. The editor of *Just Assassins: The Culture of Terrorism in Russia* (2010) and, with Peter Scotto, the translator and editor of *"I am a Phenomenon Quite out of the Ordinary" The Notebooks, Diaries and Letters of Daniil Kharms* (2013), which was named the Best Literary Translation by the Association of Teachers of Slavic and East European Languages. At present, he is at work on a monograph about the life and career of Mikhail Kalatozov.

Djurdja Bartlett is Reader in the Histories and Cultures of Fashion at the London College of Fashion, University of the Arts London. She has widely published and lectured on the theme of fashion during socialism and post-socialism. Bartlett is author of *FashionEast: The Spectre that Haunted Socialism* (2010); *FashionEast: prizrak brodivshii po vostochnoi Evrope* (2011), and editor of the volume on East Europe, Russia, and the Caucasus in the *Berg Encyclopedia of World Dress and Fashion* (2010). Bartlett's new monograph *European Fashion Geographies: Style, Society and Politics* (2016) has been funded by an Arts and Humanities Research Council Fellowship grant.

Maria Belodubrovskaya is Assistant Professor of Film at the University of Wisconsin–Madison. She has published articles in *Cinema Journal*, *Slavic Review*, *Studies in Russian and Soviet Cinema*, and *KinoKultura* and is completing a book on the Soviet film industry during the Stalin period.

Birgit Beumers is Professor in Film Studies at Aberystwyth University. She completed her DPhil at St Antony's College, Oxford and from 1994 to 2012 worked in the Russian Department at the University of Bristol. She specializes on cinema in Russia and Central Asia, as well as Russian culture. Her publications include *A History of Russian Cinema* (2009) and, with Mark Lipovetsky, *Performing Violence* (2009). She has edited a number of volumes, including *Directory of World Cinema: Russia 1 and 2* (2010, 2015) and *The Cinema of Alexander Sokurov* (2011, with Nancy Condee). She is the editor of the online journal *KinoKultura* and of the journal *Studies in Russian and Soviet Cinema*, as well as co-editor of *Zeitschrift für Slavische Philologie*. With Richard Taylor, she is General Editor of the KINO series and of the KinoSputniks series. She is currently working on contemporary Russian cinema and on early Soviet animation.

Maria Bezenkova holds a PhD (*kandidat*) in arts. She is Associate Professor at the Russian State Institute of Cinema (VGIK), head of Nevafilm Emotion (distribution of alternative content in Russia), program director of Transbaikalia International Film Festival. She is the author of many articles on the film market, film theory and history, and contemporary Russian cinema for the journals *Russian Film Business Today*, *Cinemascope*, *Vestnik VGIKa*, *Film Sense*, and film critic for *Iskusstvo kino*, and online journals.

Robert Bird is Associate Professor in the departments of Slavic Languages and Literatures and Cinema Media Studies at the University of Chicago. His main area of interest is the aesthetic practice and theory of Russian modernism. His first full-length book *Russian Prospero* (2006) is a comprehensive study of the poetry and thought of Russian poet and theorist Viacheslav Ivanov. He is the author of two books on the filmmaker Andrei Tarkovsky: *Andrei Rublev* (2004) and *Andrei Tarkovsky: Elements of Cinema* (2008). In 2012 he published *Fyodor Dostoevsky*, a brief, critical biography. His translations of Russian religious thought include *On Spiritual Unity: A Slavophile Reader* (1998) and Viacheslav Ivanov's *Selected Essays* (2001). Recent publications include essays on Soviet wartime poetry and the work in film of Aleksandr Sokurov and Olga Chernysheva. He is presently at work on a book manuscript "Soul Machine: Socialist Realism as Model, 1932–1941."

Phil Cavendish is Reader in Russian Literature and Film at the School of Slavonic and East European Studies, University College London. He is author of *Mining for Jewels: Evgenii Zamiatin and the Literary Stylization of Rus'* (2000) and *Soviet Mainstream Cinematography: The Silent Era* (2007), followed by the monograph on the visual aesthetic of Soviet avant-garde films of the silent era, *The Men with the Movie Camera* (2013). He is the author of scholarly articles on the poetics of the camera in pre-revolutionary Russian cinema (2004); the theory and practice of camera operation within the units of the Soviet avant-garde (2007); and the poetics of the photo-film in Andrei Zviagintsev's *The Return* (2013).

Nancy Condee is Professor of Slavic and Film Studies at the University of Pittsburgh. Recent publications include *The Cinema of Alexander Sokurov*, (ed. with

Birgit Beumers, 2011); and *The Imperial Trace: Recent Russian Cinema* (2009), which won the 2011 MLA Scaglione Slavic Prize and the 2010 Kovács Book Award from the Society for Cinema and Media Studies. Other volumes include *Antinomies of Art and Culture: Modernity, Postmodernity, Contemporaneity* (ed. with Terry Smith and Okwui Enwezor, 2008) and *Soviet Hieroglyphics* (1995). Her articles have appeared in *The Nation, The Washington Post, October, New Left Review, PMLA, Sight and Sound*, as well as Russian journals.

Julian Graffy is Professor Emeritus of Russian Literature and Cinema at University College London. He has written widely on Russian film and is the author of *Bed and Sofa: The Film Companion* (2001) and *Chapaev: The Film Companion* (2010). He is currently completing a study of the representation of foreign characters in a century of Russian film.

Seth Graham is Senior Lecturer in Russian at SSEES, University College London, where he teaches courses on Russian literature and language, cultural studies, and gender studies. Before coming to UCL in 2006, he taught at Stanford University and the University of Washington. His publications include numerous articles and chapters on Russian cinema, Central Asian cinema, and Russian humour. His monograph *Resonant Dissonance: The Russian Joke in Cultural Context* was published in 2009. He is co-editor of the online journal *KinoKultura*.

Jeremy Hicks is a Reader in Russian Culture and Film at Queen Mary University of London. He is the author of *Dziga Vertov: Defining Documentary Film* (2007) and *First Films of the Holocaust: Soviet Cinema and the Genocide of the Jews, 1938–46* (2012), which won the ASEEES Wayne C. Vucinich Prize, for most important contribution to the field of Slavic, East European and Eurasian Studies. The research for this book has informed a number of documentary films, including André Singer's *Night Will Fall*. He has also published various articles on Russian and Soviet film, literature, and journalism in *Russian Review, History, Studies in Russian and Soviet Cinema, Kinovedcheskie zapiski, Iskusstvo kino, Revolutionary Russia*, and *Historical Journal of Film, Radio and Televison*. He is a co-editor of *KinoKultura*, as well as an advisor on the editorial board of *Vestnik VGIKa*, and *Studies in Russian and Soviet Cinema*.

Lilya Kaganovsky is Associate Professor of Slavic, Comparative Literature, and Media & Cinema Studies, and the Director of the Program in Comparative and World Literature at the University of Illinois, Urbana-Champaign. Her publications include *How the Soviet Man was Unmade* (2008); articles on gender and sexuality in Soviet and post-Soviet cinema; and two co-edited volumes: *Mad Men, Mad World: Sex, Politics, Style and the 1960s* (with Lauren M. E. Goodlad and Robert A. Rushing, 2013), and *Sound, Speech, Music in Soviet and post-Soviet*

Cinema (with Masha Salazkina, 2014). She serves on the editorial board of the journal *Studies in Russian and Soviet Cinema*, and contributes film reviews to *Slavic Review* and *KinoKultura*. She is currently completing a book on Soviet cinema's transition to sound.

Anna Kovalova graduated from the philological faculty of St Petersburg State University (2007). From 2005 to 2008 she worked as editor for local television. From 2009 until 2015 she was a researcher at the philological faculty of St Petersburg State University. Since 2015 she is an assistant professor of philology at the Higher School of Economics (Moscow). She has published in the journals *Seans, Kinovedcheskie zapiski, Russian Review* and *Studies in Russian and Soviet Cinema*; she is the author of *Dovlatov* (with L. Lur'e, 2009), *Kinematograf v Peterburge 1896–1917* (with Yuri Tsivian, 2011) and *Kinematograf v Peterburge 1907–1917. Kinoproizvodstvo i fil'mografiia* (2012). She is editor of a volume of writings by Nikolai Erdman (2010).

Xenia Leontyeva holds a PhD (*kandidat*) in economics, and is senior analyst of the Russian film market and head of Nevafilm Research, as well as a teacher at the producers' department at St. Petersburg State Institute for Film and Television. She has been working in cinema since 2004. Editor-in-chief of the reports on the Russian film industry for the European Audiovisual Observatory (since 2009) and for the Ministry of Culture of the RF, as well as for Nevafilm.

Jamie Miller specializes in the relationship between politics and film in the USSR under Lenin and Stalin. He is the author of *Soviet Cinema: Politics and Persuasion under Stalin* (2010), journal articles and book chapters about Soviet film in the 1930s and beyond. He is currently researching the history of the Mezhrabpom film studio over the period 1923–1936.

Stephen M. Norris is Professor of History and Assistant Director of the Havighurst Center for Russian and Post-Soviet Studies at Miami University, Ohio. His teaching and research interests are in modern Russian history, with a focus on visual culture since 1800. His first book, *A War of Images: Russian Popular Prints, Wartime Culture, and National Identity, 1812–1945* (2006), examines the *lubok* as an important medium for articulating Russian nationhood. His second book, *Blockbuster History in the New Russia: Movies, Memory, and Patriotism* (2012), argues that recent Russian historical films sparked a revival of nationalist and patriotic sentiments. Norris is also the co-editor of *Preserving Petersburg: History, Memory, Nostalgia* (with Helena Goscilo, 2008); *Insiders and Outsiders in Russian Cinema* (with Zara Torlone, 2008); and *Russia's People of Empire: Life Stories from Eurasia, 1500–Present* (with Willard Sunderland, 2012). He is presently working on a biography of Boris Efimov (1900–2008), the Soviet caricaturist.

Kevin M. F. Platt is Edmund J. and Louise W. Kahn Term Professor in the Humanities, Professor of Slavic Languages and Literatures and Graduate Chair of the Comparative Literature Program at the University of Pennsylvania. He works on representations of Russian history, history and memory in Russia, Soviet film, Russian lyric poetry, and global post-Soviet Russian culture. He is the author of *Terror and Greatness: Ivan and Peter as Russian Myths* (2011) and *History in a Grotesque Key: Russian Literature and the Idea of Revolution* (1997; Russian edition 2006), and the co-editor (with David Brandenberger) of *Epic Revisionism: Russian History and Literature as Stalinist Propaganda* (2006). His current projects include a critical historiography of Russia and a study of contemporary Russian culture in Latvia.

Elena Prokhorova is Associate Professor of Russian at the College of William and Mary, where she also teaches in the Film and Media Studies program. Her research focuses on identity discourses in late Soviet and post-Soviet television and cinema. Her publications have appeared in *Slavic Review, Slavic and East European Journal, KinoKultura, Russian Journal of Communication,* and in edited volumes. She is currently finishing a book project (co-authored with Alexander Prokhorov) on film and television genres of the late Soviet era.

Peter Rollberg is Professor of Slavic Languages, Film Studies, and International Affairs at George Washington University in Washington, DC. He earned his PhD in 1988 at the University of Leipzig and came to GWU in 1991 after teaching at Duke University. His publications include articles on nineteenth- and twentieth-century Russian literature and Soviet cinema. In 1999–2001 he chaired the German and Slavic department and in and 2006–2009, the Department of Romance, German, and Slavic Languages and Literatures. In 2000–2010, he directed the GWU Film Studies Program. He has been Director of the Institute for European, Russian, and Eurasian Studies since 2012. In 2009, Rollberg published the *Historical Dictionary of Russian and Soviet Cinema.*

Masha Salazkina is Concordia University Research Chair in Transnational Media Art and Culture, and Associate Professor of Film Studies at the Mel Hoppenheim School of Cinema (Montreal, Canada). She is the author of *In Excess: Sergei Eisenstein's Mexico* (2009) and has recently co-edited the collection *Sound, Speech, Music in Soviet and Post-Soviet Cinema* (2014). Her current book project traces a trajectory of materialist film theory through the discourses of early Soviet cinema, institutional film cultures of the 1930s–1950s Italy, and critical debates surrounding the emergence of New Cinemas in Latin America.

Oksana Sarkisova is permanent Research Fellow at Blinken Open Society Archives at Central European University (Budapest), co-founder of the Visual Studies Platform at CEU (2014), and Director of the International Human Rights Documentary

Film Festival Verzio. She earned her PhD in History at CEU, and published widely on Soviet and Russian cinema and amateur photography. She has co-edited *Past for the Eyes: East European Representations of Communism in Cinema and Museums after 1989* (2008). Her monograph *Screening Soviet Nationalities: Kulturfilms from the Far North to Central Asia* is forthcoming in 2016.

Dawn Seckler is the Associate Director at the University of Pittsburgh's Center for Russian and European Studies (REES) and the Executive Director of the Slavic, East European, and Near Eastern Summer Language Institute (SLI). She earned her MA and PhD degrees from Pitt's Department of Slavic Languages and Literatures. Before returning to Pittsburgh in 2013 to join REES, she held Visiting Assistant Professorships at Sewanee: University of the South (2009–2010) and Williams College (2010–2012). Her scholarly interests center on the contemporary Russian film making industry with a particular focus on genre cinema.

Richard Taylor is Emeritus Professor of Politics at Swansea University in Wales. He is the author of numerous articles and books on Soviet cinema, including *The Politics of the Soviet Cinema, 1917–1929, Film Propaganda: Soviet Russia & Nazi Germany* and studies of Eisenstein's films, *The Battleship Potemkin* and *October*. He co-edited *The Film Factory: Russian & Soviet Cinema in Documents, 1896–1939, Inside the Film Factory: New Approaches to Russian & Soviet Cinema, Eisenstein Rediscovered* and *Stalinism and Soviet Cinema* and edited and part-translated Eisenstein's *Selected Works* in English and is General Editor of the Tauris KINO series.

Emma Widdis is associate professor in Russian Studies at the University of Cambridge, and a Fellow of Trinity College. Her publications include *Visions of a New Land: Soviet Film from the Revolution to the Second World War* (2003), and *Alexander Medvedkin* (2004); she is the editor, with Simon Franklin, of *National Identity in Russian Culture* (2004; Russian edition 2014), as well as numerous articles on Soviet cinema and culture. Widdis is currently completing a monograph tracing the hidden history of the Soviet project for the "re-education of the senses" and film's part in that project. She has recently set up the Cambridge Russian Sensory History Network (www.crush.group.cam.ac.uk), an international research forum for scholars of 'sensory history' in Russia.

Denise J. Youngblood is Professor of Russian History at the University of Vermont, specializing in the history of Russian and Soviet cinema, especially the relationship between popular films and Soviet society. She has published numerous articles and seven books, the most recent of are *Russian War Films: On the Cinema Front, 1914–2005* (2007), *Cinematic Cold War: The Soviet and American Struggle for Hearts and Minds* (2010, ed. with Tony Shaw), and *Bondarchuk's War and Peace: Literary Classic to Soviet Cinematic Epic* (2014). She is presently writing a critical history of Russian cinema with Olga Klimova.

Eugénie Zvonkine is a senior lecturer in cinema in University Paris 8. She has published a monograph *Kira Mouratova, un cinéma de la dissonance* (2012) as well as many chapters in edited volumes and papers in peer-reviewed journals on films by Kira Muratova and on other filmmakers from the stagnation period, as well as on contemporary Russian cinema. She has published *Watch your Films Attentively*, Kira Muratova's unrealised script (*Studies in Russian and Soviet Cinema* 8.1, 2014). She is currently co-editing two volumes on the cinema of perestroika and on contemporary Russian cinema, and is writing a monograph on Aleksei Gherman Senior.

Acknowledgments

I would like to thank above all, the staff at Wiley Blackwell – Jayne Fargnoli and Julia Kirk first and foremost – for venturing on this project and for their incredible patience. This has been a challenging and exciting project, and my thanks go to all the contributors who have delivered in style. And I thank my late mother, without whose encouragement I would probably not have taken on this daunting task.

Notes on Transliteration and References

Transliteration

Transliteration from the Cyrillic to the Latin alphabet is a perennial problem for writers on Russian subjects. I have followed the Library of Congress transliteration systems throughout, with a few exceptions for the main text (not the references): all film studios have dropped the soft sign in the "-fil'm," so we have Mosfilm, Lenfilm, *kulturfilm*, etc.; I have used accepted English spelling for place names (Nevsky Prospect, the town of Gorky, etc.) and borrowed names (Meyerhold, Iosseliani, etc.); we have used the spelling Gherman for the director's name, to distinguish from the "German" soldiers who appear in his films; however, in the references these names are transliterated according to Library of Congress (e.g. Ioseliani, German).

References

All references to archives are abbreviated as follows: fond, inventory [opis'], document number: sheet.

Introduction

Birgit Beumers

Rather than ambitiously aim at the impossible – a comprehensive account of Russian cinema – this *Companion to Russian Cinema* is designed to provide different histories of Russian and Soviet cinema. It deliberately refrains from using an overarching chronological approach, while covering the cinema of pre-Revolutionary Russia, of the Soviet era, as well as post-Soviet cinema. The volume offers a range of lenses or prisms through which films, filmmakers, and film history/histories are viewed. Thus, I hope, the book will cater for a variety of disciplines beyond the traditional Film Studies and Russian Studies.

The *Companion* provides five sets of studies – of films, periods, production mechanisms, cultural and historical contexts, and filmmakers in Russia and the Soviet Union. It refers to Russian-language films of the Soviet republics only in passing, without aiming at a wider coverage of these interesting cinematographies: after all, that would be a different companion altogether. This volume does not aim to rewrite either Soviet film history into Soviet-Russian film history, or turning post-Soviet cinematic history into that of the now independent republics. Furthermore, this book deals primarily with feature films, and therefore neglects the areas of documentary film and animation, as well as television production.

The Field

Let us first look at the field of scholarship on Russian and Soviet cinema, which has grown fast and substantially over the past 25 years. While Soviet/Russian cinema tended to be rather understudied, recent years have seen a surge in publications on the topic.

A Companion to Russian Cinema, First Edition. Edited by Birgit Beumers.
© 2016 John Wiley & Sons, Inc. Published 2016 by John Wiley & Sons, Inc.

Above all, there are several directories, providing brief information on films and filmmakers, such as *The BFI Companion to Eastern European and Russian Cinema* (2000), and the *Directory of World Cinema: Russia* (2011) and its sequel *Directory of World Cinema: Russia 2* (2015), as well as Peter Rollberg's *A-Z / Historical Dictionary of Russian and Soviet Cinema* (2009). In terms of history, the field already becomes thinner: for almost half a century Jay Leyda's *Kino: A History of the Russian and Soviet Film* (1960) was the only text that offered a "history" of Russian and Soviet cinema. In 1991, *The Illustrated History of the Soviet Cinema* by the eminent Soviet film scholar Neya Zorkaya complemented and updated Leyda's book. Beumers' *A History of Russian Cinema* (2009) provides a chronological survey of the various periods of Soviet and Russian film history, highlighting the key events, films, and filmmakers. Moreover, there are several textbooks on Russian cinema, including David Gillespie's *Russian Cinema* (2003), which follows a thematic approach to the study of Russian cinema, and Beumers' *24 Frames: The Cinema of Russia and the Former Soviet Union* (2007), with 24 case studies of Russian and Soviet films.

Distinct historical periods have been covered quite unevenly in scholarship: quite significant and profound research (and cataloguing) has been accomplished on the early period of pre-Revolutionary cinema, especially by Yuri Tsivian in *Early Cinema in Russia and its Cultural Reception* (1994) and Denise Youngblood in *The Magic Mirror. Moviemaking in Russia, 1908–1918* (1999). Likewise, the 1920s have received focused attention in Phil Cavendish's *Soviet Mainstream Cinematography: The Silent Era* (2007) and *The Men with the Movie Camera* (2013) and David Gillespie's *Early Soviet Cinema: Innovation, Ideology and Propaganda* (2000). Individual filmmakers of this era have also been studied in monographs, such as Jeremy Hicks's *Dziga Vertov: Defining Documentary Film* (2007), Anne Nesbet's *Savage Junctures. Sergei Eisenstein and the Shape of Thinking*, (2003), Mike O'Mahony's *Sergei Eisenstein* (2008), Masha Salazkina's *In Excess: Sergei Eisenstein's Mexico* (2009), Amy Sargeant's *Vsevolod Pudovkin: Classic Films of the Soviet Avant-Garde* (2001), George Liber's *Alexander Dovzhenko: A Life in Soviet Film* (2002), and Emma Widdis's *Alexander Medvedkin* (2005). Documents pertaining to the period and the writings of Eisenstein and Vertov have been published, most notably in editions by Annette Michelson and Richard Taylor; and film politics of the 1920s (and beyond) have been studied extensively in such works as Richard Taylor's *Film Propaganda: Soviet Russia and Nazi Germany* (1998 [1979]), Denise Youngblood's *Soviet Cinema in the Silent Era, 1918–1935* (1985) and *Movies for the Masses: Popular Cinema and Soviet Society in the 1920s* (1992), and Peter Kenez's *Cinema and Soviet Society, 1917–1953* (1992).

The Stalin era has been the subject of a range of monographs, including Emma Widdis's *Visions of a New Land: Soviet Film from the Revolution to the Second World War* (2003), John Haynes's *New Soviet Man: Gender and Masculinity in Stalinist Soviet Cinema* (2003), Evgeny Dobrenko's *Stalinist Cinema and the Production of History* (2008), Jamie Miller's *Soviet Cinema: Politics and Persuasion under Stalin* (2010), and Lilya Kaganovsky's *How the Soviet Man was Unmade* (2008), as well as Jeremy Hicks's pioneering study *First Films of the Holocaust: Soviet Cinema and the Genocide of the Jews, 1938–46* (2012).

The Thaw and the Stagnation period are, in a sense, the "stepchildren" of Soviet film history: apart from Josephine Woll's seminal study of Thaw cinema, *Real Images: Soviet Cinema and the Thaw* (2000), there are only a few publications in Russian, such as Alexander Prokhorov's *Inherited Discourse* (2007), and a huge number of articles and books on Andrei Tarkovskii, but very little on other filmmakers of the period, aside from two monographs on Kira Muratova (Taubmann, 2005; Zvonkine 2012), one on Sergei Paradjanov (Steffen 2013), and a book on the comedy filmmaker El'dar Riazanov by David MacFadyen (2004). However, these studies focus largely on auteur filmmakers rather than mainstream directors.

The perestroika era, on the contrary, has received more attention than it might deserve when looking at that brief period from 1986 to 1991 with hindsight: this trend reflects more the general enthusiasm at the time for the liberalization of the arts in the Soviet Union and Eastern Europe than the genuine value of the films made. Think, for example, of Vasilii Pichul's *Little Vera* [*Malen'kaia Vera*, 1988], a cult film of the time, which seems quite ordinary and straightforward when watched today without an explanation of the various taboos that are being broken. There are several works devoted to the institutional changes, including George Faraday's *Revolt of the Filmmakers: The Struggle for Artistic Autonomy and the Fall of the Soviet Film Industry* (2000), which investigates the administrative reforms and the collapse of the industry. Andrew Horton and Michael Brashinsky put together the first volume on the "new" cinema, entitled *The Zero Hour: Glasnost and Soviet Cinema in Transition* (1992), and Anna Lawton wrote a seminal study of the era with her *Kinoglasnost: Soviet Cinema in Our Time* (1992), which remains a standard reference book.

The chaotic Yeltsin years (1990s), which saw first a massive increase in film production on the basis of money-laundering, followed by the collapse of the entire infrastructure of production and distribution, have been addressed in Beumers' collection *Russia on Reels: The Russian Idea in Post-Soviet Cinema* (1999) and in Anna Lawton's *Imaging Russia 2000: Film and Facts* (2004). The emergence of a post-Soviet cinema and its development under Putin in the 2000s have formed fertile ground for publications, which include such volumes as Yana Hashamova's monograph *Pride and Panic: Russian Imagination of the West in Post-Soviet Film* (2007) on images of the west in cinema, or *Russia and its Other(s) on Film* (2008), edited by Stephen Hutchings, which explores the image of Russia created in foreign film and Russia's images of abroad – a topic also investigated in Stephen Norris and Zara Torlone's edited collection *Insiders and Outsiders in Russian Cinema* (2008). Norris also published *Blockbuster History in the New Russia* (2012), investigating mainstream cinema of the 2000s and the representation of history on screen in the Putin era.

Some themes have drawn the attention of scholars, such as the father/son relation, which is studied in Helena Goscilo and Yana Hashamova's collection *Cinepaternity: Fathers and Sons in Soviet and Post-Soviet Cinema* (2010). Denise

Youngblood has published an excellent and comprehensive study of the war film, *Russian War Films: On the Cinema Front, 1914–2005* (2007), and Nancy Condee's groundbreaking study of the cultural ambitions of the 1990s and 2000s, *The Imperial Trace: Recent Russian Cinema* (2009) offers discussions of the most significant auteurs of the past 20 years, focusing on their attitude to national identity. There are hardly any monographs on individual filmmakers of the period (and one might argue it is too early for that), with the exceptions of Nikita Mikhalkov (Beumers 2005) and Aleksandr Sokurov (edited volume by Beumers and Condee 2011; Szaniawski 2014).

Within this field we can therefore identify several areas that could usefully be complemented and explored in depth: first, there is a dearth of writing on the Thaw and Stagnation cinema (1960s and 1970s), a period which saw the emergence of popular, mainstream cinema and the rivalry between silver and blue screens. Second, there is an over-emphasis in scholarship on the filmmakers Eisenstein, Paradjanov, and Tarkovskii followed closely by Sokurov, Mikhalkov, and – recently – Muratova, while there is hardly anything in English on key figures, such as Iakov Protazanov or Boris Barnet from the early Soviet era; on the comedy and mainstream filmmakers of the Stagnation era, such as Leonid Gaidai; on the auteurs Aleksei Gherman and Andrei Zviagintsev; and many others. There is also an absence of studies on popular and mainstream cinema (or "cinema for the masses") beyond the 1920s, and thus also on genre cinema.

The *Companion* aims to fill some of those gaps by adopting a range of prisms, which allow wider coverage. In order to accomplish this task of "filling gaps" by using a number of lenses with which to view film history, I have opted for a structure that avoids an overall chronology, but highlights the most important aspects of film production and consumption, without attempting a full coverage of single themes or individual periods.

The Project and its Structure

The *Companion* is divided into five Parts, which are organized thematically to cover a variety of aspects that are traditionally neglected in film histories and scholarship. Each of these Parts attempts, within itself, to observe some chronological order or sense of progression, although the sections are not intended to offer full coverage of a particular aspect through the essays they contain. Therefore, the *Companion* will no doubt have gaps, precisely in those areas that have already received scholarly attention, while it aims to fill some gaps and, at the same time, open new areas for investigation.

Part 1 is devoted to institutional structures of production and exhibition, formation and training in the film sector. Since these structures were established in the early years of the emerging film industry, the section focuses on the first part of the twentieth century – the defining moment when the agendas were set. An institutional history of the Russian and Soviet film industry at large has still to be written, especially the history of individual film studios. Publications in this field have so far tended to focus on the early (pre-Revolutionary) period, with a focus on the emergence of cinemas in Moscow and St Petersburg (Mikhailov 2003; Kovalova and Tsiv'ian 2011; both in Russian), and on the later, Soviet era (Golovskoy and Rimberg 1986). The chief concern of this Part, therefore, is the relationship between the state as producer and the product film: how is the institutional infrastructure shaped, before and after the Revolution – through the establishment of a cinema network, through training, and through the foundation of film studios. Specifically, the section investigates the formation of film studios, both at a local level (Leningrad), with a remit of addressing a specific target audience (children), and of developing a genre (the documentary expedition film); and it delves into the formative years of the Film Institute VGIK, one of the oldest film schools in the world. The study of the history of central and regional film studios is only beginning, as for example through articles on Buryat and Yakut cinema (Damiens 2015; Dobrynin 2015) or the edited volume on Mezhrabpomfilm (Agde and Schwarz 2012, in German). Of course, there are the excellent Russian-language editions of documents on the history of Lenfilm, published in the 1970s (Gornitskaia 1968, 1970, 1973, 1975), or on the history of the Film Institute (Vinogradov and Bondarenko 2006; Vinogradov and Ognev 2000, 2004; Vinogradov and Riabchikova 2013). Petr Bagrov has ventured into the field with a publication of the curriculum of KEM, the experimental workshop set up by Fridrikh Ermler in the 1920s in Leningrad (Bonitenko and Georgievskaya 2012). Indeed, each chapter here covers a key moment or a key location, to offer a glimpse into areas that might attract further attention and scholarship.

The Part opens with a chapter on the film palaces on Nevsky Prospect, St Petersburg's main artery, during the pre-Revolutionary era. Anna Kovalova, who has done extensive research into this period, examines early Russian film culture through a history of the cinemas on Nevsky Prospect: their audiences, their distribution system, and their architectural development as entertainment venues competing with the imperial theaters. Since St Petersburg was not only the capital but also a cultural center, this analysis reveals the way in which the cinema developed from a fairground attraction to a solid artistic medium, and how it suffered from trade restrictions during the Great War. By focusing on venues, Kovalova allows us to retrace the history of cinema locations, as many of these palaces survived into the Soviet era and beyond. The Aurora (formerly Piccadilly), the Khudozhestvennyi (formerly Saturn) and the Neva operate on Nevsky to the present day, while the Parisiana and the Coliseum recently closed, because these central cinemas could no longer compete with the multiplexes. Through the prism of the development of these cinemas we see the emergence of a film culture that would change and perish, but ultimately define the spectatorship of the cinema for a century to come, appealing to almost all classes. Moreover, we see the role of film as a means for propaganda, and the interventions of the censor for both political and ethical reasons.

If cinema was born before the Revolution, the institutions for training people in the trade and the art were formed only after the nationalization of the industry with the famous State Film Institute VGIK, the first specialized film school in the world. With courses led by the key figures of Soviet cinema, including Lev Kuleshov and Sergei Eisenstein, VGIK soon shaped the reputation of film education. Masha Salazkina's chapter explores the early stages of the school's development in administrative and pedagogical terms. VGIK is still a leading film school today: consider for a moment the strange fact that the 2015 Oscar nominee for Best Foreign-Language Film Abderrahmane Sissako (for the film *Timbuktu*) is a graduate of VGIK, while his fellow competitor Andrei Zviagintsev (representing Russia with *Leviathan*) is not. Indeed, other graduates include Siddiq Barmak (Afghanistan) and Anders Banke (Sweden), alongside Konrad Wolf (GDR, brother of the Stasi spy Markus Wolf), whose family had left Germany when the Nazis took power in 1933 – like so many left-wing artists, including Erwin Piscator. Salazkina reconstructs the institutional history of the emerging film institute, ascertaining its role in early Soviet film culture. The chapter focuses on changes in the organizational structure and curriculum of the Institute in relation to the political and cultural shifts in the Soviet Union; pedagogical practices and cultural ideologies; the role of the pioneers of early Soviet cinema in the pedagogical and curricular development; the relationship between film production and film education; experimental projects associated with the institute, and the institutionalization of film studies as a scholarly discipline. Thus, Salazkina sheds light on the role of VGIK in the defining years of Soviet cinema, the 1920s and 1930s. Her chapter has particular resonance at a time when new, independent film schools are on the rise, such as Moscow's School of New Cinema, with a liberal agenda and a series of high-profile invited speakers, producing a new generation of filmmakers whose professional competence remains to be tested against the traditional, state-run Film Institute (which has the status of a university).

There follow three chapters on film studios: on Lenfilm and the Gorky Children's Film Studio, both formed in the early years of the Soviet film industry; and the studio Vostokfilm that was largely responsible for the production of the *kulturfilm*, an important genre for Soviet cinema in the late 1920s and designed largely to provide a view on the new territories of the Soviet empire and thus to shape a Soviet identity. Lenfilm is the country's second-largest studio, after Mosfilm in Moscow – which awaits its own history to be written. Both studios were established in the 1920s, and they distinguished themselves with their association with the city and their specific styles – Mosfilm associated more with serious acting techniques (based on the psychologism prevalent at the Moscow Art Theatre) and Lenfilm functioning as the cradle for the experimental FEKS (Factory of the Eccentric Actor), famous for its exaggerated body movements, comedic acting and extrovert character psychology. Robert Bird identifies the characteristics of Lenfilm and surveys the studio's output over the twentieth century in order to define the studio's handwriting and signature. Bird discusses to what degree Lenfilm possessed a distinctive aesthetic face and functional autonomy at different moments of its history, and how the studio managed to bring forth a number of auteur filmmakers, including Kira Muratova, Aleksei Gherman and Aleksei Balabanov. In the 1930s the studio gained a reputation for its politically loyal films with mass appeal, including the Vasil'ev brothers' *Chapaev* (1934) and the more serious work of Fridrikh Ermler. In recent years Lenfilm has made the headlines, because the studio base has been crumbling, in bad need of repair, and appeals from its key modern-day auteurs Aleksandr Sokurov and Aleksei Gherman have done nothing to ensure the studio's survival. The Gorky Film Studio, on the other hand, played a significant role in creating children's film as one of the world's first studios to be devoted to producing films for children – and often with child actors. Jeremy Hicks explores the establishment and development of Soiuzdetfilm, which later became the Gorky Film Studio, tracing the studio's defining moments through the Maksim Gor'kii trilogy films of Mark Donskoi, which led to the studio being named after the famous writer. Hicks explores the Soviet attitudes to children and children's entertainment as seen through these productions. Oksana Sarkisova traces the genealogy of the kulturfilm and its development in the Soviet Union in the 1920s and early 1930s. The concept, originally transferred from the German film industry, was applied in the Soviet Union to non-fiction films with an educational or agitational value, although filmmakers often moved between non-fiction and fiction. For the industry these films were of small significance, because they had limited public appeal, but they were made to justify the educational mission of cinema and acquaint audiences with the newly acquired Soviet territories in the Far East and Central Asia, as such providing some unique ethnographic footage.

This Part therefore opens avenues for further exploration of studio and institutional histories as areas that allow a fuller understanding of the mechanisms and motivations behind the production of certain film genres in the early Soviet period. The history of early animation, for example, is one such area that is in need of research, as is the story of the republican and regional studios.

Part II explores film "consumption" and addresses issues of audience taste and genre expectations, but also the way in which critics can manipulate audience taste. The chapters delve into different genres, ranging from the mass musical of the Stalin era to the popular comedies of the 1960s, and from questioning the role of auteur cinema in the Soviet film industry to the concept of the blockbuster in its Russian definition "blokbaster" – in order to investigate changes in cinema's relationship to the audience. Finally, the section presents a sociological analysis of the tropes that dominate Russian cinema, and to what extent their national features fit into the international (and co-production) market. This chapter draws extensively on research by Nevafilm Research, a company that compiles statistical data for the European Audiovisual Observatory, and the analysis has been carried out by two sociologists, thus adding a genuinely different angle to the established discourses on cinema as an industry.

If early Soviet film audiences had already voted with their feet for the American, fast-paced action movie over the complex montage work in Eisenstein's *Potemkin* (1925), then audience taste has dominated production issues even in the nationalized film industry that only seemingly could afford not to care about revenues. Indeed, the Soviet film industry cared a lot not only about meeting targets and fulfilling plans, but also about the profit that films made through ticket sales. Film criticism played a crucial role both in ideological terms, but also in the defense of auteur cinema when it arose in the post-war era, echoing similar developments in European cinema (Italian Neorealism, French New Wave). A topic that we her only touch upon in passing is the role of the film critic in Soviet film history – one that would also provide an interesting lens for the study of film history: is the critic's voice that of the state or of the viewer? In the post-Soviet era, mainstream commercial, or genre, cinema – the antagonists of high culture in the Soviet discourse – came to the fore, and now dominates Russian screens, with Russia having developed to be the sixth largest film market in the world.

Therefore, the Part focuses in a sense on what we might call "genre" cinema: Richard Taylor examines the Stalinist musical as a paradigm of Soviet cinema as an art "intelligible to the millions," following the failure of the revolutionary avant-garde to engage successfully with the audiences in the 1920s. The method of Socialist Realism, adopted officially in 1934, looked forward to a bright socialist future, to a fairy tale that would (actually never) become true. The advent of sound made possible a different form of mass entertainment from what had prevailed in the silent era, and the genre of the "musical comedy," partly adopted from American cinema, played a significant role in that appeal, powerfully combining words and music. A catchy and uplifting tune meant that audiences would remember the songs and repeat with them the film's ideological message. Taylor examines the major themes of these Stalinist musicals and the influence of Hollywood, which was indeed used as a template even in the organization of film production, aiming at the creation of a "Soviet Hollywood." Seth Graham further explores the genre of the film comedy in the Soviet Union and the shape it took after Stalin's death. The comedy of the 1950s and 1960s differed from its predecessor of the 1920s, and played an important role during the liberalization indicated by Khrushchev's Thaw, and in particular the emergence of popular culture (as opposed to high-brow Soviet art) of the post-Stalinist era. Graham's chapter goes beyond the traditional key figures of El'dar Riazanov and Leonid Gaidai, paying attention to such filmmakers as Elem Klimov, Georgii Daneliia, and the master of Stalinist film comedy, Grigorii Aleksandrov, whose later films are a good example of how comedy films of the time announced a new era. The cinematic Thaw that privileged comedy ended with the Stagnation, which is characterized by a more cynical outlook on life.

While musicals and comedies were part of mainstream culture, following genre conventions and attracting large audiences, the post-war era also saw the rise of auteur cinema's best known figures, including Andrei Tarkovskii, Kira Muratova and Sergei Paradjanov. Eugénie Zvonkine discusses the notion of auteur cinema as set out by the *Cahiers du Cinéma* group in the late 1950s with reference to Soviet practices. The "auteur theory" stresses the signature of the cinematic author, an idea which at first sight appears to contradict the collective spirit of socialist work. The rise of the "auteur" can be considered as part of a larger counter-culture movement that took shape during the late 1950s and 1960s and is also manifest in concepts such as *avtorskaia pesnia* [auteur song] and *avtorskii teatr* [auteur theater]. Moreover, it profoundly breaks with the totalitarian approach to Soviet cinema that imagines the Soviet film industry as a single monolithic block. Non-linear storytelling, often presenting events out of chronological order, as well as striking experimental camera-work are some of the characteristics of auteur cinema that substantially undermine the conventions of Socialist Realism with its requirement for a linear narrative and realistic shots.

If auteur cinema dwelt on the right for the artist to express himself, and frequently got filmmakers into trouble with censorship, then the collapse of the Soviet Union – and with it of the cinema infrastructure and the film industry – necessitated a sharp turn: indeed, filmmakers seemed to have almost forgotten about audiences and their taste while continuing (especially in the early 1990s) to make films for an ever-dwindling number of people who visited the few remaining cold cinemas. This decline in film production and the divide between filmmaker and his/her audience continued until the film industry landed back on its feet in the 2000s, notably with the watershed blockbuster *Night Watch* [*Nochnoi dozor*, 2004; dir. Timur Bekmambetov]. Dawn Seckler examines the epithet "blockbuster," which describes a big-budget film, commonly a Hollywood product, within the Russian context. Nikita Mikhalkov's *Barber of Siberia* [*Sibirskii tsiriul'nik"*, 1998] was the first post-Soviet film that was styled as a Hollywood blockbuster, even if it was a box-office flop. Seckler's chapter scrutinizes the Russian blockbuster as a historically determined mode of film production marked by a distinct narrative, certain stylistic and production features, as well as marketing strategies employed to launch films into stratospheric popularity. She also sets out the debates surrounding the concept of the blockbuster as a savior to the once fledgling film industry and reversing the effectual demise of Russian cinema in the 1990s. The final chapter in Part II offers a sociological analysis of data compiled by one of the leading analytical agencies for Russian cinema, Nevafilm Research, whose staff members Xenia Leontyeva and Maria Bezenkova have kindly contributed to this volume in order to provide a different view on the way in which new Russian cinema is developing in a global context. The globalization of information and the entertainment industries has played a significant part after the collapse of the Soviet Union, which coincided with the start of a new phase in the global revolution in communications. This chapter explores tropes that articulate a national identity for the new, post-Soviet Russia in the face of an intensification of globalizing trends. Four distinct modes define the way in which post-Soviet Russian cinema addresses "national" themes: international co-productions of films with Russian directors; Russian-produced films aimed specifically at a global audience; Russian films pitched to a domestic audience but dominated by global genres, tropes and formats; and films drawing on domestic cinematic traditions, but enjoying nevertheless success at international film festivals.

Part II thus addresses in chronological order the issue of genre: to what extent genre fits with ideology, to what extent it helps relate to an audience. As a consequence, the chapters raise questions about the lack of a discussion of genre during the Soviet era, when the concept of genre was regarded by critics as a value-deflating term for films that failed to express their dissent with the system through coded visual language and metaphors, and therefore appealed to mass audiences. This aspect of the "genre" debate has been discussed by Dawn Seckler in her introduction to the – genre driven – first edition of the *Directory of World Cinema: Russia* (in Beumers 2011, 28–33).

Part III investigates (or rather, creates) the history of technical developments in Russian cinema, an area that is often neglected in scholarship, although recent years have seen some attention focus on such aspects as camera work (Cavendish 2007, 2013a, 2013b) and sound (Kaganovsky and Salazkina 2014). Part III looks at the technological infrastructure, especially the way in which sound and color have changed the way in which films were made and shown, but also the role of other film crew in the creation of the film. Thus, the chapters discuss the role of the scriptwriter in the production process; the work of the production designer and costume designer; the work of cinematographers and how they frequently transferred their experience into the profession of the filmmaker; and the role of sound technology. Through an investigation of the technical infrastructure, which is a key part of the cinematic process, the chapters shed a different light on the way in which cinema developed in its early years; therefore, most chapters are concerned with developments in the formative years of the film industry – the 1920s and 1930s.

The script is maybe the single, most neglected aspect in Soviet film history, as history has traditionally focused on directors (especially auteurs) and actors, even neglecting commercial, mainstream cinema. Maria Belodubrovskaya addresses this key area, analyzing the perpetual shortage of film scripts during the Stalin era – a condition known as the "script crisis." She argues that, rather than the script crisis being the result of an inability to write ideologically suitable scripts, it was the result of a lack of a Hollywood-style division of labor in film production and writing. Studios kept no staff writers, and film directors often wrote their own shooting scripts or rewrote original screenplays that had been approved for production. As a result, studio outputs were unpredictable and many films banned upon completion. The Soviet film industry therefore considered the screenplay as an independent work of literature, written by established, freelance writers. This worsened the situation, as writers insisted on their authorship and resisted censorship; and once their screenplays had been rejected, they were reluctant to submit new works. This peculiar status of the scriptwriter had a long-lasting impact on the Soviet and post-Soviet film industry, and to some extent continues until the present day, where scriptwriters write "literary" scripts rather than shooting scripts, while directors continue to adapt the texts for their own purposes. An obvious case would be the rewriting of the original script for a film such as Andrei Zviagintsev's *The Return* [*Vozvrashchenie*, 2003], originally written as a crime drama.

Similar constraints apply to the development of sound and color in the Soviet Union, as it had to invent its own technology and patents when imports from the West became impossible because of Stalin's isolationism in the 1930s. Thus, for example, Technicolor's three-color system was not available for the Soviet film industry, while the production of film stock and cameras in the USSR lagged behind and the country depended largely on imported tools. While tinting and toning of film stock was widely practiced in pre-Revolutionary Russian films as well as in other film industry, the development of additive and subtractive processes for color films took a different turn in the USSR to the rest of the world. Phil Cavendish studies the history of color cinematography in Soviet cinema in the 1930s, which was barely known in Europe and North America at the time, and is even less well known in relation to Soviet film history. The chapter looks at the two-color processes used in the late 1920s and early 1930s to create the first Soviet color film; at experiments with other methods that produced color films that have been relegated to the archives because they depend on obsolescent projection equipment; and at the acquisition of the Agfa three-color process as a "spoil of war" thanks to the Red Army in 1945. Soviet color film stock was produced only during the 1950s and 1960s, following the move to Russia of the production base from Agfa's Wolfen plant after the war. On the other hand, Lilya Kaganovsky explores the arrival of sound in Soviet cinema: she delves into experiments with drawn sound before studying the impact of sound on the aesthetics of the films of the 1930s. The role of music is not discussed in Part III since this topic has been studied separately elsewhere, receiving the full and chronological exploration it deserves: some of the seminal studies here are Tatiana Egorova's *Soviet Film Music* (1997), Kevin Bartig's *Composing for the Red Screen: Prokofiev and Soviet Film* (2013) and John Riley's *Dmitri Shostakovich* (2005). Part III also neglects the development of special effects in Soviet cinema – a hitherto neglected area of scholarship, yet one that was once ahead of the American industry (see Kapterev 2016; Beumers 2016).

The following two chapters focus on the role of costume and set design in the 1920s, exploring some rare archival films and materials. Emma Widdis considers the evolution of the role of the set designer, the particularities of pre-Revolutionary set design, and the evolution of the discipline in the Soviet era. She addresses two issues: first, theoretical enquiries into the nature of the filmic representation of reality and how the camera could capture and/or transform reality; and second, the role of set design and dress in developing models of the film-making collective. Djurdja Bartlett continues this exploration of costume designs by exploring the looks of film actresses on screen and in public life during the 1920s and 1930s. Politically and aesthetically, these two decades differed considerably and therefore informed different styles in dress and looks on and off the screen. Thus, in the 1920s, the aesthetics of the avant-garde were echoed in the costumes designed by Aleksandra Ekster for *Aelita* in 1924, while the influence of western cinema is visible in the costumes of Aleksandra Khokhlova, whose extravagant and geometrically cut dresses by Nadezhda Lamanova reflect a modernist kind of glamour. In the 1930s, such glamour acquired a new guise, serving the Stalinist need to mask a rather harsh reality. The most famous star Liubov' Orlova played parts where she covered the grim reality through costume and glamour, cultivating a star-like appearance off the screen as well. Through an analysis of costume and set we can see the way in which a new reality was shaped on screen and guises were used to conceal the problems in the implementation of socialism in everyday life. The issue of concealment, and of creating utopian visions on the screen, will return in a different context in the discussion of the way in which urban spaces were molded to form specific visions of nationalism and internationalism in Part IV.

In the final chapter in Part III, Peter Rollberg explores the role of some outstanding cinematographers, or cameramen, who – at some point in their careers – decided to turn to directing. While the reasons for such role changes behind the camera varied, the directorial outputs of former cameramen share a heightened attention to visual aspects of filmmaking, sometimes even at the expense of narrative cohesion, acting, or psychological verisimilitude. Rollberg explores, among others, the work of Sergei Eisenstein's cameraman Eduard Tissé, who co-directed the war drama *The Immortal Garrison* (1958), and of the legendary Sergei Urusevskii, who served as cameraman on Mikhail Kalatozov's *The Cranes Are Flying* (1957), inspiring a generation of cameramen with his expressive and dynamic style. Thus, Rollberg takes the excellent and thorough work by Philip Cavendish on the men behind the camera one step further, looking at their – almost always failed – attempts to translate their technical experience into artistic language. This, in turn, reflects the strong role of the director as author (and the concept of auteurism) discussed in the previous Part.

Part IV investigates place – center and periphery, Moscow and Leningrad/St Petersburg – and time – the settings of films in specific historical periods. Soviet cinema, like any other world cinema, has always turned to the past to explore the present. The prominence of the past, and patterns revealed in such returns to the past, as well as issues related to the absence of the present from the silver screen, form a curious subject for investigation. These issues have been addressed partly in scholarly publications, most notably Youngblood's *Russian War Films: On the Cinema Front, 1914–2005* (2007) and Norris' *Blockbuster History in the New Russia* (2012). This Part focuses on two crucial moments of Soviet history: the Revolution (and Civil War), and World War II. Only here we have inverted the roles: Denise J. Youngblood examines three of the most important revolutionary films of the 1930s: Georgii and Sergei Vasil'ev's *Chapaev* (1934), Efim Dzigan's *We are from*

Kronstadt [*My iz Kronshtadta*, 1936], and Aleksandr Dovzhenko's *Shchors* (1939). Youngblood demonstrates that Soviet directors worked within various strictures of Socialist Realism in this era. In the heyday of the revolutionary genre in the 1920s, the emphasis was overwhelmingly on mass action rather than individual heroes. In the 1930s, revolutionary films were not as numerous as they had been in the preceding decade, but each film made a greater impact, especially *Chapaev*, Stalin's favorite film and a benchmark for film production to come, which highlights that it was possible to incorporate the Party line in an entertaining film. With the advent of the Great Terror, however, the stakes for producing a politically correct film were much higher. These films represent an evolving view of the foundation myth of Soviet history over the 1930s through heroes ranging from an anarchic, barely literate Civil War commander to a bunch of sailors to the revolutionary hero Shchors. In his turn, Stephen Norris examines the war film, which traditionally occupies an important place in the history of Russian cinema. The chapter surveys a handful of important war films in order to chart the ways in which they have stressed the defense of the motherland as a quintessential aspect of Russian nationhood. If the Soviet Civil War film had offered audiences the possibility to empathize with heroes defending their socialist motherland, this function gained significance in the Great Patriotic War (1941–1945), when movies tended to cast a Soviet heroine to represent Mother Russia. Post-war films explored this patriotism further, while also delving into the price of the conflict. Stagnation-era films tended to stress once again the patriotic defense of the motherland, a theme that continued into post-Soviet cinema. Thus, the Russian war film has served as an important site where nationhood gets constructed, rebuilt, and disseminated.

The Part continues by exploring locations for films, a topic that received some interest recently with the publication of a series on *World Film Locations* (intellect books). The images of cities and regions, of the provinces and foreign lands, and what these images tell us about the geographies of life lie at the heart of these investigations. Thus, for example, the city of St Petersburg (formerly Leningrad) is largely absent from the screen in the Soviet era, while Moscow dominates the screen and is usually associated with a movement towards the center rather than away from it; similarly, the provinces and outskirts are only used for certain kinds of narrative: adventure films, especially the "Red Western" often filmed in the wilderness of Central Asia. When, however, we look at western settings, the Soviet film industry (not wishing to engage in co-productions with Europe at the height of the Cold War), often used the Baltic states, especially Riga and Tallinn, as locations to represent "the West." These last chapters in Part IV explore two locations, on the periphery and the center, that played an important role in Soviet cinema: the city of Riga as an image of the "Other," as it often served as a setting for scenes supposedly taking place in the west; and the centre, Moscow, as an image of control, grandeur, and dominance. Kevin Platt examines the representation of Riga in post-war Soviet cinema, with special attention to Soviet center-periphery relations and to filmic representation of the West. When the Soviet Union annexed Latvia, Estonia, and Lithuania in 1940, it gained new urban centers; the Latvian capital Riga, with its range of typical European architectural elements, came to serve as one of the most important shooting locations for films set in "the West," a prominent location for spy thrillers, war films, and films comparing the socialist and capitalist worlds, from Grigorii Aleksandrov's *Meeting on the Elbe* [*Vstrecha na El'be*, 1949] to Igor' Maslennikov's popular television serial *Adventures of Sherlock Holmes and Dr. Watson* (1979–1986). At the same time, the Riga Film Studio emerged as a leading producer for documentary filmmaker Frank Herz and for Juris Podnieks' perestroika cult documentary film, *Is It Easy to be Young?* [*Vai viegli but jaunam?* 1987]. Platt explores how these developments fit onto the geo-political map of the Cold War and reflect the opposition between center and peripheries. In turn, Birgit Beumers focuses her attention on the center, Moscow, and examines the pivotal role of the capital in early Soviet cinema, before studying its temporary disappearance from the screen during the stagnation period and its reemergence as "Luzhkov's Moscow" in the late 1990s. Through an examination of the cinematic representation of urban locales, the chapter traces the shifts in political power and dominance, as well as the echo of social developments in an emphasis of center vs. suburbia and the characters' movements towards the capital or away from it. Ultimately, Beumers argues, the screen image of Moscow at key points in history is a utopia, a construction, or a vision, and – in more recent example – merely computer-generated images that replaces an apparently blank spot where power once converged.

Through an analysis of the way in which histories and geographies are constructed on the silver screen the authors of these chapters assess the guises created for absences of the "real thing": the real hero, the real Self/Other.

Part V of this *Companion* provides five portraits of key figures in Soviet and Russia film history, whose work has been somewhat neglected in film histories. One obvious example might have been Iakov Protazanov, whose name has been flagged up by Youngblood in her study of the 1920s (1992): he deserves closer investigation, which is possible now that many more of his films are accessible. Similarly, Fridrikh Ermler, who transformed from a Secret Police commissar to a popular filmmaker, forming his own workshop (KEM) in Leningrad in the 1920s, would surely make for an interesting study. There are numerous publications on cinematic heroes from the pre-Revolutionary era and key filmmakers of the avant-garde; the Stalinist musicals have been explored in a variety of studies (see especially Taylor 1996, 1999, 2000; Salys 2009); the key auteurs have had numerous publications devoted to their work – with the exception of Aleksei Gherman, who completed only five films; and Andrei Zviagintsev, whose career is still in progress. One might argue that filmmakers such as Marlen Khutsiev or Sergei Solov'ev also deserve more focused attention. The list of understudied filmmakers can be quite long, and the names will no doubt vary from individual to individual. I have no ambition of reaching a consensus here that the chosen five filmmakers are the "right" ones: the selection is ultimately dependant on individual contributors. So, the section offers five portraits of "understudied" directors, and they are presented in chronological order. Julian Graffy discusses the work of Boris Barnet, a professional boxer who began his cinematic career as an actor in Kuleshov's *The Extraordinary Adventures of Mr West in the Land of the Bolsheviks* [*Neobychainye prikliucheniia mistera Vesta v strane bol'shevikov*, 1924]. By 1926 he was working as co-director and co-scriptwriter with Fedor Otsep on the ideological adventure drama *Miss Mend*. His first independent film as a director, *The Girl with the Hatbox* [*Devushka s korobkoi*], followed in 1927. Over the course of the following 40 years, he made 25 feature films in a wide range of genres, from light romantic comedies to war films, from spy thriller to historical melodrama. The analysis of his oeuvre that spans from NEP (New Economic Policy) to the Thaw facilitates an examination of the relationship between politics and culture through the experience of a leading Soviet filmmaker. His combination of lyricism and social observation echoes the relationship between the Soviet cinematic process and an individual authorial voice. Jamie Miller discusses the work of Iulii Raizman, whose career spans a similar, but even longer, period than that of Barnet: Raizman made movies throughout the entire communist era. Miller examines Raizman's concern for the private space of families and individuals in a state preoccupied with collectivist ideology and his study of the relationship between the private and public. Raizman also sought to offer continuity with the pre-Revolutionary Russian cinematic traditions, dwelling on detailed character psychology and realistic and authentic set designs.

While Barnet and Raizman are interesting as filmmakers working over a long period of time, the "king of comedy," Leonid Gaidai, was the highest-grossing filmmaker of Soviet cinema, working mostly in the 1960s and 1970s. He made slapstick comedy the most popular genre on Soviet screens, even though his films are often shunned by critics as non-auteur stock. Elena Prokhorova discusses Gaidai's use of physical comedy and engagement with the "sacred cows" that he attacks in his ideologically not always impeccable films. Gaidai successfully created characters who became iconic figures; among them are the "three stooges" – the Coward, the Dumb One, and the Experienced One (played by the trio ViNiMor (Georgii Vitsyn, Iurii Nikulin and Evgenii Morgunov)). These comic icons linked official Soviet cinema with underground culture: Gaidai's stooges brought prison jargon, drinking jokes, and thieves' songs to Soviet cinemas and broadened the limits of what was permissible on Soviet screens. Prokhorova examines the key elements of Gaidai's style and the evolution of his reception in Soviet and post-Soviet culture.

Finally, we turn to two auteurs, both neglected in English-language scholarship. Anthony Anemone investigates the work of Aleksei Iur'evich Gherman (Gherman Senior), whose reputation stands, essentially, on five films made over four decades. In all these films Gherman is engaged in a double project: to represent Russian history of the twentieth century without any ideological presuppositions, while totally remaking the stylistic and narrative techniques of Russian cinema. A favorite of the Russian cultural elite, Gherman's career was hindered by the

Soviet authorities that rejected both his revisionist reinterpretation of the past and his revolutionary cinematic techniques. Hence, his films were delayed, shelved, or simply rarely shown in Soviet cinemas. Gherman's films are challenging, because they require the audience's familiarity with Soviet society and history, which may also account for his relative neglect in scholarship. Gherman tends to focus on aspects of the Soviet past that were either omitted or falsified in official historiography. Rejecting the style and narrative typical of Soviet historical cinema, Gherman combines episodic plots, hand-held cameras that are neither objective nor expressive, little or no non-diegetic music, overlapping dialog, and random noise with an almost fanatical insistence on getting the look, sound, and feel of the past right. Nancy Condee explores the work of the youngest auteur in Russian cinema, Andrei Zviagintsev, whose first feature film *The Return* won the Golden Lion at the Venice International Film Festival in 2003. His subsequent films have all gained international acclaim, right up to an Oscar nomination as Best Foreign Language Film for *Leviathan* in 2015 (which he lost to Pawel Pawlikowski's *Ida*), and have all had international distribution. Condee argues that Zviagintsev's feature films are all preoccupied with survival in a fallen world, rife with omens and portents that are no longer legible to the modern and secular protagonists. While not explicitly religious, his films are infused with a spiritual nostalgia that ties his work to the legacy of Tarkovskii. Eternal questions of elusive faith, uncertain loyalty, and family love beyond human competence recur in Zviagintsev's world, where characters often seem like outcasts from an earlier time when the state provided ethical guidance.

By offering, as it were, five alternative histories of Russian cinema – of its production infrastructure, its genre choices and audience relationship, its technological advances, its relationship to history and location, and through a series of filmmakers' portraits – taste, the *Companion* hopes to uncover new areas for investigation, and trigger exciting new research to fill, in turn, the gaps that will no doubt arise from this publication. The more holes we have laid bare, the better.

References

Agde, Günter and Alexander Schwarz, eds. 2012. *Die rote Traumfabrik. Meschrabpom-Film und Prometheus 1921–1936* [The Red Dream-Factory: Mezhrabpom and Prometheus, 1921–1936]. Berlin: Deutsche Kinemathek and Bertz+Fischer.

Bartig, Kevin. 2013. *Composing for the Red Screen: Prokofiev and Soviet Film*. New York: Oxford University Press.

Beumers, Birgit, ed. 1999. *Russia on Reels: The Russian Idea in Post-Soviet Cinema*. London: I. B. Tauris.

Beumers, Birgit. 2005. *Nikita Mikhalkov* (Kino Companion 1). London: I. B. Tauris.

Beumers, Birgit, ed. 2007. *24 Frames: The Cinema of Russia and the Former Soviet Union*. London and New York: Wallflower Press.

Beumers, Birgit. 2009. *A History of Russian Cinema*. Oxford and New York: Berg.

Beumers, Birgit, ed. 2011. *Directory of World Cinema: Russia*, Bristol and Chicago: intellect, University of Chicago Press

Beumers, Birgit, ed. 2015. *Directory of World Cinema: Russia 2*, Bristol and Chicago: intellect, University of Chicago Press

Beumers, Birgit. 2016. "Spatial/Special Effects in Soviet Cinema." In *Russian Aviation, Space Flight and Visual Culture*, edited by Vlad Strukov and Helena Goscilo, Abingdon and New York: Routledge.

Beumers Birgit and Nancy Condee, eds. 2011. *The Cinema of Alexander Sokurov*, London: I. B. Tauris.

Bonitenko, Adia and Larissa Georgievskaya, eds. 2012. "The Cinema-Experimental Workshop [Kinoeksperimental'naia masterskaia] in Documents," Preface by Peter Bagrov. *Studies in Russian and Soviet Cinema* 5.2: 277–326.

Cavendish, Phil. 2007. *Soviet Mainstream Cinematography: The Silent Era*. London: UCL Arts and Humanities Publications.

Cavendish, Phil. 2013a. "The Delirious Vision: The Vogue for the Hand-held Camera in Soviet Cinema of the 1920s." *Studies in Russian & Soviet Cinema* 7.1: 5–24.

Cavendish, Phil. 2013b. *The Men with the Movie Camera. The Poetics of Visual Style in Soviet Avant-Garde Cinema of the 1920s*. New York, Oxford: Berghahn.

Condee, Nancy. 2009. *The Imperial Trace: Recent Russian Cinema*. Oxford and New York: Oxford University Press.

Damiens, Caroline. 2015. "Cinema in Sakha [Yakutia] Republic: Renegotiating Film History." *KinoKultura* 48, http://www.kinokultura.com/2015/48-damiens.shtml (accessed October 30, 2015).

Dobrenko, Evgeny. 2008. *Stalinist Cinema and the Production of History*. Edinburgh: Edinburgh University Press.

Dobrynin, Sergey. 2015. "New Buryat Cinema: Developments So Far and Challenges for the Future." *KinoKultura* 48, http://www.kinokultura.com/2015/48-dobrynin.shtml (accessed October 30, 2015).

Egorova, Tatiana. 1997. *Soviet Film Music. An Historical Survey*. Amsterdam: Harwood, OPA.

Faraday, George. 2000. *Revolt of the Filmmakers: The Struggle for Artistic Autonomy and the Fall of the Soviet Film Industry*. University Park, PA: Pennsylvania State University Press.

Gillespie David. 2000. *Early Soviet Cinema: Innovation, Ideology and Propaganda*. London: Wallflower Press.

Gillespie, David. 2003. *Russian Cinema*. New York: Longman

Golovskoy, Val and John Rimberg. 1986. *Behind the Soviet Screen*, Ann Arbor: Ardis.

Gornitskaia, Nina, ed. 1968. *Iz istorii Lenfil'ma* [From the History of Lenfilm] vol. 1. Leningrad: Iskusstvo.

Gornitskaia, Nina, ed. 1970. *Iz istorii Lenfil'ma* [From the History of Lenfilm] vol. 2. Leningrad: Iskusstvo.

Gornitskaia, Nina, ed. 1973. *Iz istorii Lenfil'ma* [From the History of Lenfilm] vol. 3. Leningrad: Iskusstvo.

Gornitskaia, Nina, ed. 1975. *Iz istorii Lenfil'ma* [From the History of Lenfilm] vol. 4. Leningrad: Iskusstvo.

Goscilo, Helena and Yana Hashamova, eds. 2010. *Cinepaternity: Fathers and Sons in Soviet and Post-Soviet Film*. Bloomington: Indiana University Press.

Hashamova, Yana. 2007. *Pride and Panic: Russian Imagination of the West in Post-Soviet Film.* Bristol and Chicago: Intellect Books.

Haynes, John. 2003. *New Soviet Man: Gender and Masculinity in Stalinist Soviet Cinema.* Manchester and New York: Manchester University Press.

Hicks, Jeremy. 2007. *Dziga Vertov: Defining Documentary Film.* London and New York: I.B. Tauris.

Hicks, Jeremy. 2012. *First Films of the Holocaust: Soviet Cinema and the Genocide of the Jews, 1938–46*, Pittsburgh: University of Pittsburgh Press.

Horton, Andrew and Michael Brashinsky. 1992. *The Zero Hour: Glasnost and Soviet Cinema in Transition.* Princeton: Princeton University Press.

Hutchings, Stephen, ed. 2008. *Russia and its Other(s) on Film: Screening Intercultural Dialogue.* Basingstoke: Palgrave Macmillan.

Kaganovsky, Lilya. 2008. *How the Soviet Man was Unmade: Cultural Fantasy and Male Subjectivity under Stalin.* Pittsburgh: University of Pittsburgh Press.

Kaganovsky Lilya and Masha Salazkina, eds. 2014. *Sound, Speech, Music in Soviet and Post-Soviet Cinema.* Bloomington: Indiana University Press.

Kapterev, Sergei. 2016. In *Russian Aviation, Space Flight and Visual Culture*, edited by Vlad Strukov and Helena Goscilo, Abingdon and New York: Routledge.

Kenez, Peter. 1992. *Cinema and Soviet Society, 1917–1953.* Cambridge: Cambridge University Press.

Kovalova, Anna and Iurii Tsiv'ian. 2011. *Kinematograf v Peterburge 1896–1917: kinoteatry i zriteli* [The Cinema in St Petersburg from 1896–1917: Movie Theaters and Audiences]. St Petersburg: Masterskaia Seans and Skriptorium.

Lawton, Anna. 1992. *Kinoglasnost: Soviet Cinema in Our Time.* Cambridge: Cambridge University Press.

Lawton, Anna. 2004. *Imaging Russia 2000: Film and Facts.* Washington, DC: New Academia Publishing.

Leyda, J. 1960. *Kino: A History of the Russian and Soviet Film.* Princeton: Princeton University Press.

Liber, George. 2002. *Alexander Dovzhenko: A Life in Soviet Film.* London: British Film Institute.

MacFadyen. David. 2003. *The Sad Comedy of El'dar Riazanov.* Montreal and London: McGill-Queen's University Press.

Mikhailov, V. 2003. *Rasskazy o kinematografe staroi Moskvy* [Tales about the Cinema of the Old Moscow]. Moscow: Materik.

Miller, Jamie. 2010. *Soviet Cinema: Politics and Persuasion under Stalin.* London: I. B. Tauris.

Nesbet, Anne. 2003. *Savage Junctures: Sergei Eisenstein and the Shape of Thinking.* London: I. B. Tauris.

Norris, Stephen M. 2012. *Blockbuster History in the New Russia: Movies, Memory, and Patriotism.* Bloomington: Indiana University Press.

Norris, Stephen M. and Zara M. Torlone, eds. 2008. *Insiders and Outsiders in Russian Cinema.* Bloomington: Indiana University Press.

O'Mahony, Mike. 2008. *Sergei Eisenstein.* London: Reaktion Books.

Prokhorov Aleksandr. 2007. *Unasledovannyi diskurs: paradigmy Stalinskoi kul'tury v literature i kinematografe 'ottepeli'* [Inherited Discourse: Stalinist Tropes in Thaw Literature and Cinema]. St Petersburg: Akademicheskii proekt.

Riley, John. 2005. *Dmitri Shostakovich*. (Kino Companion 3). London: I. B. Tauris.

Rollberg, Peter. 2009. *A-Z / Historical Dictionary of Russian and Soviet Cinema*, Scarecrow Press.

Salazkina, Masha. 2009. *In Excess: Sergei Eisenstein's Mexico*. Chicago: Chicago University Press.

Salys, Rimgaila. 2009. *The Musical Comedy Films of Grigorii Aleksandrov. Laughing Matters.* Bristol: Intellect Books.

Sargeant, Amy. 2001. *Vsevolod Pudovkin: Classic Films of the Soviet Avant-Garde*. London: I.B. Tauris.

Steffen, James. 2013. *The Cinema of Sergei Parajanov*. Madison: University of Wisconsin Press.

Szaniawski, Jeremi. 2014. *The Cinema of Alexander Sokurov: Figures of Paradox*. London: Wallflower Press.

Taubman, Jane. 2005. *Kira Muratova* (Kino Companion 4). London: I. B. Tauris.

Taylor, Richard. 1996. "The Illusion of Happiness and the Happiness of Illusion: Grigorii Aleksandrov's *The Circus*." *Slavic and East European Review* 74.4: 601–620.

Taylor, Richard. 1998 [1979]. *Film Propaganda: Soviet Russia and Nazi Germany*. London: I. B. Tauris.

Taylor, Richard. 1999. "Singing on the Steppes for Stalin: Ivan Pyr'ev and the Kolkhoz Musical in Soviet Cinema." *Slavic Review* 58.1: 143–159.

Taylor, Richard. 2000. "But Eastward, Look, the Land is Brighter: Towards a Topography of Utopia in the Stalinist Musical." In *100 Years of European Cinema: Entertainment or Ideology?*, edited by Diana Holmes and Alison Smith, 11–26. Manchester: Manchester University Press.

Taylor, Richard, with Nancy Wood, Julian Graffy, and Dina Iordanova, eds. 2000. *The BFI Companion to Eastern European and Russian Cinema*. London: British Film Institute.

Tsivian, Yuri. 1994. *Early Cinema in Russia and its Cultural Reception*. Chicago and London: University of Chicago Press, 1994.

Vinogradov, Vladimir and V. Bondarenko, eds. 2006. *K istorii VGIKa (1946–1955)* [About VGIK's History, 1946–1955]. vol. 3, Moscow: VGIK.

Vinogradov, Vladimir and Konstantin Ognev, eds. 2000. *K istorii VGIKa (1919–1934)* [About VGIK's History, 1919–1934]. vol. 1, Moscow: VGIK.

Vinogradov, Vladimir and Konstantin Ognev, eds. 2004. *K istorii VGIKa (1935–1945)* [About VGIK's History, 1935–1945]. vol. 2, Moscow: VGIK

Vinogradov, Vladimir and Natal'ia Riabchikova, eds. 2013. *K istorii VGIKa (1956–1965)* [About VGIK's History, 1956–1965]. vol. 4, Moscow: VGIK.

Widdis, Emma. 2003. *Visions of a New Land: Soviet Film from the Revolution to the Second World War*. New Haven: Yale University Press.

Widdis, Emma. 2005. *Alexander Medvedkin* (Kino Companion 2). London: I. B. Tauris.

Woll, Josephine. 2000. *Real Images. Soviet Cinema of the Thaw*. London: I. B. Tauris

Youngblood, Denise J. 1985. *Soviet Cinema in the Silent Era, 1918–1935*. Austin: University of Texas Press.

Youngblood, Denise J. 1992. *Movies for the Masses: Popular Cinema and Soviet Society in the 1920s*, Cambridge: Cambridge University Press.

Youngblood, Denise J. 1999. *The Magic Mirror. Moviemaking in Russia, 1908–1918*. Madison, WI and London, University of Wisconsin Press.

Youngblood, Denise J. 2007. *Russian War Films. On the Cinema Front 1914–2005*. Lawrence: University of Kansas Press.

Zorkaya, Neya. 1991. *The Illustrated History of the Soviet Cinema*. New York: Hippocrene Books.

Zvonkine, Eugénie. 2012. *Kira Muratova: un cinéma de la dissonance* [Kira Muratova: A Cinema of Dissonance]. Lausanne: L'Age d'Homme.

Part I

Structures of Production, Formation, and Exhibition

1

The Film Palaces of Nevsky Prospect: A History of St Petersburg's Cinemas, 1900–1910

Anna Kovalova

"Fog … and a solid wall of lights from the electro-theatres on Nevsky" (P. 1915) – this is what a Muscovite would remember in the first instance after a visit to St Petersburg in the mid-1910s. Since Moscow was the center of the film press before the Revolution, the cinemas on Nevsky Prospect (Avenue) were first of all seen through Moscow's eyes, and this picture is quite fantastic: "A continuous strip of cinemas extends from Nikolaev Station to Anichkov Bridge. For all the money in the world, I couldn't list all of them by name. In almost every house there are two cinemas" (Rex 1915).

This information may nonplus us: where were all these innumerable cinemas? On pre-Revolutionary photographs of Nevsky Prospect, quite a few of which have been preserved, they are rather difficult to spot. This is no surprise: almost all the cinemas were situated either within the buildings, or in courtyards, because it was just impossible to build up the capital's central street with new cinemas. For the Edison, which was popular in the late 1900s, an entire covered gallery was built, which led visitors into the courtyard; this was distinct from the other "yard" cinemas on Nevsky (Anon. 1909). The smart entrance of the Crystal Palace [Kristall-Palas] cinema was visible from within the courtyard that could be accessed through tall and splendidly decorated gates (Khronika 1910c).

Indeed, a similar picture can be observed today. However, Nevsky Prospect was, and remains, St Petersburg's main cinema street. During the pre-Revolutionary era, when St Petersburg hugely surpassed Moscow by the number of cinemas, the Nevsky was the largest cinematic center in the whole of Russia: in the evenings, the projectors showed films to thousands of spectators. Thus the history of cinemas on Nevsky goes far beyond the study of local lore and has a direct relation to the hermeneutics of early Russian cinema. Imagining the cinemas on Nevsky

A Companion to Russian Cinema, First Edition. Edited by Birgit Beumers.
© 2016 John Wiley & Sons, Inc. Published 2016 by John Wiley & Sons, Inc.

means imagining the world of the film viewer in Russia at the beginning of the twentieth century.

According to available data, the first cinema opened on Nevsky in the spring of 1897, the year following the first film screenings in Russia in the Aquarium Park and the Hermitage Gardens. Boris Diushen, a pioneer of Russian cinema, left his memoirs about this cinema, which was located in the Passage [Passazh]:

> Occasional events would take place in this venue: an exhibition of wax figures, a visiting magician guest-performer, etc. The venue held no more than 50–60 persons. Curiously, it was called "Edison's Hall" before it became a cinema, and you could listen there to a tremendous novelty: Edison's phonograph. In those days people would listen by inserting small rubber tubules into their ears that connected to the phonograph, since a loud-speaking sound record did not yet exist. The cinema, which was referred to as "living photograph," opened almost unnoticed, and it was mainly children who visited it. They showed three films. The first was shown all around the world: a gardener watering the lawn and a boy stepping on the hose. In perplexity the gardener examines the end of the hose to find out why the water had stopped. The boy takes the foot from the hose, and a strong jet of water hits the gardener's face. Overall delight! The gardener rushes after the boy and scolds him. The second film showed Nevsky Prospect with a horse-drawn tram and carriages. And the last, third film, showed the arrival of a train. The steam locomotive came directly towards the audience. The spectators were frightened. Then the session was over. There was no musical accompaniment. The session lasted no more than 30 minutes, with two intervals. The first cinema in Russia quickly went bust. (Diushen 2003, 175)

The famous fire in Paris at the annual Charity Bazaar (1897) killed about two hundred people and led to the first big cinema crisis, which continued in Russia until the first Russian revolution of 1905. The demonstration of the "living photograph" created a huge public resonance in 1896, but the cinema soon disappeared onto the periphery of Russian cultural life. Films were shown off and on, more often in the provinces than in the capitals.

The cinema returned to Nevsky Prospect in the middle of the 1900s when house owners, who had earlier reluctantly rented their premises to cinemas, readily handed them over so they would be reconstructed. Between 1904 and 1908, a cinema consisted of one room only, without foyer or lobby. If, as was most often the case, the cinema was a converted apartment with the partitions removed, the spectators entered from the public staircase, obtaining tickets in the hall, at a small table by the door. Thus cinemas located on the premises of stores were set up, as Viktor Shklovskii remembered: "Small cinemas appeared in empty shops in quiet streets, where the doorbell rang all the time, indicating that the screening was about to begin. Actually they let people in at any time [...]. The bell rang with a thin, continuous electric jingle" (Shklovskii 1966, 46).

The transformations of the first Russian cinemas are described in detail and analyzed in Iurii Tsiv'ian's monograph (1991, 14–69), and his concept is applicable to the history of St Petersburg cinemas. In the second half of the 1900s the above-mentioned smaller cinemas began to move from the center to the suburbs, leaving Nevsky Prospect which had become a street for film palaces only.

Boris Diushen remembered: "Somehow, 'suddenly' some cinemas opened on Nevsky, some rather 'magnificently' furbished" (Diushen 2003, 176). Feozva Vasil'eva, the daughter of the famous gold producer from Omsk, distributed on charitable terms films from Pathé in Russia and opened several cinemas; the actor Nikolai Orlov remembers the details of such an event: "The first cinema which received the name 'As in Paris' was in a cozy, private residence in a courtyard of Nevsky Prospect. The exterior was decorated with huge, colorful Parisian posters, and the entrance was garnered with flowers in the summer and fir-trees in the winter. The public entered a splendid foyer along a magnificent carpet. The second cinema was called 'As in Nice' and was located opposite, on the corner of Nevsky and Liteiny. It had two halls: on the ground floor they showed serious, scientific films. The setting was rather smart: gilded furniture, huge mirrors in golden frames, wonderful carpets, the walls upholstered with silk, and the doors also" (Orlov 1999, 204). Orlov emphasized that these cinemas served, as Vasil'eva said, for rendezvous: they were a meeting place for rich visitors. After midnight special screenings of the "Parisian kind" were arranged for very important persons – showing openly pornographic films.

At this time the writer Ivan Shcheglov-Leont'ev wrote a malicious feuilleton, in which he likened cinematography to the image of the cheap German cocotte Bertha Kukelvan, and called the St Petersburg Royal Vio cinema a "grandiose pissoir." Shcheglov, once a protégé of the writer Mikhail Saltykov-Shchedrin and the historian and journalist Mikhail Stasiulevich, had the reputation of being a weird old man, almost a city madman, in St Petersburg at the beginning of the century: he was afraid of steamships, trams, and even carriages. Nobody paid particular attention to his words, yet in more than one way Shcheglov was right: in the 1900s the magnificent cinema was associated with the brothel. The entrepreneur Vasil'eva ran her cinema business together with her husband Vasilii Ipatovich, and they owned some ten impressive cinemas, of which – according to the journal *Artist i ststena* – only one was "decent": the Casino de Paris at the corner of Nevsky and Liteiny. The monopolists Vasili'ev occupied a visible place in the film-process of the capital, and their business approach in many respects reflected the shape of St Petersburg's film distribution of those years.

The first film theater owners in the capital were parvenus and enterprising merchants, and usually did not distinguish themselves by intelligence or a high level of culture. A repulsive scene took place in the Folies Bergère theater on Nevsky at the end of the 1900s: the wife of the owner Nakhman-Geev attacked Vera G-n, whom she suspected of an affair with her husband. The girl was beaten up and suffered bruises and concussions. Vera G-n brought a court case against both Geevs (Anon. 1910b). The feuilleton published in the magazine *Artist i stsena* also gives some clues about the social origin of the first generation of St Petersburg theatre owners: "Conversation of a doctor without practice and a merchant without credit in a mossy small restaurant," where the opening of a cinema is described simply: "Let's stop arguing and get to business. And business is good: we shall open it on Nevsky, we shall arrange it in the Parisian fashion, and it won't be business but a red mill that will spin money" (Anon. 1910a). A red mill was the emblem of the well-known cinema, the Moulin Rouge, which operated on Nevsky Prospect 51 for over ten years.

The press quite often bantered at the manners of the cinema owners, who were clearly unable to communicate with the visitors. The *Vestnik kinematografii* gave theater owners ironical advice that reflected, apparently, the true state of affairs:

> Make sure that in your theatre orange peel, sunflower seeds, stubs and boxes roll about on the floor. It very much brings alive the general view of the theatre and eloquently proves that it is visited by numerous spectators. [...] On the whole, if to you are asked any question, it is recommended, for self-respect, to inspect the customer from head down to the feet with a contemptuous look and to say through clenched teeth: "get off"; it is also good to stare point blank and growl: "piss off." (Anon 1911c)

Such theater owners would continue for a long time to dominate film culture in the provinces, while in the capital cinemas had been pushed out of the center. In the summer of 1910 Vasilii Vasil'ev died of cholera (Khronika 1910b), and his widow quickly sold all the cinemas and left the cinematic life of the capital. Although it was of course impossible to eradicate the "Parisian genre," the time of serious film palaces, which were managed by new people, had come. The cinemas on Nevsky at the turn of the 1900s and 1910s passed into the hands of "cultured" (as they were called in the press) entrepreneurs.

Above all, this concerns the owners of the Edison (Malaia Koniushennaia St 3) and The Royal Star (Nevsky Pr. 48) cinemas – the best St Petersburg cinemas of that time: "At the Edison and The Royal Star people 'dress up to go there', as they do for the ballet or the drama theatre, and during the intervals the magnificent foyers and grandiose halls of these two cinemas represent a vivid picture of the beau monde, who have come to the cinema as if it were the theater" (Obozrenie teatrov 1910). Contrary to the tradition to have several screenings per day in a cinema, the administration of the Edison held only one screening, and that was set to the "theater time" and lasted usually from 8.30 pm until 11.30 pm (Obozrenie teatrov 1911b). The press wrote that this cinema played to a full house of "its audience" every day: "The white hall of the Edison reminds us of a subscription performance at the Mariinsky. There is the habitual audience, on their favorite places, strutting before their friends in their tuxedos and gowns" (Obozrenie teatrov 1911a). There are, it is true, also unexpected visitors: in the spring of 1910 the Minister of Finance V.N. Kokovtsev made an appearance at the Edison to look at the new program and discuss the success of cinematography and state of this industry in Russia with the administration (Khronika 1910a).

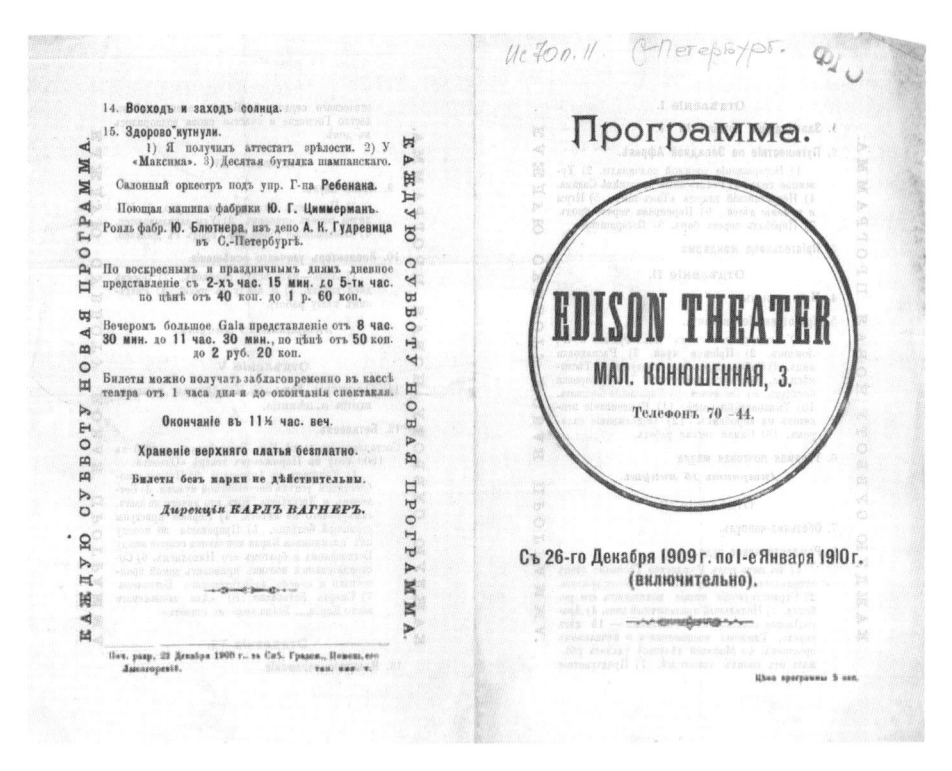

Figure 1.1 Program of the Edison Theater, December 1909–January 1910.

The Royal Star did not have a long life-span (1909–1911); however, during this time its sparkling star had become a new symbol of Nevsky Prospect: "In the evening, when the noisy, brightly lit Nevsky Prospect hardly contains an infinite flow of people, among the uncountable lights of cinemas the bright electric star on one of the enormous central buildings of the needle-shaped avenue remains visible from the distance. This star is the 'mark' of one of the best cinemas in Russia, The Royal Star" (Khronika 1910d). This cinema was located in the building of the Passage (Nevsky Prospect 48): on the third floor there was a large auditorium, on the second – a foyer and a bar, and for the services of the public there was a special "elevating machine," a lift. The furniture of the cinema was expensive, but austere and refined: hall and foyer were decorated in black-and-white tones with black drapery. The Royal Star belonged to the joint-stock company Apollo, a St Petersburg film firm which released mainly newsreels (Kovalova 2012, 44–49).

Apollo's films defined the repertoire of The Royal Star: fiction films were rare, but the transfer speed of the city's news was unusual for those times: what was filmed in the capital in the morning was shown in the cinema by the evening (Khronika 1911). Even Grand Duke Mikhail Aleksandrovich once visited this cinema (Khronika 1909b). Apollo's bankruptcy led to the closure of The Royal Star; however, the Passage remained the major cinema center on Nevsky: a new fashionable cinema opened soon after, called the Soleil, which had an elongated hall with 1000 seats, magnificently equipped boxes and a symphonic orchestra from the Imperial theatres (Anon. 1911a).

Talking about the well-known cinemas on Nevsky, we must also mention the Saturn, popular in its time, which was located at Nevsky Prospect 67, on the site now occupied by the Khudozhestvennyi [Arts] cinema. At first it was a small cinema with a single hall, and the annual turnover was 30,000 rubles. By the time of its closure in 1914 the Saturn had three halls and a revenue of 200,000 rubles (Khronika 1914e). The cinema had a magnificent foyer decorated with tropical plants. In 1909 the owner of the Saturn, Iaroslav Krynskii, was one of the first to rent films (instead of buying them), and to change the program twice a week (Khronika 1909a). Within two years such a repertoire approach became common practice for all cinemas. The popularity of the Saturn was legendary. Judging by reports in the press, the well-known actor Konstantin Varlamov was a regular visitor of this cinema.

The closure of the cinema, which for over eight years enjoyed exclusive popularity and authority, was a sad event for the town: "Three halls perish with the Saturn where, like in a mirror, the whole cinema life was reflected until recently, all the creativity of world cinema; where on three screens for several seasons the best, most beautiful, most gripping events took place before the eyes of spectators" (Khronika 1914h). The Saturn had passed to the well-known theater owners Mullert, who were going to reconstruct it, apparently, and open an even more grandiose cinema. However, the Mullerts hugely suffered from the anti-German campaign during World War I (Kovalova and Tsiv'ian 2011, 128) and they never opened a new cinema on Nevsky 67. At this time the Mullerts were seriously in danger of being expelled from Russia, and it was a miracle that they managed to keep their cinemas on Nevsky: the Union (Nevsky 88), the Khudozhestvennyi (Nevsky 102) and the Crystal Palace (Nevsky 72). These cinemas, following the Edison and The Royal Star, were guided by a model of luxurious and cultural cinema for an intelligent audience. About the Crystal Palace, which opened in 1910, the papers wrote: "The auditorium, with a height over both circles [two floors], is held in a strict Empire style and it is especially beautiful because of its whiteness and absence of all those ornaments, portieres, upholsteries and so on, which most of our cinemas strut with" (Anon. 1910c). Obviously the Mullerts tried to depart from the pretentiousness of film palaces in the mid-1900s; however, the love for external effects stayed with the vigorous Natalia Frantsevna Mullert. In 1913, when she opened the Khudozhestvennyi, the press savored the purchase of an incredible crystal luster for the new cinema which cost 6000 rubles (Khronika 1913).

In 1913, a year which became for Russia's economy the most successful in all its history, two magnificent film palaces were constructed on Nevsky, which could not be surpassed in splendor neither before nor after the Revolution: the Piccadilly (Nevsky 60) and the Parisiana (Nevsky 80). They instantly drew the attention of the public, and in 1915 they had already confidently settled in the center of cinema life on Nevsky:

> The Piccadilly sees motor cars at its entrance, there are representatives of our beau monde. If a film has been shown at the Piccadilly, the distributors say, it is already in high demand, and they make all reasonable efforts for the film to be shown first in this cinema. But, on the other hand, the audience has strict rules here. They say that once a film seemed too frank for one of the influential visitors, and, on her insistence, the censors made cuts as suggested by this same visitor. Next to the Piccadilly comes the Parisiana in terms of the quality of the audience. And here, too, there are motorcars. (Obozrenie kinematografov 1915)

Nevsky 60 is probably the most English cinema address on Nevsky Prospect. In 1900, long before the Piccadilly opened, there was a cinema called Bristol here. Foreign names were characteristic for Russian cinemas of that time, but on the whole these were French names: Moulin Rouge, Folies Bergère, Casino de Paris, Mon Plaisir, and many others. However, the Bristol occupied probably several

Figure 1.2 Entrance to the Piccadilly Cinema (Nevsky Prospect 60), 1913.

Figure 1.3 Auditorium of the Piccadilly Cinema (Nevsky Prospect 60), 1913. Photo by Viktor Bulla.

apartments in the house on Nevsky 60, while the new Piccadilly was located in a purpose-built house in the court yard. Today, with the building gone, it is difficult to imagine the architectural shape of Nevsky. The cinema, with columns, bas-reliefs, statues in niches surprised the St Petersburger of the 1910s (Khronika 1914b: 26). The building was not huge (otherwise it would not have fitted into a courtyard of Nevsky), but graceful and therefore the townspeople called the Piccadilly the *bonbonniere* [chocolate box] (A-fer 1914).

The construction of the cinema cost Iurii Iablonskii, who also owned the Majestique on Nevsky 50, some 200,000 rubles (A-fer 1914). Iablonskii, who had two large central cinemas, became a new kind of "owner of the Nevsky": he was not a casual businessman, but a well-known publisher in the city, the owner of a large printing house, where the Leningrad branch of the publishing house Molodaia Gvardiia [Young Guard] opened after the Revolution (Anon. 1910d).

The two-storey auditorium of the Piccadilly had also been planned in a special manner: the screen was equally well visible from any row, and any seat (Khronika 1914b, 26–27). The interior was in the style moderne, the hall had been decorated with yellow silk, and the "charming foyer and spectacular lobby," in the opinion of the correspondent from the *Vestnik kinematografii*, could "transport you straight to Europe" (Khronika 1914f). The projection booth of the Piccadilly had been equipped along the latest standard of technology, as is visible on a photograph that has been preserved, probably the only picture showing the projection equipment in pre-Revolutionary St Petersburg.

The composer Dmitri Tiomkin left his memoirs about the musical life at the Piccadilly; in his youth he had worked there as ballroom pianist:

> St Petersburg had many cinemas. One of the most luxurious was called the Piccadilly, since Western names were considered smart. The piano player there was Barere, a great virtuoso whose rapid fingers would play Chopin's Minute Waltz in fifty-six seconds. He was much applauded in concerts, but he had a knack of not being able to get along financially, and so he made his living in the movie house, where he was also able to keep up his keyboard technique. While the screen showed scenes that evoked tears or laughter, he would practice complicated passages, finger exercises, studies in how to surmount technical problems, regardless of whether the film was Vera Cold in a love scene, a comic skit, or a moment of tragic peril.
>
> I couldn't take such liberties. As a mere boy in a humbler theater I had to make music to fit the picture, more or less. One night I was playing to a farce of Max Linder, a popular French comic actor. There was a close-up scene of a woman being choked, her head going back and back. As I played the music, I couldn't help throwing my head back and emitting terrible grunts and roars. The audience broke into laughter. The theater manager told me I must do it at every performance. So I also became the sound effects. (Tiomkin and Buranelli 1959, 24)

However, usually those working in the magnificent cinemas had no time for jokes. Remembering life in pre-Revolutionary St Petersburg, Dmitrii Likhachev noted: "Once we were on Nevsky in the Parisiana or Piccadilly, I can't remember. We were amazed at the valets in liveries and with wigs" (Likhachev 2007, 18). Apparently, he is talking about the Parisiana, because a similar response to its employees comes from the correspondent of *Kino-kur'er* after his first visit to this cinema: "My fur coat was almost pulled off me by court lackeys in long stockings, dense and beautifully skin-tight around the leg, dandy shoes with buckles, short trousers and colored camisoles; they made the coat quickly disappear somewhere into a vault and after several seconds of anxiety gave me a coupon. The same men guarded the entrances to the stalls and the balcony" (A-fer 1914, 9).

The Parisiana opened after the Piccadilly, at the very beginning of 1914 (Khronika 1914d). St Petersburgers soon learnt about the magnificence of the new cinema, because it could be appreciated even without coming inside: "A sea of lights, which fills the magnificent entrance that is situated in a semicircle and looks onto Nevsky Prospect, involuntarily draws attention" (Khronika 1914f). The colonnade of the Parisiana, filled with light, was decorated with bright electric images of laughter and satire (Khronika 1914f); however, this luxury even nonplused the townspeople: "the lobby of new theatre constantly attracts huge crowds of spectators, who cannot bring themselves to step across the tempting threshold (as is well known, cleanliness and comfort always inspire in a Russian man above all fear: suddenly one must not spit?)" (A-fer 1914).

The furniture inside the Parisiana matched the exterior. The hall was enormous for the times, decorated in the style of Louis XVI with rich stucco. The wide marble

Figure 1.4 Entrance to the Parisiana Cinema (Nevsky Prospect 80), 1915. Photo by Viktor Bulla.

staircase led to a spacious balcony, and the boxes were isolated from each other, so everyone had a separate entrance; and they were equipped with phones (A-fer 1914). The cinema had an enormous ceiling which could be opened automatically to either side. Iurii Tsiv'ian remarked that such a cinema features in the films *Moon* (*Luna*, 1979) by Bernardo Bertolucci and *Splendor* (1989) by Ettore Scola (Tsiv'ian 1991, 39). The novelty of the Parisiana also gave rise to ironic comments: it was alleged that the ceiling could douse the smart public in St Petersburg rain, while the phones in the boxes also naturally led to questions: "I keep thinking how convenient it will be to use this phone during the interval, let alone during the screening, and would I not become the center of attention if, during the most pathetic point in the drama, I'd start a business call or an intimate conversation, or I receive a call …" (A-fer 1914).

So far my concern here has been the architecture of cinemas on Nevsky, and little has been said about the program. If the best cinemas at the end of the 1900s and early 1910s placed their stake on newsreels, then the emphasis distinctly shifted onto fiction films later. During the first months of the war, newsreels regained their former popularity, but as Russia was drawn into the international conflict, the military theme moved to the periphery: scared, the townspeople were looking for oblivion in the "illusions."

In 1910 the journal *Artist i stsena* remarked that Nevsky's cinemas were all supplied by the same distribution office, therefore frequently all the cinemas showed the same films, only occasionally changing the titles. During the 1910s the situation was complicated further and began to change; however, the satirist and playwright Arkadii Averchenko produced a feuilleton, parodying a typical film program. It certainly has not lost its bite and is quite applicable to all the fashionable cinemas in the capital.

PROGRAM[1]
Electro-magnetic illusory-realistic kinemo-biograph
(the real cinematic miracle of the twentieth century CE)

Section I

CATCHING FLEAS IN NORWAY
(useful)

That's what the insects are called which live not only in night rests of the workers, but also on the body, causing great anxiety among the inhabitants of this small vigorous country. Old and young are busy catching these small, brisk animals, and although the hunt is on without profit (their meat cannot be used in food, and the skin is useless because of their size), nevertheless these predators are caught by brave Norwegians, young and old, all along the coast.

KITTY RESCUED! OR A HEART IS NO STONE
(touching, 400 meters)

In the apartment of the rich merchant Gribul everybody is asleep; but the impudent robbers, who have thought of stealing the Gribul's fireproof wooden casket in which the landlord stacks his fortune, are not asleep... And here come, knifes between their teeth, the two convicts Jules and Ivan; with shameful skill they climb up. But foresight has not been asleep and placed on their way, near the casket, the favorite doll of Kitty, the juvenile merchant and daughter of the old Gribul. So the robbers drop the knifes, moved by the doll's show: remembering their youth, they shower the doll with kisses. But the young mistress Yvonna, having heard the noise, jumps from her bed and rushes towards the robbers. The latter want to kill her, but then they don't want to kill her and caress the little girl, and she caresses them. Some sergeants with revolvers come along and throw themselves at the murderers; Yvonna goes between them and meekly murmurs that they must not..., that they are kind, and she forces the robbers to make peace with the policemen. The latter kiss the first, daddy Gribul kisses his darling naughty little girl. The latter kisses the doll which has saved their life, and everyone cries.

Section II

THE HILARIOUS ADVENTURES OF COLLEGIATE ASSESSOR TUPITSYN
(very comic! A load of laughter, 500 meters)

Having donned coat and hat, our Tupitsyn goes for a walk. But here he encounters disaster. He overtakes a porter who is carrying empty boxes and drops them on the head of our Tupitsyn. But here comes another woe: the yard keeper waters the street and pours water over this odd fellow. It is clear that now the porter, the yard keeper and the indignant public latch onto our Tupitsyn and beat him up. This picture makes the audience laugh unremittingly.

FATAL MISUNDERSTANDING, OR HAND AND HEART OF AN INNOCENT GIRL
(tragic)

The young count George, having met the modest Madeleine on a walk, is enamored – but no! The latter has vowed to enter a monastery. But the count is persistent and always gets his way. He writes to his friend de Planchette: "Dear Planchette, go to the above-mentioned Madeleine and demand her hand and heart for me in memory of our friendship. You shall do this with perfect respect, yours count George Gvozdilin." De Planchette, carrying out the last will of his friend, goes to the girl, but here a fatal misunderstanding occurs: the persistent Planchette, taking the will of his friend literally, cuts off the unfortunate and meek Madeleine's hand and heart, and brings them to a shaken count. The latter runs to Madeleine, but too late! She dies in his arms, blessing the count because she secretly loved him. The erroneous Planchette sobs inconsolably.

PENCIL SHARPENING IN CENTRAL RUSSIA
(ethnographic)

Teenagers of central Russia, and occasionally adults, engage in this business. The sharpening of pencils demands great skill and dexterity, as it is very easy to cut oneself when holding the knife in one hand, or to cut someone who stands nearby. Look how dexterously the teenager in our picture carries out the task. This picture, both scientific and decent, can be recommended for pupils of middle schools.

THE SECRET OF THE COURTESAN
(Drama in color from Roman life)

People who lived in Greece and had aggressive bents to debauchery are referred to as Romans. So their courtesans (girls) fell in love and repeatedly took up relationships without being married or betrothed. Here on the screen we see the story of the courtesan Epikharisa who acted from her heart, and what came of that.

Epikharisa made a living by selling herself, until she met the Greek young Roman Bitullio. She lost her young heart, but that was not what the Greek Patrician Centurion thought, to whom she sold herself earlier and who loved with an animalistic passion. So what? Having learned about her love for Bitullio, whom she appointed a meeting at six o'clock, Centurion rushes to kill the brave young man. But his sand-glass lags behind, and consequently he comes to the well when the happy lover has already left and only Epikharisa remains there, this unfortunate victim of the public temperature. So what? In the dark, he snatches the ancient gun and kills her, mistaking her in her white clothes for Bitullio. The courageous girl falls like a sheaf, and Centurion, realizing his sad mistake, pierces his body with his own sword. The two victims of public temperature lay side by side. So, as they say, bad deeds follow you, the good ones flee.

FINAL SENSATIONAL FILM: MOTHER-IN-LAW HAS ARRIVED!
(Hermetic laughter!! 300 meters)

Upon hearing about the imminent arrival of his mother-in-law, Adolf instigates the servants to poison the life of this malicious Shrew. She has hardly arrived when misfortunes happen. From the roof an automobile falls on her, then the cook throws her in a tub with boiling water, then the children beat her on the head with batons in a dream and all this comes to an end when, persuaded by her son-in-law, the mother-in-law examines a thresher in the floor, gets her head in there and has it chopped off to the general laughter of all participants.

Unable to bear these jokes and mockeries, the old woman collects her things and returns home on the first bus.

Composed from sources
Arkadii Averchenko (Anon. 1912)[2]

Actually, it was largely the program and the content of the screenings that preoccupied the audience in the capital. Now it seems axiomatic, but in the 1910s such an approach to cinema was unusual and it was the topic for an entire physiological sketch, which a Moscow journalist wrote about the St Petersburg film public:

> The enormous crowd, scurrying back and forth along Nevsky Prospect, pours in a huge wave through the doors of the cinema and back again. This enormous demand shown in the attraction of the Petrograd population to the cinema is the best proof of the status that cinematography has assumed in Petrograd. For the cinematograph to achieve the audience sympathy in Moscow, it had to resort to significant 'collateral expenditure'. A lot of enormously costly film palaces had to be built, expensive orchestras employed, massive advertising campaigns launched. In Petrograd things are not as acute. Would it be possible to imagine a cinema in Moscow somewhere in a courtyard? [...] The expense of the premises forced cinemas to be located in courtyards, even such theatres as the Piccadilly and the Crystal Palace. [...] One just has to visit the Piccadilly and the Parisiana to understand that the foyers of these theatres are miles away from the foyers of the Moscow film palaces. Hence, the public is reconciled with inconveniences to which Muscovites would not accustom, or else it appreciates the cinema not for the appearance or the furnishing or structure of orchestras as in Moscow, but mainly for the content of the programs. (Rex 1915)

In memoirs, letters, diaries, and also in works of art where the old St Petersburg cinemas are mentioned (for example, in Vladimir Nabokov's novel *Other Shores* [*Drugie berega*, 1954]), their architecture and furniture is indeed hardly touched upon; there are only descriptions of old films, often in great detail. The same can be said about those few responses that appeared in the film-press of those years. Nobody complains about the deficiencies of cinemas, but what gave rise to questions and doubts was the program. Surprisingly, the questions raised by this cinemagoer in 1911 are still valid today.

> Sir, Mister Editor
>
> I'm a simple fan, often visiting electro-theaters. The backstage of the cinema business is completely unknown to me, and therefore I ask you out of ignorance to explain to me: why do the majority of electro-theaters present such terribly monotonous programs during the same period?
>   It is sufficient to compare the programs of the local cinemas, well, on Nevsky from Znamensky Square up to Liteiny and Vladimirsky Prospects. I take this area, because I live nearby and normally visit these theatres. During the week their programs are identical like two drops of water, and if not all the films are the same then nearly two or three of the most interesting ones. Therefore, instead of going to the cinema three times a week, you go only once, because there is no joy in watching a picture which you have already seen, even at another theatre. On the other side, if circumstances prevent you from watching a battle film during one week, then the next week you can already not find it anywhere: it has disappeared completely from all theatres. So it happened with *The Divine Comedy*, *The Fall of Troy*, *The Foreman*

(or *The Sergeant*, I can't remember) *Roland, Victim of Alcoholism*. All of them appeared simultaneously at all theatres, and I did not get around to seeing them, but they have already vanished completely. Though there were even queues.

Theatres think in vain that they compete with each other that way. The audience will be satisfied, and such a system only cuts the number of visits by half, even three times.

Please accept, etc.

    A film buff (Anon. 1911b)

The film audiences of St Petersburg at the beginning of the century are a topic for another study. Undoubtedly, though, in a short period the audience underwent significant evolution. In 1915 the writer Arkadii Bukhov remarked: "The type of spectator nibbling seeds and guffawing during the drama is already dying out. In the cinemas you find the same people who also go to the theatres. The audience develops its taste, if you like, and even fandom for one or another actor … The public who initially came to the cinema in passing and who very much liked that they could 'not take off their galoshes and overcoats,' as the posters alerted, is now already beginning to watch film series and follow a story over two and three evenings …" (Bukhov 1915). One might say that the public had grown and developed along with the cinemas. However, if in the capital – even on Nevsky Prospect (for example in the nameless cinema in house No. 86) (Rex 1915) – there were still plain cinemas of the old type, and the audience traditions concerning cinema easily went side by side with the custom "to dress up and go to the movies." In 1913 the star of the Russian stage Konstantin Varlamov explained his love for the cinema simply: "Say, I get called to the theatre, and I think: is it worth it? I have to dress up, don a tuxedo, put on a collar, clasp on the cufflinks. I'm better off in the cinema. I can just go in what I am wearing" (Varlamov 1913).

Sometimes it is argued that the simple audience before the Revolution was content with cinemas on the outskirts, and that the palaces on Nevsky were visited by capital's beau-monde. This is not quite true. In the Parisiana a box cost eight rubles, but for the same screening people could buy an ordinary ticket for 30 kopecks (A-fer 1914). The film historian Edgar Arnoldi remarked in his *Memoirs of a Bicycle Era* [*Vospominaniia o velosipednoi epokhi*]:

The cinema, like the tram, the record player and the bicycle, was a product that displayed the triumph of democracy. Despite the gravitation of cinemas towards class stratification, the spectators both in the center and on the periphery were a rather motley crowd. The cost of tickets on Nevsky certainly blocked access for the "common people," but in the halls of first-rate cinemas an officer and a milliner, a student and a salesman, an official and a lady of light conduct would sit next to each other. Such combinations were most of all characteristic for the tram. And away from the center, the broad masses dominated. But here also, alongside caps and peak-caps, bowler hats, kerchiefs and even hats with veils could be seen. In front of the screen everyone had equal rights, and class and property distinctions were insignificant.

> Thus cinema sharply differed from the theatre, where certain categories of spectators clearly prevailed. The regulars of the Mariinsky opera theatre were not typical in any way of the Passage or Suvorin's Maly Theatre, and the visitors of the Farces or Bouffe would not appear at the Aleksandrinsky Theatre. (RIII 12/1/5a: 10)[3]

About the cinema Soleil, which was traditionally considered one of the best and dearest in the city, a contemporary wrote: "In the hall the soft ring of heels and pleasant French speech can be heard. But right there, you may see a merchant and a student in a raincoat" (Argus 1915b). The audience of the famous Crystal Palace was also motley: "You can meet a street fairy, who has come to entertain herself with a melodrama and share the heroine's woe; next to her a grammar-school boy, admiring the feats and boldness of the detectives; and somewhere in a corner, a maid released from her duties, affectionately smiling at the gallantry of Polidor" (Argus 1915b).

The sometimes polyvalent structure of the Petersburg cinema audience was shrouded in troubles. The press wrote about a scandalous case at the Piccadilly, where a mink fur coat with beaver collar (price: 6000 rubles) was stolen from a British citizen, along with valuable documents. The thieves acted artfully: they simply retrieved the fur coat of the unlucky man under a false ticket from the wardrobe, and then, taking advantage of the general panic, frisked the pockets of the other visitors (Khronika 1915b).

The social composition of the cinema audience on Nevsky was truly varied and practically showed a cross-section of the capital's society as a whole. However, preferences and tastes of these cinema-goers apparently did not differ greatly. Travel films and scientific films were a success even in the 1900s, when the phenomenon of the "living photo" amazed and engaged the spectator. In the 1910s the chronicle was much less popular than comedies and dramas, which gained in popularity. The aristocratic public, hesitant in its love for the cinema, usually denied it: "I go to the cinema only because of the pictures of outstanding real events. The cinema is a live magazine for me," said one intellectual (K-vich 1916). In audience conversations one could hear impatient, but more sincere attitudes to travel and science films which were still included in the programs: "Awfully interesting [...] Why should I know how galoshes are made when I buy them ready-made in a shop all the same!" (G.M. 1910).

Another important factor for the cinemagoer was the novelty of the film. There is no doubt that new films are more interesting than old ones, at least those that have not yet been seen are more interesting than ones already watched. In this sense, the cinemas on Nevsky were in an advantageous position, because usually (with rare exceptions) they functioned as "first screens," that is they specialized on premiers and showed films that had not previously been shown in the city. The beginning of World War I hugely changed that situation.

The capital was hit by a genuine repertoire famine. Because of the political situation, distributors had a hard time obtaining new foreign films, and prices soared. The import of films from Germany stopped altogether.

In the conditions of a film crisis everybody had to "freshen up" films and show old titles, purchased a long time ago and already forgotten by the spectator, under the guise of new releases. The concept of "first screen" became rather relative. In the summer of 1915 St Petersburg cinema-owners faced an unprecedented problem: the complete absence of new films. Russian producers, considering the summer to be a dead season, usually prepared their novelties for the autumn. But western firms could hardly offer anything new, except for some Italian films and some ten pictures of the Society of Swedish Biograph. The Danish firm Nordisk, which had earlier delivered some popular films, presented only a few pictures. And nothing at all came from France: the branches of the French firms Gaumont and Pathé Frères rented other companies' films. As a result, the Piccadilly and the Union presented films that had been shown in Udelny a month and a half ago under the guise of new releases. Some dramas, which adverts had been shouting about on Nevsky, also turned out to be an old product accidentally found in the stacks of a city monopolist (Argus 1915a). For want of something better and against the tradition of changing the program twice a week, the Moulin Rouge showed Petr Chardynin's sensational film *Mar'ia Lus'eva* (1915) for a whole month (Khronika 1915a).

Censorship was reinforced as early as spring 1914, when the pre-war tension heightened. The Belgian film of Pathé Frères, *Maudite soit la guerre* (1914), directed by Alfred Machin, was shown in the spring of 1914 in Russian cinemas; the popular *Kino* magazine even placed the advert for this film on the cover. However, in May, even before the beginning of military action, its pacifistic pathos raised serious concerns. The Russian State Archive of History [RGIA, Rossiiskii gosudarstvennyi istoricheskii arkhiv] preserves the curious correspondence between two censors about the anti-war film (as it appeared to them); it was released in the cinemas of the capital under the title *Krovavaia niva* [*The Bloody Field*], *Uzhasy voiny* [*Horrors of War*] and *Smertel'nye uzhasy voiny* [*Fatal Horrors of War*]. The Official with Special Assignments Rebrov retells the quite ordinary plot of this film about the young soldier Khardef, who tragically dies in the war, and his young bride who has entered a monastery: "Here is the content of the drama, which, as your Highness can see, is tendentious. This tendentiousness is emphasized by the conditions of the cinema, constantly changing images, which are selected with skill. [...] I cite some inscriptions to the drama: 'the friendship of people,' 'the opportunity of a war which has arisen from an insignificant border incident,' 'Khardef, obeying strict discipline, goes to war and sows the death of people for whom he feels no hatred.' Certainly, the tendency which can be characterized with the very words of the cinema 'Damnation of War,' without any note of patriotism, is undesirable and on the cinema screen sounds like a sermon of antimilitarism" (RGIA 776/25/1123: 5–6). This film was, nevertheless, not pulled from the screens; however, all the intertitles that so disturbed the censor were removed.

During the war the cinema-owners of the capital, and especially those on Nevsky, took an active part in charities and voluntarily contributed substantial sums from their profits to the treasury. The law about a military tax on cinema

Figure 1.5 Poster for the film *Maudite soit la guerre* [*War is Hell*, 1914], directed by Alfred Machin.

tickets came into force on 1 February 1916, and it became a new stable source for the army's income. In 1916 the government had, apparently, the absolutely mad idea to requisition the largest cinemas of the city as hospitals. While in Petrograd dozens of hotels and tea rooms were empty, the best cinemas – such as the Piccadilly and the Parisiana on Nevsky, and Molniia [Lightning] on the Petrograd side, were required to close – precisely those cinemas that had brought in huge sums for the treasury through the military tax (Anon. 1916). However, the actions of the authorities were possibly not so reckless. Apparently it was assumed that the owners of large theatres would do anything to keep their premises and build infirmaries in another place. And precisely that happened. The government received both free infirmaries and the military tax.

All these burdens of military life led to a mass closure of smaller cinemas, which caused serious fears among filmmakers as Russian distribution was indissolubly connected with small cinemas and the move was thus directly connected to production. The cinemas of Nevsky would get through this crisis, but in the second half of the 1910s not a single new cinema opened there. The war prevented the further growth of the film industry on Nevsky; in fact, in February 1914, although the capital's main artery boasted a great variety of cinemas, this was insufficient for spectators: "Despite the huge number of cinemas, on holidays, especially on Nevsky Prospect, they are besieged by crowds of people so there is a serious danger of all sorts of accidents. […] The box offices of cinemas sell an unlimited quantity of tickets, not at all taking into account the number of available seats after each film. As a result, people are crushed in the foyer. When the doors open, the crowd energetically rushes into the hall, and it emerges there are no seats. They start to put additional chairs in the aisles which are almost blocked. Those people who have not got into the hall roughly protest, demanding the return of their money, and the box office has to deal with a number of misunderstandings" (Khronika 1914g).

In May 1914 Eduard Mullert specially went abroad to learn more about the way in which the best film-palaces in Europe are set up: together with his wife he planned to open a grandiose cinema on Nevsky as soon as possible, on the most prominent place he could think of: house No. 67 where the well-known Saturn had been situated earlier (Khronika 1914a). This and many other plans for the creation of new film-palaces on Nevsky would not come true.

During the Soviet era the cinema map of Nevsky Prospect changed drastically. The owners of Nevsky cinemas (the Mullerts, Madame Iablonskaia who, after the death of her husband, owned the Piccadilly) emigrated or were out of work. In rare cases a former cinema owner was allowed to head his now "Soviet" cinema as managing director. The directors of Soviet cinemas on Nevsky were the former managers. So, Nikolai Grigor, who had worked with Iablonskii, headed for many years the Piccadilly, which would subsequently become the Aurora (Bagrov 2004, 10–11). But there could be no renewal of the tradition of the film-palaces of the 1910s. The concept of the palace, the idea to build a grandiose cultural institution decorated with ornaments and accessories for the citizens was perfectly integrated into the Soviet model of life in a big city. However, the genuine life and development of film-palaces was possible only in conditions of competition, when cinema-owners, wishing to attract audiences, repaired endlessly, went to Europe for new ideas, thought up more and more attractions. During NEP (New Economic Policy) there was no money for this, and when the film industry was finally nationalized, competition between cinemas came to naught.

There were fewer cinemas, though the main venues on Nevsky remained: on the place of old, pre-Revolutionary cinemas there were new, Soviet ones. The names, of course, changed in most cases: the Parisiana became the October, the Piccadilly changed to Aurora, and on the place of the Saturn, a cinema with the rhetorical name Cinema For The Masses opened. Some cinemas returned to their old names in the 1990s: The Crystal Palace does not do badly today on Nevsky. Sadly, the Parisiana has not survived: this once magnificent cinema, half-empty, dark and cold, awaited reconstruction for a long time until it eventually closed in 2009. Contrary to the promises of the municipal authorities to keep the ancient cinema, Nevsky 80 now accommodates a huge H&M store. However, this does not worry the townspeople, since St Petersburg has long lost that selfless love of cinema for which it was famous in the 1910s.

When the Piccadilly opened in 1913, its charming building was compared to an "ancient Greek temple" (Khronika 1914c). Since Shcheglov-Leont'ev named the large

Royal Vio a "grandiose pissoir" less than ten years passed for the cinemas on Nevsky to live through more than one era. At first, the narrow illusion-halls of the store type, then the Parisiana-style cinemas with a doubtful reputation, and finally the film-palaces, the new cultural centers of the capital. The evolution of cinemas in the 1900s and 1910s reminds us of the evolution of cinema, which in less than a decade turned from the attraction of the "living photograph" to a new art. And this is not surprising: at the beginning of the century film production and cinemas were connected as tightly as never before and lived a single life. That is why the study of early cinemas is not only study of local lore, but first of all of the history of cinema.

Translated by Birgit Beumers

Notes

1. "This program was prepared for the ball 'Satirikon' and could not be implemented due to circumstances beyond the organizers' control."
2. The first version of this feuilleton was published in *Vestnik kinematografii* (Anon. 1911d). Later Averchenko reworked the feuilleton and included the novella "The Courtesan's Secret" into the text, which is missing in the original version.
3. Ob osmotre Chinovnikom Osob[ogo] Poruch[eniia] pri Gl[avnom] Upravl[enii] po d.p. Stat[skim] Sov[etnikom] Rebrovym nekotorykh peterburgskikh kinematografov; Russian Institute for Art History RIII [Rossiiskii institut istorii iskusstv].

References

A-fer. 1914. "Novye teatry" [New Theaters]. *Kino-kur'er* [Cine-Courier] 1: 8.
Anon. 1909. "Edison-teatr" [The Edison Theater]. *Sine-fono* [Cine-Phono] 3: 14.
Anon. 1910a. "Fel'eton. Istoriia odnogo kinematografa" [Feuilleton. The History of One Cinema]. *Artist i stsena* [Artist and Stage] 17: 21.
Anon. 1910b. "Krugom i okolo" [Around and Nearby]. *Artist i stsena* [Artist and Stage] 12–13: 31.
Anon. 1910c. "Otkrytye teatra 'Cristal Palace'" [Opening of the Cinema "Crystal Palace"]. *Artist i stsena* [Artist and Stage] 22–23: 29.
Anon. 1910d. "Raznye izvestiia" [Various News]. *Artist i stsena* [Artist and Stage] 22–23: 30.
Anon. 1911a. "Otkrytye teatra 'Soleil'" [The Opening of the Cinema "Soleil"]. *Artist i stsena* [Artist and Stage] 18: 21.
Anon. 1911b. "Pis'mo v redakstsiiu" [Letter to the Editors]. *Kinematograficheskii teatr* [Cinematic Theater] 13: 16.
Anon. 1911c. "Poleznye sovety nachinaiushchim predprinimateliam i vladel'tsam elektro-teatrov" [Useful Advice for Beginning Entrepreneurs and Owners of Electro-Theaters]. *Vestnik kinematografii* [Cinema Herald] 1: 13 and 2: 25.

Anon. 1911d. "Stranichka smekha" [Pages of Laughter]. *Vestnik kinematografii* [Cinema Herald] 8: 23.

Anon. 1912. "Otdel khudozhestvennoi kinematografii" [Artistic Cinema Section]. *Vestnik kinematografii* [Cinema Herald] 55: 12–13.

Anon. 1916. "Rekvizitsiia petrogradskikh teatrov" [Requisition of Petrograd Cinemas]. *Sine-fono* [Cine-Phono] 17–18: 74.

Argus. 1915a. "Net fil'm!" [No Film!]. *Obozrenie teatrov* [Theater Review] [Petrograd], July 21: 7.

Argus. 1915b. "O posetiteliakh kinemo" [About Visitors of the Cinema]. *Obozrenie teatrov* [Theater Review] [Petrograd], July 15: 7.

Bagrov, Petr. 2004. "Pervyi direktor Nikolai Grigor" [The First Director Nikolai Grigor]. *Ot "Pikadilli" do "Avrory"* [From the "Piccadilly" to the "Aurora"]. [Jubilee edition]. St Petersburg: Kinoteatr "Avrora", pp. 10–11.

Bukhov, Arkadii 1915. "O kinematograficheskikh avtorakh" [About Cinematographic Authors]. *Kinematograf* [Cinematograph] 1: 9.

Diushen, Boris. 2003. "Beglye vospominaniia" [Cursory Recollections]. *Kinovedcheskie zapiski* [Film-Scholars' Notes] 64: 175–184.

G.M. 1910. "Nashe razvlechenie [rasskaz]" [Our Entertainment (A Tale)]. *Kine-zhurnal* [Cine-Journal] 13: 6–9; also in *Kinemakolor* 1: 11.

K-vich. 1916. "Provintsial'nye vpechatleniia" [Provincial Impressions]. *Pegas* 4: 99.

"Khronika" [Chronicles]. 1909a. *Sine-fono* [Cine-Phono] 1: 12.

"Khronika" [Chronicles]. 1909b. *Sine-fono* [Cine-Phono] 3: 9.

"Khronika" [Chronicles]. 1910a. *Kine-zhurnal* [Cine-Journal] 5: 9.

"Khronika" [Chronicles]. 1910b. *Sine-fono* [Cine-Phono] 22: 9

"Khronika" [Chronicles]. 1910c. *Sine-fono* [Cine-Phono] 5: 15.

"Khronika" [Chronicles]. 1910d. *Sine-fono* [Cine-Phono] 8: 11.

"Khronika" [Chronicles]. 1911. *Sine-fono* [Cine-Phono] 14: 6.

"Khronika" [Chronicles]. 1913. *Vestnik kinematografii* [Cinema Herald] 1: 10.

"Khronika" [Chronicles]. 1914a. *Kine-zhurnal* [Cine-Journal] 10: 53.

"Khronika" [Chronicles]. 1914b. *Sine-fono* [Cine-Phono] 10: 26–27

"Khronika" [Chronicles]. 1914c. *Sine-fono* [Cine-Phono] 8: 26.

"Khronika" [Chronicles]. 1914d. *Sine-fono* [Cine-Phono] 9: 26.

"Khronika" [Chronicles]. 1914e. *Vestnik kinematografii* [Cinema Herald] 1 (81): 30.

"Khronika" [Chronicles]. 1914f. *Vestnik kinematografii* [Cinema Herald] 3 (83): 34.

"Khronika" [Chronicles]. 1914g. *Vestnik kinematografii* [Cinema Herald] 4 (84): 29.

"Khronika" [Chronicles]. 1914h. *Vestnik kinematografii* [Cinema Herald] 12 (92): 22

"Khronika" [Chronicles]. 1915a. *Obozrenie teatrov* [Theater Review] (Petrograd), July 25: 8.

"Khronika" [Chronicles]. 1915b. *Vestnik kinematografii* [Cinema Herald] 8 (110): 44.

Kovalova, Anna. 2012. *Kinematograf v Peterburge 1907–1917. Kinoproizvodstvo i fil'mografiia* [Cinema in Petersburg 1907–1917. Film Production and Filmography]. St Petersburg: Skriptorium.

Kovalova, Anna and Iurii Tsiv'ian. 2011. *Kinematograf v Peterburge 1896–1917. Kinoteatry i zriteli* [Cinema in Petersburg 1986–1917. Movie Theaters and Audiences]. St Petersburg: Masterskaia SEANS, Skriptorium.

Likhachev, Dmitrii. 2007. *Vospominaniia* [Recollections]. Moscow:

Vagrius."Obozrenie kinematografov" [Cinema Review]. 1915. *Obozrenie teatrov* [Theater Review] [Petrograd], July 11: 7.

"Obozrenie teatrov" [Theater Review]. 1910. *Artist i stsena* [Artist and Stage] 18–19: 32.
"Obozrenie teatrov" [Theater Review]. 1911a. *Artist i stsena* [Artist and Stage] 3: 23.
"Obozrenie teatrov" [Theater Review]. 1911b. *Artist i stsena* [Artist and Stage] 17: 14.
Orlov, Nikolai. 1999. "Pervye kinos"emki v Rossii. Vospominanie" [The First Films Shot in Russia. Recollections]. *Kinovedcheskie zapiski* [Film-Scholars' Notes] 42: 203–208.
P. 1915. "Okhota.... pushche nevoli" [Getting in Over One's Head]. *Kine-zhurnal* [Cine Journal] 23–24: 91.
Rex. 1915. "Nevskii. (Iz petrogradskikh nabliudenii)" [Nevsky: Petrograd Observations]. *Kine-zhurnal* [Cine-Journal] 7–8: 125–129.
Shklovskii, Viktor. 1966. *Zhili-byli*. [Once upon a Time]. Moscow: Sovetskii pisatel'.
Tiomkin, Dimitri and Prosper Buranelli. 1959. *Please Don't Hate Me*. New York: Doubleday & Company.
Tsiv'ian, Iurii. 1991. *Istoricheskaia retseptsiia kino. Kinematograf v Rossiii 1896–1930*. Riga: Zinātne. In English as Yuri Tsivian, *Early Cinema in Russia and its Cultural Reception*, translated by Alan Bodger, edited by Richard Taylor and with a foreword by Tom Gunning, London: Routledge 1994.
Varlamov, Konstantin. 1913. "Kak ia smotriu na kinematograf" [How I look at cinema]. *Kino-teatr i zhizn'* [Film-Theater and Life] 5: 7.

2

(V)GIK and the History of Film Education in the Soviet Union, 1920s–1930s

Masha Salazkina

Film Education in the Soviet Union

The history of film education in the Soviet Union is deservedly celebrated as the earliest example of the formation of a new discipline. With a highly developed and effective organizational structure, it managed to produce successful filmmakers, technicians, and critics/theorists, while contributing to the development of the film industry and the emerging academic field of film studies. Elsewhere in Europe and North America, the process of institutionalizing film training – both academic and professional – took place gradually over the course of the 1930s through the 1960s, while in the Soviet Union, by the late 1920s/early 1930s, such a formation was nearly complete and served as a model for many film educational structures around the world, especially those where the state played an important part in the development of cinema.

There is no doubt that the direct involvement of the state, which assigned high priority not only to the development of cinema but also to its didactic role, is one of the key factors accounting for this early solidification of the film education apparatus in the Soviet Union. The direct involvement and critical support of the state combined with both the existing lively cinematic and near-cinematic culture of modernist and avant-garde arts, and a highly developed intellectual and critical apparatus (themselves often already interconnected by artistic self-theorization articulated in manifestos, and the affiliation of intellectuals, critics, and scholars with specific cultural and artistic associations), creating the conditions for the development of the new discipline. In the case of cinema, its status as an industry in 1920s Soviet Union was what made the otherwise common interaction between

A Companion to Russian Cinema, First Edition. Edited by Birgit Beumers.
© 2016 John Wiley & Sons, Inc. Published 2016 by John Wiley & Sons, Inc.

the new state and new cultural formations, unique. The state's primary goal in supporting film was, as was the case with all other industries, to ensure that it developed a qualified cadre, which was lacking after the Revolution when most of the film industry practitioners left Russia. Thus much of the official discourses around the creation of film educational institutions in the 1920s and 1930s mirror the state rhetoric on "qualified cadre," and the ideological and economic pressures connected to production problems. The creation of this cadre was a particular challenge for a new industry, and a new art; the only existing training models were for apprenticeship and theater. The former was not possible precisely because the experienced practitioners and older structures were either deemed ideologically inappropriate or were simply unavailable, and the latter was not effective in addressing the industrial and technical specificities of cinema.

Intense and continual institutional restructuring marked the history of film education in general, and (V)GIK in particular, during the first decades of its existence. This restructuring is illustrated by the number of times the institution changed its name between 1919 and 1934: beginning as the First State Film School in 1919 [Goskinoshkola], it was renamed State Technical College of Cinematography (GTK) in early 1922 and by the end of that year changed its name again to State Practical Institute of Cinema (GIK). From there it went back to the State Technical College [Gosudarstvennyi tekhnikum kinematografii, GTK] in 1925, becoming the State Institute of Cinematography [Gosudarstvennyi institut kinematografii, GIK], adding "Higher" to the name in 1934 to indicate the addition of the graduate school (VGIK), only to remove the graduate school and settle finally on All-Soviet Institute of Cinematography 1938, keeping the same acronym, VGIK, by which it is known to this day.[1]

This constant change in the institutional status reflected both the challenge of creating a brand new educational apparatus and the country's political and economic shifts. In that sense, the history of VGIK goes hand in hand with the larger history of the country and of the film industry. Thus many aspects of these changes throughout those crucial decades between 1919 and 1936 tell a story that is very similar to other cultural spheres in the Soviet Union of the time, such as the gradual but relentless centralization of power resulting in the rise of (V)GIK as the primary site for film education in the Soviet Union, and a constant reshuffling of administration, teachers, and methods reflecting the shifting ideological and political struggles, growing dominance of narrowly defined Marxist-Leninist doctrines, and eventual elimination of any intellectual and artistic diversity in the service of the ideals of Socialist Realism. This particular story, however, is not without surprises – demonstrating how the development of film education was anything but linear, and despite the tight control, not always completely in line with the dominant political culture. Thus, for example, even though (V)GIK is consistently associated with Stanislavsky's "method" of actor training, which in the 1930s became implicated in the shift from avant-garde theory and practice to the institutionalization of Socialist Realism, it was not until the 1940s that this method became institutionalized at VGIK. Similarly, the otherwise dominant and successful policy of quotas that formed part of the social mobility that characterized the "Great Turn" in the cultural revolution (as famously described by Sheila Fitzpatrick, 1979) largely failed in film education (see Miller 2010, 142–144) – and it was not until after World War II that the influx of newly returned war veterans changed that dynamic. In the course of the 1920s to 1930s, (V)GIK served as a, however temporary, safe haven for many artists and intellectuals. At the same time, the "support" provided by the state to the educational structures turns out to have been largely rhetorical – while closely scrutinized and even more widely internationally celebrated, there was very little financial backing offered to the film schools, and despite the constantly emphasized importance of close ties between the academy and the industry, the actual relationship between (V)GIK and the film industrial organization(s) remained at best tense, and at worse openly hostile throughout the 1920s and 1930s.

What is important to emphasize in drawing out this early history of film education in the Soviet Union is that unique intellectual, methodological, and institutional challenges were presented from its very early stages by its radically new conception of what constituted education. Unlike any other film educational institution of that period, Soviet training was understood to combine practice with theory, and embrace artistic experimentation as a way to produce knowledge about cinema – that is, experimental research. (V)GIK is, therefore, a rare early example of a film school that quickly achieved the status of higher education, not vocational training – redefining the "craft" of filmmaking as a "discipline." This meant the inseparability of practice-based learning from the abstract models and an explicit discussion and constant debate about theory and methodology – of both filmmaking and film education. Because of this emphasis on theory as part of the praxis, questions of disciplinary method(s) were foregrounded from the first years of its existence. Of course, no such method existed as cinema was not only a new art form, but had not been embraced by the Academy as a proper object of higher learning. It would need to be invented and developed, and this became one of the key issues unique to the debates about film education that shaped the institutional discourses in the Soviet Union. Thus significantly earlier than anywhere else in the world, film education moved towards the notion of cinema as an academic and scholarly discipline. In the course of the 1920s and 1930s (in different ways), state film educational institutions became centers for the production of film theory and methodology.

Unlike elsewhere in the world during the 1920s, film instruction in the Soviet Union fairly quickly "coalesce[d] into a coherent field solidified around fixed questions and sets of practices," corresponding exactly to what Thomas Kuhn refers to as the "pre-paradigmatic phase" of disciplinary development characterized by conflicts between different groups claiming the primacy of their method for the institutionalization of the subject (Polan 2007, 6). The status of film education as not only professional training but foundational for the development of film as an academic and critical discipline with a highly developed methodological, theoretical, and pedagogical apparatus, makes it an important object of study not only for scholars of Soviet culture and cinema, but for the history and epistemology of film studies.

While the relationship between the wide range of educational institutions that existed in the Soviet Union during that period, and the history of (V)GIK specifically, deserves greater scholarly attention and poses a great number of interesting problems, due to the limitations of the scope of this chapter, I will focus on the history of (V)GIK in the 1920s to 1930s as paradigmatic of the development of film education in the Soviet Union with the hope that new scholarship will soon construct a much-needed larger picture.

Foundational Years: 1919–1924: Striving for the Method and the Victory of the Academic Model

The need for the state organization of cinematic education was articulated very soon after the victory of the Revolution. As early as 1918, the newspaper *Pravda* published an article on the intended opening of a Film School by the Photo- and Cinematographic Committee [Kinofotokabinet] of the People's Commissariat of Enlightenment [Narkompros]. This decision was the result of a report given to the Committee by Vladimir Gardin, who was then appointed the first director of the new State School of Cinematography (Vinogradov and Ognev 2000, 8). Gardin was in some ways an unlikely figure for the propagation of the new Soviet film education – he was one of the important and successful directors of pre-Revolutionary Russia, specializing in the adaptation of the Russian classics (see Zhdan 1951) – in other words, exactly the kind of artistic production the new Soviet cinema was meant to disavow. But he was also one of the few artists of the Russian film scene who actively supported the Revolution, and in 1918 Gardin was head of the fiction film section of the Photographic and Cinematographic division of Narkompros. His proposal to the Film Committee presented a powerful argument for the creation of the School as a way to address the "production crisis" of cinematography: the need to mass produce specialists. Gardin emphasized that for successful film production the country needed not a handful of individual, talented artists but thousands and tens of thousands of them: "Film production begins with the training of these thousands and tens of thousands. When we have the masters in the numbers which are needed for the state film army – then we will see the results of the labor of this army" ("Iz vospominanii V.R.Gardina" in Vinogradov and Ognev 2000, 232). His proposal was to keep film education inseparable from film production itself while at the same time providing "serious production-based research into the problems of film art and the search for the new paths" (Vinogradov and Ognev 2000, 232). Education as he envisioned it would take four years, combining academic training with production experience, and he hoped that after the first four years, with at least ten such schools, the Soviet film industry could count on those tens of thousands of highly trained artists to bring Soviet film to international recognition.

Ironically, within just another decade the Soviet film industry would indeed achieve international recognition – including that of its pioneering efforts in film education, despite the fact that the actual development of this training was quite different from Gardin's vision, both conceptually and practically. Conceptually, his idea of fusing the academic and production processes was never fully realized, despite being debated throughout the 1920s. And practically, the kind of scale he envisioned fell even further from what became the reality. Instead of the "army of film artists" smoothly mass-produced on an enormous scale through a unified method technically and infrastructurally supported by the state and the film industry, the successes of the Film School were the result of a small group of teachers and students battling abysmal conditions in an intellectually heterogeneous environment full of creative, intellectual, personal, and political conflict and never-ending restructuring.

The question of whether the Film School should be directly linked to the film industry or have an independent academic status became one of the key points of contention throughout this early period, and continued throughout the 1920s and 1930s. The other "problem" was the status of actor training in the School, as well as the method for such training.

Gardin's initial plan for the School was to include workshops for directors, screenwriters, and editors. Their goal would be to "develop new directions, new methods of work and solve artistic problems" (Vinogradov and Ognev 2000, 232). The main problems he identified were: montage, the script and standardization of scriptwriting, scientific research, technological experimentation, and the rationalization of work. It is clear that the scientific organization of labor and production, and specifically problems of industrial mass production were at the core of the organization of education and its intellectual and ideological mission. According to Gardin, the goal of this School was to raise the level of the Soviet film industry to the "heights of the world accomplishments," which, like everything else in the country, envisioned itself as large scale industrial production. The role of the auteur within this discourse was similar to that of an artisan: insufficient at best, and dangerous at worst. He warns that: "[if you give us film now] we won't create an industry but instead will produce flawed product [*brak*] and shine with single pictures which prove only the talent of their authors and not their leaders/managers [*rukovody*]" (Vinogradov and Ognev 2000, 232).

In seeming contradiction to their notion of film production on an industrial scale was the practical emphasis on actor training. In fact, despite the ambitious plans outlined above, most of the educational activity in the early days of the School centered on work with the actors. The method for actor training in the first decade of the School was not based on Stanislavsky's model, for which VGIK became later known, but on the Volkonsky "system of expressive man," which – when applied to cinema – produced the notion of the model actor [*naturshchik*], as theorized and practiced in the early 1920s by Lev Kuleshov and Vsevolod Pudovkin. This system of actor training famously rejects the interiority of the actor's creative process (which characterizes Stanislavsky's method) understanding acting, instead, as a fully exteriorized grammar of rhythmically exact, perfectly controlled muscular movements, which constitute a given emotional signification. The origins of this method were in the theories of François Delsarte and Émile Jaques-Dalcroze, and through its popularization by Prince Volkonsky became very popular in Russia in pre-revolutionary cultural circles (see Yampolsky 1995). This "new anthropology of the actor" with its absolute control over the body and its communicative abilities, was closely tied to the theories of rationalization of labor both in its origins and especially in its reception in the Soviet Union,[2] creating a paradigm that was theoretically consistent and distinctly avant-garde.

In the first years of its existence, the School faced the most basic challenges, which had to do with abysmal infrastructure (not surprisingly, in the years of War Communism), which made the functioning of the School almost impossible. The total lack of cameras or film made any kind of technical training for cameramen or directors impossible, giving an additional rationale for favoring actor training. Working against even this, however, was the fact that model-actor training was largely based on a series of physically demanding athletic exercises (including fencing, dance, and acrobatics), poorly accommodated by the tiny size of the first School's building. Even more challenging was the fact that despite the leaders of the School's emphasis on the specificity of training actors for cinema, the School was not equipped with any film technology, making the notion of film acting rather abstract. In response to this challenge, Gardin famously came up with a method of training actors for the screen by having them perform literally inside a frame – velvet curtains were moved up and down a frame lit with electric light bulbs, to mark the borders of an imaginary shot – and model actors performed inside it. This method focused on the understanding of actors' facial expressions (in particular simulating the experience of a cinematic "close up" as necessitating a different apparatus of expressions).

In addition to internal difficulties, the School was immediately under attack from the outside as well. The strongest criticisms were leveled by the film industry itself, which was not interested in providing its resources for the School's use. While the School requested the cooperation of all the film studios to provide space and equipment for the first student production (to be directed by Gardin), no studio agreed to do so. As a result, the School performed theatrical sketches based on intended future films as a way of demonstrating its training methods. It was only when the Photo- and Cinematographic Committee made a decision to involve the School in the production of "agitational (poster) films"[3] that students gained direct experience in the filmmaking process. Lev Kuleshov, who by 1920 was leading the montage section of the School, accepted this assignment to shoot on location with his students' assistance, which in reality meant that the instruction of his section of the School came to a halt. In the meantime, Gardin was successful in directing the first full-length feature film produced entirely by students and teachers of the School: *Sickle and Hammer* [*Serp i molot*, 1921].

In the meantime, the School came under attack from the Cinema Committee of Narkompros, which strongly advocated the academic direction of film education and criticized the School for its inability to "resolv[e] philosophical-aesthetic questions of film art," or organize institutional structures that would "synthesize the experimental solutions to the questions of instruction, foundation and coordination of curriculum and methods of instruction" (Vinogradov and Ognev 2000: 249). As a result of a series of institutional reorganizations, the State Film School changed its status and was renamed several times between 1921 and 1925, and also changed its reporting structure from the Film Committee to the Section for Professional Selection [Glavprofotbor], which was in charge of professional education. This was indicative of a changed attitude: the state demanded a more rigorous didactic, theoretical, and methodological basis for film education – and Gardin's "practical," industry-based approach was insufficient to meet such demands. At the same time, even the supporters of his ideas around the integration of studio experience with theoretical learning – such as Kuleshov and Pudovkin, who was studying at that time in Kuleshov's montage studio at the School – were opposed to Gardin's more traditional ideas of acting rooted in theater, favoring a more radically film-specific version of model-actor system.

Gardin left the School under pressure, and by 1922 Vasilii Il'in took up the position of Dean [*rektor*]. Il'in was one of the key figures who shaped the first decade of the School's development and its theoretical orientation, a fascinating and largely forgotten figure in the history of Russian and Soviet cinema. He had worked as an architect, stage-designer, and actor in the pre-Revolutionary Russian cinema, then graduated from the Higher Art and Technical Studios Vkhutemas [Vysshie khudozhestvenno-tekhnicheskie masterskie], and from the first years after the Revolution became involved in the political work surrounding the organization of cinema and the development of some of the key decrees governing cinematic production and education between 1918 and 1926. He was an old friend of Gardin from both their pre-Revolutionary work in cinema and their political organizational work (Il'in, in fact presided in the Cinema Committee of Narkompros, which approved the foundation of the School). He was also one of the seminal ideologues of the Volkonsky system and of the model-actor training propounded by Kuleshov and Pudovkin. However, unlike them, Il'in was a firm believer in the academic and scholarly mission of the School and opposed the merger between film studios and the educational process. This lead to a series of conflicts, and when Kuleshov left the School in 1923 (at that point already renamed GIK – the State Institute of Cinematography) to set up his own studio, he took the best students with him, among them Pudovkin and Aleksandra Khokhlova.

By then, the public and official debates over the inefficiency of the School were in full swing, resulting in a decision to close it down in 1923, and move it to Petrograd, where the Institute of Screen Arts had existed since 1918 and was by that time successfully graduating students. Due, however, to the overwhelming, negative response by the faculty and students of the Institute, the decision was overturned later that year, and after a series of re-organizations, (V)GIK re-opened.

Centralization and Reorganization: 1924–1930

In 1924, Sovkino was formed and became the main organization overseeing film and distribution, claiming a monopoly over all imports and exports, and giving tax exemptions to all film activities. At the same time, Narkompros started on a new reorganization policy, eliminating competing and experimental educational institutions. Both of these developments were geared toward greater centralization of the state's control over the various sites of production (including that of film and education). They targeted a wide variety of film studios, workshops, and schools across the country, which were deemed to be falling short of the state's demands for professionalization.

(V)GIK, too, was first closed, then reorganized and reopened as a technical college (under the acronym of GTK, which it would keep until 1930), modeled on such organizations as Vkhutemas. The institution's status as a technical college meant that it was equated with that of secondary education, and had a number of negative implications: it reduced the School's budget, making professorial salaries consistent with those of secondary school teachers, and it reduced the level of education required for admissions to only seven years of primary and secondary schooling.

At this point, the program of education was still fully committed to the Volkonsky method of actor training, while slowly starting to form other cinematic directions. In 1923, the "film-engineering" department was formed (which included sections for film technicians and cameramen), and in 1924, three new workshops became part of the School's structure: directing, animation, and "photocomposition." The animation workshop in particular had a distinct status within the School – unlike the other workshops which had a largely educational/academic function, it was formed by a group of former students of Vkhutemas, and facilitated experimental production. This group included most of the prominent early Soviet animation artists: Ivan Ivanov-Vano, Vladimir Suteev, Iurii Merkulov, and others. It was as a result of this development that many of the first Soviet animated films were made – and the animation workshop existed as a semi-independent part of the School until 1928, when it was moved directly to the film studio.

In the years between 1924 and 1928 the School gradually changed, slowly but steadily starting to eliminate the vestiges of the earlier cinematic and theatrical culture, including the theoretical and practical experiments in acting, which characterized its first decade, and bringing in greater systematization of the curriculum and allowing for greater access to film production, while at the same time creating tighter ideological control over the educational bases. In 1925 Il'in, who had been at the intellectual core of the School, was first demoted to Head of the Pedagogical Section, and eventually forced out of the School. As Party control tightened, the orientation of the School changed again – dismissing the "theoretical experimental lab" approach as no longer viable for meeting the increasing needs of the industry, to which the Party demanded it have greater ties. In 1926, in order to address these concerns, Abram Room, who had at that point just started his cinematographic career, was brought in as the new Head of the Pedagogical Section to orchestrate this vision. It was at this point that the famous – and still existing – model of establishing director's workshops as the main organizational structure of the School was formed. Abram Room, Kuleshov and Pudovkin, who returned to the Institute to pursue their vision of closer ties between education and production, began their workshops in 1926, when the first pavilion for film production opened. The presence of the three directors, who at that point had already established themselves on Soviet and international screens, temporarily lifted the morale of the School with the promise of "real" cinematic work. However, it also signaled a total shift from Il'in's method, which had demanded a common theoretical method of study across specific disciplines. With Il'in's departure, the new structure, which relied on the individual leader of the workshop (i.e., Room, Kuleshov or Pudovkin) to provide a teaching methodology and curriculum to its students, meant that any search for a systematic study of cinema was replaced with a practice-based approach.

However, despite all the official rhetoric about the direct ties between education and the production process, the budget of the School was such that it did not allow any practice-based work for its students. The relationship with the big studios was still extremely strained, and at best students' "practice" consisted of passive observation during the shooting of a film, as the commercial directors did not trust the students to handle any tasks or be involved in the film production in any way. For example, Mezhrabprom-Rus' studio (with whom the School shared a space in the same building) signed an agreement in 1927 to supply five feature films a year to be produced by the School – an agreement that never materialized, although the studio did pick its actors and cameramen from among the students in the School (Anon. 1927, 65). The most successful branch of the School at this point was the training of cameramen, who were finally equipped with real film – though only 100–150 m per year per student of the upper years, and they had to undertake the study of the variety of camera and light equipment by studying foreign instruction manuals. To raise funds, the school attempted to lead semi-private commercial initiatives, such as the opening of a movie theater and commercial photo studio in its building, and the production and sale of photo albums. However, none of these proved profitable, except for the production and sale of ink, which was done through the cashier's office of the School's union (Lebedev 1974, 343).

Given the financial difficulties and constant reorganization of its structure, location (the School moved physically six times between 1919 and 1927), and curriculum, it is not surprising that the School did not graduate its first students until 1927 (eight years from its foundation). By this point any of the School's "successes" were difficult to see, and pressure to close it was stronger than ever and fueled by a lively debate in the press where many established filmmakers spoke out against the very idea of academic film education (Trauberg 1927). A momentous shift in the state policy towards cinema in 1928/29 and the greater state control it brought about, however, and perhaps paradoxically, allowed for a new series of developments in the School solidifying its status as the center of film education in the Soviet Union and increasing its resources.

1928 was a fateful year for the All-Soviet Party Conference on Cinema, which harshly criticized Sovkino for failing to develop the industry. Along with the well-known call for "cinema for the millions," the resolutions of the conference emphasized the importance of expanding the industry, denounced the ideological unreliability of the leaders of the film industry, and demanded more cadres with worker and peasant backgrounds to be shifted from theater and literature to cinema in order to ensure the correct ideological orientation for the industry. This was quickly followed in early 1929 by the Central Committee decree "On the Strengthening of Cinema Cadre."

Two sets of consequences for the School resulted from these laws. The first was the introduction of quotas for students of working class and peasant origins. The initial proposal indicated that 75 percent of students were to represent these social groups. This decision was implemented until 1934 when it was reversed due to the failure of students to graduate. The other consequence was a result of the centralization of education: all private film workshops and schools were closed down, and the functions of the Moscow and Leningrad schools became fully differentiated with Moscow's role to prepare a creative/artistic cadre, while Leningrad's was to train technical support (which meant practically disbanding the highly successful School for Screen Arts). GTK was to be given significantly greater support financially and in terms of its faculty: bringing in successful filmmakers and writers to teach and develop the curriculum. In addition to the technical infrastructure, attention was also paid to the need to publish specialized scholarly and instructional material (A. Zh. 1928). These measures were designed to develop a unified systematic scholarly and methodological approach for the teaching and study of cinema, (needless to say, in line with objectives of the state and the Marxist doctrine), with an understanding that such an approach would be able to bridge the gap between scholarly efforts and production needs. As noted earlier, it is somewhat paradoxical that the very decrees that began the curtailing of formal and ideological diversity and experimentation in early Soviet cinema, leading in turn to the establishment of Socialist Realism as the official aesthetic doctrine, also allowed for the development of a systematic study of cinema and its legitimization as a scholarly discipline.

Decisive in this larger process was the involvement of Sergei Eisenstein, who in 1928 formally joined the faculty. Upon his arrival, he immediately organized teaching-research workshops [instruktorsko-issledovatel'skie masterskie] on a par with director's workshops led by Room, Pudovkin, and Kuleshov. The screenwriter Natan Zarkhi (who wrote the script adapting Maksim Gor'kii's novel for Pudovkin's *Mother* [*Mat'*, 1926]) was also brought into faculty, and screenwriting established as a subject.

As this group coalesces as the core faculty, we can more clearly trace the shift of the School's theoretical ideology away from the experimental lab approach centered around the theory of "expressive moment" actor training that characterized Il'in's theoretical and pedagogical platform along with the early Soviet avant-garde (as embodied in Kuleshov and Pudovkin's early work), towards the more recognizable formation symptomatic of accommodations to a broader shift towards psychological realism.

For GTK it meant that Il'in's method, which was at the core of the training for most of the students, was almost completely phased out. This change, imposed from above, was not met favorably by most of the students. In fact, 26 students from the first graduating class in 1927 signed and published a petition calling for the rejection of the workshop structure and for the return of Il'in and his method which, they argued, was integral to film education (Belostotskii, Bronshtein, Vasil'chikov et al., 1928). These demands were met with harsh criticism by the School's faculty and administration who, in an open letter, presented this conflict as one between a charismatic individual vs the collective: "we, the leaders of GTK, respond to the tactless and irresponsible challenge with our work and call for collective creative labor, rejecting the monopoly of an individual" (Sharikian 1928).

The period of internal strife and search for a systematic method was now over, and the theoretical legacy of Il'in, Gardin and other proponents of the model actor training could now only be glimpsed through its influence on the early work of Kuleshov and Pudovkin. Mikhail Yampolsky makes the well-substantiated claim that "we might [...] be justified in talking about the specific GTK-GIK film theory" as that of a collective production centered around the Film School in its first decade, and not reducible or merely equivalent to its role in the formation of Kuleshov and Pudovkin's discursive apparatus (Yampolsky 1995, 50). Despite the consequences of this claim on our understanding of such a crucial moment in the development of film theory, it still remains largely unexplored.

The public and financial boost given to the status of GTK quickly enabled faculty to lobby the government in favor of changing its educational profile away from that of a technical college towards a university-level institution. Faculty's frustration with the low educational level and lack of artistic experience of the entering students (many of whom had just 7 years of formal schooling and were no older than 16) was conflicting with the continued emphasis on research and academic prestige. Throughout 1929, appeals for GTK to obtain the status of an institution of higher learning [VUZ, Vyshchee Uchebnoe

Zavedenie] – that is, university-equivalent, were made in the press. Eisenstein, among others, called for the conversion of GTK into a university-level institution with a research institute as part of its structure, in order to "replace the 'intuitive genius' of Soviet cinema with a Marxist scientific system of cinematic labor" (Eisenstein 1929).[4]

From GTK to (V)GIK (1930–1937)

After years of reorganizations, and following intense debates in the press and among cultural bureaucrats, in 1930 the Film School finally attained the status of an institution of higher education (VUZ), and changed its name to State Institute of Cinematography (GIK). This coincided with the reorganization of Sovkino into Soyuzkino, which was now the umbrella organization to which the new institute reported.

The size of the Institute almost tripled compared to its previous years as a result of the shift in its status. As part of the new admissions that year, 58 students were accepted to the department of cinematography (cameramen), 40 to the department of film directing, 57 to the newly formed department of screenwriting, 31 students were accepted to join the actor studio (which was already excluded from the main curriculum, and was to be dismantled the following year) and 170 students continued from GTK to GIK. The length of the program of study would now consist of three years of coursework. As based on the newly instituted quotas, the Institute reported that 76 percent of the newly registered students were from the working class or peasant background, and 68 percent were members of *komsomol* or the Party, 44 percent represented national and ethnic minorities, including 3 foreign students. Since the educational minimum was raised to 9 years of formal school education, the overall number of applicants was significantly lower than before (Anon. 1939). The admission process was being conducted under pressure to meet the required quotas while simultaneously increasing the educational and artistic standards, which unsurprisingly, would quickly prove to be quite a disastrous combination.

The demands for greater professionalization and formalization of research and scholarly goals entailed in this change also led to a change of curriculum and personnel. The program of study now included much more political education with the introduction of such required courses as Leninism, Marxist Socialist Art (different from Art History or Art Theory) as well as History and Theory of Literature, Sociology of the Arts, Political Economy, Economics, and the Rational Organization of Production. Many new professors joined the Institute; most notable perhaps was the addition of the critic Viktor Shklovskii and the writer Feofan Shipulinskii. By 1932 the scope of the subjects expanded further to include separate departments of Newsreel and Scientific/Educational Cinema.

This increased politicization of education was both motivated and exacerbated by the beginnings of intense political cleansings sweeping the country. As early as 1930 the newly reorganized GIK came under attack for its association with a certain Martem'ian Riutin – a member of the regional Krasnopresnenskii Party committee (to which GIK was reporting) who was accused of distributing a paper criticizing Stalin's policies. As a result, the regional leadership of the Party was changed, and the new Party leaders were given direct control over the Institute (which it shared with Soiuzkino). With the goal of making it "politically healthier," the new leadership asked the Institute to develop a profile of a film professional [kinospetsialist] and clear educational plans that would be distributed to and used by film educational institutions "on the periphery." Even academic debates on this topic were mandated to yield "concrete positive results" instead of "scholastic word-pushing." It was announced that the development of a technological infrastructure would be a priority, but no funds were committed. The relationship between Soiuzkino and GIK was strained: Soiuzkino regularly failed to increase the Institute's budget or provide internships and jobs to the graduates. Despite and in response to this, GIK was asked to develop a detailed plan for professional internships that tied together pedagogical academic training [uchebno-metodicheskaia rabota] with professional experience.

At the same time, a series of articles in *Kino* and *Komsomol'skaia Pravda* attacked the Institute and individual students for ideological deviations, as well as the Institute at large for not meeting the goals set for it. The legacy of actor training came under particular attack. GIK was harshly criticized for the "formalist LEF training" and for not paying enough attention to the ideological importance of actor training. Their methods were identified with Factography, and "model acting" was attacked for equating actors (playing workers!) with objects, denying them agency, and depriving them of being part of the creative process. Instead, they called on actors to be an equal participant in the creative collective on the same level with the directors, screenwriters, and cameramen (Voronov, Shukailo, Lyzlova et al., 1931). As a result of these attacks, acting was first merged with directing and dramaturgy, and then eliminated from the Institute entirely. At that point, although "biomechanics" was still taught in the School in the early 1930s, all the older acting theorists (Il'in, Gardin) had already gone, Kuleshov was thought of primarily as a theorist of montage, and Pudovkin had shifted his discussion of acting away from the "model actor" idea of the earlier period towards a model of Socialist Realism.

The establishment of film criticism and film journalism was given a new priority as a discipline to study in university-level film education, and was also conceptualized as a way to introduce, enforce, and provide greater control over a *uniform* model for film scholarship, away from the "formalist tendencies" and multiplicity of positions and points of view, towards a unified "Marxist-Leninist method." It is clear from these discussions that the term "artistic method" in this context becomes an early code word for "Socialist Realist method," used in direct opposition to "the leftist excesses" (Zarkhin 1931).

Since it was the lack of theoretical, methodological, and ideological cohesion that the Institute was constantly accused of, research and the pedagogical methodology of the study of cinema were given a new emphasis and institutional priority as a way to solidify its apparatus. While this process was obviously enforced from above, it also attracted many of the most brilliant theorists and scholars, who shared the ambition of creating an institutional space for further development of a theoretical platform for the scholarly study of cinema. The new GIK prioritized the graduate school – citing Stalin's directives to promote graduate education – which was intended as both an opportunity for people with higher education in other disciplines to receive a degree in film, and as a specialized graduate education for film professionals (Order No. 62 from GIK, June 1, 1932; Vinogradov and Ognev 2000, 162).

Eisenstein was abroad during the years of the reorganization of the Institute, but he was characteristically involved in the process even from afar, writing letters of support for a more thorough and academic curriculum. He also warned against speeding up the teaching and learning processes, pointing out that in education "the greatest art is in the ability to pose questions and achieve answers" which requires time for working through problems and more serious course of study to enable a systematic approach to the problems of Soviet cinema (Eisenstein 1968, 39–40). Upon his return in 1932 Eisenstein resumed his position in the newly reorganized Institute. It was the pedagogical and administrative work by two figures over the next decade – Sergei Eisenstein and Nikolai Lebedev – that would be fundamental to its growth and development, and the unique research status achieved by (V)GIK during the 1930s.

Thus, despite the intense political scrutiny, the constantly escalating threat of purges, and problems with the infrastructure, the years between 1932 and 1937 proved to be the most productive in the Institute's history in terms of realizing its ambitious institutional research platform. In the early 1930s (V)GIK became not only the oldest but by far the most advanced film education institution in the world with regards to developing film studies as an academic discipline. This was true in terms of theory, historiography, and methodology, as well as an institutional ability to grant advanced academic degrees, create a film archive, and plans for a museum of cinema.

Nikolai Lebedev started teaching at (V)GIK in the fall of 1931. Throughout the 1920s he had established himself as a director of educational cinema, having directed five feature-length documentary films at the studio for *kulturfilms*. He had also been actively publishing essays on various aspects of cinema and started working on a dissertation on film theory in the graduate school of the Communist Academy. He initially started teaching in the newly formed faculty of cinematography, leading its newsreel department. Given his keen interest in theoretical questions and pedagogical practices, he quickly became the head of the institute-wide committee on the methodology of cinema, whose first goal was to evaluate the programs of study for individual departments. Within a year the committee was allowed to develop its own program of study, which resulted in the creation of the first courses on the history and methodology of cinema, and eventually led to the reorganization of the committee into the department of film history and theory. In 1933, once Lebedev defended his dissertation on film theory entitled "On Cinematic Specificity," he was appointed first the Deputy Director of Research, and by 1934 succeeded as director of (V)GIK, which he remained until 1937. For many decades after his dismissal, he nevertheless continued to teach at the Institute and was instrumental in the creation and preservation of its internal archive (Lebedev 1970, 350–355).

Lebedev and Eisenstein's ambition to create a methodological and pedagogical apparatus for the systematic development of leading research in film studies at the Institute was not an easy task.

By early 1930s, perhaps the best organized – and largest – faculty was that of cinematography. Its program understood the work of cameramen as a combination of both technical and aesthetic criteria and skills, elevating it to an artistic status. From its very beginning, the faculty was able to boast many of the most famous Soviet cameramen, such as Vladimir Nil'sen or Anatolii Golovnia. It was also highly specialized, methodologically differentiating between the training of cinematographers for fiction, newsreel (documentary), and educational (especially scientific) cinema. The latter two, being in very direct ways linked to the ideological goals of Soviet cinema, were given particular institutional priority.

Dramaturgy, or scriptwriting, was also prioritized, and as a new faculty in a newly reorganized Institute brought many established scholars and pedagogues from literature, theater, and philosophy, who quickly occupied a central role in the Institute. Valentin Turkin proved to be one of the only figures who successfully made the transition from the 1920s school to its new reincarnation, refocusing his intellectual and pedagogical efforts towards dramaturgy and developing instructional materials that defended the importance of the art of screenwriting, which came back into ideological focus as Soviet montage was replaced by sound film and Socialist Realism. Scripts, of course, were also a powerful way for the state to control the early stages of film production and exercise censorship, so it is not surprising that screenwriting rose as a new area of pedagogical and theoretical priority.

The faculty of actor training, on the other hand, was in a particularly precarious state. Not only did model-actor training come under direct political attack faced with the return of a psychological realism as the dominant official paradigm, but the introduction of sound, coinciding with (V)GIK's reorganization, meant that actor training had to be reconfigured to include significant work on voice and diction among many other changes to the acting style of silent cinema. Unable to address such pressures, (V)GIK closed down its faculty of acting in 1934, transferring all of its existing students to the actors' studio at Mosfilm.

Eisenstein's return as (V)GIK's head of directing in 1932 saved the faculty from a similar fate. He was able to attract many of the famous film directors back to the

Institute, whether as permanent faculty members (such as Kuleshov) or as visiting lecturers (such as Pudovkin and Aleksandr Dovzhenko). While bringing back its social and cultural prestige by involving important and successful cineastes, he also immediately threw himself into the methodological and theoretical challenge of developing a program of systematic study of film direction. This included everything, from designing entrance exams to the evaluation process, and of course, a complex and theoretically sophisticated course of study. Unlike Lebedev, who insisted that film theory and research methodologies be treated as separate subjects constituting part of the overall curriculum, Eisenstein's approach was to include all such issues (as well as many other branches of the humanities) into his own course on film direction, reflecting both his own remarkable erudition and his synthetic approach to epistemological problems as part of the creative process. This seemingly small difference in approach points to a much greater dynamic that can be seen throughout the institutional film culture of early Soviet cinema: the tension between the prestige of individual, highly versatile, and adaptable filmmaker auteurs, and the need for industrial organization of film production and education. This meant, on the one hand, that the most powerful driving force in the industry was indeed auteurist, garnering momentum in part by the institutional weight and prestige awarded to "star" auteurs (however fragile and temporary their political clout may have been). Directors sought to retain not only a greater degree of artistic autonomy but also to resist the division of labor, including the division between artistic and intellectual labor as perhaps best represented by Eisenstein as a filmmaker-theorist-pedagogue.[5] On the other hand, primacy was assigned to the industrial organization of film and education, which necessitated increasing specialization and marked institutional divisions as exemplified by Lebedev's insistence on separating methodology and theory as distinct pedagogical subjects, as well as the divisions and specializations within the directing and cinematography departments. The system essentially demanded the mass production of auteurs – a seeming contradiction, and yet embodied fully in the foundational dilemmas of the Institute. Its very institutionalization and centralization is what simultaneously allowed for more advanced production of knowledge, and enabled it to come under greater political control – a tension reflected in the struggle over (V)GIK's research agenda.

An important step in Lebedev's program for turning (V)GIK into a major center for film research was the establishment in 1933 of the Sector for Scientific Research [Nauchno-issledovatel'skii sektor, NIS] whose goal was to coordinate all the research and development of instructional materials, as well as their publication and dissemination. In order to create the necessary additional infrastructure and personnel, Lebedev arranged for the transfer of a department of methodology and organization of production from another institution, a research center for the technological aspects of film and photography [Nauchno-issledovatel'skii kinofotoinstitut, NIKFI], to be re-established at (V)GIK. Thus NIS was set up as a semi-autonomous structure within the Institute that had its own personnel in addition to those drawn from the existing faculty across the different departments, plus other artists and scholars brought in on a short-term basis to participate in individual projects (Lebedev 1970, 365). The specific goals of NIS were organized around two clusters. The first was the development of the infrastructure for research and preservation, such as the creation of a film archive, film museum, and a research library. The second focused on the organization of research, both individual and collaborative, leading to the publication of instructional and scholarly materials to be used for teaching at the Institute and its newly created graduate school. In the years between 1933 and 1938, NIS was responsible for producing the first systematized reference sources, including filmographies and bibliographies of Soviet and foreign films, archives of scripts and other production-related materials, and press clippings and other specialized film-related collections (Ryabchikova 2014). A series of research publications also took place under their auspices, although due to publishing capacity limitations – (V)GIK did not have its own publishing house – many of the dissertations and edited collections representing their research either came out in fragments through journals and newspapers, or were not published at all. A large-scale project for translations of the works on films from other languages was also being undertaken at the same time – though that, too, was only partially realized. The creation of the first systematic film archive also took place during this time. While the archival instinct was always remarkably strong in early Soviet film culture (with the first attempts to create film archives starting as early as 1923, when GIK began collecting materials towards the creation of the museum of cinema), the regular practice at the time – in the Soviet Union, as well as everywhere else – was to destroy the film prints once they were no longer in active circulation. Because they were necessary for teaching, the Institute started collecting prints of mostly foreign films in the late 1920s to use as illustrations for courses on the history of cinema. By the mid-1930s, the collection had grown to include several thousand titles, making it the first and the largest film archive of the time.[6]

As part of NIS, Eisenstein, together with Lebedev, took an active stance towards the creation of the graduate school, eventually paving the way for another major change in the institutional structure of the Institute in 1934.

In response to attacks on the Institute for failing in its mission of supplying the industry with highly trained professionals (based on the extremely low numbers of its graduates actually working in cinema), Lebedev and Eisenstein began to petition for a new academic model. They identified the problem as stemming from the fact that young students lacking knowledge of realities either of the cinematic production or of culture generally, could not be trained to be serious film professionals in such a short period of time. For a director to get all the necessary training – academic and practical – to prepare for a successful career would require about six to eight years of education. Since the Institute did not have the existing infrastructure (material as well as pedagogical) necessary for such a prolonged course of study, and the film industry urgently needed highly qualified specialists, Lebedev proposed admitting only those students with prior professional or academic experience, limiting the number of applicants and raising the acceptance criteria, and as a result, reducing the length of this new advanced degree to two years. In effect this also meant a radical change to the fulfilling the quota system, which would now be met by having a separate track for "worker students" who were not integrated into the general curriculum. After an intense campaign, a compromise was achieved, and Lebedev succeeded in changing the status of the Institute to that of a Specialized Academy, which indicated a post-graduate university level of education (signaled by adding *vyshchii* – "highest" – to its name, now abbreviated as VGIK). In addition to the inclusion of the graduate school, this change had a particular impact on the training of directors. In order to raise the bar on quality, the Institute accepted applicants for a special advanced (academy-type) degree, who had already had significant artistic or production experience, and identified the main goal of such training to be "to master the knowledge of the treasures of the world culture and the achievements of the new, the highest and most perfect culture of the socialist period" (Andrievskii, Annenskii, Barkhudar'ian et al. 1935). After the initial screening of applications, those admitted to entrance exams had to pass a special directing assignment designed by Eisenstein. In the first year of its existence, 90 people applied to this newly formed department; only 23 of them were allowed to take the entrance exams, and 15 were accepted as a result. The program of their study was also changed considerably: for example, as part of their curriculum, students were required to attend 25 plays staged in Moscow in their first year of study as part of their required course on theater history. The program also included a two-week long trip to Leningrad to visit museums as part of their art history course. Distinguished figures such as Dovzhenko, Grigorii Roshal', Vsevolod Meyerhold, Aleksandr Medvedkin, Boris Barnet, and Béla Balázs were brought in to teach and participate in the research sector. The much contested internship program was finally established for students to be able to go through practical training at the main film studios in the country; by the late 1930s graduates, unlike in earlier years, were placed at (mostly regional) film studios with a chance to make their own films.

However, despite – or perhaps because of – the overall support from the government, the growth and reorganization of the Institute, even during Lebedev's leadership (1932–1937), was accompanied by continuous ideological attacks and political purges, which created constant pressure on all the pedagogical practices. In 1935, a special committee was set up to review all the materials at the newly formed archive in order to assess their ideological appropriateness and confiscate any counter-revolutionary content (including individual shots) (VGIK Order 51, April 19, 1935, in Vinogradov and Ognev 2004, 18). By 1936, another committee was created to review all the teaching materials, plans of study, and research produced by the Institute for any signs of "formalism and other kinds of excesses in the theory and practice of cinematic arts" (VGIK Order 24, March 17, 1936, in Vinogradov and Ognev 2004, 55), which was followed by an evening of "discussion on formalism and naturalism" intended to underscore the danger of such aesthetic phenomena and attended by most of the leading faculty of the Institute. Despite his attempts to mediate the political pressures, Lebedev ultimately failed to keep the forces of Stalinist cultural repression at bay. The final break came in 1937, when Eisenstein, following his "political and ideological artistic errors in the making of *Bezhin Meadow*", was fired (temporarily – he was reinstated in 1938) by direct order of Boris Shumiatskii, then still the head of the State Management of Cinema (Soiuzkino), who would himself be arrested and sentenced to death just a year later. Lebedev was removed from his position as director, NIS was closed down, and with it, its film archive and all the plans for the creation of a film museum.

By 1938 (V)GIK was officially reorganized once again, reversing all the changes instituted by Lebedev and getting rid of the "academy-type," two-year higher degrees in directing and cinematography. All the research in the Institute was now to be geared toward the development of textbooks, and by 1939, the acting department was brought back with a training method firmly established in the Stanislavsky tradition of psychological realism that agreed with the principles of Socialist Realism. While Eisenstein and Lebedev would continue their efforts, yet another phase of pedagogical, institutional, and intellectual experimentation at the Institute was over, leaving many of its ambitious plans unrealized and ultimately forgotten.[7]

Notes

1 When discussing the history of the institution, it is usually referred to as (V)GIK to avoid confusion; the bracketing of the letter (V) reflects a range of name changes in the early years of existence.
2 The most radical enthusiasts of this method were the constructivists, such as Aleksei Gan, for whom Kuleshov's theories of the model-actor were evidence of the ultimate machine aesthetics. For a more detailed discussion on the relationship between theories of rationalization of labor and model-actor theories, see Olenina (2011, 20–50).
3 Agitational films [*agitki*] and agitational poster films [*agitplakaty*] were two types of short films made during the period of the Civil War, 1918–1921. These were short and explicit films illustrating a specific theme or conveying a direct message intended as part of ideological mobilization of the population. For more on this, see Taylor (1998).
4 What is particularly ironic about this claim is that it in fact describes the theoretical apparatus of Gardin and Il'in quite well, while Eisenstein's own work was never concerned with the theorization of collective artistic labor.
5 This, of course, is also well represented by Eisenstein's writing from the 1930s and 1940s, and his search for a unified "Method," seeking to synthesize the differentiation of the various branches of knowledge – literature, art, science, politics – into a unified system.
6 Because of its reorganization after the demise of NIS in 1937 and the eventual transfer of holdings to Gosfil'mofond in 1948, the film archive at VGIK failed to join the International Federation of Film Archives (FIAF) formed in 1938, which at the time

consisted of the British Film Institute (BFI), the French Cinémathèque, the Museum of Modern Art in New York, and the Reichsfilmarchiv in Berlin, all of whom started their film collection in the mid-1930s and – with the exception of the Reichsfilmarchiv – had close ties to the VGIK collection.

7 For more on Eisenstein's institutional work in establishing the academic discipline of film studies in the Soviet Union, see Salazkina and Ryabchikova (Forthcoming).

References

A. Zh. 1928. "Reorganizatsiia uchebnogo otdela. Ozdorovleniie raboty G.T.K." [Reorganization of the Educational Department. Enhancement of the Work of GTK]. *Kino* 31 (July 31), in *K istorii VGIKa* 1: 98–99.

Andrievskii, A., I. Annenskii, P. Barkhudar'ian et al. "Slushateli rezhisserskogo fakul'teta VGIKa" [Visiting Students of VGIK's Directing Department]. 1935. "Otkrytoe pis'mo" [Open Letter]. *Kino-gazeta* [Film-Paper] 4 (January 22), in *K istorii VGIKa* 1, 224.

Anon. 1927. "Kino-akter" [Film-Actor]. *Kino* 21 (May 24), in *K istorii VGIKa* 1, 65.

Anon. 1939. "Itogi priema v GIK" [Summary of GIK's Intake]. *Kino* 61 (October 30), in *K istorii VGIKa* 1, 139.

Belostotskii, M., L. Bronshtein, Iu. Vasil'chikov et al. 1928. "Iz zaiavleniia 26ti" [From the Statement of the 26]. *Kino* 37 (September 11), in *K istorii VGIKa* 1, 101.

Eisenstein. Sergei. 1929. "GTK – VUZ," *Kino* 11 (March 13), in *K istorii VGIKa* 1, 120.

Eisenstein, Sergei. 1968. "Pis'mo v GIK" [Letter to GIK], in *Sobranie sochinenii v shesti tomakh*, vol. 5 [Collected Works in 6 vols], 39–40. Moscow: Iskusstvo.

Fitzpatrick, Sheila. 1979. *Education and Social Mobility in the Soviet Union, 1921–1934.* Cambridge: Cambridge University Press.

Lebedev, Nikolai. 1970. "Ot shkoly k VUZu" [From School to College], in *K istorii VGIKa* 1, 350–360.

Lebedev, Nikolai. 1974. "Snova na pravakh tekhnikuma" [Again as Technical College], in *K istorii VGIKa* 1, 342–347.

Miller, Jamie. 2010. *Soviet Cinema: Politics and Persuasion under Stalin.* London: I.B. Tauris.

Olenina, Ana. 2011. "Partitury dvizheniia: kak ni stranno, o psikhologii naturshchika u Kuleshova" [The Movement Score: Strangely, about the Psychology of Kuleshov's Model Actor], *Kinovedcheskie zapiski* [Film-Scholars' Notes] 97: 20–50.

Polan, Dana. 2007. *Scenes of Instruction: The Beginnings of the US Study of Film.* Berkeley: University of California Press.

Ryabchikova, Natalie. 2014. "When Was Soviet Cinema Born? The Institutionalization of Soviet Film Studies and the Problems of Periodization." In *The Emergence of Film Culture. Knowledge Production, Institution Building and the Fate of the Avant-garde in Europe, 1919–1945*, edited by Malte Hagener, 118–140. London, New York: Berghahn.

Salazkina, Masha and Natalie Ryabchikova. Forthcoming. "Sergei Eisenstein and the Soviet Models for the Study of Cinema, 1920s–1940s." In *Sergei Eisenstein: Notes for a General History of Cinema*, edited by Naum Kleiman and Antonio Somaini, Amsterdam: Amsterdam University Press.

Sharikian, E. 1928. "GTK osparivaet zaiavlenie 26-ti" [GTK Challenges the Statement of the 26]. *Kino* 40 (October 2), in *K istorii VGIKa* 1, 101.

Taylor, Richard. 1998. *Film Propaganda: Soviet Russia and Nazi Germany*. London: I.B. Tauris.

Trauberg, Leonid. 1927. "Doloi kino-shkolu!" [Down with the Film School!]. *Kino* 49 (December 6), in *K istorii VGIKa* 1, 78–79.

Vinogradov, Vladimir and Konstantin Ognev, eds. 2000. *K istorii VGIKa (1919–1934)*, [About VGIK's History, 1919–1934], vol. 1, Moscow: VGIK.

Vinogradov, Vladimir and Konstantin Ognev, eds. 2004. *K istorii VGIKa (1935–1945)*, [About VGIK's History 1935–1945], vol. 2, Moscow: VGIK.

Voronov, B., P. Shukailo, A. Lyzlova et al. 1931. "Boltaiushchiesia v tolpe, ili strannye rassuzhdeniia Iakovleva o podgotovke kinoakterov" [Dangling in the Crowd: Iakovlev's Strange Ideas about Preparing Film Actors]. *Komsomol'skaia pravda* (May 26), in *K istorii VGIKa* 1, 158–159.

Yampolsky, Mikhail. 1995. "Kuleshov's Experiments and the New Anthropology of the Actor" in *Silent Film*, edited by Richard Abel, 45–67. Rutgers, NJ: Rutgers University Press.

Zarkhin, L. 1931. "Prevratit' GIK v moshchnyi kino-VTUZ. O putiakh razvitiia so Vsesoiuznogo instituta kinematografii" [Turning GIK into a Powerful Film-College. Paths for the Development of the All-Union Film Institute], *Kino* 37 (July 6), in *K istorii VGIKa* 1, 146–149.

Zhdan, Vitalii. 1951. *Narodnyi artist SSSR V.R. Gardin* [People's Artist of the USSR, V.R. Gardin], Moscow: Iskusstvo.

3

Lenfilm: The Birth and Death of an Institutional Aesthetic

Robert Bird

Lenfilm styles itself as the oldest and, for much of the last century, second-largest film studio in the Soviet Union and post-Soviet Russia (after Mosfilm). A recent catalogue of its films (including shorts, documentaries, and co-productions) lists 1396 titles produced between 1918 and 2003, the credits of which include many of the most prominent names in the Russian and Soviet film industry, whether as director, cinematographer, editor, screenwriter, set designer, composer, or actor (Agrafenina 2003). A perusal of these titles and their creators confirms that, at each major juncture in the history of Soviet cinema – NEP, Socialist Realism, World War II, the Thaw, and perestroika – Lenfilm has positioned itself at the forefront of film aesthetics, as a laboratory of film art. Surprisingly, given the large scale of production and tumultuous historical landscape, the diversity of talent and the emphasis on experiment, Lenfilm has maintained the myth of a distinct Leningrad school of film-making. For many of its adherents, both filmmakers and critics, the Leningrad school is defined by its dedication to resolving social and ideological pressures as visual form. The main facilitating factor in this aesthetic has been Lenfilm's organization of film production around relatively autonomous teams of film artists; the result has been a collaborative spirit, at least when compared to the more hierarchical structure of the central film studios in Moscow. The continuity in organization and aesthetics make Lenfilm an unusual example of an institutional aesthetic.

Vernacular Eccentricity

The Soviet government's People's Commissar for Enlightenment Anatolii Lunacharskii decreed the creation of a Cinema Committee of the Union of Northern Communes (known as Kinosev) in April 1918, tasking it with the

A Companion to Russian Cinema, First Edition. Edited by Birgit Beumers.
© 2016 John Wiley & Sons, Inc. Published 2016 by John Wiley & Sons, Inc.

exclusive "coordination of all affairs and the resolution of all questions concerning the cinema in all of its fields" (Ivaneev 1970, 245). Its physical infrastructure comprised the imperial army's film office, as well as the confiscated property of commercial film companies.[1] In addition to newsreels and agitation films, Kinosev produced several feature films during the Civil War period, beginning with *Consolidation of Living Space* [*Uplotnenie*, 1918, dir. Aleksandr Panteleev], shot in great haste to a screenplay by Lunacharskii himself, which premiered on November 7, 1918, the first anniversary of the Bolsheviks' seizure of power. Over time, Kinosev's activities expanded to include filmmaking courses that eventually became the Technical College of Screen Art [Tekhnikum ekrannogo iskusstva], where several major Lenfilm artists were educated (Ivaneev 1970, 247; Bonitenko and Georgievskaya 2012, 277–326).[2]

After a couple of re-namings, on May 9, 1922 the Bolshevik government re-established the studio as The North-West Regional Agency for Photography and Cinema, or Sevzapkino for short. This re-organization came months after the cessation of hostilities in the Civil War and at the very beginning of the New Economic Policy (NEP), which promoted financial self-sustainability while permitting a degree of commercialization. Under these conditions the studio's production grew exponentially, both in newsreel and genres of fiction film. Aleksandr Panteleev's anti-religious comedy *The Miracle Worker* [*Chudotvorets*, 1922] received the personal imprimatur of Lenin, while Aleksandr Ivanovskii's historical film *Palace and Fortress* [*Dvorets i krepost'*, 1923] was the first Soviet film distributed abroad. On New Year's Day 1925 the studio moved to the site of the former entertainment pavilion Aquarium, on the Avenue of the Red Dawn, where the first film program in St Petersburg had been projected in 1896, and where the studio still resides today (though the street has reverted to its pre-Revolutionary name Kamenoostrovskii [Stony Island] Avenue, having been known as Kirov Avenue from 1934 to 1991).

According to contemporaries, the site was only superficially adapted to its new purpose:

> All around were the pealing traces of former cheap luxury: artificial marble, bronze, mirrors and even a giant stuffed bear with a tray in its paws, standing on the landing of the stairs. [...] Everything was covered, divided by temporary plywood separations [...] The auxiliary workshops – the laboratory, the prop workshop, the mechanical shop, the electrical shop, etc. etc. – were housed in small huts scattered as if at random around the territory of the film studio (Mikhailov 1970, 137).

The sense of musty, even taxidermic archaism was reflected in Sevzapkino's early output. Despite its proximity to power and revolutionary ideology, the primacy of commercial interest and the conservatism of public taste hindered any great aesthetic innovations. The original core of Sevzapkino directors were established professionals from before the Revolution. Aleksandr Panteleev was an actor who turned to film around 1909; his best-known work as director was *The Tree of*

Death, or Blood-Thirsty Susanna [*Derevo smerti, ili Krovozhadnaia Susanna*, 1915], a melodramatic spy thriller (Kovalova 2012: 39, 267).[3] Aleksandr Ivanovskii had served as assistant director to Iakov Protazanov on *Father Sergius* [*Otets Sergii*, 1918]. In Mikhail Bleiman's description, these directors' approach was betrayed by titles like *Palace and Fortress*, in which "ready images collided: the image of 'palace' and the image of 'fortress.' They were allegorical in their consummate stasis" (Bleiman 1968, 15). In stark contrast to Eisenstein, who was already at work on *Strike* [*Stachka*, 1924], these holdovers from pre-Revolutionary cinema "captured, photographed someone else's image, but didn't create their own. And the new quality of cinematic art could arise only when its masters began themselves to create an image of reality" (Bleiman 1968, 15).

In Leningrad the new masters were mostly young, well-educated newcomers from the provinces, including many from the former Pale of Settlement, who had arrived in the imperial capital amidst the disruptions of the Revolution and Civil War. Accepting the government's treatment of film as an industry, and of Sevzapkino as one of several "factories," the young filmmakers played with industrial nomenclature, for example in their formation of experimental "workshops." In this the young filmmakers of Sevzapkino found common cause with the more radical versions of Russian modernism, such as Constructivism in the visual and performing arts, and with such theorists as formalist Viktor Shklovskii, whose book *Third Factory* [*Tret'ia fabrika*, 1926] was based in part on his work for a Moscow film studio. However, the young filmmakers were also fascinated with modern urbanism or (as it was known at the time) "Americanism," which often took the form of serials, adventure films, and other forms of pulp fiction (Tsivian 1996, 39–45). Such hybrid populism received official endorsement from Bolshevik leader Nikolai Bukharin, who in 1921 called for the creation of "red Pinkertons," that is, ideologically informed entertainment.[4] At the forefront of this movement, from its beginnings Lenfilm exemplified what Miriam Hansen has called "vernacular modernism," that is, "an international modernist idiom on a mass basis" that "engaged the contradictions of modernity at the level of the senses, the level at which the impact of modern technology on human experience was most palpable and irreversible" (Hansen 1999, 68, 70).[5] This eccentric cinema relied heavily on melodrama, which allowed filmmakers to map social and ideological processes on the stories, emotions, and faces of individual human actors (Bagrov 2011, 15).

Sevzapkino's version of vernacular modernism saw its filmmakers working out the medium specificity of cinema, while also embracing productive collaborations with artists in (and theorists of) other mediums, placing cinema on equal footing with the other arts, even as they transformed the other mediums by "cinefying" them. Screenwriter Mikhail Bleiman recalled:

> The innovative approach of Ermler, Kozintsev, Trauberg, Iutkevich, and the Vasil'evs – they were perceived at the time as a unified group – was sharply contrasted to the group of prerevolutionary film direction: Gardin, Sabinskii, Ivanovskii, and

Viskovskii. [...] The issue was the nature of cinema, whether it is merely entertainment and artisanal half-art, or whether it opens up new, revolutionary horizons for all art as such (Bleiman 1973, 31–32).

A central theoretical source was Béla Balász's *Visible Man*, to which Iosif Kheifits, then a student at the Technical College of Screen Art, attributed the revelation of cinema as the art of silence, gesture, and the face (Kheifits 1996, 127–128).[6] The influence of Eisenstein and other Moscow-based filmmakers cannot be overestimated; Lenfilm productions tended to exemplify Eisenstein's notion of "vertical montage," which denotes the saturation of each frame with multiple orders of signification: mise-en-scène, camera movement, gesture, lighting, speech, music, etc.

The only other Soviet studio with a clearly-defined profile at the time was Mezhrabpom-Rus', renamed in 1928 Mezhrabpomfilm (Kherroubi 1996). Before 1928, during NEP, Mezhrabpom-Rus' specialized in commercial projects in genres ranging from science fiction (Iakov Protazanov's *Aelita*, 1924), costume dramas (Konstantin Eggert's *Ice House* [*Ledianoi dom*], 1928), to comedies (Boris Barnet's *House on Trubnaia Square* [*Dom na Trubnoi*], 1928). Lenfilm stalwart Mikhail Bleiman dismissed Mezhrabpom's productions as "slightly renovated salon drama, detectives, and quasi-historical film" (Bleiman 1968, 26). In fact, many of Mezhrabpomfilm's productions can also be regarded as a kind of vernacular modernism, particularly in their incorporation of avant-garde design in such films as *Aelita* or *The Cigarette Girl from Mosselprom* [*Papirosnitsa ot Mossel'proma*, 1924] and prominent avant-garde actors, including Vsevolod Meyerhold and several graduates of FEKS (Factory of the Eccentric Actor). Moreover, while remaining attentive to commercial demand, after 1928 the re-organized Mezhrabpomfilm also responded to the government's desire for agitprop film, as with Nikolai Ekk's *The Road to Life* [*Putevka v zhizn'*, 1931], a drama set in a correctional commune for juvenile criminals, or Dziga Vertov's *Three Songs of Lenin* [*Tri pesni o Lenine*, 1934].

The aesthetic identity of Sevzapkino and, later, Lenfilm was shaped in part by the vibrant literary and theoretical discourse in Leningrad.[7] Some of the so-called Russian formalists found an institutional home in the fledgling State Institute for the History of the Arts (GIII), which at the end of 1925 opened a Film Department that numbered the young theorists Iurii Tynianov, Boris Eikhenbaum, and Adrian Piotrovskii among its members (Kumpan 2005; Arnol'di 1968a; Arnol'di 1968b). Cinematographers Andrei Moskvin and Evgenii Mikhailov joined these theorists as contributors to *The Poetics of Cinema* (1927), a landmark collection of essays on the theory of film (Gurevich 2001, 145–164). Particularly influential was Tynianov's essay "On the Bases of the Cinema," where he argued that the cinema is defined by "camera angle and perspective [...] and lighting":

> It is not the "visible man" and the "visible thing" that are the "hero" of the cinema, but "new" man and "new" thing, people and things, transfigured in the dimension of art: the "man" and the "thing" of the cinema. The visible correlations of visible people are violated and replaced by the correlations of the "people" of the cinema. (Tynianov 1927, 63)

Several of these theorists, including Tynianov, also turned their ideas into practice as screenwriters, and Sevzapkino proved a welcoming home.

The young theorists of GIII found particularly willing collaborators in the young theatre directors Grigorii Kozintsev and Leonid Trauberg, who styled themselves The Factory of the Eccentric Actor (FEKS). After a couple of short films, Kozintsev and Trauberg debuted at Lenfilm with a production of *The Devil's Wheel* [*Chertovo koleso*, 1925], based on a screenplay by Adrian Piotrovskii, which introduced cinematographer Andrei Moskvin (1901–1961) and set designer Evgenii Enei. Moskvin's assistant Evgenii Mikhailov has written that "at Lenfilm the birth of the art of cinematography began with the picture *The Devil's Wheel* [...] Each of the director's demands required a different artistic resolution and filming" (Mikhailov 1970, 140). Many of these solutions involved a great deal of invention, given the rudimentary technical resources at their disposal. Underscoring Moskvin's importance, Kozintsev later reflected:

> When we came to work in Soviet cinema, we found the Leningrad factory full of historical pictures shot in a naïvely naturalistic principle ... All generals, tsars, soldiers, etc. were shot mainly with an emphasis on exhibiting the costume workshop, which the factory was proud of. They shot costumes and the actors in them: that was the main thing then.
>
> And we mostly wanted to replace this parade of historical costumes with a sense of the epoch, i.e., replace it with some holistic image, a style of the general, and not with a naturalism of details. In the sense of cinematography we were interested in a maximum image-quality [*obraznost'*] of photography [...] to transport the viewer into the atmosphere of the epoch. [...] Moskvin began to shoot even long shots with portrait lenses. (Kozintsev 1983, 17)

Theorizing their practice, Moskvin and Mikhailov describe the "the art of 'seeing' a thing and reproducing the materials of a shot as an individual image" as:

> the need for the cameraman to maintain an equally attentive attitude to all material of shooting, a joint effort with the director to clarify the essence of the object being shot in each scene of the picture, and in this regard the use of technical means that help him to expose and show more clearly to the viewer the inner significance of the thing, which is frequently hidden in everyday life, and its hidden features. (Mikhailov and Moskvin 1927, 181)

The art of FEKS – and, by extension, of Lenfilm – was the art of material life in its visual transfiguration. The result was, in the words of one contemporary critic, that "while remaining melodrama, *The Devil's Wheel* violates canonical techniques and, while remaining in line with traditional films, it stands on the verge of new cinematographic discoveries, on the threshold of a new style" (Bleiman 1973, 110). At its most eccentric, the FEKS style borders on the grotesque. However, as critic Vladimir Nedobrovo once wrote, "The method of FEKS is not the outward

Figure 3.1 Andrei Kostrichkin and his beloved coat in *The Overcoat*, directed by Grigorii Kozintsev and Leonid Trauberg, 1926.

stylization of the actor's movements, but their genuinely cinematic organization" (Nedobrovo 1970a, 38).

After *The Devil's Wheel* Kozintsev and Trauberg enjoyed success with *The Overcoat* [*Shinel'*, 1926], based on Iurii Tynianov's adaptation of Nikolai Gogol''s short story, and the historical drama *SVD* (1927). Kozintsev and Trauberg's silent-film style culminated in *New Babylon* [*Novyi Vavilon*, 1929], "the peak of mastery in silent film" (Mikhailov 1970, 145). Here, in Kozintsev's words: "With the help of shooting techniques we no longer photographed, but rather transfigured with photograph, and the light, density of shadows, and fuzziness of some parts of the image became the basis of our compositions" (cited in Mikhailov 1970, 142). Clearly, this style owed much to the continuing presence of Moskvin and Enei in the production team, as well as to the directors' continuing dialogue with such critics as Tynianov and Nedobrovo.

As early as 1934 Nikolai Iezuitov recognized a particular "school of Leningrad direction [and] of acting" (Iezuitov 1934, 89). Bleiman contrasted it to the Moscow studio, "where talented people worked, each by himself, each in his own way, not even feeling the need for creative contact with each other" (Bleiman 1968, 8). Petr Bagrov has argued persuasively that one key to the establishment of a house style at Lenfilm was the stability of the central production team, consisting of director, cinematographer, and production designer (Bagrov 2011, 12).[8] The unusual prominence of the designer led to another shared characteristic, namely that of a strict framing that focused on faces and objects (Bagrov 2011, 12). With the advent of sound, one could add a fourth hypostasis to this "trinity," namely that of composer. Beginning with *New Babylon* FEKS absorbed the young talent of Dmitrii Shostakovich, who composed a score to be performed at demonstrations of the film. Shostakovich scored Kozintsev and Trauberg's film *Alone* [*Odna*, 1931], the first sound film produced at Lenfilm, and remained on their production team for decades afterwards.

FEKS served as a model for another collective, led by Fridrikh Ermler and known as the Cinema Experimental Workshop [Kino-eksperimental'naia masterskaia], or KEM (Anon. 1970, 227–238; Gudkin 1970, 111–131). Fridrikh Ermler and Eduard Ioganson collaborated on the first films from KEM, *Children of the Storm* [*Deti buri*] and *Katka's Reinette Apples* [*Kat'ka – bumazhnyi ranet*], both from 1926, and both with Evgenii Enei as set designer. *Children of the Storm* dramatized the defense of Petrograd in the Civil War. *Katka's Reinette Apples* marked the debut in film of Fedor Nikitin, one of the studio's great character actors. Both Ermler and Ioganson went on to illustrious careers as directors of Lenfilm. Ermler's early masterpiece was *Fragment of an Empire* [*Oblomok imperii*, 1929], which typified for critic Adrian Piotrovskii "revolutionary cinema" as the "maximum loading of each separate shot with social meaning and ideological orientation [*mirovozzrencheskoi ustanovkoi*]" (Piotrovskii 1929, 3). Ioganson specialized in much more intimate films on a smaller scale, such as his film *The Crown Prince of the Republic* [*Naslednyi prints respubliki*, 1934], in which a group of architects come into possession of an infant who forces them to reject their avant-garde principles in favor of a new Soviet humanism.

Lenfilm's eccentricity survived into the increasingly brutal 1930s, helped by the studio's close contacts with the surrounding arts scene. Of particular interest is the participation of associates of the Union of Real Art [OBERIU, Ob"edinenie real'nogo iskusstva], best known for poets Daniil Kharms and Aleksandr Vvedenskii. Their performance *Three Left Hours* on January 24, 1928 included a film produced by Aleksandr Razumovskii and Klimentii Mints. Mints became a prolific screenwriter and directed one short film, *The Adventures of Korzinkina* [*Prikliucheniia Korzinkinoi*, 1941], at Lenfilm, which starred FEKS actress Ianina Zheimo and featured a score by Shostakovich. Associates of OBERIU included Nikolai Oleinikov and Evgenii Shvarts, who wrote the screenplay for Antonina Kudriavtseva's short *Wake Lenochka Up* [*Razbudite Lenochku*, 1934], also starring Zheimo alongside Sergei Gerasimov. Shvarts and Oleinikov also collaborated on the screenplay for Ioganson's *At Rest* [*Na otdykhe*, 1936], which takes Stalin's famous slogan "life has become better, more merry" "to the point of absurdity: life has become so merry that it borders on idiotism. The usual comedic formulas are modified and take the form of open grotesquerie. [...] Not an single Soviet comedy of the 1930s had such a exquisitely meaningless text" (Bagrov 2003, 65). As late as 1945 screenwriter Shvarts reunited with Zheimo for *Cinderella* [*Zolushka*, 1947; dir. Nadezhda Kosheverova, Mikhail Shapiro], a Russian version of the fairy tale and a perennial favorite on Soviet television.

Contemporaries attribute a particular role in the Leningrad school to Adrian Piotrovskii, a sometime member of OPOIaZ, a researcher and administrator at GIII, and contributor to *The Poetics of Cinema*. Piotrovskii was a classical philologist by training, but in the aftermath of the Revolution he had become immersed in the production and theorization of mass festivals and the Theater of the Working Youth (TRAM).[9] He has even been credited with the revolutionary name of the major thoroughfare on which Sevzapkino was located: Avenue of the Red Dawn. As late as 1921 Piotrovskii had rejected the cinema along with other manifestations of "Americanism" in the arts (Piotrovskii 1922, 5), but he gradually embraced the arts of eccentricity and in 1926 wrote a screenplay "The Sailor from the Aurora," which became the basis of Kozintsev and Trauberg's *The Devil's Wheel*.[10]

After serving as head of the screenplay section from 1926, Piotrovskii was named as artistic director of Lenfilm in 1928, an amorphous position that allowed him to bring his multifaceted talents to bear on the studio's productions. In the words of a later colleague, Piotrovskii "was capable of instantly getting fired up with the truly progressive element that was born in the depths of art itself and was evoked by the needs of life" (Messer 1973, 140). Advocating an "experiment comprehensible to the millions" (Piotrovskii 1929, 5), Piotrovskii sought to combine the formal sophistication of the Moscow avant-gardists with narrative accessibility: "Affects and passions: is this really not a more worthy and at the very least more efficient means of creating entertaining films than elaborate sets and luxuriant spectacle?" (Piotrovskii 1928, 2). He continued to fulfill this advisory role right up through Fridrikh Ermler's *The Great Citizen* [*Velikii grazhdanin*, 2 parts, 1938–1939], which was released after Piotrovskii's arrest and execution during Stalin's Great Terror.

Though he allegedly worked productively with all the screenwriters and directors at Lenfilm, in the 1920s Piotrovskii was a champion of the work of director Evgenii Cherviakov, who cut his teeth as lead actor and assistant director on Vladimir Gardin's costume drama *Poet and Tsar* [*Poet i tsar'*, 1927], a dramatization of Pushkin's final years.[11] Beginning with the *Girl from the Distant River* [*Devushka s dalekoi reki*, 1927], Cherviakov drew on French impressionist cinema (especially Jean Epstein) to pioneer a slow style, "with long close-ups, frames cleansed of everything superfluous, the static play of the human body and the expressive play of actors' eyes" (Bagrov 2011, 29); Piotrovskii christened this style "lyrical." Unfortunately, of Cherviakov's early films only two survive. *My Son* [*Moi syn*, 1928] is the story of a fireman who leaves his wife when she bears another's child, only to rediscover his love for her when he saves mother and child from a fire. Based on a novel by Konstantin Fedin, *Cities and Years* [*Goroda i gody*, 1930] reduces its literary source to a portrait of "Cherviakov's latest – and last – existential hero" (Bagrov 2011, 26).

The FEKS actor Petr Sobolevskii later listed the attributes he identified with the Leningrad silent film:

> [p]roblems of shot composition, light, and camera angle, which in some cases were the decisive moment in the meaning and emotion of the film; the magnificent techniques of editing, the dynamics of action and the symbolism of the shot; finally, simply the mundane limits of actors' exterior expression – the gestures [*mimika*] of the close-up and the expressiveness of a body in long shot. (Sobolevskii 1970, 72)

Figure 3.2 Gennadii Michurin and Anna Sten in *My Son*, directed by Evgenii Cherviakov, 1928.

For all their diversity, the hallmark of the styles pioneered by these young directors and their close-knit creative teams was a saturated image within an inventive narrative treatment. Produced on a more modest scale than films of the central studios in Moscow, their films tended to be much more intimate portrayals of individuals caught up in revolutionary society, than of that society itself. In the language of filmmakers and critics alike, they sought to resolve social and historical issues within the image. Clearly, this was a fragile project for a brutal age.

Heroic Romanticism

After several reorganizations of the Soviet film industry, on January 15, 1934 the name of the Leningrad film factory was changed to the abbreviation Lenfilm, which remains its name today, even after the renaming of its host city back to St Petersburg. Surveying the studio's first 20 years, Vladimir Nedobrovo boasted of the "impressive core of young forces, both directors […] and actors," who have rid the cinema of "theatricalism" [*teatral'shchina*] and slavish "imitation of the West" to achieve "a realist art in principle":

> This circumstance makes it possible to view Lenfilm not as something fluid in its composition, but as a unified, full-blooded creative organism, in which the personal fate of every individual worker and the personal creative biography of each member is at the same time the fate and biography of the production facility as a whole. They are fused more than in any other cinematic collective in the Soviet Union. (Nedobrovo 1970b, 244)

Given the upheavals of these 20 years – the rise and fall of NEP, the implementation of the first Five-Year Plans, the institution of socialist realism as the official mode of aesthetic production, the promulgation of the Stalin Constitution and onset of mass terror – this is a remarkable claim. But it is not as far-fetched as it may seem, since the young directors of the 1920s – eccentric, experimental, lyrical – did more than anyone to define the style of socialist realist film in the 1930s.

The first years of Stalin's Great Breakthrough [*velikii perelom*] saw a precipitous drop in Lenfilm's production, but Leningrad film culture suffered less than many other artistic communities from the ascendency of the so-called proletarian groups in the initial years of the First Five-Year Plan. It was only in 1930 that the Leningrad Association of Cinema Workers (LenARK) succumbed to the militant "anti-formalism" of its mother organization, the Association of Revolutionary Cinema Workers (ARRK) or the Russian Association of Proletarian Writers (RAPP). As soon as the Central Committee of the Communist Party cancelled the hegemony of the proletarian groups on April 23, 1932, the Lenfilm artists set off a new wave of experiments, which yielded the most authoritative models for the future cinema of socialist realism. An early statement of intent was Fridrikh Ermler and Sergei Iutkevich's *Counterplan* [*Vstrechnyi*, 1932], which entered production just as the April resolution was published and serves as a chronicle of its immediate consequences. While eager to work with Ermler and Iutkevich, screenwriter Liubashevskii recalled bristling at the constraints of its initial formula:

> Again these clichéd situations, again the usual obstacles, again the victorious tractor (in this case, a turbine) rolling out at the end, again the unconscious proletarian who reconstructs his consciousness in production and ends by applying to membership in the Party, again… – Oh Lord, to the point of numbness! – the wrecker-engineer… No, what inconceivably deadly boredom! (Kovarskii 1941, 21–22)

However, Liubashevskii continues, "The beginning of production coincided with historic April, and this helped us immensely […] The walls of official pseudo-ideology disappeared, and it became possible to paint Party members outside of any pre-determined canon" (Kovarskii 1941, 23). By taking an experimental approach to this standard agitprop fare, Ermler "enlivened" the image by "mixing comic and dramatic features in each image" (Kovarskii 1941, 22). Many critics panned *Counterplan* as a relative failure, but it showed how Lenfilm production methods could be adapted to address the changing issues facing Soviet society (Nikitin 1970, 98).

Ermler's next film *Peasants* [*Krest'iane*, 1934] concerned the collectivization of agriculture and the opposition of the so-called *kulaks*, or affluent peasants. The Party secretary Nikolai Mironovich (played by Nikolai Bogomolov) unmasks a *kulak* who tries to undermine the *kolkhoz* by (somewhat paradoxically) overproducing piglets. He inadvertently confesses his guilt to his pregnant wife, the best swineherd at the *kolkhoz*, whom he then murders. The main narrative is punctuated by eccentric moments, like a long traveling shot of the *kulak* racing through the night, a grotesque scene of the collective farmers gorging themselves on *pel'meni*, and an animated sequence showing Varvara's dream about Stalin greeting the birth of her son. In his review Piotrovskii praised the film for approaching monumental tragedy, but called upon Ermler to rid his style of its "nervousness" (Piotrovskii 1969, 263). The images of hyper-fertility and over-abundance which optically resolve the problem of socialist farming proved enigmatic, even troubling.

The same year Kozintsev and Trauberg (with their usual creative team) turned a new page with their film *Maksim's Youth* [*Iunost' Maksima*, 1934], also known as *The Bolshevik*, which was followed by the sequels *Maksim's Return* [*Vozvrashchenie Maksima*, 1937] and *The Vyborg Side* [*Vyborgskaia storona*, 1938]. The Maksim trilogy amounted to a vast *bildungsroman*: an uneducated worker rises to revolutionary consciousness, while having a good deal of fun along the way. As with *The Counterplan*, Shostakovich's theme song became a popular standard, underscoring the ability of politically informed, artistically sophisticated film to become the linchpin of a new cultural formation.

The most illustrious film of 1934, possibly the most-watched Soviet film of all time (Stalin especially enjoyed re-watching it), was *Chapaev* by Georgii and Sergei Vasil'ev, which mythologized a prominent Civil War-era military commander. Known as "the Vasil'ev brothers" although they were not in fact related, the Vasil'evs had debuted in 1930 with the musical film *Sleeping Beauty* [*Spiashchaia krasavitsa*], which poked light fun at the creation of proletarian art. Based on a memoir by the general's political commissar Dmitrii Furmanov, *Chapaev* presents its hero and his sidekicks as appealing; though lacking in sophistication, they know enough to trust Furmanov's guidance in political and even military matters. Played by the versatile Boris Babochkin, the character of Chapaev instantly became a popular hero.

Lenfilm's three major hits of 1934 defined and justified Socialist Realism in the cinema, realizing the possibility of film that would be as ideologically sound as it is pleasurable to watch. Each film took sound film to new levels of accomplishment. Surveying the year's successes, Adrian Piotrovskii was confident enough to promise even "more fruitful and rich" times ahead, drawing on "the development [and] growth of the main masters of our factory, [and] the development and growth of the entire factory on the whole as a single, holistic artistic organism" (Piotrovskii 1935, 20).

One of the directors who made good on this promise was Sergei Gerasimov, formerly an actor in FEKS, with his films *Seven of the Brave* [*Semero smelykh*, 1936] and *Komsomolsk* (1938). With an illustrious ensemble cast (led by Nikolai Bogomolov), *Seven of the Brave* follows a group of six explorers on a dangerous mission to the Arctic. The seventh is a stowaway, played by Petr Aleinikov with his usual mischief. Marking the debut of Iurii Gherman as screenwriter, *Seven of the Brave* served as a model for ways it reconciled many of the conventions of the adventure film with the ethos of a production narrative.

A key member of Lenfilm's second wave of young directors was Sergei Iutkevich, who in 1928 brought his Experimental Film Collective (known by its Russian acronym EKKIu) to Lenfilm, after making the film *Lace* [*Kruzheva*] in Moscow. Apart from *The Counterplan*, which he co-directed with Ermler, in the 1930s Iutkevich became widely known for his films *Golden Hills* [*Zlatye gory*, 1931] and *Man with a Rifle* [*Chelovek s ruzh'em*, 1938], the latter introducing Lenin (played by Maksim Shtraukh) as a character in fictional film. In 1935 Iutkevich started a directing workshop at Lenfilm, which a year later released *Girlfriends* [*Podrugi*], directed by Lev Arnshtam with a score by Shostakovich. Piotrovskii welcomed *Girlfriends* as "the first film produced by our factory in this new artistic-organizational form" (Piotrovskii 1975, 155), although Iutkevich's workshop seems largely to have been updating the experience of FEKS and KEM for the demands of Socialist Realism. Its published declaration sounds very much like a defense of Lenfilm aesthetics as they developed in the 1920s, including a call for heightened attention to the work of cinematographer, set designer, and composer within the closely knit creative team. This production history, closely linked to so-called "formalist" or "avant-garde" films of the 1920s, is evoked as the key to making socialist realism "not a vague, but really multifaceted" concept and combating the "de-individualization" [*obezlichka*] of the Soviet artist (Anon. 1975, 131).

The other newcomers were Iosif Kheifits and Aleksandr Zarkhi, who studied at the Technical College for Screen Art and emerged in the early 1930s as a tandem of young directors linked to Proletkul't and the Komsomol. They enjoyed a breakthrough with *Hot Days* [*Goriachie denechki*, 1935], after which Piotrovskii encouraged them to take on a marquee project: a fictionalized biopic of pro-Bolshevik botanist Kliment Timiriazev. Starring Nikolai Cherkasov, who gained international fame as the titular character in Eisenstein's *Alexander Nevsky* (1938) and *Ivan the Terrible* [*Ivan Groznyi*, 1943–1945], *The Baltic Deputy* [*Deputat Baltiki*, 1936] confirmed the growing dominance of the biopic in Socialist Realism under Stalin (see Dobrenko 2008, 119–162), but this was not yet the completely formulaic approach that soon took hold, for example in Kozintsev's *Pirogov* (1947) and *Belinskii* (1951). The slippage between the historical Timiriazev and the fictional Professor Polezhaev allows for the creation of a full-bodied character and dynamic staging.

Both the highs and lows of Stalinist film were showcased in Fridrikh Ermler's *The Great Citizen*, a fictionalized biopic of Sergei Kirov that demonizes the various opposition figures whom Stalin was in the process of eliminating. Stalin made direct interventions in Mikhail Bleiman and Manuel' Bol'shintsov's screenplay. In the course of production four members of the crew were arrested, and in the press Ermler and his screenwriters were obliged to condemn the "wrecker" leadership of Lenfilm, most importantly Piotrovskii. In his memoir Bleiman describes the film's task as "understanding the events that were unfolding before our eyes, making sense of them and resolving them as an image" (Bleiman 1973, 37). Despite its direct complicity in Stalin's politics of terror, the film is a fascinating study in dramatizing ideological debate and conflict. While it confirms the theatrical framing that was coming to dominate Socialist Realism, Arkadii Kol'tsatyi's camera becomes an active force within the contention of faces and voices, darting from character to character, pinning down the enemies into positions of subjection.

As the style of Socialist Realism developed in the 1930s, Lenfilm continued to operate on the basis of tightly-knit creative units that worked alongside each other in friendly competition under Piotrovskii's benevolent supervision. Mikhail Bleiman describes his team's frustration with the screenplay of *The Great Citizen*:

> I recall it was at Ol'gino, in the Pushkin Theatre's small rest home, where we were working. At the same time as us Kozintsev and Trauberg were working on *Maksim's Return* and Kheifits and Zarkhi on *Baltic Deputy*. In the mornings, at breakfast, they would share their achievements. Kheifits and Zarkhi had it easiest; they were writing the director's version of the screenplay [*rezhisserskii stsenarii*]. Kozintsev and Trauberg were reworking the literary version of their screenplay. We sat over blank pages of paper and had nothing to share. (Bleiman 1973, 38; also 428–9)

This brief anecdote gives a sense of why the films from the Lenfilm collectives became largely indistinguishable from each other by the late 1930s, and into the 1940s and 1950s. In a process occurring throughout the Soviet film industry, state commissions became increasingly specific and uninspiring, keyed largely to hagiographies of Soviet saints and the showcasing of heroic moments from national history. The screenplay became a kind of passport that had to be approved by each level of the cinematic bureaucracy, from the studio to the central government agency and even Stalin. The resulting projects – and their number dwindled from year to year – were the creations more of committee than of collective, and the process of filming became one more of limiting the screenplay's mutation than of expanding its potential.

Avant-Garde as Tradition

Throughout the 1920s and 1930s Lenfilm benefited not only from the vibrancy of the performing, visual, and literary arts in Leningrad, but also from the city's geographical and cultural distance from the center of political power, which was increasingly identified with the person of Stalin, who himself led an increasingly isolated existence behind the Kremlin walls in Moscow. Over time Stalin became paranoid regarding the northern capital. The first intense orgy of violence against the Leningrad political and cultural elite came after the assassination of Sergei Kirov, the charismatic secretary of the Leningrad party organization, on December 1, 1934 (an event dramatized in Ermler's *Great Citizen*). Although the assassin, Leonid Nikolaev, was most likely acting out of personal motives, Stalin was widely suspected of complicity; in any case he used the event to settle many old scores.

Kirov was succeeded by Andrei Zhdanov, who served in this capacity through the end of World War II, implementing the increasingly draconian cultural policies of high Stalinism. The anti-formalist campaign of early 1936 targeted such luminaries as Dmitrii Shostakovich, book illustrator Vladimir Lebedev, as well as Adrian Piotrovskii. Eduard Ioganson was imprisoned for a year and never returned to filmmaking. Stalin and Zhdanov have also been accused of mendacity in their failure to evacuate Leningrad in time to avoid the 900-day siege during World War II, which led to the death of hundreds of thousands (including such film professionals as Evgenii Cherviakov, who was killed on active duty at the front lines, animator Vladislav Tvardovskii, and Eduard Ioganson) (Bagrov 2003, 45–76). Lenfilm managed to make only several short films at the beginning of the war, before the city came under direct threat in September 1941. After that, filmmaking in the city was mostly limited to the shooting of documentary footage that was edited elsewhere, although some staged footage was also shot for the film *The Unconquerable Ones* [*Nepobedimye*, 1942], featuring Boris Babochkin among an illustrious cast, and directed by Sergei Gerasimov together with Mikhail Kalatozov. Most of the filmmakers who were able to leave Leningrad were subsequently evacuated to Alma-Ata, where they collaborated with artists from other studios under the auspices of the Central United Film Studio [TsOKS, Tsentral'naia ob"edinennaia kinostudiia, 1941–44], which was headed by Fridrikh Ermler. Here the usual alliances among film artists were disrupted, sometimes to great effect, as with the collaboration between Sergei Eisenstein and Andrei Moskvin in *Ivan the Terrible*.[12] Tellingly, the 900-day siege of Leningrad only became a major topic at Lenfilm (or any other Soviet studio for that matter) in the 1960s; before then, the events were too fraught with trauma and ambivalence for film to handle.[13]

The next major blow against Leningrad came soon after the war's end, in the autumn of 1946, when Andrei Zhdanov, now serving as Stalin's ideological chief, unleashed a new anti-formalist campaign by savaging such Leningrad-based writers as Anna Akhmatova and Mikhail Zoshchenko. These years of film-famine [*malokartin'e*] are typified by triumphal war movies and wooden biopics like Kozintsev's *Pirogov* and *Belinskii*, both of which were based on screenplays by Iurii Gherman, designed by Evgenii Enei, and shot by Andrei Moskvin (among other cinematographers). Ermler slotted in to the monumental style of late Stalinism, following up on *The Great Citizen* with more films on Soviet greatness: *The Great Breakthrough* [*Velikii perelom*, 1945] on Stalin's military genius and *The Great Force* [*Velikaia sila*, 1949] displaying a triumph of Soviet chicken-breeding. Ermler's attempt to respond to the call for a new Soviet satire, the 1953 production *Broken Dreams* [*Razbitye mechty*] with Igor' Il'inskii in the main role, was not released until 1962 under the title *The Banquet* [*Zvanyi uzhin*]. Only two feature films were completed at Lenfilm in both 1950 and 1951.

The rebirth of Lenfilm after Stalin's death was attributable less to any palpable change in its ideology than to a recuperation of some aspects of pre-1940 cinema. In a 1957 speech Grigorii Kozintsev called upon his comrades to "return to our

Figure 3.3 Boris Babochkin in *The Great Force*, directed by Fridrikh Ermler, 1949.

studio the lofty tradition of a demanding attitude towards film, not as a unit of a production plan, but as a work of art and the result of a complex creative process":

> Lenfilm is not an *atelier* being offered for let. It is an artistic organism that has formed over the course of many years, that has found its face and its peculiar features in the resolution of those general tasks that stand before all our cinema and all our culture. (Kozintsev 1983, 103, 100)

Inevitably, this desire to recuperate aesthetic sophistication involved a degree of what has, perhaps harshly, been called "academism," a temptation that is most palpable in Kozintsev's late productions, and also in the dominance of literary adaptation among Lenfilm's production in the decades after Stalin's death.

One of the first successes was *The Gadfly* [*Ovod*, 1955], based on an 1897 novel by Irish author E. L. Voynich that was revered as one of the sacred texts of Russian radicals. Its hero, Arthur (Oleg Strizhenov), is a young revolutionary in northern Italy under Austrian occupation. Betrayed by his spiritual advisor, who turns out to be his biological father, Arthur goes underground and becomes a feared revolutionary. The film was directed by the otherwise unremarkable Aleksandr Faintsimmer, but the camerawork belonged to Andrei Moskvin, the design to Evgenii Enei, and the music to Dmitrii Shostakovich. The result is far from perfect; contrasting the film to contemporary Italian neo-realism, Kozintsev complained, "Having learned magnificently to shoot hardwood floors and beautifully to convey color, we have forgotten about man" (Kozintsev 1983, 77). Without directly challenging any ideological constraints, though, and remaining in large part within a claustrophobically theatrical mode, the film suggests a complex clash of ideological and emotional motives and at times foregrounds the dense material textures of human experience, which refuse to be completely suspended by the narrative denouement.

Another notable production was *The Death of Pazukhin* [*Smert' Pazukhina*, 1957], a screen version of Grigorii Nikulin's staging of Mikhail Saltykov-Shchedrin's satirical play. Wonderfully shot by Dmitrii Davydovich Meskhiev, the best of the new generation of cinematographers and father of Lenfilm director Dmitrii Dmitrievich Meskhiev, the film gestures back to the expressionist lighting and acting styles of Eisenstein's *Ivan the Terrible*.

Nikolai Cherkasov fulfilled a long-standing dream of playing the titular role in *Don Quixote* (1957), directed by Grigorii Kozintsev together with his usual team in colorful widescreen format. Though it was merely a screen adaptation of a classic of world literature, the film served as a kind of manifesto for the possibilities – and dangers – of free imagination within the Soviet cultural system. The echoes of Cherkasov's portrayal of Ivan the Terrible in Eisenstein's eponymous biopic gave the film a comic reflection on Stalin's rule. It also allowed Kozintsev to re-engage with the eccentrism of his pre-Stalin-era work: "the scene of the battle with the windmills would hardly have come out well if I hadn't in my youth staged several quite ridiculous eccentric productions," Kozintsev later reflected (Kozintsev 1983, 148). Kozintsev followed up with *Hamlet* (1964) and *King Lear* (1970), both with scores by Shostakovich, which exceeded their times to become renowned as adaptations of Shakespeare on film and, for all intents and purposes, to represent Lenfilm in world cinema culture.

Lenfilm films challenged many boundaries during the period of the Thaw. Rezo Esadze's *Fro* (1964) was the first adaptation for film of a prose work by Andrei Platonov. Ermler's *Before the Judgement of History* [*Pered sudom istorii*, 1965] is based on interviews with Vasilii Shul'gin, a Tsarist-era politician and sworn enemy of Bolshevism who had been imprisoned for 12 years after being captured during World War II. In many respects the film follows the poetics of *The Great Citizen*, with the camera dramatizing the ideological dispute between Shul'gin and a Soviet "historian." It also presages some of Aleksandr Sokurov's patient documentary studies of such great masters as Mstislav Rostropovich and Aleksandr Solzhenitsyn in the 1990s and 2000s.

At the same time, Lenfilm found new ways to engage with the vernacular spectator. One of the greatest commercial successes of the 1960s was *Amphibian Man* [*Chelovek-amfibiia*, 1961], an adaptation by a science-fiction story by Aleksandr Beliaev, directed by Gennadii Kazanskii and Vladimir Chebotarev. In addition to glamorous young stars (especially Anastasiia Vertinskaia) and locations (the film was set in Cuba but largely shot in the Crimea), the film also featured jazz cabaret and other forbidden fruits. Another popular sci-fi comedy is *His Name Was Robert* [*Ego zvali Robert*, 1967], directed by Il'ia Ol'shvanger, in which a young scientist invents a robot in his own image and has to deal with the consequences when "Robert" gets a life of his own.

The films of the northern studio contributed less directly to the political climate of the Thaw than those of Moscow, Kiev, or even Odessa. In fact, the very absence of direct ideological discourse unites these films most. It is noteworthy that the most prominent and successful films of the post-Stalin period at Lenfilm were set in times and places so distant from contemporary Soviet life. Many notable films were also dominated by a literary source or dramatic repartee. The unmistakably saturated images of Lenfilm products in the 1920s and 1930s thus flattened out into more laconic, discursive explorations of individual psychology. The rich engagement with the Petersburg myth in films of the 1920s became narrowed into the new myth of Leningrad as the cradle of revolution, in large part through the Maksim trilogy, *The Great Citizen* and *The Baltic Deputy*. Innokentii Smoktunovskii makes an unexpectedly introspective Lenin in *On a Single Planet* [*Na odnoi planete*, 1965], the action of which takes place over a single day at the end of 1917.

The end of the Khrushchev Thaw coincided with the loss of some of Lenfilm's leading lights: Ermler died in 1967, Kozintsev in 1973. Before his death Kozintsev repeatedly struck a note of warning: "Now we have clambered out of the most difficult years, but we can easily fall back into them because as an artistic organism, in my view, Lenfilm has disappeared" (Kozintsev 1983, 235). Before disappearing for good, however, Lenfilm had one more moment of glory.

Vernacular Postmodernism

The fall of the Soviet Union revealed a vast fault line separating the country's cultural needs from the populace's desires. In 1987 critic Elena Stishova described the Leningrad school of cinema as marked by "non-conformism in years when the objective circumstances inclined most people to compromise" and by "the inner need of speaking the truth on screen" (cited in Zhezhelenko 1996, 5–6). Tat'iana Moskvina, writing a mere three years later, took a less admiring view of the "'global cinema' of the Petrograd district": "Despite its vast range our 'global cinema,' taking on various complex and enormous themes, enjoys little resonance in the consciousness of our culture, often remaining the studio's internal matter. It is a disaster at the box office" (Moskvina 1990, 71). Lenfilm's problem was how to preserve its identity as a cultural institution at a time when all institutions and culture as a whole were undergoing change. Having exemplified Soviet vernacular modernism, could Lenfilm fashion a popular style for the postmodern age?

Sergei Dobrotvorskii has identified two strands in the "new cinema" of the Leningrad school: small-scale melodramas [*Kammerspiele*] that focus on the intimate lives of rank-and-file individuals, and "neo-epic" direct cinema that captures the "chaotic and formless stream of life" (Dobrotvorskii 1990, 35–36). This distinction reflects a partial breakdown of the alliance between artistic experiment and popular genre in earlier peaks of Lenfilm production. The melodramatic tendency was typified by the later films of Dinara Asanova and Il'ia Averbakh. Asanova's best-known work was *The Thugs* [*Patsany*, 1983], in which a charismatic man reforms juvenile delinquents at a camp that combines sport and labor. The film typified her commitment to the realistic portrayal of social problems, especially those afflicting young people, which clearly marked her out among Soviet directors of her day. Averbakh's realism tended to settle around the dramas suffered by professionals in their line of work. In *The Degree of Risk* [*Stepen' riska*, 1967] the eminent actor Boris Livanov plays a crusty old surgeon performing emergency surgery on a jaded mathematician, played by Innokentii Smoktunovskii; both emerge from the drama with dignity, if not with redemption. In the meta-cinematic *Voice* [*Golos*, 1982], Averbakh's final feature, a film crew struggles to cope with a series of breakdowns, including the illness of the lead actress. On his last films Averbakh relied on a stable crew, featuring cameraman Dmitrii Dolinin and designer Vladimir Svetozarov, the son of Iosif Kheifits.

The so-called "neo-epic" strand of Leningrad cinema is associated mainly with Aleksei Gherman, who began as a theatre director and built an exacting style with his controversial *Trial on the Road* [*Proverka na dorogakh*, 1971, released 1985]. Based on the prose of his father, Iurii Gherman, *Trial on the Road* follows a detachment of partisans (played by an all-star ensemble cast including Rolan Bykov, Vladimir Zamanskii and Anatolii Solonitsyn), who blow up a Nazi installation during World War II. The gritty realism is countered by Iakov Sklianskii's virtuosic camera work, but Gherman's difficulties getting the film released had more to do with the complex characterization of a young sergeant who seeks to join the partisans after having collaborated with the German occupiers. Gherman's breakthrough was

Figure 3.4 Aleksei Zharkov and Aleksandr Filippenko in *My Friend Ivan Lapshin*, directed by Aleksei Gherman, 1982.

Twenty Days without War [*Dvadtsat' dnei bez voiny*, 1976], an intense portrait of an officer on leave in Tashkent during World War II, based on Konstantin Simonov's adaptation of his own short novel, and starring the circus clown Iurii Nikulin in a rare dramatic role.

Gherman's masterpiece was *My Friend Ivan Lapshin* [*Moi drug Ivan Lapshin*, 1982, released 1984], another adaptation of his father's prose, this time focusing on NKVD officers in a provincial town who cavort with actors while fighting crime. Set in the late 1930s, the film captures the tension of the Stalinist Terror, while at the same time humanizing its agents, played by a mix of stars (Andrei Mironov and Nina Ruslanova, among others) and unknowns (particularly Andrei Boltnev). The gritty narrative is shot and recorded in a dizzyingly decentered manner, which immerses the viewer in a saturated visual and aural environment, obscuring at times the logic of the story. The confusion is exacerbated by brief explosions of eccentricity, even outright clowning by the actors. *Ivan Lapshin* was widely influential, for instance on Semen Aranovich's *Torpedo Bombers* [*Torpedonostsy*, 1983], an accomplished if somewhat derivative adaptation of work by Iurii Gherman, also starring Boltnev.

Since the advent of perestroika and the subsequent dissolution of the Soviet Union, Lenfilm has faced steep challenges for its continued existence. The basic challenge was formulated by editor Frizheta Gukasian in her contribution to the catalogue for a Lenfilm retrospective in Rotterdam in 1990, when she admitted that "[a]ll of our previous experience and our tradition rebels against commerce; at Lenfilm, we always fought with commercial cinema and the entertainment industry" (Gukasyan 1990, 11). The solution, as Gukasian predicted at the time, has been to use select commercial successes to continue to fund the production of art cinema addressed more to the international festival circuit. Under studio director Aleksandr Golutva (who served in the post from 1986 until 1996), the perestroika-era reorganization saw the creation of six independent studios under the aegis of Lenfilm: Golos [Voice], Troitskii most [Trinity Bridge], Ladoga, Diapazon [Spectrum], Neva and Petropol [Petropolis]. Kozintsev's fears have finally come to pass; the studio no longer presented itself as an organism, but as a set of facilities for let. Still, artistic experimentation continued to occur under the aegis of Lenfilm, especially in the Workshop for Debut and Experimental Film, under the stewardship of Aleksei Gherman (see German and Pavlov 1990, 15–20). One of its successes was Maksim Pezhemskii's absurdist send-up of Soviet aesthetics *Comrade Chkalov's Crossing of the North Pole* [*Perekhod tovarishcha Chkalov cherez severnyi polius*, 1990]. Gherman's Workshop also sponsored the debut of Aleksei Balabanov (a loose adaptation of Samuel Beckett's *Happy Days*, entitled *Schastlivye dni*, 1991).

In this new economic environment, Lenfilm artists found new forms of eccentricity. As if in tribute to its collaborations with OBERIU and other experimental groups of the late 1920s, Lenfilm also extended a hand to the so-called "parallel culture" of the experimental art scene and produced what has been called "parallel cinema." The group Mitki produced a semi-animated film in 1992. Lenfilm also was home to collaborations with Soviet new music culture. Experimental composer Sergei Kurekhin starred in *Sucker, the Conqueror of the Water* [*Lokh, pobeditel' vody*, 1991], a kind of post-Soviet *Devil's Wheel*. In Sergei Sel'ianov's *All Soul's Day* [*Dukhov den'*, 1988] rock singer Iurii Shevchuk starred as a man investigating his family's supernatural powers. Elements of gritty realism (with nods to Gherman and Tarkovskii) alternate with moments of visual effects and narrative discontinuities; at one moment, having escaped from assassins dressed in digitally-enhanced crimson clothes, the hero jumps from a St Petersburg rooftop and lands on the rooftops of Paris; he swims back to his home village via the Atlantic Ocean.

Joining Gherman at the artistic helm of Lenfilm was Aleksandr Sokurov, whose film *The Lonely Voice of a Man* [*Odinokii golos cheloveka*, 1978] was given its first release by Lenfilm in 1987. Sokurov's first production at Lenfilm, *Mournful Unconcern* [*Skorbnoe beschuvstvie*, 1986], loosely based on George Bernard Shaw's *Heartbreak House*, was controversial and divisive at the studio, but his next film, *Days of Eclipse* [*Dni zatmeniia*, 1988], based on a science-fiction novel by the brothers Strugatskii, was widely acclaimed. Both films featured Sergei Iurizditskii as cinematographer and Iurii Arabov as screenwriter; Sokurov has since worked with a range of different cinematographers (even shooting *Taurus* [*Telets*, 2000] himself), but Arabov has remained a near-constant as screenwriter for Sokurov's feature films. Svetlana Proskurina identified Sokurov as the key to "the resurrection, or return ... of the legendary Lenfilm of the twenties" (Proskurina 1990, 24), though many of his films were no more than a rumor for the Russian public, as the film distribution system collapsed. As early as 1990 Tat'iana Moskvina complained about the disjuncture between Sokurov's subject matter and visual style, a disjuncture she found typical of the Leningrad school: "the result is a most curious phenomenon: a visuality-in-itself, that endures even when the events fail to evoke either feeling or thought" (Moskvina 1990: 79).

Figure 3.5 Aleksei Ananishnov in *Days of Eclipse*, directed by Aleksandr Sokurov, 1988.

Drawing in part on the grittier aspects of Gherman's and Sokurov's film aesthetics, Lenfilm directors indulged heavily in late-Soviet *chernukha*, – a fascination with the darker sides of Soviet life which, having become admissible for public discourse, suddenly seemed to be swallowing the society up in a macabre apocalypse. The unwatchable (and largely unwatched) *Chekist* (1991) by Aleksandr Rogozhkin consists mostly of executions by firing squad in a bleak basement, shot as if through a hallucinatory haze. Evgenii Iufit, the most visible of the so-called "necro-realists," produced two films at the studio: the short *Knights of the Sublunar Sphere* [*Rytsari podnebes'ia*, 1989] and the feature *Daddy, Santa Claus Is Dead* [*Papa, umer ded moroz*, 1991], the latter in Gherman's Studio for Debut and Experimental Film.

In addition to producing such art films as Sokurov's *Days of Eclipse*, Lenfilm's Troitskii Most was responsible for some of the greatest commercial successes of the immediate post-Soviet period: Pavel Lungin's *Taxi Blues* (1990), which garnered the prize for best direction at Cannes, and Iurii Mamin's *Window to Paris* [*Okno v Parizh*, 1993]. In addition, Lenfilm was home to Aleksandr Rogozhkin's spectacularly successful *Peculiarities of the National Hunt* [*Osobennosti natsional'noi okhoty*, 1995], a slapstick comedy in which the outing of a group of Russian hunters and a visiting Finn devolves into a drinking binge. The film generated sequels and became a profitable franchise. These films also saw Lenfilm step, perhaps belatedly, into the home video market, which underscored the changing nature of the film industry in post-Soviet Russia.

After 1995 Lenfilm descended into crisis. As the six sub-studios each ceased to function, directors began to work independently and cobble together funding and resources for their productions. In 1997 both Aleksei Gherman and Aleksandr Sokurov released major new work, *Khrustalev, My Car!* [*Khrustalev, mashinu!*] and *Mother and Son* [*Mat'i syn*] respectively. Though both were critical successes, neither garnered much public attention. German then spent nearly 20 years producing his final feature, *It's Hard to Be a God* [*Trudno byt' bogom*], which was released posthumously in 2014. In recent years Lenfilm's most notable product may have been the cinema journal *Séance*, founded in 1990 by critic Liubov' Arkus and then-director of the studio Aleksandr Golutva.

On the other side, after directing two early features at Lenfilm, Aleksei Balabanov produced his first major hit *Brother* [*Brat*, 1997] with the private company CTB, which he co-founded with the director Sergei Sel'ianov. With such films as *Brother-2* [*Brat-2*, 2000] and *Cargo 200* [*Gruz 200*, 2007], Balabanov went on to become not only the most respected director in post-Soviet cinema, but also a pioneer of what one might call vernacular post-modernism and therefore a worthy successor to the mantle of FEKS and Lenfilm's other eccentrics. All of this, however, occurred outside of Lenfilm, which remained committed to an obsolete ideal of art cinema and failed not only to transform post-Soviet film culture, but even to exert any noticeable influence on the rapidly changing media landscape.

Conclusion

In the decade since 2003 Lenfilm's level of production has dwindled almost to zero, as the very notion of a state-run film studio has been subjected to a variety of pressures, many of them issuing from the emerging global marketplace in the digital age. The death in 2013 of Aleksei Gherman, one of the studio's two world-renowned directors and a stalwart of its traditions, and also of Aleksei Balabanov, its prodigal son, merely underscored the sense of crisis. The government of the Russian Federation has responded with a plan for the studio's radical re-invention under the leadership of a new director, board of trustees, and artistic advisory council, all made possible by a significant infusion of state funds that have made possible the renovation of its physical plant. Lenfilm has proven indispensable as an institution, even though its aesthetic might have become obsolete. Concurrently, in 2014 Lenfilm decided to celebrate its centenary four years earlier than expected, now tracing its origins not to the young Soviet government, but to the film agency created by the Russian imperial army on the eve of World War I. Eduard Pichugin, director of the studio, has recently reaffirmed Lenfilm's identity as a "production company" aiming to "multiply the studio's 'golden collection' of [classic] films" (Mazurova 2014). Any optimism that Lenfilm may yet survive into a second century as a production facility is balanced by a sense of sadness that it can do so only by ceasing to exist as a coherent aesthetic institution.

Notes

1. The Skobelev Committee (1904–1914) began to make military films in 1913 and coordinated newsreel production during World War I; see Malysheva (2012) and Pozdniakov (2014). For the fullest account to date of filmmaking in pre-Revolutionary Petersburg see Kovalova (2012). On film culture in the pre-Revolutionary period see Kovalova and Tsiv'ian (2011).
2. The graduates of the State Technical College of Screen Art also included the future Ayn Rand.
3. On Panteleev and his role in the early history of Lenfilm see Glovatskii (1968, 68–80).
4. No direct source has been documented for Bukharin's original statement. In a follow-up from late 1922 Bukharin dates it to "a year and a half ago," that is, mid-1921 [*Vestnik rabotnikov iskusstv*, nos. 3–4, 1922], but only after this reiteration did it become widely reported and discussed; see for example Anon. 1923: "Programma: LEF i MAPP."
5. Hansen writes "Russian cinema became Soviet cinema by going through a process of Americanization" (1999, 61).
6. Gordanov (1970, 174) also identifies *Visible Man* as an influence on the "Leningrad school of cinematography."
7. The best account of this intellectual and artistic ferment remains Clark (1995).

8 As an additional unifying characteristic of the Leningrad school Bagrov proposes the attention paid to minor characters.
9 On Piotrovskii's activities before cinema see von Geldern (1993) and Clark (1995).
10 Piotrovskii also co-wrote with Nikolai Erdman the screenplay for Semen Timoshenko's film *Turbine 3* [*Turbina No. 3*, 1927], also known as *Conquerors of the Night* [*Pobediteli nochi*], which has not survived.
11 On Cherviakov see Iurenev (1972).
12 I owe this observation to Petr Bagrov.
13 Lenfilm productions about the siege of Leningrad are: *Naval Battalion* [*Morskoi batal'on*, 1944], *Baltic Sky* [*Baltiiskoe nebo*, 1961], *Winter Morning* [*Zimnee utro*, 1966], *Izhorsk Battalion* [*Izhorskii batal'on*, 1972] and *Blockade* [*Blokada*, 1973].

References

Agrafenina, Ol'ga, ed. 2003. *Lenfil'm: Annotirovannyi katalog fil'mov 1918–2003* [Lenfilm: An Annotated Catalog 1918–2003]. St Petersburg: Kinostudiia Lenfil'm, Anikushin.

Anon. 1923. "Programma: LEF i MAPP" [Program of LEf and MAPP]. *LEF: Zhurnal levogo fronta iskusstv* [LEF: Journal of the Left Front of Art] 4: 3–11.

Anon. 1970. "Iz arkhiva F.M. Ermlera" [From F. Ermler's Archive]. In *Iz istorii Lenfil'ma* [From the History of Lenfilm], edited by Nina Gornitskaia, vol. 2, 223–238. Leningrad: Iskusstvo.

Anon. 1975. "Deklaratsiia Pervoi Khudozhestvennoi masterskoi pod khudozhestvennym rukovodstvom S. Iutkevich" [Declaration of the First Artistic Workshop of S. Iutkevich]. In *Iz istorii Lenfil'ma* [From the History of Lenfilm], edited by Nina Gornitskaia, vol. 4, 128–137. Leningrad: Iskusstvo.

Arnol'di, Edgar. 1968a. "Iz vospominanii o pervykh shagakh nashego kinovedeniia" [Recollections of the First Steps of Our Film Scholarship]. In *Iz istorii Lenfil'ma* [From the History of Lenfilm], edited by Nina Gornitskaia, vol. 1, 220–237. Leningrad: Iskusstvo.

Arnol'di, Edgar. 1968b. "Slovo imeiut dokumenty" [Let the Documents Speak]. In *Iz istorii Lenfil'ma* [From the History of Lenfilm], edited by Nina Gornitskaia, vol. 2, 246–252. Leningrad: Iskusstvo.

Bagrov, Petr. 2003. "Eduard Ioganson i vse-vse-vse" [Eduard Ioganson and All-all-all]. *Kinovedcheskie zapiski* [Film-Scholars' Notes] 65: 45–76.

Bagrov, Petr. 2011. *Osnovnye tendentsii leningradskogo kinoavangarda 1920-kh godov* [na materiale tvorchestva Evgeniia Cherviakova] [The Main Trends of the Leningrad Film-Avantgarde of the 1920s (On the Material of Evgenii Cherviakov)]. PhD dissertation, Research Institute of Film Art.

Bleiman, Mikhail. 1968. "Nachalo iskusstva" [The Beginning of Art]. In *Iz istorii Lenfil'ma* [From the History of Lenfilm], edited by Nina Gornitskaia, vol. 1, 7–27. Leningrad: Iskusstvo.

Bleiman, Mikhail. 1973. *O kino – svidetel'skie pokazaniia* [About Cinema: Eyewitness Testimonies]. Moscow: Iskusstvo.

Bonitenko, Adia and Larissa Georgievskaya, eds. 2012. "The Cinema-Experimental Workshop [Kinoeksperimental'naia masterskaia] in Documents," preface by Peter Bagrov. *Studies in Russian and Soviet Cinema* 5.2: 277–326.

Clark, Katerina. 1995. *Petersburg: The Crucible of Revolution*. Cambridge, MA: Harvard University Press.

Dobrenko, Evgenii, 2008. *Muzei revoliutsii: Sovetskoe kino i stalinskii narrativ* [Museum of the Revolution: Soviet Cinema and the Stalinist Narrative]. Moscow: Novoe literaturnoe obozrenie.

Dobrotvorskii, Sergei. 1990. "Leningradskoe kino: evoliutsiia avtorskoi traditsii" [Cinema in Leningrad: The Evolution of an Auteur Tradition]. In *Peterburgskoe "Novoe kino"* [Petersburg's "New Cinema"], edited by Marina Zhezhelenko, 34–46. St Petersburg: MOL.

German, Aleksey and Yuri Pavlov, 1990. "The Workshop for First Films." In *Lenfilm en de bevrijding van de Sovjet-cinema* [Lenfilm and the Liberation of Soviet Cinema], catalogue, 15–20. Netherlands: Film Festival Rotterdam.

Glovatskii, B.S. 1968. "Pervyi sovetskii kinorezhisser A. P. Panteleev" [The First Soviet Filmmaker A. Panteleev]. In *Iz istorii Lenfil'ma* [From the History of Lenfilm], edited by Nina Gornitskaia, vol. 2, 68–80. Leningrad: Iskusstvo.

Gordanov, Viacheslav. 1970. "Iz zapisok kinooperatora (1928–1932)" [From the Notes of a Cameraman, 1928–1932]. In *Iz istorii Lenfil'ma* [From the History of Lenfilm], edited by Nina Gornitskaia, vol. 2, 154–190. Leningrad: Iskusstvo.

Gudkin, Iakov. 1970. "Riadovoi kemovskogo otriada" [A Soldier of the KEM Detachment]. In *Iz istorii Lenfil'ma* [From the History of Lenfilm], edited by Nina Gornitskaia, vol. 2, 111–131. Leningrad: Iskusstvo.

Gukasyan, Frizheta. 1990. "Lenfilm Today." In *Lenfilm en de bevrijding van de Sovjet-cinema*, catalogue, 8–14. Netherlands: Film Festival Rotterdam.

Gurevich, Stella. 2001. "Vokrug 'Poetiki kino': Zubovskii osobniak, 20-e gody" [Around the "Poetics of Cinema": The Zubov Mansion in the 1920s]. In *Poetika kino. Perechityvaia "Poetiku kino"* [Poetics of Cinema. Re-Reading the 'Poetics of Cinema'], edited by Roza Kopylova, 145–164. St Petersburg: Rossiiskii institut istorii iskusstv.

Hansen, Miriam. 1999. "The Mass Production of the Senses: Classical Cinema as Vernacular Modernism." *Modernism/Modernity* 6.2: 59–77.

Iezuitov, Nikolai. 1934. *Puti khudozhestvennogo fil'ma, 1919–1934* [The Paths of the Fiction Film 1919–1934]. Moscow: Kinofotoizdat'.

Iurenev, Rostislav. 1972. *Kinorezhisser Evgenii Cherviakov* [The Director Evgenii Cherviakov]. Moscow: Soiuz kinematografistov SSSR, Biuro propagandy sovetskogo kinoiskusstva.

Ivaneev, Dmitrii. 1970. "Kratkaia spravka po istorii Leningradskoi ordena Lenina kinostudii 'Lenfil'm' [1918–1934 g.g.]" [A Brief History of the Leningrad Studio Lenfilm]. In *Iz istorii Lenfil'ma* [From the History of Lenfilm], edited by Nina Gornitskaia, vol. 2, 244–255. Leningrad: Iskusstvo.

Kheifits, Iosif. 1996. *Poidem v kino! Zhizn', trud, opyt* [Let's Go to the Cinema! Life, Work and Experience]. St Petersburg: Iskusstvo.

Kherroubi, Aïcha, ed. 1996. *Le studio Mejrabpom ou l'aventure du cinéma privé au pays des bolcheviks* [The Mezhrabpom Studio or the Adventure of Private Cinema in the Land of the Bolsheviks]. Paris: Réunion des Musées Nationaux.

Kovalova, Anna. 2012. *Kinematograf v Peterburge, 1907–1917: Kinoproizvodstvo i fil'mografiia* [Cinema in Petersburg 1907–1917. Film Production and Filmography]. St Petersburg: Skriptorium.

Kovalova, Anna and Iurii Tsiv'ian. 2011. *Kinematograf v Peterburge, 1896–1917. Kinoteatry i zriteli* [Cinema in Petersburg 1986–1917. Movie Theaters and Audiences]. St Petersburg: Masterskaia Seans.

Kovarskii, Nikolai. 1941. *Fridrikh Ermler*. Moscow: Goskinoizdat.

Kozintsev, Grigorii. 1983. *Sobranie sochinenii v piati tomakh* [Collected Works in 5 vols] vol. 2. Leningrad: Iskusstvo.

Kumpan, Kseniia. 2005. "K istorii vozniknoveniia kinokomiteta pri GIII" [A History of the Emergence of the Film Committee]. In *Shipovnik: Istoriko-filologicheskii sbornik k 60-letiiu R. D. Timenchika* [Historical-Philological Volume to Celebrate the 60th Anniversary of R. Timenchuk], edited by Iurii Leving, Aleksandr Ospovat, and Iurii Tsiv'ian, 175–201. Moscow: Vodolei.

Malysheva, Galina. 2012. "K istorii kinematograficheskoi deiatel'nosti Skobolevskogo komiteta 1913–1914 gg." [The History of the Cinematic Activity of the Skobolev Committee in 1913–1914]. *Vestnik arkhivista* [Archivist's Herald] 1: 3–17. http://vestarchive.ru/istochnikovedenie/1674-k-istorii-kinematograficheskoi-deiatelnosti-skobelevskogo-komiteta-1913-1914-gg.html [last accessed August 23, 2014].

Mazurova, Svetlana. 2014. "Kak proiti na ulitsu Kharmsa" [How to Get to Kharms Street]. *Rossiiskaia gazeta* [Russian Gazette] August 21. http://www.rg.ru/2014/08/14reg-szfo/lenfilm.html [last accessed August 23, 2014].

Messer, Raisa. 1973. "A. I. Piotrovskii i stsenarnyi otdel 'Lenfil'ma' [30-e gody]" [A. Piotrovskii and the Script Department of Lenfilm, 1930s]. In *Iz istorii Lenfil'ma* [From the History of Lenfilm], edited by Nina Gornitskaia, vol. 3, 139–150. Leningrad: Iskusstvo.

Mikhailov, Evgenii and Andrei Moskvin, 1927. "Rol' kino-operatora v sozdanii fil'my" [The Role of the Cameraman in the Creation of the Film]. In *Poetika kino* [Poetics of Cinema], edited by Boris Eikhenbaum, 110–121. Leningrad and Moscow: Kinopechat'.

Mikhailov, Evgenii. 1970. "O stanovlenii operatorskogo iskusstva na studii 'Lenfil'm'" [About the Emergence of the Art of the Cameraman at Lenfilm Studio]. In *Iz istorii Lenfil'ma* [From the History of Lenfilm], edited by Nina Gornitskaia, vol. 2, 137–145. Leningrad: Iskusstvo.

Moskvina, Tat'iana. 1990. "'Global'noe kino' petrogradskoi storony" [Global Cinema]. *Iskusstvo kino* [Art of Cinema] 7: 70–80.

Nedobrovo, Vladimir. 1970a. "Iz knigi 'FEKS'" [From the FEKS Book]. In *Iz istorii Lenfil'ma* [From the History of Lenfilm], edited by Nina Gornitskaia, vol. 2, 32–38. Leningrad: Iskusstvo.

Nedobrovo, Vladimir. 1970b. "Plan issledovaniia po istorii 20-letnego razvitiia kinostudii 'Lenfil'm'" [The Research Plan for Lenfilm's Twenty Years' History]. In *Iz istorii Lenfil'ma* [From the History of Lenfilm], edited by Nina Gornitskaia, vol. 2, 239–244. Leningrad: Iskusstvo.

Nikitin, Fedor. 1970. "Iz vospominanii kinoaktera" [From the Recollections of a Film Actor]. In *Iz istorii Lenfil'ma* [From the History of Lenfilm], edited by Nina Gornitskaia, vol. 2, 73–111. Leningrad: Iskusstvo.

Piotrovskii, Adrian. 1922. "Doloi Ameriku!" [Down with America!]. *Zhizn' iskusstva* [Life of Art] 40 [October 10]: 5.

Piotrovskii, Adrian. 1928. "Kino romantiki i geroiki [V poriadke diskussii]" [A Romantic and Heroic Cinema]. *Zhizn' iskusstva* [Life of Art] 31 [July 29]: 2.

Piotrovskii, Adrian. 1929. "Dialekticheskaia forma v kino i front kino-reaktsii" [Dialectical Film Form and the Front of Reactionary Film]. *Zhizn' iskusstva* [Life of Art] 41 (October 13): 3.

Piotrovskii, Adrian. 1929. "Pravyi i levyi uklon v kinematografii" [Left and Right Bent in Cinema]. *Zhizn' iskusstva* [Life of Art] 7 (February 10): 5.

Piotrovskii, Adrian. 1935. "Nashe tvorcheskoe zavtra" [Our Artistic Tomorrow]. *Rabochii i teatr* [Worker and Theater] 2: 20–21.

Piotrovskii, Adrian. 1969. *Teatr, kino, zhizn'* [Theater, Cinema. Life]. Leningrad: Iskusstvo.

Piotrovskii, Adrian. 1975. "Pervyi fil'm molodoi masterskoi" [The First Film of a Young Workshop]. In *Iz istorii Lenfil'ma* [From the History of Lenfilm], edited by Nina Gornitskaia, vol. 4, 155–156. Leningrad: Iskusstvo.

Pozdniakov, Aleksandr. 2014. *List'ia akanta. Istoriia i predystoriia "Lenfil'ma." 1914-2014* [Acanthus Leaves. The History of the Pre-History of Lenfilm]. St Petersburg: Kinostudiia "KinoMel'nitsa."

Proskurina, Svetlana. 1990. "The Troitsky Most Studio." In *Lenfilm en de bevrijding van de Sovjet-cinema*, catalogue, 21–26. Netherlands: Film Festival Rotterdam.

Sobolevskii, Petr. 1970. "Prigotovilis', nachali!" [Get Ready, Go!]. In *Iz istorii Lenfil'ma* [From the History of Lenfilm], edited by Nina Gornitskaia, vol. 2, 60–73. Leningrad: Iskusstvo.

Tsivian, Yuri. 1996. "Between the Old and the New: Soviet Film Culture in 1918–1924." *Griffithiana* 55–56: 39–45.

Tynianov, Iurii. 1927. "Ob osnovakh kino" [On the Basics of Cinema]. In *Poetika kino*, [Poetics of Cinema] edited by Boris Eikhenbaum, 39–59. Moscow and Leningrad: Kinopechat'.

von Geldern, James, 1993. *Bolshevik Festivals, 1917–1920*. Berkeley, CA: University of California Press.

Zhezhelenko, Marina. 1996. "'Novaia volna' ili 'deviatyi val'" [New Wave of Ninth Wall]. In *Peterburgskoe "Novoe kino"* [Petersburg's "New Cinema"], edited by Marina Zhezhelenko, 5–18. St Petersburg: MOL.

4

The Adventures of the *Kulturfilm* in Soviet Russia

Oksana Sarkisova

On June 9, 1926 Nikolai Lebedev signed a contract with the Kinopechat' publishing house, undertaking to write the monograph *Kul'turfil'ma* (MK 26/2/280).[1] The manuscript was submitted in October 1926, but by the end of the year the disaffected author received a biting review from the director of the publishing house, Viacheslav Uspenskii. Uspenskii frowned not only on the author's stylistic flaws, but first and foremost on his ambiguous take on the subject. The frustrations with the ambiguity of the term – which in the 1920s was spelt in the feminine gender as *kul'turfil'ma* (Riabchikova 2006)[2] – were not only Uspenskii's; in fact, they were expressed by most writers on the subject, including those who, like Lebedev, argued for an increase in *kulturfilm* production (RGALI 2494/1/32: 18).[3]

The dynamics of *kulturfilm* production highlight the emergence of new investment priorities in early Soviet cinema. Although only a few *kulturfilms* brought financial rewards to the studios, their number grew throughout the 1920s, helping the studios to emphasize the "edifying" dimension of filmmaking. Since the mid-1920s, *kulturfilms* were used as a rhetorical "weapon" deployed in the competition for state support, and later against the competitors on the film market (Iangirov 1997, 54–60). Moving further away from the imported German concept of *Kulturfilm*, their Soviet counterparts gradually came to be seen as the guarantee of ideological complicity, "justifying" the profit from commercial distribution. The evolution of *kulturfilm* as a production type and a notion expands the understanding of Soviet cultural policy through the prism of the economic and rhetorical strategy of studios' self-positioning.

This chapter looks into the short but dynamic lifespan of this notion; it covers the period of the second half of the 1920s and the early 1930s, when the first *kulturfilms* were in broad circulation, up to the time when they were gradually replaced by the ideas of "documentary" and "scientific" cinema. The first part introduces the semantic context of the idea, borrowed from the German film industry and appropriated by film professionals in the Soviet Union; the second part surveys the studio landscape, *kulturfilm* production practices, and cinematographic highlights of the genre, focusing specifically on the films that, through their survey of the Soviet periphery, contributed to the shaping of Soviet identity discourses. Finally, I conclude by looking into the debates criticizing the concept of *kulturfilm* which foregrounded its gradual withdrawal from film reviews and studio production plans.

Cultural, Enlightening, Useful: The Elusive Film Classification

While awkwardly dated today, the concept of *kulturfilm*, transferred from the German film industry to the Soviet context, was in active use in the 1920s and early 1930s.[4] In the Soviet Union, the imported concept drew on the pre-Revolutionary tradition of "rational" or "sensible" cinema [*razumnyi kinematograf*] (Aleinikov 1912–1914; Aleinikov 1996). Understood as films made for cultivating and educating broad masses of primarily adult viewers, and presented as objective, universal, and truthful, *kulturfilms* were made with the primary aim of shaping and ordering the audience's ideas about the world.[5] The discussion on *kulturfilm* production and distribution and its envisioned audience collided with a lively debate on the role and principles of nonfiction while the two terms were regularly used interchangeably or as synonyms (Iangirov 1997, 54–60).[6]

Reconstructing the history of *kulturfilm* in Russia poses numerous challenges that have to do only partially with the scarcity and dispersal of primary sources. The notion of *kulturfilm* continuously evaded clear-cut definitions. There is no lack of practical difficulties faced by the researcher into this extinct, elusive film form. *Kulturfilms* downplayed the notion of individual authorship, often carried no credits, used unattributed, found footage, and were overshadowed by high-budget fiction productions. Distribution took place primarily through the network of workers' clubs or as supplements to feature films, and as such was rarely documented. *Kulturfilms* spurred few reviews that could extend our understanding of reception patterns. And yet this short-lived film form shaped the way in which both early Soviet documentary and scientific cinema is still remembered and defined to this day.

Lebedev's attempt to define *kulturfilm* went by way of negation, distinguishing it from everything that it was not – not fiction, not chronicle, and not advertisement. His career in cinema started with a passionate Bolshevik article in *Pravda*, "Attention to Cinema."[7] His later writings and administrative work strove to establish and justify *kulturfilm* production in the Soviet Union, following the German example, as outlined in a small monograph, *Across German Cinema* (Lebedev 1924).

Challenged by the editor's expectation of a clear-cut definition in his manuscript on *kulturfilm*, Lebedev identified it as "any film, which aims at organizing our thoughts, irrespective of the methods it uses – scientific, pedagogical, popularizing, or many others," emphasizing the stylistic and genre variety implied by the term (MK 26/2/3; Lebedev 1927). Similar views were expressed and further developed by journalist and film critic Vladimir Erofeev (1898–1940), another key figure in the history of Soviet *kulturfilm* and Lebedev's associate during their early journalist years; Erofeev, too, encountered the German *kulturfilm* during his stay in Berlin and later attempted to adapt this form to the Soviet filmmaking context. His monograph, *The Film Industry in Germany* (1926), emphasized the popularity and profitability of "cultural films," and praised a successful mix of education and entertainment (Erofeev 1926a; 1926b; 1926c).[8] Erofeev actively published on *kulturfilm* in *Sovetskii ekran* and other professional and general periodicals, arguing for the importance of *kulturfilm* production in the Soviet Union (Erofeev 1925; 1926a; 1926c). This position was echoed by many others, such as Nikolai Aseev who quoted the German example arguing for the advancement and importance of "factographic" filmmaking and thus connecting the discussion on *kulturfilm* with that on promoting nonfiction filmmaking:

> *Kulturfilm* is represented by the biggest corporations of European film production. They are working of course not for the philanthropic moral views on future cinema. Their participation shows that they took into account all the aspects of future production, and their interest towards *Kulturfilm* speaks of the only commercially correct way of moving from "anecdote" to "fact" on the whole film front. (Aseev 1926)

The importance of the cinematic "thought-organizer" was further acknowledged by a broad circle of film professionals, from filmmakers to administrators. The Soviet professional film guild, the Association of Revolutionary Cinematographers (ARK, later ARRK), which was established with the active participation of Erofeev and Lebedev, created a "Sector of Scientific and Cultural Cinema." The 1926 discussion in ARK attempted to "purify" the definition of *kulturfilms* as films "of political-enlightening, scientific-educational, or newsreel character, without fictional plots, aimed at introducing viewers to various branches of sciences and knowledge, as well as social, political, and cultural life and working conditions" (GARF 7816/1/2: 120). The meeting concluded with appeals for the further institutionalization of *kulturfilm* production and distribution.

The campaign "to organize public opinion about *kulturfilm*" (RGALI 2494/1/32: 18) peaked in the second half of the 1920s, when the first "histories" of Soviet *kulturfilm* were written. Looking back from 1927 at the short history of the Soviet cinema, Kirill Shutko, who supervised cinema affairs in the Central Committee of the Communist Party, dated the start of systematic *kulturfilm* production in the Soviet Union to 1922, ascribing it to the period when the actual concept was not yet in use by the Soviet film industry (Shutko 1927, 12). But already by the mid-1920s, *kulturfilm* production had gained momentum and was seen as a potentially profitable undertaking for both home and foreign markets. Discussing the prospects of Soviet cinema exports, Soviet officials emphasized the attractiveness of Soviet ethnographic and geographic *kulturfilms*, which were perceived as free from ideological implications, as a welcome export product (RGALI 2494/1/212: 18).[9]

Despite the growing film production, a professional consensus on what constituted a proper *kulturfilm* was still lacking. Not everyone necessarily shared the ARK conviction of *kulturfilms* as being free from "fictional plots." On the contrary, looking for a recipe to make attractive *kulturfilms*, some suggested arranging the footage according to a pre-existing plan using "montage thinking":

> Real life should not be just secretly peeped at, but *filmed after having being understood in a certain way*. Those moments of real life should be selected, which from various sides demonstrate different social phenomena, everyday life, or facts that we want to record and show in a certain way. At some point a certain phenomenon should be *brought to life*, a real event organized and tacitly directed. In a word, one should organize the editing of the filmed material, approach all aspects of filming in an organized way, one should *edit and not simply report on life*. (N. Sh. 1925; emphasis in the original)

The promiscuousness of the genre continued to distress those filmmakers who sought a clear-cut separation between "fiction" and "reality." The advocates of "life-construction" in literature and the arts saw nonfiction as a conceptual and visual alternative to *kulturfilm*. In 1923 *LEF*, the journal of the Left Front of the Arts, published an editorial manifesto calling on filmmakers to "organize real life" (Anon. 1923). Writer, critic, and *LEF* editor Sergei Tret'iakov advanced the idea of the "industry-production screenplay" [*proizvodstvennyi stsenarii*] as the primary source for film production. His *LEF* associate, the writer Nikolai Chuzhak, identified the promotion of "art as construction of life" among the tasks of the day (Chuzhak 1923, 145–146). Dziga Vertov and his group of Kinoks prioritized the role of the chronicle and the newsreel in filmmaking, which they defined in opposition to "acted" or "played" cinema, and prescribed different working methods for the "organizers of visible life" (Vertov 1923, 138). Yet for many film administrators in the mid-1920s, such as Il'ia Trainin, Board Member of the largest Soviet studio, Sovkino, *kulturfilm* provided a convenient, albeit loose, form for packing knowledge into an easily consumable visual form, which, as he saw it, "could be done not only in nonfiction mode, but also as fiction" (RGALI 2494/1/123: 2).

The proportions of the "authentic" and the "re-enacted" in *kulturfilms* remained contentious. Lebedev, for one, attempted to provide a tentative classification, dividing *kulturfilms* into "agitational-propagandistic, scientific-popular, educational, and research films" and called for an open crossing of the fiction/nonfiction boundary (MK 26/2/3). Shutko reiterated the importance of the "documentary, chronicle basis" as a central element of *kulturfilms*, which he described as "authentic ideologically-streamlined enlightenment [*dostovernoe ideologicheski-vyderzhannoe prosveshchenie*]" (Shutko 1927, 13).

All the emphasis on the "streamlined ideology" notwithstanding, the primary examples to follow, which the critics offered to their fellow-filmmakers, came from among the imported films. The Sovkino official and film critic Konstantin Fel'dman, among others, lauded the new possibilities offered by the modern technologies:

> The development of modern film technique allows us to open before the viewer all the secrets of the universe and on the other hand the mastery [*izobretatel'nost'*] of contemporary filming allows to show on the screen the wonderful, astonishing and previously unknown beauty of things and nature. Travels to lake Chad, to the underwater kingdom, to the South Pole, to Central Africa, and the Shackleton expedition – all these are wonderful scientific [*nauchnye*] films which run for months in large cinemas, attract millions of viewers, and can compete financially with the best foreign action films. (Fel'dman 1928, 43; quoted in Deriabin 2001, 57–58)

Similarly, the critic Ippolit Sokolov identified *kulturfilm* as "a realm of reality, an area of science, reason, logic" (Sokolov 1930, 15), yet quoted as exemplary the films that excited viewers' emotions and senses by projecting a dramatized narrative to remote and exotic lands:

> It is much easier to make an interesting *kulturfilm* on a "concrete" geographic and ethnographic topic with exotic material than on an "abstract" social issue with everyday and disadvantageous [*nevyigryshnyi*] material. *Chang*, *Nanook*, or *Moana* are easier to make than a technical or political film. (Sokolov 1930, 15–16)

Sokolov's examples included not only successful film imports such as Robert Flaherty's *Nanook of the North* (1922), Merian C. Cooper and Ernest B. Schoedsack's *Grass: A Nation's Battle for Life* (1925) and *Chang* (1927), but their Soviet counterparts as well, namely Erofeev's *Heart of Asia* [*Serdtse Azii*, 1929], Shneiderov's travel films on Mongolia and China (*The Great Flight*, [*Velikii perelet*] 1925) and the Pamir (*Foot of Death* [*Podnozhie smerti*], 1929). At the same time, Sokolov and other Soviet critics expected not to screen exotic travels but to shape the identity of the viewers. Tret'iakov demanded of the filmmakers that they should "turn the screen of random chronicle into a wide window through which we can observe with the eyes of the master [*khoziaiskim glazom*] our country in construction" (Tret'iakov 1928, 28). The eyes of masters were not to see some "random" images but to become transformed by the very act of viewing. *Kulturfilms* were seen by many as the right form to survey and popularize the riches of the country and as such played a central role in formatting the way of seeing the Soviet space (Widdis 2003).

How to represent the national minorities in *kulturfilm* remained an open question. In the absence of home-made blueprints, Lebedev's manuscript singles out Flaherty's *Nanook of the North* as an ideal *kulturfilm*, and recommended that the

Figure 4.1   *A Sixth Part of the World* (1926): Learning to see the Soviet Union.

Soviet filmmakers follow Flaherty's example (MK 26/2/3). The example of *Nanook* helped to establish the concept of "ethnographic cinema" in the public discourse on filmmaking. Ethnographic cinema was applied to the recording of "unfamiliar" and "archaic" practices and traditional habits performed without stage design or professional actors.[10] In the context of accelerated modernity, cinema was considered as the most suitable instrument, rushing to collect and preserve the "disappearing" cultural traces:

> We have to send cameramen to all the corners of our USSR and their footage will be of enormous importance. Many of the poorly studied peoples are dying out. And perhaps even in a few years not a trace will be left of them. It is all the more important to preserve them on film. (Oganezov 1925)

Anatolii Terskoi's 1930 book on ethnographic cinema exemplifies the emergence of "fully Soviet" ethnography, which "could not be limited to a simple representation" but was expected to organize the viewers' opinions by "exploring the causal connection of facts" in line with the "historical-materialistic character" of Soviet ethnography (Terskoi 1930, 26).

Terskoi combined the overview of ethnographic theories undertaken from a Marxist perspective with practical recommendations on filming techniques, and provided a list of Soviet nationalities for the convenience of the filmmakers. He set the role of the filmmaker as "forcing the whole mass of the viewers to become Marxists, to see what he [the filmmaker, masculine] wants and in the way he wants it." In the hands of the filmmaker, Terskoi argued, "ethnographic material stops being a simple recording of facts. It becomes a torrent of water for the mill of materialistic understanding of history of human culture" (Terskoi 1930, 87). To this end, ethnographic cinema could be produced by taking the shape of "educational, popular-scientific, and so-called fiction film" (Terskoi 1930, 79).

The tension between commercially profitable and ideologically relevant topics remained a point of contention in evaluating the perspectives of *kulturfilm* in the Soviet context. Many, Osip Brik among them, rejected the importance of financial gains altogether. Brik stated that filmmakers "should not occupy [themselves] with the financial matters of the studio [...] We shall say: your money problems are of no concern to us. We insist on the cultural line" (Anon. 1927b, 69). But the studios required a motivation stronger than the critics' calls. How and why did the Soviet studios finance and support *kulturfilm* production?

Kulturfilms in the Soviet Studio Landscape

To understand the rapid rise and fall of *kulturfilm* production in the Soviet film industry, one has to grasp the role that the film studios played in shaping the Soviet cultural policies of the 1920s–1930s. During this time, the field of film production constituted a diversified landscape where state ownership coexisted with both private and foreign investment, and market competition mechanisms functioned in the context of state-imposed limitations on distribution. Centralizing tendencies and the striving for regional autonomy, market rationality and ideological control made the state and Party regulatory policies adjust and react to the market logic of the industry, while competition for material and symbolic capital among the studios took place during the gradual monopolization of the cinematographic infrastructure (Kenez 1992; Youngblood 1991; Taylor and Christie 1991; Fomin and Deriabin 2004, 298–299; Listov 1995; Lawton 1992, 22).

The centralization of the Soviet film industry was gradual (Youngblood 1991; Taylor 1979; Kepley 1994, 60–79). The first modest and inefficient State Film Committee was closed after the scandalous Cibrario affair, during which a large amount of budget money intended for purchasing raw film stock was stolen.[11] Its successor, the All-Russian Photo and Film Organization (VFKO) was established in January 1919. VFKO had a scientific sub-department which produced several promotional and popularizing films commissioned by state agencies like Mossel'prom, but did not turn this activity into a regular or reliable source of income or reputation (Riabchikova 2010, 92–93). VFKO's successor, Goskino State Film-Photo Organization, was formed in 1922 and invested with a distribution monopoly over the whole territory of the Russian Federation (RGASPI 17/60/263: 4–15). Existing without state subsidies in the years of the New Economic Policy (NEP), Goskino sold and rented out the nationalized facilities, including six film studios, two photographic-plate factories, film stock and storage facilities, a photo laboratory with approximately 120,000 negatives, and additional buildings (GARF 4085/12/712: 3–4). In 1923, Goskino opened a Cultural Department, which later received the status of an autonomous studio: Kul'tkino.[12] The most popular films produced by Kul'tkino addressed problems of sexual behavior: *Abortion* [*Abort*, dir. Grigorii Lemberg and Nikolai Baklin, 1924] and *Truth of Life. Syphilis* [*Pravda zhizni. Sifilis*, dir. Vladimir Karin, 1925]. In 1925, the studio undertook two promising commissions, setting out to produce films on the occasion of the Moscow Soviet anniversary and another one popularizing the activities of the State Trade Monopoly (Gostorg). Both films were directed by Dziga Vertov and released (by Sovkino which meanwhile incorporated Kul'tkino) as *Stride, Soviet!* [*Shagai, Sovet!*, 1925] and *A Sixth Part of the World* [*Shestaia chast' mira*, 1926].

A 1923 inspection at Goskino identified multiple failings, including an overgrown staff, uncatalogued collections, poor storage conditions, faulty accounting, corruption, and censored films in distribution (GARF 4085/12/712: 3–13, 65, 154–155). The management was accused of keeping no systematic record of the available film stock, allowing a great deal of it to go missing. An inspector wrote: "By chance I went to the storage facility of the negatives and there, again by chance, I found a list of negatives, sorted by Iurii Zheliabuzhskii. This is the only document that remains from the social chronicle department" (GARF 4085/12/712: 12, 75). Following the inspection and an intensifying tendency towards centralization and tighter control over distribution, Goskino's distribution monopoly was transferred to a new company, Sovkino, in the summer of 1924. Sovkino was headed by Konstantin Shvedchikov, an old Bolshevik and an experienced administrator. While originally established for distribution only, Sovkino soon started its own production and became the leading film studio in the Soviet Union. The existing competition among the studios throughout the 1920s was repeatedly branded in the press as "squabbling," and used as a pretext for centralizing the industry in order to bring "harmony" to the relationship between different production and distribution entities.[13] Sovkino was originally not supposed to be involved in film production and was expected to treat all studios equally in order "to help the toilers of the borderlands to catch up with the toilers of the center" (Trainin 1925, 12).[14] But only a year later, Sovkino announced the beginning of its own production, aiming to make films which were "100 per cent ideological and 100 per cent commercial" (GARF 8638/2/11: 11; GARF 8638/2/30: 5–6; Efremov 1925; 1929; Shapovalenko 1925). The ambitious studio plans were to reach out through a growing network of film theaters and working clubs to the most remote parts of the country as well as to expand to the markets abroad, to "the toiling masses of China, Persia, Turkey, and so on, who are looking at the Soviet Union with special inspiration" (Trainin 1925, 12). Sovkino's 1927 catalogue of "scientific cinema" listed 746 titles which, however, included primarily pre-Revolutionary, imported films (Kristol' 1927).

By entering the production field, Sovkino lost the status of an impartial institution and became one of the main targets of criticism for "profiteering." The studio management found it important to increase investment into *kulturfilm* production, which made Sovkino one of the largest producers of *kulturfilms* in the second half of the 1920s. Sovkino absorbed Kul'tkino and completed the production of the commissioned films under its own name. Throughout its existence it increased *kulturfilm* (and later *politprosvetfilm*, the political enlightenment film) production and sent filmmakers such as Erofeev, Lebedev, Esfir' Shub, Aleksandr Litvinov, and Vladimir Shneiderov to film in diverse parts of the Soviet Union. At the same time, Sovkino remained a target of regular attacks for paying insufficient attention to *kulturfilms* and the "enlightening" mission of cinema (GARF 8638/2/31: 34).

Throughout the second half of the 1920s, other studios also increased budgets allotted to *kulturfilm* production (GARF 4085/12/718: 109–110; Mikhailov 1995, 10; Kepley 1996, 344–356). Among successful early Soviet film studios was Sevzapkino, founded in Leningrad on May 9, 1922 (GARF R-8326/1/1: 17–18; Bratoliubov 1976, 44–45, 135–141; Mukhin 1924, 9–10), and originally distributing films in north-western Russia in partnership with German, Danish, Italian, Austrian, and North American companies (Bratoliubov 1976, 46; 51; 56; RGASPI 17/60/529: 2–5; GARF 8638/2/31: 8). In 1923, Sevzapkino established a scientific-agitation department and became actively involved in the distribution of *kulturfilms*. Its first screenings were the German *Kulturfilme Relativity Theory*, shown in the prestigious Piccadilly Cinema on the central Nevsky Prospect, and *Versailles Peace Treaty*, donated by the German Embassy and screened in the new 150-seat VAI-Sevzapkino cinema on the Nevsky Prospect, opened in cooperation with the All-Russian Engineers' Union and intended specifically for distributing *kulturfilms* (Bratoliubov 1971, 56–68; 1976, 71–72). Several years later, Sevzapkino was merged with Sovkino. Another short-lived studio with ambitious plans was Proletkino, which strove for a monopoly over workers' clubs and non-commercial distribution networks (Riabchikova 2010, 102). Proletkino produced the first Soviet expedition feature *The Great Flight*, filmed by the aspiring Vladimir Shneiderov and cameraman Georgii Blium. Another "enlightening" film in the studio's portfolio was *What For?* (*Za chto?*, dir. Valerii Inkizhinov, 1926), a mix of dramatic reenactment and medical information presented with the use of animation, exposing the dangers of improper treatment of venereal diseases (GARF R-8326/1/3: 24–25).

In 1928, a new studio called Vostochnoe Kino [Eastern Cinema] was established to serve the interests of national minorities.[15] The goal of the studio was the production of "truly eastern" films, the promotion of cinematographic culture and cinema networks in the national republics, and the development of local film production and distribution. Vostokfilm declared its commitment to portraying "the East without embellishment" (RGALI 2489/1/13: 5, 15, 103, 166), and produced a large number of *kulturfilms* on the national minorities in the Soviet Union. Among its most memorable releases was Viktor Turin's *Turksib* (1929), an acclaimed dramatized account of the railway construction between Turkestan and Siberia which became one of the central Soviet media campaigns at the end of the 1920s (Payne 2001a; 2001b).

Figure 4.2 *Turksib* (1929): Remapping Central Asia.

Perhaps the most extensive production of *kulturfilms* was carried out at Mezhrabpom-Rus' (after 1928 Mezhrabpomfilm). In the summer of 1924, Mezhrabpom-Rus' opened a scientific production department and began to compete with Kul'tkino, and later Sovkino, in *kulturfilm* production scope and distribution (Iangirov 1997, 56). The unique position and role of this studio and its intricate role as mediator between the Western (especially German) film market and the local film market has been systematically explored (Bulgakova 1995, 185–187; Kherroubi 1996; Agde and Schwarz 2012; also Chochlowa 1995). The studio came closest to adopting the German concept of *kulturfilm*, actively investing in the production of scientific, popularizing, and expedition films, and even running (for a short while) its own cinema, Artes, specialized in *kulturfilm* (Yangirov 1996; Agde and Schwarz 2012). Mezhrabpom-Rus'/Mezhrabpomfilm releases were diverse in scope and theme: they introduced the basics of industrial production, such as *How to Build an Engine* [*Kak stroit' parovoz*, 1928] or *From Cotton to Fabric* [*Ot khlopka do tkani*, 1928]; they popularized the metric system with *For All Times to All People* [*Na vse vremena, dlia vsekh narodov*, script by Valentin Turkin, director Iakov Poseil'skii, 1926]; and they offered help in choosing a career as in *Scientific Choice of Profession* [*Nauchnyi vybor professii*, script by I. Shpil'rein and Aleksandr Dubrovskii, director Aleksandr Dubrovskii, 1927]. Among the studio's releases are highlights of early Soviet *kulturfilms* such as Vsevolod Pudovkin's *Mechanics of the Brain* [*Mekhanika golovnogo mozga*, 1926] and Vladimir Shneiderov's explorations of Pamir in *The Foot of Death*, which received international acclaim. *Kulturfilms* were made both for specific and general audiences, ranging from educating the peasants

(*Exploitation of a Tractor, Ways of Storing and Using Manure*, 1930) to warning the broad masses of the dangers of alcoholism (*Alcohol, Work, and Health*, dirs. Boris Barnet and Aleksandr Tiagai, 1927). Mezhrabpom did not shy away from producing promotional films for state institutions and agencies, which brought the studio a modest income: *The State Trust of North-Belomor Forest Industry* [*Gosudarstvennyi trest severo-belomorskoi lesnoi promyshlennosti*], *Leningradodezhda*, *Nizhnii Novgorod Local Manufacturing* [*Nizhegorodskaia mestnaia promyshlennost'*], all 1926 (Anon. 1997, 62). In the second half of the 1920s, the studio increased the number of agitprop films, exemplifying the overall growing militarization of society as well as the changing structure of the film market: *Armed Komsomol* [*Vooruzhennyi komsomol*, dir. Georgii Bobrov]; *Kill the Old Times* [*Dob'em staroe*, dir. T. Sumarokova], *Not Fearing the Enemy* [*Ne strashen vrag*, dir. Anatolii Zhardin'e], all made in 1930 (Anon. 1997, 67, 69). Until its dissolution in 1936, Mezhrabpomfilm produced *kulturfilms* for both internal and external markets, altogether releasing several hundred titles, most of which, however, did not survive the massive purges of the film collection by the State Repertory Committee in 1933.[16]

Escalating tension between Mezhrabpomfilm and Sovkino, fueled by the insistence of the former on preserving its autonomy and the desire of the latter to incorporate a profitable studio with its assets, staff, and networks, generated a number of negotiation strategies that made instrumental use of *kulturfilm* production. Analysis of the studio conflict demonstrates that *kulturfilm* was repeatedly used as a rhetorical weapon in the competition for state support. In one of the many complaints sent to the Central Committee by Mezhrabpomfilm in 1929, Shvedchikov (head of Sovkino) was characterized as "harsh, tactless, shallow-hearted, applying *kulak* persistence [...] He hates *kulturfilms* as he believes they bring no profit..." (GARF 7816/2/4: 98 verso). Similar but reversed accusations were applied by Sovkino to Mezhrabpomfilm, the studio whose original dependency on the private capital of Rus' studio was never forgotten. And yet, Mezhrabpomfilm survived Sovkino, which was reorganized into Soiuzkino in early 1930 in yet another step towards the centralization of the film industry.[17] The closing of Sovkino was preceded by harsh criticism from Platon Kerzhentsev, at the time the deputy head of the Department of Agitation, Propaganda, and Press of the Central Committee of the Party, whose report blamed the studio for its "disdainful attitude towards *kulturfilm*" and "commercialization of the distribution policy" (RGASPI 17/113/873: 85–90 verso).

Despite regular rhetorical attacks on the commercialization of the film industry, the new head of the studio, Boris Shumiatskii, made the production of "films understandable for the millions" the studio's priority (Shumiatskii 1935). At the same time, more and more cultural bureaucrats began to replace the loose concept of *kulturfilm* with the straightforwardly ideological notion of *agitpropfilms*. By the time Soiuzkino was reorganized into the Principal Directorate for the Cinema and Photographic Industry (GUKF), directly subordinated to the Council of People's Commissars in February 1933, the notion of *kulturfilm* was no longer in use either in the studio production plans or by the film critics who had earlier insisted on its primary importance (Taylor 1979, 201).

Creative Interpretations

What were the most remarkable *kulturfilms* produced within less than a decade of the upholding and promoting of this concept and category of production? The flexibility of the term encouraged a permanent re-negotiation of its boundaries, allowing filmmakers to experiment with new forms defying strict genre conventions. An early and somewhat anecdotal example is Fridrikh Ermler's debut *Scarlet Fever* [*Skarlatina*, 1924], commissioned by the Municipal Health Department [Gorzdravotdel], which Ermler and his colleagues produced at Sevzapkino's experimental workshop KEM [Kino-Eksperimental'naia Masterskaia]. The group used this opportunity to experiment with cinematographic tricks reanimating the dead and performing eccentric dances, which were despised by the commissioning agency (Zorkaia n.d). Other films also experimented with merging fiction and non-fiction filming conventions, and repeatedly used *kulturfilms* to integrate animation within the film's narrative structure.

Some filmmakers refused the application of the concept *kulturfilm* to their work. Dziga Vertov, for example, insisted on the primarily non-fiction character of his films and came up with a novel genre of cine-race [*kino-probeg*]. Rather than emphasizing the distance between a "cultured" filmmaker and his/her audience in need of enlightenment, Vertov saw film as a community-making experiment, striving to eliminate the boundary between the participants of cine-races and their viewers. Vertov not only repeatedly included the act of filming and the cinemagoers in his films, but equaled the viewers and participants of the film with the whole population of the country.

Contemplating the principles of scientific filmmaking, Pudovkin rejected Vertov's "kino-eye" method, advocating instead thoroughly planned and scripted filming to achieve the required degree of "authenticity" and comprehensibility (Pudovkin 1925; 1927). Pudovkin's overview of Pavlov's research into conditioned and unconditioned reflexes in his *Mechanics of the Brain* started with the presumption of the experiments' universal impact which put animals and humans on the same plane. Emphasizing the social conditioning of human behavior, the film demonstrated the effects of a nervous system trained to produce predictable behavioral results. In order to achieve the most "convincing" and photogenic results during the experiments with frogs, dogs, and children, each experiment was rehearsed and repeated several times, and the film sequences were assembled from scenes recorded on different occasions. According to Pudovkin, the use of synthetic editing was the key element of "scientific" filmmaking, which favored the controlled outcome over the spontaneity of recording (Pudovkin 1925).

Similarly to Pudovkin, Aleksandr Gavronskii described his *Earth and Sky* [*Nebo i zemlia*, 1926], which popularized the basics of astronomy, as a search for "organic ways of explaining the laws of nature" to "experience gratitude and respect to the scientific method and scientific conclusions" (Anon 1927a). Soviet animators cooperated on many Soviet *kulturfilms* producing animated maps, simulated experiments, and satirical episodes. Especially remarkable in the early Soviet context is the work of animator Ivan Ivanov-Vano who cooperated productively with Pudovkin on *Mechanics of the Brain*, created abstract geometrical imagery visualizing the power of electricity for Lev Kuleshov's *Forty Hearts* [*40 serdets*, 1931] and came up with grotesque animations for the concepts of global capitalism for Aleksandr Lemberg's *From the Darkness of Centuries* [*Iz t'my vekov*, 1931], providing a memorable visual idiom for parodying the malevolent *kulaks* (Sargeant 2000; Shlegel' 2002).

A whole arsenal of "scientific" visual conventions emerged in the expedition films of the time. They ranged from animated maps to the inclusion of detailed statistical data and expert opinions. Soviet expedition films made extensive use of cinematographic mapping. Travelogues regularly opened with animated maps, demonstrating the new borders, names, and other forms of ideological domination of space. Animated maps also made it possible to establish new connections and allegiances across space as well as to formulate claims about desired political changes. Shneiderov's *The Great Flight* was a pioneering portrayal of a Chinese uprising metonymically standing for the proletarian world revolution. Erofeev's montage film, *Beyond the Arctic Circle* [*Za poliarnym krugom*, 1927], naturalized the

Figure 4.3 *From the Darkness of Centuries* (1931): Animating ideological enemies.

montage principles to create an image of a culturally mixed area, irreducible to politically driven identities. *Beyond the Arctic Circle* combined travelogue, adventure, and ethnographic modes, and featured the Nordic landscape as a space of diverse habitual, economic, and ethnic practices, functioning at once as a mastered and challenging space of different cultures.

The Soviet Far East featured as another frontier of the cinematographic "motherland," first explored by Aleksandr Litvinov with his *Forest People* [*Lesnye liudi*, 1928] and *Through the Ussuri Area* [*Po Ussuriiskoi taige*, 1928] which led the viewers from civilization into wilderness, from multicultural urban texture to archaic and exotic minorities stretched on a progressive "scale" from savagery to civilization (Deriabin 2003, 59–62; 1999; Golovnev 2012, 156–167). As the viewers were transported over thousands of kilometers, they simultaneously undertook a journey back through time to the "primordial" forests, emphasizing exploring and taming, with extensive attention to the indigenous population. Dramatized *kulturfilms* with the inclusion of studio reenactments were made by Vladimir Shneiderov during the shooting of the exploration of the Soviet Arctic. His *Two Oceans* (*Dva okeana*, 1932) placed humans in competition with nature, dramatized natural vistas, and called for individual heroism exemplified by Otto Schmidt as a romantic, larger-than-life polar explorer. One of the best internationally acclaimed Soviet *kulturfilms* was Viktor Turin's *Turksib*, which was ascribed a pioneering role in developing new cinematic language (Stollery 2000). Combining scripted narrative with location footage, the film focused on the conquest of nature through the construction of a railway that embodied ideas of Soviet technological progress and ideological superiority. Turin's personification of the natural forces clashing with technology created a dramatic narrative that transformed reportage into an emotionally charged and poignant film that marginalized the role of the indigenous population as backward and belonging to the thinning traditional culture.

The increasingly prominent role of reenactment in *kulturfilm* comes to the fore in close viewing of *From the Darkness of Centuries*. Lemberg's film focused on the life of the Mordvins, a Finno-Ugrian minority in the Soviet Union, and used *typage* acting to provide a historical "overview" combined with eccentric animation scenes that parodied and ridiculed the "class enemy." Kuleshov's *Forty Hearts* also made extensive use of animation, which was used to represent both the abstract ideas of electricity and a visionary image of the socialist future. Kuleshov combined animation with historical reenactments to exemplify the linear nature of science and progress. His contrast of a low-efficiency past and a utopian future used animated episodes to refer to a civilizational leap expected of the Soviet power as well as to vilify those opposing the changes. *Forty Hearts* adopted as a starting point Lenin's notorious definition of socialism as "electrification of the whole country" and made abundant use of abstract imagery, which reinforced accusations against Kuleshov as a "formalist." Misleadingly described by David Bordwell as "faux-naïve animation" (Bordwell 2008), Ivanov-Vano's attempt to visualize a non-centralized energy network that homogenizes and unifies the Soviet space in *Forty Hearts* stands out as a unique time experiment. The following year, Esfir' Shub made another take on the idea of electrification in one of the first sound films, *KShE* (*Komsomol–shef elekstrifikatsii*, 1932). Both Kuleshov and Shub portrayed electricity as a unifying force of modernity, visualized as a stand-in for the abstract forces of progress and science. Shub created a complex polyphony of sounds that opened with the symphonic orchestra, where a *termenvox*, the modern wonder of the Soviet musical avant-garde, is accompanied by an orchestra in a harmonic unison of high culture and modern science paradigmatic for the experimental Soviet arts and promoted by the ideology of linearly directed progress. While no longer referred to as *kulturfilm*, Shub's *KShE* had many parallels with Kuleshov's film, including the criticism that both works received for "distorting" reality (Shub was later accused of praising a power plant which after the release of the film failed to fulfill its production plan). With the gradual transition to the notion of *agitpropfilm*, the constitutive principles of *kulturfilm* came under suspicion and gradually gave way to less polysemic works that straightforwardly visualized their ideological agenda.

The Death of the Concept

The debate on *kulturfilm* peaked at the All-Union Party Conference on Cinema Affairs in March 1928, which searched for new ideological uses of cinema. Most of the film professionals shared the conviction of ARRK member Vladimir Sillov, who lamented "the situation when, as soon as our viewer realizes that he is being agitated, the shutters [*klapany*] automatically grow on his ears."[18] The ARRK members and the conference participants stressed the need to find new methods for education and political propaganda. The top Party politicians became increasingly involved with designing film policies. The Plenum of the governmental Kino-Committee, convened on May 8, 1929 and headed by the Party functionary Yan Rudzutak (Janis Rudzutaks), authorized the creation of a working group on *kulturfilm*. It included a diverse mix of filmmakers (Pudovkin, Eisenstein) and administrators (Pavel Bliakhin, Konstantin Shvedchikov, and Kirill Shutko), who were given the task of studying the audience and its education, and identifying "useful" themes for future films and new cadres, as well as looking into the creation of a special studio for "cultural cinema" (GARF 7816/1/3: 6–7). The resolution of the conference on "Workers' Audience and Cinema," organized in Moscow on July 5–6, 1929, was signed by over 200 conference participants and requested further promotion for *kulturfilms* (Levman 1930, 17–22; also Solev 1929).

In the early 1930s, the notion of *kulturfilm* was used interchangeably with the notion of *politprosvet* films (literally standing for political enlightenment films). On February 3–5, 1930, Sovkino organized the first meeting of film workers involved in the production and distribution of *politprosvet* and *kulturfilms*, where the representatives of Tsentrsoiuz, VTsSPS, Kolkhoztsentr, NKP, and other institutions took part (Vishnevskii and Fionov 1974, 58). And although the notion of *kulturfilm* was still in use at the time – Soiuzkino Third Factory, for example, was renamed the Moscow Factory for *kulturfilms* – nevertheless, it was gradually being replaced by new concepts: at first the transitional bulky and awkward-sounding *politprosvet-kulturfilm*, later shortened to *politprosvetfilm*.

The insistence on the political content of *kulturfilms* resulted in demands for the ideological message to be incorporated into the very structure of each film beyond the level of textual commentary. The imperative images of change and development were to leave no doubt about the film's ideological message. The First Moscow conference of agitation-propaganda, scientific-educational, instructional films and chronicles, convened by ARRK and Soiuzkino on April 18–22, 1931, abandoned references to *kulturfilm* with its seemingly universal notion of culture and instead stressed the importance of political enlightenment. Vladimir Sutyrin, at that time the General Secretary of the All-Union Association of Proletarian Writers and an active commentator on cinema affairs, spoke of the importance of "so-called political-enlightenment films" [*politprosvetfilmy*]," calling on filmmakers to replace "shy" [*stydlivye*] *kulturfilms* with shameless [*besstyzhie*] political enlightenment films" (Anon. 1931, 21).

Filmmakers who preferred the concept of nonfiction to that of *kulturfilm* sided with this opinion. "*Kulturfilm* does not exist," argued Esfir' Shub, inviting her fellow filmmakers to pay attention to the "reality of the nonfiction film today." She further contemplated the importance of editing for nonfiction:

> Emphasis [*ustanovka*] on the fact, not only to show the fact, but to enable it to be examined, and, having examined it, to remember, having remembered it – to grasp it [*osmyslit'*], to give the space, the context, to give a human in this space and context with maximum clarity, working with facts, collecting this material in such meaningful associative and generalizing sequences, which would clearly communicate to the viewer the attitude of the author to the facts shown – these are the tasks of montage, which the workers of nonfiction and intellectual cinema face. (Shub 1929, 10)

Erofeev, who in the mid-1920s was an active supporter of *kulturfilm*, this time sided with Shub, claiming that the opposition of fiction cinema and *kulturfilm* is "ungrounded" and "ideologically false" (Erofeev 1930). The discussion on the role of newsreel, initiated by the Department of Agitation and Mass Campaigns of the Central Committee of the Bolshevik Party and Soiuzkino, at that time the largest Soviet film studio, further contributed to the marginalization of the notion of *kulturfilm*, replacing its educational mission with the idea of using newsreel for "elevating the tastes" of the audience (Anon. 1930).

The long-term frustration with the loose definition of *kulturfilm* led to the search for meaningful replacements for the term (Anon. 1928, 3; Naumov 1929; Kazigrass 1929, 17–18). Lazar' Sukharebskii's contribution to the collected volume *Kul'turfil'ma*, edited by Kirill Shutko, included six articles on various aspects of *kulturfilm* and educational cinema. He fragmented the notion of *kulturfilm*, and preferred to speak of its sub-types such as scientific film, pedagogical film, propaganda film, chronicle, and art-historic [*iskusstvovedcheskie*] films" (Sukharebskii 1929, 93). This classification was to have practical consequences as Sukharebskii argued for the establishment of five separate film studios, one for each film type (Shutko 1929). Shutko, the editor of the volume which marked "the beginning of an end" of the concept of *kulturfilm* in the Soviet context, contributed 3 out of the 12 articles to the volume, gradually but consistently replacing the notion of *kulturfilm* with "political-enlightening film," as indicated in the subtitle of the volume.

The terminological transformation polarized the "fiction" and "nonfiction" supporters, fueling the campaign against so-called "documentarism" of 1930–1932, which revisited the notions of "document" and "fact." The pages of *Proletarskoe kino* and other Soviet film journals as well as discussions at professional meetings demonstrate a dramatic change in the use of the concepts of "nonfiction," "reality," and "document" in the context of film production which coincided with the search for conceptual alternatives to the notion of *kulturfilm*. Esfir' Shub, for example, argued for a heightened attention to documentary cinema, which she framed together with newsreel:

> The so-called 'documentarists' also conduct newsreel work, but we are referred to as a movement outside newsreel. This is wrong. There could not be a documentary film – there is documentary or chronicle footage. That is why nonfiction film grew out of newsreel and is organically connected to it. But now we have it this way: there is a newsreel studio, which produces only Sovkino-journal and separate editions of agitation-propagandist value for this or that campaign. And there are nonfiction filmmakers, outside of the newsreel studio, who [...] exist outside the normal conditions of production (Anon. 1931, 95–96).

Echoing Shub and Erofeev, Vertov stated that "nonfiction film is not a direction in cinema, but a branch of the film industry. Documentary nonfiction film is confused with facticism [*faktitsizm*], documentarism, and so on. And yet, documentarism and the production of documentary films are not the same thing" (Anon. 1931, 110).

Erofeev's position was formulated in his article "Technological innovation of documentary cinema," published in the journal *Proletarskoe kino* shortly before the conference. Erofeev abandoned the use of *kulturfilm* and revisited the definition of nonfiction while arguing for a new concept of "documentary cinema," which he defined as a "technical innovation in film production [...] which allowed us to replace reenactment of life events, as performed in fiction film [...] with the recording of authentic reality [*podlinnoi deistvitel'nosti*]" (MK 26/2/73: 134). While emphasizing the imperfections of the proposed classification, he insisted on distinguishing between documentary cinema, fiction, and newsreel. At the same time, he asserted that the concept of documentary does not imply "objective" or "unbiased" film:

> Any film (including documentary) is a tendentious film, since there could be no objective art or objective science. More than that, every frame, which records a

separate fact, is also tendentious, since already in the choice of this (and not another) fact for recording and in the perspective of the camera there is an attitude of the cameraman (and director-organizer) towards this fact.

Does this however reduce the technical innovation of documentary film, which allows us to record life events without their artificial reconstruction? Not in the least. (MK 26/2/73: 136–137)

The ARRK conference of 1931 became a turning point after which the notion of *kulturfilm* came to be replaced by the notion of "documentary" both by the defenders and the critics of the concept of nonfiction. In the closing speech, an official of proletarian literature used a casuistic logic to undermine and condemn the activities of those who began to identify themselves as documentary filmmakers:

many films which documentarist comrades did not consider fiction could be defined as such. The point is that documenarists don't understand a very simple thing, that there could be a document distorting reality and there could be fiction which documents this reality. [...] The main problem of the comrade-documentarists is that they fetishize the document as such. They did not understand that the point is not how an artist approaches reality but what comes out of it. [...] I will say more: as a rule, reenacted material more successfully represents reality than non-reenacted material. [...] Thus, comrade-documentarists, the fact that you film document and not fiction does not save you from making a faulty film. And if it is so, then what is it worth? That is how a huge cinematographic fetish, created by documentarists, is unveiled. (Anon. 1931, 126–129; MK 26/1/70)

"Unveiling the fetish," Sutyrin aimed at reinstating the state's authority not only over the interpretation of the represented events, but over the image of the past as well.

Erofeev and Vertov were found guilty of lacking "dialectical materialism" in their films and became the central targets of the attack on "documentarism." The campaign unfolded both in the press and at various discussion forums; the minutes of the "Evening of documentary cinema" on February 24, 1932 exemplify best the scope of criticism and the main arguments advanced against "documentarism." The discussion also highlighted emerging generational ruptures as film students of the State Institute of Cinematography held their teachers accountable for "faulty methods." One of them, Ol'ga Podgoretskaia, criticized Erofeev's approach to filmed footage and claimed that "by material we mean a certain attitude towards it" (MK 26/1/70: 41). Vertov, in his turn, came under attack for "abstracting the events," and was criticized for the metaphoric montage, particularly the sequence which paired the announcement of Lenin's death with the working machines (MK 26/1/70: 41–42). In response, Erofeev accused his critics of confusing ideological and technical arguments and insisted on a more detailed analysis of the works in question. Nevertheless, both sides advocated the importance of the ideological function of the newsreel and documentary footage.

On July 5, 1931, Soiuzkino closed its *kulturfilm* department. In the course of the year, the use of the term was abandoned. Originally perceived as an "ideological tax" on the film studios, *kulturfilms* stopped bringing sufficient ideological dividends to the state ideologues. Blurred conceptual definitions of the genre, which incorporated promotional and educational cinema on an equal footing, and also – albeit indirectly – its foreign roots, decided its fate. Along with *politprosvet* films, divisions into chronicle, educational, and scientific films became a new set of notions which replaced *kulturfilm*, allowing for further specialization as well as for a higher degree of ideological control. Ironically, with the waning of the anti-documentarism campaign, the concept of documentary replaced the notion of "political enlightenment" and emerged as an institutionally autonomous production and distribution network.

Notes

1. All references to archives are abbreviated as follows: for the Russian State Archive for Literature and the Arts [*Rossiiskii Gosudarstvennyi Arkhiv Literatury i Iskusstva*, RGALI], the Russian State Archive for Social and Political History [*Rossiiskii Gosudarstvennyi Arkhiv Sotsial'no-politicheskoi istorii*, RGASPI] and the State Archive of the Russian Federation [*Gosudarstvennyi arkhiv Rossiiskoi Federatsii*, GARF]: fond, inventory (opis'), document number: sheet; for the Archive of the Film Museum Moscow [*Arkhiv "Muzei Kino"*, MK]: fond/inventory (opis') and case (delo) and sheet number.
2. From here on, we have used the simplified transliteration *kulturfilm*, without the apostrophes for the soft sign.
3. "Protokol zasedania chlenov ARK po voprosy o kul't-fil'me [sic]," December 10, 1926.
4. In Germany, as demonstrated by a comprehensive edited volume, *Das Kulturfilmbuch* in 1924, the notion *Kulturfilm* was firmly established by the mid-1920s both as a concept and a production category (Beyfuss and Kossowsky 1924).
5. For the general development of *kulturfilm* as a concept and practice see Uricchio (1990); also Shlegel' (2002) and Sarkisova (2002).
6. Iangirov includes fiction *kulturfilms* in the catalogue of Mezhrabpom-Rus'/ Mezhrabpomfilm non-fiction cinema. See Anon. (1997, 60–75).
7. Lebedev 1922. On Lebedev's early career in cinema see Riabchikova (2010, 90–108) and Karaseva (2002, 380–381).
8. On the reception of German film culture and industry in Soviet Russia see Deriabin (2002, 239–285).
9. The same opinion was expressed in 1928 by Erofeev, representing the *kulturfilm* section of ARRK (RGALI 2494/1/123: 22, 26; Sukharebskii 1929, 55–56).
10. On the relationship of ethnography and filmmaking see Oksiloff (2001), Griffiths (2002), and Amad (2010).

11 Jacques Cibrario was a private film dealer hired by the Moscow Cinema Committee and sent abroad with a large hard currency subsidy provided by the All-Russian Central Executive Committee to purchase raw film stock; Cibrario disappeared with the money, never completing his mission (RGASPI 17/60/263: 36–62; Liberman 1922; Listov 1995, 66; Iangirov 2011, 125–150; Thompson 1992, 20–21).
12 The Third Factory of Goskino was reformed into Kul'tkino in October 1924; the new studio started its activities on November 3, 1924 (Sukharebskii 1929, 56).
13 Sovkino's charters were approved in December 1924, and in February 1925 the decision to hand over the distribution monopoly to the newly created entity was made, although its activities did not start until March 1925. By August 1926, Goskino was fully merged with Sovkino (Mikhailov 1995, 10–11; Youngblood 1991, 43–47).
14 On the conflict of Sovkino with VUFKU see also Youngblood (1991, 44–45).
15 A shareholding company formed in March 1926, though it did not start operations until 1928 (RGALI 2489/1/1: 91). Its founding members were the Commissariat for Enlightenment of the RSFSR, Autonomous Republics (ASSR) of Bashkiria, Chuvashia, Crimea, Karelia, Kazakhstan, Kirgizia, Tatarstan, Yakutia, Buriat-Mongolia, Dagestan, Volga Germans, and Autonomous Oblasts (AO) of Adygeia, Chechnya, Ingushetia, Kalmykia, Karachaevo, Komi, Mari, and North Ossetia, as well as a number of federal organizations. The charter of the shareholding society "Vostochnoe Kino" was approved on March 13, 1926 (Vishnevskii and Fionov 1974, 38; Skachko 1925).
16 Iangirov (1997, 59) mentions 64 surviving films. See also, Wurm (2012, 120–129), Agde and Schwarz (2012, 213-248), and Razumnyi (1975, 116–118).
17 Its first Head, Martem'ian Riutin, was also removed from his position and later arrested for criticizing Stalin, after which the studio too underwent a series of purges (Getty and Naumov 1999, 52–61; Zalesskii 2000, 398–399).
18 Sillov's speech at the debate "On Crisis in Cinema," at ARRK on November 22, 1928 (RGALI 2494/1/125: 12).

References

Agde, Günter and Alexander Schwarz, eds. 2012. *Die rote Traumfabrik. Meschrabpom-Film und Prometheus 1921–1936* [The Red Dream-Factory: Mezhrabpom and Prometheus, 1921–1936]. Berlin: Deutsche Kinemathek and Bertz+Fischer.

Aleinikov, Moisei, ed. 1912–1914. *Razumnyi Kinematograf*, 2 vols [Sensible Cinema]. Moscow: Izdatel'stvo M. Aleinikova.

Aleinikov, Moisei. 1996. "Zapiski kinematografista" [Notes of a Filmmaker]. *Iskusstvo kino* [Art of Cinema] 7: 104–115.

Amad, Paula. 2010. *Counter-Archive: Film, the Everyday, and Albert Kahn's Archives de la Planète*. New York: Columbia University Press.

Anon. 1923. "Tovarishchi – formovshchiki zhizni!" [Comrades – Molders of Life!] *LEF* 2: 3.

Anon. 1927a. "Zemlia i nebo. Beseda s A. O. Gavronskim" [Earth and Heaven. Conversation with A. Gavronsky]. *Sovetskoe kino* [Soviet Cinema] 1: 5.

Anon. 1927b. "LEF i kino. Stenogramma soveshchaniia" [LEF and Cinema. Minutes of a Meeting]. *Novyi LEF* 11/12: 50–70.

Anon. 1928. "Kul'turfil'mu na ekrany" [Kulturfilm on the Screens]. *Sovetskii ekran* [Soviet Screen] 16 (April 17): n.p.

Anon. 1930. "Kakoi dolzhna byt' sovetskaia kino-khronika" [What the Soviet Film Chronicle Should Be Like]. *Kino i zhizn'* [Cinema and Life] 29: 7.

Anon. 1931. *Za fil'my rekonstruktivnogo perioda. Moskovskaia Assotsiatsiia Rabotnikov Revoliutsionnoi Kinematografii* [For Films of the Reconstruction Period. Moscow Association of Workers of Revolutionary Cinema]. Moscow: Bibliotechka ARRK, Steklografiia "Drug detei."

Anon. 1997. "'Neigrovye fil'my 'Mezhrabpom-Rus'/Mezhrabpomfil'm (1923–1936). Katalog" [Nonfiction Films of Mezhrabpom-Rus/Mezhrabpomfilm 1923–1926. Catalog]. *Kinovedcheskie zapiski* [Film-Scholars' Notes] 33: 60–75.

Aseev, Nikolai. 1926. "V poiskakh kul'turnoi fil'moi" [In Search of Kulturfilm]. *Sovetskii ekran* [Soviet Screen] 2: 4.

Beyfuss, Edgar and Alexander Kossowsky, eds. 1924. *Das Kulturfilmbuch* [The Book of Kulturfilms] Berlin: Carl P. Chryselius'scher Verlag.

Bordwell, David. 2008 "Observations on Film Art," David Bordwell's website on cinema, July 8, http://www.davidbordwell.net/blog/category/directors-kuleshov/ (accessed May 5, 2014).

Bratoliubov, Sergei. 1971. "Daesh' rabochuiu fil'mu" [Give us a Work Film]. In *Zhizn' v kino: Veterany o sebe i svoikh tovarishchakh* [Life in Film: Veterans about Themselves and Their Comrades], edited by N. Klado, 56–68. Moscow: Iskusstvo, http://educate-m.ru/sitemap.html (accessed January 6, 2013).

Bratoliubov, Sergei. 1976. *Na zare sovetskoi kinematografii: iz istorii kinoorganizatsii Petrograda-Leningrada, 1918–1925* [At the Dawn of Soviet Cinema: From the History of the Film Organizations of Petrograd–Leningrad]. Leningrad: Iskusstvo.

Bulgakova, Oksana, ed. 1995. *Die ungewöhnlichen Abenteuer des Dr. Mabuse im Lande der Bolschewiki* [The Extraordinary Adventures of Dr Mabuse in the Land of the Bolsheviks]. Berlin: Freunde der Deutschen Kinemathek.

Chochlowa, Jekaterina. 1995. "Meshrabpom. Dokumente." In *Die ungewöhnlichen Abenteuer des Dr. Mabuse im Lande der Bolschewiki*, edited by Oksana Bulgakova, 195–206. Berlin: Freunde der Deutschen Kinemathek.

Chuzhak, Nikolai. 1923. "K zadacham dnia" [Tasks of the Day]. *LEF* 2: 145–146.

Deriabin, Aleksandr. 1999. "O fil'makh-puteshestviakh i Aleksandre Litvinove" [About Travel-Films and Aleksandr Litvinov]. *Zelenoe Spasenie* [Green Salvation] 11, http://www.greensalvation.org/old/Russian/Publish/11_rus/11_02.htm (accessed March 25, 2013).

Deriabin, Aleksandr. 2001. "'Nasha psikhologiia i ikh psikhologiia sovershenno raznye veshchi': 'Afganistan' Vladimira Erofeeva i sovetskii kul'turfil'm dvadtsatykh godov" ["Our Psychology and Their Psychology are Completely Different": "Afghanistan" by Vladimir Erofeev and the Soviet Kulturfilm of the 1920s]. *Kinovedcheskie zapiski* [Film-Scholars' Notes] 54: 53–71.

Deriabin, Aleksandr. 2002. "'Tam ia uvidel neobychainye veshchi.' Sovetskie kinematografisty o svoikh poezdkakh v Germaniiu" ["There I Saw Unusual Things": Soviet Filmmakers about Their Travel to Germany]. *Kinovedcheskie zapiski* [Film-Scholars' Notes] 58: 239–285.

Deriabin, Aleksander. 2003. "Alexandr Litvinov und der sowjetische Expeditionsfilm" [Aleksandr Litvinov and the Soviet Expedition Film]. In *Die überrumpelte Wirklichkeit: Texte zum sowjetischen Dokumentarfilm der 20er und frühen 30er Jahre*, [Reality

Overpowered: Texts about Soviet Documentary Cinema of the 20s and Early 30s], edited by Hans-Joachim Schlegel, 59–62. Leipzig: Leipziger Dok-Filmwochen.

Efremov, Mikhail. 1925. "O prokatnoi deiatel'nosti Sovkino" [About Sovkino's Distribution Activity]. *Sovetskoe kino* [Soviet Cinema] 4–5: 42–45.

Efremov, Mikhail. 1929. "O prokatnoi politike Sovkino" [About Sovkino's Distribution Policy]. *Kino i kul'tura* [Cinema and Culture] 4: 3–9.

Erofeev, Vladimir. 1925. "Chemu uchit nas Germaniia. O proizvodstve i prokate spetsial'noi fil'my" [What Germany Teaches Us: About Production and Distribution of Special Films]. *Sovetskii ekran* [Soviet Screen] 23: n.p.

Erofeev, Vladimir. 1926a. "Ob ekspeditsiakh voobshche i v chastnosti" [About Expeditions in General and in Particular]. *Sovetskii ekran* [Soviet Screen] 25: 8–9.

Erofeev, Vladimir. 1926b. "O fil'makh 'vtorogo sorta'" [About "Second Rate" Films]. *Sovetskii ekran* [Soviet Screen] 29: 4.

Erofeev, Vladimir. 1926c. *Kinoindustriia Germanii* [The Film Industry in Germany]. Moscow: Kinopechat'.

Erofeev, Vladimir. 1930. "Ot kustarshchiny k fabrike" [From Craft to Factory]. *Kino i zhizn'* [Cinema and Life] 20: 10.

Fel'dman, Konstantin. 1928. "Pamir." *Repertuarnyi biulleten' Glaviskusstva RSFSR* [Repertoire Bulletin of the Art Department of the RSFSR] 5–6: 43.

Fomin, Valerii and Aleksandr Deriabin, eds. 2004. *Letopis' rossiiskogo kino 1863–1929* [Annals of Russian Cinema 1863–1929]. Moscow: Materik.

Getty, J. Arch and Oleg Naumov. 1999. *The Road to Terror: Stalin and the Self-Destruction of the Bolsheviks, 1932–1939*. New Haven: Yale University Press.

Golovnev, Ivan. 2012. "Pervoe etnokino. Aleksandr Litvinov" [The First Ethno-Cinema: Aleksandr Litvinov]. *Vestnik Ural'skogo otdeleniia RAN* [Herald of the Ural Section of the Russian Academy of Sciences], 156–167.

Griffiths, Alison. 2002. *Wondrous Difference: Cinema, Anthropology, and Turn-of-the-Century Visual Culture*. New York: Columbia University Press.

Iangirov, Rashit. 1997. "Neigrovoe kino 'Mezhrabpom-Rus'/Mezhrabpomfilm. Materialy k katalogu" [Nonfiction Film of Mezhrabpom-Rus and Mezhrabpomfilm. Notes to the Catalog]. *Kinovedcheskie zapiski* [Film-Scholars' Notes] 33: 54–60.

Iangirov, Rashit. 2011. "Pervyi kinobiograf vozhdia. Iz istorii partiino-gosudarstvennogo rukovodstva sovetskim kinoiskusstvom v 20-e gody" [The First Film-Biographer of the Leader. From the History of the Party-State Leadership over Soviet Film Art of the 1920s]. In *Drugoe kino. Stat'i po istorii otechestvennogo kino pervoi treti XX veka* [Another Cinema: Articles on the History of Domestic Cinema of the First Third of the 20th Century], edited by Rashit Iangirov, 125–150. Moscow: Novoe Literaturnoe Obozrenie.

Karaseva, Marina. 2002. "'Ot aziatskikh proizvodstvennykh agitok k nauchno-populiarnoi i uchebnoi fil'me!" [From Asian Agit-Sketches on Production to Popular Science and School Films], *Kinovedcheskie zapiski* [Film-Scholars' Notes] 58: 380–381.

Kazigras, Aleksandr. 1929. "Kul'turfil'ma" [Kulturfilm]. *Kino i Kul'tura* [Cinema and Culture] 4: 10–23.

Kenez, Peter. 1992. *Cinema and Soviet Society, 1917–1953*. New York: Cambridge University Press.

Kepley Vance Jr. 1994. "The Origins of Soviet Cinema: A Study in Industry Development." In *Inside the Film Factory: New Approaches to Russian and Soviet Cinema*, edited by Richard Taylor and Ian Christie, 60–79. London: Routledge.

Kepley, Vance Jr. 1996. "Federal Cinema: The Soviet Film Industry, 1924–32." *Film History* 8: 344–356.

Kherroubi, Aïcha, ed. 1996. *Le studio Mejrabpom ou l'aventure du cinéma privé au pays des bolcheviks* [The Mezhrabpom Studio or the Adventure of Private Cinema in the Land of Bolsheviks]. Paris: Réunion des Musées Nationaux.

Kristol', M. ed. 1927. *Nauchnoe kino* [Scientific Cinema]. Moscow: Teakinopechat'.

Lawton, Anna, ed. 1992. *The Red Screen: Politics, Society, Art in Soviet Cinema*. London and New York: Routledge.

Lebedev, Nikolai. 1922. "Vnimanie kinematografu" [Attention to Cinema]. *Pravda*, July 14.

Lebedev, Nikolai. 1924. *Po germanskoi kinematografii* [Across German Cinema]. Moscow: Kino-Moskva.

Lebedev, Nikolai. 1927. "Tipy kul'turfil'm" [Types of Kulturfilm]. *Kino-Front* 1: 4 and *Kino-Front* 2: 5–7.

Levman, Boris. 1930. *Rabochii zritel' i kino: itogi 1-oi rabochei kino-konferentsii* [The Workers' Audience and Cinema: Summary of the First Working Film Conference]. Moscow: Teakinopechat'.

Liberman, Lev. 1922. "K voprosu o kino" [The Question of Cinema]. *Pravda* August 1.

Listov, Viktor. 1995. *Rossiia, Revoliutsiia, Kinematograf* [Russia, Revolution, Cinema]. Moscow: Materik.

Mikhailov, Vladimir. 1995. "Stalinskaia model' upravleniia kinematografom" [Stalin's Model for the Management of Cinema]. In *Kino: Politika i liudi* [Cinema: Politics and People], edited by L. Mamatova, 9–25. Moscow: Materik.

Mukhin, N. 1924. "Pervye gody Sevzapkino" [The First Years of Sevzapkino]. *Kino-nedelia Leningrad-Moskva-Berlin* [Film-Week] 35 (September 30): 9–10.

N. Sh. 1925. "Montazh khroniki" [Montage of Newsreels]. *Sovetskii ekran* [Soviet Screen] 22: n.p.

Naumov, Ivan. 1929. "Verno li? (O kult'urfil'me)" [Is it True? About the Kulturfilm]. *Sovetskii ekran* [Soviet Screen] 18: 4.

Oganezov, Konstantin. 1925. "Kino i etnografiia" [Cinema and Ethnography]. *Sovetskii ekran* [Soviet Screen] 19: n.p.

Oksiloff, Assenka. 2001. *Picturing the Primitive: Visual Culture, Ethnography, and Early German Cinema*. Basingstoke: Palgrave Macmillan.

Payne, Matthew J. 2001a. "Viktor Turin's *Turksib* and Soviet Orientalism." *Historical Journal of Film, Radio, and Television* 21.1: 37–62.

Payne, Matthew J. 2001b. *Stalin's Railroad: Turksib and the Building of Socialism*. Pittsburgh: University of Pittsburgh Press.

Pudovkin, Vsevolod. 1925. Montazh nauchnoi fil'my" [The Montage of Scientific Films]. *ARK* 9: 10–11.

Pudovkin, Vsevolod. 1927. "Kak delaetsia kulturfil'ma. Mekhanika golovnogo mozga. Beseda s Pudovkinym" [How the Kulturfilm is Made. The Mechanics of the Brain. Conversation with Pudovkin]. *Sovetskoe kino* [Soviet Cinema] 1: 5.

Razumnyi, Aleksandr. 1975. *U istokov...* [At the Source...]. Moscow: Iskusstvo.

Riabchikova, Natal'ia. 2006. "'Etot chuzhdyi nam termin.' K istorii leksemy 'fil'ma'" [This Strange Term. The Lexeme "Film"]. *Kinovedcheskie zapiski* [Film-Scholars' Notes] 77: 147–162, http://kinozapiski.ru/ru/article/sendvalues/1022 (accessed January 25, 2014).

Riabchikova, Natal'ia. 2010. "'Proletkino': ot 'Goskino' do 'Sovkino'" [Proletkino: From Goskino to Sovkino]. *Kinovedcheskie zapiski* [Film-Scholars' Notes] 94–95: 90–108.

Sargeant, Amy. 2000. *Vsevolod Pudovkin: Classic Films of the Soviet Avant-Garde*. London and New York: I. B. Tauris.

Sarkisova, Oksana. 2002. "Archäologie eines vergessenen Konzepts: diskursive und institutionelle Entwicklung des Kulturfilms in Russland" [Archeology of a Forgotten Concept: Discursive and Institutional Development of the Kulturfilm in Russia]. *Spurensuche* ('Zauber der Exotik': Aspekte ihrer Popularisierung), 13.1–4: 64–89.

Shapovalenko N. 1925. "Ekonomicheskii analiz kino-seansa" [Economic Analysis of the Film Screening]. *Sovetskoe kino* [Soviet Cinema] 2–3: 73–74.

Shlegel', Ganz-Ioakhim (Schlegel, Hans-Joachim), 2002. "Nemetskie impul'sy dlia sovetskikh kul'turfil'mov 20kh godov" [German Impulses for the Soviet Kulturfilm of the 1920s]. *Kinovedcheskie zapiski* [Film-Scholars' Notes] 58, http://kinozapiski.ru/article/313/ (accessed January 25, 2014).

Shub, Esfir'. 1929. "Neigrovaia fil'ma" [Nonfiction Film]. *Kino i kul'tura* [Cinema and Culture] 5–6: 6–11.

Shumiatskii, Boris. 1935. *Kinematografia millionov* [Cinema of the Millions] Moscow: Kinofotoizdat.

Shutko, Kirill. 1927. "Kul'turnaia fil'ma k desiatiletiiu" [Kulturfilms for the Tenth Anniversary]. *Sovetskii ekran* [Soviet Screen] 45: 12–13.

Shutko, Kirill, ed. 1929. *Kul'turfil'ma. Politiko-prosvetitel'naia fil'ma* [Kulturfilm. Films of Political Enlightenment]. Leningrad: Teakinopechat'.

Skachko, A. 1925. "Vostochnoe Kino" [Eastern Cinema]. *Sovetskoe kino* [Soviet Cinema] 2–3: 85.

Sokolov, Ippolit. 1930. "Put' kul'turfil'my" [The Path of the Kulturfilm]. *Kino i zhizn'* [Cinema and Life] 21: 15–16.

Solev, Vladimir. 1929. "Govorit kinozritel'" [The Spectator is Speaking]. *Sovetskii ekran* [Soviet Screen] 21: 10–12.

Stollery, Martin. 2000. *Alternative Empires: European Modernist Cinemas and the Cultures of Imperialism*. Exeter: University of Exeter Press.

Sukharebskii, Lazar'. 1929. "Nauchno-prosvetitel'skoe kino v SSSR" [Scientific-Educational Cinema in the USSR]. In *Kul'turfil'ma* [Kulturfilm], edited by Kirill Shutko, 55–100. Leningrad: Teakinopechat'.

Taylor, Richard. 1979. *The Politics of the Soviet Cinema, 1917–1929*. Cambridge: Cambridge University Press.

Taylor, Richard and Ian Christie, eds. 1991. *Inside the Film Factory: New Approaches to Russian and Soviet Cinema*. London: Routledge.

Terskoi, Anatolii. 1930. *Etnograficheskaia fil'ma* [Ethnographic Film]. Leningrad-Moscow: Teakinopechat'.

Thompson, Kristin. 1992. "Government Policies and Practical Necessities in the Soviet Cinema of the 1920s." In *The Red Screen*, edited by Anna Lawton, 19–42. London: Routledge.

Trainin, Il'ia. 1925. "Na puti k vozrozhdeniiu" [On the Path to Rebirth]. *Sovetskoe kino* [Soviet Cinema] 1: 8–14.

Tret'iakov, Sergei. 1928. "Chem zhivo kino" [What Cinema Lives By]. *Novyi LEF* 5: 28.

Uricchio, William. 1990. "The Kulturfilm: A Brief History of an Early Discursive Practice." In *Before Caligari: German Cinema, 1895–1920*, edited by Paolo Cherchi Usai and Lorenzo Codelli, 356–378. Pordenone: Edizioni Biblioteca dell'Immagine.

Vertov, Dziga. 1923. "Perevorot". [A Revolution] *LEF* 3: 135–143.

Vishnevskii, Veniamin and Petr Fionov, eds. 1974. *Sovetskoe kino v datakh i faktakh (1917–1969)* [Soviet Cinema in Dates and Figures 1917–1969]. Moscow: Iskusstvo.

Widdis, Emma. 2003. *Visions of a New Land: Soviet Film from the Revolution to the Second World War.* New Haven: Yale University Press.

Wurm, Barbara. 2012. "Von Mechanik des Gehirns zu Vierzig Herzen. Meschrabpom-Film und der Kulturfilm" [From *Mechanics of the Brain* to *Forty Hearts*: Mezhrabpom and the Kulturfilm]. In *Die rote Traumfabrik* [The Red Dream-Factory], edited by G. Agde and A. Schwarz, 120–129. Berlin: Deutsche Kinemathek and Bertz+Fischer.

Yangirov, Rachit. 1996. "Le cinéma non joué" [Nonfiction Cinema]. In *Le studio Mejrabpom ou l'aventure du cinéma privé au pays des bolcheviks* [The Mezhrabpom Studio or the Adventure of Private Cinema in the Land of Bolsheviks], edited by A. Kherroubi, 85–92. Paris: Réunion des Musées Nationaux.

Youngblood, Denise. 1991. *Soviet Cinema in the Silent Era, 1918–1935.* Austin: University of Texas Press.

Zalesskii, Konstantin. 2000. *Imperiia Stalina. Biograficheskii entsiklopedicheskii slovar'* [Stalin's Empire. Biographical Encyclopedia]. Moscow: Veche.

Zorkaia, Neia. n.d. "Sevzapkino na beregakh Nevy" [Sevzapkino on the Banks of the Neva]. *Slovo,* http://www.portal-slovo.ru/art/35966.php?ELEMENT_ID=35966&SHOWALL_1=1 (accessed January 5, 2013).

5

Soiuzdetfilm: The Birth of Soviet Children's Film and the Child Actor

Jeremy Hicks

From the beginnings of the medium, children have been among the most passionate cinemagoers, and children have been ubiquitous in film (Dolinskii 1959, 495; LeBeau 2008, 12). Nevertheless, it was not until 1936 that the first film studio devoted entirely to the production of films for children was founded: Soiuzdetfilm, in Moscow. With this initiative, the USSR initiated a new stage in film entertainment for children (Field 1952, 135).

Film screenings specifically for children, and films made in part for children predate the 1917 Revolution, with the potential of cinema for children's upbringing recognized in Russia as early as 1908, but from the very early years of the Bolshevik film industry, the Soviets deliberately strove to make films that appealed to children (Riabchikova 2009, 231; Miloserdova 2006, 8). Throughout the 1920s, there was a focus on extending the film network so as to reach children with weekend matinees and get cinema into schools. However, despite enthusiasm for the creation of films for children, results were sporadic, until the June 1936 decision to create a film studio, Soiuzdetfilm, with a remit specifically to make films for children. This is partly due to the particular insistence of director Margarita Barskaia, who wrote a number of letters calling for such a production unit, including one to Stalin. She was duly made artistic director of the new studio (Beumers *et al.* 2009, 245–253). She was pushing at an open door though, as is evident from wider shifts in attitudes towards the production of culture for children in the mid-1930s: a December 1935 First All-Union Conference on Children's Cinema, and linked to the creation, with the active involvement of Maksim Gor'kii, in 1936, of Detgiz, a publisher of books for children, and a central (i.e. Moscow-based) children's theatre (Dolinskii 1959, 514–518). The prioritization of children's cinema was thus a logical consequence of a highly ideological approach to children's literature, where the

---

A Companion to Russian Cinema, First Edition. Edited by Birgit Beumers.
© 2016 John Wiley & Sons, Inc. Published 2016 by John Wiley & Sons, Inc.

revolution changed the corpus more radically than with literature for others (Balina 2008, 7). In this context the Soviets' ideological focus on education, funded by the state rather than the box office, meant that they fully grasped the differing needs of the child audience before others (Miloserdova 2006, 9).

Yet this fact is routinely overlooked in discussions of the depiction of children in cinema and the making of films for children. Cary Bazalgette and Terry Staples refer to a Summer 1936 *Sight and Sound* editorial that discusses the importance of children's films without reflecting upon the Soviet inspiration for this discussion: the Soviets' creation that year of a studio dedicated to children's film (Bazalgette and Staples 1995, 94). Similarly, Pierre Sorlin has argued that "in films, childhood was an invention of the 1940s": whereas previously few films had child protagonists, with the war, the image of children, of child protagonists as symbols of their nation, and as images of suffering, became widespread on the screens of the world, marking a profound cultural shift. But he does not see this as relating especially to Russia (Sorlin 2008, 109). This neglects the Soviet initiative in inaugurating Soiuzdetfilm, a children's film studio, and one that pioneered the children's film, with child protagonists, thereby opening up similar possibilities for filmmakers in a number of countries, including in 1940s Italian Neorealism, alluded to by Sorlin.

This chapter analyses how the Soviets pioneered children's cinema, how they attempted to confront the problems associated with this form, and to mobilize the symbolic potential of the child to shape films to their own ideological requirements in the pre-World War II period through the Soiuzdetfilm studio. To do so, I shall look at the workings of Soiuzdetfilm, its search for generic models and a workable style for films for children, and illustrate this through a case study of the studio's greatest success in this era: Mark Donskoi's *The Childhood of Maxim Gorky* [*Detstvo Gor'kogo*, 1938], seen in the wider context of the studio, the problem of the child actor, and the influence of Soviet children's film internationally.

The Creation of Soiuzdetfilm

The decision to focus the efforts of a single studio on children was significant, and it was symbolic that the studio that turned to the production of children's films had previously been Mezhrabpomfilm, which made films destined for export, in particular to Germany, which embodied hopes for an international revolution. With the 1933 triumph of the National Socialist regime in Germany, the opportunities for the export of world revolution had entirely disappeared. The shift towards making specifically children's films marked a sharp contrast with the studio's previous emphasis: the new audience was national, or Soviet.

This is perhaps no surprise: Evgenii Margolit sees the child as the key symbol of the Soviet cinema, employed so as to incarnate the future, to which Soviet ideologues made special claims, frequently representing it as a land of children (Margolit

2002, 76). The focus on children may seem natural, given the Bolsheviks' emphasis on education and literacy from the outset, and the dominance of a didactic paradigm in Soviet culture: as Catriona Kelly has argued, "[t]he Soviet state placed children's affairs at the heart of its political legitimacy" (2007, 1). Yet the decision to make this the remit of a whole studio at that moment in time, one of inward refocus, may be seen as an attempt to foster deeper and firmer bonds of Soviet patriotism through cinematic means. Ernest Gellner contends that nationalism makes nations, and not the other way around, and the key institutions for engendering nationalism are education and the media (Gellner 1983, 127). This was all the more true for the pedagogically focused Soviet cinema. For children's cinema, this task had to be rethought following the coming of sound, which led to dialogue-dominated films that were too verbose for child audiences (Bazalgette and Staples 1995, 93; Riabchikova 2009, 234–235).

The fact that this model of a state-subsidized children's cinema making low-budget films for national audiences was later emulated around the world as a strategy for resisting US cultural influences paradoxically seems to corroborate the notion that there was a nationalist purpose behind the creation of Soiuzdetfilm. Hollywood in the classic studio era, by contrast, concluded that it was not commercially viable to make films specifically for children, who represented around 8 percent of the population; instead they should be offered family films (Field 1952, 98). This essentially was the Disney model for films in the early years of the studio – films that the whole family would enjoy, even if that meant elements of horror and the erotic aimed more at adults (Davies 2006, 26–27). The key distinction between the children's film and the US notion of the family film was that there are substantial adult parts in a family film, where the focus is the adults' struggles in coping with children, whereas the thrust of a children's film is children and their coping with adults. Furthermore, unlike in US family films, in children's films the heroes were not stars, but cast to suggest a more realist ordinariness, something also implied through other elements of film style too (Bazalgette and Staples 1995, 17, 95). Placing children at the center of a film was difficult, and appealing to younger children, whose needs differ most from an adult audience was a particular challenge requiring a conscious commitment to please children. This entailed a difficult transition from the studio's previous priorities, to a search for models and templates that the studio might adopt to standardize its productions efficiently (Nemoliaev 1986, 205).

Getting Inside the Child's Head

Soiuzdetfilm director, Vladimir Shneiderov, talks about the complete honesty of children's audiences, and consequently the great anxiety the crew always experienced before showing the finished film to children (Maksimova 1940, 103).

According to Shneiderov, it was not the screenings for the censorship committee or his colleagues at the studio whom he and his associates feared, but those for child spectators, implying that entertainment rather than ideology was his first concern.

Aleksandr Razumnyi, while working on the classic Soviet children's film, *Timur and his Gang* [*Timur i ego komanda*, 1940], criticized previous Soviet children's films for being made in the same way as those for adults, without what he calls "romanticism": children's stronger impressions and their investing of the world around them with a kind of fantasy. Adult directors often fail to understand that, and instead: "see all the events of children's lives through adult eyes; they evaluate and decode them from the standpoint of their own sensibility" (1940, 25–26). Razumnyi argues that this imposition of an adult vision on children is evident even from the visuals in such films – the camera angles suggest an adult perspective – such as when we see an adult from the child's point of view, we have a straight-on and not a low-angle shot. By contrast, in working on his previous film *A Private Affair* [*Lichnoe delo*, 1939], the whole crew made a special effort to consider a child's way of perceiving things (1940, 28). Razumnyi's rethinking of children's film is a reason for the enormous success of *Timur*, as Iosif Dolinskii comments: "Together with the cameraman and the set designer, Razumnyi strove to create an environment for Timur's gang: the attic, the gardens, the streets, the roads and the rooms – everything was how the main characters perceived it" (1959, 534). Razumnyi was praised for his efforts to get inside a child's head (1940, 13). A particularly important means of doing this, was through the use of a child performer.

Children Performing Children

The specific use of the child actor in cinema marks a sharp contrast with children's theater where there had long been a tradition of adults playing the role of children in "travesty." Margarita Barskaia's film, *Torn Boots* [*Rvanye bashmaki*, 1933] had set a benchmark for the use of child actors in sound cinema, pioneering an original method for working with infant performers, in which she rehearsed over a long period, involving them in games they perform for the camera (Miloserdova 2006, 30). Nevertheless, there were still examples in Soviet children's films where adults played children such as Soiuzdetfilm's adaptation of *Treasure Island* [*Ostrov sokrovishch*, 1937], directed by Vladimir Vainshtok, where the 30-year old Kapitalina Pugacheva plays the role of a child, Jenny Hawkins, changed to a girl from the original's Jack. Building on Barskaia's work, Soiuzdetfilm soon evolved "a specific method of acting for young actors" (Dolinskii 1959, 494–495). This became so widespread that by 1949 it became necessary to criticize the "theory" that all films for children must have child protagonists played by child actors (Begak and Gromov 1949, 15–16).

Before analyzing precisely what that specific method is, let us first consider what the film director is trying to elicit from the child actor. Despite the initial plurality in Soviet approaches to acting, by the mid-1930s, the Stanislavsky method had become dominant, with its emphasis on training, experiences and memories that can be drawn on and reworked. Reflecting on the broader category of the children's film, Karen Lury argues that, for the child actor, this kind of training was unlikely to be effective, because they have so small a sum of experiences and memories:

> [the] belief that the child is defined precisely by his or her lack of self-consciousness and innocence (a relative lack of complex emotional experience) would suggest that the Method is not readily available to child actors as a tactic that would allow them to control or claim authorship of their performance. (Lury 2010, 156)

Consequently, Lury asks, whether children can really be said to be acting at all: "[i]f children performing in films are not acting then what is it that they are doing?" It is the uncertainty of responses to this question that makes children's acting performances so appealing (Lury 2010, 10). It is precisely the perceived spontaneity, and non-performance of children's performances that was valued by Soviet filmmakers, especially at Soiuzdetfilm.[1] But how did Soiuzdetfilm directors set about attempting to elicit this quality of spontaneity?

Razumnyi stressed that the director must explain in broad terms what he or she wants, and then leave the child space to come to their own conclusions:

> In working with children, the director should not show how they need to act. Usually the child, trying to emulate him, will produce a poor copy of the scene the director has shown him. Children are highly sensitive to such fakery. Instead, after explaining what he wants, the director needs to give the child a chance to improvise. It is essential to unleash the child's fantasies, and he will think up his own original interpretation of the scene. He will bring to it a great deal from his own child's world, a world unknown to the director. We are grateful to our young actors for dozens of marvelous suggestions. In some places they enriched the language of the screenplay and brought it to life. (Razumnyi 1940, 33)

Another approach, termed "mixed associations" entailed the director telling stories and drawing analogies to stimulate the child's imagination (Dolinskii 1959, 519). Razumnyi also used distraction as he sought to find specific ways for each child to remove their fear of being in front of a camera and settling them down – for one boy they chatted about football, and the boy became excited and forgot to worry about being filmed (Razumnyi 1940, 30, 32).

These techniques were calculated to coax an apparently natural and spontaneous performance from the child, as Soiuzdetfilm directors from Barskaia onwards sought to avoid the studied and mannered performance of the self-consciously aspiring child actor: "The calculated ham acting of a little actor can be more

Figure 5.1 Cover of the collection *Children and Cinema* [*Deti i kino*], 1940.

repellent than the worst adult hamming" (Lukashevich 1940, 45). Yet Soviet ideology, especially in the Stalinist era formula of Socialist Realism, was famous for its need to control and discipline nature, to curb the spontaneous and elemental. It seems strange that it permitted such apparent freedom in children's acting performances, and reconciled it with the imperative to discipline and educate.

Childhood, Difference, and Ideology

The discourse of childhood specificity coexisted, in discussions of Soviet children's film, with calls to treat children seriously, introduce them to big themes: to fulfill Soviet cinema's central educational mission. Indeed, the writer Aleksandr Brunshtein denounced filmmakers who tried to drive children into "the ghetto" [*cherta osedlosti*] of specifically children's themes (Brunshtein 1938). This didacticism provokes the critique that children in Stalin-era children's films act in an unchild-like way, resembling mini-bureaucrats, since "ideological maturation" is the key thing, and is not age-specific (Prokhorov 2008, 138).

There are many examples in Soviet film of children acting like adults and such undermining of childhood's wildness was a tendency within Soviet culture, especially marked in the post-war late Stalinist era: Vladimir Sukhobokov and Mariia Sauts's film, The Red Scarf [Krasnyi galstuk, 1948] would be a good illustration of such prematurely political characterizations. Such a stance is reflected in the criticism, such as Begak and Gromov's condemnation of escapism or of attempts to create a specifically children's world, and their assertion that children cannot be separated off from politics: "The bringing up of children is, in the final analysis, always a party matter" (1949, 40–41).

This tension between Stalinist films' coveting of childhood spontaneity, and their didacticism may be said to be a specific instance of a contradiction that pervades films with child actors in general, as the child is habitually figured as the other to the rational, civilized, grown up human being, but the film must tame and capture this quality of the child's nature in performance, requiring the child actor to enact the paradoxical command: "act natural."

Essentially, as with other films using child actors, the narrative trajectory of a Soviet children's film needed to encompass a certain wild and natural dimension of childhood, a hint of hooliganism, a forgivably not-yet-Marxist existence evident even if solely in the acting, but show how that was overcome through a form of mentoring and education, curbed to the benefit of all. This was potentially tricky, especially with a film set in the Soviet present, where the politics were highly prescribed. While a film like Timur and His Gang [Timur i ego komanda] was perceived as depicting but resolving this conflict satisfactorily, the tension between the appeal to children and the political message was not always resolved to the satisfaction of the Soviet authorities, as Natalia Miloserdova suggests of the censoring of Margarita Barskaia's film Father and Son [Otets i syn, 1937]. Here, the son of hard-working party member and factory director fails to pay enough attention to his 13-year old son, who in turn neglects his education, turning to a life of delinquency and petty crime. While the son realizes what he is getting into, renounces his associates and is reconciled with a contrite father, the frank depiction of teenage revolt had gone too far, especially when it was partly caused by the father's excessive devotion to work and the party. Although it has been suggested that the film may have been banned because of Barskaia's association with Karl Radek, who had been arrested, (Miloserdova 2009, 244; Margolit 2012, 153), Miloserdova also persuasively points to the fact that the surviving print of the film has no sound for the sensitive scenes, including the one depicting a party meeting where the father finds out his son has run away from home while giving a speech on the upbringing of children (Miloserdova 2006, 31).

While an adaptation of a work set before the revolution, Mark Donskoi's Childhood of Maxim Gorky maybe seen as Soiuzdetfilm's most successful use of the child actor, shrewdly balancing a certain spirit of youthful revolt with the required political message. As a result it was popular with spectators young and old, as well as receiving widespread and enthusiastic critical acclaim for its political and historical vision, to such an extent that the studio was subsequently named after Maksim Gor'kii in 1948. Yet, while it may be seen as exceptional, Donskoi's film drew on the experience in working with the child actor developed by Barskaia, and his colleagues at Soiuzdetfilm. Donskoi's success lay in his skillful resolution of the conflict between delinquency and the correct politics.

Donskoi's Approach to Acting

Mark Donskoi's broad approach to acting from the outset combined a special method of rehearsal with improvisation on set (Deriabin 2001, 185). Thus, while he initiated extensive discussion at the read-through stage, on set Donskoi made a special effort to overcome the tendency of the cumbersome sound technology in the 1930s to kill spontaneity because the actors had to wait for the equipment to warm up: instead he ensured that the crew were ready to record the moment the actors were. As a result, they almost always ended up using the first take (Donskoi 1938). This approach likewise influenced Donskoi's approach to the child actors:

> As soon as the director succeeded in getting the desired result from the actor, without letting the actor cool off, we immediately began filming. Several scenes with Alesha were shot without the director's customary command: "Ready? Camera... action!" The actors weren't even aware that the scene had been shot. (Ermolov 1938: 4)

This approach is reminiscent of Dziga Vertov's approach to documentary in the 1920s, and the method of filming caught-off-guard, where the subjects were filmed while their attention was diverted. Indeed the scenes in *Childhood* where Gypsy does tricks with a mouse recall episodes in Vertov's *Kino-Eye* [*Kinoglaz*, 1924] and *Man with a Movie Camera* [*Chelovek s kinoapparatom*, 1929] where children are filmed, unselfconsciously fascinated, watching a magician also make a white mouse appear. Donskoi's child actor, Aleksei Liarskii, is perhaps at his most childlike, and least studied, when watching these tricks, even if giving the handicapped boy, Lenia the mouse may be seen as a renunciation of childhood (Erikson 1963, 387).

Nevertheless, Donskoi's method of working with children did involve rehearsals, but never on the day of the shoot for fear of undermining the immediacy. He recounts the incident with Lenia, as an example of the great danger of children rehearsing:

> On the whole, when working with child-actors, there is a danger of rehearsing them too much, teaching them too much. That was the situation with another gifted child-actor, Igor Smirnov, who played the role of Lenia. Igor himself aspired to "act", and on top of that his mother interfered and began to rehearse with him at home.

As a result of this "preparation," the boy came to the set so "trained" that he "overacted" in front of the camera. All the immediacy and freshness of performance had completely disappeared. We had to "break" Igor; we had to work hard to bring him back to childish immediacy. (Donskoi 1939, 235–360)

Here we see an example of precisely the need to elicit a performance of spontaneity, referred to by Lury, above. It is important to note that this danger of over-rehearsal is associated with what is said to be an incorrect approach to acting, a flawed method. Indeed, in contrast to the expectations that a child does not have a method or memories on which to draw, Donskoi explains how effectively it was his own understanding of method acting and the technique of emotional memory that unlocked Liarskii's memories enabling his expression of strong feelings:

> The director should not show the child-actor how he should act, otherwise the child-actor will imitate the director, whereas the primary task of the director consists in using the *immediacy* of the child's performance. He should only indicate by hinting, so as to, as it were, give the child-actor a thread he can grasp and take his performance further independently.
>
> That's how I worked with Aleksei Liarskii who played the role of Alesha Peshkov. For instance, it was very hard for me to get more emotion from him in the episodes that called for the display of a stormy temperament. Liarskii possesses great, albeit hidden, innate strength, and during our preliminary work I had to elicit from him some personal memories to create the right mood, for him to show strong emotions in his performance. (Donskoi 1939, 235–236; emphasis in the original)

Childhood manages to achieve a childish spontaneity in the actors' performances, but this lightness is something that had to be worked on. Curiously, this style also parallels the literary source: this is an autobiography written by a mature author, and as with all such works contains two voices. What Donskoi achieves, through his use of child actors, is to give us a sense of the child as the witness, the one experiencing the episodes, whereas the older author's voice, as Maksim Gor'kii, appears in the intertitles and the juxtaposition of episodes.

The film's technical solution to the problems of the child actor through what might be called "a calculated spontaneity," is echoed in its themes, such as delinquency: while it shows street fights, they reflect Tsarist Russia and are therefore implicitly "pro-Soviet." Key to the incredible appeal of Donskoi's film is that it both creates an image of delinquency reminiscent of the street kids that plagued 1920s Russia, and that formed the subject matter of many films, the most famous of which is Nikolai Ekk's *The Road to Life* [*Putevka v zhizn'*, 1931] but also shows these unruly kids to be precursors of socialism.

Donskoi achieved this in part by tellingly altering the episode of the street fighting in which Alesha stands up for a mentally handicapped tramp, in the original called Igosha, against one group of street urchins, and is aided and befriended by

Figure 5.2 Production still from Mark Donskoi's *Childhood of Maxim Gorky* (1938). Mark Donskoi rehearses with child actors.

another such group. In Gor'kii's narrative, Alesha does not intervene, but merely observes and disapproves of this victimization at the hands of kids who also tease him. Evgeny Dobrenko has suggested the change from passive witnessing of injustice to active resistance to it imposes an orthodox Stalinist narrative of struggle upon Gor'kii's more diffuse story of growth (Dobrenko 2008, 155). This is to overstate the case: as with his approach to child actors, instead of insisting, Donskoi tweaks things so as to ensure spectators get the hint towards the intended Soviet interpretation.

However, this scene is also linked to another plot line changed by Donskoi more overtly so as to ensure the film portrays childhood in accordance with Stalinist norms: the fight is observed by Alesha's neighbor, Good Idea [Khoroshee Delo], thus establishing a connection between him and the children: both symbols of the new world of the future, described by Margolit as a "land of children who will decide the fate of the world" (Margolit 2002, 79). Their symbolic connection explains why, although we never see them meet him, the other children also accompany Good Idea when he has to leave.

By introducing a mentor figure, Good Idea, Donskoi turns a character who is peripheral in the original literary source, into an inspirational revolutionary, in accordance with the classic Socialist Realist narrative, in which the spontaneously rebellious individual or group encounter a mentor figure usually associated with the Bolshevik Party that stands for the true path of revolt (Clark 2000, 167–176).

Curiously, even in 1938, this gesture seemed unwarranted to some, such as Soviet critic F. Levin, who commented:

> It is hard to understand why the authors of the film had to turn him (Good Idea), actually a very lonely man, into a revolutionary, who is wanted by the police and whom we see later in shackles among a group of prisoners ... Was it worth politicizing the character of "Good Idea" so obviously, when Alexei Maksimovich himself did not deem necessary to develop him in full? (Levin 1938, 164)

The other main mentor figure is Alesha's grandmother, whose importance is grasped likewise by Good Idea. The intercutting of the image of the barge-haulers with Good Idea's exclamation as to how wonderful this land is and his advice to Alesha to study, to write down his grandmother's words all accentuate the message: Alesha's role in life (pointed out by someone he barely knows) is to become a writer, and to transcribe the people's genius in order to liberate them. As if to emphasize that the message has struck home, Alesha is pictured, standing and looking above the horizon, metaphorically into the future.

Donskoi carefully interweaves this theme of mentorship with that of rebellion, in such a way as to suggest that it is not just a knee-jerk defiance of authority as such, but rather a rebellion that prefigures the Revolution somehow. Thus, while, in yet another departure from Gor'kii's narrative, Alesha stands up to his grandfather explicitly to a greater extent, he does so to stop the grandfather from beating his

Figure 5.3 Production still from Mark Donskoi's *Childhood of Maxim Gorky* (1938). Donskoi (back row, fifth from the left) with cast.

Figure 5.4 Production still from Mark Donskoi's *Childhood of Maxim Gorky* (1938). Mark Donskoi, unidentified female assistant and assistant director, Rafael Perelshtein, with child actors.

grandmother, then asserts that he will not put up with and persevere (striking another visionary horizon eye-balling pose, shot from low angle) before cutting up his grandfather's images of saints and threatening to chop off his beard. This is pointedly punctuated by a visit from the police looking for Good Idea, who it turns out is against the Tsar. Thus the rebellion becomes more explicitly ideological, as refusal to submit to the patriarchal structure at home is connected through juxtaposition with political revolt.

The addition of mentors and their coding as of the people (Grandmother) or anti-Tsarist (Good Idea) introduces a political subtext into the plot. But this political plotline is made much more effective because it mobilizes the image of the child as pure potential, as an image suggesting a time and world yet to come, and the child actor embodies this sense of process and possibility best of all. In contrast to the monumental and unquestionable authority of Stalin era, the child actor possesses a certain resistance to fixity, which has been described as "a temporality of 'not yet,' a temporality of differing and deferral" (McMahon 2012, 476).

The later episodes of the trilogy were not as successful because they lacked precisely this quality. One 15 year old (Sergei Semenov) criticized the third part of the *Gorky Trilogy*, *My Universities* in the following terms:

> I didn't like how Gor'kii was depicted in the film, like a prophet of some kind, who walks around preaching to everyone. He was still young at that time, no more than

18 or 19. Gor'kii describing his youth, always stressed that he tried to learn from life. He was very hungry for knowledge, whereas the film shows that already at 19 Gor'kii knew everything, wasn't interested in anything but just walked around pronouncing various important speeches. There is no youth in the young Gor'kii that the author of this film shows us. (Maksimova 1940, 104)

Lury argues that the characters and the performance become less interesting as the story progresses in a number of such narratives of education (2010, 11). However, in *Childhood*, this sense of not-yet, and of process, was still palpable. Such a concrete sense of a future evoked by the child actor is precisely the temporality of utopia: Donskoi is able to suggest the fluid, optimistic temporality of hope and a coming utopia despite adapting the monumental, officially sanctioned works of Gor'kii. Once again there is a clever balancing act going on here and children have a very special role to play in making it work.

Reception

Donskoi's resolution of the conundrum of the child actor succeeded in marrying the child actor's popular appeal with an acceptable political subtext, a mix ensuring the film's warm reception: released to universally positive reviews on June 18, 1938, the film was still running three months later in Moscow. When we add to that the fact that the film was also made very quickly and inexpensively, shot for the most part on location, we see why it became the studio's calling card, and a model for subsequent children's films, both in the Soviet Union and beyond.

For all its domestic orthodoxy, Donskoi's film was widely acclaimed abroad. The high esteem in which it has been held is evident from the results of critics' favorite film polls held by influential British film journal, *Sight and Sound*, where, after the first part was shown in 1943 (Anon. 1955), it figured in the top 12 consistently in the 1950s and 1960s (Anon. 1962), with the 1955 Edinburgh film festival presenting its inaugural "Richard Winnington Film Award" to Donskoi on the basis of his *Gorky Trilogy*, which was frequently described as "the high point of Russian cinema in the 1930s" (Anon. 1961).

It was Donskoi's sensitivity to the child's take upon the world that impressed British critics such as Catherine de la Roche:

Donskoi sees children as they see themselves... The children in his film bring their world with them intact, and therefore remain slightly mysterious. They have nature's elusive quality. One feels their eyes *see* something more than they express. (De la Roche 1948, 24; emphasis in the original)

One British filmmaker on whom the film made a deep impression was Lindsay Anderson, whose inspirational tirade against the class-bound nature of British cinema cited Donskoi's *Childhood* as a prime example of the kind of "popular" subject matter "with working class characters all through" that the snobbery and escapism of British film ensured could never be made (Anderson 1957, 159). It thus became a model for the ground-breaking, more social emphasis in 1960s British cinema. In an indication of his esteem for Donskoi, Anderson's response to Satyajit Ray's *Pather Panchali* was immediately to measure it against the films of Donskoi (Anderson 1956).

Yet Russian critics insist on Donskoi's influence on Italian Neorealism. Certainly, Giuseppe De Santis praised Donskoi's *The Rainbow* [*Raduga*, 1944] in an April 1945 review. Its effect may be seen as compounding that of *Childhood* which made its Italian premiere earlier that year, and was closer than *The Rainbow* to the neorealist aesthetic in its loose plotting, privileging of location shooting, use of child actors, as well as in its combining of social, political, and religious themes. Even if the direct influence of *Childhood* on neorealism is widely asserted in Russia (Turovskaia 1992; Margolit 2012), it is hard to prove, especially since key works such as *Obsession* (Luchino Visconti, 1942) and *Rome Open City* (Roberto Rossellini, 1945) were made before Donskoi's films had been digested, there can be little doubt that Donskoi's example encouraged and emboldened the Italians to continue their new direction in the knowledge that they were not alone in world cinema.

However, apart from in Russia, the role played by Donskoi and Soiuzdetfilm has been substantially forgotten, so that neorealist use of non-professional child actors for their "apparent spontaneity and lack of self-consciousness" is seen as innovative and unprecedented (Lury 2010, 159–160). Moreover, there was a need to stress, along with its novelty, the Italian-ness of the new movement, so that the suggestion of Russian links would have been unwelcome (Gelley 2012, 4). Furthermore, there was little cultural prestige for the participants in recalling the influence of someone who came to be considered a marginal figure in Soviet filmmaking, so that even for film historians, this was an obscure link to a forgotten dimension of Soviet filmmaking (it was not Eisenstein). Thus Bert Cardullo (2011, 35) asserts that Soviet cinema since 1931 had used only professionals.

Soiuzdetfilm: Setting Generic Models

The impact of *Childhood* following its release in Europe can only be explained by the fact that there were so few films like it, and that this specifically children's sensibility was something that cinema had difficulty in capturing. Yet, much that was distinctive and influential in Donskoi's approach was the product less of an individual genius, or an alternative voice "favoring the child's point of view" (Prokhorov 2008, 139) than of the wider orientation of the studio in this period.

But while *Childhood of Maxim Gorky* was appreciated the widest, and remained memorable for longer, it was far from alone among Soiuzdetfilm productions to be appreciated abroad. Fairy tale films such as *The Magic Fish* [*Po shchuchemu veleniiu*, dir. Aleksandr Rou, 1938] *The Land of Toys* [*Zolotoi kliuchik*, dir. Aleksandr Ptushko, 1939], *The Little Hump-backed Horse* [*Konek-gorbunok*, dir. Rou, 1941] were widely appreciated in the United Kingdom, at special Saturday cinema clubs run by J. Arthur Rank. The ideological subtexts of these reworkings of fairy tales were apparently lost on audience and informed commentator alike in Britain. Thus, Mary Field, founder of the Children Educational Film (CEF) organization described their purpose as:

> to provide first-class entertainment, well-made, while at the same time introducing as a background to the story, the kind of conduct that is universally admired. The Russian films deal with patience, hard work, collaboration, kindness and good temper. (1952, 98–99)

In actual fact, as with *Childhood*, they doctored the fairytales to emphasize themes of class war and economic exploitation in ways consonant with distinctly Soviet political goals. The politics were not lost on Soviet audiences, of whatever age: one 5-year-old boy watching *The Magic Fish* understood the happy ending where the peasant hero and the princess get together as meaning that the peasant would now take the unhappy princess to his "collective farm," where she would become happy (Maksimova 1940, 98).

Across various genres and movies, the appeal to children and the ideological demands were combined in different ways. The inherently layered quality of fairy tales, long popular with children, made productive material for emphasizing class struggle and work. Adventure stories were often made acceptable by weaving a political strand into the plot, such as in the 1937 *Treasure Island*, which transposed the West of England setting to Ireland, and made the search for treasure a mission to fund the Irish struggle against British Imperialism. Conversely, Vladimir Legoshin's film, *Lonely White Sail* [*Beleet parus odinokii*, 1937] took the opposite approach, and retold the explicitly political story of the 1905 Battleship "Potemkin" mutiny through the eyes of children, in an adventure plot. Prokhorov adds further examples – films of scientists' travels, children's versions of production films – and asserts that these films mapped out generic models, which functioned as the staple of Soviet children's cinema until the state's demise (2008, 133, 138). The most influential models, however, were the adventure and fairy tale films: the Soviet model for live-action fairy-tale films, with implicitly political and social subtexts legitimizing Socialism, was adopted across the Warsaw pact countries, most notably in East Germany (Creeser 1993).

The fact that the Soviets had been first to focus filmmaking specifically upon children gave them an enormous advantage, and engendered widespread sympathy. While they had to compete with the products of Disney, the "family" orientation of Disney meant that the violence and adult sexuality of their films disturbed many, and, for those worried by this, enhanced the attraction of the Soviet films' de-eroticized world.

The extraordinary opportunity presented by this lead the Soviets gained on film industries elsewhere was one granted them by the state-funded, educational model of filmmaking that they had pioneered since 1919. It seems that the very same factors that stole them a march on the rest of the world prevented them from exploiting it, as there was no economic incentive to produce films for export, only an ideological imperative: as post-war reconstruction restricted finances for film and the political focus turned ever inwards, or to Eastern Europe, the impulse to export further afield faded. To fill the vacuum, the British set up their own organization, the second in the world, after Soiuzdetfilm, to produce films specifically for children (Field 1952, 99). They were followed by Denmark and Iran, both of whom still maintain strong children's film industries intended to cultivate national cultures in opposition to Hollywood and the English language (Bazalgette and Staples, 1995).

Earlier, when the war sent the Soviet film industry into disarray, Soiuzdetfilm was among the studios evacuated East, in their case to Dushanbe (then Stalinabad), Tajikistan and, as Donskoi and other top directors were moved to other studios, Soiuzdetfilm descended into fractious chaos in the challenging new circumstances. While the studio eventually found its feet and made important and successful films, immediately after the war, in the Zhdanov retrenchment, a Soiuzdetfilm production, *A Great Life, Part 2* [*Bol'shaia zhizn'*, dir. Leonid Lukov, 1945] was condemned for its young adult protagonists' vulgar and rowdy behavior: it had failed to negotiate the tension between the wild spirit of youth and the more severe political imperatives of the new era (Bol'shakov et al. 1999). In 1948 the studio's name was changed to "Moscow's M. Gorky Film Studio for the Production of Fiction Films," and it no longer had a remit specifically to make children's cinema, although some productions already under way, such as *The Young Guard* [*Molodaia gvardiia*, 1948], where the influence of the party was shown to be ever present even during the occupation, were still oriented towards young people or children. Instead, its new remit was specifically the dubbing of foreign films into Russian, especially the so-called "trophy films" and of Soviet films into foreign languages, particular for the Warsaw pact countries (RGALI 2468/1/215: 1).[2]

The reasons why the specific emphasis on children's films was taken away are not clear, but finances were probably a factor, given that such films were not profitable. We further might surmise that certain features of children's films did not sit well with the Stalinist retrenchment: they aimed to entertain their audiences rather than insist on the political message, and often did so by at first portraying unruly behavior to be overcome. But this was a period where conflict and the portrayal of negative phenomena were greatly circumscribed; no one was trusted to draw the correct conclusions (Begak and Gromov 1949, 30–32). Moreover, the spontaneity and sense of children as a work in progress, an intimation of a not-yet, which meant the portrayal of behavior that needed to improved, seemed to valorize the future more than the present in a way that was inconvenient and anti-pathetical to the self-congratulatory chorus of late Stalinism, where glorification of Soviet achievements was paramount. Certainly the portrayal of unacceptable behavior was part of the criticism of *A Great Life, Part 2*.

Yet the studio was not closed, and in the post-Stalin years Mark Donskoi returned to the studio after a spell as artistic director of Kiev studios, sometimes referred to as exile. He announced his homecoming in 1962 with *Hello Children!* [*Zdravstvuite deti!*], a film that was not only addressed to children: they were its subject matter and the main actors. Moreover, these were children from all over the world, and it was again "Gorky Studio," which had enjoyed prior existences as the most international and most entertainment oriented studio, that was reaching out abroad: seminal African filmmaker Ousmane Sembene came to Moscow in 1962 and learnt his trade from Mark Donskoi, observing him at work on the film's set (Budiak 1983, 118).

The following year, in 1963, the studio was re-named "M. Gorky Central Studio for Children's and Young People's Films," regaining its original purpose. The privileging of the child's perspective is seen as characteristic of "Thaw" era cinema, and restoring the studio's focus on children echoed the wider culture (Prokhorov 2007, 115). While the institutional and aesthetic forms for Soviet children's films had been established in the late 1930s, they were revived and reinvigorated in the early 1960s, and persisted until the state's demise in 1991. Their enduring power is testament to Soiuzdetfilm's early and deep engagement with the profound challenges of children's cinema.

Notes

1 With older teenagers, lengthy rehearsals were used, for example by Kuleshov in *Sibiriaki*, but the results were widely criticized (Dolinskii 1959, 519).
2 Kinostudiia im. M. Gor'kogo: Statutes and changes to statutes of Moscow's M. Gor'kii Film Studio for the Production of Fiction Films (1948).

References

Anderson, Lindsay. 1956. Quoted on (2003) *The Apu Trilogy: Satyajit Ray (Pather Panchali, Aparajito & Apur Sansa)*. London: Seagull.
Anderson, Lindsay. 1957. "Get Out and Push!" *Declaration*, edited by Tom Maschler, London: Macgibbon & Key.
Anon. 1955. "Winnington Award Won by Russian," *Daily Film Renter*, August 30.
Anon. 1961. *Times*, November 2.
Anon. 1962. "Sight and Sound Poll 1962: Critics," http://alumnus.caltech.edu/~ejohnson/sight/1962.html (accessed September 18, 2009).

Balina, Marina. 2008. "Creativity Through Restraint: The Beginnings of Soviet Children's Literature." In *Russian Children's Literature and Culture*, edited by Marina Balina and Larissa Rudova, 3–17. New York and London: Routledge.

Bazalgette, Cary and Terry Staples. 1995. "Unshrinking the Kinds: Children's Cinema and the Family Film." In *In Front of the Children: Screen Entertainment and Young Audiences*, edited by Cary Bazalgette and David Buckingham, 92–126. London: British Film Institute.

Begak, Boris and Iurii Gromov. 1949. *Bol'shoe iskusstvo dlia malen'kikh. Puti detskogo khudozhestvenogo fil'ma* [Great Art for the Little Ones: The Paths of the Children's Fiction Film]. Moscow: Goskinoizdat.

Beumers, Birgit, Nikolai Izvolov, Natalia Miloserdova, and Natalia Riabchikova, eds, 2009. "Margarita Barskaia and the Emergence of Soviet Children's Cinema." (Document Cluster). *Studies in Russian and Soviet Cinema* 3.2: 229–262.

Bol'shakov, Ivan et al. 1999. "Vsesoiuznoe soveshchanie rabotnikov khudozhestvennoi kinematografii po obsuzhdeniiu resheniia TsK VKP(b) o kinofil'me 'Bol'shaia zhizn'' (2 seriia), 14–15 oktiabria 1946 goda" [All-Union Conference of Fiction Film Workers for a Discussion of the Decision of the CC of the CP(b) on the film 'Great Life', October 14–15, 1946]. In *Zhivye golosa kino. Govoriat vydaiushchiesia mastera otechestvennogo kinoiskusstva (30-e–40-e gody). Iz neopublikovannogo* [Living Voices of Cinema: The Masters of Domestic Film Art (1930s and 1940s) Speak. From Unpublished Materials], edited by Lev Parfenov, 308–384. Moscow: Belyi bereg.

Brunshtein, Aleksandr. 1938. "Kakim dolzhen byt' detskii stsenarii" [What the Children's Script Should Be Like]. *Kino* July 23.

Budiak, Liudmila. 1983. *Kino stran Azii i Afriki* [Cinema of Asia and Africa]. Moscow: Znanie.

Cardullo, Bert. ed. 2011. *André Bazin and Italian Neorealism*. New York and London: Continuum.

Clark, Katerina. 2000 [1981]. *The Soviet Novel: History as Ritual*. Bloomington and Indianapolis: Indiana University Press.

Creeser, Rosemary. 1993. "Cocteau for Kids: Rediscovering *The Singing Ringing Tree*." In. *Cinema and the Realms of Enchantment: Lectures, Seminars and Essays by Marina Warner and Others*, edited by Duncan Petrie, 111–124. London; British Film Institute.

Davies, Amy M. 2006. *Good Girls and Wicked Witches: Women in Disney's Feature Animation*. Eastleigh: John Libbey.

De la Roche, Catherine. 1948. "Mark Donskoi." *Sequence*, 5.

De Santis, Giuseppe. 1945. "Arcobaleno." *Settimana* April 12. Reprinted in Albert Cervoni, *Marc Donskoï. Le Cinéma d'aujourd'hui*, 42 [Mark Donskoi: Cinema of Today]. Paris: Seghers, 1966, 175–177.

Deriabin, Aleksandr, ed. 2001. "'My poniali, chto nastupil period akterskogo kino…' Obsuzhdenie 'Pesni o schast'e' v leningradskom ARRKe, 1934 g" ["We Understood That the Time of Actors' Cinema Had Come." Discussion of the Film "Song about Happiness" at Leningrad's ARRK, 1934]. *Kinovedcheskie zapiski* [Film-Scholars' Notes] 51: 171–188.

Dobrenko, Evgeny. 2008. "(Auto/Bio/Hagio)graphy: Peshkov – Gorky – Donskoi." In E. Dobrenko, *Stalinist Cinema and the Production of History: Museum of the Revolution*, 142–166, Edinburgh: Edinburgh University Press.

Dolinskii, Iosif. 1959. "Razvitie detskogo kino" [The Development of Children's Cinema]. In *Ocherki istorii sovetskogo kino* [Studies in the History of Soviet Cinema] 3 vols, edited by Iu. Kalashnikov, N. Lebedev, L. Pogozheva, and R. Iurenev; vol. 2 (1935–1945), 494–544. Moscow: Iskusstvo.

Donskoi, Mark. 1938. "Kinotrilogiia o velikom pisatele" [The Film-Trilogy about a Great Writer]. *Kino*, June 17.

Donskoi, Mark. 1939. "Stenogramma obsuzhdeniia fil'ma 'Detstvo Gor'kogo' v tvorcheskom klube Vsesoiuznogo Instituta Kinoiskusstva 17 oktiabria 1938" [Minutes of the Discussion of the Film 'Gorky's Childhood' in the Creative Club of the All-Union Film Institute, October 17, 1938]. In *Kinorezhissura. Khrestomatiia* [Film Directing. A Reader], compiled and annotated by Iu. Genika, edited and with a foreword by E. Dzigan, 235–236. Moscow: Goskinoizdat.

Erikson, Erik. 1963. "The Legend of Maxim Gorky's Youth." In E. Erikson, *Childhood and Society*. 358–402. New York: W.W. Norton.

Ermolov, Petr. 1938. "Po ukazaniiam Gor'kogo" [On Gorky's Order]. *Kino*, July 5.

Field, Mary. 1952. *Good Company: The Story of the Children's Entertainment Film Movement in Great Britain, 1943–1950*. London: Longmans Green.

Gelley, Ora. 2012. *Stardom and the Aesthetics of Neorealism: Ingrid Bergman in Rosselini's Italy*. New York and London: Routledge.

Gellner, Ernest. 1983. *Nations and Nationalism*. Oxford: Blackwell.

LeBeau, Vicky. 2008. *Childhood and Cinema*. London: Reaktion.

Levin, F. 1938. "'Detstvo' Gor'kogo" [Gor'kii's 'Childhood']. *Literaturnyi kritik* 7: 161–171.

Lukashevich, Tat'iana. 1940. "Piatiletniaia aktrisa" [A 5-Year-Old Actress]. In *Deti i kino*, [Children and Cinema], edited by L. Voitolovskaia and A. Amasovich, 38–51. Moscow: Goskinoizdat.

Lury, Karen. 2010. *The Child in Film: Tears, Fears and Fairytales*. London: I.B. Tauris.

Kelly, Catriona. 2007. *Children's World: Growing Up in Russia, 1890–1991*. New Haven and London: Yale University Press.

Maksimova, A. 1940. "Posle prosmotra fil'ma" [Following the Screening]. In *Deti i kino*, [Children and Cinema], edited by L. Voitolovskaia and A. Amasovich, 97–106. Moscow: Goskinoizdat.

Margolit, Evgenii. 2002. "Prizrak svobody: strana detei. Detskaia tema v sovetskom kino" [The Ghost of Freedom: The Land of Children. The Children's Theme in Soviet Cinema]. *Iskusstvo kino* [Art of Cinema] 8: 76–86.

Margolit, Evgenii. 2012. *Zhivye i mertvye. Zametki k istorii sovetskogo kino 1920–1960kh godov* [The Living and the Dead. Notes on the History of Soviet Cinema of the 1920s–1960s]. St Petersburg: Masterskaia "Seans."

McMahon, Laura. 2012. "Suspended Moments: Child Performance in *Ratcatcher*." *Screen* 53.4: 471–476.

Miloserdova, Natal'ia. 2006. "Detskoe kino" [Children's Cinema]. In *Stranitsy istorii otechestvennogo kino* [Pages from the History of Domestic Cinema], edited by L. Budiak and D. Karavaev, 6–133. Moscow: Materik.

Miloserdova, Natal'ia. 2009. "Margarita Barskaia and the Organization of Film Studios," *Studies in Russian and Soviet Cinema* 3.2: 240–245.

Nemoliaev, Vladimir. 1986. "Sorok let spustia" [Forty Years Later]. In *Zhizn' v kino. Veterany o sebe i svoikh tovarishchakh* [Life in Film: Veterans about Themselves and Their Comrades], vol. 3, 205–227. Moscow: Iskussvo.

Prokhorov, Alexander. 2007. "The Adolescent and the Child in the Cinema of the Thaw." *Studies in Russian and Soviet Cinema* 1.2: 115–129.

Prokhorov, Alexander. 2008. "Arresting Development: A Brief History of Soviet Cinema for Children and Adolescents." In *Russian Children's Literature and Culture*, edited by Marina Balina and Larissa Rudova, 129–152. New York and London: Routledge.

Razumnyi, A. 1940. "Liubimye roli" [Favorite Roles]. In *Deti i kino* [Children and Cinema], edited by L. Voitolovskaia and A. Amasovich, 23–37. Moscow: Goskinoizdat.

Riabchikova, Natalia. 2009. "Children's Cinema in the 1920s." *Studies in Russian and Soviet Cinema* 3.2: 231–35.

Sorlin, Pierre. 2008. "Children as War Victims in Post-War European Cinema." In *War and Remembrance in the Twentieth Century*, edited by Jay Winter and Emmanuel Sivan, 104–124. Cambridge: Cambridge University Press.

Turovskaia, Maia. 1992. "Mark Donskoi v dvoinom svete" [Mark Donskoi in Dual Light]. *Kinovedcheskie zapiski* [Film-Scholars' Notes] 13: 45–51.

Part II
For the State or For the Audience? Auteurism, Genre, and Global Markets

Part II

6

The Stalinist Musical: Socialist Realism and Revolutionary Romanticism

Richard Taylor

For most of the Soviet period the conventional view, both within and outside the Soviet Union, was what we might call the "heroic" view, namely that Soviet cinema consisted largely, if not entirely, of heroic aesthetic masterpieces along the lines of Sergei Eisenstein's *The Battleship Potemkin* [*Bronenosets Potemkin*, 1925], Dziga Vertov's *A Sixth Part of the World* [*Shestaia chast' mira*, 1926], or Vsevolod Pudovkin's *Storm over Asia* [*Potomok Chingis-khana*, 1928] and their successors in subsequent decades. The undoubted aesthetic achievements of these films were almost never, if indeed ever, matched by their success with audiences. Until 1927–28, for example, the box-office receipts from imported films (largely from the United States or Germany) exceeded those from Soviet films, heroic or otherwise (Taylor 1979, 74).

In the 1930s information about audiences is somewhat murkier, but the clear demand from the March 1928 Party Conference on Cinema for a "cinema that is intelligible to the millions" (Taylor and Christie 1988, 212), suggests a change of emphasis, at least on the part of the authorities, who felt increasingly that the rapidly industrializing and collectivizing country could no longer afford the luxury of what Lenin had allegedly described as the "most important of all the arts" (Taylor and Christie 1988, 57) when it failed to mobilize the mass audience. In that decade of brutal and quasi-revolutionary change there were perhaps two heroic films that did attract mass audience reaction: *Chapaev* (1934) and *Alexander Nevsky* [*Aleksandr Nevskii*, 1938], although, at least in the first instance, there is some evidence that audiences were officially 'encouraged' to attend.

More spontaneously enthusiastic responses were elicited by films of another genre, which did not, and could not, have existed in the 1920s: the musical. The emergence of this new genre was, obviously, mainly a result of technological developments that led to the introduction, rather slow in the Soviet context, of

A Companion to Russian Cinema, First Edition. Edited by Birgit Beumers.
© 2016 John Wiley & Sons, Inc. Published 2016 by John Wiley & Sons, Inc.

sound cinema, without which the pre-recorded sound track essential to a musical would not have been possible. One other factor was the dawning realization that montage cinema, which had dominated aesthetic debates in the 1920s, was less accessible to the mass audience of workers and peasants than the Hollywood "boy meets girl" model from which the star system evolved. There had, of course, been film stars in Russian cinema before the Revolution (such as Ivan Mozzhukhin (Mosjoukine), Vera Kholodnaia or Vera Karalli); there had even been Soviet film stars in the 1920s – Igor' Il'inskii, Vladimir Fogel', Nikolai Batalov, Sergei Komarov, Nato Vachnadze, Liudmila Semenova, and Anna Sten, for example (Youngblood 1992, 90–104) – but the glittering star names of the decade were not home-grown, rather they were part of the *inostranshchina* (Youngblood 1992, 50–67): Charlie Chaplin, Mary Pickford and Douglas Fairbanks, Lillian Gish, Rudolph Valentino, Buster Keaton from the United States; and Emil Jannings and Harry Piel, from Germany. Beside these, Soviet film stars had merely twinkled.

As sound cinema was gradually introduced in the USSR, first in the larger cities and eventually in the countryside, increasing emphasis was placed on the central role of the actor, and of acting, rather than montage, although montage was being downgraded rather than sidelined altogether. This paralleled an ideological move towards a greater stress on the individual as part of the collective and this in turn echoed the development of the Stalinist cult of personality, where a single man-god was identified with the country and its people as a whole. His "star quality" was imitated, although never quite duplicated, by leading film actors, some of whom successfully basked in Stalin's reflection, and indeed his shadow, while the secondary characters very definitely lived in the relative shadows – of both the Great Leader and the new stars of Soviet sound cinema.

For at least the latter part of the 1930s Soviet cinema had to operate within the framework of the guidelines promulgated under the doctrine of Socialist Realism adopted by the First Congress of Soviet Writers in August 1934 and subsequently applied to all areas of public artistic activity, including, of course, "the most important of all the arts": cinema. Socialist Realism was based upon two principles: critical realism, which derived partly from the kind of realism associated with Maksim Gor'kii, who not surprisingly endorsed it at its inception, and "revolutionary romanticism," an aspect that has all too often been overlooked, underestimated, or completely ignored by historians and critics.

Andrei Zhdanov, who was effectively Stalin's cultural commissar, claimed that Socialist Realism meant depicting reality "not [...] in a dead, scholastic way, not simply as 'objective reality,' but [...] as reality in its revolutionary development" (Zhdanov 1934, 4). Anatolii Lunacharskii, who had been in charge of Soviet cultural policy in the 1920s, tellingly remarked that "the Socialist Realist [...] does not accept reality as it really is. He accepts it as it will be [...] A Communist who cannot dream is a bad Communist. The Communist dream is not a flight from the earthly but a flight into the future" (Lunacharskii 1933).

The application of the doctrine of Socialist Realism, and in particular this aspect, dubbed "revolutionary romanticism," fell to the man who had taken responsibility for Soviet cinema in October 1930, Boris Shumiatskii, an Old Bolshevik who had first realized the power of cinema when, as Soviet Plenipotentiary in Teheran, he had shown newsreel film of unveiled women to rapt male audiences (Taylor 1991, 194). Shumiatskii was a forceful proponent of the view that cinema, above all the Soviet cinema that he was responsible for, should be "intelligible to the millions," echoing the resolution of the March 1928 Party Conference on Cinema (Taylor and Christie 1988, 212). He looked to the most successful cinema in history, Hollywood, and sought to create a Soviet equivalent. The plans to build a studio complex in the Crimea (where the climate allegedly resembled that of Los Angeles), known generally as Soviet Hollywood [*Sovetskii Gollivud*] were a central, but by no means the only, part of the overall project. Shumiatskii's intention was to make and show films in large numbers that audiences might actually *want* to see, rather than being transported or "persuaded" to see. This involved a varied diet, which included "historical-revolutionary" films, such as the "Maxim Trilogy" (directed by Kozintsev and Trauberg, 1935–1939), science-fiction films like *Cosmic Flight* [*Kosmicheskii reis*, dir. Vasilii Zhuravlev, 1936], with Sergei Komarov, one of the stars of Soviet silent film, in the leading role, but above all that genre that was popular throughout the industrialized world, the musical [*miuzikl'*], or "musical comedy" [*muzykal'naia komediia*], as it was known in the Soviet period to distinguish it from its bourgeois equivalent.

In his aptly entitled book, *Kinematografiia millionov* [*A Cinema for the Millions*], Shumiatskii argued that "neither the Revolution nor the defense of the socialist fatherland is a tragedy for the proletariat. We have always gone, and in future we shall still go, into battle singing and laughing" (Shumiatskii 1935, 239–240). As James von Geldern has shown (1992, 62), "in the mid-1930s, Soviet society struck a balance that would carry it through the turmoil of the purges, the Great War and reconstruction. The coercive policies of the Cultural Revolution were replaced or supplemented by the use of inducements." The credibility of revolutionary romanticism, the "flight into the future," was enhanced by the audience's apparent complicity in the exercise. Political speeches, newspaper articles, poster campaigns, official statistics and, above all, "the most important of all the arts" depicted life not as it actually was but as they hoped it was becoming. The media furnished what Sheila Fitzpatrick has memorably described as "a preview of the coming attractions of socialism" (Fitzpatrick 1994, 262). If the Great Terror of the 1930s was to become the stick with which to modernize the Soviet Union, entertainment cinema was to provide the carrot.

The musical comedy was in many ways the perfect vehicle for the depiction and promulgation of the Socialist Realist utopia. This is especially true if we bear in mind Richard Dyer's argument that the central thrust of entertainment is utopianism and that, while "Entertainment offers the image of 'something better' to escape into, or something we want deeply that our day-to-day lives don't provide," it "does not, however, present models of utopian worlds ... Rather the utopianism is contained in the feelings it embodies" (Dyer 2002, 20). In fact, the Stalinist musical did both: it presented models of utopian worlds (in the case of the kolkhoz musical the "Potemkin village") while also embodying the utopian feelings that stimulated audience identification. The task of Soviet cinema in the 1930s and 1940s was to convince audiences that, whatever their current hardships, life *could* become as it was depicted on the screen: life not as it is, but as it will be. In this reel utopia, if not in everyday reality as then experienced by cinema audiences, the Stalinist slogan "Life has become happier, comrades, life has become more joyous" (1935) was made real.

The reel realization of utopia was achieved by both representational and non-representational signs. Dyer's observation that we pay more attention to the former at the expense of the latter is still largely true (Dyer 2002). The non-representational signification in the Stalinist musical lies primarily in three areas: the use of fairy-tale narrative conventions; the music itself; and the topographical conventions of the image of utopia, all of which weakened audience resistance to the reception of the utopian model depicted on screen. As Dyer (2013, 2) remarks, "[s]ong is often apprehended as something magical [...] Yet we may all the same apprehend song as a direct line to feeling;" compare this with his earlier observation (2002, 20) that "the utopianism is contained in the feelings it embodies." So song provides audiences with an *entrée* into experiencing for themselves the utopian world depicted in the Stalinist musical.

I shall focus on the work of the two leading directors of "musical comedies," Grigorii Aleksandrov and Ivan Pyr'ev, while arguing that their films need to be seen in their historical and cultural context, so that the works of other film-makers will occasionally also be discussed where relevant. Aleksandrov founded the Soviet musical comedy genre with *The Happy Guys* [*Veselye rebiata*, aka *Jolly Fellows*, 1934] and went on to make *The Circus* [*Tsirk*, 1936], *Volga-Volga* (1938) and *The Radiant Path* [*Svetlyi put'*, 1940] in the same mold. Pyr'ev's first musical comedy was *The Rich Bride* [*Bogataia nevesta*, 1938], which established the model for the "kolkhoz musical." This was followed by *Tractor Drivers* [*Traktoristy*, 1939], *The Swineherdess and the Shepherd* [*Svinarka i pastukh*, 1940] and *The Kuban Cossacks* [*Kubanskie kazaki*, 1949], the apotheosis of what Khrushchev, in his Secret Speech to the delegates to the Twentieth Party Congress in February 1956 was to call the "varnishing of reality" that characterized Soviet cinema's depiction of the Potemkin village of the Stalin period.

Maia Turovskaia has perceptively analyzed the way in which Pyr'ev in particular used the conventions of the Russian fairy tale to project his "folklorised" vision (see Miller 1990) of the Potemkin village, and Masha Enzensberger has extended this analysis to Aleksandrov's *Radiant Path* (Enzensberger 1993). The use of these conventions enabled the Soviet musicals to act, in Turovskaia's own words, "not so much as the reflection of their time's objective reality, but rather as the reflection of the reality of its image of itself" (Turovskaia 1988, 132).

The plots of these films almost invariably center on what the Russians call a "love intrigue" [*liubovnaia intriga*]: but it is not "tainted" by sexual or erotic impulses, rather it is a "pure" romantic love based almost entirely on its object's labor proficiency. In the conventions of the Soviet musical – as indeed of its Hollywood equivalent – it is clear from the beginning when "boy meets girl." But the resolution of this "inevitable" liaison is usually retarded by a misunderstanding and/or by competition between two male "suitors," one of whom is in terms of his own labor productivity "worthy" of the heroine, the other is not. The plot develops around the heroine's journey towards an understanding of which is which. Sometimes, as in *The Circus*, this is obvious from the beginning and the plot therefore revolves around the heroine's discovery of the true path – the Soviet path – towards that understanding. The exceptions to this rule are the last two films by each director listed above. In *The Radiant Path* – drawing on the Cinderella story and based on a newly staged play of the same name so that the working title of Aleksandrov's film was in fact *Zolushka/Cinderella*, but this was changed at Stalin's suggestion (Salys 2009, 289–291) – the heroine has to prove to *herself* that *she* is worthy of *her* suitor by successfully emancipating herself through a Party-sponsored training program. In *The Kuban Cossacks* the hero has no rival in love: his battle is with his own Cossack male chauvinist pride and the ultimate victor is the patient heroine.

In almost all these films, and in all the kolkhoz musicals, the central character, who eventually resolves the difficulties, is in fact a woman. There are no

Figure 6.1 The romantic triangle of Ivan Pyr'ev's *Kuban Cossacks*, 1949.

fundamentally weak or evil women in these films. The only evil characters are foreign men, such as the Hitler look-alike von Kneischitz in *The Circus* (Mamatova 1995, 65), or those forces threatening the frontiers of the USSR off-screen in *Tractor Drivers*, where the three male leads ("crewmates in the vehicle of war") sing of returning from fighting the "samurai" in the Far East. The weak Soviet characters are either marginalized (the bourgeois women in *The Happy Guys*, or Kuzma and his associates in *Swineherdess*) or won over to the work ethic (Aleksei the book-keeper – a truly bourgeois because "unproductive" profession – in *The Rich Bride* and Nazar the idler in *Tractor Drivers*). In utopia, weakness is therefore redeemable: evil is not, but it is externalized.

The principal characters are de-personalized and universalized as in a fairy tale. They are symbolic figures, and the frequent use of choral singing helps this process of generalization: in both *The Rich Bride* and *Kuban Cossacks*, for instance, the "battle of the sexes" is fought out in choral form. The 1930s Soviet version of the star system helped in this: all Aleksandrov's films starred his wife Liubov' Orlova (1902–1975), the prima donna of Stalinist cinema (Nikolaevich, 1992), and all Pyr'ev's starred his wife Marina Ladynina (1908–2003). Their appearance in a series of films with similar plot structures but different settings in different parts of the Soviet Union and with different casts helped audiences all over the country to identify with them more directly, on the one hand, while broadening the appeal of the films and their message on the other. It must also be said that neither Orlova nor Ladynina conformed to the traditional stereotype of "femininity." While Ladynina in the kolkhoz musicals sometimes appeared in folk costume, both she and Orlova also appeared in "masculine" clothing (Ladynina in *The Rich Bride* and *Tractor Drivers*, Orlova in *The Circus*, *Volga-Volga* and *The Radiant Path*) which de-sexualized them (*pace* Enzensberger 1993). For Soviet women caught in the "double bind" of housework and motherhood on the one hand and collective labor on the other, this must have represented truly utopian wish fulfillment. The heroine is always depicted in the workplace, be it kolkhoz, circus, or spinning mill, and only in the home when it is a workplace, like the Cinderella heroine of *Radiant Path*. Some critics have argued that the Soviet musical heroine is a mother figure, but this is not true in the conventional sense: domesticity is absent and there is no family but the collective as workplace in microcosm or the collective as country in macrocosm. This elision between the two is effected partly by the use of folklore and partly through the music, which we shall come back to.

The characters are introduced to one another "accidentally," sometimes through the fairy-tale medium of a picture, updated as a photograph (*Tractor Drivers*, *Swineherdess*). The accident of their initial encounter reinforces the sense of the inevitability of their romance, as if it has been ordained from "on high." Often this is reinforced by a direct or indirect "blessing" from that same source. In *The Circus* the heroine "understands" her situation when she joins the May Day parade in Red Square and implicitly sees Stalin, here signified as God by the icon-like image carried at the head of the procession in the immediately preceding shot. In *Tractor*

Figure 6.2 Marion's son (Jimmy Patterson), Marion Dixon (Orlova) and Ivan Martynov (Sergei Stoliarov) in Grigorii Aleksandrov's *Circus*, 1936.

Drivers the wedding-feast finale is accompanied by toasts and choral oaths of allegiance to Stalin. In *The Radiant Path* the heroine is summoned to a fairy-tale Kremlin for an "unforgettable encounter" to receive the Order of Lenin from someone whose aura reflects light upon her face: this would be the titular head of state, Mikhail Kalinin, as Salys argues (2009, 301), but the aura suggests that he is merely acting as the agent of Stalin, because in a Soviet film in 1940 the reflection could hardly derive from anybody else.[1]

These "unforgettable encounters" occur in numerous other Soviet films, posters, paintings, and newspaper articles of the period[2]: they form a central thread in the fairy tale of Stalin as "Father of the People" [*otets naroda*], the genius who has time for everyone, who keeps constant watch from his office in the Kremlin, who can solve everybody's problems; this thread exists even when Stalin's divinity is mediated through another Party or state official such as the Soviet President Kalinin or the local Party secretary (*The Radiant Path* or *Kuban Cossacks*). Stalin is the omniscient and implicitly omnipresent father of the collective Soviet family, the avuncular patriarch of the peoples (Günther 1997a). Participation in this larger family sublimates the need for the heroines, and indeed the heroes, to participate in nuclear domesticity: sex is absent, and even the kissing is "innocent" (*The Happy Guys*, *Volga-Volga*). The family is the country itself (Günther, 1997b) in which all are equal, or at least all have equal opportunity.

A central part of the fairy tale in Aleksandrov's films, though not in Pyr'ev's, is the idea that any Soviet citizen, however humble, timid or wretched at the *beginning* of the film, can make a success of life and rise to the heights that socialist society has to offer by the *end* of the same film. In *Volga-Volga* the heroine, a local letter carrier, overcomes numerous obstacles to win the All-Union Olympiad of Song. In *The Radiant Path* the heroine receives the Order of Lenin and later becomes a deputy to the Supreme Soviet, a sure sign that she has "arrived." These closures are in fact also openings allowing the audience to participate in the action (Anderson 1995). *The Radiant Path* has perhaps the most interesting, and certainly the most bizarre, ending of any Stalinist musical and I shall return to it later.

Other films use festivals or mass scenes to draw the audience into the action and, above all, the emotional uplift: the "storming" of the Bolshoi Theatre against all obstacles by the hero and heroine of *The Happy Guys*, the Olympiad of Song at the end of *Volga-Volga*, the wedding feast at the end of *Tractor Drivers*, the implied weddings that conclude both *Swineherdess* and *Kuban Cossacks*. But the device that really involves the emotions of the audience is the use of popular music in its various forms.

The music for all the Aleksandrov and the first and last of the Pyr'ev musicals was written by the most prolific composer of Soviet popular music, Isaak Dunaevskii, director of the Leningrad Music Hall from 1929 to 1934, after which he devoted his time mainly to writing operettas and film music. He was awarded

Figure 6.3 The musicians from Grigorii Aleksandrov's *Happy Guys*, 1934.

his first Stalin Prize in 1941 for the music to Aleksandrov's *The Circus* and *Volga-Volga* and his second, ten years later, for the score to Pyr'ev's *Kuban Cossacks*. One of the songs from *The Circus*, the "Song of the Motherland" [*Pesnia o rodine*], became the call sign for Moscow Radio and the unofficial state anthem of the Soviet Union until an official anthem was introduced in 1943.

The music played a crucial part in the films because it played to the emotions of the audience and helped to weaken any intellectual resistance they may have had to the message of the films (Anderson 1995; Dyer 2013, 2–3). As I have already suggested, the scores made widespread use of choral singing, which helped to universalize the characters and the situations in which they found themselves. Furthermore, the combination of catchy tunes – and Dunaevskii had an ear above all for the catchy tune – and ideologically loaded texts (mostly by Vasilii Lebedev-Kumach, 1898–1949) meant that, when the audience left the cinema humming the tune, it also carried with it the message of reel reality into the real reality outside. This helped make audiences feel that they were part of the world depicted on the screen: it elided the actual with the utopian ideal, collapsing the "fourth wall" in the auditorium (Anderson 1995).

In *The Happy Guys* the first verse of the theme song extolled the uplifting popularity of song, while the refrain made clear the use to which this uplift was to be put:

> A song helps us build and live,
> Like a friend, it calls and leads us forth.
> And those who stride through life in song
> Will never ever fall behind.

Further verses enjoined the audience: "When our country commands that we be heroes / Then anyone can become a hero" and finally warned that any enemy threatening "to take away our living joy" would be resoundingly rejected with "a battle song, staunchly defending our Motherland." The idea of song as a central and necessary part of life is echoed in "Three Tank Drivers" by Boris Laskin and the Pokrass brothers, written for *Tractor Drivers*: "There they live – and singing guarantees it – As a tight, unbroken family." That family was not the nuclear family, but the Motherland: the word *rodina* – deriving from the Russian verb *rodit'*, to give birth to – was resurrected to reinforce this metaphor (Günther 1997a; 1997b). This was the Motherland of "socialism in one country," a land whose vast size and variety [*edinoe, mnogonatsional'noe* – single, multinational] was constantly extolled (*The Circus*, *Volga-Volga*, *Tractor Drivers*, *Swineherdess*), a land that was largely hermetically sealed against apparently hostile outside forces (*The Circus*, *Tractor Drivers*).

Dunaevskii's music carefully reflected the setting of each film. For Pyr'ev's kolkhoz musicals he wrote scores that were heavily influenced by folk music, Ukrainian or Russian as appropriate. The Aleksandrov musicals, on the other hand, were urban-orientated and the scores drew upon urban musical forms such as jazz, music hall, and military marches, however unlikely that combination may appear.

All three are evident in *The Happy Guys* and *The Circus*. *Volga-Volga* centers on a musical "civil war" (the device used here for narrative retardation) between the heroine, who has written the "Song of the Volga" which eventually wins the Olympiad of Song, and the hero, who prefers to rehearse classical music with his brass band. For him the music of Wagner is a sign of culture and civilization: in 1938 this was a clear indication of "false consciousness." In these three musicals popular or "low" culture triumphs over "high" culture. In *The Happy Guys* the respectable buffet party literally becomes a "carnival of the animals" while later on the jazz band ends the film taking the Bolshoi Theatre audience by storm; in *The Circus* the action largely takes place within the confines of a "low" cultural form; in *Volga-Volga* it is the popular *amateur* song that triumphs over *professional* classical music, and a child maestro who out-conducts the adults. Similarly in *The Radiant Path*, in some ways the least *musical* of the Stalinist musicals, it is Tania/Cinderella who outstrips her "ugly sisters." These films provided confirmation that "When our country commands that we be heroes / Then anyone can become a hero" – "and singing guarantees it"!

The texts of the songs in the Stalinist musicals tell us a great deal about the topography of utopia and clarify some of the confusions and errors committed by those critics and scholars who have ignored them. The Stalinist utopia is hermetically sealed against the outside world: the only depiction of "abroad" (the lynch mob at the start of *The Circus*) is unflattering, and other references are boldly defensive (*Tractor Drivers*). Some have argued that in this utopia gender construction was quite straightforward: the man was identified with the city, with industry,

Figure 6.4 Making music in Ivan Pyr'ev's *The Tractor Drivers*, 1939.

defense, modernity, with the rational and, therefore, with progress; the woman, by contrast, was identified with the countryside and the land, with agriculture, nurture, nature, the emotional and, therefore, also with backwardness. This construction reaches its apotheosis in the Vera Mukhina statue mentioned previously, "a syntactically symmetrical pair but with the man wielding the mace of modernity: the industrial hammer" (Stites 1992, 84).[3] This characterization is, however, an oversimplification and each musical explored different parts of the Stalinist utopia. We must, therefore, construct our topography of that utopia by pulling together those parts into a coherent whole.

Utopia exists in these films at two levels which may be broadly characterized as the periphery and the center. Aleksandrov's musicals are geographically centripetal, Moscow-orientated, Pyr'ev's are not: but they are not, as Evgeny Dobrenko has argued, centrifugal films in which the movement is *away* from the capital (Dobrenko 1996a, 109). Pyr'ev's films merely explore the periphery and validate it as part of utopia.

The Aleksandrov musicals begin at the periphery: in *The Happy Guys* it is a resort in the Crimea; in *The Circus*, for once, it is overseas, the United States; in *Volga-Volga* it is the small provincial town of Melkovodsk (meaning literally "little waters"); and in *The Radiant Path* it is a small town in the Moscow region. In the course of each film the action moves to Moscow, where it ends: in the Bolshoi Theatre, in Red Square, in the Olympiad of Song, and in the All-Union Agricultural Exhibition respectively. The ties that link the periphery to the center vary: the translation of the main characters from the one to the other is the principal of these links, but boats provide the principal method of interurban transport in *The Happy Guys* (although a train is mentioned but not seen) and in *Volga-Volga*, where the postal system is also crucial, as it is in Pyr'ev's *Tractor Drivers*, where the postman sings a song encapsulating the variety and breadth of his vast country. In *The Circus* trains offer a means of arrival and (interrupted) departure from and to abroad, but not within the USSR itself. Telegrams act as catalysts in both *Volga-Volga* and *Radiant Path*, while in the latter the first link between Melkovodsk and the capital occurs when the radio announces "Moscow calling" and the last is effected through the fairy-tale mirror device discussed earlier. The use of radio is familiar from other films of the period but the virtual absence of aircraft and trains as means of *internal* communication and linkage, when they featured so strikingly elsewhere, is curious.

It is almost as if the periphery is in some ways "living in the past," which would have been present reality for most audiences of the time. The presence of the bourgeois ladies early in *The Happy Guys* strengthens this interpretation. In *The Radiant Path* the heroine Tania is employed as a domestic servant, as is Aniuta in *The Happy Guys* – a most un-Soviet occupation even if still widespread in the 1930s: both liberate themselves from this drudgery as the plot develops. Similarly Melkovodsk in *Volga-Volga* is initially depicted in a very unflattering light: the ferry breaks down, the telephones do not work, the telegram from Moscow "slows down" when it arrives in the provinces and the population of the town seems to

Figure 6.5 "Cinderella" Tania Morozova (Orlova) in Grigorii Aleksandrov's *Radiant Path*, 1940.

spend its time either petitioning the local bureaucrat Byvalov (meaning "nothing new," hilariously played by the leading comic actor Igor' Il'inskii, another star from the 1920s "living in the past"), or practicing their music (Turovskaia 1998). Yet this is itself depicted as a caricature: whereas Byvalov, who regards his recent posting to Melkovodsk as a mere staging post on his long career track to journey's end in Moscow, claims that "[t]here can be no talent in such a dump," Strelka ["little arrow"] the letter carrier insists there is "no lack of talented people" and goes on to prove her point by singing Tchaikovsky and reciting Mikhail Lermontov. It is, however, the retarded telegram from Moscow announcing the "socialist competition" of the Olympiad of Song that breaks the log-jam of stagnation and in a deliberate irony it is through Strelka's efforts that Byvalov, despite his own efforts to obstruct her, eventually arrives in Moscow with the entire local musical talent.

In Pyr'ev's films the kolkhoz is largely a self-sufficient microcosm, a closed world of "social claustrophobia," to use Dobrenko's term (Dobrenko 1996a; 1996b). In *Tractor Drivers* the hero does, it is true, enter from outside, but he comes from the fighting in the Far East, which is therefore no longer peripheral but strategically significant (see, for example, films like Dovzhenko's *Aerograd*, 1935). Furthermore, while in transit to Moscow, this time by train, he has chosen to travel to the Ukrainian kolkhoz *rather than to the capital*. In *The Kuban Cossacks* the outside world hardly intrudes either, although it is referred to obliquely, as is the war, fought only a short time earlier on this very terrain. The plot in all three films is characterized by what became known as "conflictlessness" [*beskonfliktnost'*]: in other words it is confined to microcosmic personal rivalries expressed in differing personal labor contributions rather than to macrocosmic forces like class conflict or war, which were all too evident in other Soviet films of the period, but officially no longer existed within the frontiers of the USSR.

The leading characters in the periphery are almost invariably women. It is they who organize and produce, they who resolve the love intrigue by recognizing, albeit somewhat belatedly, the production achievements of the hero and therefore his suitability as a partner in labor and love. The exceptions are in Aleksandrov's *The Happy Guys*, where it is the hero who effects the resolution through his talent for improvising in the most adverse circumstances; Pyr'ev's *Swineherdess*, where the heroine weakly accepts her fate at the hands of the deceitful locals (although her weakness is really the result of the deception wrought upon her and therefore not really "her fault") while the hero has to ride like a knight on horseback to rescue her at the eleventh hour. One reason for the privileging of women in the countryside was the need to encourage them to play a greater part in collective, as opposed to domestic, labor in the light of male migration to the cities and the consequent labor shortage in rural areas. Another resulted from the context in which these musicals were made: by male directors to showcase the acting, singing and dancing talents of their wives. Yet another was to emphasize that women were equal and thus to underline the superiority of the Soviet way of life in the international context. For these reasons women were never villains: the villainous characters were always men, but they could be cured of their villainy by the intervention of women, unless they were foreigners, like von Kneischitz in *The Circus*.

Moscow constituted the fairyland at the heart of the Stalinist utopia. It was where unusual, even magic, things happened: the triumph of the jazz band in *The Happy Guys*; the journey to understanding of the American heroine in *The Circus*; the victory of the underdog in the singing competition in *Volga-Volga*; the translation of Cinderella into the Snow Maiden (or Fairy Princess) in *The Radiant Path*; and the labor of love/love of labor that blossoms in *Swineherdess*.

It was to Moscow that characters went to improve their lives and to be rewarded with recognition for their achievements. Within Moscow the Kremlin and the newly opened Exhibition of Agricultural Achievements played significant and separate roles. The Kremlin was the seat of government and can be seen as a synonym for Party-state power and thus for Stalin. Sometimes this is explicit (*The Circus* or *The Radiant Path*), although the general context of contemporary propaganda images rendered such explicitness hardly necessary. The role of the Exhibition is more complex: it features prominently in both Pyr'ev's *Swineherdess* and Aleksandrov's *Radiant Path*. Dobrenko argues that in the first of these 'the Exhibition represents not Moscow but the "Country"' (Dobrenko 1996a, 112). I think that this is an oversimplification. In both films the Exhibition offers a dual representation: to the periphery it represents Moscow, while in Moscow it represents the country in all its diversity, including ethnic. In *Swineherdess* the hero and heroine sing "The Song of Moscow," which opens:

> Everything's fine in spacious Moscow,
> The Kremlin stars shine against the blue sky,
> And, just as rivers meet in the sea,
> So people meet here in Moscow.

The refrain includes the lines: "I shall never forget a friend / Whom I've met in Moscow." Moscow is therefore *special*, even *magic*. We must remember that most Soviet citizens had never visited Moscow: internal passport controls and sheer cost made the journey impossible except as a special, officially sponsored reward. Most people "knew" Moscow only from screen images, and for propaganda reasons only parts of the "great stone city" were shown: the Kremlin and/or Red Square, because of their historical and political associations; the Exhibition, because it was very much a "preview of the coming attractions of socialism;" the "New Moscow:" the construction projects, such as the Hotel Moskva (*The Circus*), the river station (*Volga-Volga*) or the showcase metro (*The Circus*). As Oksana Bulgakova has pointed out, "[e]ven more frequently real Moscow was replaced by a painted backdrop, a set" (Bulgakova 1996, 57): this applies to *The Happy Guys* and *The Circus* and some of the representations of the Agricultural Exhibition (*Radiant Path*) and it increased the air of unreality for those familiar with the city from personal experience. But most of the audience had nothing real to compare to this reel image, and that enhanced its magic power.

The Stalinist musical thus presented a cinematic microcosm of the Soviet Union in macrocosm, not as it actually was, but as it was one day to be. Let us recall Lunacharskii's words: "The Socialist Realist [...] does not accept reality as it really is. He accepts it as it will be." The renewed interest in the West in the Soviet musical film, provoked by Anderson's question, "Why Stalinist Musicals?" (1995), built upon a pre-existing interest in the USSR itself by such pioneering scholars as Maia Turovskaia (Turovskaia 1988) and Sergei Nikolaevich (1992), which has flowered in post-Soviet times. Much of the work published in the post-Soviet West has been written, or inspired, by the research done by scholars from a Soviet background, such as Dobrenko, Enzensberger or, more recently, Rimgaila Salys, fruitfully diminishing, if not yet necessarily actually bridging, the academic gap between East and West. But much work still needs to be done. There is little published work on the history of film imports into the Soviet Union after the 1920s, and especially in the 1930s; little comparison between the musical films of the Soviet Union and those of the West, including, or perhaps especially, Nazi Germany;[4] little work on audiences and film reception. There are still so many blank spots in the history of Soviet cinema, above all "entertainment" film, that cry out to be explored.

To conclude, I should like to return to the final sequence of *The Radiant Path* that I mentioned earlier. The film is in many ways a Soviet version of the Hollywood "rags to riches" bio-pic. At the start of *Radiant Path* Tania/Cinderella is housemaid to her "ugly sisters" and in no position to be noticed by her Prince Charming. A *woman* (N.B.) Party worker, Pronina, takes her in hand, sends her to literacy classes and then to a spinning mill, where she eventually becomes a record-breaking Stakhanovite worker. Following the richly deserved award of the Order of Lenin, Tania finds herself in a Kremlin ante-room decorated only with chandeliers and a mirror. Scarcely able to believe that what has happened and is happening to her is real, she checks in the mirror. She sees her own reflection and therefore, according to fairy-tale convention, "knows" that it is real. Then she turns her face back to the camera and sings a duet with mirror images of her earlier selves reflected in the mirror behind her. She remarks that she knows what has happened in the past but now she wants to know what the future holds. The image in the mirror then turns into the figure of Tania as the Snow Maiden of Russian fairy tale, complete with tiara.[5] This Tania opens the frame of the mirror and invites Tania the prize-winning weaver into the world of mirror (reel?) reality. The image within the mirror frame becomes the Kremlin and, against this backdrop, the two Tanias are seated in a car that takes off on a whirlwind aerial tour of the Soviet Union, flying over the Kremlin, then Moscow, then high mountains, and then back to Moscow to the showpiece All-Union Agricultural Exhibition (later the All-Union Exhibition of Economic Achievements, VDNKh), landing at the foot of Mukhina's famous statue of "The Worker and the Collective Farm Woman."

This sequence is accompanied by song, or perhaps we should say that the song is accompanied by the images: Dyer remarks that "Songs in films take up literal but also temporal and sometimes metaphorical space. They impose musical time and length on spoken and acted narration" (2013, 30). Tania's inquisitiveness about her future is answered by a song beginning *"V staroi skazke govoritsia"* [An old fairy tale tells us], which has previously been sung at the beginning of the film (Enzensberger 1993, 100). Now the words have changed (Enzensberger 1993, 105):

> The fairy tale come true is being created by us,
> And the inventions of old fairy tales
> Grow pale before the truth of our time.

As the car begins its flight over Soviet space, the lyrics blend reel fairy-tale fantasy with real reality:

> Everything that was a song,
> What we dreamed of and what we loved,
> Has become even more marvelous,
> As today's living Soviet reality.
>
> And there is no land more beautiful,
> No land that's happier,
> May you flourish, my beloved, vast
> Invincible land!

In mid-flight the mirror frame disappears, as does Tania the Snow Maiden, so that Tania the weaver takes the wheel of the car as it makes its magic descent back into the Soviet capital. Symbolically she is now confident enough to realize her full potential.

The final scene of the film takes place in the Exhibition itself and the one-time Cinderella figure, now crowned with success, re-encounters her Prince Charming against a magic background of fountains and other symbols of abundance, including several statues of Stalin. Implicitly, now that that Cinderella and Prince Charming have both established their equality in successful careers, they *may* have time for domesticity, but this is by no means made explicit and it would in any case be a political and social arrangement, rather than a romantic episode – macrocosmic rather than microcosmic As Pronina, Tania's mentor, remarks, "What miracles humans can perform."

Against this imagery we hear the "March of the Enthusiasts" (see von Geldern and Stites 1995, 327–328):

> Hello, country of heroes,
> Country of dreamers, country of scholars.
> Across the steppe, across the forests,
> From the tropics to the Pole
> Spread out, my boundless,
> Indestructible native land.

Some of these sentiments echo those in the Dunaevskii's earlier songs, but the final verse and refrain are specific to this film:

> Our world was created for glory.
> We have done centuries' of work in years,
> We take our happiness by right,
> We love with passion and sing like children.
> Our scarlet stars
> Sparkle, as never before,
> Over all countries, over oceans,
> Like a dream that has come true.
>
> We know no obstacles on land or sea,
> We don't fear ice or cloud,
> We bear our spirit's flame,
> Our country's flag through worlds and ages!

In 1920, Iulii Khait and Pavel German had written a popular song, later adopted by the Soviet Air Force as its anthem and known as the "Aviators' March" [*Aviamarsh*] (see von Geldern and Stites 1995, 257–258). It expressed similar sentiments to the film song 20 years later and began:

> We were born to make the fairy tale come true,
> To conquer space and distance.
> Reason gave us steel wings as hands,
> And a roaring engine as a heart.

Twenty years later, at least in Soviet cinema, the fairy tale had come true, the dream had become reality. Stalin, the "Kremlin censor," is once supposed to have remarked, "cinema is an illusion, but it dictates its own laws to life itself" (Volkogonov 1988, 11). Therein lay the power and the magic of revolutionary romanticism. After all, as we have already noted, Lunacharskii had observed in 1933, "[a] Communist who cannot dream is a bad Communist. The Communist dream is not a flight from the earthly but a flight into the future."

Notes

1. These analyses are based almost entirely on the versions currently available on DVD, either from Polart and Facets in the United States or on off-air recordings from Russian television. These are often the versions restored and de-Stalinized in the 1960s and 1970s. A tantalizing sequence from the original version of *Tractor Drivers* was included in Dana Ranga's film *East Side Story* (1997), and I have myself seen yet another, more overtly military ending from the archives of Gosfilmofond.
2. Perhaps the most famous example is the painting of this title from 1936–1937 by Vasilii Efanov; it now hangs in the State Tret'iakov Gallery in Moscow.
3. This was the world's first welded sculpture, made of stainless steel, 24 m high and weighing 75 tons, originally welded for the 1937 Paris International Exhibition to make the Soviet pavilion taller than the Nazi one opposite it. The statue had such enormous propaganda value that it became the symbol of the Mosfilm studios.
4. *The Circus*, for example, was, with the character of von Kneischitz toned down, dubbed into German by Tobis in Berlin in 1936; copies exist in film archives in Berlin and Lausanne.
5. The Snow Maiden [*Snegurochka*] had been resurrected as the granddaughter of Grandfather Frost (the Soviet equivalent of Father Christmas) after the New Year holiday was reintroduced in 1936 as a Soviet substitute for the Christmas festival, which in the Orthodox calendar always came *after* the New Year.

References

Anderson, Trudy. 1995. "Why Stalinist Musicals?" *Discourse* 17.3: 38–48.

Bulgakova, Oksana. 1996. "Prostranstvennye figury sovetskogo kino 30-kh godov" [Spatial Figures in Soviet Cinema of the 1930s]. *Kinovedcheskie zapiski* [Film-Scholars' Notes] 29: 49–62.

Dobrenko, Evgenii. 1996a. "'Iazyk prostranstva, szhatogo do tochki', ili estetika sotsial'noi klaustrofobii" ["The Language of Space, Compressed to a Point", or the Aesthetics of Social Claustrophobia]. *Iskusstvo kino* [Art of Cinema] 9: 108–117.

Dobrenko, Evgenii. 1996b. "'Iazyk prostranstva, szhatogo do tochki', ili estetika sotsial'noi klaustrofobii" ["The Language of Space, Compressed to a Point", or the Aesthetics of Social Claustrophobia]. *Iskusstvo kino* [Art of Cinema] 11: 120–129.

Dyer, Richard. 2002. "Entertainment and Utopia." In *Hollywood Musicals. The Film Reader*, edited by Steven Cohan, 19–30. London: Routledge; original publication in *Movie* 24 (1977): 2–13.

Dyer, Richard. 2013. *In the Space of a Song. The Uses of Song in Film*. London and New York: Routledge.

Enzensberger, Masha. 1993. "We Were Born to Turn a Fairy Tale into Reality." In *Stalinism and Soviet Cinema*, edited by Richard Taylor and Derek Spring. 97–108. London & New York: Routledge.

Fitzpatrick, Sheila. 1994. *Stalin's Peasants: Resistance and Survival in the Russian Village after Collectivization*. New York and Oxford: Oxford University Press.

Günther, Hans. 1997a. "Wise Father Stalin and His Family in Soviet Cinema." In *Socialist Realism without Shores*, edited by Thomas Lahusen and Evgeny Dobrenko. 178–190. Durham NC and London: Duke University Press.

Günther, Hans (Kh. Giunter). 1997b. "Poiushchaia rodina. Sovetskaia massovaia pesnia kak vyrazhenie arkhetipa materi" [The Singing Motherland: The Soviet Mass Song as Expression of the Maternal Archetype]. *Voprosy literatury* [Questions of Literature] 4: 46–61.

Lunacharskii, A.V. 1933. "Synopsis of a Report in the Tasks of Dramaturgy (Extract)." In *The Film Factory. Russian & Soviet Cinema in Documents, 1896–1939*, edited by Richard Taylor and Ian Christie, 237. London: Routledge & Kegan Paul and Cambridge MA: Harvard University Press, 1988.

Mamatova, L. 1995. "Model' kinomifov 30-kh godov" [The Model of Cinematic Myths of the 1930s]. In *Kino: politika i liudi (30-e gody)* [Film: Politics and People (1930s)], edited by L. Mamatova. 52–78. Moscow: Materik.

Miller, F. J. 1990. *Folklore for Stalin: Russian Folklore and Pseudofolklore of the Stalin Era*, Armonk NY: Sharpe.

Nikolaevich, S. 1992. "Poslednii seans, ili Sud'ba beloi zhenshchiny v SSSR" [The Last Screening, or The Fate of the White Woman in the USSR]. *Ogonek* 4: 23.

Salys, Rimgaila. 2009. *The Musical Comedy Films of Grigorii Aleksandrov. Laughing Matters*. Bristol: Intellect.

Shumiatskii, Boris. 1935. *Kinematografiia millionov* [Cinema for the Millions]. Moscow, Kinofotoizdat.

Stites, Richard. 1992. *Russian Popular Culture. Entertainment & Society since 1900*, Cambridge: Cambridge University Press.

Taylor, Richard. 1979. *The Politics of the Soviet Cinema, 1917–1929*. Cambridge: Cambridge University Press.

Taylor, Richard. 1991. "Ideology as Mass Entertainment: Boris Shumyatsky and Soviet Cinema in the 1930s." In *Inside the Film Factory. New Approaches to Russian & Soviet Cinema*, edited by Richard Taylor and Ian Christie. 193–216. London & New York, Routledge.

Taylor, Richard and Ian Christie, eds. 1988. *The Film Factory. Russian & Soviet Cinema in Documents, 1896–1939*, London: Routledge & Kegan Paul and Cambridge MA: Harvard University Press.

Turovskaia, Maia. 1988. "I.A. Pyr'ev i ego muzykal'nye komedii. K problemu zhanra" [I. Pyrev and his Musical Comedies: The Problem of Genre]. *Kinovedcheskie zapiski* [Film-Scholars' Notes] 1: 111–146.

Turovskaia, Maia. 1998. "Volga-Volga i ego vremia" [*Volga-Volga* and its Time]. *Iskusstvo kino* [Art of Cinema] 3: 59–64.

Volkogonov, Dmitrii. 1988. "Stalin." *Oktiabr'* (October) 11.

von Geldern, James. 1992. "The Centre and the Periphery: Cultural and Social Geography in the Mass Culture of the 1930s." In *New Directions in Soviet History*, edited by Stephen White, 62–80. Cambridge: Cambridge University Press.

von Geldern, James and Richard Stites, eds. 1995. *Mass Culture in Soviet Russia*, Bloomington IN: Indiana University Press.

Youngblood, Denise J. 1992. *Movies for the Masses. Popular Cinema and Soviet Society in the 1920s*. Cambridge: Cambridge University Press.

Zhdanov, Andrei. 1934. (Speech to the First Congress of Soviet Writers). In *Pervyi vsesoiuznyi s"ezd sovetskikh pisatelei 1934. Stenograficheskii otchet*. Moscow, Sovetskii pisatel', 1990. English edition: *Soviet Writers' Congress 1934. The Debate on Socialist Realism and Modernism*, London: Lawrence & Wishart, 1977, 21.

7

Soviet Film Comedy of the 1950s and 1960s: Innovation and Restoration

Seth Graham

"That director is a brave man to do a humorous moving picture."
(Stalin on Grigorii Aleksandrov, after viewing Aleksandrov's *Happy Guys* in 1935)[1]

The formidable Soviet film industry produced nearly 7000 motion pictures between 1918 and 1991 (Zemlianukhin and Segida 1996, 6). Approximately 13–15 percent of them were comedies.[2] The comedy genre's popularity among viewers was proportionally greater: comedies accounted for four of the ten (indeed, four of the seven) all-time highest-grossing Soviet films, three of them so-called "eccentric comedies" directed in the 1960s and 1970s by Leonid Gaidai, the fourth a musical comedy entitled *A Wedding in Malinovka* [*Svad'ba v Malinovke*, dir. Andrei Tutyshkin, 1967]. If we dig further into the numbers, comedies accounted for 29 of the 100 top-grossing Soviet films (Kudriavtsev 2006). The popularity of film comedy in the USSR is hardly surprising or even noteworthy: Soviet filmgoers, like those of every other country in the world, enjoyed a laugh. The sources and significance of popular laughter, however, change with the given society over time, and in the Soviet Union (arguably more than elsewhere), the production and reception of comic texts – especially, although not only, texts with contemporary settings – cannot be usefully analyzed without contextualizing them in the socio-political atmosphere in which they were produced and consumed. This chapter will attempt to do just that, focusing on the post-Stalin period, that is, the 1950s and 1960s. After a look at the trajectory of film comedy in the Soviet Union during the preceding periods, I will discuss how the comedy genre was (and was not) reinvented after Stalin's death, its role in the larger cultural processes of the Thaw, and the importance of comedy in the formation of the post-Stalinist popular film

A Companion to Russian Cinema, First Edition. Edited by Birgit Beumers.
© 2016 John Wiley & Sons, Inc. Published 2016 by John Wiley & Sons, Inc.

spectator. While not ignoring the two giants of the period – El'dar Riazanov and the aforementioned Gaidai – I will attempt a more representative survey than is normally encountered. This means giving attention to other filmmakers such as Elem Klimov, lesser-known but audience-pleasing directors such as Tutyshkin and Iurii Chuliukin, and even the veteran master of the Stalin-era film comedy, Grigorii Aleksandrov, whose film *Russian Souvenir* [*Russkii suvenir*, 1960] is a good example of how comedy films of the time were highly multivalent, and could simultaneously embrace the new Thaw *Zeitgeist*, hark back to the aesthetics of the 1920s, and continue to deploy the lingering formal and thematic strategies of the Stalin period itself. These various native influences were in addition to the newfound acceptability of adopting and adapting elements of foreign filmmaking, especially European.

In her monograph on the cinema of the Thaw period (defined as 1954 to 1967), Josephine Woll writes that Soviet audiences in the heady years following the death of Stalin in 1953 were vocal in their demand for new popular genre films, and that they singled out comedy and romance as particularly desirable after several years in which no Soviet comedies (and very few Soviet films at all) were produced. The film journal *Iskusstvo kino* [Art of Cinema] reported on a large audience at a film festival in the summer of 1956: "'More comedies!' they cried with one voice" during the question-and-answer session (Woll 2000, 50). Although this was a full three years into the post-Stalin period, the pace of the response to the new era had varied across media. Film comedy, and cinema in general, had been slower to respond in 1954 and 1955 to the palpable changes in the political atmosphere than other areas of cultural production such as literature, music, and art (Woll 2000, 4–5). This was in part due to the time and expense involved in making feature films, which created a natural lag between the announcement of new official cultural policies and their reflection on screen, and also the state's long-established awareness of the ideological importance and influence of the film industry; voices raised by conservatives against the nascent liberalization of cultural production frequently singled out cinema in their criticisms, acknowledging the perceived strength of that medium's effect on public consciousness among other mass media: "Nearly everyone took for granted cinema's pedagogic-*cum*-propagandistic power" (Woll 2000, 7). The inertia of the filmmaking process (from script approval to release) also meant that the pace of the culture-wide evolution of attitudes was reflected more sluggishly on screen than on the pages of newspapers or literary journals.

Despite the slow start, however, and although "Thaw film" is often discussed primarily in relation to works from 1956 onward, already in the first year or two after Stalin's death in 1953, the Soviet film industry arguably began to respond to viewers' desire for more entertaining and palatable popular movies. This desire was heightened by the unsatisfying offerings of post-War Soviet cinema, with its calcified Stalinist aesthetics and abysmally low production numbers of the film famine [*malokartin'e*]. New films such as *Variety Stars* [*Veselye zvezdy*, dir. Vera

Stroeva, 1954], *We've Met Somewhere Before* [*My s vami gde-to vstrechalis'*, dir. Nikolai Dostal' and Andrei Tutyshkin, 1954], and *The Lady Tiger-Tamer* [*Ukrotitel'nitsa tigrov*, dir. Aleksandr Ivanovskii and Nadezhda Kosheverova, 1954] rather quietly heralded a return to light comedy; yet despite their seeming innocuousness, all three of these films would have been vulnerable to accusations of Hollywood-style "idea-lessness" or "ideology-lessness" [*bezideinost'*] just a year or two earlier (Kovalov 2004).

This is not to say that 1956 was not as much a watershed for Soviet screen comedy as it was for Soviet politics. Nikita Khrushchev's de-Stalinization campaign began in earnest after the so-called Secret Speech to the Twentieth Party Congress in February of that year, giving the implicit go-ahead to cultural producers to echo the policy shift in their fictional works, and in general to be much bolder in both content and form than artists had dared to be since the early-1930s. Late-1956 saw the release of Riazanov's musical comedy *Carnival Night* [*Karnaval'naia noch'*], the best-known and most successful comic film of the early Thaw. Even in this epoch-marking movie, however, the freshness and light satire of Stalin-era attitudes was accompanied by the obvious influence of Stalinist film comedy. As Evgeny Dobrenko has written, Riazanov's debut feature is as much a "continuation" of Aleksandrov's musical comedy *Volga-Volga* (1938) as it is a post-Stalinist departure from the earlier work (1995, 49). The villain in both films is an inflexible bureaucrat (played by the same actor, Igor' Il'inskii) whose stubborn resistance to change and dislike of frivolity are obstacles to be overcome by the youthful, creative protagonists. The bureaucrat in *Carnival Night*, Ogurtsov (whose name, evoking "cucumber" or "pickle," indicates his negative valence, as did the name of the bureaucrat Byvalov – roughly evoking the notion of "nothing new" – in *Volga-Volga*) most clearly shows just how out of step he is with the Thaw spirit of enthusiasm, innovation, and joviality in the famous scene in which he previews a clown performance to be included in a New Year's Eve variety show in the House of Culture of which he is director. The clowns come onto stage in typical clown garb, announce their typical clown names and begin an absurd conversation about why one of them is in tears (so many that his handkerchief is soaking wet):

> "Hello, Top!"
> "Hello, Tip!"
> "Top, why are you crying?"
> "I'm getting married!"
> "Congratulations! [wrings out Top's hanky over an umbrella Top is holding] Congratulations to you and your fiancée!"
> "Ssshhh! Quiet! For goodness sake, don't tell anyone!"
> "Why not?"
> "Because she doesn't know yet."
> "What? Why not?"
> "Because I'm marrying someone else entirely!"

Figure 7.1 Clown Top (Vladimir Zel'din) and Clown Tip (Boris Petker) in Riazanov's *Carnival Night*, 1956.

Ogurtsov then didactically gives them creative notes, chipping away at all of the elements of the act that he finds illogical, irresponsible, or otherwise un-Soviet, including their clownish pseudonyms, their costumes, the fact that nobody could ever cry enough tears to saturate a handkerchief, and the central joke of the bit. The final redaction sees the pair, now wearing suits and ties, walking onto the stage and addressing the audience:

> Comrades! In our society, unfortunately, we still encounter isolated incidences of irresponsible attitudes towards marriage and family. We wish to affirm in the most direct and strongest way possible that this is completely unacceptable.

Ogurtsov is thus temporarily placated, and satirized as a moralistic pedant. The scene is also, however, an indictment of the entire official approach to the comic mode that had defined film comedy and other comic genres and media since the 1920s. The authors of the script of *Carnival Night* described their foil in terms that recall the inflexible and humor-killing suspicion of the comic on the part of Party cultural ideologues in the preceding two decades: "[Ogurtsov] is prone to analyze any burst of laughter in terms of its expediency and immediate usefulness" (Woll 2000, 52). This and other issues that fueled the debates around film comedy in the transition from Stalinist to post-Stalinist culture – the ease with which comedy slips into the "ideological quicksand of 'pure' entertainment" (Woll 2000, 50), the problematic role of satire, the influence of foreign films, the ambiguous figure of the comic protagonist, and the trepidation on the part of some Ogurtsov-like

Party officials at the prospect of genuine popular laughter – had also dominated discussions of the genre at the no-less-transitional beginning of the Stalin period three decades earlier, a period worth pausing on here before taking a closer look at Thaw comedy.

The production of comic films, like other fields of creative production in the USSR, had a history of ideology-influenced stops and starts. In 1935 the Soviet film industry's head Boris Shumiatskii declared Aleksandrov's recent film *Happy Guys* [*Veselye rebiata*, 1934] "a good start to a new genre, the Soviet film comedy" (1935, 367). In fact, in its 18-year existence to that point, Soviet cinema had produced at least 165 comedies (Youngblood 1985, 244). Shumiatskii's implicit negation of a proportionally significant (and extremely popular) trend in Soviet cultural production officially reconfirmed the definitive resolution of a debate that had surrounded the genre over the course of the 1920s: could domestically produced films so clearly influenced by a foreign form (the American comedy) really be considered "Soviet?" Underlying Shumiatskii's resounding reply in the negative to that question was not only a new, Stalinist definition of "film comedy," but a new official understanding of "Soviet" and its manifestation on the screen. The comedies of the previous decade – the cultural production of which had been contaminated, according to the logic of the new cultural politics, both by the bourgeois apoliticism of the partial retreat to market economics known as the New Economic Policy (NEP, 1921–1927) and the radical excesses of "proletarianism" in the late-1920s – were as anathema to the concept of a Soviet national cinema as the "bourgeois" salon melodramas of the late tsarist period had been to the ideals of revolutionary cinema in the early 1920s.

At first glance, it appears that comedy should have been highly suited to the task of replacing what Soviet cultural politics quickly denounced as the obsolete, stultified cinema of the pre-Revolutionary period. Film comedy's signature formal features were a clear departure from the hallmark devices of the salon melodramas that had dominated Russian screens from 1912 to 1917, and those features would provide a similar corrective to the calcified, "conflictless" films of the late-Stalinist period decades later. In contrast to long takes and stationary bodies, comedy relies on speed, both within and between frames. Moreover, comedy's emphasis on physicality – visual interaction of bodies and objects – precluded the abstract, un-cinematic psychologism so roundly denounced in film discourse of the 1920s. Again, this process would repeat itself in the 1950s, when audiences would embrace comedy and other highly visual film genres as a more desirable alternative to the logocentrism, static cameras, and complete dominance of content over form that was endemic to late-Stalinist films. Both periods also saw a welcome evolution of the film protagonist. In the case of the Thaw, the new film hero/heroine was (re-)humanized in appearance, behavior, and speech: "very gradually the preternaturally sharp outlines of character and characterization typical of Stalinist cinema blurred and thickened into something closer to human beings, just as the irreproachably clear diction of actors slurred into something resembling normal speech" (Woll 2000, 12–13).

Not everyone during the Cultural Revolution of the late-1920s and early-1930s agreed that the use of a non-native cinematic model posed an ideological problem for the genre; comedy's compositional and stylistic debts to foreign models (films featuring Mack Sennett's Keystone Cops, André Deed, Max Linder, Charlie Chaplin, Buster Keaton, Harold Lloyd, and the like) could be, and were, "counterbalanced" with unmistakably Soviet thematics. Soviet Commissar of Enlightenment Anatolii Lunacharskii stated this outright, acknowledging the effectiveness of foreign cinema in "capturing" audiences and the need to harness that power for Soviet purposes: "all the best means of artistic captivation used in masterpieces of world cinema would work very well with our [Soviet] content" (1965, 14–15). Lunacharskii's views represented the moderate position in the socio-political debates surrounding cinema in the 1920s. Opposed to it were the ideas of the so-called proletarianists, who were intolerant of "entertainment films" and viewed genre cinema in general as bourgeois and out of step with the revolutionary spirit, as an impediment to cinema's fulfillment of the "social charge" [*sotsial'nyi zakaz*] of enlightening the masses (Youngblood 1991, 36–37). The tension created for artists by the dual task of entertainment and enlightenment would, of course, be keenly felt throughout the Soviet period, including during the Thaw, when powerful voices began to speak out against the Stalinist practice of creating art "to order," but creating art with no apparent relevance to Soviet reality, as defined by the Party, was still anathema, especially when it came to the complex and costly production of motion pictures (Woll 2000, 50).

Comedy film was not "perennial sore spot" in cultural politics (Youngblood 1992, 74) solely because of its foreign provenance. There is a semiotic ambivalence in early Soviet film comedies – as there arguably is in most film comedies, and perhaps even most films, worldwide – that became increasingly incompatible with state cultural ideology, and made them vulnerable to attack. Critics were typically displeased either (sometimes both) by filmmakers' extensive use of politically neutral or overtly Western subject matter, narrative patterns and cinematic techniques, and by a perceived lack of semantic transparency, all criticisms that would also be made two decades later in the late-Stalinist period, most notoriously by Andrei Zhdanov in his 1946 resolutions denouncing specific cultural producers (including such filmmakers as Sergei Eisenstein and Leonid Lukov) for departing from, or ignoring, Soviet artistic and social values in their works, and even in the subsequent Thaw period, which had its share of shelved films and castigated filmmakers.

The tendency towards double meanings has long been identified as an essential, even definitive, characteristic of the comic. Arthur Koestler detected a kind of paradox in the human reaction to humor, pointing out that a genuine moment of comic perception involves a rare interaction of the physical (laughter) and the intellectual, or cerebral (cognition of a funny image or utterance). Humor, he writes, "is the only domain of creative activity where a stimulus on a high level of complexity produces a massive and sharply defined response on the level of physiological reflexes" (1964, 31). This observation would seem on first thought to correspond well to materialist theories of artistic perception. It becomes (indeed, became) problematic, however, on the level of actual humor as a mode of cultural production, and the question of how to harness the energy of the comic stimulus-response process to the goal of revolutionary social progress. Koestler, in fact, sees in laughter only one possible "utilitarian function" – to "provide temporary relief from utilitarian pressures" (1964, 31), that is, to *distract* one from societal concerns.

Koestler goes on to describe the moment of comic perception, the immediate cause of the laughter response, as "the perceiving of a situation or idea […] in two self-consistent but habitually incompatible frames of reference," a phenomenon he dubs "bisociation" (1964, 35). In a narrative text, bisociation is achieved by a purposeful, mischievous redirecting of the expected cause-and-effect chain. Thus, according to this theory, the very nature of a humorous text would impede the representation of a logical chain of phenomena. And the "explosion" at the end of the bisociative chain – the punch line, the comic climax – can interfere with the teleological goals of those who want to make a text a delivery system for a didactic message. The potential conflict between comedy and "cinema of enlightenment" is clear.

Like the Stalinist and early-Thaw focus on recalcitrant bureaucrats, early Soviet film comedies tended to favor ideologically safe targets. The most purely satirical Soviet silent comedies were early anti-religious satires, and show the lingering spirit of the period of Civil War and War Communism: *The Miracle Worker* [*Chudotvorets*, dir. Aleksandr Panteleev, 1922] – famous for being Lenin's favorite film (Youngblood 1991, 39) – and *Brigade Commander Ivanov* [*Kombrig Ivanov*, dir. Aleksandr Razumnyi, 1922].[3] The expectation was that the ridicule in satirical films would be directed at stereotypical representatives of the undeniably risible elements of society. This made the portrayal of generalizable "types" essential. Iakov Protazanov's comedy *Don Diego and Pelageia* [*Don Diego i Pelageia* 1928], for example, was criticized for portraying "the great evil of bureaucratism" in an overly "individualised" way (Youngblood 1999, 166). Failure to represent vice (or virtue, for that matter) in clear, exemplary fashion not only impeded comprehension by the masses (or, in the parlance of the times, "the millions"), it was unacceptable also because it represented a waste of scarce film resources on a text with questionable revolutionary utility. While Thaw satirical and other comedies would sometimes deal with similar "problems" – excessive bureaucratism in particular – one of its main departures from the film comedies of the late-1920s – early-1950s was its frequent and stubborn refusal to make its heroes into types, into walking metaphors, and its tendency instead to give the heroes a degree of individuality and even agency that they had not enjoyed since the silent age. They were also allowed to come down off the pedestal, to resemble the flawed people that audience members encountered in their daily lives, rather than archetypes who did not exist off the screen or page. Thaw cinema was populated by "fallible, puzzled, ambivalent heroes and heroines" (Woll 2000, xiii).

Among these newly humanized comic protagonists were Shurik, the befuddled student protagonist of Gaidai's *Operation "Y" and Other Adventures of Shurik* [*Operatsiia "Y" i drugie prikliucheniia Shurika*, 1965] and *The Captive of the Caucasus* [*Kavkazskaia plennitsa*, 1966] the young dentist Chesnokov from Klimov's *Adventures of a Dentist* [*Prikliucheniia zubnogo vracha*, 1965] and even the title character of Ivan Lukinskii's comedy *Soldier Ivan Brovkin* [*Soldat Ivan Brovkin*, 1955]. Brovkin was an early-Thaw attempt to thread a needle that had presented problems for filmmakers for decades: "how to create a protagonist who was amusing yet identifiably heroic" (Woll 2000, 14). Such attempts continued in the Thaw period, and even led to the resurgence of a subgenre known as the "heroic comedy," which flourished in the 1960s. Examples of this type of comedy were Riazanov's *Hussar's Ballad* [*Gusarskaia ballada*, 1962] and Genrich Gaibai's *The Green Van* [*Zelenyi furgon*, 1959], and the joint Soviet-Czechoslovakian adaptation of Jaroslav Hašek's comic novel *The Good Soldier Švejk*, *The Long Road* [*Bol'shaia doroga*, dir. Iurii Ozerov, 1962]. The heroic comedy combined an "ironic intonation" with a plot depicting war and revolution, often in a farcical manner, which, according to Kovalov, had the effect of nudging audiences towards a "pacifist" view (2004). Another "solution" to the problem of depicting positive characters in a genre so prone to cynicism and carnivalesque mischief was to focus on youthful protagonists. This was the strategy of Georgii Daneliia, whose lyrical comedy *Walking the Streets of Moscow* [*Ia shagaiu po Moskve*, 1962] showed the clear influence of the Youth Prose movement represented by such authors as Vasilii Aksenov and Iurii Gladilin, whose stories in the journal *Iunost'* [Youth] defined the early Thaw.

Returning for a moment to the late-1920s, the representational multivalence that drew fire from ideological purists was partly a result of the stylistic eclecticism of an intensely experimental – and relatively ideologically de-centered – cultural moment, but was also related to the artistic process of elaborating theories of the comic and its possible cinematic manifestations. This process, combined with the sheer variety of extrinsic influences on representational art in the 1920s (and again after the death of Stalin), resulted in a multiplicity of comic loci, even within individual film texts. In its representational strategies and constitutive devices, film comedy had much in common with the cinematic theory and practice of the technical innovators of the age: Lev Kuleshov, Sergei Eisenstein, Vsevolod Pudovkin, Aleksandr Dovzhenko, and Dziga Vertov, and their admirers in the 1950s and 1960s who found inspiration in their works. It was ultimately the deeply-rooted avant-garde and formalistic aspects of 1920s Soviet film comedy – in addition to or even more than its resemblance to bourgeois cinema – that resulted in its growing disfavor, its eventual dismissal by the state in the person of cultural officials like Shumiatskii, and its replacement by "simpler" films like Aleksandrov's string of musical comedies (see chapter 6).

When proletarianist criticism of cinema began its fever pitch in 1927, three types of films were especially attacked: experimental films; social satires (with their implicit premise that the society is flawed); and representations of contemporary life.

Comedy was heavily invested in all three of these categories. However, it was not merely the choices made by comedic directors that led to the genre's problems; the very nature of the comic ensured that film comedy would prove more controversial than other filmic modes of representation such as documentary, adventure film, and even melodrama. The fact that comedy had supplanted melodrama as the cinematic genre of choice for depicting contemporary Soviet society begs the question of film comedy's relationship to modernity. That question, and specifically the problem of the relationship between man and machine, has been central to discussions of American film comedy in the West. The general question of modernity is certainly germane to its Soviet counterpart; silent comedies in the Soviet Union engaged with the issue implicitly and explicitly, and on more than one level (e.g., images of the city vs. the country in Boris Barnet's *The Girl with the Hatbox* [*Devushka s korobkoi*, 1927] and *The House on Trubnaya* [*Dom na Trubnoi*, 1928]; and the centrality of the cinema apparatus in Iurii Zheliabuzhskii's *The Cigarette Girl from Mosselprom* [*Papriosnitsa iz Mossel'proma*, 1924] and Sergei Komarov's *Mary Pickford's Kiss* [*Potselui Meri Pikford*, 1927]). Moreover, the very nature of film comedy has much in common with constitutive characteristics of "the modern," in particular speed, which is a feature of the genre on the level of acting and editing.

Again, a similar contrast with the obsolete cinema of the immediately preceding period would account for the success of a particular kind of filmmaking in the Thaw. Alexander Prokhorov attributes Gaidai's vast popularity in the 1960s to the radical way in which he rejected many of the devices of Stalinist film: "Gaidai's comedies of the 1960s owed their phenomenal success to the visual style of his humor, with its stark contrasts to the verbal instantiations of official Soviet ideology within narrative-driven Soviet cinema" (2003, 456). Saša Milić reads Gaidai's sight-gag-filled comedies as even more ideologically resonant, writing that the director's *Operation "Y"* "constructs an alternative 'situation' model for Soviet viewers, which strongly engages their working models of reality in the interpretation of the narrative" (2004).

Questions of modernity and technology were present in the debate over Soviet film comedy – and in some Soviet film comedies – in large part due to the prominent role of the Russian formalists, who were interested in such issues as the "mechanical" nature of comic acting (under the direct influence of Henri Bergson's famous notion of the comic as "something mechanical encrusted on the living" (1911, 39)) and the need to exploit the specificity of the cinema apparatus to achieve a corresponding specificity of cinema art. Bergson's premise that the incongruous superimposition of machinistic movements and behavior onto human beings is a fundamental source of humor certainly found confirmation in Western comedies, most famously in Chaplin's *Modern Times*, US, 1936). As the issue of the human body, labor, and the machine evolved in Soviet socio-political and cultural discourse, their representation in art increasingly precluded the comic.[4] Although Chaplin's reputation in the Soviet Union was always good, later Soviet film history drew a clear distinction between the Western and the Soviet treatments of the working man's relationship to the machine, as it was a subcategory of the very serious category of labor: "in Soviet comedies there are no gags involving production-line conveyer belts, since the nature of labor in socialist society is different from the nature of labor in bourgeois society" (Ioskevich 1982, 8).

In general, comedy's utility as a mode in which to represent contemporary Soviet society was questionable. As a genre in which hyperbole and distortion are not only common, but expected, comedy's capacity to re-present real-life relations – physical, sexual, social, or international – is very broad. The comic refraction of reality can even take the form of pure inversion, of a world represented in "a state of liminality where the everyday is turned upside down and where cause and effect can be triumphed over and manipulated" (Horton 1991, 5). The link between comedy and the avant-garde, reestablished after 1953, was a direct one; the holy trinity of the Soviet cinematic avant-garde – Eisenstein, Pudovkin, and Dovzhenko – had all begun their film careers in the realm of comedy. Eisenstein's first directing effort was a short film that was used in a production at Meyerhold's theater, and the early association between Aleksandrov and Eisenstein, which would come to seem so distant when viewing the former's canonical Stalinist comedies of the 1930s and 1940s, would become once again relevant in 1960 with Aleksandrov's *Russian Souvenir*. Pudovkin co-directed the memorable comedy short, *Chess Fever* [*Shakhmatnaia goriachka*, dir. with Nikolai Shpikovskii, 1925].

Lev Kuleshov, the "father" of Soviet avant-garde cinema, was among those who berated the psychological film as un-cinematic and literary. He called it a genre that represents "the external inertia of the plot" (1922, 73). Indeed, Kuleshov's first feature-length film, *The Extraordinary Adventures of Mister West in the Land of the Bolsheviks* [*Neobychainye prikliucheniia mistera Vesta v strane Bol'shevikov* 1924], is a study in cinematic exteriority. The film privileges the visual, especially the movement of bodies and facial expressions, two important categories in film comedy, which drew on the non-cinematic comedic traditions of pantomime and slapstick. Kuleshov stated outright his debt to foreign cinema, noting with approval American films' "maximum degree of cinema specificity [...] maximum amount of movement [...] primitive heroism [...] organic link with contemporary life" (1922, 73). Although it draws eclectically on numerous film genres, this first full-length manifestation of Kuleshov's theories into praxis is particularly relevant to questions of film comedy as a genre, and not only because the film itself is described in its first title as "a comedy about a yankee's curiosity and his rewards," but also because it engages those other genres in an essentially parodic fashion. The irony exhibited towards such genres as the detective film, the western, and the Griffith-esque cliffhanger does not merely serve the goal of satirizing the bourgeois content of American cinema; it also represents a critical, perspectival step back from those genres and towards cinematic innovation as Kuleshov envisioned it. Thus, if comedy as a medium for supporting socio-political revolution is problematic, as a medium in which to effect an artistic revolution, it was much more suitable.

Again, Grigorii Aleksandrov would use a similar technique in his attempt at a Thaw comedy, *Russian Souvenir*, in 1960. The film is an eclectic mix of avant-garde camera techniques, stereotypical buffoonery, cartoonish archetypes, and the motif of a group of bourgeois visitors to the Soviet Union who are pleasantly surprised to find out that their prejudices about the country are completely false. In one memorable scene, a group of foreign tourists stranded in Siberia come across a prison, from the inside of which they hear voices singing mournful songs. At first they believe they've found evidence of their image of the USSR as one big prison camp populated by desperate, unhappy people. When they investigate, however, they discover that the prison is abandoned, and has become a popular camping spot for young, enthusiastic Soviets who, moreover, enjoy singing American spirituals (hence the "sad" music).

The representation of social ills and discredited types and behaviors in satirical comedies, perceived as semiotically vague in the 1920s, would soon be approached in a new way by Aleksandrov in his famous musical comedies of the pre-war 1930s. In *Volga-Volga* (1938), for example, the satirized social element (the bureaucrat Byvalov) is the single negative presence on the screen, and is represented against a background of contrastive positive examples (Prokhorov 2003; Taylor, chapter 6, this volume). The Manichean simplicity of Stalinist satires was thus a corrective to the comedic multivalence on the screen in the 1920s, a period of volcanic activity in the Soviet arts that culminated by the early 1930s in the congealed, canonized cultural ideology of Socialist Realism.

A 1948 article in *Iskusstvo kino* entitled "On Conflict in Film Comedy" stated outright that what was needed was "not a satirical spectacle [*zrelishche-satira*], but a carnival spectacle [*zrelishche-karnaval'*]," and that directors should strive to depict the life of Soviet people as an endless holiday (Eremin 1948, quoted in Kovalov 2004). One of the most "conflictless" comedies of the late-Stalin period was the collective farm comedy *Generous Summer* [*Shchedroe leto*, 1950], directed by one of the most talented silent comedy directors of the 1920s, Boris Barnet. Ivan Pyr'ev's *Kuban Cossacks* [*Kubanskie kazaki*, 1949] became the most notorious example of late-Stalinist filmmaking's aggressive "varnishing of reality" [*lakirovka deistvitel'nosti*]. Even in this film, made during the apogee of Stalinist socialist realism, however, some critics have detected hints of the talent on the part of some directors for entertainingly capturing the joyous, "celebratory" laughter that would become a key element of Thaw culture, including cinema. Indeed, Pyr'ev would soon play an essential role in ensuring that *Carnival Night* made it to the screen in 1956, and advised Riazanov (whom Pyr'ev had hand-picked to direct the film) to make it more of a "colourful film spectacle," with "buffoonery and grotesquerie" to "enhance the satiric impact" (Woll 2000, 52–53).

Although comedy was a thoroughly moribund genre for most of the period between the end of the War and the death of Stalin, some comedies managed to be made and, arguably, even showed traces of the aesthetic revolution (or resurrection) that would define the genre from 1956. One of the very last films produced during

Figure 7.2 Igor' Il'inskii as Ogurtsov in Riazanov's *Carnival Night*, 1956.

Stalin's lifetime, Fridrikh Ermler's *Broken Dreams* [*Razbitye mechty*, 1953], was a comedy, although it was promptly shelved and released only in 1962 under the title *The Dinner Party* [*Zvanyi uzhin*]. The film's satirical depiction of a bureaucrat (played by the ubiquitous comedy actor Igor' Il'inskii, who would soon play a more famous bureaucrat, Ogurtsov in *Carnival Night*), and its history on the borderline of two different socio-political eras, testifies to an under-acknowledged continuity of content between films of the Stalin period and the Thaw. Oleg Kovalov speculates that the iconography of the protagonist also contributed to the film's shelving: Il'inskii resembles Stalin's Foreign Minister Viacheslav Molotov in the film (Kovalov 2004).

The native sources of inspiration that informed the reinvention of film comedy in the Khrushchev era were accompanied by the once-again acceptable influence of foreign film, and especially the French New Wave. Although that influence is usually traced in the works of auteur Soviet filmmakers such as Andrei Tarkovskii, Saša Milić (2004) writes that the aesthetics of the New Wave influenced Soviet comedy in particular:

> In stylistic terms, Soviet comedies of the 1960s firmly belong to the international tradition that appeared in the wake of Truffaut's *Tirez sur le pianiste* (1960) and other French New Wave films, which consciously appropriated features of early silent cinema. New Wave films have never exclusively dealt with comic topics, but in large part it was their playfulness and the introduction of their new stylistic devices in popular comedies that made them successful. A light touch, foregrounded reflexivity, episodic structure and cartoonish characters became the hallmark of mainstream

popular European cinema in the 1960s. These innovations were very quickly and successfully taken up in Eastern Europe. Their appearance coincided with a gradual loosening of control over the arts that had already begun with the Thaw before the emergence of the New Wave. Under these conditions, filmmakers in Eastern Europe found such stylistic innovations useful in trying to combine the irreverent nature of satire with lightheartedness, which appealed to wider audiences. Thus, perhaps even more than in the West, popular comedy opened a possibility for filmmakers to engage in debate about important social matters.

This eclecticism of influence is a marker of post-Stalinist film comedy that, among other features, links it aesthetically to the silent age of Soviet film comedy, and thus makes it a potential site for the oft-discussed restoration of pre-Stalinist aesthetics during the Thaw. The combination of "satire" and "lightheartedness" that Milić attributes to attempts to appeal to broader audiences was also a way for filmmakers to couch satirical content in more officially acceptable genre traditions such as physical comedy and romantic comedy.

Another key foreign influence was Italian neorealism, which, in Soviet cinema and elsewhere, "brought back the poetics of the everyday" by sending "the camera out into the street [...] into the communal kitchen and the crowded streetcar, past shop queues and through apartment courtyards" (Kovalov 2004). Such films as *Behind the Department Store Window* [*Za vitrinoi univermaga*, dir. Samson Samsonov, 1955], *The Streets are Full of Surprises* [*Ulitsa polna neozhidannostei*, dir. Samsonov, 1957], and Riazanov's second feature *Girl without an Address* [*Devushka bez adresa*, 1957] combined this new attentiveness to everyday life with the Thaw's privileging of the experiences of the young generation, which, like the demand for more comedies, had been consistently requested by audiences, and even by the Komsomol (Woll 2000, 7).

Another signature innovation of the Thaw period, the "return to lyricism," was as apparent in film comedy as it was in poetry, auteur cinema, fiction, theater, and other areas of cultural production, although, again, truly innovative work was to appear a bit later on screens than it did on the page or stage. Mikhail Kalatozov, who would soon direct the early Thaw's most famous film, *The Cranes are Flying* [*Letiat zhuravli*, 1957], made perhaps the first "lyrical comedy" of the period, *Loyal Friends* [*Vernye druz'ia*, 1954]. With a script co-authored by the future dissident Aleksandr Galich, the film helped return to Soviet screens a "heartfelt, spontaneous tone" that had been absent for almost two decades (Kovalov 2004), with the exception, perhaps, of certain moments in wartime films. The plot of *Loyal Friends* follows three men who have been pals since childhood, all of whom have achieved prominent positions in their given fields, especially the architect and Academy of Sciences fellow Nestratov. The trio decide to fulfill a promise they had collectively made as children to take a river rafting trip together. Amidst a whole series of comic and dramatic adventures, they each experience a change in worldview. Nestratov's is the most telling: as he becomes more and more self-aware, and under the influence of his good-natured friends, he sheds the arrogance and sense of importance characteristic of the Soviet *nomenklatura*. He is thus a symbol both of the lyrical individuality that would come to mark Thaw cultural texts and of the culture-wide process of criticizing the calcified socio-political structures that had been partly responsible for the excesses of the Stalin period. The theme of lost but recoverable youth also resonated with the overall premium on the value of sincere idealism, expressed with a sense of optimism and "joviality" [*vesel'e*], as a means of acknowledging and overcoming past mistakes (Vail' and Genis, 1998, 142). *Loyal Friends* also contains subtle jabs at some of the hallmarks of Stalinism that would not be officially denounced until 1956: exaggerated paranoia and overzealous interrogators.

One of the most popular films of the era, Chuliukin's *Gals* [*Devchata*, 1961], is also one that is seldom analyzed by cultural historians of the Thaw. This may be because of the film's relatively simple "romcom" plot: Tosia, a young, newly trained cook, arrives at a snowy Ural mountain logging settlement. She quickly falls for the local Don Juan/Stakhanovite. When she discovers that he had made a bet with his friend that he could make her fall in love with him, she tells him off, leaving him to realize that he too is in love with her and that he must win her back. This, of course, he does. Much of the film's wild popularity is attributable to its irresistibly energetic lead actress, Nadezhda Rumiantseva, who is reminiscent of Fellini's muse, Giulietta Masina, as well as a native star, the Soviet actress Ianina Zheimo. The seemingly innocuous film does, however, show signs of the edginess that would be much more pronounced in Klimov's *Welcome, No Trespassing* [*Dobro pozhalovat', ili Postoronnim vkhod vopreshchen*, 1964], Riazanov's *Beware of the Car* [*Beregis' avtomobilia*, 1966], and other satirical comedies of the decade. When Tosia arrives, for example, the director showing her around pauses to point out a secluded corner of the settlement where, he says, young lovers go to be alone. "They call it Kamchatka," he tells her, anticipating an even bolder reference to Siberia (and thus the Gulag) in Gaidai's blockbuster, *Diamond Arm* [*Brilliantovaia ruka*, 1968], in which a criminal nearly chokes on his drink when a tourist from the far east innocently tells him to "look us up if you're ever in Kolyma."[5]

This is not to say that overt or even muted socio-political satire had suddenly become permissible. On the contrary, especially after a minor retreat from Thaw liberalism by the state (the first of several) following the 1956 Soviet military intervention in Hungary, true social satire (i.e., systemic criticism) was met with suspicion or outright censorship. The young Gaidai, whose later "eccentric comedies" would go on to become the most popular films in Soviet history, directed a satire of bureaucratism, *Fiancé from the Netherworld* [*Zhenikh s togo sveta* 1958], that was shelved by the censors for "tarnishing reality" [*ochernenie deistvitel'nosti*] (Kovalov 2004). This was despite recent other jabs at bureaucratism such as *Carnival Night* and, of course, satires of the same "social ill" in Stalinist comedies such as the aforementioned *Volga-Volga*. Vladimir Padunov (1998, personal communication) has argued that social satire was actually in very short supply on the Thaw silver screen, and that only two major films were constructed around that brand of satirical engagement (call it Juvenalian rather than Horatian satire): Klimov's *Welcome…* and Riazanov's *Beware of the Car*. The satire in Riazanov's film is directed at so many different social problems that the film encountered resistance from the censor.[6]

Klimov's *Welcome* was even more pointed, inviting the viewer in almost every scene to perceive the setting – a Young Pioneers' camp – as a microcosm of the USSR. Kovalov (2004) calls *Welcome* the "riskiest and sharpest satire of the 1960s" and describes how Klimov took a trope from a different genre and gave it teeth:

> The Pioneer camp, familiar from the "children's film" [*detskoe kino*] here becomes a model of a society rife with gaudy totalitarianism and bureaucratic tyranny over the individual. The film is also notable for its excellent ensemble cast of children and the sheer number of gags, the likes of which had not been seen since the silent era, and which meant that nearly every frame offers the potential for dangerous multiple readings.

The "positive hero" of the film is Kostia Inochkin, an independent-minded 11-year-old boy attending the summer camp. He is disobedient from the first scene, in which he literally breaks through the established boundaries of the camp by tearing a hole in a net demarcating the swimming area in order to cross the river and swim (without boundaries) with the local village boys. The discipline-obsessed camp director, Dynin, decides to make an example of Inochkin by publicly denouncing and expelling him in front of the whole camp. The two antagonists are established as adversaries by their very names: Dynin evokes the mundane and comically bucolic image of a melon [*dynia*], which the director is frequently shown metonymically eating, and also recalls the name of another inflexible film foil, the bureaucrat Ogurtsov (from *ogurets*, "cucumber" or "pickle") in *Carnival Night*. The name Inochkin hints at his iconoclasm and outsiderness (*inoi*, "other" is also the root of the word *inakomysliashchii*, "dissident"). The name is apt, as Inochkin is forced "underground" when he returns clandestinely to the camp after being expelled (he can't bear to go home to his grandmother and tell her what happened, in fear that it will kill her). This sets the stage for a flood of microcosmic allusions to Soviet life: a petty tyrant camp director, a child artist forced to compromise his morals by having to draw a propaganda poster denouncing Inochkin, a sinister informant, blatant censorship of a movie shown to the campers (a counselor holds his hands over the heroine's décolletage), and even a jab at Khrushchev's corn fetish in the final scene, when Inochkin returns triumphantly to public life in the camp after having been disguised as a giant ear of corn for a pageant. Expecting to see the daughter of a powerful official inside the costume, Dynin is defeated completely when he sees his nemesis emerge. He is unceremoniously exiled from the camp on a milk truck.

Figure 7.3 Evgenii Evstigneev as Dynin in Klimov's *Welcome...*, 1964.

The film's implicit and explicit jabs at not only totalitarian inflexibility, but at a specific policy of the current leader, Khrushchev, make it seem a few years ahead of its time; most directors would not turn its satirical attention to the current status quo until a bit later. That shift in focus would signal the beginning of the end of the Thaw, and in particular the period of fragile accord between the ideologues who set the agenda for mass culture texts and the audiences who consumed them. At times the state-sanctioned generic "wall of honor" in the USSR substantially coincided with the unofficial, organic generic hierarchy, for example: nationalistic songs, literature, visual art, and even folk humor during the Great Patriotic War (World War II); lyric poetry and certain forms of youth culture at the height of the Thaw; and documentary film and *publitsistika* [essays on political topics] during perestroika. During such moments, popular sentiment and state ideological priorities shared constituent tropes. The episodes of apparent polar harmony were typically precipitated by a weakening of ideological supervision of cultural production by the Party, which had the wisdom to modify its cultural policies periodically for politically pragmatic reasons. The liberalization of cultural policy, in all three of the above-mentioned periods, was undertaken at least in part to give cultural producers (and consumers or "reproducers") creative latitude to express a newly emergent idea in the ruling ideology, with the ultimate goal of alleviating a crisis in, fortifying, and/or preserving that ideology. In the case of the Thaw, the new values originating from the Party under Khrushchev were fundamentally aimed at reinvigorating the progressive socialist society after the anomalous, reactionary Stalinist period. The "new idea" was de-Stalinization, with a concomitant adjustment of aesthetic emphasis from the epic to the lyrical, from the "fathers" to the "sons" (i.e., to those who came of age after Stalin's death), and, in certain, limited respects, from the masses to the individual. As I have discussed, all of these priorities found reflection in film comedy, and resonated with audiences who by and large shared the priorities.

Genres, of course, can serve just as (or more) readily as means of expressing resistance to a new policy turn. The emergence of irony as a key component in popular culture and literature of the post-Thaw period reflects the popular disillusionment in the face of renewed manipulation of cultural production – as well as renewed socio-political repression, though in a mostly non-lethal form – under Brezhnev.[7] The transition from a palpable sense of optimism and enthusiasm on the part of citizens in the wake of Stalin's death to a widespread penchant for cynicism, irony, and satire by the late 1960s (Vail' and Genis 1998, 142) – as well as a palpable reining in of artistic experimentation and variety in the mass media – was also reflected in film comedy.

The popular cynicism characteristic of Stagnation was in particularly stark contrast to the preceding period of enthusiasm and consensus, with its celebration of youth and especially its premium on sincerity and good humor. The heady enthusiasm of the Thaw made adaptation to the subsequent period of reactionism all the more complex a maneuver for the Soviet cultural consumer, who had to effect an intellectual and behavioral retreat from public *vesel'e* and sincere self-expression as the state itself retreated from reformism. To put it another way, the Thaw mentality lingered (festered?), but with ever fewer discursive outlets; Lev Anninskii (1991) contrasts the "open freedom" of the Thaw to the "secret freedom" of Stagnation. The latter period saw a revised understanding of the concept of "public," a widespread formation of smaller collectives, and the emergence of more hermetic chronotopes, both within cultural texts (on the level of plot) and as the favored environments for cultural consumption itself. The shift to television from cinema as the most influential mass medium was one of the clearest signs of this evolution.

The cinematic Thaw, for the purposes of the chapter, had already symbolically ended by the late-1960s, as exemplified by the new types of protagonists to be found in such films as *White Sun of the Desert* [*Beloe solntse pustyni*, dir. Vladimir Motyl', 1969], an adventure film with comic elements (Kovalov calls it an example of the heroic comedy, 2004), *Shine, Shine, My Star* [*Gori, gori moia zvezda*, dir. Aleksandr Mitta, 1969], and Daneliia's *Don't Be Sad!* [*Ne goriui!* 1969]. These films show signs of the more cynical Stagnation period that followed the Thaw and lasted until the opening up of Soviet culture in the glasnost era, more than a decade and a half later. By the second half of the 1960s, writes Alexander Prokhorov, literary and cinematic satirists had begun to focus their critical lens not only on the mistakes of the Stalinist past, but also on the deficiencies of the current historical moment. Here, as in much of Soviet cultural history, the hero was a key locus of meaning in fictional texts: "During the late Thaw, the writers and filmmakers of the younger generation created works in which the protagonist's main function was to produce the ironic effect of de-heroicizing not only Stalinist values, but also those of the Thaw" (Prokhorov 2002, 302). As cultural producers began to brandish the artistic freedom they had been given after 1953 towards contemporary targets, rather than at the receding mistakes and isolated vestiges of the Stalin period, the negative attention that the ideologically problematic combination of the cinematic medium and the comic mode had been attracting from the state since the 1920s once again began to nudge the form in a new direction. Post-1968 film comedy protagonists had lost most of the enthusiasm, playfulness, and idealism of Thaw heroes and heroines that populated the early films of Riazanov, Gaidai, Klimov, Daneliia, and others. Most of these artists would continue to thrive in the 1970s and beyond, but the nature of their output would change with the times.

Notes

1. According to the rest of this legend cited by Margaret Bourke-White, Stalin subsequently insisted that Aleksandrov be awarded the Order of the Red Star for his "bravery" in making the film (158, quoted in Christie 1993, 156).
2. I was not able to break down Zemlianukhin and Segida's comprehensive list of Soviet feature films by genre, but a search of the Internet Movie Database (IMDb) produced 5443 Soviet-produced feature films, with 728 (just over 13 percent) of them comedies. Also, of the 4266 Soviet and post-Soviet (1991–1996) films included in the CD-ROM database *Kinomaniia 97*, 644 (15 percent) are classified as comedies
3. According to Ioskevich, one-third of Soviet comedies produced in 1924 were satirical exposes of NEPmen, sometimes combined with ridicule of the Western bourgeoisie (Ioskevich 1982, 55). Other social issues addressed in film comedies of the time were the exploitation of domestic servants, as in Iakov Protazanov's *The Tailor from Torzhok* [*Zakroishchik iz Torzhka*, 1925], Barnet's *House on Trubnaya*; unscrupulous manipulation of housing regulations in *Girl with a Hatbox*; anti-religious themes in an "agit-kite" in *The Tailor* that reads "Religion is the Opiate of the People" and Protazanov's *Holiday of St Jorgen* [*Prazdnik sviatogo Iorgena*, 1930], and simple greed (*The Tailor*, *The Girl with a Hatbox*, and especially Protazanov's *Three Thieves* [*Protsess o trekh millionakh* 1926].
4. Indeed, machinery and labor in early Soviet cinema were arguably represented not in a comedic, but *erotic* mode. Recall the repeated shots of turbines, rods, rhythmic metallic penetration, and so on, in Dziga Vertov's *Enthusiasm* [*Entuziazm* 1930]. The repeated visual emphasis on the dormant smokestack in Eisenstein's *Strike* [*Stachka*, 1924] – as well as the centrality of a deliberately-set fire in the plot – makes the factory workers' strike in that film appear metaphorically lysistratic.
5. The term "Kamchatka" also referred to the last row of seats in a classroom, where the less-well-behaved pupils tended to sit.
6. Prokhorov (2002) has thoroughly analyzed this film.
7. The Brezhnevian retrenchment was a policy shift exemplified most dramatically by the 1968 suppression of the Prague Spring, but which was nascent in cultural

politics years before, the widely publicized persecution of Iosif Brodskii in 1964 and Andrei Siniavskii and Iulii Daniel' in 1965–1966 being the best-known examples. There were spasms of reactionism even during the Khrushchev years, of course (the 1956 intervention in Hungary and the 1957 persecution of Pasternak, for example), but with Brezhnev's ascent to power the conservatism became sustained and systemic.

References

Anninskii, Lev. 1991. *Shestidesiatniki i my. Kinematograf, stavshii i ne stavshii istoriei* [The 1960's Generation and Us: Cinema that Became, and Did Not Become, History]. Moscow: Kinotsentr.

Bergson, Henri. 1911. *Laughter: An Essay on the Meaning of the Comic*. Translated by Cloudesley Brereton and Fred Rothwell. London: Macmillan and Co.

Christie, Ian. 1993. "Canons and Careers: The Director in Soviet Cinema." In *Stalinism and Soviet Cinema*, edited by Richard Taylor and Derek Spring, 142–170. London: Routledge.

Dobrenko, Evgeny. 1995. "Soviet Comedy Film, or The Carnival of Authority." *Discourse: Journal for Theoretical Studies in Media and Culture* 17.3: 49–57.

Eremin, Dmitrii. 1948. "O konflikte v kinokomedii" [About the Conflict in Film Comedy]. *Iskusstvo kino* [Art of Cinema] 5: 9–12.

Horton, Andrew, ed. 1991. *Inside Soviet Film Satire: Laughter with a Lash*. Berkeley: University of California Press.

Ioskevich, Iakov Borisovich. 1982. *Sotsiokul'turnye usloviia rozhdeniia i evoliutsii kinokomedii: Uchebnoe posobie* [Socio-Cultural Conditions of the Birth and Evolution of Film Comedy. A Reader]. Leningrad: LGITMiK.

Kinomaniia 97: Entsiklopediia rossiiskogo kinoiskusstva [Encyclopaedia of Russian Film Art]. 1997. CD-ROM. Moscow: Cominfo.

Koestler, Arthur. 1964. *The Act of Creation*. London: Arkana.

Kovalov, Oleg. 2004. "Komediia v sovetskom kino" [Comedy in Soviet Cinema]. *Entsiklopediia otechestvennogo kino* [Encyclopedia of Domestic Cinema], http://russiancinema.ru/glossary/text44/ (accessed November 13, 2013).

Kudriavtsev, Sergei. 2006. "Otechestvennye fil'my v sovetskom kinoprokate" [Domestic Films in Soviet Distribution], *LiveJournal* April 7, http://kinanet.livejournal.com/14172.html#cutid1 (accessed December 16, 2013).

Kuleshov, Lev. 1922. "Americanism." In *The Film Factory: Russian and Soviet Cinema in Documents, 1896–1939*, edited by Richard Taylor and Ian Christie, 72–73, London: Routledge and Cambridge: Harvard University Press, 1988.

Lunacharskii, Anatolii. 1965. *O kino* [About Cinema]. Moscow: Iskusstvo.

Milić, Saša. 2004. "Sight Gags and Satire in the Soviet Thaw: *Operation Y and Other Shurik's Adventures*." *Senses of Cinema* 33, http://sensesofcinema.com/2004/33/operation_y/ (accessed November 12, 2013).

Prokhorov, Alexander. 2002. *Inherited Discourse: Stalinist Tropes in Thaw Culture*. PhD Dissertation. University of Pittsburgh.

Prokhorov, Aleksandr. 2003. "Cinema of Attractions versus Narrative Cinema: Leonid Gaidai's Comedies and El'dar Riazanov's Satires of the 1960s." *Slavic Review* 62.3: 455–472.

Shumyatsky, Boris (Shumiatskii). 1935. "A Cinema for the Millions (Extracts)." In *The Film Factory: Russian and Soviet Cinema in Documents, 1896–1939*, edited by Richard Taylor and Ian Christie, 358–369. London: Routledge and Cambridge: Harvard University Press, 1988.

Vail', Petr and Aleksandr Genis. 1998. *60-e. Mir sovetskogo cheloveka* [The 1960s. The World of Soviet Man]. Moscow: Novoe literaturnoe obozrenie.

Woll, Josephine. 2000. *Real Images: Soviet Cinema and the Thaw*. London: I. B. Tauris.

Youngblood, Denise J. 1985. *Soviet Cinema in the Silent Era, 1918–1935*. Ann Arbor: UMI Research Press.

Youngblood, Denise J. 1991. "'We don't know what to laugh at': Comedy and Satire in Soviet Cinema (from *The Miracle Worker* to *St. Jorgen's Feast Day*)." In *Inside the Film Factory: New Approaches to Russian and Soviet Cinema*, edited by Richard Taylor and Ian Christie, 36–47. London: Routledge.

Youngblood, Denise J. 1992. *Movies for the Masses: Popular Cinema and Soviet Society in the 1920s*. Cambridge: Cambridge University Press.

Youngblood, Denise J. 1999. *The Magic Mirror: Moviemaking in Russia 1908–1918*. Madison: University of Wisconsin Press.

Zemlianukhin, Sergei and Miroslava Segida. 1996. *Domashniaia sinemateka: Otechestvennoe kino 1918-1996* [Home Cinematheque: Domestic Cinema 1918–1996]. Moscow: Dubl'-D.

8

Auteur Cinema during the Thaw and Stagnation

Eugénie Zvonkine

> You know, as Maiakovskii put it [...]:
> "I want to be understood by my country,
> but if I fail to be understood,
>   – what then?
> I will pass through my native land
>   to one side,
> Like a shower
>   of slanting rain."
> Here you go, it is very beautiful and very clear.
>
> (Kira Muratova, 2005)[1]

This chapter explores the rise and decline of auteur cinema in the post-war USSR. We shall see how auteur cinema has been defined in the specific context of the Soviet Union and how its evolution is subjected to Western influences. Thus we shall establish how the classical opposition between mainstream and auteur cinema can be understood in this specific context and how the Soviet industry assessed such issues as the responsibility for the film (who is in charge of the film's ideological and aesthetical result – the crew, the studio or the director) and the relationship to the spectator.

Toward the Idea of a Director as an "Auteur"

The periods that interest us in this chapter are the Thaw and Stagnation, but in order to understand the concept fully, the analysis extends into the years of perestroika. The Thaw and Stagnation were troubled and complex periods for the Soviet film industry, but at the same time they represent a moment in Soviet film history that

---

A Companion to Russian Cinema, First Edition. Edited by Birgit Beumers.
© 2016 John Wiley & Sons, Inc. Published 2016 by John Wiley & Sons, Inc.

witnessed the emergence of a number of auteur filmmakers, including Andrei Tarkovskii, Andrei Konchalovskii, Marlen Khutsiev, Kira Muratova, Aleksei Gherman, Otar Iosseliani, Elem Klimov, Larissa Shepit'ko, Sergei Paradjanov, Aleksandr Sokurov, and Artavazd Peleshian.

The most obvious Western influence at the time is the concept of "camera-pen" introduced by Alexandre Astruc in 1948, as well as the notion of the *politique des auteurs* defined by François Truffaut in an essay published in February 1955. While Astruc underlined that the new cinematic forms allow the thoughts and emotions of the director to be expressed like those of a writer – "That is why I would like to call this new age of cinema the age of camera-pen" (Astruc 1948) – Truffaut affirms that he is more interested as a critic in a film that is a failure to some, but that expresses a singular point of view, rather than in a film well made, but without personal vision: "Even if *Ali Baba* were a failure, I would still defend it by virtue of the auteur theory to which I and my fellow critics subscribe. This theory, based on Giraudoux's statement "There are no works, there are only authors," consists in denying the axiom dear to our elders, which maintains that films are like mayonnaise, you either succeed in making them or fail" (Truffaut 1955; English translation from de Baecque and Toubiana 1999, 99). These debates echoed in the Soviet Union, even though they were sometimes discussed in contradictory ways. For instance, even though André Bazin was one of the authors who laid the ground for Truffaut's *politique des auteurs* by considering the director as essayist and philosopher, the Russian introduction to the first translation of his work *What is cinema?* (1972) argues that his theory "doesn't leave room for the embodiment of the author's thought, of the author's relationship to the subject he is depicting" (Vaisfel'd 1972, 26).

The same questions and preoccupations are present in other Soviet arts at the time. The emergence of the "auteur song" [*avtorskaia pesnia*] during the 1950s points to the importance of the idea of art as a mode of individual expression in the artistic circles of the post-Stalinist era:

> The essence of the auteur song is not at all in the "author rights" to the poems, the melody, or the performance, but rather in the affirmation [...] of a position towards life, of the author's perception and of his right to bring the meaning of his statement to the listener without any intermediaries and any loss, through the use of the entire spectrum of oral communication – words, music intonations, timbre of the voice, articulations, mimics, gestures, etc. (Levin 2004, 8)

Theater went through similar reflections with such new tendencies in the art of directing as Iurii Liubimov, voicing the concept of an *avtorskii teatr* where "the director assumes the responsibilities of an author both in writing or assembling texts, poems and songs [...] and directing the production," (Beumers 1997, 6) and where "the director must ensure both the construction and the articulation of the production" (Liubimov 1985, 78).

Yet the issue arises to what extent it is pertinent to speak about auteur cinema in the Soviet Union, when the concept of the *politique des auteurs* was born in France in the 1950s in a completely different context? As Andrei Andreev reminds us, "nowadays, the main problem of understanding the concept of 'auteur cinema' in our [Russian] film studies lies in the fact that this word is not applied to a historically formed concept, linked to a specific period in the history of cinema theory, but as a method for analyzing films" (Andreev 2014, 169). The word "author" was, however, applied to filmmakers during these years, so we should start by analyzing how it was used and what was at stake around this concept in the Soviet film industry at the time.

In a comprehensive study of the notion of auteur in Soviet cinema in the years 1956 to 1967, Irina Tcherneva notes that during this epoch film directors claimed their rights to be called authors. Although film directors had fought for their rights and obtained some of them in the late 1920s and early 1930s, the beginning of the Stalinist era gave priority to the scriptwriter. Even during the first years of the Thaw, most specialists do not consider the film director as an author in terms of his rights and obligations (Gordon 1955; Antimonov and Fleishits 1957).

Tcherneva is accurate in saying that the Thaw is remarkable for its attempts to emphasize and enhance the autonomy of directors and establish them as artists.[2] In 1957, for instance, the organizing committee of the Union of Filmmakers was created, even if the Union itself was not established until 1965. Martine Godet has argued that that "the Thaw witnessed the structuring of the cultural elite that resisted power" (Godet 1996, 782). Many of the efforts of this Union – one of the few to be set up in a spontaneous way, without any incentive "from above" – would be directed towards defending the rights of artists against the industry.[3] For instance, a reform would be proposed to separate all studios in two distinct parts: a technical base with employees, called "cine-factory" [*kinofabrika*]; and a studio [*kinostudiia*], where the artistic members of the crew would work; this would never be implemented. Another suggested reform was to abolish the directors' status of an employee in order to transform the relationship between the director and the studio into a temporary partnership involving specific projects (Tcherneva 2013, 191–192).

As a result of these efforts, in some texts of the 1960s the idea of the director as the film's author, who is also responsible for the outcome (the success or the ideological, technical or aesthetic failure of the film) becomes more common: "The filmmaker whose work results in an independent product that can be reproduced [as opposed to the theater director], should be considered as the author of the *mise-en-scène*" (Vaksberg and Gringol'ts 1961, 47). But obviously many elements of the system opposed this idea: the censorship bodies, present both in the studios and in the central authority of Goskino, and also the yearly "thematic plan" that influenced the decision about which films would be made, as well as the idea that the film was a collective enterprise where the director's talent was an important, but not the crucial component.[4]

What makes it relevant to use the term auteur cinema is that even in official committees the word "author" for the film director is used on a regular basis.

In contemporary film studies, the concept of auteur cinema is often brushed aside as irrelevant, since it doesn't seem to include the industrial, economic, and political aspects of the context that allowed films to become what they are. Though this argument may be valuable to remind us of the shortcomings of the *politique des auteurs* as introduced by François Truffaut (Truffaut 1955, 45–47), it would also seem erroneous to completely ignore the way some of the directors viewed themselves at a certain period and how it influenced their relationship with the film industry.

The concept of auteur cinema is relevant to this period of Soviet cinema, since the filmmakers are clearly inspired by the French example and theories. Valerii Fomin recounts an episode involving the film critic Viktor Bozhovich in 1959: he wrote a text entitled "Discussions with Soviet directors of the new generation" and sent it to the French magazine *Cinema 60*. The manuscript was seized and an account sent to the Central Committee of the CPSU by Pavel Romanov, head of the General Directorate for the Protection of Military and State Secrets in the Press, making obvious the seriousness of the situation. In this account, he underlines as disquieting the fact that "the author of the manuscript tries to convey the impression that something like a 'new wave' has appeared in our cinema" (Romanov in Fomin 1998, 4: dated October 21, 1959).

Clearly, the concept of the New Wave strongly influenced the way in which filmmakers and critics perceived the *mise-en-scène*. Sergei Iutkevich, one of the founding fathers of the Factory of the Eccentric Actor (FEKS) in the 1920s and a renowned teacher at the Film Institute VGIK and the Higher Courses for Directors and Scriptwriters in Moscow during the 1950s and 1960s, offers the following reflections in his notes for one of his directors' courses:

> In cinema, the filmmaker is also called a "director." But the script is written by a scriptwriter, the parts are performed by the actors, the production designer creates the sets, the cameraman shoots, the sound designer records the sound, the editor sticks together the reels, the distributors put the film on the screens. But nevertheless the critics often call the director an "author." So what makes him the "author" of his film? (Iutkevich 2004)

Later in the text, it becomes clear what influenced Iutkevich's ideas: "A limited revolt in Western Europe – the so-called 'new wave' in France [...] Alexandre Astruc and his theory of the 'camera-pen' [...] and the appearance of the expression 'auteur cinema,' as a protest to the depersonalisation of the functions of the film director…" (Iutkevich 2004).

Iutkevich goes back to Leonardo da Vinci to distinguish what he calls "skill" from "art" – the latter comprising *inventio*, which he translates into Russian as "design, idea, invention, fiction" [*zamysel, zadumka, vymysel, vydumka*] (Iutkevich 2004).

Actually, these notes emphasize Iutkevich's main ideas as presented in his 1960 book *The Director's Counterpoint*, where he affirms that, even though the "profession of the director is polyphonic by nature" (Iutkevich 1960, 9), since he uses the talents of many people for the purpose of the film, being a film director is close to other creators, such as painters or music composers:

> It appears that what is more important [...] are not the technical instruments, but the creative thought of the artist, his imagination... the worlds that he carries within him... The world that he has discovered, seen, thought through and thoroughly experienced before transporting it into the film, on canvas, or on musical sheets. (Iutkevich 1960, 16)

It is exactly this conception of a filmmaker's unique and personal point of view as the key moment of art that Goskino opposed.

During the Thaw, the tension increased between the state apparatus and directors, who saw themselves more and more as "auteurs." Contrary to what Iutkevich told his students ("in the USSR and other socialist countries the film director is, in fact and by law, the rightful author of the film"; Iutkevich 2004), the idea of a film made objectively good and useful through a collective effort and the idea of an artist solely responsible for its thematic and aesthetic coherence stand in constant confrontation during this period. The number of films that were shelved or badly received by Goskino is very significant during the Thaw.[5]

As noted the historian Valerii Fomin noted, the Thaw was not a smooth period of liberalization in cinema:

> On the one hand, the cinematic muse was stimulated to a prompter and more intensive development; on the other hand, the frequent falling out of ranks [...] worried and irritated the authorities which constantly tried to set insolent filmmakers straight and put them back in line. (Fomin 1998, 10)

This complex period witnessed the appearance of several new filmmakers, who were identified as "auteurs" in the West, such as Mikhail Kalatozov or Andrei Tarkovskii. Both directors' films *The Cranes are Flying* [*Letiat zhuravli*, 1957] and *Ivan's Childhood* [*Ivanovo detstvo*, 1962] were distinguished with the most prestigious European awards: the Palme d'Or at the Cannes Film Festival and the Golden Lion in Venice. The films were perceived not only as exceptional for their visual qualities, but as very personal interpretations of World War II, moving away from the traditional Soviet representation of this historical event. *The Cranes are Flying* was discussed in *Cahiers du cinéma* in terms of "auteur cinema" and the discussion is quite amusing, since the critic Jacques Doniol-Valcroze indulged in a debate about the "real author" of the film, typical for this epoch and this magazine:

> Let's settle the first point: the paternity of the film. In the previous film by Kalatozov, a solid craftsman of Soviet cinema, nothing foretold this flamboyant explosion. Two hypothesis come into conflict when we try to elucidate this mystery: 1. the real

author of the film would be Sergei Urusevskii, the most famous Soviet cinematographer [...]; 2. Kalatozov would be the real author and I was told that this script had been stowed away in his drawer for 15 years, already 'story-boarded' like that, and that he had always wanted to make films in this style, but was not allowed to do so by the very rigid state intervention in the Soviet cinema. (Doniol-Valcroze 1958, 46–47).[6]

In his famous review of *Ivan's Childhood*, Jean-Paul Sartre considers Tarkovskii an auteur and compares him to the New Wave directors who introduced the concept of "auteur cinema":

In a sense, I think that the author, this very young man, wanted to talk about himself and his generation. [...] I would even say this is the Soviet version of *400 Blows*, but only to better underline their differences. A child is destroyed by his parents: this is a bourgeois tragicomedy. Thousands of children are innerly destroyed by the war, this is one of the Soviet tragedies. (Sartre 1986, 10)

The criteria applied to the films are the same as suggested by Iutkevich: originality, a personal cinematic universe, and aesthetic coherence of the œuvre. Later on, when Tarkovskii's *Andrei Rublev* would receive the FIPRESCI prize at the Cannes Film Festival in 1969, it would be for "the exceptional quality of the work that celebrates the greatness of art and emphasizes the responsibility of the artist" (Vinicio Beretta, May 22, 1969; in Fomin 2006, 174). The periods of the Thaw and Stagnation would see the emergence of many other important directors, but the focus of this chapter is not so much listing them all, as to try to understand their place and their way of positioning themselves in the Soviet film industry.

But how can we determine whether directors are part of the "auteur" cinema or not? The initial idea would be to include in this group all directors who were victims of censorship, who had their films shelved or projects consistently rejected. This, however, does not seem conclusive, since it is impossible to systematically explain the troubles that some films faced, even more so since some projects were censored at the studio level, others by Goskino – both at republican and Union level, while yet others were censored for still more private and obscure reasons, such as the "telefonnoe pravo,"[7] so the private and public interests at play are various and often conflicting. In the same way, some quite innovative films would elude censorship, while others would be forbidden despite their apparent inoffensiveness.[8] Moreover, many of the films that were shelved did not present aesthetic or thematic coherence and did not remain as important works in Soviet film history ("they were just bad films," as Elem Klimov would bluntly put it later, when 250 films were rehabilitated during perestroika; Godet 2010, 228). It seems that the most effective principle would be to include in the group those directors whose works present some similarities, not in style but in their relationship to the standard Soviet production of the period, while at the same time sharing similar ideas on their position towards the system.

For instance, in the famous case of censorship of Mikhail Shveitser's *The Tight Knot* [*Tugoi uzel*, 1956] the contrast between the liberty that the director expected to enjoy and the real reception by the state is striking:

> At the time, it seemed that all the roads were open for the truth ... A month passed, and the answer came. The film had been seen "at the top" (Kaganovich, Molotov, Shepilov, who at the time was responsible for ideological questions) and was savagely criticized. In Gnezdnikovskii pereulok [the site of Goskino], they immediately came to the conclusion that the film was ideologically flawed. [...] My wife was told: "you are talking about such trifles as keeping episodes in the film, while the national security organs have doubts about your husband's loyalty!.." (Miloserdova 1988, 10)[9]

The Tolerated Margin

Therefore, during the years of Stagnation many directors emerged, each with unique cinema aesthetic and thematic preoccupations, who would be tolerated but would be in constant tension with the apparatus. Maybe one of the most enlightening quotes about the place directors were allowed in the system comes from Martine Godet. She describes her interview with Igor' Sadchikov, a former *redaktor* who once worked on Muratova's film.[10] This is what he had to say about the relationship between the system and Muratova:

> In our repertoire, here is the place of Kira Muratova, at the extremity (on his office desk that he takes as a representation of the global repertoire of Soviet cinema, Sadchikov draws with his hand a small triangle at the desk corner). She had to be held at the extremity – and that is what we did – as something exotic, as an exception to the rule. And I reckon that we were right. [...] we kept her at the periphery of art. (Sadchikov in Godet 2010, 273)

Otar Iosseliani reminds us of this complex relationship between officials and "auteur" directors: "I have to admit that some officials respected us. Sometimes they covered up for us, gave us advice on how to defend our work. Thanks to these people *April* [*Aprel'*, short, 1962], *Falling Leaves* [*Listopad*, 1966], *There once was a Singing Bird* [*Zhil pevchii drozd*, 1970], and *Pastorale* [*Pastoral'*, 1975] were made" (Ioseliani in Fedina 2008). Another revealing quote comes from an appraisal of a script by Sergei Paradjanov, written by Mikhail Bleiman, an "extremely experienced member of the Goskino committee":

> We have to decide in principle and definitively whether our cinema can be so generous as to make films with such an individual style as Paradjanov's. If not – then it must be declared, we must tell Paradjanov that there will be no place for him in our cinema. (Bleiman quoted in Fomin 2006, 136)

Figure 8.1 Marlen Khutsiev's *Ilyich's Gate*, 1964.

The works of "auteurs" have in common not only problems with the apparatus, but also several similar characteristics that help understand how and why this cinema challenged the conceptions of the Soviet apparatus. All of these directors, in one way or another, seemed to challenge and reinvent Soviet aesthetic and ideological norms.

Marlen Khutsiev, even though he was a convinced communist and a typical *shestidesiatnik* [man of the 1960s], in his films such as *Ilyich's Gate* [*Zastava Il'icha*, 1964] and *July Rain* [*Iiul'skii dozhd'*, 1967] conveys a very Antonionesque melancholy, a sense of meaninglessness and difficulty of relating to others. He loves to shoot fluid, hand-held movements and plays with the documentary style. The heroine of *July Rain* emerges in the first sequences, which show Moscow streets shot from a moving car, and seems just one of many possible persons which the camera follows.

Elem Klimov defined his style through his diploma film, *Welcome, or No Trespassing* [*Dobro pozhalovat' ili postoronnym vkhod zapreshchen*, 1964] where he mocks the bureaucratic and demagogical organization of a youth holiday camp and disrupts the hypocritical order through the character of the young Inochkin, who does not fit in this closed and rigid micro-society. The realistic narration unexpectedly breaks several times into fantastic and joyous digressions (Inochkin imagining his death; the children of the camp flying in the air). His second film, *Adventures of a Dentist* [*Pokhozhdeniia zubnogo vracha*, 1965], tells in the same whimsical and parabolic way the story of a magically talented dentist, whose talent is suffocated by jealousy and bureaucracy. His later films, shot during the Stagnation era, would take him elsewhere, to harsher and more violent narratives, but they are still made with the same inclination for parables.

Since her first film, *Brief Encounters* [*Korotkie vstrechi*, 1967], Kira Muratova has introduced a unique narrative structure that turned the initially simple and even banal plot of a love triangle into an intricate and heteroglossic narrative from multiple points of view and frequent flash-backs (see Larsen 1995). As early as this film she introduces off-center frames and renounces the establishing shot, thus unsettling the spectators' habits and certainties.

The Individual and the Collective

The start of the Stagnation period reinforces censorship, and the new guidelines are clearly opposed to the ideas and desires expressed by directors and some – daring – film critics such as Bozhovich. Maksim Medvedev assessed that "cinema is the cultural domain that succumbed least to the 'long hibernation' of the end of Brezhnev era" (Medvedev 2001); in fact, during this period many film directors emerge, whose names will remain in the history of Soviet cinema. But the administrative documents and the official reception in the Soviet Union undoubtedly show that, even though the word "author" is applied to the filmmaker, it is done so in a narrow sense. The study of these documents outlines the criteria applied to films and the way cinema creation was perceived at an official level.

When writing about films, journalists first of all quote the studio where a film is produced ("the new film of the Odessa studio"; Shatina 1968). The development of a film is seen not only as collective work, but also as a studio matter; this is what has been written about a film shot at the Dovzhenko studio: "Of course, the collective of 'Dovzhenkovians' was concerned by the production, they did their best to make it modern" (Virina 1965). When a film is attacked, the responsibility is assigned to the director, but also to the entire studio: "It is not so much the young filmmakers' mistake, but that of the collective of the Odessa studio, where its experimented masters could have helped correct the flaws in time" (Klevtsova 1964).

As early as the scandal around *The Tight Knot*, the studio, even one as powerful as Mosfilm, was under fire for the "flawed" film: "A major denunciation campaign started in Mosfilm. The studio desperately tried to save its political reputation, so the administration considered it its duty to dictate random changes" (Shveitser in Miloserdova 1988).

The most virulent press reports against Muratova's *Long Farewells* [*Dolgie provody*, 1971] put to shame the Odessa studio for allowing such a bad film to be made under its supervision:

> Could a film as defective artistically and ideologically as *Long Farewells* have seen the light of day if real criticism had existed at the Odessa studio, if the aesthetical-ideological education of the collective of creative workers had been intimately

linked to the work of the Party, and if the work of the Party had intervened at all stages of the artistic process? It is undisputable that such a film – rejected by the audience – would not have appeared. (Vinokurov 1972)

From the start, the discussions around the work of K. Muratova were not conducted with sufficient inflexibility, without the insistence and the frankness necessary in such cases. The critical remarks were usually accompanied by gallant reassurances about the talent of the director. [...] Where such indulgence leads has been made clear by the sad and instructive story of K. Muratova's film. (Sychevskii 1972)

Analyzing the long censorship story of *Ilyich's Gate*, Martine Godet sheds light on the complex relationship of artistic responsibility as understood at the time:

The Creative Union [*tvorcheskoe ob"edinenie*] functions really as a collective that takes to heart the destiny of the film and considers the speech of the First Secretary as a disapproval of the entire studio and not only of the directing crew [...]. Reciprocally, Khutsiev and his scriptwriter Shpalikov feel responsible towards the whole studio. (Godet 1996, 786)

Cinema in a Logo-Centric System

If the script is no longer as important as it was in the first years of the Stalinist era, it is still crucial enough that the scriptwriter often appears in the administrative reports as one of the authors of the completed film. This reflects the logo-centric concept typical of Soviet cinema. The ambiguous relationship to the scriptwriter, often considered on a par with the director, is echoed in Nikita Khrushchev's comment about *The Tight Knot* (directed by Mikhail Shveitser and scripted by Vladimir Tendriakov): "I don't understand where the authors of the film had seen what they showed" (Godet 1996, 786). The conclusion of the Artistic Council of the First Creative Union at Mosfilm concerning *Walking the Streets of Moscow* [*Ia shagaiu po Moskve*, dir. Georgii Daneliia, 1963] runs as follows: "The noble ideas – of camaraderie, solidarity, and mutual assistance – are presented by the authors in a very elegant and original form" (RGALI 2944/2/9: 22; December 24, 1963). In the remainder of the text, the director of photography Vadim Iusov is also referred to as one of the film's authors (RGALI 2944/2/9: 22; December, 24 1963). In his diploma for the Film Institute VGIK, Elem Klimov uses the plural (authors) when talking about his scriptwriter and himself (Klimov 2004). In the same way, the scriptwriter of a part of *Brief Encounters*, Leonid Zhukhovitskii, also a well-known Soviet writer, is often mentioned in critical reviews as co-author of the film ("the authors of the film L. Zhukhovitskii and K. Muratova"; Kovarskii 1968, 50).

This ambiguity was so common that Aleksei Gherman smartly used it to defend his own interests. Working at Lenfilm, the director had a rough start: after an already

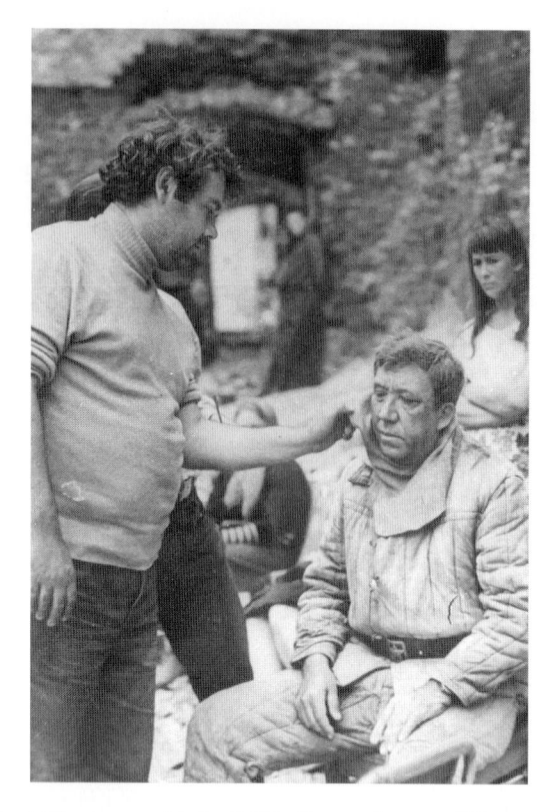

Figure 8.2 Aleksei Gherman with Iurii Nikulin on the set of *Twenty Days without War*, 1975. Courtesy of Svetlana Karmalita, from her personal archive.

controversial first film co-directed with Grigorii Aronov (*The Seventh Satellite* [*Sed'moi sputnik*], 1967), his first feature directed alone, *Trial on the Roads* [*Proverka na dorogakh*, 1971] was forbidden and shelved, even though it was an adaptation of a novel by his late father, Iurii Gherman, an officially celebrated Soviet writer. For his next film, *Twenty Days without War* [*Dvadtsat' dnei bez voiny*, 1976], he chose to adapt another Soviet classic, Konstantin Simonov, who was still alive at the time and had decided to help Gherman get the film made.

The archival documents show in full color the ways in which Gherman, the young and problematic film director, pretended to leave the "authorship" of the film to the writer. Not only did Simonov frequently intervene on account of the film and the director, before and after the shooting, but he also pretended that the casting of Iurii Nikulin in the main part was his personal initiative: "I asked Iurii Nikulin to play the main part in this film. [...] Now I ask you for help, because I really want this man to play the principal character of this novel, since he is the one I see in the part" (Konstantin Simonov, January 7, 1975; RGALI 2944/4/3499: 26). The letter to the director of the Circus Union Soiuzgostsirk, who had to decide whether Nikulin could participate in the shooting, written by the head of cinema production, also mentions "the authors of the film" who "cannot imagine another performer for the part" (G. Sokolov, October 1, 1975; RGALI 2944/4/3499: 27). In reality, the idea of Nikulin for the part of Lopatin was Gherman's and Svetlana Karmalita's (his wife and closest collaborator) and he suggested it to Simonov and convinced him to support this choice.[11] During the entire shooting period, while Goskino and the studio tried to temper the budget which got increasingly out of hand, Gherman did not hesitate to use Simonov's reputation to defend himself when asked to give up. He wrote to Eskin, the executive producer, as well as to the studio administration that he was not at liberty to cut entire sequences from the script:

> Working not with a simple scriptwriter, but with a major Soviet writer, I am obliged to thoroughly coordinate all the cuts in the script with K. M. Simonov. (Gherman, October 5, 1975, RGALI 2944/4/3499: 166)

> I will ask the author to relinquish the shooting of the sequences [...]. I cannot conceal the fact that the omission of these sequences is a loss for the storyline. It will be necessary to replace the author's ideas and accented themes in adjacent sequences, if K. Simonov agrees. (Gherman, May 1975, RGALI 2944/4/3499: 170)

Amazingly, when directors want to adapt famous and celebrated texts for the screen, they appear too liberal for Goskino. For instance, Iurii Gherman's novel *Operation "New Year"*, which his son decided to transform into a film (*Trial on the Roads*), was published in 1964 and openly denounced the Stalinist era. But for the negative character, a dishonest careerist, Goskino demanded many changes in the script and then in the film itself, to make the character appear more excusable and less high-ranked (RGALI 2944/4/2168: 79). Even earlier, during the Thaw, Georgii Daneliia recalls the distrust of Goskino towards literary classics and their subversive potential, even though most works had been published and celebrated in the USSR:

> I thought about it and decided to adapt *Dead Souls* by Gogol.
> At Goskino, they told me: "Don't." I asked: "Why?" They answered: "Because." [...]
> I thought about it and decided to adapt *The Winter of our Discontent* by Steinbeck. At Goskino, they told me: "Don't." I asked: "Why?" They answered: "Because."
> I thought a little more and decided to adapt *Crime and Punishment* by Dostoevskii. [...]
> Then they told me: "Write the script. Then we'll see." (Daneliia 2005)

The Unbearable Sadness of Life

One of the recurrent reproaches made to auteur film directors of the Thaw and Stagnation era would be their pessimism. Just as Khrushchev couldn't fathom where "the authors" of *The Tight Knot* could have seen what appeared on screen, a

Figure 8.3 Asia Kliachina (Iia Savvina) with her infant child and his father Stepan (Aleksandr Surin) in Andrei Konchalovskii's *The Story of Asya Klyachina*, 1966.

constant preoccupation throughout the 1960s, 1970s and the first half of the 1980s was that the director's personal point of view deformed the enthusiastic and happy Soviet reality by showing it in a grim and depressing way. Among frequent terms used in Soviet censorship and critical writings of the time is the word *mrachnost'*, which could be translated as "gloominess, drabness, everyday life represented in a sad light" (Godet 2010, 308). This term had already appeared during the Thaw, in connection with such films as *Ivan's Childhood*, considered as defeatist (since it shows the irreparable damages of war on the individuals), or *Ilyich's Gate*, regarded as a too somber representation of the youth of the early 1960s. The cultural historian Evgenii Gromov (1993) insists on the lack of optimism in the censored films as important for the censors' decisions. *The Story of Asya Klyachina* [*Istoriia Asi Kliachinoi, kotoraia liubila, da ne vyshla zamuzh*, 1966] is a film about a young woman with a clubfoot living in a kolkhoz, caught between a man she loves and whose child she bears but who doesn't love her, and a man who seems honest enough and wants to marry her but whom she doesn't love. The narrative rhythm is relaxed and the director lingers on the everyday life in the kolkhoz; most of the kolkhoz members were performed by real peasants. Qualified in the studio's appraisal as "decidedly new for our cinema" (Zorkaia 1989, 68), the film was then censored through "telefonnoe pravo."

Along with a long monologue by a man who had returned from the Gulag, one of the most problematic sequences in the film was a seemingly ordinary scene of a party where the peasants gather around a modest meal. While the real peasants filmed by Konchalovskii behave in a quite natural way, exchange jokes and even slightly vulgar verses, a small radio in the background plays a Soviet song that goes:

> Our songs will be sung when communism comes!
> Through these songs we will be remembered,
> We, the ordinary craftsmen of Soviet life,
> Who today build our future.

One of the characters then tunes down this perfect Soviet song about the contribution of simple workers to the common goal, while the group starts singing a popular Russian song:

> Saturday, the day of bad weather,
> It's impossible, impossible,
> Impossible to work the fields,
> Impossible to work the fields.

This moment is quite significant: a minor key wins over a major key, the popular melancholic song – far from celebrating hard work – takes preference over the enthusiastic, life-affirming, ideologically approved song.

Usually, this reproach of pessimism or *mrachnost'* from censors and journalists goes along with the accusation of an ill-digested influence of Western cinema. In 1965 *Iskusstvo kino* published an article that explained the perception of these influences:

> But try to find the capacity for happiness among the characters of Godard, Chabrol [...]. It is not the fault of these talented people that the heroes of their films are so unhappy, so unable to enjoy life. [...] Man cannot be happy in a poorly organized society. Soviet art absorbed this conclusion of world history and will never forget it. (Varshavskii 1965, 53)

Whereas the pessimism and depression among the heroes of the New Wave is considered quite natural, since they live in a capitalist society, for Soviet heroes these qualities are viewed as unjustifiable. The protagonists of *Brief Encounters* were accused of being "tired, ill at ease, weak" (Zbandut 1969, 71). *Long Farewells*, considered as particularly bleak in its representation of Soviet reality, provoked the following judgment: "the concentration of attention only on the somber aspects of life [...] is clearly unacceptable for a film director who obeys the principles of socialist realism" (Sychevskii 1972). Another critic wrote about the same film:

> It could have been an interesting film [...]. But how did Muratova treat this theme? She started talking about lack of communication and estrangement, about impersonality and lack of faith in the environment where her heroes live. [...] The film is

> shot like a chronicle, a documentary. [...] By trying to be fashionable, along with the "documentary-style," the young director seizes in a non-critical way on the aesthetic principles of certain foreign film directors and, alas, forgets the social reasons that determine their art. (Solov'ev 1972)

It is obviously the pessimism and not specifically the foreign influence that is pinned down as the key problem. The studio's appraisal of *Walking the Streets of Moscow*, comprises praise that reveals that, on the contrary, Western influence – applied in a lighthearted and optimistic film – is seen as positive:

> By its entire structure, *Walking the Streets of Moscow* is different from foreign films about youth – films about failure, unhappiness, inner discord, and depression. Such a film could only be made by Soviet artists and only about Soviet youth. [...] The elegance of the *mise-en-scène* is combined with the desire to make it look documentary. Many episodes were shot with a hidden camera. The background of many sequences is not composed of extras (as it is usually done), but of real life in a real street, or a shop, or the subway (RGALI 2944/2/9: 22–23).

One of the sequences in *Trial on the Road* that the state apparatus considered to be unsatisfactory is the final one, where the spectator sees Lokotkov, the chief of the partisan group, at the end of the war: he has not been honored with a medal or a higher rank. This moment was considered problematic from the start, as it supposedly adds "a shade of disappointment and melancholy" to the film (RGALI 2944/4/2168: 7; December 17, 1969). Goskino repeatedly refused to release the film, claiming that the partisans "appear as broken, depressed people" (RGALI 2944/4/2168: 59; March 24, 1972).

The Persistent Point of View

Directors were frequently castigated for being too much of an auteur. Any too obviously personal style in the *mise-en-scène* was assessed as formalism. The effects were viewed as gratuitous and even detrimental, since they were supposedly driven by individualism: the director puts himself forward instead of blending his personality and efforts in with the collective product that a Soviet film is supposed to be. Muratova and her husband were accused of such egocentrism for their first feature film, *Our Honest Bread* [*Nash chestnyi khleb*, 1964]: "it is no bigger truth that the directors were aiming at; they only affirmed their right to have a 'unique' point of view on the events, to have their 'personal' style" (Virina 1965). The quotation highlights the ridiculousness of such claims. The same viewpoint is emphasized by Solov'ev in his article on *Long Farewells*:

> As a matter of fact, it sometimes happens that young scriptwriters or directors understand the autonomy of their quest only as a means to express themselves,

to express their artistic tendencies, without relating them to any real problems of contemporary life. [...] Experience for the sake of experience is unacceptable in cinema. (Solov'ev 1972)

It is not just the gratuitous stylistic effect that would not enhance the understanding which is condemned here, but any visible style that contravenes the habits of the Soviet spectator. For instance, another frequent reproach made to auteur directors, which logically results from the previous one, is the lack of clarity and the didacticism in their films. When *Brief Encounters* was released, Nikolai Kovarskii fustigated it in an article for *Iskusstvo kino*: "The perception of the main character by viewers is quite ambiguous. I heard spectators (even though they were quite positive towards the film) interpret her in two radically opposed ways" (Kovarskii 1968, 50). The film is also qualified as "longish, overloaded, and motley" (Ivanov 1968).

Another frequent problem for the "auteurs" is their tendency to make films that are considered too universal, and therefore not Soviet enough. Muratova's *Long Farewells* was accused of being but a pale "imitation" (Anon. 1972) of contemporary Soviet life:

In the beginning of the film there is a star on a tomb. And that is the only element that makes it possible to determine where this mother is arguing with her son. Of course, people speak mostly (however not exclusively) Russian, the names are Russian too, but otherwise – it's the spitting image of France! (Nechiporuk 1972)

Iosseliani recalled the same kind of reproach leveled at his films of the Stagnation period: "In your films, there is no sign of Soviet governance. If they were anti-Soviet, it would be understandable, but there is not even a hint at socialism. Don't you notice us at all?" (Iosseliani in Fedina 2008). In his memoirs of Elem Klimov, Iosseliani described his friend and film director as "a-Soviet" (Iosseliani in Plakhov, 2008) and thus partially explained his problems with Goskino.

Metacinema

In his article on late-Soviet auteur cinema, Maksim Medvedev observes that another specificity was its interest in analyzing the cinematic process itself:

"Auteur" cinema, which was so enthusiastically welcomed by perestroika, emerged at the junction of the seventies and eighties and was a characteristic example of cinema, in which [...] the author was acting as a subject, thereby making cinema aware of its own nature. Its first explorations are associated with the study of cinematic self-representation, [...] inter- and auto-textuality. (Medvedev 2001)[12]

Almost all of Tarkovskii's films can be considered a parable of the artist's place in society: *Andrei Rublev* shows two major figures of artists: Rublev struggles with the idea of creating beauty in a violent and unjust world; the

Figure 8.4 The bell-founder in Andrei Tarkovskii's *Andrei Rublev*, 1966.

young bell-founder – obviously the director's alter ego – is younger than most of his crew (just like Tarkovskii when he started directing), pretends to have 'the secret' of bell-founding from his famous father (Tarkovskii's first years were overshadowed by his father's renown as a poet) and he has to impose his will and his decisions even though the crew tends to resist his ideas, trying to make him follow the usual rhythm and procedures, while he wants to try something more daring and exceptional. The end of this episode can be seen as a metaphor of filmmaking: it shows how Tarkovskii perceived his own place as a director, imposing his *inventio* to create the final miracle, while the rest of the world seems to resist his design.[13]

In Muratova's unrealized script *Watch Your Dreams Attentively* [*Vnimatelno smotrite sny*, 1969; see Muratova and Zuev 2014] she breaks down the Soviet habits and the bureaucratic jargon associated with the film industry. In the same way, Gherman shows in *Twenty Days without War* how Soviet cinema distorts both the written text and reality: Lopatin attends the shooting of a short film, based on his novel about a traumatic experience in Stalingrad, where he desperately observes how all his attempts to correct the *mise-en-scène* and the good will of the filmmaker do not change the fact that the film is a total and complete lie, a polished and heroicized version of what actually happened. Gherman demonstrates the stark opposition between film and reality by juxtaposing in the editing the artificial *mise-en-scène* and the hero's gripping memories, shot in a documentary style with a minimalistic soundtrack.

The Forgotten Audience

Another characteristic common to most auteurs of this period is their desire to implement their ideas, irrespective of their future audience. Medvedev observed that "since the seventies, the spectator ceased to interest the majority of Soviet directors, who had only a vague idea of the audience's interests and priorities" (Medvedev 2001). Iosseliani speaks about his 'shelved' films in a way that seems to confirm this: "In the USSR, I [...] tried to circumvent censorship in order to make 'my' cinema. But the films were forbidden anyway. [They] ended up on the shelf, but I did what I had meant to do" (Iosseliani in Fedina 2008).

In the same way, Muratova claimed that the most important thing for her was to finish her films as close as possible to her initial vision, even if it meant that the film would be "shelved" and never seen by anyone.[14] During the Stagnation it became common among auteurs to give Goskino a false script in order to get the authorization to shoot, which proves again that their goal wasn't making a film that would find a general consensus; they felt they were authors and did their best to follow their individual *inventio*,[15] in spite of the system. As Klimov writes: "This is how you can mislead Goskino: submit a 'false' script, get an authorization to start production, and then shoot the film based on the real script" (Klimov in Godet 2010, 227). As Muratova would word it later: "In the first place I must like what I do and then I would enjoy if mankind likes it, too" (Muratova in Desiaterik 2002).

The contrast between the situation in the late Soviet Union and the post-Soviet era shows how little directors cared about the audience during the Stagnation. For instance, Iosseliani noted that in contemporary cinema ideological issues are replaced by the obligatory concern of pleasing the audience,[16] meaning that previously he had never been worried by this aspect. When *Cahiers du cinema* put together a special issue on perestroika, they summed up their impressions collected through interviews with Aleksei Gherman, Iurii Norshtein, Aleksandr Kaidanovskii and others:

> In this too big a country, the isolation of the artist is something like a historical fatality, endured, accepted, even yearned for. The artist here always defines himself vis-à-vis authority and has a weak, even negative notion of the other, demanding, side that we, at home, call the "audience." (Daney and Toubiana 1990, 4)

The Fresh Breeze of Perestroika[17]

During the V Congress of Filmmakers, some speakers were indignant about the lack of authors' rights belonging to filmmakers. The director Vitalii Mel'nikov commented on the striking difference between the goals of the Union of Filmmakers and what it really does:

> For instance, [in our statutes] in the fourth section, we have clause 2: "The union board attends to the defense of the authors' rights of its members."' What rights? The main creators of the films – the directors, the cameramen, the designers – apart from the scriptwriters, do not have any authors' rights. Last time we confirmed our statutes

[…] exactly 15 years ago. At the time, we must have thought that one day we would get these rights and that we would have to defend them. (Mel'nikov in Anon. 1986, 31)

The idea of the collective work as an objective tool for making better films is scrutinized, because "it is very complicated to distinguish the collective responsibility from a collective irresponsibility" (Mikhalkov in Anon. 1986, 63) and the necessity of the artist to oppose the state apparatus in order to create is reaffirmed loudly and clearly: "There always has been a struggle between the artist and the bureaucrat" (Mikhalkov in Anon. 1986, 63).

In May 1986, just a few days after the Congress, the Conflict Commission was created,[18] which was in charge of the rehabilitation of censored films and their directors.[19] It is significant that one of the goals of the Commission was to "restore films in their author's version," which could be translated as the Soviet equivalent of the concept of the "director's cut" – in other words, the version wanted by the director and not the one obtained at the end of the censorship process. For instance, for Khutsiev's *Ilyich's Gate*, the Commission's conclusion stated: "Considering that *Ilyich's Gate* is undoubtedly a major piece of cinematic art of the beginning of the sixties, the committee considers it an urgent necessity to restore the author's version of the film" (Musskii 2005, 251).

Then, for a short period, a blessed period began for directors who had been castigated and censored during the stagnation period, but had managed to obtain recognition as auteurs now.[20] As Muratova summed up: "Yesterday, I was told: 'Idiot, moron, short-sighted, get out of here!' And all of a sudden: 'You are a genius! Everything you do is admirable!' Black has become white. 'Start working immediately, shoot whatever you want'" (Muratova in Taubman 1991).

The importance of the concept of auteur cinema throughout perestroika makes us understand to what degree this concept, though not part of official film production and ideology, was present in earlier years and to what extent it determined the existence of many films and directors.

Notes

1. Muratova (2005, 22); the poem she quotes is "Back Home" by Vladimir Mayakovsky, 1926. (Ia khochu byt' poniat moei stranoi / A ne budu poniat' – chto zh? / Po rodnoi strane proidu storonoi, / Kak prokhodit kosoi dozhd'.)
2. Tcherneva (2013, 185) notes that in the Soviet Union the word "artist" [*khudozhnik*] is used more often than "author" [*avtor*].
3. Tcherneva (2013, 186) underlines that, by initially not accepting in its midst all the film professions, the "Union of Filmmakers operates a notable classification of professions and individuals", separating them into categories of makers and artists.
4. The law of March 31, 1959 confirmed that the filmmaker did not have any author's rights: "The author's rights for the film belong to the production company that has produced it. The scriptwriter keeps the right to receive a monetary fee" (Vaksberg and Gringol'ts 1961, 259).

5   More films were shelved up until 1968, when the number of shelved films decreased, while preliminary control mechanisms on all levels increased (Arkus 2002).
6   For more details on the reception of the film in France see Chartreux (2007, 151–167).
7   The "telephone right" was the right exercised by high-ranking administrators to call after a private screening and demand for the film to be shelved.
8   For example, Elem Klimov's *Welcome…* was authorized despite its provocative aspects (and the mockery of Nikita Khrushchev's corn cult) because Khrushchev liked it; Klimov's next film, *Adventures of a Dentist* was shelved.
9   The film was finally released, completely re-edited and partly reshot under a new title – *Sasha Enters Life* [*Sasha vstupaet v zhizn'*] in 1957
10 They "worked together" or rather against each other, on *Getting to Know the Big, Wide World* (1978), the only Soviet film by Muratova to be produced at Lenfilm rather than the Odessa studio.
11 Gherman recalls: "It is quite a strange thing – Svetlana and I had the idea of Nikulin [for the part of Lopatin] at the same time! […] We went to see Simonov; talking with Nikulin without Simonov was useless. 'Konstantin Mikhailovich, we have one candidate – Nikulin. If you do not agree, we have no other actor in view.' And he says: 'Fantastic!'" (Gherman in Dolin 2013, 155).
12 For René Prédal (2001, 15), it is the epitome of "auteur cinema" to reflect on cinema itself: "The nature, the history and the future of auteur cinema put forward a continuous interrogation of the seventh art by itself, maintaining it in auto-analysis from the very beginning and extending a mirror, sometimes an accurate one and sometimes a distorted one."
13 All of Tarkovskii's texts, reunited in the volume *Sculpting in Time* (Tarkovsky 1986), were written from the position of a unique author of the film, using others' talents for his purposes.
14 "I make no effort to know the destiny of my films. It never really interested me" (Muratova in Kolodizhner 1993, 40).
15 An example shows how strongly the directors felt about this: Muratova, who was known to never soften her wording for any officials she had to work with, once expelled the chief editor [*glavnyi redaktor*] of Odessa Studio from her sound studio, telling her: "Making the sound track is a pleasure for me. Your presence is not. Please do not come to my sound studio, it unnerves me" (Izvolova 2006, 98–99).
16 "In the Soviet Union, the director was torn between his design and the demands of censorship. In the West, he is torn between his design and the audience, which he absolutely needs, otherwise the project collapses" (Iosseliani in Fedina 2008).
17 At the V Congress of Filmmakers the director Iurii Ozerov started his speech with the following words: "The Twenty-seventh Party Congress, quoting the popular established expression, brought a fresh breeze, and opened the vents to freshen up our lives" (Anon. 1986, 65).
18 The composition of the Commission was determined on May 19, with Andrei Plakhov at the head and including such directors as Ali Khamraev, Aleksei Gherman, Georgii Danelia (Miloserdova 1999, 184).
19 "The committee prepares an expert conclusion about each film; this conclusion is sent to the Union of Filmmakers, and from there to Goskino. There, independently or after consulting with the Central Committee (if the order to "interdict" was given at the highest level), the decision was made to release the film for the screen" (Arkus 2002).

20 The *Cahiers du Cinema* team confirmed their names as "relevant" in 1990: "When one speaks with directors there, it is obvious that they confirm what we assumed. That Tarkovskii and Paradjanov, Muratova and Gherman, Sokurov and Peleshian (and others) are in fact the names that count" (Daney and Toubiana 1990, 4).

References

Andreev, Andrei. 2014. "*Auteurism, art house* i *art-cinema*. Istoki poniatiia 'avtorskoe kino' v zarubezhnoi kinovedcheskoi traditsii" [Auteurism, Art House and Art Cinema. The Origins of the Term "Auteur Cinema" in Foreign Film History]. *Kinovedcheskie zapiski* [Film-Scholars' Notes] 102–103: 168–194.

Anon. 1972. "Gliadia vperëd..." [Looking Ahead...]. *Sovetskaia kul'tura* [Soviet Culture] March 2.

Anon. 1986. "V s"ezd kinematografistov SSSR" [At the Congress of Soviet Filmmakers]. *Iskusstvo kino* [Art of Cinema] 10: 4–133.

Antimonov, Boris and Fleishits, Ekaterina. 1957. *Avtorskoe pravo* [Authors' Rights]. Moscow: Iuridicheskaia literatura.

Arkus, Liubov' (ed.). 2002. *Noveishaia istoriia otechestvennogo kino. 1986–2000. Kino i kontekst* [New History of Domestic Cinema, 1986–2000. Cinema and its Context]. vol. 4. St Petersburg: Seans, http://old.russiancinema.ru/template.php?dept_id=3&e_dept_id=5&e_chr_id=33&e_chrdept_id=2&chr_year=1986 (accessed January 29, 2015).

Astruc, Alexandre. 1948. "Naissance d'une nouvelle avant-garde: la caméra-stylo" [The Birth of a New Avant-Garde: The Camera-Pen]. *L'Ecran français* [French Screen] 144 March 30.

Beumers, Birgit. 1997. *Yury Lyubimov at the Taganka Theatre 1964–1994*. Amsterdam: Harwood Academic Publishers/OPA.

Chartreux Félix. 2007. "La sortie du film *Quand passent les cigognes* en France. Configuration d'un succès cinématographique soviétique en 1958" [The Release of the Film *The Cranes are Flying* in France: Configuration of a Soviet Film Success in 1958]. *Bulletin de l'Institut Pierre Renouvin* 2 (26): 151–167, http://www.cairn.info/zen.php?ID_ARTICLE=BIPR_026_0151#no27 (accessed January 29, 2015).

Daneliia Georgii. 2005. *Tostuemyi p'et do dna* [He Who Has a Toast Proposed to Him Drinks "Bottom Up"']. Moscow: Eksmo, http://royallib.ru/book/daneliya_georgiy/tostuemiy_pet_do_dna.html (accessed January 29, 2015).

Daney, Serge and Serge Toubiana. 1990. "Le rideau déchiré" [The Torn Curtain] *Cahiers du cinéma* 427 (Spécial URSS, Ciné-Perestroïka): 4–5.

de Baecque, Antoine and Serge Toubiana. 1999. *Truffaut. A Biography*. Translated by Catherine Temerson. New York: Alfred Knopf.

Desiaterik, Dmitrii. 2002. "V pervuiu ochered' ia khochu nravit'sia sebe samoi" [In the First Instance I Want to Please Myself]. Interview with Kira Muratova. *Den'* (Kiev, Ukraine) July 1, http://www.day.kiev.ua/ru/article/kultura/kira-muratova-v-pervuyu-ochered-ya-hochu-nravitsya-sebe-samoy (accessed January 29, 2015).

Dolin, Anton. 2013. *German*. Moscow: NLO.

Doniol-Valcroze, Jacques. 1958. "Par la grâce du formalisme" [Thanks to Formalism]. *Cahiers du Cinéma* 85: 46–47.

Fedina, Anna. 2008. "Rezhisser Otar Ioseliani: 'Grammofon, lampochka i telefon s"eli nashe vremia" [The Director Otar Iosseliani: "The Gramophone the Light Bulb and the Telephone Have Eaten Up Our Time"]. *Izvestiia* [News] April 1, http://izvestia.ru/news/335004 (accessed January 29, 2015).

Fomin, Valerii, ed. 1998. *Kinematograf ottepeli: dokumenty i svidetel'stva* [The Cinema of the Thaw: Documents and Testimonies]. Moscow: Materik

Fomin, Valerii, ed. 2006. *"Polka": dokumenty, svidetel'stva, kommentarii* [The "Shelf": Documents, Testimonies, Comments] vol. 3. Moscow: Materik.

Godet, Martine. 1996. "L'œuvre dénaturée. Un cas de censure cinématographique dans l'URSS de Khrouchtchev" [The Dehumanized Work. A Case of Cinematic Censorship in Khrushchev's USSR]. *Annales. Histoire, Sciences Sociales* 4: 781–804.

Godet, Martine. 2010. *La pellicule et les ciseaux, la censure dans le cinéma soviétique du Dégel à la perestroika* [Film and Scissors: Censorship in Soviet Cinema from the Thaw to Perestroika]. Paris: CNRS.

Gordon, Mikhail. 1955. *Sovetskoe avtorskoe pravo* [Soviet Author's Rights]. Moscow: Gosiurizdat.

Gromov, Evgenii. 1993. "K probleme pessimizma v otechestvennom iskusstve" [The Problem of Pessimism in Domestic Art]. In *Iskusstvo sovetskogo vremeni. V poiskakh novogo ponimaniia*, [Art of the Soviet Time: In Search for a New Understanding], edited by N. Iastrebova, 160–188. Moscow, Rossiiskii institut iskusstvoznaniia.

Iutkevich, Sergei. 1960. *Kontrapunkt rezhissera* [The Director's Counterpoint]. Moscow: Iskusstvo.

Iutkevich, Sergei. 2004. "Osnovy rezhissury (kratkii konspekt kursa lektsii)" [Basics of Directing: A Short Outline of a Lecture Cycle]. *Kinovedcheskie zapiski* [Film-Scholars' Notes] 70, http://www.kinozapiski.ru/ru/article/sendvalues/222/ (accessed January 25, 2015).

Ivanov B., 1968. "Pochti zabytaia vstrecha" [An Almost Forgotten Meeting]. *Molodoi dal'nevostochnik* [Young Far-East] May 2.

Izvolova Irina, 2006. "Sredi serykh kamnei" [Among Grey Stones…]. In *"Polka": dokumenty, svidetel'stva, kommentarii* [The 'Shelf': Documents, Testimonies, Comments] vol. 3 edited by Valerii Fomin, 98–99. Moscow: Materik.

Klevtsova, Larisa 1964. "K glubinnym plastam. Zapisi k II plenumu rukovodstva soiuza kinematografistov" [To the Deeper Layers: Notes of the II Plenum of the Board of the Filmmakers' Union]. *Rabochaia gazeta* [Working Gazette] November 25.

Klimov, Elem. 2004. "Teoreticheskaia chast' diplomnoi raboty – fil'ma 'Dobro pozhalovat' ili postoronnim vkhod vospreshchen' (1964)" [Theoretical Part of the Diploma Work for the Film "Welcome, or No Trespassing" (1964)]. *Kinovedcheskie zapiski* [Film-Scholars' Notes] 68, http://www.kinozapiski.ru/ru/article/sendvalues/22/ (accessed January 25, 2015).

Kolodizhner, Asia. 1993. "Ia prelstilas' sladkimi rechami, no menia soblaznili i obmanuli" [I Was Charmed by Sweet Talk, But I Was Seduced and Betrayed]. Interview with Kira Muratova. *Seans* 9: 40.

Kovarskii, Nikolai. 1968. "Chelovek i vremia" [Man and Time]. *Iskusstvo kino* [Art of Cinema] 10: 49–56.

Larsen, Susan. 1995. "Encoding Difference. Figuring Gender and Ethnicity in Kira Muratova's *A Change of Fate*." In *Soviet Hieroglyphics. Visual Culture in Late 20th-Century Russia*, edited by Nancy Condee, 113–129. London: British Film Institute.

Levin, Lev. 2004. "Avtorskaia pesnia" [The Author's Song]. In *Estrada v Rossii, XX vek. Entsiklopedia* [Variety Theatre in Russia, 20th Century. Encyclopedia], 8–13. Moscow: Olma-Press.

Liubimov, Youri. 1985. *Le Feu Sacré* [The Sacred Fire]. Paris: Fayard.

Medvedev, Maksim. 2001. "Pozdnesovetkii 'avtorskii' kinematograf" [Late-Soviet Auteur Cinema]. *Kinovedcheskie zapiski* [Film-Scholars' Notes] 53, http://www.kinozapiski.ru/ru/article/sendvalues/736/ (accessed January 25, 2015).

Miloserdova, Natal'ia. 1988. "Kak zatiagivalsia tugoi uzel" [How the Knot got Tighter]. Interview with Mikhail Shveitser. *Sovetskii ekran* (Soviet Screen) 18: 10.

Miloserdova, Natal'ia. 1999. "Konets sovetskogo kino" [The End of Soviet Cinema]. *Kinostsenarii* [Film Scripts] 1: 180–191.

Muratova, Kira. 2005. "To, chto my nazyvaem 'kich' ili 'bezvkusitsa', mne ne chuzhdo" [I'm no Stranger to what we call Kitsch or Tasteless]. *Iskusstvo kino* [Art of Cinema] 1, http://kinoart.ru/archive/2005/01/n1-article2 (accessed January 25, 2015).

Muratova, Kira and Vladimir Zuev. 2014. "*Watch Your Dreams Attentively*, or *The Touch*." *Studies in Russian and Soviet Cinema* 8.1: 51–96.

Musskii Igor'. 2005. *100 velikikh otechestvennykh kinofil'mov* [100 Great Domestic Films]. Moscow: Veche.

Nechiporuk, Vikentii. 1972. "Chei zhe eto mir?" [Whose is This World?]. *Znamia kommunizma* [Banner of Communism] May 2.

Plakhov, Andrei. 2008. "Predpisannaia tragediia" [A Set Tragedy]. Interview with Otar Iosseliani. *Iskusstvo kino* [Art of Cinema] 4, http://kinoart.ru/archive/2008/04/n4-article20 (accessed January 25, 2015).

Prédal, René. 2001, *Le cinéma d'auteur, une vieille lune?* [Auteur Cinema: An Old Hat?] Paris: Cerf.

Sartre, Jean-Paul. 1986. "Discussion sur la critique à propos de *L'Enfance d'Ivan*" [Discussion on the Criticism of *Ivan's Childhood*]. *Etudes cinématographiques*, [Cinematographic Studies] 135–138. Paris: Lettres Modernes. First published in *Unità*, October 9. 1963; republished in *Lettres Françaises* December 26, 1963.

Shatina, Zinaida. 1968. "Korotkie vstrechi" [Short Encounters]. *Luberetskaia pravda* [Pravda of Luberets] February 3.

Solov'ev, Vladimir, 1972. "V polët za *Beloi ptitsei*" [The Flight of the *White Bird*]. *Literaturnaia gazeta* [Literary Gazette] February 23.

Sychevskii, Vasilii, 1972. "Byt' trebovatel'nei" [Being Demanding]. *Literaturnaia gazeta* [Literary Gazette] March 8.

Tarkovsky, Andrey. 1986. *Sculpting in Time*. Austin: University of Texas Press.

Taubman, Jane. 1991. "Kinematograf Kiry Muratovoi" [Kira Muratova's Cinema]. Interview with Kira Muratova. *Literaturovedcheskie teksty* [Texts in Literary Studies], http://www.az.ru/women_cd1/html/preobrazh_2_1994_ge.htm#note4 (accessed January 25, 2015).

Tcherneva, Irina. 2013. "L'auteur, le créateur et le salarié en Union soviétique" [Author, Creator, and Employee in the Soviet Union]. In *L'auteur de cinéma, Histoire, généalogie, archéologie* [Film author: History, Genealogy, Archaeology], edited by Christophe Gauthier and Dimitri Vezyroglou, 185–194. Paris: AFRHC.

Truffaut, François. 1955. "*Ali Baba* et la Politique des Auteurs" [*Ali Baba* and the Politics of Auteurs]. *Cahiers du cinéma* 44: 45–47.

Vaisfel'd, Il'ia. 1972. "Introduction." In *Chto takoe kino?* [What is Cinema?] 2–38. Moscow: Iskusstvo.

Vaksberg, Arkadii and Isidor Gringol'ts. 1961. *Avtor v kino* [Author and Film]. Moscow: Iskusstvo.

Varshavskii, Iakov. 1965. "Ot pokoleniia k pokoleniiu" [From Generation to Generation]. *Iskusstvo kino* [Art of Cinema] 6: 50–57.

Vinokurov M. 1972. "Shliakhom bezprintsipnosti" [The High Road of Lack of Principles]. *Radjanska Ukraina* February 19.

Virina, L. 1965. "Idti k iarkomu svetu. Zametki o tvorchestve molodykh v ukrainskom kino" [Towards the Bright Light. Notes about Young Filmmakers in Ukrainian Cinema]. *Pravda Ukrainy* October 25.

Zbandut, Gennadii. 1969. "Trebovaniia k sebe" [Demands to Oneself]. *Iskusstvo kino* [Art of Cinema] 6: 67–78.

Zorkaia, Neiia. 1989. "Ne stoit selo bez pravednitsy. Iz istorii odnoi kartiny, sniatoi v 1966 godu. Vospominaniia ochevidtsa, zametki kinokritika, arkhivnye dokumenty" [No Village Without Just Women. From the History of a Film Made in 1966. Recollections of a Witness, Notes of a Film Critic, Archival Documents]. *Iskusstvo kino* [Art of Cinema] 1: 56–68.

9

The *Blokbaster*: How Russian Cinema Learned to Love Hollywood

Dawn Seckler and Stephen M. Norris

Phenomenally successful cinematic hits are not new to Russian filmmaking. A quick review of Soviet cinema across the decades provides ample examples of popular movies. For example, in 1927 more than one million Soviets filed into cinemas to see Abram Room's *Bed and Sofa* [*Tret'ia Meshchanskaia*] (Graffy 2001, 93). The Stalinist-era mandate to make "movies for the masses" was fulfilled – indeed, over-fulfilled – by the Vasili'ev Brothers' *Chapaev* (1934); reportedly, Stalin watched it no fewer than 38 times and it attracted 50 million audience members (Graffy 2010, 67–81). In the latter half of the 1960s, Leonid Gaidai's comedies kept cinema seats filled. *Operation "Y" and Other Adventures of Shurik* [*Operatsiia "Y" i drugie prikliucheniia Shurika*] was the most viewed movie of 1965 with 70 million spectators; its sequel, *The Captive of the Caucasus, or Shurik's New Adventures* [*Kavkazskaia plennitsa ili novye prikluchenia Shurika*, 1966], surpassed it, selling 77 million tickets. *The Diamond Arm* [*Brilliantovaia ruka*, 1968] again had 77 million viewers. Just over a decade later, the Academy Award-winning *Moscow Doesn't Believe in Tears* [*Moskva slezam ne verit*, dir. Vladimir Men'shov 1980] drew 85 million viewers, while Boris Durov's *Pirates of the 20th Century* [*Piraty XX veka*, 1979] had 87.6 million viewers, making it the most popular Soviet film of all time.

In the article "Soviet and Russian Blockbusters: A Question of Genre?" (2003) Birgit Beumers theorizes these films as examples of Russian blockbuster cinema. She writes that while "the concept of the blockbuster may […] not be relevant in the Soviet context in terms of profitability, […] it is relevant on the level of a film's popularity, which can be measured with data on the number of spectators (number of tickets sold)" (2003, 442). For Beumers, the retrospective labeling of Soviet-era hits as "blockbusters" provides a framework within which one can find

---

A Companion to Russian Cinema, First Edition. Edited by Birgit Beumers.
© 2016 John Wiley & Sons, Inc. Published 2016 by John Wiley & Sons, Inc.

commonality among the range of cinematic genres represented by an adventure film of the 1930s (i.e., *Chapaev*), Gaidai's comedies of the 1960s, and *Moscow Doesn't Believe in Tears*, the melodrama that emerged with the 1980s. Attributing these films' popularity, at least in part, to their use of "conventional [cinematic] patterns" and reliance on genre (Beumers 2003, 441), and proceeding from Thomas Schatz's definition of genre films as those that "portray our culture in a stable, invariable ideological position" (1981, 31), Beumers deftly demonstrates a relationship between what she terms blockbusters and moments of Soviet political or ideological crisis. In other words, genre conventions that convey a sense of familiarity and political stability provide comfort and "suggest certainty in times of upheaval" (Beumers 2003, 442), thus their tremendous popularity.

While we emphatically agree with Beumers that Soviet-era genre films are used precisely to such ends (Seckler 2010), and I certainly will not deny the quantitative fact of box office data, we nonetheless find this use of the term "blockbuster" anachronistic. Film historians identify 1975 – the year Steven Spielberg's *Jaws* was released – as the start of the blockbuster era in Hollywood (Bach 1985; Bates 1978; Hoberman 1985; Keyser 1981; and Madsen 1975). In the book *Directed by Steven Spielberg: Poetics of the Contemporary Hollywood Blockbuster*, Warren Buckland writes that "[f]rom 1975 on, blockbusters increasingly became Hollywood's standard or *dominant* practice of filmmaking" noting that directors "recycled classical Hollywood films, especially B-movie genres, which they remade using A-movie budgets" (Buckland 2006, 11; emphasis in the original). Referencing the same historical timeframe, sometimes labeled "New Hollywood," David Bordwell (2006) and Thomas Elsaesser (2012) draw attention to the parallel development of studios' new emphasis on marketing strategies used to capitalize on the blockbuster as a phenomenon indicative of this new era. The rise of the blockbuster parallels a rise in the development of deals with distributors, orchestrated commercial tie-ins (e.g., soundtracks, video games), and the rise of sequels – material with previous proven commercial success.

Insofar as Russian cinema borrows the term *blokbaster* from its Californian colleagues, does it make sense to describe the Soviet Union's most beloved and popular films of the 1930s or 1960s as blockbusters? This chapter contends that it does not, and limits the discussion of Russian blockbuster cinema to a specific historical moment. In Russia the blockbuster era begins around the turn of the millennium – the very late 1990s – and is spurred into existence as a reaction to the overwhelming presence of Hollywood blockbuster movies that entered the Russian market. Speaking in 2005 on a roundtable titled "Blockbuster: Translated into Russian," Daniil Dondurei, editor in chief of the influential journal *Iskusstvo kino* opened the conversation with the following statements:

> Even a year and a half ago there were no films in Russia which could be called blockbusters – films with big budgets, stars, special effects, full-fledged budgets. [There were] no films that could compete in our market with Hollywood's products. […]

> I propose to speak about cinema as a system and to look at how blockbusters – *as a new phenomenon for us* – affect mainstream and art house cinema (Dondurei at "Kruglyi stol" 2005; emphasis added).

As Dondurei's comments reveal, in contemporary Russia, Hollywood's most pervasive global product – the blockbuster – is something with which the Russian market has had to contend and against which it has had to compete.

Of course, the dominance of Hollywood in the international arena is nothing new. In 1987 Elsaesser wrote, "Hollywood can hardly be conceived […] as totally other, since so much of any nation's film culture is implicitly 'Hollywood'" (Elsaesser 1987, 166), and the Russian film industry is no exception. Hollywood's influence on Russian filmmaking dates at least as far back as 1918, when avant-garde director Lev Kuleshov wrote of his admiration for Hollywood's use of rapid montage, which he imitated to heighten the fast-paced action of his adventure film, *The Extraordinary Adventures of Mr. West in the Land of the Bolsheviks* [*Neobychainye prikliucheniia mistera Vesta v strane bol'shevikov*, 1924] (Kuleshov 1974). It is the latter half of the twentieth century, however, that has witnessed Hollywood's increasing hegemonic presence across the globe. Though there are few – perhaps no – places untouched by Hollywood, most of Europe experienced a creeping infiltration of American movies into their cinemas. Closed as it was to capitalist products, Soviet Russia was by and large untouched by Hollywood's influence. Following the Soviet empire's collapse that situation changed quickly and forcefully.

In the mid-1990s, when the post-Soviet film industry hit its nadir,[1] Hollywood rushed in to stake a claim in Russia's desolate cinema landscape. There were movie theaters, but they were run down, unheated, and empty. There were directors, actors, even studios, but film production had come to a near complete halt (a lowly 34 films, few of them memorable, were made in 1996).[2] With few domestic films available and an economic crisis that made film tickets a luxury, pirated videos of Hollywood hits became the country's main cinematic diet. By the turn of the millennium, this had taken a toll on film-watching habits. Data on the demographics of Russia's film-going audience reveal that because potential consumers lacked sufficient economic resources, the Russian film industry of the early 2000s could only rely on an audience of approximately five million people, of whom "70 percent are young people from fourteen to twenty-four years old." This segment had grown up on a steady diet of Hollywood blockbusters whether watched in theaters, at video clubs, on pirated videos, or downloaded onto home computers (Fomina in Anon. 2007).

As early as 1994 "U.S. films would account for 73 percent of screening time in [Russian] theaters" (Karakhan, quoted in Condee 2009, 59). And while total box-office receipts grew from a mere $6 million in 1997 (Holson and Myers 2006) to a phenomenal $830 million in 2008 (Dondurei 2009), throughout this period tickets to Russian films have only accounted for a maximum 25 to 27 percent of these totals (Dondurei 2009). While these figures show an admirable 200 percent increase in tickets sold for Russian films in the course of a decade, they simultaneously reveal that Hollywood's growth far outpaced domestic products: with 75–80 percent of sales going to Hollywood films, this data reveals an approximate 600 percent increase in sales for Hollywood films screened in Russia during this time period. Always keen to find the best markets, Hollywood paid attention to Russia's rising incomes, which by the end of the first decade of the 2000s, helped make the country the fifth largest film market in the world (Gosling 2011).

Given the dominance of Hollywood in the Russian market, it is perhaps unsurprising that its influence extends beyond the exportation of hits. Throughout the late 1990s and early 2000s, Hollywood-based media holding companies swept in and began building American-style multiplex theaters, many of them in retail malls (Maternovsky 2003). Unlike the French, who famously negotiated the 1993 General Agreement on Tariffs and Trade (GATT) to limit Hollywood imports and thus minimize "the perceived Americanization of French film culture implied by the multiplex model" (Hayes 2005), the Russian film industry was unable to curtail – and, it would seem, was not unanimously interested in curtailing – the onslaught of Hollywood.[3] Hollywood's largest movie producers, such as Paramount, Sony, 20th Century Fox, Universal Pictures and Walt Disney, all have teamed up with local partners for distribution of their films and co-production of local films.[4] As a result, Hollywood is both contemporary Russian cinema's greatest rival and most-admired model. This bifurcated attitude has produced a contradictory cultural landscape, exemplified by three tensions. First, among Russian directors and film critics there are those who celebrate Russian blockbuster cinema for its ability to bring audiences back to the theaters for Russian films, and there are those who loathe this appropriation of commercial, mass-market Hollywood-style production. Second, periodic efforts made by the government to curtail Hollywood's domination have spurred government-led calls for patriotic film projects and quotas on Hollywood imports, which strike a nationalistic tenor. At the same time, Russia's leading blockbuster directors – most notably, Timur Bekmambetov and Fedor Bondarchuk – make such nationalistic films and partner with Hollywood production companies in an effort to provide their films with more technological savvy and a greater marketing reach. And third, while it has become almost commonplace to characterize popular post-Soviet Russian film of the 2000s as anti-American, pro-Russian, and increasingly xenophobic and patriotic, the proven success of Hollywood films in the Russian market has led to an opposite reaction, one that has gone by-and-large overlooked in scholarship: rather than articulate a hostile stance, mass-market Russian blockbusters – for example the *Lovey-Dovey* [*Liubov'-morkov'*] trilogy produced by Real Dakota Films – increasingly showcase an idealized self-image derived not from Russian culture, but from the American myths of upper-middle class suburban bliss, the traditional nuclear family, and fairytale-like romances ingrained by Hollywood movies. Pushing American films out of the Russian market – or displacing their dominant presence

– is therefore unlikely. Hollywood is increasingly interwoven into Russian film production and distribution, and one can now imbibe Hollywood's dominant myths by watching Russian blockbusters.

Keeping these three conflicts in mind, this chapter considers the Russian blockbuster as a historically determined mode of film production. As a phenomenon that characterizes not simply individual films, but, more precisely, modes of filmmaking, distribution and marketing, film consumption, film style, and even narrative myths, the Russian blockbuster is most logically presented in the context of Hollywood's post-Soviet invasion.

Goodbye America, Hello Hollywood: The Rise of the Russian Blockbuster in the Late 1990s

> Goodbye America
> Where I've never been.
> Goodbye forever.
> Grab the banjo
> And play me farewell.
>
> Your torn jeans
> Have become too small.
> We were taught for so long
> To love your forbidden fruit.
>
> Goodbye America
> Where I will never be,
> Will I hear the song
> That I'll remember forever.
> (Nautilus Pompilius "Goodbye America" 1997)

At least among some, the allure of America's "forbidden fruit," as the rock band Nautilus Pompilius put it in their hit, "Goodbye America," had palpably waned by the mid to late 1990s. Those watching movies had little choice but to consume American culture: it was precisely at this same time that the post-Soviet Russian film industry bottomed out and Hollywood held its greatest disproportionate sway over the Russian cine-market. It is also at this moment that the first post-Soviet films that might be conceived of as blockbusters – Aleksei Balabanov's *Brother* [*Brat*, 1997], its sequel, *Brother 2* [*Brat 2*, 2000], and Nikita Mikhalkov's *The Barber of Siberia* [*Sibirskii tsiriul'nik*, 1999] – hit the scene (Beumers 2003; Larsen 2003; Rampton 2008; Condee 2009; Norris 2012).

In ways both fortuitous and prescient, these films exemplify two key features of early Russian blockbusters. First, they reveal a certain non-intuitive quantitative fact: namely, films of the late 1990s need not have been phenomenal box office hits to qualify as blockbusters. And second, while Hollywood techniques influenced both films, the early Russian blockbuster's narratives articulate a kind of hostility toward America in order to reject its hegemonic influence on Russian culture. This rebuff often comes across as an articulation of xenophobic patriotism needed to protect the sanctity of Russia, its history, and its people.

For the simple reason that blockbusters tend to be defined in terms of superlatives – the biggest, the most expensive, the most profitable – and because the conversion of the post-Soviet economy into a market economy caused rapid inflation and a devalued ruble, it is misleading to rely solely on box office receipts when defining the Russian blockbuster. Inflation during the mid-1990s led ticket prices to double from an average of 50 cents per ticket in 1994 to $1 in 1996, which, in turn, drove further down already dismal film attendance: a pathetic average of 26.9 spectators per film screening in 1994 fell in 1996 to 15.8 spectators per screening (Venzher quoted in Beumers 1999, 884). Dilapidated cinemas paired with dilapidated incomes kept seats nearly empty. For these reasons, Russian producers at the time had no delusions about the difficulty of getting audiences into cinemas. It is, therefore, necessary to reframe how we confer blockbuster status during this period.

Balabanov's *Brother* films and Mikhalkov's *The Barber of Siberia* would hardly seem to fulfill the most basic definition of the blockbuster: films with substantial production and marketing budgets meant to generate huge revenues. For example, though deemed Russia's "first genuine Russian blockbuster" (Beumers 2007, 233) and identified as a box-office hit (Lawton 2004, 128; Condee 2009, 220), box office figures are not available for *Brother*. *Brother*, made on a modest budget of $250,000,

Figure 9.1 Danila Bagrov (Sergei Bodrov Jr) in Aleksei Balabanov's *Brother*, 1997.

Figure 9.2 Tsar Aleksandr III (Nikita Mikhalkov) in Mikhalkov's *The Barber of Siberia*, 1999.

barely had a box-office presence, but sold approximately "400,000 *legal* video copies in the first five months of its release" (Condee 2009, 220, emphasis in the original). Each video cassette sale returned one dollar to the producers' pockets (Anon. 2005). Thus, video sales, and not box office sales reveal a substantial audience. *Brother 2* was made for a modest $1.5 million, of which only $1.08 million was recouped in domestic ticket sales (Beumers 2007, 233). Nonetheless, its ability to gather over a million dollars in ticket sales during this period was unprecedented, leading Yana Hashamova to claim that it "is one of the early Russian box office successes, which [though] nothing compared to Western returns, [...] was a history making sum for the post-Soviet film industry" (Hashamova 2007, 297).

On the other end of the spectrum is Mikhalkov's *The Barber of Siberia*. With a price tag totaling a staggering $45 million, it was, at the time of its production, Russia's most expensive film ever.[5] It also lost more money than any Russian film in recent memory. The Russian government, which supplied $10 million in funding, and Mikhalkov's French financial co-backers likely did not expect to turn a profit on their investments, but no doubt they hoped for better than the $2.6 million it earned at the box office or its publically embarrassing reception at the 1999 Cannes Film Festival (Bradshaw 1999). However, the film earned a phenomenal amount given the state of the industry at the time of its release: it ranked "[n]umber one at the Russian box office in 1999–2000, and number two in video sales for 2000" (Larsen 2003, 498). Furthermore, "according to one recent report, [it is] the only Russian film to place (eighth) in the all-time top 20 films at the Russian box-office" (Larsen 2003, 498). It was inconceivable that the film would make back its $45 million costs, and, presumably, given a budget so grossly out-of-proportion with its market, no investor could have thought that it would. The goal of this grandiose project was, therefore, not to make millions of rubles, but to sell millions of tickets and reach millions of viewers in order to convey a particular sentiment, which it did.

The Russian blockbuster was born to conjure feelings of national pride and patriotism, or as Stephen Norris provocatively puts it, "to give birth to a new nation" (Norris 2012, 31). Audiences of Mikhalkov's *The Barber of Siberia* were enraptured by the exuberant displays of Russian nineteenth-century grandeur set during the reign of Tsar Aleksandr III. Within the film, Mikhalkov, a director who likes to star in his own films, plays the imperial role infusing it with un-ironic proud superiority, grandeur, and strength in such a way as to "fuse the patriarchal tsar's [supposed] greatness with his love for his son, family, and nation" (Hashamova 2007, 67). The lavish sets and costumes serve to link Russia with aristocratic cultural superiority and buttress the film's plot, which, although it is as convoluted as it is contrived, pits Russian soulfulness against American opportunism. Most prosaically, the film follows an American woman, Jane Callahan (played by British actress Julia Ormond), who masquerades as the daughter of a whacky American inventor, McCracken (played by the British actor Richard Harris), who seeks Russian financing for this latest contraption – a timber cutting machine with the capability of clear cutting Siberian forests and thus turning enormous profits. Jane's role is to seduce the necessary aristocrats of the Russian court into opening their wallets. Before she has begun her mission, while still on the train into Moscow, Jane meets Andrei Tolstoy (Oleg Men'shikov); the combination of his famous last name and their meeting on the train announces as though through a megaphone broadcasting the obvious that their imminent romance is fated for disaster, and that like Lev Tolstoy's *Anna Karenina*, that this disaster will be the fault of the woman's weak morals and overly sexualized nature. Indeed, when the passion-filled and desperately-in-love Tolstoy later spies her flirtatiously reeling in a financial suitor, he leaps to fight this man, his superior. Judged as having attempted murder, Tolstoy is sent off to his fate: a Siberian prison. By assigning the roles of opportunistic businessman-inventor and debauched seductress to Americans, Mikhalkov establishes a binary division between American immortality and Russian superiority afforded by their emotional depth and romantic love of country. Mikhalkov employs Ormond's and Harris's roles as schemers to advance the stereotype of Americans as two-faced hypocrites, whose superficial friendliness and romantic gestures are nothing more than typical tactics of greedy capitalists. Ironically, in an extra-diegetic role reversal, Mikhalkov had hoped to get in the wallets of some of those greedy capitalists himself. The prominent use of English-language dialogue in the film, most assume, was meant to make the film appealing on the American market. Needless to say, with its notoriously bad reviews, the film did not garner any international market presence.

Although the film's narratives and styles couldn't be more different, Balabanov also got domestic audiences to cheer on displays of Russian superiority. Danila (Sergei Bodrov Jr), the vigilante warrior of *Brother* and *Brother 2*, squashed his enemies in the mafia-ridden world of St Petersburg, Moscow, and even in the mythical home of gangsters, Chicago. Mikhalkov shows the danger of letting American motives sway Russian power, while Balabanov goes a step further: he not only highlights the danger, but his hero, Danila, acts from a motivation to destroy such villainous powers, whether in Russia or abroad, that wreak havoc against the common Russian people. The combination of action, indiscriminate violence, and nationalism proved successful: Balabanov's films received acclaim in the box offices, at international film competitions, and in scholarly journals.

As in *Barber of Siberia*, this success was accomplished – at least in part – via a rejection of displays of American dishonor. For example, in Chicago Danila saves a Russian prostitute from a violent and exploitative pimp (is there any other kind?), and at the film's end, takes the woman home to Russia. As *Brother 2* concludes, Danila with his no-longer-in-distress damsel, sit in the first-class section of an Aeroflot plane departing from Chicago and heading home, to Moscow. The Nautilus Pompilius song "Goodbye America," quoted at the beginning of this section, plays as Danila stares out the window where he has just waged his final battle against an American businessman – the suggestively-named Mennis (i.e., menace) – whom he blames for a friend's murder.

In its narrative, *Brother 2* posits Russian nationalism in opposition to American capitalism – symbolized most explicitly by the defeat of Mennis, the embodiment of American capitalist greed, by Danila, the embodiment of Russian patriotism and good will. The frequently-quoted final dialogue between the two opponents encapsulates the film's ideological message. Upon entering Mennis's office, Danila shoots a guy who had been playing chess with Mennis and takes that man's seat. Lying his gun on the table and happily pouring two shots from a bottle of Stolichnaya, Danila asks Mennis: "Tell me, American, what is power? Is it really money? [...] I think power comes from being right. Whoever is right is more powerful. You deceived someone, and made a lot of money, but so what? Have you become more powerful? No, you have not. Because you're not in the right."

Susan Larsen presents a superb argument that links Mikhalkov's and Balabanov's films' success to their revitalization of proud and patriotic Russian characters on screen.

> [M]uch of the pathos of these films derives from a common anxiety about what it means to be Russian at the end of the twentieth century, and most of the films articulate that anxiety in terms of threats to masculine "honor" and "dignity" (Mikhalkov) or national "might" and "right" (Balabanov). The conflation of national identity with masculine authority is a key component of these films' appeal to Russian viewers in a decade in which it often seemed as if Russian filmmakers had lost both their market share and their claim to the nation's imagination. (Larsen 2003, 493)

On the one hand, it is hardly surprising that post-Soviet popular film projected, at times, an anti-American stance. The antagonistic reaction responds to the rise of American consumerist culture and an enormous influx of Hollywood films into

Russian cinemas beginning in the mid-1990s. However, on the other hand, the film's producers and filmmakers appear to be quite comfortable with capitalist economies. Sergei Sel'ianov, to take one important example, takes advantage of the fiscal benefits provided by post-Soviet Russia's new capitalist economy: in addition to producing the blockbuster films, *Brother* and *Brother 2*, he has overseen the production of various money making tie-ins to the films. Continuing with the focus on the film's soundtrack begun above, Sel'ianov produced a promotional concert on October 9, 2000 featuring many of the bands included on the soundtrack. This was a first for the post-Soviet Russian cinema industry, and, as such, is an important indicator of how Russia's earliest blockbusters followed production-level strategies learned from Hollywood blockbuster cinema. There is no question that the concert and resulting soundtrack were conceived on a western model; the *Brother 2* website states that:

> The idea for this [the concert] sprung from the company Real Records immediately following the release of the soundtrack to Aleksei Balabanov's *Brother 2*. This event, in principle, is typical for Western record companies; among domestic [i.e., Russian] entertainment business practices, it is unique. First of all, for the first time, a soundtrack was released simultaneously with the film – as is done in the West.[6]

It has become almost commonplace to characterize popular post-Soviet Russian film as having a propensity for being anti-American, pro-Russian, and increasingly xenophobic and patriotic. Andryi Zayarnyuk, writing on Balabanov's *Brother 2*, claims that the film's success lies in its novel portrayal of Russian identity and the "realization that there are some essential and insurmountable differences between Russia and the West, and between Russian and Western identities" (2003, 270–271). Yana Hashamova locates "Russia's imagination of the West as it developed at the turn of the millennium" in cinematic examples (Hashamova 2007, 112). She argues that, while there are few "openly aggressive anti-western, and especially anti-American, films," those that do exist "have become cult films and have reached large audiences" (Hashamova 2007, 112) and locates their popularity as occurring within a new, broad nation-building project that seeks to "glorify Russia's uniqueness in history, art, and religion" (Hashamova 2007, 113).

The over-determination of Hollywood in the international arena has long been acknowledged. A 1937 British editorial "denounced the transformation of British film-goers into beings who 'talk America, think America, and dream America'" (quoted in Maltby 1998, 104). And while attempts to preserve national cinemas have persisted throughout the twentieth century, as long ago as 1987 Thomas Elsaesser cautioned of such attempts' futility, declaring that every other nation's film culture was implicitly Hollywood-like. (Elsaesser 1987, 166). Equal to the ubiquity of Hollywood's hegemonic presence are antagonistic responses to it. Certainly, this reaction fits into what Andrew Higson calls an inevitable "strategy of cultural [...] resistance, a means of asserting national autonomy in the face of [...] Hollywood's international domination" (Higson 1989, 37). At the same time, though, these "narratives of national authority," exist awkwardly alongside production tactics that emulate the adversary's models. Russia's turn toward the blockbuster captures these tensions perfectly.

Lovey Dovey: Importing the American Dream

The Russian production company composed of Renat Davlet'iarov, Aleksandr Kotelevskii, and Ermek Amanshaev goes by the name Real Dakota. Dakota is nothing more than an amalgam of the first syllable of each of the producers' last names, but the coincidental allusion to a Native American tribe is fortuitous. Their most successful films are modeled on Hollywood genres and Hollywood myths, and, despite being domestic Russian products, they appear to be more natively American.

None of the Dakota films employ spectacular special effects, epic narratives, or necessitated a tremendous production budget. Moreover, when compared to the top-grossing films in post-Soviet cinema history – for example, Timur Bekmambetov's *Night Watch* [*Nochnoi dozor*, 2004], *Day Watch* [*Dnevnoi dozor*, 2006], or *The Irony of Fate. A Continuation* [*Ironiia sud'by: Prodolzhenie*, 2007] – Real Dakota's films' profits are modest. However, Bekmambetov's hits are the exception; the rule, unfortunately, is that the vast majority Russian films do not turn a profit. Of the approximately 100 films made annually between 2000 and 2010, only 70 (on average) are released each year, and "very few of them make enough to cover production costs, let alone any profit" (Vorotnikov 2010). Therefore, that the Dakota films succeeded in making profits two to six times greater than their production budgets, reveals that in their own market, Real Dakota knows how to make epic hits.[7] Commenting on the decision to partner with Real Dakota, Fox International Production's director of development said, *Lovey-Dovey* "is one of the best testaments to the commercial success of Russia's film industry" (quoted in Kay 2010). Indeed, in terms of making a substantial return on investment, Real Dakota enjoys blockbuster-level success.

The first of the *Lovey-Dovey* trilogy, released in 2007, was made on a budget of $3 million and earned approximately $11.5 million. *Lovey-Dovey 2*, also made on a modest $3 million budget, surpassed all expectations pulling in a hefty $17.8 million in ticket sales. This tremendous return on investment got the attention of Twentieth-Century Fox, who joined Real Dakota to produce *Lovey-Dovey 3*. Though decreasing in profitability in part because of the 2008 economic crisis, *Lovey-Dovey 3* more than doubled its $4 million budget (it grossed $8.5 million), and, *Irony of Love* listed among Russia's six most profitable films for the period from December 2009 through August 2010 (Anon. 2010).[8]

Figure 9.3 Gosha Kutsenko and Kristina Orbakaite in *Lovey-Dovey*, 2007.

So, given a market where Russian films typically lose money, what is Real Dakota's recipe for success? In short, they employ a risk-adverse strategy by adopting tried-and-tested narratives that sell tickets. Real Dakota's body swap franchise *Lovey-Dovey* as well as its romantic comedy, *Irony of Love* [*Ironiia liubvi*, 2010] rely on narrative models familiar in Hollywood and familiar to young Russian audiences who have grown up watching Hollywood hits. The *Lovey-Dovey* movies feature idealized images of a traditional nuclear family, and *Irony of Love* advances the romantic variant of America's myth of easy upward class mobility – namely, that love can triumph over economic inequity. The awkward result are Russian films that project American cultural mythologies onto the screen which, as the eminent Russian film critic Nina Tsyrkun (2012) metaphorically puts it, is like "an attempt to cross an American donkey with a [Russian] horse."

Both the *Lovey-Dovey* trilogy and *Irony of Love* provide a snapshot of contemporary upper middle-class life in Russia. Gosha Kutsenko stars in both: in *Irony of Love* he has a limited cameo appearance as a meditative police chief who leverages his authority to help romantic ploys and in *Lovey-Dovey* he plays Andrei, a successful divorce attorney, opposite Kristina Orbakaite as his wife Marina, a successful art dealer and gallery director. These actors bring upper-class swagger and privilege with them to their roles. Orbakaite, the highly-recognizable daughter of Russian pop legend and songstress, Alla Pugacheva, made a name for herself as a child, when she starred in Rolan Bykov's critically acclaimed film *Scarecrow* [*Chuchelo*, 1984], and in her adult life has cultivated a successful music career releasing eight albums and winning a most-selling Russian artist award at the 2000 World Music Awards. Gosha Kutsenko is more of a traditional post-Soviet movie star whose filmography also includes Egor Konchalovskii's *Antikiller* hits (2002 and 2003) as well as director Timur Bekmambetov's wildly popular *Night Watch* and *Day Watch* blockbusters. Thus, their familiarity as pop culture icons – one as a star in the world of pop rock, the other a familiar face on the popular screen – functions to offer audiences a type of brand recognition.

In the first of the popular *Lovey-Dovey* movies, the couple is growing apart after seven years of marriage. They decide to meet with a successful psychiatrist for one last shot at making it work. When they wake up the following morning, the unexpected has happened: they have switched bodies. The two subsequent movies' narratives similarly employ the slapstick potential that accompanies a bewildering body swap. In the second film, the parents end up in their children's bodies and vice versa; in the third, Andrei and Marina literally become their parents, who, of course, are forced to walk a mile, so to speak, in their children's shoes. Despite employing different directors for each of the three films (Aleksandr Strizhenov, Maksim Pezhemskii, and Sergei Ginzburg, respectively), all three films look the same: they have the same slick production values, same upper-class settings (e.g., law offices, private art galleries, spas, upscale restaurants), the characters are well-dressed, well-quaffed, and live in an improbable world of like-wise affluent Russians. Perhaps unsurprisingly, these characters occupy settings that evoke a level of wealth far above the vast majority of Russians' annual income. For example, in the first of the three films, the central family lives in a large new-construction home surrounded by a picket fence that encloses a yard with a swing set and a disproportionate number of scenes in a glimmering new shopping mall.

Body swap comedies have long been popular in Hollywood.[9] As family comedies, the *Lovey-Dovey* movies – and in particular the second and third of the series – are most closely modeled on the parent/child body swap version of the genre and strike much more than just a family resemblance to *Freaky Friday* (Mark Waters 2003), starring Jamie Lee Curtis and Lindsay Lohan. Writing on Hollywood family comedies, Andrew Horton (2008, 46) notes that the typical representation of the nuclear family includes "some grouping of parents (or a parent) and children (or a child) and 'other relatives,' be they grandparents, uncles, aunts, or cousins, and of course, friends of the family and in-laws." He goes on to note that "the American family comedy is what we can call a 'cross-generational' form of comedy, for it involves characters of different ages and generation who often demonstrate conflicting values and attitudes whose contention with one another over some issue of value and attitude, indeed, is the motor element of the ongoing joke that the film recounts." Indeed, *Lovey-Dovey* mimics this cross-generational strategy. Unlike any number of great Soviet films that employ generational conflict to comment on shifting cultural values, these simple entertaining movies prefer a generic (i.e., not historically determined) battle between parents and children.[10]

Lovey-Dovey neither assimilates nor retrofits Hollywood's story-telling conventions to accommodate a Russian setting; it replicates the body-swap film and, in so doing, essentially provides a sophisticated version of a dubbed film. Such slapstick behaviors as an expectant father in the delivery room, who goes from filming to fainting, to a chaos-ridden house where busy parents trip over one another and the children, and from the initial misunderstanding between the two parties who will eventually teleport into one another, to the rhythmically-timed sequence of events that signal that the swap has occurred are stereotypical of American comedies.

The production group's *Irony of Love* is a similarly rudimentary genre film; it is a romantic comedy based on the legendary story of beauty and the geek at its most derivative and banal. In this installment, Kazakh actress and model Asel' Sagatova plays a version of herself. In the film she is also named Asel', and likely doesn't have to do much acting to portray a young woman who has it all – beauty, fantastic clothes, access to Moscow's most exclusive restaurants and clubs, a car, and a millionaire fiancé. The crux of the film's narrative is Asel''s desire for one more thing: to be cast as the hostess of a television talk show. Her friend offers her a chance at the job, but with a catch: she has to make the next man to walk through the door of the café where they're sitting fall in love with her. That man happens to be the dorky Ivan (Aleksei Chadov). The film proceeds as one expects: Asel' is determined, Ivan confused; Asel' brings Ivan into her gilded world, Ivan knocks stuff over. The basic plot – a beautiful woman ensnares a man with an ulterior motive and ends up falling in love – is taken from any number of Hollywood movies, from *How to Marry a Millionaire* (Jean Negulesco 1953) to *How to Lose A Guy in 10 Days* (Donald Petrie 2003) and individual scenes are poached from Hollywood films of the same ilk: for example, the fantastically raunchy scene of the tiny dog attacking Ben Stiller in the Farrelly Brothers' 1998 classic *There's Something About Mary* appears in *Irony of Love*, but is turned into a lackluster battle between Ivan and Asel''s parrot.

The irony referred to in the title is that love trumps money, more romantically expressed as love conquers all. Hollywood has told this story in melodramas – for example, *All that Heaven Allows* (Douglas Sirk 1955), *Titanic* (James Cameron 1997), *The Notebook* (Nick Cassavetes 2004) as well as in countless comedies, such as *My Fair Lady* (George Cukor 1964), *Pretty Woman* (Garry Marshall 1990), and *Maid in Manhattan* (Wayne Wang 2002) – to name just a few. In his book *The American Dream and Contemporary Hollywood Cinema* (2007), John Emmett Winn writes that in such movies "members of the cross-class relationship benefit [and] become a symbolic microcosm of the myth of a classless America" (Winn 2013, 13). This adopted narrative mythology fits together oddly with the film's emphasis on flagrant displays of wealth (e.g., a Lamborghini Murciélago, Asel''s Audi A5, bottles of Dom Perignon) used to characterize contemporary Moscow.

Tsyrkun (2012) explains that "because these nations have [...] different mythological roots, it is impossible to talk about Americans and Russians being similar. They are absolutely dissimilar, they have polar opposite mentalities, [and] completely different histories." It is this inherent dissimilarity between cultures in general, and between cinema cultures specifically, that makes these films feel more American than Russian. With no intention of arguing for distinct national cinemas in this global age of transnational influence, it is nonetheless undeniable that these Russian calques of the Hollywood blockbuster project modern American mythologies that normalize, even moralize material culture to Russia's remaining audiences.

From Blockbusters to *Blokbusters*: Russifying Content

Certain opponents of Russian cinema's Hollywoodization take offense at the commercial nature of the post-Soviet industry, which seeks profit through star-studded casts, marketing campaigns, and film-franchises. For this group, such a commercial focus demeans the artistic value of cinema. Consider the following rant from the young film scholar Vasilii Stepanov. In the ominously titled article "Our Crisis, We as the Crisis, the Crisis in Us," published in the highly esteemed Russian film journal *Seans*, Stepanov writes the following of today's industry: "This is what you call 'Russian Hollywood.' A product." He continues to decry the state of Russian cinema, charging that, "It's stagnation when 'Best Film' is a measurement of box office success. [...] It's stagnation when there's a lack of theaters showing so-called art house [films]. [...] It's stagnation when we're addicted to money" (Stepanov 2009).

Other critics have lamented the death of the director. In 2005 film critic Viktor Matizen reported that four of the top ten grossing films from the first half of that year were Russian films: in first place was *Turkish Gambit* [*Turetskii gambit*, dir. Dzhanik Faiziev, $18.5 million], *Shadow Boxing* [*Boi s ten'iu*, dir. Aleksei Sidorov, $7.4 million] took fourth place, *State Councilor* [*Statskii sovetnik*, dir. Filipp Iankovskii, $7.4 million] took fifth, and in tenth place was *Dead Man's Bluff* [*Zhmurki*, dir. Aleksei Balabanov, $4.1 million]. This would seem to be good news, signaling the resurgence of domestic production over Hollywood imports. Matizen, however, interpreted this news as indicating the "end of the era of the director," describing the first three of the four films listed above as "characteristically producer projects," which is to say what used to be an art is now just a commodity. If in 2005 Matizen announced the death of a director's cinema, seven years later the filmmaker Nikolai Khomeriki would seem to be stuck in mourning. Speaking on a roundtable comprised of Russian film directors and dedicated to the topic of commercial cinema, Khomeriki commented: "[n]owadays there is a problem with the stories, but this problem is not the fault of the scenarists, they write what they are told to write; it is the fault of the producers, who order and insist on specific plots that, seem to them, to be the right plots. [...] In short, I have one main complaint in regard to popular cinema – it is cinema made by producers, and not directors" (Khomeriki 2012).

While there may be some truths to these criticisms, a discussion of the contemporary Russian blockbuster would be incomplete without mention of two directors, who, in particular, have successfully navigated the new commercial industry, adapted the form, and Russified its content: Timur Bekmambetov and Fedor Bondarchuk. Bekmambetov and Bondarchuk competently assert their unique and distinct directorial styles, and though not entirely alone in this category, they, more so than others, exemplify the post-Soviet blockbuster director. Each began his career in other commercial visual media – Bekmambetov spent 15 years directing ad campaigns, including "the most celebrated financial advertisement of the pre-default 1990s" for *Bank Imperial* (MacFadyen 2004), while Bondarchuk, who earned a film directing degree in 1991 when the industry was in near total collapse, employed his skills shooting music videos. Each is firmly established in the contemporary Russian cinema industry – both Bekmambetov and Bondarchuk run production companies, Bazelevs and Glavkino respectively – and, at the same time, both unabashedly partner and promote their films with US-based production companies. Hollywood's Fox Searchlight production company, for example, released Bekmambetov's *Night Watch* (2005) in the West, while Sony Pictures released Bondarchuk's *Stalingrad* (2013).

Bekmambetov's breakthrough blockbuster was *Night Watch*, a movie based on Sergei Luk'ianenko's best-selling fantasy novel. The story of an eternal struggle between the forces of Light and the forces of Dark, and the tenuous truce that keeps each side in their place, *Night Watch* fused cutting-edge special effects and a "Russian" plot set against the backdrop of the new Moscow. As David MacFadyen aptly described it, Bekmambetov's plot mixed *Star Wars*, *The Matrix*, Rembrandt's painting *Abraham and Isaac*, and conceptions of good and evil straight out of Dostoevsky or Bulgakov (MacFadyen 2004). The film became the first Russian blockbuster to beat Hollywood at the domestic box office, prompting Nikita Mikhalkov to declare that it was "our answer to Tarantino." Konstantin Ernst, the film's producer, went even further when he declared at the film's premiere that "this is our cinema, and whoever isn't with us is against us."

In response to the phenomenally successful release of *Night Watch* (made on a budget of $4.2 million, the film grossed $34 million), Daniil Dondurei makes comments

Figure 9.4 The magician Dar'ia Schulz (Rimma Markova) and Anton (Konstantin Khabenskii) in Bekmambetov's *Night Watch*, 2004.

infused with the competitive (perhaps even militaristic) spirit of rivalry. He begins, "[o]nly a year and a half ago there were no films in Russia that could be called blockbusters – films which compete in our market with Hollywood products. With the arrival of *Night Watch* a new era has begun. [...] The active, mighty, even aggressive blow by one film onto all of the country's screen for Russia sounded like an echo of an all-union Soviet premier" (Dondurei at "Kruglyi stol" 2005). *Night Watch*'s director, Bekmambetov, admits that he anticipated the film's phenomenal success because "we know how to use American film language with a Russian accent to tell a Russian story" (Salisbury 2005). In his book *Blockbuster History in the New Russia*, Stephen Norris convincingly demonstrates that, somewhat ironically, the dominant tactic employed has been to adapt "Hollywood [blockbuster] technique to Russian themes" (Norris 2012, 3).

Bekmambetov's sequel ensured that *Night Watch* was no fluke and only furthered the "Watch phenomenon." Made on a budget of $4.2m, *Day Watch* would gross $38m, becoming the highest-grossing Russian film in history up to that point. Bekmambetov would follow up this success by making a sequel to one of the most popular Soviet films of all time, El'dar Riazanov's New Year's classic *Irony of Fate* [*Ironiia sud'by*, 1976]. Featuring the same cast, who now have children, and roughly the same plot as the original, Bekmambetov's *Irony of Fate: The Continuation* earned $49m. Iurii Bogomolov has suggested that the film perfectly captured what he called a two-part Ernst/Bekmambetov "Stakhanovite plan" to get Russians back to the movies and to propagate a new form of patriotic culture centered on consuming Russian products (Bogomolov 2008). Bekmambetov's success in adapting Hollywood-like special effects to audience-friendly fare caught the attention of American studios: he would go on to direct *Wanted* (2008, Russian release as *Osobo opasno*), starring Angelina Jolie and James McAvoy, and *Abraham Lincoln, Vampire Killer* (2012). Ernst, for his part, produced a host of blockbusters over the course of the 2000s and 2010s, and stated that their success was a direct result of studying Hollywood productions: "We all have to be eternally grateful to Hollywood [which] forced our lazy, fat Russian moviemakers to make films, to edit them, to do special effects, to talk in a language that teenagers understand. [...] We are grateful, but now we will make our cinema ourselves" (Ernst 2006).

Bondarchuk has been just as successful at adapting Hollywood techniques to Russian themes. The son of the famous director, Sergei Bondarchuk, who won an Oscar for his epic version of *War and Peace* [*Voina i mir*, 1965–1967], Fedor spent the better part of the 1990s making music videos with Stepan Mikhalkov, Nikita Mikhalkov's son. In 2005, he directed *Ninth Company* [*Deviataia rota*], a film set in the last year of the Soviet-Afghan War. The story traces the history of the Ninth Company of the 345th Guards Airborne Regiment, which took part in one of the last Soviet offensives of the war. Bondarchuk adapts it by fusing it with tropes from American Vietnam movies, most notably Stanley Kubrick's *Full Metal Jacket* (1987) and Oliver Stone's *Platoon* (1986). Bondarchuk's cast experience a sadistic training regime only to arrive in a war that was already lost. While critics and audiences

Figure 9.5 *Inhabited Island* by Fedor Bondarchuk, 2009.

members all noted the resemblance between *Ninth Company* and American Vietnam movies, the film earned strong praise and cleaned up at the box office, earning $25.6m, temporarily becoming the highest-grossing Russian film of all time (Bekmambetov's *Day Watch* and then *Irony of Fate: Continuation* would both surpass it).

Bondarchuk followed up his initial success by adapting the Strugatskii brothers' 1969 science fiction novel, *Inhabited Island* [*Obitaemyi ostrov*, 2009] in two parts. A dystopian tale set on a Gulag-like planet, *Inhabited Island* and *Inhabited Island 2* cost $36m to make and only earned $30m back. As a follow-up, Bondarchuk filmed the first-ever Russian movie using 3D IMAX, the blockbuster *Stalingrad* (2013). Again the budget was enormous by Russian standards – $30m – but this time Bondarchuk's film dominated the box office. *Stalingrad* earned over $68m, wresting the title of highest-grossing Russian film away from Bekmambetov. The movie, set amidst the rubble of Stalingrad in 1942 and told through the eyes of a group of five Soviet soldiers and the 19-year old woman they rescue, divided critics. Most reviews, however, praised the "look" of Stalingrad recreated in 3D and noted that Bondarchuk's special effects were just as good as those associated with Hollywood blockbusters. Valerii Kichin effectively summarized Bondarchuk's epic and other recent blockbusters when he concluded his review of the film: "it is a creation of a new epoch and for a new generation" (Kichin 2013).

Conclusion

The cover story of *Time Out Moscow* (March 3, 2014) was entitled "America in Moscow: Why Do We Love All Things American?" In its pages, the magazine's writers argued that Russia had "surrendered to America" because American restaurants, American music, American fashion, and American artistic trends dominate the Russian capital's various scenes. Above all, however, the magazine's feature article declared that Russians flock to Hollywood blockbusters and to the stories told in them.

In many ways, the *Time Out* feature perfectly captures how Russian cinema has learned to stop worrying about Hollywood and instead embraced its techniques. The mid-1990s crisis, when Russian moviemakers struggled to make anything at all, is long gone. Hollywood films may continue to do well at the Russian box office, but a homegrown form of the *blokbaster* has successfully married Hollywood-like effects, stories, star-driven movies, marketing campaigns, commercial tie-ins, and technologies to "Russian" themes. Russian consumers may love American things, but they have also demonstrated their love for Russian blockbusters.

Notes

1 For a detailed explanation for the events leading up to and reasons for the post-Soviet film industry's collapse, see Condee (2009, 49–84).
2 Sergei Bodrov's *Prisoner of the Caucasus* [*Kavkazskii plennik*], stands out as a notable exception.
3 The Russian film industry has periodically entertained the idea of increasing taxes on Hollywood films or forcing theater exhibitors to screen a minimum quota of 20 percent of Russian films in order to support the domestic industry (Holdsworth 2013). Such measures, though, have not been implemented.
4 "In 2008, Paramount Pictures International (PPI) signed a distribution and co-production agreement with Moscow-based Central Partnership, one of Russia's largest film distribution and production companies. Sony Pictures Entertainment also has a strong presence in Russia. In 2006, the US company and the Moscow-based Patton Media Group established a joint venture called Monumental Pictures, which produces and distributes Russian-language films in Russia and the CIS. Sony is involved in Monumental through the company's motion picture production and distribution unit, Columbia Pictures. Also in 2006, an official subsidiary of the Walt Disney Company, Disney Company CIS, was established. Its director general, Marina Zhigalov-Ozkan, says that after its first local production *The Book of Masters*, the company is poised to shoot two to three films in Russia per year going forward." (Vorotnikov 2010)
5 As with all superlatives and records, this accolade holds true only until it is beaten. Mikhalkov bested himself with his 2010 two-part sequel *Burnt by the Sun 2: Exodus* and *Citadel*, which cost a combined $55 million.
6 See the website http://brat2.film.ru/olimpisky.asp (accessed November 9, 2015)
7 In fact, *Lovey-Dovey 2* was one of only two Russian films released in 2009 to make a profit.
8 *Kinopoisk.ru* lists *Irony of Love*'s budget at $2 million budget and its earning at just over $4 million, http://www.kinopoisk.ru/film/276261/ (accessed January 23, 2015).
9 Examples of the body swap genre across the decades include Disney's original *Freaky Friday* film (Gary Nelson, 1976), *All of Me* (Carl Reiner, 1984) starring Steve Martin and Lily Tomlin, and *13 Going on 30* (Gary Winick, 2004).

10 Examples from Soviet cinema include those featuring intimate collectives of young characters such as Aleksei Sakharov's *Colleagues* [*Kollegi*, 1962], Aleksandr Zarkhi's *My Younger Brother* [*Moi mladshii brat*, 1962], Georgii Daneliia's *I Walk around Moscow* [*Ia shagaiu po Moskve*, 1963], Mikhail Kalik's *Goodbye, Boys!* [*Do svidaniia, mal'chiki*, 1964], and Marlen Khutsiev's *I am Twenty/Lenin's Guard* [*Mne dvadtsat' let/Zastava Il'icha* 1964/1988]. In these films, young men of the post-war generation all struggle with the stringent demands and heroic legacy of the older, war-era generation.

References

Anon. 2005. "Otets 'brata'" [The Bro's Father]. *Forbes* March 3, http://www.forbes.ru/node/18773 (accessed October 16, 2014).

Anon. 2007. "Pochemu rossiiskoe kino ne konvertiruetsia?" [Why is Russian Cinema not Convertible?]. *Iskusstvo kino* [Art of Cinema] 10, http://kinoart.ru/archive/2007/10/n10-article2 (accessed October 16, 2014).

Anon. 2010. "Dolia rossiiskogo kino v prokate padaet" [The Share of Russian Films in Distribution is Dropping]. *Sostav.ru*, August 12, www.sostav.ru/print/rus/2010/12.08/news/s5 (accessed October 16, 2014).

Bach, Steven. 1985. *Final Cut*. New York: New American Library.

Bates, William. 1978. "Hollywood in the Era of the 'Super-Grosser.'" *New York Times* December 24.

Beumers, Birgit. 1999. "Cinemarket, or the Russian Film Industry in 'Mission Impossible.'" *Europea-Asia Studies* 51.5: 871–896.

Beumers, Birgit. 2003. "Soviet and Russian Blockbusters: A Question of Genre?" *Slavic Review* 62: 441–454.

Beumers, Birgit. 2007. "Brat". In *24 Frames. The Cinema of Russia and the Former Soviet Union*, edited by B. Beumers, 233–241. London and New York: Wallflower Press.

Bogomolov, Iurii. 2008. "Ironiia sud'by Konstantina Ernsta" [Konstantin Ernst's Irony of Fate]. *Novaia gazeta* [New Gazette] January 28, http://www.novayagazeta.ru/arts/41769.html (accessed October 16, 2014).

Bordwell, David. 2006. *The Way Hollywood Tells It*. Berkeley: University of California Press.

Bradshaw, Peter. 1999. "Barber of Siberia." *The Guardian*, May 13, http://www.theguardian.com/film/News_Story/Critic_Review/Guardian/0,4267,49681,00.html (accessed October 16, 2014).

Buckland, Warren. 2006. *Directed by Steven Spielberg: Poetics of the Contemporary Hollywood Blockbuster*. New York: Continuum.

Condee, Nancy. 2009. *The Imperial Trace*. New York: Oxford University Press.

Dondurei, Daniil. 2009. "Sochi-2009. Kak my gotovili krizis v kino. Kruglyi stol prodiuserov" [Sochi 2009: How We Prepared the Crisis in Cinema. Producers' Round-Table]. *Iskusstvo kino* [Art of Cinema] 8, http://kinoart.ru/ru/archive/2009/08/n8-article16 (accessed October 16, 2014).

Elsaesser, Thomas. 1987. "Chronicle of a Death Retold: Hyper, Retro or Counter-Cinema." *Monthly Film Bulletin* 54: 164–167.

Elsaesser, Thomas. 2012. *The Persistence of Hollywood*. New York: Routledge.

Ernst, Konstantin. 2006. "Sobesednik: Konstantin Ernst" [Interlocutor: Konstantin Ernst]. *Seans* December 15, http://seance.ru/n/29-30/portret-konstantin-ernst/sobesednik-konstantin-ernst/ (accessed October 16, 2014).

Gosling, Tim. 2011. "Russia's Film Distribution Market Soars." *The Telegraph* February 24, http://www.telegraph.co.uk/sponsored/rbth/culture/8345866/Russias-film-distribution-market-soars.html (accessed October 16, 2014).

Graffy, Julian. 2001. *Bed and Sofa: KINOfiles Film Companion*. London: I. B. Tauris.

Graffy, Julian. 2010. *Chapaev: KINOfiles Film Companion*. London: I. B. Tauris.

Hashamova, Yana. 2007. *Pride and Panic: Russian Imagination of the West in Post-Soviet Film*. Bristol: Intellect.

Hayes, Graeme. 2005. "Regulating Multiplexes: The French State between Corporatism and Globalization." *French Politics, Culture and Society* 23: 14–33.

Higson, Andrew. 1989. "The Concept of National Cinema." *Screen* 30: 36–47.

Hoberman, J. 1985. "Ten Years That Shook the World." *American Film* 10: 34–59.

Holdsworth, Nick. 2013. "Russian Industry Debates Expected Box Office Quotas for Homegrown Films." *The Hollywood Reporter* June 4, http://www.hollywoodreporter.com/news/russian-industry-debates-expected-box-562463 (accessed October 16, 2014).

Holson, Laura and Steven Lee Myers. 2006. "The Russians are Filming! The Russians are Filming!" *The New York Times* July 16, http://www.nytimes.com/2006/07/16/business/yourmoney/16russia.html?pagewanted=all&_r=0 (accessed February 14, 2015).

Horton, Andrew. 2008. "Is It a Wonderful Life?: Families and Laughter in American Film Comedies." In *A Family Affair: Cinema Calls Home*, edited by Murray Pomerance, 45–62. London: Wallflower Press.

Kay, Jeremy. 2010. "Fox goes Lubby Dubby for Russian Comedy." *Screen Daily*. February 14, http://www.screendaily.com/news/production/fox-goes-lubby-dubby-for-russian-comedy/5010808.article (accessed October 16, 2014).

Keyser, Les. 1981. *Hollywood in the Seventies*. San Diego: A. S. Barnes.

Khomeriki, Nikolai. 2012. "Anketa IK. Rossiiskie rezhissery ob otechestvennom kommercheskom kino" [Questionnaire: Russian Directors about Domestic Commercial Cinema]. *Iskusstvo kino* [Art of Cinema] 2, http://kinoart.ru/archive/2012/02/anketa-ik (accessed October 16, 2014).

Kichin, Valerii. 2013. "V okopakh 'Stalingrada'" [In the Trenches of Stalingrad]. *Rossiiskaia gazeta* [Russian Gazette] October 14 http://www.rg.ru/2013/10/10/stalingrad-site.html (accessed October 16, 2014).

"Kruglyi stol." [Roundtable Discussion] 2005. "Blokbaster: perevod na russkii" [Blockbuster: Translation into Russian]. *Iskusstvo kino* [Art of Cinema] 12, http://kinoart.ru/archive/2005/12/n12-article2 (accessed October 16, 2014).

Kuleshov, Lev. 1974. "Art of Cinema." In *Kuleshov on Film: Writings*, edited by Ronald Levaco, 41–125. Berkeley: University of California Press.

Larsen, Susan. 2003. "National Identity, Cultural Authority, and the Post-Soviet Blockbuster: Nikita Mikhalkov and Aleksei Balabanov." *Slavic Review* 62.3: 491–511.

Lawton, Anna. 2004. *Imaging Russia 2000. Film and Facts*. Washington DC: New Academia Publishing.

MacFadyen, David. 2004. "Timur Bekmambetov: *Night Watch* [*Nochnoi dozor*] (2004)." *KinoKultura* 6, http://www.kinokultura.com/reviews/R104dozor.html (accessed October 16, 2014).

Madsen, Axel. 1975. *The New Hollywood: American Movies in the '70s*. New York: Thomas Y. Crowell.

Maltby, Richard. 1998. "'D' for Disgusting: American Culture and English Criticism." In *Hollywood and Europe: Economics, Culture, National Identitiy: 1945–1999*, edited by Geoffrey Nowell-Smith and Steven Ricci, 104–118. London: British Film Institute Publishing.

Maternovsky, Denis. 2003. "US Giant Joins the Battle of the Multiplexes." *The Moscow Times* September 23, http://www.lexisnexis.com.pitt.idm.oclc.org/hottopics/lnacademic/?verb=sr&csi=145252 (accessed October 16, 2014).

Matizen, Viktor. 2005. "Konets epokhi rezhisserov" [The End of the Directors' Era]. *Novye izvestiia* [New News] July 13, http://www.newizv.ru/culture/2005-07-13/28047-konec-epohi-rezhisserov.html (accessed October 16, 2014).

Norris, Stephen. 2012. *Blockbuster History in the New Russia: Movies, Memory, and Patriotism*. Bloomington: Indiana University Press.

Rampton, Vanessa. 2008. "'Are you Gangsters?' – 'No, We're Russians': The *Brother* Films and the Question of National Identity in Russia." In *eSharp*, Special Issue: Reaction and Reinvention: Changing Times in Central and Eastern Europe: 29–68.

Salisbury, Mark. 2005. "'Night Watch' Q&A with Timur Bekmambetov." Interview with Timur Bekmambetov. *Time Out Movie Blog* October 4.

Schatz, Thomas. 1981. *Hollywood Genres: Formulas, Filmmaking, and The Studio System*. New York: Random House.

Seckler, Dawn. 2010. "What Does *Zhanr* Mean in Russian?" In *Directory of Russian Cinema*, edited by B. Beumers, 28–33. Bristol: Intellect.

Stepanov, Vasilii. 2009. "Krizis s nami, krizis kak my, krizis uzhe v nas" [Our Crisis, We as Crisis, the Crisis in Us]. *Seans* July 28, http://seance.ru/n/37-38/subjectcrisis/krizis-s-nami/ (accessed October 16, 2014).

Tsyrkun, Nina. 2012. "Zhivye i mertvye. O rossiiskikh fil'makh – chempionakh prokata" [The Living and the Dead: About Russian Box-Office Hits]. *Iskusstvo kino* [Art of Cinema] 2, http://kinoart.ru/archive/2012/02/box-office-champions (accessed October 16, 2014).

Vorotnikov, Evgeny. 2010. "Russia Set for $1bn Moment." *Screen Daily* November 25, http://www.screendaily.com/territories/europe/russia-set-for-1bn-moment/5020917.article (accessed October 16, 2014).

Winn, John Emmett. 2007. *The American Dream and Contemporary Hollywood Cinema*. New York: Continuum.

Zayarnyuk, Andriy. 2003. "From Russian with Truth: Traveling to America in the Post-Soviet Russian Imagination." *Ports of Call: Central European and North American Culture/s in Motion* 1: 269–281.

10

The Global and the National in Post-Soviet Russian Cinema (2004–2012)

Maria Bezenkova and Xenia Leontyeva

The post-Soviet period of the history of Russian cinema can be divided into several stages. In the beginning, immediately after the collapse of the USSR, all internal links of communication in the sector were ruptured, leading to the destruction of the economy of film production and a loss of audience trust in the works of filmmakers, who increasingly failed to sense the needs of the people and lacked the technological and economic opportunities to satisfy them. Then, in the mid 1990s, film exhibition and distribution gradually returned to a normal function, thus creating the conditions for a revival of film production on a large scale, not only through state finances but also through private investments.

Nancy Condee (2009), investigating the phenomenon of Russian cinema after perestroika, has described the period of the early 1990s, discussing traditional themes for analysis and the development of auteur cinema at large, while separate chapters are devoted to the creativity of some key auteurs. The progressive revelation of tendencies in the development of Russian auteur cinema and the careful analysis of the historical and cultural context connected with these films command respect. However, the text does not attempt to reveal tendencies in the development of global trends in new Russian cinema, since Condee remains within a film-studies milieu, offering research on the different styles and ideologies of the selected filmmakers. Of great interest is the chapter "How Russia forgot to go to the movies," where Condee attempts to track the cause and effect of the drop in audience interest in cinema as a whole and Russian cinema in particular. Her conclusions concern the general downturn of the quantity in films produced, the relative quality of Russian films, and the absence of strict genre norms. Indeed, this situation was characteristic for the first decade of perestroika reforms (1985–1995); however, the further development of Russian cinema was not as

A Companion to Russian Cinema, First Edition. Edited by Birgit Beumers.
© 2016 John Wiley & Sons, Inc. Published 2016 by John Wiley & Sons, Inc.

linear, when considering the strategy for the development of the film-business, distribution, and exhibition.

If 1996, with the first modern Kodak cinema in Moscow, became a starting point for the revival of the film business in the Russian Federation, then 2004 laid the foundation for the box-office breakthrough for domestic producers and directors in the Russian exhibition sector. In 2004 the share of box-office receipts of Russian films increased sharply, from 5 percent to 12 percent, becoming a springboard for an even more powerful move over the following years when producers gathered practically a third of the Russian box office. It is rightly assumed that the catalyst for this breakthrough was Timur Bekmambetov's *Night Watch* [*Nochnoi dozor*, 2004], showing domestic audiences that "we can do just as well as Hollywood": build a plot and, most importantly, create special effects.

With *Night Watch* Russia got accustomed to global methods of film production that lay at the basis of the first increased interest of the Russian cinemagoer to a domestic cinematic product; strangely enough, their misuse against the background of more competitive foreign films by 2010 became the reason for a no less significant drop of this interest, when 3D swept the market with James Cameron's *Avatar* (2009).

At the same time, distinctive plots and cinematic techniques had traditionally led to Russian and Soviet cinema's popularity all over the world. However, the interruption of this tradition during a time of political and economic shifts shook domestic cinema production. With the breakdown of stable film production, contemporary structures of unique national tropes could not be generated. The use of universal methods and plots, the reliance on canonical systems became the

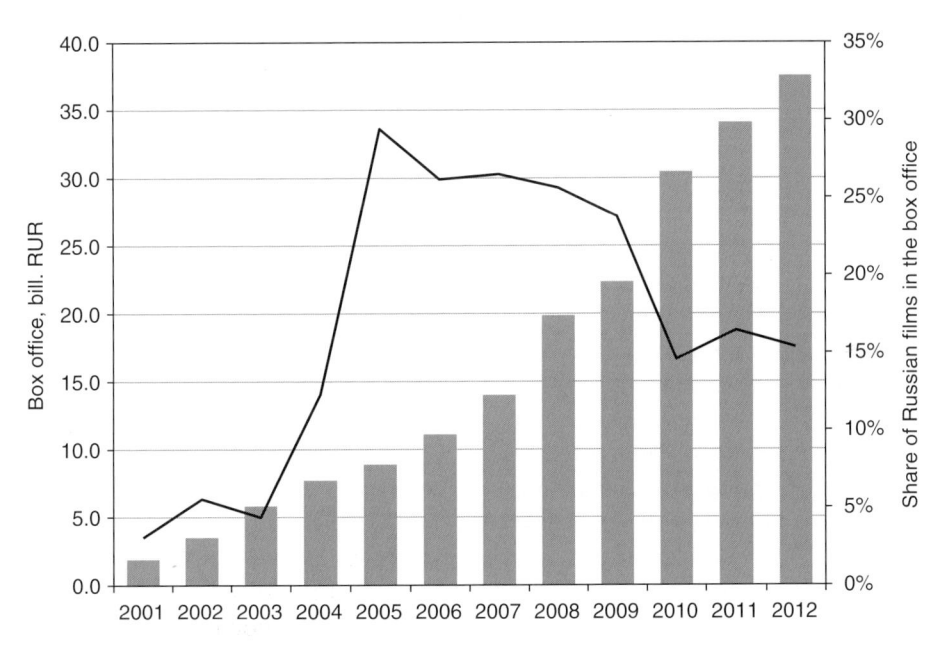

Figure 10.1 Box office of Russian film exhibition and share of domestic films.

foundation for Russian directors and producers. Nevertheless, the question of the audience and the world community's acceptance of this new way has, until now, been poorly studied.

Research Methods

In order to try to address this question, we consider films from 2004 to 2012 – the period of a sudden blossoming and gradual decline of domestic filmmakers on the internal market – from four positions: (1) film distribution within Russia; (2) co-operation of Russian producers/directors with foreign partners (co-production and work outside Russia); (3) international release of Russian films; and (4) the success of Russian films at leading international film festivals.

Let us explain the principle and the approach to each of these areas, and the sources of our primary data. First, for the internal consumption of Russian films we have used listings of films in Russian distribution published by the trade papers *Kinobiznes segodnia* [Film Business Today] and *Biulleten' kinoprokatchika* [Film Bookers' Bulletin] which have been analyzed by experts at Nevafilm Research. Thus we surveyed 635 domestic films that were released between 2004 and 2012. From this list we selected for further analysis those films which, in our opinion, reflected the trends of each year; for the study of specific tropes we selected 190 films, which took between $25,000 and $50 million on the domestic market.

Second, the list of films co-produced by Russian and foreign producers is based on data from the Ministry of Culture of the Russian Federation (official co-production in the framework of international contracts about joint film production), the European Audiovisual Observatory (http://www.obs.coe.int), Nevafilm Research and the site Kinopoisk.ru; this list includes films by Russian producers that were filmed abroad without the participation of Russian authors and film crews. Also, the filmographies of directors who had experience of international co-operation or festival recognition have been considered in order to reveal any films such directors may have shot abroad without Russian capital. As a result, 110 films that fit these criteria were selected for the period 2004 to 2012; from these, the 33 most significant titles were singled out for further analysis.

Third, since the collapse of the USSR, Russian cinema has not yet managed to inscribe itself into the global film-market: the co-production system is not well developed and is poorly supported – the arrival of Vladimir Medinskii as Minister of Culture in spring 2012 saw it being completely rejected by the state structures. The release of films in international distribution is limited by the low competitiveness of Russian film production that is, in the first instance, oriented at the internal market. Besides, an in-depth analysis of this sphere is hampered by the absence of intelligible, centralized statistics not only about the distribution figures of Russian films abroad, but even about the sales figures for foreign territories. We have used data about the attendance rates for Russian films in the European Union as presented by the European Audiovisual Observatory in their Lumière database (lumiere.obs.coe.int), as well as statistics of box office figures in the United States that are published in *Kinobiznes segodnia*, using for the calculation the average ticket price as indicated by the Motion Pictures Association of America (2013). Overall, there were 200 such films, of which only those that have gathered at least 15,000 viewers in the United States and European Union have been considered for analysis, leaving about 40 films.

For an estimation of the results of films in Russian and international distribution, different parameters have been applied: for the domestic market these are box-office returns in US dollars; for the foreign market these figures are based on attendance. Such an approach has been necessitated by the primary data: in Russia there are no viewer figures before 2009, while for European markets all data are based on attendance, and across the United States on box-office figures; however, they are based on the quantity of visits on the average ticket price to compare to European data.

Finally, the recognition of Russian filmmakers in the professional environment is assessed by main or special awards, as well as FIPRESCI awards at some of the leading international film festivals: Venice, Cannes, Berlin, Toronto, Moscow. Also, nominations for the American and European Film Academies have been considered, although during the specified period this is not applicable to any Russian film. In total, the period from 2004 to 2012 has brought forth 25 such films, of which 19 have undergone further analysis.

Since some Russian films fall into several of the above-stated four rubrics, the final number of the films selected for analysis of the period 2004 to 2012 is 210.

Global Tropes

The basic method of our research is the study of films by contemporary Russian directors from the point of view of the presence of global tropes. We aim to understand how these tropes are treated by Russian filmmakers, by domestic and foreign audience, and by the global film community.

Global tropes, which can be singled out in every historically significant period of artistic development, have for a long time crossed the framework of traditional literary analysis, where a word or phrase would be used in a figurative sense to strengthen the artistic effect of the language.

Indeed, modern tropes in visual art (above all in cinema) cover all spheres of expressiveness, from ideological to aesthetic aspects. For an initial classification of tropes, we can use structuralist principles as set out by Roland Barthes (1994) and Tsvetan Todorov (1975), where the *metaphor* is the initial and basic trope. Among the linguistic paradigms of global tropes in cinema we can highlight the *synecdoche* (*pars pro toto*) and the *menippea* (a term suggested in a modern meaning by Mikhail Bakhtin, 1975).

Furthermore, global tropes record changes of the thematic layer and of the image of the hero. Here we may single out the so-called "migrating plots," which suggest the repeatability of a motif or/and character, and the appearance of basic, cultural-philosophical directions of the twentieth century: *existentialism* and *nihilism*.

A special part in the analysis of global tropes is taken up by audiovisual tendencies in the development of the expressive means of cinema; they appear in *postmodernism*, with its system of hyperlinks. *Visual symbolism* occupies all innovations of visual language, including the developing system of sign-symbols, the system of camera skills, and the general light-color composition. Two key associative elements run through all stages of the development of film art: *carnival* and the *road*.

The historical context of modern cinema leads to the emergence of global tropes connected with ideological components, such as *gender* and *propaganda*. Industrial aspects, decisions on distribution and promotion, form the last component of the existing structures of cinematic tropes. One concerns the genre opportunities of the *screen adaptation*, while the second characterizes the *mainstream* cinematic output.

We now consider these basic global tropes with reference to contemporary Russian cinema.

Rhetorical Figures: Metaphor, Synecdoche, Menippea

Metaphor is a basic trope, where association by similarity or analogy is most important: modern Russian cinema is characterized not by the classical metaphor (figurative meaning), but its modern reading, when the figurative supersedes the basic meaning, and the visual or verbal image is understood only in the figurative sense. New elements appear outside the plot, which is characteristic for Russian films of the last decade. Film-metaphors are closer to a comprehensive poetic structure that assumes the totality of the image, adding an emotional and suggestive touch. Also typical is the development of a general metaphorical line of the film that leads to long, associative chains and symbolical structures, thus creating the basis for the film's atmosphere.

The classical example of the synecdoche, presenting a part instead of the whole, is a separate trope in modern Russian cinema. In this case the transfer of meaning from one phenomenon to another through a quantitative equivalent allows the reduction of the general statement before the demonstration of detail or de-facto recognition of a part of the plot through the author's basic statement. Reticence and an open ending are also manifestations of *pars pro toto*, that is, they assume to a significant degree the author's trust in the spectator and offer a high level of spectator freedom, which can be seen in the different interpretations of the plot and the film's general idea.

The use of a plot with threaded episodes, linked to the protagonist or another subject, suggests the simplified variant of menippea, which often appears in modern Russian films. The novella character of the overall composition unfolds the characteristics of the hero and reveals the deeper philosophical meaning of the film. From menippea, the following components may appear in a film: a combination of the high (philosophical) and the low-brow (everyday); the presence of characters created by this trope (comic copies of the hero); and the carnivalizing approach towards man and the world. Comprehension of the world's and man's imperfection motivate the artist's creation of menippea.

Migrating Plots, Existentialism, Nihilism

The trope of "migrating plots," emerging from general mythology, concerns plots which can be found in different cultural layers and different art forms, some born from the iconography cinema itself. Modern authors aspire to a maximal recognition of their plots and heroes, and use eternal paradigms of Cinderellas, Tarzans, Carmens, knights, and so forth; paired structures are also frequent, such as Romeo and Juliet. The formal, generic character of migrating plots allows filmmakers to find new content while preserving the formal aspects.

The classical, philosophical polysemantic trope of existentialism directly corresponds to its key concern with man's loneliness in the world. Contemporary Russian cinema is burdened with a pessimistic outlook on mankind due to the collapse of an era, which has led to the use of elements of this cultural-philosophical model to define the general vector of development of the filmic hero. Concepts of existence and temporariness, and their link to death, are also important characteristics of the world view of modern Russian filmmakers. Sometimes the general conceptual model of a film betrays connections to other major definition of existence: transcendence, that is, a move beyond limits. This is typical, above all, for directors with a concisely declared position outside of genre cinema.

The trope of nihilism, characteristic for art in a transition period, is widespread in new Russian cinema. Nihilism assumes the denial of moral standards of culture and society, of ideals in general; in art this is above all manifest in the classical conflict of "fathers and sons," in the demonstration of the illusoriness of modern economic-political structures. For filmmakers nihilism is often shown through the absurdity of modern life, its abnormality and chaos.

Postmodernism and Visual Symbolism

The broadest trope is connected with the culture of entropy, aesthetic changes in film formats over the last 25 years, the diffusion of grand styles and the mixture of classical forms. The basic idea of postmodernism in modern Russian cinema is the idea of deconstruction and hyperlinks, typical for Jacques Derrida and Jacques Lacan. Structures of psychoanalysis (Gilles Deleuze and Félix Guattari) and semiotics are actively used. Constant references to classical works of art with shifted emphases are possible on the thematic level of cinema and in the visual language. The structure of the labyrinth does not suggest a search of primary meanings; the main thing for artists is the demonstration of the cultural context, the breadth of the ego. Marginality becomes a method, revealing the elements of the creative work; descriptiveness and lack of evaluation therefore frequently occur.

The special visual language, which had appeared in the USSR during the Thaw with such films as Mikhail Kalatozov's *The Cranes are Flying* [Letiat zhuravli, 1957] Grigorii Chukhrai's *Ballad of a Soldier* [Ballada o soldate, 1959] and Andrei Tarkovskii's *Ivan's Childhood* [Ivanovo detstvo, 1962] and which had practically disappeared during the period of perestroika and the 1990s, began to manifest itself more and more frequently in the work of Russian filmmakers with the revival of national festivals. The skill to use subject elements for the construction of associative lines, symbolical components which are built into the figurative movement of the plot, and generously scattered visual signs with references to the classics of other arts appeared more often in Russian cinema. The visual symbolism extends to technical innovations, such as the use of slow motion, dolly zoom, micro-macro shots, and foreshortening. For modern Russian filmmakers there are no borders between the arts, as there were 60 years ago; therefore, cultural and artistic connotations reach into all kinds of disciplines, clearly showing the synthetic character of cinema.

The carnival is one of the most permanent tropes and appeared at the dawn of cinema. However, we understand it in a narrow terminological key as suggested by Mikhail Bakhtin (1975). This allows us to distinguish the carnivalesque "upside down" in film, excluding general thematic directions of this potentially theatrical genre. The carnival as trope in modern Russian cinema is interesting first of all as displacement or destruction of existing social and public norms, as the move of the antihero to the hero, as the demonstration of perversive elements of reality. The playful nature of the carnival perfectly combines with the search of young Russian filmmakers, allowing them to connect various elements of culture and style, art and religion.

The most ancient trope in art, the road, assumes variability and changeability of the spatial/temporal continuum of film due to the dynamical change of elements in reality. Modern Russian cinema keenly reacts to changing political conditions in the country, and willingly uses the road as a replaceable element of the screen image of the world, thus showing both the mythological and authentic essence of the spatial/temporal features of the screen model. Movement, which has become cinema's basic invention (as it was at the birth of this art) is the fundamental unit of the episodic structure. The road is present in the character features and in the compositional structure of the film as a whole. It is the continuing element of reality, revealing temporal characteristics, which is extremely important for modern Russian motion picture arts as they try to find ways for the presentation of reality.

Ideological Tropes: Gender and Propaganda

Gender is a new designation of a canonical trope of the 1930s. The totality of social and cultural norms typical for people of a certain gender was fully realized in the concept of the social hero of classical Soviet cinema of the 1930s ("the Stakhanovite", "the shock worker", etc.). Modern Russian cinema expands this concept, asserting that psychological models of behavior and non-standard activities define gender roles. The redistribution of classical gender roles is the basic form of this multi-layered phenomenon. This allows Russian filmmakers to find asymmetric cultural references to social roles in other types of social attitudes, and to form the structure of a new social hierarchy.

Opportunities for propaganda in the neo-mythologies of contemporary Russian cinema are practically boundless. The author's ideological accents, placed along the image of heroes, their actions and the general conclusion, give a clear indication of the author's message. Propaganda in Russian cinema is a direct dialogue of the director with the spectator, an attempt to convince the audience of his position and influence the spectator in all possible ways. Frequently classical elements of Sergei Eisenstein's "montage of attractions" are used, as well as internal monologue, direct address of the author's alter ego, explanatory inter-titles, the manipulation of classical ethic and legal rules in the plot, and moral principles in the emotional suggestive parts.

Industrial Aspects: Mainstream and Adaptation

For Russian cinema the concept of "mainstream" has changed over the last 10 years to the concept of genre cinema. The observance of the canonical norms of a genre guarantees a steady spectator interest, raises the box office, and leads producers to continue established plots. The concept of genre is directly connected to a precise structure, which is characteristic for the majority of mainstream films in the world. Most important is the presence of a precise opposition set out in archetypal terms: good and evil, truth and lie, top and bottom, right and left. The mainstream always uses known plots and basic characters; most important for the spectator is the effect of recognition and narrative simplicity. The maximal involvement in the plot is achieved due to the dramaturgic canon (using the classics of literature and theatre: beginning, development, culmination, resolution).

The adaptation of classical works of literature is convenient for the cinema, and tested for the cinematic task. In modern Russian cinema the screen adaptation allows for a visible dramaturgic structure. It is in high demand among debutant directors and the so-called producers' cinema, initially focused on commercial profit. However, auteur cinema also resorts to screen adaptations, but such films tend to be based on some motifs of a novel. This allows the filmmaker to preserve the dramaturgic structure, but simultaneously to go beyond classical stories and forms.

232   *Maria Bezenkova and Xenia Leontyeva*

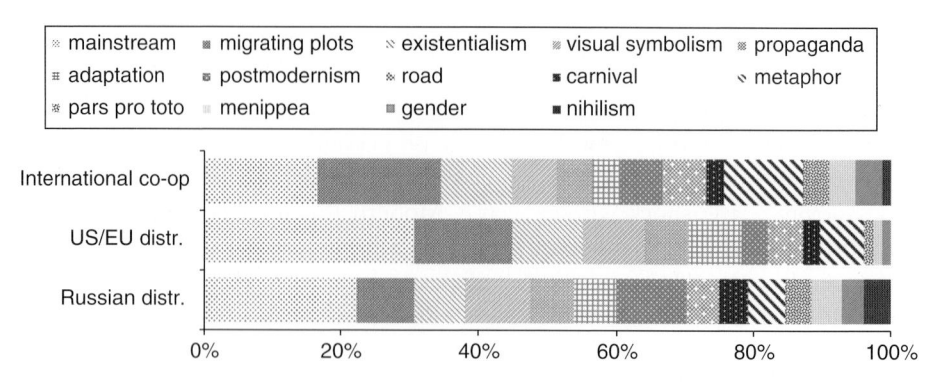

Figure 10.2 Presence of tropes in Russian films: share of the general supply (2004–2012).

Results of Research

We have compared the presence of these global tropes in Russian films in two directions, from the point of view of supply and demand, adopting a market approach.

At the basis of the analysis of supply lies the quantity of films which have been released on Russian or European/American screens, and works made in cooperation between Russian and foreign filmmakers. These three parameters are the equivalents of industrial indicators, although not all films are released both in Russia and abroad. Nevertheless, in this manner we can assess how often this or another trope is used.

At the basis of the analysis of demand we have focused not on the quantity of released films, but the reaction to these films from the audience and the international critical community. In this case, the criterion of the estimate for popularity of certain tropes is the box office in Russian distribution, the attendance figures for the United States and European Union, and also the number of films that have received awards at film festivals and a nomination for the American and European Film Academy.

Let us begin with the most widespread trope in modern Russian cinema: the mainstream. It is widely presented on the home market, appearing in a quarter of domestic films (dominating in the highest-grossing films in Russian distribution, where it is present in 15 of the Top20; see Table 10.1). The same trope appears in Russian exports: a third of the films in international distribution exploit the mainstream structure, which is recognized and accepted around the world. At the same time, in co-productions Russian directors/producers resort to the mainstream trope to a lesser extent: it appears in only 17 percent of surveyed co-produced films. Mainstream is the most successful trope on the internal and foreign market;

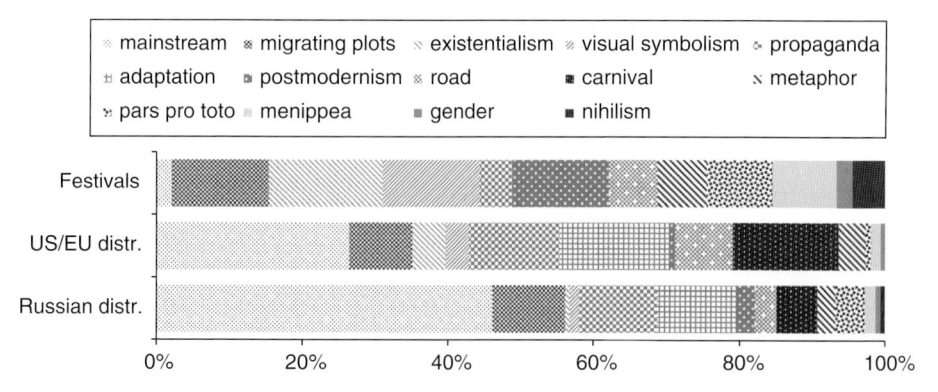

Figure 10.3 Presence of tropes in Russian films: share of the general demand (2004–2012).

it involves the greatest number of spectators in cinemas. But it has least success among film critics: as a rule, Russian mainstream films do not receive prizes at leading festivals. At the same time, the share of films that contain this trope constantly increases in the period under consideration, both in supply and demand (including from festival critics: in 2012 at the Moscow IFF the award for best direction went to Andrei Proshkin's *The Horde* [*Orda*]).

A vivid example of the link between the Soviet and Russian paradigm of cinema and of spectator expectations is the film *Irony of Fate. Continuation* [*Ironiia sud'by. Prodolzhenie*] by Timur Bekmambetov, where mainstream features are quite clearly shown: the use of a known plot (it is a continuation of a hugely popular New Year film of several generations of Soviet and Russian viewers), precisely set genre forms (comedy and melodrama), a high-quality ensemble. Moreover, the film correctly visualizes signs of modern Russian society (it actively uses product placement), without immersing the viewer in excessive realism, but, on the contrary, with a touch of prettiness and the figurative system of a "modern fairy tale." The classical linear dramaturgy continues the story from the first film, *Irony of Fate* [*Ironiia sud'by*, dir. El'dar Riazanov, 1975], and allows practically any spectator to spread their expectations across the entire plot. Predictability is the norm of mainstream production, and in the given plot the finale follows the genre laws.

Perhaps the supply and demand concerning films which follow the trope of migrating plot is most evenly distributed. Although on the internal market these plots occur less intensively than on the international or co-production market, the demand from Russian spectators is no less than from abroad. The blossoming of this trope comes in the 2005 to 2007 period, with *Day Watch* [*Dnevnoi dozor*] by Timur Bekmambetov, *12* by Nikita Mikhalkov, *1612* by Vladimir Khotinenko, *Prince Vladimir* [*Kniaz' Vladimir*] by Iurii Kulakov and, by the end of the first decade of the 2000s, the enthusiasm has essentially decreased both from filmmakers as well as from spectators and critics.

Table 10.1 Top 20 Russian films in domestic distribution (2004–2012)

Original Russian title	English title	Year	Director	Country of production	Tropes	Russian box office in million USD
Ирония судьбы. Продолжение	Irony of Fate 2	2008	Timur Bekmambetov	Russia	mainstream	49.9
Адмиралъ	The Admiral	2008	Andrei Kravchuk	Russia	propaganda	33.7
Дневной дозор	Day Watch	2006	Timur Bekmambetov	Russia	migrating plot, carnival, mainstream, adaptation	32.0
Самый лучший фильм	The Best Movie	2008	Kirill Kuzin	Russia	mainstream	27.6
9 рота	9th Company	2005	Fedor Bondarchuk	Russia	metaphor, pars pro toto, migrating plot	23.6
Ёлки	Six Degrees of Celebration	2011	Timur Bekmambetov, Aleksandr Voitinskii et al.	Russia	mainstream	22.8
Наша Russia. Яйца судьбы	Our Russia: The Balls of Fate	2010	Gleb Orlov	Russia	mainstream	22.2
Обитаемый остров. Фильм первый	The Inhabited Island. Pt I	2009	Fedor Bondarchuk	Russia	mainstream, adaptation	21.8
Иван царевич и серый волк	Ivan Tsarevich and the Grey Wolf	2012	Vladimir Toropchin	Russia	mainstream	20.7
Волкодав из рода серых псов	Wolfhound	2007	Nikolai Lebedev	Russia	not analysed	20.0
Черная молния	Black Lightning	2010	Aleksandr Voitinskii, Dmitri Kiselev	Russia	not analysed	19.7

Три богатыри и Шамаханская царица	How Not to Rescue a Princess	2011	Sergei Glezin	Russia	mainstream	19.0
Турецкий гамбит	Turkish Gambit	2005	Djannik Faiziev	Russia, Bulgaria	adaptation	18.5
Любовь-морковь 2	Lovey-Dovey 2	2009	Maksim Pezhemskii	Russia	mainstream	17.9
Каникулы строгого режима	High Security Vacation	2009	Igor' Zaitsev	Russia	mainstream	17.6
Тарас Бульба	Taras Bulba	2009	Vladimir Bortko	Russia	mainstream, adaptation	17.0
Стиляги	Hipsters	2009	Valerii Todorovskii	Russia	mainstream	16.8
Ночной дозор	Night Watch	2004	Timur Bekmambetov	Russia	carnival, propaganda, mainstream, adaptation	16.0
Жара	The Heat	2007	Rezo Gigineishvili	Russia	mainstream	15.7
Кандагар	Kandahar	2010	Andrei Kavun	Russia	mainstream	14.9

Sources: Nevafilm Research, Kinobiznes segodnia, Biulleten' kinoprokatchika

It is indicative that the active exploitation of the trope of migrating plots has fallen precisely into the period of an active rise of large-budget, producers' cinema in Russia. The use of archetypal components, the reference to a collective unconscious – all this allowed directors to draw the attention of a passive audience. For example, Nikita Mikhalkov's *12* runs the well-known American plot about the search for the innocent among the guilty from Sidney Lumet's *12 Angry Men* (1957). However, for the realization of the task, Mikhalkov "overturns" the plot onto the modern Russian reality, thus toughening and intensifying the basic dramatic conflict. Precisely following the plot allows him to concentrate as much as possible on the visualization of accented details and to display his authorial idea through the protagonists.

Russian directors traditionally have a penchant to the existential trope: it is present both on the internal and foreign market, although the Russian spectator is much less sympathetic to this message than the foreign viewer. Most of all existentialism in Russian cinema is appreciated by critics: it is the dominant trope among films that have received awards at film festivals between 2004 and 2012 (see Table 10.2). At the same time the production of such films is extremely susceptible to the economic situation in the country: during the global financial crisis in 2009, concurrent in Russia with the reform of the system of state support for cinema (when the Cinema Fund [Fond Kino] was established to develop commercial rather than auteur cinema; see Leontyeva 2012), the number of films with this trope fell sharply. However, by the end of the surveyed period the balance was restored and films were released such as *How I Spent this Summer* [*Kak ia provel etim letom*, dir. Aleksei Popogrebskii, 2010] *Anton's Right Here* [*Anton tut riadom*, dir. Liubov' Arkus, 2012], and *The Conductor* [*Dirizher*, dir. Pavel Lungin, 2012]. A classical example of existentialism in cinema is the work of the theatre directors Ivan Vyrypaev and Kirill Serebrennikov, who have turned to cinema. Vyrypaev's film *Euphoria* [*Eiforiia*, 2006] is composed on a reading of the philosophy of existentialism: lack of communication. Despite a variety of forms of dialogue, the protagonists have no link with each other; they do not hear each other, nor do they wish to listen to each other, which leads to the collapse of their most basic reference points in life.

Visual symbolism is no less popular in Russian cinema, and traditionally it holds a strong position in all categories of domestic film production: it is aimed at the internal and foreign market, but also at international co-production. However, the unsophisticated spectator is not greatly enthusiastic about the symbolical visuals of some Russian films, unlike the critics who appreciate it almost as highly as existentialism. This form of expressiveness is less subjected to economic factors, and its manifestation does not stop during a crisis. Among the clearest examples of this type are Andrei Zviagintsev's *The Banishment* [*Izgnanie*, 2007], Karen Shakhnazarov's *The White Tiger* [*Belyi tigr*, 2012], Rashid Nugmanov's *The Needle. Remix* [*Igla. Remiks*, 2010], Garik Sukachev's *The House in the Sun* [*Dom solntsa*, 2010], and Garri Bardin's animation feature *Ugly Duckling* [*Gadkii utenok*, 2010]. Zviagintsev's *The Banishment* (DoP Mikhail Krichman) possesses an amazing, suggestive impact. In

Table 10.2 Success of Russian films at international film festivals (2004–2012)

Original Russian title	English title	Year	Director	Country of Production	Tropes	Festival awards
Время жатвы	The Time of the Harvest	2004	Marina Razbezhkina	Russia	not analysed	Moscow IFF: FIPRESCI award
Свои	Our own	2004	Dmitrii Meskhiev	Russia	not analysed	Moscow IFF: Golden St George (Best Film); Silver St George (Best Director)
Итальянец	The Italian	2005	Andrei Kravtsov	Russia	not analysed	Berlin IFF: Crystal Bear
Космос как предчувствие	Dreaming of Space	2005	Aleksei Uchitel'	Russia	visual symbolism, existentialism, road, postmodernism	Moscow IFF: Golden St George (Best Film)
Первые на луне	First on the Moon	2005	Aleksei Fedorchenko	Russia	pars pro toto, nihilism, postmodernism	Moscow IFF: Golden St George
Эйфория	Euphoria	2006	Ivan Vyrypaev	Russia	existentialism, postmodernism	Venice IFF: Little Golden Lion
12	12	2007	Nikita Mikhalkov	Russia	migrating plot	Venice IFF: Special Jury Prize; OSCAR nomination for Best Foreign Language Film
Ничего личного	Nothing Personal	2007	Larisa Sadilova	Russia	not analysed	Moscow IFF: FIPRESCI award
Путешествие с домашними животными	Travelling with Pets	2007	Vera Storozheva	Russia	migrating plot, road	Moscow IFF: Golden St George
Изгнание	The Banishment	2007	Andrei Zviagintsev	Russia	not analysed	Cannes IFF: Best Actor

(*Continued*)

Table 10.2 (Continued)

Original Russian title	English title	Year	Director	Country of Production	Tropes	Festival awards
Бумажный солдат	Paper Soldier	2008	Aleksei German Jr.	Russia	metaphor, migrating plot, visual symbolism	Venice IFF: Silver Lion (Best Director)
Все умрут, а я останусь	Everybody Dies But Me	2008	Valeriia Gai-Germanika	Russia	pars pro toto, existentialism, nihilism, gender, propaganda	Cannes IFF: Special Prize of Golden Camera jury; Regards Jeune Prize
Однажды в провинции	Once in the Provinces	2008	Katia Shagalova	Russia	not analysed	Moscow IFF: FIPRESCI award
Русалка	Mermaid	2008	Anna Melikian	Russia	visual symbolism	Berlin IFF: FIPRESCI award
Тюльпан	Tulpan	2008	Sergei Dvortsevoi	Russia	not analysed	Cannes IFF: Special Jury Prize, Un Certain regard
Петя по дороге в царствие небесное	Pete on the Way to Heaven	2009	Nikolai Dostal'	Russia	not analysed	Moscow IFF: Golden St George
Чудо	The Miracle	2009	Aleksandr Proshkin	Russia	not analysed	Moscow IFF: Special Jury Prize –Silver St George
БАгИ	Bugs	2010	Andrei Bogatyrev	Russia	postmodernism	Moscow IFF: Special Mention, Perspectives Competition Jury
Овсянки	Silent Souls	2010	Aleksei Fedorchenko	Russia	visual symbolism, existentialism, road, postmodernism	Venice IFF: FIPRESCI award; Ecumenical Jury Award
Да здравствуют антиподы	¡Vivan las Antipodas!	2011	Victor Kosakovskii	Germany, Argentina, Netherlands, Chile	pars pro toto, menippea, migrating plot, visual symbolism	EFA nomination as Best Documentary
Елена	Elena	2011	Andrei Zviagintsev	Russia	metaphor, visual symbolism, nihilism	Cannes IFF: Special Jury Prize, Un Certain Regard

Фауст	Faust	2011	Aleksandr Sokurov	USA, Russia, Germany, France, Japan, UK, Italy	metaphor, menippea, migrating plot, existentialism	Venice IFF: Golden Lion
Шапито-шоу	Chapiteau-Show	2011	Sergei Loban	Russia	pars pro toto, menippea, migrating plot, postmodernism	Moscow IFF: Special Jury Prize Silver St George
Антон тут рядом	Anton's Right Here	2012	Liubov' Arkus	Russia	existentialism	Venice IFF: FIPRESCI award; Silver Mouse
В тумане	In the Fog	2012	Sergei Loznitsa	Russia, Germany, Netherlands, Belarus, Latvia	not analysed	Cannes IFF: FIPRESCI award
Орда	The Horde	2012	Andrei Proshkin	Russia	menippea, propaganda, mainstream	Moscow IFF: Silver St George (Best Director)

Sources: Ministry of Culture of the RF, festival and award sites, FIPRESCI

many respects, this is thanks to the visual side, filled with references to classical painting of the early Renaissance, the Dutch Golden Age and nineteenth-century German Romanticism. For the spectator such a cultural layer creates additional depth and challenge as it forces the viewer to read not only the standard dramatic rhetoric, but also the references to art history with their additional semantic value.

Propaganda is one of the most successful tropes among films released in the European Union and the United States, in many respects thanks to Timur Bekmambetov's *Night Watch*, which collected the greatest number of foreign spectators for the entire period surveyed here: 1.7 million (see Table 10.3). This artistic method also finds a response in the domestic market; and even critics don't bypass the film as they assess the director's intent. The most successful years for this trope were between 2004 and 2008 when, apart from *Night Watch*, the following films were released: *Driver for Vera* [*Voditel' dlia Very*, dir. Pavel Chukhrai, 2004], *The Admiral* [*Admiral*, dir. Andrei Kravchuk, 2008], *We are from the Future* [*My iz budushchego*, dir. Andrei Maliukov, 2008], *Alexander. The Neva Battle* [*Aleksandr. Nevskaia bitva*, dir. Igor' Kalenov, 2008], and *Everyone will Die but Me* [*Vse umrut a ia ostanus'*, dir. Valeriia Gai Germanika, 2008]. These were successful both in the festival world and among audiences. The propaganda model is perfectly realized in the films with a historical orientation such as *Admiral*. The biographic model of a film-portrait allows Kravchuk to accentuate the activity of the historical character depending on the given ideological paradigm. As a result, for the modern Russian spectator, not weighed down with an in-depth knowledge of the history of his own country, the historical context of the film is formed through propaganda influence due to the accent on separate fragments and actions of the protagonist.

One of the most reliable film types is the screen adaptation, which gives Russian producers the guarantee of success among domestic and foreign audiences, although it rarely brings dividends at film festivals. Sergei Lukianenko's books (*Night Watch* and *Day Watch*) and Boris Akunin's novels (*Turkish Gambit* and *State Counselor*) lie at the basis of the highest-grossing pictures in the mid-2000s and are convincing proofs for this hypothesis. Nevertheless, the last successful year for screen adaptations in Russia was 2009, which saw the release of Fedor Bondarchuk's *Inhabited Island* [*Obitaemyi ostrov*] and Vladimir Bortko's *Taras Bulba*; since 2010 there has been a noticeable drop in the interest in screen versions of literature. The screen adaptation of contemporary national literature, such as Boris Akunin's *State Counselor* [*Statskii sovetnik*, 2005], allows directors to work on the educational function of cinema. Acquainting the reader with an already established cult novel about the adventures of Erast Fandorin, the director Filipp Iankovskii offers a rigid form of stylization in the manner of early twentieth-century cinema. This allows him to show interesting visual details, and to produce narrative cinema with lyrical digressions.

The phenomenon of postmodernism, like visual symbolism and existentialism, is peculiar to Russian cinema. These three tropes are closest to the national film tradition, and are still most appreciated by critics. The films with postmodernist

Table 10.3 Top 10 Russian films in EU and US distribution (2004–2012)

Original Russian title	English title	Year	Director	Country of Production	Tropes	EU/US admissions in 1000
Ночной дозор	Night Watch	2004	Timur Bekmambetov	Russia	carnival, propaganda, mainstream, adaptation	1746.4
Последнее воскресение	The Last Station	2009	Michael Hoffmann	Germany, Russia, UK	not analysed	882.7
Монгол	Mongol	2007	Sergei Bodrov	Kazakhstan, Russia, Mongolia, Germany	road, mainstream	829.9
Дневной дозор	Day Watch	2006	Timur Bekmambetov	Russia	migrating plot, carnival, mainstream, adaptation	499.1
Белка и Стрелка: звездные собаки	Belka & Strelka. Star Dogs	2010	Sviatoslav Ushakov, Inna Evlannikova	Russia	road, mainstream	238.6
Фауст	Faust	2011	Aleksandr Sokurov	US, Russia, Germany, France, Japan, UK, Italy	metaphor, menippea, migrating plot, existentialism	209.9
Елена	Elena	2011	Andrei Zviagintsev	Russia	metaphor, visual symbolism, nihilism	187.5
Ирония судьбы. Продолжение	The Irony of Fate 2	2007	Timur Bekmambetov	Russia	mainstream	159.1
9 рота	9th Company	2005	Fedor Bondarchuk	Russia	metaphor, pars pro toto, migrating plot	112.7
1612	1612	2007	Vladimir Khotinenko	Russia	migrating plot	104.2

Sources: Nevafilm Research, Kinobiznes segodnia, European Audiovisual Observatory

features are released with an enviable regularity into domestic distribution, despite the low interest from the public. However, from time to time they charge into international film festivals, collecting bales of awards, as was the case in 2005, 2006, and 2010 with the films *Dreaming of Space* [*Kosmos kak predchuvstvie*, dir. Aleksei Uchitel', 2005], *Euphoria* by Ivan Vyrypaev, *First on the Moon* [*Pervye na lune*, dir. Aleksei Fedorchenko, 2004] and *Silent Souls* [*Ovsianki*, dir. Fedorchenko, 2010], and *BuGS* [*BAgI*, dir. Andrei Bogatyrev, 2011]. Fedorchenko's *Silent Souls* possesses the basic attributes of postmodernism: every frame, each episode is a hyperlink, a model or quotation of an existing artistic paradigm. The plot, which leans on mythology, allows the director to string together additional meanings on existing lines of action.

The archetype of the road – one of bases of cultural traditions – regularly attracts Russian filmmakers and finds a response, above all, on the global scene, in international distribution and on film festivals. Surges of interest in the trope were marked in 2005, 2007, and 2010. Among the films that have clearly embodied these tropes are *Bimmer 2* [*Bumer 2*, dir. Petr Buslov, 2005], *Garpastum* (dir. Aleksei Gherman Jr., 2005), *The Nomad* [*Kochevnik*, dir. Sergei Bodrov, 2006] and *The Mongol* (dir. Sergei Bodrov, 2007), *Travelling with Pets* [*Puteshestvie s domashnymi zhivotnymi*, dir. Vera Storozheva, 2007], and even the 3D-animation *Belka and Strelka. Space Dogs* [*Belka i Strelka. Lunnye prikliucheniia*, dirs. Sviatoslav Ushakov and Inna Evlannikova, 2013].

Storozheva's *Travelling with Pets* realizes the trope of the road in an absolutely canonical key peculiar to the films of Federico Fellini. The infinite movement of the plot and the protagonists simultaneously seems linear and closed, aimed at progress and repeatability. The protagonists show a development of character in changeable temporal and spatial characteristics of the film, which allows the spectator near to an understanding of the heroes and their problems.

Carnival is an approach that is degenerative: on the wave of its use in the screen adaptations of Lukianenko's books in 2004 and 2006, there was a revival of domestic film production; however, the public is now less interested. Filmmakers use it mainly without reflection in youth genres, examples include: *Pregnant* [*Beremennyi*, dir. Sarik Andreasian, 2011], *The Witch* [*Ved'ma*, dir. Oleg Fesenko, 2006], *Indigo* (dir. Roman Prygunov, 2008), and *On the Hook* [*Na igre*, dir. Pavel Sanaev, 2009].

Night Watch and *Day Watch* by Timur Bekmambetov fully reflected the opportunities of this trope with reference to the fantasy genre. The active use of special effects, the visualization of invented gadgets and new technologies raise the performativity in the films, maximally realizing their spectator potential. The involvement of the fan audience in the process of the viewing became possible thanks to one of the basic components of this trope: the exit into social reality over the borders of the work of art.

Another trope in Russian cinema that is traditionally highly rated by critics is the metaphor. Contemporary Russian filmmakers quite guardedly, though, regularly use it in their works, basically in co-productions and films intended for the international market. A depression occurred in 2009–2010, when both the financial crisis and the change in the support system of the Russian cinema affected this trope. In the other years quite a few striking metaphoric works were released, including *Ninth Company* [*9 rota*, dir. Fedor Bondarchuk, 2005], *Paper Soldier* [*Bumazhnyi soldat*, dir. Aleksei Gherman Jr., 2008], *Alive* [*Zhivoi*, dir. Aleksandr Veledinskii, 2006], *Faust* (Aleksandr Sokurov, 2011), *The Banishment* and *Elena* (dir. Andrei Zviagintsev, 2010), *The Tuner* [*Nastroishchik*, dir. Kira Muratova, 2004], and *It's not Me* [*Eto ne ia*, dir. Maria Saakyan, 2013]. Muratova's *The Tuner* relies on metaphor as an alternative to a plot, as is typical for the majority of her films. Each of the heroes presented in this chamber drama is a metaphor of some social process or a trend in the development of modern society. The metaphorical approach to the plot development is an obligatory super-reality in Muratova's film, adding meaning to the plot and appealing to the spectator's figurative thought process.

Most popular of the less widespread tropes in Russian cinema is the synechdoche. This approach has its greatest value in the assessment of festival critics, although it is not alien to the Russian public either. The interest in this trope has grown in the early half of the 2000s: its traces are even more appreciable in the box office successes that are concerned with "heroes of our time:" *Dukhless* (dir. Roman Prygunov, 2011), *August, Eighth* [*Avgust. Vos'mogo*, dir. Djannik Faiziev, 2012], *Glamour* [*Glianets*, dir. Andrei Konchalovskii, 2007], *Chapiteau-Show* [*Shapito-shou*, dir. Sergei Loban, 2011], and *KoKoKo* (dir. Avdot'ia Smirnova, 2012). The reticence and incompleteness of the images of protagonists is typical for Sergei Loban's auteur project *Chapiteau Show*, which permits the use of a part instead of the whole as active genre unit, entering into a dialogue with the spectators, endowing them with the power of the actual authorial position. The open ending of each short story prolongs its significance for the audience, increasing the film's cultural trace.

The trope of the menippea is new to Russian cinema; however, it has been developing swiftly and finding supporters both among directors and critics, as well as audiences. The majority of the Russian films using this approach were released between 2010 and 2012; among them we should note *Fortress of War* [*Brestskaia krepost'*, dir. Aleksandr Kott, 2010], the almanac *Moscow, I Love You* [*Moskva, ia liubliu tebia*, dir. Viacheslav Kaminskii, 2010], *The Stone* [*Kamen'*, dir. Kaminskii, 2011], Andrei Proshkin's *The Horde*, *1812: The Ballad of Ulan* [*1812: Ulanskaia ballada*, dir. Oleg Fesenko, 2012] and Timur Bekmambetov's Hollywood project *Abraham Lincoln: Vampire Hunter* (2012).

The literary origin of the menippea allows this trope to be integrated into almost any genre structure, but traditionally it appears in films with a comedy element. For example *1812: The Ballad of Ulan* maximally exploits this trope, building rows of demoted heroes, each of whom possesses a double in classical Russian literature.

Gender is the least esteemed trope in Russian cinema: although it attracts the attention of directors and critics, the spectator responds extremely poorly to films that raise questions about man's social role in relation to gender. In the rather traditional Russian society this problem does not stand in the foreground either.

Among the clearest successes in domestic cinema on this topic are the films *It Doesn't Hurt* [*Mne ne bol'no*, dir. Aleksei Balabanov, 2006], *Two Days* [*Dva dnia*, dir. Avdot'ia Smirnova, 2011], *Once There was an Old Woman* [*Zhila-byla odna baba*, dir. Andrei Smirnov, 2011], *Goddess: How I Fell in Love* [*Boginia. Kak ia poliubila*, dir. Renata Litvinova, 2004], and *Alexandra* [dir. Aleksandr Sokurov, 2007]; in the same group stands Timur Bekmambetov's Hollywood work *Wanted* (2008). The gender structures presented in the film *Goddess: How I Fell in Love* are the most organic and qualitative example of the use of this trope in the contemporary, conservative Russian tradition. The social norms of female existence in society are exposed to reproach and reconsideration in Litvinova's plot, representing female egoism as the main demiurgic component of the story. Together with the expressive dialogues written in blank verse, the general atmospheric space and time of the film, as well as the gender double-dealing, are attractive to the audience.

Finally, the least significant trope for domestic cinema of recent years is nihilism, which is, however, a sign of the end of the existential crisis in which Russia found itself after the collapse of the USSR. Russian directors continue to use this approach only with a view to festival recognition, where almost by inertia such films are actually sometimes well received. However, since 2008 Russia has had no great success on this level. As examples of nihilistic films we may consider *Generation P* (dir. Viktor Ginzburg, 2011), *Junk* [*Zhest'*, dir. Denis Neimand, 2006], *Cargo 200* [*Gruz 200*, dir. Aleksei Balabanov, 2007], and *Buben, Baraban* (dir. Aleksei Mizgirev, 2009). Balabanov's *Cargo 200* maintains nihilism as a formal feature in a specific historical context: the pre-perestroika era described in the film possessed the rigidity of denial and the anarchy that is peculiar to the nihilistic model of public and inner life. This allowed Balabanov to immerse the spectator maximally in the realities of the former Soviet Union, and to show the dying society and the chaos of the individual's inner life.

In summary we note that from the mid-2000s Russian directors have rarely been invited to shoot films abroad: only three have worked at foreign studios during the period under consideration (see Table 10.4). Pavel Lungin has traditionally been involved in a Francophone environment: he is known for films that have been made in co-production with France, and he has made a Russian-language film in Luxemburg (*The Lilac Branch* [*Vetka sireni*], 2007). Andrei Konchalovskii is one of the first to have conquered Hollywood, having emigrated from the USSR to the United States where he continued his career, making his first film in America in 1984. Since the 1990s Konchalovskii has filmed both in Russia and abroad. In 2000 his involvement in the global film-process led to his participation in the almanac *Each his Own Cinema* and the European New-Year fairy tale *The Nutcracker: The Untold Story* [*Shchelkunchuk i krysinyi korol'*, 2011], which made its box office largely on the Russian market, where the film was released at the end of 2010 and grossed US$ 13.8 million (with an overall global box office of US$ 16 million). Finally, the new Russian star on the international film market is Timur Bekmambetov who led Russian films back to box-office gains on the domestic market. Since the end of the first decade of the new millennium he and his studio Bazelevs have actively cooperated with Hollywood producers: his

Table 10.4 Russian directors working abroad (2004–2012)

Russian title	Original title	Yr	Director	Country of Production	Tropes
Ветка сирени	Lilacs	2007	Pavel Lungin	Luxemburg	not analysed
У каждого свое кино	Chacun son cinéma ou Ce petit coup au coeur quand la lumière s'éteint et que le film commence	2007	Andrei Konchalovsky et al.	France	pars pro toto, menippea, migrating plot
Особо опасен	Wanted	2008	Timur Bekmambetov	US, Germany	gender, mainstream
Щелкунчик и Крысиный король	The Nutcracker	2009	Andrei Konchalovsk	UK, Hungary	migrating plot, carnival, adaptation
Президент Линкольн: Охотник на вампиров	Abraham Lincoln: Vampire Hunter	2012	Timur Bekmambetov	US	menippea, propaganda, mainstream

films *Abraham Lincoln, Vampire Hunter* and *Wanted* appeared on global screens. Both had a world-wide release and collected US$ 207 million worldwide (of which US$ 26.4 million in Russia) and US$ 37.5 million worldwide (of which US$ 12 million in Russia) respectively.

Thus, despite a low level of involvement of Russian filmmakers in the global film industry, reflected in the small number of films in international distribution which attract not too many spectators, and Russia's active opposition to co-produce films with state support, as well as the minimal participation of Russian filmmakers in foreign projects, modern Russian cinema develops pretty much along the same lines that can be observed in world cinema. The acceptance of key global tropes facilitates the expansion of film audiences both inside the country and beyond its borders. At the same time, however, internal and external demand (and supply) do not coincide; moreover, the views of film critics on the achievements of Russian cinema differ.

On the internal market the most frequent global trope in the 2000s is the mainstream, which has enormous success with the public. Besides, between 2004 and 2012 spectators preferred screen adaptations, propaganda, and migrating plots. Among the favorite approaches of Russian directors catering for the domestic market are postmodernism, visual symbolism, and existentialism, which have been adopted from earlier traditions of Soviet film schools.

The demand on the foreign market differs: there is greater interest here in carnival tropes and screen adaptations, caused by the leading role of *Night Watch* in international distribution against the background of a very small number of Russian films that reach the foreign spectator. This confirms the similarity of modern Russian and foreign cinema, which receive a similar response from any audience. This kinship is caused first of all by the high level of loaned global tropes and structural principles by Russian directors and producers, aiming at high profits. However, one clear difference between film production focused on an external and a home market nevertheless exists: co-productions reveal a noticeably more frequent presence of the of metaphor and existential tropes.

The existential trope is most of all appreciated by critics, as well as the presence of migrating plots, visual symbolism, and postmodernism. Award-winning films at leading international festivals tend to contain more tropes than other films; their artistic level is richer and more varied.

In summary, we can conclude that modern Russian cinema of the period 2004–2012 preserves its artistic variety and original features, which are traditionally highly valued by the world film community. This is true not only for films oriented towards festival success, but also commercial films. At the same time, the success of domestic cinema on the home market has been helped by the perception and adaptation of global tropes (above all a mainstream and migrating plots), positively apprehended by domestic and foreign audiences. Despite the progressing closure of the system of Russian cinema and the separation of filmmakers from the global film community, Russian cinema today reflects global cultural traditions from which new generations of directors take their inspiration.

References

Bakhtin, Mikhail. 1975. *Voprosy literatury i estetiki. Issledovaniia raznykh let* [Questions of Literature and Aesthetics. Research from Various Years]. Moscow: Khudozhestvennaia literatura.

Barthes, Roland. 1994. *Izbrannye raboty. Semiotika. Poetika* [Selected Works: Semiotics. Poetics]. Moscow: Progress, Univers.

Condee, Nancy. 2009. *The Imperial Trace: Recent Russian Cinema*. New York: Oxford University Press.

European Audiovisual Observatory. http://www.obs.coe.int/ (accessed March 21, 2014).

Leontyeva, Xenia, ed. 2012. *The Film Industry in the Russian Federation: A Report by Nevafilm*. Strasbourg: European Audiovisual Observatory, http://publi.obs.coe.int/documents//205595/552774/ru+film+industry+2012+nevafilm+en.pdf/2a99cc4b-6946-44c3-954e-accda3e942b2 (accessed March 31, 2014).

Nevafilm Research. http://nevafilm.ru/english/reports (accessed March 21, 2014).

Todorov, Tsvetan. 1975. "Poetika" [Poetics]. In *Strukturalizm: "za" i "protiv"* [Structuralism: Pro and Contra], edited by E. Basin and M. Poliakova, 37–113, translated from French by A. Zholkovskii. Moscow: Progress. Original 1971 publication as *Poétique de la prose*, Paris, Le Seuil.

Part III
Sound – Image – Text

11

The Literary Scenario and the Soviet Screenwriting Tradition

Maria Belodubrovskaya

When the Soviets took over the Czech film industry in 1949, one of the changes they introduced to Sovietize it was the literary scenario. By then, the literary scenario had become the central fixture of the Soviet mode of film production: it was a fundamental element of any film project, as well as the Soviet approach to production organization and planning. It was also a distinct feature of the Soviet film industry. The Czechs soon transformed this cumbersome prose format into a more practical document resembling a shooting script (Szczepanik 2013). It was also less important in Hollywood under the studio system (1920s–1950s), where most films started with a literary property – a novel, short story, or play that a studio purchased as potential material for a film – or with a story idea generated in the studio story department. Only after, based on a synopsis, the decision was made to produce a property or an idea into a film, was a literary treatment ordered. After a number of revisions, the studio heads approved the final version of the treatment, and, based on this version, a special studio department prepared a shooting script for the director to film. In other words, in Hollywood, the literary treatment was where only the details of the future film were worked out. The primary decisions on the story were made based on the original material not yet written up in the screenplay format. Then, it was the shooting script, not the treatment, that was actually filmed. However important for the finished film, the literary write-up was just an intermediate, working step in the process of the film's preparation. In the Soviet film industry, in contrast, the literary scenario was for all practical purposes the primary, decisive document in the production process. The synopsis that preceded it and the director's shooting script, which was actually filmed, both played subsidiary roles.

A Companion to Russian Cinema, First Edition. Edited by Birgit Beumers.
© 2016 John Wiley & Sons, Inc. Published 2016 by John Wiley & Sons, Inc.

Elsewhere I have discussed the industrial logic behind the primacy of the literary scenario in Soviet filmmaking. From the perspective of practical industry considerations, the literary scenario emerged in the 1930s as a solution to the permanent shortage of suitable screenplays. In consultation with the cultural authorities, the industry leadership decided to alleviate the shortage by tapping into a major resource of writing talent: legitimate writers. The writers expected to maintain substantial authorship credit over their works, and the literary scenario emerged as a format that would make this possible. As a result, in the mid-1930s, the literary scenario was inaugurated as an independent work of literature and became the primary focus of the Soviet screenwriting effort (Belodubrovskaya 2011a). However, the phenomenon of the literary scenario also had a socio-political logic. It was thought of as a uniquely and appropriately Soviet approach to film conception and execution. As such, it evolved as an alternative to other theoretical and practical possibilities, including those used in Hollywood and other contemporary film cultures, which were considered, tried, and ultimately rejected by the Soviets.

This chapter traces this conceptual history of the Soviet screenplay: from the iron scenario to the authored literary scenario. From the pragmatic point of view, the literary scenario became the (very flawed) answer to the question of how to generate a sufficient quantity of controllable screenplays. From the ideological and theoretical perspective, it provided a solution to the problem of better-quality films. It was in the debate about what produced good films and what role writing and writers played in the cultural process that the literary scenario emerged and established itself as a distinctive feature of Stalinist filmmaking and of Soviet filmmaking more generally.

The Iron Scenario and the Emotional Scenario

The initial condition of Soviet screenwriting was that its formats were not fully standardized. Up for debate also were the role of the screenplay in the production process and the status of the screenwriter as a creative force behind the film. Was the screenplay a subservient or an independent form? Who was the primary author of the film: the director or the screenwriter? Three leading formats that emerged in discussions of these issues during the 1920s and 1930s were the iron scenario, the emotional scenario, and eventually the literary scenario. These three were not parallel forms: one was a not necessarily an equivalent of another, as, for instance, the literary scenario could coexist with the iron-scenario shooting script based on it. Debates about which format was most appropriate for the Soviet film industry centered on the notions of production organization, controllability, and authorship.

Throughout this period two practices remained standard. First, every film had a screenplay: a prose write-up of the story or theme authored either by a screenwriter or by the director. Even if theories such as Dziga Vertov's "life caught unawares" stipulated that films were only recordings of captured events, the vast majority of actual productions, including Vertov's own, started with some sort of a screenplay. The decision on whether to produce a film was also based on this write-up. Second, most films also had a shooting script. This was a more technical write-up typically divided up into numbered shots, and directors prepared it for themselves. Since Soviet directors – as opposed to editors or producers – were fundamentally in charge of the Soviet film's final cut, the preliminary editing structure of the film to be drawn up in a shooting script was up to them as well. The primacy of Montage thinking, with its emphasis on editing as the key creative element in filmmaking, clearly had a role in this. This practice of director-authored shooting scripts, called director's scenarios [*rezhisserskii stsenarii*], from the onset made the Soviet film industry different from its Hollywood and other Western counterparts. As opposed to these other industries, where the primary responsibility of the director was to "direct" the actual shooting and actors, Soviet screenwriting and directing tended to overlap, and film directors often participated in screenwriting to a significant degree. To use Stephen Maras's terminology, the Soviet film industry did not clearly delimit film conception from film execution (Maras 2009). The creative process – the process of the formation of the film's story and its cinematic rendition – continued sometimes from early pre-production to post-production and even to censorship review. This feature of the Soviet film industry produced major problems of organization, controllability, and authorship and spurred the call for the iron scenario.

In Hollywood a standard shooting script, called the continuity script, was the production's overall blueprint, which was used by every studio department to prepare sets, cast, costumes, and everything else ahead of shooting (Bordwell, Staiger, and Thompson 1985). In the Soviet film industry, in contrast, director's shooting scripts were not standardized across the industry or even within one studio. Moreover, productions were green-lighted and started before shooting scripts were ready, making it hard for these scripts to serve as a tool for planning and organization. All details of a production were not set in stone before the production started, changes had to be made en route, shot-to-used footage ratios were high, and films often ran over budget. The iron scenario (also sometimes referred to as the steel scenario, the numbered scenario, and the technical scenario) emerged as a solution to this problem. In its original formulation, it was simply a type of shooting script that was fixed ahead of production (Cherkasov 1926; Zhemchuzhnyi 1933).

The iron scenario was explicitly modeled on the Hollywood continuity script (as well as its rough equivalent, the German *Drehbuch* (Sokolov 1926; Turkin 2007). At the minimum, like these Western equivalents, it was to contain a detailed and finalized description of the film's action and titles (or dialogue in sound cinema), and it was to be written in a numbered shot-by-shot format. Not only could the iron scenario allow filmmakers to work out the film in advance for their own convenience, the argument went, it could also enable them to demand that their studios deliver all the personnel, supplies, and equipment required for their productions. Based on such a document, the studio in turn could precisely estimate its investment in each production, making proper planning a reality. There is evidence to suggest that some Soviet productions did utilize something approximating the iron scenario in the 1930s, particularly at the semi-independent and foreign-financed studio Mezhrabpomfilm (Nikol'skaia 1936). However, on the whole the iron scenario as an organizational method did not take hold in the Soviet film industry.

One reason for this was that the industry was not a commercial enterprise where cost control was paramount. Neither was the volume of Soviet film production ever high enough to demand strict organizational efficiency. Yet, the iron scenario had another advantage that potentially made it very attractive for the industry: it could provide for effective content control. From the 1920s on, all Soviet screenplays were censored both for conventional matters, such as state secrets and basic morality, and for the ideological message of the final film. If the screenplay approved by the censors was in fact fixed and filmed as written, then censors would have little work to do after the film was completed. This, again, was the case in Hollywood, where most sensitive issues were worked out at the screenplay stage. However, what made it possible for the Hollywood screenplays to be censored and then followed, was that the censorship guidelines were fixed and specific, and that the shooting scripts were prepared by specialized staff experienced in doing just that. This separation of tasks between scripting and directing (the separation of conception from execution) made it a lot harder or natural for directors to change film conception as scripted and thus stray away from the censored and agreed-upon content. In fact, from the point of view of censorship alone, Hollywood continuity scripts were true "iron scenarios." It was extraordinarily costly for studios to have their films banned by one of the country's censorship boards, and thus, although rewrites and retakes were not uncommon during production and post-production, they tended not to affect the film's overall tendency. Moreover, since the preparation of the continuity script was often merely a technical task of converting the prose treatment into a shooting-ready format, censorship issues rarely arose at that stage.

In contrast, the Soviet shooting script, the director's scenario, was part of the creative process. In fact, the director's scenario, as the term itself makes explicit, was the time and place where the director could *interpret* the screenwriter's material and assert his or her own authorship. The director was not creating a technical write-up, an "iron" and ironed-out version of what was already censored, but his own, *new* treatment of the censored material. To quote Vsevolod Pudovkin, speaking in 1937, "the [director's] scenario is not just a mere technical rendition, but a further creative development of the literary screenplay. The elaboration of the screenplay by the director is the actual definitive and total completion of the screenplay" (Genika 1939, 79). Only after all the casting, rehearsals, and the formal work on the rhythmical structure of the film were done, and just before the shooting was to commence, could the iron shooting scenario be prepared, according to Pudovkin (Genika 1939, 188).

This creative nature of the director's scenario was why it was difficult for it to become "iron" early in the process and to assume the control function it had in Hollywood. Censors had to occasionally review the director's scenarios as well, and multiple versions of these were written. As the Stalin period (1928–1953) progressed, the shooting scripts began to match the final films more and more closely. Yet, this did not make them "iron" or equivalent to their Western counterparts in terms of content control. A film shot following a thoroughly censored director's scenario was always yet another "take" on the vetted material and could still fail to satisfy the censors. Because Soviet censorship was unpredictable and because Soviet directors saw themselves as authors of their films (see Belodubrovskaya 2011a), every Soviet film was just another version of the original material rather than a cinematic rendition of the agreed-upon text. To give just one example, Grigorii Kozintsev's biopic *Belinskii* (released in June 1953) was first scripted in August 1947. Between that time and the film's completion in 1951, at least seven versions of the literary scenario were written (two different writers, Elena Serebrovskaia and then Iurii German, were hired to write the screenplay, and eventually their efforts were combined, with Kozintsev also receiving screenwriting credit). Still, censors (members of the Ministry of Cinema Artistic Council) were unsure of the films suitability; the director's scenario was censored as well, and Kozintsev wrote at least five versions of it. Near the film's completion, portions of the film, as well as its rough cut, were reviewed multiple times, and at least three times changes were requested before the final cut was finally approved (TsGALI 257/17/114: Delo o podgotovke stsenariia "Belinskii" [File on the Preparation of the Script "Belinskii"], 1951).

In the end, "iron-ness" was in conflict with both director authorship and censorship uncertainty. One way to deal with the multiple versions was to take the shooting script out of the directors' hands, as was the case in Hollywood. However, even as ambitious a reformer as Boris Shumiatskii, the head of the Soviet film industry between 1930 and 1937, would not go this far. Following his trip to Hollywood in 1935, Shumiatskii proposed to reform Soviet screenwriting by instituting Hollywood-style story departments in Soviet studios. Yet he never suggested that shooting scripts be prepared by anyone other than the director. Shumiatskii knew that presumption of director authorship had been a norm in Soviet cinema, and that no director would agree to a reform that would impinge on this norm. If the director's scenario was never going to become "iron," the alternative was to try turning the original literary screenplay into an iron scenario, thus preventing the director from "interpreting" it. This was much harder to implement, but it was precisely what the Soviet film industry attempted.

How could a literary write-up, which could not be filmed directly, become the final and fixed version of the future production? The answer was: it should become an equivalent of a theater play. As opposed to cinema, where a screenplay only existed so a film could be made out of it, theater plays were independent literary works. They could be staged multiple times by multiple directors and not lose their original identity. In 1929, cinema executive Vladimir Sutyrin proposed this theatrical model for the Soviet screenplay. According to Sutyrin, the goal for Soviet screenwriters was to produce play-like screenplays, "completed creative works," finalized "cinematographic texts" with fully thought-out "concrete visual representations." Such screenplays would be so perfect that any intervention by the director as a coauthor would only hurt the final product (Sutyrin 1929). This language reflected an urgent need to introduce a strong counterweight to the director's authority and to fix the film's conception in a written and censorable text. Essentially, this was a proposal for the iron literary scenario. By 1929, the Soviet film industry had had experience with a potential prototype for this idea: the emotional scenario.

The concept of the emotional scenario is usually associated with Aleksandr Rzheshevskii, who collaborated with Sergei Eisenstein on *Bezhin Meadow* [*Bezhin lug*, 1937] and with Vsevolod Pudovkin on *A Simple Case* [*Prostoi sluchai*, 1930] and had the reputation as one of the most talented scriptwriters of his generation. In his 1929 article on the screenwriter, Vsevolod Pudovkin said that Rzheshevskii's work provided the director with bold and specific emotional and intellectual tasks, which was not the case with any other screenwriter (Pudovkin 1974, 81). However, the theoretical origin of the concept goes back to Eisenstein's 1929 essay "O forme stsenariia" [On Screenplay Form]. In this essay, Eisenstein wrote that the role of the screenplay was to supply a general impulse, an "emotional requirement," a shape that the director filled with his own means. (This could serve as a definition of the emotional scenario.) To Eisenstein, the language of a screenplay was different from film language. For instance, Eisenstein wrote, a screenplay could read, "Dead silence." This phrase was expressive: it clearly communicated the emotional content of the scene. However, there were multiple ways of conveying this content on screen. All that mattered was that when watching a scene the spectator thought, "Dead silence." Eisenstein added that the better, more literary or poetic the description in the screenplay, the easier it was for the director to express it in images (Eizenshtein 1964, 297–298).[1]

The emotional scenario was seriously considered by Soviet cinema because it could answer to the problem of director authorship: it was an inspired literary work good enough that a director had to respect it in his/her own treatment. Yet, as Eisenstein's discussion plainly suggests, the emotional scenario allowed the director plenty of room for interpretation, which was why both he and Pudovkin promoted it. In reality, emotional scenarios were extraordinarily imprecise and ambiguous. As one *Kino* critic put it, referring to Rzheshevskii's unrealized screenplay "Okean" [Ocean], when the screenplay says, "there go 200 wonder boys," he refers to the Young Pioneers. But how do we know that these are Young Pioneers? Raphael's angels are also "wonder boys" (Mikh. 1931). In the end the emotional scenario was rejected because, as Shklovskii put it, given its highly literary ("emotional") prose, it made the distance between the screenplay and the film, already quite large, even more substantial (Shklovskii 1931, 69). As another critic put it, to adapt an emotional scenario meant adapting "a system of adjectives" (Otten 1937). In 1937, *Bezhin Meadow* was banned, and this marked the end of the emotional scenario.

Nevertheless, the emotional scenario contributed to the emergence of the literary scenario and, as Iosif Dolinskii and Irina Grashchenkova have suggested (Rzheshevskii and Dolinskii 1982, 15), was closer to the latter than critics tend to believe. The emotional scenario was a finalized literary work, and in the hands of a director willing to submit him- or herself to the screenwriter's version, could in principle produce a faithful adaptation. In other words, it could potentially bridge the gap between conception and the final film. This was the logic behind the literary scenario and Sutyrin's seemingly oxymoronic notion that an authored screenplay could be an iron scenario. In the absence of a division of screenwriting labor that existed in Hollywood, the only way to challenge the director was to boost the screenwriter and his contribution to the film. Making the screenplay more "iron," that is less subject to director intervention, was to give the screenplay the status of an independent work of literature, which had to be respected as such. This in turn meant that the task of writing screenplays should be assigned to established authors.

The Establishment of the Literary Scenario

In the 1930s the Soviet film industry approached Soviet writers and invited them to write screenplays. As I have argued, this phenomenon had a pragmatic underpinning. The Soviet film industry suffered from a constant shortage of good screenplays and was under constant pressure to improve both the quality and quantity of its output. What it needed was to train an army of screenwriters, as Shumiatskii proposed in 1935. However, this was a long-term solution, which was never implemented. The short-term option was to tap into available writing talent: Soviet writers. This choice to call on existing writers, as opposed to training new screenwriters, was determined by the special status of the writer in Stalinist society.

As Katerina Clark has written, in the 1930s, the Soviet authorities elevated the art of literature to the status of the most important of the arts. She explains that this elevation had to do with the belief in the reifying nature of writing (as opposed to the spoken word, not to mention other, more fleeting art forms such as music or architecture). Writing had the ability to both give expression to ideas and preserve that particular expression at the same time (Clark 2011, 78–104; see also Khennig 2006). This logocentrism, perhaps, was also related to the Bolshevik preoccupation with the newspaper as the universal means of propaganda, as well as the fact that historically the passage of ideas occurred through written texts. The Stalinists seemed to believe that if they harnessed the textual medium, they could harness everything else.[2] Therefore, when they decided to unify and Sovietize the arts under the umbrella of Socialist Realism in 1932, they started with literature, and therefore in 1934 the Writers' Union Congress became a major cultural intervention. The call on writers, "the engineers of human souls," to work for cinema was another manifestation of this general process.

Fundamentally, the appeal to the writers was a matter of quality in every meaning of the word. The Soviet film industry continued to rely on freelance screenwriters to deliver screenplays through the process derogatively referred to as *samotek* – literally self-drift, a disorganized submission of solicited and unsolicited screenplays by authors to studios. Screenplay planning was imperfect to say the least, and many submitted screenplays were of substandard quality. One way to boost quality was to improve the pool of screenplay authors. Few professional screenwriters worked in Soviet cinema (Mikhail Bleiman, Evgenii Gabrilovich, Georgii Grebner, Aleksei Kapler, Sergei Ermolinskii, Iosif Prut, Boris Chirskov, Oleg Leonidov, Vladimir Shveitser, and Georgii Mdivani, among others) and although they produced quality screenplays, they could not produce enough of them. Since writers wrote legitimate literature, it was assumed that they could also produce better-quality screenplays. Tapping into the talent of playwrights and novelists for quality product was a strategy not unique to Stalin-era cinema. When the Finnish film industry decided in the 1930s that it wanted to produce better films for the international market, it too invited legitimate writers to write for the screen (Talvio 2010). The same was done in Hollywood, where writers were often employed not only for their writing talent but also for the prestige their names could grant. Even early Russian producers in the 1910s had recruited such writers as Aleksandr Kuprin, Fedor Sologub, and Dmitrii Merezhkovskii to work for the screen, presumably for all these reasons (Kovalova 2012, 23).

The writer as screenwriter was also a measure of ideological quality and security for Soviet cinema. In the first half of the 1930s dozens of Soviet films were banned as ideologically flawed, but it was hard to know how to avoid political mistakes. Appealing to the writers was the film administrators', censors', and directors' way of outsourcing the responsibility for the final ideological message of the film elsewhere. Since the Stalin leadership was clearly spending time and effort on communicating its wishes to writers, it could be assumed that the writers knew better what the leadership wanted and, therefore, could help the film industry make more censorable films. In the production process, the literary scenario functioned in Soviet cinema as a direct equivalent of the Hollywood synopsis. Indeed, this is how Valentin Turkin classifies it in his 1938 screenwriting textbook, *Dramaturgiia kino* [Screen Dramaturgy] (Turkin 2007, 47–48, 51). The only difference was that it was a fully expanded synopsis. Both film industries needed some initial written version of the film that could be vetted. Since in Hollywood censorship was a relatively simple and predictable matter, a short synopsis was sufficient. In the Soviet case, censorship guidelines were very complex and never transparent; therefore, a longer, more detailed written version was necessary for censorship purposes.

Another way of attaining censorship security was the literary adaptation. If a novel or a play was already successfully sold, performed, and reviewed, it could provide for a more secure investment. At least half of all Hollywood films in the 1930s originated from existing literary or theatrical properties. However, the literary adaptation was looked upon with disdain by Soviet authors because it required a mere "technical" reworking of someone else's text as opposed to authoring your own original. Given that screenwriters shunned such work, the next best thing was to have the original authors adapt their own work for the screen. One such author was writer Aleksei Tolstoi, whose novel became the basis of Vladimir Petrov's very successful two-part *Peter the First* [*Petr pervyi*, 1937–1938]. Another, later example was Konstantin Simonov, who wrote screenplays for *Lad from Our Town* [*Paren' iz nashego goroda*, dirs. Aleksandr Stolper, Boris Ivanov, 1942], *In the Name of the Motherland* [*Vo imia rodiny*, Vsevolod Pudovkin, Dmitrii Vasil'ev, 1943], *Wait for Me* [*Zhdi menia*, dirs. Aleksandr Stolper, Boris Ivanov, 1943], and *Days and Nights* [*Dni i nochi*, dir. Aleksandr Stolper, 1944], all based on this own works.

To make screen work more attractive for the legitimate writers, who preferred to write original screenplays, the screenplay was given the status of a legitimate and independent work of literature. In 1940, the venerable screenwriter Katerina Vinogradskaia wrote:

> [t]he screenplay in Soviet cinema is establishing itself as a fact of Soviet literature, and is executed by means of literature, with the only caveat being its special objective: visual presentation. Its dialogues, landscapes, and authored texts – even if they do not make their way into the film and could even be skipped in quick and technical reading – are still important for the culture of the screenplay and have to be carefully written at the level of the great tasks of Soviet literature. (Vinogradskaia 1940, 26)

She proceeded to praise some of the oversized literary scenarios, major portions of which would never be filmed, as budding literature, and argued that what mattered was not their formal readiness for the screen but the civic quality of their authors and ideas (Vinogradskaia 1940, 27).

Attempts were also made to inaugurate the literary scenario as a new literary genre. When established writer Iurii Olesha wrote his first-ever screenplay for Abram Room's *A Strict Young Man* [*Strogii iunosha*, 1936], he called it *p'esa dlia kinematografa* [a play for the cinema]. Vsevolod Vishnevskii named his screenplay for Efim Dzigan's 1936 *We Are from Kronstadt* [*My iz Kronshtadta*] a "Sound-Film Poem" [*Poema. Tonfil'm*]. These gestures, however, went nowhere, when *A Strict Young Man* was banned, and Vishnevskii's screenplay faced administrative resistance. Yet, the "literary" term *kinopovest'* [screen-novella], for instance, already used occasionally in the 1920s and applied to some films of the 1930s, such as *Baltic Deputy* [*Deputat Baltiki*, dirs. Aleksandr Zarkhi, Iosif Kheifits, 1936] and *Miners* [*Shakhtery*, Sergei Iutkevich, 1937], became a standard genre designation in later Soviet cinema (see Liubimov 2007).

Screenplays started to get published in literary journals and screenplay collections. In the pre-Revolutionary cinema such publications were primary done for advertisement purposes and, after the Revolution, to expose potential film stories to public scrutiny. Now, however, this was an effort to show that the screenplay could and should be consumed as literature, and to add to the screenwriters' status, publication counts, and royalties. The screenwriter's name now appeared before the director's in the film opening credits. The special status of the literary scenario (also referred to as the authored [*avtorskii*] scenario) was reflected in the wide use of the term *kinodramaturgiia* [screen dramaturgy] in reference to Soviet screenwriting and *kinodramaturg* (as opposed to *stsenarist*) in reference to the screenwriter.

The flip side of the elevation of the literary scenario was the marginalization of the director's scenario as an element of censorship control. Although many directors' scenarios and their versions, especially for important films, continued to be censored, it was the literary scenario that had to pass censorship if the film was to be produced. For a brief moment in 1938–1939, under Shumiatskii's replacement Semen Dukel'skii, it looked as if the director's scenarios were about to become the focus of censorship. Dukel'skii was appointed Chairman of the Committee for Cinema Affairs in January 1938. In March 1938 he issued a decree that stipulated three innovations pertaining to screenwriting. First, it ordered studios to confine director responsibilities to "primarily" the director's scenarios (i.e., studios were discouraged from letting directors write screenplays for themselves). Second, studios were to begin productions only after Dukel'skii's office approved their director's scenarios. Third, no changes were to be made in the approved director's scenarios unless permission was obtained from Dukel'skii himself (Lebedev 1939, 138–142; Babitsky and Rimberg 1955, 295–297).

The effects of this ruling, however, were short-lived. The archives do contain director's "iron" scenarios where every change bears Dukel'skii signature. Moreover, while Dukel'skii was in charge, the director's scenarios approved by him translated into successful releases more often than before. Between 1930 and 1937, on average eight films were banned every year; under Dukel'skii, in 1938–1939, that number dropped to only one film per year. In addition, Dukel'skii's ruling made it more likely that directors followed their own director's scenarios while filming (although, arguably, this would have happened anyway, simply as a matter of production convenience). However, as soon as Dukel'skii was replaced in June 1939, and his replacement, Ivan Bol'shakov, took office, the censorship focus shifted back to the literary scenario, and the pressure for the iron director's scenario subsided.

In 1941, Bol'shakov prepared a resolution on cinema (that was never officially passed due to the start of World War II) that explicitly stipulated that the production plans of studios be based of the literary scenarios approved by his office, and that the centralized censors (the Committee for Cinema Affairs and, in some cases, the Communist Party Central Committee Propaganda Department) approve only the literary scenarios. The director's scenarios were subjected to censorship by the office of the studio director. Moreover, studios could start production immediately after the literary scenario was approved in Moscow, without waiting for the director's scenario to be prepared and passed (Iumasheva and Lepikhov 1993–1994, 139). This was indeed what the Soviet film industry generally practiced to the end of the Stalin period. The problem with this system was that the director's scenarios, which diverged from the literary scenarios, were not always censored by Moscow, and the film administration could never know exactly what the finished film's message would be.

The need to introduce the legitimate writer to Soviet screenwriting led to the establishment of the literary scenario as the basis of Soviet film production. Conceived as it was as a finished text written by an established writer, the literary scenario was to function as the "iron" scenario. As such, it was to contain both the finalized story and the final ideological message of the film. Its filming was to be a mere translation of the literary scenario into filmic expression. As it turned out, however, due to the unchallenged role of the director in the film production process and the prose format, the literary scenario never became iron.

The Implications of the Literary Scenario

It can be argued that movement toward the iron scenario was an attempt at professionalization and standardization in Soviet screenwriting, whereas movement away from it interfered with the process of professionalization. If implemented, the iron scenario might have solved the problems of inefficient production organization, overarching director authorship, and uncertain censorship control. It is perhaps fortunate for the Soviet film industry that it was never implemented. Without the challenge of producers and staff-screenwriters, the director remained at the center of filmmaking for the rest of the Soviet period. The failure of the iron scenario, however, meant that there was no need to invest in mid-level screenwriters. Together with the call on writers to work for the screen, this made it unnecessary to promote screenwriting as a profession. Although VGIK, the Moscow Film Institute, had been training screenwriters since the 1920s, very few of its graduates worked as screenwriters. The volume of Soviet film production was too low to support a steady inflow of new talent, and the focus on the established author only made this situation worse.

Deprofessionalization also affected the screenplay as a form. The literary scenario was nothing but a prose narrative intended for studio consideration. This was not an ideal form for planning or production. In fact, at least some industry practitioners were happy to get rid of the format altogether even before it gained prominence. In 1930, top executives at the Leningrad film studio (later Lenfilm), Veniamin Vol'f and Adrian Piotrovskii, appealed to Glavrepertkom, the state censorship authority, to abolish the then version of the literary scenario. They argued that practical experience had shown the "complete production inexpediency of the preparation of the literary scenario." First, in the majority of the cases the censorship authority failed to make decisions based on the literary write-up and requested the director's scenario as well, making the censorship of the literary scenario an unnecessary step. Second, the literary write-up was redundant for the director, who could as easily write the director's scenario based on the synopsis ("libretto"). Third, the literary scenario was too cumbersome a format for "public evaluation": it was too long for the mass reader. Fourth, its development took up to two months, delaying the production process. Vol'f and Piotrovskii requested that Glavrepertkom change its rules to allow studios to submit synopses instead for censorship purposes and additionally review of the director's scenarios when necessary (TsGALI 257/7/27, 33–34: Perepiska s GRK po stsenarnym voprosam [Correspondence with GRK on Questions of Scripts],1930). In 1930, this appeal reflected what I have mentioned already: given that the directors wrote their own versions of the original material, there was little point in principle in censoring the literary treatment.

The most problematic was the fact that the literary scenario was not standardized. It was not set what its length was to be or how its pages translated into minutes of film or meters of footage. In 1937 literary critic and screenwriter Victor Shklovskii noted that screenplays were so excessively long that it would have been cheaper to frame them in diamond-encrusted gold than to film them as written (Shklovskii 1937). It was assumed that each paragraph line stood for a different shot, but such division was included more for presentation purposes than for replication in subsequent versions or accountability. Some literary scenarios included shot numbers, others did not, and, even when included, the numbers were typically superficial. As Turkin mentions in his 1938 textbook, the literary format, which lacked any indication on exterior and interior scenes or the number of sets involved, made it very difficult for studios to determine the scale and footage of the future production (Turkin 2007, 50–51). Not surprisingly, it was very common to refer to the literary scenarios as only "raw material" [syr'e] requiring substantial reshaping before they could be used.

When the literary scenario became the focus of the Soviet screenwriting effort, it undermined not just the authority of the director's scenario but also every other type of script that was useful in film planning, production, and censorship. According to critic and early screenplay theorist Ippolit Sokolov, in 1936 Mosfilm spent 1,129,000 rubles (i.e., almost 25,000 rubles per screenplay, a substantial but typical sum for the period) on 46 literary scenarios of which it used only eight. This low usability ratio (17 per cent), Sokolov implied, resulted from the fact that the studio did not require that the authors it contracted provide any kind of synopsis or short description of the future screenplay prior to Mosfilm's financial commitment (Sokolov 1938). As the synopsis lost its validity, industry professionals lost an important intermediate (and far cheaper) step of sifting through material. It is not that the synopsis was eliminated: the material submitted to the studios included both librettos and screenplays. However, it appears that a heavy proportion of unsolicited submissions processed by the screenplay departments at Soviet studios was made up of lengthy manuscripts, and screenplay editors wasted a lot of time reading and writing rejections to literary scenarios in particular (TsGALI 257/15/57: Perepiska so stsenaristami o stsenariiakh [Correspondence with Scriptwriters on Scripts], 1938; TsGALI 257/16/1146: Perepiska s avtorami stsenariev po samotechnym zaiavkam [Correspondence with Screenwriters on Screenplay Proposals], 1941). Even if it is conceivable that a synopsis was too short for censorship purposes (and all screenplay editors were also censors), operating with the much longer prose format must have made the process very inefficient and undoubtedly discouraged unsuccessful solicitors from tackling screenplay writing again.

Finally, the major problem was that literary scenarios, especially whose authored by non-professional screenwriters, were simply, well, too literary to be useful in the production process. Complaints about the untenability and imperfection of the literary scenario as a genre came from all corners. Sokolov maintained, for instance, that Mosfilm's 1936 authors were more likely to work on literary and thematic qualities than on plot development, undermining the latter. Neither were they aware enough of the film production process to take into account such factors as the number of sets that it was practical to build for a certain type of film at any particular studio (Sokolov 1938). This trend away from "cinema specificity" to literature, apparently affected even professional screenwriters. According to Turkin, in the attempt to compete with legitimate writers, they lost their sense of what kind of stories and volume of material were appropriate for a film. Screenwriters had forgotten how to structure plots around a progression of actions as opposed to mere recounting of a series of events. Many screenplays lacked dramatic conflict, skillful dialogue, and character motivation and development (Turkin 1938).

One goal accomplished by the literary scenario in the 1930s was a redistribution of screenwriting responsibilities. With some notable exceptions (e.g., Aleksandr Dovzhenko), Soviet film directors stopped writing screenplays for themselves. In 1934, for instance, out of 87 screenplays approved for production, 27 were written by professional screenwriters, 33 by novelists and playwrights, and 17 by directors themselves (the source does not state who authored the remaining 10, but it must have been either a combination of authors or some unknown names) (Abul-Kasymova *et al.* 1973, 13). In 1947, to take just one relatively fruitful year for comparison, out of 22 films produced, only one was scripted by a director: Mikhail Romm's *The Russian Question* [*Russkii vopros*]. However, even in this case the film was an adaptation: it was based on a play by Konstantin Simonov. One other film was scripted by director Leonid Trauberg, but for someone else. Professional screenwriters wrote the majority of the screenplays, and seven screenplays were written by writers. One may even conclude from this only somewhat representative sample that the writers did not get a complete hold in the Soviet film industry, and in the end the majority of films were written by the few professional screenwriters who were active. However, such a conclusion requires additional confirmation.

What we do know is that the literary scenario stayed; and so did both its virtues and problems. Soviet screenwriting continued to be a prestigious and well-compensated occupation beyond the Stalin period. And the Soviet film directors sustained their position as the primary intelligence behind the film despite all the censorship. In fact, both director-authors and screenwriter-authors continued to make it difficult for the Soviet film industry to effectively censor itself, and conflicts, broken careers, and bans continued. On the other hand, the literary nature of the screenplay continued to provide for production difficulties.

In the end, even though the goal of the literary scenario was to produce better, more predictable (censorable, iron), and more readily adaptable material for the cinema, the outcome was largely the opposite. Instead of bridging the gap between the screenplay and the film, the literary scenario expanded this gap, or, as some writers argue, attempted to turn film into literature (Kozlov 1957, 53–54). With hindsight possible after the death of Stalin in 1953 and Khrushchev's anti-Stalin revelations of 1956, critic Leonid Kozlov, writing in 1957, summarized the status of the literary scenario as follows: "the [Soviet literary] screenplay is a type of literature, closely related to prose and play in its artistic means and principles, independent and equal [to them], created both for reading and for realization on screen, which [the latter] stipulates that it needs to take into account the visual means of cinematic art" (Kozlov 1957, 53). He added that the "literariness" was considered this screenplay's paramount quality that made it lose all connection to its actual *raison d'être*: cinema. In what ways later Soviet cinema was "literary" (and Kozlov suggests that it was) is a major research question that goes beyond the scope of this chapter. However, the idea that cinema was somehow close to literature fits well with Vladimir Papernyi's definition of Stalinist culture. Whereas in pre-Stalinist culture (Culture One) of the 1920s, it was the difference, the "untranslatability" between the arts that mattered, in Stalinist Culture Two all arts were to merge in some socialist realist message-focused whole (Papernyi 2006, 218; see also Bulgakova 2000).

Another post-Stalinist critic, Anri Vartanov, lamented that the reason Soviet films diverged from their original screenplays was because the screenplays contained everything (descriptions) but core information that was to be included in the film (actions). Although the author himself denies this link, his discussion of the literary scenarios of the 1950s reminds one of the criticisms leveled against the emotional scenario in the 1930s. As if recycling these earlier debates, Vartanov writes that the "technical" scenario (i.e., the iron scenario) is a better format, because even if the director wanted to change the conception of the technical scenario he would be unable to do so, as "the entire system of images" of the work would be fully determined by the original. At the same time, he says, "in case there is even a minimal creative difference between the director and the screenwriter, an 'emotional scenario' and a screen-novella or a screen-play [*stsenarii-p'esa*] immediately lose their core qualities: the treatment of the images becomes entirely dependent on the director, who interprets them and translates from the language of literature to the language of cinema" (Vartanov 1959, 150). He concludes that in order for the Soviet screenplay to become filmable again – in other words, to attain the form stipulating not only the film's conception but also its execution – the Soviet practice has to go back to the more cinematic format all but abandoned with the advent of the literary scenario (Vartanov 1959).

Conclusion

The primacy of the literary scenario was an anomaly of Soviet cinema. Moreover, in that cinema itself it was a diversion from alternative forms of screenplay that were both more practical and more cinematic, a diversion that was nevertheless adopted for specific historical and ideological reasons. The literary scenario emerged when the "ideological" message of the film and the availability of this message for censorship evaluation became more important than the film's director, story, setting, plot, stars, or visual style. Its emergence was part and parcel of the general "literarization" of the Stalinist culture that occurred in the mid-1930s, when the primary effort to Sovietize Soviet culture and to assure its ideological purity focused on the writer (see Heller 2003). It was the writer who was to assure this purity, and the writer required the adoption of the literary-scenario format. The phenomenon of the literary scenario is, therefore, secondary to the phenomenon of the elevation of Soviet writer and Soviet literature to the status of the primary cultural force in Soviet society. The literary nature of the Soviet screenplay was never a goal in itself. It was an accidental result of the pressure to put the legitimate writer at the center of the Soviet screenwriting effort.

Neither was the emergence of the literary scenario necessarily a direct outcome of the introduction of sound (Gerasimov 1952, 12). An iron scenario and even the director's scenario as actually practiced in the Soviet film industry were as appropriate for the censorship of text and speech as was the literary scenario. In fact, the director's scenario was a lot closer to the finished film than the literary scenario could ever hope to be, and it is a great irony of Soviet cinema that the debate on the precise iron scenario led to what was formally its exact opposite: a literary screenplay.

Scholars tend to connect the rise of the literary scenario to Stalin personally. In particular, they interpret one of his comments as suggesting that to him the director was secondary to the screenwriter and the film text was secondary to the literary text (Kenez 2001, 219; Bulgakova 2000, 150). In August 1940, the Central

Committee banned Aleksandr Stolper and Boris Ivanov's film *The Law of Life* (*Zakon zhizni*, 1940), scripted by Aleksandr Avdeenko. In September 1940, Stalin called Avdeenko and others to the Kremlin to explain why the film failed. After the meeting, Stalin reportedly said that it was the screenwriter who was responsible for the film's flaws; the directors only "cranked" what was written for them (Simonov 1988, 71–72, cited in Bulgakova 2000, 150). As already mentioned, there is no doubt that Stalin believed in the power of the written word and spent a lot of time molding the course of Soviet literature. However, the causal link between this supposed belief by Stalin and the primacy of the literary scenario in the Soviet filmmaking tradition went perhaps not directly from word to screenplay or from Stalin to screenplay. It was mediated instead by Stalin's relationship to the writer and literature. In other words, it is not that the screenplay was important because the word was important in Stalinist culture; it is that the word was important, therefore writers were important, and therefore the literary scenario became important as a format in which writers could work.

We know that Stalin both read theater plays and went to judge them in the theater. He told Eisenstein in 1947 that he did not want to see the new version of his screenplay for *Ivan the Terrible* Part Two because "[i]n general it is hard to judge based on the screenplay; it is easier to talk about the finished work" (Mar'iamov 1992, 90). We also know that he read very few screenplays but liked to watch films (Belodubrovskaya 2011b). Perhaps, it depended on the case. In the case of *The Law of Life*, it was Avdeenko, the writer, who was supposed to be astute enough to know how to avoid ideological blemishes. Yet, only months later, Andrei Zhdanov, Stalin's close associate, said that everyone was ultimately responsible for a bad film, as "everyone created the film, that is directors, set designers, actors." The screenplay was only where one was to look for the origins of the problems (Fomin 2005, 51). Thus it is possible to interpret Stalin's comment as simply saying that Avdeenko's screenplay was already problematic, and Stolper and Ivanov only replicated his mistakes. That said, it is also possible that Stalin expected that writers (and writer-screenwriters), "the engineers of human souls," would have become perfect mediums of socialist ideas by 1940, allowing the directors to only crank the camera. After all, it was writers and not filmmakers who were invited to that meeting with Stalin (Anderson et al. 2005, 573–604). This same idea of the ready translatability of the written material into a film was behind Sutyrin's conception of the literary scenario. As Sutyrin put it, the ideal screenplay was a screenplay that the director "developed" like a strip of film (TsGALI 257/6/19, 30: Stenogramma 1-go Vserossiiskogo soveshchaniia po stsenarnomu delu [Minutes of the First All-Union Meeting on Scripts], 1929).

Ultimately, despite its production inefficiency and poor susceptibility to censorship, the literary scenario had one clear advantage. Its emergence as a stand-alone literary genre allowed the film industry to share the responsibility for the final ideological message of its product with the screenplay author, the writer. The adoption of the iron scenario – an internal industry document – would have placed the blame for ideological failures squarely onto the directors, who filmed it, and the industry executives, who approved it. The literary scenario gave industry practitioners a chance to effectively protect themselves under tremulous and extremely dangerous conditions of Stalinist reality (Mikhail Iampol'skii (1990, 29) makes a similar argument). When Stalin said that Stolper and Ivanov were not responsible for the flaws of *The Law of Life*, this was precisely what the directors wanted to hear.

Notes

1. At the end of the essay Eisenstein says that the first attempt at an emotional scenario was his own 1926 screenplay for *Old and New* [*Staroe i novoe*, 1929] (Eizenshtein 1964, 299).
2. On the importance of the word in Stalinist culture see also Tertz (1976) and Dobrenko (2008).

References

References to TsGALI [Central Archive for Literature and Art] in St Petersburg are by fond, inventory [opis'], and document, followed by the file name and year.

Abul-Kasymova, Khandzhara, S. Ginzburg, I. Dolinskii et al., eds. 1973. *Istoriia sovetskogo kino, 1917–1967* [History of Soviet Cinema]. Vol. 2. Moscow: Iskusstvo.

Anderson, Kirill, Leonid Maksimenkov, L. Kosheleva, and L. Rogovaia, eds. 2005. *Kremlevskii kinoteatr, 1928–1953. Dokumenty* [The Kremlin's Cinema, 1928–1953]. Moscow: ROSSPEN.

Babitsky, Paul and John Rimberg. 1955. *The Soviet Film Industry*. New York: Praeger.

Belodubrovskaya, Maria. 2011a. "Politically Incorrect: Filmmaking Under Stalin and the Failure of Power." PhD Diss., University of Wisconsin-Madison.

Belodubrovskaya, Maria. 2011b. "The Jockey and the Horse: Joseph Stalin and the Biopic Genre in Soviet Cinema." *Studies in Russian and Soviet Cinema* 5.1: 29–53.

Bordwell, David, Janet Staiger, and Kristin Thompson. 1985. *The Classical Hollywood Cinema: Film Style and Mode of Production to 1960*. New York: Columbia University Press.

Bulgakova, Oksana. 2000. "Sovetskoe kino v poiskakh 'obshchei modeli'" [Soviet Cinema in Search for a "Common Model"]. In *Sotsrealisticheskii kanon* [Socialist-Realist Canon], edited by Hans Günther and Evgenii Dobrenko, 146–165. St Petersburg: Akademicheskii proekt.

Cherkasov, A. 1926. "Zheleznyi stsenarii" [The Iron Script]. *Kino-front* [Cinema-Front] 9–10: 3–4.

Clark, Katerina. 2011. *Moscow, the Fourth Rome: Stalinism, Cosmopolitanism, and the Evolution of Soviet Culture, 1931–1941*. Cambridge, MA: Harvard University Press.

Dobrenko, Evgeny. 2008. *Stalinist Cinema and the Production of History: Museum of the Revolution*. New Haven: Yale University Press.

Eizenshtein, Sergei. 1964. "O forme stsenariia" [On Screenplay Form]. In *Izbrannye proizvedeniia v shesti tomakh* [Collected Works in 6 vols]. Vol. 2, 297–299. Moscow: Iskusstvo.

Fomin, Valerii. 2005. *Kino na voine: Dokumenty i svidetel'stva* [Cinema at War: Documents and Testimonies]. Moscow: Materik.

Genika, Iurii. 1939. *Kinorezhissura* [Film Directing]. Moscow: Goskinoizdat.

Gerasimov, Sergei. 1952. "O professii kinorezhissera" [On the Profession of the Director]. In *Voprosy masterstva v sovetskom kinoiskusstve* [Questions of Mastery in Soviet Film Art], edited by B. Kravchenko, 7–42. Moscow: Goskinoizdat.

Heller, Leonid. 2003. "Cinéma à lire. Observations sur l'usage du "scénario litteraire" à l'époque de Jdanov" [Cinema for Reading. Observations on the Use of a "Literary Script" during the Zhdanov Era]. In *Le Cinéma "stalinien": questions d'histoire*, edited by Natacha Laurent, 57–70. Toulouse: Presses universitaires du Mirail – La Cinémathèque de Toulouse.

Iampol'skii, Mikhail. 1990. "Kak byt' khudozhnikom" [How to be an Artist]. *Iskusstvo kino* [Art of Cinema] 3: 25–36.

Iumasheva, Ol'ga and Lepikhov, Il'ia. 1993/94. "Fenomen 'totalitarnogo liberalizma' (opyt reformy sovetskoi kinematografii)." [The Phenomenon of "Totalitarian Liberalism" (The Experience of Soviet Cinema)]. *Kinovedcheskie zapiski* [Film Scholars' Notes] 20: 125–144.

Kenez, Peter. 2001. *Cinema and Soviet Society from the Revolution to the Death of Stalin*. London, New York: I. B. Tauris.

Khennig (Hennig), Anke. 2006. "Obobshchenie kinodramaturgii. Ot kinodramaturgii do dramaturgii iskusstv" [The Generalization of Scriptwriting. From Film Dramaturgy to Dramaturgy of Art]. In *Sovetskaia vlast' i media: Sbornik statei* [Soviet Power and Media: A Collection of Articles], edited by Hans Günter and Sabine Hänsgen, 430–449. St Petersburg: Akademicheskii proekt.

Kovalova, Anna. 2012. "Kinodramaturgiia N.R. Erdmana: evoliutsiia i poetika" [The Film Dramaturgy of Nikolai Erdman: Evolution and Poetics]. Candidate diss., St Petersburg State University.

Kozlov, Leonid. 1957. "O kinematograficheskoi prirode stsenariia" [About the Cinematic Nature of the Script]. *Voprosy kinoiskusstva* [Questions of Film Art]. Vol. 2, 51–76. Moscow: Izdatel'stvo Akademii nauk SSSR.

Lebedev, Nikolai. 1939. *Partiia o kino* [The Party on Cinema]. Moscow: Goskinoizdat.

Liubimov, Boris. 2007. "Fenomen kinopovesti" [The Phenomenon of the Film Novella]. *Kinovedcheskie zapiski* [Film Scholars' Notes] 84: 335–360.

Maras, Steven. 2009. *Screenwriting: History, Theory, and Practice*. London, New York: Wallflower Press.

Mar'iamov, Grigorii. 1992. *Kremlevskii tsenzor: Stalin smotrit kino* [The Kremlin Censor. Stalin Watches Cinema]. Moscow: Kinotsentr.

Mikh., B. 1931. "Kuda zovet Rzheshevskii?" [Where's Rzheshevskii Calling?]. *Kino* 69 (December 12): 3.

Nikol'skaia, Iu. 1936. "Za pravil'nuiu organizatsiiu proizvodstvennoi raboty v s"emochnykh gruppakh" [For the Right Organization of the Production Work in Film Crews]. *Rotfront* 11 (June 10): 3.

Otten, Nikolai. 1937. "Snova ob 'emotsional'nom stsenarii'" [Again about the Emotional Script]. *Iskusstvo kino* [Art of Cinema] 5: 30–35.

Papernyi, Vladimir. 2006. *Kul'tura Dva* [Culture Two]. Moscow: Novoe literaturnoe obozrenie.

Pudovkin, Vsevolod. 1974. "Tvorchestvo literatora v kino. O kinematograficheskom stsenarii Rzheshevskogo" [The Work of the Writer in Cinema. About the Firm Script by Rzheshevskii]. In *Sobranie sochinenii v trekh tomakh* [Collected Works in 3 vols]. Vol. 1, 79–84. Moscow: Iskusstvo.

Rzheshevskii, Aleksandr and Iosif Dolinskii. 1982. *A.G. Rzheshevskii – zhizn', kino.* [A. Rzheshevskii. Life and Cinema]. Moscow: Iskusstvo.

Shklovskii, Viktor. 1931. *Kak pisat' stsenarii* [How to Write a Script]. Moscow: GIKhL.

Shklovskii, Viktor 1937. "Bol'she i luchshe" [Bigger and Better]. *Kino* 59 (December 22): 3.

Simonov, Konstantin. 1988. "Glazami cheloveka moego pokoleniia" [With the Eyes of My Generation]. *Znamia* 4: 48–121.

Sokolov, Ippolit. 1926. *Kino-stsenarii. Teoriia i tekhnika* [The Film Script. Theory and Technique]. Moscow: Kinopechat'.

Sokolov, Ippolit. 1938. "Literaturnyi i s"emochnyi stsenarii" [The Literary and the Shooting Script]. *Kino* 31 (July 5): 3.

Sutyrin, V. 1929. "O stsenarii i stsenariste" [About the Script and the Scriptwriter]. *Sovetskii ekran* [Soviet Screen] 16 (April 16): 8.

Szczepanik, Petr. 2013. "How Many Steps to the Shooting Script? A Political History of Screenwriting." *Iluminace* 25.3: 73–98.

Talvio, Raija. 2010. "'First of All, the Screenplay Problem Has to Be Solved' – The Public Debate on Screenwriting in 1930s Finland." *Journal of Screenwriting* 1.2: 325–342.

Tertz, Abram. 1976. "The Literary Process in Russia," trans. Michael Glenny, in *Kontinent 1: The Alternative Voice of Russia and Eastern Europe*, edited by Vladimir E. Maximov, 73–110. London: Andre Deutsch.

Turkin, Valentin. 1938. "O proizvodstvennoi kul'ture avtorskogo stsenariia" [About the Production Culture of Original Scripts]. *Kino* 31 (July 5): 3.

Turkin, Valentin. 2007. *Dramaturgiia kino* [Screen Dramaturgy]. Moscow: VGIK (reprint of the original 1938 edition).

Vartanov, Anri. 1959. "O kinematograficheskoi obraznosti stsenariia" [About the Cinematic Image of the Script]. *Voprosy kinodramaturgii* [Questions of Film Dramaturgy]. Vol. 3, 123–201. Moscow: Iskusstvo.

Vinogradskaia, Katerina 1940. "Fabrikanty siuzhetov" [Makers of Subjects]. *Iskusstvo kino* (Art of Cinema) 9: 26–29.

Zhemchuzhnyi, Vitalii. 1933. "Zheleznyi stsenarii" [The Iron Script]. *Sovetskoe kino* (Soviet Cinema) 7: 31–40.

12

Ideology, Technology, Aesthetics: Early Experiments in Soviet Color Film, 1931–1945

Phil Cavendish

Color is essential for the expression of joyfulness and happiness. Our festivals are bright and saturated with color. All our folk art dazzles with the richness of its palette. Color is an essential element in the multinational art of the USSR.

(Aleksandrov 1940)

Introduction

The epigraph derives from an article by Grigorii Aleksandrov, the former assistant to Sergei Eisenstein who directed several popular musical comedies during the 1930s. Written some nine years after the first home-grown color experiment in the Soviet Union, and in anticipation of the approaching twenty-fifth anniversary of the October Revolution, Aleksandrov was lending his weight to a growing and influential lobby within the Soviet film industry which had been arguing for several years that the acquisition and perfection of a color-film technology should be regarded as an ideological priority, if not a utopian aspiration, for the Soviet state. The notebooks of Boris Shumiatskii, the head of the Main Directorate of the Film and Photo Industry [GUKF, Glavnoe upravlenie kino-foto-promyshlennosti; from August 1936 the Main Directorate of the Film Industry, GUK], indicate that Stalin himself was interested in the phenomenon of color. During private screenings at the Kremlin between 1934 and 1937, he was shown fragments of documentary footage in color from the 1934 May-Day parade; praised a Disney Technicolor cartoon; requested viewings of the first animation short to be filmed with a Soviet three-color process; and drew Shumiatskii's attention to the "urgent task" of developing

A Companion to Russian Cinema, First Edition. Edited by Birgit Beumers.
© 2016 John Wiley & Sons, Inc. Published 2016 by John Wiley & Sons, Inc.

a reliable color-film technology (Troshin 2002, 286; Troshin 2003, 147, 155, 159, 160). The official interest in color at this time is also reflected in the decision to screen several Technicolor films as part of the first Moscow International Film Festival in February 1935, *La Cucaracha* (1934), directed by Lloyd Corrigan, and three of Walt Disney's "Silly Symphonies," all of them advertisements for the corporation's three-color dye-transfer and imbibition process (Masurenkov 2006, 301). Recognition of the ideological importance of color is further suggested by the decision to document in color the two physical-culture parades that took place on Red Square in 1938 and 1939. It is difficult to imagine two more prestigious commissions. The parades in question were meticulously choreographed and grandiose spectacles which involved tens of thousands of sporting representatives and athletes from different Soviet republics marching past the Kremlin, with Stalin and other members of the Party leadership in attendance. Not only did these parades embody the energetic promotion of physical fitness and sporting prowess during the 1930s, but also, thanks to the involvement of the GTO program ["G̲otov k t̲rudu i o̲boronel!" – "Prepared for Work and Defense!"] from March 1931, they reflected the importance attached to military preparedness (O'Mahony 2006, 126–127). Unlike other state celebrations, the annual physical-culture parades were designed to be colorful events, with the costumes of the participants, some of them clearly drawing on the national traditions of the republics, bright and vibrant, if not extraordinarily flamboyant. Foreign observers at the time, for example the American ambassador, Joseph Davies, were struck by the gaiety of these spectacles (Schlögel 2012, 248–249). Thanks to the availability of color-film technology, such events could be captured on film for the first time and presented to a Soviet public which, owing to their exclusive nature (O'Mahony 2006, 86), would not have been able to witness them first-hand.

The existence of these two documentaries, while certainly attesting to the increasing prioritization of color on the part of the Soviet authorities during the 1930s, nevertheless conceals the complexity of the challenge that color posed for the film industry, and the fact that, on balance, the imperative to acquire a reliable color technology was met by relative failure, rather than success, as official ambition remained unmatched by actual achievement. Something approaching the reality can be gauged from the film press of the time. Newspapers reported regularly on the latest color experiments. They explained the science of the processes, offered profiles of the key researchers, and acted as a conduit for debates which not infrequently criticized official policies in relation to color: the lack of a coherent organizational strategy on the part of the GUKF/GUK; the bureaucratic inertia, if not obstruction, on the part of certain figures at studio-management level; the persistent delays in the supply of technical equipment; the excessive secrecy and rivalries of individual research teams; and the glaring discrepancies between planned production quotas and actual numbers of releases. In relation to the two documentaries mentioned above, the particular nature of the challenge can be illustrated by the fact that the first, *Blossoming Youth* [*Tsvetushchaia molodost'*, 1938], directed by Nikolai Solov'ev, has survived only as a seven-minute fragment: it is poor in terms of its natural color rendition, and was filmed according to a two-color process which, in its Soviet manifestation, had been pioneered in the early 1930s and thus could hardly be regarded as an occasion for official self-congratulation. In relation to the second, *The Blossoming Young: Parade of Physical Culture, 18 July 1939* [*Tsvetushchaia iunost', Fizkul'turnyi parad 18 iiulia 1939g.*, 1939], directed by Aleksandr Medvedkin, while much more impressive in terms of its natural color rendition, and filmed according to a more complicated three-color process, only 15 minutes of footage has survived, which is presumably only a fraction of the material recorded. Both documentaries serve as useful illustrations of the potential hazards that face the film historian seeking to investigate the "narrative" of Soviet color film in its early phases. These consist of the technological complexities of color processes generally, the difficulty of establishing with precision the scientific methods adopted by Soviet research teams, the occasional unreliability of archival documents in relation to the color processes adopted for individual films or fragments of film, and the fact that the majority of the experiments dating from this period have either not survived, or are not accessible as original positives. It is symptomatic of these challenges that, while there has been a recent revival of interest in the color experiments of the 1930s, and while several works of animation and some examples of documentary material have been digitally restored on the basis of surviving negatives (Maiorov 2011), the problems of acquiring a viable process before 1945 have been glossed over, if not ignored completely, largely due to the fact that contemporary sources have not been consulted. These not only indicate that the Soviet "color narrative" was complex at this time, they also suggest that the recent restorations of animations, because they are based on insufficient appreciation of authorial intent, may misrepresent the stylistic nuances of the originals. These sources also demonstrate that the debates around the challenges of color were prompted not only by practical considerations, but also by issues relating to the ways in which color was being exploited artistically. These debates were conducted for the most part within the sphere of the filmmaking community, but they also included significant interventions from a broader, film-interested public: art historians, practicing artists, and members of the creative intelligentsia generally. This culminated in a conference at the Moscow House of Cinema in September 1945, which was convened specifically to discuss the technical and aesthetic challenges of color film, and the delegates to which were treated to examples of Soviet films that had been made possible by the Red Army's acquisition of Agfa color-film patents as a "spoil of war" and non-Soviet color films that had been confiscated from the Reichsfilmarchiv in Berlin (Germanova 1991). The transcripts of this conference reveal that, even on the threshold of Soviet international success in the arena of color film, one made possible largely through the acquisition of these Agfa patents, there was continuing resistance to the advent of color on the part of certain delegates, and thus, by extension, to the ideological prerogatives of the state.

Ideology, Technology, Aesthetics

This chapter seeks to examine the intricacies and complexities of color-film technology in the Soviet Union during the 1930s and early 1940s. It will identify the inventors of the first color experiments, the scientific methods which they adopted in pursuit of their goal, the institutional support that they received, and the stages by means of which their experiments were eventually brought to fruition. A skeptical position will be adopted in relation to the official rhetoric of the period. Furthermore, the patriotic tendencies that characterize some of the recent writing on the subject in Russian, this reflected most baldly in Nikolai Maiorov's assertion that the Soviet Union's three-color process was somehow unique, the Soviet "answer" to Technicolor (Maiorov 2011, 201), will be strongly contested. This chapter will argue that, on the contrary, Soviet researchers during the 1930s were heavily reliant on color processes pioneered abroad; indeed, they would have made little progress without foreign equipment, in particular film stock, which was being imported right up to the Nazi invasion in June 1941. Mapping the chronology of the Soviet "color narrative" during the 1930s and early 1940s serves a much-needed purpose in the sense that, despite the recent revival of interest, it is still very much uncharted territory. Such an enterprise casts a revealing light on the dynamics of Soviet light industry during the first five-year plans, in particular on the tensions between spontaneous initiative from below and *dirigiste* official decree from above. Investigation into the cultural discourse around color during this period is also important in the sense that it reveals tensions within the creative intelligentsia in relation to the theory and practice of color cinematography. Some commentators reacted with barely concealed distaste to the arrival of color: this position was famously encapsulated in Formalist critic Viktor Shklovskii's dismissal of color film as "half-crazed fruit drops" [*vzbesivshiisia landrin*].[1] It is significant, however, that in the years immediately preceding the war there emerged a sophisticated dialogue between filmmakers and artists about how color might be handled within the medium of film. This dialogue not only featured interventions from Eisenstein (Eizenshtein 1940), but also contributions from such figures as Eduard Tissé, his first-choice camera operator, who raised concerns that the lack of technical proficiency on the part of film-directors generally was inhibiting engagement with the creative challenge of color (Tisse 1941).

Initial Explorations

According to Aleksandr Deriabin (2002), some 75 color films were made in the Soviet Union between 1931 and 1945. It is unclear, however, how many of these works were sufficiently acceptable in terms of technical quality to merit general distribution. Research into the possibilities of color film had been pursued for several years before 1931, but for the most part this took the form of a series of spontaneous initiatives on the part of individual film-industry employees, the vast majority of them camera operators. During this early phase, the phenomenon acquired momentum in the absence of official encouragement or support; even those enjoying the patronage of the Institute of Scientific Film and Photo Research (NIKFI), a body established in 1929 to develop a self-sufficient technological base for the Soviet film industry, felt themselves to be working on the margins. Nikolai Agokas, for example, one of the pioneers of the Soviet two-color process at NIKFI, referred to the general ignorance about color that prevailed at this time within the film industry and the "legends" which were circulating about NIKFI's "color laboratory" (Agokas 1934). In a later reminiscence, he recalled the sense of being marooned like "Robinson Crusoe" (Agokas 1936a).

In the folklore of Soviet color film, Agokas and his colleagues are regarded as mavericks and eccentrics, enthusiastic pioneers pursuing a private obsession, if not a utopian fantasy, in conditions that can only be described as a "cottage industry" (Zusman 1931). Collectively, although they were not collaborating with each other, and indeed were criticized in the early days for excessive secrecy and competitiveness (Anon. 1931), they were known as *tsvetniki* [colorists], and it was only when the pursuit of a commercially viable color process began to enjoy official support from 1934 onwards that they were saluted as heroes and given financial prizes for their work, albeit relatively modest ones (Anon. 1936a).

One of the key figures in these early days was Nikolai Anoshchenko, a camera operator by training who had spent a year on secondment in Berlin and on his return produced a book that detailed the latest technological developments in the Weimar film industry; this included a short chapter on the color processes that he had encountered during his stay (Anoshchenko 1927). His own invention, a two-color additive process called Spektrakoler, was a variation of the Kinemacolor system, and required specially designed filters to be fixed to the obturators of both camera and projector: its first public demonstration, a short documentary entitled *A Festival of Work* [*Prazdnik truda*], took place on August 1, 1931 and coincided with the opening of Moscow's Vostokkino film-theater (Anoshchenko 1931; K. V. 1931).[2] Another seminal figure was Fedor Provorov, a camera operator who, along with Agokas and N. Skavronskii, developed a two-color subtractive process at NIKFI.[3] This was first tested on *A Carnival of Colors* [*Karnaval tsvetov*, 1935], an experimental "film-revuc" which lasted around 45 minutes and included five different types of color "study," and was then adopted for *Grunia Kornakova*, also known as *Nightingale, My Little Nightingale* [*Solovei-Solovushko*], a full-length feature directed by Nikolai Ekk and released by the studio of Mezhrabpomfilm in 1936. A third important figure was Pavel Mershin, another camera operator by training, who was employed at Sovkino and Mosfilm during the 1920s and early 1930s and subsequently developed the Soviet Union's first three-color "hydrotype" process. Mershin most accurately fits the description of "maverick" in the sense that his initial researches were carried out in the privacy of his own home, and apparently with his own money. The lack of official support for his research is illustrated by the fact that, after he was invited to join Mosfilm in 1935, some 10 years after beginning his experiments, space for his "laboratory" could only be found in the studio's latrines (Mershin 1936; Tikhonravov 1938; Luchanskii 1939, 8–12).

A whole host of other figures are mentioned in the film press of these years in relation to experiments in color, but their contributions are relatively marginal by comparison. They are: Grigorii Kabalov, a camera operator employed at Mezhrabpomfilm, who photographed a single two-color episode for a special screening of Lev Kuleshov's *The Great Consoler* [*Velikii uteshitel'*, 1933] (Khokhlova and Kuleshov 1975, 155, 159); Iurii Zheliabuzhskii, the director and cameraman best known in the 1920s for his screen adaptations of literary classics, whose pioneering book on the art of camera operation, *Iskusstvo kinooperatora*, featured an entire chapter on recent developments in color film (Zheliabuzhskii 1932, 144–58); Georgii Reisgof, a cameraman working alongside Provorov at Mezhrabpomfilm, who photographed a short two-color documentary entitled [*Pioneer Camp in Artek* (*Artek*, 1936)] before being transferred to Soiuzdetfilm, where he shot a number of color animations and documentary shorts; Vladimir Nil'sen, a camera operator who collaborated with Aleksandrov (Tissé acted as consultant) on *The Internationale* [*Internatsional*, 1932], a two-reel *feuilleton* which used the two-color subtractive process developed at NIKFI (Deriabin 2002, 326–327); and Evgenii Sholpo, the inventor of the Variophone (a system of graphic sound production), who in 1932, alongside the animators Viktor Grigor'ev ("Gri"), Vladislav Tvardovskii, and Vitalii Siumkin, shot a two-color animated cartoon, *Symphony of the World* [*Simfoniia mira*], for the Leningrad-based Rosfilm studio (Sholpo 1933; Deriabin 2002, 326). It is important in this context not to ignore the group of scientists attached to the Leningrad State Optical Institute (GOI), who developed a three-color "hydrotype" method similar to Mershin's. This was tested on *Dance Suite* [*Tantseval'naia siuita*], a brief montage of song-and-dance routines directed by Adol'f Bergunker and photographed by Viacheslav Gordanov in 1938 (Deriabin 2002, 333–334); and also, it would appear, on *Autumn* [*Osen'*], a series of short, live-action sequences around six minutes in length, which was directed by Fridrikh Ermler and shot by Gordanov in the environs of the summer palace at Peterhof two years later (Deriabin 2002, 339–340).

The Importance of Color Processes Pioneered Abroad

Judging from the available evidence, it would appear that the enthusiasm for color on the part of the *tsvetniki* derived in part from their encounters with color film while working or travelling abroad. In his monograph on the Weimar film industry, for example, Anoshchenko (1927, paragraphs 2–3) details his encounter, quite by chance, with an ethnographic documentary, shot "either on the island of Java or somewhere in Africa," which had been released by Emil Busch AG and had used a two-color additive method. Although he claimed to know about this method already, Anoshchenko was sufficiently impressed by the quality of the color rendition to seek an audience with its inventor, Jan Szczepanik, the "Polish Edison." During their meeting, which was facilitated by industry contacts and took place several days later, Anoshchenko was given the opportunity to inspect Szczepanik's latest invention, a three-color additive process, at close quarters. With the inventor's permission, Anoshchenko later described the new process in his book and cited the view circulating among German specialists that "color cinematography can now be regarded as created" (1927, paragraph 6). Although this description mostly takes the form of a translated excerpt from an article that Szczepanik himself had published three years earlier in the pages of *Die Kinotechnik*, the in-house journal of the German Cameramen's Club (Szczepanik 1924), its importance lies in the fact that it constitutes the first scientific account in Russian of a foreign three-color process, albeit one which, because of the inventor's death only one year after Anoshchenko's meeting with him, did not achieve widespread popularity.

It was not absolutely necessary to travel abroad in order to experience the latest color experiments, however. During the early 1930s, foreign films in color were occasionally showcased at public venues in the Soviet Union. One such screening, organized by the Malaia Dmitrovka Theater on August 18, 1931, and advertised as the "first screening of a color film in the Soviet Union!," witnessed the showing of *Redskin* [in Russian, *Dolina goriashchikh skal*], a film directed by Victor Schertzinger in 1928 and marketed as the first full-length exhibition of the Technicolor two-color dye-transfer and imbibition method; although difficult to verify, it was rumored that the secrets of the Technicolor process had been offered to the Soviet authorities for the princely sum of one million dollars (K. V. 1931). Closed screenings for industry insiders were also being organized at this time. Zheliabuzhskii (1932, 153) mentions one such screening, *King of Jazz* (1930), a film directed by John Murray Anderson, which showcased Paul Whiteman's famous jazz orchestra (its most celebrated sequence is the orchestra's rendition of George Gershwin's *Rhapsody in Blue*). The 1935 International Moscow Film Festival, as indicated earlier, offered a further opportunity for the film-industry establishment and the wider public to gauge the advances made by the Technicolor Corporation; indeed, the three "Silly Symphonies," among them the hugely popular *Three Little Pigs* (1933), impressed the jury sufficiently to be awarded a special prize (Anon. 1935). Throughout the decade the Soviet film press monitored closely the progress of color technology in other countries, in particular the United States; in one instance (Shik 1936), statistics were cited which showed that in 1936 alone there had been 124 color productions released in North America, among them 14 full-length features. Although it may be speculated that reports about individual films were derived from announcements in the film press rather than actual screenings, the correspondents in question display a relatively extensive knowledge of recent color productions. The same correspondent (Shik 1936) refers to the seven Disney Technicolor films either released or planned for release during the 1936–1937 season, as well as to Lloyd Corrigan's *The Dancing Pirate* (1936) and Henry Hathaway's *Trail of the Lonesome Pine* (1936). Other correspondents (Sokolov 1936) reveal an impressive knowledge of the history of Technicolor's technological advances from 1916 to the time of writing. Such was the level of interest that it was not uncommon for correspondents based abroad to send reviews of recent color productions, for example Disney's *Snow White and the Seven Dwarfs* (1937) (Anokhina 1938).

The literature published at the time suggests that the *tsvetniki* were intimately familiar with the two- and three-color processes that made such releases possible. This is illustrated not only by Anoshchenko's description of the Szczepanik three-color method, but also by the seminal article which Provorov, Agokas, and Skavronskii published in *Proletarskoe kino* in 1931. Here they refer to a number of additive and subtractive processes pioneered abroad: the chromatized gelatin matrix and dye-transfer method (i.e., Technicolor's 1928 two-color process); Multicolor, a two-color subtractive process developed in 1928 by the Fox Film Corporation; Magnacolor, another two-color subtractive process, but this time developed by Consolidated Laboratories in Great Britain; and the "lenticular" or "mosaic" method, which had been adopted by Kodak for its Kodacolor process (Skavronskii, Agokas, and Provorov 1931, 52, 53). This article also makes clear that color films released by foreign companies in Europe and North America had been acquired by representatives of the Soviet state and their film stocks thoroughly investigated (Skavronskii, Agokas, and Provorov 1931, 56). Other sources (Zheliabuzhskii 1932; Agokas 1936b; Luchanskii 1939) confirm this familiarity. So, also, do the reports on color experiments in the Soviet film press during much of the decade. Such is the degree of knowledge that it is questionable how protected the foreign color patents were in actual practice. Reports surfacing in 1934, for example, associate the "hydrotype" method being researched at the State Optical Institute in Leningrad with the 1928 two-color Technicolor process, the latter supposedly an aggressively protected commercial secret (Agokas 1934). Quite astoundingly in view of this secrecy, at around this same time a technical drawing of the Technicolor "three-strip" camera appeared in the film journal *Sovetskoe kino* (Kliorin 1935). Almost as if indicative of Soviet ingenuity, and without the slightest degree of embarrassment, Luchanskii (1939, 10) later claimed that Mershin uncovered the secret of the three-color Technicolor process thanks to having been presented with an actual print of *La Cucaracha*, from which he was able to divine with relative ease the use of chromatized gelatin matrices. It is important to bear in mind that, despite the principle of self-reliance which had been enshrined in the first five-year plan, and which was reflected in the decision to establish, with French assistance, a chemical-processing factory in Shostka, Ukraine, the *tsvetniki* were heavily dependent on European and US film stock, in particular the bi-pack and dipo combinations necessary for the successful exploitation of two-color and three-color subtractive processes. This can be gauged by reports published at the time (Rozenfel'd 1940a), but also by the illustrations that accompany the English-language translation of Maiorov's article on his recent digital restorations (Mayorov 2012, 249, 251). These demonstrate that, even in the late 1930s and early 1940s, Dupont and Kodak emulsions were still being used to make color-film positives.

Of the various color processes to which Soviet researchers had gained access, it would appear that it was largely on grounds of cost and relative technical simplicity that the *tsvetniki* working at NIKFI recommended a two-color subtractive method. Judging by their detailed explanation of its scientific method, this process permitted a degree of flexibility in relation to color temperature and spectral range. Furthermore, it produced reliable results in a relatively quick space of time. Such was the enthusiastic reception of materials filmed with this method when they were exhibited at the First All-Union Conference of Scientific Photography in December 1932 (Agokas 1934) that Provorov was transferred with immediate effect to Mezhrabpomfilm and started working with Ekk on the production of *Grunia Kornakova*. This film was conceived as the first in a three-part series – part of an ambitious plan to kick-start investment in color technologies by producing a box-office "blockbuster" (Ignat'eva 1934; Gri-g 1934) – but the scale of the production had to be radically curtailed in light of the problems that arose during the lengthy production phase. Newspaper reports blamed the delays on the lack of technical and financial support on the part of the studio management; the lack of adequate organization and planning, which resulted in two fruitless trips to the Russian South in search of suitable locations; the spiraling production costs (at one point, with only 35 percent of the film completed, 5000 m of foreign film stock had been used, and the cost had reached 75,000 rubles); the serious disagreements on set, which led to the successive removal of seven directors in charge of the budget; and the decision to switch from Agfa bi-pack to another unspecified foreign film stock on the grounds that the former, according to Provorov, had been "insufficiently stable" in terms of its levels of contrast, sensitivity, and latitude (Gri-g 1934; Provorov 1936). The sniping directed at the cost of *Grunia Kornakova* suggests that strategic investment in a two-color process was not without its opponents within the studios and the GUKF. The film itself, however, despite nearly three years in the making, was regarded as a success (Sokolov 1936; Golovnia 1936). Furthermore, it contributed significantly to the campaign in favor of a more ambitious program of color-film productions. This campaign began to gather momentum in the summer of 1936. On June 4, for example, *Kino* reported on a special meeting convened by Shumiatskii, and attended by senior figures from the republican studios, in order to agree a union-wide strategy (Anon. 1936b). This was followed on July 22 by a robust editorial in the same newspaper, which called for the challenge of color to be "overcome," and announced that it would be hosting a conference on July 28 to examine the relevant issues (interestingly, as well as senior figures from the GUKF and the major film studios, invitations were extended to important figures from the world of art, among them Aleksandr Deineka, a leading Socialist-Realist painter; Anon. 1936c). It should be pointed out that the "dash for color" was characterized by a specific set of imperatives: the *Kino* editors were referring not to the perfecting of a two-color process, but rather to the development of a three-color method, which had the advantage of being able to reproduce the full color spectrum. It was the struggle to take command of this particular

Ideology, Technology, Aesthetics 279

Figure 12.1 *Tale of the Fisherman and the Fish*: Three-strip positive and the composite color image after digital restoration. Courtesy of Nikolai Maiorov.

strategic height, however, and the relative failure of the attempt, that characterizes the Soviet color-film "narrative" from 1936 onwards.

Warning signals that the Soviet film industry might not be in a position to produce a commercially viable three-color process beyond the sphere of animation – and even here the achievements are questionable – are encountered at frequent intervals from mid-1936 onwards; most glaringly, the failure can be gauged by the fact that, *pace* the description in archival documents (Deriabin 2002, 337), Ekk's second full-length color feature, *Sorochintsy Fair* [*Sorochinskaia iarmarka*, 1939], was not filmed with Mershin's three-color "hydrotype" process, but rather with NIKFI's tried-and-tested two-color method (Maiorov 2011, 198).

Periodic announcements during the first eight months of 1936 suggest that good progress was being made. In August, for example, one month after the release of *Grunia Kornakova*, Aleksandr Ptushko (1936) announced a forthcoming program of puppet animations that would be filmed by his team of specialists at Mosfilm and processed according to Mershin's "hydrotype" method: *The Fox and the Wolf* [*Lisa i volk*, dir. Sarra Mokil', 1937]; *The Testament* [*Zaveshchanie*, dir. Iosif Skliut, 1937]; and *The Tale of the Fisherman and the Fish* [*Skazka o rybake i rybke*, Ptushko, 1937]. This was followed by an anonymous report in early 1937 that claimed that the members of his team had not only "fully familiarized" themselves with the Mershin method, but they had also managed to over-fulfill their plan by some 180 percent (Anon. 1937b). Eight months later, however, according to a report in the same newspaper (Lukashevich 1937), some of these anticipated works had yet to reach the general public. According to the correspondent in question, who was relying on unnamed sources within Mosfilm, *The Fox and the Wolf* and *The Testament* were still "imperfect" and "unlikely to see the light of day" (Deriabin [2002, 329] confirms in relation to the former that this prediction would later prove to be accurate). Furthermore, *The Wolf and the Seven Kids* [*Volk i semero kozliat*, dir. Mokil'], another previously announced animation, was still in the process of being filmed; according to Deriabin (2002, 331), it was released only in July 1938. This situation was particularly galling in view of the symbolic significance of 1937, the twentieth anniversary of the October Revolution, which had been designated a crucial breakthrough year in terms of three-color filming. As revealed by Shumiatskii in January 1937, the GUK was planning the release of several three-color fictional shorts and animations, their length in total amounting to some 80 minutes of screen time (Anon. 1937a). In the event, judging by archival sources (Deriabin 2002, 329–330), only 50 percent of this target was actually met.

One of the reasons for the delays, it subsequently emerged, were Mershin's processing machines, which were insufficiently advanced to produce multiple copies of individual films. Lukashevich (1937) claims that, as well as being a fire hazard, the machines were difficult to operate and had ruined 11,000 m of imported film stock in the past year; indeed, the director of NIKFI, V. I. Gol'dshtein, later estimated that the total cost of Mosfilm's investment in the machines amounted to around one million rubles, most of it, in his view, wasted (Gol'dshtein 1938). Elsewhere, press reports identified delays in the manufacture of a Soviet "three-strip" camera, the TsKS-1 [Tsvetnoi kino-s"emochnyi apparat-1], which was being designed by Avenir Min at the Leningrad KinAp factory, and modeled on the Technicolor original (Azarin 1936; Provorov 1937). Frustration was also expressed in relation to serious delays in the production of a domestic film stock to replace the imported (and expensive) bi-packs and dipo combinations (Provorov 1937); in the supply of arc lights with the necessary amperage for successful "live-action" three-color filming within the studio (Provorov 1937); and in the installation of a new optical printing machine, which had apparently been lying idle for six months in Mosfilm because the management had apparently not found space for it (Provorov 1938). Lukashevich (1937) lambasted the secrecy surrounding the "hydrotype" process. Also criticized was the GUK's failure to establish a single organizing center for color-film research and production, with the result that work was being unnecessarily duplicated and funds wasted (Gol'dshtein 1938). Persistent problems with technology meant that Aleksandrov and Provorov's planned three-color documentary on the 1938 physical-culture parade, which was filmed on July 24 (Anon. 1938), could not be released because of its poor technical quality (Kabalov 1941; Deriabin 2002, 334). Awareness of these problems eventually prompted the GUK to revoke its original decision, taken shortly after the release of *Grunia Kornakova*, to abandon two-color production in favor of a three-color method. In the middle of this year, Provorov (1938) was forced to concede that the Soviet Union had fallen a long way behind the United States, and that urgent action needed to be taken in order to regain momentum.

To some extent, it is necessary to approach these criticisms with a degree of caution. They were voiced at a time of extraordinary tension within the world of

Soviet institutional structures as a result of the show trials of oppositional figures throughout 1937 and 1938; these had triggered multiple waves of purges within the *nomenklatura*, ostensibly on grounds of sabotage [*vreditel'stvo*], and had given rise to an all-pervasive climate of hysteria and fear. It is striking that during the second half of 1937, in the months preceding the arrests of Boris Babitskii, the director of Mosfilm, and Shumiatskii, who was arrested in January 1938 and executed six months later, there were several denunciations of saboteurs operating within the management structures of Mosfilm, Lenfilm, and the GUK, allegedly on the grounds that there had been insufficient support for the development of a three-color process; although they did not name names, even quite respectable figures (e.g., Lukashevich 1937; Gol'dshtein 1938; Kin 1938; Provorov 1938) succumbed to the temptation (or pressure) to adopt the official rhetoric of the period.

These caveats notwithstanding, however, it would appear that, whether the result of deliberate sabotage or bureaucratic inertia, the Soviet Union struggled to perfect both two-color and three-color processes. It is symptomatic of these ongoing problems that *Happy-Go-Lucky Artists* [*Veselye artisty*], a two-color "musical revue" directed by Iurii Fradkin and released in September 1938, and Solov'ev's *Blossoming Youth*, which was released one month later, were both criticized for the inferior quality of their color (Popov 1938; Agapov 1938). Furthermore, there is little evidence that the problems identified with Mershin's "hydrotype" process had been overcome even by the beginning of the 1940s (Irskii 1940). This can be illustrated by the fact that the first Soviet stereoscopic film, Aleksandr Andrievskii's *The Land of Youth* [*Zemlia molodosti*, 1941], which was initially announced as a three-color production (Anon. 1940b), was presented for the most part in black and white, with only the occasional (two-color) episode; and the fact that two films initially planned as three-color full-length features, *May Night* [*Maiskaia noch'*, 1940], directed by Mykola Sadkovych for Ukrainfilm, and *The Little Humpbacked Horse* [*Konek-Gorbunok*, 1941], directed by Aleksandr Rou for Soiuzdetfilm (Anon. 1940e), were eventually only released as two-color works (Krasnogub 1941; Deriabin 2002, 341). Reading between the lines of press reports dating from these years, it might be speculated that other three-color productions might have met a similar fate. Ekk's *The Blue Bird* [*Siniaia ptitsa*], for example, a screen adaptation of the play by Maurice Maeterlinck, seemed to be experiencing problems even before the Nazi invasion brought its production abruptly to a halt (Anon. 1940c; Aleksandrov 1940). In the case of the two "film-novellas" directed by Aleksandr Macheret and put into production in December 1940 – *The Swineherd* [*Svinopas*] and *Heaven and Hell* [*Nebo i ad*] – it would seem that, despite being conceived as three-color works (Anon. 1940d), they may also only have been released in two colors (Tisse 1941). An editorial in *Kino* on May 23, 1940 revealed that "disorientation" in relation to color cinematography was still persisting (Anon. 1940e). Indeed, despite apparently strenuous efforts, a reliable Soviet "bi-pack" had still not been manufactured by the late spring of that year (Tiurin 1940). This perhaps explains Aleksandrov's rather curious and paradoxical response to the screened fragments of *Autumn*, ostensibly the first color experiment to be photographed with this "bi-pack" (Anon. 1940a): on the one hand, it is hailed as a demonstration of the "enormous and miraculous possibilities of color film"; on the other, as he confesses, it is as yet "technically imperfect" (Aleksandrov 1940). Eisenstein, by contrast, who attended an evening dedicated to color film only one month after Aleksandrov's article had been published (Anon. 1940f), and who was seriously investigating the possibility of making a color biography of Aleksandr Pushkin, was less equivocal; as he writes, albeit to himself, privately, "Technically, it seems, we are not in a position to make color films" (1964 [1940–1941], 499).

Critical Reception of Early Soviet Color Films

If the *tsvetniki* and their supporters experienced difficulties in persuading the film authorities to make the necessary investment in color, their initial works provoked a number of theoretical and aesthetic debates within the wider filmmaking community and the creative intelligentsia as a whole. While the achievement of developing color processes was politely applauded, concerns were nevertheless expressed in relation to the tendency to exploit the new phenomenon as little more than a novelty or "attraction" aimed at mass audiences. For their part, art historians and practicing artists reacted with barely concealed distaste, if not a degree of sarcasm, to the brightly saturated and unvariegated use of color in the early experiments. They drew attention to the tendency of the new processes to produce separated, well-defined, and "local" blocks of color, rather than a more natural merging of colors; the failure to render adequately the complex tonal gradations of the natural world; the overly "polished" and "shiny" quality of the images, which gave an impression of severity, hardness, and sharpness; their "oleographic" quality; and the lack of emotional or psychological expressivity in the handling of color generally. The problem for these observers lay partly in the limitations of the color processes themselves, in other words, their lack of realism, but also, or so it was argued, the lack of a systematic aesthetic approach. In short, they accused filmmakers of lacking taste and artistic sensitivity, and criticized the tendency to dazzle the viewer with "cheap" color effects.

The creative challenges posed by the new technology were identified relatively early in response to *Grunia Kornakova*. Aleksandr Tyshler, a painter, theater designer, and sculptor, criticized what he argued was an absence of a "color dramaturgy" in the film; in his view, there was no color as such, only "decoration" [*raskraska*] (Tyshler 1936). Four years later, his view was echoed by Mikhail Tsekhanovskii, a well-known graphic designer, illustrator, and animator who himself had experimented with color, most notably in his short animation *The Tale of the Silly Mouse* [*Skazka o glupom myshonke*], which was released by Lenfilm in 1940 with a musical accompaniment by Dmitrii Shostakovich (Deriabin, 2002, 340).

Tsekhanovskii drew attention to the problem of the inaccurate rendering of flesh tones in live-action color films; expressed the view that unvariegated use of color quickly wearied the eye; and voiced his conviction that, because the color within the medium of film was essentially a product of the complementary dyes used in the chemical processing, the recent releases differed little in principle from the hand-colored or tinted-and-toned films of the pre-revolutionary era (Tsekhanovskii 1940). The delegates at the Moscow conference on color five years later were equally unimpressed. For Aleksei Fedorov-Davydov, an art historian who was basing his response on the screenings of US and German trophy films brought back from Berlin, color had become merely a "mechanical addition" to dramaturgy: scenes with different emotional registers were shot in the same, unvarying, and, to use his words, "parrot-like" colors (Fedorov-Davydov 1945, 132). Other delegates openly mused whether color cinematography could ever accurately or adequately reproduce the colors of nature, or indeed elevate film to the status of fine art. Abram Efros, another art historian, invoked the recent history of color still-photography to demonstrate his conviction that technological progress did not inevitably lead to greater aesthetic sophistication. For Efros, color still-photography and print technology, both Soviet and non-Soviet, were stuck in a creative rut, hence the reason why, in his view, monochrome was associated in the public mind with artistic seriousness, whereas color had become synonymous with the cheap, vulgar, and mass produced (Germanova 1991, 138–142). For many of the delegates, color appeared to be operating not only as a "mechanical" addition to dramaturgy; it was actually determining the subject-matter altogether.

The vast majority of delegates at the Moscow conference, however, whether positively or negatively inclined towards the new technology, drew distinctions between the spheres of feature film, documentary, and animation. As a stylized art form, and one, moreover, that was aimed primarily at the imaginative world of the child, animation was accepted as a genre that could deploy bright and decorative color legitimately. It is difficult to establish with absolute confidence the palettes of the early animation works in color because very few of the original positives have survived, but statements made by animators at the time suggest that their decorative ornamentation was not only rich, but also varied. In his programmatic statement published in August 1936, for example, Ptushko admitted that his team of animators had not yet learnt how to use color technology "with moderation" [*umerenno*], and that therefore, to some extent, they had fallen victim to what he termed a "childish disease" (Ptushko 1936). Nevertheless, he asserted, in future the approach to color would vary according to the subject-matter. Thus, for example, *The Testament*, which had been adapted from a *facetiae* [humorous text] by the fifteenth-century Italian scholar and humanist, Poggio Bracciolini, would draw its visual inspiration from the practices of antique Italian gravure and the restrained palettes of Gobelin tapestries. By contrast, *The Tale of the Fisherman and the Fish*, which had been adapted from Pushkin's poem of the same title, would aim for a richer and more decorative palette evocative of the Palekh tradition; indeed,

Figure 12.2 Pavel Bazhenov's *Churilo Plenkovich*, 1934.

Figure 12.3 Underwater scene from *The Tale of the Fisherman and the Fish*.

a contemporary artist working in this style, Pavel Bazhenov, had been engaged as a set-designer and consultant. Ptushko's revelations in this article are important testimonies to the ways in which the creative challenges of color were being negotiated even in the infancy of the technology. Furthermore, they resonate with a number of articles published in 1940 (Anon. 1940e; Rozenfel'd 1940b; Shveitser 1940) which draw attention to the importance of color dramaturgy and the need to think in color. Unfortunately, however, Ptushko's remarks do call into question the authenticity of Maiorov's recent digital restorations, which were presented for the first time at the Russian State Film Archive in 2011 (Maiorov 2011, 201). These works are characterized primarily by their aesthetic uniformity, irrespective of subject matter. Thus, while there can be little doubt that the brightly colored scenes in these restorations bear some relation to the original authorial intent – compare, for example, Bazhenov's *Churilo Plenkovich* (1934), a painting, the title of which is drawn from the name of a knight [*bogatyr'*] in the traditional epic song, or *bylina*, tradition, to the underwater scenes in *The Tale of the Fisherman and the Fish* – it is unlikely that this kind of saturated color palette was typical of all the works of Ptushko's studio during the late 1930s.

If the preponderance of animations and fairy-tales or fantasy tales during the early phases of Soviet color technology suggest that it was regarded primarily as a form of entertainment, the desire to record documentary material in color, in particular state occasions, suggests the influence of a more explicitly political and ideological agenda. The possible advantages of color in relation to official occasions had been suggested as early as May 8, 1934, when Stalin was invited to watch color footage from the recent May-Day parade (Troshin 2002, 286), in all probability an episode from *A Carnival of Colors* (Sokolov 1935; Masurenkov 2006, 301; Maiorov 2012). Although these advantages would not be realized across the full spectrum of color until Medvedkin's *The Blossoming Young*, the historical value of such material cannot be overestimated. This is mainly because, unlike the black-and-white footage of the same events, the viewer gains an extraordinary insight into the emerging color discourses of 1930s Stalinist culture. In the case of *The Blossoming Young*, for example, the colors are intense and vibrant, and in the case of certain participants, for example the male athletes, perhaps unexpectedly flamboyant. Thus we encounter male gymnasts sporting violet-pink, almost fuchsia-colored shorts; male athletes marching in light-blue satin tops and straw-yellow shorts; and women athletes in yellow costumes waving brightly colored streamers. In addition, we are offered glimpses of spectators dressed in bright-yellow T-shirts with colored, cone-shaped hats on their heads, and holding orange and light-green umbrellas to protect themselves from the sun. Limitations of space prevent a detailed discussion of the ways in which these colors, if authentic, and not distorted by the restoration process, might be examined in relation to the dress codes and fashions of the 1930s, but it must be regarded as noteworthy that they are significantly more vibrant than the works depicting the same or similar subjects in the figurative art of the period, for example in the sports and physical-culture paintings of Deineka, Aleksandr Samokhvalov, and Iurii Pimenov, the last of whom in the same year produced an epic work dedicated to exactly the same parade as part of the Soviet pavilion at the world fair in New York (O'Mahony 2006, 90). Neither the poster art of the period, nor the postcards, nor the occasional color

Figure 12.4 May Day Parade in *A Carnival of Colors*. Courtesy of Gosfilmofond.

Figure 12.5 Victory Parade, shot on Agfacolor, June 24, 1945. Courtesy of Gosfilmofond.

photograph capture anything like the flamboyancy of these colors. If authentic, Medvedkin's documentary suggests that the choreographing of the spectacle and the designing of the costumes were verging on kitsch towards the end of the 1930s. It also indicates that the Socialist-Realist project, despite the somber atmosphere of international tension and the military associations of the parade, was increasingly defined in terms of the dazzlingly bright and florid. It might be speculated, especially bearing in mind Aleksandrov's presence at the 1938 parade, that it was precisely events like these that gave rise to his remark about color being an "essential element" of a "multinational" USSR.

Conclusion

If *The Blossoming Young* might be regarded as a relatively peripheral work by virtue of being a color production, the general ideological principle that it embodied was nevertheless reinforced by the Red Army's acquisition of the Agfa-color patents in the early months of 1945 (Cornwell-Clyne 1951, 358–359; Masurenkov 2006, 308–309). Not only were these patents studied by Soviet chemical specialists, eventually forming the basis for the Soviet color film stock (DS-1) that began to be manufactured from 1947 onwards, but existing stocks of Agfacolor made possible a number of works released in the Soviet Union from the summer of 1945 onwards. These included several documentaries; one work of animation (*Home Sweet Home* [*Teremok*], 1945); and, perhaps most famously, the 'Dance of the Oprichnina' sequence in the second part of Eisenstein's *Ivan the Terrible* [*Ivan Groznyi*, 1944–1946]. This sequence would not have been possible without Eisenstein's opportunity to assess the qualities of Agfacolor by virtue of a documentary directed by Sergei Gerasimov and filmed by Soviet camera operators during the Potsdam conference; entitled *Berlinskaia konferentsiia*, it was shown to delegates on the very first day of the Moscow conference on color. As Germanova (1991, 117) has pointed out, the associations of such documentaries with the Soviet victory over the Nazis meant that color film began to acquire a symbolic, "epic" resonance. The first documentary to celebrate this victory, for example, Solov'ev's *Victory Parade* [*Parad pobedy*], was shot with Agfacolor on June 24, 1945. Furthermore, despite the relatively poor weather, which resulted in the fact that the majority of its footage was rejected as technically deficient, the film did nevertheless succeed in recording the firework display with which the victory parade on Red Square culminated, and in so doing produced a remarkable and dazzling piece of footage which assured the subliminal association of color film in the public mind with the idea of ecstatic celebration. Such footage implied that color film was an official gift to the nation, a reward for the terrible deprivations and sufferings of the war, and an embodiment of the surge of optimism that coursed through the nation's veins. Indeed, the acquisition of the Agfa patents launched a new era in Soviet color cinematography, one which resulted in massive investment in color processes and the regular winning of international awards, to the extent that Kuleshov could boast quite justifiably at this time that Soviet color films were "among the best in the world" (Kuleshov 1949, 152).

Notes

1. It is not clear when exactly this expression was first coined, but it is widely cited by Soviet commentators. Aleksandrov (1940), for example, uses the expression, but it is not attributed. It is also cited, but not attributed, in the same year by an assistant director working at Lenfilm in relation to *Bal'zak v Rossii*, a planned full-length color-film feature (Menaker, 1940); this suggests that the expression may have been in wide circulation at this time. Shklovskii's authorship only becomes apparent at the 1945 Moscow conference on color, where it is cited on several occasions by delegates, and attributed directly to him. The noun *landrin* derives from the name of a Russian entrepreneur, Fedor Landrin, whose factory in St Petersburg manufactured *montpensiers*, or fruit drops, in the pre-revolutionary era.
2. Additive color is the term given to the practice in still photography and cinematography of mixing two or more primary colors. Although numerous additive processes were developed during the first decades of the twentieth century, the most popular tended to be variations on the same basic method: the placing of red, green, and blue filters in front of film stock as it passes through the camera, this giving rise to groups of two or three negative images, each of which in black and white bears the traces of a particular primary color intensity from the scene being filmed. The positive images formed from each individual negative are then projected on to the cinema screen using a similar combination of filters. The speed of their projection in quick succession gives rise to the illusion of a color image. For detailed descriptions of the additive systems developed during the 1910s and 1920s, see Cornwell-Clyne (1951) and "Timeline of Historical Film Colors."
3. Subtractive color is the term given to the practice in still photography and cinematography of subtracting or absorbing parts of the spectrum of white light, usually by means of beam-splitting prisms and/or filters, or by means of layers of different filters embedded within a single emulsion. The most successful two-color subtractive systems were created by means of double-coated or "bi-pack" systems; in other words, two film stocks (Orthochromatic and Panchromatic) glued together, and thus each one (front and back) sensitive to different parts of the spectrum. For descriptions of these systems, and the two- and three-color subtractive processes developed by the Technicolor Corporation, see Cornwell-Clyne (1951) and "Timeline of Historical Film Colors."

References

Agapov, B. 1938. "'Tsvetushchaia molodost'"" [Blossoming Youth]. *Kino* 48: 3.
Agokas, Nikolai. 1934. "'Legenda o tsvetnom kino'" [The Legend of Color Cinema]. *Kino* 16: 4.

Agokas, Nikolai. 1936a. "Sozdat' blagopriiatnuiu obstanovku" [Create Favorable Conditions]. *Kino* 36: 2.
Agokas, Nikolai. 1936b. *Tsvetnoe kino* [Color Cinema]. Moscow: Kinofotoizdat.
Aleksandrov, Grigorii. 1940. "V tsentre vnimaniia – kachestvo" [Quality at the Center of Attention]. *Kino* 46: 2.
Anokhina, O. 1938. "'Belosnezhka' Uolta Disneia" [Walt Disney's "Snow White"]. *Iskusstvo kino* [Art of Cinema] 7: 62–63.
Anon. 1931. "OZPKF v pomosh' tsvetnomu kino" [OZPKF to the Aid of Color Cinema]. *Kino* 45: 2.
Anon. 1935. "Zakrytie kinofestivalia" [The Closing of the Film Festival]. *Kino* 11: 2.
Anon. 1936a. "Premirovanie rabotnikov tsvetnogo kino" [Awards for the Workers of Color Cinematography]. *Kino* 42: 4.
Anon. 1936b. "Razvitie tsvetnogo kino" [The Development of Color Cinema]. *Kino* 28: 1.
Anon. 1936c. "Zavoiuem tsvet" [We Will Conquer Color]. *Kino* 36: 1.
Anon. 1937a. "Soveshchanie po tsvetnomu fil'mu v komitete po delam iskusstv" [Meeting on Color Cinema at the Committee for Art Affairs]. *Kino* 5: 2.
Anon. 1937b. "Uspekhi tvorcheskoi masterskoi A. L. Ptushko." [Successes of A.L. Ptushko's Creative Workshop]. *Kino* 2: 2.
Anon. 1938. "Tsvetnaia kinokhronika" [Newsreels in Color]. *Kino* 34: 2.
Anon. 1940a. "Novaia trekhtsvetnaia kartina" [A New Three-Color Film]. *Kino* 36: 3.
Anon. 1940b. "Pervyi stereoskopicheskii tsvetnoi fil'm" [The First Stereoscopic Color Film]. *Kino* 21: 1.
Anon. 1940c. "'Siniaia ptitsa'" [The Blue Bird]. *Kino* 21: 1.
Anon. 1940d. "Trekhtsvetnye kinonovelly" [Three-Color Film Novellas]. *Kino* 50: 2.
Anon. 1940e. "Tsvetnoe kino" [Color Cinema]. *Kino* 23: 1.
Anon. 1940f. "Vecher tsvetnogo kino" [An Evening of Color Cinema]. *Kino* 51: 2.
Anoshchenko, Nikolai. 1927. *Kino v Germanii* [Cinema in Germany]. Moscow. Kinopechat', http://www.rudata.ru/wiki/Anoshchenko_N._D._«Kino_v_Germanii»_Kinematografiia_v_natural'nykh_tsvetakh (accessed September 14, 2013).
Anoshchenko, N. 1931. "Spektrokoler: Novyi sposob tsvetnoi kinematografii" [Spectracolor: A New Method of Color Cinema]. *Proletarskoe kino* [Proletarian Cinema] 4: 40–45.
Azarin, A. 1936. "Laboratoriia tsvetnogo kino" [Laboratory of Color Cinema]. *Kino* 15: 1.
Cornwell-Clyne, Adrian. 1951. *Colour Cinematography*. London: Chapman.
Deriabin, Aleksandr (ed.) 2002. "Rannie otechestvennye tsvetnye fil'my 1931–1945: Fil'mografiia" [Early Domestic Color Films 1931–1945. A Filmography]. *Kinovedcheskie zapiski* [Film Scholars' Notes] 56: 322–348.
Eizenshtein, Sergei. 1940. "Ne tsvetnoe, a tsvetovoe" [Not Color, But Spectral]. *Kino*, 24: 3.
Eizenshtein, Sergei. 1964 [1940–1941]. "(Tsvetovaia razrabotka fil'ma 'Liubov' poeta')" [Color Elaboration of the Film "Love of a Poet"]. Vol. 3 of Eizenshtein, *Izbrannye proizvedeniia* [Selected Works], edited by S. I. Iutkevich, 492–499. Moscow: Iskusstvo.
Fedorov-Davydov, A. 1945. "Problemy tsvetnogo kino" [Problems of Color Cinema]. *Iskusstvo kino* [Art of Cinema] 2: 9–11.
Germanova, I. G. (ed.) 1991. "Tsvetnoe kino: Zametki na poliakh arkhivnoi stenogrammy" [Color Cinema. Notes on the Margins of Archival Minutes]. *Kinovedcheskie zapiski* [Film Scholars' Notes] 12: 112–160.
Gol'dshtein, V. I. 1938. "Likvidirovat' bezprizornost' tsvetnogo kino" [Liquidating the Neglect of Color Cinema]. *Kino* 27: 3.

Golovnia, Anatolii. 1936. "Pervye shagi" [The First Steps]. *Kino* 32: 3.

Gri-g, Mikh. 1934. "'Solovei-Solovushka'" [The Little Nightingale]. *Kino* 58: 4.

Ignat'eva, G. 1934. "Zagotovki v prok" [Ready to Use]. *Kino* 58: 4.

Irskii, G. 1940. "Eti zadachi dolzhny byt' resheny" [These Tasks Must be Solved]. *Kino* 46: 2.

K. V. 1931. "Tsvetnoe kino – Spektrokolor" [Color Cinema: Spectracolor]. *Kino* 55: 6.

Kabalov, G. 1941. "Khudozhestvennye i tekhnicheskie zadachi tsvetnogo izobrazheniia" [Artistic and Technical Tasks of the Color Image]. *Iskusstvo kino* [Art of Cinema] 4: 50.

Khokhlova, A. and Lev Kuleshov. 1975. *50 let v kino* [50 Years in Cinema]. Moscow: Iskusstvo.

Kin, A. 1938. "Tsvetnoe kino v studii 'Lenfil'm'" [Color Film at Lenfilm Studio]. *Iskusstvo kino* [Art of Cinema] 9: 53–54.

Kliorin, M. 1935. "Novoe v tekhnike amerikanskogo tsvetnogo kino" [Innovations in the Technology of American Color Cinema]. *Sovetskoe kino* [Soviet Cinema] 11: 73–75.

Krasnogub, N. 1941. "'Maiskaia noch'" [May Night]. *Kino* 11: 3.

Kuleshov, Lev. 1987 [1949]. "Tsvetnoe kino" [Color Cinema]. Vol. 1 of Kuleshov, *Sobranie sochinenii* [Collected Works], edited by N. V. Volkova et al., 151–153. Moscow: Iskusstvo.

Luchanskii, M. 1939. *Liudi sovetskogo tsvetnogo kino* [The People in Soviet Color Cinema]. Moscow: Goskinoizdat.

Lukashevich, V. 1937. "Pochemu net tsvetnykh kartin" [Why There Are No Color Films]. *Kino* 37: 2.

Maiorov, Nikolai. 2011. "Tsvet sovetskogo kino" [The Color of Soviet Cinema]. *Kinovedcheskie zapiski* [Film Scholars' Notes] 98: 196–209.

Maiorov, Nikolai. 2012. "Vtoraia zhizn' 'Karnavala tsvetov'" [The Second Life of "A Carnival of Colors"], http://tvkinoradio.ru/article/article5 (accessed November 10, 2015).

Masurenkov, Dmitrii. 2006. "Vsegda pervyi: K 100-letiiu kinooperatora Fedora Provorova" [Always the First: On the Centenary of the Cameraman Fedor Provorov]. *Kinovedcheskie zapiski* [Film Scholars' Notes] 78: 294–323.

Mayorov, Nikolai. 2012. "Soviet colours." *Studies in Russian and Soviet Cinema* 6.2: 241–255.

Menaker, I. 1940. "Razreshit' tsvetnuiu kompozitsiiu" [Solve the Problem of Color Composition]. *Kino* 36: 3.

Mershin, P. M. 1936. "Preodoleem trudnosti" [We Will Overcome the Difficulties]. *Kino* 36: 2.

O'Mahony, Mike. 2006. *Sport in the USSR: Physical Culture–Visual Culture*. London: Reaktion.

Popov, Dm. 1938. "Dosadnaia neudacha" [A Regrettable Failure]. *Kino* 45: 3.

Provorov, Fedor. 1936. "Protiv zaznaistva i samouspokoeniia" [Against Conceit and Complacency]. *Kino* 36: 2.

Provorov, Fedor. 1937. "Likvidirovat' otstavanie" [Liquidate the Backwardness]. *Kino* 37: 2.

Provorov, Fedor. 1938. "Bol'she vnimaniia tsvetnomu kino" [More Attention to Color Cinema]. *Iskusstvo kino* [Art of Cinema] 6: 62–63.

Ptushko, A. L. 1936. "Tsvet podchinit' soderzhaniiu" [Subordinate Color to Content]. *Kino* 48: 2.

Rozenfel'd, E. 1940a. "Novaia tekhnika dvukhtsvetnogo kino" [Technological Improvements in Two-Color Cinema]. *Kino* 33: 3.

Rozenfel'd, E. 1940b. "Iskusstvo dinamicheskoi zhivopisi" [The Art of Dynamic Painting]. *Kino* 46: 2 (Part 1); *Kino* 47: 3 (Part 2).

Schlögel, Karl. 2012. *Moscow 1937*. Translated by Rodney Livingstone. Cambridge. Polity Press.

Shik, M. A. 1936. "Novoe v tsvetnom kino" [Innovations in Color Cinema]. *Kino* 39: 3.

Sholpo, Evgenii. 1933. "Pochemu ne primeniaetsia tsennoe izobretenie: Eshche raz o graficheskom zvuke" [Why a Valuable Invention is Not Being Adopted: Once More about Graphic Sound]. *Kino* 14: 3.

Shveitser, Vladimir. 1940. "Dialog o tsvete" [Dialog about Color]. *Kino* 28: 3.

Skavronskii, N., Nikolai Agokas and Fedor Provorov. 1931. "Tsvetnoe kino v rabotakh NIKFI" [Color Cinema in the Work of NIKFI]. *Proletarskoe kino* [Proletarian Cinema] 12: 52–56.

Sokolov, Ippolit. 1935. "Pervyi opyt" [A First Experience]. *Kino* 41: 3.

Sokolov, Ippolit. 1936. "Rozhdenie tsvetnogo kino" [The Birth of Color Cinema]. *Kino* 30: 4.

Szczepanik, Jan. 1924. "Kinematographie in natürlichen Farben" [Film in Natural Colors]. *Die Kinotechnik* 6 (17): 293–297 and 6 (18): 322–329.

Tikhonravov, P. 1938. "Entuziast tsvetnogo kino" [An Enthusiast of Color Cinema]. *Kino* 48: 4.

"Timeline of Historical Film Colors", database created by Professor Barbara Flueckiger at the Institute of Cinema Studies, University of Zurich, http:/zauberklang.ch/filmcolors/ (accessed July 21, 2014).

Tisse, Eduard. 1941. "Pervye shagi tsvetnogo kino" [The First Steps of Color Cinema]. *Kino* 22: 2.

Tiurin, I. 1940. "Piat' tsvetnykh kartin v 1941 godu" [Five Color Films in 1941]. *Kino* 23: 2.

Troshin, Aleksandr (ed.) 2002. "'A driani podobno 'Garmon'' bol'she ne stavite? ...': Zapisi besed B. Z. Shumiatskogo s I. V. Stalinym posle kinoprosmotrov 1934g" [You Won't Stage Any More Rubbish like "Accordion"?...Notes of the Conversations between B. Shumiatskii and I. Stalin after screenings in 1934]. *Kinovedcheskie zapiski* [Film Scholars' Notes] 61: 281–346.

Troshin, Aleksandr (ed.) 2003. "'Kartina sil'naia, khoroshaia, no ne 'Chapaev'...': Zapisi besed B. Z. Shumiatskogo s I. V. Stalinym posle kinoprosmotrov 1935–1937gg" [It's a Good and Strong Film, but not "'Chapaev"...: Notes of the Conversations Between B. Shumiatskii and I. Stalin after Screenings in 1935–1937]. *Kinovedcheskie zapiski* [Film Scholars' Notes] 62: 115–188.

Tsekhanovskii, Mikhail. 1940. "Tsvet v kino" [Color in Cinema]. *Iskusstvo kino* [Art of Cinema] 7–8: 64–65.

Tyshler, A. G. 1936. "Fil'm dolzhen imet' tsvetovuiu kharakteristiku" [A Film Must Have a Color Character]. *Kino* 40: 2.

Zheliabuzhskii, Iurii. 1932. *Iskusstvo kinooperatora* [The Art of the Cameraman]. Moscow: Gizlegprom.

Zusman, E. 1931. "Ne utopit' tsvetnoe kino v more rezoliutsii" [Don't Drown Color Cinema in a Sea of Resolutions]. *Kino* 55: 6.

13

Learning to Speak Soviet: Soviet Cinema and the Coming of Sound

Lilya Kaganovsky

> *In 1912, AT&T's manufacturing subsidiary, Western Electric, secured the rights to Lee De Forest's audion tube to construct amplification repeaters for long-distance telephone transmission … Within three months of the armistice [ending World War I], one essential element for a sound system was ready, the loudspeaker. First used in the "Victory Day" parade on Park Avenue in 1919, national notoriety came during the 1920 Republican and Democratic national conventions. A year later, by connecting this technology to its long-distance telephone network AT&T broadcast President Harding's address at the burial of the Unknown Soldier simultaneously to overflowing crowds in New York's Madison Square Garden and San Francisco's Auditorium. Clear transmissions to large indoor audiences had become a reality.*
>
> Douglas Gomery (2005, 31)

In his book *The Talkies: American Cinema's Transition to Sound, 1926–1931*, Donald Crafton offers a revised and very detailed history of Hollywood's transition to sound, whose coming he sees as mainly a by-product of the different advances in electricity – what he refers to, using one of the terms common in the twenties, as "a new form of *electrical* entertainment" (Crafton 1997, 21; emphasis in the original). Electric companies, along with studios and the popular press, argues Crafton, helped to create a climate of acceptance for the coming of sound cinema. They helped to organize a discourse around sound, about progress and modernity, that made sound cinema appear not as a "natural" development from silent cinema, but as a new and completely different product: a product of a new era of technological change.

In this chapter, I want to use Crafton as a starting point for thinking about the Soviet transition to sound, which did and did not resemble that of Hollywood.

A Companion to Russian Cinema, First Edition. Edited by Birgit Beumers.
© 2016 John Wiley & Sons, Inc. Published 2016 by John Wiley & Sons, Inc.

Obviously, many of the factors that went into the innovation, production, and diffusion of the new technology functioned differently in the Soviet context than in an American one. To begin with, in the United States, the development of synchronized sound cinema was the result of forces directly related to the capitalist economy and the functioning of the market: patents, exhibition rights, small vs. large theaters, profits and market share played as large (if not the largest) role in the introduction and distribution of synchronized sound film as matters of audience response or aesthetics. It was not, in other words, the instant popularity of *The Jazz Singer* (dir. Alan Crosland, 1927), but the economic realities of the market that largely determined the "coming of sound" to US and world theaters. As Douglas Gomery puts it,

> an understanding of the conversion of the US film industry to sound is basic to any understanding of this world-wide transformation. The US film industry converted to sound primarily for economic considerations. Artistic, sociological, and psychological factors certainly affected the decision, but [...] the executives who controlled the US motion picture industry were in business primarily for one reason – to maximize the long run profits of their companies. (Gomery 2005, xi-xii)

As Gomery argues, if there is a date key to the coming of sound, it is the May 11, 1928 cooperative signing of identical contracts by Paramount and Loew's (and its production subsidiary MGM), in the same room, AT&T's New York offices, and at the same time – *not* the October 6, 1927, premiere of *The Jazz Singer* (Gomery 2005, 1). The coming of sound, he stresses, was first and foremost an *industrial* change, with vast social, cultural, and aesthetic implication.

This is perhaps especially true for Soviet cinema, whose conversion to sound, while not made out of strictly economic considerations, entailed a complete restructuring of the Soviet film industry: what had been in the 1920s a fairly heterogeneous assembly of studios and artists was transformed during the First Five Year Plan into a centrally organized and administered body. As Vance Kepley Jr. has noted, during the NEP period (New Economic Policy, 1921–1928), Soviet cinema was generally heterogeneous, with a number of regional and national film organizations participating in a growing film market. By 1927, the Soviet film industry included some 13 production organizations with a total reported capital of 21,238,000 rubles (Kepley 1996, 36). Moreover, under NEP, each national republic maintained considerable autonomy of its national film market. Each republic was allowed to create a native film organization, with a monopoly on film distribution within the borders of that republic (and thereby, to prevent "colonization" by larger distributors like Sovkino) (Kepley 1996, 38). This period of relative autonomy came to an end in 1928–1929 with Stalin's "Great Turn" [*velikii perelom*], which signaled a radical change in the economic policies of the Soviet Union, the abandoning the New Economic Policy, and the acceleration of collectivization and industrialization.[1] The years of the First Five-Year Plan (1928–1932) involved a complete restructuring and centralization of the Soviet arts, and a second "nationalization" of the film industry. To be sure, many of the conferences, meetings, congresses, and decrees passed by film workers at this time called for greater oversight by the Party. Arguments against Sovkino in particular stressed that organization's commercial interests and its reliance on the importation of foreign films, as well as on its failure to make movies for the masses or to bring cinema to the countryside. Everyone agreed that sound cinema had the potential to be the greatest tool of influence over the masses (Tager 1967–1968).

The First All-Union Party Conference on Cinema Affairs held in March 1928 focused its attention on the problems of the Soviet film industry and the "crisis in Soviet cinema": the failure to make movies accessible to the masses, the failure of the *"cinefication* of the countryside," the failure to remain a self-sustaining industry, the failure to negotiate the needs of ideology and profit. Soviet cinema had to become an "experiment, intelligible to the masses"; and moreover, it had to become a true *industry* by manufacturing its own equipment. In January 1929, following the recommendations of a special commission, the Central Committee of the Communist Party issued a decree about the reorganization and purging of current cinema cadres and the centralization of the film industry into Soiuzkino, creating a single Soviet-wide agency to oversee the film and photo industries. Thus, for the Soviet Union, the centralization and second "nationalization" of the film industry meant a change not only in the kinds of films that were being made, but also in who was making them, where, with what equipment, and for what audience.

By 1929 the Cultural Revolution was in full swing, and this meant also a change in the understanding of the nature of cinema – from cinema as a "mass art," to cinema "for the masses." The conversion to sound played a major role in this transition, allowing for a more immediate transmission of party slogans, platforms, and ideological directives. In their debates over the coming sound in the late 1920s, Soviet filmmakers, theorists, and ideologues emphasized a different set of issues than the ones that concerned the American film industry. Sergei Eisenstein, Vsevolod Pudovkin and Grigorii Aleksandrov's "Statement on Sound" (1928) outlined the ways in which the coming of sound would liberate avant-garde cinema from a series of "blind alleys." In their statement, the directors dismissed "talking pictures" as those in which "the sound is recorded in a natural manner, synchronizing exactly with the movement on the screen and creating a certain "illusion" of people talking, objects making noise, etc." They called this first period, the period of "sensations," which, though innocent in itself, would lead to cinema's "unimaginative" use for "dramas of high culture" and other photographed presentations of a theatrical order. The "mere addition" of sound to image, they claimed, would equal subordination (of sound to image), a loss of independence, and the destruction of the "culture of montage." "Sharp discord," a "hammer and tongs" approach, "counterpoint" – these are the privileged terms of the "Statement's" argument.

Adrian Piotrovskii, the head of the Lenfilm script department, similarly called for a revolutionary approach to sound film (1929): he stressed in particular the ways Soviet cinema must be different from American and European sound film, whose direction in 1929 was toward dialog and the reproduction of naturalistic sound effects. Specifically, he mentions the unheard of and unprecedented sensation created by *The Jazz Singer* (which premiered in Moscow on November 4, 1929) and Al Jolson's "cabaret" songs. For Piotrovskii, this focus on "sensation" (singing and dancing) meant that sound cinema had abandoned the editing and optical techniques of its earlier, silent years. Like Eisenstein, Pudovkin, and Aleksandrov, Piotrovskii argues specifically for contrast: non-parallel construction, confrontation, and disjuncture. He advocates the dialectical possibilities of conflict, struggle, and disagreement instead of having the sound track "passively" following the course set by the image track, which he believed would provide the new sound film with political and social value (as opposed to the merely aesthetic/naturalistic/reactionary forms of American and European sound cinema).

Perhaps in no other country was the response of major filmmakers *against* synch-sound as profound as in Soviet Russia. Synch-sound technology restricted the freedom with which film could be edited, requiring auditory and therefore visual continuity where silent film had not. Moreover, *meaning* would no longer be left to the assembly and comprehension of the viewer. The site for the production of meaning would turn away from what the formalist critic Boris Eikhenbaum (1927) had called the spectator's "internal speech" [*vnutrennaia rech'*] to the audible word addressing the spectator directly from the screen. In his "Problem of Cinema Stylistics," Eikhenbaum argued that it was precisely the *absence* of the audible word that was the central organizing principle of silent cinema, and made inner speech possible (Eikhenbaum 1927, 61). But while many Soviet filmmakers wanted sound cinema to continue the practice of avant-garde revolutionary filmmaking and montage, others saw the coming of sound as an opportunity to create a "cinema for the millions," a cinema that would directly speak to the masses. Because the introduction of sound coincided with the historical moment of the Great Turn, sound in Soviet cinema helped pave the way of the film industry toward Socialist Realism, toward an ideological program that rigidly controlled what could and could not be shown and what could and could not be said on the screen. The ideal was to show life not as it is, but as it "should be." Ideology, not the "recording of facts," was to be the philosophical underpinning of the new "realism." As Konstantin Iukov, ARRK's chairman, wrote at the end of 1928 that cinema was at last "recognized as the most essential and most important means of artistic propaganda in the hands of the Party" (Iukov 1928, 2–3; quoted in Youngblood 1980, 171).

By 1930, when the USSR declared its independence from Western economic relations and trade, the Soviet film industry had already fallen behind the United States and Western Europe in the conversion to sound. The transformation of American cinemas from almost all silent to almost all sound, as Crafton and others have shown, took about a year and a half, and by the time of the stock market crash in October 1929, "out-of-the way theaters and those servicing poor neighborhoods were the only ones still waiting for amplification" (Crafton 1997, 15). Europe took longer, with the United Kingdom moving fastest, followed by Germany and France (UK exhibitors were 63 percent wired by the close of 1930; Germany did not top 60 percent until 1932; and France moved even slower; Gomery 2005, 107). Trying to stave off the US "talkie invasion," Germany developed its own sound-on-film method that became known as Tri-Ergon, but was not successful in integrating it into German theaters until the spring of 1929, when two different companies merged to form Tobis-Klangfilm, and successfully sued for the sole right to sound film patents within Germany. In 1930, Western Electric, RCA, and Tobis-Klangfilm formed a loose cartel that divided the world into four territories. Tobis-Klangfilm secured exclusive rights for Europe and Scandinavia, while Western Electric and RCA obtained the United States, Canada, New Zealand, India, and the Soviet Union. For the British market, royalties were split one-fourth for Tobis-Klangfilm, three-fourths for Western Electric and RCA. The rest of the world was open territory (Gomery 2005, 108–109). For the Soviet film industry, beset by a lack of resources, massive bureaucratization, and rapidly shifting ideological imperatives (which greatly affected script production and approval, among other things), the conversion to sound took until 1935, with the last silent versions of current films still being released as late as 1938.

Other major transformations that directly affected the conversion to sound included the development and refurbishing the USSR's principal production, distribution, and exhibition facilities. In 1930 the USSR virtually stopped importing foreign movies, technology, or film stock. Slogans about "economic independence" and "Produce from Soviet materials with Soviet tools!" dominated the discourse around cinema and the new developments in the acquisition of sound: Soviet sound cinema was to be "home-grown" and free of foreign patent obligations (although Soiuzkino contracted foreign laboratories for technical advice). Research on the Soviet-made Shorin and Tager sound systems dated back into the 1920s; indeed, Pavel Tager names November 26, 1926 as the date when he first begins to work on sound-on-film technology, with Aleksandr Shorin's first experiments following in 1927. According to Tager, August 2, 1929 marked the date of the first Soviet recording of sound footage on the streets of Moscow, and October 26, 1929, the first Soviet radio broadcast of recorded sound footage. Tager notes specifically that the Soviet Union was only one of three countries (the others being the United States and Germany) to independently develop its own sound-on-film technology (RGALI 2690/1/91: Tager, "Ochen' kratko o sovetskom zvukovom kino" "[Very Briefly about Soviet Sound Cinema], 1967–1968).

What is more, parallel to the development of sound recording equipment, a group of Soviet innovators were also experimenting with other forms of "sound-on-film" technologies: specifically, "graphic" or "drawn" sound. As Andrey Smirnov shows, this new way of synthesizing sound from light was developed as a

Figure 13.1 Shorin's sound-recording camera. Cover of the journal *Kino i zhizn'* 14 (1930).

direct consequence of the newly invented sound-on-film technology, "which made possible access to sound as a visible graphical trace in a form that could be studied and manipulated" (Smirnov 2013, 175). Among the first Soviet sound films was Abram Room's *The Plan for Great Works* [*Piatiletka. Plan velikikh rabot*, released in March 1930] shot in the Shorin's Central Laboratory of Wire Communication in Leningrad in 1929. The group working on this film included the painter, book illustrator, and animator Mikhail Tsekhanovskii, the chief of the composer's brigade Arsenii Avraamov, and the inventor Evgenii Sholpo, who was already working on new techniques of so-called "performerless" music (Smirnov 2013, 175). Drawing directly on film stock opened up possibilities not just for the image track but for the sound track as well. And although the Canadian animator Norman McLaren is the most recognized name in this field, it was the Soviet pioneers of graphic sound that made the most significant contributions to the invention and development of this technique, also known as "designed," "drawn," "paper," "animated," "synthetic," or "artificial sound" (Izvolov 2013, 22).

Figure 13.2 Tager at work. Photo from the author's personal collection.

As Nikolai Izvolov shows, using the standard animation technology of the day, in the summer of 1930 Avraamov became the first person to create drawn sound, and he demonstrated the results of his experiments at a conference on sound in Moscow the following autumn. Each of the three remaining creators of drawn sound invented his own original device designed to facilitate the drawing of sound on film. Sholpo called his the Variophone, though his colleagues at Lenfilm Studios invariably referred to it as the Sholpograph in their various memoirs. This device enabled the cinematic capture of sound on the moving filmstrip. Acoustic engineer Boris Iankovskii and animation cameraman Nikolai Voinov were also fellow inventors. Iankovskii's device, the Vibro-exponator, was devoted to creating sounds of varying timbres, a sonic aspect that had been largely underdeveloped in the other inventions, including those of Sholpo and Voinov (Izvolov 2013, 23–25). Unfortunately, as Izvolov notes, most of the works by the inventors of drawn sound have not survived to the present day. Avraamov's experiments were kept at his house and were accidentally destroyed. Iankovskii's inventions never left the laboratory stage and may have existed only in single copies. Voinov's films were much more fortunate. Some of them were released in theaters and exist in multiple copies. Four of his films are preserved in the Russian film archives. Probably the most well preserved archive is Sholpo's. Several dozen of his movies, along with fragments of those by other inventors, were shown for the first time at the animated film festival in Utrecht in November 2008 (Izvolov 2013, 26).

Beyond the development of the sound camera and the method of synchronous sound recording, however, the USSR also needed to build factories that could produce film stock, cameras, projectors, and other equipment, as well as theaters wired for sound. The USSR also needed a new federal system of distribution/diffusion of sound films in a multi-language environment (Kepley 1996: 45; Pozner 2014). Soiuzkino would now need to coordinate the production and distribution of sound prints in line with regional language patterns. This had not been an issue with silent films, which could rely either on multi-language intertitles or on a *bonimenteur*, that is to say, a speaker who interpreted the film for provincial audiences during projection (Kepley 1996, 47). Sound cinema required more complex plans for dubbing and subtitling to serve the USSR's multi-ethnic population, which led to the question which language Soviet cinema would speak.

As Denise Youngblood has noted, by 1930 the Soviet film industry had been completely disrupted:

> The pessimism in the film industry by the end of the decade, even before the purges were in full swing, was extraordinary ... [The Soviet film industry] had no yet mastered silent film technology, nor produced film stock or equipment, when along came a radical new development which necessitated the complete replacement of existing equipment with sophisticated and expensive devices. (Youngblood 1980, 221)

Figure 13.3   Evgenii Sholpo at work. Photo courtesy of Nikolai Izvolov.

Fears engendered by political pressures, lack of raw materials, and the confusion over the future of sound meant that film production, already weakened by debates over content, ideology, and profit, dropped even further. Conversion to sound became a top priority: according to Jay Leyda, Stalin was particularly interested in sound cinema, instructing Aleksandrov and Eisenstein and their cameraman Eduard Tissé to study European and American sound technology while abroad. "Knowing about our planned trip to America," wrote Aleksandrov in his op. ed., "A Great Friend of Soviet Cinema," "Josef Vissarionovich told us: 'Study the sound film in detail. This is very important to us. When our heroes discover speech, the influential power of films will increase enormously'" (Aleksandrov 1939; quoted in Leyda, 1960, 269). As Ian Christie has argued, "Soviet sound cinema is effectively a 'new apparatus' by the late '30s" (Christie 1982, 36).

In 1930 the first Soviet sound films went into production, including Room's *The Plan for Great Works*; and by 1931, the first feature sound films appeared on the Soviet screen. Their appearance did not so much mark the end of silent film (an end that was in any case prolonged by the lack of sound theaters around the country, ensuring that silent films continued to play on Soviet screens until 1935, while all sound films were released in "silent" versions), but rather, the end of the silent film era, an era of experimentation, intellectual montage, and radical avant-garde filmmaking. The massive cultural upheaval that accompanied the First Five-Year Plan led, among other things, to a complete restructuring of the Soviet arts, including the cinema. As Kepley notes, this new nationalization of the film industry did not mean that the Soviet central government took over day-to-day film affairs; rather, the government created a new bureaucratic layer, represented by Soiuzkino, to run the industry, which bureaucracy would be periodically accountable to government oversight. Soiuzkino was responsible for "all matters concerning production of the movie-photo apparatus (for filming, projecting, lighting, and so on), movie-photo accessories and materials (films, records, papers, photochemicals, and so on), as well as all matters concerning motion-picture production, rental, and exhibition" (Kepley 1996, 42–43). Beyond politics and economics, the creation of this "all-union combine" translated into the massive bureaucratization of the Soviet film industry: the two-year personnel plan was to provide cinema with more than 7,000 new administrators: over three and a half times more than the number of creative personnel slated to join the industry in the same interval.

It is vital to underscore, therefore, that unlike that of the United States or of Western Europe, the Soviet film industry's transition from silence to sound was technological and economic – but also, and perhaps, primarily – it was ideological and aesthetic. The coming of sound demanded a thorough rethinking of cinematic technique (particularly evident with acting, where a highly gestural and iconic acting style gave way to a more naturalistic style), including montage with its rapid cross-cutting and dialectical construction. But for the Soviet film industry, this purely technological innovation also coincided with a profound top-down shift, as the cinema industry was completely reorganized and given new ideological directives, which were easier to implement because the industry as a whole was now centralized under a single authority. This shift became most visible in the elaboration of the precepts of Socialist Realism (made into the official doctrine of all Soviet art in 1934) and the films of the 1930s, but it is already visible in the films of the period of transition that attempt to speak with a new "voice of technology," to use sound as a means of posing questions of authority, language, national identity, and the relationship between the state (the producer) and the artist (the filmmaker).

Machines Speaking to Machines

In the middle of Dziga Vertov's *Stride, Soviet!* [*Shagai, Sovet!*, 1926], we find this remarkable sequence: an election is being broadcast over radio and loudspeaker, but the participants are all machines. We watch as buses assemble in front of the city Soviet, where "instead of an orator" there is a loudspeaker; "instead of applause" there are horns honking; where cars and buses, car horns and speakers "greet us" "in the name" of the Moscow Soviet. As the program notes for Le Giornate Del Cinema Muto put it,

> What began as a commission by the sitting Moscow Soviet for a promotional movie, one which would show all the good things the Soviet had done for its city, was transformed by Vertov into something else entirely: a film experiment, an emotional film – anything but a picture that would help the Mossovet be reelected. In the end, the Mossovet refused to recognize *Stride, Soviet!*, and it was largely boycotted by film theaters. One can imagine the distress authorities must have felt when they saw what had been made of their election rally. No people are seen, just buses, cars, and various other vehicles gathered in the square to listen to the loudspeaker: one mechanical device talking to other mechanical devices about weapons and tools. (Tsivian 2008)

In their debates over the nature of the coming sound in the late 1920s, Soviet filmmakers, theorists and ideologues emphasized a different set of issues than the ones that concerned the American film industry. Theorists, critics, and practitioners were divided between ensuring that sound cinema continue the practice of avant-garde revolutionary filmmaking on the one hand, and an opportunity, on the other hand, to create a "cinema for the millions," a cinema that would directly address the masses. The final result – the end of the avant-garde and the advent of Socialist Realism – was marked in the early Soviet sound films by an emphasis on public address, on the technology of sound that made visible as well as audible the imposition of a voice (almost always non-diegetic, often marked as inhuman) onto the fabric of the film.

In early Soviet sound film, there is a preponderance of loudspeakers, radios, gramophones, and other devices for reproducing sound that underscore sound cinema's ability to directly address the viewer. As Evgenii Margolit has pointed out, the production of sound films in the USSR was tied directly to the production of the *agitka* (that is to say, non-fiction propaganda) films, rather than to fiction films, as it was for the United States or Western Europe.

> Many of the sound decisions made in early Soviet film (from about 1930 to 1932) had to do with the fact that, in contrast to the Western European and American cinema, sound came to the USSR first in non-fiction film. Hence the specific "laconic" [*nemnogoslovie*] nature of Soviet sound films of the first half of the 1930s and the prevalence of industrial noise over a speech. Radio is one of the important characters in the Dziga Vertov's *Enthusiasm* (1930), or in the *agitprop* documentary anti-war film *Maybe Tomorrow* (1931), by Dmitrii Dal'skoi and Lydia Snezhinskaia. (Margolit 2012, 131)

Film historians, concludes Margolit, have up to now paid "little attention to the unprecedented fact that, unlike other cinemas, Soviet sound film begins with the production not of art, but of non-fiction films" (Margolit 2012, 84). This meant that techniques and concerns of documentary (non-acted) films carried over into fiction films, including an emphasis on hearing and listening to technology.

Thus, for example, in the literary scenario for his first sound film *Enthusiasm* [*Entuziazm: Simfoniia Donbassa*, 1930], Vertov describes the sounds of his film in terms of an "invasion" or a "penetration" of the working class and its machines by speeches, revolutionary songs, and revolutionary slogans. He writes,

> the industrial sounds of the All-Union Stokehold *arrive* at the square, filling the streets with their machine music to accompany the gigantic festive parades; when, on the other hand, the sounds of military bands of parades, the challenge-banners, the red stars, the shouts of greeting, the battle slogans, the orators' speeches, etc., *fuse* with the sounds of the machines, the sounds of competing factory shops." (Vertov 1929)

Vertov imagined that of the different kinds of sounds recorded for the film, ideological speeches and slogans would assume a primary, active role, over the general din of the factories and machines. However, because of the numerous difficulties involved with both initially obtaining and then working with brand new, Soviet sound equipment, the stratification of the sound levels of the film did not come through.

Contemporary critics referred to *Enthusiasm* as a cacophony (a charge that Vertov greatly resented) in large part because in this film the distinction between the different kinds of recorded sounds was not given any clear hierarchy: radio, speeches, music, church bells, factories – all spoke with the same urgency, failing to prioritize human and non-human "voices." "Vertov fetishizes the machine and its sounds," wrote Petr Sazhin in *Kino-front* (March 1930), "Vertov has not given us a socialist Donbass Symphony. He has given us a cacophony of machines, he has given us crashing noise, din, hell" (Sazhin 1930). Another article in the same paper claimed that they received a letter signed by 18 film students, describing *Enthusiasm* as a chaos of sounds and formalist nonsense: "From the sides of the screen there's the nonstop nasal whistling and wheezing of the loudspeakers. There is the chaos of sounds of metal structures and machine parts, wildly spinning frames, formalist nonsense. And this is called – "The Symphony of Donbass" (Anon. 1930). The Communist leader Karl Radek wrote in an editorial in *Izvestiia,* speaking about Vertov's *Enthusiasm*: "It is my deep conviction ... that we should call it 'The Cacophony of Donbass' and never show it again" (Radek 1931). In his defense, Vertov complained that he was dealing with "deaf critics" [*glukhaia kritika*], while celebrating his picture as a film "wounded in battle," torn, with missing limbs and a hoarse voice that was nevertheless victorious in what it had tried to do" (Vertov 1931).

The difficulty of *Enthusiasm* for Soviet viewers lay in part in what Michel Chion would later refer to as cinematic "vococentrism" – Vertov's failure to prioritize the human voice over and above all other sounds in cinema. "In actual movies, for real spectators," writes Chion, "there are not *all the sounds including the human voice. There are voices, and then everything else.* In other words, in every audio mix, the presence of a human voice instantly sets up a hierarchy of perception" (Chion 1999: 5; emphasis in the original). But Vertov, like many of the major Soviet filmmakers of the 1920s, looked on the human voice with suspicion. Already in 1929, Pudovkin wrote: "It's become clear that talking film has no future [...] human speech – is also sound material. The point is that this speech should not be spoken by any person visible on the screen"; and Vladimir Erofeev noted that in the United States sound films have turned exclusively to opera and the musical, while the "talkies" have failed [*chisto-razgovornaia fil'ma ne privilas'*] (Pudovkin 1929; Erofeev 1931).

Noise rather than voice was originally privileged for Soviet sound cinema. For Piotrovskii, for example, the Hollywood focus on "sensation" (singing and dancing, exemplified by *The Jazz Singer*) meant that sound cinema had abandoned the editing and optical techniques of its earlier, silent years. He argued that for the Soviet film industry, this kind of cinema would signal a return to its pre-revolutionary bourgeois roots; instead, we must think of sound in film as independent, expressive material rather than a naturalistic effect. This way, Soviet cinema would create what Piotrovskii calls "cinefied music" [*kinofitsirovannaia muzyka*] – a combination of sound, noise, and "articulated intonations" requiring the same kinds of manipulation via montage as does the raw visual image. Piotrovskii particularly stressed that this way of making sound films would rely heavily on noise and other forms of disharmony [*negarmonizovannost'*], which, as a result, would produce a sound track that was more expressive with sounds new to the ear. In second place in terms of its importance for sound film, the critic suggests putting music and song, and only in *third place,* human speech (although he argues that even here, we should privilege non-speech – "yelps, screams, sharp intonations" – over dialog or any form of comprehensible speech) (Piotrovskii 1929). As Sabine Hänsgen has pointed out, with reference to the futurist poet Aleksei Kruchenykh, Russian futurism had similarly imagined sound in film as noise, first and foremost, and *zaum* [transrational] as the true language of cinema (Hänsgen 2006, 355). For Kruchenykh, whose ideas about noise in cinema had a direct influence on Vertov, the new stars of sound film would be airplanes, trains, and other technical inventions and "tricks" [*triuki*]. "And when the silent cinema speaks, its language – of the noise of machines, screeching and clanking of iron – would of course be transrational [*zaumnaia*]!" (Hänsgen 2006, 355), which was precisely what Vertov had managed to do in his first sound film, privileging industrial noise over human speech.

Many Soviet filmmakers working for the first time with sound equipment tried to capture the sounds of Soviet industry: Esfir' Shub does so in her first documentary sound film *KShE* [*Komsomol: Patron of Electrification*, 1932] commissioned to document the building of Dnepr Hydroelectric Station, as does Aleksandr Dovzhenko (the "poet of Ukrainian cinema") in his first sound film, *Ivan* (1932), also filmed at Dneprostroi. In each case, the sounds of the USSR's massive construction sites overwhelm its human subjects, silencing human speech. In *Ivan* this happens quite literally: the sequence showing an accident at the construction site and the death of one of the workers is followed by a loss of all sound. What had previously been a cacophony of orchestral score and industrial noise (train whistles, sounds of hammers, and the like) is cut off at the moment of the accident. The human cry is cut short and replaced with the sound of a train whistle, just as there is an abrupt cut from the site of the accident to a shot of a train receding into the distance. The rest of the sequence is shot in total silence, as the body of the worker is carried out and placed in front of the factory wall, and the mother stands over the body of her son. The sound comes back, but now in a menacing form as pure industrial noise, as the factory returns to life. We understand that the mother, made small and insignificant in comparison to the cranes, engines, and clam shell shovels of the construction site, has no voice – even as she attempts to speak to the head of the factory about the accident, she has no powers of speech to compete with those of heavy industry.[2]

But it is perhaps the role of the radio/loudspeaker in early Soviet sound films that shifts the power of speech from the human to the non-human subject. Stephen Lovell has noted that,

> When we reach the Soviet period, the relationship between orality and literacy is further complicated by innovations in communication technology. In Russia, from the early 1920s onwards, the spoken word received new kinds of amplification, both literally (in the form of the loudspeakers that were set up in public places in urban areas) and metaphorically (in the form of broadcasting). Potentially, radio was a huge blessing for the masters of Soviet culture: it offered a way of projecting the voice of authority into every workplace and communal flat in the USSR and of showing Soviet people exactly how to "speak Bolshevik." (Lovell 2013, 80)

Chion refers to the radio as one type of *acousmêtre*, a disembodied voice whose "sourcelessness" suggests "the paranoid and often obsessional panoptic fantasy [...] of total mastery of space by vision [...] Media such as the telephone and radio, which send acousmatic voices traveling and which enable them to be here and there at once, often serve as vehicles of this ubiquity" (Chion 1999, 24). In early Soviet sound cinema, radio – in the form of the loudspeaker, but also telephone, gramophone, slogans, and other forms of direct address – often acts precisely as an *acousmêtre*, bypassing the human body in favor of a voice that speaks both from within and from *beyond* the film.

We see this most clearly in Grigorii Kozintsev and Leonid Trauberg's *Alone* [*Odna*, 1931], where the invention of the new sound technology is embodied by a loudspeaker in the middle of an empty square addressing itself to passers-by: "Comrades! Today we are deciding the fate not of one, not of hundreds, but of millions of people. At this moment, we are facing the question: what have you done? What are you doing? What are you going to do?" In *Alone* the heroine hears this "voice of ideology" addressing her directly from a loudspeaker in the city square. Itself figured as technology (loudspeaker), the address is also made possible by means of technology – the technology of synchronized sound that allows us to *hear* as well as see/read the messages of the film. In answer, the actress Elena Kuz'mina responds with one of her two lines of spoken dialogue in the film: 'I'm going to complain!' [*Ia budu zhalovat'sia!*], she says.[3]

We might read this scene not only for its comic or dramatic effect (Kuz'mina, in all of her innocence, answering a piece of technology *as if* it were speaking directly to her; or, the tragedy of the modern subject in a technocratic world), but also for what it teaches us about the privileging of the non-human voice by the new sound-on-film technology. Kuz'mina tries to telephone her fiancé, but instead of her voice, we hear clacking typewriters and official voices issuing directives. This sequence is a kind of precursor to Charles Chaplin's *Modern Times* (1936) in which everything *but* the human beings makes noise. Chaplin's suggestion is that every advance in technology (and sound film being yet another leap in the technological rather than the aesthetic development of cinema) extends our capabilities while chipping away at our humanity. Kuz'mina's brief imprisonment in the telephone booth that prevents *her* voice from reaching the viewer suggests a similar understanding of the powers of technology. With her hands and face pressed against the glass of the phone booth, Kuz'mina is the human subject trapped by technology, incapable of making herself heard. Alarm clocks, radio, trams, loudspeakers, typewriters, telephones – these are the objects produce sound in *Alone*, interfering with or silencing the words of the heroine, until she herself becomes the "voice" of technology. Thus, toward the end of the film, the image of the mutilated and dying heroine (in bed with her arms bandaged up to the elbows) is synchronized with the sound of the telegraph communicating messages to all points in the USSR. The next time we see the loudspeaker in *Alone*, it is announcing the progress of Kuz'mina's illness. The same loudspeaker that hailed Kuz'mina to "do something" is now reporting on her imminent death: "'Listen, listen', it bellows, 'the teacher Kuz'mina is dying in Altai! Only an immediate operation could save her!'" In the middle of the city square, but now surrounded by a multitude of people, the loudspeaker speaks while the human figures fall silent.

Multi-Lingualism, or the Problem of Language in Soviet Cinema

Dovzhenko completed his first sound film *Ivan* on October 30, 1932, and its first public screenings were held on November 2 in Kiev and November 3 in Kharkov; and with an official premiere scheduled for November 6, 1932. Even before its official release, however, it was accused of "Ukrainian nationalism," though no one could say precisely in what way the film was "nationalist." On November 5 cuts were made by a "special commission," while Ukrainfilm administrators ordered Dovzhenko, his wife Iuliia Solntseva, and the film's editor, Grigorii Zeldovych to Moscow, to wait for the official decision, which came six weeks later as official approval from Stalin and the Politburo.

Yet even despite this approval, the film remained a kind of failure, and part of that failure lay with sound: more specifically, in the choice of language that issued from the screen. Dovzhenko chose to make his first sound film in Ukrainian, claiming, at the time, that Kiev had a dearth of actors, and the best ones spoke no Russian, and that no one could dub them. The choice may have been aesthetic or ideological – the film was about the transformation of the Ukrainian peasantry into a Ukrainian working class – but it was perceived as nationalist because the use of Ukrainian was said to unsettle the Russian-speaking audience of the film.[4] As many critics have written both at the time and after, *Ivan* had no clear message and was filled with visual and thematic ambiguities (for one, the project of building the dam remains incomplete and, therefore, the human toll and loss of life at the heart of the film remain unjustified). After its release, Dovzhenko admitted that the use of Ukrainian, because of its closeness to Russian, undermined the film's accessibility for Russian-speaking audiences. The Russian viewers, Dovzhenko suggested, assumed incorrectly that they could understand the Ukrainian: "The viewer's semi-knowledge of the language is the problem. This half-knowledge introduces to the viewer's consciousness inhibitory elements that irritate the viewer. This lowers the quality of the film" (A.D. 1932; Liber 2002, 128).

The film's "unclear" ideological message, therefore, stemmed in part from this choice of language, a language that was almost but not exactly the same as that of its audience. The audience, according to Dovzhenko, could not "abstract" itself from the language, and ended up frustrated by its proximity. (Indeed, Dovzhenko's use of Ukrainian opened up the question of language in Soviet sound cinema – which language would Soviet cinema speak?) As George Liber suggests in his biography of Dovzhenko, "the language of the film also became a message"

(Liber 2002, 128). Indeed, one can argue that the ideological message of the film was actually quite clear, it was simply not the message that the State wanted to receive. By 1932–1933, 88 percent of elementary and secondary students in Ukraine received instruction in Ukrainian. By 1930, 80 percent of all books published and 90 percent of all newspapers were written in Ukrainian. Dovzhenko wasn't precisely lying when he claimed that he could find no actors to speak Russian; rather, he was making sure that the new sound technology aided in the "Ukrainianization" of Ukrainian cinema.

Interestingly enough, as Margolit has noted, the first years of sound cinema saw the release of about a dozen films – (Soviet film studios produced about 20 sound films a year on average in the first half of the 1930s) showcasing a broad range of heteroglossic (not in the Bakhtinian sense, but in the sense of multilingualism – *raznoiazychie*) strategies: thus, for example, Mustafa-the-thief (played by Iyvan Kyrla) sings in his native Mari tongue in the finale of Nikolai Ekk's *The Road to Life* [*Putevka v zhizn'*, 1931], the first 100 percent Soviet "talkie". Characteristically, throughout the film Mustafa speaks Russian with a comical accent, but on the eve of his death he sings in his native tongue, as though returning to his origins. Similarly, in *My Native Land* [*Moia rodina*, Kheifits and Zarkhi, 1933], the mortally wounded hero-soldier Katz abruptly switches to Yiddish in his delirium. The young soldier Vas'ka from *My Native Land* never masters the Chinese phrase for "The Red Army is a friend of the poor," but the Chinese youth Wan (played by Boris Khaidarov, a Central Asian actor who did not speak Chinese) can nevertheless understand him through his inflections and facial expressions. The same tactic is echoed in *The Outskirts* [*Okraina*, Boris Barnet, 1933] released a month later: in this case, all communication between the German boy-soldier Müller and various Russian villagers takes place outside of spoken dialogue. "Foreign speech," argues Margolit, "compels the viewer to concentrate on the speaker's face, thus emphasizing their individuality and humanity, their triumph over the tyranny of the Word" (Margolit 2012, 122).

Indeed, a surprising number of early Soviet sound films, beyond those mentioned by Margolit, make use of foreign and untranslated speech. In Shub's *K.Sh.E.* we hear a radio program being recorded in English, German, and French, as well as a scene of an American specialist visiting the job site with his Russian translator. The emphasis on multilingualism and translation is coupled with a reliance on American specialists to provide instruction to the Soviet labor force. On the one hand, we hear the phrase "Workers of the World Unite!" (spoken in English by the radio announcer), followed by the same speech in German and French, whose recognizable words include "Stalin," "Lenin," "Komsomol," "Five Year Plan," and "enthusiasm." On the other hand, we see the American specialist instruct the Soviet worker in the use of the correct tool – in this case, a twelve-millimeter American machine gage – with the translator concluding, "Alright, they'll do as you say."

The emphasis on translation is particularly evident in a film like Aleksandr Macheret's *Men and Jobs* [*Dela i liudi*, 1932], which relies on the impossibility of translating the terms *sotsialisticheskoe sorevnovanie* [socialist competition] and *udarnik* [shock worker] into English. The miscommunication between the American engineer Cline and his translator leads to exactly the opposite of the intended effect: instead of understanding *sotsialisticheskoe sorevnovanie* as a superior form of "competition" unknown in the West, the American engineer misunderstands the translator's difficulties in putting the terms into English as evidence of the Soviet workers' lack of know-how. "Yes, my good friend, I quite understand," he tells her in English, "You mean these people don't know how to work. I saw this at once." This is, of course, a failure of *cultural* understanding that is marked as linguistic: while the Russian *sorevnovanie* easily translates as "competition," its true meaning is elided: indeed, the key to understanding Soviet competition turns out not to be skill, but "enthusiasm." Cline's final moment of cultural comprehension anticipates a similar moment of revelation for Marion Dixon at the end of Grigorii Aleksandrov's *Circus* [*Tsirk* 1936]: like Marion, Cline turns to Russian to express his new found appreciation for the Soviet state and to mark his integration into the Soviet community. Like Marion, however, Cline's Russian is spoken with a pronounced accent, which ensures that in this new-found community, he is forever marked as different.[5] "Udarnichestvo. Kompetishon. Sorevnovanie. Gip-gip, ura!" [shock work, competition, competition, hip-hip-hurrah] he concludes, reducing his final speech to pat slogans and "enthusiasm" (see Widdis 2014).

On the one hand, multilingualism (or, more precisely, "glossodiversity" – that is, the same words translated into different languages) speaks to the universal nature of Soviet ideology (all workers can understand each other, no matter what language they speak). On the other hand, the question of multilingualism in early Soviet sound films is also one of hierarchy: which speech deserves translation and which is allowed to remain incomprehensible to the viewer? In the first sound film released by the Georgian film studio Gruziiafilm – *The Last Crusaders* [*Poslednie krestonostsy*, dirs. S. Dolidze and V. Shvelidze, 1933] – for example, we find that the Chechens speak Russian, while the Khevsurs speak a local dialect of Georgian. The film opens with gunshots and the death of one of the Chechen shepherds, but once we move to the Khevsur side, we hear a melodious female voice singing as the camera pans across a waterfall and mountains – showing us the natural beauty of the Georgian landscape. It is clear already from the opening sequence that the Khevsurs are tied to their land and their traditional ways of life more than the Chechens, who carry the red Soviet flag and offer the Khevsurs a cream separator as a way of ending their blood feud. The Khevsurs are too backward to see the point of this new technology that they perceive as some kind of a trick of the Soviet state – and the separator becomes the way to separate out not only cream from milk (making butter that is significantly better than the one made by traditional methods), but also to divide those who embrace Soviet power from those who stand in its way. When Tsitsia's younger brother Mgelia returns to the village (wearing his city clothes in stark contrast to the traditional outfits of the Khevsur shepherds), he denounces the village's feudal system in favor of forming a *kolkhoz*, laughs at his older brother and his "horned tractors" (the two bulls he uses to plow the land), and removes the blanket and rocks from the still untried separator. His first colloquy with the Chechens involves playing "The International" on his shepherd's pipe, and exchanging the word "Komsomol!" by way of greeting. The plot of *The Last Crusaders* turns on Tsitsia's mishearing Mgelia's dying word, *"klass"* [class], as a name of a person, rather than understanding that Mgelia was killed by the "enemies of the working class." Once again, this is cultural rather than a linguistic misunderstanding, though throughout the film, the Khevsurs are marked as backward not only by their blood feuds, feudal structure, and their lack of technical knowledge, but also by their speech: their use of a Georgian dialect that is itself closer to the literary Georgian of the Middle Ages than to contemporary speech, stands in stark contrast to the pure Russian of the Chechens.

But it is perhaps in *The Return of Nathan Becker* [*Vozvrashchenie Neitana Bekkera*, 1932] – the world's first "Jewish" sound film – released simultaneously in two versions, Russian and Yiddish (or, *"russkii i evreiskii"* as the review in *Vecherniaia Moskva* put it), that we see this language dynamic spelled out most clearly: like Mustafa's singing in his native Mari, or the German soldier Katz's sudden turn to Yiddish in *My Native Land*, the Yiddish in the Russian version of *The Return of Nathan Becker* is reduced to the language of unarticulated sounds, whose meaning lies entirely outside of comprehensible speech.[6] Set in Belorussia during the First Five-Year Plan, the film centers on Nathan Becker's return to the *shtetl* (still recognizable as a Jewish settlement, little transformed by Soviet power), after 28 years as a bricklayer in New York. Like Macheret's Cline, Nathan is another American expert who must learn to understand that Soviet labor requires not only skill or effort, but also head and heart – in the USSR back-breaking labor is made joyful, with movements coordinated like a dance, and with friendly socialist competition taking place on a circus stage. In the Russian version, which is the only one that has been preserved, and even that in incomplete form, without the first and the last reel, Nathan and most of the other characters in the film speak perfect, unmarked Russian – with the exception of Nathan's father Tsale, played by the remarkable Solomon Mikhoels. Mikhoels' character is created via repetition (of certain movements and phrases), but his most notable sound is his constant singing of the *nigunim*, wordless Jewish melodies. Thus, for example, the first sounds we hear in the film are of Mikhoels singing, followed by his stuttered utterance, "N-n-n-Nosn!", the Yiddish form of the name "Nathan." Toward the end of the film, [David] Gutman as Nathan and Mikhoels as his father conduct an entire conversation by changing the intonation of the words "well," "yes," and "no," with the longest exchange accomplished by the single word *nu*, a syllable that both in Russian and Yiddish expresses a full range of meanings, from approval to doubt to impatience and everything in between (see Murav 2011, 98–102).

The film closes with Nathan's black friend and fellow bricklayer Jim (who has come with him from America to help build socialism) learning the *nigunim* from Tsale. Seated high above the construction site, Nathan looks down on the massive Soviet construction project with pride, while Tsale teaches Jim to sing. It is a remarkable conflation of Yiddish and African American culture, with Tsale clearly adopting Jim as a fellow Jew. Indeed, upon meeting him for the first time, Tsale asks if Jim is also Jewish, to which Nathan tells him that "he is a *bricklayer*," the profession standing in for an identity that was once determined by race, ethnicity, or religion. Yet, the ending of the film seems to belie this, keeping Nathan, the new *Soviet* worker to one side of the screen, while Tsale and Jim communicate in the "old tongue."

This conflation of black with Jewish has some implications for how we might read the film's language usage as a whole. In his famous essay "White," Richard Dyer (1988) considers the "Manicheism delirium" identified by Frantz Fanon as characteristic of colonialist sensibility, which takes an absolutist view of black and white cultures, and organizes its narrative around the rigid binarism that seemingly cannot be overcome. Here, "white" stands in for modernity, reason, order, stability, and "black" stands in for backwardness, irrationality, chaos, and violence. Dyer is particularly careful to pay attention to the way this binarism reproduces itself on the level of *mise-en-scène*: in a film like *Simba* (the first film Dyer examines), the whites' meeting takes place in early evening, in a fully lit room, characters that speak are shot with standard high key lighting, so that they are fully visible; everyone sits in rows, and although there is disagreement, some of it hot-tempered and emotional, it is expressed in grammatical discourse in a language the [British] viewer can understand; moreover, the meeting consists of nothing but speech. The black meeting, on the other hand, takes place at dead of night, out of doors, with all characters in shadow; even the MauMau leader is lit with extreme sub-Expressionist lighting that dramatizes and distorts his face; grouping is in the form of a broken, uneven circle; what speech there is, is ritualized not reasoned, and remains untranslated (and probably in no authentic language anyway), and most vocal sounds are whooping, gabbling, and shrieking (Dyer 1988, 51–52).

Early Soviet sound film similarly often marks non-Russian speech as incoherent or incomprehensible (song, delirium, wordless melody) and, more importantly, as "traditional" and non-modern. This perhaps explains the reception of Dovzhenko's *Ivan*, whose thematic content – Dneprostroi, Soviet construction, worker education – should have fit brilliantly into the films of the First Five-Year Plan, but whose choice of language placed it instead on the side of the traditional and anti-Soviet. If we compare the use of Ukrainian in *Ivan* with *The Last Crusaders*, or with Ivan Kavaleridze's *Koliivshchina* (1931), we can see that the use of "national" languages was tied to notions of backward and traditional cultures that needed to be reformed by the Soviet project.

Notes

1. The term was taken from the title of Joseph Stalin's article "The Year of the Great Turn," published on November 7, 1929, the twelfth anniversary of the October Revolution.
2. We are meant to understand that the head of the factory is already giving orders to prevent further accidents, but the sequence, in which the mother runs through numerous doors (again, shot in silence) only to be stopped in her tracks by the sound of a gruff male voice yelling into the phone, suggests that human emotions have no place here: in answer to the question, "What do you want, comrade?" the mother replies, "Nothing."
3. Zorkaia points out that other lines of dialogue were recorded but did not make it into the final cut of the film – such as the line "I will go!" [*Ia poedu!*], doubled and later replaced by intertitles, and the awkward "He is killing your sheep for meat!" [*on rezhet na miaso vashikh baranov*] that Kozintsev made Kuz'mina practice over and over. According to Zorkaia, Kuz'mina's voice in the film is dubbed by Maria Babanova (Zorkaia 2005, 148).
4. Actually, the majority of Kiev residents at the time spoke Russian, which was a typical division in Ukraine between the urban (Russian-speaking) and the rural (Ukrainian-speaking) populations (Liber 2002, 127–128).
5. The famous exchange at the end of *Circus* in which Raechka, for the fourth time in the film, asks Marion if now she understands – "Teper' ponimaesh'?" – is finally answered with an enthusiastic, "Teper' ponimaesh'!" suggesting in the end that the American can only parrot, but can never truly understand.
6. The film was made in Leningrad by the Belgoskino studio. Unfortunately, there is no surviving Yiddish version of the film, so we cannot know for sure how Solomon Mikhoels' Yiddish would have sounded in the context of everyone speaking the same language. The original (Russian language) release was in nine parts and 2600 m, but has survived without parts 1 and 9.

References

References to RGALI [Russian State Archive for Literature and Arts] in Moscow are by fond, inventory [opis'], and document, followed by the file name and year.

A. D. 1932. "Pochemu *Ivan*?" [Why "Ivan"?]. *Kino* November 24.

Aleksandrov, Grigorii. 1939. "Velikii drug sovetskogo kino" [A Great Friend of Soviet Cinema]. *Iskusstvo kino* [Art of Cinema] 12.

Anon. 1930. "Ideologia komnatnoi bolonki" [The Ideology of a Lap-Dog]. *Kino-Front* (March); RGALI 2091/1/91: 99.

Chion, Michel 1999. *The Voice in Cinema*. New York: Columbia University Press. Translation of Chion. Originally published as *La voix au cinéma*, Paris: Editions de l'Etoile 1982.

Christie, Ian. 1982. "Soviet Cinema: Making Sense of Sound." *Screen* 23.2: 34–49. doi: 10.1093/screen/23.2.34

Crafton, Donald. 1997. *The Talkies: American Cinema's Transition to Sound, 1926–1931*. Berkeley: University of California Press.

Dyer, Richard. 1988. "White." *Screen* 29.4: 44–65.

Eikhenbaum, Boris. 1927. "Problemy kino-stilistiki" [Problems of Film Style]. In *Poetika kino* [Poetics of Cinema], edited by B. Eikhenbaum, 13–52. Moscow: Kinopechat'. Translated as Boris Eikhenbaum, "Problems of Film Stylistics," *Screen* 15.3 (1974): 7–32; and B. Ejxenbaum "Problems of Cinema Stylistics," in H. Eagle, ed. and trans., *Russian Formalist Film Theory*. Ann Arbor: Michigan Slavic Publications, 1981, pp. 55–80.

Eisenstein, Sergei, Vsevolod Pudovkin, and Grigorii Aleksandrov. 1928. "Zaiavka" [Application]. *Zhizn' iskusstva* [Life of Art] August 5: 4–5. Translated in Richard Taylor and Ian Christie, eds, *The Film Factory*. London and New York: Routledge, 1988, pp. 234–235.

Erofeev, Vladimir. 1931. "Uroki zvukovogo kino" [Lessons of Sound Cinema]. *Sovetskoe iskusstvo* [Soviet Art] January 29.

Gomery, Douglas. 2005. *The Coming of Sound*. New York: Routledge.

Hänsgen, Sabine. (Khensgen, Sabina) 2006. "'Audio-Vision': o teorii i praktike rannego sovetskogo zvukovogo kino na grani 1930-x godov" ["Audio-Vision": About Theory and Practice of Early Soviet Sound Cinema on the Threshold of the 1930s]. In *Sovetskaia vlast' i media: Sbornik statei* [Soviet Power and Media: A Collection of Articles], edited by H. Günther and S. Hänsgen, 350–364. St Petersburg: Akademicheskii Proekt.

Iukov, Konstantin. 1928. "Novyi etap (K voprosu o 'krizise' v kino)" [A New Stage: About the "Crisis" in Cinema]. *Kino* 51: 2–3.

Izvolov, Nikolai. 2013. "From the History of Graphic Sound in the Soviet Union; or, Media without a Medium." In *Sound, Speech, Music in Soviet and Post-Soviet Cinema*, edited by Lilya Kaganovsky and Masha Salazkina, 21–37. Bloomington: Indiana University Press. Earlier, shorter version as "Moment ozhivleniia spiaschei idei" [The Moment of Reviving a Dormant Idea]. *Kinovedcheskie zapiski* [Film Scholars' Notes] 15 (1992): 290–296.

Kepley Jr., Vance. 1996. "The First 'Perestroika': Soviet Cinema under the First Five-Year Plan." *Cinema Journal* 35.4: 31–53.

Leyda, Jay. 1960. *Kino: A History of the Russian and Soviet Film*. Princeton: Princeton University Press.

Liber, George. 2002. *Alexander Dovzhenko: A Life in Soviet Film*. London: British Film Institute.

Lovell, Stephen. 2013. "Broadcasting Bolshevik: The Radio Voice of Soviet Culture, 1920s–1950s," *Journal of Contemporary History* 48.1: 78–97. doi: 10.1177/0022009412461817.

Margolit. Evgenii. 2012. *Zhivye i mertvoe. Zametki k istorii sovetskogo kino 1920-kh–1960-kh godov* [The Living and the Dead. Notes on the History of Soviet Cinema, 1920s–1960s]. St Petersburg: Seans.

Murav, Harriet. 2011. *Music from a Speeding Train: Jewish Literature in Post-Revolution Russia*. Stanford: Stanford University Press.

Piotrovskii, Adrian. 1929. "Tonfil'ma" [Sound-Film]. *Zhizn' iskusstva* [Life of Art] 30: 4–5.

Pozner, Valérie. 2014. "To Catch Up and Overtake Hollywood: Early Talking Pictures in the Soviet Union." In *Sound, Speech, Music in Soviet and Post-Soviet Cinema*, edited by Lilya Kaganovsky and Masha Salazkina, 60–80. Bloomington: Indiana University Press.

Pudovkin, Vsevolod. 1929. "K voprosu zvukovogo nachala v fil'me" [On the Issue of the Beginning of Sound Film]. *Kino i kul'tura* [Cinema and Culture] 5–6.

Radek, Karl. 1931. "Dve fil'my" [Two Films]. *Izvestiia* [News] April 23.

Sazhin, Petr. 1930. "Entuziazm." [Enthusiasm]. *Kino-front*. RGALI 2091/1/91: 99.

Smirnov, Andrey. 2013. *Sound in Z: Experiments in Sound and Electronic Music in Early 20th Century Russia*. London: Koenig Books.

Tsivian, Yuri. 2008. *Dziga Vertov and the Soviet Avant-Garde*. Program notes for a film series at Harvard Film Archive (March–April), adapted from Le Giornate Del Cinema Muto catalogue, http://hcl.harvard.edu/hfa/films/2008marchapril/soviet.html (accessed January 31, 2015).

Vertov, Dziga. 1929. "Entuziazm. Literaturnyi stsenarii" [Enthusiasm. Literary Script]. RGALI 2091/1/35.

Vertov, Dziga. 1931. "Pervye shagi" [First Steps]. (April 10); RGALI 2091/2/174.

Widdis, Emma. 2014. "Making Sense without Speech: The Use of Silence in Early Soviet Sound Film." In *Sound, Speech, Music in Soviet and Post-Soviet Cinema*, edited by Lilya Kaganovsky and Masha Salazkina, 100–116. Bloomington: Indiana University Press.

Youngblood, Denise. 1980. *Soviet Cinema in the Silent Era, 1918–1935*. Ann Arbor: UMI Research Press.

Zorkaia, Neia. 2005. "'Odna' na perekrestakh" ["Alone" at the Crossroads]. *Kinovedcheskie zapiski* [Film Scholars' Notes] 74: 143–158.

14

Cinema and the Art of Being: Towards a History of Early Soviet Set Design

Emma Widdis

Forty five or fifty years ago, when I started to work in cinema, the screen was flat. A sense of depth was achieved by movement within the frame, or by lighting. Overcoming this flatness was the achievement of set designers.

(Shklovskii 1977, 202)

Abram Room's declaration in 1925 that "the theatre is an art of 'seeming'; cinema is 'being'" could be read as a challenge to film set designers (Room 1925, 56). If film was the ultimate art of the real, then it was the art form most suited to the new Socialist aesthetic, with its call for art to engage in reflecting – and ultimately *shaping* – the lived everyday [*byt*]. As such, those with responsibility for selecting, designing, and molding that screened reality surely had a particularly important role to play.

Despite this, a critical and analytical history of Russian and Soviet set design (and of production design more generally) has yet to be written. The fullest account of the development of Russian film set design is given by Gennadii Miasnikov's multi-volume edition of *Studies of the History of Soviet Production Design* [*Ocherki istorii sovetskogo kinodekoratsionnogo iskusstva*], which describes how set designers grappled with the specific demands of the medium and provides invaluable information about the broad technical evolution of the practice of *mise-en-scène* (Miasnikov 1973; 1975; 1979). More recently, the scholarly journal *Kinovedcheskie zapiski* has dedicated a volume (no. 99: 2012) to varied explorations of Russian and Soviet production design and the publication of materials. These and other extant sources do not, however, add up to a systematic history of Soviet set design; nor has in-depth research yet begun to link these kinds of material to the larger questions that remain pertinent to our understanding of the field.

A Companion to Russian Cinema, First Edition. Edited by Birgit Beumers.
© 2016 John Wiley & Sons, Inc. Published 2016 by John Wiley & Sons, Inc.

What can a study of set design contribute to a history of cinema, and how can it inflect our readings of the films themselves that are our primary source material? What, if anything, can be identified as particular to Russian and Soviet production design? How does attention to set design support or challenge our scholarly tendency to view Soviet and Russian cinema as shaped by a wider cultural and ideological agenda?

First, attention to set design reminds us that film-making is a collective endeavor, and that no film is solely the work of a director. This was particularly important in the Soviet case, where the ideological value of "collectivity" inflected the formation of film-making groups, particularly in the decade immediately following the revolution. As Philip Cavendish has shown, recognition of the importance of other key figures in the film-making collective provides a new perspective for scholarship of Russian and Soviet cinema (Cavendish 2004; 2008; 2013).

This focus on the contribution of other members of any film-making group illuminates, also, how the development of film-making is shaped by the evolution of technical limits and possibilities. Cavendish's own work has argued convincingly for an alternative history of Soviet cinema through the figure of the camera-operator, and in turn through the evolution of the technical possibilities of the film camera. Other recent scholarship by, for example, Lilya Kaganovsky (2012), Oksana Bulgakowa (2010), and Valerie Pozner, (2012) argues that attention to the discussions surrounding Soviet cinema's transition to sound (approximately 1929–1935) provides a revealing lens on the evolution of both formal and ideological preoccupations.

A study of set design may provide similar alternative histories and new perspectives. In this case, we know of at least two instances where the set designer [*khudozhnik*] had a profound and ongoing influence in the evolution of the particular "style" of a film-maker: the influence of Evgenii Enei on the director/camera-man partnership of Grigorii Kozintsev and Leonid Trauberg with Andrei Moskvin (FEKS, the Factory of the Eccentric Actor); and the influence of Vladimir Egorov on the partnership of Vsevolod Pudovkin and Anatolii Golovnia. Sergei Eisenstein was more eclectic in his choice of *khudozhnik*, but his work with Vasilii Rakhal's can be regarded as highly distinctive, and characterizes his "revolutionary" films of the 1920s; it is well known that Eisenstein's decision to work with Iosif Shpinel' for the historical epics *Alexander Nevsky* (1938) and *Ivan the Terrible* [*Ivan Groznyi*, 1944–1946] marked a radical shift in aesthetic. Other partnerships of the 1920s also bear further investigation: Enei was also responsible for the design of most of Fridrikh Ermler's films of the 1920s; Boris Barnet worked consistently with Sergei Kozlovskii, acknowledged master of the "everyday" style in Soviet set design. Iakov Protazanov made careful selection of set designers appropriate to his aesthetic requirements for a particular film/part of a film: most famously, in his *Aelita* (1924), he worked with Kozlovskii for the Moscow sections of the film, but sought different designers to realize the scenes set in Mars.[1] In addition, the work of Aleksandr Rodchenko in film (with different directors) remains an important and under-explored element of that artist's broader *oeuvre*.

Individual personalities and partnerships aside, however, a fuller study of Soviet set design will – like parallel works on sound, color, etc. – uncover an often-overlooked element of cinema history. Such attention to technical aspects of film production marks a new stage in the scholarly field. It is linked to a growing resistance to over-simplified ideological narratives about Soviet cinema, and a recognition that its evolution need not be seen as entirely distinct from that of American and European cinema. In this way, the decades from 1917 to 1937 can be seen either as the evolution from the revolutionary avant-garde to the cinema of Socialist Realism, or as the evolution and professionalization of the film industry, and a series of formal developments that are as much linked to that professionalization as they are to the particular ideological frameworks that shaped Soviet cinematic form. In this sense, Soviet cinema is subject to the same developmental stages as Western cinema, as Cavendish shows in his chapter on color in this volume.

Finally, attention to set design may allow us to focus on core epistemological and theoretical questions relating to the film medium. Studying set design, costume, and props means learning to see a film as comprised of material, texture, and objects on screen, and to think about the impact of that material on the film's narrative and poetics. In particular, the study of set design raises questions about the relationship between camera and the material (broadly understood) of the film: the *stuff* in front of the camera. This in turn leads to consideration of the relationship between the film spectator and the filmic material.[2]

Although this chapter cannot address all of these issues in depth, it will provide an introduction to early Soviet set design, and its evolution through the 1920s and towards the Socialist Realist 1930s. In part, this is a chapter about the maturation and professionalization of the Soviet film industry. I will show, however, how preoccupations that shaped cinematic evolution across Europe and the United States did acquire particular ideological inflection in the Soviet case. In particular, the second part of the chapter will trace how film design grappled with a pressing question: the shapes, textures and objects of the new Soviet interior.

Set Design: The Scholarly Field

Outside the Russian and Soviet field, some scholarly attention has been paid to set design, but the field is still sparse. This is because, as Bergfelder, Harris, and Street point out (2007, 11–13), the set is often an "invisible" element of the film. Exceptionally, Charles and Mirella Affron have attempted to provide a classification for different types of cinematic set, ranging from "Sets as Denotation" (largely invisible, non-signifying background), through to "Sets as Artifice" (highly visual and responsible for a large part of the film's overall impact) (Affron and Affron 1995, 37–40). These categories reflect a key question, which recurs in historical and theoretical discussions of set design: is the set an independently expressive part of the film in itself, or a servant of the plot? For the Affrons, a good set is one that "serves" the narrative. Charles S. Tashiro, by contrast, is concerned to show how the impact of design can *exceed* the limits of the narrative. Citing Léon Barsacq's insistence that "one of the fundamental requirements of the cinema [is] to give the impression of having photographed *real* objects" (Barsacq 1976, 7), he suggests that "those objects have meanings of their own exploited by the designer that have nothing to do with the script" (Tashiro 1998, 6).

This tension, which Tashiro describes as a tension between "visible expression and invisible neutrality" (Tashiro 1998, xvi), underpinned the debates on the role of film production design during the first decades of the twentieth century. In their recent volume, Bergfelder, Harris, and Street have explored the development of set design in France, Britain, and Germany, focusing on the period from the late 1920s to the late 1930s, as "the moment in film history in which set design was given more prominence and attention that perhaps during any other period" (Bergfelder, Harris, and Street 2007, 25). In Hollywood, the establishment of the studio system brought ever more lavish production design; in Germany, the influence of Expressionism brought about a wholesale revolution in the role of the film designer, most famously realized in Robert Wiene's *Cabinet of Dr. Caligari* [*Das Cabinet des Dr. Caligari*, 1920]; in Paris, émigré Russian designers linked to the Albatros group were pioneering "a modern, performative conception of décor," with a new emphasis on multi-dimensional space (Bergfelder, Harris, and Street 2007, 58). Despite the influence of Russian émigrés on film design in the period under discussion, Bergfelder, Harris, and Street do not discuss Soviet cinema itself. This omission is consistent in histories of production design: Léon Barsacq, one of the only writers even to address the question of Soviet cinema, discounts its studio/interior shots, praising it instead for the "perfection of its exterior shots" (Barsacq 1976, 47).[3] The so-called "poverty" of early Soviet set design is commonly attributed to the underfunded state of film production during the 1920s. Looking more closely at interior sets of this period, however, and at the debates surrounding design in the film press, we discover a rich vein of experimentation.

The Russian Context: Background and Practicalities

The first set designers in Soviet cinema had almost all been working in film since before 1917, and the majority of them had come to cinema from the theater. As such, a broad understanding of the conditions and achievements of pre-Revolutionary set design is important.

For the very first Russian films, individually constructed sets were rare: standard painted backdrops, generally made from fabric and pertaining to particular historical periods, were used on several films; furniture, props, and costumes were taken from studio stores, or simply hired. Such "décor" was often prepared merely days – even hours – before filming (Cavendish 2004, 206). The elaboration of the so-called "fundus" system, however, in the years between 1908 and 1913, was a significant progression, moving set design from two-dimensional backdrops towards three-dimensionality. The "fundus" consisted of a series of standard partitions and screens ("flats"), together with columns, doorways, staircases etc., which enabled set designers to construct sets with multiple layers, and to create the illusion of depth, offering several different positions for the camera.[4]

This development of more complex equipment for set design reflected a growing understanding of the specificity of cinematic space. It was linked, of course, to evolving sophistication in other technical aspects of the film process – in particular, to increasing camera mobility (which enabled film sets to be photographed from different angles), and lighting technique. When not on location, very early cinema was largely filmed in so-called "glass houses," where glass roofs allowed daylight to illuminate the set from above. Although Hollywood "went dark" around 1907, introducing studio lighting, Europe, including Russia, continued to use glass roofs for some time (Bergfelder, Harris, and Street 2007, 41). By the middle of the next decade, however, techniques for artificial studio lighting were developing rapidly in Russia.[5]

This in turn placed new demands on the architecture, objects, and costumes of the *mise-en-scène* and, as film-makers were increasingly keen to create the illusion of cinematic deep space, there was more focus on the foreground and greater emphasis on the material properties of the *mise-en-scène*. This is particularly evident in the work of Evgenii Bauer, whose complex architectural interiors are usually seen as a pinnacle of pre-Revolutionary Russian set design. Bauer's "psychological" cinema was in large part dependent on the architecture of interior spaces, often positioning the spectator as voyeur, penetrating private space (Tsivian 1996; DeBlasio 2007). Vera Khanzhonkova, who was an editor in the Khanzhonkov studio, recalled how Bauer replaced solid elements of set design with drapery, curtains and tulle, and made extensive use of columns (Khanzhonkova 1962, 126). Foregrounded details (architectural shapes or single objects) were used to create a sense of perspective: the three-dimensional "relief" of real objects attracts the eye, creating the illusion of depth. Employed as a young set designer for Bauer, Lev Kuleshov's role was to find this defining detail (known as the *dikovinka*, or "curiosity") for every shot: "The foreground has to be based around some object or other, sometimes particular, sometimes ordinary, but characteristic of the style of the frame. Objects have a rather great significance in the construction of filmic material" (Kuleshov 1920, 83).[6] The foregrounded object structures the spectator's reception of the shot as a whole.

In his early films, Bauer was largely responsible for his own set design. In the years immediately preceding his death, however, Bauer worked with Kuleshov (employed by the Khanzhonkov Studio from 1916) as designer, and for *A Life for a Life* [*Zhizn' za zhizn'*, 1917] the more established *khudozhnik* Aleksei Utkin developed a complex, multi-textured set in the fashionable *style moderne*. The presence of Utkin's name in the credits for that film signals the growing role of set designers in late pre-Revolutionary cinema. Similarly, for the series of high production-value films known as the Golden Series [*Russkaia zolotaia seriia*, produced by Thiemann & Reinhardt Studio], the young Moscow Arts Theater-trained set designer Vladimir Egorov was employed (Gromov 1973, 13). Again, the fact that Egorov was listed in the credits of the films in which he participated signals the importance of his contribution, and a shifting understanding of the role of the designer, as well as of the communicative potential of the set (Ivanova et al. 2002, 509).[7] According to Gardin's memoirs, Egorov was noted for his understanding of the decorative potential of the film set (Gardin 1949, 109). He is best known for his work on Vsevolod Meyerhold's 1915 adaptation of Oscar Wilde's *Portrait of Dorian Grey* [*Portret Doriana Greia*], which was a key moment in Russian set design history (Lisakovskaia 2013, 27). Although the film itself has not been preserved, it is clear from contemporary reviews that Egorov's work on this film was an example of early expressionist design, exploiting volume, depth, and contrast.

In this respect, it is worth noting that Egorov had studied architecture at the Stroganov Institute under Fedor Shekhtel' and Ivan Zholtovskii[8] (Lisakovskaia 2013, 27; Gromov 1973, 13), and understood set design as both an architectural and a pictorial process, which must exploit both volume and texture. Untinted orthochromatic film stock offered a range of tones from deep black to extreme white; the task of the designer – in collaboration with director and cameraman – was to maximize the expressive potential of this range. As pre-Revolutionary set design evolved, textile played an increasingly important role in the patterning of the screen. As the anecdote about Bauer makes clear, drapery [*drapirovanie*] developed into a key method of demarcating the different levels of the set. Like architectural detail, the designs and textures of patterned textile were used to create contrast and variation.

The Soviet Designers

Pre-Revolutionary Russian film design was marked by a number of key influences. The majority of set designers working in Russian and Soviet cinema before the Revolution (and continuing after it) had artistic training. Many (such as Egorov and Utkin) had been educated in the Moscow Stroganov Institute for Technical Drawing [Stroganovskoe uchilishche tekhnicheskogo risovaniia]. A significant proportion (e.g., Egorov, Dmitrii Kolupaev, Czesław Sabiński) had gone on to apply that training to work in theater, in particular with the Moscow Arts Theater [MKhT, Moskovskii khudozhestvennyi teatr; after 1919 MKhAT, Moskovskii khudozhestvennyi akademicheskii teatr], where several worked directly with Konstantin Stanislavsky. As such, they had been exposed to the naturalist school of set design initiated by Stanislavsky's collaborations with Valentin Simov (who himself worked as a set designer in pre- and post-Revolutionary cinema). The influence of the Arts Theater should not be seen as solely that of naturalism, however. Egorov, for one, had worked with Vsevolod Meyerhold in the Experimental studio set up by Stanislavsky at the Arts Theater in 1905, which was an early cradle for modernist theatrical experiment in Russia. The ornamental *moderne* aesthetic, with its interest in *dekorativnost'* and patterning (exemplified in the set designs for Diaghilev's *Ballets russes*, but also evident in, for example, the designs for Meyerhold's 1917 production of Mikhail Lermontov's *Masquerade* [*Maskarad*]) is another core influence in early Russian film set design. Finally, we should note the influence of architectural/technical training: the Stroganov Institute, which provided the early education of so many of Russia's first set designers, educated them alongside architects and technical designers. In Russian modernist theatrical set design, too, there was a growing interest in the potential of the manipulation of spatial volume in the construction of stage sets (Bowlt 1977).

This blend of influences and impulses (naturalism, *dekorativnost'*/ornamentalism, and volumetric/architectural experiment) continued to be significant after 1917. Many of the most important *khudozhniki* working in film during the 1920s had been in the profession before 1917. And even those young directors – such as Eisenstein, Dziga Vertov, and Pudovkin – who came to film fresh after 1917, were often working alongside veterans in technical areas such as set construction. By the late 1920s, there were effectively three generations of designers: the first *khudozhniki* (such as Simov) remained linked to traditions exemplified by the naturalism of the Moscow Arts Theater. A second, younger group (including Sergei Kozlovskii, Egorov, and Vladimir Balliuzek) had mostly also begun their careers in theater and had worked in pre-Revolutionary cinema. A third generation of designers, many of whom came to prominence in the 1920s, consisted of men who had worked almost exclusively in film rather than theater: Kuleshov, Utkin, Rakhal's – and later, Enei. The evolution of practice and theory across these generations tracks growing understandings of the unique capabilities of film.

Although in 1917 several private production studios were successfully established in Russia, the early years of Soviet cinema were marked by difficulties of funding and technical shortages. Film studios were underequipped, and there was little or no money available for complex set design. The second half of the 1920s, by contrast, was a period of technical consolidation and professionalization in all areas of film production. This had an impact on the practices of set design. In the course of the 1920s, the pre-revolutionary "fundus" system was significantly developed and elaborated, in particular through the work of Sergei Kozlovskii, when the Mezhrabpom-Rus Studio moved to new, bigger premises in 1927 (Kozlovskii 1929, 57–58; Kozlovskii and Kolin 1930) As the organization of major studios was increasingly consolidated, Kozlovskii was named head of Art Direction at Mezhrabpom; Rakhal's filled the same role in the state-run Goskinofabrika (later Sovkino). The technical possibilities for set design were gradually improved: by 1930, for example, Mezhrabpom had six large pavilions.[9]

These improvements in technical provision were accompanied by a focus on professional training. In 1924, a so-called "architectural-decorative" [*arkhitekturno-dekorativnyi*] design department opened as part of the state film college (GTK, Gosudarstvennyi tekhnikum kinoiskusstva), which had been founded in 1922. In 1930 the college became an institute (GIK, Gosudarstvennyi institut kinematografii); and from 1938, (V)GIK had a designated Arts faculty (established and run by Fedor Bogorodskii until 1959), which incorporated set design, animation, and, later, costume design. It is the first GTK department of 1924 that principally concerns us here, however. Instructors included Sergei Kozlovskii, together with the artist-architect Konstantin Mel'nikov (Miasnikov 1975, 41); the first cohort of students graduated in 1927, and a new generation emerged into professional practice. This group included Moisei Aronson (who was employed by Mezhrabpom, and worked with Pudovkin on *Storm over Asia* [*Potomok Chingiz-Khana*] in 1929), Feliks Bogoslavskii (later designer for Leonid Lukov's *A Great Life* [*Bol'shaia zhizn'*, Part 2, 1946]), and Arnold Vaisfel'd (designer for Pudovkin's *Admiral Nakhimov*, 1946) (Miasnikov 1975, 41). In his manifesto for set design, written in 1930, Kozlovskii identified this 'new generation' of film artists and included two further recent (female) graduates as worthy of note: Valentina Khmeleva – later artistic director for Igor' Savchenko's *The Accordion* [*Garmon'*, 1934], and Liudmila Blatova, who also worked with Savchenko on his *A Chance Encounter* [*Sluchainaia vstrecha*, 1936] (Kozlovskii and Kolin 1930, 40).

Not all set designers coming to cinema during the late 1920s and into the 1930s went through the GTK/GIK training, however. Far from it. First, there were other institutes providing designated film training: the Higher Institute for Photography and Technology [Vysshii Institut Fotografii i Fototekhniki], established in Petrograd in 1919; the Institute for Screen Arts [Institut Ekrannogo Iskusstva], which specialized in training actors; and the School of Film Technicians [Shkola Kino-mekhanikov], which offered courses for future film-industry technicians (Cavendish 2013, 49, n.3). Second, it was not yet clear what kind of professional/specialist training the film artist needed. Kozlovskii was explicit in stating that "the question of who should provide the specialist training for our film artists is still not clear – GTK, VKhUTEIN, or another organization?" (Kozlovskii and Kolin 1930, 37). Many active *khudozhniki* (such as Vasilii Kamardenkov and Iosif Shpinel') graduated from VKhUTEMAS [Vysshie khudozhestvenno-tekhnicheskie masterskie, the Higher Art and Technical Studios, 1920–1926] and VKhUTEIN [Vysshii khudozhestvenno-tekhnicheskii institut, or Higher Art and Technical Institute, Leningrad, until 1930] (Miasnikov 1975, 92; Kozlovskii and Kolin 1930, 40), which had replaced the Stroganov Institute in 1920 and became a cradle for avant-garde creativity through the 1920s. Others, such as Blatova, went to GTK *after* initial broader arts training in VKhUTEIN (Kozlovskii and Kolin 1930, 38). In 1929, by the initiative of the artist and production designer Boris Dubrovskii-Eshke, a special department for film art direction was opened in the Academy of Arts. And of course, the field of influence was wider still: filmmaker and production designer Vladimir Kaplunovskii, for example, emerged from an art institutes in Kiev; Enei, who began working in cinema in 1923, had been trained in architecture, and spent time in the Budapest Academy of Arts.

In general, the story of the professional formation of set designers is one of considerable fluidity in this early period. Iakov Rivosh recalls how, after initial architectural training, when he was studying at the Institute for the History of Arts [Gosudarstvennyi institut istorii iskusstv, GIII] where a cinema department had been formed in 1927, then dean Iurii Tynianov recommended him as assistant to Evgenii Enei for the film SVD (directed by FEKS from Tynianov's screenplay) (Rivosh 2012, 245). This led to further work with Enei, and thence to an independent professional career. This kind of flexibility in professional formation points to a clear understanding, in the period, that the film set designer was primarily an artist, and that creative talent was of more significance than any professional training. Such a view is backed up by the appointment of the easel painter Fedor Bogorodskii at the head of the VGIK art department from 1938.[10]

This lack of clarity regarding professional status was reflected also in a debate about the role of the set designer that took place in the cinema press from 1925 to 1928, shortly after the opening of GTK's dedicated department (Makhlis 1925; Kozlovskii 1925; Agden 1926). Part of broader discussions about the rationalization and professionalization of the film production process, this was also a process of role definition, marking the boundaries between different members of the filmmaking collective. From the point of view of the *khudozhniki*, the main ambition of this debate was to carve out a role, and appropriate recognition, for the designer. Dmitrii Kolupaev, for example, argued that the *khudozhnik* must have overall responsibility for all "artistic-decorative elements" of the film – set, costume, props, and the much more nebulous "style" (Kolupaev 1926, 18). He claimed that the designer was a vital part of the film's creative team, that he or she should "help the director with imagination and ingenuity." Aleksandr Rodchenko called for the *khudozhnik* to have control of a film's entire "material environment" (Rodchenko 1925, 14). In the same vein, in February 1928, set designer members of ARK [Assosiatsiia revolutsionnykh kinematografistov] published a "resolution," seeking to define the role of the *khudozhnik* as a "creative" member of the production collective, insisting that the name of the the *khudozhnik* must feature on a film's promotional material (Anon. 1928, 13). The debate was not easily won, however: almost a decade later, Natan Al'tman felt the need to state that the artist "must be a fully-fledged creative partner in the process": the designer should have an input into lighting and shooting decisions, working closely with the cinematographer (Al'tman 1936, 22).

In general, the involvement of the *khudozhnik* in production of a film in this period seems to have been divided into two stages. First, responding to the screenplay, he or she was responsible for generating sketches – usually of the interior and (to a lesser extent) exterior settings envisaged for the film. Some designers (for example Enei, Rivosh, Petr Galadzhev) took an active role in envisaging costumes at this stage. The second stage of the *khudozhnik*'s work was more "hands on" – usually involving the actual construction of the film sets, responsibility for props, costume, etc. As the discipline professionalized, responsibility for different elements of the artistic design began to be more precisely apportioned. Costume design became a separately designated role in the film design process in the mid-1930s (Miasnikov 1975, 16).

Professional set designers were often employed on permanent contract with particular studios, and thus would generally work on more than one film at a time. In the course of the 1920s, however, a growing interest in maximizing the power of the set led to more frequent use of pairs of set designers, usually including one "seasoned" expert (often a permanent employee of the studio) and a newer creative voice. The pairing of Vasilii Rakhal's with young avant-gardist Sergei Iutkevich for the set design of *The Traitor* [*Predatel'*, 1926] and *Bed and Sofa* [*Tret'ia Meshchanskaia*, 1927] is a case in point here; as is the work of Aleksandr Rodchenko with Kozlovskii for Sergei Komarov's *A Doll with Millions* [*Kukla s millionami*, 1928], and with Rakhal's for Kuleshov's *Your Acquaintance* [*Vasha znakomaia*, 1927] (Widdis 2009). Other such partnerships abound. In some cases, the rationale for embedding a new creative voice is evident: for Eisenstein's *General Line* [*General'naia liniia* 1929], Rakhal's (as head of the studio and Eisenstein's accustomed collaborator) worked with the younger Vasilii Kovrigin (who had worked with Eisenstein on *October* [*Oktiabr'*, 1928] and produced detailed sketches for the rural interiors); they also drafted in constructivist architect Andrei Burov to produce a vision of a utopian future in the modernist milk production plant in the finale.[11] In other cases, such as that of Rodchenko's or Natan Al'tman's involvement, it speaks to the centrality of cinema in the Soviet avant-garde creative pantheon (Cavendish 2013, 22–26).

In Search of the Soviet Interior

Miasnikov identifies three distinct approaches to set design in the period before 1930. The first is characteristic of those *khudozhniki* who saw cinema as an extension of theater, and who transferred their understanding of theatrical space into their work for cinema, seeing cinema as a kind of staged theater. The second strand of production design (Kozlovskii, Rakhal's) is that of designers who explicitly rejected theatrical traditions, saw the essence of cinema in permitting a new proximity with reality, and were preoccupied by enhancing the "authenticity" of their interior and exterior sets, and increasingly focused on location shooting. The third direction was, according to Miasnikov, a rejection of both of these opposites, exploring the specificity of cinematic representation as such, and a view of the film set as an artistic factor in its own right, a key locus of meaning and aesthetic impact (Miasnikov 1975, 23). As representatives of this third route he names Egorov, Enei, and Balliuzek.

This diversity notwithstanding, in the course of the 1920s, as part of the struggle for a clearly defined role for the *khudozhnik*, a debate about the "appropriate" aesthetic for Soviet set design took place. Soviet set designers were under threat: in addition to complaints of poor quality work (Agden 1926, 16), the principal accusation leveled at *khudozhniki* during the 1920s was that of "excess" and "pomposity" [*pompeznost'*]. Writing in 1925, Pudovkin called for modern set design to avoid the "chaos" characteristic of pre-Revolutionary films (Pudovkin 1925, 117). Contemporary Soviet cinema must distinguish itself from that of the pre-Revolutionary years and, in particular, from the dominance of costume dramas. Much criticism was directed towards contemporary costume dramas such as Iurii Tarich's *Wings of a Serf* [*Kryl'ia kholopa*, 1926], Aleksandr Ivanovskii's *The Decembrists* [*Dekabristy*, 1926], and Vladimir Gardin, Aleksandr Gintsburg and Evgenii Cherviakov's *The Poet and the Tsar* [*Poet i tsar'*, 1927].[12]

With decorative excess eliminated, so too should Soviet set design avoid the traps of German Expressionist design. There were increasing suggestions in the critical press that good set design meant a set that was fully integrated with the film's narrative and poetics. According to Pudovkin, the task of a true *kino-khudozhnik* was to "create a calm décor, which does not attract the eye." (Pudovkin 1925, 117). A pseudonymous opinion piece in *Sovetskii ekran* dismissed the "self-indulgence" and "absurdity" of the set design of Wiene's *Cabinet of Dr. Caligari* and, closer to home, of the futuristic designs for Protazanov's *Aelita*. Instead, it praised the "reality" of Eisenstein's *The Strike* [*Stachka*, 1924], and declared, provocatively, that the Soviet realist agenda meant that perhaps it was time for the *khudozhnik* to "disappear" entirely from cinema (Irinin 1925, 32).

In response, set designers were inevitably defensive. There were regular complaints about poor quality technical equipment and suggestions that the resources available were insufficient to take enable *khudozhniki* to take on large historical projects: engineers and architects needed to work together to professionalize film design in the Soviet Union (Irinin 1925, 32). In 1925, Kolupaev bemoaned the insufficient attention – and insufficient funds – accorded to set and costume design in the Soviet production process. Using the example of "folk" and "peasant" films, he described how: "In the studio village style dominates, with its uniform huts, barns, and basic details of peasant life." He called for greater accuracy and ethnographic detail: "We need to improve our stocks with sketches and photographs of the village. We must organize an artistic/photographic commission and send them out into the countryside" (Kolupaev 1925, 34).

This quest for "authenticity" was common in discussions during the 1920s – an attempt to carve a new role for set design within the contemporary realist agenda.[13] Indeed, the fact that leading roles in design were given to Kozlovskii and Rakhal's, in Mezhrabpom and Sovkino respectively, from the early 1920s, points to the dominance of the "realistic" ambition in Soviet set design from this early stage. Such a preoccupation with "authenticity" had been pronounced in set design from its beginnings (a response to the blatant artificiality of early sets), but it acquired a particular ideological flavor in the Soviet context. Here film's "reality impulse" came together with ideological demands, particularly towards the end of the decade. In 1928, with the first Party Conference on Cinema in March, the challenge for film-makers to portray contemporary reality became much more urgent: in a much-quoted speech by Aleksandr Krinitskii at the Party Conference of 1928, Soviet cinema was called upon to reflect Soviet everyday life [*byt*] – and to model the path for its improvement. It should distinguish itself by a refusal of the suspicious pleasures of costume drama and melodrama, and careful attention to contemporary reality (Krinitskii 1928, 6).

Ideology, indeed, seemed at times to work against domestic interiors in cinema altogether: Soviet filmmakers should favor the energy of outdoor shooting, the life of the streets and the "masses." In the words of Leo Mur, "[t]he future path of Soviet cinema lies in fields, forests, seas, cities of the republic, not in cabinets – be they ordinary ones, or those of Dr. Caligari" (Mur 1926, 7). The problem, however, as Mur himself put it, was that "most of human life is spent not under the open sky, but under a ceiling." Even the revolutionary masses needed homes to live in. If Soviet cinema was to picture Soviet *byt*, then it needed to find a way to picture interior spaces. It must configure new visions of the relationship between people and the material objects of domestic space, to suit the revolutionary agenda. The studio, and with it set design, could not be rejected entirely.

Domestic interior spaces in films set in the contemporary Soviet Union during the 1920s and into the early 1930s reveal a complex picture. In schematic terms, interior spaces can be divided into three basic categories: the rural provincial interior; the bourgeois interior; the new (as yet unformed) Socialist interior. One of the key directors of the "everyday" genre in Soviet cinema of the second half of the 1920s is Boris Barnet, who worked extensively with Sergei Kozlovskii, as named *khudozhnik* for his key films of this period: *The Girl with the Hatbox* [*Devushka s korobkoi*, 1927]; *The House on Trubnaya* [*Dom na Trubnoi*, 1928]; and *Outskirts* [*Okraina*, 1933]. In Barnet's films, we can see how these three different domestic environments interacted and acquired ideological meaning. *Girl with the Hatbox*, for example, sets them clearly against one another. First, we have the traditionally furnished village home of the milliner and his daughter, the eponymous girl with a hatbox. Second, we have the modern bourgeois urban home of shop mistress Madame Irène and her husband, to which Natasha delivers hats, and where she is the nominal inhabitant of a room that is in fact used by Irène, in defiance of housing allocation laws. This space is marked by an excess of heavy furniture, drapes, carpets and ornament. Finally, we have Natasha's single room, now emptied of any furniture or decoration at all, which she offers to Il'ia, freshly arrived from the country, and which he sets out to make his home.

One of the most striking interior sequences in this film comes the morning after Il'ia has spent his first night in Madame Irène's home, in the now-denuded room that Natasha has claimed for him. The arrival of morning is signaled first by the awakening of Il'ia, and then by the telling contrast of a shot of a plump eiderdown

Figure 14.1 A bourgeois density of pattern and textile. From Boris Barnet's *The Girl with the Hatbox*, 1927.

Figure 14.2 The empty (proto-) Soviet space. From Boris Barnet's *The Girl with the Hatbox*, 1927.

and two pairs of slippers sitting on top of an oriental carpet. Feet emerge and fill the slippers: Madame Irène and her husband awaken. This collision of textures and patterns (note the corner of a lace sheet peeping beneath the eiderdown) draws the spectator's attention to the physical opulence of Irène's world, in contrast to the simplicity of that of Il'ia. The plush excesses of Mme Irène's domestic space are familiar signs of bourgeois aspiration. Heavy furniture, wall hangings, oriental carpets and a divan piled high with cushions: these act as a visual shorthand, ideologically encoded for the Soviet viewer (Barnet's next film, *House on Trubnaya*, shows bourgeois hairdresser Golikov's wife in a similar environment). In cinema of this period, bourgeois and petty-bourgeois domestic space was consistently represented by an excess of texture and pattern. In contrast, Il'ia's room is inhospitable: the anomalous crystal chandelier, remnant of the room's previous form, serves to emphasize its current lack of decoration.

The opposition between plush bourgeois space and simple worker's is not straightforward, however. Rather, the excess of Irene's spaces throws the few objects of material texture in Il'ia's almost empty room into relief. A single patterned blind covers the window, a few clothes and a towel with folk pattern hang in a corner. Il'ia sleeps with a risibly small sheet, and the pathos of his attempts to cover himself gives the spectator a tangible sense of the human body's quest for comfort. We recognize his project as one of home-making. Likewise, the implicitly sheltered, indulged bodies of Irene and her husband throw Il'ia's robust physicality into relief. After an enthusiastic set of exercises, he sets off, bare-chested, to find a washbasin. Outside, he navigates a labyrinth of sheets that have been hung out to dry and that form a network of textile walls. Il'ia's progression through the sheets, through the textile walls, before he finds a place to wash, is first comic, and reveals what we might call the underside of domestic life; but it also draws the spectator into a multi-sensory apprehension of the experience of his body, of the experience of his flesh. This is enhanced when he finally washes, placing his head beneath running water and rubbing his neck with an improvised loofah.

Il'ia's bare space reveals the new socialist interior as an unformed space in *The Girl with the Hatbox* – as it is in most of the "everyday" comedies of the 1920s. Fridrikh Ermler's *Katka's Reinette Apples* [*Kat'ka—bumazhnyi ranet*, 1927] for example, for which Enei was designer, explicitly shows its positive hero and heroine as crafting a new home in a bare space, in contrast to the heavily-furnished domestic environments of its more negative protagonists. In a sense, the characters' keenly-felt search for a space to inhabit echoes cinema's search for an appropriate socialist interior. In *The Girl with the Hatbox*, in the scene of Il'ia's awakening, it also shows how the choice of textures and objects in a film set plays a key role in meaning, and in spectatorial experience. Archival production papers for this film give us a sense of the contribution of the set designer to the final appearance of this scene in particular. The screenplay for *The Girl with the Hatbox* talks only about the "awakening" of the couple (Gosfilmofond 2 / 1 / 228). In its filmic realization, however, the impact of this scene is created by the textures of the set, and the sensory, *felt* interaction between human body and material texture. The case of *The Girl with the Hatbox* also gives an indication of the role played by the process of censorship in the evolution of the set. The documents tracing the approval process of the film include a note from the censor, which criticizes the original plan to show Il'ia in a completely empty room, noting that the room must "all the same, have a table and chairs, a cupboard, a commode and a bed" (Gosfilmofond 2/1/92). For the censor, it seems, the emergent socialist interior could not be entirely unformed – and implicitly unformable. In the film's final realization, I suggest, the sheer vitality of Il'ia's act of makeshift home-making goes some way to answering the censor's concerns.

Urban bourgeois interiors such as Madame Irene's apartment had a counterpart in Soviet cinema's other principal domestic space of the 1920s: the rural interior. In *The Girl with the Hatbox* this space is represented by the provincial home of Natasha's father, with its wooden architecture and folk style. Such rural interiors were usually distinguished by the presence of patterned textile and decoration – sometimes in excess. In Protazanov's *The Tailor from Torzhok* [*Zakroishchik iz Torzhka*, 1925], also designed by Kozlovskii, Melan'ia Ivanovna, stereotype of the Russian bourgeois merchant woman, inhabits a world of overwhelming pattern, in her clothes and her home. The traditional iconography that surrounds her was a familiar sign, in this period, of the retrograde and bourgeois. In one scene, Melan'ia Ivanovna discovers her old bridal gown in a chest, and reverently hangs it, and her headdress, on a tailor's model. Here, depth of space is articulated by pattern: different designs are layered, drawing the eye from tailor's model, through curtain, to dressing table, and then to Melan'ia Ivanovna herself, in a dress that renders her too part of the film's textural surface. In the background, we have at least five further surfaces and patterns.

Figure 14.3 Provincial patterns. From Iakov Protazanov's *Tailor from Torzhok*, 1924.

Such interiors – rural and urban – were negatively coded, clearly part of a retrograde world, far from the Socialist ideal. In the latter part of the 1920s, however, there was a growing sense that film could and should do more than simply picture Soviet life *in transition*. Perhaps it could offer models of an ideal future? This idea was taken up directly in an article published by Nikolai Lukhmanov in *Kino* in 1929, inspired by a new documentary film, *How You Live* [*Kak ty zhivesh'*, Shirokov, 1927], which pictured a clean-lined, rationalized modernist domestic environment. Lukhmanov called for fiction films to take up the challenge of picturing everyday life *"as it should be."* Cinema can picture "model," or "exemplary" [*obraztsovyi*] life (Lukhmanov 1929, 37). In this respect, Lukhmanov praised the designs produced by Aleksandr Rodchenko for Kuleshov's *Your Acqauintance*, particularly for the domestic space inhabited by the journalist Khokhlova, and the offices of the newspaper where she is employed.[14] He also praised Burov's futuristic factory in Eisenstein's *The General Line* [*General'naia liniia*, aka *Staroe i novoe*, 1929]. In another essay of 1929, provocatively entitled "Things in Cinema", Boris Kolomarov praised these interiors, and also the modernist hostel and communal dining room of Fridrikh Ermler's *Fragment of an Empire* [*Oblomok imperii*, 1929] (Kolomarov 1929, 37).

Such exhortations and exceptions notwithstanding, however, the search for a shape for the socialist worker's domestic space remained a work in progress in cinema through the early 1930s. In Ermler and Iutkevich's *Counterplan* [*Vstrechnyi*,

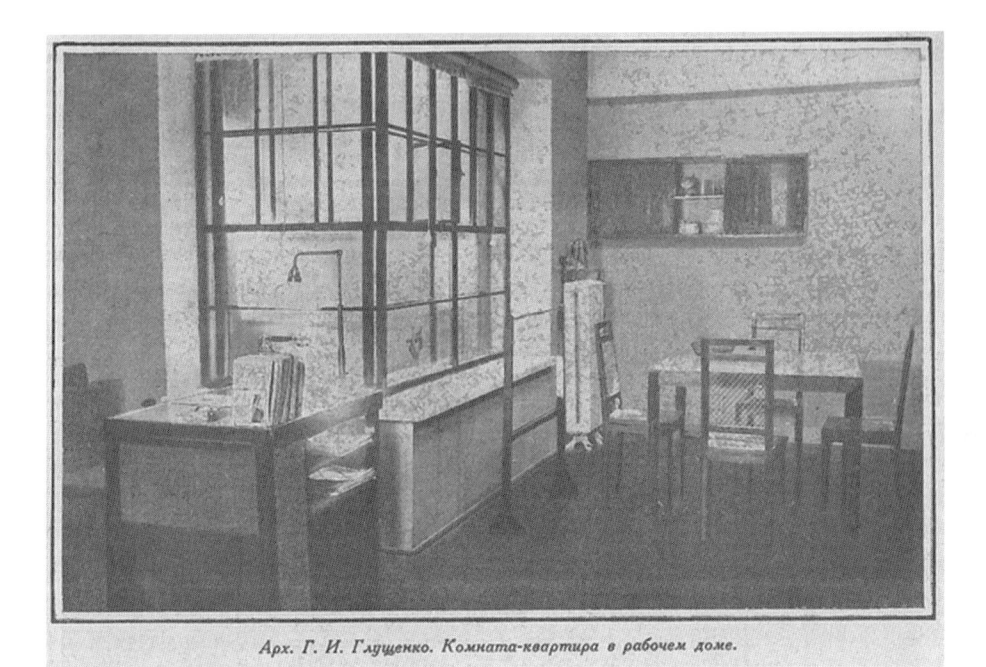

Арх. Г. И. Глущенко. Комната-квартира в рабочем доме.

Figure 14.4 Drawing of the set designed by architect G. Glushchenko for *How You Live*, 1927.

Figure 14.5 The modern factory, designed by Aleksei Burov. From Eisenstein's *The General Line*, 1927.

1932], for which Boris Dubrovskii-Eshke was *khudozhnik,* and which was frequently celebrated as a successful move towards a new model for Soviet cinema, three domestic interiors are again used in pointed contrast, but here a new socialist interior does begin to take shape. The flat of the engineer Aleksei Skvortsov is explicitly stylized as a high bourgeois space, with drapery, heavy curtains, and filigree ironwork music rest on top of the piano. By contrast, the home of Babchenko, who begins the film as a recalcitrant "remnant" of the old regime, is styled according to old provincial Russia, with its samovar and bourgeois houseplants. In the latter, extensive close ups of Babchenko and his wife at their table, drinking tea, marks the characters' resistance to the public spaces and imperatives of collectivity. The third interior space of the film is most interesting, however, for it has thematic centrality and is linked to narrative evolution. This is the living space of the young couple Pavel and Katia Il'in. The film opens with shots of their marital life, but at this point taking place in a single room, with a single bed. The plot makes explicit their need for a home of their own, and they move, eventually, into an apartment – an event emphasized in the narrative ("We have got a room!"), and even signaled by a title announcing a House Warming. Here the openness of the space, and lack of ornate decoration, marks the residence of a "new person." Yet the new space also reveals the growing separation of Pavel, an engineer, from the collective, and his failure to understand the human implications of his technical decisions. It is a sign of his withdrawal from the shared enthusiasm of the factory team; and as such, he must be reeducated.

Counterplan was a rare instance where a purely domestic environment appeared in Soviet film of this period. It is particularly interesting, therefore, that even that domestic environment failed to emerge as a model for a future domestic space for the proletariat. The problem continued into the 1930s. Indeed, Dashkova (2007; 2013) goes so far as to identify only one intimate (marital) domestic environment in cinema of the 1930s: the marital room of Irina and Grishka in Igor' Savchenko's *A Chance Encounter*, designed by Blatova. Like that of *Counterplan*, moreover, this space turns out to be an illusion: the relationship between Irina and Grisha fails, and Irina finds salvation – and a nurturing family for her baby, a real home – in the collective. Although a number of domestic environments do appear in film of this period, they are primarily *collective*: the hostel rooms of Aleksandr Macheret's *The Private Life of Petr Vinogradov* [*Chastnaia zhizn' Petra Vinogradova*, 1934], designed by Aleksei Utkin; and Eduard Ioganson's *Crown Prince of the Republic* [*Naslednyi prints respubliki*, 1934], for example. More intimate domestic space is indeed rare. In the course of the 1930s, moreover, the design of contemporary Soviet interior sets was a source of considerable debate in the cinematic press, and focus of some of the key issues relating to the development of a Socialist Realist aesthetic. In particular, it was part of a wider discussion of what became known as *kamernoe kino* [chamber cinema]. This term emerged with a force into the cinematic press out of an article written by Vsevolod Vishnevskii, published in 1937 (Vishnevskii 1937). Vishnevskii criticized directors such as Mikhail Romm, Iulii Raizman, and Aleksandr Macheret, among others, for what he called "chamber" cinema – a cinema of a small scale, which failed to capture the monumental scale [*monumental'nost'*] of Soviet heroism. There were several replies to this article. Hungarian film theorist Béla Balázs, for example, suggested that the best way to convey the *scale* of Soviet achievement, to achieve what Vishnevskii called *monumental'nost'* in cinema, was precisely through individuals, on a human scale. "Real" heroes, not faceless masses, were needed in Soviet cinema (Balash 1937).

A growing emphasis on the need for a cinema of "real" heroes, for a more intimate narrative of Socialist achievement, made the quest for an appropriate interior for the new Socialist hero ever more urgent. In practice, however, a new, appropriately socialist film interior did not emerge in Soviet film design of the 1930s – or after. Rather, the diverse spaces and styles of the films of the 1920s were maintained in the formal *bricolage* of Stalinist cinema in its first decade. *Khudozhniki* of the 1930s continued to relish the possibilities of costume drama, in the growing number of historical-biographical films produced in the latter part of the decade and into the 1940s. The columns, drapery, and textures of high bourgeois interiors returned in the domestic environments of highly placed Soviet officials, as in Ivan Pyr'ev's *The Party Card* [*Partiinyi bilet*, 1936] for example. And the patterns and decorative woodwork of the Russian provincial style returned in force in the collective-farm films of Pyr'ev and Grigorii Aleksandrov, among others. The battle for appropriate recognition for the *kino-khudozhnik*, and for appropriate resources, also continued. In 1937, in a long article, lavishly illustrated by photographs of film sets in Hollywood and Soviet productions, Dubrovskii-Eshke could still complain about the "poor quality" technical provision for set construction in Soviet cinema, suggesting that this remained an area in which Soviet production lagged far behind Hollywood and Europe. He bemoaned the lack of good fundus elements, poor organization of the production process, and called for Soviet set designers to be given the resources that would enable them to catch up with Hollywood (Dubrovskii-Eshke 1937).

This snapshot of Soviet film design during the 1920s raises more questions than it can answer. Above all, I seek to encourage further research into film set design as an overlooked part of Soviet film history. As Viktor Shklovskii affirmed in the epigraph to this chapter, film set design plays a key role in the creation of cinematic space, and in the *sensory* impact of a film on its spectators. In the development of set design through the 1920s we can trace a growing awareness of the role of material (surfaces, shapes, patterns) in creating a film's impact. And, in relation to this, certain film theorists and practitioners reveal an increasing interest in the capacity of film to make the spectator aware of the affective power of the material world. This was of central importance in Soviet film in its early years, and part of a wider project. For Kolomarov, cinema was capable of bringing about a "revolution in things" (Kolomarov 1929, 37). For Rodchenko, film must show ordinary objects "as they have never been seen before" (Rodchenko 1925). At its most ambitious, film design would seek to create a new lived environment, and to model new ways of living in it. Although the new Socialist interior never materialized on screen, its traces provide provocative evidence of the shape of utopia.

Notes

1 Constructivist artist Aleksandra Ekster was selected for Martian costume design; theater designer Isaak Rabinovich put forward designs for the scenes set in Mars, and is often credited with their final realization (although Kozlovskii's memoirs dispute this; Kozlovskii 1968, 78). Miasnikov sees in *Aelita* the "collision of two distinct directions […] the aesthetic of everyday, and the aesthetic of constructivist *dekorativnost*'" (Miasnikov 1975, 21).
2 See my article on *faktura* (Widdis 2009) for an analysis of how Soviet film practitioners were preoccupied by the impact of the materiality of objects and materials in film.
3 Berthomé (2003, 82) suggests poverty as the principle reason for the weakness of Soviet studio work, and preference for location shooting.
4 Mikhin (1979) suggests that this system was introduced in the autumn of 1911 for the sets used on Petr Chardynin's *Kreutzer Sonata* [*Kreitserova sonata*, 2011]. Sobolev, however, suggests that while Mikhin elaborated his fundus system in the Khanzhonkov studio, Czesław Sabiński was working in parallel on a similar system in the studio of Thiemann, Reinhardt, Osipov, and Co. (Sobolev 1961, 61–63).

5   This is clear in the work of Evgenii Bauer, discussed later, and in Vladimir Egorov's designs for *Portrait of Dorian Grey* (see Voevodin 1992, 224).

6   Kuleshov stresses the director's emphasis on creating depth of field. If a set was to consist of two rooms, then they must be at different levels, and connected by a staircase. In addition, columns, architectural friezes, drapery etc. were used to provide further 'relief' and contrasting volumes (Kuleshov 1920, 79). Kuleshov published other articles dealing explicitly with the role of the *khudozhnik* in cinema (Kuleshov 1917a; 1917b; 1925).

7   It was also common for Boris Mikhin to be credited as *khudozhnik* in films directed by Chardynin (e.g., *A House in Kolomna* [*Domik v Kolomne*, 1913]; *Uncle's Apartment* [*Diadiushkina kvartira*, 1913]). Fester was credited as early as 1909 in Goncharov's *The Mermaid* [*Rusalka*]; Balliuzek was credited in Protazanov's 1916 *Queen of Spades* [*Pikovaia dama*].

8   Fedor Shekhtel' is best known as a pioneer of *style moderne* architecture in pre-revolutionary Russia, and for his distinctive integration of stylized references to Russian historical architecture and contemporary international styles such as art nouveau. Ivan Zholtovskii began his career in 1908 (and worked with the more senior Shekhtel' in the Stroganov Academy from 1898); he came to particular prominence, however, in post-revolutionary Russia, and in particular in the 1930s, when his neo-classical style was celebrated as an appropriate direction for Socialist Realist architecture.

9   It was also in this period that the possibility of *kombinirovannye s"emki* – i.e., matte shots (the superimposition of filmed action onto a pre-shot setting) developed (Kozlovskii 1968, 80).

10 Indeed, Lisakovskaia goes so far as to suggest that production design became a space of refuge for artists, where they could find relative creative freedom, especially from the 1930s on (Lisakovskaia 2012, 32).

11 Kovrigin's sketches are preserved in the Museum of Cinema [Muzei kino] 5353/1–9: 28. For more information on the holdings see Iur'eva (2012, 114–120).

12 Other targets for criticism were Konstantin Eggert and Gardin's *Bear's Wedding* [*Medvezh'ia svad'ba*, 1925], Eggert's *The Ice House* [*Ledianoi dom*, 1927], and Grigorii Roshal' and Mikhail Doller's *Salamandra* (1928).

13 Kozlovskii recalls, for example, a visit to the Donbass to see coal mines; RGALI 2394/1/85, cited in Miasnikov (1975, 27).

14 Likewise, in for Komarov's *A Doll with Millions* (1928), Rodchenko designed contemporary transparent screens divide the washing and dressing areas of men and women. Rodchenko's work in cinema was confined to four films over a two-year period: Kuleshov's *Your Acquaintance*, 1927; Leonid Obolenskii's *Al'bidum* (1927), Boris Barnet's *Moscow in October* [*Moskva v oktiabre*, 1927], and *A Doll with Millions*, where he worked alongside Kozlovskii.

References

Affron, Charles and Affron, Mirella J. 1995. *Sets in Motion: Art Direction and Film Narrative*. New Brunswick: Rutgers University Press.

Agden, V. 1926. "Kino-khudozhnik na zapade i v SSSR" [The Film Artist in the West and in the USSR]. *ARK* 3: 16–18.

Al'tman, N. 1936. "Khudozhnik v kino" [The Artist in Cinema]. *Iskusstvo kino* [Art of Cinema] 3: 22.

Anon. 1928, "Rezoliutsiia sektsii khudozhnikov arkhitektorov" [Resolution of the Artist-Architects' Section]. *Kino-Front* 2: 12–13.

Balash, Bela (Balázs, Bela) 1937. "Monumentalizm ili kamernost'?" [Monumentalism or Chamber Settings]. *Kino* 22 (May 11): 2.

Barsacq, Léon 1976. *Caligari's Cabinet and Other Grand Illusions: A History of Film Design*, edited by Elliott Stein. New York: New American Library.

Bergfelder, Tim, Sue Harris, and Sarah Street. 2007. *Film Architecture and the Transnational Imagination: Set Design in 1930s European Cinema*. Amsterdam: Amsterdam University Press.

Berthomé, Jean-Pierre. 2003. *Le décor au cinéma*. [Décor in Cinema]. Paris: Cahiers du cinéma.

Bowlt, John E. 1977. "Constructivism and Russian Stage Design." *Performing Arts Journal* 1.3: 62–84.

Bulgakowa, Oksana. 2010. *Sovetskii Slukhoglas: Kino i ego organy chuvstv* [The Soviet Hearing-Eye. Film and its Organs of Perception]. Moscow: Novoe literaturnoe obozrenie.

Cavendish, Phil. 2004. "The Hand that Turns the Handle: Camera Operators and the Poetics of the Camera in Pre-Revolutionary Russian Film." *The Slavonic and East European Review* 82.2: 201–245.

Cavendish, Phil. 2008. *Soviet Mainstream Cinematography: The Silent Era*. London: UCL Arts and Humanities Publications.

Cavendish, Phil. 2013. *The Men with the Movie Camera: The Poetics of Visual Style in Soviet Avant-garde Cinema of the 1920s*. Oxford, New York: Berghahn.

Dashkova, Tat'iana. 2007. "Nevidimye miru riushi: odezhda v sovetskom predvoennom i voennom kino" [The Invisible World of Ruche: Clothing in Soviet Cinema before and during the War]. *Teoriia mody: Odezhda. Telo. Kul'tura* [Theory of Fashion: Clothing, Body, Culture] 3: 149–162.

Dashkova, Tat'iana. 2013. *Telesnost', Ideologiia, Kinematograf: Vizual'nyi kanon i sovetskaia povsednevnost'* [The Corporeal, Ideology, Cinema: The Visual Canon of the Soviet Everyday]. Moscow: Novoe literaturnoe obozrenie.

DeBlasio, Alyssa. 2007. "Choreographing Space, Time and Dikovinki in the Films of Evgenii Bauer." *The Russian Review* 66.4: 671–692.

Dubrovskii-Eshke, Boris. 1937. "Voprosy dekoratsionnoi tekhniki" [Issues of Decorative Technology]. *Iskusstvo kino* [Art of Cinema] 6: 60–64.

Gardin, V. R. 1949. *Vospominaniia* [Recollections]. Vol. 1. Moscow: Goskinoizdat.

Gromov, E. 1973. *Vladimir Egorov: Khudozhnik v kino* [Vladimir Egorov: An Artist in Cinema]. Moscow: Biuro propagandy sovetskogo kinoiskusstva.

Irinin (pseudonym). 1925. "Arkhitektura i dekoratsiia" [Architecture and Décor]. *Sovetskii ekran* [Soviet Screen] 5: 32.

Iur'eva, K. 2012. "Izobrazitel'nyi fond Muzeia kino" [The Visual Collection of the Museum of Cinema]. *Kinovedcheskie zapiski* [Film Scholars' Notes] 99: 114–120.

Ivanova, V., V. Myl'nikova, S. Skovorodnikova, Iurii Tsiv'ian, and Rashid Iangirov (eds.) 2002. *Velikii kinemo: Katalog sokhranivshikhsia igrovykh fil'mov Rossii 1908–1919* [The Great Kinemo: Catalog of Preserved Fiction Films from Russia, 1908–1919]. Moscow: Novoe literaturnoe obozrenie.

Kaganovsky, Lilya. 2012. "Elektrische Sprache: Dsiga Wertow und die Tontechnologie / Electric Speech: Dziga Vertov and the Technologies of Sound." In *Resonanz-Räume: die Stimme und die Medien* [Rooms of Resonance: Voice and the Media], edited by Oksana Bulgakowa, 41–54. Berlin: Bertz & Fischer.

Khanzhonkova, Vera. 1962. "Iz vospominanii o dorevoliutsionnom kino" [From Recollections of Pre-Revolutionary Cinema]. In *Iz istorii kino: materialy i dokumenty* [From the History of Cinema: Materials and Documents] 5: 120–131. Moscow: Akademiia nauk.

Kolomarov, Boris. 1929. "Veshch' v kino" [The Thing in Cinema]. *Kino i kul'tura* [Cinema and Culture] 9–10: 29–37.

Kolupaev, D. 1925. "O dekoratsiiakh" [About Décor]. *Kino-zhurnal ARK* [ARK Film Journal] 2: 34.

Kolupaev, D. 1926. "Khudozhnik v kino-proizvodstve" [The Artist in Film Production]. *Kino-zhurnal ARK* [ARK Film Journal] 3: 18.

Kozlovskii, Sergei. 1925. "Prava i obiazannosti kino-khudozhnik" [Rights and Duties of the Film-Artist]. *Kino-zhurnal ARK* [ARK Film Journal] 11–12: 16–17.

Kozlovskii, Sergei. 1929, "Tekhnika kinoatel'e" [The Technology of the Film Workshop]. *Kino i kul'tura* [Cinema and Culture] 4: 57–58.

Kozlovskii, Sergei. 1968. "Smysl' moei zhizni" [The Meaning of my Life]. *Iz istorii kino: materialy i dokumenty* [From the History of Cinema: Materials and Documents] 7: 63–93. Moscow: Akademiia nauk.

Kozlovskii, Sergei and N. M. Kolin 1930. *Khudozhnik-arkhitektor v kino* [The Artist-Architect in Cinema]. Moscow: Teakinopechat'.

Krinitskii, Aleksandr. 1928. "Nuzhen reshitel'nyi sdvig: k itogam partiinogo kinosoveshchaniia" [A Decisive Move is Needed: Summary of the Party's Film Meeting]. *Pravda* March 25.

Kuleshov, Lev. 1917a. "O zadachakh khudozhnika v kinematografe" [On the Tasks of the Artist in Cinema]. *Vestnik kinematografii* [Cinema Herald] 126: 15–16; reprinted in Kuleshov, *Sobranie sochinenii v trekh tomakh* [Collected Works in 3 vols]. vol. 1: 57–58, Moscow: Iskusstvo, 1987.

Kuleshov, Lev. 1917b. "Zadachi khudozhnika v kinematografe" [The Tasks of the Artist in Cinema]. *Vestnik kinematografii* [Cinema Herald] 127, 37–38; reprinted in *Sobranie sochinenii v trekh tomakh*, [Collected Works in 3 vols], vol. 1: 59–60, Moscow: Iskusstvo, 1987.

Kuleshov, Lev. 1920. "Znamia kino" [The Flag of Cinema]. In *Sobranie sochinenii*, [Collected Works], vol. 1: 63–87.

Kuleshov, Lev. 1925. "Khudozhnik v kino" [The Artist in Cinema]. *Sovetskii ekran* [Soviet Screen] 29: 6–7, reprinted in *Sobranie sochinenii* [Collected Works] vol. 1: 104–105.

Lisakovskaia, M. 2012. "Nezamechennyi avangard: khudozhniki v kino" [The Unnoticed Avant-Garde: Artists in Cinema]. *Kinovedcheskie zapiski* [Film Scholars' Notes] 99: 26–34.

Lukhmanov, Nikolai. 1929. "Zhizn', kak ona dolzhna byt'" [Life as it Should Be]. *Kino i kul'tura* [Cinema and Culture] January: 29–37.

Makhlis, Isaak. 1925. "Rol' khudozhnika v kino" [The Role of the Artist in Cinema]. *Kino-zhurnal ARK* [ARK Film Journal] 11–12: 15–16.

Miasnikov, Gennadii I. 1973. *Ocherki istorii sovetskogo kinodekoratsionnogo iskusstva (1908–1917)* [Studies of the History of Soviet Production Design 1908–1917]. Moscow: VGIK.

Miasnikov, Gennadii I. 1975. *Ocherki istorii sovetskogo kinodekoratsionnogo iskusstva (1918–1930)* [Studies of the History of Soviet Production Design 1918–1930]. Moscow: VGIK.

Miasnikov, Gennadii I. 1979. *Ocherki istorii sovetskogo kinodekoratsionnogo iskusstva (1931–1945)*. [Studies of the History of Soviet Production Design 1931–1945]. Moscow: VGIK.

Mikhin, B. 1979. "Rozhdenie fundusa" [The Birth of the Prop Store]. In *Iz istorii kino: dokumenty i materialy* [From the History of Cinema: Materials and Documents]. 9: 148–155. Moscow: Akademiia nauk.

Mur, Leo. 1926. "S"emki na nature i v atel'e" [Shooting in the Open Air or in the Pavilion]. *Kino-Front* 2: 2–7.

Pozner, Valerie. 2012. "Die Einführung des Tonfilms bei Meschrabpom-Film" [The Introduction of Sound Film at Mezhrabpom-Film]. In *Die rote Traumfabrik (1921–1936)* [The Red Dream-Factory], edited by Alexander Schwarz and Günther Agde, 91–101. Berlin: Bertz & Fischer.

Pudovkin, Vsevolod. 1925. "O khudozhnike v kino" [About Artists in Cinema]. *Kino* March 3: 2. Reprinted in *Sobranie sochinenii v trekh tomakh* [Collected Works in 3 vols], vol. 2: 117–118. Moscow: Iskusstvo, 1975.

Rivosh, Iakov. 2012. "…V etom moe schast'e! (Avtobiografiia)" [Therein is My Luck. Autobiography]. *Kinovedcheskie zapiski* [Film Scholars' Notes] 99: 245–258.

Rodchenko, Aleksandr. 1925. "Khudozhnik i 'material'naia sreda' v igrovoi fil'me" [The Artist and the "Material World" in Fiction Film]. *Sovetskoe kino* [Soviet Cinema] 5–6: 14–15.

Room, Abram. 1925. "Kino i teatr (diskussionno)" [Film and Theater]. *Sovetskii ekran* [Soviet Screen] 8: 56–7.

Shklovskii, Viktor. 1977. "O Petre Galadzheve"[About Peter Galadzhev]. In *Iz istorii kino: dokumenty i materialy* [From the History of Cinema: Materials and Documents]. 10: 201–203. Moscow: Iskusstvo.

Sobolev, R. P. 1961. *Liudi i fil'my dorevoliutsionnogo kino* [People and Films of Pre-Revolutionary Cinema]. Moscow: Iskusstvo.

Tashiro, Charles S. 1998. Pretty Pictures: Production Design and the History Film. Austin: University of Texas Press.

Tsivian, Iurii. 1996. "Two 'Stylists' of the Teens: Franz Hofer and Evgenii Bauer." In A Second Life: German Cinema's First Decades, edited by Thomas Elsaesser, 264–276. Amsterdam: Amsterdam University Press.

Vishnevskii, Vsevolod. 1937. "Protiv kamernoi kinematografii" [Against Chamber Cinema]. *Kino* 20 (April 29): 2.

Voevodin, V. 1992. "V. Egorov – Khudozhnik fil'ma V. Meierkhol'da 'Portret Doriana Greia'" [V. Egorov, the Production Designer of Meyerhold's Film "Portrait of Dorian Gray"]. *Kinovedcheskie zapiski* [Film Scholars' Notes] 13: 214–224.

Widdis, Emma. 2009. "Faktura: Depth and Surface in Early Soviet Set Design," *Studies in Russian and Soviet Cinema* 3.1: 5–32.

15

Stars on Screen and Red Carpet

Djurdja Bartlett

This chapter explores fashions and film costumes through the looks of film actresses on the screen and in their public life during the 1920s and 1930s.[1] Politically and aesthetically, these two decades differ considerably, and I investigate here how the different political circumstances – the Bolshevik rule following the 1917 Revolution, the introduction of the New Economic Policy (NEP) in the early 1920s, and the rise of Stalinism at the beginning of the 1930s – informed different styles in dress and looks. The names of costume designers were traditionally not listed in the film credits. Instead, the tasks of production designer, or film artist [*khudozhnik*], equally covered scenography, dress, and make-up. Under the economically and politically difficult circumstances in the 1920s, and later, in the different, but even more challenging 1930s, the costumes nevertheless exhibited high quality and precision, and visually enriched and contextualized film narratives. In order to explore these issues, this chapter observes film costumes in the Soviet romantic comedies and musicals within the context of sartorial cultures of the 1920s and 1930s and their practitioners, taking into account the politics and ideologies that informed them, as well as the audiences who highly enjoyed those films.

Following the 1917 Bolshevik Revolution, fashion was perceived as an endeavor embedded in the messy everyday, tainted with its connections to commerce and to inappropriate desires and pleasures, which could only lead to irrational consumption.[2] Fashion belonged to the past, and not to the new, rationalized and ordered world that the early Bolsheviks were attempting to build. Yet fashion returned to Russia with the introduction of the New Economic Policy in 1921.[3] The NEP re-introduced private ownership and retail practices, which were more efficient than state-run businesses. The fact that political power stayed firmly in the hands of the Bolsheviks, while at the same time the NEP acted as an economic system, contributed to the confusing status of fashion during the 1920s. A number of conventional fashion magazines re-appeared on the market after having been closed down following the Revolution.[4] They published numerous drawings of flapper dresses, which were literal copies of the latest western fashion trends. The commercially

A Companion to Russian Cinema, First Edition. Edited by Birgit Beumers.
© 2016 John Wiley & Sons, Inc. Published 2016 by John Wiley & Sons, Inc.

informed culture of the NEP was equally present on the screens of Soviet cinemas, both through a large number of imported films, especially from the United States,[5] and through an active domestic film production. While Soviet audiences adored glamorous western imports, they were also attracted to the contemporary Soviet romantic comedies, melodramas, and detective films. The latest fashions were a great attraction in the western films, but fashionable and luxurious ensembles often glamorized the drab reality in the Soviet popular cinematic genres as well.

In this context, film costume faithfully embodied the drawings published on the pages of the contemporary western and domestic fashion magazines. The first real fashion magazine since the Revolution, *Atel'e* [Atelier] was launched in 1923. It was a programmatic journal, which aimed to bring fashion back to the Soviet Union, justifying its rituals and adjusting them to the new socialist reality. Original contributions on fashion design in *Atel'e* presented artistic-style dresses and luxurious eveningwear. *Atel'e* was born into the flourishing NEP culture, and had to accommodate its artistic pretensions to its commercialized surroundings. The journal was in fact the mouthpiece of the fashion salon "Atelier of Fashion" [Atel'e mod], which was affiliated with the Moscow Sewing Trust [Moskvoshvei].[6] The journal proudly advertised the salon's luxuriously furnished and spacious premises in the center of Moscow with its Art Deco furniture, palms, and chandeliers. In his role as representative of a big American clothes company, the American businessman Oliver MacBright found himself precisely in this establishment in one of the best-known comedies of the period – *The Cigarette Girl from Mosselprom* [*Papirosnitsa ot Mossel'proma*].[7] Directed by Iurii Zheliabuzhskii in 1924, the film featured Zina Vesenina, a street cigarette seller who, by accident, became a film star. At the same time, pretty Zina (played by Iuliia Solntseva) was pursued by her three romantic suitors. Soviet Russia was a communist country, but, due to its huge and, even more tempting, underdeveloped market, it was an irresistible challenge to western entrepreneurs during the economically relaxed NEP period. So, MacBright visited the "Atelier of Fashion" within the Moscow Sewing Trust[8] on a couple of occasions. Once, he brought there his Soviet love interest, Zina. MacBright and Zina watched a fashion show together and he bought her an outfit. On the following visit, Zina played at being a model at the small catwalk, mingling with a couple of professional models while MacBright talked business with his Soviet counterpart. The latter was not pleased with the American's attitude. As one of the inter-titles informs us, he told the American: "You aggressively try to import everything here, even impose the mannequins. But, we make our clothes at Moscow Sewing Trust relying on our own prototypes." While the clothes which the viewer sees on the screen are not only extravagantly luxurious but also perfectly executed, there was some credibility in the claim of the Soviet official. The task of the "Atelier of Fashion" was to execute prototypes of dresses for mass-production by the Moscow Sewing Trust, as well as to design individual, custom-made outfits.

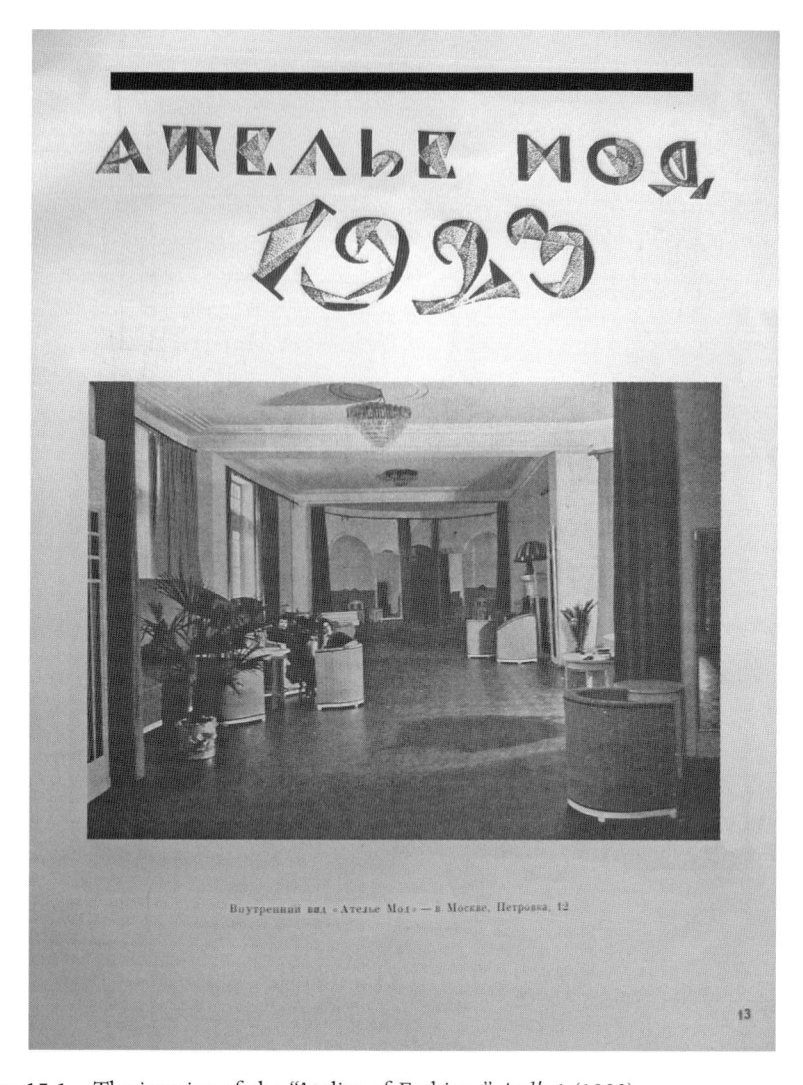

Figure 15.1 The interior of the "Atelier of Fashion," *Atel'e* 1 (1923).

A small group of fashion designers and artists – Nadezhda Lamanova, Evgeniia Pribyl'skaia, Aleksandra Ekster, and Vera Mukhina – were in charge of these two contradictory assignments at the "Atelier of Fashion."[9] They won the highest recognition for their outfits shown at the First All-Russian Exhibition of the Art in Industry which was organized in Moscow in 1923.[10] The awarded ensembles sported simple, elongated lines and were embellished either with ethnic motifs or with geometrical patterns.[11] While this engagement was supposed to bring into being a new socialist dress, the other and ideologically quite opposite task – to design and produce custom-made clothes – was much closer to the NEP reality. In this sense, the extravagant interior of the "Atelier of Fashion" provided a realistic

Figure 15.2 Evening outfits, designs by the "Atelier of Fashion," *Atel'e* 1 (1923).

idea of its customers, the rich NEP clientele, and possibly an occasional US businessman. Aleksandra Ekster developed for those customers a concept of multi-layered outfits of asymmetric cuts, designing them in brocade, satin, and silk, and adorning them with fur and leather trimmings, as shown in all her drawings and the accompanying captions in the journal *Atel'e*.[12] Indeed, these drawings cannily resembled the executed outfits paraded on the catwalk of the "Atelier of Fashion" in the film *The Cigarette Girl from Mosselprom*. Ekster was mentioned as working for the Moscow Sewing Trust in an overview of the artistic industry in the early 1920s (Vetrov 1924, 341). Moreover, an advertisement published in the journal *Atel'e* announced that the salon provided elegant off-the-peg and custom-made eveningwear, as well as film and theatre costumes.

The probability that Aleksandra Ekster designed the costumes for the film *The Cigarette Girl from Mosselprom* could be additionally supported by her equally extravagant costumes of similar asymmetrical cuts in the film *Aelita*, directed by Iakov Protazanov in 1924, and set in Moscow as well as on the planet Mars, where the hero, engineer Los, lands in his dream.[13] Sartorially, the costumes shown in the "Atelier of Fashion" scenes in *The Cigarette Girl from Mosselprom*, and those worn on Mars in *Aelita* belonged to the elitist and excessive world of haute couture. However, on both occasions, they drew on Ekster's cubist artistic practices, applying the same avant-garde technique that the art critic Iakov Tugendkhol'd had already observed in her work for the theatre: "Ekster's costumes are neither 'designed' nor 'sewn' but constructed: built up from different surfaces just like her stage decorations..." (1922, 13). The difference was that Ekster had used aluminum, metal foil, glass, and Perspex, in order to achieve futuristic boldness in her costumes for Aelita, while her Art Deco drawings in *Atel'e* and the dresses in *The Cigarette Girl from Mosselprom* made use of luxurious fabrics, and exuded an impression of fashionable luxury. Moreover, she abandoned patterns and vivacious colors in her black-and-white costumes for *Aelita*. As John Bowlt observed: "industrial materials served a definite objective: they defined form in the absence of color; in their transparency or reflectivity they joined with the space around them and created an eccentric montage of forms" (Bowlt 1976, 8).

As a pre-Revolutionary fashion designer, Nadezhda Lamanova was in a completely different position than avant-garde artist Ekster.[14] Throughout the 1920s Lamanova nevertheless enjoyed an unquestionable support by Anatolii Lunacharskii, as her professional knowledge and skills were precious in the Bolsheviks' attempts to invent a new socialist dress. Towards that goal, Lamanova was active in the dress and textile laboratories of the Academy of Artistic Sciences and the Workshop of Contemporary Dress at the Ministry of Enlightenment, as well as in the "Atelier of Fashion" of the Moscow Sewing Trust. Her contribution was officially acknowledged only in relation to the ideologically approved tasks within those state institutions, as any public acknowledgement of her involvement in costume design in commercial films could have caused only additional damage to her already fragile social standing.[15] Yet, quite possibly, Lamanova might have contributed to the design of the NEP-style costumes in the film *The Cigarette Girl from Mosselprom*, as they look precisely like the "Atelier of Fashion" outfits presented on the photographs in the journal *Atel'e*. Moreover, while she was not listed on the credits for *Aelita*, Lamanova was recognized as its costume designer in the media.[16] Ekster, quite rightly, took all the glory for the artistic and daring Martian costumes, but a professional fashion designer like Lamanova might have designed the conventionally fashionable evening dress which Los' desperate wife Natasha wears at the secret NEP ball in contemporary Moscow when she believes that he abandoned her, as well as other lavish outfits worn by the NEP women on that occasion.

Even more so, Lamanova could have been in charge of Natasha's smart leather jacket, and her feminine yet simple dress which she wore both at her busy Demobilization Centre office, as well as at home. In contrast to the queen of Mars, Aelita, whose noble status was enhanced by her amazing long dresses with sashes and trains, and extravagant headgear, Natasha was an urban Muscovite, and so she was in need of functional clothes. However, her pretty patterned dress with a discreet lace collar showed that she was more likely a socially conscious white-collar working woman than a fierce political activist. The latter was played by Vera Lopatina in the film *The Extraordinary Adventures of Mr West in the Land of the Bolsheviks* [*Neobychainye prikliucheniia mistera Vesta v strane Bol'shevikov*], directed by Lev Kuleshov in 1924. Her intense Elly was completely dedicated to liberate Mister West from the criminals who exploited his fear of the Bolsheviks. Simultaneously, Elly attempted to enlighten his bodyguard, cowboy Jeddy, as well as the US businessman himself, on the true, glorious nature of the Bolshevik project. Elly embarked on those tasks in her austere, yet perfectly cut woolen coat, looking practically the same as the one proposed by Lamanova in the journal *Krasnaia niva* in the same year.[17] In the same film, Lamanova certainly dressed Aleksandra Khokhlova for her role of the wicked countess, whom the viewer sees casually applying her make-up and perfuming herself while drying up her lavish lingerie in the shambolic lodgings she shares with her equally mean partner. Further on, she tried to seduce the American in her *femme fatale* dress of dark silk which revealed her shoulders, legs and underwear.

Aleksandra Khokhlova knew how to wear Lamanova's extravagant dresses both on film screen and in her personal life.[18] Her atypical beauty, angular body shape, and expressionist acting technique perfectly suited the modernist tendencies in the Soviet Union of the 1920s, but, on the other hand, also strongly clashed with both the hard-revolutionary and the conventional imagery of an ideal woman. Sergei Eisenstein claimed that Soviet cinema perceived Khokhlova as a decadent bourgeois relic,[19] while he wanted to put her eccentric looks into the service of a new modernist cinema. Eisenstein imagined Khokhlova as a naive peasant woman, dressed in a traditional pinafore dress [*sarafan*] and with her hair gathered in braids, getting lost on her visits to the big city in a series of grotesque and comic countryside-city movies (Shklovskii and Eisenstein 1926, 7). It would have been interesting to see Khokhlova in the roles of a country woman, but it did not happen.

Sporting an unthreatening, ordinary prettiness, quite in contrast with Khokhlova's dramatic looks, Vera Maretskaia played two most prominent roles of naïve peasant women in the Soviet romantic comedies: Katia in *The Tailor from Torzhok* [*Zakroishchik iz Torzhka*, 1925], directed by Iakov Protazanov, and Parasha in *The House on Trubnaya* [*Dom na Trubnoi*, 1928], directed by Boris Barnet. Katia works as servant for the owner of a local grocery shop who, fittingly for a NEP-man, is persistently mean to her. She is always pictured in a peasant-style wide skirt, a short white tunic made of coarse fabric, and a scarf tied below her chin. The latter was an important iconographic detail, as the way they tied their scarves on their heads differentiated women workers from peasant women. A scarf tied below the chin continued to represent a traditional peasant woman, while the dynamic working woman tied her scarf at the back of her neck. Only in one scene, when she flirts with the tailor Petia Petelkin (played by comedian Igor' Il'inskii) does she let her scarf slip on her shoulders revealing her plait, yet another sign of her genuine peasant origin. In the last scene of the film, showing Katia and Petia embarking on a new life, thanks to the winning lottery ticket,[20] her fiancée is dressed in a fashionable, smart suit while Katia still wears a headscarf tied below her chin, but on this occasion, relevant to her imminent bride-to-be role, it was long and made of white muslin. Playing Parasha Pitunova in the film *The House on Trubnaya*, Maretskaia arrives from her village to Moscow with a living duck under her arm, and also with a head-scarf tied below her chin. She again lands a maid's job, with a barber and his ghastly wife, Madame Golikova (played by Elena Tiapkina) a caricature of the NEP woman in her over-decorated yet ill-fitting silk dresses, an overtly elaborated hair-do and too much make-up on her face.

But in the over-crowded house on Trubnaia Square there were many more tenants, carefully composed so to present the complex Soviet social structure in the 1920s. In his biography of the director Boris Barnet, Mark Kushnirov (1977, 87) called *The House on Trubnaya* "a mini-encyclopedia of Moscow life." While the tenants moved up and down a huge common staircase, the role of dress in representing the messy and contradictory Soviet reality was obvious, especially as their clothes were visually precise to the tiniest detail, enabling the viewer to promptly contextualize the social and ideological standing of each character. Political activist Fenia sports a woolen military jacket worn with a striped dress of straight lines and a head-scarf tied at the back of her neck. A union activist who visits Parasha in order to inform her on her working rights and encourage her to join the Union is clad in the same style: mannish jacket, a simple dress with geometrical pattern, and the obligatory headscarf tied at the back of her neck. An austere dress worn by a female political activist was never meant to be a fashion statement but gradually became an anachronism. In contrast to the urban working women who, encouraged by the commercialized NEP climate, were already interested in fashionable and handsome clothes, the political activists belonged professionally to a system which preferred class over gender and loyalty to the Party over any expression of femininity, which limited their dress choices.[21] On the other hand, in the role of the urban maid Marisha, Anel' Sudakevich was allowed a modest cloche hat and a modish, yet functional fur coat to protect her from a harsh Moscow winter. But Maretskaia's Parasha stays loyal to her peasant clothes and her head-scarf even when she joins the Union and proudly marches in the workers' parade. As everybody goes after their business afterwards, Parasha, still holding a big flag, is left confused and alone on the suddenly empty square. Her long wide peasant skirt and her traditionally tied head-scarf only emphasize that she has not joined the Moscow urban fabric yet.

The House on Trubnaya did not only strictly divide the various social groups inhabiting busy Moscow streets and houses through their dress. It also showed the NEP-couple – the barber and his wife – living in an over-decorated home, with a bed covered with plump pillows, a table crammed with porcelain, crystal glasses, and exquisite cutlery. While dress, as an artifact visually signifying class and gender difference, worried the early Bolsheviks, they were equally anxious about other everyday objects belonging to the world of petit-bourgeois coziness, and, in this way, obstructing the advance of their functional and well-ordered new socialist world. In 1925, the Constructivist critic Boris Arvatov claimed that "the organization of things in everyday life of the bourgeoisie does not go beyond the rearrangement of things, beyond the distribution of ready-made objects in space" (Arvatov 1997, 126). In his fierce ideological attack on the NEP, another Constructivist, Sergei Tret'iakov, heatedly enumerated all the luxuries, from delicatessen to shining jewelry, furs, silk, and porcelain figurines that had sneaked back into the shop windows due to the NEP initiative (Tret'iakov 1923, 70–71). But these unwelcome reminders of the past also crept in the contemporary films, so the struggle concerning the role of things in the life of a new socialist person equally raged on Soviet screens in the 1920s.

In his film *The Girl with the Hatbox* [*Devushka s korobkoi*, 1927], Barnet sharply contrasts the corrupted NEP world with the underprivileged working-class world, through both the interiors and the dress of his female and male protagonists. Throughout the whole film, Anna Sten, in the role of a provincial milliner Natasha, hardly takes off her modest coat and her simple woolly hat while endlessly travelling, with a hatbox in hand, from her suburban home to Moscow in order to deliver her wares to the owner of a smart hat shop. The latter, Madame Irène (played by Serafina Birman) spends time at home in her lavish negligée or, smartly dressed, leisurely take the stairs to her shop on the ground floor. Equally sartorially opposed are Madame Irène's husband and the poor student-to-be Il'ia Snegirev, whom Natasha befriends. While the latter wears a simple *tolstovka* tunic (or *kosovorotka*, a peasant shirt with a skewed collar), the former enjoys, in his smart suits, all the perks one could buy with the easy-earned NEP-money. Yet the designated living spaces of the two couples point towards an even bigger difference. At the beginning of the film, Natasha fictively rents a room in the flat while in fact it is used by Madame Irène's husband; it is comfortably furnished so he can indulge in his spoilt life-style. But the NEP couple completely empty the room once Natasha lets them know that her homeless friend Il'ia would move in. Furthermore, when she misses her train home, Natasha eventually joins Il'ia, sleeping on the floor in the other corner. Presenting his film in the journal *Sovetskii ekran* (Soviet Screen), Barnet emphasized that he wanted to tackle the relationship between man and the world of objects by situating a young couple in an empty room with only a hatbox and a few other small things (Barnet 1927, 10). In contrast, Madame Irène and her husband occupy all the other rooms in the flat, crammed with expensive objects, from porcelain figurines to luxurious clothes.

Obviously, the NEP households, such as those in *The House on Trubnaya* and *The Girl with the Hatbox*, were too lavish and cozy, and thus ideologically inappropriate, but some films pictured too many, and even unsuitable, objects in the spaces occupied by working-class people. The film *Bed and Sofa* [*Tret'ia Meshchanskaia*, 1927][22] takes place in a small room suffocated by too much stuff. The film's director Abram Room insisted on the cinematic importance of things, claiming: "Things are mute in everyday life, they do not signify anything […] In the cinema, on the screen, things grow to gigantic dimensions and function with the same force (if not greater) as a person' (Room 1926).[23] There are various historical and contemporary photographs on the wall, including one of a film star, press-clipped from the magazine *Sovetskii ekran*, a bed covered with a white bed linen, a screen with a flowered pattern, a comfortable sofa, a cat figurine, pots and pans, tea glasses with metal holders, and clothes. There are some differences in dress between the husband (played by Nikolai Batalov) and his friend Vladimir (played by Vladimir Fogel'). Working as a foreman on the reconstruction of the Bolshoi theatre, Nikolai is dressed more casually in his everyday life, wearing mostly a *tolstovka* tunic and a military-style jacket, while Vladimir, who works at the printers, sports a slightly smarter and more urban style, consisting of suit jackets and cozy pullovers.

Furthermore, clothes accurately contextualized the film's heroine Liudmila (played by Liudmila Semenova), both in relation to her position within the household she shares with the two men and in the world outside. She spends most of her time observing the busy Moscow street life sitting by the window of her basement flat, looking pretty in her roomy flapper dress with a big flower pattern. While Liudmila emulates the looks of a film actress with her kohl-rimmed eyes and her hair cut in a modern bob, she covers her head with a head-scarf tied at the back of her neck while doing housework, thus symbolically providing some dignity to her socially degraded role of housewife. Her headgear is nevertheless more varied, depending on the different social situations in which she participates. For her exciting ride on the airplane with Vladimir, Liudmila wears a hat made of soft fabric shaped into a cloche, but which also resembles a headscarf with its two wide ribbons tied up at the side of her head. Without any headgear and with her bobbed hair in view, she looks like any young urban woman while sitting in the waiting room of the abortion clinic. At the end of the film, having become a stronger person, she is pictured leaving her tiny flat and the two men who neglected her, embarking on a train journey that takes her out of Moscow. On that occasion, her black leather cloche contributes to her determination to start a new life.

Contemporary audiences certainly could read all the intended meanings in Liudmila's headgear. A beret often replaced a head-scarf on the heads of urban working women towards the end of the 1920s. Obviously competing for attention with the numerous US movies, the poster for *Bed and Sofa*, designed by the Stenberg brothers, depicted a young, good-looking, and made-up woman with a beret. That small iconographic detail was enough to situate the heroine on the poster in the urban working class milieu, because the NEP woman would have worn a cloche hat. On the other hand, by publishing the basic instructions for both a cloche hat and a beret in a Do-It-Yourself column in 1926,[24] the Bolshevik-supported *Zhenskii zhurnal* [Women's Journal] announced that it had entered the public space in order to broker an ideological truce between fashionability and urban female workers.

The recognition of fashionability challenged the concept of a well-organized and streamlined modernity envisioned by the Constructivists, and acknowledged a messy, everyday one lived by the masses of urban population. As shown in the film *The Cigarette Girl from Mosselprom*, a flapper-dress sewn of Stepanova's geometrically-patterned fabric on the big body of the typist Maria Ivanovna could be matched with an outdated flower-patterned wallpaper in her flat, and those two clashing aesthetics would be additionally accompanied by an overwhelming number of trinkets, symbolizing that the old and the new adjusted to each other on an everyday level. In her witty analysis, Christina Kiaer recognizes the clownish absurdity of this specific film scene: "The film designers recognize that Stepanova's fabric is meant to signify dynamism, rationality, and mechanization, even as these meanings are used to poke mean-spirited fun at this ungainly woman clutching her pot lid, the futuristic fabric rendering her almost clownish" (Kiaer 2005, 118). To complicate things further, or rather to embed the narrative more convincingly in the everyday, Maria Ivanovna, who is in love with her office colleague, a clumsy accountant (played by Il'inskii), also wears feminine lace dresses and stylish hats in order to grab his attention from the cigarette girl Zina to herself. Those conventionally feminine ensembles were, quite likely, designed and produced within the ideologically opposite sartorial field to the Constructivist dream on the mass production of clothes – the "Atelier of Fashion," which excelled in custom-made outfits.

The film *Your Acquaintance* [*Vasha znakomaia*; aka *The Female Journalist*, 1927], directed by Lev Kuleshov and starring Aleksandra Khokhlova in the lead role, was probably most successful in applying the Constructivist aesthetics through both the costumes worn by Khokhlova and the film sets designed by Aleksandr Rodchenko. Reminiscing on their collaboration, Kuleshov stated that Rodchenko understood that he wanted simplicity, and that clogging the space with too many objects just because they would be, in real life, conventionally positioned there, would only distract from the narrative (Khokhlova 1987, 152–153). While the film as a whole has been lost, it is easy to spot in the remaining fragments how Khokhlova effortlessly fits into a newsroom office, perfectly matching Rodchenko's interiors with her geometrically-cut dress and her bobbed hair. Indeed, Khokhlova superbly embodied a modernist experience – changing gender roles, new technology, and the wit needed to survive in the metropolis with all its excesses. While unhappily in love and being fired from her journalistic post, Khokhlova still radiates a modernist glamour of the 1920s' woman who dares to be individual, different, and inspirational. In one of the remaining fragments of the film, her married love interest Petrovskii enters the "Atelier of Fashion" at the Moscow Sewing Trust – the same establishment which in 1924 hosted the US businessman MacBright in

Figure 15.3 Aleksandra Khokhlova in the film *Your Acquaintance* with film sets by Aleksandr Rodchenko, *Sovetskii ekran* 1927.

the film *The Cigarette Girl from Mosselprom* – because Petrovskii has spotted in its window a silk scarf with a bold geometrical pattern. He promptly buys it for his wife while murmuring to himself: "The same that Khokhlova has got." In their booklet on Khokhlova, Shklovskii and Eisenstein provide many references to her western counterparts, but Eisenstein specifically emphasizes that Khokhlova is definitely not the "Soviet Mary Pickford" (Shklovskii and Eisenstein, 6). But this is precisely what the Soviet audiences craved.

Mary Pickford and her husband and fellow actor Douglas Fairbanks were huge stars in the Soviet Union, as demonstrated by the feverish reports in the domestic media during their visit in 1926.[25] Director Sergei Komarov used that opportunity to shoot his romantic comedy *The Kiss of Mary Pickford* [*Potselui Meri Pikford*, 1927], with the American star herself appearing in a cameo role. The plot vividly shows the Soviet fascination with the Hollywood stars by featuring a simple film usher, Goga Palkin (played by Il'inskii) who is madly in love with a girl Dusia (Anel' Sudakevich), who on her part is madly in love with Douglas Fairbanks. Goga's appeal nevertheless suddenly goes up, not only with Dusia but with all the girls, once Mary Pickford lands a kiss on his cheek. Film historian Miriam Hansen has observed that classical Hollywood cinema "succeeded as an international modernist idiom on a mass basis" due to the ability of its films to "open up hitherto unperceived modes of sensory perception and experience" and "to suggest a different organization of the daily world" (Hansen 1999, 72). In that sense, Dusia's interest in fashionable flapper-dress topped with cloche hats, as well as her daily visits to the cinema to enjoy, over and over again, Fairbanks's screen adventures, resonated with the expressions of the contemporary urban modernity, such as pleasure and sensuality, but did not fit into the new austere and rationalized socialist way of life as imagined by the early Bolsheviks. Furthermore, thanks to Sudakevich's polished beauty and enhanced by her carefully applied make-up and her stylishly bobbed hair, Dusia looked like a Hollywood film star herself. In the last scene, after she has finally settled for Goga, Dusia wears a striped football jersey shirt (known as *futbolka*) – a visual signifier of a socially conscious young woman at the time.[26] It could have been a sartorial nod towards her return to Soviet reality and abandoning the illusionary world of Hollywood.

The romantic comedies, especially those directed by Iakov Protazanov, continued to resemble their western counterparts. Moreover, the NEP life-style scenes in Protazanov's films *The Tailor from Torzhok* and *The Three Million Trial* [*Protsess o trekh millionakh*, 1926] could have been equally produced by any western film studio. When Igor Il'inskii, as the poor provincial tailor Petia, suddenly finds himself in St Petersburg, he is transplanted into an exciting metropolitan life-style, crowded with fancy cars and people dressed in the latest and most expensive fashions. His adventure becomes even more exciting when the ticket he happens to own wins 100,000 rubles at the lottery draw taking place in a grand, over-decorated hall. Furthermore, Petia is wooed to the world of high-class NEP parties by a glamorous NEP woman, the original owner of that ticket, plotting to reclaim the award. While Il'inskii had played a poor little crook in *The Three Million Trial*, this film featured probably the most luxurious sets and costumes among the all romantic comedies of the 1920s. Dressed in rags, Il'inskii's little naïve criminal of *The Three Million Trial* was paired with a series of morally corrupted, but lavishly dressed people, from a filthy bank owner to his indecent wife Noris (played by Ol'ga Zhizhneva), who carelessly enters a passionate, extramarital relationship with a dashing thief who really stole three million from the sumptuous mansion she shares with her husband. On each occasion, from her fur trimmed travel cape to a muslin negligee encrusted with jewels and trimmed with fur that she wears while meeting her lover, and her silk oriental pajamas in which she greets her husband, Noris' clothes signal wealth and sophistication. Equally dazzling is the dancing party with tens of couples swirling in lavish eveningwear in the ballroom of the banker's mansion.

Protazanov's Soviet films were polished and expensive and, in that sense, consistent with his pre-Revolutionary work in Russian cinema and his film career in the West in the immediate post-Revolutionary period. Denise Youngblood claims that Protazanov was a bourgeois specialist who linked the pre-Revolutionary and Bolshevik Russia once he returned to his homeland in 1924 (Youngblood 1992, 120–121). Similarly, Nadezhda Lamanova was a survivor and a link to a pre-Revolutionary past in her profession. With all other pre-Revolutionary fashion designers disappearing after the Revolution, she was the only one with the experience to design the costumes in *The Three Million Trial*. In the 1920s she continued to discretely provide custom-made dresses for private clients from artistic circles and some members of the new Kremlin elite. Owing to the NEP's commercial channels, Lamanova still managed to procure machine lace and some silk to embellish her dresses with beadwork and silk ribbon tassels, but her work during that impoverished period did not match the lavishness of the best chiffon, tulle, silk, satin, sequins, and highly ornamental beaded decorations for which she was famous in the 1890s and 1910s.[27] In this context, Noris' exquisite ensembles could have come straight from Paris or, more likely, from some of the leading Berlin fashion houses.[28]

Most of the films in popular genres screened at the cinemas were foreign, but the Soviets produced 128 melodramas and 100 comedies in the period from 1921 to 1928 (Youngblood 1992, 73), with both genres attracting big audiences.[29] In 1927, even the fierce Constructivist Sergei Tret'iakov recognized that young Soviet women, at the end of a dull working day, in a mood "to escape their own lives through the familiar images of empresses, duchesses, heroines, mermaids, temptresses," would rush to the cinema. He flatly admitted that "the desire for elegance is very strong" (Tret'iakov 1927, 29). In the still pluralistic 1920s, working women could indulge in these ideologically inappropriate films, whether they were imported or produced at home. In general, cinema audiences continued to cut across the class lines throughout the 1920s, just as they did in pre-Revolutionary years, as described by Vance Kepley:

> Commercial theatre managers made a special effort to attract proletarians, knowing that many of them had access to inexpensive movies on the club circuit. Most commercial houses offered discount ticket prices for labour union members and their families. A spot check at one of Moscow's commercial cinemas revealed that 75 per cent of the audience members belonged to labour unions and were eligible to see movies at clubs. The relative comfort and the superior programme quality of the commercial houses helped explain this patronage pattern. (Kepley 1994, 273)

Indeed, even the cartoon "In the Cinema Foyer" published in *Sovetskii ekran* in 1926 confirms this claim. Differentiated by dress, body language, and attitude, members from different social classes – from workers to soldiers, members of the middle class and the NEP-couples – happily mingled in a spacious cinema lobby, plastered with the posters for Fairbanks' film *Robin Hood* (US, dir. Allan Dwan, 1922).[30] Moreover, at the end of the film *The Cigarette Girl from Mosselprom*, the new film actress Zina appears in the box of a lavishly decorated cinema palace in order to greet her fans who have gathered to watch a filmed story which takes her from a street cigarette seller to a film actress. Likewise, the scenes at the cinema palace in the film *The Kiss of Mary Pickford* take place in yet another luxuriously clad cinema space.[31]

The mass popularity of romantic comedies was accompanied by strong ideological disapproval, which only became more disparaging towards the end of the 1920s. In 1924, the critics found *The Cigarette Girl from Mosselprom* funny, but argued that it was not a Soviet comedy and claimed that it was made according to "capitalist standards" (Youngblood 1992, 75). Produced only a couple of years later, *The Girl with the Hatbox* was accused of being "in coarse taste" and "straight from Paris" (Youngblood 1992, 133), while critics attributed *The Three Million Trial*'s popularity to "its 'primitive Americanism' and its emphasis on sex and greed" (Youngblood 1992, 113), and pronounced *The Kiss of Mary Pickford* "completely alien," "vulgar," and "artless" (Youngblood 1992, 76). Those attacks on commercial films were embedded in a wider condemnation of NEP values and life-styles, which were identified as a serious threat to the social body. As the Bolsheviks tried to expel both previous sartorial history and future fashions from their Utopia, the return of fashion during the NEP period seriously disturbed the new emerging culture. On the page of fashion magazines and on the film screens, the NEP-woman reminded loyal Bolsheviks of the worst practices of capitalism, and symbolically suggested the notion of the female body as the site of consumption and pleasure. With such an avid consumer of all sorts of luxuries – from fur to cosmetics, perfumes, fashion accessories, and clothes – traditional symbols of bourgeois impurity (including make-up, nail varnish, feminine dress, and jewelry) threatened to pollute the pure proletarian body.

Yet throughout the 1920s, urban working women preferred the Westernized style of clothes and appearance to the ideological austerity in their everyday dress. Indeed, *Zhenskii zhurnal* was launched in 1926 with the idea of promoting dress that would be fashionable enough to be interesting for urban working-class women, but that would avoid the extravagant and luxurious sartorial statements that the NEP aesthetics preferred.[32] By the end of the 1920s, even the previously rigid Bolshevik strongholds, such as the journal *Rabotnitsa*, introduced advice on fashion, paper patterns, and fashion spreads. They featured simple, but nevertheless pretty, dresses with elongated lines that corresponded to contemporary Western fashion trends. On her travels through the Soviet Union in 1927, the French journalist Andrée Viollis spotted young women who "would be at home on our boulevards, for they know how to dress, how to twist the humble felt at the proper angle, and like the *Parisiennes*, how to make the utterly outmoded dress gay and fashionable with […] nothing – a fresh collar, a pocket, an unexpected flower" (Viollis 1929, 36). It could be said that, immersing themselves in the mass media images, they unfailingly spotted the latest model of hat and a cut of dress that they themselves, or some inexpensive seamstress, could easily make.

Figure 15.4 Iurii Pimenov, "Our Heroine, Heroine of Foreign Cinema", *Sovetskii ekran*, 1927.

The Soviet film audiences enjoyed watching foreign film stars, such as Pearl White, Mary Pickford, Pola Negri, Asta Nielsen, Lilian Gish, Douglas Fairbanks, Rudolph Valentino, Harry Piel, and Milton Sills, all of whom deserved paperback biographies by the Moscow publishing house Kinopechat'.[33] The Soviet public was likewise familiar with domestic film actors, such as Igor' Il'inskii, Nata Vachnadze, Aleksandra Khokhlova, and Ol'ga Tret'iakova, on whom Kinopechat' also published such booklets by 1926, and they also knew well some others, among them Vera Malinskaia, Vera Maretskaia, Anel' Sudakevich, Vladimir Fogel', and Nikolai Batalov. Additionally, the journal *Sovetskii ekran* presented domestic actors as stars through full page portraits, in a manner of their Hollywood counterparts. Wearing loads of masterfully applied make-up, perfect hair-dos and dazzling dresses, Anel' Sudakevich, Galina Kravchenko, Anna Sten, Aleksandra Khokhlova, Liudmila Semenova, and others looked the part, yet none of the Soviet actors became a film star. While in the Hollywood of the 1920s stars were the result of a carefully cultivated process within a standardized film industry in which each player, from director to screenplay writer, editor, set and costume designer had a precise and well-defined role, the director was an unquestionable authority in the young Soviet film industry.[34]

A new heroine had already started to emerge towards the end of the 1920s. The formation of the new Soviet subject runs in parallel with the demise of NEP and its cosmopolitan cultures and life-styles. This new heroine had a tough character, a strong will and a robust body, and she was increasingly becoming Soviet. In two films from that period, this woman was in fact a girl, but she was already socially conscious, belonged to the collective, and, moreover, was not bothered by the latest western fashions and looks. Played by Ada Voitsik, Marusia Ivanova, the heroine of Sergei Komarov's film *The Doll with Millions* [*Kukla s millionami*, 1928] is a 17-year-old high school student. She is clad in a *futbolka*, a simple jersey shirt with big stripes, when she studies with a group of colleagues; she wears a modern, one-piece swimming suit while training at the swimming pool with her team. Fully dedicated to her study and engaged in the sports, so properly integrated in socialist society, Marusia is not impressed when she learns that her long-lost aunt from Paris has left her a considerable inheritance; hence she is not disappointed when she is told that her inheritance, held in shares, has lost its value.

Sergei Iutkevich directed the film *Lace* [*Kruzheva*, 1928]. Its heroine Marusia is a Komsomol member, who, due to her steely determination, succeeds in defeating the hooligans in her lace-producing factory. She also imposes the wall newspaper with the current domestic content as a perfect medium for communicating the socially appropriate topics in her working environment. Played by Nina Shaternikova, Marusia does not wear any make-up and is also often dressed in a *futbolka*. Even when she wears a flapper dress, she sports a simple monochrome version and wears it underneath her mannish jacket. When she does not wear a head-scarf tied at the back of her neck, her hair is simply gathered in a small pony-tail. In contrast, the hooligan's girlfriend, a typist Tania, played by N. Mass, wears a lot of make-up, has bobbed hair, and is always presented in a flapper dress with a loud pattern. Praising the topic and acting, the weekly *Ogonek* greeted the film with the heading "The Komsomol Members on the Screen."[35] As Emma Widdis has observed, Iutkevich searched in *Lace* "for a model of cinematic individuality without bourgeois elements – a freeing of the cinematic hero from romantic complications, into a fully realized place within the new collective" (Widdis 2012, 603). The characters of Voitsik and Shaternikova were such heroines, but those young women were not only an ideological invention. Spotting many modestly but fashionably dressed women on the Moscow streets in 1927, Andrée Viollis also noticed this energetic type: "young women bareheaded, or their short curls done up in a red silk hand kerchief, their hands carried with a swagger in the pockets of modest golf jackets, their step elastic, they seem to throw out from their curls a breath of sea air and of long vacations" (Viollis 1929, 35).

Throughout the 1930s, films continued to "turn" their public Soviet by presenting new types of protagonists and their struggles to achieve new social ideals. In that sense, while Elena Kuz'mina in the role of the novice teacher Elena in *Alone* [*Odna*, dirs. Grigorii Kozintsev and Leonid Trauberg, 1931], was a beautiful, smartly dressed young woman living in a big city and planning her marriage with an equally good-looking young man, the film's plot could not have been further removed from the romantic comedies of the 1920s. Elena's hopes on married life and a cozy home full of nice objects are smashed when she is posted to a far-away mountainous province in the Altai. While she meets her fiancée, shops for furniture, and longingly inspects white porcelain in Leningrad's shop windows, Elena wears a fashionable white dress, in line with the mature elegance of the early 1930s. She changes into a smart, but more restricted style of a black skirt, white shirt and a grey cardigan when she visits the Education Office in a failed attempt to change her teaching post. Elena arrives in the Altai in her urban winter coat and without any headgear, but at the end of film she is wrapped up in a long skirt and her blond hair is covered by a big woolen headscarf. The changes in sartorial styles point towards deeper changes, as Elena slowly makes peace with her new life. After the conflicting period of the 1920s when Bolshevik austerity was challenged by the NEP-style celebration of abundance, the film *Alone* promotes a new relationship between the Soviet citizen and the world of objects. Elena not only learns to live in the countryside and dress sensibly but also realizes that she does not need all the cosy objects she earlier craved so much.

Elena's struggles to adjust to the hardship of a new life were still realistically depicted in comparison to the films that followed during the 1930s. Liubov' Orlova in the film *The Happy Guys* [*Veselye rebiata*, 1934], directed by Grigorii Aleksandrov, started her screen career as the maid Aniuta. Her apron and a peasant-style, wide, flower-patterned skirt clash with the polished beach pajamas, modernist swimsuits with geometrical patterns, and luxurious silk eveningwear worn by the elite occupying the sumptuous villa at the exclusive resort during the summer months. With the NEP purged from Soviet life, this new privileged stratum could have only been the members of the highest ranks of Stalin's *nomenklatura*. Not unlike directors of the 1920s, who could only show NEP luxuries in dress and life-style if they ridiculed them, Aleksandrov mocked the artistic pretenses and snobbish rituals of this new privileged social group. In line with the emerging Socialist Realist creed, Aniuta's natural musical talent not only enchants the audience of the Bolshoi theatre in Moscow, but also wins the heart of the shepherd Kostia. On his part, Kostia gets bored with Aniuta's musically challenged and shallow mistress, while, at the same time, amazingly advances from a simple shepherd to the leader of a jazz orchestra in Moscow. In the last scene, Aniuta appears miraculously transformed from a scruffy maid, who sang while cleaning her employers' house, into a superb performer at the most prestigious Soviet stage, wearing a glitzy dress and a top hat embellished with feathers.

Socialist Realism became the official aesthetic method once the modernist experiments were abandoned. The official brief to the artists was to aestheticize the existing reality according to the laws of beauty and harmony. Consequently, Socialist Realism created a new parallel, mythical reality, which was disseminated through mass media, from films to fashion magazines. Moreover, Stalinism granted fashion a highly representational role and eventually imposed an overdecorated style on its ideal dress, which matched the main characteristics of

Socialist Realist aesthetics, such as grandness and classicism. This aesthetics was launched in the new central fashion institution "Dom modelei" (House of Prototypes), which opened in Moscow in 1935.[36] The established fashion designer Nadezhda Makarova, who started her career under Lamanova's guidance, was its first director, while Lamanova was appointed artistic consultant. The actress Anel' Sudakevich left her film career and joined the design studio within the "Dom modelei."[37] Similarly to the earlier attempts at the "Atelier of Fashion" in the 1920s, the new fashion institution designed theatre and film costumes. However, their respective aesthetics considerably differed. In contrast to the mix of bold experiments and latest fashions that characterized dresses envisioned by the "Atelier of Fashion," the "Dom modelei," embedded as it was within the Stalinist myth, proposed dresses of conventional elegance and timeless style.

This newly approved fashion appeared in a variety of expressions, from the imposingly glamorous to the conventionally pretty; Liubov' Orlova brilliantly paraded in all of them in the film *The Circus* [*Tsirk*, 1936], directed by Grigorii Aleksandrov. It could be said almost with certainty that those costumes were produced by the newly established "Dom modelei," as many of them resembled photographs and drawings published in the first issue of the journal *Dom modelei*. They were proposed by its experienced design team, from Anel' Sudakevich, who eventually specialized in design of showy circus costumes, to Sergei Topleninov, who perfectly captured the mid-1930s urban elegance, to Lamanova's disciples Makarova and Fekla Gorelenkova, and, finally, to Lamanova herself in her consultant role. Orlova plays the US circus performer Marion Dixon who – ostracized in the West for having a mixed-race child – finds herself entertaining Soviet audiences. As Marion, Orlova glows with a polished glamour, whether she wears extravagant, over-decorated outfits during her circus performances or is dressed in exquisite, demure ensembles in her off-duty hours, combined with lady-like hats and gloves. Orlova's sumptuous clothes greatly contributed to her image of a sophisticated international diva, never more so than in the scene when her nasty manager throws the entire contents of her vast wardrobe at her: long slinky dresses, eveningwear splashed with sequins, silk ensembles, white fur and similar items which only very privileged woman would own in the USSR. Orlova was allowed to excel in such an international sartorial glamour, as very soon afterwards her character's looks and style of dress would acquire a very specific Soviet allure. With her blond hair freely flowing in the breeze and a radiant expression on her healthy-looking face, having scrubbed off the excessive stage make-up and false eyelashes, she marches in a parade on Moscow's Red Square, dressed in a white sweater and a knee-length white skirt, looking chaste and dazzling at the same time. The sartorial trajectory of the three film heroines from the late 1920s to the mid-1930s shows how the mythical was getting increasingly more important than the everyday. While Elena accepts practical clothes in her own life and Aniuta turns into a glamorous woman only on the stage, Marion's personal life merges with the public life, as her upper-class, elegant clothes give way to a simple white outfit of the collective body.

Figure 15.5 The actress Anel' Sudakevich in *Sovetskii ekran*, 1928.

In Aleksandrov's film *The Radiant Path* [*Svetlyi put'*, 1940], Orlova's character Tania Morozova is a maid, who eventually becomes a praised shock-worker in a textile factory,[38] graduates to engineer, and finally is appointed Deputy to the Supreme Soviet, the political body which governed the Soviet Union. In the 1920s, Katia in *The Tailor from Torzhok* and Parasha in *The House on Trubnaya* stayed truthful to their country-style clothes, even when their personal lives changed significantly. In contrast, Tania's incredible life trajectory is accordingly sartorially accompanied by a wide peasant skirt during her maid days, a workers' overall at the factory floor, a pretty silk dress when her career development takes her to Moscow, and reaches its climax with the most elegant ensemble once she becomes an important political figure. As pointed out by Maria Enzensberger, Tania's consecutive makeovers are signaled in the film by a dissolve of her face, showing, on each occasion, her new identity (1993, 102). Indeed, once she receives her order in the Kremlin, a jubilant Tania dances in front of gilded mirrors in the lavish ballroom, prompting each of mirrors to reflect back to her an image of one of her former selves, marked by different clothes and different hair-styles. Moreover, Tania astonishingly manages to change clothes even during the same scene. Dressed in a romantic, long muslin white dress, she boards a black limousine

Figure 15.6 Cover of *Modeli sezona*, 1938–1939.

driven by her fairy godmother. They fly over Moscow, continue their journey over a dramatic mountain range and return to the Textile Pavilion at the All-Union Exhibition of Agricultural Achievements in Moscow, where Tania lands alone and at the driving wheel, wearing now a sophisticated ensemble of black coat and silk dress. Shot during the period of the mature phase of Socialist Realism, the film perfectly fits into the framework of Stalinist mythical culture, and indeed it was initially supposed to be called *Cinderella*.[39]

The plot of this cinematic fairy tale had its roots in the Stalinist everyday reality, in its extraordinary version. During the mid-1930s, media attention focused on the Stakhanovites, the shock-workers. The daily newspapers regularly reported on their congresses in Moscow and their meetings with Stalin, but also covered their social life, including visits to the Bolshoi theatre, dancing in clubs or buying clothes in special shops with the best goods on offer. The Stakhanovites were entitled to order custom-made clothes from the best fabrics in special workshops in order to attend State celebrations in the Kremlin's grand settings. Long evening gowns were paraded in salons with chandeliers, as the regime emphasized its successes and celebrated its heroes. Magazines paid special attention to the smartly dressed young female shock workers, who were also supposed to be extraordinary mannequins. Stalinist culture delegated them to dress up for the rest of the population, and some of them, such as the sisters Marusia and Dusia Vinogradova, shock workers from the textile mills at Ivanovo-Voznesensk, became media stars. In that sense, Orlova's Tania, with her astonishing changes in dress and social status, was a convincing role model on the screen. She radiated a new Soviet glamour, whether she danced and sang in the Kremlin's sumptuous surroundings or operated an incredulous number of two hundred looms in her factory, turning even such a prosaic activity into a series of ritualized ballet movements.

Those shifts in social stratification for certain categories of citizens, marked by beautiful clothes, did not take place in the real world of ordinary people. Sheila Fitzpatrick recognized two Stalinist realities as "life as it is" and "life as it is becoming" (1993, 219–227). The luxurious goods granted to the Stakhanovites in the 1930s were not available to their co-workers, who could neither afford nor find even the simplest items of clothing in the shops. Although the daily newspapers occasionally pointed out everyday problems, films and magazines usually preferred to represent the extraordinary rather than the ordinary. The aim of constructing a radically new, utopian society was replaced by the rapid industrialization of the country, and the equally rapid production of its mythical images. Aleksandrov's films, with his wife Orlova in the leading roles, flawlessly fulfilled that task. In May 1936 the première of *Circus* took place at the newly opened outdoor cinema "Gigant" situated in Moscow's Gorky Park and seating up to 20,000 spectators. Its success with the public has been further confirmed after a record one million people saw the film during the first two weeks of its run in Moscow's cinemas, and finally sealed by 1939, when, seen by 40 million people, *Circus* became the most popular Soviet film (Salys 2009, 148–149).

Stalinism needed such huge spaces to reach the masses and initiate them in its grandiose culture. While it was not interested in the latest artistic explorations and achievements of the West, Stalinist culture was expressed through film, musicals, fashion, and new mass magazines. This move from the paradigms of the so-called high culture to the paradigms of the so-called low culture happened because Stalinism wanted to engage the masses in its project. As it could not deliver in everyday life its promises on new enchanting life and glamorous dresses that fitted it, its films provided a desired reality. Ilya Ehrenburg coined the term "Dream Factory" in 1931 in relation to the Hollywood film machinery and its capacity to produce an illusionary, much more interesting world in comparison to the real one, but the Soviet film industry embarked on the same task at the same time. The re-introduction of opulent decoration and femininity in socialist fashion held a wide appeal for the masses. The role of the films and their most famous star, Liubov' Orlova, was to embellish the everyday through the costumes fitting a new, home-grown Soviet glamour.

Within Stalinist mass-culture, elegance and femininity became desirable categories that were owned by those who deserved them, and that would soon be within the reach of every woman worker in the country. Orlova was not only their official, but also much-loved, representative. While the film actresses of the 1920s were mostly confined to their artistic circles, Orlova cultivated a glamorous appearance off the screen as well, fulfilling Stalinist efforts to offer role models to the Soviet masses. In that sense, Orlova was a marketable commodity, just as the Hollywood stars of the contemporary period. The difference was that she was not marketing specific fashion brands or particular cosmetics goods, but the socialist project itself. In the end, Stalinist fashion from the Moscow "Dom modelei" shared not only its aesthetics but also its ontological status with Socialist Realism. Its perfect beauty on a magazine page or on the film screen conjured up a life that did not exist. While the style of opulent Stalinist clothes was similar to outfits designed by the leading Hollywood costume designer Adrian, their uses differed. Ordinary US women could buy copies in a wide variety of qualities and prices. Orlova's star status was probably only heightened by the fact that these dresses and looks remained merely a dream for her Soviet film audiences.

Notes

1 The research for this chapter has been generously supported by an AHRC Fellowship, which enabled my two research trips in Moscow and other two in St Petersburg in 2012–2013. Additionally, I am very grateful to Julian Graffy and Rachel Morley from UCL, who kindly supported my request to watch most of the films I needed for writing this chapter at the UCL/SSEES Library. My gratitude extends to Gillian Long and her colleagues at the Library, who have been very helpful as usual.
2 For an overview of Soviet dress and fashion in the 1920s and 1930s, see Bartlett (2010).
3 The NEP was initiated in 1921 by Lenin in a desperate attempt to improve the supply of basic goods following the Civil War, and came to an end in 1929 with the start of Stalin's centralization of the whole economy and the introduction of the First Five Year Plan. For an overview of the political, economic and social circumstances of the NEP see Ball (1987).
4 These magazines included: *Novosti mod* [Fashion News], *Poslednie mody: Zhurnal dlia zhenshchin* [The Latest Fashions: Women's Magazine], and *Zhurnal dlia khoziaek* [The Housewives' Magazine].
5 The Soviets imported 1113 American, German, and French films in the genres of adventure, comedy, and melodrama in the years between 1921 and 1928 (Youngblood 1992, 73).
6 Although the journal *Atel'e* was aligned with the Moscow Sewing Trust, it was not initiated by the official women's organization "Zhenotdel," such as the popular weekly *Rabotnitsa* [Working Woman]. Only one issue of *Atel'e* was ever published in a modest circulation of 2000 copies.

7 The photograph of the Atelier of Fashion published in the journal *Atel'e* and the interior of the salon in the film *The Cigarette Girl from Mosselprom* are almost identical, which probably means that the salon was not constructed as a film set, but that these scenes were filmed in the existing space of the "Atelier of Fashion." Moreover, the camera shows MacBright rushing out of the building with the "Atelier of Fashion" logo once he learns that the trunk with his company's clothes and the mannequin was seized at the railway station. Similarly, the scenes taking place at the Mezhrabpom Film studio were also filmed at the studio itself.

8 All Russian textile and clothing firms were nationalized by decree in 1918, and organized in ten trusts. Comprising 32 factories, the Moscow Sewing Trust was one of them.

9 Their paths diverged after 1923. Lamanova and Pribyl'skaia stayed in the Soviet Union and both occupied a series of important functions related to fashion and theatre design, and ethnic art respectively, while Aleksandra Ekster emigrated to the West in 1924. Vera Mukhina became one of the most appreciated Soviet artists in the 1930s, with her monumental sculpture "The Worker and Peasant Woman" [Rabotnik i kolkhiznitsa] greeting visitors at the International Exhibition of the Arts and Industry in Paris in 1937.

10 The exhibition was organized by the Subsection of Art and Production within the Ministry of Enlightenment, and the State Academy of Artistic Sciences. The award was announced in the journal *Atel'e*: "Attestat I-i stepeni prisuzhdennyi 'Atel'e mod' na Vserossiiskoi khudozhestvennoi promyshlennoi vystavke" [Certificate of the First Order at the First All-Russian Exhibition of Art in Industry awarded to "Atelier of Fashion"], *Atel'e* 1923, p. 48.

11 The photographs of the display of "Atelier of Fashion" at the First All-Russian Exhibition of the Art in Industry were published in *Russkoe iskusstvo* [Russian Art] 2–3 (1923).

12 Ekster was well-informed on the colorful and ornamental shapes of the emerging Art Deco aesthetics due to her intense participation in the Western art world prior to the revolution, and her participation in the Moscow pre-Revolutionary Kamerny Theatre.

13 For an overview on *Aelita*, see Christie (1991).

14 Lamanova had opened her fashion salon in Moscow in 1885. By the 1910s, she employed twenty seamstresses, supplied haute couture dresses for her rich and sophisticated clientele which comprised gentry and famous actresses. She lost her fashion house in the aftermath of the Revolution.

15 In the original documents that I have explored on her life and work, Lamanova herself never mentions designing film costumes. Instead she emphasizes her activities at the Workshop of Contemporary Dress, which, embedded in the Subsection of Art and Production, was in charge of inventing and promoting the new socialist dress. The documents also confirm her active role at the Academy of Artistic Sciences, which was founded in 1921, and, which, among its other activities, organized the Soviet display at the Paris exhibition of the Decorative Arts in 1925, where Lamanova's outfits were included. Lamanova also designed the theatre costumes for Vakhtangov and Stanislavskii.

16 In a review on *Aelita*, both Ekster and Lamanova are credited for the costumes in the film; *Krasnaia niva* [Red Field] 42 (October 19) 1924: 1020.

17 "Prostota v odezhde" [Simplicity in Dress], *Krasnaia niva* [Red Field] 45 (November 9) 1924: 1098.
18 Ekaterina Khokhlova, film historian and grand-daughter of Aleksandra Khokhlova and Lev Kuleshev, told me that her grandmother reminisced on wearing Nadezhda Lamanova dresses, but she was unaware of any other details (Interview conducted in Moscow on September 19, 2012).
19 Khokhlova's position as a credible artist in post-Revolutionary Russia was additionally challenged by the fact that she was born into the extreme wealth and privilege of an artistic family, related to the founder of the Tretyakov Gallery.
20 Organizing their plots around the winning lottery tickets, the films *The Tailor from Torzhok* and *The Girl with the Hatbox* promoted the newly introduced state lottery.
21 For an overview of the changes in the perception of a political activist, see Wood (1997).
22 For an overview on the film, see Burns (1982); Graffy (2001); Grashchenkova (1977); Mayne (1989: 110–129); and Youngblood (1992).
23 Moreover, as stated by the film's cameraman Grigorii Giber, Room encouraged his crew to use all the household items on the set themselves (Giber 1927).
24 "Domashnie remesla" [Handicraft], *Zhenskii zhurnal* [Women's Journal] 2 (1926): 35.
25 The publishing house Kinopechat' dedicated a whole booklet to that visit, covering their careers, the enthusiastic reception they received in the Soviet Union and the excerpts from Pickford's diary during their stay (Iakovlev 1926).
26 Symbolizing a strong connection to the official support of the sports, the *futbolka* was ever more popular with young women, and often depicted in films, magazines, and the fine arts. See for example, the painting "Girl in a Football Jersey" by Aleksandr Samokhvalov, 1932.
27 The Hermitage Museum in St Petersburg has in its dress collection Lamanova's eveningwear both from the pre-Revolutionary period and the 1920s, and the difference in the quality of fabrics and embellishments is only too visible.
28 All of Protazanov's films were produced at the studio Mezhrabpomfilm, a joint Soviet-German enterprise run by the International Workers' Aid. They were made for German distribution also, and both *Aelita* and *The Three Million Trial* were successful in the West (Youngblood 1992).
29 For example, *The Cigarette Girl from Mosselprom* "came in number five in a list of 'most seen films', with overwhelmingly positive viewer reactions" (Youngblood 1992, 75), while *Bed and Sofa* was seen by 1,260,560 viewers in the first six months after its release in March 1927 (Youngblood 1992, 161). Also, according to a survey on the cinema spectator published in 1928, Protazanov's *The Three Million Trial* was the seventh most popular film (Youngblood 1992, 60).
30 Vigranskii, "V foie kino" [At the Cinema Foyer], *Sovetskii ekran* [Soviet Screen] 24 (June 15) 1926: 2. The precise depiction of the place and circumstances could be also drawn from the fact that Fairbanks' film *Robin Hood* played at 14 of Moscow's 50 cinemas simultaneously (Youngblood 1992, 52).
31 Similarly to some other sumptuous interiors, such as the salon of the "Atelier of Fashion" shown in *The Cigarette Girl from Mosselprom*, those scenes were almost certainly shot in the actual cinemas rather than on expensive sets.

32. In *Zhenskii zhurnal* [Women's Journal] numerous fashion spreads, articles on the latest Paris fashions, and regular columns "Our Dress Proposals" and "Fashion Chronicle" were balanced by articles on women scientists, on mother and child, and on women's health issues. Lamanova was one of its contributors in the first two issues in 1926, proposing simple and functional but nevertheless feminine dresses.
33. An advertisement, published in the film journal *Sovetskii ekran* [Soviet Screen], promoted a series of 22 picture biographies dedicated to these, and some other foreign and domestic film actors (*Sovetskii ekran* 33, August 17, 1926, back cover).
34. For an overview on the role of director at the technique of montage, see Thomson (2004, 358–365); Yampolsky (1991); and Youngblood (1992).
35. M. A. "Komsomol'tsy na ekrane" [Komsomol members on the screen], *Ogonek* [Little Flame] 39 (September 25) 1927: 15.
36. "Dom modelei" is often translated as the "House of Fashion," but its correct translation, the "House of Prototypes," already points to its main task: to design and produce prototypes of dresses, to be, ideally, reproduced into mass clothing in textile factories all over the country.
37. All the names, from designers to cutters, sample makers, and the members of the Artistic Board, were listed in the editorial of the first issue of the journal *Dom modelei* (Moscow, 1936), in order to demonstrate the importance of the new institution and the new role of fashion at the time. In her designer career, Sudakevich also wrote on a proper style, feminine yet simple and balanced (for example, Sudakevich 1960).
38. "Shock work" existed before, but in the mid-1930s it was accompanied by material stimuli. Known as Stakhanovism, it acquired its name from the coalminer Aleksei Stakhanov, who over-fulfilled his work quota by 1,400 percent on August 30, 1935.
39. For an excellent reading of *The Radiant Path*, see Salys (2009, 283–340). Salys also quotes Aleksandrov's claim that Stalin enjoyed the film but did not like the title *Cinderella* and went on to suggest the existing title.

References

Arvatov, Boris. 1997. "Everyday Life and the Culture of the Thing" (1925). *October* 81: 119–128.

Ball, Alan M. 1987. *Russia's Last Capitalists: The Nepmen, 1921–1929*. Berkeley and Los Angeles: University of California Press.

Barnet, Boris. 1927. "Devushka s korobkoi" [The Girl with the Hat Box]. *Sovetskii ekran* [Soviet Screen] 12 (March 19): 10.

Bartlett, Djurdja. 2010. *FashionEast: The Spectre that Haunted Socialism*. Cambridge, MA: MIT Press.

Bowlt, John. 1976. *Stage Designs and the Russian Avant-Garde, 1911–1929: A Loan Exhibition of Stage and Costume Designs from the Collection of Mr. and Mrs. Nikita D. Lobanov-Rostovsky*. Washington: International Exhibitions Foundation.

Burns, Paul, E. 1982. "An NEP Moscow Address: Abram Room's Third Meshchanskaia (Bed and Sofa) in Historical Context." *Film and History* 12.4: 73–81.

Christie, Ian. 1991. "Down to Earth: *Aelita* Relocated." In *Inside the Film Factory: New Approaches to Russian and Soviet Cinema*, edited by R. Taylor and I. Christie, 80–102. London: Routledge.

Ehrenburg, Ilya, 1931. *Fabrika snov* [Dream Factory]. Berlin: Petropolis.

Enzensberger, Maria. 1993. "'We were Born to Turn a Fairy-tale into Reality': Grigori Alexandrov's *The Radiant Path*." In *Stalinism and Soviet Cinema*, edited by R. Taylor and D. Spring, 97–108. London: Routledge.

Fitzpatrick, Sheila. 1993 *The Cultural Front: Power and Culture in Revolutionary Russia*. Ithaca and London: Cornell University Press.

Giber, G. 1927. "Kak snimalas' 'Tret'ia Meshchanskaia'" [How "Bed and Sofa" Got Filmed]. *Sovetskii ekran* [Soviet Screen] 5 (January 29): 4.

Graffy, Julian. 2001. *Bed and Sofa*. London: I. B. Tauris.

Grashchenkova, Irina. 1977. *Abram Room*. Moscow: Iskusstvo.

Hansen, Miriam. 1999. "The Mass Production of the Senses: Classical Cinema as Vernacular Modernism." *Modernism/Modernity* 6.2: 59–77.

Iakovlev, N. M. 1926. *Meri Pikford i Duglas Ferbenks v SSSR* [Mary Pickford and Douglas Fairbanks in the USSR]. Moscow: Kinopechat'.

Kepley, Vance 1994. "'Cinefication': Soviet Film Exhibition in the 1920s." *Film History* 6.2: 262–277.

Khokhlova, Ekaterina, ed. 1987. *Lev Kuleshov: Fifty Years in Films*. Moscow: Raduga Publishers.

Kiaer, Christina. 2005. *Imagine No Possessions*. Cambridge, MA: MIT Press.

Kushnirov, Mark. 1977. *Zhizn' i fil'my Borisa Barneta* [Life and Films of Boris Barnet]. Moscow: Iskusstvo.

Mayne, Judith. 1989. *Kino and the Woman Question: Feminism and Soviet Silent Film*. Ohio State University Press.

Room, Abram, 1926. "Moi kinoubezhdeniia" [My Cinema-Convictions], *Sovetskii ekran* [Soviet Screen] 8: 5.

Salys, Rimgaila. 2009. *The Musical Comedy Films of Grigorii Aleksandrov: Laughing Matters*. Bristol and Chicago: Intellect

Shklovskii, Viktor and Sergei Eizenshtein. 1926. *Khokhlova*. Moscow: Kinopechat'.

Sudakevich, A. A. 1960. "Odevaites' krasivo" [Let's Dress Smartly], in *Vam, devushki* [To You, Girls], edited by G. Popova and L. Seregina, 207–224. Moscow: Medgiz.

Thomson, Kristin. 2004. "Early Alternatives to the Hollywood Mode of Production: Implications for Europe's Avant-gardes." In *The Silent Cinema Reader*, edited by Lee Grieveson and Peter Krämer, 349–367. London: Routledge.

Tret'iakov, Sergei. 1923. "LEF i NEP" [Left Front of Art and New Economic Policy]. *LEF* 2: 70–78

Tret'iakov, Sergei. 1927. "Khoroshii ton" [Good Form]. *Novyi LEF* [New LEF] 5: 26–30.

Tugendkhol'd, Iakov. 1922. *Alexandra Exter*. Berlin: Sarja Edition.

Vetrov, A. 1924. "Khudozhestvennaia promyshlennost' za gody revoliutsii" [Artistic Production during the Revolution]. *Sovetskaia kul'tura: itogi i perspektivy* (Supplement to *Krasnaia niva*), [Soviet Culture: Summary and Perspectives] Moscow: Izdatel'stvo Izvestii TsIK i SSSR i VTsIK, 334–342.

Viollis, Andrée. 1929. *A Girl in Soviet Russia*. New York: Thomas Y. Crowell Company.

Widdis, Emma. 2012. "Socialist Senses: Film and the Creation of Soviet Subjectivity." *Slavic Review* 71.3: 590–618.

Wood, Elizabeth, A. 1997. *The Baba and the Comrade: Gender and Politics in Revolutionary Russia*. Bloomington, Indiana University Press.

Yampolsky, Mikhail. 1991. "Kuleshov's Experiments and the New Anthropology of the Actor." In *Inside the Film Factory: New Approaches to Russian and Soviet Cinema*, edited by R. Taylor and I. Christie, 31–50. London: Routledge.

Youngblood, Denise. 1992. *Movies for the Masses: Popular Cinema and Soviet Society in the 1920s*. New York: Cambridge University Press.

16

Revenge of the Cameramen: Soviet Cinematographers in the Director's Chair

Peter Rollberg

Photography is a moderately complex technology, accessible to many people; direction is an art, denied to most.

(David Thomson[1])

Conventional wisdom among film critics has it that cameramen rarely become good directors. Yet the list of accomplished cinematographers, who at some point in their career risked the transition to direction, is long and diverse, including Jack Cardiff, Nicholas Roeg, Sven Nykvist, Andrzej Bartkowiak, and Jan de Bont, to name but a few. Russian and Soviet cinema, too, boasts a good number of excellent cinematographers-turned-directors, with varying degrees of success. Some gained international fame as cameramen before transitioning, yet their later directorial output remained largely unknown. Others undertook the decisive step so early that their juvenile beginnings as cinematographers were sometimes completely forgotten.

Why do cameramen turn to direction? Is this "career switch" intended as an act of liberation from the authority of overpowering directors, a step toward greater creative freedom? Or is it perhaps the result of collegial envy because the final film is always considered the creation of the director? Have the transitions resulted in extraordinary films that justified the step from an aesthetic point of view? An examination of various biographies shows that the majority of directorial careers of former cameramen is largely unremarkable, and most have been treated unkindly by film historians; from the above list the only exception is Roeg, who developed a critically acclaimed, albeit controversial body of work, always staying true to the deep sense of visual magic acquired in his first career. In Soviet cinema, most transitions took place in the 1960s. Why was that period more open to cameramen turned directors than others?

A Companion to Russian Cinema, First Edition. Edited by Birgit Beumers.
© 2016 John Wiley & Sons, Inc. Published 2016 by John Wiley & Sons, Inc.

The present chapter – the title of which alludes to the animation short *Revenge of the Cameraman* [*Mest' kinematograficheskogo operatora*, 1912] by Władysław Starewicz, a filmmaker who also moved from cinematography to direction – discusses five accomplished Soviet cinematographers who moved to directing: Iurii Zheliabuzhskii, Eduard Tissé, Mikhail Kalatozov, Boris Volchek, and Sergei Urusevskii.[2] Each in his own way made an indubitable impact on Soviet cinema, and, in the case of Tissé and Kalatozov, on world cinema. This chapter seeks to determine the nature of that impact. It also discusses the foundation of long-lasting partnerships between cinematographers and directors, using the examples of Romm/Volchek and Kalatozov/Urusevskii, and asks what motivated the cameramen to break out of that partnership. It further discusses the relative flexibility of normative Soviet aesthetics, proposing a reevaluation of some of the lesser known films of cinematographers cum directors, whose aesthetic exceptionality warrants renewed scholarly attention. The following discussion of Soviet filmmakers whose careers began behind the camera is not a survey and by no means exhaustive; rather, the selected cases are intended as a typology of cameramen/directors, highlighting a variety of career paths, where the switch from one function to the other allows for a deeper understanding of the aesthetics of Soviet cinema. This is because the differences between individual cases are rooted in the artists' psychological and aesthetic dispositions as well as in the changing function of the cinematographer and the director in the evolution of Soviet cinema.

The Versatile Professional: Iurii Zheliabuzhskii

In the early days of silent cinema, the camera was treated strictly as a technical device, subjugated to screenplay and acting. The Soviet avant-garde of the 1920s made a point of changing that hierarchy, placing supreme value on angle, composition, lighting, and montage. The cinematographer was elevated to the role of second-in-command and became the director's supreme partner, whose skills proved decisive for the artistic quality of the final outcome. The 1930s saw yet another shift in emphasis back to acting, first and foremost, since it dominated audiences' perception of sound film. That shift was regarded by many as a regression from the high artistry of the camera-dominated classical silent film.

The early silent period, in which the cinematographer's role was predominantly technical, shaped the professional identity of Iurii Zheliabuzhskii, one of the first cameramen who risked the switch to direction while often simultaneously serving as cinematographer on the same film. Zheliabuzhskii's example is especially noteworthy since he was one of the few to master the transition from Russian bourgeois to Soviet communist cinema comparatively smoothly. Born in Moscow to a family of leftist intellectuals, Zheliabuzhskii began in 1916 to work as a screenwriter and cameraman, joining the company Rus' in 1917. His debut as director was the mystical drama *The Virgin Hills* [*Dev'i gory*, 1919], co-directed with Aleksandr Sanin, with whom Zheliabuzhskii also created the famous Tolstoi adaptation *Polikushka* (1919–1923), his most lasting contribution to cinema. Zheliabuzhskii[3] learned all technical aspects of filmmaking from scratch, subsequently combining screenwriting, cinematography, and direction and effortlessly meandering between genres, from literary adaptation (*The Collegiate Registrar* [*Kollezhskii registrator*], 1925) to historical drama (*Petr and Aleksei*, 1919), from newsreel to fairy-tale (*Morozko*, 1924), and from comedy (*The Cigarette Girl of Mosselprom* [*Papirosnitsa ot Mossel'proma*], 1924) to animation. As Philip Cavendish wrote, "Zheliabuzhskii never relinquished his training as a cameraman, and his technical expertise was widely recognized within the industry" (Cavendish 2007, 69). In addition, Zheliabuzhskii was a valued pedagogue, one of the founders of the State Film Institute (GTK/GIK, later VGIK) in 1919, and a talented administrator who protected the school during the hardships of World War II. But he never gained the reputation of a great artist, neither as cameraman, nor as director.

One of the paradoxes of Zheliabuzhskii's biography is the fact that, although a lifelong Bolshevik, he was not considered part of the Soviet avant-garde. Worse yet, as a result of his indifference toward radical aesthetic innovation he was often dismissed as part of the "old school" of Russian cinema, an attitude that was at least partially justified due to his aesthetic moderation and common sense approach to the role of cinema in society.[4] Zheliabuzhskii's cinematography was always technically reliable and sometimes inventive, but rarely artistically daring, and never an aim in itself. The same can be said about his direction. Zheliabuzhskii's primary goal was to captivate and entertain the audience. But the aesthetics of his films remained conventional and the political dimension was naïve at best. Thus, while undoubtedly one of Soviet cinema's founding fathers, Zheliabuzhskii was not on the long list of honored filmmakers during the state celebrations of Soviet cinema in 1935.

One of the surviving silent pictures in which Zheliabuzhskii acted both as cameraman and director is *Polikushka*. It caused a sensation at the time of its release in Western Europe in 1923, primarily due to its cast that was recruited from the Moscow Arts Theater, with which Zheliabuzhskii was closely associated. At the visual level, Zheliabuzhskii uses predominantly medium close shots to capture the interior of a typical Russian peasant hut, achieving a high degree of verisimilitude. This was the first time that the everyday life of Russian peasants was visualized with such claustrophobic authenticity. Still, its realism notwithstanding, the depiction of class relations could not have pleased the young Soviet iconoclasts who regarded the film as retrograde: the peasant Polikushka appears as a pious fatalist while his landowner, far from being the required stock exploiter and sadist, is genuinely concerned about him. Loyal to Tolstoi's patriarchal worldview, *Polikushka*'s theme is not class struggle but the mentality of the Russian peasantry – their humility, awkwardness, and piety, on the one hand, and debauchery and hard drinking on the other. As director of photography, Zheliabuzhskii demonstrates his inventiveness by introducing a subjective visual element: in the moment before his suicide, Polikushka is shown out of focus, as if to visualize his despair and loss of rational control. This method was later adopted by avant-garde filmmakers but never attributed to the underappreciated film pioneer (Sobolev 1963, 73).

Zheliabuzhskii continued his career into the beginning of the sound era, but his output became increasingly patchy. He often switched studios and, despite obvious accomplishments, never found adequate official appreciation. In the late 1940s, he delivered some remarkable documentaries about nineteenth-century Russian painters, where the usage of color was innovative, proving once again his technical skill and fine taste. As always, Zheliabuzhskii's was inventive but not radical in his approach. In his case the combination of cinematographer and director was simply registered as a vocational choice, a "Jack of all trades" phenomenon, not the display of a unique combination of gifts.

Too Little, Too Late: Eduard Tissé

For great Soviet directors such as Sergei Eisenstein, Vsevolod Pudovkin, Mikhail Romm, and Mark Donskoi finding a kindred spirit in a cinematographer who would help them develop the visual dimension of their films and maintain it over long periods, or even throughout their careers, was an essential part of their artistic self-definition.[5] Whenever possible these filmmakers tried to cultivate and continue their partnership with the one cameraman who understood them best. Whenever they were forced to work with others, the visual element of their films changed considerably, and often these works are regarded their weakest.

Eduard Tissé, arguably the best-remembered cinematographer of Soviet cinema due to his cooperation with Sergei Eisenstein, made two directorial efforts, one early in his career, the other at the end. In 1929, during a stay in Switzerland,[6] Tissé got the chance to direct *Misery and Fortune of Women* (aka *Women's Plight – Women's Happiness*; German title *Frauennot – Frauenglück*), a semi-documentary, semi-fictitious picture about one of the most tabooed issues of its time – abortion. Tissé approached the risqué project with the libertarian attitude that was characteristic of the early Soviet era, a time when virtually all restrictions regarding sexuality and marriage were lifted. The Swiss producer, Lazar Wechsler, provided him with documentary footage that local cinematographer Emil Berna had shot earlier that year at the gynecological clinic of Zurich University. With input from Eisenstein and Aleksandrov, Tissé directed a number of fictitious episodes that were then blended with the pre-made documentary material. In the resulting film, Eisenstein's influence, especially on montage, is hard to overlook: shots are polemically juxtaposed to generate a sense of outrage; politically explicit intertitles channel viewers' emotions in the needed direction; sharply contoured metonymies contrast the lifestyles of rich and poor women, thus explaining their different attitudes toward abortion, and so on.

But the film also features a number of elements that were new and can be attributed to Tissé as a director in his own right. Thus, the atmosphere of a modern Western city with endless lines of cars is impressively captured – the city appears as a blind monstrosity, oblivious to the needs of women, one of whom is about to give birth to her fifth child while she cannot afford to feed her family. The interior scenes are characterized by an attention to psychological subtleties that is rarely found in Eisenstein. In the non-fictional introduction, the film bases its arguments on statistical data prior to their visualization, following a strict cause-effect line. Clearly, Tissé the director knew how to effectively present a sociopolitical argument. *Misery and Fortune of Women* made a splash in Switzerland and abroad, but was prohibited in many countries. Tissé's surefooted direction leaves little doubt of this great cameraman's ability to helm a film on his own, yet it took almost 30 years before he got another chance.[7]

After Eisenstein's passing, Tissé focused mainly on his pedagogical work at VGIK, while also serving as director of photography on a number of prestigious pictures, whose content may be dubious from today's point of view, but whose cinematographic quality is superb.[8] Then, profound changes in the Soviet film industry got him another opportunity to direct. During the mid-1950s, when the Soviet government sharply increased the number of feature films and a dramatic shortage of directors led to dozens of recent graduates' debuts, Tissé – by that time a universally recognized master – was appointed chief cameraman and co-director with Zakhar Agranenko on *The Immortal Garrison* [*Bessmertnyi garnizon*, 1956], a film about the 1941 defense of the Brest fortress. It received little attention abroad but was important for Soviet society as one of the first efforts to revise the Stalinist version of the Great Patriotic War.

Based on a screenplay by Konstantin Simonov, *The Immortal Garrison* tells the story of a border unit that, against all odds, held out for a month after Germany's blitzkrieg attack on the Soviet Union on June 22, 1941. In many respects, the film is typical of the Thaw's approach to World War II: Stalin's name is not mentioned once, the Soviet people face the Nazis as one egalitarian family, and the ultimate victory is solely the result of rank-and-file self-sacrifice. Simonov's plot is at times unrealistic, reflecting underlying ideological compromises, but the film stands out stylistically, bearing the mark of classic Tissé: action sequences are split into minuscule shots, establishing a logical cause-and-effect relationship; in battle scenes, the frequency of cuts is noticeably higher than in the typical sound picture of that period, creating a sense of dramatic urgency not unlike that in silent pictures. During dialogue scenes, time and time again, Tissé presents series of static, often low-angle portrait shots lit in a monumental manner that resemble sculptures and elicit the viewers' admiration for the heroes of Brest. These series of sharply contoured close shots yield an effect of individualization vis-à-vis the usual composite masses of soldiers and officers, salvaging them from the facelessness of newsreels. These shots, in combination with similarly static group compositions of soldiers and officers conferring in the basement, as well as long tracking shots of the fortress's ruins – awe-inspiring petrified witnesses to the tragic events – generate pathos akin to that in the silent pictures made under Eisenstein's direction. Still, *The Immortal Garrison*'s overall artistic caliber falls short of those predecessors, primarily due to an indecisive historical approach.

The film's implied rehabilitation of Soviet Prisoners of War is rendered in a manner not entirely truthful – after all, in reality tens of thousands of these prisoners were treated as traitors and sent to the gulag after surviving the ordeal as POWs in Nazi Germany. Here, Tissé's camera serves as a conceptual corrective. Given the difficulty of dealing with these issues verbally at the time, the cinematography provides implicit visual arguments for their moral rehabilitation whenever the explicit discourse remains half-hearted. As is often the case in Soviet cinema, the film's true daring can only be understood in the context of its time: to depict Soviet confusion, chaos, and despair in the face of a determined aggressor at the beginning of the war was directly opposed to the triumphal war cinema of the late 1940s. But that cautious revisionism is one of subject-matter, not of tone, which remains uncompromisingly pathos-filled, with the sole difference that *The Immortal Garrison* shifts the pathos from the previously hailed central figure of Stalin toward rank-and-file personnel. It is this shift, sensitively reflected by Tissé's direction, that justifies the film's return to the visual pathos of classical silent cinema that, too, was profoundly egalitarian. While *The Immortal Garrison* was not a cinematic breakthrough, it demonstrated the vitality and legitimacy of camera techniques of the silent avant-garde in a new context. Its monumental approach is doubtless worthy of the subject.

The Immortal Garrison became Tissé's last work. One might speculate what exactly his individual contribution to the project in relation to his young co-director was[9] and how he would have continued his directorial career if given an opportunity. On the one hand, for both of Tissé's films, the decision to direct seems to have been the result of happenstance, not long-term strategy; moreover, while sharing social pathos, both films are stylistically sufficiently different. On the other hand, the fact that a great cameraman risked the role of co-director at that late a stage in his life, following a hiatus of almost three decades after his directorial debut, is significant in itself. The film's subject-matter legitimized a heightened pathos that allowed for a return to some elements of classical silent cinema – it was precisely in this respect that Tissé's responsibility both for camera and direction proved to be an ideal combination.

Passion and Restraint: Mikhail Kalatozov

Almost exactly at the time when Tissé made his directorial debut in Switzerland, Mikhail Kalatozov embarked on direction in Georgia, yet unlike Tissé he never went back to working as a director of photography. A high-school dropout, car mechanic, and film projectionist, Kalatozov began his career in the budding Georgian film industry in 1923 in a variety of jobs. At Tbilisi film studio, he shot newsreels and was behind the camera in Lev Kuleshov's unfinished project *Locomotive B 1000* [*Parovoz B 1000*, 1926]. In feature film, Kalatozov made his debut as cinematographer on Nikoloz Shengelaia's *Giulli* (1927).

Giulli, a feature-length drama about a young Muslim woman who loves a Christian, but is sold to an old wealthy man who eventually kills her, contains ample proof of Kalatozov's professional prowess – nothing in it feels like a beginner's work. However, on the visual level, the film rarely goes beyond mainstream conventions. Surely, the many beautifully composed extreme long shots conveying the majestic harmony of the Georgian countryside and its bucolic, peaceful nature establish a noticeable contrast to the lawlessness and disarray of human relations. No less important are the close shots, in particular of the legendary Nato Vachnadze in the title role, capturing subtle psychological changes. But nothing in *Giulli* predicts the eruption of visual energy that became Kalatozov's trademark. It was the encounter with the Russian avant-garde and its radically new approach to camera and montage that profoundly reshaped Kalatozov's style. In 1928, he made his directorial debut with *Their Kingdom* [*Mati samep/Ikh tsarstvo*], a compilation documentary depicting the historical development of Georgia between 1918 and 1928, polemically exposing the machinations of the Georgian Menshevik Party. The experience of working entirely with pre-made footage gave Kalatozov a clearer sense of the enormous potentials of montage. His next film as cameraman and director, *Salt for Svanetia* [*Jim Shvante/Sol' Svanetii*, 1930], raised eyebrows.

Made from footage of two unfinished older projects,[10] it contained all the qualities for which his greatest films in the late 1950s and 1960s became famous: a relatively simple theme – the catastrophic lack of salt in the secluded mountains inhabited by the tribe of Svans – is treated in a visually sophisticated manner that engages and overwhelms the viewer by its sheer passion. Kalatozov's main instrument for expressing passion was the camera that dominates all other elements of the film. It is the camera work that endows this narrative documentary about a small backward people's liberation from religious and economic oppression with unbridled pathos and visual inventiveness that transforms propaganda into art. Although the film was accused of "formalism," it was eventually recognized as a groundbreaking masterpiece and has since achieved the status of a classic. Kalatozov's being both cinematographer and director was a condition for this success.

Kalatozov was only able to make such a unique picture using a brief window of opportunity in the late 1920s. Taking inspiration from the Russian-Soviet avant-garde (both Sergei Tret'iakov and Viktor Shklovskii were directly involved as authors, while the influence of Aleksandr Rodchenko's photography is clearly recognizable in the imagery), Kalatozov was welcomed with open arms by the leftist intelligentsia that held influential positions in Soviet culture. Thus, *Salt for Svanetia*'s dynamic camera movement, extreme angles, and expressively rhythmic montage were also a reflection of the freedom to experiment that was still granted

(a)

(b)

Figure 16.1a and 16.1b Fear in *Giulli*, directed by Lev Push and Nikoloz Shengelaia, DoP Mikhail Kalatozov, 1927.

during that period. Unfortunately, Kalatozov's directorial career had just begun when this freedom was about to wane. The early 1930s marked a solidification of the cultural system, with the center of control in Moscow and the degree of individual artistic freedom rapidly shrinking. Kalatozov experienced these changes first-hand, when his next film as director, the 50-minute *A Nail in the Boot* (*Gvozd' v sapoge*, aka *The Country Is in Danger* [*Strana v opasnosti*], 1932) which criticized inefficiency in the Red Army, was banned as too controversial. The main charge against it was not thematic but aesthetic – it was "formalism," a charge that became *de rigueur* against all avant-garde artists during the aesthetically restrictive 1930s. The fiasco almost ended Kalatozov's career; he left Georgia for Russia where he eventually became an accomplished director and administrator, representing the Soviet film industry in Hollywood in World War II and rising to the position of Deputy Minister of Cinema in the late 1940s. As for Kalatozov's directorial output from the late 1930s to the mid-1950s, it was professionally solid throughout but not aesthetically exceptional; the breathtaking early years when his direction and camerawork formed a seamless and highly original unity seemed to have been forgotten both by critics and the artist himself.

Then, *The Cranes are Flying* [*Letiat zhuravli*, 1957] demonstrated in an astonishing way that this director was able to rejuvenate himself as an artist and return to his avant-garde origins. The romantic story of loyalty and tragic loss during the Great Patriotic War revealed an uncompromising humanity that spoke to millions of viewers worldwide. For western connoisseurs, however, the film's expressive cinematography was the most unexpected element, a true shock. After years of stolid Stalinist officialdom, suddenly the hand-held camera was given the status of an active participant in the unfolding story, acquiring a near-independent subjectivity, incessantly interacting with the main characters yet seemingly following a plotline of its own, sometimes transcending the realistic dimension and reaching a metaphysical level. Immediately, the exceptional cinematography was attributed to Kalatozov's cameraman, Sergei Urusevskii. Yet Urusevskii's previous films – including *The Country Teacher* [*Sel'skaia uchitel'nitsa*, 1947] for Mark Donskoi and *The Forty-First* [*Sorok pervyi*, 1956] for Grigorii Chukhrai – while beautifully executed, were far from the exaltation of *The Cranes Are Flying*. Kalatozov's film must be seen as a rare case when all elements fell in place: A director, himself a former cameraman, who was willing to take the risk and return to his avant-garde beginnings; a cinematographer who enthusiastically responded to this challenge; and a fundamental relaxation in Soviet cultural policies that allowed for a degree of formal experimentation not seen for 30 years. It is fair to say that, through Urusevskii, Kalatozov had the opportunity to realize his vision to the same degree as 30 years earlier with *Salt for Svanetia*.

The director/cinematographer team used the sudden international fame to go even further with their next projects. Both *The Unsent Letter* [*Neotpravlennoe pis'mo*, 1960], an existentialist parable about self-sacrifice for a higher cause, and *I Am Cuba* [*Ia – Kuba*, aka *Soy Cuba*, 1964], a Cold War ballad of sorts, took the camera's freedom of mobility to extremes. In the latter, the cinematic acrobatics literally go over the top, creating a formal brilliance that belies the verbal one-dimensionality. *The Unsent Letter* is arguably Kalatozov's most accomplished masterpiece in which all of his preferred themes are expressed in their purest form. Not only is political propaganda absent from the story of a geological expedition – the literal cleansing of the central characters by fire and ice conveys a metaphysical respect for nature, free of any attached optimism from which even *Cranes* had suffered. However, it was the Communist litany *I Am Cuba* that received an unexpected endorsement from Francis Ford Coppola and Martin Scorsese in the early 1990s, and since acquired cult status among Western cinema buffs. Both films' flamboyant, fluid black-and-white cinematography is undoubtedly spectacular but proved insufficient to attract domestic audiences at the time. Perhaps unintentionally, Kalatozov and Urusevskii had managed to create art-house pictures in a society that never accepted such an elitist notion. In the 1930s, Kalatozov surely would have been taken to task for his "formalism," but in the 1960s, his national and international status served as protection.

From the point of view of cinematographic sophistication and narrative pathos, *I Am Cuba* was hard to surpass within the framework of Kalatozov and Urusevskii's artistic partnership. Therefore, it did not come as a surprise that the cameraman decided to move into direction himself, while the director embarked on his next film, *The Red Tent* [*Krasnaia palatka*, aka *La Tenda Rossa*, 1969], with a different

Figure 16.2 Adversity in *Giulli*, directed by Lev Push and Nikoloz Shengelaia, DoP Mikhail Kalatozov, 1927.

Figure 16.3 Adversity in *The Unsent Letter*, directed by Mikhail Kalatozov, DoP Sergei Urusevskii, 1959.

cinematographer. This Soviet-Italian coproduction about the 1928 Nobile expedition revisits several of Kalatozov's favorite themes, but does so without the previous visual finesse or passion. How would Urusevskii have shot it? Would he have acquiesced to the pressures of narrative conventions, enforced by a Western producer? Clearly, he had reached the ceiling of what was artistically doable in Soviet cinema even with a likeminded experimenter such as Kalatozov – at 60, Urusevskii was eager to finally test his own artistic boundaries. Kalatozov had used the unique opportunity of meeting a likeminded camera artist during a liberal period of Soviet history to realize his artistic potential to a maximum, after it had been dormant for three decades. Sadly, his swan song *sans* Urusevskii, although a hit with Soviet audiences, was a far cry from the cinematographic audacity of their joint pictures. Yet, there can be no doubt that the partnership of the former cinematographer and the soon-to-be director helped to widen the aesthetic boundaries of Soviet cinema in the 1960s and beyond.

The Betrayed Loyalist: Boris Volchek

Kalatozov's and Urusevskii's breakup was regrettable but not a personal drama – both artists had gained the maximum from their collaboration. The breakup of cinematographer Boris Volchek and director Mikhail Romm took place under much more dramatic circumstances. While it ultimately led to Volchek's successful directorial career, his status in film history, just like that of Tissé,[11] is still almost exclusively defined by his work for Romm.[12]

Figure 16.4 Harmony in *Giulli*, directed by Lev Push and Nikoloz Shengelaia, DoP Mikhail Kalatozov, 1927.

Figure 16.5 Harmony in *The Letter Never Sent*, directed by Mikhail Kalatozov, DoP Sergei Urusevskii, 1959.

Romm and Volchek formed a partnership on the Maupassant adaptation *Boule de Suif* [*Pyshka*, 1934], the success of which was in no small part due to the cameraman's ability to creatively respond to the director's ideas. Like many cameramen who later took the director's helm, Volchek learned important skills from his close interaction with an outstanding director at all stages of the production, from observing his work with the cast to his exceptional managerial talent.[13] Likewise, for Romm, Volchek proved an ideal choice as cinematographer because of his adaptability and their shared, unconditional pro-Soviet worldview.[14] Within its framework, cinema's supreme mission in a society building communism was to actively and consistently engage with this society, addressing the most burning sociopolitical issues and combining stringent didacticism with entertaining stories. For Romm and Volchek, there could be no contradiction between individual artistic strivings and societal needs; a split into art-house and mainstream cinema was unthinkable. Even those of Romm's films that display a more personal, melancholic touch, such as The Dream [Mechta, 1941], were intended for mass audiences, their encoded political and moral messages being in exact congruence with the general line of the Communist Party and Stalin personally. It is telling that in the 1960s, when Volchek started his own directorial career, his credo as filmmaker was no different – its social determinacy and thematic choices were identical with those of Romm, ranging from the heroicized history of the Soviet secret service to the Great Patriotic War and contemporary moral problems.

Volchek's stylistic evolution as cinematographer betrays an exceptional ability to adapt cinematic means to the specific needs of each new project. At the same time, Romm gave Volchek sufficient room for technical experimentation so as to enhance the effects that he was after, such as anti-bourgeois satire in *Boule de Suif* or documentary authenticity in *Lenin in October* [Lenin v oktiabre, 1937] and *Lenin in 1918* [Lenin v 1918 godu, 1937]. The latter two catapulted Romm to the Olympus of Soviet cinema, also because Volchek was able to achieve a sense of objectivity and to generate maximum verisimilitude so that the hagiographic portrayal of Lenin and Stalin appeared historically truthful. Indeed, hagiography masking as historic objectivity was the underlying principle that turned Romm's films into mainstays of Soviet cinema for the next half century and secured his status as a Soviet classic.

Volchek's ambition to achieve three-dimensional effects on screen was accomplished by his trademark sophisticated lighting schemes and a deliberate manipulation of foreground and background. In Romm's Cold War films of the late Stalin period – *The Russian Question* [Russkii vopros, 1948] and *Secret Mission* [Sekretnaia missiia, 1950] – the sharpness of focus supports the films' analytical claim, covering up their inherent aggressive propaganda. While the primary effects were caused by the performances, the polemical dialogues, and extremely one-sided political characterizations, Volchek's camera was tasked with creating the desired visual framework of objectivity and documentary authenticity. On a subconscious level, the cinematography was intended to shape the viewer's political and emotional attitude toward characters and their statements. The carefully designed shot compositions situated the performers within a clearly defined, politically charged space, producing an effect of determinacy. Characters are shaped by their surroundings, that is, by objective reality, whether they themselves are aware of it or not. This profoundly Marxist approach to human behavior supplied Romm's and Volchek's films of the late Stalin period with a pseudo-analytical effectiveness that fully supports their political agenda.

The duo's trademark analytical-political pamphlet style in *Murder on Dante Street* [*Ubiistvo na ulitse Dante*, 1956] once again resulted in a hit. However, this time Romm was uneasy about the success. From debates with his VGIK students he realized that this was not the cinema needed for the new grass-root democratization period that the Thaw was widely hoped to be. Romm's and Volchek's style of the 1940s and early 1950s had become an anachronism. After publicly and at times sarcastically denouncing his own film – including the work of his cinematographer[15] – Romm's breakup with Volchek was inevitable. For Volchek, the separation was a catastrophe. Romm, however, managed to reinvent himself: in the following six years, he undertook a revision of his artistic and political principles. It is telling that the split between director and cinematographer happened at a time of systemic crisis: Romm, who had contributed to Soviet cinema of the 1930s–1950s a lucid, politically passionate yet rationally driven body of work, had to redefine himself in the turbulence of post-Stalinism. As one of Stalin's favorite and most reliable filmmakers, he was forced to formulate a new socio-cultural position resulting in aesthetic shifts. Consequently, for his next project, the scientist drama *Nine Days of a Year* [*Deviat' dnei odnogo goda*, 1963], Romm chose a different cameraman.

Boris Volchek, deeply hurt by the separation from Romm,[16] likewise reexamined his career, a process that eventually took him into the director's chair. On the three completed pictures that he shot in the course of the following ten years, Volchek chose to work both as director and as chief cameraman – a rare combination, bringing back a whiff of Zheliabuzhskii's versatility. His first film, the potboiler *Shot in the Fog* [*Vystrel v tumane*, aka *Sotrudnik ChK*, 1964], was an effective Civil War drama that became a hit, as did his last, the grand-scale *Commander of the Happy Pike* [*Kommandir schastlivoi shchuki*, 1973] about a submarine in the Great Patriotic War. Of Volchek's directorial efforts, the most artistically interesting, particularly from the viewpoint of combined responsibilities as cameraman and director, is *Accused of Murder* [*Obviniaiutsia v ubiistve*, 1969].

The film's introductory shots are panoramic city vistas, conveying an idyllic image of modern urbanity with shining white apartment blocks, monotonous but orderly and friendly; the accompanying relaxed score underlines the harmonious impression. Suddenly the opening sequence of modern socialist life comes to a halt – the same city images are now shown through a grid, as if from within a cage, while the music turns dark and ominous. A militia truck is taking four juvenile delinquents to the courthouse. The viewer realizes: what he just saw was the world through the eyes of the accused. Next, four freeze frames introduce the suspects, while a stern voice announces their identity and the crime they are accused of. This introductory sequence sets the tone for the film as a whole: the smooth façade of a functioning society is contrasted against four isolated individuals who are threatening the social order. Another series of close-ups introduces the officers of the court as well as the people in the courtroom. The crime is announced in a dry, unspectacular tone: the four defendants killed a young man. Now, without transition or explanation, Volchek cuts to the recent past: the viewer is about to witness the crime.

Aleksandr, a decently dressed and polite young man, walks with his girlfriend near a kindergarten. Four hooligans, obviously under the influence, verbally harass him, provoking a fistfight. Within a second, the previously neutral camera style changes to frenzied motions, following and imitating the body language of the enraged youngsters. One of the aggressors hits the girl, who falls to the ground; another one attacks Aleksandr with a bottle – with deadly force. The visual shock value of the scene is enhanced by shots of neighbors who observe the crime but hastily close their blinds and hide in their apartments. Back in the present, the court tries to establish which defendant played exactly what role in the crime. Since the death penalty for murder was still mandatory in the Soviet Union, the question of which of the four men dealt the deadly blow is vital – literally. Each defendant describes what he did on that fateful day, claiming to have slid into violence by mere chance and accusing the victim of having himself caused the clash. As if in response to these claims, the camera shows what really happened prior to the fight: the four drank together, danced in the streets, and mocked bystanders – typical everyday hooliganism, all too often ignored by citizens.

The contradiction between the humanity of the accused and the violent crime they committed becomes ever harder to explain. Again, a chain of close-ups shows the reactions of the audience. When the sentence is finally announced, the film breaks off after just one word – "Imenem…" [In the name of…]. Indeed, the viewer never learns what exactly the final sentence handed down to the four criminals is. The visual circle closes with the harmonious panoramic shots of happy living quarters in a modern socialist city.

Accused of Murder is a profoundly analytical film, its underlying credo one of social enlightenment. The narrative structure, defined by elaborate flashbacks, reveals the truth to the viewer whenever testimonies in the courtroom fail to do so. Not only does Volchek's camera support the analytical approach – it acts as its main agent. The entire range of shot types – from extreme long in the city panoramas to close-ups of officers of the court, observers, witnesses, and the defendants – helps viewers form their opinion, especially when the verbal plane is too treacherous and ambiguous to identify the factual and moral truth. This truth-seeking function of the camera and the pathos that derives from it at times resemble Tissé's direction in *The Immortal Garrison*, although Volchek's pathos is generally toned down. Regarding its connections with Romm's films, Volchek the director/cameraman makes a point of singling out the perpetrators, separating them from the overall societal space. He does not apply Romm's method of demonstrating social determinacy used to denounce the enemy: since crime by definition could never be the product of Soviet society, its carriers had to be singled out – indeed, literally cut off from their environment through editing – as alien elements that disturb an inherently harmonious picture and must be removed from it. While the criminals are shown as hopeless deviants, the most polemical approach is that toward the indifferent bystanders. Here, the camera acts as an exploring agent, first showing the façades and then looking behind them; in other words, Volchek uses the camera as a social and psychological investigative tool, but also as a marker for positive and negative values, not unlike its function in his films with Romm.

On the visual plane, the main goal is to expose the causality of actions, demonstrating to the viewer a greater evidentiary prowess than the verbal assessment, since the latter is prone to moral relativism.[17] In a number of scenes, the camera quickly pans back and forth between the debating characters, engaging the viewer in the pro and contra argumentation. However, while Volchek's social stance is uncompromising and straightforward, the purported search for truth is not entirely objective: the defendants never have a real chance. Two of the witnesses explicitly associate them with Nazis, that is, enemies and intruders. As a result, open-mindedness and forgiveness appear as precarious weaknesses of judgment that must be resisted and overcome. The film locates such ambiguity in wavering eyewitnesses, cowardly bystanders, and the victim's father, who resigns without fighting for his son's reputation.

In delivering an uncompromising ideological message, Volchek the director and Volchek the cameraman act in functional unity. Thus, within the Soviet context, *Accused of Murder* can serve as a fine example of the redeeming potential that lies in the transition of a first-rate cinematographer to the director's chair: Volchek's approach to direction is inventive and dynamic while remaining utterly functional, using a broad range of cinematographic solutions without ever making camera art an aim in itself. This approach secured Volchek's films a firm position in Soviet mainstream, each of them garnering over 30 million viewers – a sure sign that he had a good sense of what Soviet audiences were looking for in a film. And yet, despite his remarkable popular success as director in the last decade of his life, Volchek's reputation in film history to this day is defined solely by his partnership with Romm, on the one hand, and his pedagogical skill and generosity, on the other.[18] His directorial career appears as an appendix at best, most likely because Volchek was unable or unwilling to develop a recognizable *individual* style, once again resembling the hapless Zheliabuzhskii. Volchek settled for solid professionalism and aesthetic functionalism, serving social-patriotic and civic [*grazhdanskie*] values that were dear to him throughout his career. His aesthetic ambition never went beyond mainstream standards.

If one were to identify a common element in all of Volchek's directorial output, it is the notion of self-sacrifice: in *Shot in the Fog*, Maria, the young secret agent, is killed when exposing a gang of "whites"; in *Accused of Murder*, Aleksandr is killed when he tries to protect his girlfriend from attacking hooligans; and in *Commander of the Happy Pike*, captain Strogov saves his crew by consciously sacrificing his own life. It might be worthwhile to reflect on the theme of self-sacrifice not just in relation to Soviet society and ideology, where it always played a fundamental role, but also in regards to the careers of cinematographers who give their all to serve the vision of a director who is regarded the sole "author" of a film. For this ethos of sacrificing one's personal authorial ambitions for the sake of another artist, Volchek is an excellent example. His self-liberation when becoming a director cum cinematographer was an act of professional self-respect and survival, first and foremost. Aesthetically Volchek did not transcend the framework set by his former master.

The Camera Purist: Sergei Urusevskii

Sergei Urusevskii[19] turned to direction in the late 1960s, at about the same age as Volchek. And like Volchek, he retained the responsibility for the camera work in his two films. His reputation as one of the most innovative and original Soviet cinematographers had emerged in the late 1940s; it solidified in the 1950s[20] and grew further – sometimes acquiring a controversial undertone – in the mid-1960s.[21] Conspicuously, Urusevskii's directorial work in the last years of his life added little to his fame which had been hugely advanced by his partnership with Kalatozov.[22] Their joint output won the most undivided recognition in *The Cranes are Flying*;[23] it was the most aesthetically balanced in *The Unsent Letter*, and the most spectacular in *I Am Cuba*. Yet, the high hopes that Urusevskii and many of his admirers had for his subsequent directorial work went largely unrealized.

Indeed, while Urusevskii's posthumous fame as an outstanding cinematographer has grown internationally since the 1990s, his two independently made pictures, *Run of the Pacer* [*Beg inokhodtsa*, 1969] and *Sing Your Song, Poet...* [*Poi pesniu, poet...*, 1972], did not benefit from this phenomenon, remaining unknown in the West and forgotten in Russia. However, when Urusevskii set out to make his directorial debut in the late 1960s, this event was eagerly expected by the Soviet film community, especially since the master-cinematographer had selected a literary source by a recent literary shooting star: Chingiz Aitmatov's novella *Farewell, Gulsary!* (Merkel' 1980: 118).

Urusevskii approached the text with utmost respect, trying to capture its letter and spirit. To him, Aitmatov's prose was poetry, whose adequate adaptation required innovative visual means, from the manipulation of color to extreme viewpoints and image distortions achieved by the usage of anamorphous lenses. Thus, when the old shepherd Tanabai talks to his ailing horse, Gulsary, not only is the sky kept in a cold dark blue – so is the entire frame. When a flashback shows Tanabai's first encounter with young, playful Gulsary, the shot scintillates as if seen through a rainbow. The switch from monochromatic to a rich color spectrum conveys a juxtaposition of old age to youth, from resigned suffering to euphoric happiness. It also alerts the viewer to the aesthetic dimension of the film; indeed,

Urusevskii's direction, putting the visual plane markedly above all others, makes the viewers conscious of the viewing act itself – always under the condition that they choose to accept this kind of cinema and engage with it.

It must be added, though, that in his first film as director, despite abundant visual experimentation, Urusevskii does not compromise on the realistic nature of the story or soften Aitmatov's criticism of power abuse and cruelty in the post-war years. What viewers experienced as frustrating is the unsteadiness of the narrative flow – the frequent slow-pace segments are not justified by the logic of the narrative but by the director's striving for maximum poetic effect in virtually every episode. As a result, the viewer's senses are constantly challenged in multiple ways, having to focus on psychological aspects (Tanabai's love for the widow Bibizhan, his marriage crisis), social issues (the tyranny of the new kolkhoz chairman), and ethnic traditions (Kyrgyz horse races), while still appreciating the haunting beauty of the imagery. Such viewing prevents viewers from a convenient immersion in the world of the film, requiring a different, self-aware kind of perception that is not part of mainstream conventions.

The critical response to *Run of the Pacer* was mixed. But it was Urusevskii's next – and last – film, a biopic of the poet Sergei Esenin that became a near-total critical failure. While its disastrous reception[24] can be understood in the context of Soviet mainstream film aesthetic of the 1970s which Urusevskii actively undermined, its uniqueness deserves an analytical reassessment by itself.

From the opening shots, *Sing Your Song, Poet...* is recognizable as a cinematographer's film: its dominating plane is visual, not verbal. The imagery is structured in the form of motif chains interacting with Kirill Molchanov's musical score and Esenin's verses. At the beginning, the film displays an epigraph, a quote from Sergei Esenin praising the sound of the word "Russia" [Rossiia] and its inherent poetic meaning. Immediately following the epigraph, images and music take over and keep their dominating role until the end, leaving no room for a clearly outlined plot, dialogues, or any sort of verbal discourse, let alone explanations. Almost the entire verbal plane consists of quotes from Esenin poems related to the chain of images on screen; the biographical facts behind these scenes have to be known in order to be understood. The conventions of the biographical genre are only served insofar as a roughly chronological order is maintained. Omitted are all allusions to Esenin's alcoholism, his womanizing and scandal-mongering, his marriage to American dancer Isadora Duncan, the ideological controversies surrounding his poetry and personal life in the early 1920s when he was attacked as a champion of patriarchy, and his suicide. Not only does Urusevskii keep the factual information to a minimum, he deliberately obscures it, explaining nothing and requiring the viewer to surrender to the hypnotic fluidity of dream-like images.

The opening sequence is dominated by bluish fields seemingly emanating a mystical energy; a lake is the setting of romantic encounters with Tania, "the prettiest girl in the village"; underwater shots motivate image distortions that continue even when the fields above water are featured; subsequent sequences are devoted to peasant work and rest that are described in a bucolic manner. These images of life in the Russian countryside convey an incredible tenderness: Urusevskii manipulates the color spectrum to achieve pastel-like softness, most importantly mild tones of yellow, green, and blue, forming a harmonious unity and embracing the white clothes of the young protagonists. World War I, to which Esenin's father was drafted, is depicted through montage sequences of multiple shots of about half a second, resembling Aleksandr Dovzhenko's *Arsenal* (1928) or Boris Barnet's *Outskirts* [*Okraina*, 1933]. Suddenly, westernized urbanity appears in stark contrast to the preceding rural idyll: in a salon, Esenin stands dressed like a dandy, accepting the blasé admiration of elegant upper-class ladies and gentlemen. The artificiality of this milieu is emphasized by countless projectors hanging from the ceiling, as if this were a television studio, and by the shining – and perhaps slippery – floor. Esenin is a proud outsider in this milieu and obviously will remain so forever. When the snobbish audience leaves the room, the poet is all by himself. The archetypal productivity of the rural world is represented by an old miller whom the poet visits repeatedly – he stands for the Russian people's silent might, their ability to perceive and understand reality without being able to express themselves. The arrangement of these episodes, together with their inner tension leave no doubt that for Urusevskii, Esenin is not the singer of bygone patriarchy but the expresser of eternal beauty that defines the very center of Russia's culture.

It is easy to dismiss *Sing Your Song, Poet...* as a failure from the point of view of genre conventions. Urusevskii's direction can certainly be judged as problematic because its innovative aesthetic means differ extremely from mainstream and are not communicated to an unprepared viewer – unlike Kalatozov's films, where the overall comprehensibility of the narrative was always secure. However, a less normative assessment allows for a more differentiated approach to Urusevskii's last film: problematic it may be, but a grandiose experiment it is nonetheless. In essence, the cinematographer/director attempted a new kind of filmmaking, one in which the narrative is carried exclusively by the visual plane and is merely supported by music, thus marginalizing all verbal elements, especially dialogues. *Sing Your Song, Poet...* denotes an inner resistance against a definition of cinematic meaning as primarily verbal. The underlying anti-textual approach made Urusevskii's two films difficult for general comprehension. While they may not have been intended as avant-garde or art-house pictures, they turned out that way due to the radical attitude of their creator. An appropriate analogue to this film would be a song, not a short story.

Sing Your Song, Poet... is best understood as an original continuation of Dovzhenko's early films, as well as a response to Paradjanov's more recent *Shadows of Forgotten Ancestors* [*Teni zabytykh predkov*, 1964]. As soon as Urusevskii acquired directorial sovereignty, he became a de facto avant-gardist. And like many in the avant-garde, he paid the price of being misunderstood during his lifetime. Of course, applying avant-garde aesthetics to a subject that is not commonly viewed as part of the avant-garde adds another irresolvable contradiction to *Sing Your*

Song, Poet... Had Urusevskii used similar innovative techniques in a film about Mayakovsky, Khlebnikov, or Mandel'shtam, perhaps at least the film connoisseur community would have embraced it. But Esenin's reputation has always precariously meandered between that of a multifaceted poetic innovator and a vulgar populist. Thus, Urusevskii was caught in the middle between mass audiences expecting a typical dramatic biopic about a beloved cult figure[25] and elites that would have preferred a subject more in line with their idols.

Sing Your Song, Poet... also demonstrates Urusevskii aim to "out-poeticize" those of his former directors – particularly Pudovkin and Donskoi – who saw the Russian countryside as a repository of poetic value.[26] Indeed, Urusevskii creates on screen the essential poetic Russian village, leaving aside almost all historical and psychological details. He does not juxtapose this idyll to the new communist order, though; his Esenin is not a reactionary but someone who greets the Soviet era enthusiastically. This interpretation assumes a fundamental harmony between the archetypal Russia and the new communist society, in which the latter is depicted as an organic product of the former. Esenin's embrace of communism dominates the final part of the film, a celebration of popular power, again in the spirit of the finale of Dovzhenko's *Earth* [*Zemlia*, 1930]. This fundamental agreement with the Soviet project saved Urusevskii's overall reputation: he became one of the increasing number of filmmakers consciously defining their identity outside the Soviet mainstream, but not a dissident. His striving for new visual solutions went far beyond anything that the other camera artists dared when they assumed the director's chair. Because of his radically new approach to direction, and unlike Zheliabuzhskii, Tissé, Volchek, and even Kalatozov, Sergei Urusevskii as director turned out to be an unapologetic individualist and a genuine auteur.

Conclusion

Based on the five cases discussed in this article, the hypothesis that transitions from cinematography to direction rarely yield outstanding results cannot be confirmed. However, it is obvious that such transitions encounter specific problems. Without doubt, the presented five Soviet cinematographers were all solid professionals who fulfilled the function of director of photography with skill and inventiveness and made major contributions to the advancement of Soviet film art. Their transition to direction was never intended as a complete switch from one profession to another, but as a synthesis of functions. These syntheses had in common that, to a certain degree, the cinematographers' visual perceptiveness carried over to their directorial methods and choices. In the case of Zheliabuzhskii and Volchek, the synthesis was primarily functional. In the case of Tissé, Kalatozov, and Urusevskii, it was primarily artistic.

Occupying the director's chair means a higher degree of control over process and product. Zheliabuzhskii and Tissé accepted the opportunity to gain such control whenever it occurred, whereas Volchek achieved it when his longtime partnership with Romm faltered; in his case, the term "revenge" from the article's title applies in the most literal sense – he demonstrated to his former master that he had sufficient prowess to helm large-scale projects on his own. Kalatozov returned to his avant-garde origins when the cultural situation in the Soviet Union permitted it and he had found a likeminded cameraman. Urusevskii used his international reputation as cinematographer acquired with Kalatozov to move into a camera-centered method of direction. Of the five discussed cases, Urusevskii comes the closest to the notion of auteur. In his two directorial efforts, he was the most radical in realizing his idiosyncratic vision.[27]

Thus, what can be considered a matter of professional versatility in the early days of cinema represented by Zheliabuzhskii, increasingly became an existential matter of artistic self-expression. Tissé's first direction was more happenstance than planning, although his return to the pathos of his silent pictures in his second film indicates deep-seated artistic ambitions. With exceptional restraint, Kalatozov put his own aesthetic ambitions on hold when the sociopolitical situation in the Soviet Union became inhospitable to avant-garde experimentation but realized them in partnership with Urusevskii as soon as the political situation in the Soviet Union allowed him to. Yet, in none of these five cases was the search for a fuller artistic self-realization politically motivated; all listed cameramen/directors were devoted Communists. The motivation was a combination of professional and aesthetic aspects. Interestingly, the visual sensitivities of several cinematographers were formed by fine art, although only Urusevskii is widely known as an accomplished painter.

The transition of outstanding cinematographers to the director's chair in the 1960s was associated with a redefinition of artistic autonomy, a rediscovery of the poetic, a trend toward critical social analysis,[28] as well as a general move from collectivist to individualist self-realization. When settling for solid professionalism, as in the cases of Zheliabuzhskii and Boris Volchek, the transition proved to be outwardly successful and acceptable to the mainstream. Indeed, Zheliabuzhskii's output in the 1920s and Volchek's films of the 1960s demonstrate that the merger of director and cinematographer can result in a genuine synthesis yielding a high degree of narrative functionality, especially when the aesthetic goals are clearly defined and moderate. Contrary to Zheliabuzhskii's and Volchek's aesthetic moderation, Urusevskii's transition from cinematography to direction resulted in a different synthesis, characterized by aesthetic maximalism that proved to be much harder to accept for critics and audiences. Urusevskii's intention was to redefine the hierarchical relationship between the verbal and the visual by putting exclusive emphasis on the latter. Thus, when the switch to the new role of director implied a redefinition of direction as such, in other words, when the transition was accompanied by an uncompromising approach toward authorial freedom as in the case of Urusevskii, the consequences for the artist could be traumatic and even tragic.[29]

Notes

1. Thomson is one of the most skeptical critics in regards to cameramen who moved to direction (see, for example, 2002, 134).
2. In Ukraine, cameraman Iurii Il'enko's encounter with director Sergei Paradjanov in the early 1960s led to an aesthetic revolution in *Shadows of Forgotten Ancestors* (1964). None of Paradjanov's later films featured a similar camera mobility. Il'enko, too, became a director with a peculiar career, displaying uncompromising aesthetic and political principles and a sense of national distinctiveness that came to the fore in the post-Soviet period.
3. For an account of Zheliabuzhskii's career in the context of Russian and Soviet film history, see Sobolev (1963). An excellent discussion of Zheliabuzhskii's cinematographic techniques can be found in Cavendish (2007, esp. pp. 68–86).
4. For an even-handed discussion of Zheliabuzhskii's position vis-à-vis avant-garde aesthetics see Sobolev (1963, 68–69).
5. A noteworthy example is that of Andrei Tarkovskii. "His" cameraman, Vadim Iusov, helped define Tarkovskii's style from *Ivan's Childhood* [*Ivanovo detstvo*, 1962] to *Solaris* (1972). Their break made a noticeable impact on the visual plane of Tarkovskii's following pictures that were entrusted to other cinematographers, including Sven Nykvist in *Sacrifice* [*Offret*, 1986]. Ironically, Nykvist is also one of the great cinematographers who began directing late in their career.
6. Eisenstein, Tissé, and Aleksandrov were invited to the first congress of avant-garde filmmakers in the castle La Sarraz near Lausanne from 3–7 September, 1929.
7. In May 2004, I was given the opportunity to watch one of the extant versions, released by Wechsler's Praesens Film, at the Seminar für Filmwissenschaft of Zürich University.
8. Of particular interest is the underrated biopic *The Composer Glinka* [*Kompozitor Glinka*, 1952] by Grigorii Aleksandrov, shot in color.
9. Zakhar Agranenko made his directorial debut with *The Immortal Garrison*; he is also remembered for the impressive *Leningrad Symphony* [*Leningradskaia simfoniia*, 1957].
10. One was the feature film *The Blind Woman* [*Slepaia*, 1930] from a screenplay by Sergei Tret'iakov; it has not survived.
11. Boris Volchek won three Stalin Prizes: in 1946 for *Human Being #217*; in 1948 for *The Russian Question*, and in 1951 for *Secret Mission*. *Accused of Murder* was awarded a State Prize of the USSR in 1971.
12. See the excellent article by Marina Goldovskaia (1978). Goldovskaia characterizes Volchek as Romm's "friend and a likeminded person [edinomyshlennik]" (1978, 124) but leaves out the story of their break-up.
13. Romm was highly respected for his efficiency in organizing the production of his films.
14. Volchek joined the Communist Party in 1926, Romm in 1939.
15. The real story behind the end of Romm's and Volchek's partnership may be both private and professional: Romm's wife, renowned actress Elena Kuz'mina, was supposed to play the female lead in *Murder on Dante Street* when Ivan Pyr'ev, then director of Mosfilm studio, unexpectedly refused to approve her casting due to her age. Strangely, not Pyr'ev but Volchek was blamed for that decision "since he did not film Kuz'mina favorably during test shots" (see Egorov 2009).

16 According to a recent documentary about Volchek, the split was a shock and a "creative and personal drama" for the cinematographer (Egorov 2009).

17 *Accused of Murder* features a deeper, quasi-philosophical discourse on morality that is articulated in the film's dialogues.

18 The list of his accomplished students includes Vadim Iusov, Evgenii Andrikanis, Jonas Gricius, German Lavrov, Levan Paatashvili, Margarita Pilikhina, and Georgii Rerberg, all of whom developed a distinct style. On Volchek's pedagogy, see Medynskii (1986: 170–184).

19 Urusevskii graduated from the Moscow Institute of Fine Art; his teacher, Vladimir Favorskii, recommended him to Vsevolod Pudovkin and cameraman Anatolii Golovnia as an assistant on *Victory* [*Pobeda*, 1938]. He won Stalin Prizes in 1948 – for *The Country Teacher* [*Sel'skaia uchitel'nitsa*] – and 1951 for *Knight of the Golden Star* [*Kavaler zolotoi zvezdy*].

20 Urusevskii used a variety of filters and gauze to achieve natural colors at a time when many films shot in color suffered from unnatural bluishness in landscapes and reddishness in faces; this was particularly valued by Vsevolod Pudovkin who chose Urusevskii for his Thaw drama *The Return of Ivan Bortnikov* [*Vozvrashchenie Ivana Bortnikova*, 1953].

21 Urusevskii learned to work with hand-held cameras during the Great Patriotic War when he was a frontline cameraman.

22 Aleksei Batalov described Kalatozov's and Urusevskii's maximalist standards for their work – the two were in absolute agreement when it came to the realization of their vision; they would "rather not do something at all than do it in a normal way" (in Mel'man 2006).

23 Maia Merkel' (1980, 29) aptly wrote: "Beginning with *The Cranes Are Flying*, everything was principally different. This was not simply an 'astonishing' or 'wonderfully' filmed picture, but a qualitatively new type of cinema."

24 Urusevskii foresaw that his film likely would be rejected both by critics and audiences. For insights into his thinking and the shooting process, see Lipkov's text "Dvizhenie tvorchestva" in Urusevskii (2002, esp. p. 307).

25 Urusevskii's film was seen by 2.2 million viewers – a very small number by Soviet standards and given the huge popularity of Sergei Esenin.

26 Urusevskii defined the main theme of his film as "love for Russia" [*liubov' k Rossii*], see Merkel' (1980, 122). In this regard, Urusevskii's film resonated with the positive reevaluation of the Russian countryside and peasantry that took place in the late 1960s, whose main voice was the so-called "village prose."

27 Urusevskii himself was aware of that; in a conversation with Merkel' he confessed that he "was always lucky" and that "for some reason I never depended on anybody, and nobody ever put pressure on me… [With one exception] I worked with the rest easily and freely, and they accepted everything that I proposed" (Merkel' 1980, 37).

28 See the case of Petr Todorovskii, also a student of Boris Volchek, who graduated from VGIK in 1954. He proved a fine cinematographer on Marlen Khutsiev's neorealist *Spring on Zarechnaia Street* [*Vesna na Zarechnoi ulitse*, 1956] and *The Two Fedors* [*Dva Fedora*, 1958] and became an independent prolific director in 1964.

29 Viktor Kushch states in the documentary (Braga 2012) that "the majority of cameramen who switched to direction became weak directors." He also mentions that there was a debate on whether Urusevskii really made his mark as a director.

References

Braga, Bogdan. 2012. *Sergei Urusevskii. Master-khudozhnik* [Sergei Urusevskii. A Master-Artist]. Documentary for TRK "Glas."

Cavendish, Philip. 2007. *Soviet Mainstream Cinematography. The Silent Era*. London: UCL Arts & Humanities Publications.

Egorov, Andrei. 2009. *Boris Volchek. Ravnovesie sveta* [Boris Volchek. Balance of Light]. Documentary for State Channel Kul'tura, http://tvkultura.ru/brand/show/brand_id/28491 (accessed January 31, 2015).

Goldovskaia, Marina. 1978. "B.I. Volchek." In *Desiat' operatorskikh biografii* [Ten Cinematographers' Biographies], edited by M. Goldovskaia, 124–139. Moscow: Iskusstvo.

Medynskii, Sergei. 1986. "Nash master (o B.M. Volcheke)" [Our Master, B. Volchek]. *Zhizn' v kino* [Life in Cinema] vol. 3: 170–184. Moscow: Iskusstvo.

Mel'man, Leonid. 2006. *Mikhail Kalatozov. Fil'm o rezhissere* [Mikhail Kalatozov. A Film about the Director]. Documentary in 2 parts, produced by Fond Mikhaila Kalatozova.

Merkel', Maia. 1980. *Ugol zreniia (Dialog s Urusevskim)* [Angle of Vision: Dialog with Urusevskii]. Moscow: Iskusstvo.

Sobolev, Romul. 1963. *Iurii Zheliabuzhskii*. Moscow: Iskusstvo.

Thomson, David. 2002. *The New Biographical Dictionary of Film*. New York: Alfred A. Knopf.

Urusevskii, Sergei. 2002. *S kameroi i za mol'bertom* [With the Camera behind the Easel]. Moscow: Algoritm.

Part IV

Time and Space, History and Place

17

Soldiers, Sailors, and Commissars: The Revolutionary Hero in Soviet Cinema of the 1930s

Denise J. Youngblood

The 1930s were paradoxical years in Soviet history. Following the tumult of the so-called "Stalin Revolution" of 1928–1932, with its emphasis on collectivization, industrialization, and cultural revolution, Stalin sought a return to some semblance of normality, at least for the urban population. Rural life had been permanently blighted by the ravages of collectivization and the subsequent famine, particularly in Ukraine. Major public works projects – like the Moscow metro, the steel city Magnitogorsk, and the massive Dnepr dam – were intended to instill public pride in a regime that had all but abandoned its revolutionary roots. Traditional education, replete with classic Russian literary works and historic Russian heroes, returned to the schools. The 1936 Constitution, which the people were encouraged to discuss publically, was proclaimed the most democratic in the world. Anniversaries were celebrated with mass festivals. "Life has become more joyous, comrades!" Stalin famously proclaimed. Of course this manufactured joy unfurled against the backdrop of massive state terror, and in 1936 the Great Terror began. The Great Terror was initially directed toward Old Bolsheviks and other high-ranking members of the Communist Party, but by the time it wound down in 1938, intellectuals and artists, military leaders, and even ordinary people had been swept away, either to be executed or sent to languish in the vast system of prison camps known as the Gulag.

Like every other aspect of Soviet society and culture, cinema was much affected by the imposition of Stalinism. By mid-decade the film industry was fully nationalized and centralized; the glorious diversity and experimentation of the 1920s had vanished, pushing filmmakers into straitjacketed service to the state. Censorship reached new heights, with many scripts banned before they could be produced. Films were banned as well. Socialist Realism, an emphasis on aesthetically

A Companion to Russian Cinema, First Edition. Edited by Birgit Beumers.
© 2016 John Wiley & Sons, Inc. Published 2016 by John Wiley & Sons, Inc.

straightforward art that reinforced the goals of state and party, was now the official aesthetic method. Yet it was still possible to make films that were, if not aesthetically adventurous, at least artistically interesting, and sometimes entertaining. Of course there were "enemies" films intended to reinforce the fears of enemies within, engendered by the Great Terror, but there were also true entertainment films, most notably the musical comedies of Grigorii Aleksandrov and Ivan Pyr'ev.

Occupying a mediating space between the heavily political films that focused on internal enemies and the musical comedies that wore their political correctness lightly was the "historical-revolutionary" genre, a genre that was clearly political but that also had the potential to be highly entertaining. I have chosen three films about the Russian Revolution to illustrate the face of the "revolutionary hero" in a post-Revolutionary age: Georgii Vasil'ev and Sergei Vasil'ev's *Chapaev* (1934), Efim Dzigan's *We are from Kronstadt* [*My iz Kronshtadta*, 1936], and Aleksandr Dovzhenko's *Shchors* (1939). All three films received Stalin's personal imprimatur, as we shall see, and *Chapaev* was the most popular film of the decade and among the most beloved Soviet films of all time.[1] These films can, therefore, be used to illustrate the changing, and sometimes contradictory, images of the revolutionary hero in a time of troubles.

As we shall see, the revolutionary hero, whether soldier, sailor, or commissar, had to be a man of action devoted to the cause. Yet true political awakening – supporting the cause for the right ideological reasons – might take time. Until *Shchors* the hero followed the sometimes tortuous road to the development of revolutionary consciousness, aided by a commissar who might himself also be a "revolutionary hero." *Chapaev*'s Furmanov is probably too much a man of words to fit this definition of a hero, but Martynov in *We are from Kronstadt* exemplifies it. By the time Shchors makes his appearance on screen, he is presented as a ready-made hero with only minor foibles. My argument is that this evolution represents the restricted range of human characteristics and emotions that could be attributed to the revolutionary hero at the end of the Great Terror, by which time the real heroes of the revolution had essentially been wiped out.

Chapaev

Self-styled as the Vasil'ev Brothers although they were not related, directors Georgii Vasil'ev and Sergei Vasil'ev turned to Dmitrii Furmanov's *Chapaev*, a fictionalized history of his time as a political commissar with the legendary Civil War commander Vasilii Chapaev for inspiration for their second film. Furmanov's 1923 novel had been popular, restoring the exploits of Chapaev to public consciousness. The Vasil'evs wisely took the route of borrowing loosely from the book, jettisoning its more tendentious elements and adding a romantic subplot between two fictional characters: Pet'ka, Chapaev's adjutant and An'ka, a machine-gunner. The Vasil'evs also pushed Chapaev front and center, diminishing the role that Furmanov as commissar had given himself in the novel.

The plot of this famous film is simple and on the surface hews closely to the tenets of Socialist Realism. Chapaev is a man of action, a vigorous leader much loved by his men. He is appropriately suspicious of any behavior that he deems "bourgeois," even if it comes from Furmanov. He does, however, need some political education, which Furmanov is supposed to provide. Chapaev's White counterpart is Colonel Borozdin, whose mission is to kill Chapaev. Borozdin's true character as a representative of the old order is revealed when he sentences his orderly's brother to be beaten by ramrods for desertion; Borozdin considers this a kindness because the original sentence had been execution. After helping Chapaev adopt a more professional demeanor, Furmanov is called away by Frunze and replaced as commissar. Borozdin's troops surprise Chapaev's men in a night-time raid. Both Chapaev and Pet'ka are killed trying to escape the debacle. An'ka arrives with reinforcements, too late to save Chapaev but in time to rout the enemy. Although Chapaev is dead, the cause is saved, thereby mitigating the sad ending, which is unusual for a Socialist Realist film.

The contrasts between commander and commissar and their relationship with one another are essential to an understanding of this film. Taken singly, both men are rather imperfect creatures. Chapaev's energy is physical whereas Furmanov's is mental; together they bridge the mind-body divide. It is fitting that Chapaev is first seen in motion, racing down the road in a troika with Pet'ka; his men have scattered in a skirmish with the Czechs. In the best-known image from this film, Chapaev is seen straining forward, directing Pet'ka who is manning the machine gun. Chapaev's pose is reminiscent of Lenin's iconography, in which the late leader is always depicted as moving forward to the future. Chapaev harshly interrogates his men about the whereabouts of their guns, but he nevertheless allows them to fetch their guns from the river where they have thrown them away in panic. Chapaev is a man of few words; he and Pet'ka stand in silent comradery on the bridge watching the men search for the weapons.

When Furmanov arrives, Chapaev is rightfully suspicious. Why does he need this well-groomed fop? He has got along fine without a commissar. Furmanov recognizes Chapaev's suspicions, so when Chapaev, in a strategy session, announces that the brigade will attack both enemy flanks and craftily turns to Furmanov to ask what he thinks, the commissar diplomatically replies, "What the commander thinks is right. We attack on both flanks." Actually, commissars were well-known for their interference in decision-making.

Chapaev's brashness is shown in a number of ways. In the "potato scene," Chapaev illustrates tactics by moving potatoes around on a table. He lectures about the correct position of the commander, at the head at first, but then moving to the rear while the battle is ongoing. One of his men protests: "But Chapaev is always at the head!" Chapaev laughs. Another instance occurs when some doctors rush in to Furmanov clamoring for protection: "Chapaev's threatening to shoot

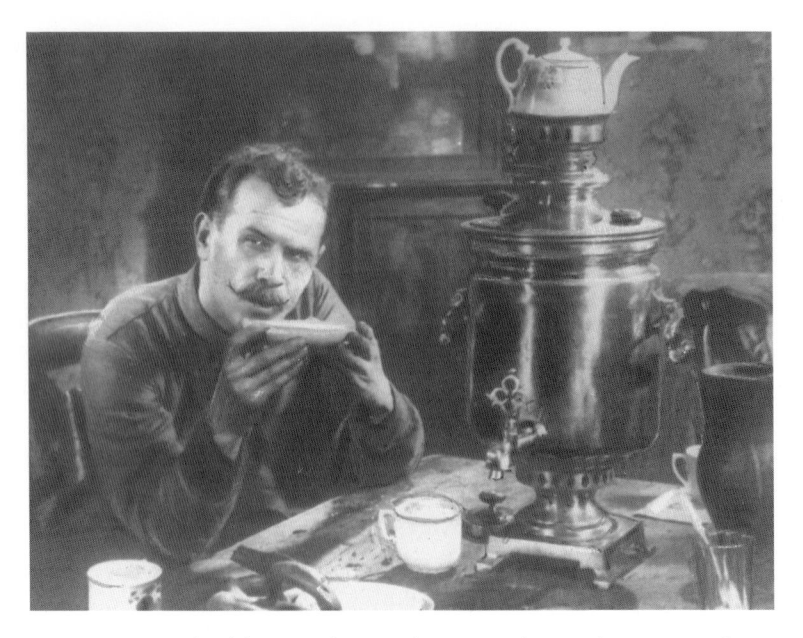

Figure 17.1 Boris Babochkin as the revolutionary hero Chapaev in the Vasil'evs' *Chapaev*, 1934.

us! Horse doctors can't be doctors!" It seems that Chapaev wanted them to certify a veterinarian as a doctor for humans. An angry Chapaev, shouting and disheveled, rushes in to headquarters to find the men cowering behind Furmanov. Chapaev accuses Furmanov of "rooting for the rotten intelligentsia." When Furmanov flashes him a smug smile, Chapaev shouts, "How dare you mock Chapaev!" and smashes a chair. Furmanov says that Alexander of Macedonia would not have behaved that way, which silences the furious Chapaev for a moment. "Aleksandr Makedonskii?" queries Chapaev, "Why don't I know him?" Furmanov's smugness reasserts itself, but the now calm Chapaev responds with dignity, "It's only been two years since I learned to read." Furmanov uses his temporary advantage to tell Chapaev to smarten himself up and tuck his shirt in his trousers, to set a good example for his men.

A final example is when Furmanov learns that the soldiers in the third platoon have been marauding and pillaging the village, a common problem during the Civil War that made the peasants hate both Reds and Whites. Furmanov, as the film's moral compass, naturally hates pillaging and issues an order for everything to be returned. He arrests the ringleader. Chapaev loses his temper when he finds out; he is incensed about the arrest of his comrade: "What he allowed only I can forbid!" When Furmanov attempts to prevent him from leaving, Chapaev says, tellingly: "I'm Chapaev! Who are you?!" and accuses Furmanov of wanting to trade on Chapaev's fame (which the real Furmanov did). Suddenly peasants from the village arrive to speak to Chapaev. They look dubiously at him, when he identifies himself, because he looks like one of his men, not a commander. Chapaev immediately tucks his shirt in. It turns out that they want to thank him for returning the booty. So in this instance, Furmanov has allowed Chapaev to claim credit for what *he* has done. Chapaev looks abashed, then says "They wouldn't send some nobody to defend Chapaev!" This scene in particular begs the question that the Vasil'evs raise throughout the film: Who is the true hero, Chapaev or Furmanov? Perhaps the "hero" is both of them when they work together for the common goal.

Chapaev's readiness to fight, whether the Whites or Furmanov, has been in evidence, but the movie, like the novel, continues to focus on the commander's ignorance. Chapaev decides to call his men together for a political lecture. He rants vaguely about fighting against exploitation. He threatens to shoot anyone caught plundering. But he is nonplussed when a peasant asks him whether he is a Bolshevik or a Communist. "I'm for the International!" he declares triumphantly. He fearfully turns to Furmanov for a cue, but the commissar refuses to extend a lifeline, asking Chapaev, "Which International? The Second or the Third?" Chapaev may be ignorant of Party ideology, but he is not as dumb as Furmanov thinks he is. He asks Furmanov cautiously, "Which International was Lenin for?" When Furmanov responds the Third, Chapaev knows that his gamble paid off. "Then I'm for the Third!"

It seems that Chapaev has been tamed by the resolute commissar. Chapaev has now adopted a spit-and-polish look and upbraids Pet'ka for his slovenly dress. Chapaev and Furmanov now sit side by side in HQ, and when the Whites plan an attack, Chapaev actually requests Furmanov's advice, although we have no evidence that the commissar possesses an ounce of military knowledge. Yet Chapaev has not lost his bravado. When Pet'ka asks him if he can command, an army, then a front, then all the armed forces, Chapaev resolutely responds, "I can." But when Pet'ka pushes him, "Can you command the world?" he replies in the negative because "I don't know foreign languages."

When Chapaev learns that Furmanov is leaving, the commander sighs, "They have hurt me by this." The two comrades have a sentimental farewell. Furmanov predictably extends his hand, but Chapaev embraces him, and they kiss.

With Furmanov gone, Chapaev's luck has run out. Furmanov has consistently been concerned about lackadaisical sentries, and when the White forces come, not only are Chapaev and his men sleeping, the sentries are, too. The Chapaev brigade is overrun, and Chapaev, manning a machine gun in a furiously burning building, is shot in the arm. Now Pet'ka is in charge. Although Chapaev protests that he never retreats, Pet'ka drags him off. They make it to the top of a bluff. Chapaev manages to get down to the river and in the water as Pet'ka covers him. Pet'ka is shot, but Chapaev is still swimming. His last words before he sinks are defiant: "No, you won't get me!"

The audience appeal of this film is obvious. Chapaev is a genuine hero: courageous, confident, and resolute. His men love him, even when he must take action against them. When a soldier is inciting men to mutiny, Chapaev quickly and decisively dispatches him. Chapaev is, however, no plastic hero. He is full of purely human flaws: his bombast, his pride, his ignorance, all these make him endearingly human. He is fundamentally a good person who cares deeply about his men.

But politically, the film fails to conform to the guidelines of Socialist Realism. Where is the political program? Chapaev evinces a severely underdeveloped class consciousness. It is never clear why he is on the side of the Reds, his few protestations against "rotten intellectuals" and "exploiters" notwithstanding. He knows nothing about ideology; he does not even know whether there is any difference between a Bolshevik and a Communist.

The commissar is supposed to be responsible for Chapaev's political education, but Furmanov is more interested in Chapaev's dress and manners. Furmanov's own beliefs remain unknown; he never says anything that would mark him as a stalwart Communist. Furthermore, he takes a smug satisfaction in lording it over Chapaev, based on what he conceives as his innate superiority, rather than his ideological superiority. Although Chapaev learns to appreciate him, and indeed, develops an unaccountable fondness for him, Furmanov is not a very likeable character.

Despite its apparent ideological shortcomings, *Chapaev* became an instant classic and opened on November 7, 1934, the seventeenth anniversary of the October Revolution. The press coverage was widespread, with the critics fawningly enthusiastic (Anon. 1934b). The only comparable press had been for Sergei Eisenstein's *Battleship Potemkin* [*Bronenosets Potemkin*, 1926]. The Leningrad studio, which had produced the film, could not keep up with the number of copies needed to satisfy the theaters. (In Leningrad, it was shown in 10 theaters; in Moscow, 16.) Two weeks after its release, *Chapaev* had already been seen by 4 million spectators, almost completely drawn from urban areas (at the time of its release, there were only 20 sound projectors in the countryside) (Anon. 1934a). By the end of the decade, the audience numbered 50 million (Turovskaia 1993, 95–107).

The film's biggest fan was Stalin. In its first six weeks. Stalin saw the film 16 times (Troshin 2002, 309–334). A year later, he was still watching it; after his twenty-seventh viewing on November 10, 1935, he observed to his cohort at one of his late night screenings that "the more one watches it, the more one likes it." Eleven screenings later, on March 9, 1936, he remarked with pleasure, "This is, of course, the best film" (Troshin 2003, 153, 168).

Chapaev's afterlife was long and enduring. Not surprisingly, it was *the* canonical Soviet film as long as Stalin was alive, considered to be the best picture about the Civil War and the model for Socialist Realist films. In a commemorative photo album of Soviet cinema published for the twentieth anniversary of the Revolution in 1937, stills from *Chapaev* were prominently featured (Anon. 1937, *passim*). The film's popularity remained strong during World War II, and it was widely shown at the front to delight reported in various sources, including the memoirs of war veterans (e.g., Beregovoi 1980; Nikulin 1980). (One wonders what lessons soldiers learned from the unruly and undisciplined Chapaev.) Soviet cinema scholars analyzed and reanalyzed *Chapaev* for the next five decades, keeping it in the public consciousness (e.g., Gerasimov 1949; Lebedev 1951; Iurenev 1964; Anon. 1974). In 1977, the fan magazine *Sovetskii ekran* [Soviet Screen] conducted a survey of old movies that should be shown again; *Chapaev* came in 25th (Anon. 1978).

When compared to Hollywood or European films from the mid-1930s, *Chapaev* is a fairly ordinary picture hampered by the poor quality of Soviet sound technology. In the context of Soviet history, however, it is an extraordinary example of how an entertainment film can shape public consciousness. *Chapaev* was an event of political as well as cultural importance.

We are from Kronstadt

No other historical-revolutionary film of the decade could possibly match *Chapaev*. Dzigan's *We are from Kronstadt* was its closest competition.[2] Based on a screenplay by the well-known playwright Vsevolod Vishnevskii, *We are from Kronstadt* concerns an assault on Petrograd (as St Petersburg was known from 1914–1924) carried out by the White general Nikolai Iudenich in fall 1919. There are two intertwined narrative threads. The first concerns Artem, a socially marginal sailor whose revolutionary consciousness is raised by a commissar, Martynov; the second is a tale of the masses: the story of how the military unites soldiers and sailors to repel the invaders. The way both stories play out is indicative of the rapidly changing cultural climate in 1936. *We are from Kronstadt* provides a telling contrast to *Chapaev*, especially in its less complex depiction of the relationship between sailor and commissar.

Right away, Artem, unlike Chapaev, is established as a totally negative character, joining his mates harassing a woman on the quay in Petrograd. The sailors surround her menacingly, mockingly referring to her as "Mademoiselle" because of her genteel appearance. When the situation has become very tense, rescue arrives in the person of a soldier, accompanied by his small son, whom he is placing in a children's home while he goes off to fight. As the two men grapple with each other, Artem takes a solid punch in the face. Mademoiselle returns with the police in tow; Artem shouts "You wait! I'll pay you back.

Artem continues to be a troublemaker on board his ship. He loudly complains about the shortage of food for the sailors and foments a mini-mutiny. The sailors call for the commissar to answer for the cut in rations. Martynov is the mysterious man seen at the beginning of the film, heading to Kronstadt at the orders of the Party Central Committee; he projects a calm authority. "Where's your revolutionary spirit?" he challenges Artem. Martynov reminds the men that they sent their bread to feed starving children and workers, and orders them to divide the single loaf that they have been given. Artem glowers at him: "I won't give up more bread!" Whereas Chapaev was an instinctive revolutionary, even if unschooled, Artem clearly needs help with his attitude.

The commissar gives a speech, with a message from Lenin: "Petrograd is the last bastion of Soviet power! Fight to the last breath! Victory is near. Victory is ours!" When Martynov asks if there are any questions, the sullen Artem says yes, with a mean look. The sailors challenge Martynov's credentials, which turn out to be impeccable. He has been a member of the Party since 1901, making him an "Old Bolshevik." He participated in the Revolution of 1905–1907. He was arrested, sentenced to death and then escaped abroad.

The next scene shows the commissar selecting sailors to go to the front with him. The sailors, eager to go, recite their own revolutionary credentials and class background. Surprisingly, Artem also steps forward. He says that he has been in the navy since 1914 and stormed the Winter Palace during the Revolution. There are immediate objections from his comrades. "He won't do; he's undisciplined"; Artem is also not a member of the Party. Martynov asks for a vote; only a few raise their hands in favor. A voice from the ranks calls out: "I wouldn't trust him." But the commissar stares at him thoughtfully, then announces "Let him show what he can do."

The sailors are assigned to defend the coastal sector, while the soldiers go to the Petrograd highway. All bivouac for the night at a "children's home" presided over by Mademoiselle, the same woman whom Artem hassled at the quay. As Artem struggles to find sleep lying in an uncomfortable position on the stairs of the former mansion, he realizes that he is next to the soldier who rescued Mademoiselle. Artem, combative as ever, gestures to hit him, but the start of bombing precludes a fight.

The next day, Martynov reveals himself to be a commissar of a new kind. Unlike *Chapaev*'s Furmanov, Martynov is as personally courageous as he is politically correct. He is a military leader as well as a political one, rushing into the fray of battle, with only his Nagan revolver for his defense, shouting "Forward!" and "Attack!" Artem seems inspired by the commissar's trust and is marching at the head of the ranks, singing.

The sailors quail before the heat of battle; when Martynov urges them forward, they hesitate. This is Artem's moment of reckoning, and he immediately jumps up to join the commissar. Another crisis occurs when a White tank arrives. Fearful, the sailors begin to run, but Martynov stops the rout with "Communists, halt!" Their orders are "not one step back," ominously foreshadowing Stalin's infamous order of the same name during World War II.

The enemy advances again. Artem has time for a joke: "It's no tea party," he deadpans. The commissar works the machine gun; the Whites temporarily retreat under the barrage of fire, but they advance again. The machine gun jams, and the sailors desperately throw grenades, to no avail. They are quickly surrounded by the Whites. "Surrender, commissars! Take some of them alive!" says the White commander. Recognizing Martynov's evident authority over his men, the commander asks Martynov who he is. The commissar tersely replies: "A communist-Bolshevik," knowing that this admission will doom him. When asked who he is, Artem sarcastically replies that he is an albatross; frustrated, the White commander

Figure 17.2 The sailors in *We are from Kronstadt*, directed by Efim Dzigan, 1936. Courtesy of Photofest.

orders: "Communists, step forward." There is silence and stillness, then Artem moves forward. The rest of the sailors follow him. "No non-Party?" queries the commander. "No," resolutely replies Artem. His awakening to revolutionary consciousness is now complete.

The sailors are marched away, to the edge of a cliff. Their hands are bound and rocks are tied around their necks. They are pushed off the cliff into the sea below. As Martynov goes over, he proclaims: "Thousands will rise for every Bolshevik you kill!" Finally, only Artem is left. He jumps, shouting "Long live the Baltic Fleet!"

Artem, however, does not drown. It is critical that he survive to carry on Martynov's cause. Artem cuts himself free with his knife, then goes back to find the commissar's body, dragging it to shore. "Commissar! Commissar! Comrade! Friend!" Artem laments. Before he buries Martynov under some rocks, Artem carefully safeguards the commissar's Party card, a holy object in the context of the mid-1930s, where a campaign was underway to sanctify this most precious form of identification.

On his own, Artem makes his way back to the children's home, which the Whites have taken over, pushing Mademoiselle and the children out. When Artem appears, asking for help, she is naturally suspicious. But a stalwart communist herself, she takes the chance that his conversion is real and offers Artem some of her clothing as a disguise. Dressed like a woman, Artem finds that his disguise is perhaps too successful as he is harassed by a White soldier, ironic considering his previous behavior. Artem kills the soldier with his knife, finds a boat, and manages to row away while under fire, headed for Kronstadt.

Now the action turns away from Artem, to demonstrate the bravery of the soldiers who have taken over the fight now that the sailors have been massacred. Draudin, the soldiers' regimental commander, is bravely leading the battle to control the Petrograd highway. Suddenly Mademoiselle appears; the Whites have forced her to serve as a decoy, to urge the Reds to surrender, which she refuses to do, crying instead: "Keep fighting, comrades! Kronstadt will send help!" Although she is standing in the line of fire, Draudin orders his men to shoot; when they hesitate because of the woman, he begins shooting anyway. It is not until the end of the movie that the portent of this action becomes clear: Mademoiselle is his wife. Everything must be sacrificed for victory. (Fortunately, she is not killed and manages to make her way down the hill to join her comrades.)

The situation is so desperate that Draudin orders all wounded men to take up arms and fight, in the name of the Party. When someone calls out "And non-Party?" a soldier responds: "They're needed, too." Just in time, the Baltic Fleet comes to the rescue, with Artem at their head. Quoting Martynov from early in the film, Artem cries out "Lenin says to fight to the last breath, comrades!" and adds "We'll wipe out all who threaten the revolution!" Artem has thereby taken over both of Martynov's roles, as military and political leader of the sailors.

The sailors come to shore at the very spot where Artem buried Martynov. This has become a site of revolutionary martyrdom, as Artem makes clear. "Never forget this place," he intones somberly. In the meantime, Draudin's regiment is still fighting bravely but is barely hanging on. Finally, the sailors join the battle; Artem hugs the soldiers that he has formerly deprecated and even hugs his old adversary (the soldier who had rescued Mademoiselle at the beginning of the film). The Whites retreat, jumping off the same cliff that had carried the sailors and Martynov to their deaths. Artem advances with determination. The film ends with a close-up of Artem and his triumphant words "Who else wants to take Petrograd?!"

Chapaev represented the politicization of Soviet life in the 1930s. Much had changed since the previous decade; the hand of the Party was now omnipresent. Yet *Chapaev* demonstrates that as late as 1934, it was still possible to make a film where both commissar and commander had many foibles, right up to the end. *We are from Kronstadt*, despite some superficial resemblance to *Chapaev*, is actually rather different. This reflects the political and cultural changes that took place over only two years, as the Party's grip tightened on the film industry.

Like *Chapaev*, *We are from Kronstadt* is a rousing adventure film, albeit with even more emphasis on the front and better-staged battle scenes. *We are from Kronstadt* also foregrounds a conversion tale of the relationship between a commissar and a military man, in this case Artem the sailor. But there the resemblances end.

The two commissars have little in common. Furmanov is almost prissy as he fusses about Chapaev's dress and manners. He is always well behind the battle lines. His only mention of the Party line is when he twits Chapaev about not knowing the difference between the Second and Third Internationals. Martynov, on the other hand, leads as much from example as from words. He is a born leader who does not even need a military commander; he takes over on the battlefield as well, charging forward into the heat of battle with his revolver in hand. Martynov models "Party-mindedness" [*partiinost'*]; he quotes Lenin and is proud to die as a Bolshevik for his country and Party. In fact, Martynov is arguably the hero of the film.

There can be no question that Chapaev is the hero of his movie, which is signified from the start by the title. Instinctive, wily, emotional, and very likeable, he is a charismatic leader and at the heart of every scene in *Chapaev*. Artem, by contrast, is an anti-hero. A distinctly unpleasant personality in the beginning, he engages in a number of dubious acts. He harasses a woman, he brawls with the man who rescued her, he nearly incites a riot on board over the shortage of bread. Furthermore, he is heartless, condemning the starving children with a sneer. All this makes his conversion much more profound than Chapaev's. (Indeed, all Chapaev really changes is to smarten his appearance.) The awakening of Artem's revolutionary consciousness is completely inspired by Martynov and his combination of courage and idealism. Artem's conversion from bad man to revolutionary hero is too quick to satisfy those who are looking for psychological underpinnings and perhaps too quick to be believable, but such is the power of the commissar.

Martynov's death in the middle of the film and the shift in focus from Artem to commander Draudin and his soldiers near the end weaken the film artistically but enhance it politically. Martyrdom was a central element of the mythology of the revolution, and the facts behind Martynov's demise heroicize the image of the commissar. With the onset of the Great Terror in 1936, the best kind of hero was a dead one (which was why Chapaev was never denounced). The movement of the narrative away from Artem (as he heads back to Kronstadt for help) and toward the soldiers still doing battle with the Whites is intended to emphasize the mass character of the revolutionary enterprise, which continued to be an important aspect of the mythology. The comradery and fighting spirit of the soldiers and their evident admiration for their commander exemplified the correct relationship between troops and officers in a militaristic society.

In sum, *We are from Kronstadt* was a solid, entertaining film that scored major political points. Efim Dzigan had directed five unremarkable films prior to *Kronstadt*, but he was elevated to prominence when he was given the commission to make this film. That it was considered a prestige project was clear from the beginning, when its production was announced six months in advance of its screening in *Pravda* (Vishnevskii 1935). This did not mean, however, that production proceeded smoothly and the reasons for its high degree of adherence to Bolshevik mythmaking lay as much in the political inference that Dzigan faced as in Vishnevskii's script (Dzigan 1961, 4–5).

The film was a big hit, not on the order of *Chapaev*, of course, but a crowd pleaser nonetheless (Dzigan 1961, 8). *Pravda* compared it favorably to *Chapaev* (Ermolinskii 1936) and it was screened in 13 Moscow theaters simultaneously, only a few less than the Vasil'evs' picture (Anon. 1936b). Stalin declared it "good and extremely interesting" and viewed it at least three times (Troshin 2003, 166–167).

Like *Chapaev*, *We are from Kronstadt* was exported and enjoyed a positive reception, particularly in France, at least as reported in *Pravda* (Anon. 1936a). *We are from Kronstadt* was also awarded a prize at an international film exhibition held in Paris in 1937. Some rival filmmakers, notably Sergei Eisenstein, privately lamented the artistic quality of the movie, at least as compared to the output of the 1920s, but such views could no longer be aired in public (Bulgakowa 2001, 182). *We are from Kronstadt* had been sanctioned by the Party through *Pravda* and by no less an authority than Comrade Stalin himself. The film was rereleased regularly in the decades that followed (Vishnevskii 1954, 56–76; Kremlev 1966, 22; Parfenov 2005, 159–164) and like *Chapaev* was shown at the front in 1942, when Soviet soldiers certainly needed their morale boosted (Strel'chenko 1985, 17). The importance of the political message in *We are from Kronstadt* had not faded.

Shchors

By the time that Aleksandr Dovzhenko's *Shchors* appeared in 1939, the USSR had suffered through the Great Terror, a period of cataclysmic upheaval that ruined millions of lives. Now Stalin's control was complete. As we shall see, the history of the making of *Shchors* cannot be understood outside its political context.[3]

Nikolai Shchors (1895–1919), the founder of the so-called Bogun brigade and commander of the First Soviet Ukrainian Division during the Civil War, was a little-known figure in 1935, when Stalin suggested to Dovzhenko that his next project should be about Shchors, in Stalin's styling the "Ukrainian Chapaev" (Kepley 1986, 121). Dovzhenko took this as a command, and the Soviet propaganda machinery immediately moved into high gear, quickly manufacturing a Shchors who was a larger-than-life hero, rather than a commander whom his superiors thought to be questionable (Liber 2002, 156).

Dovzhenko, unlike the Vasil'evs and Dzigan, was a very well-known director when he accepted this important commission. The maker of *Arsenal* (1929) and *Earth* [*Zemlia*, 1930], he was considered at home and abroad to be an artistically important director. He was not, however, an obvious choice to make a film about a Civil War hero because he had found himself in trouble during the cultural revolution for the "formalism" that was evident in his films, especially *Earth*. There was more: for a brief period during the Civil War, Dovzhenko had served under ataman Simon Petliura, a Ukrainian nationalist and an enemy of the Bolshevik Revolution – including Shchors, who fought against Petliura (Liber 2002, 158). Dovzhenko doubtless hoped that a successful *Shchors* would redeem his dubious past.

Dovzhenko took this project very seriously, studying all the available historical materials. He wanted as much historical verisimilitude as possible, and so the early versions of the script contained many real-life figures, who had fought with Shchors. One of these was Ivan Dubovyi, Shchors's right-hand man, whom

Dovzhenko invited to serve as military consultant on the picture. Dubovyi, like many other members of the Bogun brigade, was swept into the maws of the Great Terror and was executed in 1938. First arrested for alleged espionage, Dubovyi eventually confessed to murdering Shchors, who actually was killed in battle. Shortly after Dubovyi's execution, Dovzhenko was injured in a suspicious automobile accident; the steering column of his car had been severed. At the same time all this was going on, Stalin met with Dovzhenko frequently to criticize the script, with the result that virtually all the historical figures in the film had been excised by the time it came to the screen. Not surprisingly, before the filming was completed, Dovzhenko suffered a mental breakdown (Liber 2002, 157–164). The production process had taken four tortuous years.

The plots of *Chapaev* and especially *Kronstadt* appear sophisticated when compared with *Shchors*. In 1918–1919 Shchors and his men fight assorted Germans, Poles, and even their fellow Ukrainians under Petliura's leadership, and Shchors delivers lots of speeches and lectures. Its episodic nature makes constructing a coherent narrative difficult.

Unlike Chapaev, who is first seen in action, Shchors appears several minutes into the film, after a well-staged battle sequence, one of many in the picture. Neatly dressed in jodhpurs and gleaming boots, he addresses a group of partisans seeking to join the Bogun brigade. Costumes are important in this picture as they were in *Chapaev*; the next time we see Shchors, he is dressed in a leather jacket and cap, looking very much like a commissar rather than a commander. His commissar is conspicuously absent from the film, save for one comical incident. Shchors acts like Furmanov in *Chapaev*; he neatens up a soldier's uniform. Shchors's counterpoint in dress is his sidekick, the kindly, elderly hetman Bozhenko, who wears an embroidered Ukrainian shirt, the long sheepskin cloak called *burka*, and a peaked sheepskin hat. The two men sit side-by-side on a settee, a study in contrasts, Shchors with his arm around Bozhenko. Later on, they embrace and kiss; Shchors calls Bozhenko *bat'ka* (a colloquialism for "father").

Continuing the motif of Shchors as the opposite of Chapaev, the bookish commander sits down to write a speech rather than delivering it extemporaneously. Shchors speaks passionately but formulaically, standing stiffly, gesturing mechanically with his right arm. But he also displays a temper. When some soldiers come to ask him for his identity documents, he comes alive, rushing at them ferociously with a sword; in another scene he shoves a German officer. Yet another speech, this one delivered from a viewing stand. "Long live the civil war! Long live victory! Long live Lenin!" Shchors passively watches as his men, including some German defectors, march past him.

Winter arrives, and at last Shchors is seen on horseback with his soldiers. He even mans a machine gun against the Germans (recall similar scenes with Chapaev and Martynov). In the village around which the battle swirls, there is a strange sight: a wedding party. After the battle, Shchors and his men join the feast, but Shchors, quoting Lenin, uses this as an opportunity to recruit some peasants.

Figure 17.3 Evgenii Samoilov as Shchors and Ivan Skuratov as Vasil' Bozhenko in *Shchors*, directed by Aleksandr Dovzhenko, 1939. Courtesy of Photofest.

This scene is followed by yet another speech; again Shchors only moves his right hand, but here he leans forward, reminiscent of Lenin, which gives a more dynamic impression than when he is standing ramrod straight. Later, he appears on foot in a greatcoat, binoculars around his neck. "I'm a worker," he announces (which is not true; he came from a bourgeois family). He is more passionate when addressing the Cossacks. The union of Russians, Ukrainians, and Bolsheviks will be victorious: "We will drive out the Polish-German forces and destroy the Polish nobility [*panstvo*]!" This time, he carries a whip in his right hand, which gives him an appearance of enhanced power, reinforcing his words. He also reminds the viewer of the German general, who also carried a whip in his right hand.

Shchors is next seen triumphant, riding on horseback through the city of Kiev, which he has just taken. Bozhenko is at his side. The bourgeoisie are in a panic, hastily attempting to burn papers. They are herded into a theater to listen to a speech, this time by Bozhenko, not Shchors. The old man is full of bombast and emotion, much like Chapaev and distinctly unlike Shchors. By this time in Soviet history, however, a Bozhenko type cannot be a hero; rather, he is a comic foil to Shchors.

At a celebratory dinner with his men, Shchors cites Lenin yet again. Now he is wearing a side-buttoned Russian shirt. Cheerful, for once changing his stern expression, Shchors watches as the other men, including Bozhenko, imbibe alcohol. In fact, Bozhenko carries his own bottle in his greatcoat. As we learn later, when a village elder offers him liquor, Shchors is that rarity in east Slavic culture, a teetotaler. His Russian shirt may have been intended to counteract the impression that Shchors is an "other," distinct from the hard-drinking brotherhood of Russian and Ukrainian men.

One of the more bizarre scenes in the film concerns Shchors' plans to establish an officer's school. To staff it, he intends on using White officers that he has brought around to the Red cause. One such officer has been, Shchors suspects, feigning illness. The commander calls the offender into his office, tells him to disrobe, and whips out a stethoscope to listen to his heart (Shchors had been trained as a military doctor). Malingerers cannot escape Shchors; he knows everything.

Dovzhenko continues the film's pattern of alternating scenes of Shchors in battle with Shchors speechifying. Petliura's forces are coming, and Shchors's brigade is in a panic. Shchors tries to stem the panic among his men and hits one with his whip. In the heat of the nine-day battle for Berdichev, the commander is in the fray; afterwards, he has lost his cool demeanor. Exhausted, Shchors puts his head under a faucet to clean his dirty face, meanwhile *dictating* a letter to his wife, an unintentionally comic scene. The letter is wholly impersonal; he only gives her details of the battle just fought. A scene that must have been intended to humanize Shchors has the opposite effect.

Shchors learns that Bozhenko's wife has been murdered. As he is discussing this with several of his officers, one of them lights a cigarette, prompting the commander to fly into a rage and snatch the offending cigarette from the man's hand. Not only is Shchors opposed to alcohol, he prohibits smoking as well; he is the perfect ascetic.

Bozhenko is nearly in hysterics at the news of his wife's death; he lies on a divan, sobbing. Shchors, whom Bozhenko calls by his Ukrainian name, Mykola, attempts to comfort the old man. Bozhenko refuses to be consoled, crying that he will take his men to avenge his wife. This irritates the commander, who begins shouting at, and even threatening to kill, his distraught friend. Finally, Shchors presents Bozhenko with a ceremonial sword, which mollifies the old man. They embrace.

It is Bozhenko's turn to give a speech to the men that quickly becomes loud and emotional, true to his character. Shchors is beside him, calming him down. In true commissar fashion, he even feeds Bozhenko a line. This is followed by a battle with the Poles; Shchors leads the charge to Polish headquarters, gesturing with his sword: "Forward!"

In summer 1919, the end was at hand. A title informs us that Bozhenko is dying; he stills manages to be very talkative to his demise as he is carried on a stretcher. Shchors is too late; he gives a speech by Bozhenko's bier but is not particularly emotional. Shchors was killed a few days later, but the film's finale takes place as Shchors stands at a window watching a military parade. The smartly-uniformed men marching past him could not be more different from the rag-tag bands that populate *Chapaev* and *We are from Kronstadt*. They march like automatons, in precise alignment, the fantasy soldiers of 1939, not 1919. Shchors is thrilled at the sight: his face alight with ecstasy, he invokes Lenin one last time. "Lenin told me" of the victory. It seems that Shchors will live on.

Parts of this film are vintage Dovzhenko, especially the opening scene of bombs blasting a field of sunflowers. There is hand-to-hand combat, villages in flames, the riderless horses that augur death. The Germans are on the run, back to a village to take shelter. Now it is the peasants' turn to flee; those who cannot get away are executed. It is both beautiful and terrible, like *Arsenal* and *Earth*.

The nightmare is banished when Shchors appears on the screen. Well-dressed, standing tall, a neatly trimmed beard framing his handsome face, Shchors is a model Soviet soldier, if not a realistic Red commander of the Civil War era. One historian of the 1930s has written that by this time the Party "had established a strict definition of the proper values and behavior of Party members: sobriety, sexual propriety, honesty, openness, and loyalty" (Hoffman 2003, 85). As we have seen, the cinematic Shchors embodies all of these virtues, except, perhaps, "openness." He keeps his own counsel and resents being given advice.

Shchors also seems to combine with his military leadership capacity the qualities of the commissar. In his person, he is like a stiffer version of Furmanov, attentive to his own dress and to others' dress and manners. He is also an intellectual, like both Furmanov and Martynov. In fact, Shchors resembles an especially pedantic professor, with his constant hectoring and lecturing. There are books in his headquarters and a picture of Pushkin on the wall in his room. Unlike Chapaev and Artem, there is no conversion, because Shchors is already perfect: commander and commissar in one character.

Dovzhenko did, however, manage to sneak in some subversive religious imagery. Shchors, with his narrow face, neat beard, and fanatical dark eyes, strongly resembles Jesus as depicted in Russian Orthodox icons. He wears an air of martyrdom; his facial expressions, such as they are, reflect pain at the human imperfection he sees all around him. He has sacrificed his personal life for the cause. He frequently quotes the deity, Lenin. Shchors will also be martyred: although the film does not show this, the audience already knew it from the film's publicity.

The film's reception is interesting. Given that Stalin's influence is evident in virtually every scene of the heavy-handed story, it is not surprising that critics responded with adulation (Liber 2002, 164–165). Two months before the film's release January 1939, *Pravda* prepared the public and the critics for the Party line on *Shchors* by announcing that Stalin was the picture's inspiration (Arnshtam 1939). Its shortcomings were brushed aside. Stalin, the only critic who mattered, was reportedly pleased (Liber 2002, 164–165).

Yet there is no external evidence for film's success at the box office or lack thereof. Unlike *We are from Kronstadt*, no one claimed that Chapaev-ian popularity for *Shchors*. In the decades that followed, it was never cited as an important film; indeed, after Stalin's death a leading director was quick to criticize it (Gerasimov 1953, 67). *Shchors* never appeared on lists of old films that viewers wanted to watch again. Despite the fact that Germans are among the enemies seen in *Shchors*, it was apparently not revived during World War II. Finally, Dovzhenko did not enjoy a career boost as a result, and his relations with the regime continued to be fraught. The film is a perfect example of how a great director's work was deleteriously affected by Stalin's direct interference in moviemaking.

Chapaev, *We are from Kronstadt*, and *Shchors* were released in a five-year period, only two or three years separating each of them. The changes over this time are quite remarkable and illustrate the impact of encroaching Stalinization on the once vibrant film industry. The progression of these three films provides a textbook illustration of the evolution of Stalinism's drive to create a disciplined citizenry and a spit-and-polish military from the leavings of revolutionary society.

Notes

1   Much more has been written on *Chapaev* than on the other works under discussion here combined. By far the best is Graffy (2010), which combines thorough research from the most up-to-date scholarship as well as from primary sources with astute analysis.
2   Little has been written in English about *Kronstadt*; see Youngblood (2007, 43–46).
3   The best analysis of *Shchors* in English is Kepley (1986, 121–134). On its production history see Liber (2002, ch. 7).

References

Anon. 1934a. "*Chapaeva* posmotrit' vsia strana" [The Whole Country is Watching *Chapaev*]. *Pravda* November 22.
Anon. 1934b. "Vstrecha literatorov s uchastnikami fil'ma *Chapaev*" [Meeting of Writers with the Film Crew of *Chapaev*]. *Pravda* November 26.
Anon. 1936a. "*My iz Kronshtadta* na Parizhskikh ekranakh." [*We are from Kronstadt* on Parisian Screens]. *Pravda* March 22.
Anon. 1936b. "Uspekh zamechatel'nogo fil'ma: Pervyi den' demonstratsii *My iz Kronshtadta*" [The Success of a Remarkable Film: The First Day of Screenings of *We are from Kronstadt*]. *Pravda* March 22.
Anon. 1937. *Sovetskoe kino* [Soviet Cinema]. Moscow: Iskusstvo.
Anon. 1974. "Kartina zhivet!" [The Film is Alive!]. *Sovetskii ekran* [Soviet Screen] 21: 14–15.
Anon. 1978. "Konkurs-77" [Competition '77]. *Sovetskii ekran* [Soviet Screen] 13.
Arnshtam, Lev. 1939. "*Shchors*: Novyi fil'm A. Dovzhenko, proizvodstva Kievskoi kinostudii" [*Shchors*: Aleksandr Dovzhenko's New Film, a Production of the Kiev Film Studio]. *Pravda* January 25.
Beregovoi, G. 1980. "Nasha pobeda" [Our Victory]. *Sovetskii ekran* [Soviet Screen] 9: 7.
Bulgakowa, Oksana. 2001. *Sergei Eisenstein: A Biography*. Trans. Anne Dwyer. Berlin: PotemkinPress.

Dzigan, Efim. 1961. "Chetvert' veka: *My iz Kronshtadta*" [A Quarter of a Century: *We are from Kronstadt*]. *Sovetskii ekran* [Soviet Screen] 8: 4–5, 8.

Ermolinskii, I. 1936. "*My iz Kronshtadta*: Zamechatel'nyi fil'm" [*We are from Kronstadt*: A Remarkable Film]. *Pravda* March 3.

Gerasimov, Sergei. 1949. "Sila Stalinskikh idei" [The Power of Stalinist Ideas]. *Iskusstvo kino* [Art of Cinema] 6: 13–18.

Gerasimov, Sergei. 1953. "Beseda rezhissera so stsenaristom" [Conversation between Director and Scriptwriter]. *Iskusstvo kino* [Art of Cinema] 11: 67.

Graffy, Julian. 2010. *Chapaev*. London: I. B. Tauris.

Hoffman, David L. 2003. *Stalinist Values: The Cultural Norms of Soviet Modernity, 1917–1941*. Ithaca: Cornell University Press.

Iurenev, Rostislav. 1964. "*Chapaev*." *Iskusstvo kino* [Art of Cinema] 11: 10–19.

Kepley, Vance Jr. 1986. *In the Service of the State: The Cinema of Alexander Dovzhenko*. Madison: University of Wisconsin Press.

Kremlev, German. 1966. "1936-xxx-1966: *My iz Kronshtadta*." [1936-xxx-1966: *We are from Kronstadt*]. *Sovetskii ekran* [Soviet Screen] 6: 20.

Lebedev, Nikolai. 1951. "Na podstupakh k *Chapaevu*" [On the Approach to *Chapaev*]. *Iskusstvo kino* [Art of Cinema] 2: 9–14.

Liber, George. 2002. *Alexander Dovzhenko: A Life in Soviet Film*. London: British Film Institute Publishing.

Nikulin, Iurii. 1980. "*Chapaev* s nami" [*Chapaev* is with Us]. *Sovetskii ekran* [Soviet Screen] 9: 17.

Parfenov, Lev, 2003. "*My iz Kronshtadta*" [*We are from Kronstadt*]. In *Rossiiskii illiuzion*. [Russian Illusion], edited by L. Budiak, 159–164. Moscow: Materik.

Strel'chenko, A. 1985. "*Krasnye d'iavoliata* na dorogakh voiny" [*The Red Imps* on the Road to the War]. *Sovetskii ekran* [Soviet Screen] 20: 17.

Troshin, Aleksandr, ed. 2002. "'A driani podrobno *Garmon'* bol'she ne stavite? Zapiski besed B. Z. Shumiatskogo s I.V. Stalinym posle kinoprosmotorv 1934" [You Won't Stage any More Rubbish Like "Accordion?" ... Notes of the Conversations between B. Shumiatskii and I. Stalin after Screenings in 1934]. *Kinovedcheskie zapiski* [Film Scholars' Notes] 61: 281–346.

Troshin, Aleksandr, ed. 2003. "Kartina sil'naia, khoroshaia no ne *Chapaev*: Zapiski besed B.Z. Shumiatskogo s I.V. Stalinym posle kino prosmotrov, 1935–1937" [It's a Good and Strong Film, but not "*Chapaev*" ... : Notes of the Conversations between B. Shumiatskii and I. Stalin after screenings in 1935–1937]. *Kinovedcheskie zapiski* [Film Scholars' Notes] 62: 115–187.

Turovskaia, Maia. 1993. "The Tastes of Soviet Moviegoers during the 1930s." In *Late Soviet Culture: From Perestroika to Novostroika*, edited by Thomas Lahusen, 95–107. Durham: Duke University Press.

Vishnevskii, Vsevolod 1935. "*My iz Kronshtadta*" [*We are from Kronstadt*]. *Pravda* August 22.

Vishnevskii, Vsevolod. 1954. "Pisatel' i rezhisser: Iz pisem k E. Dziganu" [Writer and Director: From the letters to E. Dzigan]. *Iskusstvo kino* [Art of Cinema] 6: 56–76.

Youngblood, Denise J. 2007. *Russian War Films: On the Cinema Front, 1914–2005*. Lawrence: University Press of Kansas.

18

Defending the Motherland: The Soviet and Russian War Film

Stephen M. Norris

The war film occupies an important place, arguably *the* most important, in Russian film history. Because of its significance, the war movie established a series of "firsts" in Russian cinematic culture. The first full-length film in Russian cinematic history, Vasilii Goncharov's *The Defense of Sevastopol* [*Oborona Sevastopolia*, 1911] narrated the history of the Crimean War (1853–1856). The first "hit" of the Soviet era, Ivan Perestiani's *Little Red Devils* [*Krasnye d'iavoliata*, 1923], was about the Civil War. The first and only winner thus far of a Golden Palm at Cannes was Mikhail Kalatozov's *The Cranes are Flying* [*Letiat zhuravli*, 1957]. The first-ever 3D IMAX film in Russian history was Fedor Bondarchuk's *Stalingrad* (2013). The list could go on, and would encompass both big and small screens: the first-ever television movie, to take one more example, was the 4-part World War II drama, *We Draw Fire on Ourselves* [*Vyzyvaem ogon' na sebia*], which aired in 1964 and 1965. War films have consistently proven to be among the most popular and most critically acclaimed movies over the course of the last century. They have also been central to the ways audiences understood the past, the meanings of conflicts in the bloody twentieth century, and even their own sense of patriotism.

Despite its significance, the Russian war film has only been the subject of one comprehensive study in English and part of only a handful of others. This chapter builds on these previous works and analyzes four war films in order to chart the evolution of one important function they performed: the ways they have stressed the defense of the motherland. *The Defense of Sevastopol* focused on the heroic actions of Russian soldiers in the Crimean War and established certain themes that would reoccur in subsequent war films. The other three films examine the Great Patriotic War (1941–1945), illustrating that conflict's central importance to first Soviet and then Russian history. *She Defends the Motherland* [*Ona zashchishchaet rodinu*, dir. Fridrikh Ermler, 1943] tapped into a timeless Russian spirit and cast a Soviet heroine as a representation of Mother Russia herself. Sergei Bondarchuk's *They Fought for the Motherland* [*Oni srazhalis' za rodinu*, 1975] focused on a single battalion

A Companion to Russian Cinema, First Edition. Edited by Birgit Beumers.
© 2016 John Wiley & Sons, Inc. Published 2016 by John Wiley & Sons, Inc.

of Soviet soldiers and how they collectively helped in the fight against fascism. Finally, Aleksandr Kott's joint Russian/Belorussian feature *The Brest Fortress* [*Brestskaia krepost'*, aka *Fortress of War*, 2010] recast the importance of defending the motherland so that post-Soviet audiences would continue to receive this message. By focusing on four films each made approximately 30 years apart, this chapter will chart how the war film has served as an important site where patriotism gets constructed, rebuilt, and disseminated.

Shaping Memory: Understanding the Russian War Film

In the most sustained examination of the Russian war film's significance, Denise Youngblood (2007) analyzes Russian films about several conflicts: her study encompasses the two world wars, the Civil War (1918–1922), the Soviet-Afghan War (1979–1988), and the two Chechen Wars from the 1990s. Youngblood adopts Hayden White's concept of "historiophoty" (or the way that films engage with each other across time) in order to prove her primary argument that war films "not only reflected their times, but also shaped them" (Youngblood 2007, 1). Youngblood also stakes out what she considers to be the most significant function of the genre; namely, that they "provided a highly contested space for supporting and challenging official views of Soviet history" (Youngblood 2007, 3).

The war film, Youngblood notes, has been particularly important because wars have decisively shaped Russian history in the last 100 years. The imperial government collapsed because of a war (the Great War), the Soviet state was born amidst another (the Civil War), reforged in the Great Patriotic War, and died in part because of the Afghan conflict. The post-Soviet state also came of age during the Chechen Wars of the 1990s. The interpretations and mythologies created about these conflicts, Youngblood posits, often served as the basis for maintaining an authoritarian state. As she argues, the Russian war film should be understood as a distinctive form of historical discourse (Youngblood 2007, 3).

Evgeny Dobrenko (2008) takes this view a step further in his book on Stalinist cinema. Although not exclusively about war films, Dobrenko's work offers another important lens through which to view the role of historical cinema. "Stalinist art," Dobrenko writes, "works with time, the past, and memory," not just as part of a general style, but as a "grandiose political-aesthetic project which completes the revolutionary project" (Dobrenko 2008, 1). Put another way, Stalinist cinema "becomes the medium of 'history' itself, of the historical myth being created" (Dobrenko 2008, 5). In Dobrenko's framework, Stalinist cinema created lasting interpretations of the past and simultaneously fostered the work of memory. "Post-Soviet culture," he suggests, "cannot escape from this system of images of the past for the very reason that history comes together with ready-made images, just as thought comes with speech" (Dobrenko 2008, 2).

Both Youngblood's general theses and Dobrenko's specific argument inform this chapter's analysis. It takes up Dobrenko's concept of the "ready-made," which Helena Goscilo (2012) has also employed to examine how narratives about war are so easily slotted into preexisting notions about patriotism, national identity, and national mythologies. Goscilo argues that all nations tend to create a cultural "ready-made" that in turn generates

> certain ecumenical stereotypes within war rhetoric: "Our" rectitude, bravery, and patriotism, by contrast with the enemy's craven, brutal aggressiveness; "our" noble defense of sacrosanct values, versus "their" numerically stronger military equipment but morally weaker fighting spirit; "our" troops' defense of women and children, as opposed to "their" defilement and murder of the defenseless, and so forth. (Goscilo 2012, 135)

These general notions are marshaled whenever a nation goes to war, updating them to fit the current conflict while simultaneously deepening their historical roots.

In the case of the Russo-Soviet war film, one of the central ready-made cultural constructions has been the notion of defense of the motherland, a conception that in turn has been employed on screen and on the page to justify the idea that dying is the noblest act for a soldier to make. Although this idea is not one unique to Russia (all countries tend to produce their own version), it has served as a more explicit component to the Russian cinematic culture of war than elsewhere. The actor Nikolai Kriuchkov, who appeared in over 100 Soviet films, wrote in 1975 that one of the central components of "the Russian character" was the readiness of citizens to defend the motherland as a reflexive act of self-sacrifice (Kriuchkov 1975, 54). Kriuchkov, who often portrayed soldiers embodying this character, suggested that this act was so central to Russian self-understanding because "the love for the motherland is in our blood" (Kriuchkov 1975, 54). As the analysis below will demonstrate, Kriuchkov's comments should be understood as part of the way a particular cultural ready-made evolved; for the stress film placed on the defense of the motherland was first evoked at the beginning of Russian cinema and has continued to be called for right up to the present day.

A Patriotic Spectacle

The first full-length feature in Russian cinematic history was a war film. Released in 1911, Vasilii Goncharov's *The Defense of Sevastopol* recreated the action of the Crimean War (1853–1856) over the course of 100 minutes. The conflict with the Ottoman Empire, Britain, and France might initially seem as an odd choice for such a film because it ended in a disastrous loss for Russia and precipitated an empire-wide crisis. Alexander II (reigned 1855–1881), who had to deal with the defeat after his father, Nicholas I (reigned 1825–1855), died in the midst of the conflict, immediately understood that things had to change. Through a series of laws that came to be known as the Great Reforms, Russians witnessed the end of serfdom, the lifting of strict censorship laws, the overhauling of the military and the judicial system, and the creation of local welfare boards. The defeat, in other words, forced the Russian autocrat and his subjects to plunge into modernity.

Nicholas and his advisors had provoked the conflict with the Ottoman Empire after bullying Turkish leaders through an insistence that Orthodox believers be granted special rights in the holy lands. When Ottoman leaders refused, Russian armies occupied the Turkish principalities of Moldavia and Wallachia. Fearing a greater Russian presence in the region, France and Britain came to the Ottomans' aid. In September 1854, French and British forces landed on the Crimean Peninsula in the Black Sea, laying siege to the Russian fortress at Sevastopol. The fortress held out for a year, but the British and French forces were better armed and better supplied, eventually capturing it in September 1855. Alexander II pressed for peace. The war, a senseless one from the start, ended with the signing of the Treaty of Paris in February 1856. Russia lost over 500,000 men (more than 100,000 at Sevastopol alone) and Russian leaders came face-to-face with the system's inadequacies.

In Russian popular memory the war came to be associated with the siege at Sevastopol and the heroic, patriotic spirit its defenders demonstrated. Leo Tolstoy, a young officer who served at the front, published his *Sevastopol Sketches* as the war waged around him. His tales did much to spread the notion to the reading public that the average soldier demonstrated extreme heroism in defending Sevastopol, while Russia's newspapers and journals also focused on the spirit of soldiers and the sacrifices made by commanders such as Admiral Vladimir Kornilov, who was killed on October 17, 1854, and his successor, Admiral Pavel Nakhimov, who was killed on July 12, 1855 while defending the fortress. Russian popular prints also helped to foster the notion that the war was best understood as one where ordinary soldiers heroically defended their motherland. After the war's end, these notions became part of the ways the war got remembered. Perhaps the most significant example of how the work of memory eventually turned the defeat into a victory of sorts came in 1905, when Franz Roubaud's panorama "The Siege of Sevastopol" opened on the fiftieth anniversary of the fortress's capitulation. The panorama captures one of Russia's small wartime victories, when the fort's defenders successfully rebuffed French and British troops on June 6, 1855. Roubaud's panorama powerfully captures the essence of the war's memory culture and with it, the cultural ready-made updated after 1855: heroic Russian soldiers fight to defend their motherland, Admiral Nakhimov guides them, and everyday heroes such as the nurse Dar'ia Mikhailova (who was heroized as Dasha of Sevastopol) and Nikolai Pirogov, the surgeon who gained fame for the way he treated the wounded at Sevastopol, all find space in the work.

Roubaud's creation directly influenced Vasilii Goncharov and Aleksandr Khanzhonkov. The latter, born to a well-off Don Cossack family, served as an officer in the army but left to establish one of the first film studios in Russia. His director, Goncharov, used connections gained during his previous career working in the Ministry of Transportation to secure government support for the first-ever film about the Siege of Sevastopol. The two employed army troops and naval units as extras in their spectacle, lending a touch of realism to the film. Debuting first at a special premiere for the tsar in November 1911 and then distributed throughout the empire, *The Defense of Sevastopol* consists of a series of episodic scenes: peasants and other residents of Sevastopol cross themselves and bless the Russian fleet; Sevastopol citizens take part in a collected effort to build up the city's fortifications; the first enemy attack of October 5, 1855 features an Orthodox priest blessing the city's defenders; Admiral Kornilov heroically dies fighting; an ordinary sailor named Petr Koshka selflessly saves one of his comrades; soldiers defend a bastion on the fortress; Pirogov works on the wounded; Admiral Nakhimov delivers orders to his troops; peasants sing and dance; Russian troops heroically defend the fortress on June 28, 1855; Nakhimov dies during an attack; Russia's enemies hold a war council; the attack of July 6, 1855 features intense fighting; a Russian Captain named Ostrovskii dies defending his motherland; the last attack features still more heroism but ultimately Russian troops retreat. The film closes with lengthy shots of French, English, and then Russian veterans still alive in 1911, then the camera captures the monuments built at Sevastopol since 1855. Khanzhonkov, who praised Goncharov for his "first class skills as an organizer" as well as his energy and management in making the film, would complain that *The Defense of Sevastopol* "was a collection of separate military and domestic episodes with no internal connection between them" (Tsivian and Cherchi Usai 1989, 136).

Figure 18.1 The death of Admiral Nakhimov. Still from Vasilii Goncharov's *The Defense of Sevastopol*, 1911.

It may be best to interpret the movie as a moving picture version of the panorama and the popular prints from 1855 (which also featured Koshka, Ostrovskii, Nakhimov, citizens of Sevastopol building defenses, enemy attacks heroically rebuffed, and Orthodox priests blessing Russian forces). *The Defense of Sevastopol's* episodes collectively narrate a handful of consistent themes, particularly the willingness of all soldiers to fight and to die for the motherland and a common spirit they all possessed, largely derived from their shared Orthodox faith. The movie travelled around the empire and garnered a great deal of press coverage. Critics and audiences dubbed it a "patriotic spectacle"; in what sources about the film's reception exist, their reactions often depended upon the quality of the print they saw. Georgi Kazachenko wrote the original music for the film and insisted that the producers hold a gala performance of the film at the Moscow Conservatory. When Kazachenko's score was performed (or a score of equal gusto), audiences reportedly embraced *The Defense of Sevastopol*. One report, from the screening at the Volga town of Kineshma, provides a particularly vivid account of what the patriotic performance could be like:

> The accompanying pianist thumped frenziedly on the bass notes. Behind the screen iron sheets and other objects were hammered and rattled, and real revolver shots rang out. When the cannons opened up, muffled rifles were fired. The auditorium was thick with gunsmoke, and the shots made the viewers jump. The projection beam hardly managed to pierce the smoke and its reflection lit up the whole auditorium. (quoted in Tsivian 1998, 101)

A second report noted that one St Petersburg movie hall had to stop the film so that the venue could be ventilated after audiences complained they could not see through all the gunpowder smoke.

Because of its epic scope, its promotional campaign, and its subject matter, *The Defense of Sevastopol* generated a lot of critical reports in Russia's burgeoning newspaper culture. Writing in *Cine-phono*, Pavel Nilus noted that the episodic structure produced repetitiveness but the audience sat for "nearly two hours" transfixed by this "new view of art," concluding that "the germ of the impact lies in the rapid alternation of impressions which is presented as a value in itself" (Nilus 1911, 9). *Russkoe slovo* [The Russian Word], the most-read Russian newspaper at the time, reported on both the Moscow conservatory screening and the special screening at the Tsar's palace. At the former, the correspondent noted that while the military and symphonic orchestras added to the experience, "unfortunately, the most interesting of the episodes depicted in the picture lacked clarity, for the lighting made them blend into some sort of solid mass." The reporter concluded that the intertitles often were unreadable, causing "great displeasure among the numerous members of the audience," which let loose with "frequent whistles and shouts (Anon. 1911). The St Petersburg paper, *Golos zemli* [Voice of the Land] criticized the producers of the "highly patriotic" film for sacrificing historical accuracy and sacred patriotism to commercial needs, claiming that many audience members laughed at the pantomimed acting, particularly that depicting Nakhimov, "a national hero." The paper concluded that the filmmakers should feel shame for mocking the "great, historic defense of Sevastopol" (Anon. 1912). Reports from cities such as Riazan and Harbin did not level these sorts of charges, but instead noted that the print was so tattered audiences could barely decipher the mess that appeared onscreen.

While the film may not have been certified as fresh on Rotten Tomatoes (had it existed then), Russian reporters noted that the film was unprecedented in its scale and scope. Numerous articles noted that *The Defense of Sevastopol* was "heavily advertised," "had drawn large audiences," or was "grand" in its presentation. The film was certainly a commercial success, allowing Khanzhonov to build a movie empire by 1915. He also received the St Stanislav Cross, second degree, from Nicholas II for his "cultural services" to the nation. Russia's first-ever feature film thus established a number of important precedents that would remain for the next century (and beyond). The role of state support; the relationship between commerce and culture, particularly when historical films are involved; the nature of "patriotism" expressed onscreen; and the representation of war as a spectacle that involved heroic defense of the nation: all these subjects would be raised again and again over the course of the next decades.

Pasha's Patriotism

The rapid advance of Wehrmacht troops into the USSR during the summer and fall months of 1941 led the Soviet government to evacuate important industries. In September, the major film studios relocated to Alma-Ata, Kazakhstan. The evacuation meant that for the first year of the war, the only new films created and aired on screens were newsreels or shorts. By 1943, however, Mosfilm, now operating in the Soviet Republic of Kazakhstan in the Central United Film Studios (TsOKS), began to release feature films. One of the most significant of these films – and one Denise Youngblood has called "the canonical movie of the war years" (Youngblood 2007, 60) – was Fridrikh Ermler's *She Defends the Motherland*. The early feature films of the war, Ermler's among them, focused on partisans in general and women in particular. Soviet women could embody the concept of the "motherland" [*rodina*] best, a personification also captured in the most famous poster from the initial months of the war, Iraklii Toidze's "The Motherland Calls!" [*Rodina mat' zovet*]. Thus, with the Nazi armies on Soviet soil, filmmakers turned once again to the concept of defending the motherland, employing it this time as the best ideal to inspire the population to fight.

Ermler's film focuses on a model Soviet woman, Praskov'ia (Pasha) Luk'ianova, who initially enjoys a blissful life as a tractor driver, mother, and wife. The idyll is disturbed when the Wehrmacht invades and Luk'ianova's husband is drafted and leaves for the front. She remains and organizes the village evacuation as the enemy approaches. She is in the village when the Wehrmacht arrives: in short order she discovers her husband is dead, watches the enemy destroy her village, and witnesses the horrific death of her young boy at the hands of a sadistic Nazi who shoots him and leaves him on a road for a tank to run over. Dazed, Luk'ianova is taken away and apparently raped (the rape is not seen onscreen, but is implicitly suggested). She emerges stumbling through a forest, clearly traumatized by what she has just experienced. Praskov'ia finds her way to a group of other Soviet refugees. When her new comrades begin to suggest that they should just surrender to the Nazis, she snaps out of her stupor and shouts "Kill them! Kill the beasts!" Pasha snatches an axe and leads her fellow refugees to attack an advancing German column. Wielding her weapon, she cuts down a German soldier as her comrades also engage in hand-to-hand combat. Luk'ianova, as Youngblood has commented (2007, 61), has transformed herself from the ideal Soviet woman into the embodiment of Toidze's famous poster.

The rest of the film follows Pasha's actions in this new role. She leads her fellow partisans, becomes infamous to the Nazis, and even marries off two young comrades. Comrade P, as she calls herself, eventually meets the Nazi who killed her son and runs him over with a tank. In the dramatic end sequence, Pasha is captured by the enemy, imprisoned, and sentenced to death. As she stoically stands upon the rough gallows, Comrade P's partisans attack the enemy and rescue her. Youngblood concludes, "the message was clear and inspirational: ordinary citizens, especially women, had an essential role to play in the resistance against the fascist invaders" (Youngblood 2007, 64). With just a little dose of hyperbole, Vera Maretskaia, who played Pasha, would later claim: "I would say that in this picture, she won the War" (quoted in Youngblood 2007, 64).

Figure 18.2 Pasha as partisan. Still from Fridrikh Ermler's *She Defends the Motherland*, 1943.

Films such as *She Defends the Motherland* did inspire audiences. They also articulated some of the reasons why the USSR eventually emerged victorious: by and large, Soviet citizens responded patriotically to the Nazi invasion and, like Pasha, did their bit to turn the tide. Ermler's film also crystallized a process underway in Soviet culture since the mid-1930s; namely, the turn away from the internationalist ideas of communism and toward a more openly nationalist concept of Soviet-Russian patriotism. *She Defends the Motherland* contains many images and statements that added to the storehouse of the cultural, ready-made concept urging citizens to defend the motherland. Some Soviet citizens in Ermler's film even express an Orthodox spirit: one elderly villager clutches an icon as she is evacuated. While these themes updated preexisting ones, *She Defends the Motherland* did not offer any conciliatory messages to the enemy as *The Defense of Sevastopol* did: the Germans are uniformly beastly and evil. Ermler's movie stressed the need to fight to the death, to sacrifice everything, in order to protect the socialist motherland.

Some of the film's messages troubled Georgii Aleksandrov, the head of Soviet propaganda and agitation during the war. In an internal letter he sent to the Central Committee, Aleksandrov wrote that the filmmakers "made it their goal to create a heroic image of the Soviet partisan-revenger" and that "they were able to show the Soviet people hating the German invaders with all of their soul," but some problems remained (Fomin 2005, 352). In particular, Aleksandrov questioned Pasha's motivation for becoming a partisan, declaring that the film shows her to be "a heartbroken mother" and not the "idea of her as a conscientious soldier who defends freedom and the motherland's independence." The propaganda chief also worried that Ermler's film would not stress the war's realities enough, concluding that "Germans are portrayed as a bunch of simpletons that the guerillas, armed with clubs and sticks, can easily smash" (Fomin 2005, 352). *She Defends the Motherland* will be "useful," he wrote, but some deficiencies remained. The critic and scriptwriter Nikolai Kovarskii expressed similar sentiments when he reviewed the movie. He criticized the film's inconsistent plot, its lack of development, and the scene where Comrade P is rescued, which he dismissed as "not real life" (Kovarskii 1943, 3).

The state higher-ups, however, recognized the film's larger purpose of capturing vital emotions that would inspire audiences. The film, its director, and Maretskaia all received Stalin Prizes. In 1946, Iurii Rotov argued in the journal *Iskusstvo kino* that *She Defends the Motherland* "was able to show with disarming honesty those fine spiritual qualities of the Russian nation" while also demonstrating "the brutal environment that led to national revenge" (Rotov 1946, 18). The Russian people, he argued, have an "inherent humanism" instilled within them that led to the "need for them to defend their motherland, their sons, against evil" (Rotov 1946, 19). He concludes that the film scores "high marks" as a "truly humanistic work of art during the difficult years of the Great Patriotic War because it was joyously accepted in the hearts of all those who love their motherland and defended it" (Rotov 1946, 19).

The Responsibility for the Motherland

In an article dedicated to Fridrikh Ermler, the Soviet film director Sergei Bondarchuk praised his former teacher as a model "communist artist" in part because he believed that Ermler the artist and Ermler the man were inseparable, allowing the director to speak directly to the Soviet people. According to Bondarchuk, Ermler created "a critical atmosphere, a spiritual mood" (Bondarchuk 1973, 98) that spoke directly to his audiences and that would carry Soviet culture into the future.

Bondarchuk's article appeared after he had long cemented his own status as one of the most important directors working in the USSR. In the late 1930s, he studied to be an actor, and then fought in the Great Patriotic War. After his discharge, Bondarchuk starred in several films, winning a Stalin Prize and receiving the title People's Artist in 1952. In 1959, as the cultural Thaw had opened up new possibilities for artistic expression after Stalin's death, Bondarchuk directed and starred in *Fate of a Man* [*Sud'ba cheloveka*], the story of a veteran whose wife and children are killed in the war. The film garnered him new acclaim and perfectly captured the trends in the war film that had appeared after 1953: filmmakers still affirmed the justness of the war, but focused more on its costs. After this success, Bondarchuk lobbied for and received the chance to direct an epic adaptation of Tolstoy's *War and Peace*. The resulting four-part, seven-hour film, which used resources not seen in Russian cinema since Goncharov's *The Defense of Sevastopol*, won Bondarchuk the Academy Award for Best Foreign Language Film. It was the first Soviet film to receive this prize and it allowed Bondarchuk to make an English-language film about the Napoleonic era, *Waterloo* (1970), starring such luminaries as Orson Welles, Christopher Plummer, and Rod Steiger.

When he authored his article on Ermler and praised his mentor's qualities, Bondarchuk had begun work on another film about the Great Patriotic War. Finished and released in 1975, *They Fought for Their Motherland*, like *Fate of a Man*, was based on a story by the Nobel Prize-winning author, Mikhail Sholokhov. Released on the thirtieth anniversary of the Victory, *They Fought for Their Motherland* appeared at a time when the Soviet state had turned the victory over Nazi Germany into a full-fledged cult. Leonid Brezhnev, a Great Patriotic War veteran who became General Secretary in 1964, restored the Victory Day parade in 1965 and made it into an annual holiday. The state subsequently oversaw a number of monumental memory projects, the largest being the massive complex built at Volgograd (as Stalingrad has been renamed in 1961), culminating with the 300-foot "Motherland Calls" statue. The cinematic equivalent of these Brezhnev-era memory projects was Iurii Ozerov's massively long film, *Liberation* [*Osvobozhdenie*], which was released in five parts, lasting over eight hours. It narrated what Nina Tumarkin (1995, 134) has identified as the cult's "master plot": Stalin's industrialization policies prepared the country for war, Soviet citizens patriotically rallied to the cause after the surprise attack, the Party and Stalin led the nation well, and the massive losses of soldiers defending their motherland saved Europe from fascism.

Compared to the bombastic, ponderous *Liberation*, *They Fought for the Motherland* tackled the "they" and "the motherland" in more personal, humanistic ways. Set in July 1942, as the Red Army begins to battle at Stalingrad, the film dissects the various "they" who made up the Red Army at that point. Petia Lopakhin, played by the popular writer and actor Vasilii Shukshin (who died of a heart attack at the age of 45 while finishing the film), is a womanizing braggart who attempts to charm local peasants out of their food. Over the course of the film, the viewer sees Lopakhin's human side, particularly when he weeps after the death of a young comrade because he knows how tough the death will be for his mother (he is told to "stop whimpering" by a comrade). Bondarchuk plays Ivan Zviagintsev, a veteran who is seriously wounded in the course of a skirmish and who prays to God because he is scared of death. He survives only because of the bravery of a very young nurse who drags him to safety. The famous Soviet actor Viacheslav Tikhonov, who starred in Bondarchuk's adaptation of *War and Peace* and who had just appeared in the popular television series *Seventeen Moments of Spring* [*17 mgnovenii vesny*, dir. Tat'iana Lioznova, 1973] as a Soviet spy who has infiltrated the Nazi hierarchy, plays Nikolai Strel'tsov, a soldier who "cannot find anything to be happy about" because his wife left him on the first day of the war and who describes the war as "a catastrophe." He is wounded, but miraculously survives his ordeal. The rest of the regiment are populated by other complex characters, including a jovial private (played by Iurii Nikulin), a hardened vet (played by Georgii Burkov), and a grizzled sergeant (Ivan Lapikov) who has fought in four wars. The "they" in the movie, in other words, are broken, wounded, weary, older, complex individuals. At the outset, they are told they are to dig in and to hold the land "at all costs." They come together in order to protect their motherland. Bondarchuk (and Sholokhov) decided to have this collection of soldiers defend a small, relatively unimportant plot of land: as the narrator describes it, "the war has reached this place, a small, remote farm lost in the vast steppes near the Don." In the end, after defending far-flung locales along the Don, the regiment, which has lost all of its officers, is told they will head to Stalingrad.

In a lengthy article published in *Iskusstvo kino*, Viktor Dmitriev hailed Bondarchuk's film as the rare example of a movie that was even better than the book. *They Fought for the Motherland*, Dmitriev argues, adds a new chapter to Sholokhov's novel and breathes new life into it. The film appeared on the thirtieth anniversary of Victory and should, therefore, be understood as a chance to teach a new generation the lessons of that war. Bondarchuk's movie, while part of the war film genre that "has found a second life" in the Brezhnev era, has captured what Dmitriev considers an essential truth about the war: ordinary Soviet citizens took up "the responsibility for the motherland's fate" (Dmitriev 1975, 26). Soviet soldiers made a choice to defend their motherland, he argues, because of their "love for her, the Soviet land, and her people" (Dmitriev 1975, 26). The critic analyzed one particular scene, when the soldiers laboriously take up the "boring, mundane, and difficult" task of digging trenches, to point out both the "naturalness" of

Figure 18.3 Digging into the motherland. Still from Sergei Bondarchuk's *They Fought for the Motherland*, 1975.

Bondarchuk's movie and its major argument: digging trenches is literally an expression of defending the motherland. This soil will become "charred, wounded, and dead" over the course of the film, for, as Dmitriev concludes, "the earth is the motherland. The earth is a nurse and protector. The earth is also a mass grave" (Dmitriev 1975, 31–32). Their decisions to defend this plot, he concludes, dissolves the distance between 1945 and 1975 because "in a broad, historical sense this is our fate too, one we have inherited and carry with us hourly throughout our lives" (Dmitriev 1975, 32). Dmitriev's review built upon the narration offered onscreen. The narrator declared at the outset of *They Fought for Their Motherland* that the film was "for all those who survived, those who did not, and those who will come after," while the conclusion came accompanied with long shots of the Russian steppe and Sholokhov's words that if one kept "the love of the motherland within our hearts, as long as we are breathing," it will allow anyone to defend against enemies.

No Choice but to Defend

Filmed in time for the sixty-fifth anniversary of the Victory, Aleksandr Kott's *The Brest Fortress* was explicitly dedicated to "those who defended the motherland." A joint Russian/Belorussian production, it aimed to tell the cinematic version of a story that only truly emerged during the Thaw. The defense of the Brest Fortress in June and July 1941, when Soviet troops resisted the Wehrmacht for one month while the Nazis ran rampant elsewhere in the country, was not one Stalin wanted told because it implicitly reminded Soviet citizens of the debacle during the war's early months. By the early 1960s, however, and as the Brezhnev-era war cult grew, the story of heroic defenders who represented a number of different national groups proved to be a perfect vehicle for promoting the "brotherhood" of Soviet peoples and for reminding younger generations of the war's costs. These desires proved to be lasting ones: the film's producer declared that it should teach young people "the truth about the war" and that the victory had been won by Soviet soldiers such as those who defended the fortress. Echoing Dmitriev's review of *They Fought for Their Motherland*, he expounded that "memory about the Great Patriotic War lives in us genetically" and "is not only a key to understanding history, it is also a key to self-consciousness" (quoted in Lewis 2011, 379).

The Brest Fortress debuted in a transformed landscape. The Soviet Union's dissolution in 1991 precipitated a near collapse in the film industry. During the economic depression of the 1990s, few movies of any kind were made. By the early 2000s, however, with the Russian economy on firmer ground, Russian filmmakers and audiences desired new film narratives, particularly ones that explored the past. Not surprisingly, war films – and particularly films about the Great Patriotic War – helped to revive the film industry and with it a renewed Russian patriotism. Beginning with the film *Star* [*Zvezda*, dir. Nikolai Lebedev, 2002], itself a remake of a 1949 film (dir. Aleksandr Ivanov), Russian directors began to revise the history of the war, exploring some of the stories not told before. At the same time, a slew of films that appeared on both big and small screens revised what it meant to defend the motherland, often by focusing on what Greg Carleton (2010) has termed "annihilation narratives": that is, movies that depict the near-total decimation of Soviet soldiers in combat.

Kott's movie was filmed at the Brest Fortress and certainly focused on the extreme sacrifices individuals made there in 1941. The main character, Sasha Akimov (played by Alesha Kopashov), is a 15-year old boy who is studying at the town's military academy. Despite his brother's attempts to keep him focused on his civic duties, he is more motivated by his desire for a local girl, Anya. The film opens on June 21, 1941, with some members of the fortress's garrison worried about the rumors of an impending German attack. Sasha and Anya, meanwhile, arrange to meet up at the nearby river and stay out all night, enabling them to witness the invasion as it begins at 3:58 a.m. When the invasion begins, the audience follows Sasha and three other characters introduced in the opening scene. The first, Lt. Andrei Kizhevatov (played by Andrei Merzlikin), is Anya's father and an officer assigned to the fortress. He attempts to find his daughter, evacuate the rest of his family, and lead his troops in the defense of the fortress. The second, Commissar Efim Fomin (Pavel Derevianko), is the political officer assigned to the battalion. Once the war begins, he leads a regiment of soldiers defending one of the fortress's main gates. The third is Major Petr Gavrilov (Aleksandr Korshunov), who had been the most vociferous officer warning against impending attack. When it comes, he too gathers his men to defend the fortress. Collectively, the three officers and their men fight heroically but soon learn that the Brest Fortress is surrounded and that the main German army has already moved into Minsk. When they understand the situation, Gavrilov voices the major argument the film

Figure 18.4 The defense of the Brest Fortress. Still from Aleksandr Kott's *The Brest Fortress*, 2010.

makes, telling his men "we are soldiers of the Red Army and we will defend our motherland to the death" because "we have no other choice."

Through several intense battle scenes, the audience sees how these soldiers enact Gavrilov's words. Sasha's brother dies early on in the fighting. Fomin's forces gradually die off and he eventually surrenders. Because he is a Soviet commissar (and Jewish), he is immediately executed. Kizhevatov manages to get his family out of the fortress, but he dies in the subsequent battles. Gavrilov also surrenders after the soldiers under his command hold out for a month and die in great numbers: both he and Sasha will survive the war. The end credits inform the viewers that their fates were not entirely pleasant: Gavrilov, along with Fomin, will only receive medals in 1957, after Stalin's death, because they initially had been viewed as defeatists who surrendered. Kizhevatov was honored only in 1965, the year Brezhnev designated Brest as a "hero fortress." Before this information is shared, however, the end sequence summarizes what this defense of the motherland cost: the camera pans over thousands of bodies strewn about the fortress. The final scene has the real-life Sasha Akimov visiting the present-day memorial complex at Brest and stating he has preserved his faith in his comrades and kept their memory alive, implying that the spectator must do the same.

For the most part, film critics dismissed Kott's epic, partly because by the time it appeared cinemas had become saturated with war films and partly because *The Brest Fortress* seemed too closely associated with an attempt to reforge a "Soviet" identity. Alexander Lukashenko, the authoritarian President of Belarus, and Vladimir Putin, the authoritarian leader of Russia (at the time of the film's debut he was the country's Prime Minister) gave *The Brest Fortress* their stamps of approval. One Russian critic noted that the film was noteworthy as an educational project "in spite of the Prime Minister's strong words of support" but ultimately concluded that the film collapsed into a chaotic, bloody mess that "clearly wants to be like a great *Soviet* film about the war" (Favorov 2010; emphasis added).

A second critic noted that the narrative offered onscreen was one that did not matter much historically because, as the Soviet-era story of the defense pointed out, the Brest Fortress had already been surrounded and ultimately did not matter in terms of what transpired in 1941. He concluded his review by stating that Kott's film was apparently one meant for spectators "to fulfill their duty to honor those who died for their motherland" (Matizen 2010), a responsibility better fulfilled by laying flowers at a grave or war memorial or by having a drink at home.

By and large, audience members who posted views on various blogs and film forums liked the film and its patriotism, sentiments that sharply contrasted with the critics. One spectator who posted on a popular online forum concluded that the film was a "worthy one about our ancestors' exploits and about our nation's exploits."[1] Another posted that she came away from the film with a better sense of the "strength of spirit the people living in and around Brest" possessed, ideals that also led her to think about the patriotism and pride in their motherland the defenders possessed. At the end, she concluded that "we really are reminded that it is our Motherland" and wonder if her generation would have defended it with the same spirit.

Filmed a century apart, *The Defense of Sevastopol* and *The Brest Fortress* appeared in completely different historical contexts. The first feature-length film in Russian history debuted in Nicholas II's empire, consisted of black-and-white vignettes, and required musical accompaniment to accentuate the special effects. *The Brest Fortress* premiered as a joint production between two new nation-states formed after the Soviet experiment, was modeled on a Hollywood blockbuster, and contained state-of-the art sound and special effects. These differences can mostly be explained by the political changes and the evolution of cinema as an art form over the course of a century. The similarities they share in terms of their narratives and themes, however, are striking. Both movies recreate the siege of a fortress that ultimately resulted in defeat, both end by capturing the memory work that had occurred to commemorate those heroic actions, both capture devastating loss of life, both stress the patriotism of the ordinary soldier, and both stress that defense of the motherland is a supreme value all citizens should aspire to. Both films had special screenings for political leaders who gave the films their respective stamps of approval, endorsements that prompted critical responses. These similarities, particularly when understood along with films that appeared between 1911 and 2010 such as *She Defends the Motherland* and *They Fought for the Motherland*, powerfully capture how this cultural ready-made got constructed on film.

Conclusion: The Malleable Motherland

What is this motherland that always needs to be defended and that is worth dying for? The answer is not a simple one, but it does help to explain the role the war film has played in articulating notions of how the "motherland" exists, what it consists of, and why it needs to be preserved. In the movies surveyed above, to illustrate this complex problem, characters are identified as Russian, Ukrainian, Belorussian, Siberian, and Muscovites (to name the most prominent); demonstrating just how many possible "motherlands" there may be to defend.

The motherland during the Crimean War and represented in Goncharov's 1911 film could be understood as the Russian empire encompassing numerous different ethnic and national groups, the Russian nation made up of ethnic Russians, or some combination of the two. The film does not clarify what the "motherland" is other than it includes Sevastopol, the soldiers and residents defending it, and individuals such as Petr Koshka (a Ukrainian soldier in the imperial army), Admiral Nakhimov (a Russian officer), and others who represented the empire's diversity. This complex relationship between empire and nation, one that complicates the easy definition of the motherland only deepened in the Soviet era. The Bolsheviks openly rejected "bourgeois nationalism" in favor of a class-based entity that also encouraged former tsarist national groups to develop a sense of nationhood. By the mid-1930s, however, Stalin began to favor a more Russo-centric sense of identity. At the same time, as Emma Widdis has noted (2003), the cinema of the 1930s helped to construct an "imaginary geography" of "Sovietness." In another work, Widdis usefully notes that "Russia has been a flexible concept" in part because its borders have often changed and because various rulers have conquered so many different peoples that the imaginary geography of Russia proves hard to pinpoint (Widdis 2004, 33).

In many ways, the difficulty in pinpointing the exact nature of the nation or empire that has been constructed across vast space illustrates the reason why calls to defend the "motherland" have proven to be so important across time. Originating from the word *rod* and *rodnia* meaning "family," "kin," "relation," the *rodina* is both a more familiar, personal way to imagine your homeland and a very malleable concept. The motherland became a way to construct a dynamic entity, one to be loved and defended, and a term that could easily transition to different political situations (and changed political borders). A 1936 article in *Iskusstvo kino* helps to capture the Soviet adaptation connected to the defense of the motherland. The article, about recent films such as *The Motherland Calls* [*Rodina zovet*, dir. Aleksandr Macheret, 1936], also articulated what "Soviet patriotism" meant. Semen Ginzburg defined it as "our commitment to our motherland, the fatherland of workers, and the willingness of the Soviet people to give their lives to their country" (Ginzburg 1936, 4). This love, he stressed, "has nothing to do with bourgeois patriotism, which is based on bestial nationalism and the desire to justify imperialist policies." Instead, Soviet patriotism is based on the happiness for workers in the world, a love and boundless devotion to the people of the Soviet Union, and to their leader, Stalin. To preserve this love, Ginzburg stressed, Soviet people have to be ready "for the first call of the motherland to quit their typical work, their family, and come to its defense" (Ginzburg 1936, 4).

Ginzburg did not clarify what the "motherland" was exactly, leaving it up to the reader to decide. Filmmakers have done the same, offering a range of possibilities for audiences to embrace: from an empire of nations to newly created nations, the Russo-Soviet war film has captured a number of "motherlands" worthy of protection. The four analyzed in this chapter, along with numerous other war films made since Goncharov's film, illustrate two important conclusions: first, how movies built the cultural ready-made concept of defense of the motherland as an essential aspect of belonging to a specific society; and second, just how malleable the "motherland" can be. Characters defended the same geographical space in these films, but the "motherland" they defended could mean a Soviet one, a Russian one, or some combination of the two.

Perhaps the best way to conclude is to turn to one more film, which was the box office leader for that year: Vladimir Rogovoi's film *Officers* [*Ofitsery*, 1971]. It is the story of two friends, Aleksei and Ivan, who served in the Civil War, then became Soviet officers. The two would fight together again in Spain and the Great Patriotic War. They become generals and meet to reflect on their lives. Their memories – and one of the major messages the film presents – center on the lesson their Civil War commander taught them: "there is such a profession as defending one's motherland." Aleksei and Ivan, as Rogovoi narrates, lived these words. For over a century, Russian and Soviet directors have provided the scripts for understanding what they mean.

Note

1   This post and others noted in the chapter can be found at the *Kinopoisk.ru* site devoted to the film: http://www.kinopoisk.ru/film/436263/ (accessed January 15, 2014).

References

Anon. 1911. (untitled). *Russkoe slovo*, [Russian Word] November 15. In *Velikii kinemo: katalog sokhranivshikhsia igrovykh fil'mov Rossii: 1908–1919* [The Great Kinemo: Catalog of Preserved Fiction Films from Russia, 1908–1919], edited by V. Ivanova, V. Myl'nikova, S. Skovorodnikova, Iu. Tsiv'ian, and R. Iangirov, 93. Moscow: Novoe literaturnoe obozrenie, http://2011.russiancinema.ru/index.php?e_dept_id=2&e_movie_id=4241 (accessed February 13, 2015).

Anon. 1912. (untitled). *Golos zemli* [The Voice of the Earth], March 2. In *Velikii kinemo: katalog sokhranivshikhsia igrovykh fil'mov Rossii: 1908–1919* [The Great Kinemo: Catalog of Preserved Fiction Films from Russia, 1908–1919], edited by V. Ivanova, V. Myl'nikova, S. Skovorodnikova, Iu. Tsiv'ian, and R. Iangirov, 95. Moscow: Novoe literaturnoe obozrenie, http://2011.russiancinema.ru/index.php?e_dept_id=2&e_movie_id=4241 (accessed February 13, 2015).

Bondarchuk, Sergei. 1973. "Edinstvo" [Unity], *Iskusstvo kino* [Art of Cinema] 9: 97–99.

Carleton, Greg. 2010. "Victory in Death: Annihilation Narratives in Russia Today." *History and Memory* 1: 135–168.

Dmitriev, Viktor. 1975. "Narod na voine" [The People at War], *Iskusstvo kino* [Art of Cinema] 9: 23–37.

Dobrenko, Evgeny. 2008. *Stalinist Cinema and the Production of History*. New Haven: Yale University Press.

Favorov, Petr. 2010. "*Brestskaia krepost*'"[The Fortress of Brest], *Afisha.ru* October 25, http://www.afisha.ru/movie/195624/review/347373/ (accessed January 15, 2014).

Fomin, Valerii. 2005. *Kino na voine: dokumenty i svidetel'stva* [Cinema at War: Documents and Testimonies]. Moscow: Materik.

Ginzburg, Semen. 1936. "Rodina i ee geroi" [The Motherland and Her Heroes]. *Iskusstvo kino* [Art of Cinema] 6: 3–6.

Goscilo, Helena. 2012. "Slotting War Narratives into Culture's Ready-Made." In *Fighting Words and Images: Representing War across the Disciplines*, edited by E. Baraban, S. Jaeger, and A. Muller, 132–160. Toronto: University of Toronto Press.

Kovarskii, Nikolai. 1943. "Ona zashchishaet rodinu" [She Defends the Motherland]. *Literatura i iskusstvo* [Literature and Art] May 22: 2.

Kriuchkov, Nikolai. 1975. "Russkii kharakhter" [The Russian Character]. *Iskusstvo kino* [Art of Cinema] 3: 53–60.

Lewis, Simon M. 2011. "'Official Nationality' and the Dissidence of Memory in Belarus: A Comparative Analysis of Two Films." *Studies in Russian and Soviet Cinema* 5.3: 371–387.

Matizen, Viktor. 2010. "Pervyi sovmestnyi blin" [The First Jointly Baked Pie]. *Novye izvestiia* [New News] June 30, http://www.newizv.ru/culture/2010-06-30/129084-pervyj-sovmestnyj-blin.html (accessed January 15, 2014).

Nilus, Pavel. 1911. "Novyi vid iskusstva" [A New Art Form]. *Cine-phono* 9: 9.

Rotov, Iurii. 1946. "Ona zashchishaet rodinu" [She Defends the Motherland]. *Iskusstvo kino* [Art of Cinema] 2: 18–19.

Tsivian, Yuri. 1998. *Early Cinema in Russia and Its Cultural Reception*. Chicago: University of Chicago Press.

Tsivian, Yuri and Paolo Cherchi Usai, eds 1989. *Silent Witnesses: Russian Films, 1908–1919*. London: British Film Institute.

Tumarkin, Nina. 1995. *The Living and the Dead: The Rise and Fall of the Cult of World War II in Russia*. New York: Basic Books.

Widdis, Emma. 2004. "Russia as Space." In *National Identity in Russian Culture: An Introduction*, edited by Simon Franklin and Emma Widdis, 30–49. Cambridge: Cambridge University Press.

Widdis, Emma. 2003. *Visions of a New Land: Soviet Film from the Revolution to the Second World War*. New Haven: Yale University Press.

Youngblood, Denise J. 2007. *Russian War Films: On the Cinema Front, 1914–2005*. Lawrence: Kansas University Press.

19

Shooting Location: Riga

Kevin M. F. Platt

In her memoirs, Elena Kuz'mina, the leading lady and wife of legendary Soviet director Mikhail Romm, recounts how the shooting location for the war thriller *Secret Mission* [*Sekretnaia missiia*, 1949] was found in Riga, Latvia, which was chosen for its "little, non-Russian streets, buildings in the German style, and highways that had not been damaged by war" (Kuz'mina 1989, 523). With the annexation of the Baltic States in the course of World War II, the Soviet Union gained both new territories and new shooting locations for film. And these two results of Soviet expansion – the geopolitical and the filmic – were bound together in a complex manner. Representation of the west in film, which had certainly constituted a part of pre-war Soviet film culture, now became one of its central staples, in a reflection of the important new subjects for film derived from the history of the war and the new status of the USSR as a global hegemon (Dobrynin 2009). Conveniently, the USSR's newly acquired cities, with their "non-Russian" appearance, fitted the bill to represent the west (Frolova 2005).

While all of the Baltic cities served as shooting locations, Riga came to play this role more than perhaps any other. As we shall see below, the concerted study of films shot in and around Riga offers special insight into the structure of both the Soviet film industry and the Soviet filmic imagination of its own geography and of the geographic structure of the Cold-War globe. Larger than any other city in the Baltic, the Latvian capital and its surrounding areas are graced with a variety of typical northern European built environments: a large medieval old city, city blocks ranging from early nineteenth-century wood construction to late nineteenth-century Art Nouveau, Medieval castles, parks and baroque palaces. Up until the collapse of the USSR, these sites were crucial elements of the Soviet cinematic imagination of the western world, serving to represent London, Paris,

A Companion to Russian Cinema, First Edition. Edited by Birgit Beumers.
© 2016 John Wiley & Sons, Inc. Published 2016 by John Wiley & Sons, Inc.

the French countryside, Berlin, Sherwood Forest, Nevada, and many other locations in such classic Cold War films as Romm's *Secret Mission*, Vasilii Levin's *Last Case of Commissar Bärlach* [*Poslednee delo komissara Berlakha*, 1971] and Igor' Gostev's *European Story* [*Evropeiskaia istoriia*, 1984], as well as in highly significant serial productions for television such as Tat'iana Lioznova's *Seventeen Moments of Spring* [*17 mgnovenii vesny*, 1973] and Igor' Maslennikov's *Adventures of Sherlock Holmes and Dr Watson* [*Prikliucheniia Sherloka Kholmsa i doktora Vatsona*, 1979–86].

Yet for Soviet film culture, Riga was more than simply a Soviet city with a "European" appearance. The Baltic republics constituted a hybrid contact zone where European possibility energized Soviet cultural activity. Riga's own cultural traditions, shaped by the history of Latvia as an inter-cultural and inter-imperial space where Latvian, Russian, German, and Jewish traditions had met and intermingled for centuries, formed the basis for a unique contribution to Soviet screens. The first high-profile Soviet film to be shot in the city, Grigorii Aleksandrov's *Meeting on the Elbe* [*Vstrecha na El'be*, 1949] drew on local actors not only for mass scenes, but also in speaking roles: Iurii Iurovskii from Riga's Theater of Russian Drama – a leading dramatic institution whose pedigree reached back to the Russian Imperial era – and Harijs Avens from the Latvian National Theater. This was the foundation for a tradition of participation of Latvian actors in Soviet film shot in Riga, both in leading roles and as extras, often cast, like the city itself, to represent varieties of the European "other."

Furthermore, although in the immediate post-war era Latvia had little capacity to produce cinema in its own right, as a result of the disruptions of the war and imposition of the Soviet regime, by the end of the 1950s the Latvian film industry had been reconstituted and began to offer its own cinematic output (Abul-Kasymova et al. 1969–1978, 2: 258–270; Pērkone 2012; Novikova 2012; Tcherneva and Denis 2011). Many films produced by the Riga Film Studio contributed to the dominant Soviet filmic culture that made use of Riga to generate the image of the west. Yet Latvian film also offered distinct departures from this regime. In particular, the Latvian "Poetic Documentary School," came to be a hallmark of films produced in Riga, beginning in the 1960s with award-winning works such as Uldis Brauns' *Snowbells* [*Baltie zvani*, 1961] and continuing up through important examples of late Soviet truth-telling, such as Juris Podnicks' *Is It Easy to be Young?* [*Vai viegli būt jaunam?*, 1986], which had a tremendous impact on perestroika-era public life across the Soviet Union.

Now, it would perhaps be more intuitive in our post-Soviet age to present Soviet Latvian film production as part of a "national tradition," distinct from that of the other Soviet republics and the dominant and culturally Russian center. However, although Soviet cultural institutions did in fact recognize and enforce national distinctions in film, to take Latvian cinema of the Soviet period in isolation would be to pass over the complex imbrications of central and republican production and consumption of film.[1] As we shall see more fully later, the total *gestalt* of Soviet filmic representations of space shot in Riga presents a scene of multiple competing geographies, documentary and fictive, mapped onto the complex relations between Cold-War ideological opponents and between the "imperial" and Russian core of the USSR and the non-Russian peripheries.

Before turning to the films themselves, let us consider more closely the geo-spatial organization of Soviet culture. The structure of the Soviet film industry ensured close, yet multiply inflected relations between the institutional centers in Moscow and peripheral sites of production such as Riga. Cultural development policies dictated that every Soviet republic must have its own capacity for film production and local oversight for distribution. Each republic therefore had at least one major studio and a separate administrative structure – Goskino Latvia, for instance – that was parallel in its functions to the central Moscow Goskino, directing film production and policy in the republic in question (Golovskoy and Rimberg 1986, 43–44). Yet these republican administrative organizations and studios enjoyed only limited independence from central institutions. Personnel, especially high-ranking executives and officials in republican level studios and film administration, were often appointed via Moscow. A significant portion of film production at the republican level responded to plans and requests generated by the central Goskino and Gosteleradio, the Soviet film, television and radio broadcast administrations. The screenplays for all feature-length films produced in republican studios passed through initial censorship mechanisms located within the organizational structure of Mosfilm and were duplicated and distributed across the USSR by Goskino only after passing through central approval mechanisms once again – the Goskino Artistic Councils.

In addition to these structural linkages, the organization of film education in the USSR ensured a high degree of professional interconnectivity across republics. It was possible in Riga, especially in the first decades after the war, to enter professional film-making without special preparation – Aivars Freimanis and Herz Frank, for instance, moved from budding careers in journalism to work in subsidiary roles in the Riga Film Studio before eventually becoming legendary directors themselves. Yet these were exceptions. In later decades, specialized professional education increasingly became the norm. Because the only Soviet educational institutions devoted to film were located in Moscow and Leningrad – chiefly the All-Union State Institute of Cinematography (VGIK) in Moscow, the Leningrad Institute for Film Engineers (LIKI), and the Leningrad State Institute of Theater, Music and Cinema (LGITMiK) – the majority of leading republican film professionals passed through the center and developed a broad network of contacts (Golovsky and Rimberg 1986, 10). This was the path taken by Latvia's leading documentary filmmakers Brauns and Podnieks, both mentioned earlier.

However, despite all of this, it should also be recognized that institutional interconnections between center and periphery were sufficiently loose to allow for significant regional differentiation in the conditions for cultural activity. Due to their European character, history, and location in cultural geography as the westernmost territory of the Soviet Union, in the post-Stalin era Soviet cultural elites came to regard the Baltic States as a special zone of progressive cultural life. Cinema, as well as music, literature, design, the arts and even scholarship were granted increased liberty for experimentation in the Baltic (Platt 2013). In tourism, vacation settlements of the region, such as Latvia's Jūrmala, became favorite destinations for the Soviet party leaders and Moscow's liberal intelligentsia. In short, in Riga cultural activity was in some sense freer than was generally the rule in the USSR.

Goskino Latvia was led for a decade by Oleg Rudnev, "a supporter of liberal experimentation in film-making" (Golovskoy and Rimberg 1986, 44). Among his legacies was the film journal *Kino* – one of a set of prominent Latvian periodicals, including also *Rodnik* and *Daugava*, which became known in the last decades of the USSR for publication of materials impossible to print in Moscow. *Kino* was published in both Latvian and Russian, and although it could not be purchased outside of Latvia, the journal was distributed to industry figures across the USSR. It was these special conditions for cultural activity that underwrote the experimental élan of Latvian documentary cinema. Furthermore, collaboration with the Riga Film Studio at times appears to have licensed directors from Moscow and elsewhere to carry out more daring projects. In light of the above, one may propose that, in the case of Latvia, the polarities of center and periphery were in some aspects of cultural life reversed, rendering Latvia something of a "minor center on the periphery."

This variegated landscape is the scene of the three trajectories through late-Soviet film-making offered below, which are organized according to both chronological and thematic principles. In sum, they offer an investigation of Soviet film in and about space from the peculiar and privileged vantage point of Riga, Latvia.

Riga as Soviet West

The first minutes of Mikhail Romm's war thriller *Secret Mission* (1950) take us by stages from the most abstract and distant view of events of power and war – a map – to the most intimate and concealed – Winston Churchill's private deliberations with a British intelligence officer. As the credits fade, the map comes into view. It shows Europe, centering on Germany, with the eastern and western fronts of a late moment in World War II drawn in with heavy lines. A voiceover intones: "What you are about to see happened at the very end of the Great Fatherland War." The narrator goes on to explain that Soviet forces are marching inexorably from the east towards Germany. As the map fades to battle scenes, the voiceover tells us of the less successful course of events on the western front, where American and British forces are retreating in the face of the Ardennes Counteroffensive – the Battle of the Bulge.

Subsequent shots, still accompanied by the explanatory voiceover, present the initiating events and characters of the film: an intertitle sets the date as January 5,

1945. We see an airplane in flight, and then the two men sitting silently inside the airplane. They are flying from New York to Berlin "on a secret mission, by prior agreement with Himmler." Another title moves the scene to London. Following an aerial establishing shot of Westminster Abbey and the Houses of Parliament, we are brought to the first dialogue of the film, between Churchill (Mikhail Vysotskii) and an intelligence officer, seated around the British Prime Minister's desk. Yet at the conclusion of this dialogue, the camera returns to maps once again: Churchill and the officer stand and approach a map remarkably similar to the one shown in the film's first shot, as they discuss the Soviet advance.

Romm's map, voiceover, and title are the founding moments for an authoritative vision of the events treated in this film – secret negotiations between German and American military and political leaders. Romm, and with him, the Soviet filmic gaze, lays claim to the truth concerning the facts of history, which will be presented in open view, in distinction from the duplicitous mendacity of the western powers as they are shown in the film. Yet the return to a map at the conclusion of these initial sequences must give us pause, for it complicates the film's lines of force and vision: with his reference to maps, does Churchill also lay his own claim to an authoritative and objective viewpoint over historical events?

The question is even more complex than it seems at first glance. The front line in the upper right-hand corner of the film's initial map lies along the Vistula River in northeastern Poland. Just beyond the frame, then, lies the Baltic region and Riga, which was liberated from Nazi occupation in October, 1944, shortly before the film's action takes place. Furthermore, on Churchill's wall hang not one, but two maps – including a fuller map of Europe that includes the Baltic in plain view.

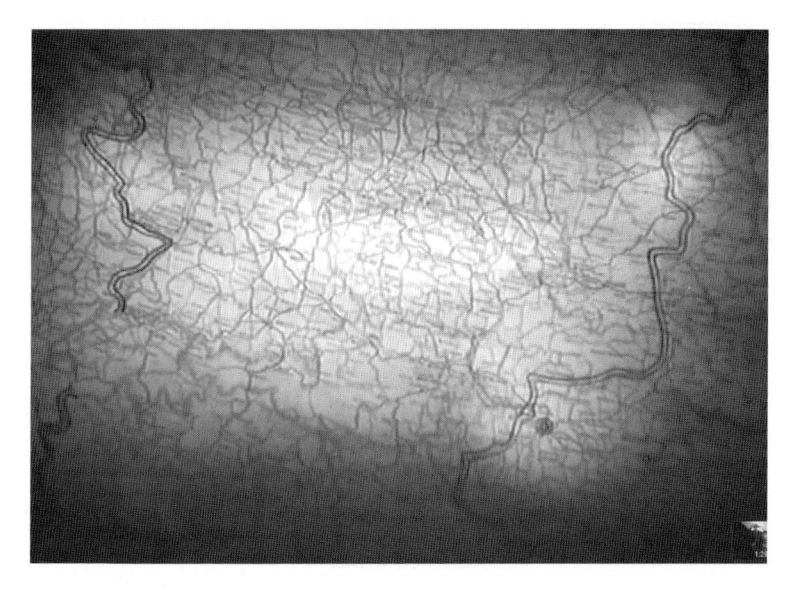

Figure 19.1 The map of Europe at the beginning of Mikhail Romm's *Secret Mission*, 1949.

Figure 19.2 Maps of Europe being viewed at the beginning of Mikhail Romm's *Secret Mission*, 1949.

However, the Baltic is not only shown on the map. It is also shown in the dramatic action itself, much of which was shot on location in Riga and Kaliningrad. How, in this light, are we to comprehend this film's claims with regard to objective gaze and geography? Are the dramatic spaces contained in the maps, or are the maps contained in the dramatic spaces? Does Romm's map show the maneuvers of Churchill's armies across geography, or does Churchill's map show the movements of Soviet borders into the Baltic area, and hence Romm's own movements?[2]

The epistemological confusion of space in *Secret Mission* projects in direct fashion onto the film's plot and action. The core of the story revolves around a battle of false and assumed identities in connection with the historical events of Operation Sunrise – negotiations over the capitulation of Nazi forces in Italy, which were held between Nazi military commanders and American and British representatives, expressly excluding Soviet representatives, in Switzerland near the close of the war in Europe. Romm's film moves these negotiations to Berlin and represents them as a prelude to Cold War antagonisms, in which western powers are scheming with Nazis and German industrialists to limit Soviet incursions into Germany and sabotage Soviet influence in Eastern Europe with the aid of Nazi intelligence agents remaining in formerly occupied territory. The positive hero of the film is Masha Glukhova (Elena Kuz'mina), a Soviet agent operating under the assumed identity of Marta Schirke, the coldly efficient, chain-smoking chauffeur assigned to the Americans in Berlin.

In sum, *Secret Mission* presents Europe as a land of false and hybrid identities, where nothing is what it seems to be. In this sense, Romm's use of Latvia as a shooting location is doubly determined: not only does Latvia present in its built environment a European scene for the film's action, it also figures as a border zone of contested identities within the Soviet Union – a place where post-war and late Soviet identity was complex, multilayered, and never identical to itself. And while to the general Soviet audience in theaters in Moscow or Irkutsk the complex imbrication of Soviet and European geography may not have been fully apparent in 1949, it would have been quite obvious to the newly Soviet audience in Riga or Vilnius. What, for instance, would such an audience have *seen* in this film's images of a military parade on the central square of Riga's old town, before the iconic Dome Cathedral: German occupying forces in an unnamed town on the western front, as announced in an intertitle, or Soviet actors, brought to Riga by the Soviet occupation of the Baltic?

Kuz'mina's memoirs, which I cited at the start of this chapter, pose these same questions in a different and starker manner. In her account, the dramatic action of the film and the scene of filming coincide in uncanny manner. As she explains: "It was the post-war era. When they pulled out of the Baltic, the Germans had left their own people behind – our fierce enemies who tried to do us harm however they could. It was impossible to search them all out at once. We were even warned not to walk in the streets alone at night" (Kuz'mina 1989, 523). Kuz'mina goes on to describe how her assigned chauffeur always held a machine-gun at the ready for an attack by anti-Soviet partisans as he would drive her to one of the film's suburban shooting locations outside of Riga in the Opel Admiral that served to represent official Nazi transportation in the film.

Of particular interest is her account of an encounter with two young men who had set their horse and cart across the road. When her chauffeur brings the Opel to an abrupt stop, Kuz'mina accidentally opens the door and tumbles out into the road:

> The surprise of the young men registered in my eyes like a snapshot. I knew only one word in German, which we would pronounce jokingly when we were bogged down in shooting. "Schnell, schnell!" I now screeched, for some reason. One of the young men grabbed the halter of his horse and the cart was soon on the shoulder of the road. Only half-conscious, I got back into the car. The engine roared and we raced onwards. When I regained my composure, the driver shot a look at me and cracked a toothless smile [...]: "Well, well! They took you for a fascist. That's the stuff!" Only then did I realize that my SS uniform for the role of the intelligence officer, along with the black cap emblazoned with the Nazi emblem, had played their role. And not only on the screen. Quite possibly, it was thanks to that uniform that we didn't wind up in a shootout (Kuz'mina 1989, 525).

Kuz'mina seems to have experienced her stay in Riga as an extension of her dramatic role as undercover agent in enemy territory. And while her fears of German agents and partisans on the loose in Riga may have been slightly exaggerated, they speak volumes concerning the geographical and spatial complexities of *Secret Mission* and of a prominent series of Soviet films like it that were shot in this same city.

These films, a significant element in Soviet representations of Cold-War conflict, tell cloak-and-dagger stories about American spies, Nazi war criminals, western manipulations of money, politics, and journalism, and other similar subjects. They include, for instance, Aleksandrov's *Meeting on the Elbe*, the plot of which revolves around clandestine and open conflicts in occupied Germany between the American forces, governed by an exploitative drive to acquire war booty and German scientific military secrets, and the Soviets, whose intentions are peaceful and directed towards the emancipation of Germany's proletariat. The iconic riverfront and bell towers of Riga's Old City feature prominently in the film, representing the Elbe river in Torgau, Germany. Other films shot in whole or part in Riga that present the mendaciousness and instability of truths and identities in the west include Romm's later work *A Murder on Dante Street* [*Ubiistvo na ulitse Dante*, 1956], concerning partisans and collaborators in occupied and post-war France, Vladimir Basov's four-part adaptation of a novel by Vadim Kozhevnikov, the wartime spy-thriller *Shield and Sword* [*Shchit i mech*, 1968], Levin's *Last Case of Commissar Bärlach*, a thriller based on Swiss author Friedrich Dürrenmatt's mystery novel *Der Verdacht* [*Suspicion*, 1951–1952], concerning a former Nazi doctor who continues his inhumane medical experiments on his patients in post-war Switzerland, and Igor' Gostev's *European Story* [*Evropeiskaia istoriia*, 1984], which tells the story of an election in a small European city in which warmongering American industrialists seek to bring neo-Nazis to power.

In the main, these Cold-War statements concerning the intersections of European and Soviet histories and identities, shot on location in the Baltic, were produced by central Soviet studios. Yet the Riga Film Studio also made important contributions to this tradition in late Soviet cinema, usually rendering these same themes more topically relevant to Latvian audiences and/or making more "literal" uses of location. Rostislav Goraev's *Nocturne* [*Noktirne*, 1966], for instance, based on a novella by Žanis Grīva, tells of the fight against fascism in the Spanish Civil War and in occupied France, yet centers its plot on the romance of a Latvian man George (Gunārs Cilinskis) and a French woman Ivetta (Pola Raksa) who work together against the common enemy. Rolands Kalniņš' *I Remember Everything, Richard!* [*Es visu atceros, Ričard!*, 1967] tells the story of Latvians conscripted into the German army – the political sensitivity of the subject matter subjected the film to a long stream of revisions and cuts before it finally reached its audience (Pērkone 2012; Tcherneva and Denis 2011). The genre of mystery thriller, which in the 1970s and 1980s became something of a staple in the output of the Riga Film Studio, also participated in representation of global conflict, projected onto the Latvian landscape (Novikova 2012, 379–380; Pērkone 2012). In particular, the director Aloizs Brenčs became known for his many detective films, which utilized shooting on location in Riga to represent far-flung settings ranging from Germany to Nevada, but which more frequently told stories set in Latvia, cast as a border space, tense with Cold-War rivalries. Notable titles in Brenčs' filmography include *Triple Scrutiny* [*Trīskārtējā pārbaude*, 1969], a film about a Soviet double agent in World

War II, *Rally* [*Rallijs*, 1978] a mystery involving an attempt to smuggle an artwork stolen during the war to the west in a racing car during an international rally, and the most watched film of 1986 in the USSR, *Double Trap* [*Dubultslazds*, 1985], another film about smuggling across the Iron Curtain set in Riga, to which I will return.

Special mention must be made here of Lioznova's *Seventeen Moments of Spring*, based on the 1970 spy novel of the same name by Iulian Semenov, which takes up some of the same historical material as Romm's *Secret Mission*. According to anecdotal accounts, virtually every television in the USSR was tuned to show this 12-part series when it first aired in 1973, emptying Soviet streets and causing spikes in electricity usage. *Seventeen Moments of Spring* tells the suspenseful, yet also surprisingly meditative and slow-paced story of the Soviet "super agent" Maksim Isaev, under cover in the Nazi intelligence services as Max Otto von Stirlitz, who against all odds informs Moscow concerning American-Nazi negotiations and undercuts them by means of intrigue. The series was created with the special oversight and consultation of the KGB, whose patronage ensured extraordinarily high production values and a massive budget (Prokhorova 2003, 82). The deep pockets of the KGB also explain Lioznova's extraordinarily involved use of shooting on location, that utilized the built environments not only of Riga, but of East Berlin, Leningrad, Soviet Georgia, and so on – often combined in a single montage. One sequence, for instance, following the steps of the character Dr Werner Pleischner (Evgenii Evstigneev) through Bern, begins with shots taken on the streets of the small city of Meissen in East Germany, then proceeds to shots in which the doctor admires animals in a zoo, taken in Tbilisi's city zoo, and finally shots that present the doctor's encounter with the members of a Gestapo cell, in which he takes cyanide and falls from a window to his death, taken in a landmark Art Nouveau building in Riga's Old City.[3] Here, the complexity of the director's subterfuge with locations matches that of the suspense plot itself.

In works such as these, Riga was multiply inscribed in the Soviet filmic imaginary as a territory where Soviet identity and geography became unstable and unfixed. The vision of the west offered by mysteries and thrillers like *Meeting on the Elbe* and *Secret Mission* was, as in all mystery films, a double exposure: an image of the falsity of western visions of time and space, superimposed by an image of the objective comprehension of human events underwritten by Socialist Realist truth-telling. Yet considering the potential interpretative destabilization wrought by the use of shooting locations like Riga, these images were double exposures twice over. These films present images of Soviet space as other than it seems, harboring depths of meaning that are not apparent on the surface. Let us recall, in this regard, a map of the Baltic region quite different from the one with which Romm begins *Secret Mission*, yet nearly contemporary with the action of the film. This other map, appended to the secret protocol of the Molotov–Ribbentrop Pact of 1939, marked out Nazi and Soviet zones of conquest across Poland and the Baltic States. Recovered from German archives and officially recognized in the USSR in 1989, it served to demonstrate the illegal nature of the Soviet annexation of the Baltic, and contributed significantly to the collapse of the worldview that supported both the place of Riga in Soviet geography and the "costuming" of Riga as a simulacrum of Europe in these films. Reading these films in our current historical context – unforeseen by their authors and first audiences – one might propose that Churchill's map ultimately triumphed over Romm's, rather than the reverse. In *Secret Mission*, we now may see not only a Soviet city dressed up as a European one, but also a European city dressed up as a Soviet shooting location.

Riga through Latvian Eyes

In 1961, Uldis Brauns shot his first film at the Riga Film Studio – a black-and-white short entitled *Snowbells* [*Baltie zvani*], directed by Ivars Kraulītis. The film features two main characters: a little girl of five or six years old and the city of Riga. The first quarter of the 24-minute film shows the city waking up on a busy working day. At five and a half minutes, the little girl appears and the point of view becomes associated with her experience of the bustling adult world. Four minutes later (well over a third of the way through the film), the engine of the plot appears: the little girl spots some flowers – the snowbells of the film's title – in a store window and is filled with desire. The next nine minutes show her adventures as she seeks to acquire flowers of her own: losing her money, encountering closed flower stores, chasing after a flower delivery truck, being picked up and given a ride by unfamiliar, yet caring adults, and finally arriving at a huge flower market where she takes, with the acquiescence of a flower-seller, a small bouquet of snowbells. The plot is seemingly resolved: her walk home is shown, with special attention to her great love for the flowers. But the film ends with one final scene of conflict: the girl drops the flowers in the middle of a busy street. It seems that they will be crushed by cars and trucks, and then, finally, by a steamroller. But the steamroller driver spots the flowers in time and the little girl emerges to claim them. The film's final seconds are devoted to a crane shot of the little girl walking away down the white line in the middle of the road, followed by a return to anonymous views of Riga.

Despite the fact that this film includes played dramatic action, it is typically seen as the origin (or as one of two candidates for the origin) of the Latvian Poetic Documentary School.[4] In subsequent years, Brauns, the cameraman and initiator of the project, went on to make a series of documentaries as director, pulling into his undertakings younger film professionals who would go on to become documentary film-makers themselves. A partial consideration of the resulting professional "genealogy," which by no means exhausts the field of figures associated with Latvian Poetic Documentary, illustrates the close relationships that tied the movement together. The scriptwriter for *Snowbells*, Herz Frank, would collaborate with Brauns on other projects, but also soon struck out on his own. Among his projects was his work as writer for the film *Report On A Year* [*Gada reportāža*, 1965], directed by Freimanis and shot by cameraman Ivars Seleckis, celebrating 25 years of Soviet Latvia. Freimanis had emerged from work on newsreels with his own debut in the new style, a short documentary about life in a Latvian fishing village entitled *The Shore* [*Krasts*, 1963]. Subsequently, both Seleckis and Frank would become major directors in their own right. In later years, Frank would initiate into the tradition a younger collaborator, Juris Podnieks, who would become one of the leading figures of Latvian Poetic Documentary in the 1970s and 1980s. Podnieks' untimely death in 1992 coincided with the end of the movement as a unified phenomenon, largely as a result of the collapse of filmmaking institutions in post-Soviet Latvia, although many of its key figures would continue to make film in one way or another in the post-Soviet era.

Clearly, documentary film shot in Riga constitutes a radically different representational regime than the fiction films discussed earlier: these documentaries present the "real" Riga, rather than Riga as France or Riga as Germany. Nevertheless, they also register in their own way the complex nature of Soviet conceptions of Baltic geography. The stylistic specificity of Latvian Poetic Documentary was characterized from its inception by an emphasis on the subjective and lyrical, rather than the objective and authoritative. Composition relied heavily on metaphoric and associative montage. The technical principles of the movement featured experimentation with the widescreen format newly introduced in Soviet film in the 1960s, allowing for a more complex representation of interrelationships and conflicts between individuals and environments (Surkova 2012). Later, in the 1970s and 1980s, hand-held cameras made possible a projection of immediacy and authenticity of perception (Sīmanis 2012). In sum, the works of the movement contributed to Soviet visual culture personal and often idiosyncratic views of and from Riga.

In a retrospective of the "Riga School" of documentary cinema delivered at the first International Symposium of Documentalists held regularly from 1977 onwards in Jūrmala, the Latvian film critic and practitioner Abram Kletskin noted that the initial impulse of Latvian Poetic Documentary was closely in tune with the overall currents of cultural life of the Thaw years. Explaining the aspiration of the movement towards "questions regarding worldview and the eternal," rather than objective documentation of everyday reality, he noted:

> It is [...] important to note that thirst for the affirmation of the human, of the humane, of the inherent worth of a human life, which permeated the entire atmosphere of the end of the 1950s and the start of the 1960s. In these circumstances, a turn in the direction of "eternal" themes was completely comprehensible, and perhaps more contemporary than a concern with concrete problems of life. (1977, 4)

As Kletskin's comments suggest, Latvian Poetic Documentary was a typical phenomenon of Soviet culture of the Khrushchev era, which ushered in a revival of neo-romantic tendencies, sanctioning the examination of subjective exaltation, rebellious passion, and aspiration towards the ideal, as long as the ideals in question were proper socialist ones. (Leighton 1983; Clark 2013).[5]

Yet Latvian Poetic Documentary, in its initial blossoming during the 1960s, was not devoted to expression of the personal or the subjective alone. Granted, these films were poetic – but they also remained documentary. As is implied by the oxymoronic tensions of the movement's name, or by the similarly oxymoronic conception of a "romantic" variant of Socialist Realism – a Socialist Romanticism – the project of these films was to bridge between the inner world of subjective impressions and emotions and the objective social order, between inspired ideals and socialist reality.[6] In this they participated in the Thaw-era drive to reintegrate Soviet society by enlisting spontaneous enthusiasm in the grand projects of the day, from the Virgin Lands campaign to the construction of the Baikal Amur Mainline (BAM), to the project of building communism itself.

To return to *Snowbells* – the articulation of such an affective and poetic passage between the subjective and the objective, the ideal and the real is the film's major theme. The start of the film, we may note, presents a homage to an earlier instance of highly metaphorical filmic language inspired by a socialist vision of the world: that of Dziga Vertov. In particular, in these images of a city waking up we recall the initial scenes of *Man With a Movie Camera* [*Chelovek s kinoapparatom*], as well as the overall tradition of city symphony films associated with Vertov's film, such as Walter Ruttman's *Berlin: Symphony of a Great City* (1927). Yet the introduction of the child's specific point of view on the city is Brauns' and Frank's own, rather sentimental innovation. The little girl's pursuit and capture of simple, white flowers, perhaps inspired by Albert Lamorisse's *Red Balloon* (1956), presents an allegory of the organic unity of the most innocent human desire with the enormous totality of a socialist city (Abul-Kasymova et al. 1969–1978, 3: 279). The city and all of its inhabitants, shown pursuing their own grand, adult, socialist ends – constructing buildings, installing cables, shipping goods, departing on journeys – nevertheless at one and the same time all help the little girl to achieve her end. The film's combination of diegetic and non-diegetic sound, integrating industrial and mechanical sounds of the city with the soundtrack by Arvīds Žilinskis, yet reducing human voices to a distant murmur, presents the child's point of view as one of lyrical integration into the humming, undifferentiated urban life. The final confrontation with the steamroller is a literally heavy-handed gesture to drive the point home: the construction of a communist city and the pursuit of childlike dreams are in fact entirely compatible processes. The girl and the snowbells are perfectly reconciled with the steamroller and the busy street.

In its mixed generic construction, *Snowbells* illustrates an analogous point: as Frank notes in his memoirs, the film was shot on location in Riga without any attempt to control the everyday action on the streets. Many of those caught on celluloid had no idea they were being filmed or were part of a planned narrative (Frank 1975, 37–40). In this generic hybridity, the oxymoronic tensions of poetic documentary are once more apparent. Just as the romantic and the real, and the subjective and the objective could be bridged, so too could the acted and the documentary. In each case, the key was affective linkage of artistic vision with socialist reality that rendered acted elements no less "real" than the document and the documentary elements no less "poetic." As Frank later wrote of this film: "the distinction between invention and reality was erased" (1975, 40).

Perhaps the most extraordinary, culminating statement of the dedication to overcoming the conceptual gulf between the poetry and document, the subjective and the collective of this initial era of blossoming in Latvian Poetic Documentary cinema was the film *235,000,000* (1967). This was an ambitious attempt to present a portrait of the entire population of the Soviet Union on the occasion of the fiftieth anniversary of the October Revolution – 235 million was the population of the Soviet Union at the time (shades here of Vladimir Maiakovskii's 1920 long poem *150 Million*). Like *Snowbells*, the project featured the work of Brauns and Frank as director and scriptwriter, yet their collaboration expanded to encompass many other figures: filming involved four separate teams – Herz Frank and cameraman Rihards Pīks; assistant director Laima Žurgina with cameraman Valdis Kroģis; assistant director Biruta Veldre with cameraman Ralfs Krūmiņš; and directors Brauns and Seleckis, and camerawoman Ruta Ubaste – who dispersed to locations across the Soviet Union and filmed during much of 1966. The mode of production of this film itself might be described as an experiment in the organic unity of individual vision with a collective undertaking in a celebration of socialist ideals.

The explicit goals of filming were codified in the "Battle Regulations" – a pamphlet written by Frank to be carried throughout the filming by all four teams, which includes key quotations from Vertov's own "Battle Regulations of the Kinoks" of 1924, including the director's famous formula "life caught unawares" (Vertov 1984). According to Frank's instructions, *235,000,000* was to combine two "lines": the "personal life of the individual" and the "eventual." The former compositional line was to seek out "the personal, intimate, reverential, the expression of feelings, the individual," whereas the latter was to strive to capture "event-ness, mass character, the collective, sensational qualities, scale" (Frank 1975, 150–152).

The final result of these efforts was an ode to the collective life of the USSR that ranged from the peripheries of Central Asia, Georgia, and the Baltic to the center of the society in the Kremlin and from the intimate sphere of courtships, weddings (and even wedding nights) in diverse ethnic traditions, births, young couples acquiring baby carriages, and children learning to walk to the public life of the society as seen at the Twenty-Third Party Congress, in an "overheard" interview with cosmonaut Valentina Tereshkova, in industrial processes and newspaper printing factories, and in military exercises involving advanced weaponry. As in *Snowbells*, *235,000,000* combined diegetic and non-diegetic sound, including a score by emerging Latvian Jazz composer Raimonds Pauls, with no documentary narration (although in this film, at times, the human voice is audible – both the voices of the film's subjects and at one point an overdub "borrowed" from some more standard "newsreel" documentary announcing the Party congress). Apart from

Pauls' score, the central glue that holds the film together is the poetic resonance of one scene with another and of one image with another – as, for instance, in a cut from a man and his children running in the snow following their ice-bath who appear seamlessly to become children running down a sand-dune, or a shot of parachutes in a military exercise that completely imperceptibly cuts to a shot of the veils of new brides – cuts that out of a series of formal analogies create a novel, filmic spatiality of the Soviet Union in which remote points of the social, ethnic, and physical landscape are brought together in one fabric. Here, the imaginative geography of Riga expanded to encompass the entirety of the USSR.

Snowbells and other previous films of Latvian Poetic Documentary presented a synthetic vision of Riga uniting the personal and emotive with the socialist and the grand. *235,000,000* applies this filmic strategy to a broader geography, linking together the entirety of Soviet space by means of the Baltic filmic vision, uniting not only individual and society, but also geographical center and periphery, distinct ethnic enclaves and cultures, and disparate climates and landscapes. The film carries out the inversion of a more intuitively obvious conception of the relationship between the individual and the collective in documentary, in which an "objective" representation of the real provides a matrix in which subjective experience finds its place. Here, it is the reverse, as is seen quite clearly in the "Battle Regulations," where Frank explains that the thematic "line" of "the personal life of the individual," is "the backbone of the film," while the "eventual" line of collective and mass events are inserts [*vstavki*] – episodic interpellations into this structure. In this, the film is an extreme expression of faith that commonalities of Soviet subjective experience could in fact be the basis for the unity of Soviet society and geography. Poetry takes priority over documentation. In contrast to the queasy uneasiness concerning false geographies of the thrillers shot in Riga discussed above, *235,000,000* is wildly optimistic about the coherence of Soviet landscapes and identities.

However, the judgment of contemporaries seems to have been that Brauns' and Frank's experiment was a failure. The film was shown in 1967 at the Leipzig Documentary Film Festival, and in Moscow in connection with celebrations of the October Revolution. At the insistence of Goskino, the original version had to be cut by nearly 30 percent before it was licensed for what appears to have been a minimal distribution anyway (Eksta 2012). Naum Kleiman asserts that the film was not so much subjected to censorship as quietly suppressed: "it was not banned, but simply removed from the screen in order to avoid making too much noise and a precedent" (Kleiman 2013). Authoritative critical voices afforded serious attention to the film in order to exorcise it as a failure. Film critic Lev Roshal' condemned *235,000,000* for its failure to organize material according to a coherent conceptual frame and refusal to employ a voice-over narration, and suggested that the film's poetic, plastic unity was insufficient to bind the documentary material together:

> The aspiration to 'hide' more deeply in the material, the consciously declared lack of organization of that material as the highest degree of documentary veracity, itself

linked supposedly with a natural rejection of speculative constructions that do violence to the facts – all of this is ultimately just as formal as the imposition of schematic constructions on the documentary evidence. For such a "retreat into the material" makes it impossible to comprehend the essence of phenomena. It does not lead to the truth, but rather away from it. (Roshal' 1973, 108).[7]

Perhaps we should interpret Roshal''s view as a statement of changing social and aesthetic circumstances of the end of the 1960s and the start of the 1970s, when a "Socialist Romanticism," or a fully Poetic Documentary style was becoming more difficult to imagine and articulate. In the 1977 retrospective cited above, Kletskin expressed similar views, critiquing the Poetic Documentary films of the 1960s in general for their aestheticization of reality, excessive concern for "eternal" problems, and rejection of the proper publicistic calling of documentary film. Poetic Documentary was a broad movement, with many practitioners and works, and certainly the quest for lyrical unity between subjective experience and collective life continued to find expression in various films of the following decades. But certain key films of the 1970s demonstrate that the school's creative impetus underwent significant modifications in this decade. Perhaps Frank's most important film of the 1970s was a prize-winning short created in 1978 in collaboration with Podnieks titled *Ten Minutes Older* [*Par 10 minūtēm vecāks*] – a single long take of a young boy watching a puppet show and passing through the gamut of human emotions, from fear to joy to boredom to surprise. This is an extraordinary, and extraordinarily beautiful, study of human subjectivity at close range, but it evinces zero interest in the integration of subjectivity in any broader social context.

If the Poetic Documentary films of the 1960s combined the subjective and the romantic with the objective and the socialist, *Ten Minutes Older* is interested in subjective experience alone. Many other works of Latvian documentary cinema of the 1970s may be seen as expressions of this same turn away from the high ideals of the common Soviet project to explore either the intimate, the deviant, or the particular – Laima Žurgina's eponymously titled documentaries on ballet dancer Māris Liepa (1971) and composer Raimonds Pauls (1977), for instance, or Frank's and Podnieks' first collaboration, their documentary on a juvenile offender's colony *Forbidden Zone* [*Zapretnaia zona*, 1975]. We may interpret this shift in attention as a corollary of the loosened bonds between personal ideals and social imperatives typical of the USSR in the 1970s and early 1980s, which has been described as a "deterritorialization" of the language and values of socialism by Alexei Yurchak (2006), or Platt and Nathans (2011) as the advent of an "imaginary private sphere." In the 1960s, it had seemed that collective and personal life, and the geographical periphery and center, could be merged in a single fabric, fused together by enthusiasm for Soviet ideals. Yet in later decades, as socialist life became, for more and more Soviet men and women, divorced from an increasingly autonomous precinct of personal values, pursuits, and goals, the central terms of Romantic aesthetic formations such as Poetic Documentary were pulled apart as well. In response to the new gulf between subjective and collective existence, and between the Latvian part and the socialist whole of Soviet geography, Poetic Documentary retained its focus on the former terms rather than the latter. It, too, became deterritorialized.

The Baltic as Soviet Little Europe

Meeting on the Elbe, Seventeen Moments of Spring, European Story and the other visions of the west as a threatening zone of false ideology and identity examined earlier in the chapter did not represent the only tradition in the late Soviet filmic imagination of capitalist geography. From the Khrushchev years on, western cultural forms, consumer goods, and modes of life increasingly constituted an object of fascination at many different levels of Soviet society: from western figures and works of art, literature and music deemed sufficiently leftist, popular, or super-ideological to pass into a Soviet canon of world culture, to jazz and rock in both officially tolerated popular culture and in the music of youth rebellion, to participation in international trends in art, fashion, and architecture, to the trade in black-market western consumer goods. Yurchak, who observes that most Soviet men and women could never travel beyond the borders of the USSR, describes these varied cultural phenomena as elements of an "imaginary west" – an amalgamation of alternative values that at times intersected with recognized Soviet cultural life, at times represented an oppositional underground, but mostly constituted an intermediate zone of relative freedoms from the cultural forms and social codes of Soviet civilization (Yurchak 2006, 158–206).

Yurchak notes that the Soviet imaginary west did not exist in "any real place" (Yurchak 2006, 159). Without disputing his analytical frame, one might offer the quibble, literally on the margins of Yurchak's argument, that in some sense it was also located in the Baltic.[8] As we have seen, Elena Kuz'mina, when filming *Secret Mission* in 1949, felt that she was penetrating enemy territory. In contrast, Mikhail Kozakov's trip to Riga six years later with the cast and crew of Romm's *Murder on Dante Street* appears to have been more of a pleasure tour. In his memoirs, the actor, who plays the young French collaborator Charles Thibault, recalls the pleasures of professional travel: "Riga. Shooting on location. How wonderful it was for me! Not a single difficult scene, and you just stroll around in a beautiful suit, sewn by the legendary [Isaak] Zatirka. [...] Often, Mikhail Il'ich [Romm] would invite me after shooting to walk through Riga with him" (Kozakov 1993, 196–197). By the late 1950s and 1960s Riga and the Baltic as a whole were acquiring their significance as a privileged tourist site, where Soviets could experience something of European history, traditions, modernity, and cultural refinement, but perhaps also something of the alternately coveted and denigrated west – so much so that by the last Soviet decades, some referred to the Baltic was as "our little Europe." One may recall, in this regard, Vasilii Aksenov's Youth Prose novella

Ticket to the Stars [*Zvezdnyi bilet*, 1961], immediately adapted for film as *My Younger Brother* [*Moi mladshii brat*, 1962], which tells the story of four friends who travel to Tallinn after graduation from school and encounter medieval architecture and historical reminiscences, Bach organ music, poker-playing "capitalist" wheeler-dealers, a bustling café culture, and, of course, love (Graffy 2005).

In short, the Baltic often served as the real landscape or theatrical screen on which the imaginary west was projected. The more positive conceptions of both the west and of the Baltic associated with this dimension of late Soviet subjectivity found expression in a range of films shot on location in Riga both by central studios and the Riga Film Studio. Most commonly, these films were in the genre of historical romance, providing Soviet viewers access to a European elsewhere charged with libidinal excitement and cultural alterity. *Robin Hood's Arrows* [*Strely Robina Guda*, 1975] can serve as a paradigmatic example of late Soviet historical romance. Directed by well-connected Moscow film professional Sergei Tarasov at the Riga Film studio, shot on location in and around Riga to take advantage of its period architecture, and involving a team of actors incorporating both Latvian and Russian stars, the film was one of the biggest hits of Soviet cinemas in 1976 with 28.9 million viewers (Razzakov 2004, 377). Of course, Robin Hood, the outlaw who takes from the rich and gives to the poor, is *prima facie* an ideologically suitable subject for Soviet moviegoers. Tarasov's version, predictably, tilts the legend even further in the direction of class struggle. Yeoman Robin Hood (Boris Khmel'nitskii) with his merry band of outlaws battles against greedy aristocrats. The outlaw's love interest is Maria (Regina Razuma), whose father, a miller, is gratuitously murdered by landlords extracting taxes.[9] However, although these plot features rendered the film politically acceptable Soviet entertainment, it is also clear to any viewer that its center of gravity in fact lay elsewhere – in the defiant individualism of its characters, their romantic interludes in pastoral settings, not to mention their hippie-inspired costumes. Undoubtedly, these aspects of the film, which evoked youth rebellion against morally compromised conventional society rather than any "correct socialist values," were the key to its success.[10]

Historical escapism, nominally politically conformist, yet pregnant with ambivalence with regard to the Soviet present, was visible in a range of other films shot at the Riga Film Studio or by other studios on location in Riga. Some, like *Robin Hood's Arrows*, were derived from west European history and culture, such as Georgii Iungval'd-Khilkevich's three-part adaptation of Alexandre Dumas' *Count of Monte Christo*, entitled *Prisoner of Castle If* [*Uznik Zamok If*, 1988]. Others, shot at the Riga Film Studio, explored a similar dynamic, yet set the action in Riga itself during various historical time periods: generically close to *Robin Hood's Arrows*, Aleksandrs Leimanis' musical comedies *Servants of the Devil* [*Vella kalpi*, 1970] and its sequel *Servants of the Devil at the Devil's Mill* [*Vella kalpi, vella dzirnavās*, 1970], about daring young people who save Riga from Swedish conquest and foil the plots of greedy merchants prepared to betray the city for personal gain (Novikova 2012, 377–378), as well as the same director's next work in this same generic category,

In the Claws of the Black Crab [*Melnā vēža spīles*, 1973], about Latvian peasants who get the better of their German landlords. Another notable Latvian historical romance was Imants Krenbergs' *In the Shadow of the Sword* [*Zobena ēnā*, 1976], a loose adaptation of Janis Rainis' play on the legend of the Rose of Turaida, which tells of a lowborn Latvian maiden who prefers death to dishonorable submission to a Polish mercenary. In all of these films, the physical boundaries of Soviet space in the Baltic peripheries, either as shooting location or as actual setting, served as a location in which Soviet film could imagine what lay beyond the temporal boundaries of Soviet history and the strictures of Soviet social life.

The most influential example of the late Soviet imaginary west in film shot on the streets of Riga was Maslennikov's *Adventures of Sherlock Holmes and Dr Watson*, adapted for the small Soviet screen by Iulii Dunskii and Valerii Frid. A series in eleven parts, produced and shown intermittently from 1979 to 1986, this was one of the most popular Soviet television productions of the first half of the 1980s. A significant number of scenes set on the streets of London were shot in Riga's Old City – in particular, 22 Jauniela iela was immortalized as the exterior of 221B Baker Street, the famous address of Holmes and Watson (played by Vasilii Livanov and Vitalii Solomin). Other locations in and around Riga were also utilized, especially in the earlier installments of the series.

As with the works examined earlier, the fundamental key to the series' success was its licensing of an apolitical historical escapism. By making a great show of faithfulness to a beloved pre-Revolutionary literary classic, *The Adventures of*

Figure 19.3 "Baker Street" – Riga's Jauniela. Still from Igor' Maslennikov's *Adventures of Sherlock Holmes and Dr Watson*, 1979–1986.

Figure 19.4 "No. 221B" on Jauniela. Still from Igor' Maslennikov's *Adventures of Sherlock Holmes and Dr Watson*, 1979–1986.

Sherlock Holmes and Dr Watson evaded the demand for ideological tendentiousness in depicting the west that was so heavily expressed in the thrillers and spy films discussed earlier.[11] Yet as with those films, there were undoubtedly special attractions to this historical fantasy that support an ideologically inflected reading at a deeper level. At the outset, we may propose that Holmes' and Watson's identities as private citizens who untangle complex concealed histories and establish truth and justice while obeying a strict code of personal morals – those qualities that rendered them archetypal literary detectives the world over – undoubtedly made them doubly attractive for viewers in the USSR in an age of increasing alienation from the epistemological, political and moral conventions of Soviet civilization.

Further, drawing on critical work that has demonstrated the importance of the British imperial project in Conan Doyle's writings, Catherine Nepomniashchy has proposed (2005) that Maslennikov's version may be seen as an allegory for the complex relations of late Soviet viewers to the imperial structures of the USSR in particular. Conan Doyle's works labor to defend the Victorian English values that justify the British Empire and ensure its stability against colonial disorder and foreign threats. The Soviet version, especially the final episodes in which Holmes foils German intelligence plots, echo at a discrete distance the very themes of espionage and assumed identity characteristic of Cold-War representations of the west discussed above. As Nepomniashchy argues (2005), the series expresses a form of nostalgia for less compromised relations between patriotic identity and the political imperatives of the state by projecting this story into a distant and

Figure 19.5 "London" in Riga. Still from Igor' Maslennikov's *Adventures of Sherlock Holmes and Dr Watson*, 1979–1986.

foreign time and place – and, we may add, by cheekily offering the British Empire, precisely the world power that appears in such films as Romm's *Secret Mission* as the personification of ideological deceit, as the figure of a bygone era of honest integration of private morality and patriotic loyalty. In short, Holmes and Watson model a form of social being that was no longer possible for many of their viewers.

And so Riga, which in Romm's film and others served as a border location in the USSR, where one could envision the falsity of western concepts of space and time, and which in Poetic Documentary films of the 1960s (such as Brauns' and Frank's *235,000,000*) served to illustrate the proper integration of the centers and peripheries of Soviet geography, in *The Adventures of Sherlock Holmes and Dr Watson* came to represent a coherence of imperial space and civilization that was increasingly felt to be absent in the USSR itself.

Conclusion

With *The Adventures of Sherlock Holmes and Dr Watson* our tour of the Soviet filmic imagination, via Riga, has come full circle, bringing us once again to an appreciation of the place of the Baltic in Soviet cultural geography as a hybrid space, on the peripheries of the USSR, at the intersection of east and west. The series also suggests that the analytical categories offered above of Cold-War mystery thriller,

Poetic Documentary and fantasy of the imaginary west intersected with one another in surprising ways as the Soviet era was drawing to a close. Brenčs' *Double Trap* of 1985 exemplifies this categorical instability. Set in contemporary Riga, the film tells the story of criminals who smuggle art treasures to the west. In return, they receive not only cash, but also pornography, which they distribute for profit through circles of young black-marketeers. Their western handlers are moved equally by desire for financial profit and by a shady geopolitical mission to corrupt Soviet youth. The hero of the film, who is introduced initially as Ferz (Algis Matulionis), a member of the underworld contracted by one crook to take revenge on another, is eventually revealed to be the KGB agent Gunar, operating deep undercover.

While *Double Trap* activates familiar themes of western mendacity and false identities laid bare and corrected by the true Soviet filmic vision and justice, that vision also lingers with suspicious relish on the Riga criminal underworld. One might suggest that the success of this film derived less from the defeat of lawbreakers and nefarious agents of the west than it did from viewers' prurient interest in scenes of glamorous night clubs with sexually explicit dance acts, luxurious dachas, parties where pornography dealers contracted young women for illicit services, and other morally compromised delights of western depravity and liberty. Ostensibly a parable of Soviet resistance to western corruption, the film may quite easily be seen as fantasy about the dangerous and delightful sexual and economic freedoms of the imaginary west. In short, by the time of Mikhail Gorbachev's appointment as General Secretary of the CPSU, Riga and films shot in it were increasingly becoming illustrations of a frank ambivalence about the integrity and significance of Soviet society and its values.

If Riga had served as a location of hybridity and mysterious double identity in the Soviet filmic imagination, it was in documentary film that this mystery was ultimately dispensed with in the last years of the USSR. As we have seen above, the directors of the Latvian Poetic School had turned away from the grand statements of the 1960s concerning the integration of lyrical vision with objective documentation of socialist reality, such as Brauns' *235,000,000*, to concentrate instead on the personal, the particular and the asocial in such films as Frank's *Forbidden Zone*. This tendency culminated in Podnieks' influential 1986 film about disaffected youth culture in Latvia, *Is it Easy to Be Young?*, which was screened to tremendous acclaim throughout the Soviet Union – a reported 28 million viewers saw it in its first year (Horton and Brashinsky 1992, 72–76, 143–146; Vitols 2008, 143–160). By the end of the 1980s, a new vision of social integration and shared collective values emerged to take the place that had been vacated by the fading of socialist ideals. This new framework was of course the project of Latvian identity and national independence, which became the central subject of late expressions of Soviet Latvian documentary film. The geography of nation accomplished the reterritorialization of the Baltic landscape. Podnieks' last completed film before his accidental death, *Homeland* [*Krustceļš*, 1990], documents the mass choral rallies of the Baltic independence movements in Latvia, Estonia, and Lithuania. Ansis Epners *I am a Latvian* [*Es esmu latvietis*, 1990] studies Latvian diaspora across the globe. In each, Riga is represented as identical only to itself and as the center of a new conception of national geography.

Unfortunately, the end of the USSR that becomes visible in these films also brought a severe crisis to the Latvian film industry. The disintegration of the institutional and economic conditions of Soviet culture made film production on a large scale nearly impossible in Latvia beginning in the early 1990s. Apart from a few independent projects, very few films have been made in Riga since that time. The Riga Film Studio, which was privatized in the 1990s, is mothballed and crumbling: rental of production facilities and equipment for shooting on soundstages and on location in Latvia is its main business, but business is scarce. Despite the noble efforts of some to continue the traditions of Poetic Documentary in an era of scarcity, the most prominent documentary film to come out of Latvia in recent years has been Edvīns Šnore's *The Soviet Story* [*Labvakar*, 2008] a ponderous documentary film about Soviet history in the Baltic and elsewhere, presented from largely nationalist positions. On a stroll through Riga's Old City, one may encounter tour guides directing the attention of groups of tourists from the former Soviet territories to "the building where Dr Pleischner plunged to his death" and "that famous address, 221B Baker St." The filmic imaginary west, shot on location in Riga, remains as a celluloid memory of a geography that never was.

Notes

1. For examples of more focused accounts of Latvian cinema in isolation, see Pērkone (2012) and Novikova (2012).
2. My interpretation of maps in the initial sequence of Romm's *Secret Mission* is inspired by Conley (2007).
3. The sequence in question is in *Seventeen Moments of Spring*, Episode 9, at 46:06.
4. The other possible initiation point for Poetic Documentary is *My Riga* [*Mana Rīga*, Riga Film Studio, 1960] by Aloizs Brenčs. It should also be mentioned that innovative documentary cinema was appearing at a number of other sites in the Soviet Union at about this time, most prominently at the Frunze Film Studio in Kirghizia and at the Leningrad Studio of Documentary Film in Russia (Sidenova 2014).
5. Consider, in this regard, the series of debates concerning Romanticism that took place on the pages of the leading literary journal *Voprosy literatury* from 1957 to 1964. A typical example of the terms of these debates is offered by critic Mikhail Kuznetsov's praise of Konstantin Paustovskii's "Romanticism": "We march in the vanguard of humanity because both our reality and our ideals are extraordinarily elevated. … For this reason, it is entirely justified in a broad historical perspective to discuss features of the literature of socialist realism such as its striving for the future, affirmation of high ideals, or Romanticism as a general, genealogical trait" (Kuznetsov 1958, 223–224).

6   My thoughts concerning "Socialist Romanticism" were stimulated by the conference convened by Serguei Oushakine at Princeton University in 2014 on "Romantic Subversions of Soviet Enlightenment: Questioning Socialism's Reason." I thank Oushakine and the other participants of that meeting for comments on my work on Poetic Documentary.

7   Roshal''s assessment was originally published in the leading journal *Iskusstvo kino* in 1968. Frank cites the original publication of this essay in Frank (1975, 176). See also Kletskin (1977, 6–7).

8   Although it is somewhat outside of the scope of this chapter, let us note that the mysterious "Zone" of paranormal activity that figures in Tarkovsky's *Stalker* (Mosfilm 1979), which Yurchak interprets as a figure for the extraterritorial dimension of the Soviet social imaginary, was also shot on location in Estonia (see Yurchak 2006, 160–161).

9   Tarasov's choices should not be taken as a distortion of the Robin Hood legend, but rather as a predictable selection from a tradition that includes many variants (perhaps historically primary ones) in which Robin and Marian are both lowborn.

10 Arguably, the core of the film's cultural significance is to be found in the six ballads about Robin Hood written and performed for the soundtrack by the bard of youth rebellion, Vladimir Vysotskii, featuring such lines as: "Now and for ever, in future and past / A debt is a debt, and guilt is just that / All will be well, if honor is saved, / And you've trusty friends shielding your back" (Vysotskii 1988, 355). However, as a result of censorship, the songs were cut from the film in post-production and replaced by new music written by Raimonds Pauls with lyrics by Lev Prozorovskii. Tarasov was able to recycle some of the original songs recorded for *Robin Hood's Arrows* in his *Ivanhoe* [*Aivengo*, 1982], which was shot largely in Ukraine, rather than the Baltic. A director's cut with the original music restored was released in 2002. See Novikov (2002, 249–257).

11 In *The Adventures of Sherlock Holmes and Dr Watson*, the most significant liberty taken in adaptation of Conan Doyle consisted in the artful combinations of plots from separate stories into unified episodes.

References

Abul-Kasymova, Khandzhara, S. Ginzburg, I. Dolinskii *et al.*, eds 1969–1978. *Istoriia sovetskogo kino* [History of Soviet Cinema]. 4 vols. Moscow: Iskusstvo.

Clark, Katerina. 2013. "'Wait for Me and I Shall Return': The Early Thaw as a Reprise of Thirties Culture?" In *The Thaw: Soviet Society and Culture in the 1950s and 1960s*, edited by Denis Kozlov and Eleonory Gilburd, 85–108. Toronto, Canada: Toronto University Press.

Conley, Tom. 2007. *Cartographic Cinema*. Minneapolis: University of Minnesota.

Dobrynin, Sergei. 2009. "The Silver Curtain: Representations of the West in the Soviet Cold War Films." *History Compass* 7.3: 862–878.

Eksta, Viktorija. 2012. "Review of *235,000,000*, by Uldis Brauns." *KinoKultura*, Special Issue 13: Latvian Cinema, http://www.kinokultura.com/specials/13/235million.shtml (accessed June 10, 2014).

Frank, Gerts (Herz). 1975. *Karta Ptolomeia: Zapiski kinodokumentalista* [Ptolemy's Map: Notes of a Documentalist]. Moscow: Iskusstvo.

Frolova, Gaļina. 2005. "Rīgas noslēpumi krievu kino" [Secrets of Riga in Russian Cinema]. *Kino Raksti* [Cinema Articles] 5: 35–43.

Golovskoy, Val S. and John Rimberg. 1986. *Behind the Soviet Screen: The Motion-Picture Industry in the USSR, 1972–1982*. Ann Arbor: Ardis.

Graffy, Julian. 2005. "Film Adaptations of Aksenov: The Young Prose and the Cinema of the Thaw." In *Russian and Soviet Film Adaptations of Literature, 1900–2001: Screening the Word*, edited by Stephen Hutchings and Anat Vernitski, 100–115. London: Routledge.

Horton, Andrew and Michael Brashinsky. 1992. *The Zero Hour: Glasnost and Soviet Cinema in Transition*. Princeton, NJ: Princeton University Press.

Kleiman, Naum. 2013. "Sovetskie 'nezavisimye': mif ili real'nost'" [Soviet "Independents": Myths and Reality]. *Seans* February 5, http://seance.ru/blog/lectures/soviet_independent_films_lecture/ (accessed June 11, 2014).

Kletskin, Abram. 1977. "'Rizhskaia shkola' i problem razvitiia documental'nogo kino" [The Riga School and Problems for the Development of Documentary Cinema]. In *Dokumental'noe kino: vchera, segodnia, zavtra…* [Documentary, Cinema: Yesterday, Today, Tomorrow…]; Manuscript Book of Materials to Conferences held in Jūrmala, Latvia from 1977 to 1989. First pagination, 1–19.

Kozakov Mikhail. 1993. "Dve fotografii" [Two Photos]. In his *Moi rezhisser Romm* [Romm, My Director] 194–204. Moscow: Iskusstvo.

Kuz'mina, Elena. 1989. *O tom, chto pomniu* [What I Remember]. Moscow: Iskusstvo.

Kuznetsov, M. 1958. "O proze romanticheskogo stilia" [About the Prose of the Romantic Style]. *Voprosy literatury* [Questions of Literature] 4: 221–228, http://dlib.eastview.com/browse/doc/12223703 (accessed June 11, 2014).

Leighton, Lauren G. 1983. "The Great Soviet Debate over Romanticism: 1957–1964." *Studies in Romanticism* 22.1: 41–64. doi: 10.2307/25600412.

Nepomniashchy, Catherine Theimer. 2005. "'Imperially, My Dear Watson': Sherlock Holmes and the Decline of the Soviet Empire." In *Russian and Soviet Film Adaptations of Literature, 1900–2001: Screening the Word*, edited by Stephen Hutchings and Anat Vernitski, 164–177. London: Routledge.

Novikov, Vladimir. 2002. *Vysotskii*. Moscow: Molodaia gvardiia.

Novikova. Irina. 2012. "Nation, Gender and History in Latvian Genre Cinema." In *A Companion to Eastern European Cinema*, edited by Anikó Imre, 366–384. Chichester, UK: John Wiley and Sons.

Pērkone, Inga. 2012. "A Brief Look at Latvian Film History." *KinoKultura*, Special Issue 13: Latvian Cinema, http://www.kinokultura.com/specials/13/235million.shtml (accessed June 10, 2014).

Platt, Kevin M. F. 2013. "Eccentric Orbit: Mapping Russian Culture in the Near Abroad." In *Empire De/Centered: New Spatial Histories of Russia*, edited by Sanna Turoma and Maxim Waldstein, 271–296. Aldershot: Ashgate.

Platt, Kevin M. F. and Benjamin Nathans. 2011. "Socialist in Form, Indeterminate in Content: The Ins and Outs of Late Soviet Culture." *Ab Imperio* 2: 301–324.

Prokhorova, Elena. 2003a. "Fragmented Mythologies: Soviet TV Mini-Series of the 1970s." PhD dissertation, University of Pittsburgh, http://etd.library.pitt.edu/ETD/available/etd-06062003-164753/ (accessed June 10, 2014).

Razzakov, Fedor. 2004. *Zhizn' zamechatel'nykh vremen, 1975–1979 gg.: vremia, sobytiia, liudi* [Lives in Remarkable Times, 1975–1979: Times, Events. People]. Moscow: Eksmo.

Roshal', Lev. 1973. *Mir i igra* [The World and the Game]. Moscow: Iskusstvo.

Sidenova, Raisa 2014. "Romanticism in Soviet Poetic Documentary as Rehabilitation of Non-Fiction Film Practice after Stalin." Paper delivered at Princeton University, May 10.

Sīmanis, Dāvis. 2012. "Untraditional Visual Forms in Latvian Cinematography: The Soviet Period." *KinoKultura*, Special Issue 13: Latvian Cinema, http://www.kinokultura.com/specials/13/235million.shtml (accessed June 10, 2014).

Surkova, Agnese, 2012. "Sight and Angle in the Cinema of Latvia: Widescreen in the 1950 and 1960s." *KinoKultura*, Special Issue 13: Latvian Cinema, http://www.kinokultura.com/specials/13/235million.shtml (accessed June 10, 2014).

Tcherneva, Irina and Juliette Denis. 2011. "Je me souviens de tout, Richard (Rolands Kalniņš, Studio de Riga, 1967): Une Manifestation Précoce d'une Mémoire Concurrente de la Grande Guerre Patriotique" [I Remember Everything, Richard (Rolands Kalniņš, Studio de Riga, 1967): A Precocious Manifestation of a Memoir Concurrent with World War II]. *The Journal of Power Institutions in Post-Soviet Societies* 12, http://pipss.revues.org/3875 (accessed June 10, 2014).

Vertov, Dziga. 1984. "Field Manual." In *Kino-Eye: The Writings of Dziga Vertov*, edited by Annette Michelson, translated by Kevin O'Brian, 162–163. Berkeley: University of California Press.

Vitols, Maruta Zane. 2008. "From the Personal to the Public: Juris Podnieks and Latvian Documentary Cinema." PhD dissertation, Ohio State University, http://rave.ohiolink.edu/etdc/view?acc_num=osu1210796660 (accessed June 10, 2014).

Vysotskii, Vladimir. 1988. *Izbrannoe* [Selected Works]. Moscow: Sovetskii pisatel'.

Yurchak, Alexei. 2006. *Everything Was Forever, Until It Was No More: The Last Soviet Generation*. Princeton, NJ: Princeton University Press.

20

Capital Images: Moscow on Screen

Birgit Beumers

> IRINA. *To go back to Moscow. To sell the house,*
> *to make an end of everything here, and off to Moscow. [...]*
> *My God, every night I dream of Moscow...*
>
> (Anton Chekhov, *The Three Sisters*)

Moscow has always been a city of desire, a place of longing: to get there has been the wish of Chekhov's Irina as much as of Soviet citizens from the provinces and of post-Soviet migrant workers from Tajikistan and Uzbekistan. Once a dream location, Moscow's cinematic image has, however, turned into a nightmare in contemporary screen versions, as for example the post-apocalyptic vision of Moscow created by Chris Gorak and produced by Timur Bekmambetov in *The Darkest Hour* (2011).

As opposed to the rare screen appearance of the beautiful architectural features of the imperial capital St Petersburg, Moscow has been a favorite location of Soviet cinema. Its screen images have projected the new Soviet capital and control center during the Stalin era, while showcasing urban life in post-war film. As the capital of the Russian Federation, Moscow has reappeared in the cinema of the 2000s after a temporary absence following the collapse of the USSR.

This chapter explores the way in which the "project" for Moscow as the capital was shown on film before the architectural designs were actually implemented, using cinema as testing ground for the Grand Reconstruction under Stalin during the 1930s. I then briefly sketch the changes and shifts in the representation of Moscow in post-war cinema, before analyzing the images of Moscow in contemporary, post-Soviet cinema. I argue that Moscow was never just a shooting location: rather, cinema has projected the city as it should be (or should have been)

A Companion to Russian Cinema, First Edition. Edited by Birgit Beumers.
© 2016 John Wiley & Sons, Inc. Published 2016 by John Wiley & Sons, Inc.

Figure 20.1 The apocalyptic vision of Moscow in Chris Gorak's *The Darkest Hour*, 2011.

onto the silver screen, and rarely, only episodically, does the real Moscow appear in film. As Svetlana Boym has astutely noted in her study of nostalgia for the Soviet past and Russia's (and Russians') inability to live in the present that "Moscow devoured the dreams of other cities" (Boym 2001, 94); it is "not so much a historical city as a kind of promised land" (Boym 2001, 96). Moscow is, then, a site of utopia, not a real city; this project originated in the 1930s and would remain relevant for the development of Moscow's screen image throughout the twentieth and into the twenty-first century. In her seminal book *Moscow, the Fourth Rome* Katerina Clark dwells on Iurii Lotman's and Boris Uspensky's suggestion that the concept of Moscow as a third Rome conflates its function as political and spiritual center (Clark 2011, 2), and she demonstrates how international influences are manifest in the design for Moscow, which she calls the "Great Appropriation" of styles (Clark 2011, 8), both from the west and from the past. This suggests that Moscow is faceless: the image(s) created are masks or projected, artificial images that do not reflect reality. I attempt to demonstrate this "loss of face" that the city undergoes in the new millennium, if not in architectural terms, then at least in its screen representation.

The Soviet Capital

In the early years of Soviet cinema, the image of Moscow is mostly created through montage; it is a city in motion, as is evident in the chase scene in Lev Kuleshov's *The Extraordinary Adventures of Mister West in the Land of the Bolsheviks* [*Neobychainye prikliucheniia mistera Vesta v strane bol'shevikov*, 1924], when the cowboy Jeddy takes flight through main streets, side streets, and over rooftops, with Moscow's landmark of the Cathedral of Christ the Savior appearing in the frame from different perspectives. The sequence assembles different views to construct an image of modernity (the police's automobile) and backwardness (the horse-drawn carriage). The Cathedral also features in Iakov Protazanov's *Aelita* (1924), where the viewing platform serves as a location for Los's rendezvous with his wife Natasha. Again, the perspective from atop the Cathedral is a rare shot, but also indicative of the time when aerial views dominated and allowed the spectator to share this view. Iurii Zheliabuzhskii's *The Cigarette Girl from Mosselprom* [*Papirosnitsa ot Mossel'proma*, 1924] opens with aerial shots of Moscow before focusing on the landmarks of the Triumphal Gate (on Tverskaia Street), the Kremlin, the Resurrection Gates, St Basil's, the Cathedral of Christ the Savior, the Bolshoi Theater, Kiev Railway Station, and the Moscow River as the character of cameraman Latugin takes shots of the new Moscow, and his love interest Zina (Solntseva). Abram Room's *Bed and Sofa* [*Tret'ia Meshchanskaia*, 1927] also contains a stunning shot by cameraman Grigorii Giber from atop the Bolshoi Theater onto Theater Square (then Sverdlov Square). The viewpoint almost matches a photograph of the Quadriga of Apollo on the front of the Bolshoi Theater by Aleksandr Rodchenko (1929), which reveals the proximity of constructivism with filmmaking, and the project of Moscow under construction. Barnet's *The Girl with the Hatbox* [*Devushka s korobkoi*, 1927] or *The House on Trubnaya* [*Dom na Trubnoi*, 1928] both feature buildings in central Moscow – living accommodation and railway stations prominently – as people from the villages arrive in Moscow and try to make a living in the city; this also serves as one of the plotlines for *Bed and Sofa*, where Kolia's friend Volodia arrives at a railway station, having come to stay in the capital. The themes of films in the 1920s often feature arrivals from the provinces of people who are impressed but also lost in this chaotic city, but who often stay there. In the 1930s such visits would still occur, but the characters were not to stay. These films often confirm the correctness of the socialist system: the American entrepreneur Mr West finds Moscow (standing in for the USSR as a whole and its socialist system) rather different than portrayed in American, anti-Bolshevik propaganda; *Aelita* asserts that the Revolution had already happened on other planets. Yet films also highlight the problems of the NEP (New Economic Policy, 1921–1928), temporarily introducing private enterprise to remedy the economic effects of the Civil War: such enterprise is shown as subversively bourgeois. The housing shortage is also prominently in evidence – problems that would disappear from the screen in the 1930s under Socialist Realism. The central roles in these films are often played by women – Aleksandra Khokhlova, Iuliia Solntseva, Anna Sten, and Vera Maretskaia: their characters come to Moscow and are trapped by the vicissitudes of urban life and corruption, even if at the end there is sometimes a way out – thanks to Soviet government plans. Railway stations are therefore a frequent site of action: they are the gates to the center. *Aelita* features the Kursk and Yaroslavl railway stations as sites of arrival for the Red Army returning to the city and villagers fleeing the countryside during and after the Civil War. Parasha (Maretskaia in *House on Trubnaya*) arrives at the Yaroslavl railway station, and Natasha (Sten in *The Girl with the Hatbox*) at the Kazan railway station.

Figure 20.2 Jeddy on the run. From the rooftop of the Cathedral of Christ the Savior in Lev Kuleshov's *The Extraordinary Adventures of Mister West in the Land of the Bolsheviks*, 1924.

This mobility of characters in the films of the 1920s would be replaced in the 1930s by a more disciplined movement of characters and camera alike. As Boym has argued:

> Moscow of the 1920s was a city of spontaneous chaotic life, multilayered and multi-centered, that cunningly escaped central control. Moscow of the 1930s was re-imagined as a city of controlled movement. Films of that era all contained some kind of a tour of Moscow – by ship or by plane (or even by flying car). The camera movement itself created a new space. (Boym 2001, 97–98)

What changes is the way in which the camera captures space: the city becomes a center of attractions, with locations such as Gorky Park, the Water Stadium [Vodnyi stadion], the banks of the Moskva-River as sites for (state-)organized relaxation. It might be helpful at this point to draw on a somewhat dated, but nevertheless useful distinction made by the architect Vladimir Paperny: in his study *Kul'tura Dva* Paperny (1985) underlines the principle of binary oppositions in twentieth-century Russian culture: Culture One destroys the past to construct a new image (1920s), whilst Culture Two appropriates the past and creates a monument to itself, using facets of the cultures it absorbs (1930s). Culture Two is not original, as it merely rehearses forms of the past and fills them with new content. While Culture One is concerned with the conquest of the periphery and oriented on the horizontal axis, Culture Two monopolizes the center and develops on a vertical axis; in other words, Culture One is centrifugal, while Culture Two is centripetal.

What Boym terms "controlled movement" is not so much echoed through static shots and a less mobile camera, but through carefully planned movements and a structured, choreographed mobility. Means of transportation – cars, ships, the metro, and trains – feature more prominently than the nodes that connect. Straight and geometrical lines of tram cables, roads and crossroads, escalators and bridges, as reflected in the symmetry of the projects designed by Stalin's prime architects Aleksei Shchusev (Hotel Moskva), Karo Alabian (Central Red Army Theater), Boris Iofan (House on the Embankment, Palace of Soviets), Vladimir Gel'freikh and Mikhail Minkus (Ministry of Foreign Affairs), Lev Rudnev (Moscow State University), Vladimir Shchuko (Lenin State Library) or Ivan Zholtovskii (Apartment Block on Mokhovaia Street) – all emphasize planned and controlled harmony.

Political leaders have used Moscow to imprint their largely center-based ideology onto the city, but also to "personify the state" (Clark 2011, 14), and these traces can be found in Moscow's topography and architecture as forged in the 1930s: "In national narratives, generally, the capital city is represented as isomorphous with the state, and indeed personifies it" (Clark 2011, 14). Access to that "persona" is regulated in the 1930s: people do not just come, but they follow a call to the city, normally by the state.

Grigorii Aleksandrov's *Happy Guys* [*Veselye rebiata*, 1934] brings two musical talents – the shepherd Kostia and the maid Aniuta (Liubov' Orlova) – to the capital for a competition at the Bolshoi, and they come *not* to stay. In *Volga-Volga* (1938) amateur musicians travel from Melkovodsk to Moscow for a competition in the Moscow Musical Olympiad; the River Station forms the portal that allows their access to the center. *Circus* [*Tsirk* 1936] brings circus artiste Marion Dixon (Orlova) from America to Moscow, where she finds happiness. The film includes a scene filmed on the rooftop of the still unfinished building of the Hotel Moskva (architect Aleksei Shchusev) and Marion, who stays in a room in the hotel offering a strangely high-angle view overlooking Red Square and the Kremlin. It culminates in a finale with the Soviet people (and Marion) marching across Red Square, facing the leader during the May Day Parade. Similar journeys occur in Konstantin Iudin's *A Girl with Character* [*Devushka s kharakterom*, 1939], where Katia Ivanova (Valentina Serova) journeys from the Soviet Far East to Moscow to seek justice over her incompetent fur farm boss. The typical site of the railway station (here the Yaroslavl station) features as the gate for arrival/departure. Katia stays in Moscow to gain experience, only to return to the Far East as a high-profile manager. Moscow is the place where women are empowered – rather than entrapped, as in the 1920s – as is perfectly evident in Aleksandrov's *The Radiant Path* [*Svetlyi put'*, 1940] where Tania Morozova (Orlova) undergoes a magical transformation from an illiterate, domestic servant to textile worker to engineer and to deputy of the Supreme Soviet. It is an encounter with Stalin that sends her on a magic journey over Moscow in a flying car, which ends at the All-Union Agricultural Exhibition (VSKhV, later Exhibition of Achievements of the People's Economy, VDNKh) – one of the projects of

Stalin's Grand Plan for Moscow – flying past Vera Mukhina's monument to the Worker and Kolkhoz Woman (1937, made for the Soviet Pavilion at the World Exhibition in Paris), and finishing with a romantic encounter at the Fountain of the Friendship of Peoples.

With few exceptions (Morozova, who has turned into a political figure; and Dixon, who is a foreigner) the characters who come to Moscow in the 1930s do not stay: Moscow is the dream space of socialism, and the hero journeys there to come in physical touch with that the utopia: "Moscow represents achieved socialism, an ideal city" (Clark 2011, 123). The characters return to the periphery which is still working towards that ideal: "Moscow therefore remains a closed, utopian space, and as with classic utopias only designated intermediaries and emissaries can breach its fortified border" (Clark 2011, 124).

Another attraction in these films is the construction of the new transport system within the urban space: the overpowering dominance of the new highrises for the elite is, as it were, set against the construction of underground palaces "for the people" in the form of the metro. As Mike O'Mahony has pointed out (2006), the stations were designed as palaces for the people, creating a grand Moscow underground, while the surface of Moscow was being redesigned and reconstructed to improve the communal habitat. Many stations resembled museums, lavishly decorated with marbles from all over Soviet Russia, bronze statues and mural decorum. One might equally argue that the beauty of the surface city is complemented by the underground network, which expresses with its radial pattern an extremely

Figure 20.3 The view from Marion's room in the Hotel Moskva in Grigorii Aleksandrov's *Circus*, 1936.

controlled mobility from center to periphery. Moscow's metro was built in the 1930s, with the first stretch opening on May 15, 1935 between Sokol'niki and Park Kul'tury, and a side branch from Okhotnyi Riad to Smolenskaia, and later (1937) Kievskaia. The second radial line opened in 1938 from Sokol to Ploshchad' Sverdlova; a third radial line from Kurskaia to Ismailovo's Stadium of Nations opened in 1944, while the circle line followed only in the early 1950s.

A key film for this period is Aleksandr Medvedkin's *New Moscow* [*Novaia Moskva*, 1938], which was banned at the time of its making. The plot revolves around the engineer Alesha, who brings from his native Siberian village a "Living Model" of the reconstruction of Moscow to the capital; when the model is set in motion, it accidentally goes into the wrong direction, returning Moscow to the ancient medieval settlement it once was, before Alesha switches it round and shows the projection of the new Moscow, including the Palace of Soviets. Cinema is used to show the city that is being constructed, to bring it to life in a controlled manner. Stalin's Moscow of the 1930s marks a climax in the history of the film location Moscow: houses are moved (the painter Fedia in *New Moscow* cannot even capture the city on canvas, so fast is its development); projects are brought to life (the "living model"); the metro is being built (*New Moscow* is one of the first films to feature a ride on the metro; see Beumers 2002); and the hotel Moskva is literally completed on the screen in *Circus*. In *New Moscow* the visitors to the capital travel on the metro, which is cheap (Alesha has only 3 kopecks and a button left), orderly (they have to wrap the pig as a baby, as animals are not permitted on the trains), and comfortable (upholstered seating in the carriages). The metro is presented as an ideal means of transport, used but not overcrowded; in *Circus*, it is a place of safety for Marion's black child, Jimmy. In this sense, Medvedkin demonstrates the object of Soviet pride without depicting it as palatial museum, but "just" as means of transport in the city. Despite intentions, Medvedkin contradicted even in this small scene the official *metrodiskurs* as defined by Mikhail Ryklin (2005). Other classic sites also remain in view, including the Bolshoi Theater as a place where high art is brought to the masses, where the center allows performances from the periphery. Some classic monuments feature as attractions in the margins: Red Square forms the frame for the parade in *Circus*; churches, cathedrals and old city gates appear in the frame but not in focus. The film *The Foundling* [*Podkidysh*, 1939] by Tat'iana Lukashevich visits a whole range of sites as the 5-year-old Natasha "strolls" around Moscow, having run away from her brother and being taken care of and guided by her large Soviet family: all the attractions are seen from the perspective of a child. Instead, railway stations and the River Station remain prime locations: they facilitate mobility to and away from the center. Thus, Stalin's General Plan for the reconstruction of Moscow has taken shape precisely through the medium of film, which tended to show new public spaces – such as the Palace of Soviets, the Hotel Moskva, the All-Union Agricultural Exhibition or metro stations – on screen before their completion, anticipating visually the achievements of the Soviet state.

This screen image of the capital represents at the same time the ideal state, a state that seeks to project an aesthetically pleasing, harmonious image of itself, incorporating styles from the west and the past. As Clark has demonstrated, beauty and harmony of the ensemble dominate the urban space of Moscow in the 1930s (Clark 2011, 12).[1] Clark highlights the role of intellectuals in the projection of the "Kunststadt" (a term she borrows from Joseph Chytry), which places beauty over functionality (Clark 2011, 106). In fact, this constructed and artificial face, which is perfected through a screen "make-up," is but a mask. The image of Moscow on celluloid echoes the political ambitions of the country, of a beautiful, perfect, loveable and universal space. The film locations and settings reflect the cultural agenda of the times, as Clark has evoked in defining Moscow as *pars pro toto* for the Soviet state at large.

"Little" Moscow

Several films of the early 1950s follow the pattern of short visits to the capital: Anatolii Granik's *Alesha Ptitsyn Forms his Character* [*Alesha Ptitsyn vyrabatyvaet kharakter*, 1953] revolves around a tour of Moscow's sights for visitors, Grandmother Olia and her granddaughter Sasha, who spent three hours in the capital; in Mikhail Kalatozov's *Loyal Friends* [*Vernye Druz'ia*, 1954] three friends meet to remember the Moscow of their childhood – and return to their suburbia; and in Viktor Eisymont's adaptation of Viktor Rozov's play, *Good Luck!* [*V dobryi chas*, 1956], Aleksei comes from Siberia to study in Moscow, and – having failed the entrance exam – returns to Siberia together with his cousin, departing from Yaroslavl station.

However, the images of Moscow in films after the war reflect a gradual shift away from the centrality of Moscow:

> For decades Moscow had been the hub of national life; Soviets dreamed of going "to Moscow, to Moscow!" no less than did Chekhov's three sisters. But as the sense of national commonality disintegrated in the mid-1960s, so did Moscow-centrism and the mental map it engendered [...] contemporary characters often found economic opportunity and personal commitment in provincial cities that no longer seemed merely inadequate substitutes for the "real" metropolis. (Woll 2000, 211–212)

Although Stalinist building projects (including the metro and the "Seven Sisters," constructed in the early 1950s) continued to feature after the war, the sites of post-war cinema differ significantly from the earlier locations: instead of showing monumental architecture, films focus on private housing, embankments, leisure parks, department stores, public squares, and the metro as a (radial) connection to suburbs, focusing on the stations at the end of the line. Throughout the Thaw and into the Stagnation era, public spaces rarely reflect state control: they are hospitals and office buildings, but most frequently private housing. Moscow is no longer the grand capital, but a city consisting of small urban and suburban communities. Khrushchev's architectural plans extended to the periphery, where he built five-storey housing estates [*khrushcheby*], creating accommodation for the people. The metro stations connecting to these new districts were plain and practical, but often identical in design. The new stations had a long central platform with trains running either side, the platform tunnels fitted with white tiles and the stations designed in plain white granite, and this is how they feature in a few rare screen appearances. But mostly films of the Thaw and the Stagnation feature Stalin's Moscow as a space that alienates – the characters, the camera, the inhabitants.

Once again, people come to the capital and stay: in Vasilii Ordynskii's *A Man is Born* [*Chelovek rodilsia*, 1956] the provincial girl Nadia Smirnova may fail her entrance exam and be disappointed in her love, but she stays in the capital, even if life there is far from a dream. El'dar Riazanov's *Girl without Address* [*Devushka bez adresa*, 1957] sees the arrival of Katia Ivanova in the capital – on the square of three stations, where she loses her Muscovite friend Pavel; unable to make a living or get into acting school, she is about to leave – this time from the Belorussian station, when Pavel finds her – and she stays. These arrivals in the capital are complicated, reflecting the complexity of Moscow.

Mikhail Kalatozov's *The Cranes are Flying* [*Letiat zhuravli*, 1957] may feature the Crimean [Krymskii] Bridge, which opened in 1938 during Stalin's massive reconstruction of central Moscow, but it never fills the frame: instead the monument is

Figure 20.4 The Crimean Bridge as a backdrop for a romantic encounter between Veronika (Tat'iana Samoilova) and Boris (Aleksei Batalov) in Mikhail Kalatozov's *The Cranes are Flying*, 1957.

minimized and serves as shelter from the rain and meeting place for Boris and Veronika. In another film of the same year, *The House I Live In* [*Dom, v kotorom ia zhivu*] by Lev Kulidzhanov and Iakov Segel', the relocation of a family to a newly-built apartment on the outskirts of Moscow happens before the war, and postwar Moscow is a silent, empty city. The attention shifts from exterior to interior spaces: even if the location is an eminent building, as for example the House of Architects on Rostov Embankment [Rostovskaia naberezhnaia] that features in Andrei Tarkovskii's student film *The Steamroller and the Violin* [*Katok i skripka*, 1960], or Tat'iana Lioznova's popular film *Three Poplars on Pliushchikha Street* [*Tri topolia na Pliushchikhe*, 1967], the action is set in the courtyard of the building. Marlen Khutsiev's *Ilyich's Gate* [aka *I am Twenty*; *Zastava Il'icha/ Mne dvadtsat' let*, 1964] predominantly shows domestic settings and courtyard scenes, capturing the atmosphere of the Thaw through public events at the Polytechnic Museum. The Moscow of the three neighbors who return from army service is "far more than a mere 'setting': the city is all-inclusive, a cosmos" (Woll 2000, 142). The May Day parade is a time when Sergei (Valentin Popov) and his friends meet and talk, and proceed (rather than march) as an "unforced, joyful procession of free people (Chernenko in Woll 2000, 143) through Lubianka Square and past the KGB headquarters, which feature as mere backdrops. These films show the intersection of private lives and public spaces: the young generation lives in a city that may be alien to them, but the camera makes it less monumental and more personal, and turns it into a private space that is habitable. In *July Rain* [*Iul'skii dozhd'*, 1966] Khutsiev's protagonist Lena (Evgeniia Uralova), realizes how alienated she has become from her boyfriend. She walks out of a pedestrian tunnel and into the spring air of Alexander Gardens by the Kremlin: the space is symbolic for her awakening and her move from darkness into light, from winter into spring, and has no further (political or ideological) purpose. The city is bustling on a spring day – it happens to be Victory Day: the past is what connects people, not the space.

> For *July Rain* [DoP] German Lavrov filmed Moscow's broad avenues and streets in long dollying shots, much as [DoP] Margarita Pilikhina had in *Ilich's Gate*, but keeps his camera much further away, observing with detachment streets clogged with traffic, people isolated in their locked cars or scurrying impatiently past one another in crowds. Instead of the camaraderie and warmth that characterized *Gate*, where the camera seemed part of the world it filmed, Lavrov's camera remains aloof and slightly intimidating. Like a voyeuristic observer it stalks the heroine… (Woll 2000, 221–222)

The Moscow of the Thaw has become a more open city: it is "increasingly international" and "constantly expanding" (Woll 2000,159). It remains a desirable destination: travel to the city still features in *Three Poplars on Pliushchikha Street* where the peasant girl Niura comes to Moscow to visit her sister-in-law, but she abandons the idea of life in the city – a potential prospect that unfolds with the romantic interest from her taxi driver. Kol'ka of Georgii Daneliia's *Walking the Streets of Moscow* [*Ia shagaiu po Moskve*, 1963] works as a metro construction worker and knows Moscow best. Having spent the day showing a visitor from Siberia round the city as the latter falls in love with a Moscow shop assistant of the State Department Store GUM (who will leave for Siberia with him), Kol'ka is left to return to his night shift, alone but happy, in harmony with the city. Daneliia's choice of a new metro station for the final frames of the film alludes to the contrast between physical work that brings happiness and study at the university (the exit is towards the university). The hero has rejected the latter in favor of hard work. *Walking the Streets of Moscow* is one of the Thaw films where "the crowded but clean streets, streams of pedestrians, river lights, statues and squares become part of the film's action, a visual means of conveying youth's mastery over their own future…" (Woll 2000, 159). Only work brings happiness and dominance in the capital, which might otherwise reject its visitors: Nina Solomatina in Tat'iana Lioznova's *Carnival* [*Karnaval'*, 1981] finds no space here as an actress; the Armenian grandfather visiting his family in Moscow in Edmond Keosayan's *When September Comes* [*Kogda nastupaet sentiabr'*, 1975] finds himself alienated in the city; and the doctor who visits family in the remote Tushino in Khutsiev's *Epilogue* [*Posleslovie*, 1983] is not only separated from his absent daughter, but also reminisces about old times on the boulevard, only to return home at the film's end. Although the city is visited and cradles its visitors, the experience is not always one that fulfils a dream. At the same time, Moscow holds a strong attraction for consumers: in Vasilii Shukshin's *Happy Go Lucky* [*Pechki-lavochki*, 1972] the main character Ivan Rastorguev (Shukshin) visits Moscow with his wife: their destination is a shopping center; a series of toy shops are the location for Valerii Kremenov's *Children's World* [*Detskii mir*, 1982] as a man tries to purchase a game as a Christmas present for his nephew. In general, locales focus more on consumer and leisure spaces: cafes, shops, concert halls, skating rinks, gardens (Hermitage Gardens, Neskuchnyi Gardens), boulevards feature prominently on screen, particularly in Mikhail Kozakov's *Pokrov Gates* [*Pokrovskie vorota*, 1982].

Without acquaintances or guides, Moscow can be an alienating city: El'dar Riazanov's *Office Romance* [*Sluzhebnyi roman*, 1977] opens with shots of a crowded and bustling city as people go to work; the film's prime location is the Statistics Office near the Central Department Store (TsUM). Vladimir Men'shov's *Moscow Does Not Believe in Tears* [*Moskva slezam ne verit*, 1979] shows the vain attempts of three student girls from the provinces who come to Moscow and try to find their feet in the city. They all have aspirations, but neither of them manages to settle in the city: Tonia returns to the countryside with her husband; Liudmila ends up in an unhappy marriage; and Katia's attempt to become a Muscovite through a relationship based on the lie that she comes from a family who lives in one of Stalin's high-rises fails miserably. Only through hard work and perseverance does she make a career, raises her daughter and obtains status symbols such as a car and an apartment – albeit in a new suburban housing complex. Other locations feature highlights of the theater and literature of the Thaw (the time when the girls first arrive in Moscow) and the leisure parks, suburban railways, embankment, and factories of the 1970s. As a city, as an aesthetically beautiful space Moscow has almost disappeared from the screen: instead, suburbia has taken its place, while the center is reserved for cultural events or to show the falsity of the décor of Stalinist architecture and its alienating effect on the young generation. Moscow is a functional space, where people rush to work, where transportation is both beautiful and fast, where housing is practical in its design, almost to the extent of anonymity, as is perfectly exemplified in the parodic references to contemporary architecture of Riazanov's *Irony of Fate* [*Ironiia sud'by*, 1975] where living spaces are reduced to identical boxes that make it impossible to distinguish even between Moscow and Leningrad. The confusion of the (drunken) Zhenia Lukashin (Andrei Miagkov), who accidentally boards a flight to Leningrad and enters there, with his key, a flat on a street with the same name, in the same building, and furnished in the same standard, Soviet manner that he inhabits in Moscow, is a perfect example for the faceless city that Moscow has become. The lack of an identity, of a face, is evident already in these late Soviet examples of the representation of Moscow on screen: Moscow is no longer a desirable destination, but a faceless, functional megapolis. This facelessness has nothing to do with the collapse of the Soviet Union, and the loss of a "Soviet" identity, but is a process that had already reached a climax by the 1980s.

"Fixing" the Image

During the perestroika period, film locations tended to be even less recognizable places, including halls of residence, boulevards, factories, or just ordinary streets. An important theme of perestroika cinema is youth culture, and therefore places where young people meet feature prominently. Karen Shakhnazarov's *The Messenger* [*Kur'er*, 1986] shows skateboarders Ivan and Kolia on Sparrow Hills[2]: the university precinct serves as a new location here, along with the river beach of the woodland in Serebrianyi bor. The Stalinist "wedding cakes" or "Seven Sisters" are similarly associated with youth culture in Pavel Lungin's *Luna Park* (1992), where a gang of bikers and punks usurp their turf on the embankment of the Hotel Ukraina. The location here forms a contrast to the new subculture and signals a dissociation of the young protagonists from the monumentalism of Moscow architecture. By contrast, Riazanov's *Dear Elena Sergeevna* [*Dorogaia Elena Sergeevna*, 1988] features the Student House of Moscow State University on Vernadskii Prospekt (DSV), built in the mid-1970s, and Pavel Lungin's *Taxi Blues* (1990) has part of the action set in the Kauchuk Factory Club on Pliushchikha Street, using more contemporary locations, thus reflecting the appropriation of alternative and modern spaces by the young generation.

Following the collapse of the USSR, two paradigms dominated the image of Moscow created on screen. I adopt a chronological approach here, although these trends practically exist in parallel for most of the 1990s. First, Moscow is frequently marked as an absent, invisible but powerful center in films that are set in the contemporary period. In the latter half of the 1990s Moscow reappears on the screen with its new shopping malls and business complexes featuring as prime locations. If in the cinema of the 1930s Moscow was the center of political and ideological power, it has now turned into a center of consumer culture and economic (often criminal) power. Second, and most frequently, the capital features in the 1990s in films that look back at the past, almost nostalgically, as cinema deconstructs the Soviet era and especially Stalinism (a topic I have discussed elsewhere; see Beumers 2012). Let us, therefore, begin here with the image of Stalin's Moscow (largely of the 1930s) in the films of the early 1990s.

Restoring the Past

With the demise of the communist state and, more importantly, the collapse of the Soviet dream of socialism, an entire value system vanished. The fairy tale that the socialist utopia had wanted to make come true in the 1930s (the line "we were born to make fairy tales come true" comes from the Aviators' March by Pavel Gherman and Iulii Khait; see von Geldern and Stites 1995, 257–258) had suddenly evaporated; man and the masses had lost any sense of location, direction, or center. In the turmoil of trying to establish a democratic system, to conduct major economic reforms, and to bring in new legislation, the state forgot about the people, who were deprived of ideals and whose expectations and hopes for a better life after communism were disappointed by the chaos and economic and social instability of the Yeltsin era that is reflected by the absence of any positive screen or media portrayals of the country in which they lived, echoed in the trend towards *chernukha* [making black]. Therefore, a nostalgia for the Soviet past informed visual arts and literature, on the one hand deconstructing Stalinist culture in postmodernist portrayals, on the other hand gleaning back at Russia's imperial past to boost morale by showing a powerful and glorious identity that contemporary Russia lacked.

The sites of Moscow's Stalinist architecture therefore abounded in films that sought to fragment and parody the period that had so much shaped post-war Soviet culture. Locations that had featured as the pride of Stalinist culture in films of the 1930s, such as the All-Union Agricultural Exhibition (VDNKh), leisure parks (such as Gorky Park) and the metro, which echoed the real and virtual achievements of the Soviet state, are revisited in the 1990s: the VDNKh has turned into a permanent trade fair; the reconstructed Cathedral of Christ-the-Savior has become an emblem of religious (spiritual) power; leisure parks have turned into theme parks; and the metro has become a place of the (criminal) underworld.

The architectural reconstruction of Moscow's former glory under Mayor Luzhkov (in office from 1992–2010) included not only reconstruction (Cathedral of Christ the Savior, Iberian Gates, etc.) and the renaming of the metro stations, streets and squares (as well as cities), returning – along with the original names of metro stations renamed in the 1960s – also pre-Revolutionary district names and cancelling out all references to the Communist past,[3] but also new projects that mark Moscow as the grand business capital: the business center "Moscow City"; the underground "Okhotnyi Riad" Shopping Mall; a Third Ring Road, extending the perimeter of the center, as well as a number of high-rises that replicate the neo-classicist style of the 1930s, labeled "Luzhkov style," such as Novinskii Passage shopping mall, or the Galina Vishnevskaia Operatic Center. The sculptures and ornaments created by Zurab Tsereteli form the decorative part of Luzhkov's reconstruction project and reflect the monumental and grand aspect of the architecture of the 1990s and 2000s. Grigorii Revzin has connected Luzhkov's construction projects to the vertical axis of Culture Two, and linked Luzhkov's towers to the toy-like character of Tsereteli's detailed sculptures:

> Let us take a look at the building of the Tokobank: the building begins with a paraphrase of the Stalin high-rises. Yet a peculiarity arises: instead of the stone portal we have its shadow, made of polarized glass, as if it were an image of negation. But the overall contour still is perceived as a greeting to Stalinism. On the top we have some cubist still-life instead of the spire. As if the spire had been broken off, leaving behind the line of the break, the rift, the ruin. (Revzin 1997)

Defining what he terms the "poetics of the Moscow style," Revzin suggests:

> the Moscow style appeared in a situation when the architecture of vernacular postmodernism began to represent the state idea. Accordingly, the postmodernist citation is a proof of the legitimacy of authority (Iurii Luzhkov with his architecture quotes Stalin, i.e. he partly inherits from him), while post-modernist irony is the proof that power is with the people [*narodnost' vlasti*]. (Revzin 2002)

As Moscow underwent a reconstruction of Soviet and pre-Revolutionary monuments, Luzhkov promoted an architectural style that imitates Stalinist monumentalism.

In the cinematic representation, this alignment with the state idea can also be sensed: if the Stalinist hero was allowed to see down from above (Zoia flies back to Alesha in *New Moscow*; Tania Morozova takes off in her limo over the skies of Moscow), and is allowed a superior perspective through an aerial view (and a view to the future), the cinema of 1990s mostly denies its characters such a perspective.

In the post-modern cinematic reassessment of the 1930s the location Moscow stresses the centrality it held in Stalinist culture: Ivan Dykhovichnyi's *Moscow*

Parade [*Prorva*, 1993]; Sergei Livnev's *Hammer and Sickle* [*Serp i molot*, 1994] and Nikita Mikhalkov's *Burnt by the Sun* [*Utomlennye solntsem*, 1994] all conform to the paradigms of Stalinist-era cinema, both in terms of controlled mobility and key locations. In *Hammer and Sickle*, set in 1936, the gender-transformed Evdokim Kuznetsov is a metro construction worker, who will marry his female equivalent, the kolkhoz farm worker Liza Voronina; both later model for Vera Mukhina's statue "Worker and Kolkhoz Worker." *Moscow Parade* is set in Moscow and features the metro (prominently foregrounding the sculptures and arches of the station Ploshchad' Revoliutsii and the inset mosaics showing Soviet achievements against a blue sky in the ceiling panels of the station Maiakovskaia) as a meeting place for the characters to discuss ideas, not to provide transportation; other locations include the River Station, the Fountain of Friendship in the All-Union Exhibition, railway stations (where the protagonist works as a porter) and the Hall of Columns, subverting previous functions. *Burnt by the Sun* opens with a scene where the protagonist Mitia arrives back home at the House on the Embankment, the building that was constructed to accommodate the Party elite, and ends with a view from the same building onto the Kremlin. These films re-create the centrality of Moscow, emphasizing its beauty and style, and focusing on locations that facilitate communication (stations, trains, metro, cars). Films of the 1930s were characterized by a centripetal movement toward Moscow, and films of the 1990s repeat this pattern: *Moscow Parade*, *Burnt by the Sun*, *Hammer and Sickle* all end in Moscow, even of the protagonists are left incapacitated or disabled: Evdokim Kuznetsov is paralyzed and exhibited in a museum; Mitia is left in the bathtub with his wrists cut. The patterns of movement and locations of Stalinist culture are extrapolated, and ironically replicated in these films.

The House on the Embankment as traumatic space appears in Vladimir Naumov's *Ten Years without the Right to Correspond* [*Desiat' let bez prava perepiski*, 1990]. A somewhat different, because comic, portrayal of the Stalinist past, again focused on the emblematic House on the Embankment, is offered in Riazanov's *Old Hags* [*Starye kliachi*, 2000], which is concerned with corruption in modern-day Moscow. The elderly Liuba (Liia Akhedzhakova) who has lived her whole life in the famous House, is being tricked out of her apartment by criminals. With the help of her girlfriends, she manages to get rid of the tricksters, using her father's gadgets: he once was Stalin's chauffeur (hence the apartment in the House), who kept an amphibious Black Maria specially equipped to deter attackers – the Soviet equivalent of a James-Bond car.

However, it is not only Stalinist Moscow that re-appears on the screen. Khrushchev's or Brezhnev's city appears occasionally, as for example in Valerii Todorovskii's *Hipsters* [*Stiliagi*, 2008], set in Moscow in the 1950s. The film reviews the *stiliagi* as a group of people protesting against uniformity. Their quest for plurality is met only in present-day Russia, which allows genuine diversity and multi-culturedness: the film ends with an ever-growing group of young

Figure 20.5 Young people strolling down Tverskaia Street in the finale of Valerii Todorovskii's *Hipsters*, 2008.

people strolling down Tverskaia Street, visually uniting Mels, the film's *stiliaga* hero of the 1950s, with modern-day punks, dandies, and hippies. The film's style with its close-ups and crane shots, musical interludes, and colorful dresses, deliberately sets itself apart from the style of the period to underline the fake quality of the historical setting and emphasize the film's performative nature: this is a deliberate and conscious revisioning of the past, without glorification and restoration, but of open myth-making that serves to promote the diversity of Putin's Russia.

Somewhat different is the approach to Moscow as historical location in Karen Shakhnazarov's *Vanishing Empire* [*Ischeznuvshaia imperiia*, 2008] which meticulously reconstruct the prime locations of 1970's cinema and culture – bookshops, leisure parks, cinema, and theater (the Taganka, the Arts [Khudozhestvennyi] cinema), as well as the new suburban district Teplyi Stan in the south of Moscow.

The nostalgia for the Stalinist era occurs through a deconstruction, mocking the sites of Stalinist culture in *Moscow Parade* and *Hammer and Sickle*. *Burnt by the Sun* instead restores the Stalinist past, defending the people's belief in the communist ideal. Svetlana Boym distinguishes "between two kinds of nostalgia: utopian (reconstructive and totalizing) and ironic (inclusive and fragmentary). The former stresses the first root of the word, *nostos* [home], and puts the emphasis on the return to that mythical place on the island of Utopia where the 'greater patria' has to be rebuilt [...] Ironic nostalgia puts the emphasis on *algia*, longing, and acknowledges the displacement of the mythical place without trying to rebuild it" (Boym 1994: 284; emphasis in the original). The post-Soviet past is deconstructed through exaggeration in Todorovskii's film about the *stiliagi*, and by a narrative framework that offers a distanced view in Shakhnazarov; neither film is "nostalgic" about the past in the above sense.

Crime Scene: Moscow

Let us turn to the absence of Moscow from films with contemporary settings. In the cinema of the 1990s, Moscow is no longer a city of pride: its facades crumble, the new buildings are designated crime scenes, and Moscow seems like a tourist attraction for its own citizens.

One of the first films where the capital moves back into focus without actually appearing on screen is Aleksei Balabanov's *Brother* [*Brat*, 1997] where Danila Bagrov (Sergei Bodrov) makes several references to Moscow as the center where power lies; in a conversation with Hoffman, he argues that it is a city only for the strong. Therefore, once he has finished with the criminal world of St Petersburg (whence he arrived from the provinces), Danila hikes to Moscow, now an accomplished killer. *Brother* defines a new type of hero who upholds no moral standards: Danila possesses skill, strength, and courage, and is ruthless to his enemies, while at the same time he is a knight (Margolit 1998, 58), who keeps his word and helps the poor. At the end of the film Danila prepares for a new screen image, the Moscow killer: he never reaches Moscow within the film, but instead the final shot shows the snow-white landscape with the road to Moscow; it is a blank page that is waiting for the hero's new image. Moscow is an absent location in *Brother*, while it represents the center where the strings of the underworld run together. *Brother 2* [*Brat 2*, 2000] begins and ends in Moscow, now Danila's base, although the action mainly unfolds in Chicago, where Danila goes to revenge the death of a comrade-in-arms. The locations in Moscow include the Historical Museum on Red Square, a residential building on the embankment and other sights, echoing the cinematic image of Moscow created in the past: central sites have now turned into hiding places for criminals and lodgings for the new (media) elite. Balabanov subverts the historical significance of buildings: the Historical Museum becomes a site for criminal action, where yesterday's weapons are wielded against today's Mafia.

Many comedies use Moscow for their setting as a crime-ridden city, from which the characters miraculously escape, often to foreign lands: Vladimir Men'shov's *Shirly-Myrli* (1995) ends on a flight to the Canary Islands, Alla Surikova's *Moscow Holidays* [*Moskovskie kanikuly*, 1995] on a flight to Rome, while Valerii Todorovskii's *The Land of the Deaf* [*Strana glukhikh*, 1997] lands both protagonists in a world without sound. An escape into a different world forms part of the plot of Todorovskii's *The Land of the Deaf*. Rita dreams of simple happiness with her boyfriend Andrei, who is a gambler and has lost the Mafia's money at the casino; unless he repays, he is a target for the Mafia. YaYa is a deaf girl, who dreams of taking Rita with her into the happy land of the deaf. The two women become involved with the Mafia in order to make money to realize their respective dreams; they survive a shoot-out of rival gangs, but here Rita turns deaf: her dream of happiness is a manifest illusion, while the (unreal) journey to the land of the deaf comes true. The everyday reality of Moscow is mainly represented in images of the city at night, while its daylight depiction in the last frames turns the buzzing city – in which YaYa is always at risk – into a quiet sea of movement under the sound of the ocean which is all that Rita can now hear (Todorovskii 1997, 102). Deafness is a retreat from reality, and turns the crime-ridden and threatening city into a sea of traffic.

The films of the 1990s subvert the centripetal pattern of mobility of Stalin-era films: they begin in the provinces only to return there, once the center has been destroyed, as is the case in Petr Lutsik's *Outskirts* [*Okraina*, 1998]. Lutsik's film reiterates the point made in earlier films with a rural setting, regarding the negative influence of the center on the provinces. Here it is not the center which wins, and forces the characters out of their native land, but they destroy the center, leaving Moscow to a nuclear disaster while they return to plough their land.

The representation of Moscow as a trap, as an unpleasant experience resurges in the 1990s, when characters from the provinces fail to make a home in Moscow. In Daneliia's *Nastia* (1993) the heroine compensates her sense of loss in the contemporary city by escaping into a fairy tale; in Riazanov's *Prediction* [*Predskazanie*, 1993] the city is in political turmoil as Oleg Goriunov visits his home town after a six-months absence, echoing his estrangement. In Daneliia's *Heads or Tails* [*Orel i reshka*, 1995] Moscow is a place of cheating and betrayal, forcing the characters to leave in the end. Luzhkov's Moscow is thus a topos of crime and alienation. While reconstructing Moscow's past – the Cathedral of Christ the Savior, the Iberian (Resurrection) Gate on Red Square, the Hotel Moscow, Gostinyi dvor – Luzhkov seemingly competes with Stalinist architecture in the replication of the Empire style in red granite for many buildings in the center, suggesting continuity. In *Moscow Holidays* the Italian lady who arrives in Moscow to bury her dead lapdog is mugged immediately; in *Shirli-Myrli* Moscow is made up of facades and appearances, and behind the collapsing scaffolding of the airport terminal reign theft and corruption. But it is primarily the business center "Moscow City," which Luzhkov projected in the late 1990s, where the Mafia shoot-outs in Aleksandr Atanesian's *24 Hours* [*24 chasa*, 2000] and Aleksandr Borodianskii and Boris Giller's *The Cheque* [*Chek*, 2000] take place: the precise location is the Bagration Bridge (opened in 1997), at the time the only completed feature of the projected City between Kutuzov Avenue (Tower 2000) and the side of the Moscow International Business Center "Mezhdunarodnaia" on Krasnopresnenskaia Embankment.

The Empty Space

Aleksandr Zeldovich's *Moscow* (2000) features a number of traditional sites of the capital and subverts their function. The autistic Olga is taken on a tour of the city by Lev, a courier for a dubious business; thus the film repeats the stereotypical tour of the capital for the visitor, only that here the visitor is a Muscovite with a handicap. The metro is part of Moscow's sights, along with the Kremlin, the Cathedral of Christ the Savior, the Lenin Stadium, the Tretyakov Gallery, the Babaev chocolate factory and others. Yet the metro is no longer a palace for the people, nor a means of transport, nor a scene of crime: it is simply a place for sex. Lev takes Olga on the "dernier metro" which goes to the depot, and once they leave the station he presses her against the door (comically, despite the written instruction: do not lean against the doors) and has sex with her. Indeed, the function of the entire city of Moscow is reduced to a location for sex: in another scene Lev cuts a hole into the map of Russia on spot where Moscow is located to have sexual intercourse with Masha, who is covered by the map. *Moscow* ultimately subverts all prime locations and turns them into empty, meaningless spaces, or places of death: Mark's suicide is staged on the ski jump; Mike is shot on the stage of the Bolshoi Theater.

In the cinema of the 2000s Moscow becomes unrecognizable, faceless, and featureless: Bakur Bakuradze's *Shultes* (2008) dwells on the issue of a forged identity and takes this search to a logical conclusion. The film's hero Lesha Shultes suffers from amnesia following a trauma: he and his wife/girlfriend have been in a car accident in which she died. Unable to come to terms with the loss, he represses his memory: Shultes effaces his past Self. Moreover, the city in which he lives has no face: all districts look alike, the metro is a place of theft, and rows of kiosks serve crime, not commerce. Similarly unrecognizable is the Moscow of Kirill Serebrennikov's *Betrayal* [*Izmena*, 2012]: the film is set somewhere on the outskirts of a featureless city, where all suburban areas look alike: they are not even stereotyped as in Riazanov's classic *Irony of Fate*, but they lack all individual features. The cityscape has no bearing on the individual.

The center of Moscow is transformed: in *Night Watch* [*Nochnoi dozor*, 2004] and *Day Watch* [*Dnevnoi dozor*, 2006] the classical spaces of metro, hotels, and television towers turn into places of horror where a battle between the forces of Light and Darkness takes place. The films choose as locations key sites: the river tour, the hotel Cosmos, the VDNKh metro station; but here horrific events occur: the former Stalinist sites are – unsurprisingly – governed by the forces of Darkness. At the same time, locations of crime and prostitution are transposed from the periphery into the center, while the periphery remains a place for marginal characters and migrants (*Shultes* lives on the periphery; Larisa Sadilova's *She* [*Ona*, 2013] and Dmitrii Mamuliia's *Another Sky* [*Drugoe nebo*, 2010] both feature the periphery as the habitat of the gastarbeiter-protagonist; see Beumers 2014). Most frequently, however, Moscow appears in darkness, at night.

The relationship between Moscow and the rest of the country, or center and periphery, has been a dominant theme in Soviet culture in general and in cinema in particular, as it tended to focus on the center, Moscow, with a centripetal movement from the periphery (see Widdis 2003). In the 1990s, however, rather than shifting to a centrifugal movement away from the center, the Moscow-centric mode of the Soviet era continued even after the collapse of the USSR (see Beumers

1999, 76–87). During the power-centric Putin-era one might expect a continuation of the depiction of Moscow, especially the new, capitalist sites such as the City: however, these new complexes serve largely as crime sites, for example in Marina Liubakova's *Cruelty* [*Zhestokost'*, 2007], where the Moscow International Business Center (Naberezhnaia Tower) features as a prime location for the revenge that the successful lawyer Zoya (Renata Litvinova) plans on her lover; her private life is focused in the real center, near Taganka Square and Solianka Street. Similarly, shopping malls reflect wealth, but serve as shelters for orphaned and homeless teenagers in Valerii Priemykhov's *Who, if Not Us* [*Kto, esli ne my*, 1998], while the old city center [Staropimenovskii pereulok] is a spot for prostitution in Iurii Moroz's *The Spot* [*Tochka*, 2006]. In Anna Melikian's *Mermaid* [*Rusalka*, 2007] Alisa (Maria Shalaeva) moves with her mother and grandmother to Moscow after a hurricane destroys her seaside house on the Black Sea. Alisa gets a job working for a mobile phone company, walking around the city dressed as a phone for advertisement purposes. She advances in her job and saves her boss's life, only to be run over by a car: the city poses a danger for the outsider. *The Star* [*Zvezda*, 2014], shows the Moscow of new riches and juxtaposes this with the hostel-like living conditions for outsiders; a similar situation can be seen in Andrei Zviagintsev's *Elena* where the rich people live in protected accommodation on Ostozhenka Street, while ordinary people inhabit a few square meters in Biriulevo. The final sequence of Roman Prygunov's *Dukhless* (2011) shows the "top manager" Maks Andreev (Danila Kozlovskii) being dumped on a landfill, thus stripping the (business) center of Moscow of any alluring attributes altogether: this is not a city that attracts, but that repels, that "wastes" humans.

The historical center is re-created through CGI images as, for example, the visualization of the (destroyed, and at the time of filming not completely restored) Cathedral of Christ the Savior in Nikita Mikhalkov's *The Barber of Siberia* [*Sibirskii*

Figure 20.6 Stalin's Moscow in 1941 as it never was: CG images of Moscow in Aleksei Andrianov's *The Spy*, 2012.

tsiriul'nik, 1998]. A perfect illusion is created in the film *The Spy* [*Shpion*, 2012] by Aleksei Andrianov, where the meeting of a German envoy to Stalin on the day before the German invasion in June 1941 takes place in the Palace of Soviets, constructed through CGI: this is the digitally perfected Moscow that Stalin planned to have by the time the war broke out. Moscow is not only repaired, but the communist utopia of the Palace of Soviets is actually achieved. It is curious that such a restoration of a utopian vision of Moscow came at time when Putin had consolidated his power, thus strengthening the vertical of power in contemporary Russia. If most films set in Moscow have been shot on actual location rather than in pavilions, then the recent CGI manipulation of the city in such blockbusters as *The Spy*, but also the apocalyptic vision in *The Darkest Hour*, would appear to suggest a change in Moscow's image from a real to a virtual one.

Conclusion

From the utopia of the 1930s, the real Moscow of the post-war period followed to be transformed into a virtual (or dark) Moscow as a prime shooting location for contemporary films. More than often the capital is either absent from films, or features as a center of theft and crime. Moscow has visitors, but they do not stay long or permanently; none of the films end in Moscow as the termination of a longer movement by the protagonist, although they may be set there as a static location. Moscow is a lost center, and this reflects the disorientation in a space where central control exists no longer. The principle of domination (by aerial shots or in architectural terms) is replaced by one of undermining and disappearance into the lower under-world that serves as a mirror image for the dominance of extreme wealth above, in the center.

The camera images produce a featureless, static Moscow that does not move or develop: as Svetlana Boym has suggested, Moscow's "mythical time is that of eternal rebirth, not of historical progression [...]; it doesn't mourn its past, it creates it anew, bigger and better" (Boym 2001, 100). Moscow is frozen on screen: it is never a living, changing, and pulsating city; instead it is immersed in darkness, stripped of identity, and drained of real life. The CG images used to create an apocalyptic future or a utopian past echo this timelessness: "Future Perfect and Distant Past merged together, destined to hypnotize the viewer into a complete oblivion of the Present" (Boym 2001, 103). Moscow is not inhabitable: protagonists who live there or come to visit tend to perish: Alisa (*The Mermaid*) and Margarita (*The Star*) die; the nameless lovers are murdered in *Betrayal*; the protagonist Maks in *Dukhless* ends up on a landfill: he is social waste, unable to run a business or his private life. If in the 1990s Moscow was the center of crime and capitalist consumerism, in the 2000s it is the center of death and annihilation; survival may be possible on the periphery, and notably for migrants. Moreover, the city has no style: the filming locations are look-alike buildings; the new Moscow is faceless (and soul-less): "For now Luzhkov's style has come to an end. It was destroyed by Putin, economically undermining the monolith of Luzhkov's construction complex. […] Vladimir Putin has not yet declared any architectural program" (Revzin 2002). Moscow is a blank page that awaits its new face to be drawn, in reality or in virtual terms.

Notes

1 Clark (2011) continues that in the latter half of the decade this aesthetic state turns from beauty to the sublime, echoed in a concern with upward movement and aerial conquest.
2 Later this location reappears in a historical context in Pavel Chukhrai's *Driver for Vera* [*Voditel' dlia Very*, 2004]; the story begins in Moscow in 1962 and involves a soldier's recruitment as driver to a general stationed on the Crimea as the latter gets sucked up in political intrigues against Khrushchev. See Beumers (2012).
3 Original names were returned to Okhotnyi Riad (1935), renamed Prospekt Marksa (1964), then Okhotnyi Riad (1990); Krasnye vorota (1935) became Lermontovskaia (1964) and reverted to Krasnye vorota (1990); Alekseevskaia was renamed Shcherbakovskaia in 1958 and reverted back to Alekseevskaia in 1990. New names were given in 1990 to Dzerzhinskaia and Ploshchad' Sverdlova (1935), which were renamed Lubianka and Teatral'naia; Gor'kovskaia (1980) was renamed Tverskaia; Kol'khoznaia (1967) was renamed Sukharevskaia; Kirovskaia (1935) became Chistye prudy, and Ploshchad' Nogina (1970s) became Kitai Gorod.

References

Beumers, Birgit. 1999. "To Moscow! To Moscow? The Russian Hero and the Loss of the Centre." In *Russia on Reels: The Russian Idea in Post-Soviet Cinema*, edited by B. Beumers, 76–87. London: I. B. Tauris.
Beumers (Boimers), Birgit. 2002. "Puteshestvie pod zemliu: metro na ekrane" [Underground Journeys: The Metro on Screen]. *Neprikosnovennyi zapas* [Emergency Reserve] 3. http://magazines.russ.ru/nz/2002/3/boi.html (accessed April 1, 2015).
Beumers, Birgit. 2012. "National Identities through Visions of the Past: Contemporary Russian Cinema." In *Soviet and Post-Soviet Identities*, edited by Mark Bassin and Catriona Kelly, 120–153. Cambridge: Cambridge University Press.
Beumers, Birgit. 2014. "A 'Hero of our Time': The *Gastarbeiter* in Recent Russian Cinema," *Zeitschrift für Slavische Philologie* [Journal for Slavic Philology] 70.1: 161–178.
Boym, Svetlana. 1994. *Common Places. Mythologies of Everyday Life in Russia*. Cambridge MA: Harvard University Press.
Boym, Svetlana. 2001. *The Future of Nostalgia*. New York: Basic Books.
Clark, Katerina. 2011. *Moscow. The Fourth Rome. Stalinism, Cosmopolitanism and the Evolution of Soviet Culture, 1931–1941*. Cambridge MA and London: Harvard University Press.

Margolit, Evgenii. 1998. "Plach po pioneru, ili Nemetskoe slovo 'Iablokitai'" [The Lament for a Pioneer, or the German Work "Iablokitai"]. *Iskusstvo kino* [Art of Cinema] 2: 57–64.

O'Mahony, Mike. 2006. *Sport in the USSR. Physical Culture – Visual Culture*. London: Reaktion.

Paperny, Vladimir. 1985. *Kul'tura Dva* [Culture Two]. Ann Arbor: Ardis.

Revzin, Grigorii. 1997. "Postmodernizm kak 'Kul'tura 2'" [Postmodernism as "Culture Two"]. *Nezavisimaia gazeta* [Independent Gazette] January 25.

Revzin, Grigorii. 2002. "Moskva. Desiat' let posle SSSR" [Moscow. Ten Years after the USSR]. *Neprikosnovennyi zapas* [Emergency Reserve] 5, http://magazines.russ.ru/nz/2002/5/revz.html (accessed April 1, 2015).

Ryklin, Mikhail 2005. "Metrodiskurs." *Topos* July 12, http://www.topos.ru/article/3805 (accessed April 1, 2015).

Todorovskii, Valerii. 1997. "Rossiia perezhivaet burnyi roman s den'gami" [Russia is in a Deep Love Affair with Money]. Interview with Roman Khrishch. *Seans* 16: 102.

von Geldern, James and Richard Stites, eds 1995. *Mass Culture in Soviet Russia: Tales, Poems, Songs, Movies, Plays and Folklore 1917–1953*. Bloomington: Indiana University Press.

Widdis, Emma. 2003. *Visions of a New Land: Soviet Film from the Revolution to the Second World War*. New Haven: Yale University Press.

Woll, Josephine. 2000. *Real Images. Soviet Cinema and the Thaw*. London: I. B. Tauris.

Part V
Directors' Portraits

21

Boris Barnet: "This doubly accursed cinema"

Julian Graffy

The 1920s saw the birth of Soviet cinema and the first films of the masters Lev Kuleshov, Sergei Eisenstein, Vsevolod Pudovkin, Dziga Vertov, and Aleksandr Dovzhenko. But while the directorial careers of all of these men were over by the time of Stalin's death in 1953, other major figures whose first films had been made in the 1920s, including Grigorii Kozintsev and Leonid Trauberg, Aleksandr Zarkhi and Iosif Kheifits, Fridrikh Ermler, Sergei Iutkevich, Mikhail Kalatozov, Iulii Raizman, and Abram Room, continued to produce films into the Thaw period, the 1960s and 1970s. Indeed, Iutkevich, Raizman, and Zarkhi were still directing in the 1980s. By paying attention to the trajectories of these men's lives in Soviet film we can shed light upon the history of Soviet cinema and on the political, social, and intellectual contexts in which they worked. One of the most remarkable (and poignant) of such lives is that of Boris Barnet, who acted in the first Soviet cinematic masterpiece, Kuleshov's *The Extraordinary Adventures of Mr West in the Land of the Bolsheviks* [*Neobychainye prikliucheniia mistera Vesta v strane bol'shevikov*, 1924] and made his last film in 1963. Though he is still neither as well known nor as appreciated as he deserves, his probing, personal interpretation of the Russian experience of the twentieth century, both on the historical and the intimate planes, his ability to coax brilliant performances out of young actors (and to turn them into stars), his compelling sense of place and his enlivening attention to cinematic detail have attracted the praise of such connoisseurs as Jean-Luc Godard, Jacques Rivette, and Otar Iosseliani, while the recent appearance of a number of his major films on good quality DVDs is bringing him to the belated attention of a broader audience across the world.

A Companion to Russian Cinema, First Edition. Edited by Birgit Beumers.
© 2016 John Wiley & Sons, Inc. Published 2016 by John Wiley & Sons, Inc.

A Moscow Youth: The "Champion of Denmark"

Barnet was born in Moscow, where his father ran a small printing house, on June 18, 1902. As his name suggests, his forefathers were not Russian. According to his main biographer (Kushnirov 1977, 4), Barnet's English – or, as he later suggested, Scottish (Kushnirovich 1995, 41) – grandfather, the typographer Thomas Barnet, arrived in Russia in the mid-nineteenth century. Barnet himself told the French film historian Georges Sadoul, perhaps fancifully, that his great-grandfather was an English soldier who set up in Russia during the Napoleonic wars (G. S. 1965). At the age of eight, Barnet started school, spending his spare time visiting the theatre and the cinema, where he enjoyed the films of Max Linder. After leaving school, in the autumn of 1916, he enrolled in the painting department of the Moscow School of Painting, Sculpture, and Architecture, where he could indulge his passion for drawing, while at the same time working as a stage-hand at the First Studio of the Moscow Arts Theatre. After the Revolution, he joined the Red Army as a medical orderly. In the summer of 1922 he fell sick with what may have been cholera, was sent to Moscow for treatment, and was demobilized. There he entered the Main Military School of Workers' Physical Education, where he later became a boxing instructor. He spent two years as a professional boxer and took part in bouts of "French" wrestling, in which he was presented as the champion of Denmark or Iceland.[1]

Working with Kuleshov

It was when Lev Kuleshov saw him fight that Barnet's life in film began. Kuleshov invited him to train the actors of his studio in movement and wrote the part of the Cowboy Jeddy in *Mr West* especially for him. Thus Barnet joined the number of remarkable actors and directors who began their careers working with Kuleshov. Barnet's charismatic comic performance as Mr West's loyal, impetuous, slightly dim bodyguard combines a shy, rueful smile with startling athleticism as he performs a succession of breath-taking chases, fights, and stunts. Indeed, it was the dangerous nature of one of these stunts, in which he was required to hang from a rope between two tall buildings "for 25–30 minutes" (Margolit and Zabrodin 1992, 8–9; Kuleshov 1934, 133–134), that led to his parting with Kuleshov. Deciding to exert more control over his cinematic fate, Barnet took a script to the Rus' Studio, where he met the scriptwriter Valentin Turkin, who invited him to collaborate on the screenplay of *Miss Mend*, a film which Fedor Otsep was slated to direct. Barnet was also offered a leading role in the film, and Kushnirov (1977, 37) reports that he was appointed as co-director to the equally inexperienced Otsep even before filming began.

First Films as a Director: The 1920s Comedies

Miss Mend (The Adventures of Three Reporters) [Miss Mend (Prikliucheniia trekh reporterov, 1926] tells the implausible story of how the eponymous heroine, a typist in a small-town American factory, along with her three male acolytes, discovers a dastardly plot by a sinister Fascist "organization" to advance its political agenda by unleashing plague bacteria on the unsuspecting people of Leningrad. Rushing across the Atlantic, they valiantly attempt to warn the Soviet authorities. The film both celebrates and pastiches the American action cinema, which, as Kuleshov (1922) had established, was enormously popular among early Soviet audiences. To add to the excitement, the depiction of the villains is steeped in ironical references to the conventions of German Expressionism, something immediately alluded to by Gusman (1926) in a reference to the Mabusian quality [*mabuzistost'*] of their leader Chiche, and examined in detail by Burch (1985).

So there are chases and fights, murders and corpses, mad scientists, greed, corruption, and lust. There are cliff-hanger endings and broad humor. To leaven the adventures there are traces of ideology, contrasting the strikes and racism in America with the daring and effective policemen in the USSR, but Soviet critics still called it "varnished barbarism" (Youngblood 1992, 130).

Though it is not possible to establish definitively what Barnet's directorial contribution was, the legacy of his work with Kuleshov is apparent in the stunts and there are motifs that will recur in his later films. On the other hand, his films would never again be so plot-driven and the hectic tone of *Miss Mend* differs greatly

Figure 21.1 Vladimir Fogel' as photo journalist in *Miss Mend*, 1926.

from that of his later work. Unlike many of his contemporaries, Barnet never wrote theoretical articles about how he made films – indeed he almost never wrote anything of any length on the subject. His one substantial piece of writing and the nearest he gets to producing an artistic credo, "Notes on film comedy" (Barnet 1954) is full of banalities and comes to life only when he talks about his own film practice, stressing the need to follow the "truth of life" rather than going all out for laughs, the fundamental importance of working well with his actors, the crucial role of the detail in bringing a scene alive, and his unwavering commitment to improvisation, a point reiterated by his fourth wife, Valentina Kozintseva:

> at the basis of his work on the set, and also when he was editing, was improvisation. He would arrive on set, latch on to any detail of the stage decoration, or a costume, or notice something in the face of an actor, and start to improvise, sometimes really moving a long way from the script. (Kozintseva 2002, 167)

Indeed this principle, which meant that his scripts were always no more than a starting point, repeatedly caused him difficulties: the Repertory Section found 13 "major and unforgiveable" deviations from the script in *The Girl with the Hatbox* [*Devushka s korobkoi*, 1927] (Kushnirov 1977, 63–64). Bela Zorich, the writer of the original script for *The House on Trubnaya* [*Dom na Trubnoi*, 1928] confessed that the "rift between the intention and the embodiment" was "painful" (Anon. 1928b), while the dramatist Fedor Knorre wrote a scathing letter of complaint about the traducing of his scenario for *One Night* [*Odnazhdy noch'iu*, 1944] (Musina 2002b, 141–143).

At the end of the decade, Barnet directed the two charming lyrical comedies, *The Girl with the Hatbox* and *The House on Trubnaya*, which began to define his unique style.[2] Both are set in the Moscow of late NEP, and in both a character from the backwoods comes to the city for the first time. In both the central figure is a spirited young woman, and such women would recur in several of Barnet's later films. There was widespread debate at the time about the cinematic representation of women. At a discussion at the Association of Workers of Revolutionary Cinematography (ARRK), on September 14, 1928, 10 days after the release of *The House on Trubnaya*, Bela Zorich asserted:

> As long as we see in our pictures a woman who is the opposite of the woman we see in life, we shall never see the Soviet woman on screen. [...] Until the social commission [*sotsial'nyi zakaz*] dictates it from outside, and until directors and scriptwriters understand this, the on-screen woman will always be false. (Ostrovskii 1994, 129, 131)

But Barnet's heroines are not this new Soviet woman. On the contrary, as Khrisanf Khersonskii (Musina 2002b, 151) noted: "Where does Barnet's strength lie? In the fact that, unlike anyone else in our cinema, he portrays very precisely the purely psychic life of the ordinary person, unusually precisely, like the most refined instrument." Like few others, Barnet could render the texture of daily life [*byt*], or, as Grashchenkova (2002, 103) has argued, not so much daily life as a simulation of daily life as a source for comedy. He made his approach clear in a short but revealing piece published a month before the release of *The Girl with the Hatbox*:

> When embarking on the production of the comedy *The Girl with the Hatbox* I was absolutely clear that it would be necessary to some extent to step on to the path of experiment, since the methods for bringing out the comic material of our contemporary life, on which the script was mainly based, have not yet been found. [...] It was necessary when organizing the material to find the comic elements that would make it possible to show the comic as an organic part of what was happening. [...] [The scriptwriters] tried to include a minimal amount of plot material.
> We developed every situation and action for the maximal exploitation of people and things. [...] In our work we discovered the amazing and pleasant fact that you can construct scenes which impress not only by montage but through the mise-en-scène itself. [...] This is my first independent work and in it I wager on the actors. (Barnet 1927a)

The film itself puts all of these principles into practice. *The Girl with the Hatbox* is ostensibly about such contemporary issues as the housing crisis and the national lottery instituted to help resolve it, but its real center of gravity is in its light, airy love story, a fact underlined by giving the two central protagonists avian surnames, Natasha Korosteleva [corncrake] and the student Il'ia Snegirev [bullfinch].[3] Moreover, the charm and conviction of the acting (Anna Sten, who plays Natasha, would later enjoy some success in Hollywood) entirely justifies Barnet's confidence in his reliance on his actors which, as Zorkaia (2000, 196) points out, departed radically from the practice of both Kuleshov and Eisenstein. Things, too, play a central role: Natasha is rarely seen without her hats or hatbox, or Il'ia without his enormous felt boots or the pile of books which are intended for his studies but which serve instead as both an impromptu seat and weights for his morning exercises. The film is peppered with visual gags and Barnet is also thrillingly innovative in his *mise-en-scène*. *The Girl with the Hatbox* opens with scenes set in a vast snowy landscape, reminiscent of a Malevich Suprematist white-on-white canvas, in which the protagonists are reduced to the size of scurrying rats, while the splendid comic sequence in which Natasha and Il'ia are forced to spend the night in her recently emptied room uses their meager possessions as the furnishings of an abstract stage set.

The Girl with the Hatbox is now acknowledged as Barnet's first masterpiece, but its initial critical reception was less enthusiastic. The Repertory Section [Glavrepertkom] called it "hack fabrication with elements of hooliganism" (Ostrovskii 1994, 105), while Nikolai Iakovlev (Iakov 1927) found it to be "dangerous" in its (ideological) "neutrality". As Barnet (1927b) contended, in a discussion of Soviet comedy, "the most complicated question (strange as it may be) is finding a theme". But Soviet audiences must have liked it, for, after a clever advertising

Figure 21.2 Anna Sten as Natasha in *The Girl with the Hatbox*, 1927.

campaign, it recouped 173 percent of its costs at the box office (Iusupova 2013, 166), making it one of the biggest native-made popular hits of the late 1920s.

In Barnet's next film, *The House on Trubnaya*, the ideological element is ostensibly more important. The heroine, Parania Pitunova, comes to Moscow to take up work as a housemaid and is mistaken for a worker delegate to the Moscow Soviet. As Neia Zorkaia has noted (Zorkaia 2000, 203), this turns her into a kind of Soviet version of Gogol''s Government Inspector, who inadvertently reveals the vices of the NEP characters who surround her, thus eventually leading to the imprisonment of her bullying employer. But this does not happen until near the end of the film, causing the journalist Shneider to complain at the Association of Workers of Revolutionary Cinematography that "the main theme has perished," since the first five reels were given over to exposition and only one to the development and dénouement of the plot (Anon. 1928a). Once again the strength and allure of the film lie in its affectionate observation of late 1920s Moscow *byt*, its imaginative deployment of a succession of brilliant gags involving plates and washing lines, and the inventive use of the possibilities of cinematic form. When Parania arrives in Moscow with a live duck, which promptly wanders on to tramlines, her back story is told through freeze-frame, rewinding the film and a comic flashback portraying her departure from her village and her increasingly confused wandering around the big city. Most original and visually exciting of all is the extraordinary sequence with which Barnet opens the film, showing morning on the common staircase of the house itself. There had been a cleverly choreographed fight on a staircase in *Miss Mend*, but here Barnet shoots simultaneous action on five landings and the five connecting flights of stairs, trumping even the Eisenstein of *The Strike* [*Stachka*, 1924].

Politics and History, Love and Levity

Between these two comedies, Barnet made *Moscow in October* [*Moskva v Oktiabre*, 1927], commissioned, like Eisenstein's *October* [*Oktiabr'*, 1927] and Pudovkin's *The End of St Petersburg* [*Konets Sankt Peterburga*, 1927], to mark the tenth anniversary of the Revolution. As its title suggests, it relates how the revolutionary events unfurled in Moscow. Barnet explained his choice of subject by the fact that "in Moscow the October days passed more profoundly, more sharply, more cinematographically interestingly than in Leningrad", adding that lack of time had prevented him from innovating (Barnet 1927c, 17). He provocatively asserted that in many ways the October Revolution had already become "a fine legend," admitting that some episodes of the film had strayed from historical accuracy, since "the cinema has its own demands" (Barnet 1927d). These statements suggest an original approach to an already canonized subject, but the film has been widely judged a failure. Alas, only three complete reels, lasting around 30 minutes, remain. Some of those who have seen them consider them to be "antithetical to his style in every way" (Youngblood 1992, 133), a Barnet film "without any Barnet" (Kushnirov 1977, 77). But Ostrovskii tantalizingly finds "ethnographic improvisations," "expressionist foreshortenings" (the designer was Aleksandr Rodchenko) and even subversive "fragments which destroy all the monumental effects" of the film, serving as "the tragic 'spoon of tar' in the ideological 'barrel of honey'" (Ostrovskii 1994, 114), while more recently Kovalov has reminded us that the Jubilee Commission approved the film and asserts that the remaining reels are consistently "fresh, unexpected and engaging," providing a hitherto unrecognized original model for making a historical film (Kovalov 2013, 271, 272).

After *The House on Trubnaya* Barnet directed two *kulturfilms* about the manufacture of musical instruments, both of them now lost. He then further expanded the genre diversity which had marked his career so far with *Icebreak* [*Ledolom*, 1931], which also developed the contemporary ideological concerns that he had first addressed in *Moscow in October* and would return to later in the decade. Set near the Volga, and telling the story of the struggle between kulaks and a new kolkhoz, *Icebreak* has many parallels with Dovzhenko's *Earth* [*Zemlia*, 1930]. Indeed, it starts with extended lyrical scenes of a loving couple in the steppe. But it is much darker than *Earth*, for when the young heroine, Anka, tells her lover, the son of a rich peasant, that she is pregnant, he abandons her. And the division between the (good) poor peasants and Party and the (bad) kulaks is not clear-cut in the way it is in *Earth*. Okulov, the Chairman of the Village Council, is a drunk who is suborned into taking much less corn from the kulaks than they can afford to give and exploiting the poor peasants. The Chairman of the Village Soviet is also lazy and corrupt in Kozintsev and Trauberg's *Alone* [*Odna*], made the same year, but in *Icebreak* the consequences of this corruption are more pervasive. The kulaks terrorize the village, smashing the windows of the hut of the pregnant Anka and killing Okulov when he seems to repent. The forces of good are represented in the film by a Komsomol member, Semen, and by Anka, who, despite prejudice among the old women that she is "fallen," is elected, along with Semen, to a new Soviet. The film ends with a stirring intertitle calling the Soviets to greater class firmness in the battle against the enemy.

Perhaps because of the rigor of its criticism of Party officials *Icebreak* seems hardly to have been noticed in the contemporary press. It differs from Barnet's earlier comedies not only through explicit political engagement but also by the absence of a love affair between Anka and Semen. But it shares with those films an admiration for a resilient young woman, and in its loving evocation of the deep Russian hinterland – *Icebreak* opens and closes with scenes on the Volga itself – it points to Barnet's next film, and his greatest achievement, *Outskirts* [*Okraina*, 1933].[4]

Set in 1914 and 1917, in a backwoods town and in the trenches of the Front, *Outskirts* tells the story of the consequences of War and Revolution for the workers in a boot factory and their families. It opens on a gloriously indolent summer's day. Loving couples are sitting on benches, while the young heroine, Man'ka Greshina, looks on contentedly. The idyll is broken by the sound of a strike whistle, with mounted Cossacks breaking down worker resistance. But this violence is merely a rehearsal for the greater disruption caused by war. Films about World War I were unsurprisingly far less common in the Soviet Union than films about the Revolution that had ushered in the Soviet state, though there are poignant sequences mourning the tragedy and horror of that war at the start of both Dovzhenko's *Arsenal* (1928) and Fridrikh Ermler's *Fragment of an Empire* [*Oblomok imperii*, 1929]. Unlike these two films, however, all of *Outskirts* is concerned with the experience of the War itself. At first patriotism provokes enthusiasm, as departing soldiers, including the Kadkin brothers, Nikolai and Sen'ka, are seen off by excited crowds and stirring martial music, though even here a black-clad mother has to be carried away prostrated by grief. But it is precisely their blinkered but mutually exclusive patriotism that causes an immediate rift between Man'ka's father and his German lodger and draughts partner, Robert Karlovich. Later, in the trenches, patriotic enthusiasm is corroded by boredom and punctured by sudden shattering violence, giving way to a fear caused by desperate vulnerability to an unseen enemy.

Time and again, Barnet humanizes his story by the inclusion of unexpected but suggestive detail. When Robert Karlovich departs Greshin's house in indignation, he passes a drunk lying in the gutter, empty bottle in hand. In the trenches it is Sen'ka Kadkin's (simulated?) toothache that prevents him from going over the top with the other soldiers, causing him to be beaten up by an officer and leading directly to his farcical, piteous death. Sometimes these details are comic. When Man'ka tries to catch the attention of the German prisoner of war Müller, she puts on her best dress, the tiered skirts of which make her look like a walking wedding cake. And the emotional intensity of the scene of the soldiers' departure is lightened by a comic episode with a little dog hanging in mid-air which Barnet included to "destroy the sense of 'premeditation' about the thickening of somber colors, to bring what is happening 'down to earth'" (Barnet 1954, 160). The boots being made throughout the film become a polysemous symbol, associated with labor for the workers, with profit for the factory owner, and with death for the soldiers. Barnet's alertness to the weft of lived experience leads Evgenii Margolit (2012, 220) to note the "almost unnoticed flow, the self-propulsion of life, its meager but distinct inner meaningfulness." Politics is less important in the film than compassion for the simple desires of ordinary people, whichever side they are on. A fragile love affair develops between Man'ka and Müller, both of them innocents, almost "infantile," in the way that Barnet's characters so often are (Ostrovskii 1994, 95), while the Kadkins' bereaved father stresses that Müller's identity as a cobbler is more important than the fact that he is German. Though the film ends with a march through the town by supporters of the Bolsheviks, their political awareness is rudimentary – in the words of a little soldier at the Front who becomes the film's mouthpiece, "they've taken some Winter…"

Figure 21.3 Man'ka and the German prisoner in *Outskirts*, 1933.

Béla Balázs (1933) praised Barnet's capacity to remove the dualism between the comic and the tragic, something that he felt even Shakespeare could not manage. Sergei Gerasimov, who, like Barnet, had begun his career as an actor, but who had by then embarked upon his own long and influential directorial career, asserted that *Outskirts* had taught Soviet artists "to understand the details of phenomena, [...] to love and value the texture of phenomena [...] to understand that art is constructed out of the tiniest facets" (Musina 2002a, 127).

But *Outskirts* was also Barnet's first sound film and is of crucial significance in the history of the development of sound cinema in the Soviet Union. That this process was considerably more complex than the mere introduction of heard speech (the "talkies") is illuminated by Emma Widdis, whose pioneering examination of sound in three important Soviet films of the early 1930s shows how they "challenge the dominance of the spoken word" (Widdis 2014, 112). In *Outskirts* there are romances, martial music, hymns, and workers' songs. There is Russian and untranslated German.[5] There is the clatter of an abacus clicking up profits, the squeak of a cupboard door being surreptitiously opened, the shattering crash of a dropped tray, church bells, a chiming pocket-watch, even the sound of a talking horse. Clever sound montage takes us from the tapping of cobblers' hammers to the shattering din of the battlefield. It is largely through the suggestive power of this complex and ambitious sound design, on which Barnet worked with his brilliant fellow-graduate of the Kuleshov studio, Leonid Obolenskii, that *Outskirts* achieves its psychological acuity and emotional intensity.

As a reward for *Outskirts*, Barnet was sent for two months to Germany and France (Margolit and Zabrodin 1992, 5) and on his return he began a number of abortive projects, including a version of Il'ia Il'f and Evgenii Petrov's classic novel *The Golden Calf* [*Zolotoi telenok*] (Musina 2002a, 139), before making his next film *By the Bluest of Seas* [*U samogo sinego moria*, 1935], where the lyric element present in all Barnet's best films is at its most pronounced. Drawing on the literary tradition of the desert island story, the film opens with the shipwreck of two young men, the mechanic Alesha and his workmate Iusuf, en route to a posting in a remote fishing kolkhoz on the Caspian Sea. Though the kolkhoz is called "Lights of Communism" and there is a huge bust of Marx in the management office, the film presents the island as an isolated, mythic place of beauty and harmony on to which the friends project their deepest desires: Margolit (1993a, 170) notes the ever greater abstraction of the settings of Barnet's pre-war films. By entering this dreamscape, which they first take to be inhabited only by women, the men bring not only technical knowledge, but also the fierce passions which threaten to destroy it (and which could, by doing so, provide the film with a plot). Time and again, however, Barnet refuses this darkly predictable course. Both men fall in love with a young work brigadier, Mashen'ka, but they are reconciled when they discover that she has a more worthy fiancé, away defending the motherland in the Pacific Fleet. A storm sweeps Mashen'ka overboard and she is assumed to be drowned, but she is washed ashore in the middle of her own memorial service. And in the film's strangest sequence, set at a meeting of kolkhoz members, Iusuf denounces his erstwhile best friend as a "fake and malingerer," who puts his love for Mashen'ka before the interests of the whole kolkhoz, refusing to mend their only motor launch and causing a five-fold fall in the fish catch. In another film of this period Alesha would be marked as an enemy and wrecker, but here the scene comes to an abrupt, inconsequential end. Barnet replaces ideology with the majesty of nature – there are many striking sequences of the waves of the Caspian, now serene, now whipped up by storm – with visual gags and witty dialogue. He explains the film's many absurd touches in his "Notes on Film Comedy" (Barnet 1954, 162–163, 173–176) as motivated by a desire to avoid melodrama and sentimentality. Some viewers were left unsatisfied by the film's fragile charm: Mark Donskoi praised its ludic quality but wanted it to be "deeper", calling on Barnet to tackle a big script on a Party theme (Musina 2002a, 121). The critic Nikolai Otten (1936, 19, 16) noted its "microscopic" ideological content and complained that you left the cinema "with nothing," while Viktor Shklovskii (Musina 2002b, 154) concluded that there was "no plot development, no dénouement, just the air of the Caspian."

Over the next three years, Barnet worked on three unrealized projects, the most intriguing of which, after the ideological evasions of *By the Bluest of Seas*, was a version of Nikolai Ostrovskii's classic novel of Soviet self-sacrifice, *How the Steel was Tempered* [*Kak zakalialas' stal'*] (Musina 2002a, 138, 139). Eventually, in 1939, he completed the production drama *A Night in September* [*Noch' v sentiabre*, 1939], inspired by the exploits of another Soviet hero, the coal-miner Aleksei Stakhanov,

Figure 21.4 Alesha and Mashen'ka in *By the Bluest of Seas*, 1935.

who served as a consultant on the film. Stakhanov's record-breaking shift took place on August 31, 1935, and the "night" of Barnet's film is in September of that year, but the film purports to look back on this heroic period from decades later, thus suggesting (as has indeed been the case) that Stakhanov's name will live in history. Though the hero, here called Stepan Kulagin, produces 14 times the norm for a shift, as played by Nikolai Kriuchkov (a favorite Barnet actor, Sen'ka in *Outskirts*, Alesha in *By the Bluest of Seas*) he remains blandly handsome and courageous, "a sort of abstract quantity whose role is to 'move' the plot" (Vaks 1939, 32). The motivation of the saboteurs who oppose him is not clear – they seem, as so often in films of this type, to be congenitally deceitful and vengeful. They are, however, drawn more fully than Kulagin and allowed the occasional full-blooded act of villainy: when Kulagin's girlfriend, Dunia reports that she has seen a man dynamiting the mine, they lock her into a straightjacket and forcibly incarcerate her in a psychiatric hospital, accusing her of having delusions. But they lack the passion of their counterpart in the classic of this genre, Ivan Pyr'ev's *Party Card* [*Partiinyi bilet*, 1936], so, almost bathetically, Dunia is eventually saved by a doctor from the state security organs, while the Party, in the person of Sergo Ordzhonikidze, defends Stepan from attack. The film contains a few moments of eccentric comedy, in the recognizable Barnet style, but his venture out of his familiar territory now seems dull and dated.

The Old Jockey [*Staryi naezdnik*, 1940], the last film Barnet made before the outbreak of the Great Patriotic War, was taken from a screenplay by Mikhail Vol'pin and Nikolai Erdman, the brilliant dramatist who had also contributed to the script of *The House on Trubnaya*. True to a revolving pattern which can be observed throughout Barnet's career, it marked a turn away from ideology and back to the genre of lyrical comedy in which he had made several of his most successful films. The film's hero, Trofimov, is a 64-year-old trainer and jockey at the Moscow racecourse whose powers are beginning to fade. Encouraged to think of retirement, he takes offence and returns to his native village, announcing that "the jockey Trofimov is dead." The village turns out to be a place of idyll, reminiscent of the settings of *Outskirts* and *By the Bluest of Seas*. The local kolkhoz is inhabited by a cast of typically loveable Barnet eccentrics, including a barber afraid to take a parachute jump and a portly lady doctor who seems congenitally unable to drive the car she has won in a lottery. Their care and concern for him give Trofimov new energy. He trains up a kolkhoz horse and eventually takes it to race in Moscow, where of course it triumphs. He has discovered that "old age doesn't exist."

The initial reception of both the script and the film was enthusiastic. The director Il'ia Trauberg wrote that Vol'pin and Erdman had written "the best comic screenplay of the year" (Erdman 2010, 712). The playwright Fedor Knorre asserted that until the film's appearance "we had not had … throughout the period of sound cinema, a comedy which didn't provoke an element of shame when we watched it" (Margolit and Shmyrov 1995, 70) and Mark Donskoi asserted that "Soviet comedy is the radiant path of Barnet" (Zabrodin 2000, 113). But in the spring of 1941 *The Old Jockey* came under sustained attack. A report from the Central Committee Directorate of Propaganda and Agitation insisted, in a phrase that familiarity did not render less threatening, that "this film is a slander on Soviet reality" (Erdman 2010, 713). Andrei Zhdanov, then the Central Committee Secretary, complained about its low ideological level (Margolit and Shmyrov 1995, 71) and the film was banned, the first of Barnet's works to suffer this fate. The charges leveled in the Central Committee report were that the representation of the racecourse was "no different from any such capitalist enterprise," a haunt of "dodgy punters, gambling and tavern merriment", while "the film's authors mock everything new that has come to the countryside with the kolkhoz system" showing the kolkhoz workers as driven by greed, rivalry, and envy (Erdman 2010, 713). Zabrodin (2000, 108), however, comes up with the more intriguing suggestion that the story of an ageing professional forced to retire against his will had angered Stalin, who had recently celebrated his sixtieth birthday. Either way, the film was not released until 1959, years after Stalin's death, to be greeted by critical indifference and a mixed reception from viewers, one of whom wrote to Barnet in a depressing echo of the attacks of 20 years earlier that it was a "repulsive libel on Soviet people and Soviet reality" (Margolit and Shmyrov 1995, 71).

The Wartime Films

With the mobilization of the Soviet film industry after the German invasion in June 1941, studios rushed to produce the short propaganda features collected together as *Fighting Film Collections* [*Boevye kinosborniki*]. Barnet, who joined the Communist Party during the War (Aldoshina 1996, 113), made two such films, *Valor* [*Muzhestvo*, 1941] made for Mosfilm in the third collection and *The Priceless Head* [*Bestsennaia golova*, 1942] in the tenth, made at the Central Studio in Alma-Ata after the studio had been evacuated to a place of safety. *Valor* is a conventionally atmospheric tale in which a laconically heroic group of Soviet soldiers penetrates behind enemy lines on a reconnaissance mission, finds and captures the concrete guard post from which the Germans have been pounding Soviet troops, and holds out against impossible odds, with every one of them being either killed or injured, until Soviet batteries can destroy it. *The Priceless Head*, set in occupied Poland, is much more ambitious. Margolit (1993b, 125) calls it "probably the best" of the films in the *Fighting Film Collections*. As it opens, Josef Grochowski, a charismatic hero of the resistance, a kind of Polish Scarlet Pimpernel who has already escaped five times from German captivity, undertakes a dramatic new act of sabotage. As the film's epilogue states, his courage inspires others to emulate him, and the main dramatic thread of the film is the playing-out of the moral journey made by the other characters. An old doctor moves from hopelessness to the explicit articulation of resistance, for which he pays with his life. Even more dramatically, a woman who had been on the point of prostituting herself in order to get food for her desperately sick child is told by Grochowski to turn him in to the Germans instead and claim the reward. Her vacillations over whether to do so are played out on the staircase of her apartment block, dramatic music building up the tension and bringing out the symbolic implications of her walking up and down the stairs. In *Valor* none of the protagonists had hesitated for a second before choosing the path of self-sacrifice, but here the temptation to collaborate is underlined by a minor figure who guides the enemy to the woman's house. Eventually the woman leads the Germans up past her door, giving Grochowski time to escape, an action which provokes her arrest. As Hicks (2012, 81–91) has shown, however, in a pioneering new study, there is another key character in the film: a Jew, whose experience, though tellingly ignored by contemporary reviewers, leads Hicks to call *The Priceless Head* "the first treatment of the theme of the Holocaust" in Soviet cinema (2012, 81). When he first appears at the beginning of the film, this character is both identified as Jewish by his Star of David armband and associated with Grochowski and resistance by his desire to read the wanted notice about him. Later he shows agency both by helping Grochowski to escape and by taking the woman's child in his arms when she is knocked to the ground. All three are then led off into an empty snowy landscape, they imagine to their deaths, in a scene which prefigures the death marches of later Holocaust films. But Grochowski's supporters save them and the woman joins him in his next underground radio broadcast. The contagion of resistance has spread.

In Barnet's first wartime feature *The Fine Fellow* [*Slavnyi malyi*, 1942] a band of partisans go about their daily tasks of cooking and cleaning in a wood full of beautiful trees, dappled light, and birdsong. Though the Germans are based in another wood, not far away, they seem to present no threat to this idyll. One of their crashed planes has become a picturesque ruin. A delicate love story develops between a young Russian woman, Katia and a downed French pilot, Claude, whose untranslated French is no barrier to their relationship (they sing a duet in two languages) and who makes miraculous strides in Russian. This is also a place where art can flourish and console – an opera singer, Doronin, who has escaped from an occupied town to avoid performing for the enemy, wanders into their camp and regales them with a beautiful Tchaikovsky romance. The camp is an island of respite, apart from the dangers and threat of the wartime world. As Margolit (1993b, 123, 124) has pointed out, authorial films were rare in Soviet wartime cinema, but Barnet has transported settings and tropes familiar from his earlier comedies – the "ark," the "enchanted island," the "reserve of harmony" – into this wartime subject matter and the world of these partisans is overtly abstract.

When they emerge into the world, the partisans meet suffering, homeless women and are themselves in mortal danger. Doronin is tortured and dies a terrifying death. Here art's function as respite gives way to a new role as stubborn resistance: before his tragic end, Doronin, now a wandering pilgrim, walks through a ravaged, smoking landscape, dressed in rags, performing Prince Igor''s aria from

Act Two of Borodin's opera in which he sings of saving suffering Russia from its enemies. This turns *The Fine Fellow* into a metafilm, a meditation both on its own working, and on the various functions of art in wartime. It is only at the end that the film's plot judders into action, as Doronin's tragically acquired knowledge, Claude's bravery, and the fearless cunning of the partisans combine to allow the Soviet air force to annihilate a hidden Fascist aerodrome. This innocent but serious divertissement was banned from wartime screens. It has not been possible to establish the reason for this decision, but one can surmise that its eccentric approach was deemed inappropriate to the dark times.

Barnet's powerful final wartime film, *One Night* [*Odnazhdy noch'iu*, 1944] revisits the resistance-to-occupation plot familiar from *The Priceless Head*, this time in the ruins of a bombed-out Russian town. Varia, a bereaved and traumatized young woman, forced to work for the German military, risks her life by feeding and nurturing the wounded pilots of a crashed Russian plane. Once again, the space of the film is, as Margolit has noted (1993a, 177), "frankly abstract," with almost every scene taking place either in the German headquarters or in a bombed building across the courtyard. Once again Barnet exploits the symbolic implications of the vertical axis, with the attic that provides a hiding place for the wounded Russians contrasted with the cellar where the Germans abuse their prisoners. Varia is repeatedly seen running up an ornate external staircase and there is further symbolism in her consistent association with water, from the drips of a tap which she patiently collects to slake the men's thirst at the start of the film, to her frenzied washing of the floors of the German building, as if to wipe out their guilt, to the laundry under which she conceals the food she takes to the pilots and which also serves to hide them from prying German eyes. The staircase, the film's moral vertical, is twice profaned, first when German soldiers penetrate the attic, and then when Varia is shot by the sadistic German commanding officer, played by Barnet himself. The film's happy ending, which incorporates the pilots into newsreel scenes of the triumphant Soviet advance and then takes one of them back to the bombed house where an initially distraught Varia recognizes and kisses him, is strangely unsatisfying, inconsistent with the heightened tragic tone of the rest of the film. Perhaps it was dictated by the optimism of the last months of the war – *One Night* was released on May 1, 1945, just a few days before Victory Day.

The Films of the Late Stalin Years: Innovation and Frustration

Barnet's first planned film after the war was an adaptation of Aleksandr Ostrovskii's 1875 play *Wolves and Sheep* [*Volki i ovtsy*] with the veteran director Iakov Protazanov, but the project was aborted on Protazanov's sudden death. Instead, with *The Spy's Exploit* [*Podvig razvedchika*, 1947], he made another war film, but in adapting the play *The Exploit Remains Unknown* [*Podvig ostaetsia neizvestnym*] by the playwright and former secret agent Mikhail Makliarskii (later responsible for the script of another such film, Mikhail Romm's gripping *The Secret Mission* [*Sekretnaia missiia*, 1950]), he invented the cinematic genre of the Soviet World War II spy thriller. *The Spy's Exploit* offers a fast-moving plot in which a master of disguise is pitted against a master of detection. The hero, Major Aleksei Fedotov, is sent into German territory to capture Hitler's operational plans for the Eastern Front, which are in the possession of General von Kühn. Standing in Fedotov's way will be General von Rummelsberg, a glacially wily figure whom he had first encountered 10 years previously in Montevideo. In order to complete his assignment Fedotov is, of course, required to assume an alias, and he becomes Heinrich Eckert, the representative of a German trading company. To cement his new identity Fedotov changes both his manner and his voice, feigning a refined incapacity to pronounce the letter "r." But in this dangerous drama of bluff and counter-bluff several other characters, agents for both sides, are also concealing their true identities. Tension is raked up by secret rendezvous and ominous nocturnal car journeys, by coded messages and a secret password ("Are you selling a Slavic cupboard?") which has since entered the Russian language as a phrase suggesting conspiratorial intent. Throughout the film the audience knows everything that Fedotov knows, which leads them to appreciate the charged double meaning of much that he says, notably when he drinks to "our victory" at von Kühn's birthday party; and much that he does not know, which alarms them when his ignorance places him in mortal danger. The action moves swiftly from one scene to another and, especially at the beginning, there is liberal use of darkness and shadow reminiscent of the noir thrillers then at their peak in Hollywood. Fedotov's vulnerability is underlined both by repeatedly putting him in places where he is under surveillance and from which there is no easy escape, and by his own frank admission of his errors. In monologue he abjures himself to "think, think, think." Yet for all his seriousness and bravery, it is chance, in the form of the incautious, drunken stupidity of a German adjutant, which finally brings about the encounter with his quarry, von Kühn. This dramatic conclusion to the film is set in the vast chambers of a grand mansion, and von Kühn (again the enemy is played by Barnet himself) is an ageing, handsome, melancholic man, completely unlike the hysterical or sadistic German enemy of the wartime films. Contemporary audiences were stunned by this break with cinematic convention ("A German, a general, an enemy – but sympathetic?"; Galiev 1995, 44). Nevertheless, as both von Kühn's ignominious capitulation and a passionate final speech from Fedotov make clear, Russian moral superiority lies in their readiness to sacrifice their lives. This heady mix of patriotism and drama made *The Spy's Exploit* the top box-office film of 1947 and Barnet's greatest popular hit.

After a diversion helping Aleksandr Macheret to salvage his Five-Year-Plan drama *Pages of Life* [*Stranitsy zhizni*, 1948], Barnet tried his hand at another unfamiliar genre, the kolkhoz musical. *The Generous Summer* [*Shchedroe leto*, 1950], like the almost contemporaneous *Kuban Cossacks* [*Kubanskie kazaki*, dir. Pyr'ev, 1949] and *Chevalier of the Golden Star* [*Kavaler Zolotoi zvezdy*, dir. Iulii Raizman, 1950] is full of the tropes of the genre: set on the *Forwards* kolkhoz, it has beautiful and abundant nature, a harvest accompanied by songs and slogans, dreams of the bright future and practical steps to achieve it, an electricity station, an agricultural exhibition, a demobbed soldier returning to his village, a cantankerous kolkhoz chairman and young lovers whose misunderstandings and partings merely delay their eventual happiness. Frankly ludicrous, and mendacious about post-war rural reconstruction, it ends with a speech announcing that "We shall name our new kolkhoz after our father, comrade Stalin," who looks down benignly from the wall. Unmoved by the "oleographs of the life of Soviet *paysans*" and the "struggle of the good with the better," Sergei Anashkin (1999, 117) finds "the hand of a great master" only in the almost wordless scenes of work. Barnet wrote about it at length in his 1954 study of film comedy in terms that echo the ideas of Vladimir Pomerantsev's December 1953 *Novyi mir* article "On sincerity in literature" [Ob iskrennosti v literature], widely seen as a harbinger of the Thaw:

> I often think how much *The Generous Summer* would have gained if all of us, the authors and the director and the actors, had not been entranced by our heroes and by the milieu in which they acted, if we had discarded the lacquered shell from Petr, and Nazar, and Oksana! How strongly the authentic rather than vaudeville troubles of the heroes would have resounded, how interestingly they would have revealed themselves in real and not operetta difficulties! But we sinned against the truth of life and passed its conflicts by, and the situations in the film turned out to be petty; we had to waste time and the efforts of the actors only in order to create and support artificial contradictions between the heroes. (Barnet 1954, 167)

Nevertheless, for Jacques Rivette, the film showed that:

> As for genius, be assured that he has it, and has it moreover in one of its most refined forms; he can even impart it to his young heroines, who climb into a lorry or a cart in a way that would have enraptured Stendhal. (Rivette 1953, 49)

In 1952, at a time when almost no new feature films were being initiated, Barnet was commissioned by the Kiev Film Studio to make *A Concert by Masters of Ukrainian Art* [*Kontsert masterov ukrainskogo iskusstva*, 1952], but, as the director Sulamif' Tsybul'nik recalls, the material was "completely alien to him" and the film was made against the constant intervention of the Ukrainian Party Central Committee (Khlebnikova 2002, 108–109). In the decade that followed Stalin's death Barnet would make another six films, but they were not personal projects and each of them was, by his own standards, a failure. Unlike many of the other leading directors of the time, Barnet had not enjoyed the luxury of a consistent group of cinematic collaborators, and, tragically, the Thaw years were not a period of renewal for him, as they were for his contemporaries Kalatozov and Kheifits, Kozintsev and Raizman, who made some of their most innovative films during these years.

Slow Fade

Liana (1955) is an old-fashioned kolkhoz musical, with several nods in the direction of Pyr'ev and Grigorii Aleksandrov, in which the primitive plot comes to a standstill for formal production numbers. One of the few original touches is the introduction into the music of a "folk" trio of Glenn Miller's "Chatanooga choo choo" from H. Bruce Humberstone's 1941 *Sun Valley Serenade*, a film popular with Soviet audiences since its inclusion in the allied wartime film exchange in 1944. Otar Iosseliani describes *Liana* as one of several films Barnet was "forced" to make, though Marlen Khutsiev, who worked as an assistant on it, recalls Barnet's conscientiousness and how "in the most insignificant part he tries to find the precise, essential details" (Khutsiev, Ioseliani, and Poloka 2002, 98, 89). It was followed by the Civil War drama *The Poet* [*Poet*, 1956], in which the titular hero narrowly escapes execution by counter-revolutionary forces. After this came *The Wrestler and The Clown* [*Borets i kloun*, 1957], which Barnet agreed to complete out of a sense of duty (Aldoshina 1996, 113) after the death of the scriptwriter and director Konstantin Iudin.[6] Set in Odessa before the Revolution, it is based on the lives of real people, the wrestler Ivan Poddubnyi and the clown and animal trainer Anatolii Durov. The finished film has an impersonal air, and watching it one feels that anyone could have made it. But it was admired by Jean-Luc Godard, who loved the regularity of the composition of Barnet's long shots and declared that "One doesn't have to be stupid to dislike Barnet's film, but one does have to have a heart of stone" (Narboni and Milne 1972, 140, 139).

In the 1950s, sensing the spirit of the times, Barnet told his wife that he felt it was his duty to make films on contemporary themes (Aldoshina 1996, 113) and each of his last three films conforms to this model. *Annushka* (1959) begins during World War II (in a story that is much more conventional than Barnet's earlier films on the subject) but is mainly a tale of the post-war reconstruction. It marks a departure from Barnet's many earlier feature films with a female protagonist in that Annushka is a mother (in the wartime episodes she heroically gives birth in a bomb crater before getting up to re-join the evacuation of her home town). Widowed by the war, she later becomes a worker, first on a kolkhoz, then on an urban building site, thus becoming a one-woman embodiment of Vera Mukhina's statue of the *Worker and the Kolkhoz Woman* [*Rabochii i kolkhoznitsa*, 1937]. *Annushka* is made more plausible by giving each of the main characters human flaws, and by Barnet's sympathy for most of them in their weakness. Perhaps the most revealing episode comes at the end of the film, when Annushka's foreman reports that she has been mentioned in an article in the paper. When it turns out that she is not in fact mentioned by name, the old man insists that she is one of those referred to at the end of the list of names by the words "and others" [*i drugie*]. Throughout his directorial career these "others" had always been at the center of Barnet's attention. But in this case, sympathy for the lives and concerns of ordinary people was not enough: the future director Gennadii Poloka, who worked as an assistant on the film, recalls that Barnet was forced by lack of money to take on this piece of "crawling Soviet Neo-Realism" which had "neither a strong plot, nor anything that Barnet loved" (Khutsiev, Ioseliani and Poloka 2002, 95).

Alenka (1961) is set during the Virgin Lands campaign. Its frame story is thin and anonymous, marred by an uplifting female voiceover that sternly reminds us that the film's protagonists are building Communism. Moreover, the film fails to avoid the sentimentality which Barnet recognized as a danger in his 1954 *Notes on Comedy*, something that is always likely when the main character is a nine-year-old girl. But *Alenka* is also a formal experiment for Barnet, since the frame story is merely the shell for a number of extensive tragi-comic flashbacks which explain why a motley group of passengers have been drawn together on the back of a truck. Best among these is an episode in which Vasilii Shukshin, in one of his very first roles, as the truck-driver Stepan, describes, in tragi-comic terms, his unlikely marriage to Lida, a would-be sophisticate who wishes she was living in Moscow. When, instead, he took her to the provincial town of Belogorsk, where he had found work on a building site, she decided that she was bored, though he could not understand why since "we lived in a cultured way, we subscribed to Ogonek". There she read Chekhov's "The Lady with the Lapdog" ["Dama s sobachkoi"], bought her own dog and took to walking around town with a pained expression on her face, evidence of her "moral exhaustion," and with the pet on a lead (summoning unlikely echoes both of Kheifits's film of Chekhov's story, released the year before Barnet made *Alenka*, and of the young lady with a dog in his own *Outskirts*). Once again, Barnet shows himself to be a masterly director of actors, and his attention to the tiny details of dialogue and action that move the stories from comedy to melancholy and back again temporarily lifts the film out of its conventional frame.

In Barnet's final film *The Halt* [*Polustanok*, 1963], the hero, a Muscovite Doctor of Technical Sciences, spends a brief summer vacation in the countryside, where he is expecting silence and peace, only to find that a busy kolkhoz is anything but quiet and tranquil. In some ways this is a re-make of *Alenka*, with winsome children to the fore; in others it is an old man's *By the Bluest of Seas*. Both title and setting continue Barnet's interest in the ordinary and the marginal, but here the plot is very thin, the jokes are predictable, the comic situations are so drawn out and the desire to make you laugh is so intense that the film ends up not funny at all. It is probably most interesting to read it, as Giuliano Vivaldi has done in his perceptive and incisive assessment of the whole of Barnet's career (Vivaldi 2011), as veiled autobiography, the story of an old craftsman worn down by hard work, who attempts to find solace by spending time with friendly, simple people, only to be torn back to the cares of the world.

In a letter to his fifth wife, Alla Kazanskaia, written from the set of *The Spy's Exploit* in April 1947, Barnet attempted "to explain myself to you":

Many times in life I have left home, gone missing, locked myself in myself and …
I have divorced my wives three times in part because of my "behavior," but mainly because I could not then act otherwise. And these things always happened when I was working exceptionally hard, it always happened when I couldn't think of

anything except this doubly accursed cinema, work which I both hate and, clearly, very much love." (Aldoshina 1996, 115–116)

He went on to write about his "physical and psychic need" for "full freedom and independence" and to explain that when he was working intensely "I need to think about it 24 hours a day" (Aldoshina 1996, 116). He told Georges Sadoul that "my ambition was also to show people in contemporary life […] I am not and never have been a man of theories. I have always taken my material from contemporary life" (G. S. 1965). His best films combine this human sympathy and psychological acuity with dazzling formal experiment. Marlen Khutsiev considered that "he saw things that others didn't see, he was a poet in his soul," adding that "all the direction was between the lines," while Gennadii Poloka noted that "in art he was endlessly alone" (Khutsiev, Ioseliani, and Poloka 2002, 90, 93). Otar Iosseliani went as far as to suggest that "he lived in the Soviet Union and acted as if it didn't exist, except as a paradox" (Iosseliani 1994, 50), but these fine and much-quoted words are belied by the many practical and ideological difficulties that plagued his work, especially in his later years.

The ousting of Nikita Khrushchev on October 14, 1964 is one of the several dates that mark the demise of the tentative optimism of the Thaw years. Two months later, in a letter to his wife and daughter of December 23, 1964 from Riga, where he was planning a new film, Barnet announced that he had lost faith in himself, that he was entirely to blame, and that he hoped that they would find the courage not to judge him (Aldoshina 1996, 126). These words recur in edited form in a note he wrote on the same day: "I have lost faith in myself, without which it's impossible to work, and, consequently, to live." On January 8, 1965, he added a postscript, "I've scarcely managed to drag on to January 8!!" (Anon. 2002). On that day Boris Barnet committed suicide.

Notes

1 This and other biographical information in this article is based on Barnet (1947), Barnet (1949), and Kushnirov (1977), which differ slightly in their details.
2 *The House on Trubnaya* is also known in English as *The House on Trubnaya Square*. The original Russian title is ambiguous as to whether it refers to the street or the square. I have preferred to retain this ambiguity since Zorkaia (2000, 202), basing her assertion on the history of the period, suggests that it is far more likely to refer to a house on Trubnaia Street (now demolished) than on the square, where there was still a market.
3 This is further developed in Natasha's grandfather's suggestion that she will "fly away" and in the name of her unsuccessful suitor Fogelev, taken from the (German) name of the actor, Vladimir Fogel' (German: Vogel = 'bird'), and the caged bird he keeps. Intriguingly, Il'ia Snegirev is also the name of one of the schoolboys befriended by Alesha in *The Brothers Karamazov*.

4 Though conventionally the film is known as *Outskirts*, a more accurate translation would be *Backwoods*.
5 Margolit (2014) examines the implications of heteroglossia in Soviet films of the 1930s.
6 Both the fact that the hero of the film is a wrestler and the general affective affinity between the work of Barnet and Iudin, noticeable, for example, in the horse-racing sequences of *The Old Jockey* and Iudin's *Bold People* [*Smelye liudi*, 1950], may also have been factors impelling Barnet to take on this task.

References

Aldoshina, Oksana. 1996. "'Bez viny vinovatyi'" [Guilty Without Guilt]. *Iskusstvo kino* [Art of Cinema] 10: 112–127.

Anashkin, Sergei. 1999. "Parad dikovin" [A Parade of Curiosities]. *Iskusstvo kino* [Art of Cinema] 3: 114–124.

Anon. 1928a. "Dom na Trubnoi" [The House on Trubnaya]. *Kino* 38 (September 18): 6.

Anon. 1928b. "V stsenarnoi kukhne 'Doma na Trubnoi'" [In the Script Kitchen of "House on Trubnaya"]. *Sovetskii ekran* [Soviet Screen] 35: 15.

Anon. 2002. "Predsmertnaia zapiska Borisa Barneta" [Boris Barnet's Death Note]. *Kinovedcheskie zapiski* [Film Scholars' Notes] 57: 174.

Balázs, Béla. 1933. "Privet tovarishchu Barnetu" [Greetings to Comrade Barnet]. *Kino* 11 (February 28): 3.

Barnet, Boris. 1927a. "Devushka s korobkoi" [The Girl with the Hatbox]. *Sovetskii ekran* [Soviet Screen] 12 (March 19): 10.

Barnet, Boris. 1927b. Contribution to "Na podstupakh k sovetskoi komedii" [Approaching Soviet Comedy]. *Kino* 16 (April 19): 3.

Barnet, Boris. 1927c. "Moskva v Oktiabre" [Moscow in October]. *Sovetskoe kino* [Soviet Cinema] 7: 16–17.

Barnet, Boris. 1927d. "Moskva v Oktiabre" [Moscow in October]. *Sovetskii ekran* [Soviet Screen] 42 (October 18): 7.

Barnet, Boris. 1947. In *Kak ia stal rezhisserom* [How I Became a Filmmaker], 34–40. Moscow: Goskinoizdat; also in *Boris Vasil'evich Barnet (1902–1905) Materialy k retrospektive fil'mov.* [Boris Barnet: Materials for a Retrospective of Films], edited by E. Margolit and V. Zabrodin. 6–9. Moscow: Muzei kino, 1992.

Barnet, Boris. 1949. "Avtobiografiia" [Autobiography]. In *Boris Vasil'evich Barnet (1902–1905) Materialy k retrospektive fil'mov.* [Boris Barnet: Materials for a Retrospective of Films], edited by E. Margolit and V. Zabrodin. 4–5. Moscow: Muzei kino, 1992.

Barnet, Boris. 1954. "Zametki o kinokomedii" [Notes on the Film Comedy]. In *Voprosy dramaturgii. Sbornik statei* [Questions of Dramaturgy. A Collection of Essays]. vol. 1, edited by I. Vaisfel'd, 156–179. Moscow: Iskusstvo.

Burch, Noël. 1985. "Harold Lloyd contre le Docteur Mabuse" [Harold Lloyd against Dr Mabuse]. In *Boris Barnet. Écrits, Documents, Études, Filmographie* [Boris Barnet: Writings, Documents, Studies, Filmography], edited by F. Albéra and R. Cosandey, 103–112. Locarno: Éditions du Festival International du Film de Locarno.

Erdman, Nikolai. 2010. *Kinostsenarii* [Film Scripts]. St Petersburg, Masterskaia Seans.

G(eorges) S(adoul). 1965. "Rencontre avec Boris Barnett" [Meeting with Boris Barnet]. *Cahiers du cinéma* 169: 13.

Galiev, Anatolii. 1995. "Velikii ozornik" [The Great Ruffian]. *Rodina* [Motherland] 2: 44–46.

Grashchenkova, Irina. 2002. "Dvoinoi portret: Boris Barnet – Abram Room" [Double Portrait: Boris Barnet – Abram Room]. *Kinovedcheskie zapiski* [Film Scholars' Notes] 61: 102–105.

Gusman, Boris. 1926. "Miss-Mend." *Pravda* 262 (December 12): 8.

Hicks, Jeremy. 2012. *First Films of the Holocaust. Soviet Cinema and the Genocide of the Jews, 1938–1946*. Pittsburgh: University of Pittsburgh Press.

Iakov, Lev (Nikolai Iakovlev). 1927. "Devushka s korobkoi" [The Girl with the Hatbox]. *Kino* 18 (May 3): 2.

Iosseliani, Otar. 1994. "A propos de Boris Barnet." *Positif* (June): 50–52.

Iusupova, Galiia. 2013. "Kassovye fenomeny kinematografa 1920-kh i legenda o 'novom zritele'" [Box Office Phenomena of the Cinema of the 1920s and the Legend of the "New Spectator"]. *Kinovedcheskie zapiski* [Film Scholars' Notes] 102–103: 151–167.

Khlebnikova, Veronika, ed. 2002. "'Rabotat' s nim bylo neveroiatno legko' (Barnet v Kieve). Vspominaiut N. A. Gebdovskaia, S. M. Tsybul'nik, E. M. Vasil'ko-Gakkebush." ["He Was Incredibly Easy to Work With". Boris Barnet in Kiev. N. Gebdovskaia, S. Tsybul'nik, and E. Vasil'ko-Gakkebush remember]. *Kinovedcheskie zapiski* [Film Scholars' Notes] 61: 106–112.

Khutsiev, Marlen, Otar Ioseliani, and Gennadii Poloka. 2002. "'On tak i ne nauchilsia snimat' po zakazu.' Vspominaia Barneta" ["He Never Did Learn to Shoot to Order." Remembering Barnet]. *Kinovedcheskie zapiski* [Film Scholars' Notes] 61: 87–99.

Kovalov, Oleg. 2013. "Iubileinoe" [Anniversary]. *Seans* [Séance] 55–56: 265–273.

Kozintseva, Valentina. 2002. "O prekrasnom cheloveke" [About a Wonderful Man]. *Kinovedcheskie zapiski* [Film Scholars' Notes] 57: 165–173.

Kuleshov, Lev. 1922. "Amerikanshchina" [Americanism]. *Kino-fot* 1: 14–15.

Kuleshov, Lev. 1934. "Nashi pervye opyty" [Our First Experiences]. *Sovetskoe kino* [Soviet Cinema] 11–12: 126–137.

Kushnirov (Kushnirovich), Mark. 1977. *Zhizn' i fil'my Borisa Barneta* [The Life and Films of Boris Barnet]. Moscow: Iskusstvo.

Kushnirovich, Mark. 1995. "Ot 'Okrainy' do 'Podviga razvedchika'" [From "Outskirts" to "The Spy's Exploit"]. *Rodina* [Motherland] 2: 41–43.

Margolit, Evgenii. 1993a. "Barnet i Eizenshtein v kontekste sovetskogo kino" [Barnet and Eisenstein in the Context of Soviet Cinema]. *Kinovedcheskie zapiski* [Film Scholars' Notes] 17: 165–180.

Margolit, Evgenii. 1993b. "'Slavnyi malyi'" [A Fine Fellow]. *Iskusstvo kino* [Art of Cinema] 6: 123–125.

Margolit, Evgenii. 2012. *Zhivye i mertvoe. Zametki k istorii sovetskogo kino 1920–1960-kh godov* [The Living and the Dead: Notes on the History of Soviet Cinema of the 1920–1960s]. St Petersburg: Masterskaia "Seans".

Margolit, Evgenii. 2014 (first 2006). "The Problem of Heteroglossia in Early Soviet Sound Cinema (1930–1935)". In *Sound, Speech, Music in Soviet and Post-Soviet Cinema*, edited by L. Kaganovsky and M. Salazkina, 119–128. Bloomington and Indianapolis: Indiana University Press.

Margolit, Evgenii and Viacheslav Shmyrov, eds 1995. *(Iz"iatoe kino) Katalog sovetskikh igrovykh kartin, ne vypushchennykh vo vsesoiuznyi prokat po zavershenii v proizvodstve ili iz"iatikh iz deistvuiushchego fil'mofonda v god vypuska na ekran (1924–1953)*. [(Excised Cinema): Catalog of Soviet Feature Films that were not Released into Distribution after Their Completion, or Excised from the Active Film Collection during the Release Year (1924–1953)]. Moscow, Dubl'-D.

Margolit, Evgenii and Vladimir Zabrodin, eds 1992. *Boris Vasil'evich Barnet (1902–1905). Materialy k retrospektive fil'mov* [Boris Barnet: Materials for a Retrospective of Films]. Moscow: Muzei kino.

Musina, Milena, ed. 2002a. "'Tebe dana takaia sila …' Diskussionnyi prosmotr kartiny 'U samogo sinego moria' 1 aprelia 1936 goda v Dome kino." ["You Have Such Power…" A Discussion Screening of the Film 'By the Bluest of Seas' on April 1, 1936 in the House of Cinema]. *Kinovedcheskie zapiski* [Film Scholars' Notes] 57: 116–139.

Musina, Milena, ed. 2002b. "'Tut Barnet pereklikaetsia s siurrealizmom!' Stenogramma zasedaniia sektsii teorii i kritiki pri Dome kino 28 maia 1945 goda o fil'me B. Barneta 'Odnazhdy noch'iu'" ["Here Barnet Resonates with Surrealism!" Minutes of a Meeting of the Department of Theory and Criticism at House of Cinema on May 28, 1945 about Barnet's Film "One Night"]. *Kinovedcheskie zapiski* [Film Scholars' Notes] 57: 140–157.

Narboni, Jean and Tom Milne, eds 1972. *Godard on Godard*. London: Secker & Warburg.

Ostrovskii, D. V. 1994. "Boris Barnet i mutatsiia kul'turnogo soznaniia kontsa 20-kh godov" [Boris Barnet and the Mutation of the Cultural Consciousness of the Late 1920s]. *Kinovedcheskie zapiski* [Film Scholars' Notes] 22: 91–133.

Otten, Nikolai. 1936. "Deistvitel'nost' i fil'm" [Reality and Film]. *Iskusstvo kino* [Art of Cinema] 5: 16–20.

Rivette, Jacques. 1953. "Un nouveau visage de la pudeur (*Un été prodigieux*)" [A New Face of Modesty. "The Generous Summer"]. *Cahiers du Cinéma* 20: 49–50.

Vaks, B. 1939. "Stsenarii 'Noch' v sentiabre'" [The Script for "A Night in September"]. *Iskusstvo kino* [Art of Cinema] 9: 30–33.

Vivaldi, Giuliano. 2011. "Boris Barnet. The Lyric Voice in Soviet Cinema." *Bright Lights Film Journal* 73 http://www.brightlightsfilm.com/73/73barnet_vivaldi.php (accessed February 14, 2015).

Widdis, Emma. 2014 "Making Sense without Speech: The Use of Silence in Early Soviet Sound Film". In *Sound, Speech, Music in Soviet and Post-Soviet Cinema*, edited by L. Kaganovsky and M. Salazkina, 100–116. Bloomington and Indianapolis: Indiana University Press.

Youngblood, Denise J. 1992. *Movies for the Masses*. Cambridge: Cambridge University Press.

Zabrodin, Vladimir, ed. 2000. "'Sovetskaia komediia – eto svetlyi put' Barneta.' Iz stenogrammy obsuzhdeniia fil'ma 'Staryi naezdnik' v Dome kino 14-go ianvaria 1941 goda" ["Soviet Comedy is Barnet's Radiant Path." From the Minutes of the Discussion of "The Old Jockey" at the House of Cinema on January 14, 1941]. *Kinovedcheskie zapiski* [Film Scholars' Notes] 45: 107–119.

Zorkaia, Neia. 2000. "'Ia delaiu stavku na aktera'. Boris Barnet v raznye gody" ["I Wager on the Actor." Boris Barnet in Various Years]. *Kinovedcheskie zapiski* [Film Scholars' Notes] 47: 186–214.

22

Iulii Raizman: Private Lives and Intimacy under Communism

Jamie Miller

Iulii Iakovlevich Raizman is one of the most remarkable film directors of the Soviet period. His career began in the 1920s and lasted until the 1980s, making him one of the few filmmakers who made movies throughout the entire communist era. Despite his importance, attention to his work throughout his career, and following his death in 1994, has been relatively limited. In the former Soviet Union, the first major study of Raizman's work was written by the film critic Mark Zak and published in 1962. Zak's work coincided with the success of the film *And What if it is Love?* [*A esli eto liubov'?*, 1962] and helped to draw more attention to the director's work. Zak points to the importance of the pre-Revolutionary influence on Raizman through figures such as Iakov Protazanov, and notes the importance of emotion in the films. However, while the book provides some informed discussion of Raizman's cinema, it lacks a coherent thread and is, at times, slightly restrained by "official" language. Within a few years the Russian film historian Neia Zorkaia developed what would prove to be an enduring interest in Raizman's work, and included the director in her study of leading Soviet filmmakers. Zorkaia sees Raizman as a director who situated himself outside the avant-garde of the 1920s, and saw himself as a maker of films that continued the pre-Revolutionary tradition of Russian "psychologism," and that are concerned with individual human thoughts and emotions. For Zorkaia, Raizman's subtle use of subtext and the expression of ideas through actions rather than words is distinctly Chekhovian. In Raizman's case the formal themes and dialogues of his films are seen as less important compared to the "chronicle of feelings" that underlies them (Zorkaia 1966, 179–219; Zorkaia 2004).

Attention to Raizman's work in the West has also been limited. In October 1984 a National Film Theatre retrospective of Raizman's work, organized by Ian Christie and John Gillet, took place (Christie and Gillet 1984, 14–17). This was an important step toward bringing the previously unheard of director's work to the attention of

---

A Companion to Russian Cinema, First Edition. Edited by Birgit Beumers.
© 2016 John Wiley & Sons, Inc. Published 2016 by John Wiley & Sons, Inc.

the British public. Since this event, references to Raizman's work started to appear more frequently in both popular and academic literature, as well as general overviews of Russian and Soviet cinema which offer interesting discussion within a broader context (Beumers 2009; Gillespie 2002). However, there are no monographs or scholarly articles dedicated to Raizman's work; therefore, this chapter seeks to fill that gap and initiate further debate on Raizman's contribution to Russian/Soviet film history.

In this chapter, I seek to emphasize the importance of Raizman's work as a crucial part of Soviet film history. I will argue that Raizman was unique in that his films sought to offer an alternative look at Soviet life by showing and defending the autonomy of private life, intimacy, and emotion in the face of an overwhelming concern with public duty and ideology, an approach that was highly unusual in the 1930s and 1940s. Indeed, as we shall observe in several cases, Raizman managed to resist attempts to make him conform to the political and artistic orthodoxies of the day. From the 1960s onwards, Raizman maintained this concern with the individual trying to find intimacy and meaning in the context of communism. However, by this time the director not only wanted to assert the autonomy of private life, but also to criticize strongly any attempt to deny the individual self-realization and freedom from collective demands.

Figure 22.1   Iulii Raizman in his home library, 1955. Source: RIA Novosti.

Raizman was born in Moscow in 1903 and grew up in the city. He later attended Moscow University where he studied art and literature. After graduation in 1924, Raizman had a brief foray in theater, but soon found himself working as a literary consultant at the Mezhrabpom studio. At this studio he laid the foundations of his long career in cinema; he soon became an assistant director to the leading filmmakers Konstantin Eggert and Iakov Protazanov (Rollberg 2009, 562–65). Raizman's first film, *The Circle* [*Krug*, 1927] was co-directed with Aleksandr Gavronskii, who was later arrested for alleged anti-Soviet activity (Anon. 1931). This film was made for the military-affiliated studio Gosvoenkino and was about an investigator who discovers that the criminal he is tracking is in fact his wife's lover. This was followed by *Penal Servitude* [*Katorga*, 1929] about protest in a Siberian prison camp, and *The Earth Thirsts* [*Zemlia zhazhdet*, 1930] about a Komsomol mission to Turkmenia to irrigate the land. In 1932 Raizman made *A Story About Omar Khaptsoko* [*Rasskaz ob Umare Khaptsoko*], a short documentary film about the efforts of a village elder to eliminate illiteracy. While these films gave Raizman crucial experience, he did not really develop his distinctive style until the production of his first major feature, *Men on Wings* [*Letchiki*, 1935]. The film told about two men who compete for the affections of a young female pilot – a battle won by the older, less attractive but disciplined of the two. The film contains many features that would be central to his cinematic style, such as subtle character psychology, the theme of intimacy, the distinctive use of lighting and a pictorial cinematography. However, it was his next film, *The Last Night* [*Posledniaia noch'*, 1936], where Raizman reached a new level.

The Apolitical Revolutionary Film: *The Last Night*

Although well-established by 1937, Raizman acknowledged that it was through the film *The Last Night* that he reached "professional maturity." The director joined up with Evgenii Gabrilovich, his contemporary from school, to develop a script version of Gabrilovich's story *Quiet Brovkin* [*Tikhii Brovkin*, 1936]. The script told of the last night of the tsarist system and the struggle between the old and new world. This clash is rendered through the experiences of the working-class Zakharkin family and the factory-owning Leont'ev family. Individuals from both families come into conflict with one another throughout the film. The heads of the families, Egor Zakharkin and Petr Leont'ev, engage in a bitter dispute and Egor is shot dead. Subsequently, the middle brother Il'ia Zakharkin, and then the youngest Zakharkin, the naive schoolboy Kuz'ma, are shot by the Whites. But the oldest, Petr Zakharkin, survives and leads the seizure of the Briansk railway station. The revolutionary soldiers then make their way towards the Kremlin accompanied by the mother of the Zakharkin family.

Indeed, both Gabrilovich and Raizman later acknowledged the difficulties that they had experienced after completing *The Last Night*. Raizman did not directly refer to problems with censorship, but suggested that they had been attacked by those who advocated "monumentalism" and grand "epic" portrayals of the October Revolution. In the 1960s Gabrilovich pointed out that the filmmakers were accused of failing to capture the "epic" and "romantic" nature of the Revolution and providing an accurate political emphasis. By "monumentalism" the film-makers were referring to films such as *Battleship Potemkin* [*Bronenosets Potemkin*, 1925], with its emphasis on the masses rather than the individual as the hero. Yet by the 1930s this sort of film was no longer the norm. The real conflict that the two men were referring to was between the idea of the Revolution as a glorified myth led by Party heroes, such as Lenin, and the idea of the Revolution from the point of view of the ordinary person which, during the late 1930s, could be an extremely controversial perspective.

Raizman and Gabrilovich's focus on the everyday and the ordinary was a pioneering step that foresaw later developments in Soviet cinema during the Thaw. Of course, in *The Last Night* the film-makers were careful to suggest that the Bolsheviks were correct, and there are elements of minor glorification. Yet the film offers a believable characterization of the ordinary man suddenly involved in a social revolution. Nikolai Dorokhin, who played the part of Petr Zakharkin, a rank-and-file sailor, did not match the traditional depiction of the muscular, smiling and confident revolutionary. On the contrary, Raizman deliberately selected an actor who could show that the average sailor empowered by the possibilities of the Revolution would be almost overawed by such an event (Zak 1962, 101–104). Here Raizman sought to develop character psychology beyond the flat, uninvolving Soviet film heroes of the time. There is an effort to see what really motivated ordinary men and women to become involved in the Revolution. Physically awkward and lacking in confidence, Petr is fully committed to the Bolshevik cause, yet it is clear that he does not really understand the political ideals which he is fighting for. In the early part of the film he attempts to quote Marx's famous phrase "material being gives rise to consciousness" and stutters in the process. When Mikhailov, the head of the Revolutionary Committee, gives him orders, he repeats words in a manner that suggests he cannot think through the strategy for himself. Petr is unemotional and driven. When he learns that his younger brother is at a dance, he angrily suggests that this is unacceptable behavior when a revolution is taking place. Petr's obtuse nature is further evidenced when he and his brothers take to the streets and, rather than embracing his mother, he shakes her hand as they leave the family home. Petr's motivation is based on anger and resentment towards his former capitalist master and the burning desire to gain revenge rather than a commitment to create a fairer society. In the scenes where Petr confronts members of the capitalist Leont'ev family for whom his father worked, he is abusive and aggressive towards them – an attitude of which his political leader, Mikhailov, approves. Mikhailov sees Petr as a potential leader; despite his hotheadedness, he tells him that during revolution "you need to hate." This suggestion that the Revolution came, to some extent, from anger and bitterness was uncommon at a time when characters in Soviet cinema tended to be motivated by the righteousness of Party ideology and learning about the inevitable course of history.

Indeed, while the wealthy Leont'ev family are broadly seen in a less favorable light than the working class Zakharkin family, *The Last Night* is also remarkable for its reluctance to *always* draw sharp distinctions between social classes. In the case of the Zakharkin family, the youngest son, Kuz'ma, is an example of an aspirational working class young man who seeks to improve his lot through education. Kuz'ma attends a Moscow lycée, an elite secondary school usually seen as a pathway into higher education. He is also romantically interested in Lena, the daughter of the Leont'ev family. Thus Kuz'ma is trapped in a grey area between the classes and his place in the Revolution is ambiguous. He is also naive and unaware of the danger that surrounds him; the Revolution is nothing more than an excuse to try to win Lena's affections by pretending to be a young Marxist, "fighting for a wonderful new life." As he wanders aimlessly through the Moscow streets, he accidentally gets caught up in crossfire and finds himself among White soldiers who expect him to fight with them. When they discover that he is from a working-class family, he runs away only to be shot. This particular element in the plot was included to show that the Revolution was not all about heroism and great feats, but also tragedy and loss of innocent life. Raizman was unique as a filmmaker in the 1930s by going beyond simplistic binary categorizations that presented the Revolution entirely as a victory of oppressed over their oppressors. For Raizman the Revolution comes across as a messier, confused historical juncture where clarity and purpose and often absent.

By the late 1930s the system of censorship that governed Soviet cinema had become too powerful and Raizman was unable to escape its pernicious influence. In 1937 a new body called Kultpros [Cultural Enlightenment] assumed control over censorship with a mandate to further tighten ideological control. In January 1937, as a result of its obsession with the sacred status of Soviet history and Party leaders, it banned the release of *The Last Night* because it did not show the "role of Stalin in the struggle for October," stressing that "Stalin's name was not even mentioned" in the film. Kultpros decided that Raizman's work could not be released without changes and that the State Directorate for the Film Industry (GUK), which was accountable for the film's "defects," would have to take a close look at the film and consider where amendments could be made (Maksimenkov 1997, 294). *The Last Night* was released two months later, on March 2, 1937, on screens throughout the USSR. During the intervening period, Raizman made minimal changes to the film. While Lenin is given an obligatory mention, the final version did not refer to Stalin's role in the October Revolution. Raizman's film was difficult to change as it was structured around the place of ordinary people in the Revolution and, therefore, it was never intended to be a film about the Bolshevik elite. Introducing such changes would have meant making a different film. It appears that the censor eventually accepted the movie in its existing form. Nonetheless, this was a warning to Raizman that his alternative view of the Revolution was not considered desirable at a time when the cult of personality was at its height. *The Last Night* received substantial publicity in the film press. The critics broadly praised the film and, according to Gabrilovich, it enjoyed "huge success," with the cinema-going public (Gabrilovich 1967, 29). Certainly, reviews in the press were largely favorable with one critic from the newspaper *Vecherniaia Moskva* observing Raizman's "natural, truthful, humane approach" (Slavin 1938, 3).

Love at a Time of War: *Mashenka*

Following an adaptation of Mikhail Sholokov's *Virgin Soil Upturned* (1939), a film that achieved limited success, Raizman went on to make one of his most popular films. *Mashenka* (1942) is a love story set before and during the Winter War with Finland in 1939. The war (especially the later battles against Germany) was typically depicted as a heroic struggle, emphasizing the military process rather than the emotional experiences of individuals and their perceptions of life during the conflict. Raizman and Gabrilovich's insistence on the primacy of emotion and intimacy provided a refreshing alternative to the more conventional Soviet war films. After submitting the script to the Mosfilm studio for approval in the autumn of 1940, the filmmakers did not have to wait long for the conclusions of Nikolai Semenov (the head of the studio's script department) and Aleksei Sazonov (the editor of that department). The reviewers commented on the film's potential to be a success based on its focus on the "creative power of love, which is one of the most fundamental elements in the development of the modern person's character and behavior." The review noted that the existing script made Mashen'ka's character too focused on her ordinariness in looks and character and her willingness to tolerate Alesha's (Mashen'ka's love interest) shortcomings to win his affection. The men were concerned that her character was purely interested in this goal, showing no concern for public matters; they wanted the emphasis of the script to change with Mashen'ka's love being about her "desire to help the person rid himself of his individual shortcomings. Herein lies the strength and educational meaning of her love." The review also demanded that the script be changed in relation to Alesha's character: he was seen as too self-interested and, in a similar way to Mashen'ka, not sufficiently interested in the world around him (RGALI 2453/2/19: 2–6). Their views on the script reveal the crux of Raizman's problematic relationship to a film industry built to serve political ideology: the criticism of the script were essentially attacks on Raizman's fundamental approach to filmmaking and his concern to create stories about private lives and individuals, their thoughts, feelings, and emotions. Raizman's dramas rarely sought to use human feelings as an educational tool to serve political or public ends, and that is precisely what made him unique as a Soviet director.

After the initial criticism of the script, the Cinema Committee's own script department looked at the work and offered a more positive critique, suggesting that the script was both ideologically and artistically strong. Interestingly, the reviewer thought the script gave the first believable depiction of love in both Soviet film and literature. Nonetheless, it concluded that the concerns of the studio's script department were justified and that the changes could be implemented in the shooting script. (RGALI 2453/2/19: 1). On March 1, 1941 the Chairman of the Cinema Committee Ivan Bol'shakov, called for further changes to be made to the language of the script. Given the concern with everyday life, it is unsurprising that many of Raizman's films contain elements of slang and street language. However, Bol'shakov was concerned with several expressions, including words derogatory to women, such as *baba* [daft woman] and *dura* [stupid woman], as well as the expression *sukin syn* [son of a bitch] (RGALI 2453/2/86: 25).

In July 1941 the director of Mosfilm wrote to the Cinema Committee, indicating that Gabrilovich and Raizman had redone the director's script to make changes to Alesha's character and that this had all been approved. However, in the final version of the film the most significant demands for change to Mashen'ka's character were not implemented. The derogatory elements of language were removed, but not entirely. The expression *sukin syn* is used twice by Alesha when referring to his driver colleague. Overall, Raizman resisted the crucial move from a purely romantic love to one aimed at human improvement. This appears to have been achieved through a clever strategy of negotiation and a small degree of compromise. Raizman was able to present his films as positive human interest stories which then appeared to be unthreatening in a political sense (RGALI 2453/2/86: 2). In the post-Soviet period artists who had worked with Raizman recalled his "iron constitution" and restraint when dealing with disgruntled Party officials and film industry bureaucrats. While Raizman did offer some ground with *Mashenka*, he never gave up on the fundamental idea. His unwillingness to back down was also crucial in the eventual release of later films almost destined for the shelf, including *And What if it is Love?* (1962), as well as *Your Contemporary* [*Tvoi sovremennik*, 1968] (Anon. 2003).

In the early stages of the film, the emphasis on Mashen'ka's ordinariness is clear. When talking to the object of her affection, Alesha, she describes herself as a "nobody." She is the epitome of averageness and is thus representative of the typical female Soviet citizen. In the early 1940s this type of heroine was very much an anomaly. Typically, women were depicted in a highly politicized manner with little interest in private or family matters. As Oksana Bulgakowa comments, the heroines of the time

> had no time for love [...] duty and work pushed it out of the picture. Intimacy and sensuality were also absent. Love was celebrated on top of a tractor, a kiss took place only on the platform where awards were being given out. This is why the heroines – emancipated and enjoying equal rights with men on the screen [...] seemed somehow "man-like", even though they were beautiful women. (Bulgakowa 1993, 149–174)

In *Mashenka*, Raizman deliberately reacted against this de-feminized and artificial new stereotype. He wanted to convey what might be perceived as believable emotions and aspirations of an ordinary Soviet female. Mashen'ka aspires to go beyond her everyday, humdrum existence at the post office, yet this aspiration is not about social mobilization within the narrow confines of Soviet ideology. On the contrary, her aspiration is about emotional fulfillment and a desire to escape from the dullness of her everyday life.

Raizman was almost always successful in finding artistic collaborators who would help him realize his creative visions. One of the key figures in the production of *Mashenka* was the highly talented cameraman Evgenii Andrikanis. He was attracted to the lyrical and intimate quality of the script and held Raizman in high esteem. Raizman invited Andrikanis to his flat where he was rehearsing with Valentina Karavaeva, and during these rehearsals the cameraman got a better understanding of Mashen'ka's essence. The men decided that, visually, it was crucial to convey the events through the heroine's young, innocent perception of the world. Indeed, the completed production suggests that this aim was realized. Raizman's films are distinguished by a concern with pictorial beauty, especially in terms of the way his actors are framed. His romantic portraiture draws in the spectator to the private world of the fictional characters, creating a subtle and nuanced sense of the self often lacking in the one-dimensional protagonists of Socialist Realism.

Andrikanis was aware that Karavaeva used her eyes to express many of the internal thoughts and emotions experienced by Mashen'ka. Here Raizman continued the pre-Revolutionary tradition which focused on character psychology. In many of his films the internal feelings of characters are conveyed through subtle gestures and especially through glances and the use of the eyes. For Raizman, the possibility of expressing the character's deepest thoughts and fears through the use of the eyes was one of the ways in which cinema could be more expressive than the theater (Raizman 1959, 108). Karavaeva was able, through the subtlest manipulation of her eyes, to express a range of emotions, including joy, sadness, forlorn hope, love, fear, surprise. Andrikanis worked carefully to capture Karavaeva's use of her eyes by applying a filter to the camera lens, which had its central section cut out so that the portraits of Mashen'ka would emphasize her ocular expressiveness. This is supported by the use of low-key lighting, often directed from below, which serves not to glamorize Mashen'ka, but to soften the face and allow certain features, including the eyes and forehead, to stand out (Andrikanis 1988, 93–96). The result is a romanticized portrait of Mashen'ka that allows the viewer to get a constant sense of the heroine's thoughts and feelings. Unlike the steely portraits of the leading ladies of wartime Soviet cinema, which served to distance the viewer from the subject, in *Mashenka* the cinematography is used to draw us in to the intimate world of the protagonist and encourage empathy and identification.

As David Bordwell has noted, the Socialist Realist style that superseded the montage of the 1920s involved an increasing use of deep-space composition in the cinematography. In most of the Soviet films from the 1930s and 1940s this was used to emphasize the "gigantomania," the monumental depiction of leading Bolsheviks and the historical events leading to communism (Bordwell 2001, 13–37). However, Raizman also adopts a significant depth of field in many of his films to a different effect: to provide painstaking detail of the physical environment and background objects that highlight the depth of character. Many of his contemporaries were simply using *mise-en-scène* in a formal way, perhaps showing more concern for rhythm, while Raizman saw *mise-en-scène* as a means of creating both a sense of authenticity and atmosphere, thus allowing the actor to express any given emotion and develop the character in a natural way. In Mashen'ka, Raizman seeks to create a lyrical mood throughout the film allowing Karavaeva to express herself to the full. This cinematic lyricism is evident throughout the film. Mashen'ka's melancholic mood can be felt when she meets her friend Klava in the park on an autumnal day. The leaves fall from the trees and, as nature dies out, so does her belief in the possibility of Alesha's love for her. The film's visual lyricism is also tangible in unexpected places, such as the scene of battle. At the end of the film, Mashen'ka and Alesha are accidentally reunited, expressing a sense of hope. The *mise-en-scène* here is characterized by the vivid contrast of white snow and black smoke from ruined buildings as exhausted soldiers return from battle. Mashen'ka expresses disbelief that her deepest desires may come true; the sense of hope is set against the backdrop of carnage: for now, at least, the war is over.

Mashenka proved to be one of Raizman's more enduring films and he continued the war theme with his next film, *Moscow Skies* [*Nebo Moskvy*, 1944] about the defense of the capital. This was followed by two documentaries: *Berlin* (1945) and *On the Truce with Finland* [*K voprosu o peremirii s Finliandiei*, 1945]. At this point Raizman was a highly respected and decorated Soviet director, yet the immediate post-war period proved to be difficult with the onset of the anti-cosmopolitan campaign, essentially an attack on Jews. The then head of the film industry, Bol'shakov, wrote an article in *Pravda* on the subject of "cosmopolitans" in the film industry, making an uncomfortable reference to Raizman's *The Train Goes East* [*Poezd idet na vostok*, 1948] as "ideologically weak." The article also referred to Raizman's favorite scriptwriter, Evgenii Gabrilovich, as being too tolerant of cosmopolitans (Bol'shakov 1949). This all came just over a year after Bol'shakov had described Raizman as one of the USSR's "leading film directors" (Bol'shakov 1948). Given this difficult context, it is perhaps unsurprising that the late 1940s was one of the less memorable periods in Raizman's filmmaking career. *The Train Goes East* threatened to undermine Raizman, but in truth it was an unremarkable romantic drama about a naval captain and his female companion as they try to make their way across the Soviet Union. It was followed by *Rainis* (1949) a film about the Latvian poet Janis Rainis, which was destined for cinematic obscurity.

1950s and 1960s: *And What if it is Love?* and *Your Contemporary*

His next film, *Chevalier of the Golden Star* [*Kaval'er Zolotoi Zvezdy*, 1950] is often referred to as Raizman's most politically orthodox film (Taylor 1999, 143–159). Despite this reputation, it nonetheless contains some impressive cinematography from Sergei Urusevskii, the future cameraman on Mikhail Kalatozov's *The Cranes are Flying* [*Letiat zhuravli*, 1957]. Raizman returned to form in his next film *The Lesson of Life* (1955), a cautionary tale of how career success can corrupt even the best Soviet citizen. This was followed by *The Communist* [*Kommunist*, 1957] a story set in the Civil War in which the central character, Vasilii Gubanov, experiences an inner conflict between his commitment to Soviet political values and the need for individual emotional expression and fulfillment. *The Communist* was certainly an important milestone in Raizman's career. However, it was the director's next work which is arguably one of his most important films. *And What If It Is Love?* was based upon the true story of a young couple at school, whose romance was subject to public exposure and the interference of parents, teachers, and peers. This eventually led to the couple's suicide. Raizman took on the basic theme of young love subject to external pressures, although the couple do not commit suicide in the film. Nonetheless, the film was highly controversial on release. While many young people could identify with its attack on the Soviet obsession with progress over the importance of private happiness, the more conservative journalists lambasted the film for its portrayal of the Soviet school and society more broadly as places of conformism and cruelty (Woll 2000, 134–136).

Raizman's films often give a distinctive portrayal of the physical characteristics of Soviet modernity and its faceless, alienating qualities in contrast to the complex psychological and emotional world of individuals who inhabit that society. In *And What if it is Love?* much of the action takes place at a massive Khrushchev-era housing complex, shown in construction during the film. It opens with a view on the site of a housing complex and the school from a private window. The camera angles are carefully set to capture the straight lines and homogeneity of the new architecture to emphasize the uniformity and conformity of life as people leave buildings in ordered, synchronous, single files. The roads are full of vehicles carrying building materials for the expanding site, and schoolchildren struggle to get past the seemingly endless convoy of trucks that almost has a military quality. The camera shows the people living in this environment, especially the young who are not in harmony with their surroundings; the buildings and machines of Soviet modernity dwarf and restrain the very people they are intended to serve. Overall, Raizman and his cinematographer Aleksandr Kharitonov create a *mise-en-scène* characterized by a grey sterility, which provides a highly effective background for the narrative.

It is in this physical environment that many of Raizman's protagonists struggle to find intimacy or some form of self-realization. The two protagonists, Boris (Igor' Pushkarev) and Kseniia (Zhanna Prokhorenko), attempt to share feelings, yet they are constantly hampered by others crushing their individuality. When they try to find forms of intimate communication in a public context, they are subject to persistent interference. The film begins with the discovery of a love letter by the German teacher. She instantly reports this to the headmistress and treats it as an object of great suspicion. The headmistress further emphasizes the insensitivity of the school environment by inserting commas in the letter. At this stage we do not know that the letter is from Boris to Kseniia, yet the teacher is determined to find the author, forcing the class groveler to find out. The girl lets others see the letter and the couple is soon exposed to ridicule among their peers.

The discovery of the letter precipitates public interest in the youngsters, who are unable to communicate in public and reduced to making physical gestures from their balconies. Boris and Kseniia decide to skip school fearing reprisals over the letter. However, when they spend the day in a nearby forest, a young child overhears their plans. Soon the local neighborhood is openly discussing why the two were not at school. Even Kseniia's mother fails to respect the teenagers' privacy, slapping Kseniia in front of a large gathering of neighbors when she learns that she has not been attending classes. Here the sacred social sphere is not lauded as a source of mutual respect and sharing as per Marxist ideology. On the contrary, ordinary people are shown as petty, preoccupied with gossip and, in some cases, determined to destroy young love which is regarded as a source of public shame.

Figure 22.2 Zhanna Prokhorenko as Kseniia and Igor' Pushkarev as Boris in Raizman's *What if it is Love?* (1962). Source: RIA Novosti.

Boris and Kseniia constantly struggle to find a private space where they can be together without interference. They are often reduced to meeting in stairwells for fear of public ridicule. Raizman uses light to great effect to express this contrast between intimacy and public exposure. When the couple finds its way to a deserted old church, there is a strong sense that Raizman is alluding to the abandonment of spirituality and old values. The young couple does a mock wedding ceremony and Boris declares his love for Kseniia. Here soft rays of light shine in through the church windows on the couple as if to confer some sort of divine blessing. By contrast, when Boris and Kseniia come together in the darkness of an urban building site near their homes, light plays a more sinister role. Here it seems that they are finally able to freely express their love for one another in the darkness, but a bright bulb swinging in the breeze periodically exposes the young couple as if acting as an investigative search light. On their last meeting, they are exposed to a punishing natural sunlight, which works effectively against the background of an empty, new building site that has a soulless, overpowering quality. Ultimately, it is the construction of communism which will determine the fate of the young couple. Kseniia plans to go to Novosibirsk to study and puts her hand out to shake Boris goodbye. He wants to go with her, but they part forever, as the need to conform is irresistible.

Your Contemporary (1968) explores the life of the son of Gubanov (the fictional protagonist from *The Communist*) who comes to Moscow to try to persuade the government to stop the construction of a factory to produce coal-based kaetan (an invented substance) and replace it with a new project using oil as a basis for production. In truth the relationship between the two films is fairly tenuous and mainly exists on a thematic level, looking at Raizman's concern with the individual and her/his relationship to Soviet modernity.

Raizman's trademark attention to a detailed *mise-en-scène* to parallel character development is very effective in *Your Contemporary*, which features a series of scenes in offices and ministries. The final meeting in a room in the Council of Ministers has a distinctly official feel. The room is surrounded by wooden paneling and an extremely Spartan interior all intended to be as authentically Soviet as possible (Rybak 1974, 78–81). It is against this staid background that Vasilii Gubanov (played by Igor' Vladimirov) asserts the vitality of initiative and the importance of the individual to realize successful ideas for the Soviet state. While Raizman portrays the environment of political power and "official interiors" as grey and static, his main characters aim to be different in one way or another, and often go against the physical environment of the *mise-en-scène* through either the dynamism of new ideas or through the assertion of individuality. Indeed, Raizman allowed a degree of improvisation with the *mise-en-scène* so that he could react during filming to the natural behavior of the actors (Rybak 1967, 61). This contrast between official sites of Soviet power and unorthodox individuals is particularly evident in Professor Nitochkin's (Nikolai Plotnikov) behavior. In the final scene Nitochkin leaves Gubanov and tries to walk across Red Square. This site was a visual symbol of Soviet communism, especially through its ordered parades. During that era the square was often regulated by policemen who could control movement with whistles. Nitochkin proceeds to walk across the square when the sound of a whistle tries to stop him in his tracks; he ignores it and proceeds anyway. This humorous moment illustrates an important aspect of Nitochkin's character: he will not conform to routines and predictability; his eccentric individualism is unchangeable.

Indeed, these themes of spontaneity versus conformism and individual free will versus social responsibility are carefully explored through the film's main characters. Gubanov is an engineer and the director of an institute; he appears to have the typical physical and behavioral characteristics of a senior bureaucrat. Gubanov believes in doing the right thing and in responsible action. His own self-reflection emerges through arguments with his son Misha. Gubanov learns that the latter has abandoned his studies to live with Katia, a young mother with whom he has fallen in love. Gubanov is furious and, after meeting Katia, he tells him about the importance of responsibility. However, Misha asserts his right to do what he wants, telling his father: "Man walks on two legs but everybody has their own gait and you believe for some reason that everyone thinks the same". He then adds: "Man is interesting in the way he differs from others, not because of his similarities."

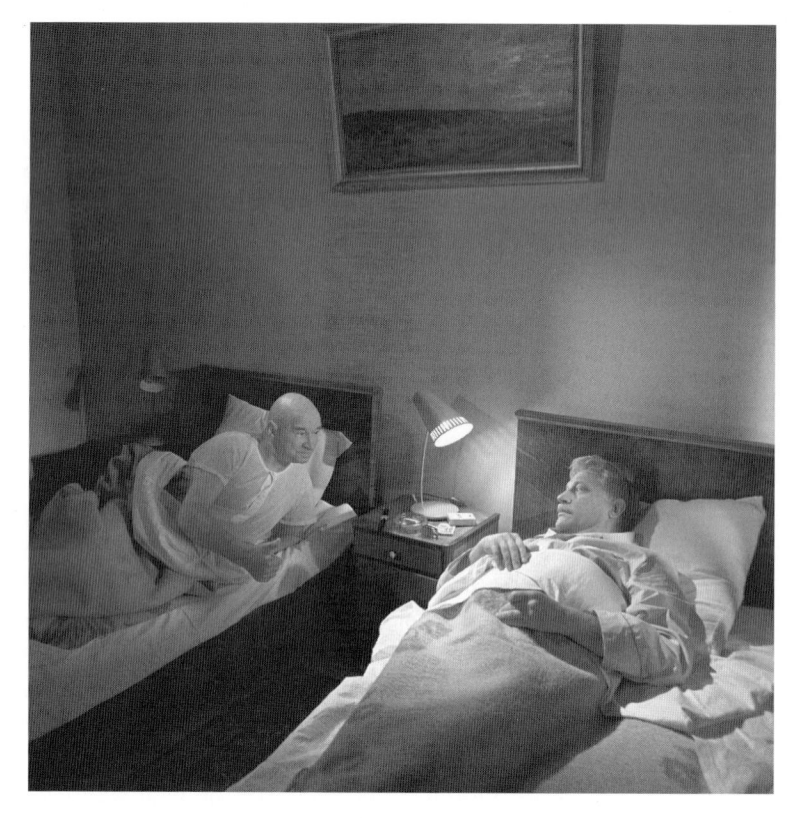

Figure 22.3 Nikolai Plotnikov as Professor Nitochkin (left), and Igor' Vladimirov as Vasilii Gubanov in Raizman's *Your Contemporary* (Mosfilm), 1967. Source: RIA Novosti.

While Gubanov strongly rejects his son's folly and irresponsible behavior, he starts to doubt himself when Misha quotes from Paul Éluard's *La Mort, L'Amour, La Vie* (1951), where the poet expresses a feeling of love not experienced since childhood. Deep down Gubanov starts to question himself and whether he has led a full and meaningful life.

This self-doubt is also encouraged by the eccentric Nitochkin. Much to Gubanov's relief, Nitochkin seems to avoid most of the meetings that concern the possible implementation of his own idea. While Nitochkin is a talented scientist, he is simply not interested in the dull process of implementation; it is the idea that excites him. While Gubanov is preoccupied with meetings, Nitochkin enjoys the adventure of visiting Moscow, with an almost childlike behavior and naiveté: he asks Misha Gubanov what TsUM (Central Universal Department Store) stands for and the latter explains, in an amused tone, that it is one of Moscow's most famous department stores. Subsequently, he quizzes a perplexed female receptionist on the existence of ladies' tights without a seam and the possibility of buying a belt with suspenders for his daughter. Nitochkin has found his happiness in freedom and spontaneity. In one scene he appears in the hotel room, shared with Gubanov, at two in the morning, merry after drinking a bottle of champagne. After hearing of Gubanov's frustration over his son's actions, Nitochkin declares that people "need to live, guided by their passions." This conversation unsettles Gubanov who sees that Nitochkin has managed to live life his own way, while Gubanov continues to question his own existence. The process of debate on whether kaetan should be based on older coal production or on Nitochkin's proposed oil-based approach parallels his own personal life; should he proceed living as before or search for something more? Gubanov heads for the hotel lobby in the middle of the night; when the night porter mentions that it is three in the morning, Gubanov replies: "yes, perhaps it is rather late." He has talked also about his inability to fundamentally change his own path in life. His expression for change can only find an outlet in the political, economic, and moral debates in which he is engaged.

Soviet Men and Women of the 1970s and 1980s: *A Strange Woman, Private Life* and *A Time of Desires*

Although the films often have women in the central roles, Raizman did not try to impose politicized visions of what a Soviet woman should be, instead offering an authentic portrayal of what it meant to be a woman in the USSR during the 1970s and 1980s. After the often ignored *Courtesy Call* [*Vizit vezhlivosti*, 1972], a film that tells of the adventures of Soviet sailors in Italy, Raizman made another three films: *A Strange Woman* [*Strannaia zhenshchina*, 1977], *Private Life* [*Chastnaia zhizn'*, 1982] and *A Time of Desires* [*Vremia zhelanii*, 1984]. The first and last of these films focused on modern Soviet women. *A Strange Woman* has an ironic title: its heroine, Evgeniia, is a lawyer; she leaves her husband and teenage son. She is tired of the insincerity of her conventional marriage to a dull diplomat and seeks a meaningful relationship. This sort of behavior would have been widely condemned in the conservative Soviet society. However, Raizman shows that a relationship is meaningless unless it is built upon genuine feelings, and Evgeniia is only truly happy when she meets a younger man who feels the same way. Yet the reality for most Soviet women was about survival and what might be described as the tragedy of necessity. Individualism and emotional expression were compromised and sometimes crushed by wider political and social burdens, which were often inescapable. In Raizman's last major film, *A Time of Desires*, the everyday life in the communist state is mercilessly dissected through the prism of female experience. Vera Alentova plays Svetlana, a woman situated at the crossroads between youth and maturity, looking for a husband who will provide material comfort and financial stability. The desired husband is nothing more than a means to an end; when she first meets Vladimir Lobanov, a rather grey bureaucrat, it is clear that she does not find him attractive or have any common ground with him. For Svetlana, Vladimir is merely another object of value to add to her growing inventory. Svetlana spends her days measuring her properties for potential sale or exchange, counting items of furniture, thinking about monetary value. Svetlana has escaped from an abusive partner, Valentina, who returns into her life in the film only to sexually assault her. She tells Vladimir that he is dead, adding to the atmosphere of falsehood and deception. When Vladimir shows Svetlana his dacha, she immediately sizes it up and suggests that they could make money out of it. When he tells Svetlana that he has had the dacha since childhood, she bluntly reminds him that "childhood is over." Svetlana pressurizes Vladimir into advancing his career, despite his reluctance. At the end of the film, Vladimir has a heart attack. As a doctor attends her husband, Svetlana reveals her indifference towards him by phoning the shop where she has purchased a new crystal lampshade to see if they will let her pick it up later in the day. Raizman is not condemning Svetlana, but identifying her as a tragic and typical example of a Soviet woman reduced to her most primal survival instincts. This is not only an illustration of individual misfortune, but an indictment of a corrupt Soviet society where meaningful human relationships have been reduced to daily transactions. Raizman's Soviet Union on the eve of perestroika is a society not only characterized by deception and material greed, but also by banality and tedium.

In *Private Life*, Sergei Abrikosov (Mikhail Ul'ianov) is a high-ranking Soviet bureaucrat, one of those men who stood at the heart of the command economic system. Before us we see an old man consumed by regret. Abrikosov is a man who has dedicated his life to communism in the form of paperwork and procedure, and realizes that he has not achieved any form of self-realization. His family life is also an unhappy one. His wife has achieved success as an academic in part thanks to Sergei's financial support; she goes as far as to tell him: "you made me." Yet their personal relations are devoid of affection. During one scene in the couple's bedroom Sergei asks her to give him her hand to which she responds: "Oh really

Sergei, don't be silly." Abrikosov does not express himself very often and the depth of his unhappiness is only hinted at through certain objects. The most notable of these is a gun which he puts at the back of his desk drawer, suggesting that he has been contemplating suicide. Abrikosov also hides a bust of Lenin away in the drawer, an outright rejection of Soviet ideology.

The life that Abrikosov wanted was undoubtedly something more spontaneous and less restricted by rules and regulations. Suddenly, Abrikosov almost finds himself like a helpless child, stating "I don't know how to live my life." At one point he crosses a road on a red light, suggestive of an inner desire to go beyond a life bereft of adventure and exploration. Sergei is controlled by petty emotions, which govern his actions. When he meets his former secretary, Nelly, he admits to her that he is jealous of his wife. While Abrikosov does not specify what he means, we can infer that he is referring to the fact that Natalia's life is full of color and joy; she enjoys music and is stunned when her husband suddenly shows an interest. She has a social life and a successful academic career. All this is in stark contrast to Abrikosov's empty existence devoid of interests and friendship and dominated by the dull career as a bureaucrat that he has come to despise. Bitterness, jealousy, and regret prevent him from relating to his own children for whom he shows very little affection.

A sense of decay and death are strongly present in *Private Life*. The action is deliberately slow and Raizman reinforces a sense of boredom that characterizes Sergei's

Figure 22.4 Mikhail Ul'ianov (right) as Abrikosov in Raizman's *Private Life*. Source: RIA Novosti.

existence. Raizman tends to use long takes and avoids fast-moving cuts, at least around Abrikosov, emphasizing stasis. He only uses faster cuts around younger characters to contrast their energy to Abrikosov's pedestrian life. There are relatively long takes of Abrikosov in his office at work, or at home sitting at his desk, tapping his fingers and writing out lists. Another method by which Raizman emphasizes age and decay is through the adoption of background sounds introduced at certain points in the film. For instance, when Abrikosov visits his secretary we hear the sound of children playing outside – the sound of youth and spontaneity which clearly irritates Abrikosov. At home he hears his son laughing with his friends in another room and asks his daughter "what is that noise?" as if laughter were something he had never experienced. At the end of the film Sergei gets ready for a return to work: the ministry has called and his services are required once more. Yet the clock ticks loudly and incessantly in the background, reminding Sergei that his own life is running out. Clocks seem to be everywhere to remind Sergei of the time ticking away, chiming loudly on the hour as a sort of disciplinary sign. In the final close-up shot he looks at himself in the mirror and the mood would seem to suggest that he is attending his own funeral as the shot fades to black.

Conclusion

The importance of Iulii Raizman's films lies not only in his alternative view on life in the Soviet past and present, but in the creative means by which he expresses that alternative. In the 1930s and 1940s ordinary people were bombarded with films that suggested that the private life was always secondary to the public sphere and the values of the Soviet system. I have argued for the importance of Raizman as a profound defender of the private and intimate world of the Soviet citizen, and later as a strong critic of those aspects of the Soviet regime which threatened individual aspiration, fulfillment, and free will.

His concern for the individual fits into the cultural paradigms of the Thaw, but extends through his entire career, making Raizman an outspoken defender of the individual. Raizman managed to carve himself an enviable position of autonomy and artistic expression which, given the substantial political, social and financial pressures of the Soviet period, was quite remarkable.

References

References to the Russian State Archive for Literature and the Arts (RGALI) are cited in the text as follows: RGALI, fond, inventory, document number, sheet. All references to RGALI in this chapter are drawn from: *Mosfilm (1938–1945): Russia's Propaganda on Film* (Reading: Primary Source Media, 1999).

Andrikanis, Evgenii. 1988. *O Presne, o Parizhe, o kino* [About Presnya, Paris, and Cinema]. Moscow: Iskusstvo.

Anon. 1931. "Iz doklada sekretno-politicheskogo otdela OGPU 'Ob antisovetskoi deiatel'nosti sredi intelligentsii za 1931 god'" [From the Report of the Secret Political Department of the OGPU "About Anti-Soviet Activity among the Intelligentsia in 1931"]. Document 72. In *Vlast' i khudozhestvennaia intelligentsia* [The Authorities and the Artistic Intelligentsia], edited by A. Artizov and O. Naumov, 161. Moscow: Demokratiia, 2002.

Anon. 2003. "Ostrova. Iulii Raizman" [Islands. Iulii Raizman]. *TV Kanal Kul'tura*, [Culture Channel] December 15 2008, http://tvkultura.ru/video/show/brand_id/20882/episode_id/379838 (accessed October 20, 2013).

Beumers, Birgit. 2009. *A History of Russian Cinema*. Oxford: Berg.

Bol'shakov, Ivan. 1948. "Pis'mo I. G. Bol'shakova E.K. Voroshilovu o nagrazhdenii S. M. Eizenshteina ordenom Lenina" [Letter by I. Bolshakov to E. Voroshilov about the Award of the Lenin Order to S. Eisenstein]. Document 283, dated January, 21. In *Kremlevskii kinoteatr, 1928–1953* [The Kremlin Cinema 1928–1953], edited by K. Anderson *et al.*, 800. Moscow: Rosspen, 2005.

Bol'shakov, Ivan. 1949. "Razgromit burzhuaznyi kosmopolitizm v kinoiskusstve" [Crushing Bourgeois Cosmopolitanism in Film Art]. *Pravda* March 3. Fond A. N. Iakovlev, http://www.alexanderyakovlev.org/fond/issues-doc/69557 (accessed October 20, 2013).

Bordwell, David. 2001. "Eisenstein, Socialist Realism and the Charms of Mizanstsena." In *Eisenstein at 100: A Reconsideration*, edited by A. Lavelley and B. P. Scherr, 13–37. New Brunswick: Rutgers University Press.

Bulgakowa, Olga. 1993. "The Hydra of the Soviet Cinema." In *Red Women on the Silver Screen*, edited by Lynne Atwood, 149–174. London: Pandora Press.

Christie, Ian and John Gillet. 1984. "Love and Conscience: The Films of Yuli Raizman." *National Film Theatre*, October/November: 14–17. London: British Film Institute.

Gabrilovich, Evgenii. 1967. *O tom, chto proshlo* [What has Passed]. Moscow: Iskusstvo.

Gillespie, David. 2002. *Russian Cinema: Inside Film*. Harlow: Longman.

Maksimenkov, Leonid. 1997. *Sumbur vmesto muzyki. Stalinskaia kul'turnaia revoliutsiia 1936–1938* [Chaos Instead of Music. Stalin's Cultural Revolution 1936–1938]. Moscow: Iuridicheskaia kniga.

Raizman, Iulii. 1959. "Vybor aktera na rol'" [Choosing an Actor for a Part]. In *Mosfi'lm, stat'i, publikatsii, izobrazitel'nye materialy* [Mosfilm: Articles, Publications, Visual Materials] edited by M. Bogdanov *et al.* Moscow: Iskusstvo.

Rollberg, Peter. 2009. *Historical Dictionary of Russian and Soviet Cinema*. Plymouth: Scarecrow Press.

Rybak, Lev. 1967. "500 chasov u Iuliia Raizmana" [500 Hours with Iulii Raizman]. *Iskusstvo kino* [Art of Cinema] 1: 61.

Rybak, Lev. 1974. *V kadre – rezhisser* [The Filmmaker in the Frame]. Moscow: Iskusstvo.

Slavin, Lev. 1938. "Posledniaia noch'" [The Last Night]. *Vecherniaia Moskva* [Evening Moscow] January 21.

Taylor, Richard. 1999. "Singing on the Steppes for Stalin: Ivan Pyrev and the Kolkhoz Musical in Soviet Cinema." *Slavic Review* 58.1: 143–159.

Woll, Josephine. 2000. *Real Images: Soviet Cinema and the Thaw*. New York: I. B. Tauris.
Zak, Mark. 1962. *Iulii Raizman*. Moscow: Iskusstvo.
Zorkaia, Neia. 1966. *Portrety* [Portraits]. Moscow: Iskusstvo.
Zorkaia, Neia. 2004. "Sgustki istorii. Portret rezhissera Iuliia Raizmana" [Clots of History. A Portrait of the Filmmaker Iulii Raizman]. *Iskusstvo kino* [Art of Cinema] 2, http://kinoart.ru/ru/archive/2004/02/n2-article13 (accessed October 20, 2013).

23

The Man Who Made Them Laugh: Leonid Gaidai, the King of Soviet Comedy

Elena Prokhorova

In a survey conducted in 1995 by the RTR television channel, audiences in Russia named Leonid Gaidai's *The Diamond Arm* [*Brilliantovaia ruka*, 1968] the best comedy ever made and he was awarded posthumously the "Golden Ticket" (Kudriavtsev 1998, 26; Brashinskii 2001, 235). By the mid-1990s post-Soviet viewers could access much of the world film culture which had been previously unavailable behind the "Iron Curtain." Whether this vote was a matter of national loyalty, an educated choice, or nostalgia for less uncertain times is beyond the point. The popular choice merits attention, if only because Gaidai ruled Soviet comedy unchallenged for over a decade, beginning with two shorts, *The Dog Barbos and the Unusual Cross* [*Pes Barbos i neobyknovennyi kross*] and *Moonshiners* [*Samogonshchiki*], both released in 1961 within film anthologies, and ending with *Ivan Vasilievich: Back to the Future* [*Ivan Vasil'evich meniaet professiiu*, 1973]. Three of his feature films from the 1960s topped the box office by a wide margin: 69.6 million spectators for *Operation "Y" and Other Adventures of Shurik* [*Operatsiia "Y" i drugie prikliucheniia Shurika*, 1965], and 76.5 and 76.7 million for *Kidnapping, Caucasian Style* [*Kavkazskaia plennitsa*, 1966] and *The Diamond Arm* respectively (Segida and Zemlianukhin 1996).[1] Until 1980 Gaidai was the absolute leader of the Soviet box office.[2] The steady revenues that Gaidai's blockbusters brought to the Soviet film industry were barely reflected in the director's salary.[3] Only once he approached Nikolai Sizov, the director of the Mosfilm Studio, with a question that, in its subversive simplicity, could serve as an epigraph to Gaidai's filmmaking: "If we live under socialism, shouldn't we be paid according to our work?" (Pupsheva, Ivanov, and Tsukerman 2002, 107).

An equally revealing but lesser known fact is that *The Diamond Arm* was released in 2079 copies (Kudriavtsev 1998, 26). The number of copies was one of the mechanisms of control of Goskino (State Committee of Cinematography), which assigned to each film a distribution category. The first category ensured the widest

---

A Companion to Russian Cinema, First Edition. Edited by Birgit Beumers.
© 2016 John Wiley & Sons, Inc. Published 2016 by John Wiley & Sons, Inc.

distribution and the highest honorarium for the film crew, and often secured an all-Union premiere, participation in Soviet and international film festivals, positive reviews in the press, state prizes, and other financial perks for the filmmakers (Zorkaia, n.d.). The number of copies for *The Diamond Arm* exceeded 2000 – the category assigned exclusively to state commissioned, ideologically important films with international distribution. In the entire history of Soviet cinema only three films were released in over 2000 copies: *War and Peace* [*Voina i mir*, dir. Sergei Bondarchuk, 1966, 2805 copies for the first part], *Liberation* [*Osvobozhdenie*, dir. Iurii Ozerov, 1970, 2202 copies; see Kudriavtsev 1998] – both spectacular epics – and Gaidai's eccentric comedy. But here the parallel ends. Gaidai's films did not receive accolades in the press or won prizes; they were almost never screened at film festivals, with one – albeit major exception: his *The Dog Barbos* was nominated for Best Short Film at Cannes and screened at the San Francisco Film Festival.

While acknowledging the popular appeal and profitability of Gaidai's comedies, Soviet film administrators and the press were reserved about praising them. The Soviet "taste police" – critics deploring the lowbrow appeal of the pictures – often compared him unfavorably to Charlie Chaplin who had "several layers and meanings" to his slapstick (Pupsheva, Ivanov, and Tsukerman 2002, 104). In other words, there was no good reason, beyond the budgetary gain, to be proud of Gaidai's films. Comedy, especially eccentric comedy, stood low in the Soviet culture's table of ranks. As Kristin Roth-Ey writes, "[b]ecause [Soviet] culture aimed to elevate everyone to connoisseurship and artistry, it was inherently, unapologetically elitist and pedagogical" (Roth-Ey 2011, 4). Gaidai's widow recounts a typical situation: a Moscow movie theater would proudly display a billboard advertising a historical-revolutionary film *Lenin in Poland* [*Lenin v Pol'she*, dir. Sergei Iutkevich, 1966] which was shown in one screening, while the other dozen showings, hypocritically tucked in inside, were of Gaidai's *Kidnapping, Caucasian Style* – a guaranteed profit maker for the cinema.[4]

Gaidai's Comedy and Soviet Culture

There are several ways to approach Gaidai's unique position in Russo-Soviet cinema. Some scholars have focused on his decisive abandonment of logos-driven narrative in favor of body language and editing. Aleksandr Prokhorov claims that Gaidai's slapstick comedies follow the aesthetics of the cinema of attractions, not narrative cinema: "Gaidai's overriding concern with the image in motion rather than with film's narrativity is what distinguishes him from the majority of Russian directors. His comic devices work against the linear flow of narrative and present the viewer with a series of 'attractions' in the form of comic turns" (Prokhorov 2003, 459). By privileging visual humor over the less ambiguous satire, Gaidai's comedies challenged and put to comic use elements of Soviet ideological narrative and its major device, the positive hero.

Other scholars have examined Gaidai's signature slapstick devices as ciphers for topical concerns of the day: corruption, alcoholism, the black market, Khrushchev's economic and social campaigns, and so on. Saša Milić argues that Gaidai's sight gags invite a double reading: the diegetic one and the one alluding to the world beyond. For example, *Operation "Y"*, according to Milić, offers not so subtle references to Khrushchev and his mass housing project, among other things. The film came out in 1965, a year after Khrushchev was ousted from office, and "knowing the number of hurdles the script had to jump through in order to go into production in the Soviet system, the complex manner in which Khrushchev features in the comedy must have been approved, and even initiated, from a higher place" (Milić 2004).

Gaidai's comedies were unique in post-1920s Soviet cinema,[5] and the focus on slapstick and sight gags as his most distinctive elements is quite justified. Contemporary Soviet comedy, according to the director, was weighed down by "stinking realism" (Pupsheva, Ivanov, and Tsukerman 2002, 359). Gaidai wanted to make eccentric comedy in the tradition of Max Linder, Mack Sennett, and Charlie Chaplin, and deplored the disappearance of the arsenal of means that made silent comedy a great international language: "Most comic pictures nowadays have only dialogue and music left. This will get you only so far … But why, as a matter of fact, can't we use devices and tools of silent cinema? It was very expressive" (Pupsheva, Ivanov, and Tsukerman 2002, 77). Gaidai and his scriptwriters, Moris Slobodskoi, Iakov Kostiukovskii, and Vladlen Bakhnov, were mostly concerned with the films' comic potential. Gaidai collected and used spontaneous jokes of his film crew; obsessively perfected his pictures for their effect, using film projectionists as his test audience; and chose actors based on their expressive body language. Iurii Nikulin, his long-time star, was a circus clown, and the main cinematic attraction of the famous ViNiMor (the three "stooges" Georgii Vitsyn, Iurii Nikulin, and Evgenii Morgunov) was the grotesque contrast of their bodies. Gaidai valued Andrei Mironov as an heir of Faina Ranevskaia, as well as Sergei Martinson and Erast Garin, who had a rare talent for the lost art of extravaganza (Pupsheva, Ivanov, and Tsukerman 2002). Aleksandr Dem'ianenko ("Shurik") was for Gaidai the epitome of a "pure soul" [*svetlaia lichnost'*], and in order to achieve the isomorphism of concept and character, the actor had to bleach his dark hair. Gaidai haunted his songwriters with demands to create popular hits and approved them only after getting confirmation from the street.

But an alternative and synthesizing approach to Gaidai's oeuvre is also possible: to consider his films from the point of view of the narrative, in which individual gags form a pattern of thematic and audio-visual motifs. This narrative is constituted by Soviet tropes and cultural common places, which were the only available material for the filmmaker to use. Precisely because Gaidai spent every waking minute trying to find the perfect stunt and sound effect rather than to build a cause-and-effect motivated narrative, the narrative of incomplete, superficial modernization suggested itself. Eager to show rather than tell, Gaidai saturated his

Figure 23.1 Leonid Gaidai (left) with his star, Iurii Nikulin, on the set of *Kidnapping, Caucasian Style*, 1966.

films with visual gags, sound effects, chase scenes, and musical numbers, and fiercely defended every line and every slapstick moment.[6] Any material could be worked into the spectacle – the voraciousness had an effect most likely not anticipated by the director himself. Having discarded realistic motivation, character psychology, and satiric didacticism, Gaidai tapped into two bottomless wells in the 1960s–early 1970s: first, the deep-seated Russian cultural attitudes, tastes, and taboos (including prison and drinking culture); second, the horrific experiences of the recent Soviet past – Stalin-era terror and World War II.

At the same time, Gaidai insisted that comedy should be contemporary, and his films up to *Twelve Chairs* [*Dvenadtsat' stul'ev*, 1971] brim with visual and auditory signs of late socialist culture: student life, ethnographic expeditions, rock climbing, space travel hype, lottery tickets, travel abroad, consumer goods, Vladimir Vysotskii's songs, Soviets' obsession with sausage and sprats, and last but not least, a score of contemporary Soviet slogans. According to Sergei Dobrotvorskii, "Gaidai created an almost journalistic style of the 1960s – plastic surfaces, light structures, brightly colored synthetic suits, twist, and streamlined automobiles" (Dobrotvotskii 1996). Yet this modern and civilized world is only skin-deep. Right under the surface is the unapologetically arbitrary and violent culture of brute force and archaic notions, the threat of arrest or mental institution. Although contemporary and familiar, Russia in Gaidai's films is decidedly not modern. As Geoff King argues, "[o]ne of the pleasures of comedy is the freedom vicariously to enjoy departure from the norm" (King 2002, 7). These "ruptures of normal expectations" are not meant to be taken too seriously (King 2002, 8), lest an implausible premise or situation might be construed as absurd or "monstrous" and thus too close to horror (King 2002, 16). In Gaidai this model is turned upside down: the signs of modernity easily dissolve, while the "norm" is constituted as "horrific."[7] The protagonist of *Kidnapping, Caucasian Style* comes to a mountainous town to collect old legends and traditions, but instead participates in an actual bride kidnapping. The "stooges" first appear in several films as independent entrepreneurs (selling goods at the market, giving dance lessons) but are instantly revealed to be thugs-for-hire, serving corrupt Soviet officials. One of the centerpieces of *Kidnapping, Caucasian Style* is a musical number "If I only were a sultan," which debates the pros and cons of polygamy. *Diamond Arm*, the most modern-looking of Gaidai's films with its foreign travel, private apartment, hotels, restaurants, fashion shows, and other signs of the "good life" traps its protagonist between gangsters and the police who use him as bait and whose ubiquitous control flickers in surveillance, doubles, and mind-reading.

The terrifying aspects of the "normal" Soviet experience – surveillance, lack of privacy, disregard for human life, state violence, arbitrariness of power – are diffused through slapstick and dialogue and transposed into the safe, consumer-oriented late socialism. This duality is different from irony, the dominant modality in comedies of El'dar Riazanov who replaced Gaidai as the reigning king of Soviet comedy in the 1970s. If ironic discourse alludes to the second meaning beyond the literal one, in Gaidai's best films the diegesis itself is duplicated. The result is what Michel Foucault describes as heterotopia, which is "capable of juxtaposing in a single real place different spaces and locations that are incompatible with each other" and which "enters fully into function when men find themselves in a sort of total breach of their traditional time" (1997, 354). Gaidai's films captured two such breaks: the 1960s and the gradual dismantling of Stalinist society, and the late 1980s and the collapse of socialist culture. Under the pressure of comedic eccentricity, the Soviet – and broadly Russian – norm itself became fluid and in the process exposed its absurd and unseemly aspects.

Dialogue in Gaidai's comedies in particular is a category of its own. It is pithy, aphoristic, or nonsensical, and, while superficially belonging to the diegetic narrative, also creates a perfect comic gag (like a series of "imitation cusses" in *Diamond Arm*) or engages the viewer with a wink. "[T]he joke disrupts the assumption of a 'natural' relation between language and meaning and, at the same time, serves as a screen for the fact that such a relation never existed in the first place" (Bloch 1986, 127–128). The origin of the film's jokes is the Soviet universe of the 1960s, which suddenly touched ground between the phantasmagoria of Stalinism and the utopian optimism of reformed socialism. It is a truly popular art, unencumbered by official didacticism or intellectual Aesopian language. But it taps into the repressed, the unspoken, and the un-processed experiences of several generations of Soviet audiences. Performed in the setting of the consumerist and peaceful late socialism (a restaurant, a prefab apartment building, a southern resort town) the jokes produce what King calls "comic hysteria [...] based on a combination of attachment and detachment" from the film's diegesis (King 2002, 10) and operate on the two planes. "You should come over and visit us in Kolyma," – innocently remarks a man at the restaurant in *The Diamond Arm*. The smuggler chokes on his beer and mumbles "Thanks, but I'd rather you visit us here." The joke simultaneously invokes the smuggler's true criminal identity and references the most notorious part of Stalin's Gulag system. In *Ivan Vasilievich*, the tsar addresses all men in the 1970s apartment building as *kholop* [serf] and *smerd* [dirty peasant]. While the dentist and the film director are outraged by the insult, the joke instantly erases centuries of Russian history and asserts the unchanging nature of Russian power.

Commenting on the director's phenomenal popularity in the 1960s, Dobrotvorskii wrote that, unlike other popular Soviet filmmakers who assumed that "people already know something about themselves [...] in his best years Gaidai never relied on this – and scored. [...] Gaidai's eccentric comedy sprang on the uncultivated patch of collective soul, where seeds of other knowledge or temptations have not yet been planted, where people's soul is still virginal and bare" (Dobrotvorskii 1996). This does not mean that Gaidai made his films from a position of higher knowledge or understanding. More than anything he resembled his own idealistic characters who, like proverbial fools-in-Christ, are entirely powerless and often nonsensical.

The Making of the King

Leonid Gaidai was born in 1923 in the Amur region of the Soviet Far East, in the town whose fate epitomized the grotesque nature of the century. The town of Alekseevsk was renamed into Svobodnyi ["free"] after the Revolution and in the 1930s became the administrative center of Bamlag [Baikal-Amur Mainline Labor Camp], one of the largest camps of the Gulag. The family moved to the city of Irkutsk from where, at the outbreak of the war in 1941, the 17-year-old Gaidai volunteered for the front. He became a scout (by exaggerating his knowledge of German); in 1944 he was seriously wounded and demobilized from the army.

After working at the Irkutsk Drama Theater, Gaidai moved to Moscow in 1949 and enrolled in the director's department at the All-Union State Institute of Cinematography (VGIK), where he studied under renowned Soviet filmmakers Mikhail Romm and Grigorii Aleksandrov. Gaidai's early cinematic career hardly presaged a comedic genius and was peppered by changes of fortune, despite the patronage of famous directors. Gaidai got hands-on training as assistant director and actor in Boris Barnet's comedy *Liana* (1955). His directorial debut, *Long Journey* [*Dolgii put'*, 1956], was a historical drama, but Romm saw comedic talent in the young director and invited him to his comedy workshop and offered him a script *The Dead Affair* [*Mertvoe delo*]. The film sets up a Gogolian situation: a Soviet bureaucrat's passport is stolen and the thief, carrying the documents, is run over by a car. The authorities and the bureaucrat's colleagues presume him dead. The very rule he defends in his official capacity ("no document – no person") turns him into a non-entity: it is impossible to prove that you are alive if the police report claims otherwise. The Minister of Culture Nikolai Mikhailov saw the completed picture as a libel of Soviet reality, and Gaidai had to cut, re-edit, and rename the film, which was released in 1958 as *Fiancé from the Netherworld* [*Zhenikh s togo sveta*]. Another famous director, Ivan Pyr'ev, offered Gaidai the project which was to serve as the director's *mea culpa*: a historical-revolutionary film *Thrice Resurrected* [*Trizhdy voskresshii*, script Aleksandr Galich, 1960], about a legendary Soviet tugboat.

Pyr'ev invited Gaidai to his newly organized comedy unit at Mosfilm. The more permissive political and cultural environment of the early 1960s was well suited for the official acceptance of Gaidai's comedic revolution. Yet in retrospect, the most paradoxical thing about Gaidai is why censors ever gave the green light to release his films, which could easily be called anti-Soviet. Gaidai did everything that Soviet film ideologues frowned upon. His characters drink, slack off, engage in brawls – and do it with gusto and with no didactic purpose. His villains, starting with the comedic trio of ViNiMor, are more relatable than positive heroes. Authorities and representatives of respectable Soviet institutions – police, doctors, housing superintendents, local administrators – are dupes of the crooks at best, or are themselves corrupt, tyrannical monsters. The dialogue – the anchor of Soviet ideological discourse – is sparse, reduced to memorable one-liners. Finally, Gaidai's films brought into broad circulation a number of songs that aroused justified suspicion on the part of the censors. Indeed, what do "The Island of Bad Luck" or "Song about Hares" (with the refrain "We Don't Care") refer to, especially since they have absolutely no connection to the eccentric narrative of *The Diamond Arm*?

After his first comedy had been butchered, Gaidai learned to anticipate censors' criticism and surround his film with a thick protective layer of politically correct discourses. His standard answer about future films was "We will use the means of satire to fight the flaws which still sometimes hinder the lives of Soviet people" (Pupsheva, Ivanov, and Tsukerman 2002, 65). Even so, accounts of Gaidai's run-ins with censors and film administrators and the resulting changes to his films are the stuff of legend. A recurring feature of these incidents is that Soviet officials ended up giving in or suggesting changes that were even more absurd than the original. For example, in the original script of *The Diamond Arm*, the vigilant superintendent tells the wife of Semen Gorbunkov, who just returned from a trip abroad: "All this is the corrupting Western influence. I wouldn't be surprised if your husband visits a synagogue on the sly." An equally vigilant Soviet censor, following the Party line (at once atheist and anti-semitic) demanded to replace the "synagogue" with "brothel." "I know we have synagogues in the USSR," – wondered Gaidai, – "but I did not know we have brothels as well" (Admin 2015).

Gaidai's early comedic oeuvre follows a very clear trajectory, which re-enacts the history of cinema: moving from shorts to feature films, and from quasi-silent films to talkies. Gaidai treated language as an object, and an unwelcome one at that. His films prior to *Kidnapping, Caucasian Style* are no more than 20 minutes in length; when dialogue appears, it is minimalist and aphoristic, nonsensical, or simply muffled. With his short films Gaidai made a test run for his approach to comedy: under the guise of satire – the space of controlled, "socially productive" laughter – he staged his carnivalesque and spontaneous flicks, where the laughter was anarchic, unmotivated, and absurdist. *The Dog Barbos* and *Moonshiners* used as their premise officially sanctioned satirical bits: a feuilleton about unlucky poachers published in *Pravda*, and a circus number satirizing bootleggers, the latter suggested by Iurii Nikulin, a professional clown who became a long-term actor in Gaidai's films. Both films thus nominally responded to Khrushchev's campaign against social loafing and unearned income through a series of gags and chases. Each film is neatly divided into two equal parts. In the first part the trio of Soviet stooges – the Coward, the Dumb One, and the Experienced One – enjoy drinking and bonding in nature's lap; in the second part the requisite punishment follows, which merely replaces imbibing and male camaraderie with the equally gratuitous slapstick violence and chase.

Figure 23.2 The three stooges (Georgii Vitsyn, Iurii Nikulin, and Evgenii Morgunov) combining alcohol production and consumption in *Moonshiners*, 1961.

Alcohol is never in short supply: in *Dog Barbos* vodka materializes out of thin air, while in *Moonshiners* the titular liquid is produced right in front of the audiences. Gaidai accelerates motion and uses trick photography to portray the magical filling of the shelves with moonshine. The camera's close-ups of the steam-gauge, coil, and sacks of sugar, with red glare on characters' inspired faces mocks work sequences in socialist realist production films, while the song extolling the pleasures of drinking parodies musical numbers in socialist realist musicals (see Prokhorov 2003, 464–465). In the "three stooges" Gaidai succeeded in creating cinematic characters who, like Chaplin's Tramp or Tati's Monsieur Hulot, became iconic masks of Russia cinema. But where Chaplin and Tati pitched their organic individuals against the oppressive, mechanized modernity and, through slapstick, exposed the inhumanity of the "norm," Gaidai's comic masks brought to Soviet cinemas the repressed aspects of culture: street talk, drinking jokes, jail songs, body (including butt and penis) jokes (Prokhorov 2003, 461–462), and sexual innuendos: ViNiMor and similar comic villains in Gaidai's films are allowed to stare at women without any romantic overtones.

In order to be able to make people laugh for an hour or more a Soviet film director needed an excuse: to produce a satire, a parody of a Western genre, a literary adaptation, etc. Gaidai transitioned from comedic shorts to feature films via the portmanteau format. In *Strictly Business* [*Delovye liudi*, 1962] and *Operation "Y"* he preserved the short as his signature feature, but this time he was the sole director of all films. *Strictly Business* consists of three adaptations of O. Henry's stories under one title: "The Roads We Take," "Make the Whole World Kin," and "The Ransom of Red Chief."[8] Gaidai tried his hand at Hollywood genres: "The Road We Take" is an imitation of a Western, "Kindred Souls," especially in the first five minutes, is executed in the film noir style, and "The Ransom of Red Chief" is slapstick comedy.

While the first two shorts are excellent stylizations, it is the third one that brought Gaidai success. "The Ransom of Red Chief" – a story of two hapless kidnappers who are terrorized by the unruly boy they hold for ransom – engages with themes and motifs that were alien to and unwelcome in Soviet culture, with its denial of individual psyche, wariness of the dark irrational forces, and the absence of the genre of horror films: dreams as nightmarish comments on rational waking reality; practical and hyper-confident men who are revealed to be half-children, and angelic children who are devilish pranksters. These themes and motifs, as well as the classic device of doubles, would become the linchpin of Gaidai's future films. For example, in "The Ransom of Red Chief," the kidnappers have nightmares about being chased, captured, and roasted by a gang of the boy's (grown-up) look-alikes. In *The Diamond Arm* the drugged Gorbunkov's dream merges the prostitute hired by the gangsters with the house superintendent, and thus aggressive sexuality with state supervision – both of which invade the character's last resort for autonomy, his sleep.

Operation "Y" used the same portmanteau format but united the three narratives through the protagonist Shurik and set the action in the contemporary Soviet

Union, not a fairy-tale forest or literary America. Just like Gaidai's early shorts fit with current socialist campaigns, so did *Operation "Y"* pay tribute to the contemporary debate about the new cinematic hero. For his protagonist, Gaidai chose the icon of the 1960s culture – a student, and on the surface the plots are perfect socialist realist miniatures. In "Workmate," Shurik tries to re-educate a thug who is sentenced to community service at a construction site for unruly behavior. In "Operation 'Y'" he single-handedly apprehends a gang of perpetrators hired by the embezzling warehouse director to create havoc and conceal the theft.

The films turn socialist sites into a pleasure fairground, revealing the comic potential of the *mise-en-scène* and preventing a reading of the shorts as satires of social vices. Instead, in the two framing novellas Gaidai focuses on the hostile social environment where criminals and thugs conspire with or successfully use authorities to achieve their goals. Gaidai surrounds his bespectacled, nerdy, and confused males with aggressive and boorish men and assertive, commandeering women. The police and the foreman in "Workmate" are oblivious to the hoodlum's manipulation of the system and his terrorizing of the student "mentor." The police deliver to the thug a three-course meal; the foreman welcomes him with an enthusiastic lecture about the successes of Soviet construction, while the thug attempts to immure the student with bricks. All in all, thugs and criminals are much better integrated into the system than Gaidai's do-gooders, students and engineers: to use Stalin-era term, the former are "social allies" [*sotsial'no blizkie*].

Despite the aphoristic and absurdist nature of dialogue in Gaidai's films, language and sound in general are central to the films' success through a carnivalistic inversion of the very role that dialogue played in Soviet cinema. The foreman's clichéd comparison of the pace of Soviet construction with that in the West is muffled by industrial sounds, and all that we hear are the words "France" and "the United States." After a good meal the hoodlum tells Shurik that it is time for him to lecture: "Go ahead, drill me on how our spaceships traverse the Bolshoi Theater," a perfectly conceptualist and absurdist merger of two standard propaganda items: Soviet dominance in space and in ballet. When the crooks in *Operation Y* inquire what exactly they are hired to steal from the warehouse, their boss explains: "Nothing. Everything has been stolen before us." Not only do such lines open the scene up to interpretation, but the use of sound crosses many ideological boundaries. For example, the "interment" of the student happens to the melody of "Gospodi pomilui" [Pray to the Lord], while the slapstick fight between Shurik and the thug is accompanied by a soundtrack imitating bomb explosions, machine gun clatter, and the characteristic howling of Katyusha rockets – unmistakable references to the Great Patriotic War. Gaidai develops the "religious" theme in *The Diamond Arm*, where one of the crooks panics when he finds himself on an island but then sees a young boy who seems to be walking on water. A nimbus appears over the boy's head, and in ecstasy the crook follows him. The scene abruptly ends when the "miracle" is revealed to be a shallow crossing.

Operation "Y" was also the first film where Gaidai used a song as neither part of the narrative, nor as a strictly atmospheric element. But unlike his later films for which he commissioned original songs, "Postoi, parovoz" [Engine, wait] is a prison song, invoking an entire repressed layer of Russo-Soviet culture, including the Gulag. As performed by the famous actor Iurii Nikulin, the song instantly identifies the trio of Stooges not just as hoodlums but as jail birds, and pioneers Gaidai's special kind of musical numbers which expand the limits of permissible in Soviet cinema. "Engine, wait!" is a Russian chanson, "Song about Bears" is a twist, "Help me!" is a passionate tango (the last two accompanied by sexually explicit dance), and so on.

The central novella, "A Spell" ["Navazhdenie"] is a romantic story, which focuses on one of Gaidai's central themes – acting outside of reason. A student follows an attractive girl home. Both are so absorbed by her lecture notes that they do not notice each other or their surroundings. In a scene rather risqué for a Soviet film, they both strip down to their underwear (the girl wears a bathing suit) and continue reading while lying side by side on the couch. After the exam Shurik and the girl get acquainted, and he ends up in her apartment. The film ends with a scene rather strange for a romantic comedy: trying to explain his feeling of *déjà vu*, Shurik invokes Wolf Messing, a famous psychic and telepathist who closely worked with the Soviet secret police before and during World War II, and advised both Stalin and Khrushchev. The novella ends with a kiss, yet the theme of mind-reading would become important for Gaidai.

The Golden Decade

By the time Gaidai started making his feature films, the permissiveness of the Khrushchev era culture gave way to the multi-level censorship of scripts and finished films of the Brezhnev era. Gaidai's move to feature-length films implied a single narrative and more reliance on dialogue. By that time Gaidai had established a reputation of a successful comedy director and managed to retain many of his signature devices and narrative features, such as long scenes of drinking, devoid of the usual Soviet moralism, and even to add some sexually suggestive scenes. The label of satire, meaningless in the case of Gaidai's oeuvres, served as a handy defense against trigger-happy censors, while the loose structure even of his feature films allowed excising scenes without serious damage to the pictures.[9]

In his feature films Gaidai's aesthetic approach remained largely unchanged: the narratives consist of a series of loosely motivated gags. But the three best films foreground and develop an emblematic figure of Russian culture: that of a tyrant. Comrade Saakhov in *Kidnapping, Caucasian Style*, the superintendent [*upravdom*] in *The Diamond Arm*, and the two Ivans (the tsar Ivan the Terrible and the superintendent) in *Ivan Vasilievich* are Gaidai's great contributions to exposing the nature of Russian/Soviet power, its arbitrariness, brutality, and disregard for both the rule of

Figure 23.3 Feudal mores: the corrupt official Comrade Saakhov is living a nightmare of "blood revenge," administered by the girl he kidnapped in *Kidnapping, Caucasian Style*, 1966.

law and individual life. The despots are comic figures but the source of laughter is very different from slapstick gags of the Three Stooges, on the one hand, and Soviet masks of Shurik and Semen Gorbunkov, on the other. It is laughter of recognition and at least a temporary release from fear and from the spell of the authoritative word.

In his memoirs, Iurii Nikulin writes that after *Operation "Y"* Gaidai decided not to film the ViNiMor trio in the central role anymore; they were becoming obsolete. The next film, *Kidnapping, Caucasian Style* had the trio simply to "animate the film" (Nikulin 2003, 499). Indeed, while most of the film's gags originate in the familiar masks, Gaidai's first feature film takes on a much more epic and audacious task: to pitch Shurik, a student collecting local folklore, not against bullies and petty criminals but against a Soviet official who de facto owns an entire region. The film's setting in "one of mountainous regions" motivates the plot of kidnapping and rescuing a girl spending her summer with a rock-climbing student group. But while the Caucasus was a safer choice for showing such "relics of the past" as "selling the bride," it also became a perfect, if unwitting, metaphor for the entire culture. Soviet critics raved about the film but emphasized that Comrade Saakhov "does not personify anybody" (Zak 1967, 83) – a coy disclaimer, which suggested that critics indeed recognized Comrade Stalin.

Ultimately, however, Saakhov and other similar figures are personifications not so much of specific historical figures but of the primordial cultural traditions. In Gaidai's films the archaic constantly erupts into the texture of the present. *Kidnapping, Caucasian Style* opens with a donkey trotting on a dusty road, while the truck would not start;[10] in *Ivan Vasilievich*, the plot literally emerges out of a sixteenth-century setting which, once the camera pulls out, turns out to be Modest Musorgskii's opera *Boris Godunov* playing on television. Time travel into the past instantly, of its own volition, extracts Ivan the Terrible. The trip to the Caucasus mutates into a trip in time, to feudalism, where a Soviet official inaugurating the modern Wedding Palace is simultaneously calculating the costs of buying a bride, according to a medieval tradition defining life in the area.

Sound in Gaidai's film has liminal status, on the border of the films' diegesis, generating its own reality. Such, for instance, is the "oriental" motif, which appears in *Kidnapping, Caucasian Style* when Saakhov sees Nina for the first time. While not explicitly diegetic, the melody anticipates Saakhov's haggling with Nina's uncle over the number of sheep to be paid as part of the dowry. The motif then develops into a series of verbal jokes, which play on the grotesque combination of two seemingly incompatible discourses: the feudal tradition of bride money, in which sheep are an equivalent of the virgin's worth, and the socialist discourses of new Soviet woman and planned economy. The uncle praises Nina's qualities as "a student, a komsomol member, an athlete, and a beauty," while Saakhov remarks that it is "shameful to demand 25 sheep when the *sovkhoz* has not yet fulfilled state quota in fleece and meat." The uncle raises the stakes, observing that Saakhov confuses "his own fleece with state fleece." The two settle on 20 sheep, a Finnish-made refrigerator, and an official commendation letter. In the next scene we see the sheep driven into the uncle's yard by the "three stooges," and the sheep's bleating echoes the original oriental sound motif.

Every comic situation has a reverse side, where the seemingly innocent, even pleasurable, everyday events threaten the hero and expose him to the manipulation of the villain. The events follow a cause-and-effect logic, which is comic and absurd on the genre level (what Dobrotvorskii (1996) called "an eccentric linking of externally logical things") but where comic exaggeration does not cancel the events' plausibility. When the hotel manager hears about Shurik's project of collecting local drinking traditions, he offers him a "toast in three copies," that is, three bottles of wine. Despite Shurik's assertions that he is a teetotaler, the manager insists that this is part of local hospitality and lures Shurik with a promise of more "research." This begins a series of comic scenes in which Shurik consumes ever-bigger portions of wine and where hospitality turns into a black hole, which sucks in the protagonist and delivers him directly to Comrade Saakhov. The scene at the police station is a small gem of cultural commentary: as the policeman reads the protocol listing Shurik's despicable actions while drunk, Saakhov, acting like a feudal lord, winks at the policeman and suggests to continue "studying toasts" with more wine. Shurik's two weaknesses – gullibility and weak alcohol tolerance – provide superficial, comic logic to the events; the deep structure is about arbitrary power, corruption, and archaic tribal relations hiding behind socialist rhetoric. When Shurik realizes that he has become an accomplice in an actual kidnapping and rushes to see the prosecutor, Saakhov sends him to another drinking party and

Figure 23.4 Iurii Nikulin in *Diamond Arm*, 1968.

from there to a mental institution where Saakhov explains to the doctors Shurik's rambling about kidnapping as *delirium tremens*.

Kidnapping, Caucasian Style ends appropriately at the border of comedy and horror in the sequence of Saakhov's punishment. Before the actual trial, the three young protagonists stage the scene of "blood revenge for sister's honor" – a fitting eye-for-eye performance belonging to the same primordial paradigm as the bride kidnapping. The collision of modernity and humor (television set, tracksuit, shooting the villain with salt in the rear) with barbarism and horror (a raven, the three young people dressed in "traditional" garb) happens as Saakhov is watching *The Swan Lake* – the Russian and Soviet claim to belonging to European civilization.

The enjoyment of slapstick originates in the distance from the comic figures who are not represented as "rounded characters" but rather as masks (King 2002, 9). Gaidai's casting of Nikulin as the positive character, Semen Gorbunkov, rather than a comic villain in *The Diamond Arm*, confused Soviet film critics who argued that, by assigning the clown to play a positive role, the director deprived the film of universal masks and the satirical spirit typical of *Kidnapping, Caucasian Style* (Kuznetsov 1969, 12). Yet Gorbunkov is the most daring mask of all – the comic mask of a Soviet citizen, and *The Diamond Arm* is a parody both of the detective genre and of the Soviet "way of life." While Gaidai's three stooges brought to the puritan Soviet screen the pleasures of alcohol, sexuality, and other forms of unruly behavior, it is Gaidai's positive heroes that are the most transgressive. Mikhail Brashinskii argues that chases and other slapstick devices were *not* the strongest aspects of Gaidai's films. "The 'real Gaidai' started when, looking closely at the social-historical circumstances, the director saw that they readily fit the laws of slapstick. [...] In the simple Soviet man Gaidai discovered the features of an ideal classical archetype" (Brashinskii 2001, 234).

Gaidai's positive hero is the Soviet viewer's perfect *alter ego*: a man who is ignorant of the rules of the world he lives in. For a good portion of every film he has no agency whatsoever; even though he has a well-defined social identity and specified occupation (a student, an engineer) things just happen to him. Gorbunkov travels abroad because his wife decided so; foreign crooks mistake him for a smuggler and put his arm in a cast loaded with gold and diamonds; once he returns home the police use him as bait to catch the smugglers who, in turn, attempt to remove the cast from the titular "diamond arm." As Prokhorov suggests, the body part hijacks the agency from the protagonist, acting in his stead (2003, 469). Gorbunkov is so positive and so Soviet that his subjectivity is objectified and shared by the collective and the authorities. He is transparent to his police handler who can read his thoughts; to his wife who speaks for him; to the housing superintendent who appears in his dream; and to the smugglers who quite correctly identify him as a "patsy." After the smugglers' failed attempt to extract diamonds with the help of a prostitute and a mickey, the wife leaves the hapless Semen. Instead of the spouse, Semen wakes up to discover a cop who, sporting the wife's apron, is cooking breakfast in Semen's apartment. In this world of cops-and-robbers, the best visual metaphor for him is the string bag [*avos'ka*], where he "hides" the gun.

By the late 1960s Gaidai had established himself as the unchallenged king of Soviet comedy and was invited to Grigorii Chukhrai's Experimental Creative Unit [Eksperimental'noe tvorcheskoe ob"edinenie, ETO] within Mosfilm. Gaidai's capacity to produce blockbusters seemed a perfect fit for the ETO which operated as a semi-commercial venture. Here Gaidai realized his dream of making an adaptation of one of the early Soviet classics, *Twelve Chairs* [*Dvenadtsat' stul'ev*], the 1928 trickster novel by Il'ia Il'f and Evgenii Petrov.[11] While the film faired better than Mikhail Shveitser's version of *The Golden Calf* [*Zolotoi telenok*, 1968], *Twelve Chairs* begins a series of Gaidai's increasingly unsuccessful films. One difficulty was the popularity of the novel – the kind of cult status that *a priori* was harmful to the film. In addition to the usual challenge of readers having their own idea about characters, Il'f and Petrov's text existed in the memory of several generations of people through verbatim quotations. And while in theory these aphoristic one-liners were exactly Gaidai's kind of dialogue, when performed on screen they turned into mere quotes. As one critic noted: "Cinema has its own gags, literature its own" (Bogomolov 1971, 51).

Another problem with the film was the casting of Archil Gomiashvili as Ostap Bender. The actor fought with the director over the meaning of the character, trying to "humanize" or psychologize him while Gaidai's concept was theatricality. The opening of the film, with the sounds of the orchestra tuning in behind the credits, and the ending – crowds of contemporary moviegoers flocking to see the premier of the film, with Ostap Bender winking from the billboard, give a taste of a very different film. Yet, unlike Mark Zakharov a few years later in his television version of *Twelve Chairs*, Gaidai stopped half way in this direction, never making the flexible and open world of the novel fresh and contemporary.

In his next film, another adaptation made at the ETO, Gaidai freed himself from the hypnosis of the text which shackled him in *Twelve Chairs*. In *Ivan Vasilievich: Back to the Future*, which is a loose adaptation of Mikhail Bulgakov's play (1934–1936; first published in 1965), two characters from the Soviet 1970s (a house superintendent and a burglar) are transported via a time machine into the sixteenth century, whereas Ivan the Terrible finds himself trapped in a Soviet apartment. While much of the humor results from the incongruence of the characters' expectations and the changed environment (e.g., Ivan the Terrible believes that he was "immured" in the elevator), an equally powerful source of effect, both comic and *horrific*, is the parallelism between the two eras and cultures. The brutal mores of medieval Russia might shock the Soviet engineer, but only in degree, not the logic of violence. The transplanted tsar suggests impaling the engineer's cheating wife and her lover; tells his host who boasts of having invented the time machine that back home he too had an inventor of a winged machine and ordered to put him on a barrel of gunpowder – "that made him really fly." Back in the sixteenth century the scribe informs the two time-travelers who, in order to save themselves, impersonate the tsar and a prince, that the only German interpreter at the court was boiled alive for being drunk at work. The fake prince's reaction is pragmatic rather than terrified ("you shouldn't be so wasteful with interpreters!"), and the shock effect is folded into the comic coda: forced to answer something in German, the superintendent produces the ultimate phrase, "Hitler kaput!"

As with their previous films, Gaidai and his fellow scriptwriters presented *Ivan Vasilievich* as a satire in order to ensure a favorable official reaction. This time, however, Goskino critics objected precisely to the satirical and parodic elements directed at the symbols of state power: Ivan the Terrible, the Kremlin and the Russian past. "Making fun [*komikovanie*] of the figure of Ivan the Terrible and his people in the Kremlin [sic!] introduces an element of mockery of Russia's history into the film" (RGALI 2944/4/1263: 16). For the early 1970s this is a remarkable objection, whether it originated in the new Russian nationalism and the search of a "usable past" beyond 1917, or in the wariness of parallels with the present. Some of these parallels emerge from the dual temporal setting, with a single location in Moscow, enhanced by the dynamic chase

Figure 23.5 Ivan the Terrible, interrogated by the Soviet police in *Ivan Vasilievich: Back to the Future*, 1973.

sequences: as the *oprichniks* pursue the fake "tsar" and "prince," the police are rushing to apprehend the real tsar who they mistake for a thief. In the script, to the standard question by the police, "Your place of residence," Ivan gives a reasonable answer: "Moscow, Kremlin." Yet this innocent line had to be changed to "palace" [*v palatakh*]: the topographical name with such symbolic weight triggered a host of dangerous associations, erasing the safe epic distance between the bloody tsar and his Soviet heirs. Other lines changed by the censors start as comic anachronisms but immediately explode into open satire. As the superintendent and the thief are about to dine in royal fashion, the camera tracks over dozens of dishes, some that long disappeared from the Russian cuisine (like pike's head stuffed with garlic), others that were deficit items in the 1970s (like black caviar). In the script the superintendent asks suspiciously, "Who is paying for this banquet?," and a servant answers "Russian people, your majesty." The last line hit too close to home and was changed to "In any case, *we* are not paying."

The film critic Iurii Bogomolov saw this erasure of the boundary between the past and the present as the focus of Gaidai's picture which he insightfully called "carnivalistic": "Time in the film is edited in a manner more radical than in the play. [...] The director made not just a satirical comedy, but an enchanted spectacle, a carnival story where everyone is in disguise – some in the garb of the future, others in the garb of the past, where everyone knows everyone else, without really recognizing them" (1973, 9). Bogomolov also draws a parallel between the thief and Ostap Bender: both are "free artists" (read: tricksters) and as such are central meaning-makers of the text. Finally, the critic observes a propos the two Ivans in the film: "Ivan the Terrible remains himself in the Soviet apartment, while the superintendent *becomes* himself when transported into the sixteenth century" (Bogomolov 1973, 9). In other words, the farcical Soviet tyrant effortlessly mutates into a sublime bloodsucking tsar of "All Russia." The nature of power has not changed – the conclusion Bogomolov stops short of making. Unlike Ivan the Terrible, however, his Soviet double wants to enjoy the power without much responsibility: he is willing to give Russian lands away to Swedes, he gets drunk and hits on a woman next to him (who is his, that is the tsar's, wife), and so on.

What keeps Gaidai's films comedic is that visual violence is conventionally farcical, while truly horrific violence is only referred to verbally. The latter, however, is ever present, always lurking as a possibility. The policeman in *The Diamond Arm* in a matter-of-fact way lectures the protagonist who serves as a bait for the smugglers that it is possible to take the precious cast off without him noticing: "A person can be drugged, knocked senseless; in short, become an unconscious body and, lastly, a corpse."

Gaidai captures the porosity of the boundary between comedy and horror with his playful ambiguities in his films' beginnings and "happy ends." If the opening sequence sets the mood and signals the film's modality, Gaidai's films send a mixed message. On the one hand, music and visual elements indicate comic modality: the crooked and uneven typeface, cheerful bright colors, etc. On the other, all of the films start with an eclectic and complex soundtrack: the eerie sound effects in *Operation Y*, followed by a scream, a shot, a jazz piece, and so on. Likewise, *Ivan Vasilievich* begins with Shurik waking up, looking at something off-screen and screaming in horror. While this comic incongruity is part of the genre, the darker notes are there.

The "happy end" in all three films involves what might be considered an assertion of privacy: having vanquished the villains, the hero is re-united with his beloved (*Kidnapping, Caucasian Style*), his family (*Diamond Arm*), or his wife (*Ivan Vasilievich*). This moment of private happiness, however, is scratched in the first one (Shurik remains with his donkey); in *Diamond Arm* Gorbunkov falls out of a trunk of an airborne car in one scene, survives, and emerges in the last sequence on crutches. The last scene is a tableau, with Gorbunkov's super blond, Aryan-looking family in a car under a sunny sky, modeled on a Stalinist "great style" painting. Finally, the ending of *Ivan Vasilievich* reveals the entire narrative of time travel and the unfaithful wife to be the hero's dream; the film switches from color to black-and-while, familiar and modest 1970s. But the portal is not shut close, and the double vision (and the double diegesis) persist. As in the dream, the superintendent and his wife harass the engineer, and as before, the black cat can at any moment morph into the Monomakh's Cap.

The Decline and the Second Life

With his instinct for cultural tropes, Gaidai was also an ideal indicator of their changes. His films from the mid-1970s to early-1980s bear all the signs of stagnation, despite the seeming continuity with his earlier work. Some of these films are literary adaptations (Mikhail Zoshchenko, Nikolai Gogol'), while others use a familiar mix of slapstick and satire. Yet none of the films could match the success of Gaidai's best films. As Dobrotvorskii quite rightly points out, his films of the 1970s and 1980s are "just Soviet comedies." The satirical element and the original literary dialogue define the diegesis and overwhelm Gaidai's strongest features, visual humor and the doubling of the film narrative, which gave contemporary viewers a point of pleasurable recognition. Instead, in It Can't Be [*Ne mozhet byt'*, 1975], what bifurcates is the texture of the film itself: Zoshchenko's laughter here exists separately from Gaidai's laughter (Zolotusskii 1976, 5), the two never fusing into an organic whole. Gaidai's eccentric style also seems too jarring for the verbal nuances of Zoshchenko's humor.

Incognito from St Petersburg [*Inkognito iz Peterburga*, 1979], an adaptation of Nikolai Gogol''s famous satire of provincial bureaucracy, marks the low point in Gaidai's career, despite the star-studded cast. The film is static and theatrical in a bad way, only occasionally animated by the director's signature "silent cinema" sequences, such as the police chasing pigs through the street in an attempt to make the town more presentable, or by gags when the Russian imperial eagle on a seal suddenly crows like a rooster. Those moments, however, are rare, and the film drags out its full delivery of Gogol''s text over a series of tableaux.

The cultural freeze of the 1970s affected Gaidai where he previously excelled the most: in seeing the comic sides of Russia's struggles with modernization. On the one hand, he chose to adapt literary works, which were focused on exactly this theme. On the other, the films never connect the literary originals to contemporary Russian culture, and thus remain thorough adaptations and nothing more. Unlike the carnivalistic worlds of *Kidnapping, Caucasian Style* and *Ivan Vasilievich*, *It Can't Be* and *Incognito from St Petersburg* do not venture beyond their original cultural context – a fact which is confirmed by the use of still frames as background for the credits: *It Can't Be* features images of issues of the satirical magazine *Krokodil* from the 1920s and 1930s as transitions between shots and *Incognito from St Petersburg* – engravings of famous sites of St Petersburg. In this respect, Gaidai's film *Borrowing Matchsticks* [*Za spichkami*, 1980], a Soviet-Finnish comedy about the adventures of several not-too-bright villagers, while not entirely successful, offers a peculiar cultural commentary on Russia's identity. The film both mocks and celebrates premodern culture transposed to Finland, a former province of the Russian empire. Here Gaidai remains true to himself, focusing on people's animalistic drives, for example, connecting marriage with discussions of cattle and reveling in a favorite Russian pastime of drinking and steam bathing.

In *Sportloto-82* (1982) Gaidai tried to revive his earlier formula: San Sanych, an idealistic young man, travels to a Crimean resort and becomes involved in a series of adventures involving a winning lottery ticket. Gaidai uses some of his tested devices: contemporary cultural references (e.g., the entire country is reading detective novels of Genian Zelenyi – a parody of Iulian Semenov); the theme of unconscious behavior (the protagonist Kostia consumes tons of food without noticing it, because he is engrossed by reading); and several successful gags that tether on the boundary of the permissible (e.g., chickens lay eggs with a Soviet quality label on them). Even though the film's attendance was quite high – 55 million viewers in 1982 – it was a far cry from Gaidai's best pictures (Segida and Zemlianukhin 1996). At least part of the reason was the choice of the "villain," a black marketeer who brings oranges from Moscow to resell them at a profit. Unlike epic despots like Saakhov and Ivan the Terrible and their lesser doubles like the *upravdom*, San Sanych is a creature from the late socialist campaign against individual entrepreneurship and, as such, a figure from an officially approved satire.

Likewise, the last pre-perestroika film *Danger, High Voltage!* [*Opasno dlia zhizni*, 1985] relies entirely on official Soviet tropes. The protagonist with the suggestive name, Spartak Molodtsov [Spartacus the Good Boy, played by Leonid Kuravlev] is a responsible person who, on his way to work, sees a loose high voltage wire and decides to wait for the repairman and warn people about the danger. While some of the gags are reminiscent of the "Gaidai of old" (e.g., corruption and bureaucracy at a Soviet institution is metonymically represented via a circulation of chocolate bars: in order to speed up their cases, clients buy chocolate bars at a cafeteria and bribe the secretary, who then returns the bars to the cafeteria), the pace of the film is lethargic and bland dialogue replaces Gaidai's visual humor. Perhaps the most telling feature of the film is that its plot rotates around the protagonist literally fixed in space, next to the loose wire – a fitting metaphor for Soviet culture frozen in time.

Gaidai's last two films, *Private Detective, or Operation "Cooperation"* [*Chastnyi detektiv, ili operatsiia "Kooperatsiia,"* 1989] and *There's Good Weather on Deribasovskaya Street, It's Again Raining on Brighton Beach* [*Na Deribasovskoi khoroshaia pogoda, na Braiton Bich opiat' idut dozhdi*, 1992] came out in a much freer cultural environment, when the carnivalization of Soviet tropes had become acceptable. In a way, cinema finally – 25 years later – caught up with Gaidai, just as the director tried to reinvent himself within the new spiral of Russian modernization, when cultural norms again became fluid. Both films feature a "pure soul" for the new times, played in both films by Dmitrii Kharat'ian. In *Private Detective* he plays a private detective, in *There's Good Weather on Deribasovskaya...* – an idealistic KGB agent. While the films were moderately successful, they had to compete with a flood of imported film and television products. The plot of *Private Detective* consists of a chain of perestroika clichés: small businesses, pay toilets, prostitutes, racketeers, corruption, informal youth organizations, and the rest. Nevertheless, Gaidai, with his characteristic straight face of a clown, questions exactly what many perestroika films celebrate as a transition to freedom, namely the superficial nature of Russia's new spiral of modernization: one of the officials declares that "[t]he foundation of bourgeois democracy are private detectives; the foundation of our democracy are exclusively the police and security forces." Gaidai captures perfectly the perennial Russian tradition of imitating change, modernizing without changing anything but the very surface.

After a long period of decline, Gaidai's last film again offers moments of great insight that originate yet again in the paradoxes of Russia's evolution. *There's Good Weather on Deribasovskaya…* tells of a joint KGB-CIA operation to combat the Russian mafia in New York. One of the scenes takes place in a theater, where a festively dressed audience enjoys a classical ballet. When the announcement is made ordering all KGB agents to report to the headquarters, half of the audience, both men and women, get up and leave, followed by members of the orchestra and the lead ballet dancer who drops his partner and marches to the exit. As KGB agent Fedor Sokolov and CIA agent Mary Star work to capture the mafia boss "Artist" (whose major talent is "reincarnation" as tyrants, from Lenin to Peter the Great to Saddam Hussein) they use help of an old Jewish man, Monia. Monia was a coder during the Great Patriotic War; now living in a tent in Brighton Beach he continues to receive coded messages from Moscow.

Gaidai died in Moscow in 1993 of pulmonary embolism, at a time when his films were just beginning their second life in popular culture: VHS releases, repeated television runs, characters and scenes used in commercials, and most recently, remakes, such as the 2014 release of Maksim Voronkov's *Kidnapping, Caucasian Style 2* [*Kavkazskaia plennitsa-2*], starring the famous standup comedian Gennadii Khazanov in the role of Comrade Saakhov. Needless to say, neither Gaidai nor his widow (and long-term actress) Nina Grebeshkova benefited much from royalties. While Gaidai's heirs do not collect high revenues from his film releases his fate as the film author is much better than that of many of his contemporaries, such as Andrei Tarkovskii or Sergei Bondarchuk. Few Russians today remember these famous auteurs of the 1960s but everyone remembers Gaidai. Like his two favorite filmmakers, Chaplin and Keaton, Gaidai was celebrated as the king of lowbrow comedy at the height of his career and became the focus of highbrow research as the ultimate film auteur after his death.

Notes

1 Gaidai's other high grossing films include *Ivan Vasilievich* – 61 million spectators; *Sportloto-82* – 55 million spectators; and *It Can't Be* – 47 million spectators.
2 In 1980 three films by other directors became blockbusters, marking simultaneously the zenith and the precipitous decline of Soviet film attendance: Boris Durov's *Pirates*

of the Twentieth Century [Piraty XX veka]; Vladimir Men'shov's Moscow Does Not Believe in Tears [Moskva slezam ne verit] and Aleksandr Mitta's The Crew [Ekipazh] hit the 87.6, 84.4 and 71 million marks respectively; see Segida and Zemlianukhin (1996).

3   The only exceptions were the films which Gaidai made at Grigorii Chukhrai's Experimental Creative Unit (ETO) which, until its closure in 1976, operated as a semi-commercial enterprise within Mosfilm.

4   Criticism in post-Soviet Russia remains equally scarce and produced little scholarly analysis of Gaidai's comedies. The best publications are articles (Dobrotvorskii 1996; Margolit 2013; Brashinskii 2001; Tsymbal 2003); the only book publication dates from 2002 (Pupsheva, Ivanov, and Tsukerman), but this, as well as the book about the trio ViNiMor (Lainer 2001), are popular readings rather than scholarly publications.

5   In fact, as Prokhorov reminds us, Gaidai's competitor for the title of the "king of Soviet comedy," El'dar Riazanov, made an attempt to create his own eccentric comedy and outperform Gaidai with gags and stunts in his The Unbelievable Adventures of Italians in Russia [Neveroiatnye prikliucheniia ital'iantsev v Rossii, 1973], a late Soviet remake of Lev Kuleshov's The Extraordinary Adventures of Mr West in the Land of Bolsheviks [Neobychainye prikliucheniia mistera Vesta v strane bol'shevikov, 1924]. Riazanov's comedy, however, did not come even close to Gaidai's spectacles, not the least because irreverent humor and slapstick disappear when characters arrive to Moscow (Prokhorov 2003, 471).

6   In Diamond Arm, censors demanded to shorten the episode at the seashore, where the Count tries various means to knock Gorbunkov senseless. The scene is pure slapstick, and Gaidai refused to sacrifice it. Instead, the director asked the composer Aleksandr Zatsepin to write dynamic music to accompany the scene. The music "sped up" the scene, and at the next screening the officials praised Gaidai for cutting it (Pupsheva, Ivanov, and Tsukerman 2002, 245–6).

7   Dobrotvorskii (1996) suggests that Gaidai's cinematic aesthetics is analogous to Hitchcock's: the latter made thrillers and horror films which, by their very calculated effect, have the potential to produce laughter; the former made comedies where horror lurked through the uncontrollable laughter.

8   O. Henry was one of only few American authors approved in the USSR. In early post-Stalin culture the author's short stories, with their humanist message and ironic twists, became popular again.

9   As is well documented, Gaidai often strategically planted entire scenes as red herrings. For example, The Diamond Arm almost lost one of its gems: the censors demanded to "soften" the figure of the upravdom. Instead, Gaidai requested the addition of a final sequence: an atomic explosion. "We live in a dangerous world," stated the director in all seriousness in his request. Goskino officials were quite taken aback by the prospect of ending an eccentric comedy on such a global scale and were relieved when Gaidai heeded their warnings and omitted the provocative ending. The rest of the film remained largely unchanged (Pupsheva, Ivanov, and Tsukerman 2002, 252–253).

10 The donkey-car coupling appears in several films: in Gentlemen of Fortune [Dzhentel'meny udachi, Aleksandr Seryi, 1971], for example, one of the characters ends up in jail for diluting automobile fuel with donkey urine.

11 For a discussion of the trickster plot in the novel see Lipovetsky (2010).

References

"Admin." 2015. "Brilliantovaia ruka: kak snimali liubimyi fil'm" [Diamond Arm: How the Favorite Film Got Shot]. *Tainy i zagadki istorii* [Secrets and Riddles of History] January 30, http://tayni.info/68092/ (accessed April 1, 2015).

Bloch, Howard R. 1986. *The Scandal of the Fabliaux*. Chicago: University of Chicago Press.

Bogomolov, Iurii. 1971. "Ravnenie na rampu" [Eyes to the Stage]. *Iskusstvo kino* [Art of Cinema] 9: 47–56.

Bogomolov, Iurii. 1973. "Karnaval'nyi den'" [Carnival Day]. *Sovetskii ekran* [Soviet Screen] 14: 8–9.

Brashinskii, Mikhail. 2001. "Leonid Gaidai." *Noveishaia istoriia otechestvennogo kino, 1986–2000* [New History of Domestic Cinema 1986–2000], vol. 1, edited by Liubov' Arkus. 233–234. St Petersburg: Seans.

Dobrotvorskii, Sergei. 1996. "I zadacha pri nem" [He has a Task]. *Iskusstvo kino* [Art of Cinema] 9; republished in *Seans* [Séance] January 30, 2008, http://seance.ru/blog/gayday/ (accessed February 14, 2015).

Foucault, Michel. 1997. "Of Other Spaces: Utopias and Heterotopias." *Rethinking Architecture: A Reader in Cultural Theory*, edited by Neil Leach, 350–356. London and New York: Routledge.

King, Geoff. 2002. *Film Comedy*. London: Wallflower Press.

Kudriavtsev, Sergei. 1998. *Svoe kino* [My Cinema]. Moscow: Dubl'-D.

Kuznetsov, M. 1969. "Komediia neozhidannostei: chto dal'she?" [Comedy of Surprises: What Next?]. *Sovetskii ekran* [Soviet Screen] 10: 10–12.

Lainer, Lev. 2001. *Veselaia troitsa: Vitsyn, Morgunov, Nikulin* [A Happy Troika: Vitsyn, Morgunov, Nikulin]. Moscow: Tsentrpoligraf.

Lipovetsky, Mark. 2010. *Charms of the Cynical Reason: Trickster in Soviet and Post-Soviet Culture*, Brighton, MA: Academic Studies Press.

Margolit, Evgenii. 2013. "Uzkii krug bytovykh problem" [A Narrow Circle of Everyday Problems]. *Seans* [Séance] January 30, http://seance.ru/blog/gayday-90/ (accessed July 18, 2014).

Milić, Saša. 2004. "Sight Gags and Satire in the Soviet Thaw: *Operation Y and Other Shurik's Adventures*. *Senses of Cinema* 33 (October), http://sensesofcinema.com/2004/33/operation_y/ (accessed July 18, 2014).

Nikulin, Iurii. 2003. *Pochti ser'ezno…* [Almost Seriously…]. Moscow: Vagrius.

Prokhorov, Aleksandr. 2003. "Cinema of Attractions versus Narrative Cinema: Leonid Gaidai's Comedies and El'dar Riazanov's Satires of the 1960s." *Slavic Review* 62.3: 455–472.

Pupsheva, Mariia, Valerii Ivanov, and Vladimir Tsukerman. 2002. *Gaidai Sovetskogo Soiuza* [The Gaidai of the Soviet Union]. Moscow: Eksmo.

Roth-Ey, Kristin. 2011. *Moscow Prime Time: How the Soviet Union Built the Media Empire That Lost the Cultural Cold War*. Durham: Cornell University Press.

Segida, Miroslava and Sergei Zemlianukhin. 1996. *Domashniaia sinemateka: otechestvennoe kino 1918–1996* [Home Cinematheque: Domestic Cinema 1918–1996]. Moscow: Dubl' D.

Tsymbal, Evgenii. 2003. "Ot smeshnogo do velikogo. Vospominaniia o Leonide Gaidae" [From Funny to Great: Recollections about Leonid Gaidai]. *Iskusstvo kino* [Art of Cinema] 10, http://kinoart.ru/archive/2003/10/n10-article20 (accessed July 18, 2014).

Zak, M. 1967. "Oboidemsia bez tamady" [We'll do Without a Toastmaster]. *Iskusstvo kino* [Art of Cinema] 7: 82–85.

Zolotusskii, Igor'. 1976. "Smekh Zoshchenko i smekh Gaidaia" [Zoshchenko's and Gaidai's Laughter]. *Sovetskii ekran* [Soviet Screen]. 1: 4–5.

Zorkaia, Neia. n.d. "Vos'midesiatye: perelom. Konets kino SSSR. Trudnye marshruty fil'ma" [The 1980s: A Turning Point. End of Soviet Cinema. Hard Paths for Film]. *Slovo* [Word], http://www.portal-slovo.ru/art/38910.php (accessed July 18, 2014).

24

Aleksei Gherman: The Last Soviet Auteur

Anthony Anemone

Aleksei Gherman's reputation stands on five films: *Trial on the Road* [*Proverka na dorogakh*, 1971; released 1986], *Twenty Days without War* [*Dvadtsat' dnei bez voiny*, 1976], *My Friend, Ivan Lapshin* [*Moi drug Ivan Lapshin*, 1981; released 1984], *Khrustalyov, My Car!* [*Khrustalev, mashinu!*, 1998] and *Hard to Be a God* [*Trudno byt' bogom*, 2013]. In all his films, Gherman was engaged in a double project: to represent twentieth-century Russian history impartially, without the myths, conventions, and ideological assumptions that distorted official Soviet versions, and to create a new cinematic language by remaking the stylistic and narrative techniques of Russian cinema. Long a favorite of the Russian cultural elite, Gherman's career was hobbled by Soviet censorship that rejected his independence, his revisionist interpretation of the past, and his inventive cinematic language. Hence, his films were delayed, shelved, or simply rarely shown in Soviet cinemas. His struggles with a benighted cultural and political establishment provide a vivid commentary on the fate of cinema in Russia from the 1960s to the present.

Gherman's stylistic experiments, perfectionism, and refusal to compromise either with Soviet censorship or the demands of the mass audience resulted in his completing a mere handful of films, while also earning him an almost legendary status among the Russian cultural elite. They have also led to inevitable comparisons with Andrei Tarkovskii. While the films of both directors were strongly influenced by avant-garde European cinema of the 1950s and 1960s, especially the great Swedish director Ingmar Bergman, there are significant differences as well. For if Tarkovskii's films use Russia to explore universal philosophical, psychological, and artistic issues, the central issue of Gherman's films has always been Soviet history, and specifically the history of Stalinism, that is, the history of his beloved father's generation and the period of his own youth. Perhaps even more so than Tarkovskii, Gherman assumes an audience open to unconventional narrative and stylistic

A Companion to Russian Cinema, First Edition. Edited by Birgit Beumers.
© 2016 John Wiley & Sons, Inc. Published 2016 by John Wiley & Sons, Inc.

techniques and with an insider's knowledge of Soviet history, culture, and life. This latter point has proven an especially serious stumbling block with international audiences. His method is to focus on aspects of the Soviet past either omitted (e.g., the wartime treatment of Soviet POWs in *Trial* and the hardships of the civilian population in *Twenty Days*) or falsified (e.g., the human cost of the utopian impulse to build a new society in *Lapshin* and *Khrustalyov*) in the official versions of the Soviet past. While rejecting the patriotic, ideological, and propagandistic myths of Soviet history, Gherman's films reflect the director's fanatical insistence on getting the look, sound, and "feel" of the past exactly right. By rejecting the narrative, ideological, and stylistic conventions of Soviet and post-Soviet cinema, Gherman has created his own cinematic language. The price of this achievement, paid also by such giants of the cinema as Eisenstein and Tarkovskii, was that his films received neither wide distribution nor popularity among a mass audience. The future will tell whether Gherman's films turn out to be the beginning of a new cinematic culture in post-Soviet Russia or the brilliant conclusion to Soviet cinema.

Born into the cultural elite of Stalinist Leningrad on July 10, 1938, the future director was the first son of Iurii Pavlovich Gherman (1910–1967), a popular and successful writer, and Tat'iana Aleksandrovna Rittenberg (1904–1995). When Aleksei was just an infant, the family moved to Arkhangelsk and later to Poliarnoe, near Murmansk, where his father was billeted as a TASS war correspondent covering the Northern Fleet. At the conclusion of the war, they moved back to Leningrad and settled into a large apartment on the Moika Canal, a few steps from Palace Square and the Hermitage, where Aleksei was raised in a large, educated, successful, and loving extended family. Family friends included such luminaries of Russian literature and cinema as Evgenii Shvarts, Konstantin Simonov, Anna Akhmatova, Iosif Kheifits, Grigorii Kozintsev, Nikolai Cherkasov, as well as high ranking military and militia officers. As befitted a member of the Stalinist elite, his father had a chauffeur-driven car, servants, and a dacha at Komarova, a leafy suburban retreat reserved for writers and intellectual outside Leningrad (Dolin 2011).

Iurii Gherman specialized in stories about the lives and adventures of *chekisty*, police investigators, border guards, doctors, partisans, and other stalwarts of official Stalinist culture.[1] Many of his works were based on friends and acquaintances, like the eponymous hero of the story "Our Friend Ivan Bodunov" (Gherman 1964), a detective and the head of the Criminal Investigative Division of Leningrad, who became one of the models for *My Friend Ivan Lapshin* (Dolin 2011, 193–194). The idea of writing about the Secret Police, the *Cheka*, was, according to family legend, suggested by none other than Maksim Gorkii, who admired Gherman's early writings and suggested that he write a book about Felix Dzerzhinskii, the founder of the Soviet Secret Police (Dolin 2011, 16–17). In the spirit of Stalinist literature, Iurii Gherman's cops and spies not only bring criminals and counter-revolutionaries to justice but rehabilitate them by teaching them the value of honest labor. He also became an accomplished writer of scripts for the cinema, the author, or co-author, of 13 scripts for some of the most important directors of

Figure 24.1 Aleksei Gherman.

the time, including Sergei Gerasimov, Grigorii Kozintsev, and Iosif Kheifits. Mixing love, duty, adventure, and melodrama, and told with the proper ideological orientation, Gherman's novels, stories, and screenplays contributed to establishing the parameters of emerging Socialist Realism in both literature and the cinema. For his services, Gherman was richly rewarded with several state prizes, including a Stalin Prize in 1947 for his screenplay for *Pirogov*, Kozintsev's exemplary Stalinist biopic of the great nineteenth-century Russian surgeon. Yet despite his official standing in the Stalinist elite, Iurii Gherman understood the true horrors of Stalinism. Memories of stories told by and to his father by friends, relatives, writers, policemen, and acquaintances who had returned from the Gulag remained the wellspring of inspiration and ideas for all of his son's movies.

While most of the leading Russian film directors of his generation studied at the All-Russian Institute of Cinematography (VGIK) in Moscow, Aleksei Gherman attended instead the Leningrad State Institute of Theater, Music and Cinema (LGITMiK) from 1955 to 1960, where he majored in theatre, his first love. Younger, more independent, and more connected to the Leningrad cultural elite than his fellow students, Gherman earned a reputation as a talented trouble-maker, yet he graduated with top honors. While still an undergraduate, Gherman was hired as an assistant by Iosif Kheifets, then directing *My Dear Man* [*Dorogoi moi chelovek*,

1958], based on Iurii Gherman's stories. After graduation, he took a position as an assistant to Georgii Tovstonogov, the legendary artistic director of Leningrad's most important theater, the Bolshoi Dramatic Theater (BDT), and a close friend of his father. For the next several years, he worked closely with Tovstonogov, although he also had the opportunity to direct several plays in various provincial theaters. Although his future in the theater seemed assured, Gherman bristled working in the shadow of an established star like Tovstonogov and, when the opportunity arose, he abandoned the theater and his mentor for the cinema, where, once again, his father's connections would prove invaluable (Dolin 2011, 69–96).

Already an experienced theater director, Aleksei studied directing with the eminent film director and pedagogue Grigorii Kozintsev, another family friend, and he quickly adapted to the new medium: within a year he had made his professional debut as assistant director on Vladimir Vengerov's film *Workers Settlement* [*Rabochii poselok*, 1965], based on a story by Vera Panova. Like William Wyler's 1946 Academy Award winning *The Best Years of Our Lives*, *Workers Settlement* tells the story of a disabled veteran's troubled adjustment to peacetime. Blinded in the war and feeling unable to contribute to the reconstruction of his town, heavily destroyed during the war, Oleg (Oleg Borisov) plays the guitar for handouts and spends all his money on alcohol. When his wife takes their son and leaves him, he hits rock bottom. In the end, he is saved by a recently returned army buddy who convinces him that, despite his blindness, he can still contribute to society and finds him a job at the local factory. Notwithstanding the unrealistic positive hero who helps Oleg rediscover his self-respect and find his place in Soviet society, *Workers Settlement* is remarkably honest in showing life in a provincial town devastated by the war: men reduced to alcoholism, women stretched to the breaking point, and overbearing all-powerful bureaucrats. Visually, the film is noteworthy for its luminous black-and-white photography, which won the award for best cinematography at the All-Soviet Film Festival in Kiev in 1966, and for another of the trademarks of Gherman's style: costume and production design that convincingly conveys the past with remarkable authenticity. Gherman's reputation soared with the film's success, allowing him to turn down offers to collaborate with Kozintsev and Kheifets in order to direct his own film (Dolin 2011, 96–104).

He began collaborating with his father on a screenplay based on the latter's 1965 story, *Operation "Happy New Year"* [*Operatsiia "S novym godom"*] but as the cancer that would eventually kill his father worsened, Gherman abandoned the project to collaborate with another experienced film director, Grigorii Aronov, in directing an adaptation of a 1927 story by Boris Lavrenev (Lavrenev 1963).[2] Set in St Petersburg during the Red Terror, *The Seventh Satellite* [*Sed'moi sputnik*, 1967] tells the story of General Adamov, a former professor of military law, who, along with other Tsarist government and military officers is being held hostage by the *Cheka* in the wake of the attempted assassination of Lenin on August 30, 1918. While most of the hostages are convinced that the "rightful" government would eventually return to power, Adamov (the first man!) feels that, although personally guilty of nothing, ultimate justice may indeed be on the side of the Revolution. During the investigation of his case, it comes to light that, while serving as a military prosecutor in 1905, he released two accused revolutionaries for lack of evidence. Although he considered this simply doing his duty, Adamov is unexpectedly released by the revolutionary *troika* and allowed to return home. While he was being held hostage, however, several workers' families have been installed in his home which has been turned into a communal apartment, and his personal possessions sold. After a day and night spent looking for help from friends terrified of giving shelter to someone just released from prison, he has no choice but to return to the prison, where the warden gives him work laundering the prisoners' and guards' clothing and a place to sleep. When a high-ranking Bolshevik comes to the prison looking for volunteers to fight against the attacking White army of General Yudenich, Adamov joins the Reds as a military lawyer. Eventually he is captured by the Whites and, when he refuses to join them in fighting the Bolsheviks, executed.

While the fate of "former people" was a central theme of much Russian literature of the 1920s and early 1930s, revisiting the history of the Revolution in the late 1960s, after the end of Khrushchev's Thaw, was fraught with difficulty. At the same time that Aronov and Gherman were working on Lavrenev's story, another young director was adapting Vasilii Grossman's story about the Civil War "In the Town of Berdichev"[3]: but while *The Seventh Satellite* was released without any controversy, Aleksandr Askol'dov's *Commissar* (1967; released 1988) was instantly banned, the director expelled from the Communist Party and fired from the film studio, and his promising career as a movie director ended almost before it began.[4] In a 1986 interview, Gherman suggested that while the minders of Soviet cinema feared the individual talent visible in every frame of Askoldov's first and only film, *The Seventh Satellite* was released without problem precisely because it was a conventional and mediocre film (Christie 1989, 50–51). Gherman's dismissal of *The Seventh Satellite* is surely one reason why the movie is rarely seen and remains underrated by both viewers and critics.[5]

Unlike *Workers Settlement*, *The Seventh Satellite* shows distinct signs of being directed by two, very different cinematic sensibilities. The first part of the film, Aronov's contribution, confined mostly to the palace interior where the hostages are being held, is dramatic but in conventionally theatrical ways: the characters sit around and discuss the meaning of the Revolution, the existence of God and other such "Russian" topics. The characters are clichés from Soviet culture: the Bolsheviks are brusque but decent; the military officers brave but cold and arrogant; the former Tsarist politicians are pompous and self-deluded; the professional criminal accepts his fate without complaint. A very different cinematic style becomes apparent as soon as Adamov returns "home" from prison and the film moves beyond the claustrophobic interiors of the palace where the hostages are being held. Gherman's signature set design is apparent in the detailed and authentic recreation of a Soviet communal apartment [*kommunalka*] in the process of being created out of

Adamov's bourgeois home. And while the suspicious, hostile, and legalistically absurd jargon spoken in the communal apartment is shocking by contrast to the elegant and polite literary Russian spoken by the hostages, it also points towards the brilliant colloquial language spoken by the characters of Gherman's mature films.[6] In the spirit of much of the best literary treatments of the Revolution in the 1920s, Gherman does not shy away from its tragic dimensions: by refusing to demonize either the newly settled workers' families or the dispossessed former owner, he conveys the human cost of the new world's destruction of the old. The film is ripe for a critical reevaluation.

The release of *The Seventh Satellite* in 1967 marked not only the last time Gherman would collaborate with an older, more established director but also the end of his brief "honeymoon" with Soviet censorship: for the next 20 years, his films would be endlessly discussed, criticized, delayed, and shelved. Following the death of his father, Gherman turned to a young scriptwriter, Eduard Volodarskii, to complete an adaptation of his father's 1964 story *Operation "Happy New Year"* about partisans in the early days of World War II. Now entitled *Trial on the Road*, the film was banned upon completion in 1971 and not shown publicly for 15 years. Once shown, however, the film became an overnight sensation[7] and one of the defining moments of Gorbachev's new policy of *glasnost'* in the arts, instantly turning Gherman into the most famous Russian director of his generation.

Like the story on which it is nominally based,[8] the movie takes place in 1942, somewhere in the "bloodlands" of the Eastern Soviet Union, where a partisan detachment is engaged in a brutal struggle with the occupying Germans. A former Red Army sergeant, Aleksandr Lazarev (played with tragic understatement by Vladimir Zamanskii),[9] in the uniform of a Wehrmacht soldier, surrenders to the partisans. Although the partisans see him as a traitor who deserves to be killed, as he tells his story, we gradually come to see him as a quintessential victim of history. Captured, along with thousands of other Soviet soldiers, by the Germans in the first days of the war, he was, as he admits, "broken" in a POW camp. When it became clear that collaborating with the Germans was the only way to survive, he reluctantly agreed, but, deeply troubled by his betrayal of the motherland, surrendered to the partisans at the first opportunity. Despite the hostility and suspicion of the detachment's fanatical political officer Major Petushkov (the great Anatolii Solonitsyn), the partisan commander Ivan Lokotkov (Rolan Bykov in one of his greatest performances) devises a "test" for Lazarev: to prove his loyalty, he must kill several German soldiers at a makeshift roadblock. After he passes the test, he is sent with several other partisans on a mission to hijack a German provision train. Thanks to Lazarev the operation succeeds but he is killed in the action. The movie ends with a scene of victorious Russian soldiers on their way to Berlin in the last days of the war.

As would be the case with most of Gherman's films, *Trial on the Road* was ahead of its time and caused immediate consternation among the ideological watchdogs of Soviet cinema (Graham 2012, 182). Despite very positive responses from such leading lights of Soviet literature, theater, and cinema as Simonov, Kozintsev, Gerasimov, Tovstonogov, and Kheifits (Lipkov 1987, 208; Dolin 2011, 148), the administration of Goskino opposed the release of a film which, in the words of one bureaucrat was "unique in that it makes every possible mistake a war movie can possibly make."[10] But if Gherman's decision to make a movie about a Russian soldier and former POW who had joined the German army before returning to the Soviet side was a daring and risky move for 1971, turning "Former Red Army Sergeant Lazarev" into a sympathetic hero and tragic victim of history truly incensed the studio administrators. Even worse was Gherman's portrayal of Major Petushkov's fanatical hatred of the Germans as more of a threat to Soviet soldiers than the Nazis. The conflict between Petushkov and Lokotkov comes to a head when the latter refuses to detonate a bridge because doing so would also kill hundreds of Russian POWs who at that time would be passing under the bridge, while Petushkov rages that war must be waged without regard for the casualties.[11] By focusing on conflicts within the partisan detachment, the critics argued, Gherman had "falsified" the war effort by relegating the struggle with the Germans to the sidelines.

In fact, the critics were not far from the truth. Gherman's focus on conflict, weakness, treachery, and error in the partisan theater, and especially his view of the characters as tragic victims of forces beyond their control,[12] were profoundly subversive to the officially sponsored myth of the Great Patriotic War canonized in innumerable books, movies, and political speeches. According to the official version of the war, the fascists were defeated as a result of the heroic struggle of all the Soviet people united under the leadership of Stalin. But by showing how actions by the partisans led to Nazi reprisals against the civilian population, Gherman implied that, from the point of view of the peasants, there was little real difference between the Soviets and the Nazis: they wanted nothing to do with either. Indeed, the film is extremely critical of the Soviet conduct of the war: the lack of concern for peasants caught between the two armies, the gross incompetence that resulted in the destruction of entire Soviet armies in the first months of the war, the profligate waste of untold numbers of ordinary Soviet soldiers for the slightest tactical advantage, and, especially, the harsh treatment of soldiers taken prisoner by the Germans.[13] More subtle, and perhaps even more dangerous, was the film's implicit argument that the German occupation would have been impossible without the active support of innumerable Soviet collaborators.

Gherman's directorial debut was both his most conventional film and the easiest for audiences to "read." Appreciably more than his later movies, *Trial on the Road* relies on the conventional elements of plot exposition, narrative development, and psychological realism, while the themes of the movie emerge directly out of actions, situational conflicts, and conversations between characters. While Gherman avoids the usual patriotic and ideological clichés of most Soviet war movies, the film is, on occasion, sentimental and manipulative, for example, in the doomed (and completely predictable) relationship between the scout Solomin and the partisan Inga.[14] At the same time, the elements of Gherman's mature style are already visible: the initial voice-over, the brilliant high-contrast black-and-white cinematography, the long takes, the tracking hand-held camera, the overlapping conversations, vivid colloquial Russian spoken by the characters, the use of both professional and non-professionals actors, and the fanatically detailed reconstruction and documentary-like recreation of the historical past. In *Trial on the Road*, Gherman begins the reexamination and "deconstruction" of the official Soviet version of the past which will be the central theme of all his movies.

Thanks to the intercession of influential members of the Soviet cultural elite who were also friends of his recently deceased father, Gherman's career did not immediately suffer when *Trial on the Road* was banned. If the argument made by some of his supporters that the problem was the script and not the director, was, on its face, implausible, the possibility of "reeducating" the talented son of Iurii Gherman in the spirit of Soviet values was a clear priority of the Lenfilm administration (Dolin 2011, 150–152). Konstantin Simonov, a close family friend and leading Soviet writer, offered to work with Gherman on adapting Simonov's story "Twenty Days without War" for his next film (Lipkov 1987, 209). Gherman and his co-writer and wife Svetlana Karmalita,[15] did prodigious research in order to reproduce the look and feel of wartime Tashkent. They supplemented Simonov's story with his diary entries, studied newsreels and photo-archives, and scouted locations tirelessly in search of neighborhoods that still retained the look of the 1940s (Lipkov 1987, 209–210). Adding to the film's authenticity was Gherman's insistence that the long introductory sequence be filmed in an old unheated train (Dolin 2011, 160–162). The result was that, rather than simply an adaptation of Simonov's story, the movie became a portrait of Russian life on the home front at the midpoint of the war.

From the very beginning, the production was a constant struggle as Lenfilm demanded changes in the script and the cast: were it not for Simonov's authority and willingness to intercede for the director, the film would never have got off the ground. Particularly upset with Gherman's choice of the Soviet Union's most famous clown, Iurii Nikulin, to play the central role of the war correspondent Lopatin, the studio demanded a more suitably heroic actor (Dolin 2011, 155–156). Thanks largely to Gherman's obstinate perfectionism, the shooting itself turned into a marathon: at a time when a typical Soviet movie with a running time of approximately 90 minutes would normally be filmed in 16–18 days of shooting, Gherman used 316 shooting days spread out over two years (Condee 2009, 194–195). When the film was finally finished, studio officials were still unhappy with Nikulin's depiction of Lopatin and, perhaps even more, with Gherman's depiction of civilian life on the home front. The release was delayed for several months (Dolin 2011, 169–170; Condee 2009, 293) before a screening at the 1977 Cannes festival was approved, followed by limited release in the Soviet Union (Lipkov 1987, 216).

Twenty Days without War follows Major Lopatin, a semi-autobiographical war correspondent in several stories by Simonov, on a short leave from the front. First

Figure 24.2 Still from Gherman's *Twenty Days without War*, 1976.

seen at the opening of the Soviet campaign to retake the Crimea, Lopatin travels on an ordinary passenger train to Tashkent on a 20-day leave. While the plot relates Lopatin's bittersweet and brief love affair with a seamstress working at the local theater, the film's main focus is on the emotional lives of soldiers and the families they have left behind. Two of the film's most famous scenes convey Gherman's brilliance in directing actors. A train travels through the Central Asian steppe at nighttime as an emotionally distraught pilot tells the story of his unfaithful wife and his inability to forgive her to Lopatin, who sits facing him, but unseen by the audience. As the captain (Aleksei Petrenko in a *tour de force* performance), his illuminated face framed by the darkness in the train compartment, tells his story to Lopatin, Gherman's camera remains fixed on his face for almost ten minutes without cutting away. Simple *mise-en-scène*, a convincingly "real" setting, magnificent acting at the limits of human expression and emotion, brilliantly crafted colloquial language, and a precisely calibrated single take combine to allow the emotional power to build to a climax and resonate long after the scene is over. Once in Tashkent, Lopatin's first order of business is to visit the wife of a friend who died at Stalingrad and to return his possessions to her. The scene rises to an almost unbearable emotional intensity as the widow's overwhelming grief turns into hostility towards the bearer of bad news: as she gives into her despair, the scene is suddenly punctuated by an absurdist non-sequitur as a noticeably matter-of-fact older woman (the widow's mother?) opens the dead man's suitcase and finds one boot. The intensity of the scene is only deepened by our realization that Lopatin's own deep grief at the death of his comrade, which we have seen in one of the film's only flashbacks, remains unexpressed. While the hardships of the home front were, of course, a traditional theme in many traditional Soviet films about the war, Gherman creates a searing, unforgettable image of the emotional toll of war on ordinary Soviet men and women.

But if the central theme of Simonov's story is the suffering of the civilian population in the rear, Gherman is ultimately more interested in revealing the truth behind the official image of the war as represented in countless Soviet movies, plays, and stories. Stripped of false heroism and patriotism by his experience of war, Lopatin is an ordinary man caught up in a historical tragedy. His matter-of-fact response when asked what soldiers feel when they kill the enemy – "when I feel like smoking, I have a cigarette. When things are frightening, I'm scared" – fails to satisfy the theater director and actors who are looking for something more suitably "dramatic" to help them portray the war on the stage. While Lopatin can shrug off their inability to understand the reality of war, he is horrified when he sees how his dispatches from Stalingrad are being made into a typical Stalinist war movie. And yet Lopatin is not only powerless to influence the theatrical and cinematic visions of the war, but is himself completely implicated in the system: his speech to the assembled workers at a war factory is full of the same heroicizing clichés that he had just objected to in the filming of his war stories.[16]

The film displays the full range of stylistic features and techniques that we associate with Gherman's poetics of the cinema: high contrast black and white cinematography that minimizes the difference between fiction film and documentary, a voice-over narrative frame, extreme long takes punctuated with an unsteady hand-held camera, the use of nonprofessionals alongside trained actors, a complex soundtrack composed of bits of overheard conversation, the "ugly" noises of everyday life, mostly diegetic music, fanatically authentic and historically resonant settings, and sparing use of flashbacks. In his last three movies, Gherman will continue to expand the use of these stylistic techniques, while gradually reducing the role of dramatic plot to the absolute minimum.

Since the late 1960s, Gherman had wanted to do a film based on his father's stories and novels about a charismatic criminal investigator in 1930s Leningrad (German 1938; 1961). Although he had drafted a screenplay as early as 1969, he enlisted Eduard Volodarskii in the late 1970s to write a new screenplay, while he and his wife did extensive research in order to reproduce the historical look of the period: they scoured document- and photo-archives, visited prisons and police stations where they were present at numerous interrogations of criminals. Still, when, after four years, *My Friend Ivan Lapshin* was finally completed, its release was initially blocked by Lenfilm: Gherman's bleak and completely deromanticized vision of provincial life in 1935 struck the studio bureaucrats as too negative a depiction of what was traditionally seen as the "golden age" of Stalinism (Condee 2009, 194). Happily, a new period was about to dawn in the Soviet Union and, shortly before Gorbachev was elected Secretary General, the film was released in 1984 (Christie 1989).

Figure 24.3 Still from Gherman's *My Friend, Ivan Lapshin*, 1981.

Framed by a prologue and epilogue set in the 1980s, the main action of *Lapshin* takes place in 1935 in the fictional provincial town of Urchinsk. Narrated by an elderly writer who calls the story "my confession of love for those people with whom I lived as a child, a five minute walk from here and half a century ago," *Lapshin* introduces us to several members of the local militia investigating a gang of brutal murderers and black marketers. The arrival of a touring theater troupe and a big-city journalist looking for material on the work of the local militia sets in motion a Chekhovian subplot of misdirected and unrequited love among the main characters. The main characters' desperately unhappy private lives, consisting largely of unhappy love affairs and grinding poverty in communal apartments, contrast powerfully with the triumphant atmosphere of Stalinism that dominates the public life of the town and its people. By the film's elegiac conclusion, while the criminals have been arrested or killed, none of the characters has found happiness and each goes back to a lonely private life. The film returns to the voiceover narrative that conveys an understated, yet profound disappointment that contemporary Russia is still so far from achieving the utopian future so confidently envisioned in the 1930s.

At the center of *Lapshin* is a remarkably realistic recreation of the look and feel of a Russian provincial town in the 1930s and of the worldview of committed Stalinists. Gherman's characters represent a "lost generation" of true believers, veterans of the Revolution and Civil War, who, the audience knows, if not destroyed by Stalin's terror will probably perish in Hitler's war. Although Gherman's approach to his characters is sympathetic and understated, he also rejects the accumulated ideological clichés and heroic myths of traditional representations of the 1930s. The film captures an essential contradiction of Stalinist life: boundless enthusiasm and optimism about Socialism's brilliant future despite political intolerance, positively primitive living standards, and callousness towards those who live outside the protection of the State.[17] By showing us not only his characters' idealism, asceticism, and willingness to sacrifice themselves for a greater cause, but also their personal and private weaknesses, Gherman succeeds in revealing the essential dishonesty of the official vision of the period while humanizing the "positive heroes" of his father's propagandistic prose works.

The title character, Ivan Lapshin (Andrei Boltnev) is a likable character, a competent policeman, and a true believer in the promise of the Revolution. Yet, scarred by his service in the Civil War, he embodies the contradictory combination of brutality and idealism of the Bolshevik legacy. Where Iurii Gherman's hero, as much psychologist and social worker as detective, was above all else concerned with the root causes of criminality and the possibility of rehabilitating criminals through labor, the title character of his son's film is a pitiless and violent defender of Soviet society. Although, on occasion, Boltnev's character pays lip service to the goal of rehabilitating criminals (the central motif of Iurii Gherman's militia stories), he is uninterested in the roots of criminality and dismissive of criminal psychology: his job is simply to eliminate criminal elements from Soviet society any way he can.[18] And yet his brutality is redeemed, at least in his own eyes, by the utopian promise of the Revolution, the ultimate purpose and justification of his violence. Lapshin's combination of brutality and idealism is most clearly expressed in the phrase "We'll clean out the scum, plant a garden and live in it," spoken as he leaves the scene of a multiple murder. As Lapshin's words echo through a lifeless winter landscape, Gherman suggests that the tragedy of an entire generation starts with the failure to imagine the complexities of realizing utopian dreams in the real world.

Perhaps Gherman's greatest achievement in the film is the seamless integration of the themes of utopia, ideology, and society with the problem of how best to represent reality in art. Inspired by the quasi-scientific neo-Lamarckian theories of Ivan Michurin and Trofim Lysenko popular at the time,[19] a local Pioneer group depicted in the film conducts an experiment of the material power of environment to change animal nature: in the lobby of the local theater, they have put a well-fed fox and hen into one cage. While the animals peacefully coexist for a while, as soon as the pioneers are late feeding the fox, its predatory instincts return and it consumes the hen. As this is happening, a touring theater company is rehearsing Nikolai Pogodin's classic Stalinist play *Aristocrats*, in which criminals and class enemies working on the White Sea Canal project are rehabilitated through the enlightened guidance of their prison wardens and the beneficent effects of forced labor. And if the audience does not yet understand, Gherman cuts to the play's intermission, when Lapshin and his colleagues agree that, although not at all realistic, Pogodin's play is ideologically correct and, therefore, necessary. By undercutting the Stalinist confidence in the priority of environment over nature and the ability of ideology to change the laws of nature, Gherman also provides comic counterpoint to the more serious issues raised by the movie.

Gherman's fortunes began to turn as the changes that would lead to Gorbachev's policy of glasnost in the arts gained momentum in the mid-1980s. After almost three years on the shelves of Lenfilm, *Lapshin*'s release in 1984 marked the beginning of the process of releasing other previously banned films, including Tengiz Abuladze's *Repentance* [*Monanieba*, 1984, released 1986] and Gleb Panfilov's *The Theme* [*Tema*, 1979, released 1986], while inaugurating a New Wave in Russian cinema (Horton and Brashinsky 1993). The film became an instant sensation, equally popular with the critics and the audience, and received numerous prestigious prizes at home and abroad, including the "Vasil'ev Brothers" Russian Federation State Prize (1987) and a State Prize of the Soviet Union (1988), as well as prizes at International Film Festivals. The reaction of the Russian audience was, if anything, even more positive: *Lapshin* was chosen one of the best Russian films of the year by the readers of the journal *Soviet Screen* (Christie 1989, 50–53). Shortly after *Lapshin* was released, Gherman was elected Secretary of the Union of Filmmakers of the USSR, and his first feature, *Trial on the Road*, was finally released in 1985 after being banned for 15 years. In 1988, at the apex of his fame and success, Gherman founded and became the first Artistic Director of Lenfilm's Studio of First and Experimental Films. He also taught, with his wife Svetlana Karmalita, graduate workshops in Moscow at the Higher Courses for Scriptwriters and Directors. Intensely caught up with the changes and new opportunities in Soviet society in the 1980s, Gherman, perhaps not surprisingly, had little time to start a new directing project. Instead, he spent much of the period writing or co-writing screenplays for other directors, notably for Semen Aranovich's *Torpedo Bombers* [*Torpedonostsy*, 1983] and Ardak Amirkulov's historical epic *The Fall of Otrar* [*Gibel' Otrara*, 1991]. With the collapse of the Soviet Union in 1991, Gherman turned to a new project, his first and only movie not based on a previously existing literary source. Working with his wife, they completed the screenplay for what would become *Khrustalyov, My Car!*, Gherman's most radical and challenging film to date.

Surprisingly, making films in the post-Soviet period ultimately proved no less challenging and Gherman's pace making movies, always extremely slow, actually decreased after 1991.[20] Raising money in a completely new environment for filmmakers and viewers turned out to be no simpler, and perhaps even more difficult, than navigating an entrenched, politically intolerant, and obtuse bureaucracy. If Gherman had been famous for his refusal to respect the sensitivities of official Soviet cinema, he was no less contemptuous of the demands of commercial film production. While financing the shooting of *Khrustalyov* was complicated by the economic difficulties of the 1990s, Gherman's intransigence made things even worse: American financiers backed out when Gherman refused their demand to use an American actor in the role of the dying Stalin (Wood 2001, 103). After a seven-year struggle, with money cobbled together from various sources, including an unidentified New Russian oligarch, the office of the Mayor of St Petersburg, and the French government, Gherman finally completed the film in 1998.

Set during the so-called "Doctors' Plot" of 1953, *Khrustalyov* tells the story of Dr Klenskii, a leading Moscow surgeon who is arrested for no good reason, brutalized, and then suddenly recalled to the Kremlin, where he witnesses the death of Stalin and the apparent ascension of the secret police chief Lavrentii Beria. At the film's end, Klenskii is seen riding the rails with an entourage of other dropouts from Soviet life, apparently having embraced the life of a Soviet hobo. More than simply depicting the nightmarish last days of Stalinism through the experiences of a family from the Stalinist elite, Gherman does everything possible to ensure that viewers feel the paranoia, brutality, uncertainty, irrationality, and terror that his characters experience. Indeed, the experience of watching *Khrustalyov* can seem very much like punishment: every single aspect of the film seems devised to frustrate the audience's desire to understand what is happening on screen: dimly-lit interiors, nighttime scenes illuminated by ordinary street lights, mumbled dialog, unidentified characters, irregular framing, apparently random camera tracking, unexplained plot connections. As numerous critics have argued (Iampol'skii 1989, 175–178, Condee 2009, 211–212), Gherman's use of the camera is perhaps the most radical aspect of his cinematic language: rather than serving as a guide to the narrative, Gherman's camera seems to function independently, equally unrelated to the subjectivity of an individual character or a privileged "objective" point of view, and often seems to be searching for significance within the frame.[21] Condee sums up this important point best when she describes the director's camera technique as a metaphor for the limited knowledge possessed by people living in any historical present:

> Gherman forces the spectator to sort out what is important, without benefit of a more traditional camera's discursive nudge. So too, by implication, his characters struggle with a world in which they operate, wherein the raw material of life only contingently and momentarily adheres to the regime of their individual desires and anticipations (Condee 2009, 206).

The result is a new cinematic language that, rather than simply "representing" the Soviet past, conveys to the audience the experience of living in the Stalinist nightmare.

In the end, Gherman's refusal to compromise with the needs and desires of the film's audience effectively insured that the film would be a commercial failure in Russia and the West. The difficulties of the film were such that even professionals, at least initially, were perplexed. At the 1998 Cannes Film Festival, for example, the audience of international film critics created a scandal by walking out during the screening, and the first reviews were devastating: in the words of Stephen Holden (1998), the film was "virtually impossible to decipher." Even more telling were the initial responses of a majority of Russian critics who complained that the film was

Figure 24.4 Still from Gherman's *Khrustalyov, My Car!*, 1998.

inaudible, unintelligible, and incomprehensible (Matizen 1998). Within a short period of time, however, most of the critics reconsidered their initial reactions: the film swept the NIKA awards in 2000, including awards for best film and best director (Condee 2009, 195). Within ten years, the film was acknowledged to be a masterpiece of world cinema and "one of the great films of the 1990s" (Hoberman 1999).

Gherman's career comes full circle with his final movie, *Hard to be a God*, an adaptation of the classic novel by Soviet Russia's greatest science-fiction writers, Boris and Arkadii Strugatskii. Originally published in 1964, the novel tells of emissaries from an advanced civilization sent as observers to a planet where a fascist dictatorship is establishing itself in the midst of a brutal civil and religious conflict reminiscent of the darkest days of the European Middle Ages. Horrified at the society's ignorance, anti-intellectualism, and brutality, the alien hero – disguised as a local warrior called Don Rumata – is tempted to disregard his orders and, by intervening in local events, accelerate this benighted society's evolution towards a more humane order. As the despairing hero eventually learns, no higher power, ideology, or technology can "speed up" history or "correct" human beings. In the context of Soviet culture of the 1960s, the novel was often seen as an implicit critique of the impulse of either superpower to intervene in the historical development of "primitive" societies, equally applicable to Vietnam, the Third World, and Eastern Europe, and the impossibility of improving human nature. And while Rumata sees Don Reba's regime as a brutal fascist dictatorship in the making, Russian readers were just as likely to think of the more recent terror of Beria and Stalin.

Originally intending that *Hard to Be a God* would be his first independent directing project after *The Seventh Satellite*, Gherman had created an adaptation in collaboration with Boris Strugatskii in the late 1960s. Although the screenplay was approved for production in the summer of 1968, it had to be abandoned following the Soviet army's intervention in Czechoslovakia to end the Prague Spring in late August 1968: the novel's skepticism that intervention could change a society for the better now raised uncomfortable questions too close to home (Wood 2001, 107). Gherman quickly moved on to make *Trial on the Road*, but he never forgot about this project.

A second chance to adapt the novel came about during the cultural thaw of Gorbachev's glasnost. But while the Strugatskiis wanted him to direct the movie, Gherman hesitated: as he admitted in an interview, the prospect of directing a political allegory in the freer conditions of the 1980s seemed much less important (Lemkin 2001). In any case, Soviet authorities eventually invited the West German Peter Fleischman to direct the film based on the novel, and a colorless jointly-produced Soviet-West German adaptation was released in 1989. Perhaps inspired by the inadequacy of Fleischman's film, Gherman continued thinking about the project, and by the late 1990s he and his wife had crafted a new adaptation that was less tied to the specifics of the novel's plot and far removed from the 1960s themes of the original (Vail' 2000). As Tarkovskii had previously done in *Solaris* (1972) and *Stalker* (1979), his adaptations of science fiction classics by Stanislaw

Figure 24.5 Still from Gherman's *Hard to Be a God*, 2013.

Lem and the Strugatskii brothers, Gherman would transform the source novel to tell his own story.

Gherman's largest and most complex project began in the Czech Republic in 2000, where, in an astonishing triumph of production and art design, his crew built the town of Arkanar around a medieval castle. Shooting continued with several breaks over the next few years and the production finally wrapped in 2006. Although several release dates were announced between 2007 and 2011, post-production took as long as the original filming. Pressured by financial backers and extraordinarily high expectations, and hindered by declining health, Gherman completed the basic editing by 2008 but was still working on the soundtrack when he died on February 21, 2013. His wife and their son, the director Aleksei Gherman Jr., completed the soundtrack and the film's official premiere took place at the Rome Film Festival on November 13, 2013, while the film's theatrical run opened in Russia three months later.

Taking little more than the general situation from the novel, Gherman immerses the viewer in the midst of the unremitting ugliness, brutality, and violence of Arkanar and, by extension, of human history. Perhaps even more than horror, the film conveys the sheer tedium of life in a world devoid of all spiritual, artistic, and intellectual values. In addition to eating, shitting, farting, and fucking, the people in Gherman's dystopian vision of a future Dark Age derive pleasure from hurting others and from witnessing others being violated. Despite the film's unrelentingly gross naturalism, the astonishing production design, the remarkable black-and-white cinematography of Vladimir Il'in and Iurii Klimenko, and the director's absolute control over every inch of every frame transform nightmarish ugliness into a remarkable, if terrifying, beauty. Building on Tarkovskii's *Andrei Rublev*, Bergman's *The Seventh Seal*, and Eisenstein's *Ivan the Terrible*, Gherman uses the familiar imagery, iconography, and architecture of the Middle Ages to create a new world (Zvonkine 2015). As he did in *Khrustalyov*, Gherman minimizes plot while maximizing the tension, paranoia, horror, tedium, and violence in which the characters wander. Rather than allowing the viewer's gaze to differentiate between the important and incidental aspects of the frame and the narrative, Gherman's restlessly tracking camera makes the viewer feel Rumata's disorientation and confusion. If Gherman's stylistic techniques (i.e., the claustrophobic close-up, the leisurely long-takes, the intentionally "clumsy" framing of the action, a screenplay composed mostly of bits and pieces of random words, phrases, and noises "overheard" by the tracking camera, lack of non-diegetic music, repeated violations of the cinematic "fourth" wall as characters acknowledge the camera's gaze, etc.) are by now familiar, he uses them here with an intensity that surpasses even *Khrustalyov* (Stishova 2014).

The central philosophical issue of the film becomes clear when, having finally succeeded in freeing Dr Budach from the clutches of Reba, Rumata asks what advice he would give to a God who wants to help humanity. One of the very few extended dialogs from the novel to survive the transition to Gherman's film confirms the viewer's fears: since anything God does would only worsen the situation, the best thing to do is nothing. In other words, Gherman rejects all ideologies – communist, capitalist, and religious – that profess to free humanity from the inevitable suffering of existence and history. While this conclusion is, broadly speaking, consistent with the anti-utopian message of much Science Fiction of the 1960s,[22] it also suggests Gherman's profound disappointment with 20 years of post-Soviet Russia. Still, the world of *Hard to Be a God* is filmed with such exquisite clarity and definition that each scene, no matter how squalid the content, approaches the nightmarish beauty of a painting of Hieronymus Bosch (Kartashov 2013). As Tarkovskii concluded in *Rublev* and Sokurov in *Russian Ark*, the only possible consolation in a world dominated by violence and brutality is art.

As numerous critics have argued, Gherman's cinema is located on the border between history and memory (Wood 2001; Condee 2009). Indeed, his movies use the memories of his own family to re-imagine Soviet history from the Revolution to the death of Stalin and beyond.[23] Initially based on prodigious research in public and family archives, the scrupulously authentic recreation of the past in his films was, obviously, only possible because the director was able to coax remarkable performances from a large number of collaborators: script writers, art, production and costume designers, cinematographers, actors, musicians, and many others. But while no one would deny the director's obsession with Soviet history, creating a visually and aurally compelling vision of the Soviet past has always been just one part of a larger project. Rather than simply restoring omissions or correcting falsifications in the historical record, Gherman wants to enlarge our understanding of the past by making the audience experience the world as it was experienced by people alive in the past. This problem is complicated since, by virtue of being alive today, we already "know" things that people actually living in the past could not have known: their (unknowable) future has already become our (known) past, as Condee argues (Condee 2009, 210–212). To allow viewers to experience the past as it was originally experienced, then, means more than simply recreating a historically accurate image on the screen: to experience the past as if it were the present, viewers must, temporarily at least, be stripped of the excess knowledge that intervening time has given them. To solve this phenomenological difficulty, Gherman would develop a radically new cinematic language capable of representing the past "as it really was experienced." The elements of that new language, contrary to all the rules of Socialist, Hollywood, and Art House cinema, were, as Condee (2009, 212) puts it, "frequently inaudible soundtrack, blocked camera angles, chaotic, handheld camera, incoherent narrative lines, visual and narrative distractions, [and] unidentified characters." To watch a movie by Gherman, then, is to confront the complexity, obscurity, incomprehensibility, even absurdity of a past that can neither be fully remembered, completely understood, nor adequately represented on the screen. The rigor with which Gherman carried out this project accounts for the notorious density and difficulty of his films.

Although other filmmakers have brought to light previously hidden aspects of the Soviet experience, none has yet equaled Gherman. However, Nikolai Dostal's television mini-series *Penal Battalion* [*Shtrafbat*, screenplay Eduard Volodarskii, 2004] and Sergei Loznitsa's brilliant *In the fog* [*V tumane*, 2012] come close. In intellectual weight, political seriousness, and aesthetic ambition, the only Russian directors comparable to Gherman are Sergei Eisenstein and Andrei Tarkovskii. Yet if he is generally acknowledged to be the greatest Russian director since the death of Tarkovskii, Gherman's influence is minimal in post-Soviet Russian cinema. Indeed, Gherman's experience since 1991 suggests that, given his uncompromising perfectionism and disdain for market realities, his style is, if possible, even less suited to capitalism than it was to socialism. Gherman may go down in history as the last great Soviet filmmaker who, despite his contribution to the end of Soviet power, was himself unable to make the transition to post-Soviet cinema.

Notes

1. Although he specialized in contemporary characters and stories, in 1954 he published an interesting historical novel about Peter the Great called *Young Russia* [*Rossiia molodaia: Istoricheskii roman*. Leningrad: Sovetskii pisatel'].
2. Probably best known today as the author of the Civil War story "The Forty-First" ["Sorok pervyi"] which was turned into popular films by Iakov Protazanov in 1927 and Grigorii Chukhrai in 1956, Lavrenev was one of the major "Fellow Travelers" of the 1920s. After studying law at St Petersburg University, he served in the Tsarist and White armies before finally coming over to the side of the Reds. One of the main themes of his stories and plays was the complex social and psychological processes of adapting to the new revolutionary reality.
3. Although the action of Grossman's story was set in the early 1920s, it was first published in *Literaturnaia gazeta* in 1934.
4. The film itself, long thought destroyed, was finally released in 1988, when it was instantly recognized as a classic of Soviet cinema of the 1960s, winning a Special Jury Prize at the Berlin Film Festival, and several NIKA awards in the Soviet Union.
5. In an "Open letter," Eduard Volodarskii (2002), the author of the screenplays for *Trial on the Road* and *My Friend Ivan Lapshin*, argues that working with Aronov on *The Seventh Satellite* was actually formative in the development of Gherman's mature style.
6. When Adamov announces to the head of the newly organized communal apartment that he was released from prison and has returned home, the latter answers that "the fact that you're still alive is a misunderstanding [*nedorazumenie*]."
7. See Padunov and Condee (1985) for a fascinating contemporary description of the film's reception among the Moscow intelligentsia at the end of the 1980s.
8. In reality, the screenplay is based more on stories that Gherman heard around the family dinner table than on his father's book. For Gherman's fascinating account of

how he learned about the fate of Russian soldiers who had fought with the Nazis from the mouths of partisans and former "Vlasovites" who stayed in the family apartment after being released from prisons camp in 1956, see Dolin (2011, 125–127).

9 Gherman saw that Zamanskii, an unknown actor who had fought in the war and done time in a military prison for striking an officer, would be able to convey the tragedy of an ordinary Russian soldier caught up in history. See Dolin (2011, 137).

10 Boris Vladimirovich Pavlenok, head of the Glavnyi komitet of Goskino, as quoted in Lipkov (1987, 206). For the fullest documentary account of the official objections to the film, see Fomin (1992, 111, 117, 121–122).

11 If Nancy Condee's contention (2009, 203–204) that the barge scene is the center of the movie and Lazarev a "McGuffin" is an exaggeration, it does suggest the remarkable intensity and power of this scene.

12 Lazarev's plight was the result of the incompetence of Soviet military and political leaders at the start of the war; Petushkov was unhinged by the deaths of his wife and son in the war; Lokotkov cannot reveal his sympathy for Lazarev without losing his authority as commander.

13 Stalin issued the infamous Order 270, making surrender, for whatever reasons, equivalent to treason, on August 16, 1941. Russian soldiers who managed to escape from encirclement, captivity, or were liberated by advancing allied armies were often sent directly to the Gulag. See Merridale (2006, 112–113).

14 The same thing can be observed even in the best Soviet revisionist war movies, such as Mikhail Kalatozov's *The Cranes are Flying* [*Letiat zhuravli*, 1957], Grigorii Chukhrai's *Ballad of a Soldier* [*Ballada o soldate*, 1959], and Andrei Tarkovskii's *Ivan's Childhood* [*Ivanovo detstvo*, 1962].

15 Since they first met in 1968, when Karmalita left graduate school to join Gherman on the set of *Trial on the Road*, she was his closest collaborator, working on each of his films, while also writing scripts for other directors. See Condee (2009, 190).

16 Lipkov (1987, 215) speaks of Gherman's rejection of the rhetoric of "grazhdanskii trudovoi podvig" [civic feat of labor].

17 In one typically understated, yet significant scene, the loneliness and alienation of an old friend of Lapshin's, whose only sin is being married to an Orthodox priest's daughter, are made apparent at Lapshin's birthday party.

18 When asked by one of the actors about the psychology of criminals, he responds with disdain: *dusheguby*, that is, "murderers" or, more literally, "soul destroyers."

19 The lobby of the theater is decorated with a famous quote from Michurin: "We cannot expect any kindness from nature. Our task is to take it by force."

20 If between 1970 and 1990, Gherman had completed three films, he made only two in the final two decades of his life, taking seven years to complete *Khrustalyov* and working on *Hard to Be a God* during the final 13 years of his life.

21 Despite their many differences, filmmakers as different as Eisenstein, Vertov, and Tarkovskii all used the camera to organize and direct the gaze of the viewer.

22 The struggle against utopianism is a major theme in the works, for example, of the great Polish science-fiction writer Stanislaw Lem.

23 The legacy of the Revolution and the 1920s in *The Seventh Satellite*, the rise of Stalinism in *My Friend Ivan Lapshin*; the Great Patriotic War in *Twenty Days without War* and *Trial on the Road*; and the death of Stalin in *Khrustalyov, My Car!*

References

Christie, Ian. 1989. "The Cinema." In *Culture and Media in the USSR Today*, edited by Julian Graffy and Geoffrey Hosking, 43–77. New York: St Martin's Press.

Condee, Nancy. 2009. *The Imperial Trace: Recent Russian Cinema*. New York: Oxford University Press.

Dolin, Anton. 2011. *German: interv'iu, esse, stsenarii* [Gherman: Interviews, Essays, Scripts]. Moskva: Novoe literaturnoe obozrenie.

Fomin, Valerii. 1992. *Polka: dokumenty, svidetel'stva, kommentarii* [Shelf: Documents, Testimonies, Commentary]. Moscow: Nauchno-issledovatel'skii institut kinoiskusstva.

German, Iurii P. 1938. *Dve povesti* [Two Tales]. ("Moi drug Ivan Lapshin" and "Andrei Zhmakin"). Leningrad: Khudozhestvennaia literatura.

German, Iurii P. 1961. *Odin God*. [One Year]. Leningrad: Sovetskii pisatel'.

German, Iurii P. 1964. "Nash drug Ivan Bodunov" [Our Friend Ivan Bodunov]. *Neva* 2: 91–131.

Graham, Alexander. 2012. "'Immersion in Time': History, Memory and the Question of Readability in the Films of Aleksei German." *Studies in Russian and Soviet Cinema* 6.2: 177–216.

Hoberman, J. 1999. "Aleksei Guerman among the Long Shadows." *Film Comment*, 35.1: 48–53.

Holden, Stephen. 1998. "The Weather is Bad, but Life is Worse." *The New York Times*, September 28.

Horton, Andrew and Michael Brashinsky. 1993. *The Zero Hour: Glasnost and Soviet Cinema in Transition*. Princeton, NJ: Princeton University Press.

Iampol'skii, Mikhail. 1989. "Diskurs i povestvovanie" [Discourse and Narration]. *Kinostsenarii* [Film Scripts] 6: 175–189.

Kartashov, Andrei. 2013. "*Hard to be a God*: Will Alexei German's Long-Awaited Final Film Secure his Place among the Greats?" *The Calvert Journal*, November 13, http://calvertjournal.com/comment/show/1693/alexei-german-hard-to-be-a-god (accessed March 15, 2014).

Lavrenev, Boris. 1963. *Sobranie sochinenii* [Collected Works]. 6 vols. Moscow: Khudozhestvennaia literatura.

Lemkin, Mikhail. 2001. "Aleksei German sobstvennymi slovami" [Aleksei Gherman in his own words]. Interview. *Chaika/Seagull Magazine* 8 (August 16), www.chayka.org/node/3972 (accessed March 15, 2014).

Lipkov, Aleksandr. 1987. "Proverka … na dorogakh" [Trial… on the Road]. *Novyi mir* [New World] 2: 202–225.

Matizen, Viktor. 1998. "*Khrustalev, mashinu!*, nevedomyi shedevr" [*Khrustalev, My Car!*, A Mysterious Masterpiece]. *KinoPark* (August): 20–21.

Merridale, Catherine. 2006. *Ivan's War: Life and Death in the Red Army, 1939–1945*. New York: Metropolitan Books.

Padunov, Volodya and Nancy Condee. 1985. "Recent Soviet Cinema and Public Responses: Abdrashitov and German." *Framework: The Journal for Cinema and Media* 29: 42–56.

Stishova, Elena. 2014. "Byt' bogom. *Trudno byt' Bogom*. Rezhisser Aleksei German" [To be a God. *Hard to Be a God*. Director Aleksei Gherman]. *Iskusstvo kino* [Art of Cinema] 1, http://kinoart.ru/archive/2014/01/byt-bogom-trudno-byt-bogom-rezhisser-aleksej-german (accessed March 15, 2014).

Vail', Petr. 2000. "'Aleksei German: *Trudno byt' bogom*,' skazal tabachnik s Tabachnoi ulitsy" ["Aleksei Gherman: *It's Hard to be a God*," Said the Tobacco Merchant from Tobacco Street]. Interview. *Iskusstvo kino* [Art of Cinema] 8: 4–20.

Volodarskii, Eduard. 2002. "Otkrytoe pis'mo k tomu, komu trudno byt' bogom" [Open Letter to Someone Who Finds it Difficult to be a God]. *Moskovskii komsomolets* [Moscow Komsomolets] August 24, http://www.mk.ru/old/article/2002/08/24/163028-otkryitoe-pismo-tomu-komu-trudno-byit-bogom.html (accessed January 15, 2014).

Wood, Tony. 2001. "Time Unfrozen: The Films of Aleksei German." *New Left Review* 7: 99–107.

Zvonkine, Eugénie. 2015. "The Artistic Process of Aleksei German." *Studies in Russian and Soviet Cinema* 9.3: 187–217.

25

Knowledge (Imperfective): Andrei Zviagintsev and Contemporary Cinema

Nancy Condee

Love never ends. But as for prophecies, they will come to an end; as for tongues, they will cease; as for knowledge, it will come to an end.
For we know only in part; and we prophesy only in part;
But when the complete comes, the partial will come to an end.

(First Epistle to the Corinthians 13: 8–10)

Though a skeptic, I have begun with biblical verses: here love is contrasted principally with prophecy and knowledge – not, at first glance, obvious choices for contrast.[1] Love's millennial associations suggest that it lies not so much along an axis of morality (good and evil) as along an axis of time: love is closer to sacred timelessness and more distant from the worldly temporalities of prophecy and knowledge. The verses' tone invokes an end when "the partial" will fall away – that is, when prophecy and knowledge, with their temporal constraints and epistemological drive, will be superseded by love, whose value lies not in the realm of foreseeing or knowing but in the realm of meaning. The worldly duo of prophecy and knowledge is like a Janus-faced pair: prophecy makes claims about the future; knowledge, about the past and present. And what about love? In the world of this biblical passage, love is exempted from these secular temporalities: "love never ends."

The Corinthians quotation does not appear in Zviagintsev's work until his second film, *The Banishment* [*Izgnanie*, 2007]. Here biblical verses are read aloud (at much greater length) by two young girls, Flora and Frida, at a critical moment: the heroine Vera ("belief," after all) is undergoing an abortion that will contribute to her death. These on-screen children, reading from the Bible, contrast with

---

A Companion to Russian Cinema, First Edition. Edited by Birgit Beumers.
© 2016 John Wiley & Sons, Inc. Published 2016 by John Wiley & Sons, Inc.

the unseen, unborn child, aborted as the Bible is read. The living girls and aborted child are a key juxtaposition in Zviagintsev's parable about the failure of family love.[2]

While Zviagintsev's second film – often considered his weakest – may be least interesting to the film critic and journalist, it is perhaps most valuable to the film scholar: here, the workings of this filmmaker's craft are more evident. Prophecy, knowledge, and love – for Zviagintsev, the states of foreseeing, secular understanding, and transcendent contemplation – inform his core enactment of our place in the moral universe.

And so while the fiercest political debates rage around Zviagintsev's drama *Leviathan* [*Leviafan*, 2014] – whether this fourth film is "anti-Putin," "anti-Church," or "anti-Russian" – any comprehensive answer must account for Zviagintsev's ambition to deliver a religious message, not a political one. The filmmaker's religious "disestablishmentarianism,"[3] if it can be called this, is not a political stance but a philosophical frame of mind. Hence, the more intensely that liberal Russian film critics (and Western journalists) attempt to extract an ideological statement from the director, the more we find him responding with an abstracted message. To this extent, Western criticism of Zviagintsev's work as "didactic" is not so much wrong as poorly conceived: it is akin to criticizing Kira Muratova for ornamentalism, Nikita Mikhalkov for nationalism, or Aleksandr Sokurov for demiurgy. Such criticism takes the text's very substance (where would Russian culture be without didacticism?) as a sign of weakness, as if it were a recipe with "too much" leavening.

In *Leviathan*, the didacticism is most evident in the Mayor, the film's most cartoonish figure who is a mere intermediary in the more significant – that is, for Zviagintsev, spiritual – battle between Bishop and Lawyer (both, in the end, negative figures).[4] Narrative details, such as the Bishop's and the Lawyer's unslaked craving for water,[5] bring these two characters into alignment as false prophecy and secular knowledge, as a corrupt spiritual leader and an atheist, as co-opted "truth" and worldly "facts" – that is to say, non-truth and non-facts. We –Western scholars, Russian critics – may prefer it to be a political film rather than a religious film; Zviagintsev has a different view.

Biographical Aside

Before saying more about this triad, let me provide brief biographical notes on Zviagintsev's work. The director comes from an artistic background initially distinct from film production.[6] Born in Novosibirsk in 1964, he was educated at the local Novosibirsk Theater School, from which he graduated in 1984. After a stint in the army (1984–1986), he moved to Moscow to study acting (1986–1990) with actor-director Evgenii Lazarev at the State Academy of Theatre Arts (GITIS). After

Figure 25.1 Andrei Zviagintsev and his DoP Mikhail Krichman. Photo by V. Mishukov. Courtesy of Intercinema.

graduation and without immediate professional success, Zviagintsev picked up minor roles as a theatre, television serial, and film actor (1992–2000), even working as a street cleaner while auditioning for parts. As he later told Erica Abeel (2004):

> 1993 was a bad year in Russia post-Perestroika and I had trouble finding work. So I took a job filming a commercial for a furniture store. I learned the craft that way, came to understand the shooting process.

In 2000, Zviagintsev was hired by Dmitrii Lesnevskii, a co-founder of REN-TV, where he directed three episodes of the television series *Black Room* [*Chernaia komnata*, 2000]: "Bushido," "Obscure," and "Choice" ["Vybor"], all with DoP Mikhail Krichman, with whom he would continue to work for all his subsequent films.

It was, therefore, a surprise to the festival and journalist communities when Zviagintsev's first feature film, *The Return* [*Vozvrashchenie*, 2003], won the Golden Lion, as well as the Luigi De Laurentiis Prize for Best Debut, at the Venice International Film Festival. After all, Zviagintsev's own technical crew (including Krichman) were also for the most part debuting their first full-length feature film. To many experts, Zviagintsev seemed to have come from "nowhere" (namely, theatre and television, not yet as intensely integrated in the 1990s into the film world as they would later become). Zviagintsev had not passed through the conventional vetting system of the State Institute of Cinematography (VGIK) or the Higher Courses of Scriptwriters and Directors (VKSR); nor had he yet worked on a full-length feature film as First Assistant Director or as a film scriptwriter who then traditionally "graduated" to shoot his own debut. Instead, he moved from a short stint in a television series directly to the Venice Golden Lion. Apart from the top award at an A-class festival, the film garnered 27 other awards and 13 nominations, including the 2003 Golden Eagle for Best Film and the 2004 NIKA for Best Film.[7] No wonder, therefore, that Zviagintsev's sudden visibility triggered considerable envy among his peers. This envy was surely magnified by the inevitable historical comparison with Russia's last Golden Lion recipient (another debutant) Andrei Tarkovskii, director of the war drama *Ivan's Childhood* (*Ivanovo detstvo*, 1962).[8] Unfavorable comparisons with the earlier filmmaker, who went on to become Russia's premiere auteur, were irresistible.

Four years later, Zviagintsev shot his second full-length feature film, the drama *The Banishment*, with a script loosely based on William Saroyan's novella *The Laughing Matter* (1953).[9] Premiering at the Cannes International Film Festival in 2007, *The Banishment* suffered from the frequent curse of second films – inflated festival expectations – and met with considerable domestic and international criticism. Nevertheless, serious scholarly interest in Zviagintsev's work originates from this same period.[10]

Zviagintsev subsequently broadened his profile, contributing to two almanac films. His short "Apocrypha" (cut from a theatrical release, but available on DVD) for the 2008 almanac *New York, I Love You*; his short "Mystery" ["Taina"] contributed to the almanac *Experiment 5IVE* [*Eksperiment 5IVE*, 2011].

Of greater interest to our discussion here is Zviagintsev's third full-length feature *Elena*, which premiered in 2011 at Cannes in Un Certain Regard, where the film was awarded its Jury Prize. *Elena* went on to win the 2012 NIKA Best Director; 2012 Golden Eagle for Best Fiction Film and Best Director.

Leviathan, Zviagintsev's fourth full-length feature film, was released to much critical acclaim and won a nomination for the Academy Award for Best Foreign Language Film (Oscar). The film (shot in the Murmansk District) tells the story of a family – father Nikolai, or Kolia (Aleksei Serebriakov), son Roma, young wife Liliia (Elena Liadova) – that lives in a small bay on the Barents Sea. Followers of Zviagintsev's work will recognize the large mythological frame, within which the profane details of gritty secular life are played out: here, a corrupt, small-town mayor who challenges Nikolai's property rights and triggers a series of retaliations.

Of the enduring contradictions in critical reception of Zviagintsev's work, this one stands out: although his films are routinely identified as social critiques – some more scathing than others – Zviagintsev passionately rejects this orientation. A plausible interpretation of *The Return*, for example, might expound on its depiction of the social deterioration of the family. Side by side to this view, Zviagintsev's interpretation is unrecognizable: "I would say that it's about the metaphysical incarnation of the soul's movement from the Mother to the Father" (Abeel 2004).

And while some critics (again, quite plausibly) might see *Elena* as a film about economic difference, Zviagintsev is scornful: "They saw socio-class struggle in the film! What class struggle!" (Matizen 2013, 671).

Coyness? Caprice? Strategic deflection? Before reverting to an explanation *ad hominem*, let us – as a thought experiment – take him at his word, resistant to "reducing" his work to such categories as social drama, political allegory, or sociological sketch. As Zviagintsev has repeatedly stressed, any viewing of his work that proceeds "from the standpoint of everyday life" is a mistake: "the mystery of the film won't reveal itself to you" (Abeel 2004).

It is evident by now that these metaphysical musings are part of an artistic outlook that situates Zviagintsev alongside other descendants of Andrei Tarkovskii in a domain that directs our attention away from the profane to the unseen world of spiritual abstraction. In this effort, Zviagintsev's work engages three specific techniques that cohere into a distinct signature and differentiate his film style from such kin as Aleksandr Sokurov. It is the intent of this chapter to capture that style. In this respect, the chapter is less interested in such self-perpetuating debates as *whether* Zviagintsev is a descendent of Tarkovskii – an argument both indisputable and contingent[11] – as it is in *how* Zviagintsev uses recognizable devices to engage with the legacy of Tarkovskii's filmmaking in contemporary world cinema.

The First Technique: Inversion

To the literalist, Zviagintsev's film titles might seem puzzling: *The Return* is less about a return than about an extended voyage *away* from home. *The Banishment* is not – as the title might imply – a Biblical couple's expulsion from Eden out into the fallen world, but the opposite: the couple's trip from the benighted cityscape to the pastoral surroundings of the original home. It is in the heart of this "Eden" that its tragedy is acted out.

These "mismatches" between title and content are neither the scriptwriter's lapses nor the critic's misinterpretations (the misattribution, for example, of a biblical reference). How do we know that Zviagintsev's *The Banishment* invokes an Edenic subtext? The protagonist's daughter is named Eva; she is offered an apple. Flora and Frida read from a Bible bookmarked with a reproduction of Masaccio's fresco *The Expulsion from the Garden of Eden* [*Cacciata dei progenitori dall'Eden*, 1425]. In an interview (if we lend credence to a director's statements), Zviagintsev has explicitly made the connection between the film title and the biblical story (Matizen 2013, 664).

Why then the odd disjuncture between title and script? Something else is in play. What we are seeing here and elsewhere in Zviagintsev's work are inversions, a series of "counter-symbols," a strategy necessary to stage the complex, deflective functions of Zviagintsev's secular world.

While these counter-symbols appear through much of Zviagintsev's work, the technique is most traceable in *The Banishment*. Here, for example, the association of the Virgin Mary with the pregnant heroine (whose blue and white clothing signals this supposition) is underscored by passages from Johann Sebastian Bach's 1723 *Magnificat* ("Song of Mary," BWV 243). The pregnant heroine's children put together a puzzle reproduction of Leonardo da Vinci's and Andrea del Verrocchio's 1472–1475 painting *Annunciation* (Luke 1: 26–39), in which Gabriel appears to Mary with news of the Christ child, whose reign will have no end. This cultural strategy is not (as we sometimes find in Sokurov) mere snobbery: Bach, da Vinci, del Verrocchio, masters of European culture who – Sokurov would have intimated – far surpass any modest cinematic competencies. Instead, the references have a larger, refractive function. Zviagintsev's intent is the creation of – among other things – a secular counter-Mary: her pregnant condition is stripped of spiritual value; her earthly child is aborted; the child's father is neither a lover nor God, but (in all likelihood) merely the husband himself. As for the husband – a kind of counter-Joseph – he does not welcome the unexpected child; instead, he kills it.

The film, therefore, functions as an inversion of two stories, Eden and the Virgin Birth,[12] revealing (through inversion) their mundane, sublunary status: the little Eve is sinless; the pregnant "Mary," by contrast, is subjected to her husband's censure. And, as if this were not capricious enough – where the Bible tells first the story of Eve and then (only much later) the story of Mary – Zviagintsev's world gives us an inverted chronology: Eve is daughter to "Mary." In conversation with critic Viktor Matizen, Zviagintsev has gone so far as to suggest that the heroine's pregnancy might be framed as modern-day sinless conception, a miracle unrecognized by the profane world. While an early version of the script had pointed to the heroine's adultery, the scriptwriters (including Zviagintsev himself) rejected that choice in favor of the implicit miracle:

> We rejected the idea of the adulteress. The rational motive disappeared; her behavior became inexplicable. After that, some [viewers] decided that she was simply an idiot, and lost interest in the film. But another group of viewers, immured into a wall of the inexplicable, into paradox, lifted their eyes upward and saw the sky. These viewers stayed with me. To those who had turned away, I have nothing to say. (Matizen 2013, 662)

Retrospectively then, let us turn backwards to Zviagintsev's first film, *The Return*. Here, the key elements cluster first around the figure of Christ. The sleeping father's resemblance to Jesus, underscored by a visual citation of Andrea Mantegna's 1480 painting *Lamentation over Dead Christ*, is reiterated near the film's end, when the father's corpse is returned in the boat (Vicks 2010). The father's association with Christ triggers a series of related choices: the children bear the names of Apostles Andrew and John (Andrei and Ivan); the family sits down to a final supper where the father shares wine with them before the trip; their journey lasts seven days, ending on Sunday, and so on.[13] And yet pushing back against these Christian conventions is Zviagintsev's signature strategy: the earthly father – neither Christ nor Christ-like – is vengeful, punitive, and unforgiving. At the moment of his death, the father's corpse – far from offering hope (as Christ does, raised from the earth) – leaves us instead with sorrowful relief, as his corpse is consigned to the water.

This is not a satanic Anti-Christ (any more than Vera, the heroine of *The Banishment*, had been a slatternly Anti-Mary), but an inverse strategy that transforms the sacred figure into a profane, earthly counterpart. By this playful logic, therefore, it is not "Christ" who walks on water in *The Return*, but the "apostles" Andrei and Ivan who appear to do so. Whether this series of inversions is caprice or philosophical statement about the secular world is never entirely offered to us as a fixed solution. I will reserve speculation about this question until the end of the chapter.

Just as *The Banishment* pairs an inverted Mary with Eve, *The Return* offers a male pair, Christ and Abraham. Discovering their sleeping father, the children run to find an old photograph, slipped into the family Bible, next to an image of Abraham. This image sets the same inversive technique in motion. Like Abraham, the film's father wields a knife, but the outcome is different: he is under no compulsion to kill his son. The young boy steals the knife; the scuffle results in the father's death. It is as if the jumbled elements of the Abraham story produced a counter-story, barely legible as such because each individual piece finds its own inverted equivalence.[14]

In *Leviathan*, the dominant text, of course, is the story of Job, the biblical prophet who loses family, health, and property in a series of trials. Spurning the false counsel of his friends, Job endures his assigned hardships as a living testimony to the limits of human understanding. Zviagintsev's most striking image – the whale skeleton washed up on the beach[15] – visually anticipates the biblical citation recited by a local priest in the closing moments of the film. It is God's final address to Job:

> Can you pull in Leviathan with a fishhook
> or tie down its tongue with a rope?
> Can you put a cord through its nose
> or pierce its jaw with a hook?
> (Job 41: 1–2)

The irony of the passage is this: God's message to Job (and the priest's message to Kolia) might equally serve as the corrupt mayor's threat: "If you lay a hand on it, you will remember the struggle and never do it again!" (Job 40: 8).[16]

The whale skeleton is in turn a visual link to the film's second member of the pair. Jonah and Job are prophets of the Hebrew Bible's two most unconventional books; they share the story of trial, endurance, and eventual recompense. In Jonah's case, refusing God's enjoinment to travel to Nineveh, the prophet is thrown overboard and swallowed by a whale, where he survives three days and three nights, returning alive. Jonah's survival and reappearance itself prefigures Christ's resurrection ("For as Jonas was three days and three nights in the whale's belly; so shall the Son of man be three days and three nights in the heart of the earth;" Matthew 12:40).

Job and Jonah (and, by implication, Christ) are thus joined in a query about the value of human suffering and the insufficiency of human knowledge to make sense of earthly torment. A strength of Zviagintsev's film is its apparent agnosticism at the climax of human suffering. That is to say, as an artifact of human creation, the film itself does not perform for us a knowledge of whether the very suffering it depicts finds redemption in a world to which it has only tenuous access. The act of filmmaking testifies to the belief that this outcome lies beyond human knowledge.

In this sense, the biblical stories of Job and Jonah are transformed from Bible stories into Zviagintsev's tale of non-eventuality: Job's wealth is not returned to him; the whale in which Jonah had sheltered lies stripped on the shore; and we as spectators are left to make whatever "higher sense" we can of what we have seen on the screen. Job and Jonah (like Mary and Eve, like Christ and Abraham) populate a cinematic world in which meaning, not knowledge – in fact, the inverse of knowledge – is the best we have.

The Second Technique: Effacement

For viewers sensitive to local particularities, *Elena*, Zviagintsev's third full-length feature film, has a distinct, dual setting: on the one hand, Moscow's wealthy Ostozhenka Street; on the other, Biriulevo, the city's poor industrial suburb. The film is so firmly grounded in the quotidian details of each locale that the misguided secular critic might well blunder into sociological commentary from these details alone. In this respect, Elena is more circumspect than the previous two films. If *The Return* and *The Banishment* accelerated rapidly into spiritual abstraction, *Elena* could plausibly be mistaken as a socially engaged text about contemporary urban class disparities. This is precisely the challenge – though "spiritual temptation" is perhaps the more accurate term – that Zviagintsev and his scriptwriter Oleg Negin have set for themselves. The success of the film lies in its capacity to transform a secularly grounded event into a plausibly universal human story of family loyalties and greed. Naum Kleiman's comment, for example, that Zviagintsev's work is "in the tradition of Greek tragedy" (Meek 2004) reveals the capacity of this talented team to move towards a larger transcendence – equipped with the classical moment

Figure 25.2 Ivan (Ivan Dobronravov, left) and Andrei (Vladimir Garin) in Zviagintsev's *The Return*, 2003.

of catharsis – that is an explicit part of the filmmaker's aesthetic credo.[17] Retaining a minimalist design and verbal restraint from the first two films, the director balances his accustomed mythic sweep with a distinct cultural particularity.

This balance of the universal with the particular may have been forged in the film's own production history: *Elena* was originally a British project with an English-language script (translated for the project). The original screenplay was produced in response to an offer (February 2009) to four directors by British producer Oliver Dungey for each to shoot a full-length, English-language feature, with a budget of about US$ 6–7 million apiece on the topic of the Apocalypse. By late March 2009, Zviagintsev's scriptwriter Oleg Negin had finished the script *Helen* about a British couple, Helen and Richard. Further progress on the project was delayed by funding complexities; by mid-May 2009, Zviagintsev had withdrawn from negotiations with Dungey. By the end of August, the director had found alternative support from Alexander Rodnyansky (Non-Stop Production) and by early October 2009 was in pre-production. The British drama had become a Russian – or rather, an Ostozhenka/Biriulevo – drama (see Zviagintsev, Negin, and Krichman 2014, 59–80).

Beyond the exigencies of its production history, however, the film is a clear example of a second dominant tendency in Zviagintsev's work: a pattern of strategic effacement. That is to say, the script, written in Russian, translated into English for a British film, then recast as a very specific Moscow drama, may transfer easily from culture to culture – some critics may argue – because it is a work of genius, deftly able to transcend cultural barriers. But this is not our concern here.

Instead, we are interested in Zviagintsev's selective withholding of certain cultural information so to throw other details into high relief, moving the work towards the moment of transcendence. In *Elena*, this technique is most evident in the wealthy protagonist Vladimir and his wife. Despite the very specific context of Ostozhenka, Vladimir remains an indeterminate figure: is he a former Soviet research scientist turned wealthy businessman? A retired security agent? A former high-ranking Komsomol functionary?[18] These questions, which haunt the film in its opening shots, fade into the background, not only because of actor Andrei Smirnov's performance. The scriptwriter and filmmaker are determined that the categories themselves – science, state security, state activism – reveal their dark, underlying compatibilities, fused into a single credible character, a filmic hieroglyph, a high-functioning abstraction. The marriage at the center of this film is doomed from its opening frames by Zviagintsev's alignment of "false knowledge" and "false love." One need not agree philosophically with Zviagintsev to appreciate this complex of elements.

The absence of information, therefore, is never simply an oversight; it is a strategy we can trace backwards in the earlier films. In retrospect, we recognize we had had similar uneasy hesitations about Zviagintsev's other male protagonists: who was the unnamed father (*The Return*) and why had he returned after 12 years? Why are most of the characters referred to only by common nouns (Mother, Father, Grandmother, Hooligan, Ringleader ["Zavodila"], Waitress)? This streamlined series is utterly compatible with the director's minimalist visual style and laconic script. But then, in strategic contrast to this dominant namelessness, the two "name-bearing" boys – Andrei and Ivan – are thereby linked to each other. Their naming encourages us to see the narrative through their eyes; their stark character differences are magnified in importance, throwing their performance into high relief.[19]

This pattern of effacement continues in *The Banishment*, where its execution finds a different strategy. Who were Alex and his brother, educated men somehow involved with the criminal underworld? Little by little, we are trained by Zviagintsev to expect no answers in an environment where more foundational information is already missing. Here, Zviagintsev's characters have proper names, but they are largely unmarked by national or ethnic identifiers – Alex (not Alek), Mark, Vera, Robert, Max, Victor, Liza – and are often chosen for their emblematic value: Alex [defender, an ironic choice], Vera [faith], Mark [warrior], and Eva [life]. National locale, too, is missing: shot in rural Moldova, urban Belgium and France, and Russia, the film in production or postproduction erases all conventional visual clues: street signs, currency, license plates, and other cultural indicators. We will not explore here the trans-European marketing and exhibition advantages for such a decision. Our interest here instead lies in the ways that erasure supports Zviagintsev's larger project of sublation and its part in cinematic significance.

The Third Technique: Indeterminacy

A third element in Zviagintsev's work is his love of indeterminacy, of loose ends or puzzles never solved: in *The Return*, what does the strongbox contain and why are we never permitted to know?[20] In *The Banishment*, why are we never given an explanation for Mark's gunshot wound? And why did Vera mislead the husband whom she loved? Critics have – quite reasonably – seen these lacunae as flaws (Bradshaw 2008). This is a critic's conversation. The interest here concerns a distinct cinematic style.

One should acknowledge immediately that this trait of indeterminacy is confoundingly akin to Zviagintsev's love of effacement. Let us pause for a moment to clarify this issue. If Zviagintsev's effacement is carried out by deleting empirical information of the past and present (origin, locale, profession, name), then here indeterminacy is sustained by withholding an anticipated revelation, the advent of which the director himself had signaled: surely in time, the film would come to reveal the contents of the strongbox (*The Return*), the reason for Mark's shooting and the motive for Vera's prevarication (*The Banishment*). Zviagintsev's men, who often have a murky past – in *The Return* and *The Banishment*, perhaps a criminal past, in *Elena*, perhaps a state-security past – are at the center of unsubstantiated intimations of a past densely correlated to the dark, unfulfilled omens of the future in ways that will remain unavailable to us. Our anticipation is frustrated; the narrative scroll does not unroll in the manner we had expected. The films all tend to mix an incomplete knowledge of the past with unreliable omens of the future.

Why, for example, are we proffered no story for the whale skeleton? It would have been an easy enough subplot; a less experienced filmmaker could not have resisted this temptation. Zviagintsev's and Negin's refusal to provide this detail is surely in part an effort to ensure no distractions from the associative value of the

Figure 25.3 Aleksandr (Konstantin Lavronenko) and Vera (Maria Bonnevie) in Zviagintsev's *The Banishment*, 2007.

image, which invites us to move conceptually from the stripped skeleton of the whale to the stripped architectural ruins of the old church to the skeletal ribs of the abandoned fishing boats. This linkage of the natural skeleton, the ruins of earlier church life, and the wreckage from a once-prosperous fishing trade leads us gradually first to a happy contrast and then to a second, mournful one. The first is Kolia's home and workplace; the second (in the same spot) is the garish new church built once the wreckage from Kolia's confiscated property is cleared. In the rolling out of this displacement in its larger significance – including the Church's false prophecies and the Law's false knowledge – the whale skeleton wisely remains an image without a story.

In this respect, Zviagintsev is a kind of counter-Chekhov. In Chekhov's work, we are often told, the gun hanging on the wall in Act One must be shot in Act Four; otherwise it has no place either on the wall or in the script.[21] In Zviagintsev's work, the gun hanging on the wall turns out to be an intimation of nothing – unless, perhaps, a knife fight in the closing scene. Surfeited with omens, his world remains increasingly unstable and unpredictable as the signs accumulate. The tower (*The Return*) from which the fearful son Ivan jumps at the film's beginning is not the tower from which his fearless father topples to his death. The photograph the children find in the film's beginning is not the photograph they find at the end. Such occasional framing devices are not signals of predictability, similarity, or even repetition, but of irrecoverable loss.

Love, Knowledge, Prophecy

These three techniques – inversion, effacement, indeterminacy – are the hallmarks of Zviagintsev's visual and narrative style. They are deployed by the filmmaker to induce the conditions within which he would like to stage his central dramas: worldly evil long in place that comes to crisis; the imperiled condition of love; the recurrent nightmare of a world without spiritual guidance. Zviagintsev arrives at his core topics by forcing the viewer to experience repeated failures: the earthly inversions of meaning render love unrecognizable; the effacement of the past confounds knowledge; the indeterminacy of the future confounds prophecy.

What unites Zviagintsev's feature films – thus far, in an unfinished career – is his preoccupation with mortal love adrift from the sacred, its incipient failure and distance from "the complete." The filmmaker's portrait of "human error and its consequences" (Bitel 2007) is not concerned with abstract error as such, but with wayward missteps of humans impaired by their distance from the divine. The attendant uncertainty of survival in a world rife with portents unintelligible to its characters exacerbates eternal questions of elusive faith, uncertain loyalty, and the demands of love beyond human competence. Zviagintsev's sublunary characters

Figure 25.4 Elena (Nadezhda Markina) and her husband Vladimir (Andrei Smirnov) in Zviagintsev's *Elena*, 2010.

often seem like exiles from an earlier time when ethical guidance had still been available. Their profane environment is replete with foreboding, but often about dire events that will not happen: the father carries a knife, but does not kill the children (*The Return*); the protagonist brings a gun, but does not kill his wife's alleged lover (*The Banishment*); the rowdy grandson is left for dead, but does not die; the toddler does not topple from the balcony (*Elena*); the meddling lawyer is brought to execution, but let go (*Leviathan*). These unexpected reprieves are not mercy but mere happenstance: they exist in a universe far too distant from the sacred original.

In *Elena*, the most distinct symbol of impending apocalypse – the white horse by the railroad tracks, as Elena travels out to see her son's family – seems to foretell the heroine's doomed future. By the film's conclusion, it is the horse itself that comes to a violent end; the heroine flourishes.[22] In some other's filmmaker's work, this inversion would be an ironic twist; in Zviagintsev's work, it is a statement about the unintelligibility of meaning in a world that has forgotten its contact to the divine.

It is against the backdrop of these dominant techniques – inversion, effacement, indeterminacy – that I would like to conclude this chapter with comments on Zviagintsev's links to the Tarkovskian tradition. The topic cannot receive exhaustive treatment here; the links are simultaneously self-evident and deserving of extensive elaboration.

It is evident that Zviagintsev is apprenticed to Andrei Tarkovskii in several stylistic respects: the director's leisurely narrative tempo (a slow camera, little movement, long takes); the minimalist script with its sparse dialogue; the extensive use of ambient sound design (water, birds, trains); the broad landscapes, with sudden changes of weather; the pervasive mood of spiritual nostalgia. Given these compatibilities, it is difficult to ignore their cultural affinities, which is more a matter of dialogue than identical repetition. Zviagintsev's selection for *The Return* of an extended passage from Wolfgang Amadeus Mozart's 1791 Requiem Mass in D minor (K626) is arguably an homage to Tarkovskii, who had selected an extended passage from Johann Sebastian Bach's 1732 Choral Prelude in F Minor ("Ich ruf zu dir Herr Jesu Christ"; BWV 639) for his science-fiction film *Solaris* [*Soliaris*, 1972]. More verifiably, Zviagintsev has spoken at length of his indebtedness to Tarkovskii – in particular, "his attitude toward the rhythm and flow of time" – and has underscored his admiration for both Tarkovskii's *Andrei Rublev* (1966) and *The Mirror* [*Zerkalo*, 1975] (Abeel 2004).

It is inevitable, therefore, that comparisons might further be made with another filmmaker 13 years Zviagintsev's senior, but equally indebted to Tarkovskii's cinema. Aleksandr Sokurov and Zviagintsev can be situated in a larger constellation of Tarkovskian descendants loosely described as Russia's transcendental cinema, a cluster that would also include the early Sergei Sel'ianov, Aleksandr Kaidanovskii, and Konstantin Lopushanskii.[23] The list is contingent; it implies a working distinction from so-called poetic cinema (Aleksandr Dovzhenko, Iurii Illienko, Leonid Osyka, Sergei Parajanov).[24] While the categories surely overlap, and the distinction must advisably remain weak, transcendental cinema is concerned less with visual style (perspectivalism, flatness, tableau aesthetics, ornament) than with philosophical states of cognition and meaning that reside in distinct historical belief systems outside the cinema text.

An accurate positioning of Zviagintsev in the contemporary cinema landscape must comment on sharp contrasts to Sokurov's work, principal among them the status of the narrative line. Sokurov is committed to that state of grace best captured through the static image and an accompanying radical suppression of narrative (see Condee 2011). By contrast, Zviagintsev's concern with secular human error and its catastrophic consequences are deeply dependent on narrative complexity. Zviagintsev's principal techniques – an inversion of cultural references; an erasure of local signs; and an insistence on loose ends – are grounded in characters with a robust and credible earthly existence, confused by debased sacred fragments. Moreover, Zviagintsev does not share Sokurov's preoccupation with death, and while Zviagintsev's cinema is compatible with Sokurov that art (including cinema) can afford us a fleeting glimpse of immortality beyond the visible world, no characters (in Zviagintsev's work) have access to this knowledge within the four sides of the cinema screen.

On a larger scale, Sokurov and Zviagintsev figure among those "transcendentalists" who share a common philosophical engagement with the later writings of

Soviet philosopher Merab Mamardashvili.[25] Mamardashvili's voice appears in Sokurov's short documentary *Demoted* [*Razzhalovannyi*, 1980]; he is cited by both Sokurov and Zviagintsev with enormous reverence (Sokurov 1994, 16; Matizen 2013, 657; also Savel'ev 1994, 60). The two directors share Mamardashvili's recurrent investment in pan-European culture as a measure of humanity.[26]

Most relevant, however, to the argument presented on these pages, it is perhaps no coincidence that Mamardashvili repeatedly returns to the trope of inverted forms to describe the ways in which humanity operates in a distorted world it has failed to understand. Arguing that "the real social connections between people take on inverted, irrational forms" (1963, 114), Mamardashvili takes up a tradition of things turned on their heads, deriving from Karl Marx's polemics on the *verwandelte Form* (Nikolchina 2014). In his most explicit treatment of this theme, his essay "Inverted Forms: On the Necessity of Irrational Expressions," Mamardashvili (1992) speaks of such inverted forms as an "enchanted world, placed on its head, and densely populated with ghosts and miracles," but (in the words of Miglena Nikolchina), "immune to a reversal, a backward inversion, so to speak, that would reveal their truth" (Nikolchina 2014, 94).

More research – such as that already begun by Alyssa DeBlasio – must be ventured to establish an explicit link between Zviagintsev's inversions and its ancestry in Mamardashvili's "Inverted Forms," in circulation in the hothouse philosophical environment of Moscow's 1970s, 1980s, and early 1990s. But these details perhaps contribute to the earlier, near-forgotten promise: are Zviagintsev's inversions a

Figure 25.5 The skeleton in Zviagintsev's *Leviathan*, 2014.

playful caprice or a philosophical statement about the secular world? More plausibly the latter. His sublunary drifters cannot set the world right; their knowledge and prophecies are insufficient to rescue their loved ones from a condition that requires something more than human competencies. It would be banal to assert that Zviagintsev's core theme is transcendent love – love beyond the secular realm – but much of his filmmaking suggests that he hopes to position the viewer for a contemplation of what precisely such an elusive state might be.[27]

Notes

1. After its initial mention, "tongues" plays no role in this rhetorical cluster.
2. It is perhaps not incidental that two of Zviagintsev's most admired directors – Ingmar Bergman in his drama *Through a Glass Darkly* [*Såsom i en spegel*, 1961]; and Krzysztof Kieślowski in his *Blue* [*Bleu*, 1993] – have also drawn on the same Corinthian passages. The Corinthians (in particular, the phrase "through a glass, darkly") is cited, of course, more broadly than these two directors, though this expedition is not relevant here. The most familiar examples include Agatha Christie's short story ("In a Glass Darkly," 1939); Isaac Asimov's collection of four short stories (*Through a Glass, Clearly*, 1967); and George Steiner's contribution to the Dutch *Huizinga Lecture* [*Huizingalezing*, 1987].
3. I do not attribute this strain of political activism to Zviagintsev or to his film; rather, I suggest that Zviagintsev directs a film where the capacity of human spirituality to approach the Divine is impaired by contact with an official Church that colludes with the State over secular concerns of property, law, money, and political power. The term itself usually refers to the effort to sever the official Church from the state. Successful outcomes to historical disestablishmentarianist movements took place in 1869 (the disestablishment of the Church of Ireland), 1920 (Church of England in Wales), and 1929 (Church of Scotland).
4. Another link between the Bishop and the Lawyer is suggested circumspectly in the Bishop's office, where the Bishop clearly functions as a "legal advisor" to the Mayor. Behind the Bishop on his mantel, a bust bearing the words "Ecce homo" ["Behold the man!"] associates the Bishop with Pontius Pilate and – by extension – the film's protagonist with the scourged Christ. While we are initially inclined to see the lawyer Dima as a rescuer, it becomes clear that he scourges the protagonist in his own way.
5. Here one might recall that the ruined church has a bonfire constantly burning in its center.
6. For greater detail, see Zviagintsev's official website http://az-film.com/ru/Bio/.
7. The NIKA Award (Russian Academy of Motion Picture Arts and Sciences), established in 1987 by Iulii Gusman and often compared with the Oscars (Academy Awards), is the country's oldest and most prestigious national film award. The Golden Eagle Award (National Academy of Motion Picture Arts and Sciences of Russia), established in 2002 by Nikita Mikhalkov, is often viewed as a competing award (but is awarded by the National Academy in both cinema and television).
8. Tarkovskii shared the Lion with Valerio Zurlini's screen adaptation *Family Diary* [*Cronaca familiare*, 1962].

9   See Beumers (2007) for an invaluable account of the relation between Saroyan's novella and the script, co-written by Artem Melkumian and Oleg Negin.
10 For example Kliueva (2010); Anokhina and Gasparov (2014). Serious Anglophone scholarship had begun already in response to *The Return* (Beumers 2003; Graffy 2004; 2008; Strukov 2007). I would like to thank Natalie Ryabchikova for alerting me to Kliueva's work.
11 See, for example, Naum Kleiman's intriguing comment on *The Return*: "This is not a Tarkovsky film. Tarkovsky's films are Protestant. This is more in the tradition of Greek tragedy" (Kleiman quoted in Meek 2004).
12 In conversation with Viktor Matizen (2013, 664), Zviagintsev mentions that he had considered both "banishment" and "annunciation" as possible film titles.
13 Zviagintsev is explicit in interviews about these religious references: "In *The Return*, I was rebuked because [in this film] a Russian man, returning home after a long absence, sets wine on the table rather than vodka. But I needed wine in the shot, precisely to point towards the biblical model. So, too, with the shot in which the father in shown from the same angle as Christ in Mantegna's picture" (Matizen 2013, 670).
14 For an elaboration of inverse value more broadly in Russian culture, see Condee (1999).
15 Considerable debate surrounds the figures of Behemoth (Job 40: 15–24) and Leviathan (Job 41: 1–34). In the Second Lesson of Chapter 40 in his *Commentary on the Book of Job* [*Expositio super Iob ad litteram*] (Aquinas n.d.), Thomas Aquinas identifies them thus: "the name Behemoth, which means 'animal,' refers to the elephant […] The name 'Leviathan' […] refers to the large whales;" ("ut hoc nomen Vehemot, quod significat animal, referatur ad elephantem […] nomen autem Leviathan […] referatur ad cete grandia"). In the second volume of his *Hierozoicon, sive hipertitum opus de animalibus Sacrae Scriturae* (5:15–16), however, Samuel Bochart takes a different view: "not an elephant, if you will, but a hippopotamus"; "Leviathan, so named, does not mean a whale, but a crocodile" ("non esse Elephantem, ut volunt, sed hippopatamum"; "Leviathanis nomine son significari Balaenam, sed Crocodilum") (Kinnier Wilson 1975, 1).
16 The biblical passage, if further "misread" as if it were the mayor's soliloquy, continues in an equally chilling vein: "Who then is able to stand against me? Who has a claim against me that I must pay? Everything under heaven belongs to me" (Job 41: 10–11).
17 "I belong to the old school of theatre and cinema and I believe that every work needs a catharsis. A film is basically another reality. It's like a dream. It's important that the viewer can give themselves [sic] to that dream and live within it, so when they enter the cinema they are in one kind of space and when the leave it they are in a different space" (Davies 2008).
18 While the director, together with lead actor Andrei Smirnov, considered these alternatives, they leaned towards the choice of "former scientist," only because Smirnov physically resembled this role more than a former KGB officer or a Komsomol functionary.
19 This technique, akin to high-contrast lighting, does not seem to be ethically marked: elements withheld from the viewer's attention are not necessarily sacred or profane. The technique seems to be deployed independent of axiological categories.

20 An earlier draft of the script contains the answer, but this fact tells us more about Zviagintsev than about the contents.
21 Chekhov's remark "If you have hung a pistol on the wall in the first act, then in the last act, it should shoot. Otherwise, don't hang it there" has taken on a life of its own over the years. It is attributed in different variants to several historical moments. One reliable source ascribes its enunciation in Yalta in summer 1889 to I. Ia. Guliand, first published in the journal *Osa* 45 (November 21, 1910): 3. For additional attribution and information, see Chekhov (1976) and Guliand (1904).
22 The Apocalypse that does not happen is perhaps a trace of Zviagintsev's and Negin's original submission to British producer Oliver Dungey, who had tendered an offer for a film on the Apocalypse. As Graffy (2012) deftly notes, an apocalyptical theme (in visual and verbal references) runs throughout the heroine's final visit to her family.
23 The term "transcendental film" has a rich history. For the major coordinates, see Efird (2007) (on Andrei Tarkovskii) and Schrader (1988) (on Yasujirō Ozu, Robert Bresson, and Carl Theodor Dreyer).
24 My argument here is indebted to Olga Kim and Joshua First, whose work has helped sharpen my thinking.
25 See the work-in-progress by Alyssa DeBlasio on Mamardashvili's impact on late Soviet culture: "The Freest Man in the USSR: Merab Mamardashvili and Russian Cinematic Consciousness."
26 Exceptions to Sokurov's putative regard for pan-European high culture, of course, are his three Japanese documentaries: *Eastern Elegy* [*Vostochnaia elegiia*, 1996]; *A Humble Life* [*Smirennaia zhizn'*, 1997]; and his *dolce… [dol'che…*, 2000]. Arguably, one might add his feature *Sun* [*Solntse*, 2005], in which Hirohito is a more amiable creature than his European counterparts Hitler in *Moloch* [*Molokh*, 1999] and Lenin in *Taurus* [*Telets*, 2001].
27 I am grateful to the following experts and scholars for their support as this chapter was being written: Sitora Alieva, Birgit Beumers, Joel Chapron, and Eugénie Zvonkine. They are not responsible for the views expressed here.

References

Abeel, Erica. 2004. "Return of the Prodigal Father: Andrey Zvyagintsev Talks about *The Return*." *Indiewire* February 2, http://www.indiewire.com/article/return_of_the_prodigal_father_andrey_zvyagintsev_talks_about_the_return. (accessed February 20, 2015).

Anokhina, Iuliia and Vladimir Gasparov, eds 2014. *Dykhanie kamnia: Mif fil'mov Andreia Zviagintseva: Sbornik statei i materialov* [The Breath of the Stone: The Myth of Andrei Zviagintsev's Films]. Moscow: Novoe literaturnoe obozrenie.

Aquinas, Thomas. n.d. *Expositio super Iob ad litteram* [Commentary on the Book of Job]. Edited by Joseph Kenny, translated by Brian Mulladay. http://dhspriory.org/thomas/SSJob.htm (accessed February 20, 2015).

Beumers, Birgit. 2003. "Review of Andrei Zviagintsev, *The Return*." *KinoKultura* 3, http://www.kinokultura.com/reviews/R14return.html (accessed February 20, 2015).

Beumers, Birgit. 2007. "Review of Andrei Zviagintsev, *The Banishment.*" *KinoKultura* 18, http://www.kinokultura.com/2007/18r-izgnanie.shtml (accessed February 20, 2015).

Bitel, Anton. 2007. "The Banishment [Izgnanie] Review." *Film4*, http://www.film4.com/reviews/2007/the-banishment (accessed February 20, 2015).

Bradshaw, Peter. 2008. "The Banishment." *The Guardian* August 14, http://www.theguardian.com/film/2008/aug/15/drama.worldcinema (accessed February 20, 2015).

Chekhov, Anton. 1976. Letter No. 707 (November 1, 1889) to A. S. Lazarev (Guzinskii). *Polnoe sobranie sochinenii i pisem* vol. 3: 273–275. Moscow: AN SSSR Nauka.

Condee, Nancy. 1999. "No Glory, No Majesty, or Honor: The Russian Idea and Inverse Value." In *Russia on Reels: The Russian Idea in Post-Soviet Cinema*, edited by Birgit Beumers, 25–33. London: I. B. Tauris.

Condee, Nancy. 2011. "Endstate and Allegory (Late Sokurov)." In *The Cinema of Alexander Sokurov*, edited by Birgit Beumers and Nancy Condee, 246–260. London: I. B. Tauris.

Davies, Rebecca. 2008. "Andrei Zviagintsev Interview." *The Telegraph* August 12, http://www.telegraph.co.uk/culture/film/3558368/Andrei-Zvyagintsev-interview.html (accessed February 20, 2015).

Efird, Robert. 2007. "*Andrei Rublev*. Transcendental Style and the Creative Vision." *Journal of Popular Film and Television* 35.2: 86–93.

Graffy, Julian. 2004. "*The Return.*" *Sight and Sound* 7: 64.

Graffy, Julian. 2008. "Film of the Month: *The Banishment.*" *Sight and Sound* 9, http://old.bfi.org.uk/sightandsound/review/4441 (accessed February 20, 2015).

Graffy, Julian. 2012. "Review of Andrei Zviagintsev, *Elena.*" *KinoKultura* 35, http://www.kinokultura.com/2012/35r-elena.shtml (accessed February 20, 2015).

Guliand, I. Ia. 1904. "Iz vospominanii ob A. P. Chekhove" [Recollections about Chekhov]. *Teatr i iskusstvo* [Theater and Art] 28 (July 11): 521.

Kinnier Wilson, J. V. 1975. "A Return to the Problems of Behemoth and Leviathan." *Vetus Testamentum*, 25.1: 1–14.

Kliueva, Liudmila. 2010. *Ot vidimogo k nevidimomu: Andrei Zviagintsev i ego kino* [From the Visible to the Invisible: Andrei Zviagintsev and his Cinema]. Moscow: GITR.

Mamardashvili, Merab. 1963. "K kritike eksistentsialistskogo ponimaniia dialektiki" [A Critique of an Existentialist Understanding of Dialectics]. *Voprosy filosofii* [Questions of Philosophy] 6: 108–120.

Mamardashvili, Merab. 1992. "Prevrashchennye formy: O neobkhodimosti neratsional'nykh vyrazhenii" [Inverted Forms: On the Necessity of Irrational Expressions]. In his *Kak ia ponimaiu filosofiiu* [How I Understand Philosophy]. 269–282. Moscow: Progress.

Matizen, Viktor. 2013. "'Iskhodit' sleduet iz vysshei pravdy o cheloveke' 2009, 2012" [You Should Depart from the Highest Truth about Man]. Two interviews with Andrei Zviagintsev. *Kino i zhizn'. 12 diuzhin interv'iu samogo skepticheskogo kinokritika*] [Cinema and Life. 12 Dozen Interviews of the Most Skeptical Film Critic]. Vol. 2: 653–674. Vinnitsa: Globus-Press.

Meek, James. 2004. "From Russia with Compassion." *The Guardian* June 25, http://www.theguardian.com/film/2004/jun/25/features.jamesmeek (accessed February 20, 2015).

Nikolchina, Miglena. 2014. "Inverted Forms and Heterotopic Homonymy: Althusser, Mamardashvili, and the Problem of 'Man.'" *boundary 2* 41.1: 79–100.

Savel'ev, Dmitrii. 1994. "Krugi razzhalovannogo" [Circles of the Degraded]. *Sokurov*, edited by Liubov' Arkus and Dmitrii Savel'ev, 59–62. St Petersburg: Seans.

Schrader, Paul. 1988. *Transcendental Style in Film*. Cambridge, MA: Da Capo Press.

Sokurov, Aleksandr. 1994. "Ten' zvuka" [The Shadow of Sound]. Television interview for TV-6 Moscow with Petr Shepotinnik, Asia Kolodizhner, and Liubov' Arkus. *Iskusstvo kino* [Art of Cinema] 12: 13–17.

Strukov, Vlad. 2007. "The Return of Gods: Andrei Zviagintsev's *Vozvrashchenie* [The Return]." *Slavic and East European Journal* 51.2: 331–356.

Vicks, Meghan. 2010. "Re-review of Andrei Zviagintsev, *The Return*." *KinoKultura* 32, http://www.kinokultura.com/2011/32rr-return.shtml (accessed February 20, 2015).

Zviagintsev, Andrei, Oleg Negin, and Mikhail Krichman. 2014. *Elena: Istoriia sozdaniia fil'ma* [*Elena*: History of a Film's Creation]. London: Cygnnet.

Appendix

Chronology of Events in Russian Cinema and History

Date	Cinema and Culture	History
1896		
May 4	Cinema at the Aquarium Park, Petersburg	
May 14		Coronation of Tsar Nicholas II
1902		
Apr 2		Assassination of Dmitri Sipiagin, Interior Minister
Sep 22	Meyerhold in Kherson, *Three Sisters*	
1904		
January		Russo–Japanese War (until Aug 1905)
Jul 15		Assassination of Viacheslav von Plehve, Interior Minister
Jul 30		Birth of Tsarevich Alexei
1905		
Jan 9		Bloody Sunday (1905 Revolution)
Feb 19	Metropol Hotel in Moscow opens	
Jun 14–25		Uprising on battleship "Potemkin"
1906		
Apr 27		First Duma elected
Dec 9	Khanzhonkov company opens	
Dec 30	Meyerhold, *The Fairground Booth*	

(*Continued*)

A Companion to Russian Cinema, First Edition. Edited by Birgit Beumers.
© 2016 John Wiley & Sons, Inc. Published 2016 by John Wiley & Sons, Inc.

(Continued)

Date	Cinema and Culture	History
1907		
Oct 28	Drankov Atelier opens	
Dec 22	Anna Pavlova dances *The Dying Swan*	
1908		
Sep 6	Tolstoy's eightieth birthday	
Oct 15	*Stenka Razin*	
Nov 1	Khanzhonkov's *Gypsy Camp*	
Nov 27	Film control introduced	
1909		
Summer	*Ballets Russes* in Paris	
Nov 29	Pathé color film *Happy-go-Lucky Merchant*	
Nov 10	Ars Cinema [Khudozhestvennyi] opens	
1910		
Nov 7	Death of Tolstoy	
	Gramophone factory near Moscow	
1911		
February	Fire in Bologoe cinema	
Sep 1		Assassination of Petr Stolypin, (chairman of council of ministers)
Oct 1	Circus opens (Nikitin Bros)	
Nov 14	*Defense of Sevastopol* shown to the Tsar	
1913		
Feb 16	Drankov and Taldykin, *300 Years of the Romanovs*	
Nov 14	Khanzhonkov opens cinema on Triumphal Square	
Dec 2	Futurist theater: *Victory over the Sun*	
Dec 26	Starewicz, *Christmas Eve*	
1914		
Mar 3	Bauer, *Child of the Big City*	
Jun 28		Murder of Franz-Ferdinand
Jul 19–24		Germany, then Austria-Hungary declare war on Russia
August		Petersburg becomes Petrograd
1915		
May 8	Prohibition of import of German films	

Chronology of Events in Russian Cinema and History

(Continued)

Date	Cinema and Culture	History
November	Meyerhold's *Portrait of Dorian Gray*	
1916		
January	0,10 exhibition of futurist abstract art	
Apr 19	Protazanov, *Queen of Spades*	
May 10	Bauer, *Life for a Life*	
Dec 17		Murder of Rasputin
1917		
Feb 23–27		February Revolution
Mar 2		Abdication of the Tsar
Mar 7–9		Arrest of imperial family
Apr 3		Lenin returns to Russia
Jul 9	Death of Evgenii Bauer	
Oct 16	Proletkult clubs for workers	
Oct 21	Protazanov, *Satan Triumphant*	
Oct 25		October Revolution: Storming of Winter Palace
December		Lunacharskii as head of Narkompros
December		Cheka [Emergency committee] established
1918		
Jan 11		Ukrainian People's Republic
Mar 3		Treaty of Brest-Litovsk (Russia loses territories but withdraws from the war)
Mar 4	Prohibition on cinema closures	
Mar 12		Moscow becomes capital
May 14	Protazanov, *Father Sergius*	
Apr 29		Hetmanate in Ukraine under Pavlo Skoropadsky
Jul 17	Kinokomitet of the Commissariat for Enlightenment [Narkompros]	Execution of imperial family in Ekaterinburg
Oct 10		new orthography introduced
November		Directorate of Ukraine under Symon Petliura
1919		
Feb 3	Death of actress Vera Kholodnaia	
Aug 27	Cinema nationalized under Narkompros	
Sep 1	Goskinoshkola [State Film School] opens	
Sep 5	Death of Chapaev	
Dec 26		Campaign against illiteracy

(Continued)

(Continued)

Date	Cinema and Culture	History
1920		
		Azerbaijan and Armenia become Soviet Republics; Independence for Latvia, Lithuania, Estonia
Jul 8		American embargo
Nov 7	Evreinov's spectacle *Storming of the Winter Palace*	
1921		
		Georgia becomes a Soviet Republic
Mar 21		New Economic Policy introduced
Feb 28–Mar 18		Kronstadt uprising against Soviet power
October	Gor'kii leaves Soviet Russia for Italy on health grounds	
1922		
	Establishment of Glavlit (Main Administration for Safeguarding State Secrets in the Press)	Campaign against the church: arrests and executions
Jan 17	Leninist proportion: 75 percent entertainment and 25 percent propaganda films	
February		Cheka renamed GPU (State Political directorate, from 1923 OGPU)
Apr 3		Stalin as General Secretary of the Party
May 25		Lenin suffers stroke
Jun 5	First newsreel of *Kinopravda*	
Jul 9	FEKS (Factory of the Eccentric Actor)	
December	Goskino (Central State Film and Photo Enterprise)	
Dec 30		Formation of USSR
1923		
	Eisenstein makes "Glumov's Diary"; publishes "Montage of Attraction"	
Jan 4		Lenin's Testament
Jul 6		Soviet Constitution
Nov 30	Perestiani, *Red Imps*	
1924		
		Uzbekistan, Tajikistan and Turkmenistan join the USSR; Kirghiz ASSR; USSR recognized by UK and France
Jan 21		Death of Lenin
Jan 24		Petrograd named Leningrad
Jan 31		Call for party membership (Leninskii prizyv)

Chronology of Events in Russian Cinema and History

(Continued)

Date	Cinema and Culture	History
Feb 3		Rykov as Premier
Jun 4	Sovkino (All-Russian Photo-Cinematographic Shareholding Company) formed	
Aug 1	Mezhrabpom-Rus formed (Mezhrabpomfilm from 1928)	
Sep 25	Protazanov's *Aelita* (first film after his return to Russia)	
Nov 23	First radios	
Dec 2	Zheliabuzhskii, *The Cigarette Girl from Mosselprom*	
Dec 9	Kozintsev and Trauberg, *Oktyabrina's Adventures*	
December		Stalin announces "socialism in one country"
1925		
	Journal *Sovetskii ekran* launched	
Apr 28	Eisenstein's *The Strike* released	
Nov 6		Yekaterinburg renamed Sverdlovsk
1926		
		Grigorii Zinoviev, Lev Trotskii, and Lev Kamenev form an opposition to Stalin
Jan 18	Eisenstein's *Potemkin* shown at Ars Cinema	
Jul 20		Death of Felix Dzerzhinsky (Cheka founder)
Oct 11	Pudovkin's *The Mother*	
1927		
Mar 14		Plan for hydro-electric power station Dneprostroi
Mar 15	Room's *Bed and Sofa*	
Nov 7	Moscow Youth Theatre and TRAM (Theatre of Working Youth) founded	
1928		
		First Five-Year-Plan 1928–1932: industrialization
		Kamenev and Zinoviev admit "mistakes" and are re-admitted to the Party
Mar 12	Eisenstein's *October*	
Mar 15–21	Conference on Cinema Affairs	
Apr 13	Dovzhenko, *Zvenigora*	
May 28	Return of Maksim Gor'kii	
Nov 10	Pudovkin, *Storm over Asia*	

(Continued)

(Continued)

Date	Cinema and Culture	History
1929		
	TEA jazz ensemble by Leonid Utesov	Lunacharskii dismissed; Bukharin and Rykov excluded from the Party
		Building of Magnitogorsk
Jan 18		Trotsky exiled to Alma-Ata
Mar 18	Kozintsev and Trauberg's *New Babylon*	
Apr 9	Vertov's *Man with a Movie Camera*	
August		Purges in the Academy of Sciences
September		First combine harvester
Oct 05	First sound cinema in Leningrad	
Oct 26		Destruction of Iberian Gates on Red Square (reconstructed 1995)
Nov 7	Eisenstein's *The General Line*	
December		Prohibition of sale of Christmas trees; no church bells
1930		
Jan 30		Liquidation of *kulaks* (campaign)
February	Soiuzkino formed	
Mar 6	Khudozhestvennyi (Ars) with sound	
Apr 8	Dovzhenko's *Earth*	
Apr 14	Suicide of poet Maiakovskii	
April	Film train departs for 16 months	
Nov 10		New Lenin Mausoleum by Shchusev
Dec 19		Rykov replaced by Molotov as Premier
December	Shumiatskii as head of cinema affairs	
1931		
Feb 9	Soiuzkino factory opens in Moscow (from 1935 known as Mosfilm)	
Mar 28		Turksib railway opens
Jun 01	*Path to Life*: first sound film	
Jul 1	Soiuzkinokhronika	
Oct 10	Kozintsev and Trauberg's *Alone*	
Nov 7	Udarnik cinema opens	
Dec 5		Cathedral of Christ the Savior blown up, reconstructed in 1995
1932		
1932–1934		Moskva-Volga Canal construction; Dneprostroi construction

(Continued)

Date	Cinema and Culture	History
Apr 23	Writers' Union formed: Socialist Realism	
Nov 9		Nadezhda Allilueva (Stalin's wife) dies
1933		Second Five-Year-Plan 1933–1937 industry and communications
Mar 25	Barnet's *Outskirts*	
Jun 20		White Sea Canal opens
Jul 12		"Cheliuskin" on arctic expedition; crushed Feb 13, 1934
Jul 15		Uralmash industry opens
Nov 25		Korolev: rocket test
Nov 16		US–USSR enter diplomatic relations
Dec 17	First children's film *Torn Boots*	
Dec 26		Lunacharskii dies
1934		
May 4	Dom Kino [House of Cinema] opens	
May 10		Iagoda heads secret service, OGPU
Jun 26	Savchenko's *The Accordion* (first musical)	
Jul 10		OGPU becomes NKVD [People's Commissariat for Internal Affairs]
Aug 17–Sep 1	Writers' Union Congress	
Oct 27		Gulags (prison camps) open
Nov 7	*Chapaev*	
Dec 1		Assassination of Leningrad Party chief Kirov
Dec 25	Aleksandrov, *Jolly Fellows*	
September	Mosfilm, Lenfilm organized	
1935		
		VSKhV, All-Union Agriculture Exhibition, opens: building complete 1939
Jan 8–13	Cinema Workers' Union: congress	
Feb 21–Mar 2	Moscow International Film Festival	
Mar 25	Ptushko, *New Gulliver*	
1935		Trial of 16 (Kamenev, Zinoviev) begins
May 15		First metro line opens
Jul 10		Plan for the reconstruction of Moscow
Sep 19		Death of Konstantin Tsiolkovskii

(Continued)

(Continued)

Date	Cinema and Culture	History
Nov 17		Stalin's phrase "Life had become better, comrades, life has become more joyous"
Dec 20		Hotel Moskva opens

1936

Date	Cinema and Culture	History
Jan 28	Attack in Pravda on Shostakovich for *Lady Macbeth of Mtsensk*	
Mar 25	First film, *The Great Citizen*, shown on television	
May 25	Aleksandrov, *The Circus*	
Jun 8	Soiuzdetfilm formed on the basis of Mezhrabpomfilm	
Jun 11	First color film *Grunia Kornakova*	
Jun 18	Death of Gor'kii	
Jun 27		Abortion prohibited
Jul 24		Chkalov's first flight to the east
Aug 25		Zinoviev and Kamenev executed
Sep 26		Ezhov as head of NKVD replaces Iagoda
Dec 5		Soviet Constitution

1937

Date	Cinema and Culture	History
January		Trial of 17: Radek, Piatakov, Sokolnikov
May–Nov	International Exhibition in Paris (Mukhina, ["Worker and Peasant"])	
Nov 5	Regular evening television from Shabolovka transmitter	
Nov 10	Death of actor Nikolai Batalov	

1938

Date	Cinema and Culture	History
		Third Five-Year-Plan 1938–1941: armament
Jan 7	Closure of Meyerhold Theater	
Mar 13		Russian language compulsory in all schools across USSR
Mar 17		Anschluss: Austria as ally to Nazi-Germany
Apr 24	Aleksandrov's *Volga-Volga*	
Jul 27		Arrest of Korolev
July		Third show trial against 21, including Bukharin, Rykov, and Iagoda: executions
August		Beriia as head of NKVD replaces Ezhov
Aug 7	Death of theater director Stanislavskii	
Dec 1	Eisenstein's *Alexander Nevsky*	
Dec 15		Death of Valerii Chkalov

Chronology of Events in Russian Cinema and History 593

(Continued)

Date	Cinema and Culture	History
1939		
Jan 18	Death in Paris of Ivan Mosjoukine	
Apr 21	Cinema "Moskva" installed in St Catherine's cathedral, Leningrad	
May 1	Dovzhenko's *Shchors*	
Jun 10		Ezhov arrested and executed on Feb 4, 1940
Jul 3	Pyr'ev's *The Tractor Drivers*	
Jul 15	Murder of Meyerhold's wife Zinaida Raikh	
Aug 23		Molotov–Ribbentrop Pact
Sep 01		World War II: Germany invades Poland; UK and France declare war on Germany
Sep 17		Soviet Army in eastern Poland; western Ukraine to USSR
Nov 30		Soviet–Finnish war (Winter War) until defeat of Russia army on Dec 26; Soviet breakthrough Feb 12, 1940
1940		
Feb 2	Meyerhold executed	
Apr/May		NKVD shoot Polish POWs in Katyn
Jun/Jul		Ultimatum to Baltic states and annexation
Aug 21		Assassination of Trotsky
1941		
May 6		Stalin as Premier
Jun 22		Germany attacks USSR
July		Evacuation of Moscow
Aug 8		Stalin as chief commander of the army
August		Deportation of Volga Germans to Siberia and Kazakhstan
Sep 8		Leningrad Blockade until Jan 18, 1943
Sep 29–30		Massacre of Baby Yar
1942		
May 4	*She Defended the Motherland*	
Jul 1942–Jan 1943		Siege of Stalingrad
August		Churchill in Moscow
September		Young Guard resistance in Krasnodon, executions in Feb 1943
1943		
		Patriarchate restored
Nov 28–Dec 1		Tehran conference with Roosevelt, Stalin, and Churchill

(Continued)

(Continued)

Date	Cinema and Culture	History
1944		
Jan 1		New Soviet hymn replaces Internationale
Jan 24	The Rainbow	
Dec 1943–Apr 1944		Deportation of Kalmyks, Ingush, and Chechens
1945		
Jan 16	Eisenstein's *Ivan the Terrible*	
Feb 4–11		Yalta conference: agreement on spheres of influence in Europe
Apr 25		Meeting of American and Soviet army on the Elbe
May 9		Victory: capitulation of Germany
Jun 24		Victory Parade in Moscow
Jul 17–Aug 2		Potsdam conference: denazification, demilitarization and decentralization of Germany
Aug 6 and 9		Nuclear bombs on Hiroshima and Nagasaki
Aug 8	Death of Protazanov	
Sep 2		Japan capitulates
Sep 26	Death of producer Khanzhonkov	
1946		
		Fourth Five-Year-Plan 1946–1950: reconstruction
Mar 5		Churchill: Fulton speech ("Cold War")
Jun 18	Death of Georgii Vasil'ev (*Chapaev*)	
Aug 9	Stalin criticizes Eisenstein	
Sep 4	Accusations leveled against *Great Life*	
1947		
		Zhdanov's Cosmopolitan Campaign
Feb 24	Meeting of Stalin and Eisenstein	
July	The Vow	
1948		
Jan 13	Solomon Mikhoels killed in Minsk	
Feb 11	Death of Eisenstein	
Jun 2		Law on layabouts [*tuneiadtsy*]
Aug 31		Death of Zhdanov
Oct 11	The Young Guard	
1949		
	Closure of Jewish Theater GOSET; closure of Pushkin Museum (western art collection)	
Mar 10	Meeting on the Elbe	

Chronology of Events in Russian Cinema and History 595

(Continued)

Date	Cinema and Culture	History
May 9	*Battle of Stalingrad*	
Aug 29		Soviet test of nuclear bomb in the Kazakh Polygon (further tests on Sep 24 and Oct 18, 1951)
1950		
	Tvardovskii as chief editor of *Novyi Mir*	Fifth Five-Year-Plan 1951–1955
Jan 19	*The Fall of Berlin*	
Dec 14	Death of filmmaker Savchenko	
1951		
	Tarzan on Soviet screens	
August	Soviet films prevented from participating in Venice IFF	
1952		
Jan 1		2.5 million prisoners in Gulags
Jul 10		Volga–Don Canal opens
1953		
January		Doctors' Plot (alleged scheme of Jewish doctors to murder Soviet officials)
Feb 11		Break of Israeli–Soviet relations
Mar 5	Death of composer Prokofiev	Death of Stalin
Mar 6		Malenkov as Premier, Khrushchev First Secretary of CPSU
Jun 17		Uprising in GDR suppressed by Soviet troops
Jun 26		Arrest of Beriia
Jun 30	Death of Pudovkin	
Sep 1	Moscow State University opens on Sparrow (Lenin) Hills	
Oct 15	Radio Iunost' launched	
Dec 23		Beriia executed
Dec 31	GUM (State Department Store) opens	
1954		
		Virgin Lands campaign
Feb 12	Death of documentary filmmaker Vertov	
Mar 13		KGB [State Security Committee] replaces NKVD
Aug 1		Opening of Agriculture Exhibition
Dec 15–26	II Writers' Union Congress: Fadeev replaced by Surkov	

(Continued)

(Continued)

Date	Cinema and Culture	History
1955		
	New Literary journals launched; Pushkin Museum reopens;	Corn campaign
Feb 8		Bulganin as Premier
Feb 12		Baikonur space center opens
February	Odessa Film Studio opens	
May–Aug	Exhibition of trophy art from Dresden Gallery before it is returned to GDR	
Jul 25	Death of composer Dunaevskii	
Nov 15		Leningrad metro opens
December	Week of French Cinema	
1956		
		Sixth Five-Year-Plan 1956–1960: living standards (lower prices; maternity leave; pension schemes; free schooling; increase in apartments)
		Furtseva in charge of Ideology at CC
Feb 14–25		XX Party Congress
Apr 15	Sovremennik Theater opens	
Oct 15	Chukhrai, *The Forty-First*	
Oct 21		Election of the liberal Władysław Gomułka as Party secretary in Poland
Oct 23–Nov 10		Anti-Soviet revolution in Budapest: Imre Nagy (1896–1958) as prime minister
Oct 25	Death of Dovzhenko	
Nov 4		Soviet troops in Budapest
Dec 29	Riazanov, *Carnival Night*	
1957		
Feb 28–Mar 7	First Congress of Artists' Union	
May 18		Decision on Academy of Sciences branch in Akademgorodok, Siberia
May 22		Khrushchev: "to catch up and overtake America"
May 25	Ukraina Hotel opens	
May		Attempt to topple Khrushchev
Jul 28–Aug 11	International Youth Festival	
Sep 29		Mayak nuclear accident near Cheliabinsk
Oct 4		Sputnik 1 launched into space
Oct 12	*The Cranes are Flying*	
November	*Doctor Zhivago* published in Milan	
1958		
Feb 28	Panorama cinema "Mir"	
Mar–Apr	Tchaikovsky competition with van Cliburn in Moscow	

Chronology of Events in Russian Cinema and History

(Continued)

Date	Cinema and Culture	History
Mar 27		Khrushchev as Premier
Jul 29	Maiakovskii statue erected on Triumphal Square	
Oct 25	Boris Pasternak accepts the Nobel Prize for his novel *Doctor Zhivago*	
Dec 20		"Iron Felix": monument to Dzerzhinskii
1959		
	Literary evenings at the Polytechnic Museum	Seventh Five-Year-Plan 1959–1965
Apr 12	*Fate of a Man* at Udarnik Cinema	
May 14	Death of filmmaker Perestiani	
May 18–23	III Writers' Congress	
Aug 3–17	Moscow International Film Festival	
Sep 15–27		Khrushchev in the United States
Dec 1	*Ballad of a Soldier*	
Dec 16	Death of filmmaker Sergei Vasiliev (*Chapaev*)	
1960		
		Furtseva as Minister of Culture (until 1974)
May 4		New ruble
May 30	Death of the writer Boris Pasternak	
Jul 16		Swimming pool Moskva opens
Sep 23		Khrushchev at the United Nations
1961		
		Stalin removed from mausoleum
January		"Khrushchevki" apartment blocks launched
Feb 28	Death of cameraman Andrei Moskvin	
April 12		Gagarin in space
May 4		Law against parasitism (lack of permanent work)
Jul 9–23	Moscow International Film Festival	
Aug 13		Berlin Wall
Oct 7		Kremlin Congress Palace opens
Oct 18	Death of cameraman Eduard Tissé	
Dec 2		Stalingrad renamed Volgograd, Stalinabad renamed Dushanbe
1962		
May 9	Tarkovskii, *Ivan's Childhood*	
May 30	Benny Goodman in Moscow	
Jun 2		Strikes in Novocherkask crushed
Sep 21–Oct 11	Igor Stravinsky in Moscow	

(Continued)

(Continued)

Date	Cinema and Culture	History
October		Cuban missile crisis
Nov 6		MKAD orbital motorway around Moscow opens
Nov 11	Solzhenitsyn's *The Life of Ivan Denisovich* published with Khrushchev's permission	
Dec 1	Manege exhibition of modern art trashed by Khrushchev	
1963		
Jan 19–28	Estrada festival in Gorky	
Mar 7–8		Kremlin Meetings with the intelligentsia
Mar 23	Cinema Committee under Romanov	
Jul 7–12	Moscow International Film Festival: Fellini's *Otto e mezzo* wins main prize	
Aug 18	Tvardovskii's *Terkin in the Other World* published with Khrushchev's permission	
Nov 4		Completion of New Arbat (Kalinin Prospekt)
1964		
Feb 18	Trial of Brodskii: five years hard labor	
Mar 30	Kozintsev's *Hamlet*	
Apr 11	*Walking the Streets of Moscow*	
Oct 14		Khrushchev ousted
Oct 23		Kosygin as Premier
1965		
Jan 8	Death of Boris Barnet	
Jan 18	Khutsiev: *I Am Twenty*	
Jul 5–20	Moscow International Film Festival	
Sep 8	Arrest of Siniavskii and Daniel'	
Nov 5	Evgenii Urbanskii dies on set in Karakum	
Nov 23–26	Congress of the Filmmakers' Union	
Dec 9		Mikoyan followed by Podgorny as chair of Supreme Soviet
1966		
		Eighth Five-Year-Plan 1966–1970
Jan 14		Death of rocket scientist Korolev
Feb 10–14		Trial of Siniavskii and Daniel'

Chronology of Events in Russian Cinema and History

(Continued)

Date	Cinema and Culture	History
Mar 18	"Illusion" as Gosfilmofond cinema	
1967		
		Andropov as head of KGB
Jan 22		Human Rights protests on Pushkin Square; arrest of Ginzburg
Mar 8		Svetlana Allilueva (Stalin's daughter) defects in India
Apr 1	Gaidai's *Kidnapping, Caucasian Style*	
May 16	Open letter by Solzhenitsyn	
Jun 5–10		Arab Israeli War (Six-Day War)
Jul 5–20	Moscow International Film Festival	
Jul 12	Death of filmmaker Ermler	
Sep 30	Color TV transmission begins	
Nov 5	Cinema "October" opens on New Arbat	
1968		
Jan 1	News program "Vremia"	
Jan 8–12		Trials against dissidents: Ginzburg and Galanskov
Feb 7	Death of Ivan Pyriev	
Mar 27		Death of Gagarin
Jun 2	Solzhenitsyn's *Gulag Archipelago* completed	
Jul 29	*The Commissar* shelved	
Aug 21–23		Soviet troops to Prague to counter Dubcek's socialism with human face
1969		
Apr 8	Gaidai's *Diamond Arm*	
Apr 15	Oscar for *War and Peace*	
May 29		Letter to UN by Human Rights Watch
Jul 7–22	Moscow International Film Festival	
Jul 20		Apollo 11 on moon
Nov 26	Solzhenitsyn excluded from Writers' Union	
1970		
Feb 3	*Novyi Mir* new editorial board without Tvardovskii	
May 29		Dissident Zhores Medvedev admitted to psychiatric clinic
Jul 7		Trial of dissident Natalia Gorbanevskaia

(Continued)

(Continued)

Date	Cinema and Culture	History
Aug 10	Death of writer Nikolai Erdman	
Aug 12		Ostverträge between USSR and FRG
Oct 8	Nobel Prize for Solzhenitsyn	
1971		
		Ninth Five-Year-Plan 1971–1975: grain imports
Feb 20	Death of jazz musician Tsfasman	
Apr 19		Salyut space station (until 1982)
Jul 20–Aug 3	Moscow International Film Festival	
Sep 11		Death of Khrushchev
Nov 1	Death of Mikhail Romm	
Nov 5	"Rossiia" concert hall opened	
Dec 24	*Andrei Rublev* released	
1972		
May		President Nixon visits Moscow
Jun 4	Brodsky expelled from USSR	
Aug 22	Goskino head: Ermash	
1973		
		Zhores Medvedev exiled; wave of emigration to Israel
Mar 6	Death of filmmaker Ptushko	
Mar 27	Death of Mikhail Kalatozov	
May 11	Death of Grigorii Kozintsev	
Jul 10–23	Moscow International Film Festival	
Aug 11	Spy serial *Seventeen Moments of Spring*	
1974		
		Sakharov establishes the Moscow Human Rights Committee with Tverdokhlebov, Chalidze, and Elena Bonner
Jan 3	Death of actor Maksim Straukh	
Feb 12–13		Arrest of Solzhenitsyn and deportation
Jun 14–Jul 8	Da Vinci exhibition in Moscow	
Sep 25	Bulldozer exhibition	
Oct 2	Death of Vasilii Shukshin	
Oct 24		Suicide of Furtseva
Nov 1	Suicide of scriptwriter Shpalikov	
Nov 12	Death of cameraman Urusevskii	
Nov 23		Brezhnev suffers stroke

(Continued)

Date	Cinema and Culture	History
1975		
		Demichev as Minister of Culture (until 1986)
Jan 26	Death of Liubov' Orlova	
Jul 3	Central State Archive for Cinema and Foto-Documentation in Krasnogorsk	
Jul 17	Death of actor Babochkin (Chapaev)	
Jul 10–23	Moscow International Film Festival	
Jul 28–Aug 1		Helsinki Accord on Security and Co-operation in Europe
Aug 9	Death of composer Shostakovich	
Oct 10		Sakharov receives Nobel Peace Prize
1976		Tenth Five-Year-Plan 1976–1981: quality and efficiency
Jan 1	Riazanov's *Irony of Fate*	
May 12		Helsinki Watch Group headed by the nuclear physicist Iurii Orlov
Jul 14	Death of filmmaker Nikolai Ekk	
Jul 26	Death of filmmaker Abram Room	
1977		
Feb 25		Fire in Hotel Rossiya
February		Arrest of Helsinki Group's members
May 3	Gherman's *Twenty Days without War*	
Jul 7–21	Moscow International Film Festival	
Sep 25	Mikhalkov's *Unfinished Piece*	
Oct 7		New Soviet Constitution
1978		
		Conductor of Bolshoi, Kondrashin, seeks political asylum in Holland
		Writer Alexander Zinoviev expelled and stripped of citizenship
Mar 15		Cellist Mstislav Rostropovich and his wife Galina Vishnevskaia stripped of Soviet citizenship
Jul 10–14		Trial of dissidents Sharansky, Filatov
Aug 17	Death of actress Vera Maretskaia	
Sep 3	Melodia record label	
Oct 17		Physicist Kapitsa receives Nobel Prize
Dec 22	Almanach Metropol (*samizdat*)	

(Continued)

(Continued)

Date	Cinema and Culture	History
1979		
Jan 12	Death of filmmaker Stolper	
Aug 14–28	Moscow International Film Festival	
Jul 2	Death of Larisa Shepit'ko	
Dec 25		Soviet troops in Afghanistan
1980		
		Priest Gleb Iakunin condemned for anti-Soviet activity (prison until 1987)
		Violinist Gidon Kremer seeks political asylum in Germany
		Kopelev, Voinovich, Aksenov exiled
Jan 22		Sakharov exiled to Gorky and placed under house arrest
Feb 11	*Moscow does not Believe in Tears*	
Mar 8	Rock festival in Tiflis	
May 19	Tarkovskii's *Stalker*	
Jul 19–Aug 3		Olympic Games in Moscow
Jul 25	Death of Vladimir Vysotskii	
Oct 23		Kosygin replaced by Nikolai Tikhonov as Premier
Dec 18		Death of Kosygin
1981		
		Eleventh Five-Year-Plan 1981–1985
		Solidarnosz movement in Poland: martial law
Mar 21	Death of filmmaker Donskoi	
Jun 4	Exhibition Moscow-Paris	
Jul 7–21	Moscow International Film Festival	
1982		
Mar 9	Death of jazz musician Utesov	
Mar 15		Moratorium on nuclear weapons
Jul 11	Death of actor Solonitsyn	
Oct 20		Luzhniki UEFA cup match: crowd crushed
Nov 10		Death of Brezhnev
Nov 12		Andropov as General Secretary of CPSU
1983		
Mar 8		Reagan calls USSR "empire of evil"
Mar 23		"Star Wars"
Jun 16		Andropov as President of Supreme Council
Jul 7–21	Moscow International Film Festival	

(Continued)

Date	Cinema and Culture	History
Sep 1		Korean aircraft shot down by USSR
Dec 16	Death of Grigorii Aleksandrov	
1984		
Feb 9		Death of Andropov
Feb 13		Chernenko as General Secretary
Apr 8		Death of Petr Kapitsa
May 8		Boycott of Los Angeles Olympics
Jul 10	Emigration of Andrei Tarkovskii	
Dec 5	Death of writer Viktor Shklovskii	
Dec 15–21		Gorbachev in the UK
1985		
Mar 10		Death of Chernenko
Mar 11		Gorbachev confirmed as General Secretary
Apr 4	Death of filmmaker Dinara Asanova	
Apr 23	Death of film critic and historian Sergei Iutkevich	
May 16		Announcement of anti-alcohol campaign
Jun 11–12		Announcement of "acceleration" (*uskorenie*) of scientific and technological progress
Jun 24		Announcement of "perestroika"
Jun 21		Iakovlev as secretary for propaganda in the CC
Jun 28–Jul 12	Moscow International Film Festival	
Jul 16		Shevardnadze as Minister of Foreign Affairs
Aug	Twelfth International Youth Festival, Moscow	Moratorium on nuclear tests (until February 1987)
Aug 22	Death of actress Aleksandra Khokhlova	
Sep 27		Tikhonov replaced by Ryzhkov (head of UralMash) as chairman of Council of Ministers
Oct 2–5		Gorbachev on state visit to France
Nov 19–21		Reagan and Gorbachev meet in Geneva
Nov 28	Death of filmmaker Sergei Gerasimov	
Dec 24		Yeltsin replaces Grishin at Moscow Party Section
1986		
		Twelfth Five-Year-Plan 1986–1990: perestroika
Feb 20		Mir space station launched
Feb 25–Mar 6		Congress of the CPSU
Mar	Melodia releases Beatles album	

(Continued)

(Continued)

Date	Cinema and Culture	History
Apr 26		Fire in reactor at Chernobyl
May 13–15	Fifth Congress of the Filmmakers' Union	
Aug 14		Law permitting co-operatives
Oct 11–12		Gorbachev–Reagan meeting in Reykjavik
Dec 3		Gorbachev meets with the creative intelligentsia
Dec 23		Andrei Sakharov returns to Moscow from exile in Gorky (Nizhnii Novgorod)
25 Dec	Aleksei Kamshalov as head of Goskino	
Dec 29	Death of filmmaker Andrei Tarkovskii	
1987		
Jan 13	Death of actor Igor' Il'inskii	
Jan 26	Release of Abuladze's film *Repentance*, and Podnieks's documentary *Is it Easy to be Young?*	
Feb 19	Rehabilitation of Boris Pasternak	
Jul 6–17	Moscow International Film Festival	
Aug 16	Death of actor Andrei Mironov	
Nov 11		Yeltsin removed from post as Moscow Party Chief
Dec 12	Nobel Prize for Literature to Joseph Brodskii	
1988		
Jan 5		Control of psychiatric clinics moved from Ministry of Interior to Ministry of Health
Feb 6		Nuclear test in Semipalatinsk (also May 4)
Mar 15	First Dali exhibition in Moscow	
May 2	Death of actor Pavel Kadochnikov	
May 29–Jun 2		Reagan in Moscow
Jun 7	First auction of modern art by Sotheby's	
Nov 29		Jamming of Radio Liberty and Radio Liberty Europe stops
Dec 30	Death of poet and dissident Iulii Daniel'	
1989		
Jan 19	Malevich exhibition	
Jan 31	First McDonalds opens in Moscow	
Feb 2	Death of actor Iurii Bogatyryov	
Feb 15		Removal of troops from Afghanistan

Chronology of Events in Russian Cinema and History

(Continued)

Date	Cinema and Culture	History
Mar 26		Election for delegates for the Congress of People's Deputies
May 25–Jun 9		First Congress of People's Deputies
Jul 2		Death of Andrei Gromyko
Jul 4	Exhibition of Vasili Kandinsky	
Jul 7–18	Moscow International Film Festival	
Nov 9		Fall of Berlin Wall
Nov 10	Rostropovich, Vishnevskaia, and Voinovich receive USSR citizenship	
Dec 2–3		Bush and Gorbachev meet in Malta
Dec 12–24		Second Congress of People's Deputies
Dec 14		Death of Andrei Sakharov
1990		
Mar 12–15		Third Congress of People's Deputies elects Gorbachev as President
May 16–Jun 2		First Congress of People's Deputies of the RSFSR
May 29		Yeltsin elected chair of the Supreme Soviet of the RSFSR
Jun 2–13		Congress of the CPSU
Jul 20	Death of filmmaker Sergo Paradjanov	
Aug 13		Rehabilitation of writers Voinovich, Kopelev, Aksenov, Solzhenitsyn
Aug 15	Death of rock singer Viktor Tsoi	
Aug 23		Gorky renamed Nizhnii Novgorod
Aug 22	Radio station Echo Moscow goes live	
Oct 25		Nobel Peace Prize for Gorbachev
Nov 14	Death of filmmaker Leonid Trauberg	
Nov 23–5		Congress on Chechen independence
Dec 17–27		Fourth Congress of People's Deputies (USSR)
Dec 20		Shevardnadze resigns as Foreign Minister
Dec 27	Jan 7 (Christmas) as official holiday	
1991		
Jan 3		Diplomatic relations with Israel
Mar 7		Gubenko as Minister of Culture
Mar 17		Referendum on USSR

(Continued)

(Continued)

Date	Cinema and Culture	History
Mar 28		Third Congress of People's Deputies if the RSFSR
May 21–26		Fourth Congress of People's deputies (RSFSR)
Jun 12		Yeltsin elected president of the RSFSR
Jun 17		Union Treaty with nine former Soviet republics
Jul 1		Warsaw Pact disbanded
Jul 10		Romanov remains exhumed
Jul 10–17		Fifth Congress of People's Deputies (RSFSR)
Jul 8–19	Moscow International Film Festival	
Aug 19–21		August Coup (GKChP) by vice-president Ianaev; Kriuchkov; Pavlov; Pugo; Iazov; etc.
Aug 22		Tricolore as flag of Russia (Yeltsin)
Aug 24		Gorbachev resigns as head of CPSU, CP is prohibited
Aug 30		Nuclear polygon closed by Kazakh president Nazarbaev
Sep 5		Sverdlovsk renamed Yekaterinburg
Sep 6		Dudaev seizes power in Chechnya
Sep 7		Independence of the Baltic States Lithuania, Estonia, Latvia recognized
Autumn		Leningrad renamed St Petersburg
Oct 28–Nov 13		Yeltsin authorized by Fifth Congress of People's Deputies of the RSFSR to form a government
Nov 6		Yeltsin as Premier
Nov 14		Novo-Ogarevo: union with Azerbaijan, Kazakhstan, Kyrgyzstan, Tajikistan, and Turkmenistan
Dec 8		CIS Treaty at Belovezhsk: Russia, Belarus, Ukraine
Dec 25		Gorbachev resigns; Yeltsin is president of the Russian Federation

1992

Date	Cinema and Culture	History
Jan 1		Economic shock therapy (Gaidai)
Mar 4	Death of actor Evgenii Evstigneev	
April		Congress of People's Deputies
Jun 1		Gavriil Popov succeeded by Iurii Luzhkov as Moscow's Mayor
Dec 14		Chernomyrdin as PM

1993

Date	Cinema and Culture	History
Jan 6	Death of dancer Rudolf Nureyev	
Mar 23		Calls for impeachment of Yeltsin
Apr 25		Referendum supports Yeltsin
Jul 1–12	Moscow International Film Festival	
Sep 21		Yeltsin dissolves parliament
Oct 3–4		Storming of White House: Rutskoi and speaker Khazbulatov oppose Yeltsin

Chronology of Events in Russian Cinema and History 607

(Continued)

Date	Cinema and Culture	History
Nov 19	Death of filmmaker Leonid Gaidai	
Dec 11		"Patriotic song" by Glinka as new national anthem
Dec 12		Parliamentary Elections: LDP 23 percent, Vybor Rossii 15 percent, CP 12 percent, Union&Accord 7 percent
Dec 12		Referendum ratifies Russian constitution
1994		
Mar 6	Death of filmmaker Tengiz Abuladze	
Apr 28	Death of actor Oleg Borisov	
May 23	*Burnt by the Sun* wins Grand Prix in Cannes	
May 27	Solzhenitsyn returns to Russia	
Aug 3	Death of actor Innokenti Smoktunovskii	
Sep 26		Cathedral of Christ the Savior to be rebuilt
Oct 20	Death of filmmaker and Oscar-winner Sergei Bondarchuk	
Dec 11	Death of filmmaker Iulii Raizman	Russian Army to Chechnya
1995		
Mar 27	Oscar for Mikhalkov's *Burnt by the Sun*	
Apr 25	Death of filmmaker Iosif Kheifits	
May 12	Death of actor Andrei Boltnev	
Jul 11		Yeltsin in hospital: heart attack
Jul 17–28	Moscow International Film Festival	
Oct 26	Iberian Gates open on Red Square	Yeltsin suffers second heart attack
Autumn	Rogozhkin: *Peculiarities of the National Hunt*	
Dec 3	Death of actor Kaidanovskii	
Dec 17		Parliamentary Elections: NDR, 9 percent; CP, 22 percent; LDPR, 11 percent; Yabloko, 7 percent
1996		
Mar 15	Release of Bodrov's *Prisoner of the Mountains*	
May 27		Ceasefire in Chechnya
Jun 11		Terrorist attacks on metro and buses in Moscow
Jun 16		Presidential elections: Yeltsin 35 percent, Ziuganov 32 percent
Jul 3		Second round of presidential elections: Yeltsin 53.7 percent, Ziuganov 40 percent

(Continued)

(Continued)

Date	Cinema and Culture	History
Jul 10	Death of musician Sergei Kurekhin	
Jul 25	Death of composer Mikhail Tariverdiev	
Aug 31		Lebed and Maskhadov sign peace accord
Oct 17		General Lebed resigns
Nov 5–Dec 23		Yeltsin has bypass operation
Nov 23	Death of composer Edison Denisov	
Dec 1		Troops withdrawn from Chechnya

1997

Date	Cinema and Culture	History
Jan 27		Maskhadov elected Chechen president
May 12	Release of Balabanov's *Brother*	Peace agreement with Chechnya
Jun 9	Death of actor Evgenii Lebedev	
Jul 19–29	Moscow International Film Festival	
Aug 21	Death of clown Iurii Nikulin	
Nov 5	RAPO anti-piracy organization	

1998

Date	Cinema and Culture	History
Jan 4	*Streets of Broken Lights* on TV	
Mar 23		Kirienko replaces Chernomyrdin as PM
Jul 17		Interment of the Tsar's family in Petersburg
Aug 3	Death of composer Alfred Schnittke	
Aug 17		"Default" (devaluation of ruble): 90-day moratorium on bank transactions
Aug 23		Chernomyrdin replaces Kirienko as interim PM;
Sep 11		Primakov replaces Chernomyrdin
Oct 6	Death of actor Rolan Bykov	
September		Camilla Carr and John James freed from Chechen captivity (held since July 1997)

1999

Date	Cinema and Culture	History
Feb 20	Premiere of *The Barber of Siberia*	
Mar 18	Release of Rogozhkin's *Checkpoint*	
Mar 29		Putin as head of FSB (Federal Security Bureau)
May 12		Stepashin replaces Primakov as PM
May 15		Impeachment against Yeltsin fails
Jun 25	Death of comedian Evgenii Morgunov	
Jul 19–29	Moscow International Film Festival	

(Continued)

Date	Cinema and Culture	History
Aug 7		Beginning of Second Chechen campaign
Aug 9		Stepashin dismissed; succeeded by Putin (Aug 16)
Aug 31		Bomb explosion in Okhotnyi Riad
Sep 8		Bomb in Moscow apartment block in Pechatniki
Sep 13		Bomb in Moscow apartment block on Kashirkoe Chausee
Dec 19		Duma elections: CPRF, 24 percent; Unity, 23 percent; OVR, 13 percent
Dec 31		Yeltsin resigns, leaving Putin as acting president
2000		
Mar 26		Putin elected president
May 11		Search of Media Most (NTV) offices
May 11	Release of Balabanov's *Brother 2*	
May 7		Kasianov as PM
May 24	Death of actor and director Oleg Efremov	
Jun 12		Kadyrov designated president of Chechnya
Jul 19–29	Moscow International Film Festival	
Aug 8		Bomb explosion in Pushkin Square pedestrian subway
Aug 12		Explosion on the Kursk submarine
Aug 25	Death of filmmaker and actor Valerii Priemykhov	
Aug 27		Fire on Ostankino television tower
December		Soviet national anthem re-introduced
2001		
Apr 4		NTV journalists strike; new management
May 10	Release of Bodrov's *Sisters*	
Jun 21–30	Moscow International Film Festival	
Oct 28	Death of filmmaker Grigorii Chukhrai	
2002		
Mar 14	Release of Balabanov's *War*	
Jun 9		Riots after Russia–Japan soccer match
Jun 21–30	Moscow International Film Festival	
Sep 20	Death of Bodrov Jr and his film crew	
Oct 23–26		800 hostages at Moscow Theater (*Nord Ost*): 120 dead

(Continued)

(Continued)

Date	Cinema and Culture	History
2003		
Jun 28	Release of Buslov's *Bimmer*	
Jun 20–29	Moscow International Film Festival	
Jul 6		Suicide bomb at rock festival in Tushchino, Moscow
Sep 6	Zviagintsev's *The Return* wins the Golden Lion in Venice	
Oct 25		Arrest of Yukos manager Mikhail Khodorkovskii (fraud, tax evasion)
Oct 27	Death of filmmaker Elem Klimov	
Dec 7		Duma elections: CP 12.5 percent; United Russia 37.5 percent; LDPR 11.5 percent; Rodina 9 percent
Dec 9		Suicide bomb at National Hotel, Moscow
2004		
Jan 22	KinoPark multiplex opened	
Feb 6		Terrorist attack in the Moscow metro station Avtozavodskaia
Feb 24		Putin dismisses PM Kasyanov
Mar 9		PM Mikhail Fradkov
Mar 14		Presidential elections: Putin 57 percent
Apr 3	First IMAX in Moscow	
May 9		Kadyrov killed in Grozny
Jun 18–27	Moscow International Film Festival	
Jul 11	Release of Bekmambetov's *Night Watch*	
Aug 24		Two airliners crash as a result of terrorist attacks
Sep 1–3		Beslan siege of school no.1
2005		
Feb 27	Release of Faiziev's *Turkish Gambit*	
Mar 8		Aslan Maskhadov, Chechen separatist leader, killed
Mar 20	Release of Sidorov's *Shadowboxing*	
May		Khodorkovskii sentenced
Jun 17–26	Moscow International Film Festival	
Sep 29	Release of Bondarchuk's *Ninth Company*	
2006		
Jan 1	Release of Bekmambetov's *Day Watch*	
Jun 23 – Jul 2	Moscow International Film Festival	

(Continued)

Date	Cinema and Culture	History
Jul 10		Shamil Basaev killed
Nov 23		Alexander Litvinenko dies in London of polonium poisoning
Oct 7		Murder of Anna Politkovskaya
2007		
Feb 15		Ramzan Kadyrov as Chechen president
Apr 23		Death of Yeltsin
Apr 27		Death of cellist Rostropovich
May 27	Zviagintsev's *The Banishment* wins Best Actor at Cannes	
Jun 21–30	Moscow International Film Festival	
Sep 14		Fradkov dismissed; Viktor Zubkov as PM
Dec 02		Duma Elections: United Russia 64 percent, CP 11.5 percent, LDPR 8 percent
2008		
Jan 1	Release of Bekmambetov's *Irony of Fate 2*	
Mar 2		Election of Dmitrii Medvedev as president (70.5 percent)
May 25	Golden Camera's jury prize for Gai-Germanika's *Everybody Dies but Me*	
May 25	Cannes UCR Jury Prize for Dvortsevoi's *Tulpan*	
Jun 19–28	Thirtieth Moscow International Film Festival	
Aug 7–16		South Ossetia War
Sep 6	Venice Silver Lion for Aleksei A. Gherman's *Paper Soldier*	
Oct 9	Release of Kravchuk's *Admiral* ($34 mill.)	
Dec 19	Release of Todorovskii's *Hipsters* ($16 mill.)	
2009		
Jan 1	Release of Bondarchuk's *Inhabited Island* ($21 mill.)	
Jun 19–28	Moscow International Film Festival	
Nov 27		Nevsky Express train bombing
2010		
29 Mar		Moscow metro bombings (Lubianka, Park Kultury)
Jun 17–26	Moscow International Film Festival	

(Continued)

(Continued)

Date	Cinema and Culture	History
Nov 3		Death of former PM Viktor Chernomyrdin
Dec 16	Release of Bekmambetov's *Yolki* ($22 mill.)	
2011		
Jan 24		Domodedovo Airport bombing
Mar 30	Death of actress Liudmila Gurchenko	
May 22	Cannes UCR special prize for Zviaginstev's *Elena*	
Jun 23–Jul 2	Moscow International Film Festival	
Aug 27	Death of actress Iia Savvina	
Sep 10	Venice Golden Lion for Sokurov's *Faust*	
Sep 29	Death of filmmaker Tatiana Lioznova	
December		Election protest marches –Jul 18, 2013
Dec 4		Duma Elections: United Russia 49 percent; CP 19 percent, JustRussia 13 percent, LDPR 11 percent
Dec 15	Release of *Yolki 2* ($26 mill.)	
2012		
Feb 4		Protest march
Feb 21		Pussy Riot performance at Cathedral of Christ the Savior
Mar 3		Arrest of Pussy Riot members Tolokonnikova and Alekhina; Samutsevich arrested 16 March
Mar 4		Election of Putin as President, 63.6 percent
May 6		"March of Millions," Bolotnaya Square
May 7		Putin's inauguration
Jun 3–4		EU–Russia summit in St Petersburg
Jun 21–30	Moscow International Film Festival	
Oct 4	Release of Prygunov's *Dukhless* ($13 mill.)	
2013		
Feb 15		Meteorite strike near Cheliabinsk
Feb 21	Death of filmmaker Aleksei Iu. Gherman	
Mar 23		Death of Boris Berezovsky
Apr 18	Release of Lebedev's *Legend No. 17*, ($29 mill.)	
May 18	Death of filmmaker Aleksei Balabanov	

(Continued)

Date	Cinema and Culture	History
Jun 20–29	Moscow International Film Festival	
Oct 10	Release of Bondarchuk's *Stalingrad* ($53 mill.)	
Oct 21		Volgograd bombing (bus)
Nov 21		Euromaidan: protests against pro-Russian and anti-EU politics of Ukrainian president Viktor Yanukovich (>Feb 23 2014)
Dec 23		Amnesty for Pussy Riot members; Mikhail Khodorkovskii
Dec 26	Release of *Yolki 3* ($37 mill.)	
Dec 29–30		Volgograd bombings (station, bus)
2014		
Jan 23		Release from prison of magnate Platon Lebedev
Jan 29		"Dozhd" independent TV channel disconnected
Feb 7–23		Winter Olympics in Sochi
Feb 22		Yanukovich resigns as president of Ukraine
Feb 24–25		Protests in Moscow
Feb 27		Crimean crisis
Mar 16		Referendum on Crimea to rejoin Russia (republic declared Mar 17)
Mar 21		Ukraine signs accord with EU
April–May		Pro-Russian protests in Eastern Ukraine
Jun 7		Petro Poroshenko becomes Ukrainian president
Jun 19–28	Moscow International Film Festival	
Jul 17		MH17 flight from Amsterdam to Kuala Lumpur shot down over Eastern-Ukrainian territory
16 Dec		Russian financial crisis

Notes

- Dates used follow the old calendar until January 31, 1918, when Russia switched to the new style, noting that date as February 14, 1918.
- Names: St Petersburg became Petrograd from August 1914 until January 24, 1924, when it was named Leningrad.
- Premier: Chairman of the Council of People's Commissars until 1946; then Chairman of Council of Ministers of the USSR.

Bibliography

Arkus, Liubov', ed. 2001. *Noveishaia istoriia otechestvennogo kino 1986–2000. Kinoslovar'* [New History of Domestic Cinema 1986–2000. A Film Dictionary]. 3 vols. St Petersburg: Seans.

Arkus, Liubov', ed. 2002–2005. *Noveishaia istoriia otechestvennogo kino 1986–2000. Kino i kontekst* [New History of Domestic Cinema 1986–2000. Cinema and its Context]. 4 vols. St Petersburg: Seans.

Beumers, Birgit, ed. 2011. *Directory of World Cinema: Russia*, Bristol and Chicago: intellect, University of Chicago Press.

Beumers, Birgit, ed. 2015. *Directory of World Cinema: Russia 2*, Bristol and Chicago: intellect, University of Chicago Press.

Iutkevich, S., ed. 1986. *Kinoslovar'* [Film Dictionary]. Moscow: Sovietskaia Entsiklopediia.

Kudriavtsev, Sergei. 1998. *Svoe kino* [My Cinema]. Moscow: Dubl' D.

Razlogov, Kirill, ed. 2006. *Pervyi vek nashego kino* [The First Century of our Cinema]. Moscow: Lokid Press.

Segida, Miroslava and Sergei Zemlianukhin, eds. 1996. *Domashniaia sinemateka: otechestvennoe kino 1918–1996* [Home Cinemathèque: Domestic Cinema 1918–1996]. Moscow: Dubl' D.

Segida, Miroslava and Sergei Zemlianukhin, eds. 2001. *Fil'my Rossii. Igrovoe kino. 1995–2000* [Films from Russia. Fiction Films. 1995–2000]. Moscow: Dubl' D.

Segida, Miroslava and Sergei Zemlianukhin, eds. 2004. *Fil'my Rossii. Igrovoe kino. TV. Video. 1992–2003* [Films from Russia. Fiction Films, Television, Video. 1992–2003]. Moscow: Dubl' D.

Taylor, Richard, with Nancy Wood, Julian Graffy, and Dina Iordanova, eds. 2000. *The BFI Companion to Eastern European and Russian Cinema*. London: British Film Institute.

★★★

A Companion to Russian Cinema, First Edition. Edited by Birgit Beumers.
© 2016 John Wiley & Sons, Inc. Published 2016 by John Wiley & Sons, Inc.

Agde, Günter and Alexander Schwarz, eds. 2012. *Die rote Traumfabrik. Meschrabpom-Film und Prometheus 1921–1936* [The Red Dream-Factory: Mezhrabpom and Prometheus, 1921–1936]. Berlin: Deutsche Kinemathek and Bertz+Fischer.

Alaniz, José. 2008. "'Nature', Illusion and Excess in Sokurov's *Mother and Son*." *Studies in Russian & Soviet Cinema* 2.2: 183–204.

Alpert, Erin. 2013. "Reinventing Soviet Visual Memory: A Case Study of Marina Goldovskaya's Documentary *Solovki Power*." *Studies in Russian & Soviet Cinema* 7.2: 207–226.

Anderson, Trudy. 1995. "Why Stalinist Musicals?" *Discourse* 17.3: 38–48.

Andrew, Joe. 2007. "Birth Equals Rebirth: Space, Narrative and Gender in *The Commissar*." *Studies in Russian & Soviet Cinema* 1.1: 29–44.

Apostolov, Andrei. 2014. "The Enemy at the Gate: The Soviet Goalkeeper in Cinema, Culture, and Policy." *Studies in Russian & Soviet Cinema* 8.3: 200–217.

Attwood, Lynne, ed. 1993. *Red Women on the Silver Screen: Soviet Women and Cinema from the Beginning to the End of the Communist Era*. London: Pandora.

Aumont, Jacques. 1987. *Montage Eisenstein*. London: British Film Institute Publishing and Bloomington, IN: Indiana University Press.

Balina, Marina with Evgenii Dobrenko, and Iurii Murashov, eds. 2002. *Sovetskoe bogatstvo: Stat'i o kul'ture, literature i kino* [Soviet Riches: Articles about Culture, Literature and Cinema]. St Petersburg: Akademicheskii proekt.

Baraban, Elena. 2007. "*The Fate of a Man* by Sergei Bondarchuk and the Soviet Cinema of Trauma." *Slavic and East European Journal* 51.3: 514–534.

Barker, Adele Marie, ed. 1999. *Consuming Russia: Popular Culture, Sex, and Society since Gorbachev*. Durham, NC: Duke University Press.

Barna, Yon. 1973. *Eisenstein*. London: Secker & Warburg.

Barta, Peter and Stephen Hutchings. 2002. "The Train as Word-Image Intertext in the Films 'Ballad of a Soldier' and 'Thief.'" *Intertexts* 6.2: 127–144.

Bartig, Kevin. 2013. *Composing for the Red Screen: Prokofiev and Soviet Film*. New York: Oxford University Press.

Batalin, Viktor. 2002. *Kinokhronika v Rossii, 1896–1916gg.: Opis' kinos"emok, khraniashchikhsia v RGAKFD* [Newsreels in Russia, 1896–1916. List of Filmic Recordings Preserved in the Russian State Archive for Film and Photo Documentation]. Moscow: Olma-Press.

Beardow, Frank. 1991. "Soviet Cinema, Past, Present and Future." *Rusistika* 3: 19–25.

Beardow, Frank. 1993. "Soviet Cinema: Coming to Terms with the Past." *Rusistika* 7: 31–36 and 8: 2–18.

Beardow, Frank. 1994–1995. "Soviet Cinema: Women – Icons or Individuals?" *Rusistika* 9 (1994): 22–42; 10 (1994): 2–13; and 11 (1995): 35–42.

Beardow, Frank. 1997. "Soviet Cinema – War Revisited." *Rusistika* 15: 19–34 and 16: 8–21.

Beardow, Frank. 2003. *Little Vera* (KinoFile 8). London: I. B. Tauris.

Beilenhoff, Wolfgang and Sabine Hänsgen. 2008. "Speaking about Images: The Voice of the Author in *Ordinary Fascism*." *Studies in Russian & Soviet Cinema* 2.2: 141–153.

Belodubrovskaya, Maria. 2011. "The Jockey and the Horse: Joseph Stalin and the Biopic Genre in Soviet Cinema." *Studies in Russian & Soviet Cinema* 5.1: 29–53.

Bernstein, Seth. 2015. "Wartime Filmmaking on the Margins: Soiuzdetfilm in Evacuation in Stalinabad, 1941–1943." *Studies in Russian & Soviet Cinema* 9.1: 24–39.

Berry, Ellen E. and Anessa Miller-Pogacar, eds. 1995. *Re-Entering the Sign: Articulating New Russian Culture*. Ann Arbor: University of Michigan Press.

Beumers, Birgit. 1999. "Cinemarket, or the Russian Film Industry in 'Mission Possible.'" *Europe–Asia Studies* 51.5: 871–896.

Beumers, Birgit, ed. 1999. *Russia on Reels: The Russian Idea in Post-Soviet Cinema*. London: I. B. Tauris.

Beumers, Birgit. 2000. *Burnt by the Sun* (KinoFile 3). London: I. B. Tauris.

Beumers, Birgit. 2000. "Father Frost on 31 December: Christmas and New Year in Soviet and Russian Cinema.," in *Christmas in the Movies*, edited by Mark Connelly, 185–209. London: I. B. Tauris.

Beumers, Birgit. 2003. "Soviet and Russian Blockbusters: A Question of Genre?" *Slavic Review* 62.3: 441–454.

Beumers, Birgit. 2005. *Nikita Mikhalkov* (Kino Companion 1). I. B. Tauris, London.

Beumers, Birgit. 2005. *Popular Culture Russia!* Santa Barbara, Denver, and London: ABC Clio.

Beumers, Birgit, ed. 2007. *24 Frames: The Cinema of Russia and the Former Soviet Union*. London and New York: Wallflower Press.

Beumers, Birgit. 2009. *A History of Russian Cinema*. Oxford and New York: Berg.

Beumers Birgit and Nancy Condee, eds. 2011. *The Cinema of Alexander Sokurov*, London: I. B. Tauris.

Beumers, Birgit, Stephen Hutchings, and Natalya Rulyova, eds. 2009. *The Post-Soviet Russian Media: Conflicting Signals*. London: Routledge.

Biltereyst, Daniel. 2008. "'Will We Ever See Potemkin?': The Historical Reception and Censorship of Eisenstein's *Battleship Potemkin* in Belgium (1926–1932)." *Studies in Russian & Soviet Cinema* 2.1: 5–19.

Bird, Robert. 2004. *Andrei Rublev*. London: British Film Institute Classics.

Bird, Robert. 2008. *Andrei Tarkovsky: Elements of Cinema*. London: Reaktion Books.

Bohlinger, Vincent. 2011. "Engrossing? Exciting! Incomprehensible? Boring! – Audience Survey Responses to Eisenstein's *October*." *Studies in Russian & Soviet Cinema* 5.1: 5–27.

Bohlinger, Vincent. 2013. "The Development of Sound Technology in the Soviet Film Industry During the First Five-Year Plan." *Studies in Russian & Soviet Cinema* 7.2: 189–205.

Bonitenko, Adia and Larissa Georgievskaya, eds. 2012. "The Cinema-Experimental Workshop [Kinoeksperimental'naia masterskaia] in Documents," Preface by Peter Bagrov. *Studies in Russian and Soviet Cinema* 5.2: 277–326.

Bordwell, David. 1972. "The Idea of Montage in Soviet Art and Film." *Cinema Journal* 11.2: 9–17.

Bordwell, David. 1993. *The Cinema of Eisenstein*. Cambridge, MA and London: Harvard University Press.

Boym, Svetlana. 1994. *Common Places: Mythologies of Everyday Life in Russia*. Cambridge, MA and London: Harvard University Press.

Boym, Svetlana. 1995. "Post-Soviet Cinematic Nostalgia: From 'Elite Cinema' to 'Soap Opera.'" *Discourse* 17.3: 75–84.

Boym, Svetlana. 2001. *The Future of Nostalgia*. New York: Basic Books.

Brashinsky, Michael and Andrew Horton, eds. 1994. *Russian Critics on the Cinema of Glasnost'*. Cambridge: Cambridge University Press.

Brooks, Jeffrey. 1991. "Russian Cinema and Public Discourse, 1900–1930." *Historical Journal of Film, Radio and Television* 11.2: 141–148.

Budiak, Liudmila. "We Cannot Live This Way: Reflections on the State of Contemporary Soviet Film." *Film Quarterly* 44.2 (1990–91): 28–33.

Bulgakowa, Oksana. 2001. *Sergei Eisenstein: A Biography*. Berlin and San Francisco: Potemkin Press.

Carleton, Greg. 2009. "A Tale of Two Wars: Sex and Death in *Ninth Company* and *Cargo 200*." *Studies in Russian & Soviet Cinema* 3.2: 215–228.

Casula, Philipp. 2015. "*Five Days of War* and *Olympus Inferno*: The 2008 South Ossetia War in Russian and Western Popular Culture." *Studies in Russian & Soviet Cinema* 9.2: 110–125.

Cavendish, Phil. 2007. *Soviet Mainstream Cinematography: The Silent Era*. London: UCL Arts and Humanities Publications.

Cavendish, Phil. 2013. "The Delirious Vision: The Vogue for the Hand-Held Camera in Soviet Cinema of the 1920s." *Studies in Russian & Soviet Cinema* 7.1: 5–24.

Cavendish, Phil. 2013. *The Men with the Movie Camera. The Poetics of Visual Style in Soviet Avant-Garde Cinema of the 1920s*. New York, Oxford: Berghahn.

Challis, Clare. 2015. "'The Piano is Not Tuned': Music in Two Films by Kira Muratova." *Studies in Russian & Soviet Cinema* 9.1: 40–60.

Chapman, Andrew. 2013. "Performing 'Soviet' Film Classics: Tajik Jimmy and the Aural Remnants of Indian Cinema." *Studies in Russian & Soviet Cinema* 7.2: 227–242.

Cherchi Usai, Paolo, et al., eds. 1989. *Silent Witnesses. Russian Films, 1908–1919*. coordination by Yuri Tsivian. London: British Film Institute.

Chernetsky, Vitaly. 2008. "Visual Language and Identity Performance in Leonid Osyka's *A Stone Cross*: The Roots and the Uprooting." *Studies in Russian & Soviet Cinema* 2.3: 269–280.

Chernyshova, Natalya. 2011. "Philistines on the Big Screen: Consumerism in Soviet Cinema of the Brezhnev Era." *Studies in Russian & Soviet Cinema* 5.2: 227–254.

Christie, Ian and Richard Taylor, eds. 1993. *Eisenstein Rediscovered*. London: Routledge.

Clark, Katerina. 1981. *The Soviet Novel: History as Ritual*. Chicago: Chicago University Press.

Condee, Nancy, ed. 1995. *Soviet Hieroglyphics: Visual Culture in Late Twentieth-Century Russia*. London/Bloomington: British Film Institute/Indiana University Press.

Condee, Nancy. 2009. "Rape and Medium Specificity in *The Cranes are Flying*." *Studies in Russian & Soviet Cinema* 3.2: 173–183.

Condee, Nancy. 2009. *The Imperial Trace: Recent Russian Cinema*. Oxford and New York: Oxford University Press.

Crofts, S. 1977. "Ideology and Form: Soviet Socialist Realism and Chapayev." *Essays in Poetics*, II.1: 43–57.

Damiens, Caroline. 2015. "Cinema in Sakha (Yakutia) Republic: Renegotiating Film History." *KinoKultura* 48, http://www.kinokultura.com/2015/48-damiens.shtml (accessed October 30, 2015).

DeBlasio, Alyssa. 2008. "The New-Year Film as a Genre of Post-War Russian Cinema." *Studies in Russian & Soviet Cinema* 2.1: 43–61.

Dobrenko, Evgeny. 1995. "Muzyka vmesto sumbura: Narodnost' kak problema muzykal'noi kinokomedii stalinskoi epokhi" [Music Instead of Chaos: Narodnost as a Problem in the Musical Film Comedy of the Stalin Era]. *Revue des Études slaves* 67.2–3: 407–433.

Dobrenko, Evgeny. 2001. "The Russia We Acquired: Russian Classics, the Stalinist Cinema, and the Past from the Revolutionary Perspective." *Russian Studies in Literature* 37.4: 61–91.

Dobrenko, Evgeny. 2003. "Late Stalinist Cinema and the Cold War: An Equation without Unknowns." *Modern Language Review* 98.4: 929–944.

Dobrenko, Evgeny. 2007. "Creation Myth and Myth Creation in Stalinist Cinema." *Studies in Russian & Soviet Cinema* 1.3: 239–264.

Dobrenko, Evgeny. 2008. *Stalinist Cinema and the Production of History*. Edinburgh: Edinburgh University Press.

Dobrynin, Sergey. 2015. "New Buryat Cinema: Developments So Far and Challenges for the Future." *KinoKultura* 48, http://www.kinokultura.com/2015/48–dobrynin.shtml (accessed October 30, 2015).

Doubivko, Lena. 2011. "No Nailing Fins to the Floor: Ambivalent Femininities in Anna Melikian's *The Mermaid*." *Studies in Russian & Soviet Cinema* 5.2: 255–276.

Drobashenko, S. ed. 1984. *Sovetskoe kino 70-e gody* [Soviet Cinema of the 1970s]. Moscow: Iskusstvo.

Dumančić, Marko. 2012. "De-Stalinizing Soviet Science: Rethinking the Moral Implications of Scientific Progress in Khrushchev-Era Film." *Studies in Russian & Soviet Cinema* 6.1: 75–92.

Dunne, Nathan, ed. 2008. *Tarkovsky*. London: Black Dog Publishing.

Dymshits, N. and Aleksandr Troshin, eds. 1990. *Iz proshlogo v budushchee: Proverka na dorogakh* [From the Past to the Future: Trial on the Roads]. Moscow: VNII Kinoiskusstva.

Dzhulai, Liudmila. 2001. *Dokumental'nyi illiuzion: Otechestvennyi kinodokumentalizm. Opyty sotsial'nogo tvorchestva* [Documentary Illusion: Domestic Film Documentalism. Experiences of Social Work]. Moscow: Materik.

Eagle, Herbert, ed. 1981. *Russian Formalist Film Theory*. Ann Arbor: Michigan Slavic Publications.

Eagle, Herbert. 1989. "Soviet Cinema Today: On the Semantic Potential of a Discredited Canon." *Michigan Quarterly Review* 28.4: 743–60.

Eagle, Herbert. 1993. "Pavel Lungin's *Taxi Blues*," *Slavic Review* 52.2: 353–354.

Efird, Robert. 2009. "Dreams, Mirrors and Subjective Filtration in *Ivan's Childhood*." *Studies in Russian & Soviet Cinema* 3.3: 289–308.

Efird, Robert. 2014. "Amorphous Forms: Time and Subjectivity in *Shadows of Forgotten Ancestors*." *Studies in Russian & Soviet Cinema* 8.1: 24–40.

Egorova, Tatiana. 1997. *Soviet Film Music. An Historical Survey*. Amsterdam: Harwood, OPA.

Eikhenbaum, Boris, ed. 1927. *Poetika kino* [Film Poetics]. Moscow, Leningrad: Kinopechat'.

Eisenstein, Sergei. 1987. *Nonindifferent Nature*. Cambridge: Cambridge University Press.

Engel, Christine, ed. 1999. *Geschichte des sowjetischen und russischen Films* [History of Soviet and Russian Film]. Stuttgart und Weimar: Metzler.

Etkind, Alexander. 2010. "The Tale of Two Turns: *Khrustalev, My Car!* and the Cinematic Memory of the Soviet Past." *Studies in Russian & Soviet Cinema* 4.1: 45–63.

Etkind, Alexander. 2011. "Mourning the Soviet Victims in a Cosmopolitan Way: Hamlet from Kozintsev to Riazanov." *Studies in Russian & Soviet Cinema* 5.3: 389–409.

Faraday, George. 2000. *Revolt of the Filmmakers: The Struggle for Artistic Autonomy and the Fall of the Soviet Film Industry*. University Park, PA: Pennsylvania State University Press.

First, Joshua. 2008. "Making Soviet Melodrama Contemporary: Conveying 'Emotional Information' in the Era of Stagnation." *Studies in Russian & Soviet Cinema* 2.1: 21–42.

Fomin, Valerii. 1976. *Peresechenie parallel'nykh: Lotianu, Il'enko, Ioseliani, Mansurov, Okeev, Panfilov, Shukshin* [Crossing of Parallels. Lotianu, Illienko, Iosseliani, Mansurov, Okeev, Panfilov, Shukshin]. Moscow: Iskusstvo.

Fomin, Valerii. 1992. *Polka* [The Shelf]. Moscow: NII Kinoiskusstva.

Fomin, Valerii. 1993. *Zapreshchennye fil'my* [Forbidden Films]. (vol 2 of *Polka*). Moskva: NII Kinoiskusstva.

Fomin, Valerii. 1996. *Kino i vlast': sovetskoe kino, 1965–1985 gody: dokumenty, svidetel'stva, razmyshleniia* [Cinema and the Authorities: Soviet Cinema 1965–1985: Documents, Testimonies, Thoughts]. Moscow: Materik.

Fomin, Valerii, ed. 1998. *Kinematograf ottepeli: Dokumenty i svidetel'stva* [The Cinema of the Thaw: Documents and Testimonies]. Moscow: Materik.

Fomin, Valerii. 2001. *Pravda skazki. Kino i traditsii fol'klora* [The Truth of the Fairy Tale: Cinema and Folk Traditions]. Moscow: Materik.

Fomin, Valerii and Aleksandr Deriabin, eds. 2004. *Letopis' Rossiiskogo kino, 1863–1929* [Annals of Russian Cinema, 1863–1929]. Moscow: Materik.

Fomin, Valerii and Aleksandr Deriabin, eds. 2007. *Letopis' Rossiiskogo kino, 1930–1945* [Annals of Russian Cinema, 1930–1945]. Moscow: Materik.

Fomin, Valerii and Aleksandr Deriabin, eds. 2010. *Letopis' Rossiiskogo kino, 1946–1965* [Annals of Russian Cinema, 1946–1965]. Moscow: Kanon.

Fomin, Valerii, ed. 2015. *Letopis' Rossiiskogo kino, 1966–1980* [Annals of Russian Cinema, 1966–1980]. Moscow: Reabilitatsiia, Kanon+.

Foster, David. 2010. "Where Flowers Bloom but Have No Scent: The Cinematic Space of the Zone in Andrei Tarkovsky's *Stalker*." *Studies in Russian & Soviet Cinema* 4.3: 307–320.

Furman, Yelena. 2008. "*Shamara*: Writing and Screening the Female Body." *Studies in Russian & Soviet Cinema* 2.2: 167–181.

Galichenko, Nicholas. 1991. *Glasnost: Soviet Cinema Responds*. Austin: University of Texas Press.

Gershenson Olga. 2013. *Phantom Holocaust: Soviet Cinema and Jewish Catastrophe*. New Brunswick, NJ: Rutgers University Press.

Gillespie, David. 1996. "Identity and the Past in Recent Russian Cinema." In *European Identity in Cinema*, edited by Wendy Everett, 53–60. Exeter: Exeter University Press.

Gillespie David. 2000. *Early Soviet Cinema: Innovation, Ideology and Propaganda*. London: Wallflower Press.

Gillespie, David. 2003. *Russian Cinema*. New York: Longman

Gillespie, David. 2003. "The Sounds of Music: Soundtrack and Song in Soviet Film." *Slavic Review* 62.3: 473–490.

Gillespie, David. 2006. "Confronting Imperialism: The Ambivalence of War in Post-Soviet Film." In *Military and Society in Post-Soviet Russia*, edited by Stephen Webber and Jenny Mathers, 80–93. Manchester: Manchester University Press.

Ginzburg, Semen. 1963. *Kinematografiia dorevolutsionnoi Rossii* [The Cinema of Pre-Revolutionary Russia]. Moscow: Iskusstvo.

Givens, John. 1999. "Vasilii Shukshin and the 'Audience of Millions': *Kalina krasnaia* and the Power of Popular Cinema." *Russian Review* 58: 268–285.

Golovskoy, Val and John Rimberg. 1986. *Behind the Soviet Screen*, Ann Arbor: Ardis.

Goodwin, James. 1993. *Eisenstein, Cinema & History*. Urbana and Chicago, IL: University of Illinois Press.

Gornitskaia, Nina, ed. 1968. *Iz istorii Lenfil'ma* [From the History of Lenfilm] vol. 1. Leningrad: Iskusstvo.

Gornitskaia, Nina, ed. 1970. *Iz istorii Lenfil'ma* [From the History of Lenfilm] vol. 2. Leningrad: Iskusstvo.

Gornitskaia, Nina, ed. 1973. *Iz istorii Lenfil'ma* [From the History of Lenfilm] vol. 3. Leningrad: Iskusstvo.

Gornitskaia, Nina, ed. 1975. *Iz istorii Lenfil'ma* [From the History of Lenfilm] vol. 4. Leningrad: Iskusstvo.

Goscilo, Helena. 2010. "Between the Sword and the Scales, or Celluloid Justice." *Studies in Russian & Soviet Cinema* 4.2: 137–145.

Goscilo, Helena and Yana Hashamova, eds. 2010. *Cinepaternity: Fathers and Sons in Soviet and Post-Soviet Film*. Bloomington: Indiana University Press.

Goscilo Helena and Vlad Strukov, eds. 2011. *Celebrity and Glamour in Contemporary Russia: Shocking Chic*. London: Routledge.

Goulding, Daniel J. ed. 1989. *Post New Wave Cinema in the Soviet Union and Eastern Europe*. Bloomington: Indiana University Press.

Graffy, Julian. 2001. *Bed and Sofa* (KinoFile 5). London: I. B. Tauris.

Graffy, Julian. 2007. "History, Memory, Water: The Reclamation of Georgian Identity in Irakli Kvirikadze's *The Swimmer*." *Studies in Russian & Soviet Cinema* 1.3: 299–327.

Graffy, Julian. 2012. "'An Unpretentious Picture'? – Igor' Savchenko's *A Chance Encounter*." *Studies in Russian & Soviet Cinema* 6.3: 301–318.

Graffy, Julian and G. Hosking, eds. 1989. *Culture and the Media in the USSR Today*. London: Macmillan.

Graham, Alexander. 2012. "'Immersion in Time': History, Memory and the Question of Readability in the Films of Aleksei German." *Studies in Russian & Soviet Cinema* 6.2: 177–216.

Graham, Seth. 2000. "*Chernukha* and Russian Film." *Studies in Slavic Culture* 1: 9–27.

Gromov, E. 1989. *Komedii i ne tol'ko komedii* [Comedy and Not Only Comedy]. Moscow: Soiuz kinematografistov SSSR.

Günther, Hans and Evgenii Dobrenko, eds. 2000. *Sotsrealisticheskii kanon* [Socialist-Realist Canon]. St Petersburg: Akademicheskii proekt.

Günther, Hans and Sabine Hänsgen, eds. 2006. *Sovetskaia vlast' i media* [Soviet Power and the Media]. St Petersburg: Akademicheskii proekt.

Gurga. J. J. 2011. "Remembering (in) Ukrainian Cinema of the 1960s: Rolan Serhiienko's *White Clouds* (1968)." *Studies in Russian & Soviet Cinema* 5.3: 353–370.

Halperin, Charles J. 2013. "Ivan the Terrible Returns to the Silver Screen: Pavel Lungin's Film *Tsar*." *Studies in Russian & Soviet Cinema* 7.1: 61–72.

Harte, Tim. 2005. "A Visit to the Museum: Aleksandr Sokurov's Russian Ark and the Framing of the Eternal." *Slavic Review* 64.1: 43–58.

Hashamova, Yana. 2007. *Pride and Panic: Russian Imagination of the West in Post-Soviet Film*. Bristol and Chicago: Intellect Books.

Haynes, John. 2003. *New Soviet Man: Gender and Masculinity in Stalinist Soviet Cinema*. Manchester and New York: Manchester University Press.

Haynes, John. 2007. "Film as Political Football: *The Goalkeeper*." *Studies in Russian & Soviet Cinema* 1.3: 283–297.

Hicks, Jeremy. 2007. *Dziga Vertov: Defining Documentary Film*. London and New York: I. B. Tauris.

Hicks, Jeremy. 2009. "Confronting the Holocaust: Mark Donskoi's *The Unvanquished*." *Studies in Russian & Soviet Cinema* 3.1: 33–51.

Hicks, Jeremy. 2012. *First Films of the Holocaust: Soviet Cinema and the Genocide of the Jews, 1938–46*, Pittsburgh: University of Pittsburgh Press.

Hilton, Marjorie. 2014. "Gender and Ideological Rivalry in *Ninotchka* and *Circus*: The Capitalist and Communist Make-over." *Studies in Russian & Soviet Cinema* 8.1: 2–23.

Holmgren, Beth. 2007. "The Blue Angle and Blackface: Redeeming Entertainment in Aleksandrov's Circus." *Russian Review* 66: 5–22.

Horton, Andrew. 1993. *Inside Soviet Film Satire*. Cambridge: Cambridge University Press.

Horton, Andrew and Michael Brashinsky. 1992. *The Zero Hour: Glasnost and Soviet Cinema in Transition*. Princeton: Princeton University Press.

Hughes, Angela Ungoed and Howard Riley. 2007. "The Multi-Modal Matrix – A Laboratory of Devices: Film and the Formalist Legacy." *Studies in Russian & Soviet Cinema* 1.2: 191–209.

Hutchings, Stephen. 2000. "Word and Image in El'dar Riazanov's *S legkym parom*. Or, The Irony of (Cinematic) Fate." *Essays in Poetics* 25: 236–255.

Hutchings, Stephen. 2002. "Tchapaiev: l'homme de tous les temps, l'homme de tous les medias" [Chapaev: A Man of All Times, of All Media]. *La Revue Russe* 21: 9–16.

Hutchings, Stephen, ed. 2008. *Russia and its Other(s) on Film: Screening Intercultural Dialogue*. Basingstoke: Palgrave Macmillan.

Hutchings, Stephen and Anat Vernistski, eds. 2005. *Russian and Soviet Film Adaptations of Literature, 1900–2001. Screening the Word*. London: Routledge.

Isakava, Volha. 2009. "The Body in the Dark: Body, Sexuality and Trauma in Perestroika Cinema." *Studies in Russian & Soviet Cinema* 3.2: 201–214.

Iurenev, Rostislav. 1985. *Sergei Eizenshtein. Zamysli. Fil'my. Metod. Chast' pervaia: 1898–1929* [Sergei Eisenstein: Thoughts. Films. Method. Part I: 1898–1929]. Moscow: Iskusstvo.

Iurenev, Rostislav. 1997. *Sovetskoe kinoiskusstvo tridtsatykh godov* [Soviet Film Art of the 1930s]. Moscow: VGIK.

Ivanov, Viacheslav and Anna Kovalova. 2013. "Boris Glagolin and the Cinema." *Studies in Russian & Soviet Cinema* 7.3: 265–293.

Ivanova, V. with V. Myl'nikova, S. Skovorodnikova, Iu. Tsiv'ian, and R. Iangirov, eds. 2002. *Velikii Kinemo: Katalog sokhranivshikhsia igrovykh fil'mov Rossii, 1908–1919* [The Great Kinemo: Catalog of Preserved Fiction Films from Russia, 1908–1919]. Moscow: Novoe literaturnoe obozrenie.

James, Vaughan. 1973. *Soviet Socialist Realism: Origins and Theory*. New York: St Martin's Press.

Jameson, Fredric. 2006. "History and Elegy in Sokurov." *Critical Enquiry* 33: 1–12.

Johnson, Vida T. and Graham Petrie. 1994. *The Films of Andrei Tarkovsky: A Visual Fugue*. Bloomington: Indiana University Press.

Kaganovsky, Lilya. 2007. "The Voice of Technology and the End of Soviet Silent Film: Grigorii Kozintsev and Leonid Trauberg's *Alone*." *Studies in Russian & Soviet Cinema* 1.3: 265–281.

Kaganovsky, Lilya. 2008. *How the Soviet Man was Unmade: Cultural Fantasy and Male Subjectivity under Stalin*. Pittsburgh: University of Pittsburgh Press.

Kaganovsky, Lilya. 2009. "The Cultural Logic of Late Socialism." *Studies in Russian & Soviet Cinema* 3.2: 185–199.

Kaganovsky, Lilya. 2012. "The Homogenous Thinking Subject or Soviet Cinema Learns to Sing." *Studies in Russian & Soviet Cinema* 6.3: 281–299.

Kaganovsky Lilya and Masha Salazkina, eds. 2014. *Sound, Speech, Music in Soviet and Post-Soviet Cinema*. Bloomington: Indiana University Press.

Kapterev, Sergei. 2008. *Post-Stalinist Cinema and the Russian Intelligentsia, 1953–1960: Strategies of Self-Representation, De-Stalinization, and the National Cultural Tradition*. Saarbrücken: VDM Verlag Dr. Müller.

Kapterev, Sergei. 2012. "The War as Spectacle: Images of Warfare in the Films of Igor' Savchenko." *Studies in Russian & Soviet Cinema* 6.3: 333–345.

Kelly, Catriona and David Shepherd. 1998. *Russian Cultural Studies*. Oxford: Oxford University Press.

Kenez, Peter. 1985. *The Birth of the Propaganda State: Soviet Methods of Mass Mobilization, 1917–1929*. New York: Cambridge University Press.

Kenez, Peter. 1992. *Cinema and Soviet Society, 1917–1953*. Cambridge: Cambridge University Press.

Kenez, Peter. 1998. "Jewish Themes in Stalinist Films." *Journal of Popular Culture* 31.4: 159–169.

Kepley, Vance. 1979. "Foreign Films on Soviet Screens, 1922–1931." *Quarterly Review of Film Studies* 4.4: 429–442.

Kepley, Vance. 1983. "The Workers' International Relief and the Cinema of the Left, 1921–1935." *Cinema Journal* 23.1: 7–23.

Kepley, Vance. 1985. "The Origins of Soviet Cinema: A Study in Industry Development." *Quarterly Review of Film Studies* 4: 22–38.

Kepley, Vance. 1987. "Building a National Cinema: Soviet Film Education, 1918–1934." *WideAngle* 9.3: 4–20.

Kepley, Vance, ed. 1990. "Contemporary Soviet Cinema" (special issue). *WideAngle* 12.4.

Kepley, Vance. 1994. "Dovzhenko and Montage: Issues of Style and Narration in the Silent Films." *Journal of Ukrainian Studies* 19.1: 29–44.

Kepley, Vance. 2003. *The End of St Petersburg* (KinoFile 10). London: I. B. Tauris.

Khitrova, Daria. 2011. "Eisenstein's Choreography in *Ivan the Terrible*." *Studies in Russian & Soviet Cinema* 5.1: 55–71.

Kovalova, Anna. 2012. "Nikolai Erdman and the Poetics of Children's Film-Scripts." *Studies in Russian & Soviet Cinema* 6.2: 163–175.

Kovalova, Anna. 2012. *Kinematograf v Peterburge 1907–1917. Kinoproizvodstvo i fil'mografiia*. [Cinema in Petersburg 1907–1917. Film Production and Filmography]. St Petersburg: Skriptorium.

Kovalova, Anna and Iurii Tsiv'ian. 2011. *Kinematograf v Peterburge 1896–1917: kinoteatry i zriteli* [Cinema in Petersburg 1986–1917. Movie Theaters and Audiences]. St Petersburg: Masterskaia Seans and Skriptorium.

Kozintsev, Grigorii. 1977. *King Lear: The Space of Tragedy. Diary of a Film Director*. London: Heinemann.

Krukones, James H. 2010. "Peacefully Coexisting on a Wide Screen: Kinopanorama vs. Cinerama, 1952–1966." *Studies in Russian & Soviet Cinema* 4.3: 283–305.

Kujundzic, Dragan. 2004. "After 'After': The Arkive Fever of Alexander Sokurov." *Quarterly Review of Film and Video* 21: 219–239.

Kukulin, Il'ia. 2011. "A Prolonged Revanche: Eisenstein and Solzhenitsyn." *Studies in Russian & Soviet Cinema* 5.1: 73–103.

Kunichika, Michael. 2012. "'The Ecstasy of Breadth': The Odic and the Whitmanesque Style in Dziga Vertov's *One Sixth of the World* (1926)." *Studies in Russian & Soviet Cinema* 6.1: 53–74.

Kunze, Peter C. 2013. "Child's Play: Nadia and Romantic Childhood in Nikita Mikhalkov's *Burnt by the Sun*." *Studies in Russian & Soviet Cinema* 7.1: 25–38.
Lahusen, Thomas, ed. 1997. *Socialist Realism without Shores*. Durham, NC: Duke University Press.
Lahusen, Thomas with Gene Kuperman, eds. 1993. *Late Soviet Culture: From Perestroika to Novostroika*. Durham, NC: Duke University Press.
Larsen, Susan. 1999. "In Search of an Audience: The New Russian Cinema of Reconciliation." In *Consuming Russia: Popular Culture, Sex, and Society since Gorbachev*, edited by Adele Barker, 192–216. Durham, NC: Duke University Press.
Larsen, Susan. 2000. "Melodramatic Masculinity, National Identity, and the Stalinist Past in Postsoviet Cinema." *Studies in 20th Century Literature* 24.1: 85–120.
Larsen, Susan. 2003. "National Identity, Cultural Authority and the Post-Soviet Blockbuster: Nikita Mikhalkov and Aleksei Balabanov." *Slavic Review* 62.3: 491–511.
Laurent, Natacha. 2000. *L'oeil du Kremlin: cinema et censure en URSS sous Staline* [The Kremlin's Eye: Cinema and Censorship in Stalin's USSR]. Toulouse: Privat.
Lawton, Anna. 1992. *Kinoglasnost: Soviet Cinema in Our Time*. Cambridge: Cambridge University Press.
Lawton, Anna. 1992. *The Red Screen: Politics, Society, Art in Soviet Cinema*. London and New York: Routledge.
Lawton, Anna. 2002. *Before the Fall: Soviet Cinema in the Gorbachev Years*. Washington, DC: New Academia Publishing.
Lawton, Anna. 2004. *Imaging Russia 2000: Film and Facts*. Washington, DC: New Academia Publishing.
Le Fanu, Mark. 1987. *The Cinema of Andrei Tarkovsky*. London: British Film Institute.
Lewis, Simon M. 2011. "'Official Nationality' and the Dissidence of Memory in Belarus: A Comparative Analysis of Two Films." *Studies in Russian & Soviet Cinema* 5.3: 371–387.
Leyda, J. 1960. *Kino: A History of the Russian and Soviet Film*. Princeton: Princeton University Press.
Leyda, Jay and Zina Voynow, eds. 1985. *Eisenstein at Work*. London: Methuen.
Liber, George. 2002. *Alexander Dovzhenko: A Life in Soviet Film*. London: British Film Institute.
Listov, Viktor. 1991. "Early Soviet Cinema: The Spontaneous and the Planned, 1917–1924." *Historical Journal of Film, Radio and Television* 11.2: 121–127.
Listov, Viktor. 1995. *Rossiia. Revoliutsiia. Kinematograf: K 100–letiiu mirovogo kino* [Russia. Revolution, Cinema. For the Centenary of World Cinema]. Moscow: Materik.
Listov, Viktor and Elena Khokhlova, eds. 1996. *Istoriia otechestvennogo kino: dokumenty, memuary, pis'ma* [The History of Domestic Cinema: Documents, Memoirs, Letters]. Vol. 1. Moscow: Materik.
Livers, Keith A. 2005. "Empty is My Native Land: The Problem of the Absent Center in Aleksandr Zel'dovich's *Moscow*." *Russian Review* 64: 422–39.
MacFadyen. David. 2003. *The Sad Comedy of El'dar Riazanov*. Montreal and London: McGill-Queen's University Press.
MacFadyen, David. 2005. *Yellow Crocodiles and Blue Oranges: Russian Animated Film since WWII*. Montreal: McGill-Queen's University Press.
MacFadyen, David. 2007. "*Moscow Does Not Believe in Tears*: From Oscar to Consolation Prize." *Studies in Russian & Soviet Cinema* 1.1: 45–67.

Makoveeva, Irina. 2010. "The Woman-Avenger on the Post-Soviet Screen." *Studies in Russian & Soviet Cinema* 4.2: 147–159.

Mal'kova, Liliana. 2002. *Sovremennost' kak istoriia: Realizatsiia mifa v dokumental'nom kino* [The Contemporary World as History: The Realization of a Myth in Documentary Cinema]. Moscow: Materik.

Mamatova, Lidiia, ed. 1983. *Aktual'nye problemy sovetskogo kino nachala 80–kh godov* [Current Issues of Soviet Cinema of the early 1980s]. Moscow: NII Kinoiskusstva.

Mamatova, Lidiia, 1995. *Kino: politika i liudi: 30–ye gody* [Cinema: Politics and People, the 1930s]. Moscow: Materik.

Margolit, Evgenii and Viacheslav Shmyrov. 1995. *iz"iatoe kino* [Cinema Withdrawn]. Moscow: Dubl' D.

Mar'iamov, Grigorii. 1992. *Kremlevskii tsenzor: Stalin smotrit kino* [The Kremlin Censor: Stalin Watches Films]. Moscow: Kinotsentr.

Martin, Michel. 1993. *Cinéma soviétique: de Khrouchtev à Gorbatchev* [Soviet Cinema: From Khrushchev to Gorbachev]. Lausanne: L'Age d'homme.

Mayne, Judith. 1989. *Kino and the Woman Question: Feminism and Soviet Silent Cinema*. Columbus: Ohio State University Press.

McReynolds, Louise. 2000. "The Silent Movie Melodrama: Evgenii Bauer Fashions the Heroine's Self." In *Self and Story in Russian History*, edited by Laura Engelstein and Stephanie Sandler, 120–139. Ithaca and London: Cornell University Press.

McReynolds, Louise. 2002. "Home Was Never Where The Heart Was: Domestic Dystopias in Russia's Silent Movie Melodrama." In *Imitations of Life: Two Centuries of Melodrama in Russia*, edited by L. McReynolds and J. Neuberger, 127–151. Durham and London: Duke University Press.

McReynolds, Louise. 2009. "Demanding Men, Desiring Women and Social Collapse in the Films of Evgenii Bauer, 1913–1917." *Studies in Russian & Soviet Cinema* 3.2: 145–156.

Menashe, Louis. 2001. "Moscow Believes in Tears: The Problems (and Promise?) of Russian Cinema in the Transition Period." *Cineaste* 26.3: 10–17.

Menashe, Louis. 2010. *Moscow does not Believe in Tears: Russians and Their Movies*. Washington, DC: New Academia Publishing.

Merrill, Jason. 2009. "Gender and Nationality in Iurii Kuzin's *The Ark*." *Studies in Russian & Soviet Cinema* 3.3: 335–352.

Merrill, Jason. 2012. "Brothers and Others: Brotherhood, the Caucasus, and National Identity in Post-Soviet Film." *Studies in Russian & Soviet Cinema* 6.1: 93–111.

Michelson, Annette, ed. 1984. *Kino-Eye: The Writings of Dziga Vertov*. Berkeley: University of California Press.

Mihailova, Mihaela. 2014. "'The Tender Beasts': Peasant Mythology in Petr Lutsik's *The Outskirts*." *Studies in Russian & Soviet Cinema* 8.2: 120–137.

Mikhailov, V. 2003. *Rasskazy o kinematografe staroi Moskvy* [Stories about Cinema in the Old Moscow]. Moscow: Materik.

Miller, Jamie. 2006. "Soviet Cinema, 1929–41: The Development of Industry and Infrastructure." *Europe–Asia Studies* 58. 1: 103–124.

Miller, Jamie. 2007. "Educating the Filmmakers: The State Institute of Cinematography in the 1930s." *The Slavonic and East European Review* 85.3: 462–490.

Miller, Jamie. 2007. "The Purges of Soviet Cinema 1929–1938." *Studies in Russian & Soviet Cinema*, 1.1: 5–26.

Miller, Jamie. 2010. *Soviet Cinema: Politics and Persuasion under Stalin*. London: I. B. Tauris.

Mjolsness, Lora Wheeler. 2008. "Dziga Vertov's *Soviet Toys*: Commerce, Commercialization and Cartoons." *Studies in Russian & Soviet Cinema* 2.3: 247–267.

Monastireva-Ansdell, Elena. 2014. "Trapped in the Prisoner Scenario: The First Chechen War and Sergei Bodrov's *Prisoner of the Mountains*." *Studies in Russian & Soviet Cinema* 8.2: 98–119.

Moore, Tiffany Ann Conroy. 2012. *Kozintsev's Shakespeare Films: Russian Political Protest in* Hamlet *and* King Lear. Jefferson, NC: MacFarland.

Morley, Rachel. 2003. "Gender Relations in the Films of Evgenii Bauer." *Slavonic and East European Review* 81.1: 32–69.

Morley, Rachel. 2016. *Performing Femininity: Woman as Performer in Pre-Revolutionary Cinema*. London: I. B. Tauris.

Moss, Anne Eakin. 2009. "Stalin's Harem: The Spectator's Dilemma in Late 1930s Soviet Film." *Studies in Russian & Soviet Cinema* 3.2: 157–172.

Mulcahy, Robert. 2013. "A Not-So-Thrilling Thriller: Adapting Boris Akunin's *State Counsellor*." *Studies in Russian & Soviet Cinema* 7.3: 311–335.

Nesbet, Anne. 2003. *Savage Junctures: Sergei Eisenstein and the Shape of Thinking*. London: I. B. Tauris.

Neuberger Joan. 2003. *Ivan the Terrible* (KinoFile 9). London: I. B. Tauris.

Neuberger, Joan. 2012. "Strange Circus: Eisenstein's Sex Drawings." *Studies in Russian & Soviet Cinema* 6.1: 5–52.

Norris, Stephen M. 2005. "Tsarist Russia, *lubok* Style: Nikita Mikhalkov's *Barber of Siberia* (1999) and Post-Soviet National Identity." *Historical Journal of Film, Radio and Television* 25.1: 101–118.

Norris, Stephen M. 2007. "Guiding Stars: The Comet-Like Rise of the War Film in Putin's Russia." *Studies in Russian & Soviet Cinema* 1.2: 163–189.

Norris, Stephen M. 2012. *Blockbuster History in the New Russia: Movies, Memory, and Patriotism*. Bloomington: Indiana University Press.

Norris, Stephen M. and Zara M. Torlone, eds. 2008. *Insiders and Outsiders in Russian Cinema*. Bloomington: Indiana University Press.

O'Mahony, Mike. 2008. *Sergei Eisenstein*. London: Reaktion Books.

Oukaderova, Lida. 2010. "The Sense of Movement in Georgii Daneliia's *Walking the Streets of Moscow*." *Studies in Russian & Soviet Cinema* 4.1: 5–21.

Papazian, Elizabeth Astrid. 2009. *Manufacturing Truth: The Documentary Moment in Early Soviet Culture*. Evanston: Northern Illinois University Press.

Petric, Vlada. 1987. *Constructivism in Film: The Man with the Movie Camera*, Cambridge: Cambridge University Press.

Pozefsky, Peter. 2008. "Russian Gangster Films as Popular History: Genre, Ideology and Memory in Pavel Lungin's *Tycoon*." *Studies in Russian & Soviet Cinema* 2.3: 299–325.

Pozefsky, Peter. 2010. "Childhood and the Representation of the History of Stalinism in Russian Cinema of the Transition Period." *Studies in Russian & Soviet Cinema* 4.1: 23–44.

Pozner Valérie and Natacha Laurent, eds. 2012. *Kinojudaica: Les représentations des Juifs dans le cinéma de Russie et d'Union soviétique des années 1910 aux années 1980* [Representations of the Jews in Rusisan and Soviet Cinema of the 1910s–1980s]. Toulouse: Cinematheque de Toulouse.

Prokhorov Aleksandr. 2007. *Unasledovannyi diskurs: paradigmy Stalinskoi kul'tury v literature i kinematografe "ottepeli"* [Inherited Discourse: Stalinist Tropes in Thaw Literature and Cinema]. St Petersburg: Akademicheskii proekt.

Prokhorov, Alexander. 2002. "Soviet Family Melodrama of the 1940s and 1950s: From *Wait for Me* to *The Cranes Are Flying*." In *Imitations of Life: Two Centuries of Melodrama in Russia*, edited by L. McReynolds and J. Neuberger, 208–231. Durham, NC: Duke University Press.

Prokhorov, Alexander. 2003. "Cinema of Attraction versus Narrative Cinema: Leonid Gaidai's and El'dar Riazanov's Satires of the 1960s." *Slavic Review* 62.3: 455–472.

Prokhorov, Alexander. 2007. "Revisioning Alexandrov's Circus: Seventy Years of the Great Family." *Russian Review* 66: 1–4.

Prokhorov, Alexander. 2007. "The Adolescent and the Child in the Cinema of the Thaw." *Studies in Russian & Soviet Cinema* 1.2: 115–129.

Prokhorova, Elena. 2003. "Can the Meeting Place Be Changed? Crime and Identity Discourse in Russian Television Series of the 1990s." *Slavic Review* 62.3: 512–524.

Quart, Barbara. 1988. "Between Mysticism and Materialism: The Films of Larisa Shepitko." *Cineaste* 16.3: 4–11.

Raiklin, Benjamin E. 2009. "Soviet Cinema in the Wake of the Terror: The Artistic Council at Mosfilm, 1939–1941." *Studies in Russian & Soviet Cinema* 3.3: 267–288.

Ratchford, Moira. 1992. "Post-*Glasnost* Shock in the Russian Film Industry: The Euphoria is Past. Now Comes the Tough Part." *New Outlook* 3.1–2: 102–114.

Redwood, Thomas. 2010. *Andrei Tarkovsky's Poetics of Cinema*. Newcastle: Cambridge Scholars Publishing.

Reeder, R. 1989. "Agit-Prop Art: Posters, Puppets, Propaganda and Eisenstein's *Strike*." *Russian Literature Triquarterly* 22: 255–278.

Renfrew, Alastair. 2013. "Facts and Life: Osip Brik in the Soviet Film Industry." *Studies in Russian & Soviet Cinema* 7.2: 165–188.

Rifkin, Benjamin. 1993. "The Christian subtext in Bykov's 'Čučelo'." *Slavic and East European Journal* 37.2: 178–193.

Riley, John. 2005. *Dmitri Shostakovich*. (Kino Companion 3). London: I. B. Tauris.

Rimberg, John. 1973. *The Motion Picture in the Soviet Union, 1918–1952: A Sociological Analysis*. New York: Arno Press.

Roberts, Graham. 1999. *Forward Soviet. History and Non-Fiction film in the USSR*. London: I. B. Tauris.

Roberts, Graham. 2000. *The Man with the Movie Camera* (KinoFile 2). London: I. B. Tauris.

Roberts, Tom. 2013. "'Simply an Anachronism': Repetition and Meaning in Kira Muratova's Chekhovian Motifs." *Studies in Russian & Soviet Cinema* 7.1: 39–59.

Rollberg, Peter. 2009. *A–Z/Historical Dictionary of Russian and Soviet Cinema*, Lanham, MD: Scarecrow Press.

Rouland, Michael, with Gulnara Abikeyeva, and Birgit Beumers, eds. 2013. *Cinema in Central Asia: Rewriting Cultural Histories*. London: I. B. Tauris.

Ryabchikova, Natalie. 2015. "Eisenstein's First Auto/Biography." *Studies in Russian & Soviet Cinema* 9.2: 74–93.

Salazkina, Masha. 2009. *In Excess: Sergei Eisenstein's Mexico*. Chicago: Chicago University Press.

Salys, Rimgaila. 2007. "Art Deco Aesthetics in Grigorii Aleksandrov's The Circus." *Russian Review* 66: 23–35.

Salys, Rimgaila. 2009. *The Musical Comedy Films of Grigorii Aleksandrov. Laughing Matters*. Bristol: Intellect Books.

Salys Rimgaila, ed. 2013. *The Russian Cinema Reader*, vol. 1, *1908 to the Stalin Era* and vol. 2, *The Thaw to the Present*. Boston: Academic Studies Press.

Sandomirskaia, Irina. 2008. "A Glossolalic Glasnost and the Re-Tuning of the Soviet Subject: Sound Performance in Kira Muratova's *Asthenic Syndrome*." *Studies in Russian & Soviet Cinema* 2.1: 63–83.

Sargeant, Amy. 2001. *Vsevolod Pudovkin: Classic Films of the Soviet Avant-Garde*. London: I. B. Tauris.

Sarkisova, Oksana. 2010. "Folk Songs in Soviet Orchestration: Vostokfilm's *Song of Happiness* and the Forging of the New Soviet Musician." *Studies in Russian & Soviet Cinema* 4.3: 261–281.

Sarkisova, Oksana. 2015. "Taming the Frontier: Aleksandr Litvinov's Expedition Films and Representations of Indigenous Minorities in the Far East." *Studies in Russian & Soviet Cinema* 9.1: 2–23.

Schmulevitch, Éric. *Réalisme socialiste et cinéma: Le cinéma stalinien (1928–1941)* [Socialist Realism and Cinema: Stalinist Cinema 1928–1941]. Paris: Editions L'Harmattan, 1996.

Schuckman, Emily Matthews. 2011. "Reclaiming 'The Spot': The Prostitute as Entrepreneur in Iurii Moroz's *The Spot*." *Studies in Russian & Soviet Cinema* 5.2: 205–225.

Seton, Marie. 1978. *Sergei M. Eisenstein. A Biography*. London: Dennis Dobson.

Shaw, Tony and Denise J. Youngblood. 2010. *Cinematic Cold War: The American and Soviet Struggle for Hearts and Minds*. Lawrence: University Press of Kansas.

Shlapentokh, Dmitry and Vladimir Shlapentokh. 1993. *Soviet Cinematography, 1918–1991*. New York: Aldine de Gruyter.

Skakov, Nariman. 2009. "The (Im)possible Translation of *Nostalgia*." *Studies in Russian & Soviet Cinema* 3.3: 309–333.

Skakov Nariman. 2012. *The Cinema of Tarkovsky: Labyrinths of Space and Time*. London: I. B. Tauris.

Smorodinska, Tatiana. 2010. "Rule of Law vs. 'Russian Justice': Nikita Mikhalkov's *12*." *Studies in Russian & Soviet Cinema* 4.2: 161–170.

Sobolev, R. 1961. *Liudi i fil'my russkogo dorevoliutsionnogo kino* [People and Films of Russian Pre-Revolutionary Cinema]. Moscow: Iskusstvo.

Steffen, James. 2013. *The Cinema of Sergei Parajanov*. Madison: University of Wisconsin Press.

Stishova, Elena. 2001. *Territoriia kino: Postsovetskoe desiatiletie* [Territory of Cinema: The Post-Soviet Decade]. Moscow: Pomatur.

Stites, Richard. 1992. *Russian Popular Culture. Entertainment and Society since 1900*. Cambridge: Cambridge University Press.

Strukov, Vlad. 2010. "'For All Who Draw the Sword Will Die By the Sword': The Symbolism of Filipp Iankovskii's *The Sword Bearer*." *Studies in Russian & Soviet Cinema* 4.2: 171–185.

Strukov, Vlad and Helena Goscilo, eds. 2016. *Russian Aviation, Space Flight and Visual Culture*. Abingdon and New York: Routledge.

Synessiou Natasha. 2001. *Mirror* (KinoFile 6). London: I. B. Tauris.

Szaniawski, Jeremi. 2007. "Historic Space in Sokurov's *Moloch*, *Taurus* and *The Sun*". *Studies in Russian & Soviet Cinema* 1.2: 147–162.

Szaniawski, Jeremi. 2014. *The Cinema of Alexander Sokurov: Figures of Paradox*. London: Wallflower Press.

Tarkovskii, Andrei. 1994. *Time Within Time: The Diaries, 1970–1986*. London: Faber.
Tarkovsky, Andrey. 1986. *Sculpting in Time*, Austin: University of Texas Press.
Taubman, Jane. 1993. "The Cinema of Kira Muratova." *Russian Review* 52: 367–381.
Taubman, Jane. 2005. *Kira Muratova* (Kino Companion 4). London: I. B. Tauris.
Taylor, Richard. 1979. *The Politics of the Soviet Cinema, 1917–1929*. Cambridge: Cambridge University Press.
Taylor, Richard, ed. 1982. *The Poetics of Cinema. Russian Poetics in Translation*, 9. Oxford: RPT Publications.
Taylor, Richard. 1983. "A 'Cinema for the Millions': Soviet Socialist Realism and the Problem of Film Comedy." *Journal of Contemporary History* 18: 439–461.
Taylor, Richard. 1996. "The Illusion of Happiness and the Happiness of Illusion: Grigorii Aleksandrov's *The Circus*." *Slavic and East European Review* 74.4: 601–620.
Taylor, Richard. 1998 (1979). *Film Propaganda: Soviet Russia and Nazi Germany*. London: I. B. Tauris.
Taylor, Richard, ed. 1998. *The Eisenstein Reader*. London: British Film Institute.
Taylor, Richard. 1999. "Singing on the Steppes for Stalin: Ivan Pyr'ev and the Kolkhoz Musical in Soviet Cinema." *Slavic Review* 58.1: 143–159.
Taylor, Richard. 2000. "But Eastward, Look, the Land is Brighter: Towards a Topography of Utopia in the Stalinist Musical." In *100 Years of European Cinema: Entertainment or Ideology?*, edited by Diana Holmes and Alison Smith, 11–26. Manchester: Manchester University Press.
Taylor, Richard. 2000. *The Battleship Potemkin* (KinoFile 1). London: I. B. Tauris.
Taylor, Richard. 2002. *October*. London: British Film Institute.
Taylor, Richard, ed. 2006. *The Eisenstein Collection*. London, New York, and Calcutta: Seagull Books.
Taylor, Richard, ed. 2006. *Vsevolod Pudovkin: Selected Essays*. London and Calcutta: Seagull Books
Taylor, Richard and Ian Christie, eds. 1988. *The Film Factory. Russian and Soviet Cinema in Documents 1896–1939*. London and New York: Routledge.
Taylor, Richard and Ian Christie, eds. 1991. *Inside the Film Factory. New Approaches to Russian and Soviet Cinema*. London and New York: Routledge.
Taylor, Richard and Derek Spring, eds. 1993. *Stalinism and Soviet Cinema*. London: Routledge.
Tode, Thomas and Barbara Wurm, eds. 2006. *Dziga Vertov: The Vertov Collection at the Austrian Film Museum*. Vienna: SYNEMA.
Toropova, Anna. 2011. "'If We Cannot Laugh Like That, Then How Can We Laugh?': The 'Problem' of Stalinist Film Comedy." *Studies in Russian & Soviet Cinema* 5.3: 335–351.
Troianovskii, Vitalii, ed. 1996. *Kinematograf ottepeli. Kniga pervaia*. Moscow: Materik.
Tsivian, Yuri. 1994. *Early Cinema in Russia and its Cultural Reception*. Chicago and London: University of Chicago Press.
Tsivian, Yuri. 2001. *Ivan the Terrible*. London: British Film Institute Classics.
Tsivian, Yuri, ed. 2005. *Lines of Resistance: Dziga Vertov and the Twenties*. Pordenone: Giornate del Cinema Muto.
Tsyrkun, Nina. 2013. "Film Comics in Russia and Their Genesis." *Studies in Russian & Soviet Cinema* 7.3: 295–310.
Tupitsyn, Margarita. 2002. *Malevich and Film*. New Haven: Yale University Press.

Turovskaya, Maya. 1989. *Tarkovsky: Cinema as Poetry*. London: Faber.

Usuvaliev, Sultan. 2014. "The Godfathers of Mikhail Kuznetsov." *Studies in Russian & Soviet Cinema* 8.3: 184–199.

Vail', Petr. 1999. "60–e: sovetskoe kino i stil' epokhi. Razmyshleniia i kommentarii" [The 1960s: Soviet Cinema and the Style of an Era. Thoughts and Comments]. In *Close-Up: Istoriko-teoreticheskii seminar vo VGIKe: Lektsii 1996–1998 gody* [Close-Up: Historico-Theoretical Seminar at the Film Institute VGIK. Lectures 1996–1998], edited by Aleksandr Troshin, 230–233. Moscow: VGIK.

van Geldern, James and Richard Stites, eds. 1995. *Mass Soviet Culture in Soviet Russia*. Bloomington: Indiana University Press.

Vinogradov, Vladimir and Konstantin Ognev, eds. 2000. *K istorii VGIKa (1919–1934)* [About VGIK's History, 1919–1934], vol. 1, Moscow: VGIK.

Vinogradov, Vladimir and Konstantin Ognev, eds. 2004. *K istorii VGIKa (1935–1945)* [About VGIK's History, 1935–1945], vol. 2, Moscow: VGIK.

Vinogradov, Vladimir and V. Bondarenko, eds. 2006. *K istorii VGIKa (1946–1955)* [About VGIK's History, 1946–1955], vol. 3, Moscow: VGIK.

Vinogradov, Vladimir and Natal'ia Riabchikova, eds. 2013. *K istorii VGIKa (1956–1965)* [About VGIK's History, 1956–1965], vol. 4, Moscow: VGIK.

White, Frederick H. 2008. "*Of Freaks and Men*: Aleksei Balabanov's Critique of Degenerate Post-Soviet Society." *Studies in Russian & Soviet Cinema* 2.3: 281–297.

White, Frederick H. 2015. "*Cargo 200*: A Bricolage of Cultural Citations." *Studies in Russian & Soviet Cinema* 9.2: 94–109.

Widdis, Emma. 1996–1997. "An Unmappable System: The Collapse of Public Space in Late Soviet Film." *Film Criticism* 21.2: 8–24.

Widdis, Emma. 2003. *Visions of a New Land: Soviet Film from the Revolution to the Second World War*. New Haven: Yale University Press.

Widdis, Emma. 2005. *Alexander Medvedkin* (Kino Companion 2). London: I. B. Tauris.

Widdis, Emma. 2009. "*Faktura*: Depth and Surface in Early Soviet Set Design." *Studies in Russian & Soviet Cinema* 3.1: 5–32.

Widdis, Emma. 2012. "Child's Play: Pleasure and the Soviet Hero in Savchenko's *A Chance Encounter*." *Studies in Russian & Soviet Cinema* 6.3: 319–331.

Wilmes, Dusty. 2014 "National Identity (De)Construction in Recent Independent Cinema: Kirill Serebrennikov's *Yuri's Day* and Sergei Loznitsa's *My Joy*." *Studies in Russian & Soviet Cinema* 8.3: 218–232.

Woll, Josephine. 2000. *Real Images. Soviet Cinema of the Thaw*. London: I. B. Tauris.

Woll Josephine. 2003. *The Cranes are Flying* (KinoFile 7). London: I. B. Tauris.

Woll, Josephine and Denise J. Youngblood. 2001. *Repentance* (KinoFile 4). London: I. B. Tauris.

Yampolsky, Mikhail. 1991. "Reality at Second Hand." *Historical Journal of Film, Radio and Television* 11.2: 161–171.

Yangirov, Rashit. 1991. "Soviet Cinema in the Twenties: National Alternatives." *Historical Journal of Film, Radio and Television* 11.2: 129–139.

Youngblood, Denise J. 1985. *Soviet Cinema in the Silent Era, 1918–1935*. Austin: University of Texas Press.

Youngblood, Denise J. 1991. "'History' on Film: The Historical Melodrama in Early Soviet Cinema." *Historical Journal of Film, Radio and Television* 11.2: 173–184.

Youngblood, Denise J. 1991. "The Fate of Soviet Popular Cinema During the Stalin Revolution." *The Russian Review* 50: 148–162.

Youngblood, Denise J. 1992. *Movies for the Masses: Popular Cinema and Soviet Society in the 1920s*, Cambridge: Cambridge University Press.

Youngblood, Denise J. 1995. "Repentance: Stalinist Terror and the Realism of Surrealism." In *Film and the Construction of a New Past*, edited by Robert Rosenstone, 139–154. Princeton: Princeton University Press.

Youngblood, Denise J. 1996. "Andrei Rublev: The Medieval Epic as Post-Utopian History." In *The Persistence of History: Film, Television, and the Modern Event*, edited by Vivian Sobchack, 127–143. New York: Routledge.

Youngblood, Denise J. 1999. *The Magic Mirror. Moviemaking in Russia, 1908–1918*. Madison, WI and London, University of Wisconsin Press.

Youngblood, Denise J. 2003. "The Cosmopolitan and the Patriot: The Brothers Mikhalkov-Konchalovsky and Russian Cinema." *Historical Journal of Film, Radio & Television* 23.1: 27–41.

Youngblood, Denise J. 2007. *Russian War Films. On the Cinema Front 1914–2005*. Lawrence: University of Kansas Press.

Zhabskii, M., ed. 1997. *Ispytanie konkurentsiei: Otechestvennoe kino i novoe pokolenie zritelei* [Experiencing Competition: Domestic Cinema and the New Generation of Spectators]. Moscow: VNII Kinoiskusstva.

Zorkaia, Neia. 1974. *Èl'dar Riazanov: Sbornik* [Eldar Riazanov. A Collection]. Moscow: Iskusstvo.

Zorkaia, Neia, and Anri Vartanov, eds. 1991. *Ekrannye iskusstva i literatura: nemoe kino* [Screen Art and Literature: Silent Cinema]. Moscow: Nauka.

Zorkaya, Neya. 1991. *The Illustrated History of the Soviet Cinema*. New York: Hippocrene Books.

Zvonkine, Eugénie. 2007. "The Structure of the Fairy Tale in Kira Muratova's *The Sentimental Policeman*." *Studies in Russian & Soviet Cinema* 1.2: 131–145.

Zvonkine, Eugénie. 2012. *Kira Muratova: un cinéma de la dissonance*. [Kira Muratova: A Cinema of Dissonance]. Lausanne: L'Age d'Homme.

Index

12 2007 *see* Mikhalkov
1612 2007 *see* Khotinenko
235,000,000 1967 *see* Brauns

Abortion (*Abort*, Grigorii Lemberg and Nikolai Baklin, 1924), 99
Abraham, 217, 571, 572
Abraham Lincoln, Vampire Killer 2012 *see* Bekmambetov
Abuladze, Tengiz, 604, 607
   Repentance (*Monanieba*, 1984), 555
Academy Award, 202, 418, 546, 568, 580
Accordion, The 1934 *see* Savchenko
Accused of Murder 1969 *see* Volchek
Admiral Nakhimov 1946 *see* Pudovkin
Admiral, The 2008 *see* Kravchuk
adventure film, 13, 68, 76, 166, 174, 203, 204, 400
Adventures of a Dentist 1965 *see* Klimov
Adventures of Korzinkina, The 1941 *see* Mints
Adventures of Sherlock Holmes and Dr Watson 1979–86 *see* Maslennikov
Aelita 1924 *see* Protazanov
Aerograd 1935 *see* Dovzhenko
Affron, Charles and Mirella, 316, 317
Afghan War (1979–1988), 218, 410
Agfa, 11, 272, 278, 287
agitka (agitational film), 302
Agokas, Nikolai, 274, 277, 278
Agranenko, Zakhar, 368, 385
   The Immortal Garrison (*Bessmertnyi garnizon*, with Tissé 1956), 368
Aitmatov, Chingiz, 380
Akhedzhakova, Liia, 466
Akhmatova, Anna, 79, 544

Aksenov, Vasilii, 165, 442, 602, 605
Akunin, Boris, 240
Alabian, Karo, 456
Aleinikov, Petr, 73
Aleksandrinsky (theatre), 38
Aleksandrov, Georgii, 417
Aleksandrov, Grigorii, 8, 14, 142–147, 149–151, 158–160, 162, 165, 167–168, 175, 270, 275, 280–282, 287–288, 294–295, 300, 308, 311, 353–355, 357, 361, 367, 385, 392, 417, 428, 434, 456–457, 494, 524, 591–592, 603
   The Circus (*Tsirk*, 1936), 142–144, 147–149, 151, 152, 354, 592
   Happy Guys (*Veselye rebiata*, aka *Jolly Fellows*, 1934), 142, 144–149, 151, 152, 158, 162, 353, 456
   Meeting on the Elbe (*Vstrecha na El'be*, 1949), 14, 428, 434
   The Radiant Path (*Svetlyi put'*, 1940), 142–146, 148, 149, 151, 152, 355, 456
   Russian Souvenir (*Russkii suvenir*, 1960), 159, 167, 168
   Volga-Volga (1938), 142, 144–149, 151, 152, 160, 168, 456, 567
Alenka 1961 *see* Barnet
Alentova, Vera, 514
Alesha Ptitsyn forms his Character 1953 *see* Granik
Alexander II, 411, 412
Alexander III, 208, 209
Alexander Nevsky, 1938 *see* Eisenstein
Alexander of Macedonia, 394
Alexander. The Neva Battle 2008 *see* Kalenov
Alexandra 2007 *see* Sokurov
Alive 2006 *see* Veledinskii
All Soul's Day 1988 *see* Sel'ianov

A Companion to Russian Cinema, First Edition. Edited by Birgit Beumers.
© 2016 John Wiley & Sons, Inc. Published 2016 by John Wiley & Sons, Inc.

All that Heaven Allows (Douglas Sirk, 1955), 215
All-Union Agricultural Exhibition *see* VDNKh
All-Union Party Conference on Cinema Affairs, 106, 294
Alma-Ata, 79, 415, 489, 590
Alone 1931 *see* Kozintsev, Trauberg
Al'tman, Natan, 322, 323
American Film Academy, 232
Americanism (*amerikanshchina*), 68, 73, 350
Amirkulov, Ardak, 555
   The Fall of Otrar (*Gibel' Otrara*, 1991), 555
Amphibian Man 1961 *see* Chebotarev; Kazanskii
Ananishnov, Aleksei, 85
Anderson, Lindsay, 129, 130
Andreasian, Sarik, 242
   Pregnant (*Beremennyi*, 2011), 242
Andreev, Andrei, 180
Andrei Rublev 1966 *see* Tarkovskii
Andrianov, Aleksei, 471, 472
   The Spy (*Shpion*, 2012), 471, 472
Andrievskii, Aleksandr, 281
   The Land of Youth (*Zemlia molodosti*, 1941), 281
Andrikanis, Evgenii, 507
And What if it is Love? 1962 *see* Raizman
Anemone, Anthony, 15, 543–562
12 Angry Men 1957 *see* Lumet
Animation, 1, 7, 52, 100, 103–105, 236, 270, 272, 275, 279, 280, 282, 283, 285, 287, 298, 321, 365, 366
Anninskii, Lev, 174
Annushka 1959 *see* Barnet
Anoshchenko, Nikolai, 274–277
Another Sky 2010 *see* Mamuliia
Antikiller 2002–3 *see* Konchalovskii E.
Anton's Right Here 2012 *see* Arkus
Apollo (company), 27, 454, 599
Apostles, 570, 571
April (short) 1962 *see* Iosseliani
Aquarium Park, 24, 585
Arabov, Iurii, 85
Aranovich, Semen, 84, 555
   Torpedo Bombers (*Torpedonostsy*, 1983), 84, 555
Archive, archival, 11, 39, 58, 59, 61–63, 188, 260, 272, 279, 280, 285, 298, 327, 435, 560, 601
ARK (Association of Revolutionary Cinematographers), 94, 95, 322 *see also* ARRK
Arkus, Liubov', 86, 236, 239
   Anton's Right Here (*Anton tut riadom*, 2012), 236
Arnoldi, Edgar, 37
Arnshtam, Lev, 77, 406
   Girlfriends (*Podrugi*, 1936), 77, 406
Aronov, Grigorii, 188, 546, 547, 561
   The Seventh Satellite (*Sed'moi sputnik*, with Gherman, 1967), 188, 546, 547
Aronson, Moisei, 321
ARRK (Association of Workers of Revolutionary Cinema), 75, 94, 106, 107, 109, 295, 480, 482

Arsenal 1928 *see* Dovzhenko
Art Deco, 338, 341
Artek (*Pioneer Camp in Artek*, 1936), 275
Art Nouveau, 427, 435
Asanova, Dinara, 82, 603
   The Thugs (*Patsany*, 1983), 82
Aseev, Nikolai, 94
Askol'dov, Aleksandr, 547
   Commissar (1967/1988), 547
Astruc, Alexandre, 179, 181
Atanesian, Aleksandr, 469
   24 Hours (*24 chasa*, 2000), 469
Atelier of Fashion, 338–341, 346, 354
At Rest, 1936 *see* Ioganson
AT&T, 292, 293
August, Eighth 2012 *see* Faiziev
Aurora (cinema), 5, 41, 73
auteur cinema, auteurism, 7–9, 170, 178–198, 224, 231, 236
avant-garde, 2, 12, 45, 46, 50, 69, 72, 77–82, 106, 165, 167, 168, 294, 295, 300, 301, 316, 321, 323, 341, 365–367, 369, 370, 372, 382, 384, 500, 543
Avatar (James Cameron, 2009), 225
Avdeenko, Aleksandr, 266
Avens, Harijs, 428
Averbakh, Il'ia
   The Degree of Risk (*Stepen' riska*, 1967), 83
   Voice (*Golos*, 1982), 83
Averchenko, Arkadii, 33, 35
Avraamov, Arsenii, 297, 298

Babochkin, Boris, 76, 79, 80, 394, 601
Bach, Johann Sebastian, 570, 578
Bagrov, Petr, 5, 41, 68, 71–73, 79
Bakhnov, Vladlen, 521
Bakhtin, Mikhail, 227, 230
Bakuradze, Bakur, 470
   Shultes (2008), 470
Balabanov, Aleksei, 7, 84, 86–87, 206–207, 209–211, 216, 244, 468, 608–609, 612
   Brother 2 (*Brat 2*, 2000), 86, 206, 209–211, 468, 609
   Brother (*Brat*, 1997), 86, 206, 207, 209, 211, 468, 608
   Cargo 200 (*Gruz 200*, 2007), 86, 244
   Dead Man's Bluff (*Zhmurki*, 2005), 216
   Happy Days (*Schastlivye dni*, 1991), 84
   It Doesn't Hurt (*Mne ne bol'no*, 2006), 244
Balázs, Béla, 62, 331, 486
Ballad of a Soldier 1959 *see* Chukhrai G.
Ballets russes, 320, 586
Balliuzek, Vladimir, 320, 323
Baltic Deputy, The, 1936 *see* Kheifits, Zarkhi
Baltic States, 13, 427, 430, 435, 593, 606
BAM (Baikal Amur Mainline), 438
Banishment, The 2007 *see* Zviagintsev
Banke, Andres, 6

Banquet 1962 *see* Ermler
Barber of Siberia, The 1998 *see* Mikhalkov
Bardin, Garri, 236
    Ugly Duckling (Gadkii utenok, 2010), 236
Barmak, Siddiq, 6
Barnet, Boris, 4, 15, 62, 69, 102, 166, 168, 175, 307, 315, 325–327, 333, 342–344, 382, 454, 477–497, 525, 591, 598
    Alenka (1961), 495
    Annushka (1959), 494
    By the Bluest of Seas (*U samogo sinego moria*, 1935), 486–488, 495
    A Concert by Masters of Ukrainian Art (*Kontsert masterov ukrainskogo iskusstva*, 1952), 493
    The Fine Fellow (*Slavnyi malyi*, 1942), 490, 491
    The Generous Summer (*Shchedroe leto*, 1950), 492, 493
    The Girl with the Hatbox (*Devushka s korobkoi*, 1927), 15, 166, 325, 344, 454, 480
    The Halt (*Polustanok*, 1963), 495
    House on Trubnaya (*Dom na Trubnoi*, 1928), 69, 166, 325, 342, 454, 480
    Liana (1955), 494, 525
    Miss Mend (*The Adventures of Three Reporters*) (*Miss Mend* (*Prikliucheniia trekh reporterov*), with Otsep, 1926), 479
    Moscow in October (*Moskva v oktiabre*, 1927), *Icebreak* (*Ledolom*, 1931), 483
    A Night in September (*Noch' v sentiabre*, 1939), 487
    The Old Jockey (*Staryi naezdnik*, 1940), 488, 489
    One Night (*Odnazhdy noch'iu*, 1944), 480, 491
    Outskirts (*Okraina*, 1933), 307, 382, 484–486, 488, 495, 591
    The Priceless Head (*Bestsennaia golova*, 1942), 489–491
    The Spy's Exploit (*Podvig razvedchika*, 1947), 491, 492, 495
    Valor (*Muzhestvo*, 1941), 489, 490
    The Wrestler and The Clown (*Borets i kloun*, 1957), 494
Barsacq, Léon, 317
Barskaia, Margarita
    Father and Son (*Otets i syn*, 1937), 123
    Torn Boots (*Rvanye bashmaki*, 1933), 120
Barthes, Roland, 227
Bartig, Kevin, 11
Bartkowiak, Andrzej, 364
Bartlett, Djurdja, 11, 337–361
Basov, Vladimir, 434
    Shield and Sword (*Shchit i mech*, 1968), 434
Batalov, Nikolai, 140, 345, 351, 592
Battleship Potemkin 1926 *see* Eisenstein
Bauer, Evgenii, 318–319, 333, 586–587
    A Life for a Life (*Zhizn' za zhizn'* 1917), 318, 586, 587
Bazelevs, 217, 244
Bazhenov, Pavel, 284
Bazin, André, 179

BDT (Bolshoi Dramatic Theater), 546
Bed and Sofa 1927 *see* Room
Before the Judgement of History, 1965 *see* Ermler
Behind the Department Store Window 1955 *see* Samsonov
Bekmambetov, Timur, 9, 205, 212–213, 216–219, 225, 233–235, 240–245, 452, 610–612
    Abraham Lincoln, Vampire Killer (2012), 218
    Day Watch (*Dnevnoi dozor*, 2006), 212, 233, 470
    The Irony of Fate. A Continuation (*Ironiia sud'by: Prodolzhenie*, 2007), 212
    Night Watch (*Nochnoi dozor*, 2004), 9, 212, 225
    Wanted (2008, *Osobo opasno*), 218
Beliaev, Aleksandr, 81
Belinskii 1953 *see* Kozintsev
Belka and Strelka. Space Dogs 2013 *see* Evlannikova, Ushakov
Belodubrovskaya, Maria, 10, 251–267
Bergman, Ingmar, 543
Bergson, Henri, 166
Bergunker, Adol'f, 275
Berlin 1945 *see* Raizman
Berlin IFF, 237, 238
Berlin: Symphony of a Great City 1927 *see* Ruttman
Berna, Emil, 367
Bertolucci, Bernardo–*Moon* (1979), 32
Betrayal 2012 *see* Serebrennikov
Beumers, Birgit, 4, 10, 11, 14, 117, 179, 202, 203, 206–208, 452–473, 501
Beware of the Car 1966 *see* Riazanov
Beyond the Arctic Circle, 1927 *see* Erofeev
Bezenkova, Maria, 9, 224–247
Bezhin Meadow see Eisenstein
Bimmer 2 2005 *see* Buslov
Biograph, 33–42
Bird, Robert, 6, 7, 66–88
Birman, Serafina, 344
Blatova, Liudmila, 321, 331
Bleiman, Mikhail, 68–71, 77, 78, 184, 258
Bliakhin, Pavel, 106
Blium, Georgii, 100
blockbuster [blokbaster], 7, 9, 171, 202–221, 278, 423, 472, 519, 533
Blossoming Young: Parade of Physical Culture, 18 July 1939 see Medvedkin
Blossoming Youth 1938 *see* Solov'ev, N.
Blue Bird 1940 *see* Ekk
Bodrov, Sergei Jr, 207, 209, 609
Bodrov, Sergei Sr, 220, 241–242, 607, 609
    The Mongol (2007), 242
    The Nomad (*Kochevnik*, 2006), 242
    Prisoner of the Caucasus (*Kavkazskii plennik*, 1996), 220
Bogatyrev, Andrei, 238, 242
    BuGS (*BAgI*, 2011), 242
Bogomolov, Iurii, 218, 533, 535

Bogomolov, Nikolai, 75, 76
Bogorodskii, Fedor, 321, 322
Bogoslavskii, Feliks, 321
Bol'shakov, Ivan, 132, 260, 506, 508
Bolshevik, The, 1934 *see Maksim's Youth*, Kozintsev and Trauberg
Bolshevism, Bolshevik, 81
Bol'shintsov, Manuel', 77
Bolshoi Theater, 454, 458, 470, 528
Boltnev, Andrei, 84, 554, 607
Bondarchuk, Fedor, 205, 216–219, 234, 240–241, 243, 409, 610–611, 613
   Inhabited Island (*Obitaemyi ostrov*, 2009), 219, 240, 611
   Ninth Company (*Deviataia rota*, 2005), 218, 243, 610
   Stalingrad (2013), 217, 219, 409, 613
Bondarchuk, Sergei, 218, 409, 418–420, 520, 539, 607
   Fate of a Man (*Sud'ba cheloveka*, 1959), 418
   They Fought for the Motherland (*Oni srazhalis' za rodinu*, 1975), 409, 419, 420
   War and Peace (*Voina i mir*, 1965–1967), 218, 520
Bonnevie, Maria, 575
Bordwell, David, 105, 203, 253, 508
Borisov, Oleg, 546, 607
Borodianskii, Aleksandr, 469
   The Cheque (*Chek*, with Giller, 2000), 469
Borrowing Matchsticks 1980 *see* Gaidai
Bortko, Vladimir, 235, 240
   Taras Bulba 2009, 235, 240
Boule de Suif 1934 *see* Romm
Bowlt, John, 320, 341
Boym, Svetlana, 453, 455, 456, 467, 472
Bozhovich, Viktor, 181, 186
Brashinsky, Michael, 3, 447, 555
Brauns, Uldis, 428, 429, 436, 438–440, 446, 447
   235,000,000 (1967), 428, 429, 436, 438–440, 446, 447
Brenčs, Aloizs
   Double Trap (*Dubultslazds*, 1985), 435, 447
   Rally (*Rallijs*, 1978), 435
   Triple Scrutiny (*Trīskārtējā pārbaude*, 1969), 434
Brest Fortress, The 2010 *see* Kott
Brezhnev era, 186, 418–420, 529
Brief Encounters 1967 *see* Muratova
Brigade Commander Ivanov 1922 *see* Razumnyi
Brik, Osip, 98
Brodskii, Iosif, 176
Broken Dreams [*Banquet*, 1962] 1953 *see* Ermler
Brother 2 2000 *see* Balabanov
Brother 1997 *see* Balabanov
Brunshtein, Aleksandr, 122
Buben, Baraban 2009 *see* Mizgirev
Buckland, Warren, 203
BuGS 2011 *see* Bogatyrev
Bukharin, Nikolai, 68
Bukhov, Arkadii, 37
Bulgakov, Mikhail, 534

Bulgakowa [Bulgakova], Oksana, 315, 402, 506
Bulla, Viktor, 30, 32
Burnt by the Sun 1994 *see* Mikhalkov
Burov, Andrei, 323
Buslov, Petr, 242, 610
   Bimmer 2 (*Bumer 2*, 2005), 242
Bykov, Rolan, 83, 213, 608, 548
   Scarecrow (*Chuchelo*, 1984), 213
By the Bluest of Seas 1935 *see* Barnet

Cabinet of Dr. Caligari 1920 *see* Wiene
Cahiers du Cinéma, 9, 182, 195, 198
Cameraman, cameramen, 12, 50, 52, 53, 56, 57, 59, 70, 83, 97, 100, 109, 120, 181, 195, 275, 276, 298, 300, 319, 364–386, 436, 437, 439, 454, 507, 509, 597, 600
Cannes Film Festival, 182, 183, 208, 556
Captive of the Caucasus, The [aka *Kidnapping, Caucasian Style*] 1966 *see* Gaidai
Cardiff, Jack, 364
Cargo 200 2007 *see* Balabanov
Carleton, Greg, 421
carnival, 168, 228, 230, 234, 235, 241, 242, 245, 246, 535
Carnival 1981 *see* Lioznova
Carnival Night 1956 *see* Riazanov
Carnival of Color, A (*Karnaval tsvetov*, 1935), 274, 285, 286
Cathedral of Christ the Savior, 453–455, 464, 465, 469–471, 590, 607, 612
Cavendish, Phil, 2, 10–12, 270–288, 315, 316, 318, 321, 323, 366
Censorship, 9, 10, 39, 59, 120, 171, 172, 180, 183, 184, 186, 187, 190, 195–197, 253–255, 258–266, 328, 391, 412, 429, 440, 449, 503, 504, 529, 543, 548
Central Committee, 54, 75, 94, 102, 107, 181, 197, 261, 294, 397, 489, 493
chamber cinema, 331
Chance Encounter, A 1936 *see* Savchenko
Chang, 1927 *see* Cooper and Schoedsack
Chapaev 1934 *see* Vasil'ev G. and S.
Chapiteau-Show 2011 *see* Loban
Chaplin, Charlie, 140, 163, 166, 305, 520, 521, 527, 539
   Modern Times (1936), 166, 305
Chardynin, Petr, 39, 332, 333
   Mar'ia Lus'eva (1915), 39
Chebotarev, Vladimir
   Amphibian Man (*Chelovek-amfibiia*, 1961), 81
Chechen War, 410
Chechnya, Chechen, 606, 607–608, 609
Cheka (Secret Police), 544, 546
Chekhov, Anton, 452
Chekist, 1991 *see* Rogozhkin
Cheque, The 2000 *see* Borodianskii, Giller
Cherkasov, Nikolai, 77, 81, 544
chernukha, 86, 464

Index

Cherviakov, Evgenii, 73–74, 79, 324
   Cities and Years (*Goroda i gody*, 1930), 73
   Girl from the Distant River (*Devushka s dalekoi reki*, 1927), 73
   My Son (*Moi syn*, 1928), 74
   The Poet and the Tsar (*Poet i tsar*, with Gardin and Gintsburg, 1927), 324
Chess Fever 1925 *see* Pudovkin, Shpikovskii
Chevalier of the Golden Star 1950 *see* Raizman
Childhood of Maxim Gorky, The 1938 *see* Donskoi
Children of the Storm 1926 *see* Ermler and Ioganson
Children's World 1982 *see* Kremenov
Chion, Michel, 303, 305
Chirskov, Boris, 258
Christie, Ian, 98, 139, 141, 300, 500, 547, 552, 555
Chukhrai, Grigorii, 230, 372, 533, 540, 561–562, 596, 609
   Ballad of a Soldier (*Ballada o soldate*, 1959), 230
   The Forty-First (*Sorok pervyi*, 1956), 372, 596
Chukhrai, Pavel, 240, 473
   Driver for Vera (*Voditel' dlia Very*, 2004), 240
Chuliukin, Iurii, 159, 171
   Gals (*Devchata*, 1961), 159, 171
Churchill, Winston, 430
Chuzhak, Nikolai, 95
Cibrario, Jacques, 111
Cigarette Girl from Mosselprom, The 1924 *see* Zheliabuzhskii
Cinderella, 143, 144, 148, 150–152, 154, 229, 356
Cinderella, 1947 *see* Kosheverova, Shapiro
Cinema Fund [Fond Kino], 236
Circle, The 1927 *see* Gavronskii, Raizman
Circus, The 1936 *see* Aleksandrov
Cities and Years 1930 *see* Cherviakov
Civil War, 12, 13, 67, 68, 72, 76, 148, 164, 377, 392, 394, 396, 402, 403, 406, 409, 410, 425, 434, 454, 494, 509, 547, 553, 554
Clark, Katerina, 126, 257, 438, 453, 456, 457, 459
Cold, Vera *see* Kholodnaia, Vera
Cold War, 13, 14, 372, 376, 427–429, 432, 434, 445, 446, 594
Coliseum (cinema), 5
Collectivization, 75, 293, 391
Collegiate Registrar, The 1925 *see* Zheliabuzhskii
color film (technology), 11, 270–288, 586, 592
color process, additive, 11, 274, 276, 277
color process, subtractive, 11, 274, 275, 277, 278
comedy, 3, 4, 8, 15, 67, 72, 81, 86, 141, 142, 158–176, 213–215, 233, 243, 347, 350, 366, 481, 488, 493, 495, 519–540
Commander of the Happy Pike 1973 *see* Volchek
Commissar 1967/1988 *see* Askol'dov
Commissar of Enlightenment, 163
Committee for Cinema Affairs, 260, 261
Communist Party, 75, 94, 261, 294, 376, 391, 489, 547

Comrade Chkalov's Crossing of the North Pole 1990 *see* Pezhemskii
Conan Doyle, Arthur, 445
Concert by Masters of Ukrainian Art, A 1952 *see* Barnet
Condee, Nancy, 4, 16, 204, 206–208, 224, 550, 552, 556, 557, 560, 565–582
Conductor, The 2012 *see* Lungin
conflictlessness (*beskonfliktnost'*), 151
Congress of Filmmakers, 195
Congress of Soviet Writers, 140
Consolidation of Living Space 1918 *see* Panteleev
Constitution (1936), 391
Constructivism, constructivist, 68, 454
Cooper, Merian C (with Ernest B. Schoedsack)
   Chang (1927), 96
   Grass: A Nation's Battle for Life (1925), 96
Coppola, Francis Ford, 373
Corinthians, 565, 580
Cosmic Flight 1936 *see* Zhuravlev
Counterplan 1932 *see* Ermler, Iutkevich
Country Teacher, The 1947 *see* Donskoi
Courtesy Call 1972 *see* Raizman
Crafton, Donald, 292, 295, 296
Cranes are Flying, The 1957 *see* Kalatozov
Crimean War (1853–1856), 409, 411, 424
Crown Prince of the Republic, The 1934 *see* Ioganson
Cruelty 2007 *see* Liubakova
Crystal Palace (cinema), 23, 28, 36, 38, 41
CTB (film company), 86
Cultural Revolution, 47, 141, 163, 294, 391, 402
Culture Two, 264, 455, 465
Curtis, Jamie Lee, 214

3D, 219, 225, 242, 409
Daddy, Santa Claus Is Dead see Iufit
Dancing Pirate, The (Lloyd Corrigan, 1936), 276
Daneliia, Georgii, 8, 165, 174–175, 187, 189, 221, 462, 469
   Don't Be Sad! (*Ne goriui!* 1969), 174
   Heads or Tails (*Orel i reshka*, 1995), 469
   Nastia (1993), 469
   Walking the Streets of Moscow (*Ia shagaiu po Moskve*, 1962), 165, 187, 462
Danger, High Voltage! 1985 *see* Gaidai
Daniel', Iulii, 176, 604
Davies, Joseph, 271
da Vinci, Leonardo, 181, 570, 600
Days and Nights 1944 *see* Stolper
Days of Eclipse 1988 *see* Sokurov
Day Watch 2006 *see* Bekmambetov
Dead Man's Bluff 2005 *see* Balabanov
Dear Elena Sergeevna 1988 *see* Riazanov
Dear Man 1958 *see* Kheifets
Death of Pazukhin, The 1957 *see* Nikulin
DeBlasio, Alyssa, 318, 579
de Bont, Jan, 364

Decembrists, The 1926 *see* Ivanovskii
Defense of Sevastopol, The 1911 *see* Goncharov
De Forest, Lee, 292
Degree of Risk, The 1967 *see* Averbakh
dekorativnost', 320
Delsarte, François, 50
del Verrocchio, Andrea, 570
Dem'ianenko, Aleksandr, 521
Demoted 1980 *see* Sokurov
Deineka, Aleksandr, 278, 285
Derevianko, Pavel, 421
Deriabin, Aleksandr, 96, 98, 105, 124, 273, 275, 279–282
Derrida, Jacques, 229
De Santis, Giuseppe, 130
Devil's Wheel, The 1925 *see* Kozintsev and Trauberg
Diaghilev, Serge, 320
Diamond Arm, The 1968 *see* Gaidai
Dinner Party, The 1962 *see* Ermler
Directorate of Propaganda and Agitation, 489
Disney, 119, 131, 132, 205, 270, 271, 276, 277
Dissidence, dissident, 170, 172, 383, 599, 601, 604
distribution, 3, 5, 16, 25, 32, 40, 52, 85, 92–94, 98–102, 106, 110, 205, 206, 224–228, 232–234, 241, 242, 246, 273, 293, 296, 299, 344, 429, 440, 519, 520, 544
Diushen, Boris, 24, 25
Dmitriev, Viktor, 419, 420
Dnepr Hydroelectric Station; Dneprostroi, 304
Dobrenko, Evgeny [Evgenii], 2, 126, 149, 160, 410
Dobronravov, Ivan, 573
Dobrotvorskii, Sergei, 82, 522, 524, 531, 537
Doctors' Plot, 556, 595
documentarism, 108, 109
Dog Barbos and the Unusual Cross 1961 *see* Gaidai
Dolinin, Dmitrii, 83
Dolinskii, Iosif, 117, 120, 121, 257
Doll with Millions, A 1928 *see* Komarov
Don Diego and Pelageia 1928 *see* Protazanov
Dondurei, Daniil, 203–205, 217, 218
Don Quixote 1957 *see* Kozintsev
Donskoi, Mark, 7, 118, 123–130, 132–133, 367, 372, 383, 487–488, 602
  The Childhood of Maxim Gorky (*Detstvo Gor'kogo*, 1938), 118
  The Country Teacher (*Sel'skaia uchitel'nitsa*, 1947), 372
  Hello Children! (*Zdravstvuite deti!*, 1962), 133
  The Rainbow (*Raduga*, 1944), 130
Don't Be Sad! 1969 *see* Daneliia
Dostal', Nikolai N., 238, 561
  Penal Battalion (*Shtrafbat*, 2004), 561
Dostal', Nikolai V., 160
  We've Met Somewhere Before (*My s vami gde-to vstrechalis'*, with Andrei Tutyshkin, 1954), 160
Double Trap 1985 *see* Brenčs

Dovzhenko, Aleksandr, 13, 60, 62, 150, 165, 167, 186, 263, 304, 306–307, 310, 382–383, 392, 402–407, 477, 483–484, 578, 589–590, 593, 596
  Aerograd (1935), 150
  Arsenal (1928), 382, 484
  Earth (*Zemlia*, 1930), 383, 402, 483
  Ivan (1932), 304
  Shchors (1939), 13, 392
Dreaming of Space 2005 *see* Uchitel'
Dream, The 1941 *see* Romm
Driver for Vera 2004 *see* Chukhrai, P.
Dubrovskii, Aleksandr, 101
Dubrovskii-Eshke, Boris, 321, 330, 332
Dukel'skii, Semen, 260
Dukhless 2011 *see* Prygunov
Dunaevskii, Isaak, 146, 147
Duncan, Isadora, 381
Dupont, 277
Durov, Anatolii, 494
Durov, Boris, 202, 539–540
  Pirates of the 20th Century (*Piraty XX veka*, 1979), 202, 539
Dürrenmatt, Friedrich, 434
Dyer, Richard, 141, 142, 147, 153, 310
dye-transfer, 271, 276, 277
Dykhovichnyi, Ivan, 465–466
  Moscow Parade (*Prorva*, 1993), 465–466
Dzerzhinskii, Felix, 544, 597
Dzigan, Efim, 12–13, 259, 392, 397, 399, 401, 402
  We Are from Kronstadt (*My iz Kronshtadta*, 1936), 12–13, 259, 392, 397, 399, 401

Earth 1930 *see* Dovzhenko
Earth and Sky, 1926 *see* Gavronskii
Earth Thirsts, The 1930 *see* Raizman
Edison (cinema), 23, 26–28
Efros, Abram, 283
Eggert, Konstantin, 69, 333, 502
  Ice House (*Ledianoi dom*, 1928), 69
Egorova, Tatiana, 11
Egorov, Vladimir, 315, 319
Eikhenbaum, Boris, 69, 295
Eisenstein, Sergei, 2, 4, 6, 8, 12, 55–56, 58–64, 68–69, 77, 79, 81, 106, 139, 163, 165, 167, 175, 231, 256, 266–267, 270, 273, 282, 287, 294–295, 300, 315, 320, 323–324, 329–330, 342, 347, 367–369, 385, 396, 402, 477, 481, 483, 544, 559, 561–562, 588–590, 592, 594
  Alexander Nevsky (1938), 77, 139, 315, 592
  Battleship Potemkin (*Bronenosets Potemkin*, 1926), 139, 396
  Bezhin Meadow (*Bezhin lug*, 1937), 256
  The General Line (*General'naia linia* [*Staroe i novoe*] 1929), 329
  Ivan the Terrible (*Ivan Groznyi*, 1944–1946), 287, 315
  October (*Oktiabr'*, 1928), 323
  Strike (*Stachka*, 1924), 68, 324, 483

Eisymont, Viktor, 459
  Good Luck! (*V dobryi chas*, 1956), 459
Ekk, Nikolai, 69, 125, 274, 278–279, 281, 307, 601
  The Blue Bird (*Siniaia ptitsa*, 1940), 281
  Grunia Kornakova, [*Nightingale, My Little Nightingale*] (*Solovei-Solovushko*, 1936), 274
  The Road to Life (*Putevka v zhizn'*, 1931), 69, 125, 307
  Sorochintsy Fair (*Sorochinskaia iarmarka*, 1939), 279
Ekster, Aleksandra, 12, 339–341
Elena 2010 *see* Zviagintsev
Elsaesser, Thomas, 203, 204, 211
Eluard, Paul, 513
Emil Busch AG, 275
End of St Petersburg, The 1927 *see* Pudovkin
Enei, Evgenii, 70–72, 79, 80, 315, 320, 322, 323, 327
Enlightenment, 48, 66, 96, 100, 103, 106, 107, 110, 163, 164, 341, 378, 504, 587
Enthusiasm 1930 *see* Vertov
Enzensberger, Maria, 355
Epilogue 1983 *see* Khutsiev
Epners, Asnis, 448
  I am a Latvian (*Es esmu latvietis*, 1990), 448
Erdman, Nikolai, 488, 489, 600
Ermler, Fridrikh, 5, 7, 14, 68, 72–73, 75–82, 103, 169, 275, 315, 327, 329, 409, 415–418, 477, 484, 599
  Broken Dreams (*Razbytie mechty*, 1953; aka *The Dinner Party* /*Zvanyi uzhin*, 1962), 79, 169
  Children of the Storm (*Deti buri*, with Ioganson, 1926), 72
  Counterplan (*Vstrechnyi*, with Iutkevich and Arnshtam, 1932), 75, 329–330
  Fragment of an Empire (*Oblomok imperii*, 1929), 72, 329, 484
  The Great Breakthrough (*Velikii perelom*, 1945), 79
  The Great Citizen (*Velikii grazhdanin*, 1938–39), 73
  Before the Judgement of History (*Pered sudom istorii*, 1965), 81
  Katka's Reinette Apples (*Kat'ka–bumazhnyi ranet*, with Ioganson, 1926), 72
  Peasants (*Krest'iane*, 1934), 75
  Scarlet Fever (*Skarlatina*, with Ioganson, 1924), 103
  She Defends the Motherland (*Ona zashchishchaet rodinu*, 1943), 409, 416
Ermolinskii, Sergei, 258
Erofeev, Vladimir, 94, 96, 100, 104, 107–110, 303
  Beyond the Arctic Circle (*Za poliarnym krugom*, 1927), 104, 105
  Heart of Asia (*Serdtse Azii*, 1929), 96
Esadze, Rezo, 81
  Fro (1964), 81
Esenin, Sergei, 381
ETO (Experimental Creative Unit), 533, 534, 540
Euphoria 2006 *see* Vyrypaev
European Audiovisual Observatory, 7, 226, 227, 241
European Film Academy, 232
European Story 1984 *see* Gostev
Everyone will Die but Me 2008 *see* Gai Germanika

Evlannikova, Inna, 241, 242
  Belka and Strelka. Space Dogs (*Belka i Strelka. Lunnye prikliucheniia*, with Ushakov, 2013), 241, 242
Exhibition of Agricultural Achievements *see* VDNKh
existentialism, 228, 229, 236–240, 246
Experimental Film Collective (EKKIu), 77
Experiment 5IVE (almanac, 2011), 568
Expressionism, expressionist, 317, 479
Extraordinary Adventures of Mister West in the Land of the Bolsheviks, The 1924 *see* Kuleshov

Factory of the Eccentric Actor (FEKS), 6, 69, 70, 72, 73, 76, 77, 86, 181, 315, 322, 588
Faintsimmer, Aleksandr, 80
  The Gadfly (*Ovod*, 1955), 80
Fairbanks, Douglas, 140, 347, 351
Faiziev, Dzhanik, 216, 235, 243, 610
  August, Eighth (*Avgust. Vos'mogo*, 2012), 243
  Turkish Gambit (*Turetskii gambit*, 2005), 216
Falling Leaves 1966 *see* Iosseliani
Fall of Otrar 1991 *see* Amirkulov
Faraday, George, 3
Fascism, fascist, 410, 418, 434
Fate of a Man 1959 *see* Bondarchuk, S.
Father and Son 1937 *see* Barskaia
Father Sergius 1918 *see* Protazanov
Faust 2011 *see* Sokurov
Fedin, Konstantin, 73
Fedorchenko, Aleksei, 237–238, 242
  First on the Moon (*Pervye na lune*, 2004), 242
  Silent Souls (*Ovsianki*, 2010), 242
Fedorov-Davydov, Aleksei, 283
FEKS *see* Factory of the Eccentric Actor (FEKS)
Fellini, Federico, 171, 242, 598
Fesenko, Oleg, 242–243
  1812: The Ballad of Ulan (*1812: Ulanskaia ballada*, 2012), 244
  The Witch (*Ved'ma*, 2006), 242
Festival of Work, A (*Prazdnik truda*, 1931), 274
Fiance from the Netherworld 1958 *see* Gaidai
Field, Mary, 117, 119, 131, 132
Fighting Film Collections (*Boevye kinosborniki*), 489
Filippenko, Aleksandr, 83
film education, film schools, 6, 45–64, 429
Film Institute (VGIK), 5, 6, 181, 187, 261, 366
Fine Fellow, The 1942 *see* Barnet
FIPRESCI, 183, 227, 237–239
First on the Moon 2004 *see* Fedorchenko
Fitzpatrick, Sheila, 47, 141, 357
Five-Year Plan, 75, 273, 277, 293, 300, 307, 309, 310, 492, 589, 591, 592, 594, 595, 596, 597, 598, 600, 601, 602, 603
Flaherty, Robert, 96, 97
  Nanook of the North (1922), 96
Fleischman, Peter, 558
Fogel', Vladimir, 140, 345, 351, 479

Folies Bergère, 25, 29
Fomin, Valerii, 98, 181–184, 266, 417
Foot of Death 1929 *see* Shneiderov
Forbidden Zone 1975 *see* Frank
Forest People 1928 *see* Litvinov
Formalism, formalist, 62, 192, 370, 372, 373, 402
Fortress of War, 2010 [*Brest Fortress*] *see* Kott
Forty-First, The 1956 *see* Chukhrai, G.
Forty Hearts, 1931 *see* Kuleshov
Foucault, Michel, 523
Foundling, The 1939 *see* Lukashevich
Fox and the Wolf, The 1937 *see* Mokil'
Fox International, 212
Fradkin, Iurii, 281
  Happy-Go-Lucky Artists (*Veselye artisty*, 1938), 281
Fragment of an Empire 1929 *see* Ermler
Frank, Herz, 14, 429, 436–441, 446–447, 449
  Forbidden Zone (*Zapretnaia zona*, 1975), 441, 447
  Ten Minutes Older (*Par 10 minūtēm vecāks*, 1978), 441
Freaky Friday (Mark Waters, 2003), 214
Freimanis, Aivars, 429, 437
  Report on a Year (*Gada reportāža*, 1965), 437
  The Shore (*Krasts*, 1963), 437
French New Wave, 8, 169
Fro, 1964 *see* Esadze
From the Darkness of Centuries 1931 *see* Lemberg
Full Metal Jacket (Stanley Kubrick, 1987), 218
Furmanov, Dmitrii, 76, 392–396, 398, 400, 403, 406

Gabrilovich, Evgenii, 258, 502, 503, 505, 506, 508
Gadfly, The, 1955 *see* Faintsimmer
Gags, visual, 481, 487, 521
Gaibai, Genrich, 165
  The Green Van (*Zelenyi furgon*, 1959), 165
Gaidai, Leonid, 4, 8, 15, 158–159, 165–166, 171, 175, 202–203, 519–540, 599, 607
  Borrowing Matchsticks (*Za spichkami*, 1980) *Sportloto-82* (1982), 538
  Danger, High Voltage! (*Opasno dlia zhizni*, 1985), 537
  The Diamond Arm (*Brilliantovaia ruka* 1968), 202, 519
  The Dog Barbos and the Unusual Cross (*Pes Barbos i neobyknovennyi kross*, 1961), 519
  Fiance from the Netherworld (*Zhenikh s togo sveta*, 1958), 525
  Incognito from St Petersburg (*Inkognito iz Peterburga*, 1977), 537
  It Can't Be (*Ne mozhet byt'*, 1975), 537
  Ivan Vasilievich: Back to the Future (*Ivan Vasil'evich meniaet professiiu*, 1973), 519, 534, 535
  Kidnapping, Caucasian Style [aka *The Captive of the Caucasus*, or *Shurik's New Adventures*] (*Kavkazskaia plennitsa, ili novye prikliucheniia Shurika*, 1966), 165, 202
  Long Journey (*Dolgii put'*, 1956), 525
  Moonshiners (*Samogonshchiki*, 1961), 519
  Operation "Y" and Other Adventures of Shurik (*Operatsiia "Y" i drugie prikliucheniia Shurika*, 1965), 165, 202, 519
  Private Detective, or Operation "Cooperation" (*Chastnyi detektiv, ili operatsiia "Kooperatsiia,"* 1989), 538, 539
  Strictly Business (*Delovye liudi*, 1962), 527
  There's Good Weather on Deribasovskaya Street, It's Again Raining on Brighton Beach (*Na Deribasovskoi khoroshaia pogoda, na Braiton Bich opiat' idut dozhdi*, 1992), 538
  Thrice Resurrected (*Trizhdy voskresshii*, 1960), 525
  Twelve Chairs (*Dvenadtsat' stul'ev*, 1971), 522, 534
Gai Germanika, Valeriia, 238, 240, 611
  Everyone will Die but Me (*Vse umrut a ia ostanus'*, 2008), 238, 240, 611
Galadzhev, Petr, 322
Galich, Aleksandr, 170, 525
Gals 1961 *see* Chuliukin
Gardin, Vladimir, 48, 49, 50, 51, 55, 57, 63, 68, 73, 319, 324
  The Poet and the Tsar (*Poet i tsar*, with Gintsburg and Cherviakov, 1927), 324
Garin, Erast, 521
Garin, Vladimir, 573
Garpastum 2005 *see* Gherman A.A.
Gaumont, 39
Gavronskii, Aleksandr, 104, 502
  The Circle (*Krug*, with Raizman, 1927), 502
  Earth and Sky (*Nebo i zemlia*, 1926), 104
Gel'freikh, Vladimir, 456
Gellner, Ernest, 119
gender, 2, 92, 148, 228, 231, 238, 244, 245, 343, 344, 346, 466
General Agreement on Tariffs and Trade (GATT), 205
General Line, The 1929 *see* Eisenstein
Generation P 2011 *see* Ginzburg
Generous Summer, The 1950 *see* Barnet
Genre, 4–8, 10, 13, 15, 16, 26, 67, 69, 82, 93–95, 103, 110, 131, 139, 141, 142, 158, 159, 161–163, 165–168, 170, 172, 174, 203, 212, 214, 215, 224, 228–231, 233, 242–243, 259, 260, 263, 266, 283, 325, 338, 349, 366, 381, 382, 392, 410, 419, 434, 443, 483, 488, 492, 493, 527, 531, 533, 536
Georgia, 308, 309, 369, 370, 372, 439, 588
Gerasimov, Sergei, 72, 76, 79, 287, 486, 545, 549, 603
  Komsomolsk (1938), 76
  Seven of the Brave (*Semero smelykh*, 1936), 76
  The Unconquerable Ones (*Nepobedimye*, 1942), 79
  The Young Guard (*Molodaia gvardiia*, 1948), 132
German, Pavel, 154
Gershwin, George, 276
Gherman, Aleksei A. (Jr), 242–243, 559
  Garpastum (2005), 242
  Paper Soldier (*Bumazhnyi soldat*, 2008), 243, 611
Gherman, Aleksei Iu. (Sr), 4, 7, 14–16, 79, 83–87, 179, 187–189, 194–195, 197–198, 543–562, 601, 611–612

Hard to Be a God (*Trudno byt' bogom*, 2014), 86
Khrustalyov, My Car! (*Khrustalev, mashinu!*, 1998), 543, 555, 557
My Friend, Ivan Lapshin (*Moi drug Ivan Lapshin*, 1981), 543, 553
The Seventh Satellite (*Sed'moi sputnik*, with Aronov, 1967), 546
Trial on the Road (*Proverka na dorogakh*, 1971), 83, 543
Twenty Days without War (*Dvadtsat' dnei bez voiny*, 1976), 84, 188, 543
Gherman, Iurii, 76, 79, 83, 84, 188, 189, 544–546, 550, 554
GIII (State Institute for the History of Arts), 69, 70, 72, 322
GIK *see* VGIK
Giller, Boris, 469
The Cheque (*Chek*, with Borodianskii, 2000), 469
Gintsburg, Aleksandr, 324
The Poet and the Tsar (*Poet i tsar*, with Gardin and Cherviakov, 1927), 324
Ginzburg, Sergei, 214
Ginzburg, Victor, 244
Generation P (2011), 244
Giornate Del Cinema Muto, 301
Girlfriends 1936 *see* Arnshtam
Girl from the Distant River 1927 *see* Cherviakov
Girl with Character, A 1939 *see* Iudin
Girl without Address 1957 *see* Riazanov
Girl with the Hatbox, The 1927 *see* Barnet
Gish, Lillian, 140, 351
GITIS (State Academy of Theatre Arts), 566
Giulli 1927 *see* Shengelaia
Gladilin, Iurii, 165
Glamour 2007 *see* Konchalovskii A.
Glavkino, 217
Glavrepertkom, 262, 481
Godard, Jean-Luc, 477, 494
Goddess: How I Fell in Love 2004 *see* Litvinova
Godet, Martine, 180, 183, 184, 187, 190, 195
Gogol', Nikolai, 71, 537
Golden Calf, The 1968 *see* Shveitser
Golden Calf, The (*Zolotoi telenok*) *see* Il'f and Petrov
Golden Eagle Award, 580
Golden Hills 1931 *see* Iutkevich
Golovnia, Anatolii, 59, 278, 315
Golutva, Aleksandr, 84, 86
Gomery, Douglas, 292, 293, 296
Goncharov, Vasilii, 409, 411–413, 418, 424, 425
The Defense of Sevastopol (*Oborona Sevastopolia*, 1911), 409, 411–413, 418
Good Luck! 1956 *see* Eisymont
Goraev, Rostislav, 434
Nocturne (*Noktirne*, 1966), 434
Gorak, Chris, 452, 453
The Darkest Hour (2011), 452, 453

Gorbachev, Mikhail, 447
Gordanov, Viacheslav, 275
Gorelenkova, Fekla, 354
Gor'kii, Maksim, 7, 55, 117, 124, 129, 140
Gorky Film Studio (Children's Film Studio), 7, 132
Gorky Park, 357, 455, 464
Goscilo, Helena, 3, 411
Gosfilmofond, 286, 327, 328, 599
Goskino, 98, 99, 180, 182–184, 189, 192, 193, 195, 429, 430, 440, 519, 534, 549, 588, 600, 604
Gostev, Igor', 428, 434
European Story (*Evropeiskaia istoriia*, 1984), 428, 434
Gostorg (State Trade Monopoly), 99
Gosvoenkino, 502
Graffy, Julian, 15, 202, 443, 477–497
Graham, Seth, 8, 158–176
Granik, Anatolii, 459
Alesha Ptitsyn forms his Character (*Alesha Ptitsyn vyrabatyvaet kharakter*, 1953), 459
Grashchenkova, Irina, 257, 481
Grass: A Nation's Battle for Life, 1925 *see* Cooper and Schoedsack
Great Breakthrough (*velikii perelom*), 75, 79
Great Breakthrough, The 1945 *see* Ermler
Great Citizen, The 1938–39 *see* Ermler
Great Consoler, The 1933 *see* Kuleshov
Great Flight, The 1925 *see* Shneiderov
Great Life, A 1939, 1945 *see* Lukov
Great Patriotic War (WWII), 13, 173, 368, 372, 376, 377, 409, 410, 417, 418, 421, 425, 488, 528, 539, 549
Great Terror, 13, 73, 141, 391, 392, 401–403
Great Turn, 47, 293, 295
Great War (WWI), 5, 141, 410
Grebner, Georgii, 258
Green Van, The 1959 *see* Gaibai
Grigor'ev, Viktor, 275
Grigor, Nikolai, 41
Grossman, Vasilii, 547
Grunia Kornakova 1936 *see* Ekk
Gruziiafilm, 308
GTK (State Technical College of Cinematography), 46, 52, 54–63, 321, 322, 366
GUK (Directorate for Cinema/Film Industry), 270, 271, 280, 281, 504
Gukasian, Frizheta, 84
GUKF (Directorate for the Film and Photo Industry), 102, 270, 271, 278
Gulag, 171, 190, 219, 369, 391, 524, 529, 545, 595, 601, 608
GUM (State Department Store), 462, 595
Gutman, David, 309

Hamlet 1964 *see* Kozintsev
Hammer and Sickle 1994 *see* Livnev
Hansen, Miriam, 68, 348

Hänsgen, Sabine, 304
Happy Days, 1991 see Balabanov
Happy Go Lucky 1972 see Shukshin
Happy-Go-Lucky Artists 1938 see Fradkin
Happy Guys, The [Jolly Fellows] 1934 see Aleksandrov
Harris, Richard, 209
Hasek, Jaroslav, 165
Hashamova, Yana, 3, 208, 209, 211
Haynes, John, 2
Heads or Tails 1995 see Daneliia
Heart of Asia 1929 see Erofeev
Hello Children! 1962 see Donskoi
Hermitage (museum), 360
Hermitage Gardens, 24, 462
Herz, Frank, 14, 429, 436, 439
Hicks, Jeremy, 2, 7, 117–133, 490
Higher Courses for Directors and Scriptwriters (VKSR), 181
Hipsters 2008 see Todorovskii, V.
His Name Was Robert 1967 see Ol'shvanger
historiophoty, 410
Holiday of St Jorgen 1930 see Protazanov
Hollywood, 8–10, 119, 132, 140, 141, 143, 152, 160, 202–221, 225, 244, 251–255, 257–259, 292, 303, 317, 318, 332, 347, 348, 351, 357, 358, 372, 397, 423, 481, 492, 527, 560
Homeland 1990 see Podnieks
Horde, The 2012 see Proshkin, Andrei
Horton, Andrew, 3, 167, 214, 447, 555
Hot Days 1935 see Kheifits and Zarkhi
24 Hours 2000 see Atanesian
House I Live In, The 1957 see Kulidzhanov, Segel'
House in the Sun, The 2010 see Sukachev
House on the Embankment, 456, 466
House on Trubnaya, The 1928 see Barnet
How I Spent this Summer 2010 see Popogrebskii
How the Steel was Tempered see Ostrovskii N.
How to Lose A Guy in 10 Days (Donald Petrie 2003), 215
How to Marry a Millionaire (Jean Negulesco 1953), 215
Hussar's Ballad 1962 see Riazanov
Hutchings, Stephen, 3
hydrotype method, 275, 277, 279

Iablonskaia, Madame, 41
Iablonskii, Mr, 30, 41
I am a Latvian 1990 see Epners
I Am Cuba 1964 see Kalatozov
I am Twenty 1964 see Khutsiev
Iankovskii, Boris, 298
Iankovskii, Filipp, 216, 240
   State Councilor (*Statskii sovetnik*, 2005), 216, 240
Icebreak 1931 see Barnet
Ice House 1928 see Eggert
Ida 2015 see Pawlikowski
Iezuitov, Nikolai, 71

Il'f, Il'ia, 486, 533
Il'inskii, Igor', 79, 140, 150, 160, 169, 343, 346–348, 351
Il'in, Vasilii, 51, 55, 57
Il'in, Vladimir, 559
Illienko, Iurii, 578
Ilyich's Gate 1964 see Khutsiev
IMAX, 219, 409, 610
imbibition, 271, 276
Immortal Garrison, The 1956 see Tissé, Agranenko
Incognito from St Petersburg 1977 see Gaidai
Indigo 2008 see Prygunov
Inhabited Island 2009 see Bondarchuk, F.
Institute for Screen Arts, 321
In the Claws of the Black Crab 1973 see Leimanis
In the Fog 2012 see Loznitsa
In the Name of the Motherland 1943 see Pudovkin, Vasil'ev D.
In the Shadow of the Sword 1976 see Krenbergs
Iofan, Boris, 456
Ioganson, Eduard, 72, 79, 331
   Children of the Storm (*Deti buri*, with Ermler 1926), 72
   The Crown Prince of the Republic (*Naslednyi prints respubliki*, 1934), 72
   Katka's Reinette Apples (*Kat'ka–bumazhnyi ranet*, with Ermler 1926), 72
   At Rest (*Na otdykhe*, 1936), 72
Iosseliani, Otar, 179, 184, 193, 195, 477, 494, 496
   April (*Aprel'*, short, 1962), 184
   Falling Leaves (*Listopad*, 1966), 184
   Pastorale (*Pastoral'*, 1975), 184
   There once was a Singing Bird (*Zhil pevchii drozd*, 1970), 184
I Remember Everything, Richard! 1967 see Kalniņš
Iron Curtain, 435, 519
Irony of Fate 1976 see Riazanov
Irony of Fate. A Continuation 2007 see Bekmambetov
Is It Easy to be Young? 1986 see Podnieks
Italian Neorealism, 8, 118, 130, 170
It Can't Be 1975 see Gaidai
It Doesn't Hurt 2006 see Balabanov
It's Hard to Be a God 2014 see Gherman
It's not Me 2013 see Saakyan
Iudenich, Nikolai, 397
Iudin, Konstantin, 456, 494, 497
   A Girl with Character (*Devushka s kharakterom*, 1939), 456
Iufit, Evgenii, 86
   Daddy, Santa Claus Is Dead (*Papa, umer ded moroz*, 1991), 86
   Knights of the Sublunar Sphere (*Rytsari podnebes'ia*, short 1989), 86
Iukov, Konstantin, 295
Iungval'd-Khilkevich, Georgii, 443
   Prisoner of Castle If (*Uznik Zamok If*, 1988), 443
Iurizditskii, Sergei, 85

Iurovskii, Iurii, 428
Iutkevich, Sergei, 68, 75, 77, 181–183, 260, 323, 329, 352, 477, 520, 603
   Counterplan (Vstrechnyi, with Ermler, 1932), 75, 329–330
   Golden Hills (Zlatye gory, 1931), 77
   Lace (Kruzheva, 1928), 77, 352
   Lenin in Poland (Lenin v Pol'she, 1966), 520
   Man with a Rifle (Chelovek s ruzh'em, 1938), 77
   Miners (Shakhtery, 1937), 260
   The Traitor (Predatel', 1926), 323
Ivanov, Aleksandr–Star (Zvezda, 1949), 421
Ivanov, Boris, 259, 266–267
   Lad from Our Town (Paren' iz nashego goroda, 1942), 259
   The Law of Life (Zakon zhizni, 1940), 266
   Wait for Me (Zhdi menia, 1943), 259
Ivanovskii, Aleksandr, 67–68, 160, 324
   The Decembrists (Dekabristy, 1926), 324
   The Lady Tiger-Tamer (Ukrotitel'nitsa tigrov, with Nadezhda Kosheverova, 1954), 160
   Palace and Fortress (Dvorets i krepost', 1923), 67, 68
Ivanov-Vano, Ivan, 52, 104, 105
Ivan's Childhood 1962 see Tarkovskii
Ivan the Terrible, 1943–45 see Eisenstein
Ivan Vasilievich: Back to the Future 1973 see Gaidai
Izvolov, Nikolai, 297–299

Jannings, Emil, 140
Jaques-Dalcroze, Émile, 50
jazz music, 147
Jazz Singer, The (Alan Crosland, 1927), 293
Job (book of), 57, 215, 307, 343, 370, 471, 546, 554, 567, 571, 572
Jolie, Angelina, 218
Jonah, 571, 572
July Rain 1966 see Khutsiev
Junk 2006 see Neimand

Kabalov, Grigorii, 275, 280
Kaganovsky, Lilya, 2, 10, 11, 292–311, 315
Kaidanovskii, Aleksandr, 195, 578
Kalatozov, Mikhail, 12, 79, 170, 182–183, 230, 365, 369–375, 380, 382–384, 386, 409, 459–460, 477, 493, 509, 562, 600
   The Cranes are Flying (Letiat zhuravli, 1957), 12, 170, 230, 372, 380, 409, 460, 509
   I Am Cuba (Ia–Kuba, aka Soy Cuba, 1964), 372
   Loyal Friends (Vernye Druz'ia, 1954), 170
   A Nail in the Boot (Gvozd' v sapoge [aka The Country is in Danger/ Strana v opasnosti], 1932), 372
   Salt for Svanetia (Jim Shvante/Sol' Svanetii, 1930), 370, 372
   Their Kingdom (Mati samep/Ikh tsarstvo, 1928), 370
   The Unconquerable Ones (Nepobedimye, 1942), 79

The Unsent Letter (Neotpravlennoe pis'mo, 1960), 372, 373, 380
Kalenov, Igor', 240
   Alexander. The Neva Battle (Aleksandr. Nevskaia bitva, 2008), 240
Kalinin, Mikhail, 145
Kalniņš, Rolands, 434
   I Remember Everything, Richard! (Es visu atceros, Ričard!, 1967), 434
Kamenoostrovskii Prospect, 67
Kaminskii, Viacheslav, 243
   Moscow, I Love You (Moskva, ia liubliu tebia, 2010), 243–244
   Stone (Kamen', 2011), 243
Kapler, Aleksei, 258
Kaplunovskii, Vladimir, 321
Karalli, Vera, 140
Karavaeva, Valentina, 507, 508
Karmalita, Svetlana, 188, 189, 550, 555
Katka's Reinette Apples, 1926 see Ermler and Ioganson
Kavaleridze, Ivan, 310
   Koliivshchina (1931), 310
Kazachenko, Georgi, 414
Kazanskii, Gennadii, 81
   Amphibian Man (Chelovek-amfibiia, 1961), 81
Keaton, Buster, 140, 163, 539
Kelly, Catriona, 119
KEM (Cinema Experimental Workshop), 5, 14, 72, 77, 103
Kenez, Peter, 2, 98, 265
Keosayan, Edmond, 462
   When September Comes (Kogda nastupaet sentiabr', 1975), 462
Kepley, Vance, 98, 100, 293, 299, 300, 349, 402
KGB (Committee for State Security), 435, 447, 461, 539, 595, 599
Khabenskii, Konstantin, 217
Khait, Iulii, 154, 464
Khanzhonkov, Aleksandr, 318, 412, 413, 585, 586, 594
Khanzhonkova, Vera, 318
Khanzhonkov Studio, 318
Kharat'ian, Dmitrii, 538
Kharms, Daniil, 8, 72
Khazanov, Gennadii, 539
Kheifets, Iosif, 545–546
   Baltic Deputy (Deputat Baltiki, with Zarkhi, 1936), 77
   Dear Man (Dorogoi moi chelovek, 1958), 545–546
   Hot Days (Goriachie denechki, with Zarkhi 1935), 77
   My Native Land (Moia rodina, with Zarkhi, 1933), 307
Khersonskii, Khrisanf, 480
Khevsur (people, language), 308, 309
Khmeleva, Valentina, 321
Khokhlova, Aleksandra, 12, 51, 275, 329, 342, 346, 347, 351, 454, 603

Kholodnaia, Vera, 140, 587
Khomeriki, Nikolai, 216
Khotinenko, Vladimir, 233, 241
　1612 (2007), 233, 241
Khrushchev, Nikita, 160, 187, 496
Khrustalev, My Car! 1997 see Gherman A. Iu.
Khudozhestvennyi (cinema); formerly Saturn,
　5, 28, 467
khudozhnik, 315, 318, 320–325, 330, 331, 337
Khutsiev, Marlen, 14, 179, 185, 187, 196, 221, 386,
　461–462, 494, 496, 598
　Epilogue (Posleslovie, 1983), 462
　Ilyich's Gate (aka *I am Twenty; Zastava Il'icha/ Mne dvadtsat' let*, 1964), 185, 196, 461
　July Rain (Iul'skii dozhd', 1966), 461
Kidnapping, Caucasian Style! 2014 see Voronkov
Kidnapping, Caucasian Style [also as *Captive of the Caucasus*] 1966 see Gaidai
Kinemacolor, 274
King Lear, 1970 see Kozintsev
King of Jazz (John Murray Anderson, 1930), 276
Kino-Eye 1924 see Vertov
Kinoks, 95, 439
Kirov, Sergei, 67, 77–79, 591
Kleiman, Naum, 440, 572
Kletskin, Abram, 437, 441
Klimenko, Iurii, 559
Klimov, Elem, 8, 159, 165, 171–173, 175, 179, 183, 185,
　187, 193, 195, 197, 610
　Adventures of a Dentist (Prikliucheniia zubnogo vracha,
　1965), 165, 185
　Welcome, No Trespassing (Dobro pozhalovat', ili Postoronnim vkhod vopreshchen, 1964), 171
Knights of the Sublunar Sphere 1989 see Iufit
Knorre, Fedor, 480, 488
Kodacolor, Kodak, 277
Koestler, Arthur, 163, 164
KoKoKo 2012 see Smirnova
Kokovtsev, V.N., 26
Koliivshchina 1931 see Kavaleridze
kolkhoz, 75, 144, 150, 190, 309, 381, 457, 466, 483,
　486–489, 493–495
kolkhoz musical, 142–144, 147, 492, 494
Kolupaev, Dmitrii, 319, 322, 324
Komarov, Sergei, 140–141, 166, 323–333, 347,
　352, 544
　A Doll with Millions (Kukla s millionami, 1928), 323
　Mary Pickford's Kiss (Potselui Meri Pikford,
　1927), 166
Komsomol, 56, 77, 102, 170, 304, 307, 309, 352, 484,
　502, 531, 574
Komsomolsk 1938 see Gerasimov
Konchalovskii, Andrei, 179, 190–191, 243–244
　Glamour (Glianets, 2007), 243
　The Nutcracker: The Untold Story (Shchelkunchuk i krysinyi korol', 2011), 244

The Story of Asya Klyachina (Istoriia Asi Kliachinoi, kotoraia liubila, da ne vyshla zamuzh, 1966), 190
Konchalovskii, Egor, 213
　Antikiller, 2002–3, 213
Kopashov, Alesha, 421
Kornilov, Vladimir (Admiral), 412, 413
Korshunov, Aleksandr, 421
Kosheverova, Nadezhda, 72, 160
　Cinderella (Zolushka, 1947), 72
　The Lady Tiger-Tamer (Ukrotitel'nitsa tigrov, with Aleksandr Ivanovskii 1954), 160
Kostiukovskii, Iakov, 521
Kostrichkin, Andrei, 71
Kott, Aleksandr, 243, 410, 420, 421, 422, 423
　The Brest Fortress (Brestskaia krepost', aka *Fortress of War*, 2010), 410, 420, 422
Kovalova, Anna, 5, 23–42, 68, 258
Kovalov, Oleg, 160, 165, 168–172, 174, 483
Kovrigin, Vasilii, 323
Kozakov, Mikhail, 442, 462
　Pokrov Gates (Pokrovskie vorota, 1982), 462
Kozintsev, Grigorii, 68, 70–71, 77, 79–82, 84, 255, 311,
　493, 544–546, 549, 598, 600
　Belinskii (1953), 255
　Don Quixote (1957), 81
　Hamlet (1964), 81
　King Lear (1970), 81
　Pirogov (1947), 77, 79
Kozintsev, Grigorii and Trauberg, Leonid,
　70–73, 76, 78, 141, 305, 315, 352, 477, 484,
　589, 590
　Alone (Odna, 1931), 72, 305, 352
　The Devil's Wheel (Chertovo koleso, 1925), 70,
　71, 73
　Maksim's Return (Vozvrashchenie Maksima,
　1937), 76
　Maksim's Youth (Iunost' Maksima, 1934; aka *The Bolshevik*), 76
　New Babylon (Novyi Vavilon, 1929), 71, 590
　The Overcoat (Shinel', 1926), 71
　SVD (1927), 71
　The Vyborg Side (Vyborgskaia storona, 1938), 76
Kozlov, Leonid, 264
Kozlovskii, Danila, 471
Kozlovskii, Sergei, 315, 320–325, 328
Kraulītis, Ivars, 436
　Snowbells (Baltie zvani, 1961), 436
Kravchenko, Galina, 351
Kravchuk, Andrei, 234, 240, 611
　The Admiral (Admiral, 2008), 234, 240, 611
Kremenov, Valerii, 462
　Children's World (Detskii mir, 1982), 462
Kremlin, 78, 145, 151–153, 155, 266, 270, 271, 349,
　355, 357, 439, 454, 456, 461, 466, 470, 502, 535,
　556, 597, 598

Krenbergs, Imants, 444
   In the Shadow of the Sword (*Zobena ēnā*, 1976), 444
Krichman, Mikhail, 236–237, 567, 573
Kriuchkov, Nikolai, 411, 488
Krūmiņš, Ralfs, 439
Kroģis, Valdis, 439
Krokodil, 537
Kruchenykh, Aleksei, 304
Krynskii, Iaroslav, 28
KShE 1932 *see* Shub
Kuban Cossacks, The 1949 *see* Pyr'ev
Kudriavtseva, Antonina, 72
   Wake Lenochka Up (*Razbudite Lenochku*, short, 1934), 72
Kukelvan, Bertha, 25
kulak, 75, 76, 102, 104, 483, 484, 590
Kulakov, Iurii, 233
   Prince Vladimir (*Kniaz' Vladimir*, 2006), 233
Kuleshov, Lev, 6, 15, 50–51, 53, 55, 57, 60, 63, 104–106, 133, 165, 167, 204, 275, 288, 318, 320, 323, 329, 333, 342, 346, 370, 453, 455, 477–479, 481, 486, 540
   The Extraordinary Adventures of Mister West in the Land of the Bolsheviks (*Neobychainye prikliucheniia mistera Vesta v strane bol'shevikov* 1924), 167, 453, 455
   Forty Hearts (*40 serdets*, 1931), 104, 105
   The Great Consoler (*Velikii uteshitel'*, 1933), 275
   Your Acquaintance (*Vasha znakomaia*, 1927), 323, 346, 347
Kulidzhanov, Lev, 461
   The House I Live In (*Dom, v kotorom ia zhivu*, with Segel', 1957), 461
Kul'tkino, 99–101
Kultpros (Cultural Enlightenment), 504
kulturfilm, 6, 7, 58, 92–111, 483
Kuprin, Aleksandr, 258
Kuravlev, Leonid, 538
Kurekhin, Sergei, 85, 608
Kutsenko, Gosha, 213
Kuz'mina, Elena, 305, 306, 352, 427, 432, 433, 442
Kyrla, Iyvan, 307

Lacan, Jacques, 229
Lace 1928 *see* Iutkevich
La Cucaracha (Lloyd Corrigan, 1934), 271, 277
Lad from Our Town 1942 *see* Stolper, Ivanov B.
Ladynina, Marina, 144
Lady Tiger-Tamer, The 1954 *see* Ivanovskii, Kosheverova
Lamanova, Nadezhda, 12, 339, 341, 342, 349, 354
Lamorisse, Albert, 438
   Red Balloon (1956), 438
Land of the Deaf, The 1997 *see* Todorovskii, V.
Land of Toys 1939 *see* Rou

Land of Youth, The 1941 *see* Andrievskii
Laskin, Boris, 147
Last Case of Commissar Bärlach 1971 *see* Levin
Last Crusaders, The (*Poslednie krestonostsy*, S. Dolidze, V. Shvelidze, 1933), 308
Last Night, The 1936 *see* Raizman
Lavrenev, Boris, 546
Lavronenko, Konstantin, 575
Law of Life, The 1940 *see* Stolper, Ivanov B.
Lawton, Anna, 3, 98, 207
Lazarev, Evgenii, 566
Lebedev-Kumach, Vasilii, 147
Lebedev, Nikolai A., 53, 58–63, 92–96, 100, 110, 260, 397
Lebedev, Nikolai I., 234, 421
   Star (*Zvezda*, 2002), 421
Lebedev, Vladimir, 79
LEF (Left Front of Art), 57, 95
Legoshin, Vladimir, 131
   Lonely White Sail (*Beleet parus odinokii*, 1937), 131
Leimanis, Aleksandrs, 443
   In the Claws of the Black Crab (*Melnā vēža spīlēs*, 1973), 444
   Servants of the Devil (*Vella kalpi*, 1970), 443
   Servants of the Devil at the Devil's Mill (*Vella kalpi dzirnavās*, 1970), 443
Leipzig Documentary Film Festival, 440
Lemberg, Aleksandr, 104, 105
   From the Darkness of Centuries (*Iz t'my vekov*, 1931), 104, 105
Lenfilm (studio), 6, 7, 66–88, 187, 262, 281, 282, 295, 298, 550, 552, 555, 595
Leningrad siege, 79
Lenin in 1918 1937 *see* Romm
Lenin in October 1937 *see* Romm
Lenin in Poland 1966 *see* Iutkevich
Lenin, Vladimir, 456
Leonidov, Oleg, 258
Leontyeva, Xenia, 9, 224–247
Lermontov, Mikhail, 150, 320
Lesnevskii, Dmitrii, 567
Lesson of Life, The 1955 *see* Raizman
Leviathan 2014 *see* Zviagintsev
Levin, Vasilii, 428, 434
   Last Case of Commissar Bärlach (*Poslednee delo komissara Berlakha*, 1971), 428, 434
Leyda, Jay, 2, 300
LGITMiK (Leningrad State Institute of Theater, Music and Cinema), 429, 545
Liadova, Elena, 568
Liana 1955 *see* Barnet
Liberation 1968–71 *see* Ozerov
Liber, George, 2, 306
Liepa, Maris, 441
life caught unawares, 253, 439
Lilac Branch, The 2007 *see* Lungin

Linder, Max, 31, 163, 478, 521
Lioznova, Tat'iana, 419, 428, 435, 461–462, 612
    Carnival (*Karnaval*, 1981), 462
    Seventeen Moments of Spring (*17 mgnovenii vesny*, 1973), 419, 428, 435
    Three Poplars on Pliushchikha Street (*Tri topolia na Pliushchikhe*, 1967), 461
Liteiny Prospect, 25, 36
Little Humpbacked Horse, The 1941 see Rou
Little Red Devils 1923 see Perestiani
Little Vera 1988 see Pichul
Litvinov, Aleksandr, 100, 105
    Forest People (*Lesnye liudi*, 1928), 105
    Through the Ussuri Area (*Po Ussuriiskoi taige*, 1928), 105
Litvinova, Renata, 244, 471
    Goddess: How I Fell in Love (*Boginia. Kak ia poliubila*, 2004), 244
Liubakova, Marina, 471
    Cruelty (*Zhestokost'*, 2007), 471
Liubimov, Iurii, 179
Livanov, Boris, 83
Livanov, Vasilii, 444
Livnev, Sergei, 466
    Hammer and Sickle (*Serp i molot*, 1994), 466
Lloyd, Harold, 163
Loban, Sergei, 239, 243
    Chapiteau-Show (*Shapito-shou*, 2011), 239, 243
Loew, 293
Lohan, Lindsay, 214
Lonely Voice of a Man, The 1978 see Sokurov
Lonely White Sail 1937 see Legoshin
Long Farewells 1971 see Muratova
Long Journey 1956 see Gaidai
Long Road, The 1962 see Ozerov
Lopatina, Vera, 342
Lopushanskii, Konstantin, 578
Lotman, Iurii, 453
Lovell, Stephen, 304
Lovey-Dovey (*Liubov'-morkov'*, 2007–2010, dirs. A. Strizhenov, M. Pezhemskii, S. Ginzburg), 205, 212–214
Loyal Friends 1954 see Kalatozov
Loznitsa, Sergei, 239, 561
    In the Fog (*V tumane*, 2012), 239, 561
Luigi De Laurentiis Prize, 567
Lukashevich, Tat'iana, 122, 458
    The Foundling (*Podkidysh*, 1939), 458
Luk'ianenko, Sergei, 217, 240
Lukinskii, Ivan, 165
    Soldier Ivan Brovkin (*Soldat Ivan Brovkin*, 1955), 165
Lukov, Leonid, 132, 163, 321
    A Great Life (*Bol'shaia zhizn'*, 2 parts: 1939, 1945), 132, 321
Lumet, Sidney, 236
    12 Angry Men (1957), 236

Lunacharskii, Anatolii, 66, 67, 140, 152, 155, 163, 341, 587, 590, 591
Lungin, Pavel, 86, 236, 244–245, 463
    The Conductor (*Dirizher*, 2012), 236
    The Lilac Branch (*Vetka sireni*, 2007), 246
    Taxi Blues (1990), 86, 463
Lutsik, Petr, 469
    Outskirts (*Okraina*, 1998), 469
Luzhkov, Iurii, 465, 606
Lysenko, Trofim, 554

MacFadyen, David, 3, 217
Macheret, Aleksandr, 281, 307, 309, 331, 424, 492
    Men and Jobs (*Dela i liudi*, 1932), 307
    Pages of Life (*Stranitsy zhizni*, 1948), 492
    The Private Life of Petr Vinogradov (*Chastnaia zhizn' Petra Vinogradova*, 1934), 331
Machin, Alfred, 39, 40
    Maudite soit la guerre (1914), 39, 40
Maeterlinck, Maurice, 291
Magic Fish, The 1938 see Rou
Magnacolor, 277
Magnitogorsk, 391, 590
Maiakovskii, Vladimir, 439
Maid in Manhattan (Wayne Wang 2002), 215
Maiorov, Nikolai, 272, 273, 279, 285
Makarova, Nadezhda, 354
Makliarskii, Mikhail, 492
Maksim's Return 1937 see Kozintsev and Trauberg
Maksim's Youth 1934 see Kozintsev and Trauberg
Malaia Dmitrovka Theatre, 276
Malinskaia, Vera, 351
Maliukov, Andrei, 240
    We are from the Future (*My iz budushchego*, 2008), 240
Mamardashvili, Merab, 579
Mamin, Iurii, 86
    Window to Paris (*Okno v Parizh*, 1993), 86
Mamuliia, Dmitrii, 470
    Another Sky (*Drugoe nebo*, 2010), 470
Man is Born, A 1956 see Ordynskii
Mantegna, Andrea, 570
Man with a Movie Camera 1929 see Vertov
Man with a Rifle 1938 see Iutkevich
Maras, Stephen, 253
Maretskaia, Vera, 342, 343, 351, 416, 417, 454, 601
Margolit, Evgenii, 118, 123, 126, 130, 302, 307, 468, 478, 485, 486, 488–491
Mari (people), 307, 309
Mar'ia Lus'eva 1915 see Chardynin
Mariinsky Theater, 26, 38
Markina, Nadezhda, 577
Martinson, Sergei, 521
Marxism, Marxist doctrine, 54
Marx, Karl, 579
Mary (Virgin), 570
Mary Pickford's Kiss see Komarov

Mashenka 1942 *see* Raizman
Masina, Giulietta, 171
Maslennikov, Igor', 14, 428, 444–446
    Adventures of Sherlock Holmes and Dr Watson (Prikliucheniia Sherloka Kholmsa i doktora Vatsona, 1979–86), 14, 428, 444–446
Matizen, Viktor, 216, 423, 557, 569, 570, 579
Maudite soit la guerre 1914 *see* Machin
Maupassant, Guy de, 375
May Night 1940 *see* Sadkovych
McAvoy, James, 218
McLaren, Norman, 297
Mdivani, Georgii, 258
Mechanics of the Brain 1926 *see* Pudovkin
Medinskii, Vladimir, 226
Medvedev, Maksim, 186, 193–195
Medvedkin, Aleksandr, 62, 272, 285, 287, 458
    The Blossoming Young: Parade of Physical Culture, 18 July 1939 (Tsvetushchaia iunost', Fizkul'turnyi parad 18 iiulia 1939g., 1939), 272
    New Moscow (Novaia Moskva, 1938), 458
Meeting on the Elbe 1949 *see* Aleksandrov
Melikian, Anna, 238, 471
    Mermaid (Rusalka, 2007), 471
    The Star (Zvezda, 2014), 471
Mel'nikov, Konstantin, 321
Mel'nikov, Vitalii, 195
Men and Jobs 1932 *see* Macheret
Menippea, 227–229, 238, 239, 241, 243–245
Men on Wings 1935 *see* Raizman
Menshevik Party, 370
Men'shikov, Oleg, 209
Men'shov, Vladimir, 202, 462, 468, 540
    Moscow Doesn't Believe in Tears (Moskva slezam ne verit, 1980), 202
    Shirly–Myrli (1995), 468
Merezhkovskii, Dmitrii, 258
Merkulov, Iurii, 52
Mermaid 2007 *see* Melikian
Mershin, Pavel, 274, 275, 277
Merzlikin, Andrei, 421
Meskhiev, Dmitrii Davydovich, 81
Meskhiev, Dmitrii Dmitrievich, 81
Messenger, The 1986 *see* Shakhnazarov
metaphor, 147, 194, 227–229, 234, 238, 239, 241, 243, 246, 530, 533, 538, 556
Metro, Moscow metro, 152, 391, 456–460, 462, 464–466, 470, 591, 596, 607, 610, 611
Meyerhold, Vsevolod, 62, 69, 167, 319, 320, 585, 587, 593
    Portrait of Dorian Grey (Portret Doriana Greia, 1915), 319
Mezhrabpom (Mezhrapom-Rus', Mezhrabpomfilm), 69, 101
Miasnikov, Gennadii, 314, 321, 323
Michelson, Annette, 2
Michurin, Gennadii, 74

Michurin, Ivan, 554
migrating plot, 228, 229, 234, 236–239, 241, 245–246
Mikhail Aleksandrovich, Grand Duke, 27
Mikhailov, Evgenii, 69–71
Mikhailov, Nikolai, 525
Mikhalkov, Nikita, 4, 9, 206–210, 217, 220, 233, 236–237, 466, 471, 566, 580, 601, 607
    12 (2007), 236, 237
    Barber of Siberia (Sibirskii tsiriul'nik, 1998), 471–472
    Burnt by the Sun (Utomlennye solntsem, 1994), 466
Mikhoels, Solomon, 309, 594
Milić, Saša, 166, 169, 170, 521
Miller, Glenn, 494
Miller, Jamie, 2, 15, 47, 500–516
Min, Avenir, 280
Miners 1937 *see* Iutkevich
Ministry of Culture of the Russian Federation, 226
Minkus, Mikhail, 456
Mints, Klimentii, 72
    The Adventures of Korzinkina (Prikliucheniia Korzinkinoi, 1941), 72
Miracle Worker, The 1922 *see* Panteleev
Mironov, Andrei, 84, 521, 604
Mirror, The 1975 *see* Tarkovskii
mise-en-scène, 69, 180, 181, 192, 194, 310, 318, 481, 508, 509, 511, 528, 551
Misery and Fortune of Women 1930 *see* Tissé
Miss Mend 1926 *see* Otsep, Barnet
Mitki, 85
Mitta, Aleksandr, 174, 540
    Shine, Shine, My Star (Gori, gori moia zvezda, 1969), 174
Mizgirev, Aleksei, 244
    Buben, Baraban (2009), 244
Modern Times, 1936 *see* Chaplin
Mokil', Sarra, 279–280
    The Fox and the Wolf (Lisa i volk, 1937), 279
    The Wolf and the Seven Kids (Volk i semero kozliat, 1938), 280
Molniia (cinema), 40
Molotov–Ribbentrop Pact (1939), 435, 593
Molotov, Viacheslav, 169, 184, 590
Mongol, The 2007 *see* Bodrov S. Sr
Monsieur Hulot, 527
montage, 8, 49–51, 57, 59, 69, 95, 104, 107, 109, 140, 204, 231, 253, 275, 294, 295, 300, 303, 341, 365, 367, 370, 382, 435, 437, 453, 481, 486, 508
Moon 1979 *see* Bertolucci
Moonshiners 1961 *see* Gaidai
Morgunov, Evgenii, 15, 521, 526, 608
Moroz, Iurii, 471
    The Spot (Tochka, 2006), 471
Morozko 1924 *see* Zheliabuzhskii
Moscow 2000 *see* Zeldovich
Moscow Arts Theater (MKhAT, MKhT), 319, 320
Moscow Doesn't Believe in Tears 1980 *see* Men'shov

Moscow Holidays 1995 *see* Surikova
Moscow IFF, 233, 237–239
Moscow, I Love You 2010 *see* Kaminskii
Moscow in October 1927 *see* Barnet
Moscow Parade 1993 *see* Dykhovichnyi
Moscow Sewing Trust, 338, 340, 341, 346
Moscow Skies 1944 *see* Raizman
Mosfilm (studio), 6, 59, 66, 186, 187, 262, 263, 274, 279–281, 415, 429, 489, 505, 506, 512, 519, 525, 533, 590, 591
Moskva (river), 455
Moskva, hotel, 152, 456–458, 592
Moskvin, Andrei, 69–71, 79, 80, 315, 597
Moskvina, Tat'iana, 82, 85
Mossel'prom, 98
Mother 1926 *see* Pudovkin
Mother and Son 1997 *see* Sokurov
Motherland, 13, 105, 147, 259, 409–425, 486, 548, 593
Motyl', Vladimir, 174
   White Sun of the Desert (*Beloe solntse pustyni*, 1969), 174
Moulin Rouge, 26, 29, 39
Mournful Unconcern 1986 *see* Sokurov
movies for the masses, 2, 202, 294
Mozart, Wolfgang Amadeus, 578
Mozzhukhin, Ivan (Mosjoukine), 140
MPAA (Motion Pictures Association of America), 227
Mukhina, Vera, 149, 153, 339, 457, 466, 494
Mullert, Natalia and Eduard, 28, 41
Multicolor, 277
Muratova, Kira
   Brief Encounters (*Korotkie vstrechi*, 1967), 186
   Long Farewells (*Dolgie provody*, 1971), 186
   Our Honest Bread (*Nash chestnyi khleb*, 1964), 192
   The Tuner (*Nastroishchik*, 2004), 243
   Watch Your Dreams Attentively (*Vnimatelno smotrite sny*, script, 1969), 194
Murder on Dante Street 1956 *see* Romm
Mur, Leo, 325
My Fair Lady (George Cukor, 1964), 215
My Friend Ivan Lapshin 1982 *see* Gherman
My Native Land 1931 *see* Kheifits and Zarkhi
My Son 1928 *see* Cherviakov
My Younger Brother 1962 *see* Zarkhi

Nabokov, Vladimir, 36
Nail in the Boot, A 1932 *see* Kalatozov
Nakhimov, Pavel (Admiral), 412
Nanook of the North 1922 *see* Flaherty
Narkompros (People's Commissariat of Enlightenment), 48
Nastia 1993 *see* Daneliia
Naumov, Vladimir, 466
   Ten Years without the Right to Correspond (*Desiat' let bez prava perepiski*, 1990), 466

Nautilus Pompilius, 206, 210
Nazi (army), 415
Necro-realism, necro-realist, 86
Nedobrovo, Vladimir, 70, 71, 74
Needle. Remix 2010 *see* Nugmanov
Negin, Oleg, 572, 573
Negri, Pola, 351
Neimand, Denis, 244
   Junk (*Zhest'*, 2006), 244
Neorealism, Italian, 8, 118, 130, 170
NEP (New Economic Policy), 15, 41, 66, 67, 69, 75, 98, 162, 293, 337–345, 348–350, 352, 353, 454, 480, 482, 589
Nepomniashchy, Catherine, 445
Nesbet, Anne, 2
Neva (cinema), 5, 84, 240
Nevafilm Research, 7, 9, 226, 235, 241
Nevsky Prospect, 5, 23–42, 100
New Babylon 1929 *see* Kozintsev and Trauberg
New Moscow 1938 *see* Medvedkin
Newsreel, 27, 32, 56, 58, 59, 67, 94, 95, 107, 108, 110, 141, 366, 368, 370, 415, 437, 439, 491, 550, 588
New Wave, French, 8, 169
New York, I Love You (almanac, 2008), 568
Nicholas I, 412
Nicholas II, 415, 423, 585
Nielsen, Asta, 351
Night in September, A 1939 *see* Barnet
Night Watch 2004 *see* Bekmambetov
nihilism, 228, 229, 237, 238, 241, 244
NIKA (Russian Academy of Motion Picture Arts Award), 557, 568
NIKFI (Scientific Institute of Film and Photo Research), 60, 274, 275, 278–280
Nikulin, Grigorii, 81
   The Death of Pazukhin (*Smert' Pazukhina*, 1957), 81
Nikulin, Iurii, 15, 84, 188, 189, 396, 419, 521, 522, 526, 529, 530, 532, 550, 608
Nil'sen, Vladimir, 59, 275
Nine Days of a Year 1963 *see* Romm
Ninth Company 2005 *see* Bondarchuk F.
NIS (Sector for Scientific Research), 60, 61, 63
NKVD, 84, 591–593, 595
Nocturne 1966 *see* Goraev
Nomad, The 2006 *see* Bodrov Sr
nomenklatura, 171, 281, 353
Nordisk (Denmark), 39
Norris, Stephen, 3, 13, 202–221, 409–425
Norshtein, Iurii, 195
Nostalgia, 16, 445, 453, 464, 467, 519, 578
Notebook, The (Nick Cassavetes 2004), 215
Nugmanov, Rashid, 236
   The Needle. Remix (*Igla. Remiks*, 2010), 236
Nutcracker: The Untold Story 2011 *see* Konchalovskii A.
Nykvist, Sven, 364

OBERIU (Union of Real Art), 72, 84
Obsession (Luchino Visconti, 1942), 130
October 1928 see Eisenstein
Office Romance 1977 see Riazanov
Officers 1971 see Rogovoi
Old Hags 2000 see Riazanov
Old Jockey, The 1940 see Barnet
Oleinikov, Nikolai, 72
Olesha, Iurii, 259
Ol'shvanger, Il'ia, 81
　His Name Was Robert (*Ego zvali Robert*, 1967), 81
　On a Single Planet (*Na odnoi planete*, 1965), 82
Olympiad of Song, 146, 148–150
O'Mahony, Mike, 2, 271, 285, 457
On a Single Planet, 1965 see Ol'shvanger
Once There was an Old Woman 2011 see Smirnov
One Night 1944 see Barnet
On the Hook 2009 see Sanaev
On the Truce with Finland 1945 see Raizman
Operation "Y" and Other Adventures of Shurik 1965 see Gaidai
OPOIaZ (Society for the Study of Poetic Language), 72
Orbakaite, Kristina, 213
Order of Lenin, 145, 146, 153
Ordynskii, Vasilii
　A Man is Born (*Chelovek rodils'ia*, 1956), 460
Orlova, Liubov', 12, 144, 145, 150, 353–355, 357, 358, 456, 601
Orlov, Nikolai, 25
Ormond, Julia, 209
Ostozhenka Street, 471, 572
Ostrovskii, Aleksandr, 491
Ostrovskii, Nikolai, 487
Osyka, Leonid, 578
Otsep, Fedor, 15, 478
　Miss Mend (*The Adventures of Three Reporters*) (*Miss Mend* (*Prikliucheniia trekh reporterov*), with Barnet, 1926), 15, 478
Otten, Nikolai, 257, 487
Ottoman (empire), 411, 412
Our Honest Bread 1964 see Muratova
Outskirts 1933 see Barnet
Outskirts 1998 see Lutsik
Overcoat, The 1926 see Kozintsev and Trauberg
Ozerov, Iurii, 165, 197, 418, 520
　Liberation (*Osvobozhdenie*, 1968–71), 418, 520
　The Long Road (*Bol'shaia doroga*, 1962), 165

Pages of Life 1948 see Macheret
Palace and Fortress 1923 see Ivanovskii
Palace of Soviets, 456, 458, 472
Palekh, 283
Pale of Settlement, 68
Panfilov, Gleb, 555
　The Theme (*Tema*, 1979), 555

Panova, Vera, 546
Panteleev, Aleksandr, 67, 87, 164
　Consolidation of Living Space (*Uplotnenie*, 1918), 67
　The Miracle Worker (*Chudotvorets*, 1922), 164
　The Tree Death, or Blood-Thirsty Susanna (*Derevo smerti, ili Krovozhadnaia Susanna*, 1915), 67–68
Papernyi, Vladimir, 264
Paper Soldier 2008 see Gherman A. Jr
Paradjanov, Sergei, 3, 4, 9, 179, 184, 198, 382, 385, 605
　Shadows of Forgotten Ancestors (*Teni zabytykh predkov*, 1964), 382, 385
Paramount, 133, 205, 254, 264, 293
Parisiana (cinema), 5, 28, 29, 31, 32, 36, 37, 40, 41
Party Card, The 1936 see Pyr'ev
Party Conference on Cinema (All-Soviet), 54, 139, 141, 294, 325
Pasternak, Boris, 597, 604
Pastorale 1975 see Iosseliani
Pathé Frères, 39
Pauls, Raimonds, 439, 441
Pawlikowski, Pavel, 16
　Ida (2015), 16
Peasants, 1934 see Ermler
Peculiarities of the National Hunt 1995 see Rogozhkin
Peleshian, Artavazd, 179
Penal Battalion 2004 see Dostal' N.N.
Penal Servitude 1929 see Raizman
Perestiani, Ivan, 409, 588, 597
　Little Red Devils (*Krasnye d'iavoliata*, 1923), 409
perestroika, 3, 14, 66, 84, 173, 178, 183, 193, 195–196, 224, 230, 463, 514, 603
Peterhof, 275
Petker, Boris, 161
Petliura, Symon, 587
Petr and Aleksei 1919 see Zheliabuzhskii
Petrenko, Aleksei, 551
Petrov, Evgenii, 486, 533
Petrov, Vladimir, 259
　Peter the First (*Petr pervyi*, 1937–1938), 259
Pezhemskii, Maksim, 84, 214, 235
　Comrade Chkalov's Crossing of the North Pole (*Perekhod tovarishcha Chkalov cherez severnyi polius*, 1990), 84
Piccadilly (cinema), 5, 28–31, 36, 38–41, 100
Pichugin, Eduard, 87
Pichul, Vasilii, 3
　Little Vera (*Malen'kaia Vera*, 1988), 3
Pickford, Mary, 140, 166, 347, 348, 350, 351
Piel, Harry, 140, 351
Pimenov, Iurii, 285, 351
Piotrovskii, Adrian, 69, 70, 72, 73, 76–79, 262, 295, 303, 304
Pirates of the 20th Century 1979 see Durov
Pirogov 1947 see Kozintsev
Pirogov, Nikolai, 412, 413

Pīks, Rihards, 439
Plan for Great Works, The 1930 *see* Room
Platonov, Andrei, 81
Platoon (Oliver Stone, 1986), 218
Platt, Kevin M., 13, 14, 427–449
Plotnikov, Nikolai, 511, 512
Plummer, Christopher, 418
Poddubnyi, Ivan, 494
Podnieks, Juris, 14, 428–429, 437, 441, 447, 604
  Homeland (*Krustceļš*, 1990), 447
  Is It Easy to be Young? (*Vai viegli būt jaunam?*, 1986), 428
Poet and the Tsar, The 1927 *see* Gardin, Gintsburg, Cherviakov
Poetic Documentary School (Latvian), 428, 436–442, 446–448
Pogodin, Nikolai, 554
Pokrass brothers, 147
Pokrov Gates 1982 *see* Kozakov
Polikushka 1919–1923 *see* Zheliabuzhskii
Poloka, Gennadii, 494–496
Pomerantsev, Vladimir, 493
Popogrebskii, Aleksei, 236
  How I Spent this Summer (*Kak ia provel etim letom*, 2010), 236
Portrait of Dorian Grey 1915 *see* Meyerhold
postmodernism, 82–86, 228–230, 237–239, 242, 246, 465
Pozner, Valerie, 299, 315
Prague Spring, 558
Prediction 1993 *see* Riazanov
Pregnant 2011 *see* Andreasian
Pre-Revolutionary, 1, 2, 5, 11, 14, 15, 23, 30, 31, 41, 48, 50, 51, 67, 68, 93, 99, 162, 260, 283, 303, 317–320, 324, 341, 348, 349, 444, 465, 500, 507
Pretty Woman (Garry Marshall 1990), 215
Pribyl'skaia, Evgeniia, 339
Priceless Head, The 1942 *see* Barnet
Priemykhov, Valerii, 471, 609
  Who, if Not Us (*Kto, esli ne my*, 1998), 471, 609
Prince Vladimir 2006 *see* Kulakov
Prisoner of Castle If 1988 *see* Iungval'd-Khilkevich
Prisoner of the Caucasus 1996 *see* Bodrov Sr
Private Affair, A 1939 *see* Razumnyi
Private Detective, or Operation "Cooperation" 1989 *see* Gaidai
Private Life 1982 *see* Raizman
Private Life of Petr Vinogradov, The 1934 *see* Macheret
Prokhorenko, Zhanna, 509, 510
Prokhorova, Elena, 15, 435, 519–540
Prokhorov, Alexander, 123, 130, 131, 133, 166, 168, 174, 175, 520, 527, 533
Proletkino, 100
Proletkul't, 77
propaganda, 2, 6, 102, 106, 107, 151, 152, 172, 228, 231, 234, 235, 238–241, 245, 246, 258, 261, 295, 302, 370, 373, 376, 402, 417, 454, 489, 528, 588, 603
Proshkin, Andrei, 233, 239, 243
  The Horde (*Orda* 2012), 233, 239, 243
Proskurina, Svetlana, 85
Protazanov, Iakov, 4, 14, 68–69, 164, 175, 315, 324, 328, 333, 341–342, 348–349, 360, 454, 491, 500, 502, 561, 587, 589, 594
  Aelita (1924), 69, 315, 324, 341, 342, 454, 589
  Don Diego and Pelageia (*Don Diego i Pelageia* 1928), 164
  Father Sergius (*Otets Sergii*, 1918), 68, 587
  Holiday of St Jorgen (*Prazdnik sviatogo Iorgena*, 1930), 175
  The Tailor from Torzhok (*Zakroishchik iz Torzhka*, 1925), 175, 328, 342
  Three Thieves [aka *The Three Million Trial*] (*Protsess o trekh millionakh* 1926), 175
Provorov, Fedor, 274, 275, 277, 278, 280, 281
Prut, Iosif, 258
Prygunov, Roman, 242–243, 471, 612
  Dukhless (2011), 243, 471, 612
  Indigo (2008), 242
Ptushko, Aleksandr, 131, 279, 283–285, 591, 600
  The Land of Toys (*Zolotoi kliuchik*, 1939), 131
  The Tale of the Fisherman and the Fish (*Skazka o rybake i rybke*, 1937), 279, 283, 285
Pudovkin, Vsevolod, 50, 51, 53, 55, 57, 60, 101, 103–104, 106, 139, 165, 167, 254–256, 259, 294–295, 303, 315, 320–321, 324, 367, 383, 386, 477, 483, 589, 595
  Admiral Nakhimov (1946), 321
  Chess Fever (*Shakhmatnaia goriachka*, with Nikolai Shpikovskii, 1925), 167
  The End of St Petersburg (*Konets Sankt Peterburga*, 1927), 483
  Mechanics of the Brain (*Mekhanika golovnogo mozga*, 1926), 101, 104
  Mother (*Mat'*, 1926), 55
  In the Name of the Motherland (*Vo imia rodiny*, 1943), 259
  A Simple Case (*Prostoi sluchai*, 1930), 256
  Storm over Asia (*Potomok Chingis-khana* 1928), 139, 321, 589
Pugacheva, Alla, 213
Pushkarev, Igor', 509, 510
Pushkin, Aleksandr, 282
Push, Lev, 371, 373, 375
Putin, Vladimir, 422, 473
Pyr'ev, Ivan, 142–144, 146–151, 168, 331, 385, 392, 488, 492, 494, 525, 593
  The Kuban Cossacks (*Kubanskie kazaki* 1949), 142
  The Party Card (*Partiinyi bilet*, 1936), 331
  The Rich Bride (*Bogataia nevesta* 1938), 142
  The Swineherdess and the Shepherd (*Svinarka i pastukh* 1940), 142
  Tractor Drivers (*Traktoristy* 1939), 142, 148, 149, 593

Radek, Karl, 123, 303
Radiant Path, The 1940 *see* Aleksandrov
Rainbow, The 1944 *see* Donskoi
Rainis, Janis, 444, 508
Raizman, Iulii, 15, 331, 477, 492–493, 500–516, 607
   Berlin (doc., 1945), 508
   Chevalier of the Golden Star (*Kavaler Zolotoi zvezdy*, 1950), 492, 509
   The Circle (*Krug*, with Gavronskii, 1927), 502
   Courtesy Call (*Vizit vezhlivosti*, 1972), 513
   The Earth Thirsts (*Zemlia zhazhdet*, 1930), 502
   The Last Night (*Posledniaia noch'*, 1936), 502
   The Lesson of Life (*Urok zhizni*, 1955), 509
   Mashenka (1942), 505
   Men on Wings (*Letchiki*, 1935), 502
   Moscow Skies (*Nebo Moskvy*, 1944), 508
   Penal Servitude (*Katorga*, 1929), 502
   Private Life (*Chastnaia zhizn'*, 1982), 513
   A Story About Omar Khaptsoko (*Rasskaz ob Umare Khaptsoko*, 1932), 502
   A Strange Woman (*Strannaia zhenshchina*, 1977), 513
   A Time of Desires (*Vremia zhelanii*, 1984), 513
   The Train Goes East (*Poezd idet na vostok*, 1948), 508
   On the Truce with Finland (*K voprosu o peremirii s Finliandiei*, doc., 1945), 508
   Virgin Soil Upturned (*Podniataia tselina*, 1939), 505
   And What if it is Love? (*A esli eto liubov'?*, 1962), 500, 506
   Your Contemporary (*Tvoi sovremennik*, 1968), 506, 511
Rakhal's, Vasilii, 315, 323
Rally 1978 *see* Brenčs
Ranevskaia, Faina, 521
Rank, J. Arthur, 131
RAPP (Russian Association of Proletarian Writers), 75
Razumnyi, Aleksandr, 120–121, 164
   Brigade Commander Ivanov (*Kombrig Ivanov*, 1922), 164
   A Private Affair (*Lichnoe delo*, 1939), 120
   Timur and his Gang (*Timur i ego komanda*, 1940), 120, 123
Razumovskii, Aleksandr, 72
Real Dakota, 205, 212, 213
Red Balloon 1956 *see* Lamorisse
Red Scarf, The 1948 *see* Sukhobokov, with Sauts
Redskin (Victor Schertzinger, 1928), 276
Red Square, 144, 149, 152, 271, 287, 354, 456, 458, 468, 469, 511, 590, 607
Red Tent, The 1969 *see* Urusevskii
Red Terror, 546
Red Western, 13
Reichsfilmarchiv (Berlin), 64, 272
Reisgof, Georgii, 275
Renaissance, 240
Repentance 1984 *see* Abuladze
Report on a Year 1965 *see* Freimanis

Return of Nathan Becker, The (*Vozvrashchenie Neitana Bekkera*, dir. Rashel' Mil'man, Boris Shpis 1932), 309
Return, The 2003 *see* Zviagintsev
Revenge of the Cameraman 1912 *see* Starewicz
Revolution (October Revolution, Bolshevik Revolution), 5, 6, 9, 12, 23, 24, 28, 30, 37, 46–48, 51, 67, 68, 73, 82, 104, 117, 118, 123, 127, 140, 141, 163, 165, 167, 168, 260, 270, 280, 294, 315, 317, 319, 332, 337, 338, 349, 391, 392, 396, 398, 400–402, 439, 440, 454, 478, 483, 484, 494, 503, 504, 525, 547, 548, 553, 554, 560, 585, 587, 596
Revzin, Grigorii, 465, 473
RGIA (Russian State Archive of History), 39
Riazanov, El'dar, 3, 8, 159–161, 165, 168–172, 175, 218, 233, 460, 462–463, 466, 469–470, 523, 540, 596, 601
   Beware of the Car (*Beregis' avtomobilia*, 1966), 171, 172
   Carnival Night (*Karnaval'naia noch'*, 1956), 160, 161, 168, 169, 596
   Dear Elena Sergeevna (*Dorogaia Elena Sergeevna*, 1988), 463
   Girl without Address (*Devushka bez adresa*, 1957), 460
   Hussar's Ballad (*Gusarskaia ballada* 1962), 165
   Irony of Fate (*Ironiia sud'by*, 1976), 218
   Office Romance (*Sluzhebnyi roman*, 1977), 462
   Old Hags (*Starye kliachi*, 2000), 466
   Prediction (*Predskazanie*, 1993), 469
Rich Bride, The 1938 *see* Pyr'ev
Riga Film Studio, 14, 428–430, 434, 436, 443, 448
Riley, John, 11
Rittenberg, Tat'iana, 544
Rivette, Jacques, 477, 493
Rivosh, Iakov, 322
Road to Life, The 1931 *see* Ekk
Robin Hood (Allan Dwan, 1922), 349, 443
Robin Hood's Arrows 1975 *see* Tarasov
Rodchenko, Aleksandr, 315, 322, 323, 329, 332, 346, 347, 370, 454, 483
Rodnyansky, Alexander, 573
Roeg, Nicholas, 364
Rogovoi, Vladimir, 425
   Officers (*Ofitsery*, 1971), 425
Rogozhkin, Aleksandr, 86, 607–608
   Chekist (1991), 86
   Peculiarities of the National Hunt (*Osobennosti natsional'noi okhoty*, 1995), 86, 607
Rollberg, Peter, 2, 12, 364–384, 502
Romanov, Pavel, 181
Romanticism, 74–78, 120, 139–155, 240, 438, 441
Rome Film Festival, 559
Rome Open City (Roberto Rossellini, 1945), 130
Romm, Mikhail, 263, 331, 365, 367, 374–377, 379, 384–385, 427–428, 430–432, 434–436, 442, 446, 448, 492, 524–525, 600

Romm, Mikhail (cont'd)
  Boule de Suif (Pyshka, 1934), 375, 376
  The Dream (Mechta, 1941), 376
  Lenin in 1918 (Lenin v 1918 godu, 1937), 376
  Lenin in October (Lenin v oktiabre, 1937), 376
  Murder on Dante Street (Ubiistvo na ulitse Dante, 1956), 377, 434
  Nine Days of a Year (Deviat' dnei odnogo goda, 1963), 377
  The Russian Question (Russkii vopros, 1948), 263, 376
  Secret Mission (Sekretnaia missiia, 1950), 376, 430, 492
Room, Abram, 53, 55, 202, 259, 297, 300, 314, 345, 360, 454, 477, 589, 601
  Bed and Sofa (Tret'ia Meshchanskaia, 1927), 202, 323, 345, 454, 589
  The Plan for Great Works (Piatiletka. Plan velikikh rabot, 1930), 297
  A Strict Young Man (Strogii iunosha, 1936), 259
Roshal', Grigorii, 62
Roshal', Lev, 440, 441
Rostropovich, Mstislav, 81, 601, 605, 611
Rotterdam IFF, 84
Rou, Aleksandr, 131, 281
  The Little Hump-backed Horse (Konek-gorbunok, 1941), 131, 281
  The Magic Fish (Po shchuchemu veleniiu, 1938), 131
Roubaud, Franz, 412
Royal Star (cinema), 26–28
Royal Vio (cinema), 25, 42
Rozov, Viktor, 459
Rudnev, Lev, 456
Rudnev, Oleg, 430
Rudzutak, Yan [Janis Rudzutaks], 106
Rumiantseva, Nadezhda, 171
Run of the Pacer 1969 see Urusevskii
Ruslanova, Nina, 84
Russian Ark 2003 see Sokurov
Russian Question, The 1948 see Romm
Russian Souvenir 1960 see Aleksandrov
Ruttman, Walter, 438
  Berlin: Symphony of a Great City (1927), 438
Ryklin, Mikhail, 458
Rzheshevskii, Aleksandr, 256, 257

Saakyan, Maria, 243
  It's not Me (Eto ne ia, 2013), 243
Sabinski, Czeslaw, 319
Sadchikov, Igor', 184
Sadilova, Larisa, 237, 470
  She (Ona, 2013), 470
Sadkovych, Mykola, 281
  May Night (Maiskaia noch', 1940), 281
Sadoul, Georges, 478, 496
Sagatova, Asel', 215
Salazkina, Masha, 2, 6, 10, 45–64

Salt for Svanetia 1930 see Kalatozov
Saltykov-Shchedrin, Mikhail, 25, 81
Samokhvalov, Aleksandr, 285
Samsonov, Samson, 170
  Behind the Department Store Window (Za vitrinoi univermaga, 1955), 170
  The Streets are Full of Surprises (Ulitsa polna neozhidannostei, 1957), 170
Sanaev, Pavel, 242
  On the Hook (Na igre, 2009), 242
San Francisco Film Festival, 520
Sanin, Aleksandr, 366
  The Virgin Hills (Dev'i gory, with Zheliabuzhskii, 1919), 366
Sargeant, Amy, 2, 104
Sarkisova, Oksana, 7, 92–111
Saroyan, William, 568
Sartre, Jean-Paul, 183
Satire, 31, 79, 160, 161, 164, 165, 168, 170–172, 174, 376, 520, 526–528, 529, 534, 537, 538
Sauts, Mariia, 123
Savchenko, Igor', 321, 331, 591, 595
  The Accordion (Garmon', 1934), 321
  A Chance Encounter (Sluchainaia vstrecha, 1936), 321
Sazonov, Aleksei, 505
Scarecrow 1984 see Bykov
Scarlet Fever 1924 see Ermler
Scenario (literary scenario; iron scenario; director's scenario), 251–267, 302, 480
Schatz, Thomas, 203
Schmidt, Otto, 105
Schoedsack, Ernest B see Cooper, Merian
School of New Cinema (Moscow), 6
Scola, Ettore, 32
  Splendor (1989), 32
Scorsese, Martin, 373
Seckler, Dawn, 9, 10, 202–220
Secret Mission 1950 see Romm
Secret Speech, 142, 160
Segel', Iakov, 461
  The House I Live In (Dom, v kotorom ia zhivu, with Kulidzhanov, 1957), 461
Seleckis, Ivars, 437
Sel'ianov, Sergei, 85, 211, 578
  All Soul's Day (Dukhov den', 1988), 85
Sembene, Ousmane, 133
Semenova, Liudmila, 140, 345, 351
Sennett, Mack, 163, 521
Serebrennikov, Kirill, 236, 470
  Betrayal (Izmena, 2012), 470
Serebriakov, Aleksei, 568
Serebrovskaia, Elena, 255
Servants of the Devil 1970 see Leimanis
Servants of the Devil at the Devil's Mill 1970 see Leimanis
Seven of the Brave, 1936 see Gerasimov

Seventeen Moments of Spring 1973 *see* Lioznova
Seventh Satellite, The 1967 *see* Gherman A.Iu., Aronov
Sevzapkino (North-West Regional Agency for Photography and Cinema), 67
Shadow Boxing 2004, 2007 *see* Sidorov
Shadows of Forgotten Ancestors 1964 *see* Paradjanov
Shakhnazarov, Karen, 236, 463, 467
   The Messenger (*Kur'er*, 1986), 463
   Vanishing Empire (*Ischeznuvshaia imperiia*, 2008), 467
   The White Tiger (*Belyi tigr*, 2012), 236
Shalaeva, Maria, 471
Shapiro, Mikhail, 72
   Cinderella (*Zolushka*, 1947), 72
Shaternikova, Nina, 352
Shaw, George Bernard, 85
Shcheglov-Leont'ev, Ivan, 25, 41
Shchors 1939 *see* Dovzhenko
Shchors, Nikolai, 402
Shchuko, Vladimir, 456
Shchusev, Aleksei, 456, 590
She 2013 *see* Sadilova
She Defends the Motherland 1943 *see* Ermler
Shekhtel', Fedor, 319
Shengelaia, Nikoloz, 370–371, 373, 375
   Giulli (1927), 370
Shepit'ko, Larissa, 179, 602
shestidesiatnik (man of the 1960s), 185
Shevchuk, Iurii, 85
Shield and Sword 1968 *see* Basov
Shine, Shine, My Star see Mitta
Shipulinskii, Feofan, 56
Shirly–Myrli 1995 *see* Men'shov
Shklovskii, Viktor, 24, 68, 214, 257, 262, 273, 332, 342, 347, 370, 487, 603
Shneiderov, Vladimir, 96, 100–101, 104–105, 119–120
   Foot of Death (*Podnozhie smerti*, 1929), 96, 101
   The Great Flight, (*Velikii perelet*, 1925), 96, 100, 104
   Two Oceans (*Dva okeana*, 1932), 104
Sholokhov, Mikhail, 418–420
Sholpo, Evgenii, 275, 297–299
Sholpograph, 298
Shore, The 1963 *see* Freimanis
Shorin, Aleksandr, 296
Shostakovich, Dmitrii, 11, 72, 77, 79–81, 282
Shostka, 277
Shot in the Fog 1964 *see* Volchek
Shpikovskii, Nikolai, 167
   Chess Fever (*Shakhmatnaia goriachka*, with Pudovkin, 1925), 167
Shpinel', Iosif, 315, 321
Shtraukh, Maksim, 77
Shub, Esfir', 100, 106, 107, 108, 304, 307
   KShE (*Komsomol: Patron of Electrification*, 1932), 106, 304, 307
Shukshin, Vasilii, 419, 462, 495, 600
   Happy Go Lucky (*Pechki-lavochki*, 1972), 462

Shul'gin, Vasilii, 81
Shultes 2008 *see* Bakuradze
Shumiatskii, Boris, 63, 102, 141, 162, 165, 255, 257, 260, 270, 278, 280, 281, 590
Shutko, Kirill, 94–96, 106–108
Shvarts, Evgenii, 72, 544
Shvedchikov, Konstantin, 99, 102, 106
Shveitser, Mikhail, 184, 187, 533
   The Golden Calf (*Zolotoi telenok*, 1968), 486, 533
   The Tight Knot (*Tugoi uzel*, 1956), 184
Shveitser, Vladimir, 258, 285
Sidorov, Aleksei, 216, 610
   Shadow Boxing (*Boi s ten'iu*, 2004, 2007), 216
Sight and Sound, 118, 129
Silent Souls 2010 *see* Fedorchenko
Sillov, Vladimir, 106
Sills, Milton, 351
Silly Symphonies, 271, 276
Simonov, Konstantin, 84, 188, 189, 259, 263, 266, 368, 544, 550
Simov, Valentin, 319, 320
Sing Your Song, Poet. 1972 *see* Urusevskii
Siniavskii, Andrei, 176
Sissako, Abderrahmane, 6
   Timbuktu (2014), 6
Siumkin, Vitalii, 275
   Symphony of the World (*Simfoniia mira*, 1932), 275
Sixth Part of the World, A 1926 *see* Vertov
Sizov, Nikolai, 519
Skliut, Iosif, 279
   The Testament (*Zaveshchanie*, 1937), 279
Slapstick, 15, 86, 167, 214, 520–522, 526, 527, 528, 530, 532, 533, 537
Sleeping Beauty, 1930 *see* G. & S. Vasil'ev
Slobodskoi, Moris, 521
Smirnova, Avdot'ia, 243–244
   KoKoKo (2012), 243
   Two Days (*Dva dnia*, 2011), 244
Smirnov, Andrei, 574, 577, 581
   Once There was an Old Woman (*Zhila-byla odna baba*, 2011), 574, 577
Smirnov, Andrey (book), 296, 297
Smoktunovskii, Innokentii, 82, 83, 607
Šnore, Edvīns, 448
   The Soviet Story (*Labvakar*, 2008), 448
Snowbells 1961 *see* Kraulītis
Snow White and the Seven Dwarfs (Disney, 1937), 277
Sobolevskii, Petr, 73
socialism in one country, 147, 589
Socialist Realism, Socialist Realist, 8, 9, 13, 46, 54, 57, 59, 63, 66, 75–78, 122, 126, 139–155, 168, 191, 258, 264, 278, 287, 295, 301, 316, 331, 353, 354, 356, 358, 391, 393, 396, 435, 438, 454, 507, 508, 527, 528, 545, 591
Soiuzdetfilm, 7, 117–133, 275, 281, 592

Soiuzkino, 57, 63, 102, 107, 294, 296, 299, 300, 505, 506, 590
Sokolov, Ippolit, 96, 253, 262, 263, 276, 278, 285
Sokurov, Aleksandr, 4, 7, 81, 85–86, 179, 198, 239, 241, 243–244, 560, 566, 569–570, 578–579, 582, 612
   Alexandra (2007), 244
   Days of Eclipse (*Dni zatmeniia*, 1988), 85
   Demoted (*Razzhalovannyi*, 1980), 579
   Faust (2011), 239, 243
   The Lonely Voice of a Man (*Odinokii golos cheloveka*, 1978), 85
   Mother and Son (*Mat' i syn*, 1997), 85
   Mournful Unconcern (*Skorbnoe beschuvstvie*, 1986), 85
   Russian Ark (*Russkii kovcheg*, 2003), 560
   Taurus (*Telets*, 2000), 85
Solaris 1972 *see* Tarkovskii
Soldier Ivan Brovkin 1955 *see* Lukinskii
Soleil (cinema), 28, 38
Solntseva, Iuliia, 306, 338, 404, 454
Sologub, Fedor, 258
Solonitsyn, Anatolii, 83, 548, 602
Solov'ev Nikolai
   Blossoming Youth (*Tsvetushchaia molodost'*, 1938), 281
   Victory Parade (*Parad pobedy*, 1945), 287
Solov'ev, Sergei, 14
Solzhenitsyn, Aleksandr, 81
Song of the Motherland, 147
Sony Pictures, 217
Sorlin, Pierre, 118
Sorochintsy Fair 1939 *see* Ekk
sound cinema, 120, 140, 253, 292–296, 299–301, 303, 305–307, 486, 488, 590
Soviet Hollywood, 8, 141
Soviet Story, The 2008 *see* Snore
Sovkino, 52, 54, 56, 95, 96, 99–102, 106, 108, 274, 293, 294, 320, 324, 589
Spektrakoler, 274
Spielberg, Steven, 203
   Jaws 1975, 203
Splendor 1989 *see* Scola
Sportloto-82 1982 *see* Gaidai
Spot, The 2006 *see* Moroz
Spy's Exploit, The 1947 *see* Barnet
Spy, The 2012 *see* Andrianov
Stagnation, 3, 4, 8, 14, 150, 174, 178–198, 216, 459, 460, 537
Stakhanov, Aleksei, 487
Stakhanovite, 153, 171, 218, 231, 356, 357
Stalingrad 2013 *see* Bondarchuk, F.
Stalin, Iosif, 77
Stalinism, Stalinist, 79, 133, 171, 337, 353, 357, 391, 407, 464, 465, 524, 543, 545, 552, 553, 556
Stalinist musical, 8, 14, 139–155
Stalin Prize, 147, 417, 418, 545
Stalker 1979 *see* Tarkovskii
Stanislavsky, Konstantin, 63

Star 1949 *see* Ivanov A.
Star 2002 *see* Lebedev N.
Starewicz, Władysław, 365, 586
   Revenge of the Cameraman (*Mest' kinematograficheskogo operatora*, 1912), 365
Star, The 2014 *see* Melikian
Stasiulevich, Mikhail, 25
State Councilor 2005 *see* Iankovskii F.
State Optical Institute, Leningrad (GOI), 275, 277
State Repertory Committee (Glavrepertkom), 102
Steamroller and the Violin, The 1960 *see* Tarkovskii
Steiger, Rod, 418
Sten, Anna, 74, 140, 344, 351, 454, 481, 482
Stenberg, Vladimir and Georgii ("Brothers"), 345
Stepanova, Varvara, 346
Stiller, Ben, 215
Stoliarov, Sergei, 145
Stolper, Aleksandr, 259, 266–267, 602
   Days and Nights (*Dni i nochi*, 1944), 259
   Lad from Our Town (*Paren' iz nashego goroda*, 1942), 259
   The Law of Life (*Zakon zhizni*, 1940), 266, 267
   Wait for Me (*Zhdi menia*, 1943), 259
Stone 2011 *see* Kaminskii
Storm over Asia 1928 *see* Pudovkin
Storozheva, Vera, 237, 242
   Travelling with Pets (*Puteshestvie s domashnymi zhivotnymi*, 2007), 237, 242
Story About Omar Khaptsoko, A 1932 *see* Raizman
Story of Asya Klyachina, The 1966 *see* Konchalovskii A.
Strange Woman, A 1977 *see* Raizman
Streets are Full of Surprises, The 1957 *see* Samsonov
Strictly Business 1962 *see* Gaidai
Strict Young Man, A 1936 *see* Room
Stride, Soviet! 1926 *see* Vertov
Strike 1924 *see* Eisenstein
Strizhenov, Aleksandr, 214
Strizhenov, Oleg, 80
Stroeva, Vera, 159–160
   Variety Stars (*Veselye zvezdy*, 1954), 159–160
Stroganov Institute, 319–321
Strugatskii, Boris and Arkadii, 557
Sucker, the Conqueror of the Water 1991 *see* Tigai
Sudakevich, Anel', 343, 347, 351, 354, 355
Sukachev, Garik, 236
   The House in the Sun (*Dom solntsa*, 2010), 236
Sukharebskii, Lazar', 107, 108
Sukhobokov, Vladimir and Marriia Sauts, 123
   The Red Scarf (*Krasnyi galstuk*, 1948), 123
Sun Valley Serenade (H. Bruce Humberstone, 1941), 494
Surikova, Alla, 468
   Moscow Holidays (*Moskovskie kanikuly*, 1995), 468
Suteev, Vladimir, 52
Sutyrin, Vladimir, 107, 109, 256, 266
SVD 1927 *see* Kozintsev and Trauberg
Swineherdess and the Shepherd, The 1940 *see* Pyr'ev

Symphony of the World 1933 see Grigor'ev, Siumkin, Tvardovskii
synchronized sound (synch-sound), 293, 305
synecdoche, 227–229
Szczepanik, Jan, 276

Tager, Pavel, 294, 296, 298
Tailor from Torzhok, The 1925 see Protazanov
Tale of the Fisherman and the Fish, The 1937 see Ptushko
Tale of the Silly Mouse, The 1940 see Tsekhanovskii
Taras Bulba 2009 see Bortko
Tarasov, Sergei, 443, 449
    Robin Hood's Arrows (*Strely Robina Guda*, 1975), 443
Tarich, Iurii, 324
    Wings of a Serf (*Kryl'ia kholopa*, 1926), 324
Tarkovskii, Andrei, 3–4, 9, 16, 85, 169, 179, 182–183, 193–194, 197–198, 230, 385, 461, 539, 543–544, 558–562, 568–569, 578, 580, 582, 597, 602–604
    Andrei Rublev (1966), 183, 194, 559, 578
    Ivan's Childhood (*Ivanovo detstvo*, 1962), 230, 568
    The Mirror (*Zerkalo*, 1975), 578
    Solaris (1972), 558, 578
    Stalker (1979), 558, 602
    The Steamroller and the Violin (*Katok i skripka*, 1960), 461
Tashiro, Charles, 317
Tati, Jacques, 527
Taurus 2000 see Sokurov
Taxi Blues 1990 see Lungin
Taylor, Richard, 2, 8, 14, 98, 103, 139–155, 168, 509
Tchaikovsky, Petr, 150, 490, 596
Tcherneva, Irina, 180, 428, 434
Technical College of Screen Art, 67, 69
Technicolor, 11, 270, 271, 273, 276, 277, 280
Tendriakov, Vladimir, 187
Ten Minutes Older 1978 see Frank
Ten Years without the Right to Correspond 1990 see Naumov.
Tereshkova, Valentina, 439
Terskoi, Anatolii, 97, 98
Testament, The 1937 see Skliut
Thaw, the, 3, 4, 8, 15, 66, 81, 82, 133, 158–160, 162–166, 168–175, 178–198, 230, 368, 377, 418, 420, 437, 459–463, 477, 493, 496, 503, 516, 547, 558
theatricalism (*teatral'shchina*), 74
1812: The Ballad of Ulan 2012 see Fesenko
Their Kingdom 1928 see Kalatozov
Theme, The 1979 see Panfilov
There once was a Singing Bird 1970 see Iosseliani
There's Good Weather on Deribasovskaya Street, It's Again Raining on Brighton Beach 1992 see Gaidai
There's Something About Mary (Farrelly Brothers, 1998), 215
They Fought for the Motherland 1975 see Bondarchuk S.
Thiemann & Reinhardt Studio, 319
Three Little Pigs (Disney, 1933), 276

Three Million Trial, The [aka *Three Thieves*] 1926 see Protazanov
Three Poplars on Pliushchikha Street 1967 see Lioznova
Three Songs of Lenin 1934 see Vertov
Three Thieves 1926 see Protazanov
Thrice Resurrected 1960 see Gaidai
Through the Ussuri Area 1928 see Litvinov
Thugs, The 1983 see Asanova
Tiagai, Aleksandr, 102
Ticket to the Stars (*Zvezdnyi bilet*, 1961), 443
Tigai, Arkadii, 85
    Sucker, the Conqueror of the Water (*Lokh, pobeditel' vody*, 1991), 85
Tight Knot, The 1956 see Shveitser
Tikhonov, Viacheslav, 419
Timbuktu 2014 see Sissako
Time of Desires, A 1984 see Raizman
Timiriazev, Kliment, 77
Timur and his Gang, 1940 see Razumnyi
Tiomkin, Dmitri, 31
Tissé, Eduard, 12, 273, 275, 300, 365, 367–369, 374, 378, 383–385, 597
    The Immortal Garrison (*Bessmertnyi garnizon*, with Zakhar Agranenko, 1956), 368
    Misery and Fortune of Women (*Frauennot–Frauenglück*, 1930), 367, 368
Titanic (James Cameron 1997), 215
Tobis-Klangfilm, 296
Todorovskii, Valerii, 235, 466–469, 611
    Hipsters (*Stiliagi*, 2008), 467
    The Land of the Deaf (*Strana glukhikh*, 1997), 468
Todorov, Tsvetan, 227
Tolstoi, Aleksei, 259
Tolstoy, Lev, 209
Torn Boots 1933 see Barskaia
Toronto IFF, 227
Torpedo Bombers 1983 see Aranovich
Tovstonogov, Georgii, 546, 549
Tractor Drivers 1939 see Pyr'ev
Trail of the Lonesome Pine (Henry Hathaway, 1936), 276
Train Goes East, The 1948 see Raizman
Trainin, Il'ia, 95, 99
Traitor, The 1926 see Iutkevich
TRAM–Theater of the Working Youth, 73, 589
Trauberg, Il'ia, 488
Trauberg, Leonid see Kozintsev and Trauberg
Travelling with Pets 2007 see Storozheva
Treasure Island 1937 see Vainshtok
Treaty of Paris, 412
Tree Death, The 1915 see Panteleev
Tret'iakova, Ol'ga, 351
Tret'iakov, Sergei, 95, 96, 344, 349, 370
Tretyakov Gallery, 470
Trial on the Road 1971 see Gherman
Triple Scrutiny 1969 see Brenčs

Triumphal Gate, 454
Troitskii Most, 84, 86
Truffaut, François, 179, 181
Truth of Life. Syphilis (*Pravda zhizni. Sifilis*, dir. Vladimir Karin, 1925), 99
Tsar, Tsarist, 70, 73, 125, 128, 162, 208, 209, 324, 413, 414, 424, 502, 524, 529, 534–536, 546, 547, 585, 586, 587, 608
Tsekhanovskii, Mikhail, 282, 283, 297
  The Tale of the Silly Mouse (*Skazka o glupom myshonke*, 1940), 282, 283
Tsivian, Yuri [Tsiv'ian, Iurii], 2, 5, 24, 28, 32, 68, 301, 318, 413, 414
TsOKS (Central United Film Studios), 79, 415
TsUM (Central Department Store), 462, 513
Tsyrkun, Nina, 213, 215
Tugendkhol'd, Iakov, 341
Tuner, The 2004 *see* Muratova
Turin, Viktor, 100, 105
  Turksib (1929), 100, 105
Turkin, Valentin, 59, 101, 253, 258, 262, 263, 478
Turkish Gambit 2005 *see* Faiziev
Turksib, 1929 *see* Turin
Turovskaia, Maia, 130, 142, 150, 152, 396
Tutyshkin, Andrei, 158–160
  A Wedding in Malinovka (*Svad'ba v Malinovke*, 1967), 158
  We've Met Somewhere Before (*My s vami gde-to vstrechalis'*, with N. Dostal', 1954), 160
Tvardovskii, Vladislav, 79, 275, 595, 598, 599
  Symphony of the World (*Simfoniia mira*, 1932), 275
Tverskaia Street, 454, 467
Twelve Chairs 1971 *see* Gaidai
Twelve Chairs 1976 *see* Zakharov
Twentieth Party Congress, 142, 160
Twenty Days without War 1976 *see* Gherman
Two Days 2011 *see* Smirnova
Two Oceans 1932 *see* Shneiderov
Tynianov, Iurii, 69–71, 322
Tyshler, Aleksandr, 282

Ubaste, Ruta, 439
Uchitel', Aleksei, 237, 242
  Dreaming of Space (*Kosmos kak predchuvstvie*, 2005), 237, 242
Ugly Duckling 2010 *see* Bardin
Ukrainfilm, 281, 306
Ul'ianov, Mikhail, 514, 515
Unconquerable Ones, The 1942 *see* Gerasimov and Kalatozov
Union of Filmmakers, 180, 195, 555
Unsent Letter 1960 *see* Kalatozov
Urusevskii, Sergei, 12, 183, 365, 372–375, 380–384, 386, 509, 600
  The Red Tent (*Krasnaia palatka*, aka *La Tenda Rossa*, 1969), 373

Run of the Pacer (*Beg inokhodtsa*, 1969), 380
Sing Your Song, Poet. (*Poi pesniu, poet*, 1972), 380, 382, 383
Ushakov, Sviatoslav, 241, 242
  Belka and Strelka. Space Dogs (*Belka i Strelka. Lunnye prikliucheniia*, with Evlannikova, 2013), 241, 242
Uspenskii, Viacheslav, 92
Uspensky, Boris, 453
Utkin, Aleksei, 318–320, 331

Vachnadze, Nato, 140, 351, 370
Vainshtok, Vladimir–*Treasure Island* (*Ostrov sokrovishch*, 1937), 120
Vaisfel'd, Arnold, 321
Valentino, Rudolph, 140
Valor 1941 *see* Barnet
Vanishing Empire 2008 *see* Shakhnazarov
Variety Stars 1954 *see* Stroeva
Variophone, 275, 298
Varlamov, Konstantin, 28, 37
Vartanov, Anri, 264, 265
Vasil'eva, Feozva, 25
Vasil'ev, Dmitrii, 259
  In the Name of the Motherland (*Vo imia rodiny*, 1943), 259
Vasil'ev (Brothers), Sergei and Georgii, 7, 12, 68, 76, 392–395, 401–402, 555
  Chapaev (1934), 7, 12, 202, 392
  Sleeping Beauty (*Spiashchaia krasavitsa*, 1930), 76
Vasil'ev, Vasilii Ipatovich, 25
VDNKh (Exhibition of Agricultural Achievements), 151, 153, 356, 456, 467, 470
Veldre, Biruta, 439
Veledinskii, Aleksandr, 243
  Alive (*Zhivoi*, 2006), 243
Vengerov, Vladimir, 546
  Workers Settlement (*Rabochii poselok*, 1965), 546
Venice Film Festival, 16, 182, 227, 567
Vertinskaia, Anastasiia, 81
Vertov, Dziga, 2, 69, 95, 99, 103, 108, 124, 139, 165, 175, 253, 301–304, 320, 438–439, 477, 562, 590, 595
  Enthusiasm (*Entuziazm: Simfoniia Donbassa* 1930), 302
  Kino-Eye (*Kinoglaz*, 1924), 124
  Man with a Movie Camera (*Chelovek s kinoapparatom*, 1929), 124, 438, 590
  A Sixth Part of the World (*Shestaia chast' mira*, 1926), 139
  Stride, Soviet! (*Shagai, Sovet!*, 1926), 99, 301
  Three Songs of Lenin (*Tri pesni o Lenine*, 1934), 69
VFKO (All-Russian Photo and Film Organization), 98
VGIK/GIK (All-Union State Institute of Cinematography), 5, 6, 46, 47, 49, 62, 181, 187, 261, 322, 366, 368, 377, 429, 524, 545, 568
Victory Day, 292, 418, 461, 491

Victory Parade 1945 *see* Solov'ev N.
ViNiMor *see* Georgii Vitsyn, Iurii Nikulin, Evgenii Morgunov
Vinogradskaia, Katerina, 259
Viollis, Andrée, 350, 352
Virgin Hills, The 1919 *see* Sanin, Zheliabuzhskii
Virgin Lands, 438, 495, 595
Virgin Soil Upturned 1939 *see* Raizman
Vishnevskii, Vsevolod, 259, 331, 397, 401, 402
Vitsyn, Georgii, 15, 521, 526
VKhUTEIN (Higher Art and Technical Institute, Leningrad), 321
VKhUTEMAS (Higher Art and Technical Studios), 51, 52, 321
VKSR (Higher Courses of Scriptwriters and Directors), 568
Vladimirov, Igor', 511, 512
Voice, 1982 *see* Averbakh
Voinov, Nikolai, 298
Voitsik, Ada, 352
Volchek, Boris, 365, 374–380, 383–386
  Accused of Murder (*Obviniaiutsia v ubiistve*, 1969), 377
  Commander of the Happy Pike (*Kommandir schastlivoi shchuki*, 1973), 377
  Shot in the Fog (*Vystrel v tumane*, aka *Sotrudnik ChK*, 1964), 377, 379
Vol'f, Veniamin, 262
Volga-Volga 1938 *see* Aleksandrov
Volkonsky, Prince, 50
Volodarskii, Eduard, 548, 552, 561
Vol'pin, Mikhail, 488
von Geldern, James, 141, 154, 464
Voronkov, Maksim, 539
  Kidnapping, Caucasian Style! (*Kavkazskaia plennitsa!*, 2014), 539
Vostokfilm (Studio), 6, 100
Vostokkino, 274
Voynich, E. L., 80
Vvedenskii, Aleksandr, 72
Vyborg Side, The 1938 *see* Kozintsev and Trauberg
Vyrypaev, Ivan, 236, 237, 242
  Euphoria (*Eiforiia*, 2006), 236, 237, 242
Vysotskii, Mikhail, 431
Vysotskii, Vladimir, 522, 602

Wagner, Richard, 148
Wait for Me 1943 *see* Stolper, Ivanov B.
Wake Lenochka Up, 1934 *see* Kudriavtseva
Walking the Streets of Moscow 1962 *see* Daneliia
Wanted 2008 *see* Bekmambetov
War and Peace 1965–1967 *see* Bondarchuk S.
War Communism, 164
We are from Kronstadt 1936 *see* Dzigan
We are from the Future 2008 *see* Maliukov
Wechsler, Lazar, 367
Wedding in Malinovka, A 1967 *see* Tutyshkin

We Draw Fire on Ourselves (*Vyzyvaem ogon' na sebia*, TV, 1964–5), 409
Weimar, 274
Welcome, No Trespassing 1964 *see* Klimov
Welles, Orson, 418
Western Electric, 292, 296
We've Met Somewhere Before 1954 *see* Tutyshkin, Dostal'
When September Comes 1975 *see* Keosayan
White, Hayden, 410
White, Pearl, 351
White Sea Canal, 554, 591
White Sun of the Desert 1969 *see* Motyl'
White Tiger, The 2012 *see* Shakhnazarov
Who, if Not Us 1998 *see* Priemykhov
Widdis, Emma, 2, 11, 96, 308, 314–333, 352, 424, 470, 486
Widescreen, 81, 437
Wiene, Robert, 317, 324
  Cabinet of Dr. Caligari (*Das Cabinet des Dr. Caligari*, 1920), 317, 324
Wilde, Oscar, 319
Window to Paris 1993 *see* Mamin
Wings of a Serf 1926 *see* Tarich
Winter Palace, 398, 587, 588
Witch, The 2006 *see* Fesenko
Wolf and the Seven Kids, The 1938 *see* Mokil'
Wolf, Konrad, 6
Wolf, Markus, 6
Woll, Josephine, 3, 159, 161–165, 168, 170, 459, 461, 462, 509
Wolves and Sheep *see* Ostrovskii, A.
Workers Settlement 1965 *see* Vengerov
World War I, 28, 38, 87, 292, 382, 484 *see also* Great War
World War II, 12, 47, 66, 79, 81, 83, 84, 118, 173, 182, 260, 366, 368, 372, 396, 398, 407, 409, 427, 430, 492, 494, 522, 529, 548, 593 *see also* Great Patriotic War
Wrestler and The Clown, The 1957 *see* Barnet
Wyler, William, 546

Yampolsky, Mikhail (Iampolskii), 50, 55
Yeltsin, Boris, 3, 603, 604, 605–609, 611
Yeltsin era, 464
Youngblood, Denise, 2–4, 12–14, 98, 140, 162–164, 295, 299, 348–350, 391–407, 410, 411, 415, 416, 479, 483
Young Guard, The 1948 *see* Gerasimov
Young Pioneers, 172, 256
Your Acquaintance 1927 *see* Kuleshov
Your Contemporary 1968 *see* Raizman
Yurchak, Alexei, 441, 442

Zakharov, Mark, 534
  Twelve Chairs (*Dvenadtsat' stul'ev*, TV, 1976), 534
Zak, Mark, 500, 503, 530
Zamanski, Vladimir, 83, 548

Zarkhi, Aleksandr, 55, 77–78, 221, 260, 307, 477
  Baltic Deputy (*Deputat Baltiki*, 1936), 77, 260
  My Native Land (*Moia rodina*, with Kheifits, 1933), 307
  My Younger Brother (*Moi mladshii brat*, 1962), 443
Zarkhi, Natan, 55
zaum, 304
Zel'din, Vladimir, 161
Zel'dovich, Aleksandr, 469
  Moscow (2000), 469
Zeldovych, Grigorii, 306
Zharkov, Aleksei, 83
Zhdanov, Andrei, 79, 132, 140, 163, 266, 489, 594
Zheimo, Ianina, 72, 171
Zheliabuzhskii, Iurii, 99, 166, 275–277, 338, 365–367, 377, 379, 383–385, 454, 589
  The Cigarette Girl from Mosselprom (*Papriosnitsa ot Mossel'proma*, 1924), 69, 166, 338, 454, 589
  The Collegiate Registrar (*Kollezhskii registrator*, 1925), 366
  Morozko (1924), 366
  Petr and Aleksei (1919), 366
  Polikushka (1919–1923), 366
  The Virgin Hills (*Dev'i gory*, with Sanin 1919), 366
Zhizhneva, Ol'ga, 348
Zholtovskii, Ivan, 319, 456
Zhukhovitskii, Leonid, 187
Zhuravlev, Vasilii, 141
  Cosmic Flight (*Kosmicheskii reis*, 1936), 141
Zilinskis, Arvids, 438
Zorkaya, Neya [Zorkaia, Neia], 2, 103, 190, 481, 482, 500, 520
Zoshchenko, Mikhail, 79, 537
Žurgina, Laima, 439, 441
Zviagintsev, Andrei, 4, 6, 11, 14, 16, 236–238, 241, 243, 471, 565–582, 610–611
  The Banishment (*Izgnanie*, 2007), 236, 565, 575, 611
  Elena (2010), 243, 471, 572, 577
  Leviathan (*Leviafan*, 2014), 568, 579
  The Return (*Vozvrashchenie*, 2003), 11, 567, 573, 575, 610
Zvonkine, Eugénie, 3, 9, 178–198, 559